AF819888

All in One®

Recommended by **Teachers** Trusted by **Toppers**

# BIOLOGY

## Class 11

**EVERYTHING YOU NEED TO SCORE**

- Simplified NCERT Theory
- In-text & Chapter Exercises
- All Types of Exam Pattern Questions
- CBQs; MCQs, A-R, Case Based
- Sample Question Papers

**CBSE Exams 2026**

All in One

Recommended by **Teachers** Trusted by **Toppers**

# BIOLOGY

Class 11

**EVERYTHING YOU NEED TO SCORE**

- Simplified NCERT Theory
- In-text & Chapter Exercises
- All Types of Exam Pattern Questions
- CBQs; MCQs, A-R, Case Based
- Sample Question Papers

**CBSE Exams 2026**

*Authors*

Samiksha Gupta
Manvi Sirohi

arihant
SUCCESS AND NOTHING LESS

**arihant**
SUCCESS AND NOTHING LESS

# ARIHANT PRAKASHAN

(School Division Series)

All Rights Reserved

卐 *© PUBLISHER*

No part of this publication may be re-produced, stored in a retrieval system or by any means, electronic, mechanical, photocopying, recording, scanning, web or otherwise without the written permission of the publisher. Arihant has obtained all the information in this book from the sources believed to be reliable and true. However, Arihant or its editors or authors or illustrators don't take any responsibility for the absolute accuracy of any information published and the damage or loss suffered thereupon.

All disputes subject to Meerut (UP) jurisdiction only.

卐 *ADMINISTRATIVE & PRODUCTION OFFICES*

*Regd. Office*

'Ramchhaya' 4577/15, Agarwal Road, Darya Ganj, New Delhi -110002
Tele: 011- 47630600, 43518550; Fax: 011- 23280316

卐 *Head Office*

Kalindi, TP Nagar, Meerut (UP) - 250002, Tel: 0121-7156203, 7156204

卐 *SALES & SUPPORT OFFICES*

Agra, Ahmedabad, Bengaluru, Bareilly, Chennai, Delhi, Guwahati, Hyderabad, Jaipur, Jhansi, Kolkata, Lucknow, Nagpur & Pune.

*PO No : TXT-XX-XXXXXXX-X-XX*

Published By Arihant Publications (India) Ltd.

For further information about the books published by Arihant, log on to www.arihantbooks.com or e-mail at info@arihantbooks.com

Follow us on

卐 *PRICE* ₹525.00

**PRODUCTION TEAM**

| Publishing Managers | Cover Designer | Inner Designer |
|---|---|---|
| Mahendra Singh Rawat & Keshav Mohan | Salman Shaikh | Ankit Tyagi |
| *Project Head* | *Page Layouting* | *Proof Reader* |
| Shiva Choudhary | Naresh Kumar | Nidhi |

# Index *cum* Study Planner

# One Book- Endless Features

## *to Help you Succeed*

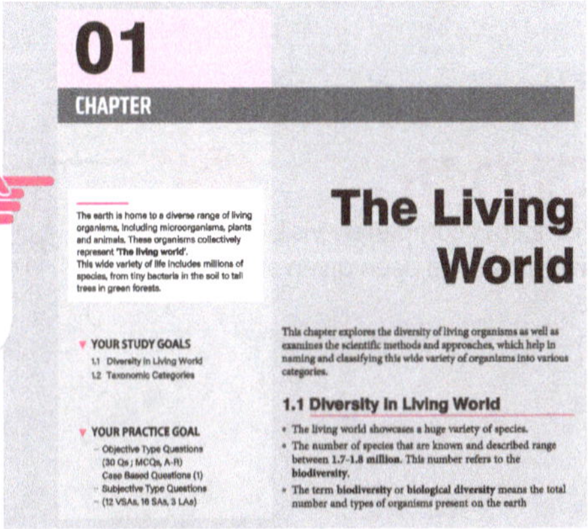

01

CHAPTER

The earth is home to a diverse range of living organisms, including microorganisms, plants and animals. These organisms collectively represent **'The living world'**.
This wide variety of life includes millions of species, from tiny bacteria in the soil to tall trees in green forests.

**The Living World**

YOUR STUDY GOALS
1.1 Diversity in Living World
1.2 Taxonomic Categories

YOUR PRACTICE GOAL
– Objective Type Questions (30 Qs ; MCQs, A-R) Case Based Questions (1)
– Subjective Type Questions – (12 VSAs, 16 SAs, 3 LAs)

This chapter explores the diversity of living organisms as well as examines the scientific methods and approaches, which help in naming and classifying this wide variety of organisms into various categories.

**1.1 Diversity in Living World**

- The living world showcases a huge variety of species.
- The number of species that are known and described range between **1.7-1.8 million**. This number refers to the **biodiversity**.
- The term **biodiversity** or **biological diversity** means the total number and types of organisms present on the earth

**Chapter Intro**

A quick information about the coverage of the chapter to explain students about what they are going to study.

### 1.1 Diversity in Living World

- The living world showcases a huge variety of species.
- The number of species that are known and described range between **1.7-1.8 million**. This number refers to the **biodiversity**.
- The term **biodiversity** or **biological diversity** means the total number and types of organisms present on the earth.
- As we continue to explore new areas and even old ones, new organisms are continuously being added. This huge available variety cannot be studied without the use of taxonomy.

Taxonomy

- It is the branch of science that deals with characterisation, identification, classification and nomenclature of organisms.

TEACHER'S TIP
Species are groups of organisms that can interbreed and produce fertile offspring. This ability to reproduce sets them apart from larger categories like genus, family and order, where members may not be able to breed with each other. This shows that species are the basic level of classification, based on how they reproduce.

**Simplified Theory**

It contains the necessary study material well supported by Definitions, Facts, Figures, Flow Charts, etc.

**Teacher Tips**

Important Points related to given concept to bring students focus on important points.

### Quick Test 1

1. Name the branch of science that was primarily based on observable characters.
2. State True or False.
   Systematics studies show how different living things are connected through their evolutionary relationships.
3. Mention the process of describing an organism and assigning the correct name to it.
4. Name the scientist that developed the formal system of naming species of living organisms using two Latin-based names.
5. State True or False.
   In the system of binomial nomenclature, it is standard for the genus name to be lowercase, while the species name is typically written in capitalised.

**Quick Tests**

To make students understand the chapter in a smooth part-by-part manner, Quick Tests have been given in each chapter. These Exercises help students to assess the understanding of related concepts at regular interval.

# One Book- Endless Features
## *to Help you Succeed*

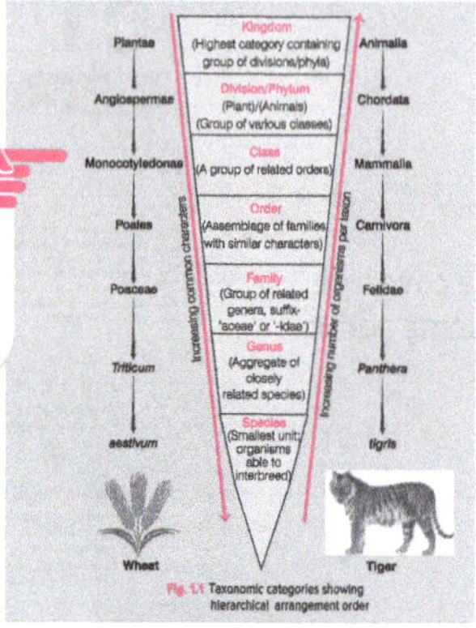

Fig. 1.1 Taxonomic categories showing hierarchical arrangement order

**Illustrative Figures**

To make the concepts completely visible, illustrative diagrams have been given at various place.

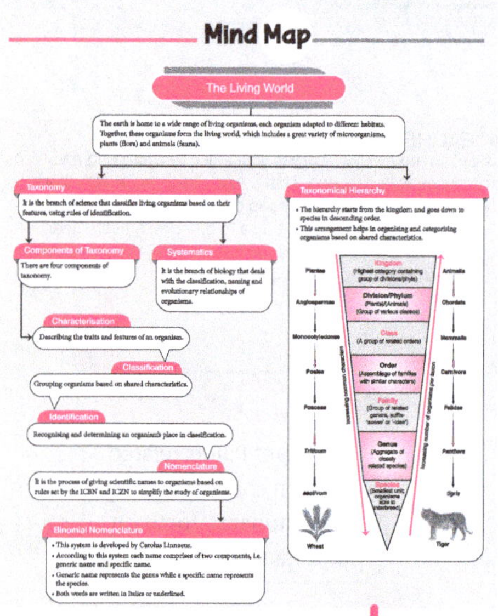

**NCERT Questions**

To make students completely understand NCERT books, answers of selected NCERT questions have been given in each chapter.

**2. Which are the basic processes in the taxonomy?**

**Ans.** The basic processes in taxonomy are
(i) Characterisation (ii) Identification
(iii) Classification (iv) Nomenclature (½ × 4)

**3. What different criteria would you choose to classify people that you meet often?** **NCERT**

**Ans.** Different criteria that can be used to classify individuals we frequently encounter include behaviour, geographic location, physical appearance, gender and family relationships, among others.

**4. Why is it difficult to assign common names to all living organisms?**

**Ans.** It is difficult to assign common name to all organisms because the organism may have several names in given language. It can create confusion to the people while recalling organism.

**5. How are living organisms divided into different taxa? What is the name given to this process?**

**Ans.** Living organisms can be divided into different taxa based on their characteristics. This process of classification is called taxonomy. (½ + ½)

**Mind Map**

A quick revision visual tool for the complete chapter.

# One Book- Endless Features

*to Help you Succeed*

## NCERT Exemplar Problems

NCERT Exemplar Problems are considered to be the best problem books for School/Board Examinations. To make students practice of exemplary questions given in this book, each chapter has selected problems from NCERT Exemplar.

**10.** Brinjal and potato belong to the same genus- *Solanum*, but two different species. What defines them as separate species? **NCERT Exemplar**

**Ans.** Brinjal and potato belong to same genus as they share some common correlated characters.

They belong to different species because they have
(i) different morphological features. (½)
(ii) reproductive isolation (inability to interbreed). (½)

**11.** Cats and dogs belong to different families, but are classified under the same order–Carnivora. Based on which characteristics are they placed in the order–Carnivora? **Competency Based Que.**

**Ans.** Cats and dogs are placed in the order–Carnivora due to shared traits like large canine teeths, strong claws for hunting and a digestive system specialised for meat consumption.

## Exam Pattern Exercise

To make students completely prepared for examination, this Exercise contains Exam Pattern Questions. This exercise covers all types of questions, like; MCQs, Case Based Questions, Assertion-Reason, VSA, SA & LA Type Questions.

SAMPLE QUESTION PAPER 1

A Highly Simulated Sample Question Paper for CBSE Class XI Examination

**BIOLOGY**

Time : 3 Hours | Max. Marks : 70

***General Instructions***

1. All questions are compulsory.
2. The question paper has five sections and 33 questions.
3. Section-A has 16 questions of 1 mark each; Section-B has 5 questions of 2 marks each; Section-C has 7 questions of 3 marks each; Section-D has 2 case-based questions of 4 marks each; and Section-E has 3 questions of 5 marks each.
4. There is no overall choice. However, internal choices have been provided in some questions. A student has to attempt only one of the alternatives in such questions.
5. Wherever necessary, neat and properly labelled diagrams should be drawn.

**SECTION-A**

**1.** Diagrams A and B indicate the shape of leaves in larkspur and buttercup, respectively. Choose the correct option.

(a) The juvenile and adult leaf of larkspur differ in size due to genetic and plant growth regulator factors
(b) Both leaf of buttercup differ in size due to genetic and intercellular factors
(c) Both larkspur and buttercup leaf size variation is due to habitat plasticity
(d) None of the above

**2.** Male frogs can croak louder than female frogs because of
(a) vocal sacs
(b) strength
(c) large size
(d) large sound box

**3.** 'Bakane' (foolish seedling) disease of rice seedlings, was caused by *Gibberella fujikuroi*, which is a
(a) fungi (b) protozoans
(c) bacteria (d) virus

**4.** Given below are some related pairs of bone.

| | Column I | | Column II |
|---|---|---|---|
| A. | Flat bones | 1. | Sternum |
| B. | Irregular bones | 2. | Ear ossicles |
| C. | Glenoid cavity | 3. | Shoulder joint |
| D. | Clavicle | 4. | Collar bone |

Observe them carefully and find how many of them are correctly match?
(a) 3 (b) 2
(c) 1 (d) 4

**5.** What happens when pacemaker is non-functional?
(a) Only the auricle will contract rhythmically
(b) The cardiac muscle do not contract in a coordinated manner rhythmically
(c) Only ventricles will contract rhythmically
(d) Cardiac muscle will contract in a coordinated manner

## Sample Question Papers

To make students practice of examination in real sense, there are 3 Sample Question Papers at the end. All these Sample Questions Papers are exactly prepared on the latest syllabus & pattern of examination.

## Exam Pattern Questions

### Objective Type Questions

**Multiple Choice Questions**

**1.** The number and types of organisms present on earth are referred to as
(a) biodiversity (b) ecology
(c) population (d) biogeography

**Ans.** (*a*)

**2.** The basic rule of taxonomy is
I. a new taxon cannot be framed if the organism is different from the existing taxa.
II. orgainsms are described on the basis of morphology and other characteristics.

Choose the correct option. **Competency Based Que.**
(a) Statement I is correct, but II is incorrect
(b) Statement I is incorrect, but II is correct
(c) Both statements I and II are correct
(d) Both statements I and II are incorrect

**Ans.** (*b*) Statement I is incorrect, but II is correct. The incorrect statement can be corrected as

A new taxon can be framed if a new organism, different from existing taxa is discovered.

**3.** The term 'systematics' refers to **NCERT Exemplar**
(a) identification and study of organ systems
(b) identification and preservation of plants and animals
(c) diversity of kinds of organisms and their relationship
(d) study of habitats of organisms and their classification

**Ans.** (*c*)

**4.** Which of the following option is incorrect with respect to need for classification?
(a) Understanding adaption
(b) Determine life span of an organism
(c) Discovery of new organisms
(d) Convenience in study

**Ans.** (*b*)

**5.** Which of the following is not a characteristic of binomial nomenclature?
(a) The genus name is always capitalised.
(b) The specific epithet is unique to each genus.
(c) Names are often derived from Latin.
(d) Both parts of the name can be used interchangeably.

**Ans.** (*d*)

**6.** Which of the following is against the rules of ICBN? **Competency Based Que.**
(a) Handwritten scientific names should be underlined.
(b) Every species should have a generic name and a specific epithet.
(c) Scientific names are in Latin and should be Italicised.
(d) Generic and specific names should start with small letters.

**Ans.** (*d*)

**7.** What do *X*, *Y* and *Z* represent in a scientific name?

| *Mangifera* | *indica* | Linn |
|---|---|---|
| *X* | *Y* | *Z* |

(a) Specific epithet, generic name and authors name.
(b) Generic name, specific epithet and authors name.
(c) Specific epithet, authors name and generic name
(d) Authors name, generic name and specific epithet.

**Ans.** (*b*)

**8.** Consider the following statements.
I. Classification is not a single step process, but involves hierarchy of steps in which each step represents a rank or category.
II. Taxonomic hierarchy constitutes taxonomic categories.

Choose the correct option.
(a) Statement I is correct, but II is incorrect
(b) Statement I is incorrect, but II is correct
(c) Both statements I and II are correct
(d) Both statements I and II are incorrect

**Ans.** (*a*)

**9.** As we go from species to kingdom in a taxonomic hierarchy, the number of common characteristics **NCERT Exemplar**
(a) will decrease (b) will increase
(c) remain same (d) may increase or decrease

**Ans.** (*a*)

**10.** Arrange the following in ascending order of similar characteristics.
I. Family II. Genus
III. Class IV. Species

# Latest Course *Structure*

Time: 3 Hrs

Total Marks : 70

| Units | Title | Marks |
|---|---|---|
| I | Diversity of Living Organisms | 15 |
| II | Structural Organisation in Plants and Animals | 10 |
| III | Cell: Structure and Functions | 15 |
| IV | Plant Physiology | 12 |
| V | Human Physiology | 18 |
| | **Total** | **70** |

## UNIT I Diversity of Living Organisms

**Chapter 1 : The Living World**

Biodiversity; Need for classification; three domains of life; taxonomy and systematics; concept of species and taxonomical hierarchy; binomial nomenclature

**Chapter 2 : Biological Classification**

Five kingdom classification; Salient features and classification of Monera, Protista and Fungi into major groups; Lichens, Viruses and Viroids.

**Chapter 3 : Plant Kingdom**

Classification of plants into major groups; Salient and distinguishing features and a few examples of Algae, Bryophyta, Pteridophyta, Gymnospermae (Topics excluded – Angiosperms, Plant Life Cycle and Alternation of Generations)

**Chapter 4 : Animal Kingdom**

Salient features and classification of animals, non-chordates upto phyla level and chordates upto class level (salient features and at a few examples of each category).

*(No live animals or specimen should be displayed in school.)*

## UNIT II Structural Organisation in Plants and Animals

**Chapter 5 : Morphology of Flowering Plants**

Morphology of different parts of flowering plants: root, stem, leaf, inflorescence, flower, fruit and seed. Description of family Solanaceae

**Chapter 6 : Anatomy of Flowering Plants**

Anatomy and functions of tissue systems in dicots and monocots.

**Chapter 7 : Structural Organisation in Animals**

Morphology, Anatomy and functions of different systems (digestive, circulatory, respiratory, nervous and reproductive) of frog.

## UNIT III Cell : Structure and Functions

### Chapter 8 : Cell-The Unit of Life

Cell theory and cell as the basic unit of life, structure of prokaryotic and eukaryotic cells; Plant cell and animal cell; cell envelope; cell membrane, cell wall; cell organelles - structure and function; endomembrane system, endoplasmic reticulum, Golgi bodies, lysosomes, vacuoles, mitochondria, ribosomes, plastids, microbodies; cytoskeleton, cilia, flagella, centrioles (ultrastructure and function); nucleus.

### Chapter 9 : Biomolecules

Chemical constituents of living cells: biomolecules, structure and function of proteins, carbohydrates, lipids, nucleic acids; Enzyme - types, properties, enzyme action. (Topics excluded: Nature of Bond Linking Monomers in a Polymer, Dynamic State of Body Constituents – Concept of Metabolism, Metabolic Basis of Living, The Living State)

### Chapter 10 : Cell Cycle and Cell Division

Cell cycle, mitosis, meiosis and their significance.

## UNIT IV Plant Physiology

### Chapter 13 : Photosynthesis in Higher Plants

Photosynthesis as a means of autotrophic nutrition; site of photosynthesis, pigments involved in photosynthesis (elementary idea); photochemical and biosynthetic phases of photosynthesis; cyclic and non-cyclic photophosphorylation; chemiosmotic hypothesis; photorespiration; C3 and C4 pathways; factors affecting photosynthesis.

### Chapter 14 : Respiration in Plants

Exchange of gases; cellular respiration - glycolysis, fermentation (anaerobic), TCA cycle and electron transport system (aerobic); energy relations - number of ATP molecules generated; amphibolic pathways; respiratory quotient.

### Chapter 15 : Plant - Growth and Development

Seed germination; phases of plant growth and plant growth rate; conditions of growth; differentiation, dedifferentiation and redifferentiation; sequence of developmental processes in a plant cell; growth regulators - auxin, gibberellin, cytokinin, ethylene, ABA.

## UNIT V Human Physiology

### Chapter 17 : Breathing and Exchange of Gases

Respiratory organs in animals (recall only); Respiratory system in humans; mechanism of breathing and its regulation in humans - exchange of gases, transport of gases and regulation of respiration, respiratory volume; disorders related to respiration - asthma, emphysema, occupational respiratory disorders.

**Chapter 18 : Body Fluids and Circulation**

Composition of blood, blood groups, coagulation of blood; composition of lymph and its function; human circulatory system - Structure of human heart and blood vessels; cardiac cycle, cardiac output, ECG; double circulation; regulation of cardiac activity; disorders of circulatory system - hypertension, coronary artery disease, angina pectoris, heart failure.

**Chapter 19 : Excretory Products and Their Elimination**

Modes of excretion - ammonotelism, ureotelism, uricotelism; human excretory system – structure and function; urine formation, osmoregulation; regulation of kidney function - renin - angiotensin, atrial natriuretic factor, ADH and diabetes insipidus; role of other organs in excretion; disorders - uremia, renal failure, renal calculi, nephritis; dialysis and artificial kidney, kidney transplant.

**Chapter 20 : Locomotion and Movement**

Types of movement - ciliary, flagellar, muscular; skeletal muscle, contractile proteins and muscle contraction; skeletal system and its functions; joints; disorders of muscular and skeletal systems - myasthenia gravis, tetany, muscular dystrophy, arthritis, osteoporosis, gout.

**Chapter 21 : Neural Control and Coordination**

Neuron and nerves; Nervous system in humans - central nervous system; peripheral nervous system and visceral nervous system; generation and conduction of nerve impulse.

**Chapter 22 : Chemical Coordination and Integration**

Endocrine glands and hormones; human endocrine system - hypothalamus, pituitary, pineal, thyroid, parathyroid, adrenal, pancreas, gonads; mechanism of hormone action (elementary idea); role of hormones as messengers and regulators, hypo - and hyperactivity and related disorders; dwarfism, acromegaly, cretinism, goiter, exophthalmic goitre, diabetes, Addison's disease.

*Note: Diseases related to all the human physiological systems to be taught in brief.*

# Practicals

**Practicals should be conducted alongside the concepts taught in theory classes**

## LIST OF EXPERIMENTS

Time : 3 Hrs **Max Marks : 30**

| Evaluation Scheme | | Marks |
|---|---|---|
| One Major Experiment Part A (Experiment No- 1,3,7,8) | | 5 |
| One Minor Experiment Part A (Experiment No- 6,9,10,11,12,13) | | 4 |
| Slide Preparation Part A (Experiment No- 2,4,5) | | 5 |
| Spotting Part B | | 7 |
| Practical Record + Viva Voce | (Credit to the student's work over the academic session may be given) | 4 |
| Project Record + Viva Voce | | 5 |
| **Total** | | **30** |

### A. List of Experiments

1. Study and describe locally available common flowering plants, from family Solanaceae (Poaceae, Asteraceae or Brassicaceae can be substituted in case of particular geographical location) including dissection and display of floral whorls, anther and ovary to show number of chambers (floral formulae and floral diagrams), type of root (tap and adventitious); type of stem (herbaceous and woody); leaf (arrangement, shape, venation, simple and compound).
2. Preparation and study of T.S. of dicot and monocot roots and stems (primary).
3. Study of osmosis by potato osmometer.
4. Study of plasmolysis in epidermal peels (e.g. Rhoeo/lily leaves or flashy scale leaves of onion bulb).
5. Study of distribution of stomata on the upper and lower surfaces of leaves.
6. Comparative study of the rates of transpiration in the upper and lower surfaces of leaves.
7. Test for the presence of sugar, starch, proteins and fats in suitable plant and animal materials.
8. Separation of plant pigments through paper chromatography.
9. Study of the rate of respiration in flower buds/leaf tissue and germinating seeds.
10. Test for presence of urea in urine.
11. Test for presence of sugar in urine.
12. Test for presence of albumin in urine.
13. Test for presence of bile salts in urine.

## B. Study and observer the following (Spotting):

1. Parts of a compound microscope.
2. Specimens/slides/models and identification with reasons - Bacteria, *Oscillatoria, Spirogyra, Rhizopus,* mushroom, yeast, liverwort, moss, fern, pine, one monocotyledonous plant, one dicotyledonous plant and one lichen.
3. Virtual specimens/slides/models and identifying features of - *Amoeba, Hydra*, liverfluke, *Ascaris*, leech, earthworm, prawn, silkworm, honey bee, snail, starfish, shark, rohu, frog, lizard, pigeon and rabbit.
4. Mitosis in onion root tip cells and animals cells (grasshopper) from permanent slides.
5. Different types of inflorescence (cymose and racemose).
6. Human skeleton and different types of joints with the help of virtual images/models only.

01

CHAPTER

# The Living World

The earth is home to a diverse range of living organisms, including microorganisms, plants and animals. These organisms collectively represent '**The living world**'.
This wide variety of life includes millions of species, from tiny bacteria in the soil to tall trees in green forests.

**YOUR STUDY GOALS**

1.1 Diversity in Living World
1.2 Taxonomic Categories

**YOUR PRACTICE GOAL**

- Objective Type Questions (30 Qs ; MCQs, A-R)
  Case Based Questions (1)
- Subjective Type Questions
- (12 VSAs, 16 SAs, 3 LAs)

This chapter explores the diversity of living organisms as well as examines the scientific methods and approaches, which help in naming and classifying this wide variety of organisms into various categories.

## 1.1 Diversity in Living World

- The living world showcases a huge variety of species.
- The number of species that are known and described range between **1.7-1.8 million**. This number refers to the **biodiversity**.
- The term **biodiversity** or **biological diversity** means the total number and types of organisms present on the earth.
- As we continue to explore new areas and even old ones, new organisms are continuously being added. This huge available variety cannot be studied without the use of taxonomy.

### Taxonomy

- It is the branch of science that deals with characterisation, identification, classification and nomenclature of organisms.

- In early days, the taxonomy was primarily based on observable characters. In contrast, modern taxonomy studies rely on
  - **External** and **internal structures** (comparative morphology),
  - **Structure of cells** (cytology),
  - **Development process** (embryology)
  - **Ecological information of organisms** (ecology).

Taxonomy is the subset of systematics and together they provide comprehensive understanding of classification and evolutionary relationships of life forms.

## Systematics

- The word '**systematics**' is derived from the Latin word *Systema*, which means systematic arrangement of organisms.
- **Linnaeus** used ***Systema Naturae*** as the title of his publication.
- Systematics combines taxonomy with the study of evolutionary relationships to classify and name organisms.
- The scope of systematics was later enlarged to include identification, nomenclature and classification.
- In order to group the organisms we need to follow the following steps

### 1. Identification

- It is the process of recognising and determining the identity of an organism by examining its characteristics and comparing them to known species.
- It involves identifying an organism and comparing its similarities and dissimilarities with other known organisms.
- The morphological and anatomical characters are examined for proper identification.

### 2. Classification

- It is the process by which organisms are grouped into convenient categories based on similarities and dissimilarities in some easily observable characters. The scientific term for these categories is **taxa**.
- For example, insects, cats and dogs are grouped as animals based on their visible features, whereas wheat and rice are classified as plants.

#### Need for Classification

Classification is necessary for organisms due to following reasons

- Convenience in study
- Understanding adaptations
- Tracing evolutionary sequence
- Knowledge of phylogenetic relationships
- Discovery of new organisms

### 3. Nomenclature

- The system of naming living organisms in a way that a particular organism is known by the same name all over the world is called **nomenclature**.
- These names can be **common/local** or **scientific**.

#### Common/Local Names

- The common names or local names are given to an organism in a specific language in a particular region. There are different names of the same organism in different regions, even within a country.
- For example, rose is called 'Gulab' in Hindi, 'Golap' in Bengali, 'Oja' in Tamil.
- Various languages use different names for the same organism. Therefore, it is important to standardise the naming of organisms.

#### Scientific Names

- A scientific name is given by biologists.
- Each name represents a particular organism in all parts of the world.
- The system of providing scientific names is called **binomial nomenclature**.

## Binomial Nomenclature

- Binomial nomenclature was first developed by **Carolus Linnaeus.**
- It is the system of providing distinct and appropriate names to organisms, each name consisting of two components, first **generic name** (i.e. name of genus) and second **specific epithet** (i.e. name of species).
- For example, scientific name of mango is written as *Mangifera indica.*

- In this name, *Mangifera* represents the genus and *indica* is a particular species or specific epithet.
- The principle and criteria of naming plants and animals have been established by
  - **International Code of Botanical Nomenclature** (ICBN).
  - **International Code of Zoological Nomenclature** (ICZN).

### Rules of Binomial Nomenclature

Nomenclature of organisms follow certain universal rules, which are as follows

- The names are generally in **Latin** and written in **Italics**.
- They are Latinised or derived from Latin irrespective of their origin.
- The first word in a biological name represents the **genus**, while the second word denotes the **specific epithet**.
- Both the words in a biological name, when handwritten, are separately **underlined** or printed in **Italics** to indicate their Latin origin.
- The first word denoting the genus starts with a **capital letter**, while, the specific epithet starts with a **small letter**, e.g. *Mangifera indica*.
- Name of the author appears after the specific epithet, i.e. at the end of the biological name and is written in an abbreviated form, e.g. *Mangifera indica* Linn, Linn is for Linnaeus.
- This indicates that this species was first described by Linnaeus.
- The following figure provides a clearer explanation of the concept.

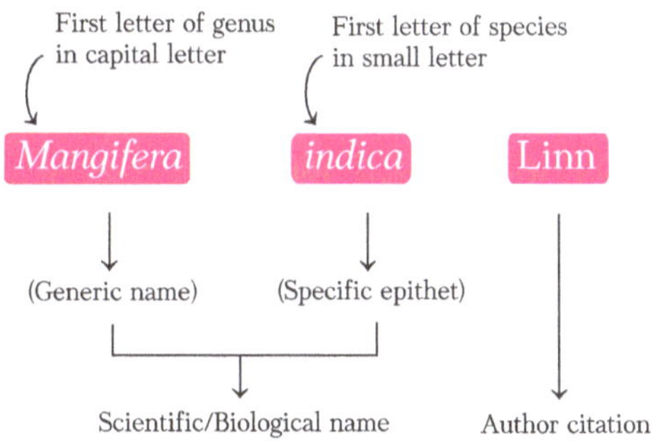


### Quick Test 1

1. Name the branch of science that was primarily based on observable characters.
2. **State True or False.**
   Systematics studies show how different living things are connected through their evolutionary relationships.
3. Mention the process of describing an organism and assigning the correct name to it.
4. Name the scientist that developed the formal system of naming species of living organisms using two Latin-based names.
5. **State True or False.**
   In the system of binomial nomenclature, it is standard for the genus name to be lowercase, while the species name is typically written in capitalised.

## 1.2 Taxonomic Categories

- Classification is not a single step process.
- It involves hierarchy of steps in which each step represents a **rank** or **category**.
- Each category, in fact, represents a rank and is commonly termed as **taxon**.
- Since, the category is a part of overall taxonomic arrangement, it is called the **taxonomic category** and all categories together constitute the **taxonomic hierarchy**.

### Taxonomic Hierarchy

- The system of arranging taxonomic categories in specific order is called **taxonomic hierarchy**.
- Taxonomic category and hierarchy can be demonstrated by the following example.
  - Insects represent a large group of organisms sharing common features like three pair of jointed legs.
  - It means that insects are recognisable concrete objects which can be classified and therefore were given a **rank** or **category**.
  - Groups represent **category** and category further denotes **rank**.
  - Each rank or taxon represents a unit of classification.

- The taxonomic categories which are universally used in hierarchical classification of organisms are seven in number.
- In descending order, these are– kingdom, phylum or division (for plants), class, order, family, genus and species.
- These categories are also divided into **sub-categories**, which facilitate more accurate and scientific classification of various taxa.
- This system not only organise organisms systematically but also highlights shared traits within each group.
- All the members of taxonomic categories possess some similar characters, which are different from those of others.
- Similarity of characters decreases with the rise in hierarchy.
- Thus, the maximum similarity occurs in species, which is also the **lowest category** in the hierarchy of categories.

## 1. Species

- It is a group of individual organisms with fundamental similarities.
- One species can be distinguished from other closely related species, based on distinct morphological differences.
- The member of one species resemble each other more closely than the individuals of other species.
- Each species is identifiable by unique characteristics. For example, *Mangifera indica* (mango), *Solanum tuberosum* (potato) and *Panthera leo* (lion) are separate species. In these scientific names *indica, tuberosum* and *leo* represent the specific epithets while, the first words *Mangifera, Solanum* and *Panthera* are genera and represent another higher level of taxon or category.
- Each genus may have one or more than one specific epithets representing different organisms, but having morphological similarities, e.g. *Panthera* has another specific epithet called *tigris, Solanum* includes species like *nigrum* and *melongena.*
- Human beings belong to the species-*sapiens*, which is grouped in genus–*Homo*. The scientific name, thus for human beings is written as *Homo sapiens.*

**TEACHER'S TIP**
Species are groups of organisms that can interbreed and produce fertile offspring. This ability to reproduce sets them apart from larger categories like genus, family and order, where members may not be able to breed with each other. This shows that species are the basic level of classification, based on how they reproduce.

## 2. Genus

It comprises a group of related species, which has more characters in common in comparison to species of other genera. For example,

- Among plants, potato and brinjal are two different species that belongs to the genus–*Solanum.*
- Among animals, lion (*Panthera leo*), leopard (*P. pardus*) and tiger (*P. tigris*) all belong to the genus–*Panthera.*
- Genus panthera differs from another genus–*Felis* which includes cats.

## 3. Family

- It is a group of related genera with less number of similarities as compared to genus and species. For example,
  - Among plants, the genera–*Solanum, Petunia* and *Datura* are placed in the family– Solanaceae.
  - Among animals, the genus–*Panthera* (Lion, tiger and leopard) and *Felis* (Cat) belong to the same family- Felidae.
- Similarly, cats and dogs show similarities in feeding habits, but belong to different families-Felidae and Canidae, respectively.
- In case of plants, the genera of one family are separable from genera of a related family by important differences in both vegetative and reproductive features.

## 4. Order

It is a group of one or more related families, containing fewer shared characteristics than those found in a family or genus. For example, as

- Plant families are grouped into order based on floral characters as Convolvulaceae, Solanaceae are included in the order-Polymoniales.

- Animal families like Felidae and Canidae are included in the order-Carnivora.

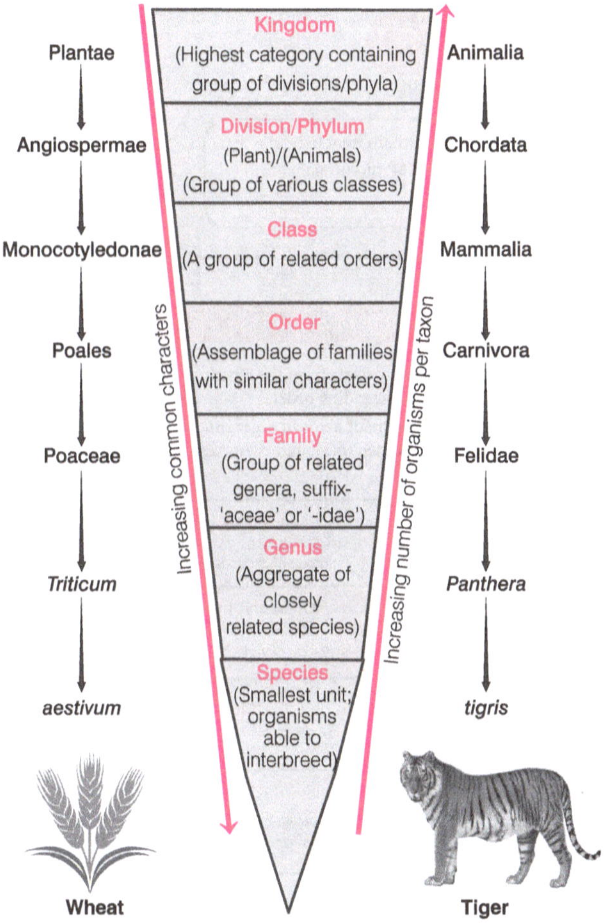


**Fig. 1.1** Taxonomic categories showing hierarchical arrangement order

## 5. Class

- It is a major category which includes related orders.
- For example, the order-Primata comprising monkey, gorilla and gibbon along with the order-Carnivora, that includes animals like tiger, cat and dog, are placed in class-Mammalia, which has other orders also.

## 6. Phylum or Division

- It is a taxonomic category higher than class and lower in rank to kingdom. The term phylum is used for animals, while division is commonly used for plants.
- Different classes having some specific and common characters are placed in a phylum or division.
- For example, based on presence of notochord and dorsal hollow neural system animals of phylum-Chordata contains following classes– Pisces, Amphibia, Reptilia, Aves and Mammalia.

## 7. Kingdom

- It is known to be the highest category in taxonomy.
- This includes all the organisms which share a set of distinguished characters, e.g. all the animals belonging to various phyla are assigned the highest category called kingdom– Animalia. Similarly, all the plants are kept in kingdom–Plantae.
- At the highest taxonomic level (kingdom), classification becomes more complicated as the groups lacks the shared characteristics seen in lower taxa.

**Organisms with their Taxonomic Categories**

| Common Name | Man | Housefly | Mango | Wheat |
|---|---|---|---|---|
| **Scientific Name** | *Homo sapiens* | *Musca domestica* | *Mangifera indica* | *Triticum aestivum* |
| **Species** | *sapiens* | *domestica* | *indica* | *aestivum* |
| **Genus** | *Homo* | *Musca* | *Mangifera* | *Triticum* |
| **Family** | Hominidae | Muscidae | Anacardiaceae | Poaceae |
| **Order** | Primata | Diptera | Sapindales | Poales |
| **Class** | Mammalia | Insecta | Dicotyledonae | Monocotyle-donae |
| **Phylum/ Division** | Chordata | Arthropoda | Angiospermae | Angiospermae |
| **Kingdom** | Animalia | Animalia | Plantae | Plantae |

### Quick Test 2

1. What term describes the hierarchical levels used by scientists to systematically classify and identify organisms?
2. At which taxonomic level will the common characteristics between a lion and a leopard be the greatest?
3. **State True or False.**
   In the context of the taxonomic hierarchy, it is important to note that the family falls under the order, indicating that the order is a broader classification.
4. In exploring the various levels of classification in taxonomy, which rank is recognised as the most inclusive?
5. Provide the scientific names for the tiger and the potato.

# Mind Map

## The Living World

The earth is home to a wide range of living organisms, each organism adapted to different habitats. Together, these organisms form the living world, which includes a great variety of microorganisms, plants (flora) and animals (fauna).

### Taxonomy

It is the branch of science that classifies living organisms based on their features, using rules of identification.

### Components of Taxonomy

There are four components of taxonomy.

### Systematics

It is the branch of biology that deals with the classification, naming and evolutionary relationships of organisms.

### Characterisation

Describing the traits and features of an organism.

### Classification

Grouping organisms based on shared characteristics.

### Identification

Recognising and determining an organism's place in classification.

### Nomenclature

It is the process of giving scientific names to organisms based on rules set by the ICBN and ICZN to simplify the study of organisms.

### Binomial Nomenclature

- This system is developed by Carolus Linnaeus.
- According to this system each name comprises of two components, i.e. generic name and specific name.
- Generic name represents the genus while a specific name represents the species.
- Both words are written in Italics or underlined.

### Taxonomical Hierarchy

- The hierarchy starts from the kingdom and goes down to species in descending order.
- This arrangement helps in organising and categorising organisms based on shared characteristics.

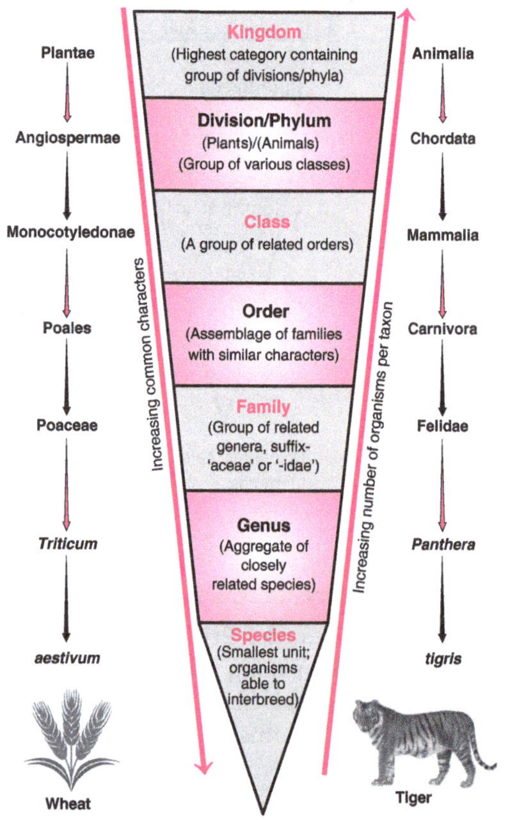

# Exam Pattern Questions

## Objective Type Questions

### Multiple Choice Questions

**1.** The number and types of organisms present on earth are referred to as

(a) biodiversity (b) ecology
(c) population (d) biogeography

**Ans.** (*a*)

**2.** The basic rule of taxonomy is

**I.** a new taxon cannot be framed if the organism is different from the existing taxa.

**II.** orgainsms are described on the basis of morphology and other characteristics.

Choose the correct option. **Competency Based Que.**

(a) Statement I is correct, but II is incorrect
(b) Statement I is incorrect, but II is correct
(c) Both statements I and II are correct
(d) Both statements I and II are incorrect

**Ans.** (*b*) Statement I is incorrect, but II is correct. The incorrect statement can be corrected as

A new taxon can be framed if a new organism, different from existing taxa is discovered.

**3.** The term 'systematics' refers to **NCERT Exemplar**

(a) identification and study of organ systems
(b) identification and preservation of plants and animals
(c) diversity of kinds of organisms and their relationship
(d) study of habitats of organisms and their classification

**Ans.** (*c*)

**4.** Which of the following option is incorrect with respect to need for classification?

(a) Understanding adaption
(b) Determine life span of an organism
(c) Discovery of new organisms
(d) Convenience in study

**Ans.** (*b*)

**5.** Which of the following is not a characteristic of binomial nomenclature?

(a) The genus name is always capitalised.
(b) The specific epithet is unique to each genus.
(c) Names are often derived from Latin.
(d) Both parts of the name can be used interchangeably.

**Ans.** (*d*)

**6.** Which of the following is against the rules of ICBN? **Competency Based Que.**

(a) Handwritten scientific names should be underlined.
(b) Every species should have a generic name and a specific epithet.
(c) Scientific names are in Latin and should be Italicised.
(d) Generic and specific names should start with small letters.

**Ans.** (*d*)

**7.** What do *X*, *Y* and *Z* represent in a scientific name?

| | | |
|---|---|---|
| *Mangifera* | *indica* | Linn |
| *X* | *Y* | *Z* |

(a) Specific epithet, generic name and authors name.
(b) Generic name, specific epithet and authors name.
(c) Specific epithet, authors name and generic name
(d) Authors name, generic name and specific epithet.

**Ans.** (*b*)

**8.** Consider the following statements.

**I.** Classification is not a single step process, but involves hierarchy of steps in which each step represents a rank or category.

**II.** Taxonomic hierarchy constitutes taxonomic categories.

Choose the correct option.

(a) Statement I is correct, but II is incorrect
(b) Statement I is incorrect, but II is correct
(c) Both statements I and II are correct
(d) Both statements I and II are incorrect

**Ans.** (*a*)

**9.** As we go from species to kingdom in a taxonomic hierarchy, the number of common characteristics **NCERT Exemplar**

(a) will decrease (b) will increase
(c) remain same (d) may increase or decrease

**Ans.** (*a*)

**10.** Arrange the following in ascending order of similar characteristics.

**I.** Family **II.** Genus
**III.** Class **IV.** Species

(a) Class < Family < Genus < Species
(b) Family < Class < Genus < Species
(c) Species < Genus < Family < Class
(d) Class < Genus < Species < Family

**Ans.** (*a*)

**11.** **Can you identify the correct sequence of taxonomical categories?** **NCERT**

(a) Species → Order → Phylum → Kingdom
(b) Genus → Species → Order → Kingdom
(c) Species → Genus → Order → Phylum
(d) None of the above

**Ans.** (*c*)

**12.** **Species is considered as .....*A*..... . One is able to distinguish one species from other closely related species based on .....*B*..... .** **NCERT Exemplar**

| | *A* | *B* |
|---|---|---|
| (a) | Smallest taxon of classification | Habitat |
| (b) | Highest taxon of classification | Anatomical characters |
| (c) | Smallest taxon of classification | Morphological differences |
| (d) | Highest taxon of classification | Mode of nutrition |

**Ans.** (*c*)

**13.** **Genus represents** **NCERT Exemplar**

(a) an individual plant or animal
(b) a collection of plants or animals
(c) group of closely related species of plants or animals
(d) None of the above

**Ans.** (*c*)

**14.** **If a newly discovered organism is placed in the genus–*Felis*, which of the following statement must also be true?**

(a) It is a member of the kingdom-Plantae.
(b) It belongs to the family-Canidae.
(c) It shares the genus with domestic cats.
(d) It is a species of plant.

**Ans.** (*c*) If an organism is placed in the genus– *Felis*, it is related to domestic cats. This genus is specific to the cat family, distinguishing it from plants and other animal families.

**15.** **Which of the following is not correctly matched with its family?**

(a) Man – Hominidae (b) Wheat – Anacardiaceae
(c) Housefly – Muscidae (d) Cat – Canidae

**Ans.** (*d*)

**16.** **Choose odd-one-out from the series given below.**

**Series I Primata, Poales, Sapindales and Insecta**

**Series II *Mangifera, Solanum, Datura* and *Petunia***

**Competency Based Que.**

(a) Insecta and *Mangifera*
(b) *Datura* and Poales
(c) Primata and *Petunia*
(d) Sapindales and *Solanum*

**Ans.** (*a*) Insecta and *Mangifera* are odd-one-out from series I and II, respectively.

In series I, Primata, Diptera and Sapindales represent order, while Insecta represents a class.

In series II, *Solanum, Petunia* and *Datura* represents the genera that belong to family-Solanaceae, while *Mangifera* belongs to family-Anacardiaceae.

**17.** **Go through the statements given below and choose the option with all incorrect statements.** **Competency Based Que.**

I. **Cats and dogs belong to same order.**
II. **Species is less general in characters as compared to genus.**
III. **Lions and cats belong to same family.**
IV. **The number of common characters decrease from kingdom to species.**

Codes

(a) I and III (b) II, III and II
(c) Only IV (d) I and IV

**Ans.** (*c*) Statement IV is incorrect and can be corrected as

The number of common characters increase from kingdom to species.

**18.** **Identify the incorrect statements from the following.** **Competency Based Que.**

I. **The lower the taxon, the fewer characteristics the members within the taxon share.**
II. **A family is an assemblage of orders that exhibit similar characteristics.**
III. **The class-Mammalia includes orders like Carnivora and Primata.**

IV. **Binomial nomenclature was introduced by Carolus Linnaeus.**

V. **The order-Carnivora includes families such as Felidae and Canidae.**

Select the correct answer from the options given below.

(a) I and II (b) III, IV and V
(c) IV and V (d) II and III

**Ans.** (*a*) Statements I and II are incorrect and can be corrected as.

I. Higher the taxon, the fewer characteristics the members within the taxon share.
II. A family is an assemblage of genus that exhibit similar characteristics.

**19. The taxonomic unit 'phylum' in the classification of animals is equivalent to which hierarchical level in classfication of plants?** **NCERT Exemplar**

(a) Class (b) Order
(c) Division (d) Family

**Ans.** (*c*)

**20. Choose the incorrect match.**

(a) Order – a group of related families
(b) Genus – a group of related species
(c) Class – a group of related orders
(d) Division – a group of related phyla

**Ans.** (*d*) The match pair given in option (d) is incorrect. It can be corrected as
The term division is commonly used for plants to represent a group of related classes.

**21. The correct ascending order of taxonomic categories of housefly is given by**

(a) *Musca* Insecta Diptera Muscidae
(b) Muscidae Diptera *Musca* Insecta
(c) *Musca* Muscidae Diptera Insecta
(d) Muscidae *Musca* Diptera Insecta

**Ans.** (*c*)

**22. Match the following columns.**

| | Column I (Taxonomic Hierarchy) | | Column II (Examples) |
|---|---|---|---|
| A. | Family | 1. | Diptera |
| B. | Order | 2. | Arthropoda |
| C. | Class | 3. | Muscidae |
| D. | Phylum | 4. | Insecta |

**Codes**

| | A | B | C | D |
|---|---|---|---|---|
| (a) | 3 | 1 | 4 | 2 |
| (b) | 3 | 2 | 4 | 1 |
| (c) | 4 | 3 | 2 | 1 |
| (d) | 4 | 2 | 1 | 3 |

**Ans.** (*a*)

**23. Match the following and choose the correct option.** **NCERT Exemplar**

| | Column I | | Column II |
|---|---|---|---|
| A. | Family | 1. | *tuberosum* |
| B. | Kingdom | 2. | Polymoniales |
| C. | Order | 3. | *Solanum* |
| D. | Species | 4. | Plantae |
| E. | Genus | 5. | Solanaceae |

**Codes**

| | A | B | C | D | E |
|---|---|---|---|---|---|
| (a) | 4 | 3 | 5 | 2 | 1 |
| (b) | 5 | 4 | 2 | 1 | 3 |
| (c) | 4 | 5 | 2 | 1 | 3 |
| (d) | 5 | 3 | 2 | 1 | 4 |

**Ans.** (*b*)

## Assertion-Reason Questions

**Direction** (Q. Nos. 1-7) *In each of the following questions, a statement of Assertion (A) is given followed by corresponding statement of Reason (R). Of the statements, mark the correct answer.*

(a) Both A and R are true and R is the correct explanation of A.
(b) Both A and R are true, but R is not the correct explanation of A.
(c) A is true, but R is false.
(d) A is false, but R is true.

**1. Assertion** (A) Taxonomy helps scientists to organise and understand the diversity of life by grouping organisms in a systematic way.

**Reason** (R) Systematics and taxonomy are used interchangeably by the biologists.

**Ans.** (*b*)

**2. Assertion** (A) Taxonomic studies require correct classification and identification of organisms.

**Reason** (R) Taxonomic studies are useful in knowing bioresources and their diversity.

**Ans.** (*b*) Both A and R are true, but R is not the correct explanation of A.

Taxonomic studies focus on accurately classifying and identifying organisms, which is essential for understanding the variety of life. This clarity helps scientists to communicate and study different species more effectively.

**3.** **Assertion** (A) The higher the category, easier it is to determine the relationship to other taxa at the same level.

**Reason** (R) In higher taxa there are more characteristics that the members within the taxa share.

**Ans.** (*c*) A is true, but R is false. R can be corrected as

In higher taxa there are fewer characteristics that the members within the taxa share.

**4.** **Assertion** (A) The genus–*Panthera* includes multiple species such as *Panthera leo* and *Panthera pardus*.

**Reason** (R) Each genus may have one or more than one specific epithet.

**Ans.** (*a*)

**5.** **Assertion** (A) Species is a group of individuals with fundamental similarities.

**Reason** (R) *indica, leo, tuberosum* represent such group of individuals.

**Ans.** (*b*) Both A and R are true, but R is not the correct explanation of A.

A species is defined as a group of individuals that share fundamental similarities, such as physical characteristics, behaviour as well as genetic makeup and can breed with each other to produce fertile offspring.

**6.** **Assertion** (A) There are seven major categories in the hierarchy of taxonomy.

**Reason** (R) Sub-categories facilitate sound and scientific placement of various taxa.

**Ans.** (*b*)

**7.** Given below is the taxonomic category showing arrangement in descending order.

Study this figure and comment upon the appropriateness of the Assertion and the Reason.

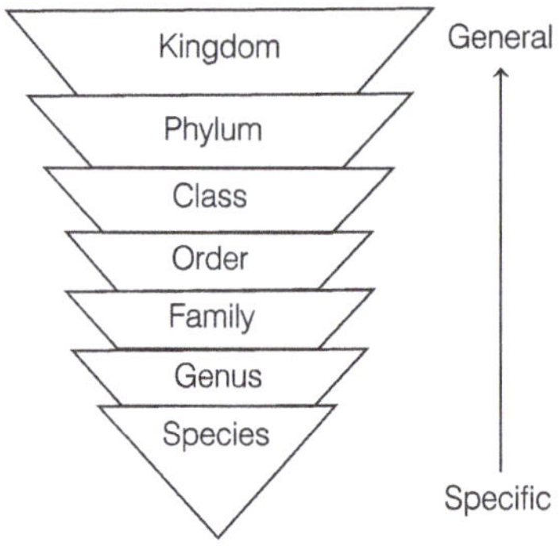


**Assertion** (A) As we go from species to kingdom in a taxonomic hierarchy, the number of common characteristic will decrease.

**Reason** (R) Any lower grade of classification (genus) has members with more similarities as compared to higher grade of classification (family).

**Ans.** (*a*)

# Subjective Questions

## Very Short Answer Type Questions

**1. All the organisms are not yet identified on the earth. Justify the statement.**

**Ans.** There are diverse habitats on earth hosting millions of living organisms. Due to limited number of taxonomists, absence of thorough survey of different areas and occurrence of several inaccessible regions, e.g. hot springs, underwater reefs, etc, it is difficult to identify all the organisms.

**2. Which are the basic processes in the taxonomy?**

**Ans.** The basic processes in taxonomy are

(i) Characterisation (ii) Identification

(iii) Classification (iv) Nomenclature (½ × 4)

**3. What different criteria would you choose to classify people that you meet often?** NCERT

**Ans.** Different criteria that can be used to classify individuals we frequently encounter include behaviour, geographic location, physical appearance, gender and family relationships, among others.

**4. Why is it difficult to assign common names to all living organisms?**

**Ans.** It is difficult to assign common name to all organisms because the organism may have several names in given language. It can create confusion to the people while recalling organism.

**5. How are living organisms divided into different taxa? What is the name given to this process?**

**Ans.** Living organisms can be divided into different taxa based on their characteristics. This process of classification is called taxonomy. (½ + ½)

**6. What does ICZN stands for?** NCERT Exemplar

**Ans.** ICZN stands for International Code of Zoological Nomenclature.

**7. Given below is the scientific name of Mango, identify the correctly written name.**
***Mangifera Indica, Mangifera indica*** NCERT

**Ans.** The correctly written scientific name of Mango is *Mangifera indica*.

**8. Write the hierarchical rank group in which the members are capable of interbreeding or exchanging genes among themselves.**

**Ans.** The group in which the members are capable of interbreeding or exchanging genes among themselves is species. It is considered as the lowest taxonomic category.

**9. Write species of each genus.**

| Common name | Genus | Species |
|---|---|---|
| Leopard | *Panthera* | ......... |
| Brinjal | *Solanum* | ......... |

**Ans.** *Panthera pardus* (leopard).

*Solanum melongena* (brinjal). (½ + ½)

**10. Brinjal and potato belong to the same genus- *Solanum*, but two different species. What defines them as separate species?** NCERT Exemplar

**Ans.** Brinjal and potato belong to same genus as they share some common correlated characters.

They belong to different species because they have

(i) different morphological features. (½)

(ii) reproductive isolation (inability to interbreed). (½)

**11. Cats and dogs belong to different families, but are classified under the same order–Carnivora. Based on which characteristics are they placed in the order–Carnivora?** Competency Based Que.

**Ans.** Cats and dogs are placed in the order–Carnivora due to shared traits like large canine teeths, strong claws for hunting and a digestive system specialised for meat consumption.

**12. Which of the following possess more characters in common?**

**(i) Phylum or family (ii) Species or genus**

**(iii) Class or order**

**Ans.** (i) Family, (ii) Species, (iii) Order

## Short Answer Type Questions

**1. In a given habitat we have 20 plant species and 20 animal species. Should we call it as 'diversity' or 'biodiversity'? Justify your answer.**
NCERT Exemplar, Competency Based Que.

**Ans.** In a given habitat, there are existing 20 plant species and 20 animal species. They will of course exhibit the biodiversity of that given habitat because diversity refers to variation in a broad term and can be applied to any area. Whereas biodiversity is a degree of variation of life forms within a specified area.

**2. Why are living organisms classified?** NCERT

**Ans.** Living organisms are classified because

(i) There are millions of organisms on the earth, which need a proper system of classification for their easy identification and methodical studies.

(ii) A number of new organisms are discovered each year. They require a particular system to be identified and placed in correct position in a group. (1 + 1)

**3. Why there is a need to standardise the system of naming of living organisms?**

**Ans.** There are millions of living organisms in the world. Often, these organisms are known by their local names that vary from place to place, even within a country. Hence, the naming process of living organism is standardised in a way that a particular organism is known by the same name all over the world in the scientific community.

**4. A plant may have different names in different regions of the country or world. How do botanists solve this problem?** **NCERT Exemplar**

**Ans.** Botanists use binomial nomenclature to solve this problem. A scientific name is given to the plant based on certain principles and criteria. The scientific name of a particular plant is same all over the world and is not given to any other plant.

**5. Why are classification systems changing every now and then?** **NCERT, Competency Based Que.**

**Ans.** Now-a-days, biologists use several principles and criteria to classify the organisms. These are based on morphology, anatomy, cytology, physiology, phylogeny, reproduction, evolution, biochemistry and genetics. Thus, there are several characteristic differences which help in classification. This is the reason of change in classification systems every now and then.

**6. Distinguish between taxonomy and systematics.**

**Ans.** Differences between taxonomy and systematics are as follows

| Taxonomy | Systematics |
|---|---|
| It is related to identification, nomenclature and classification of organisms. | It is the science of identification, nomenclature and classification of organisms, focusing on evolutionary relationships. |
| Taxonomic studies are based on rules and principles of classification. | Systematics use phylogenetic methods to study evolutionary relationships between organisms. |

(1+1)

**7. What do we learn from identification of individual and populations?** **NCERT**

**Ans.** Identification of individuals and populations categorise them into a specific species. Each species has unique characteristic features. On the basis of these features, organisms can be distinguished from other closely related species, e.g.

| Genus | Species | |
|---|---|---|
| *Solanum* | *tuberosum* | Both are two different species included in genus - *Solanum*. |
| *Solanum* | *nigrum* | |

**8. Discuss in detail the binomial nomenclature of living organisms as given by Carlous Linnaeus.**

**Ans.** Refer to text on page no. 2 and 3.

**9. *Mangifera indica* Linn.**

(i) Give the common name of the plant.

(ii) What do the first two parts of the name denote?

(iii) Why are they written in Italics?

(iv) What is the meaning of Linn written at the end of the name?

**Ans.** (i) **Common name** Mango. (½)

(ii) First part represents the genus or generic name, while the second part represents the specific epithets. (1)

(iii) They are written in Italics in order to highlight their Latin origin. (½)

(iv) Linn written at the end of the name is the abbreviation of the name of scientist Linnaeus, who described the species. (1)

**10. What makes species a basic taxonomic category?**

**Ans.** Species is the lowest of a population or basic taxonomic category which consists of individuals that resemble one another more closely than individuals of other species.

The members of a species interbreed freely and are reproductively isolated from members of other species. These features make the species basic taxonomic category.

**11. Distinguish between taxon and category.**

**Ans.** Differences between taxon and category are as follows

| Taxon | Category |
|---|---|
| A taxon deals with real biological objects. | A category is an abstract term that simply represents a rank or level in classification. |
| Taxon may belong to any ranking. | It belongs to one particular ranking. |

(1 × 2)

**12. Write the relation between taxonomic category and taxonomic hierarchy. Fill in the missing category in following hierarchical arrangement in ascending order.**

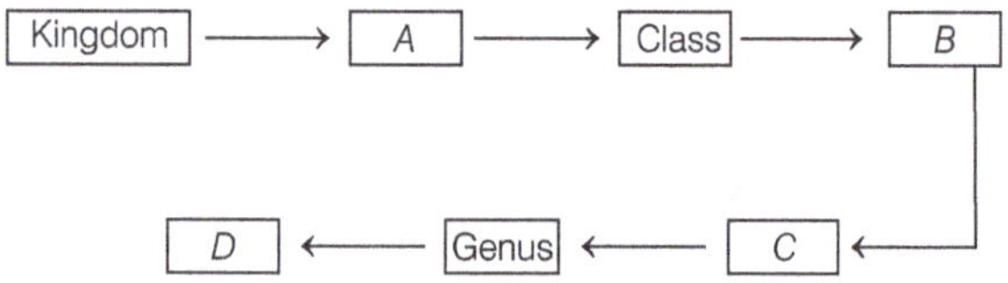

**Ans.** The category is a part of overall taxonomic arrangement called taxonomic category. All the categories together constitute the taxonomic hierarchy.

*A*–Phylum, *B*–Order, *C*–Family, *D*–Species (1 + 2)

**13. Define a taxon. Give some examples of taxa at different hierarchical levels.** **NCERT**

**Ans.** A taxon is a group of one or more organisms that share common characteristics and are classified together at any taxonomic level. (1)

Some examples of taxa at different hierarchial levels are as follows

**Kingdom** : Animalia
**Phylum** : Chordata
**Class** : Mammalia
**Order** : Carnivora
**Family** : Felidae
**Genus** : *Panthera*
**Species** : *tigris* (2)

**14. Illustrate the taxonomical hierarchy with suitable examples of a plant and an animal.** **NCERT**

**Ans.** Taxonomical hierarchy for plants is as follows

**Kingdom** : Plantae
**Phylum** : Angiospermae
**Class** : Dicotyledonae
**Order** : Solanales
**Family** : Solanaceae
**Genus** : *Solanum*
**Species** : *melongena* (1½)

Taxonomical hierarchy for animals is as follows

**Kingdom** : Animalia
**Phylum** : Chordata
**Class** : Mammalia
**Order** : Carnivora
**Family** : Felidae
**Genus** : *Felis*
**Species** : *catus* (1½)

**15. Try to collect all the currently accepted meanings for the word 'species'. Discuss with your teacher the meaning of species of case of higher plants and animals on one hand and bacteria on the other hand.** **NCERT**

**Ans.** The term 'species' refers to a group of organisms that can interbreed and produce fertile offspring, which is commonly used for higher plants and animals. However, for bacteria, which reproduce asexually, the definition is based on genetic similarity rather than interbreeding. Therefore, the meaning of species can vary depending on the organism, with sexual reproduction being a key factor for higher plants and animals, while genetic similarity is more relevant for bacteria.

**16. Place the following species in their respective categories.**

**(i) Housefly** **(ii) Mango**

**(iii) Man**

**Ans.** Refer to text on page no. 5. (1 × 3)

## Long Answer Type Questions

**1. (i) A scientist has come across a plant, which he feels is a new species. How will he go about its identification, classification and nomenclature?**

**(ii) Distinguish between taxon and genus.**

**Ans.** (i) The scientist has to study the morphological and anatomical characters of the plants/plant parts, compare the characteristic features with the similar information available in the scientific literature and after that he can decide the exact systematic position of the plant, name it according to the rules of binomial nomenclature and fix it's systemic position. (2½)

(ii)

| | Taxon | Genus |
|---|---|---|
| (a) | Taxon is a group of organisms classified together based on shared characteristics. | A genus is a taxonomic rank that groups closely related species sharing common characteristics. |
| (b) | It refers to groups like kingdom Animalia and family–Felidae. | It includes specific groups like *Homo* (humans) and *Panthera* (lions) |

(2½)

**2. Define a taxon. What is meant by taxonomic hierarchy? Give a flow diagram from the lowest to highest category for a plant and an animal. What happens to the number of individuals and numbers of shared characters as we go up the taxonomical hierarchy?** **NCERT Exemplar**

**Ans.** Taxon is a scientific term used for different categories of classification. (1)

Taxonomic hierarchy is the arrangement of different taxonomic categories in ascending order with respect to number of shared characters. It describes the complete systematic position of any living organism. (1)

Given below is the flow diagram of taxonomic hierarchy

**Flowchart for Plant Species**

Species → Genus → Family → Order → Class → Division → Kingdom. (½)

**Flowchart for Animal Species**

Species → Genus → Family → Order → Class → Phylum → Kingdom. (½)

As we move up in the taxonomic hierarchy, from species to kingdom, the number of shared characters decrease.

At lower taxonomic levels, the organisms tend to have more shared characters. Higher the taxonomic level greater is the difficulty in determining the relationship of one taxa to other taxa at the same level.

The number of individuals increase from lower to higher taxonomic categories. (2)

**3. Define and understand the following terms.**

**(i) Phylum** **(ii) Class**
**(iii) Family** **(iv) Order**
**(v) Genus** NCERT

**Ans.** (i) **Phylum** A category, which is higher than class and consisting of one or more related classes with certain common features. Botanists use the term division instead of phylum.

(ii) **Class** A taxonomic category higher in rank than order and consisting of one or more related orders with some common features.

(iii) **Family** A category having one or more related genera with some similar common features.

(iv) **Order** (Cohort) A category consisting of one or more related families having some common or correlated characters.

(v) **Genus** A taxonomic category higher in rank than species having one or more assemblage of related species, having a common ancestory and similar correlated characters. (1 × 5)

## Source Based/ Case Based/ Passage Based Question

**1. A research team studying a remote rainforest discovers a new species of orchid that blooms only during the rainy season. This orchid has a unique structure that attracts a specific type of bee for pollination and displays vibrant colours that differ from other known orchids in the region. The team aims to classify this new species within the existing taxonomic framework.**

**(i) Identify the taxonomic level that would be most affected by this discovery and explain why.**

**(ii) What distinctive feature of the orchid's structure is important for its identification?**

**(iii) What key factors should the research team consider when classifying this new orchid species?**

*Or* **(iii) Discuss two reasons why the classification and naming of this new orchid species are essential following its discovery.**

**Ans.** (i) The taxonomic level most affected would be the genus. Discovering a new species may lead to the creation of a new genus or an adjustment in the existing classification of related species to accommodate this unique orchid. (1)

(ii) The unique floral structure that attracts a specific type of bee is crucial for its identification. (1)

(iii) The research team should consider both morphological and evolutionary traits when classifying the new orchid species. Morphological traits, such as flower shape and colour, help in identifying and distinguishing the species. Evolutionary traits, including genetic relationships with related orchids, provide insights into its lineage and adaptive strategies, ensuring a more accurate classification. (2)

*Or*

(iii) (a) Proper classification and naming allow scientists and conservationists to communicate effectively about the orchid, ensuring that discussions about its ecological role and conservation needs are clear and standardised across the scientific community. (1)

(b) Naming the new species enables researchers to document and study its characteristics, distribution and interactions with other organisms. This is crucial for ongoing ecological studies and for developing conservation strategies tailored to protect the newly identified species and its habitat. (1)

# SELF ASSESSMENT TEST

## Multiple Choice Questions

**1.** What does binomial nomenclature refer to?

(a) Naming of an organism using species and variety.
(b) Naming of an organism using family and genus.
(c) Naming of an organism using order and family.
(d) Naming of an organism using genus and species.

**2.** Select the correctly written scientific name.

(a) *Homo* sapiens (b) *Triticum Aestivum* (c) *musca domestica* (d) *Mangifera indica*

**3.** In the classification of organisms, what is the correct order of taxonomic groups from smallest to largest?

(a) Family, Genus, Class, Order and Phylum
(b) Genus, Phylum, Order, Family and Class
(c) Genus, Family, Order, Class and Phylum
(d) Species, Genus, Order, Family and Phylum

**4.** The common characteristics between lion and cat will be minimum at the level of

(a) genus (b) kingdom (c) phylum (d) species

**5.** Which of the following is incorrectly matched with its respective taxonomic group?

(a) Human – Primata (Order)
(b) Mango - Anacardiaceae (Family)
(c) Wheat – Poales (Order)
(d) Housefly – Primata (Order)

**6.** Which of the following taxonomic categories ranks immediately above "genus"?

(a) Species
(b) Order
(c) Class
(d) Family

## Assertion-Reason Questions

**Direction** (Q. Nos. 7-11) *In each of the following questions, a statement of Assertion (A) is given followed by corresponding statement of Reason (R). Of the statements, mark the correct answer.*

(a) Both A and R are true and R is the correct explanation of A.
(b) Both A and R are true, but R is not the correct explanation of A.
(c) A is true, but R is false.
(d) A is false, but R is true.

**7.** **Assertion** (A) Plant families like Convolvulaceae, Solanaceae are included in the order–Polymoniales mainly based on the vegetative characters.

**Reason** (R) An order is an assemblage of families that exhibit similar characters.

**8.** **Assertion** (A) In higher taxonomic categories, it is difficult to understand the relationships between different taxa.

**Reason** (R) From species to kingdom, the number of specific characteristics increase.

**9.** **Assertion** (A) Binomial nomenclature uses two Latin or Latinised words to name an organism.

**Reason** (R) The first word in the binomial name indicates the species and the second word indicates the genus.

**10.** **Assertion** (A) In taxonomy, species is the most specific level in the hierarchy of classification.

**Reason** (R) Species is the only level of classification that can interbreed and produce fertile offspring.

**11.** **Assertion** (A) The scientific name of mango, *Mangifera indica,* is standardised globally, ensuring accurate identification across different and regions.

**Reason** (R) In binomial nomenclature, both the genus and species names are always derived from Latin.

## Very Short Answer Type Questions

**12.** What are the advantages of using scientific names instead of local names?

**13.** Name the international codes used for the naming of plants and animals?

**14.** Differentiate between a taxa and a species.

**15.** What is the purpose of nomenclature in biology?

## Short Answer Type Questions

**16.** What is the primary need for classifying organisms in science?

**17.** Why are the species considered as dynamic group?

**18.** Why is it important to standardise the naming of living organisms?

## Long Answer Type Questions

**19.** Explain the rules of binomial nomenclature.

**20.** Explain the taxonomical hierarchy with example.

**21.** Discuss the importance of taxonomy in the study of living organisms. Include how taxonomy aids in the identification, nomenclature, and classification of organisms.

## Case Based Question

**22.** Scientists studied the plant genera–*Petunia* and *Datura*, examining their morphological and biochemical traits, such as flower structure, leaf arrangement, and alkaloid content. Both genera are known for their ornamental and medicinal properties but differ in habitat and growth habits. The researchers classified them into the same plant family based on shared characteristics, while noting their distinct traits. The study also highlighted the role of genetic analysis in refining traditional taxonomic classification.
Based on this case, answer the following questions:

(i) Considering the study of the plant genera–*Petunia* and *Datura*, what family do they share, and what are some key characteristics that define this family?

(ii) What criteria are used to classify plants in a taxonomic hierarchy and how do these apply to plants?

(iii) What common traits do these plants share that helped scientists put them in the same plant family?

## Answers

**1.** (d) **2.** (d) **3.** (c) **4.** (b) **5.** (d) **6.** (d) **7.** (d)
**8.** (c) **9.** (c) **10.** (a) **11.** (b)

# 02

# CHAPTER

Biological classification is the scientific procedure of arranging organisms in a hierarchical series of groups and sub-groups on the basis of their similarities and dissimilarities.

# Biological Classification

▼ **YOUR STUDY GOALS**



▼ **YOUR PRACTICE GOAL**

- Objective Type Questions (40 Qs ; MCQs, A-R) Case Based Questions (4)
- Subjective Type Questions
- (10 VSAs, 40 SAs, 14 LAs)

- Living organisms need to be classified because of the following reasons.
- Classification helps in knowing the relationship amongst different groups of organisms.
- It helps in the study of evolutionary relationship between organisms.

In this chapter, we will study the classification of organisms into various kingdoms, highlighting the key features of each kingdom and discuss about lichens, prions, viruses and viroids.

## 2.1 Classification of Organisms

- There have been many attempts to classify living organisms since ancient times.
- **Aristotle** was the earliest to attempt a scientific basis of classification.
- He used simple morphological characters to classify plants as trees, shrubs and herbs.
- He also classified animals into **two groups**, those which had **red blood** and those **that did not**.

- Similarly, various classification systems have been proposed by different scientists over time. Some of these are discussed as follows

## 1. Two Kingdom Classification System

- It is one of the oldest system of classification proposed by **C Linnaeus** (the father of taxonomy).
- He divided all the living organisms into two kingdoms–**Plantae** and **Animalia.**
- Classification of organisms into plants and animals was easily done and was easy to understand, but a large number of organisms did not fall into either category.
- This system did not distinguish between the eukaryotes and prokaryotes, unicellular and multicellular organisms and photosynthetic (green algae) and non-photosynthetic (fungi) organisms.
- Hence, this system used for long time was found inadequate.

> **TEACHER'S TIP**
> After the two-kingdom classification system, **Ernst Haeckel** proposed a **three-kingdom classification** consisting of kingdoms Plantae, Animalia and Protista. Later, **Copeland** introduced a **four-kingdom classification** system that included the kingdom–Monera, in addition to the other three.

## 2. Five Kingdom Classification System

- This classification was proposed by **RH Whittaker** in 1969.
- In this classification system, he divided all living organisms into kingdom- **Monera, Protista, Fungi, Plantae** and **Animalia**.
- The main criteria for classification used by him were as follows
  - **Cell Structure** Prokaryotes or eukaryotes
  - **Mode of Nutrition** Autotrophs or heterotrophs
  - **Body Organisation** Unicellular or multicellular
  - **Reproduction** Sexual or asexual
  - **Phylogenetic relationships**

The comparative account of different characteristics of the five kingdoms is given

**Characteristics of the Five Kingdoms**

| Characters | Monera | Protista | Fungi | Plantae | Animalia |
|---|---|---|---|---|---|
| **Cell type** | Prokaryotic | Eukaryotic | Eukaryotic | Eukaryotic | Eukaryotic |
| **Cell wall** | Non-cellulosic (polysaccharide + amino acid) | Present in some | Present with chitin | Present (cellulose) | Absent |
| **Nuclear membrane** | Absent | Present | Present | Present | Present |
| **Body organisation** | Cellular | Cellular | Multicellular/loose tissue | Tissue/organ | Tissue/organ/organ system |
| **Mode of nutrition** | Autotrophic (chemosynthetic and photosynthetic) and heterotrophic (saprophytic/parasitic) | Autotrophic (photosynthetic) and heterotrophic | Heterotrophic (saprophytic/parasitic) | Autotrophic (photosynthetic) | Heterotrophic (holozoic/sapro-phytic, etc.) |

### Need for Five Kingdom Classification

- Earlier classification systems included bacteria, blue-green algae, fungi, mosses, ferns, gymnosperms and the angiosperms under **'plants'** due to the presence of cell wall in their cells.
- This has brought together the **prokaryotic bacteria** and the **blue-green algae** (cyanobacteria) with other groups that were eukaryotic.
- It has also grouped together the unicellular organisms and the multicellular organism. For example, *Chlamydomonas* and *Spirogyra* were placed together under **algae**.
- The earlier classification also failed to differentiate between the **heterotrophic group** – fungi and the **autotrophic green plants**, despite their distinct wall compositions—fungi have chitin in their walls, while green plants have a cellulosic cell wall.
- When such characteristics were considered, the fungi were placed in a separate kingdom; kingdom–Fungi.

- In five kingdom system, all prokaryotic organisms were grouped together under kingdom–Monera and the unicellular eukaryotic organisms were placed in kingdom–Protista.
- Kingdom–Protista has brought together *Chlamydomonas*, *Chlorella* (earlier placed in algae within plants and both having cell walls) with *Paramoecium* and *Amoeba* (which were earlier placed in the animal kingdom which lack cell wall).
- Five kingdom classification system has put together organisms, which in earlier classifications, were placed in different kingdoms due to change in the criteria for classification.
- Over time, an attempt has been made to evolve a classification system which reflects not only the morphological, physiological and reproductive similarities, but is also phylogenetic, i.e. is based on evolutionary relationships.

### 3. Six Kingdom Classification System

- This system is also named as **three domain system**.
- In this system, organisms are classified into three domains, i.e. **Archaea**, **Bacteria** and **Eukarya**.
- It mainly used basic principles of five kingdom system, but divides Monera into two domains, leaving the remaining eukaryotic kingdom in the third domain.

**Quick Test 1**

1. The father of taxonomy divide all the living organisms into how many kingdoms? Name them.
2. State True or False.
   The two kingdom system of classification included bacteria, blue-green algae, fungi, mosses, ferns, gymnosperms and angiosperms under 'Plants'.
3. In the five kingdom system of Whittaker, how many kingdoms are eukaryotes? *NCERT Exemplar*
4. In five kingdom system of classification, which group comprises single celled eukaryotes only?
5. State True or False.
   The six kingdom system of classification, divided the eukaryotic group into two domain.

## 2.2 Kingdom-Monera

This kingdom includes unicellular prokaryotic organisms. Bacteria are the sole members of this kingdom. They are the most abundant microorganism that occurs almost everywhere.

### General Characters of Monera

The characteristic features of kingdom–Monera are given below

1. **Habitat** They are present in soil and also live in extreme habitats such as hot springs, deserts, snow and deep oceans where very few other life forms can survive. Many of them live in or on other organisms as parasites.
2. **Shape** On the basis of their shape bacteria are grouped under four categories.
   - **Coccus** (pl. cocci) The bacterium is spherical in outline.
   - **Bacillus** (pl. bacilli) The bacterium is rod-shaped.
   - **Spirillum** (pl. spirilla) The bacterium is spiral–shaped.
   - **Vibrium** (pl. vibrio) The bacterium is comma-shaped.

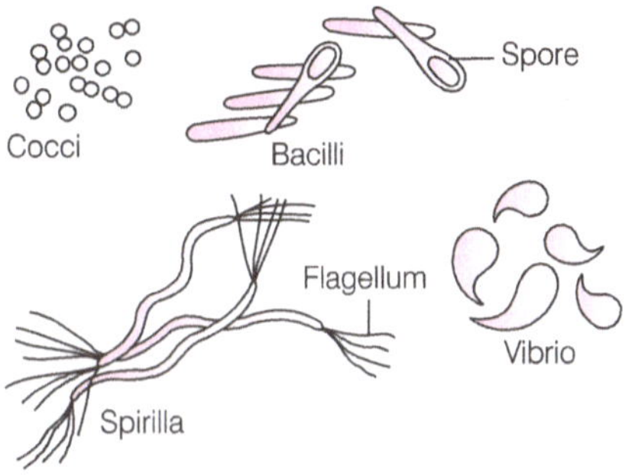


Fig 2.1 Bacteria of different shapes

**Note** Although the bacterial structure is very simple, they are very complex in behaviour

3. **Nutrition** Bacteria as a group show the most extensive metabolic diversity. On the basis of mode of nutrition, bacteria are of two types
   - **Autotrophic Bacteria** These bacteria synthesise their own food from inorganic

substrate. These may be **photosynthetic autotrophic** or **chemosynthetic autotrophic**.

- **Heterotrophic Bacteria** These bacteria are not capable of synthesising their own food. Instead, they are dependent on other organisms or on dead organic matter for food. These are most abundant in nature.

4. **Reproduction** Bacteria reproduce by asexual and sexual processes.
   - **Asexual reproduction** occurs mainly by binary fission. However, under unfavourable condition they also reproduce by spore formation.
   - **Sexual reproduction** occurs by a primitive type of DNA transfer from one bacterium to the other.

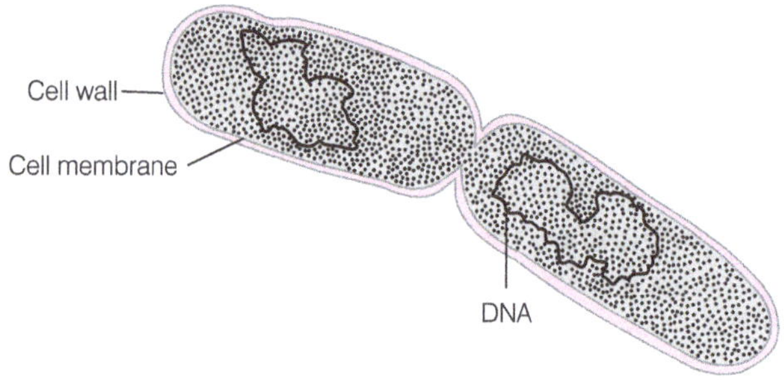


Fig 2.2 A dividing bacterium

## Classification of Monera

The monerans are majorly classified as follows

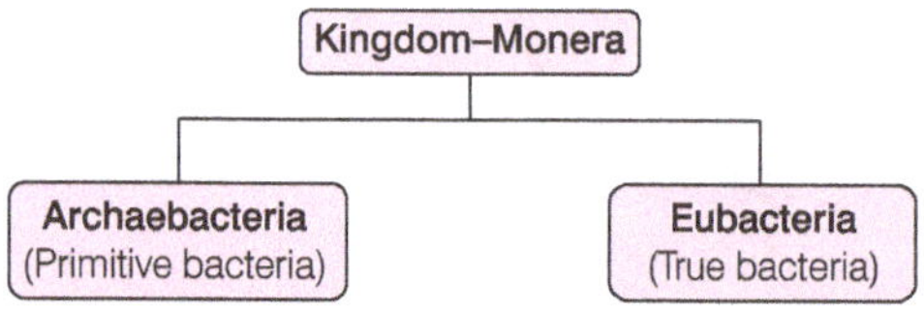


These are described as follows

## Archaebacteria

- These are the group of most primitive prokaryotes.
- They differ from other bacteria in having a unique cell wall structure, which is responsible for their survival in extreme conditions.
- They live in some of the most harsh habitats such as
  - **Extreme salty areas** (halophiles)
  - **Hot springs** (thermoacidophiles)
  - **Marshy areas** (methanogens)
- Methanogens live anaerobically in the gut of several ruminants such as cows and buffaloes. These bacteria have been exploited for the production of methane (biogas) from the dung of these animals.

## Eubacteria

- They are called **'true bacteria'** and are characterised by the presence of a rigid cell wall and if motile they have a flagellum.
- They show both autotrophic and heterotrophic mode of nutrition.

### Autotrophic Bacteria

- These bacteria can produce their own food using inorganic substances.
- Autotrophic bacteria includes photosynthetic autotrophs and chemosynthetic autotrophs.

### 1. Photosynthetic Autotrophic Bacteria

- They use light energy to convert carbon dioxide into organic compounds, through photosynthesis.
- These include **cyanobacteria** (also referred to as **blue-green algae**). They have chlorophyll-*a* which is similar to green plants.
- General characters of cyanobacteria are as follows
  - They are predominantly **aquatic** (freshwater/marine), but many species are known to be **terrestrial** also.
  - They could be unicellular, colonial or filamentous. The colonies are generally surrounded by gelatinous sheath.
  - They often form blooms in polluted water bodies.
  - Some cyanobacteria (*Nostoc, Anabaena)* possess special type of cells called **heterocysts** that are the sites of nitrogen fixation.

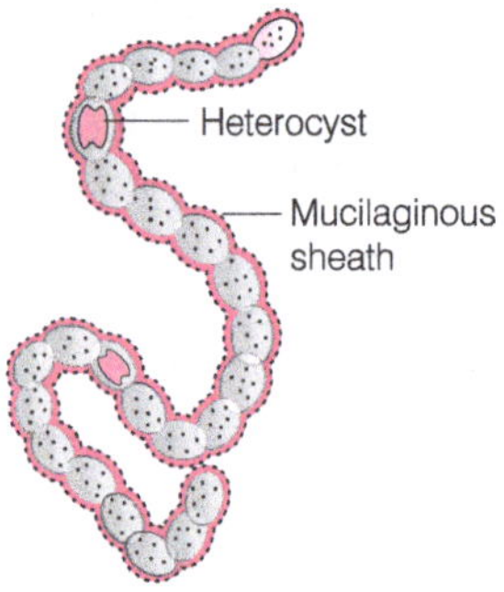


Fig 2.3 A filamentous blue-green algae; *Nostoc*

### 2. Chemosynthetic autotrophic bacteria

- These bacteria obtain energy by oxidising various inorganic substances such as nitrates, nitrites and ammonia to convert carbon dioxide into organic compounds.
- They play a great role in recycling nutrients like nitrogen, phosphorus, iron and sulphur, e.g. nitrogen fixing bacteria, iron and sulphur oxidising bacteria.

### Heterotrophic Bacteria

- These bacteria obtain their energy by consuming organic compounds, as they cannot synthesise their own food from inorganic sources.
- These are most abundant in nature. The majority of them are important **decomposers**. They can have both harmful and useful impacts on human affairs. For example,
  - Some of them are helpful in making curd from milk, producing antibiotics, fixing nitrogen in legume, roots, etc.
  - Some of them are **pathogens**, causing damage to human beings, crops, farm animals and pets. Cholera, typhoid, tetanus, citrus canker are well known diseases caused by different bacteria.
- The **mycoplasma** are smallest living cells that completely lack cell wall and can survive without oxygen. Many mycoplasma are pathogenic in plants and animals.

### Quick Test 2

1. Name the organisms living in salty areas.
2. Give the scientific term used for organisms that produce biogas.
3. Are chemosynthetic bacteria-autotrophic or heterotrophic? *NCERT Exemplar*
4. Bacteria 'X' oxidises inorganic substances for ATP production. Identify 'X'.
5. Name the smallest living bacteria that is pathogenic in plants and animals.

## 2.3 Kingdom-Protista

- Kingdom–Protista includes all **single-celled eukaryotes,** but the boundaries of this kingdom are not well-defined.
- Members of kingdom–Protista acts as a connecting link between the kingdom–Monera and the complex multicellular kingdoms–Fungi, Plantae and Animalia.

### General Characters of Protista

The general characteristic features of kingdom–Protista are given below

- These are mostly **aquatic organisms**. Some protists also live in the bodies of animals as parasites.
- They contain well-defined nucleus and membrane bound cell organelles like mitochondria, Golgi complex, endoplasmic reticulum, etc.
- Some members have flagella and cilia that are used for locomotion and feeding.
- Protists reproduce asexually and sexually by a process involving cell fusion and zygote formation.

### Classification of Protista

The organisms of this kingdom are classified as chrysophytes, dinoflagellates, euglenoids, slime moulds and protozoans.

### Chrysophytes

This group includes **diatoms** and **golden algae** (desmids). The general characteristic features of chrysophytes are as follows

- They are found in **freshwater** as well as in **marine** environment.
- They are microscopic and float passively in water currents (planktons).
- Most of them are photosynthetic in nature.
- In diatoms, the cell walls form two thin overlapping shells, which fit together as in a soap box.
- The cell walls are embedded with glass-like silica. This property makes these cells simply indestructible.

- Diatoms leave behind a large amount of cell wall deposits in their habitat that pile up at the bottom of water reservoirs and form big heaps called **diatomaceous earth**. Being gritty this soil is used in polishing, filtration of oil and syrups.
- Diatoms are the chief producers in the oceans.

## Dinoflagellates

The general characteristic features of dinoflagellates are listed below

- These are mainly **marine** and photosynthetic organisms.
- They appear yellow, green, brown, blue or red colour depending on the main pigments present in their cells.
- The cell wall of dinoflagellates is composed of number of plates that is made up of cellulose on the outer surface.
- Most of them have two flagella, i.e. one lies longitudinally and other transversely in a furrow between the wall plates.
- Some dinoflagellates like *Gonyaulax* undergo rapid multiplication and make the water appear red and form '**red tide**'.
  Toxins released by such large numbers may even kill other aquatic animals such as fishes.

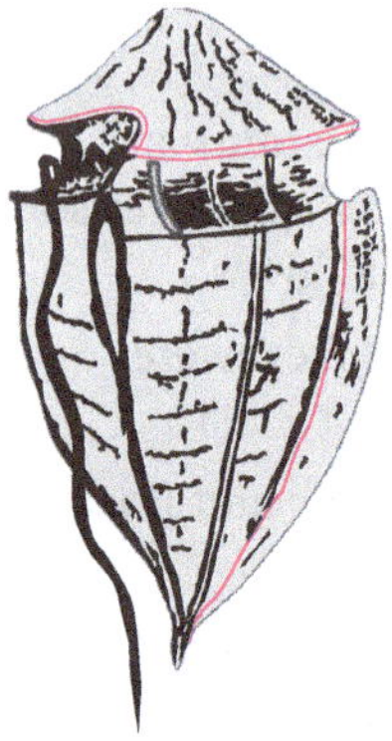

Fig 2.4 Dinoflagellates

## Euglenoids

The characteristic features of euglenoids are described below

- These are **freshwater** organisms that occur mostly in stagnant waters.
- They are unicellular flagellate protists.
- Instead of cell wall, their body is covered by a thin protein rich layer called **pellicle**, which makes their body flexible.
- They have two flagella, usually one long and one short.
- Euglenoids are autotrophic in the presence of sunlight. If deprived of sunlight, they behave like heterotrophs by predating on other smaller organisms.
- The pigments found in euglenoids are similar to those in higher plants, e.g. *Euglena*.

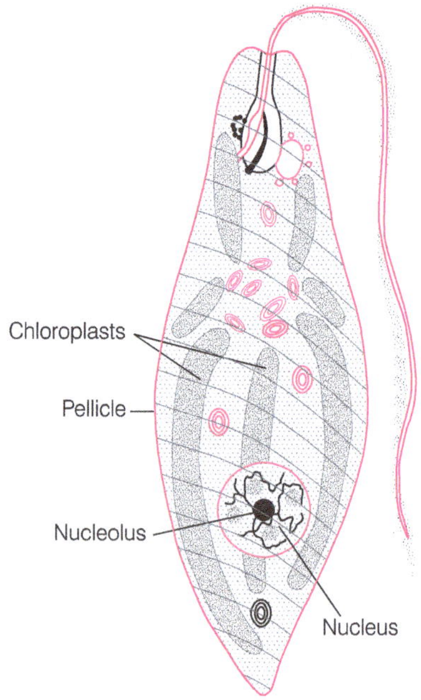


Fig 2.5 *Euglena*

> **TEACHER'S TIP**
> *Euglena* is considered as plant as well as animal.
> This is because it can photosynthesise like plants and can move and consume food like animals.

## Slime Moulds

The general features of slime moulds are discussed below

- These are saprophytic protists that are widely distributed and grow in **damp** and **moist places**.
- They are found in moist terrestrial places rich in decaying organic material.

- They move along decaying twigs and leaves engulfing organic material.
- Under favourable conditions, they form an aggregation known as **plasmodium**, which can grow and extend over several feet.
- During unfavourable conditions, the plasmodium differentiates and forms fruiting bodies bearing spores at their tips. The spores possess true walls.
- Spores are extremely resistant and survive for many years under adverse conditions. They are carried away by air currents.

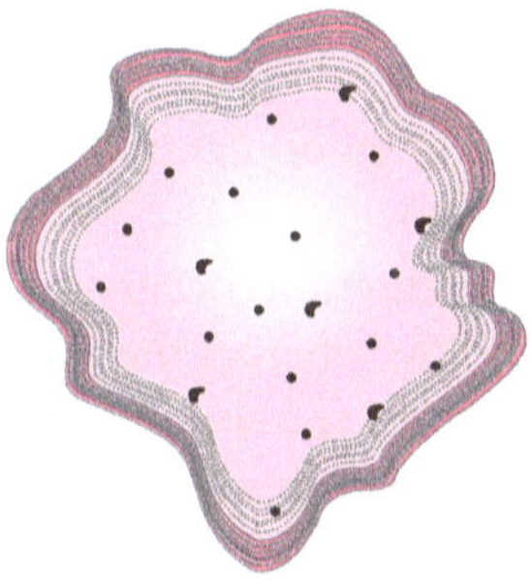

Fig 2.6 Slime mould

## Protozoans

All protozoans are heterotrophs and live as predators or parasites. They are thought to be primitive relatives of animals.

There are four major groups of protozoans

### 1. Amoeboid Protozoans

- These organisms live in freshwater, sea water or moist soil.
- Amoeboid protozoans move and capture their prey by putting out **pseudopodia** (false feet) as in *Amoeba* (as mouth is absent).

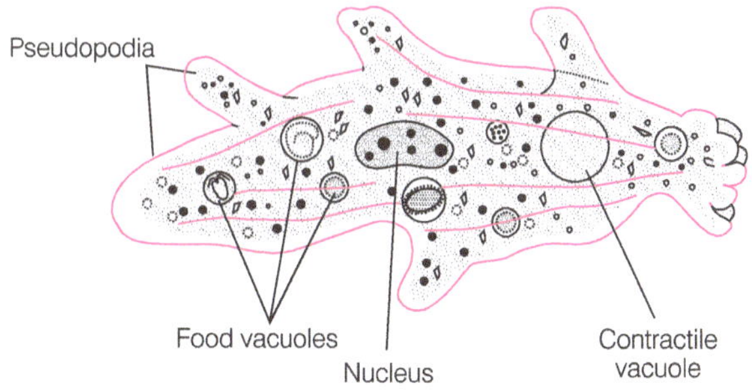


Fig 2.7 Microscopic view of *Amoeba proteus*

- Marine forms have silica shells on their surface.
- Some of them such as *Entamoeba* are parasities.

### 2. Flagellated Protozoans

- The members of this group are either free-living or parasitic.
- They have flagella for locomotion.
- Various species of these protozoans are parasitic and cause diseases in humans. For example, sleeping sickness is cause by *Trypanosoma.*

### 3. Ciliated Protozoans

- These are aquatic, actively moving organisms because of the presence of thousands of cilia, e.g. *Paramoecium.*
- Ciliated protozoans have a **cavity** (gullet) that opens to the outside of the cell surface. The coordinated movement of rows of cilia causes the water laden with food to be steered into the gullet.

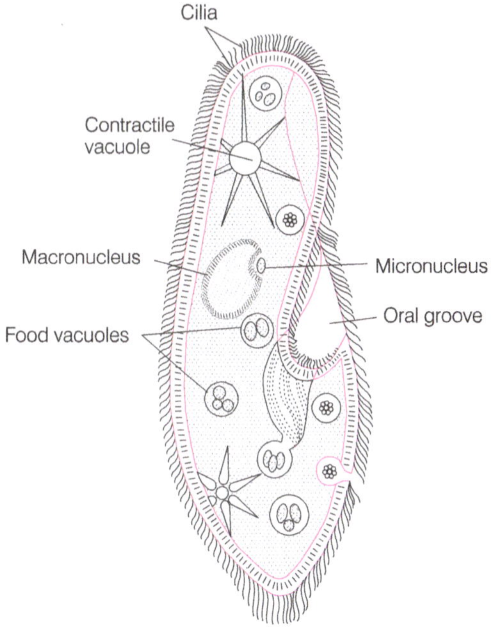


Fig 2.8 *Paramoecium*

### 4. Sporozoan Protozoans

This group includes organisms that have an infectious spore-like stage in their life cycle, e.g. *Plasmodium* (malarial parasite), which causes malaria in humans.

## Quick Test 3

1. Name any two cell organelles that are present in Protista, but are absent in monerans.
2. **State True or False.**
   Red algae grows in large number in sea and makes water look bright red.
3. Name the structure that helps *Euglena* to maintain its flexibility.
4. What observable features in *Trypanosoma* would make you classify it under kingdom-Protista? *NCERT Exemplar*
5. Name three structures that assist locomotion in protists.

## 2.4 Kingdom-Fungi

- These constitute a unique group of heterotrophic organisms and show great diversity in morphology and habitat.
- These are **cosmopolitan in distribution** and occur in air, water, soil and on plants and animals. They grow in warm and humid places.
- Some unicellular fungi, such as yeast are used to make bread and beer, while some, e.g. *Penicillium*, are important source of antibiotics.
- Certain fungi also causes diseases in plant and animals, e.g. wheat rust is caused by *Puccinia*.

### General Characters of Fungi

The characteristic feature of kingdom-Fungi are given below

#### Fungal Structure

- The fungal body is an assemblage of long, thin, tubular, threads or filaments filled with protoplasm and covered by wall, called **hyphae**.
- Numerous hyphae are twined around one another to form **mycelium** (pl. mycelia).
- The hyphae in fungi are of the following types
  - **Coenocytic Hyphae** These hyphae are continuous tubes filled with multinucleate cytoplasm.
  - **Septate Hyphae** In this type, cross walls or septae are present in the hyphae.
- Their cell wall is made up of **chitin** and **polysaccharide**.

#### Nutrition

- Fungi are mostly **heterotrophic** due to the absence of chlorophyll.
- Some fungi are dependent on living plants and animals and hence are called **parasites**.
- Some of them absorb soluble organic matter from dead substrates and hence are called **saprophytes**.
- Some fungi grow in **symbiotic association** with algae to form **lichens**. Some other forms grow in close association with the roots of higher plants and form **mycorrhiza**.

#### Reproduction

- Reproduction in fungi occurs by vegetative, asexual and sexual methods.
- **Vegetative reproduction** occurs by fragmentation, fission and budding, whereas the asexual reproduction occurs by **zoospores**, **sporangiospores** or **conidia**.
- The **sexual reproduction** occurs by oospores, ascospores and basidiospores.
- The various spores are produced in distinct structures are called **fruiting bodies**.
- The sexual cycle involves the following three stages
  - **Plasmogamy** It is the first stage in which the protoplasm of gametes either two motile or non-motile fuse together.
  - **Karyogamy** It is the stage in which two compatible nuclei fuse together resulting in the formation of diploid nucleus.
  - **Meiosis** It is the stage in which the diploid zygote divides resulting in the formation of haploid spores (reduction division).

**Dikaryophase**

- In most of the lower fungi, the fungus reproduces sexually by compatible mating of two haploid hyphae, i.e. **plasmogamy**. It is immediately followed by **karyogamy** and **meiosis**.
- In some fungi, the fusion of two haploid cells immediately results in diploid cells ($2n$).
- However, in some higher forms (Ascomycetes and Basidiomycetes), karyogamy is delayed and an intervening dikaryotic stage ($n+n$, i.e. two nuclei per cell) occurs. Such a condition is called a **dikaryon** and the phase is called **dikaryophase** of fungus.
- After that, the parental nuclei fuse and the cell becomes diploid.
- The fungi form fruiting bodies in which reduction division occurs, leading to the formation of haploid spores.

## Classification of Fungi

Kingdom–Fungi can be divided into various classes on the basis of morphology of mycelium, mode of spore formation and fruiting bodies.
These are given below

### 1. Phycomycetes

The members of Phycomycetes are found in **aquatic habitats** and on **decaying wood** in moist and damp places or as obligate parasites on plants.

General characteristics of this class are as follows

- The mycelium is **aseptate** and **coenocytic**.
- Asexual reproduction takes place by **zoospores** (motile) or by **aplanospores** (non-motile).
- Asexual reproduction involves the endogenous formation of spores in sporangium.

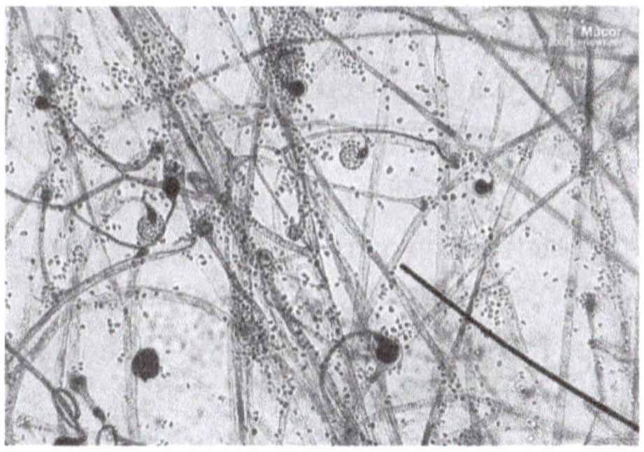

Fig 2.9 *Mucor* (Fungi)

- During sexual reproduction, a zygospore is formed by the fusion of two gametes.
- These gametes are similar in morphology **(isogamous)** or dissimilar (**anisogamous** or **oogamous**).
- Some common members are *Mucor, Albugo* (parasitic fungi on mustard that causes white spots on its leaves), *Rhizopus* (the bread mould).

### 2. Ascomycetes

The members of Ascomycetes are commonly called as **sac fungi**. They are mostly multicellular (*Penicillium*) and rarely unicellular (yeast).

The common features of Ascomycetes are described below

- They are saprophytic, decomposers, parasitic or coprophilous (growing on dung).
- The mycelium is **branched** and **septate**.
- The asexual spores are conidia produced exogenously on the special mycelium called **conidiophores**. Conidia on germination produce mycelium.
- Sexual spores are called **ascospores** which are produced endogenously in sac-like **asci** (sing. ascus). These asci are arranged in different types of fruiting bodies called **ascocarps**.
- Some of the examples are *Penicillium, Aspergillus, Claviceps, Neurospora,* yeast (*Saccharomyces*), etc.
- *Neurospora* is used extensively in biochemical and genetic work.
- Some members like morels and truffles are edible and are considered delicacies.

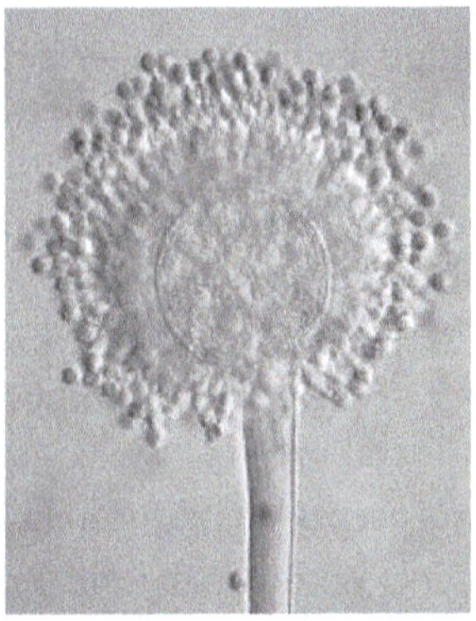

Fig 2.10 *Aspergillus*

### 3. Basidiomycetes

The members of Basidiomycetes grow in soil, on logs and tree stumps and in living plant bodies as parasites, e.g. rusts and smuts.

The common features of Basidiomycetes are described below

- The mycelium is **branched** and **septate**.
- The asexual spores are generally not found, but vegetative reproduction by fragmentation is common.
- The sex organs are absent, but **plasmogamy** occurs by the fusion of two vegetative or somatic cells of different strains or genotypes. The resultant structure is a **dikaryon** which ultimately gives rise to **basidium**.
- Karyogamy and meiosis take place in basidium producing four basidiospores.
- The basidiospores are exogenously produced on the basidium (pl. basidia). The basidia are arranged in fruiting bodies called **basidiocarps**.

- Some examples are *Agaricus* (edible mushroom), *Puccinia* (cause rust), *Ustilago* (cause smut diseases), toad stools, bracket fungi and puffballs.

Fig 2.11 *Agaricus*

### 4. Deuteromycetes

These are commonly known as **imperfect fungi** because only the asexual or vegetative phases of these fungi are known.
The characteristic of Deuteromycetes are described below

- Some members are **saprophytes** or **parasites**, while a large number of them are **decomposers** of litter and help in mineral cycling.
- The mycelium is **septate** and **branched**.
- Asexual reproduction occurs by the formation of **conidia**.
- Sexual reproduction is not certain.
- Once the perfect (sexual) stage of certain Deuteromycetes were identified, they were often moved to Ascomycetes and Basidiomycetes.
- Some examples are *Alternaria, Colletotrichum* and *Trichoderma.*

## 2.5 Kingdom–Plantae

- Kingdom–Plantae includes all eukaryotic, chlorophyll containing organisms called plants.
- Some of these members are partially heterotrophic, such as insectivorous plants or parasites. For example, Venus flytrap and bladderwort are insectivorous plants and *Cuscuta* (dodder) is a parasite.
- The plant cell has an eukaryotic type structure with prominent chloroplasts and cell wall containing cellulose.
- This kingdom includes following divisions
  - Algae
  - Bryophytes
  - Pteridophytes
  - Gymnosperms
  - Angiosperms
- The members of kingdom–Plantae have two distinct phases in their life cycle i.e. the diploid sporophytic and haploid gametophytic phase, which alternate with each other. This is called **alternation of generation.**
- The details of this kingdom will be discussed in chapter 3.

## 2.6 Kingdom-Animalia

- The animal kingdom contains heterotrophic, eukaryotic organisms that are multicellular and their cells lack cell wall. They directly or indirectly dependent on plants for food.
- The food is digested in an internal cavity and is reserved as **glycogen** or **fat**.
- Their mode of nutrition is holozoic, i.e. by ingestion of food.
- They have definite growth pattern and grows into adults that have definite shape and size.
- The higher forms have well-developed sensory and neuromuscular mechanism.
- Locomotion is present in majority of organisms.
- Sexual reproduction occurs by copulation followed by fertilisation of gametes and embryonic development.
- The details of this kingdom will be discussed in chapter 4.

### Quick Test 4

1. Fungi 'X' is parasitic on a mustard plant. Identify 'X'.
2. Both zoospores and zygospores are associated with the reproduction in a fungi. State any one difference between them.
3. Name the class of fungi that obtain nutrition from the faeces of animals.
4. Plants are autotrophic. Can you think of some plants that are partially heterotrophic? *NCERT*
5. **State True or False.**
   The members of kingdom-Plantae have distinct phases in their life cycle, i.e. the diploid gametophytic and haploid sporophytic phase.

## 2.7 Viruses, Sub-viral Pathogens and Lichens

The five kingdom classification of **RH Whittaker** has not classified viruses, viroids, prions and lichens in any group. These are discussed below

### Viruses

- They did not find a place in any classification system, since they are not truly living. Virus means venom or poisonous fluid.
- The viruses are non-cellular organisms that are characterised by having an inert crystalline structure outside the living cell.
- These are **obligate parasites** and do not have their own biosynthetic machinery.
- Once they infect a living host cell, they take over the machinery of the host cell to replicate themselves, killing the host.
- They cause a variety of diseases in animals like mumps, small pox, herpes, influenza and AIDS (in humans). In plants, viral infections can lead to symptoms such as mosaic formation, leaf curling and rolling, yellowing and vein clearing, dwarfing and stunted growth.

### Discoveries Related to Virus

- **Dmitri Ivanovsky** (1892) recognised certain microbes as causative organism of the mosaic disease of tobacco. These were found to be smaller than bacteria because they passed through bacteria proof- filtres.
- **MW Beijerinck** (1898) demonstrated that the extract of the infected plants of tobacco could cause infection in healthy plants. He called the fluid as *contagium vivum fluidum* (infectious living fluid).
- **WM Stanley** (1935) showed that viruses could be crystallised and crystals consist largely of proteins. They are inert outside their specific host cells.
- The discovery of characteristics of viruses revealed their unique structures that distinguished them from other living organisms.

### Structure of Viruses

A virus structure has mainly two parts

- **Capsid** It is a protein covering around the genetic material. Capsid protects the nucleic acid and is made up of small protein subunits called **capsomeres.** These capsomeres are arranged helically or in polyhedral geometric forms.
- **Genetic Material** It consists of is either DNA or RNA, but never both.
  - It is generally infectious in nature.
  - Most of the bacterial viruses (or bacteriophages) have double-stranded DNA as genetic material.
  - Majority of plant viruses have single-stranded RNA as genetic material.
  - Some animal viruses may have either single or double-stranded RNA or double- stranded DNA.

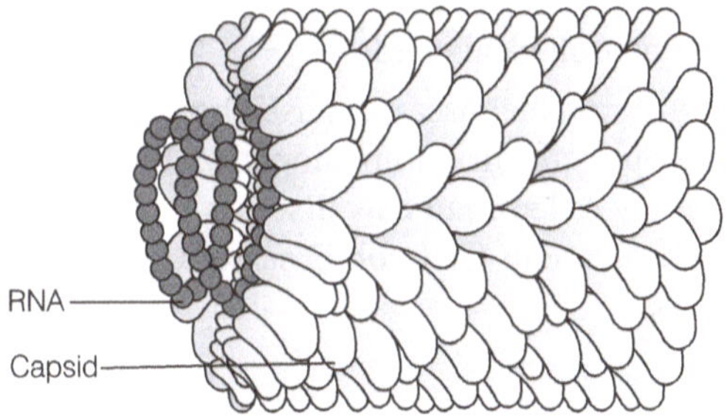


Fig 2.12 Tobacco mosaic virus

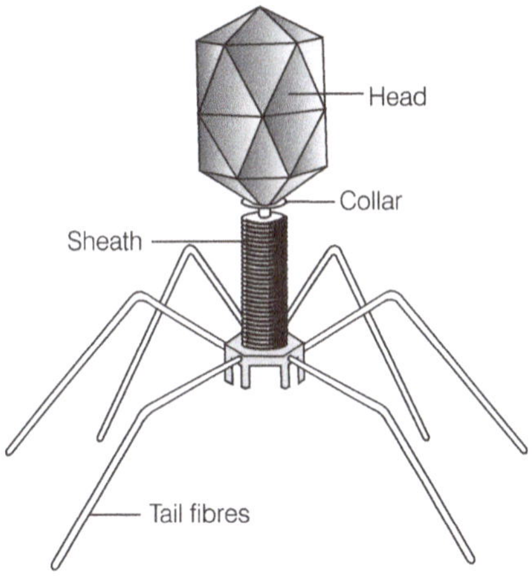


Fig 2.13 Structure of a bacteriophage

## Sub-viral Pathogens

**Viroids** and **prions** belong to this category.

### Viroids

- **TO Diener** (1971) discovered a new infectious agent that was smaller than viruses and caused potato spindle tuber disease.
- These are small circular RNAs similar to viruses, but lacked protein coat that is found in virus.
- The RNA of the viroid has low molecular weight.

### Prions

- These are obligate parasites made of abnormally folded proteins.
- These are similar in size to viruses, but causes certain neurological diseases.
- The most notable diseases caused by prions are Bovine Spongiform Encephalopathy (BSE) commonly called **mad cow diseases** in cattle and analogous variant Cr-Jacob Disease (CJD) in humans.

## Lichens

- These are symbiotic associations, i.e. mutually useful associations between algae and fungi.
- The algal component (autotrophic) is called **phycobiont** and fungal component (heterotrophic) is **mycobiont.**
- Algae prepare food for fungi and fungi provide shelter, absorb mineral and water for its partner.
- Lichens are best indicators of pollution. They do not grow in polluted environments.

### Quick Test 5

1. Viruses rely on host organisms for reproduction? Given one reason.
2. **State True or False.**
   Bacteriophages are unique in their structures and contain both DNA and RNA.
3. It is difficult to a certain whether viruses are living or non-living write one character of virus that confirms its non-living nature.
4. Bovine spongiform encephalopathy caused by prions is analogous to which disease in humans?
5. Lichens are called dual organisms. What kind of relationship is observed between the two organisms present in the lichens?

# Mind Map

## Biological Classification

### Classification of Organisms

- **Two kingdom classification** given by **Linnaeus** (1735) in the book *Systema Naturae*, divided organisms into plant and animal kingdoms.
- **Five kingdom classification** given by **RH Whittaker** (1969), divided living organisms into five kingdoms, i.e. Monera, Protista, Fungi, Plantae and Animalia based on the complexity of cell structure, body structure and mode of nutrition.

### Kingdom-Monera

- Include all prokaryotes.

**Bacteria**

**Archaebacteria** (primitive bacteria)

- Most primitive prokaryotes.
  - **Halophiles** (salty/marine bacteria)
  - **Methanogens** (methane producing bacteria)
  - **Thermoacidophiles** (present in acidic sulphur springs)

**Eubacteria** (true bacteria)

- They are true bacteria, lacking a well-organised nucleus, membrane bound cell organelles.
- Reproduce asexually as well as sexually.
- Cyanobacteria are Gram negative photosynthetic prokaryotes.
- Mycoplasma is the smallest free living prokaryote.

### Kingdom-Protista

- It consists of all single-celled eukaryotes.
- Mostly aquatic and show both autotrophic and heterotrophic (parasitic) mode of nutrition.
- Reproduces both sexually and asexually.
- Protista are classified as follows

**Protozoans**

- **Flagellated protozoans** (Possess flagella, e.g. *Trypanosoma*).
- **Amoeboid protozoans** (Develop pseudopodia, e.g. *Amoeba*).
- **Sporozoans** (Locomotory organelles absent, e.g. *Plasmodium*).
- **Ciliated protozoans** (Locomotory organelles are cilia, e.g. *Paramecium*).

**Slime Moulds**

- True cell wall is present.
- Forms an aggregation called **plasmodium** on favourable conditions.
- Under unfavourable condition, plasmodium differentiates into fruiting bodies.

**Chrysophytes**

(i) **Diatoms**

- Form diatomite or diatomaceous earth.
- They do not possess flagella (except reproductive stage).

(ii) **Desmids**

- Unicellular golden algae.
- Found in freshwater and are indicators of clean water.

(iii) **Dinoflagellates**

- Cell wall is cellulosic.
- Mostly marine and autotrophic.
- Possess two flagella-one transverse and one longitudinal.
- e.g. *Gonyaulax* (causes red tides).

**Euglenoids**

- Body is covered by pellicle instead of a cell wall.
- Possess two flagella.
- e.g. *Euglena*.

### Kindom-Fungi

- Achlorophyllous, heterotrophic, spore-forming, non-vascular, eukaryotes with chitinous cell wall.
- Body is generally in the form of long thread like structures

**Phycomycetes**

- Aseptate, cenocytic mycelium
- Reproduces asexually as well as sexually.
- Fruiting body-Absent.

**Ascomycetes**

- Septate, branched and multicellular mycelium.
- Reproduces sexually and asexually.
- Fruiting body-Ascocarp.

**Basidiomycetes**

- Branched, septate mycelium.
- Fruiting body-Basidiocarp.
- Reproduces sexually and by fragmentation; asexual spores generally absent.

**Deuteromycetes**

- Branched, septate mycelium.
- Reproduces only asexually.
- Fruiting body-Absent.

### Kingdom–Plantae

- Includes all eukaryotic, chlorophyll-containing organisms.
- Some are partially heterotrophic (insectivorous/parasite) in nature.
- Presence of cellulosic cell wall and prominent chloroplasts.

### Kingdom–Animalia

- Heterotrophic, multicellular eukaryotes lacking cell wall.
- Holozoic mode of nutrition and store food reserves as glycogen/fat.
- Sexual reproduction involves embryological development.

### Viruses

- Considered as neither living nor non-living.
- They are an obligate parasites and remain inert outside the host cell.
- A virus consists of following parts

1. **Nucleoid** (Viral chromosome)
2. **Capsid** (Proteinaceous covering consisting of a number of subunits called **capsomeres**).
3. **Envelope** (A loose membranous covering present in some animal viruses).

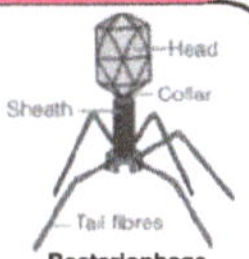

Bacteriophage

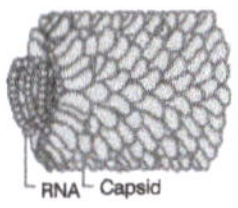

TMV

- **Viroids** are infectious RNA particles devoid of protein coat.
- **Prions** are highly infectious agents made up of abnormally folded proteins.

### Lichens v/s Mycorrhiza

Lichen (Algae+Fungi)

- Algal part (phycobiont) provides food to fungi.
- Fungal part (mycobiont) provides shelter to algae.

Mycorrhiza (Fungi + Roots of higher plants)

- The fungus helps in absorbing water, minerals and inorganic salts from the soil.
- The plant provides shelter and food to fungi.

# Exam Pattern Questions

## Objective Type Questions

### Multiple Choice Questions

**1. Five kingdom system of classification suggested by RH Whittaker is not based on the**

(a) presence or absence of blood
(b) mode of reproduction
(c) mode of nutrition
(d) complexity of body organisation

**Ans.** (*a*)

**2. Which of the following statement given below is correct?**

(a) Biological classification is the scientific ordering of organisms in a hierarchical series of groups on the basis of their relationships, i.e. morphological, evolutionary and others
(b) Whittaker classified organisms on the basis of multiple factors including mode of nutrition
(c) In five kingdom system of classification, living organisms can be divided into prokaryotic and eukaryotic cells on the basis of cell structure
(d) All of the above

**Ans.** (*d*)

**3. Bacteria are grouped under four categories based on their shape. Refer to the given figures and identify *A*, *B*, *C* and *D*.**

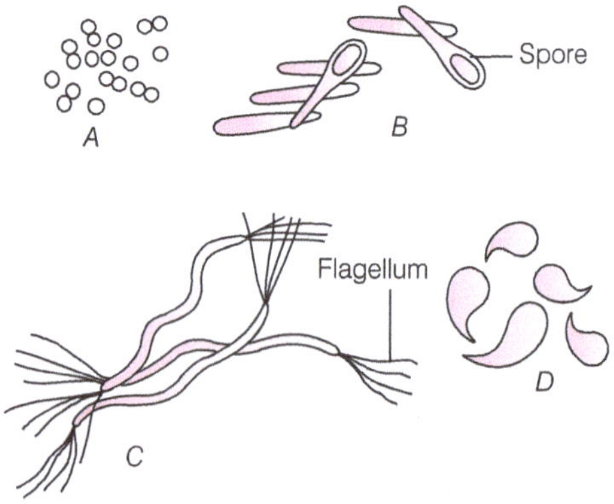


(a) *A*–Vibrio, *B*–Cocci, *C*–Bacilli, *D*–Spirilla
(b) *A*–Cocci, *B*–Bacilli, *C*–Spirilla, *D*–Vibrio
(c) *A*–Bacilli, *B*–Spirilla, *C*–Vibrio, *D*–Cocci
(d) *A*–Spirilla, *B*–Vibrio, *C*–Cocci, *D*–Bacilli

**Ans.** (*b*)

**4. Archaebacteria differ from Eubacteria in**

(a) cell wall structure (b) mode of nutrition
(c) cell shape (d) mode of reproduction

**Ans.** (*a*)

**5. Which of the following is not grouped with Archaebacteria?**

(a) Methanogens (b) Cyanobacteria
(c) Thermophiles (d) Halophiles

**Ans.** (*b*)

**6. Which of the following option is correctly belong to the *Nostoc* and *Anabaena*?**

(a) Actinomycetes (b) Cyanobacteria
(c) Mycoplasma (d) Rickettsia

**Ans.** (*b*)

**7. Select the incorrect statement.**

(a) Bacterial show most extensive metabolic diversity
(b) Bacteria are multicellular prokaryotes
(c) Cyanobacteria lack flagellated cells
(d) Mycoplasma is wall-less microorganism

**Ans.** (*b*)

**8. Which of the following organisms are known as chief producers in the oceans?**

(a) Cyanobacteria (b) Diatoms
(c) Dinoflagellates (d) Euglenoids

**Ans.** (*b*)

**9. Which of the following is/are the characteristic feature(s) of dinoflagellates?**

(a) They are unicellular and motile
(b) They can display a wide range of colours
(c) They possess two flagella
(d) All of the above

**Ans.** (*d*)

**10. Which of the following statements about *Euglena* is false?**

(a) Euglenoids bear flagella
(b) Their body is covered by pellicle
(c) The pigments of *Euglena* are similar to those in higher plant
(d) *Euglena* is a marine protist

**Ans.** (*d*)

**11.** **Naked cytoplasm, multinucleated and saprophytic are the characteristics of** **NCERT Exemplar**

(a) Monera (b) Protista
(c) Fungi (d) Slime moulds

**Ans.** (*d*) Slime moulds are saprophytic protists, moving along the dead leaves engulfing organic material. These are multinucleated and do not possess cell wall and have naked cytoplasm.

**12.** **Consider the following statements about amoeboid protozoans.** **Competency Based Que.**

I. They live in freshwater, sea water or moist soil.
II. They have pseudopodia for locomotion and capturing prey.
III. They have silica shells on their surface in marine forms.
IV. Some of them are parasities

Which of the statements given above are correct?

(a) I and II (b) III and IV
(c) II and III (d) I, II, III and IV

**Ans.** (*d*)

**13.** **Identify the incorrect statement regarding kingdom–Protista.** **Competency Based Que.**

(a) Sporozoans have an infectious spore like stage in their life cycle.
(b) Euglenoids have pellicle instead of cell wall.
(c) Dinoflagellates forms plasmodium under unfavourable conditions.
(d) Amoeboids capture their prey by pseudopodia

**Ans.** (*c*)

**14.** **An association between roots of higher plants and fungi is called**

(a) lichen (b) fern (c) mycorrhiza (d) BGA

**Ans.** (*c*)

**15.** **The spores that help fungi to undergo asexual reproduction during favourable conditions is**

(a) zoospores (b) sporangiospores
(c) conidia (d) All of these

**Ans.** (*d*)

**16.** **With respect to fungal sexual cycle, choose the correct sequence of events** **NCERT Exemplar**

(a) karyogamy, plasmogamy and meiosis
(b) meiosis, plasmogamy and karyogamy
(c) plasmogamy, karyogamy and meiosis
(d) meiosis, karyogamy and plasmogamy

**Ans.** (*c*) Plasmogamy means fusion of protoplasm and karyogamy means fusion of nucleus. These two events lead to the formation of zygote ($2n$), which is diploid structure where meiosis takes place.

**17.** **A dikaryon is formed when** **NCERT Exemplar**

(a) meiosis is arrested
(b) two haploid cells do not fuse immediately
(c) cytoplasm does not fuse
(d) None of the above

**Ans.** (*b*) Dikaryon is a cell containing two nucleus. This results when two somatic cells fuse but their nucleus does not fuse immediately.

**18.** **Members of Phycomycetes are found in** **NCERT Exemplar**

(i) aquatic habitats
(ii) on decaying wood
(iii) moist and damp places
(iv) as obligate parasites on plants

Choose from the following options.

(a) (i) and (iv) (b) (ii) and (iii)
(c) All of these (d) None of these

**Ans.** (*c*) Phycomycetes are the members of fungi that can thrive well on dead and decaying wood as saprophytes. These prefer to live in moist and damp places.

Few members of Phycomycetes are obligate parasites like *Phytophthora infestans* causing late blight of potato.

**19.** **Unicellular fungi belongs to**

(a) Phycomycetes
(b) Ascomycetes
(c) Deuteromycetes
(d) Basidiomycetes

**Ans.** (*b*)

**20.** **Deuteromycetes are called imperfect fungi because**

(a) sexual reproduction has not been observed
(b) they lack zygospore
(c) they form conidia
(d) All of the above

**Ans.** (*a*)

**21.** **Which of the following statement is incorrect?**

(a) *Neurospora* is used extensively in biochemical and genetic work
(b) *Agaricus* and *Puccinia* reproduce sexually by basidiospores
(c) *Albugo* and *Mucor* are parasitic fungi on mustard
(d) The asexual phase of Deuteromycetes is absent

**Ans.** (*c*)

**22.** **Which of the following bacterial features is also a plant character?**

(a) Heterotrophic nutrition
(b) Prokaryotic organisation
(c) Presence of flagella
(d) Rigid cell wall

**Ans.** (*d*)

**23.** **Match the following columns and choose the correct combination from the given options.** Competency Based Que.

| Column I (Kingdoms) | | Column II (Classes) | |
|---|---|---|---|
| A. | Plantae | 1. | Archaebacteria |
| B. | Fungi | 2. | Euglenoids |
| C. | Protista | 3. | Phycomycetes |
| D. | Monera | 4. | Algae |

**Codes**

| | A | B | C | D | | A | B | C | D |
|---|---|---|---|---|---|---|---|---|---|
| (a) | 4 | 3 | 2 | 1 | (b) | 1 | 2 | 3 | 4 |
| (c) | 3 | 4 | 2 | 1 | (d) | 4 | 2 | 3 | 1 |

**Ans.** (*a*)

**24.** **Higher organisms of kindom-Animalia**

I. are capable of locomotion.

II. have specialised sensory and neuromotor sytem.

III. show sexual reproduction by copulation of male and female followed by embryological development.

**Which of the statements given above is/are correct?**

(a) I and II (b) I and III

(c) Only I (d) I, II and III

**Ans.** (*d*)

**25.** **Viruses are non-cellular organisms, but replicate themselves once they infect the host cell. To which of the following kingdom do viruses belong to?** NCERT Exemplar

(a) Monera (b) Protista

(c) Fungi (d) None of these

**Ans.** (*d*) In five kingdom classification of Whittaker, non-cellular organisms like viruses and viroids are not mentioned. Viruses did not find a place in classification since they are not truly 'living' and are non-cellular.

**26.** **Which of the following is not a feature of virus?**

(a) Acellular (b) Saprophytes

(c) Inert outside body of host (d) Highly pathogenic

**Ans.** (*b*)

**27.** **Which of the following shows coiled RNA strand and capsomeres?**

(a) Poliovirus (b)Tobacco mosaic virus

(c) Potato spindle tuber virus (d) Retrovirus

**Ans.** (*b*)

**28.** **Difference between virus and viroid is** NCERT Exemplar

(a) absence of protein coat in viroid, but present in virus

(b) presence of low molecular weight RNA in virus, but absent in viroid

(c) Both (a) and (b)

(d) None of the above

**Ans.** (*a*) Virus contains DNA or RNA as genetic material and a protein coat, whereas viroids have no protein coat, but only RNA as their nucleic acid.

**29.** **Read the given statements that describe certain infectious agent.**

I. It is responsible for transmitting neurological diseases.

II. They cause mad cow disease in cattle.

III. These are responsible for causing Cr-Jacob disease in humans.

IV. These are misfolded proteins.

**Which of the following is referred to here?**

(a) Virus (b) Viroids

(c) Prions (d) Bacteriophages

**Ans.** (*c*)

**30.** **Which of the following organism is a pollution indicator?**

(a) moss (b) lichen (c) fern (d) grass

**Ans.** (*b*)

## Assertion-Reason Questions

**Direction** (Q. Nos. 1-10) *In each of the following questions, a statement of Assertion (A) is given followed by corresponding statement of Reason (R). Of the statements, mark the correct answer as*

(a) If both A and R are true and R is the correct explanation of A.

(b) If both A and R are true, but R is not the correct explanation of A.

(c) If A is true, but R is false.

(d) If A is false, but R is true.

**1.** **Assertion** (A) The two kingdom classification, used for a long time, was found to be inadequate.

**Reason** (R) Two kingdom system of classification did not distinguish between the eukaryotes and prokaryotes, unicellular and multicellular organisms and green algae and fungi. Competency Based Que.

**Ans.** (*a*)

**2.** **Assertion** (A) *Euglena* is a plant due to the presence of chlorophyll.

**Reason** (R) *Euglena* cannot be classified on the basis of two kingdom system.

**Ans.** (*d*) A is false, but R is true. A can be corrected as *Euglena* is a Protista because it is a single cell organism with a well defined nucleus.

**3.** **Assertion** (A) Five kingdom system of classification did not differentiate between the heterotrophic group, fungi and the autotrophic green plants.

**Reason** (R) Fungal cell wall contains chitin, while green plants have a cellulosic cell wall.

**Ans.** (*d*) A is false, but R is true. A can be corrected as

Two kingdom system of classification did not differentiate between the heterotrophic group, fungi and the autotrophic green plants.

**4.** **Assertion** (A) Three domains system classifies kingdom–Monera into two domains.

**Reason** (R) The three domains are, i.e. Archaea, Bacteria and Eukarya.

**Ans.** (*b*)

**5.** Observe the diagram and comment upon the appropriateness of the Assertion and Reason.

**Competency Based Que.**

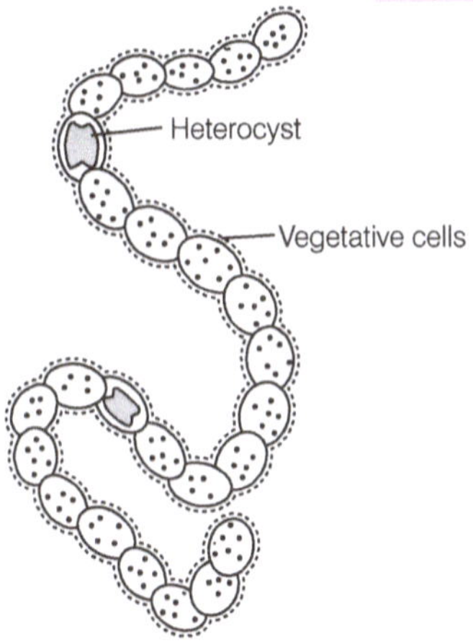


**Assertion** (A) The given organism is prokaryotic and are often grouped with bacteria.

**Reason** (R) They play an important role in recycling nutrients like iron, sulphur, etc.

**Ans.** (*b*)

**6.** **Assertion** (A) Diatoms are placed under Protista.

**Reason** (R) Diatoms do not have cell wall.

**Ans.** (*c*) A is true, but R is false. R can be corrected as

Diatoms are placed under Protista because they are unicellular and eukaryotic organisms.

**7.** **Assertion** (A) Fungi are wide spread in distribution.

**Reason** (R) Fungi can occur in air, water, soil and on animals and plants.

**Ans.** (*a*)

**8.** **Assertion** (A) Fungi are mostly heterotrophic.

**Reason** (R) Fungi lacks chlorophyll.

**Ans.** (*a*)

**9.** **Assertion** (A) Kingdom–Plantae includes all eukaryotic, chlorophyll containing organisms.

**Reason** (R) Few of its members are partially heterotrophic.

**Ans.** (*b*)

**10.** **Assertion** (A) Viruses cause diseases and replicate when they are inside the host cell.

**Reason** (R) Viruses do not replicate outside the host.

**Ans.** (*b*)

# Subjective Questions

## Very Short Answer Type Questions

**1. Name the five kingdoms proposed by Whittaker.**

**Ans.** Monera, Protista, Fungi, Plantae, Animalia.

**2. Name the smallest microorganism that completely lack cell wall.**

**Ans.** Mycoplasma

**3. Write the scientific name of fungus that causes**

**(i) bread mould**

**(ii) smut diseases**

**Ans.** (i) *Rhizopus*

(ii) *Ustilago* (½ × 2)

**4. Name the group of fungi which is commonly called as imperfect fungi.**

**Ans.** Deuteromycetes

**5. What does the 'perfect' stage of a fungus indicate?**

**Ans.** It indicates that the fungi is able to form perfect sexual spores.

**6. What type of genetic material is found in tobacco mosaic virus?**

**Ans.** RNA

**7. Name the viruses that are capable of attacking bacterial cells.**

**Ans.** Bacteriophages (1)

**8. Identify *A* in the figure shown given below and mention its function.**

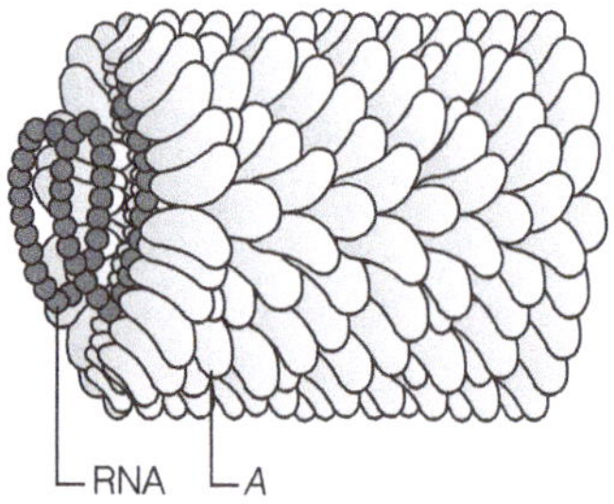


**Ans.** *A* represents the capsid. It is a protein covering around the genetic material which protects the genetic material.

**9. Name a disease which is caused by viroids.**

**Ans.** Potato spindle tuber disease

**10. Give the technical term for the symbiotic association of fungi with**

**(i) algae** **(ii) roots of higher plants**

**Ans.** (i) Lichens

(ii) Mycorrhiza (½ × 2)

## Short Answer Type Questions

**1. The two kingdom classification system placed bacteria, algae, blue-green algae, fungi, mosses, ferns, gymnosperms and angiosperms, together under one single kingdoms–Plantae. According to you, what could have been the basis of such classification.** **Competency Based Que.**

**Ans.** The two kingdom classification system was given by Linnaeus in 1758. Lesser number of organisms were known than in comparison to what the world knows today. He classified all the known living beings into two categories–Animalia and Plantae on the basis of the gross morphology. As bacteria, blue-green algae, fungi, algae, mosses, ferns, gymnosperms and angiosperms have their cells surrounded by cell walls, unlike animals, they were placed together under kingdom– Plantae.

**2. Who gave five kingdom classification? What was the criteria used for such classification?**

**Ans.** RH Whittaker gave five kingdom classification.

The main criteria used by him includes cell structure, body organisation, mode of nutrition, reproduction and phylogenetic relationship. (1 + 1)

**3. How is the five kingdom classification advantageous over the two kingdom classification?** **Competency Based Que., NCERT Exemplar**

**Ans.** The two kingdom system is divided into Plantae and Animalia solely on the basis of their gross morphology. On the other hand, the five kingdom classification is based upon more specific characters like cell structure, body structure, nutrition, evolutionary relationships, etc.

**4. Gamete formation and fusion are absent in bacteria. How do then bacteria undergo sexual reproduction?** **Competency Based Que.**

**Ans.** Reproduction in bacteria occurs by conjugation. It involves transfer of genetic material from one bacterium to another through cell to cell contact.

**5. How does a nucleoid differ from a nucleus?**

**Ans.** Nucleus is membrane-bound structure located in centre of eukaryotic cell, while nucleoid is a membraneless structure found in prokaryotic cell.

**6. What is the principle underlying the use of cyanobacteria in agricultural fields for crop improvement?** **NCERT Exemplar**

**Ans.** The principle behind using cyanobacteria in agriculture for crop improvement is their ability to fix atmospheric nitrogen. Cyanobacteria convert nitrogen gas ($N_2$) into a form that plants can use, enriching soil fertility naturally.

This process reduces the need for chemical fertilisers, promotes sustainable farming and enhances crop growth by supplying essential nitrogen to plants.

**7. Cyanobacteria and heterotrophic bacteria have been clubbed together in Eubacteria of Kingdom–Monera as per the five kingdom classification even though the two are vastly different from each other. Is this grouping of the two types of taxa in the same kingdom justified? If so, why?** Competency Based Que., NCERT Exemplar

**Ans.** Although cyanobacteria and heterotrophic bacteria are vastly different from each other, they still bear some common characters, on the basis of which they are introduced in Eubacteria of kingdom–Monera. (1½)

These characters are as follows

(i) Both the groups do not possess well-defined nucleus.
(ii) Nucleus lacks nucleolus and nuclear membrane.
(iii) DNA (genetic material) lies freely in the cytoplasm.
(iv) They possess 70S type of ribosomes. (1½)

**8. Polluted water bodies have usually high abundance of plants like *Nostoc* and *Oscillatoria*. Give reasons.** NCERT Exemplar

**Ans.** Polluted water bodies possess high algal growth due to the presence of nutrient. These nutrients increase the rapid growth of blue-green algae especially *Nostoc* and *Oscillatoria*, etc., and result in colonies. These colonies are generally surrounded by a gelatinous sheath and further leads to the formation of blooms in water bodies.

**9. What is the mode of reproduction in bacteria?**

**Ans.** Refer to text on page no. 20.

**10. State two economically important uses of**
**(i) Heterotrophic bacteria.**
**(ii) Archaebacteria.** NCERT

**Ans.** (i) **Heterotrophic Bacteria** They decompose dead bodies of plants and animals so, they are nature's scavengers. The organic content of sewage is broken down by these bacteria. They also generate humus which is used in agriculture. (1½)

(ii) **Archaebacteria** They are used in gobar gas (biogas) production and are helpful in causing fermentation of cellulose in ruminants. (1½)

**11. List out the differences between Monera and Protista.**

**Ans.** Differences between Monera and Protista are

| Monera | Protista |
|---|---|
| Cell wall is made up of Polysaccharide and amino acid. | Cell wall is made up of cellulose. |
| Ribosomes are 70S type. | Ribosomes are 80S type. |
| These are prokaryotic and have naked circular DNA. | Eukaryotic, linear DNA is present in nucleus. |
| Extra chromosomal DNA is present in the form of plasmids. | Extra chromosomal DNA is present in organelles like mitochondria and chloroplast. |

**12. Describe the cell structure of a typical protist.**

**Ans.** Refer to text on page no. 21.

**13. What is the nature of cell wall in diatoms?** NCERT

**Ans.** Cell wall in diatoms is made up of cellulose and silica compounds. It is double-walled layer called frustule.

**14. Diatoms are called as pearls of ocean. Why? What is diatomaceous earth?** NCERT Exemplar

**Ans.** Diatoms have a shinning silicified double-walled covering or frustule. Because of their distinctive cell walls these are sometimes called as the pearls of ocean. (1)

**Diatomaceous earth** is a pile of siliceous skeletons of diatoms which accumulates at the bottom of sea or oceans, being resistant to decay. (1)

**15. Find out what do the terms algal blooms and red tides signify.** NCERT

**Ans.** Algal bloom refers to the excessive growth of algae especially blue-green algae in polluted waters. Red tides refer to the red colour imparted to the seawater by the rapid multiplication of dinoflagellates like *Gonyaulax*. (1 + 1)

**16. Suppose you accidently find an old preserved permanent slide without a label. In your effort to identify it, you place the slide under microscope and observe the following features.**
**(i) Unicellular**
**(ii) Well-defined nucleus**
**(iii) Biflagellate, one flagellum lying longitudinally and other transversely.**

**What would you identify it as? Can you name the kingdom it belongs to?** Competency Based Que.

**Ans.** Dinoflagellates are unicellular, motile, photosynthetic protists. They have a well-defined nucleus and possess two different flagella one transverse and the other is longitudinal. They belong to kingdom–Protista. (1 + 1)

**17. Give the general characteristics of dinoflagellates.**

**Ans.** Refer to text on page no. 22.

**18. Justify the statement *Euglena* is a taxonomic puzzle.**

**Ans.** *Euglena* is a taxonomic puzzle since, it shows both plant and animal characters. Absence of cell wall is an animal feature and presence of chloroplast is a plant character of *Euglena*. It have mixotrophic nutrition. In the presence of sunlight, it can photosynthesise its food and in the absence of sunlight, it behaves like a heterotroph by predating on other smaller organisms.

**19. What are the characteristic features of euglenoids?** NCERT

**Ans.** Refer to text on page no. 22.

**20. How do dinoflagellates differ from euglenoids?**

**Ans.** Differences between dinoflagellates and euglenoids are

| Dinoflagellates | Euglenoids |
|---|---|
| They are mostly marine. | They are freshwater forms found in stagnant water. |
| They have a cell wall with stiff cellulose plates on the outer surface. | They have no cell wall, but have a pellicle layer which gives shape and flexibility to body. |
| They are always photoautotrophic. | They may be photoautotrophic or heterotrophic. |
| They have two flagella, one transverse and one longitudinal. | They have two flagella and both are anterior. |

**21. Describe briefly the four major groups of Protozoa.** NCERT

**Ans.** Refer to text on page no. 23.

**22. Study the table and fill in the blanks (*a*), (*b*), (*c*) and (*d*).**

| Protozoan | Habitat | Examples |
|---|---|---|
| Amoeboid | (*a*) | (*b*) |
| Flagellated | Free-living or parasitic | (*c*) |
| (*d*) | Aquatic | *Paramoecium* |

**Ans.** (a) Freshwater, sea water or moist soil.

(b) *Entamoeba*

(c) *Trypanosoma*

(d) Ciliated (½ × 4)

**23. On what basis was fungi removed from the plant kingdom?**

**Ans.** Refer to text on page no. 18.

**24. Describe the structure of fungus in detail.**

**Ans.** Refer to text on page no. 24.

**25. Briefly describe the sexual cycle of fungi.**

**Ans.** Refer to text on page no. 24.

**26. Reproduction in fungi can occur sexually as well as asexually. Explain.**

**Ans.** Reproduction in fungi occurs by asexual and sexual methods. Asexually, it takes place either by formation of motile spores (zoospores) or by formation of non-motile spores (sporangiospores, conidia). Sexual reproduction occurs by oospores, ascospores and basidiospores. Ascomycetes and Basidiomycetes produce fruiting bodies by sexual process, which contain sexual spores called ascospores and basidiospores, respectively.

**27. Explain the following terms in relation to Phycomycetes.**

**(i) Hyphae (ii) Asexual reproduction.**

**Ans.** (i) **Hyphae** They are thread-like structures that make up the mycelium of fungi. It may be coenocytic and non-septate or aseptate.

(ii) **Asexual Reproduction** It involves the endogenous formation of spores in sporangia. (1+1)

**28. Write a short note on Phycomycetes.**

**Ans.** Refer to text on page no. 25.

**29. *Neurospora*, an Ascomycetes fungus has been used as a biological tool to understand the mechanism of plant genetics much in the same way as *Drosophila* has been used to study animal genetics. What makes *Neurospora* as a genetic tool?** Competency Based Que., NCERT Exemplar

**Ans.** *Neurospora* is often called *Drosophila* of plant kingdom because it can be easily grown under laboratory conditions. It is haploid in nature which helps in immediate expression of every mutation. Beadle and Tatum used it as an experimental tool to find out that genes express their effect through synthesis of specific enzymes.

**30. What is the characteristic feature of *Claviceps*?**

**Ans.** Ascospore formation is the characteristic feature of *Claviceps* that belong to class–Ascomycetes. Ascospores are a type of non-motile meiospores which are produced inside special sacs called asci (sing. ascus).

**31. What makes Phycomycetes and Ascomycetes two different classes?**

**Ans.** Differences between Phycomycetes and Ascomycetes are

| Phycomycetes | Ascomycetes |
|---|---|
| Hyphae are aseptate and coenocytic. | Hyphae are septate and branched. |
| Asexual spores are zoospores or aplanospores. | Asexual spores are conidia. |

(1 + 1)

**32. Explain the terms**

**(i) Basidiocarp (ii) Basidia (iii) Basidiospores**

**Ans.** (i) **Basidiocarp** It is a fruiting body which bears basidia. (1)

(ii) **Basidia** These are special reproductive bodies of Basidiomycetes where karyogamy, meiosis and basidiospore formation occurs. (1)

(iii) **Basidiospores** These are meiospores of Basidiomycetes. Basidiospores are borne exogenously basidium.

**33. What are the main differences between Ascomycetes and Basidiomycetes?**

**Ans.** Refer to text on page no. 25.

**34. Why the members of class–Deuteromycetes are considered as the fungi imperfecti?**

**Ans.** Deuteromycetes is an artificial class of fungi which has been created to include all those fungi (fungi imperfecti) in which sexual stage is either absent or not known. It is believed that most members of Deuteromycetes are actually Ascomycetes in which sexual reproduction is either absent or yet to be discovered. Hence, are considered as fungi imperfecti.

**35. What is capsid and how is it useful for viruses?**

**Ans.** Capsid is a proteinaceous covering around the material. It protects the genetic from damage from physical and chemical agents. (1+1)

**36. How are viroids different from viruses?** NCERT

**Ans.** Differences between viroids and viruses are

| Viroids | Viruses |
|---|---|
| Protein coat is not present. | Protein coat is present. |
| These are short segments of free RNA which are infectious. | The genetic/infectious material is RNA or DNA. |
| RNA is small. | RNA is comparatively larger in size. |

(1 × 3)

**37. What are viroids and prions?**

**Ans.** Refer to text on page no. 28.

**38. Write a short note on lichens.**

**Ans.** Refer to text on page no. 28.

**39. Explain the physiological relationships between the algal and fungal components of lichen.**

**Ans.** Refer to text on page no. 28.

**40. What do the terms phycobiont and mycobiont signify?** NCERT

**Ans.** Phycobiont and mycobiont are parts of lichens. The phycobiont is the algal partner in lichens and mycobiont is the fungal partner in lichens. (1+1)

## Long Answer Type Questions

**1. Explain the criteria used for the two kingdom system of classification. Briefly explain the demerits of two kingdom classification.**

**Ans.** Refer to text on page no. 18.

**2. Biological classification is a dynamic and ever evolving phenomenon which keeps changing with our understanding of life forms. Justify the statement by taking any two examples.** NCERT Exemplar

**Ans.** Biological classification keeps changing with our understanding of life forms.

As more and more knowledge gathered for delimitation of taxa, the ways for natural system of classification became clear. (1)

This can be understood by following examples

(i) Two kingdom classification was replaced by three kingdom classification when Haeckel (1866) proposed the kingdom–Protista.

(ii) It was converted into four kingdom classification by Copeland when he proposed the kingdom–Monera.

(iii) Whittaker in 1969 proposed five kingdom classification.

(iv) As the information about biochemistry of Archaebacteria gathered, Carl Woese in 1990 raised another kingdom–Archaea. (4)

**3. Discuss how classification system have undergone several changes over a period of time.** NCERT

**Ans.** Changes in classification system over a period of time are as follows

(i) Biological classification of living organisms was first done by Aristotle. On the morphological basis, he gave the broad classification of plants and animals. He further divided plants into trees, shrubs and herbs. The animal classification was done on the basis of the presence or absence of red blood into Enaima or Anaima, respectively.

(ii) The first proper classification system was proposed by Linnaeus who divided living beings in two kingdoms–Plantae (all plants) and Animalia (all animals). Although this system of classification had been accepted for a long time, but eventually it was rejected due to its inadequancies.

(iii) Later, more criteria for classification were implemented that include, cell structure, body organisation, mode of nutrition and reproduction, evolutionary relationships.

(iv) Classification on the basis of these criteria led to the creation of three more kingdoms which are now part of the five kingdom system of classification given by Whittaker in 1969. The five kingdoms are—**Monera** (prokaryotes), **Protista** (single-celled eukaryotes), **Fungi**, **Plantae** and **Animalia**.

(v) The six kingdom classification system is the latest system introduced by Carl Woese in 1990. It divides Monera into two kingdoms–Archaebacteria and Eubacteria. (1×5)

**4. Make an outline of the five kingdom classification.**

**Ans.** Refer to text on page no. 18.

**5. In which organisms heterocyst is present? Mention two features of heterocysts. Which features make it suitable for nitrogen-fixation?** Competency Based Que.

**Ans.** **Heterocysts** are present in some cyanobacteria. It is a large-sized, pale coloured, thick-walled cell which occurs in terminal, intercalary or lateral position, e.g. *Nostoc*. (2)

Features of heterocyst are

(i) Mucilage sheath is present.

(ii) Thylakoids lack phycobilins. Therefore, photosynthesis is absent.

(iii) Heterocyst is dependent for its nourishment on adjacent vegetative cells.

The thick wall is impermeable to oxygen, but permeable to nitrogen. It has enzyme nitrogenase which is specialised to perform nitrogen-fixation. (3)

**6.** **(i) Write a short note on nutrition in fungi.**

**(ii) List some common feature of sac fungi.**

**Ans.** (i) Refer to text on page no. 24.

(ii) Refer to text on page no. 25.

**7.** **Give a comparative account of the classes of kingdom–Fungi under the following**

**(i) Mode of nutrition**

**(ii) Mode of reproduction.** NCERT

**Ans.** Classes of kingdom–Fungi are

(i) **Mode of Nutrition**

**Phycomycetes** Saprotrophic and parasitic.

**Ascomycetes** Saprotrophic, decomposers, coprophilous and parasitic.

**Basidiomycetes** Saprotrophic and parasitic.

**Deuteromycetes** Parasitic and saprotrophic. (2)

(ii) **Mode of Reproduction**

**Phycomycetes** Asexual reproduction occurs by zoospores (motile) or by aplanospores (non-motile). Sexual reproduction is by gametangial fusion and gametic fusion.

**Ascomycetes** Asexual reproduction is by conidia and sexual reproduction is by ascospores.

**Basidiomycetes** Asexual spores are generally not found, but vegetative reproduction by fragmentation is common. Sexual reproduction is by basidiospores.

**Deuteromycetes** Reproduce only by asexual spores called conidia. Sexual reproduction is not reported. (3)

**8.** **Write differences between ascocarp and basidiocarp.**

**Ans.** Refer to text on page no. 25.

**9.** **(i) Write a short note on kingdom–Plantae.**

**(ii) Describe alternation of generation.**

**Ans.** Refer to text on page no. 26.

**10.** **Given a brief account on kingdom–Animalia.**

**Ans.** Refer to text on page no. 26.

**11.** **Differentiate between kingdom–Plantae and Animalia in detail.** DIKSHA

**Ans.** **Kingdom–Plantae**

(i) It includes all eukaryotic chlorophyll containing organisms commonly called plants.

(ii) Plants are autotrophs, but a few members are partially heterotrophic such as the insectivorous plants or parasites.

(iii) Plant contain chloroplasts and cell wall is mainly made of cellulose.

(iv) Plants are immobile and cannot move from one place to another. (2½)

**Kingdom–Animalia**

(i) This kingdom is characterised by heterotrophic eukaryotic organisms that are multicellular and their cells lack cell walls.

(ii) Animals are hetetrotrophs they directly or indirectly depend on plants for food.

(iii) Animals lack chloroplasts and cell wall.

(iv) Higher forms show elaborate sensory and neuromotor mechanism. Most of them are capable of locomotion. (2½)

**12.** **How do viruses resemble non-living things?**

*Or*

**Organise a discussion in your class on the topic 'Are viruses living or non-living'?** NCERT

**Ans.** Viruses are intermediate between living and non-living objects.

They resemble non-living objects in

(i) Lacking protoplast.

(ii) Ability to get crystallised.

(iii) Absence of respiration and energy storing system.

(iv) Absence of growth and division.

(v) Cannot live independent of a living cell. (1 × 5)

**13.** **Give a brief account of viruses with respect to their structure and nature of genetic material. Also name four common viral diseases.** NCERT

**Ans.** Viruses are nucleoproteins. The genetic material is protected within a protein coat, called capsid. The capsid consists of a number of subunits called capsomeres. These capsomeres are arranged in helical, polyhedral or geometric form. (3)

The genetic material, i.e. DNA or RNA may be single-stranded or double-stranded. (1)

The four common viral diseases are mumps, AIDS, small pox, herpes. (1)

**14.** **Explain the structure of bacteriophage with the help of well-labelled diagram.**

**Ans.** A bacteriophage consists of two main parts, i.e. head and tail.

**Head** It consists of proteinaceous membrane enclosing a core of viral DNA. The DNA is double-stranded.

**Tail** It is cylindrical. It has four components are

(i) A central core

(ii) A protein sheath surrounding the core.

(iii) A sheath connected to head by a collar and at distal end to a hexagonal basal plate.

(iv) Basal plate also bears six long tail fibres which are the organs of attachment to the bacterial surface. (3)

**For diagram** Refer to fig no. 2.13 on page 27. (2)

## Source Based/Case Based/Passage Based Questions

**1.** A student observed polluted water bodies. He found green gelatinous organisms which spread all over the water. He studied some of these organisms under microscope and discussed with his teacher.

(i) What are these green gelatinous organisms?

(ii) The given organism belong to which kingdom?

(iii) Write any two features of the given organism.

(iv) Write any one similarity between the given organism and plants.

**Ans.** (i) Cyanobacteria are generally surrounded by gelatinous sheath. They form blooms in polluted water bodies. (1)

(ii) The given organism belongs to kingdom–Monera. (1)

(iii) The given organism (cyanobacteria) is photosynthetic prokaryote and can survive in wide variety of habitats such as freshwater or marine water. (1)

(iv) Cyanobacteria have chlorophyll-*a* similar to green plants. (1)

**2.** Study the diagram given below and answer the questions that follows

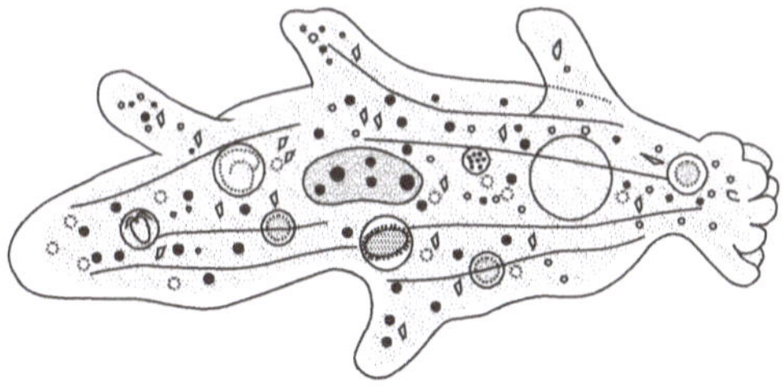

(i) Name the organism shown in the above picture.

(ii) To which kingdom does it belongs to?

(iii) Write any one characteristic feature of the kingdom to which it belongs.

(iv) How do these organisms capture their prey?

**Ans.** (i) *Amoeba*

(ii) It belongs to kingdom–Protista.

(iii) The members of this kingdom are single-celled eukaryotes.

(iv) They capture their prey by putting out pseudopodia. (1 × 4)

**3.** Read the following passage and answer the questions that follows

Viruses are non-cellular organisms that are characterised by an inert crystalline structure surrounding the genetic material. These are obligate parasites and do not have a biosynthetic machinery. Therefore, they use host machinery to replicate themselves.

Viruses are ultra-microscopic nucleoprotein entities having variable size and shape.

The basic structure of virus is composed of envelope, capsid and nucleoid.

(i) Name the viruses which do not contain DNA.

(ii) What is the features of virus capsid?

(iii) Name the kingdom under which they are placed.

(iv) Name a virus that affects plants.

**Ans.** (i) Human Immunodeficiency Virus (HIV) do not contains DNA.

(ii) Capsid surrounds the genetic material of virus. It is proteinaceous and is composed of several capsomeres.

(iii) Viruses are not given any place in five kingdom classification

(iv) Tobacco Mosaic Virus (TMV).

**4.** Given below is a graphical representation of abundance of lichens in a given area for a period of 10 years.

**Competency Based Que.**

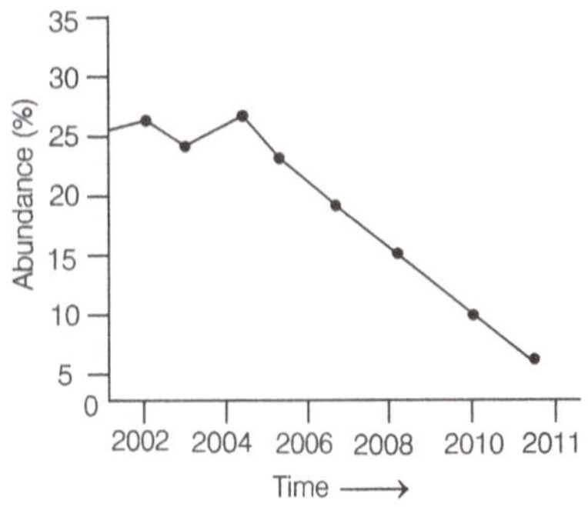


Study the graph carefully and answer the following questions

(i) What observation can be drawn from the graph?

(ii) Give reason for your answer in (i).

(iii) Comment upon the components that make up lichens.

*Or*

(iii) Write two economic importance of lichens that makes it valuable for industry purpose.

**Ans.** (i) The graph shows decline in abundance of lichens from the year 2004 onwards. (1)

(ii) Lichens show decline abundance due to increasing pollution in the area as they do not grow in polluted areas. (1)

(iii) Each lichen comprises of two components a fungus (mycobiont) and an alga (phycobiont). The fungal component of lichens either belongs to Ascomycetes or Basidiomycetes. The algal component is either a green alga or a cyanobacteria. (2)

*Or*

(iii) (a) **Food and Fodder** Some lichens are used as food by catterpillars, mites and snails, etc.

(b) **Medicinal Use** Some lichens have great significance in medicine and treatment of various diseases. (2)

# SELF ASSESSMENT TEST

## Multiple Choice Questions

1. Archaebacteria found in marshy areas are also present in
   (a) gut of cows and buffaloes
   (b) intestine of humans
   (c) cold and freshwater ecosystems
   (d) aerobic environment

2. Among the following protists, which one is responsible for appearance of red sea?
   (a) *Euglena*, euglenoid
   (b) Diatoms, chrysophytes
   (c) *Gonyaulax*, dinoflagellates
   (d) Planktons, slime moulds

3. Which of the following match pair is incorrect?
   (a) Phycomycetes – Asexual reproduction occurs by aplanospores.
   (b) Deuteromycetes – Isogamous type of sexual reproduction takes place
   (c) Basidiomycetes – Vegetative reproduction occur by fragmentation
   (d) Ascomycetes – Asexual reproduction occurs by conidia

4. Match the following columns.

| | Column I | | Column II |
|---|---|---|---|
| A. | Saprophyte | 1. | Symbiotic association of fungi with plant roots. |
| B. | Parasite | 2. | Decomposition of dead organic materials |
| C. | Lichens | 3. | Grow on living plants or animals |
| D. | Mycorrhiza | 4. | Symbiotic association of algae and fungi |

**Codes**

| | A | B | C | D | | A | B | C | D |
|---|---|---|---|---|---|---|---|---|---|
| (a) | 1 | 2 | 3 | 4 | (b) | 3 | 2 | 1 | 4 |
| (c) | 2 | 1 | 3 | 4 | (d) | 2 | 3 | 4 | 1 |

5. Which of the following represents an insectivorous and a parasitic plant, respectively?
   (a) Venus flytrap and bladderwort
   (b) *Cuscuta* and *Rafflesia*
   (c) Bladderwort and *Cuscuta*
   (d) *Rafflesia* and venus flytrap

6. Identify the phycobiont and mycobiont components of a lichen.
   (a) Algae and fungi, respectively
   (b) Plant and animal, respectively
   (c) Fungi and algae, respectively
   (d) Animal and plant, respectively

7. Identify the label *A*, *B*, *C* and *D* in the following figure.

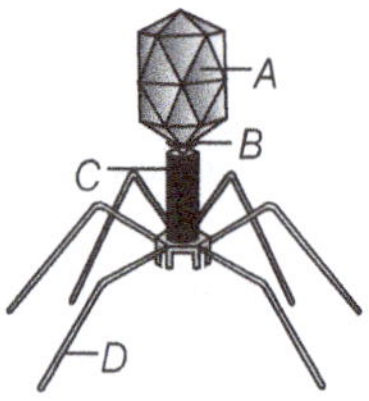


   (a) *A*– Head, *B*–Collar, *C*–Sheath, *D*–Tail fibres
   (b) *A*–Collar, *B*–Head, *C*–Sheath, *D*–Tail fibres
   (c) *A*–Head, *B*–Collar, *C*–Tail fibres, *D*–Sheath
   (d) *A*–Collar, *B*–Tail fibres, *C*–Head, *D*–Sheath

## Assertion-Reason Questions

**Direction** (Q. Nos. 8-11) *In each of the following questions, a statement of Assertion (A) is given followed by corresponding statement of Reason (R). Of the statements, mark the correct answer as*

(a) Both A and R are true and R is the correct explanation of A.
(b) Both A and R are true, but R is not the correct explanation of A.
(c) A is true, but R is false.
(d) A is false, but R is true.

8. **Assertion** (A) Archaebacteria have a distinct cell wall structure compared to other bacteria.

**Reason** (R) Archaebacteria thrive in extreme conditions.

9. **Assertion** (A) Slime moulds are saprophytic protists.

**Reason** (R) Slime moulds form plasmodium under, unfavourable conditions.

10. **Assertion** (A) In some Ascomycetes, the conidia are borne on specialised structures known as conidiophores.

**Reason** (R) Conidiophores are produced during sexual reproduction.

11. **Assertion** (A) Prions can cause neurodegenerative diseases like mad cow disease and Creutzfeldt-Jakob disease.

**Reason** (R) Prions induce changes in the DNA of the affected organism, leading to cellular damage.

## Very Short Answer Type Questions

12. Give two characteristics of smallest known living organism.
13. Do dinoflagellates have a cell wall? If yes, what is it made of?
14. What is the most common method of reproduction in Basidiomycetes?

## Short Answer Type Questions

15. What are the three main types of Archaebacteria and what are their key characteristics?
16. What is the function of the fruiting body in slime moulds?
17. Describe any two major groups of protozoan.

## Long Answer Type Questions

18. **(i) What are the key features of the kingdom–Monera?**

**(ii) Explain the classification of Monera with examples.**

19. **(i) Write the characteristic features of the diatoms.**

**(ii) Explain the role of diatoms in the ecosystem.**

20. **(i) Write the distinct characters of fungi.**

**(ii) Differentiate between Phycomycetes and Basidiomycetes.**

## Case Based Question

21. Study the diagram given below and answer the question that follows.

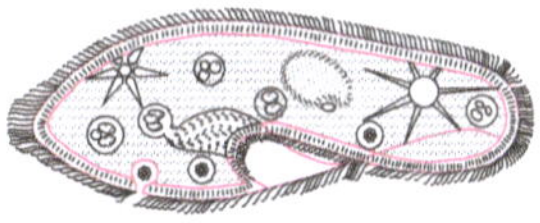

(i) Name the organism shown in the above picture.

(ii) To which kingdom does it belongs?

(iii) Write any two characteristic feature of the organism shown in the above picture.

# Answers

| | | | | | | | |
|---|---|---|---|---|---|---|---|
| 1. (a) | 2. (c) | 3. (b) | 4. (d) | 5. (c) | 6. (a) | 7. (a) | 8. (b) |
| 9. (c) | 10. (c) | 11. (c) | | | | | |

# 03

CHAPTER

According to Whittaker's classification system, plants are classified under kingdom–Plantae.
Kingdom–Plantae includes all multicellular, eukaryotic organisms that contain chlorophyll. These organisms are generally autotrophic in nature and serve as the main producers on land and in water.

**YOUR STUDY GOALS**

3.1 Basis of Classification
3.2 Algae
3.3 Bryophytes
3.4 Pteridophytes
3.5 Gymnosperms
3.6 Angiosperms

**YOUR PRACTICE GOAL**

- Objective Type Questions (37 Qs ; MCQs, A-R) Case Based Questions (3)
- Subjective Type Questions
- (13 VSAs, 24 SAs, 10 LAs)

# Plant Kingdom

In this chapter, we will study the classification of the plant kingdom in detail, exploring its major groups, key characteristics, and economic significance.

## 3.1 Basis of Classification

- In earlier classifications, fungi and members of Monera and Protista having cell walls were included in Plantae. However, these groups have now been excluded from this kingdom, highlighting their distinct traits.
- The kingdom–Plantae now includes **algae**, **bryophytes, pteridophytes, gymnosperms** and **angiosperms**.
- The first classification system took only a few vegetative characteristics into account for classifying plants. However, modern taxonomic studies are more detailed and take into account various factors such as **evolutionary relationships, morphological characteristics**, etc.
- All these led to the development of various systems of plant classification.

## Types of Classification System

The various systems used in classification of plants are discussed below.

### 1. Artificial System of Classification

- This system was given by **Linnaeus** and was based on comparison of one or few gross **superficial morphological characteristics** such as habit, colour, number and shapes of leaves, etc.
- They were mainly based on vegetative characters or on the androecium structure.

#### Disadvantages

- It gave equal weightage to **vegetative** and **reproductive/sexual characters** which is not acceptable as vegetative characters get more easily influenced by the environmental factors.
- It separates the closely related species as they were based on a few characteristics.

### 2. Natural System of Classification

- This classification was given by **George Bentham** and **Joseph Dalton Hooker** for flowering plants.
- This classification was based on **natural affinities** among the organisms.
- It considers not only external features but also the internal features like ultrastructure, anatomy, embryology and phytochemistry.

### 3. Phylogenetic System of Classification

- This system of classification was initiated by **Engler** and **Prantl**.
- It is based on the **evolutionary relationships** among organisms and assumes that organisms belonging to the same taxa have a common ancestor.
- It utilises fossil records to provide evidence of these relationships. In the absence of supporting fossil evidence, this system gathers evidences from various branches of taxonomy.

## Types of Taxonomy

To classify plants into various categories, different branches of taxonomy are used. These branches help in understanding plant diversity and their relationships. The various type of taxonomy are discussed below.

#### Numerical Taxonomy

- It is based on all **observable characteristics** and is easily carried out by using computers.
- Number and codes are assigned to all the characters and the data are then processed. In this way, each character is given equal importance and at the same time hundreds of characters can be considered.

#### Cytotaxonomy

- It is based on **cytological information** like chromosome number, structure and behaviour.
- Behaviour of chromosomes was used by taxonomists during pairing and banding patterns to understand the relationships between species, e.g. origin of humans from apes, origin of wheat, etc.

#### Chemotaxonomy

- It is based on the information about **chemical constituents** of plants body such as secondary metabolites, nature of proteins, etc. To resolve confusions, they are widely used by taxonomist these days.

  All these methods of taxonomy help in better classification, allowing for a more accurate understanding of the relationships among organisms. This information prepares us to discuss the different divisions of the plant kingdom in detail.

## Classification of Plants

- As discussed in previous chapter, **RH Whittaker** classified all organisms into a five-kingdom system: Monera, Protista, Fungi, Plantae, and Animalia.
- Within this classification, various types of algae, including blue-green algae, red algae, brown algae, and green algae, were initially placed in the **kingdom-Plantae**.
- However, later research revealed that blue-green algae are prokaryotic organisms. This discovery resulted in the reclassification of blue-green algae, shifting them from the kingdom–Plantae to the kingdom–Monera. This change highlights how our understanding of plant classification has evolved.

- An overview of the classification of kingdom–Plantae is demonstrated below in the flowchart.

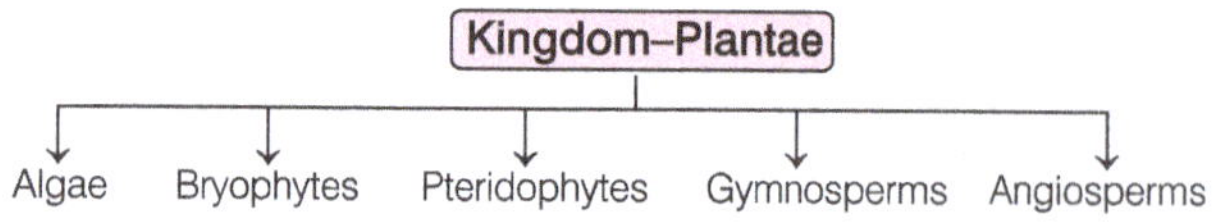


## Quick Test 1

1. Name the method of classification that relies primarily on observable external features like colour, shape, or size, rather than evolutionary relationships.
2. Mention the classification system proposed by Bentham and Hooker.
3. Name the classification system that assumes organisms within the same taxon share a common ancestor.
4. **State True or False**
   Cytotaxonomy is based on information like the genetic makeup of organisms.
5. In which kingdom blue-green algae classified?

## 3.2 Algae

These are chlorophyll containing simple, thalloid, autotrophic and largely aquatic organisms.

### General Characteristics

The important general characteristics of algae are given below.

- **Habitat** These are found in both **freshwater** and **marine habitats**. Some algal forms are also found in variety of habitats like moist stones, soil, wood, etc. Some of them are also found in close association with fungi (lichen) and animals (e.g. on sloth bear).
- **Thallus Structure** It is highly variable and ranges from **filamentous form** (e.g. *Ulothrix* and *Spirogyra*) to **colonial forms** (e.g. *Volvox*). Some of the marine forms such as kelps, forms massive plant bodies.
- **Reproduction** The algae reproduce vegetatively, asexually and sexually.
  - **Vegetative reproduction** occurs by fragmentation. Each fragment gets developed into an independent plant body (thallus).
  - **Asexual reproduction** occurs by production of different types of spores. The most common are **zoospores**, which are flagellated (motile) and on germination gives rise to new plants.
  - **Sexual reproduction** occurs by fusion of two gametes.
- On the basis of morphology of reproductive cells, sexual reproduction is of three types.
  - **Isogamous** In this method, two morphologically similar gametes fuse to form a zygote. Gametes can be flagellated and similar in size (e.g. *Ulothrix*) or non-flagellated, but similar in size (e.g. *Spirogyra*).
  - **Anisogamous** This method involves fusion of two dissimilar gametes that differ in size, e.g. *Eudorina*
  - **Oogamous** In this method, fusion between one large, non-motile(static) female gamete and a smaller, motile male gamete takes place, e.g. *Volvox, Fucus.*

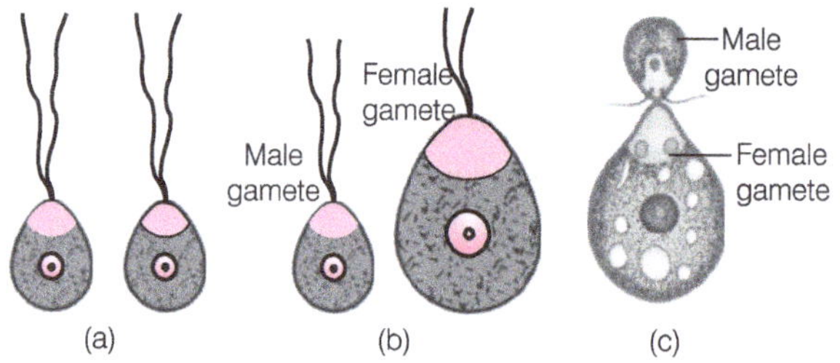


Fig. 3.1 (a) Isogamy, (b) Anisogamy, (c) Oogamy

### Classification of Algae

Algae are divided into various classes based on pigmentation, type of stored food materials, cell wall and type of flagellation. The three main classes are Chlorophyceae, Phaeophyceae and Rhodophyceae.

### 1. Class–Chlorophyceae (Green Algae)

The members of Chlorophyceae are commonly called **green algae**. They are commonly found in freshwater, brackish water, and marine environments.

The characteristic features of Chlorophyceae are discussed below.

- **Cell Organisation** The plant body may be unicellular, colonial or filamentous. They have rigid cell wall that is usually made up of cellulose (inner layer) and pectose (outer layer).
  The chloroplasts may be discoid, plate-like, reticulate, cup-shaped, spiral or ribbon-shaped in different species.
- **Photosynthetic Pigments** The chloroplasts contain photosynthetic pigments. They are usually grass green due to dominance of pigments chlorophyll-*a* and *b*.

- **Food Reserve** Most of the members have one or more storage bodies called pyrenoids located in the chloroplasts. Pyrenoids contain protein besides starch. Some algae may also store food in the form of oil droplets.
- **Reproduction** It occurs by following type
  - **Vegetative reproduction** occurs through fragmentation or by formation of different types of spores.
  - **Asexual reproduction** occurs by flagellated zoospores, produced in zoosporangia.
  - **Sexual reproduction** shows considerable variation in the type and formation of sex cells and it can be isogamous, anisogamous or oogamous.
- Some common forms are *Chlamydomonas, Volvox, Ulothrix, Spirogyra* and *Chara.*

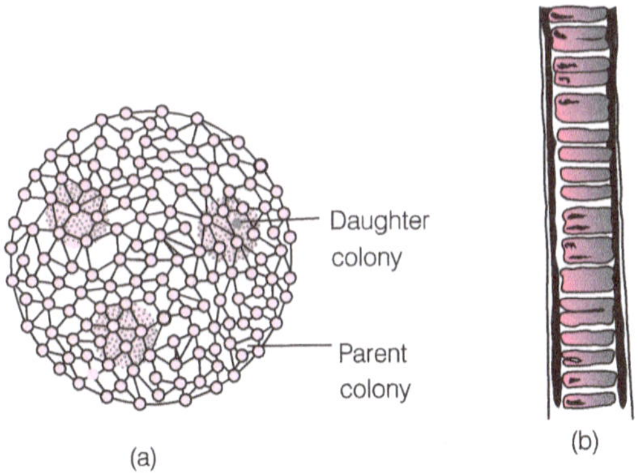


Fig. 3.2 Green algae : (a) *Volvox*, (b) *Ulothrix*

## 2. Class–Phaeophyceae (Brown Algae)

The members of Phaeophyceae are commonly called **brown algae** and are primarily found in **marine habitats.**

The characteristic features of Phaeophyceae are discussed below.

- **Size and Form** They show great variation in size and form. They range from **simple branched, filamentous** forms (*Ectocarpus*) to profusely branched forms as represented by kelps (may reach a height upto 100 metres).
- **Cell Organisation** The vegetative cells have cell wall that is composed of cellulose and is usually covered on the outside by a gelatinous coating of algin.
  The protoplast contains a centrally located vacuole and nucleus, in addition to plastids.
- **Photosynthetic Pigments** The major photosynthetic pigments include chlorophyll-*a, c,* carotenoids and xanthophyll.
  They range in colour from olive green to various shades of brown depending upon the amount of the xanthophyll pigment, fucoxanthin present in them.
- **Food Reserve** The food is stored in the form of complex carbohydrates such as laminarin or mannitol.
- **Thallus Organisation** The plant body of large forms is often differentiated into a **holdfast** (which is attached to the substratum), a stalk called the **stipe** and a leaf like **frond** (which is photosynthetic).
- **Reproduction** It is occurs by following type
  - **Vegetative reproduction** occurs through fragmentation.
  - **Asexual reproduction** takes place by biflagellate zoospores, which are pear-shaped having two unequal laterally attached flagella.
  - **Sexual reproduction** is performed by isogamy, anisogamy and oogamy. Union of gametes may take place in water or within the oogonium (oogamous species). The gametes are pyriform (pear-shaped) and have two laterally attached flagella.
- Some common forms are *Ectocarpus, Dictyota, Laminaria, Sargassum* and *Fucus.*

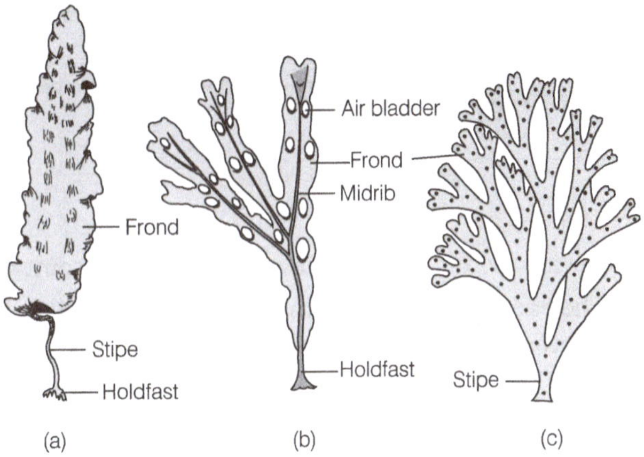


Fig. 3.3 Brown algae : (a) *Laminaria*, (b) *Fucus*, (c) *Dictyota*

## 3. Class–Rhodophyceae (Red Algae)

The members of Rhodophyceae are commonly called **red algae.** Majority of the red algae are **marine** with greater number found in the **warmer areas.**

They are found in both well-lighted regions close to the surface of water and also at great depths in oceans where relatively little light penetrates.

The characteristic features of Rhodophyceae are discussed below

- **Thallus Organisation** The red thalli of most of the algae are multicellular. Some of them have complex body organisation.
- **Photosynthetic Pigments** The major photosynthetic pigments include chlorophyll-*a*, *d*, and *r*-phycoerythrin (red pigment).
- **Food Reserve** The reserve food is floridean starch which is similar in constitution to glycogen and amylopectin.
- **Reproduction** It is occur by
  - **Vegetative reproduction** occurs by fragmentation.
  - **Asexual reproduction** occurs by non-motile spores.
  - **Sexual reproduction** occurs by non-motile gametes and is oogamous type. Fertilisation is accompanied by complex post-fertilisation developments.
- The common members are: *Polysiphonia, Porphyra, Gracilaria* and *Gelidium*.

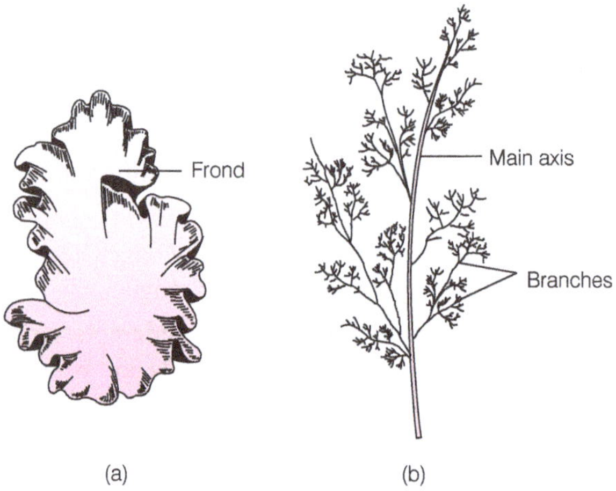


Fig. 3.4 Red algae : (a) *Porphyra*, (b) *Polysiphonia*

**Divisions of Algae and their Main Characteristics**

| Classes | Common Name | Major Pigments | Stored Food | Cell Wall | Flagellar Number and Position of Insertions | Habitat |
|---|---|---|---|---|---|---|
| Chlorophyceae | Green algae | Chlorophyll-*a*, *b* | Starch | Cellulose | 2-8, equal, apical | Freshwater, brackish water, salt water |
| Phaeophyceae | Brown algae | Chlorophyll-*a*, *c*, fucoxanthin | Mannitol, laminarin | Cellulose and algin | 2, unequal, lateral | Freshwater (rare), brackish water, salt water |
| Rhodophyceae | Red algae | Chlorophyll-*a*, *d*, phycoerythrin | Floridean starch | Cellulose, pectin and polysulphate esters | Absent | Freshwater (some), brackish/salt water (most) |

## Economic Importance of Algae

Algae are useful to humans in a variety of ways, some of them are listed below.

- They are responsible for carrying out about a half of the total carbon dioxide fixation on earth by the process of **photosynthesis**. They increase the level of dissolved oxygen in their immediate environment.
- They are of paramount importance as **primary producers** of energy-rich compounds which form the basis of food cycles of all aquatic animals.
- About 70 species of marine algae are **used as food**, e.g. *Porphyra, Laminaria* and *Sargassum*.
- Some forms of marine brown and red algae produce large amounts of hydrocolloids (water holding substance), e.g. are **algin** (brown algae) and **carrageen** (red algae), which have many commercial uses.
- The algae *Gelidium* and *Gracilaria* are used to produce **agar**, which is used to grow microbes and in preparation of ice creams and jellies.
- Some protein rich unicellular algae, like *Chlorella* are used as **food supplements** by **space travellers**.

**Quick Test 2**

1. Identify the algae
   (a) Present in filamentous form
   (b) Present in colonial form
2. **State True or False**
   The plant body of chlorophyceae have rigid cell that is made up of cellulose and hemicellulose.
3. Give two examples of algae having phycoerythrin as major pigment.
4. Name the pigment present in the algae that does not have flagella.
5. Which natural organism is used in the production of agar and hydrocolloids?

## 3.3 Bryophytes

These are non-vascular plants, characterised by the presence of an independent gametophyte and parasitic sporophyte. Bryophytes include various mosses and liverworts.

### General Characteristics

General characteristics of bryophytes are as follows.

- **Habitat** Bryophytes commonly grow in **moist, shaded areas** in **hills**. They usually occur in damp humid and shaded localities and play a important role in plant succession on bare rocks/soil. These are also called **amphibians of the plant kingdom** because these can live in soil but are dependent on water for sexual reproduction.
- **Thallus Organisation** The plant body of bryophytes is more differentiated than that of algae.
  - It is thallus-like and prostrate or erect and attached to the substratum by unicellular or multicellular **rhizoids**.
  - The thallus lacks true roots, stems, and leaves but possesses root-like, leaf-like, or stem-like structures.
- The main plant body of the bryophyte is **haploid**. It produces gametes, hence it is called a **gametophyte**.
  - **Sex Organs** The gametophyte develops sex organs which are multicellular.
  - The male sex organ is called **antheridium**, which produces biflagellate **antherozoids**. The female sex organ, known as the **archegonium**, is flask-shaped and produces a single egg.
- **Reproduction** Bryophytes shows both asexual and sexual reproduction.
  - **Asexual reproduction** is quite common through fragmentation, gemmae, etc.
  - **Sexual reproduction** in bryophytes occurs as follows
    - At maturity, the antherozoids are released into water where they come in contact with archegonium.
    - Only one antherozoid fuses with an egg and produces a diploid zygote.
    - Zygotes do not undergo reduction division immediately. Instead, they produce a multicellular body called **sporophyte**.
    - The sporophyte is not free-living, but attached to the photosynthetic gametophyte, deriving nourishment from it.
    - Some cells of the sporophyte undergo reduction division (meiosis) to produce **haploid** spores which germinate to produce gametophyte.

### Classification of Bryophytes

The bryophytes are further classified into two main groups- liverworts and mosses.

#### 1. Liverworts

They usually grow in moist, shady places such as banks of streams, marshy ground, damp soil, bark of trees and deep in the woods.

Some important characteristic features of liverworts are as follows.

- **Plant Body** The plant body of a liverwort is thalloid, e.g. *Marchantia*.
  - The thallus is dorsiventral and closely appressed to the substrate.
  - Some leafy members have tiny **leaf-like appendages** in two rows on the stem-like structures.
- **Reproduction** It shows both asexual and sexual reproduction.
  - **Asexual reproduction** occurs by fragmentation of thalli or by the formation of specialised structures called **gemmae** (sing. gemma). These are green, multicellular, asexual buds which develop in small receptacles called **gemma cups** located on the thalli.

The gemmae become detached from the parent body and germinate to form new individuals.

- **Sexual reproduction** is accomplished by the formation of male and female sex organs, either on the same or on different thalli.

- **Sporophyte** It develops from zygote which continues to grow on gametophyte. It is differentiated into a **foot**, **seta** and **capsule**. After meiosis, spores ($n$) are produced within the capsule. These spores germinate to form free-living gametophytes.

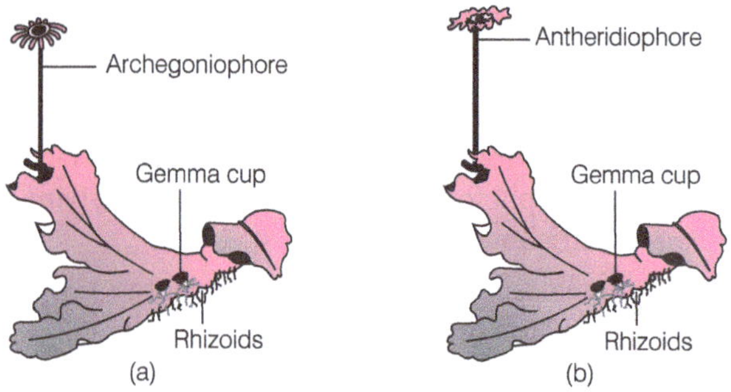


Fig. 3.5 A liverwort (*Marchantia*): (a) Female thallus, (b) Male thallus

## 2. Mosses

They grow in dense mats over moist shady places, especially during rainy seasons.

Some important characteristic features of mosses are as follows

- **Plant Body** The predominant stage of life cycle of a moss is the gametophyte which consists of two stages i.e. **protonema** and **leafy stage**.
  - The **first stage** is the **protonema stage**, which arises directly from a spore. This stage is marked by a creeping, green, branched structure that is often filamentous.
  - The **second stage** is the **leafy stage** which develops from the secondary protonema as a lateral bud. They consist of upright, slender axis bearing spirally arranged leaves. This stage bears rhizoids and sex organs.
    The rhizoids are long, multicellular branched structures that attaches the plant body to the soil.
- **Reproduction** It can be done by following ways
  - **Vegetative reproduction** occurs by fragmentation and by budding in the **secondary protonema**.
  - **Sexual reproduction** takes place by formation of gametes in the sex organs, **antheridia** (male) and **archegonia** (female). They are produced at the apex of the leafy shoots.
  - After fertilisation, the zygote develops into a sporophyte, consisting of **foot, seta** and **capsule** (containing spores).
- **Sporophyte** The sporophyte in mosses is more elaborate than that in liverworts. It derives its nutrition from gametophyte for its development.
- They also have an elaborate mechanism of spore dispersal.
- Some common members are *Funaria*, *Polytrichum* and *Sphagnum*.

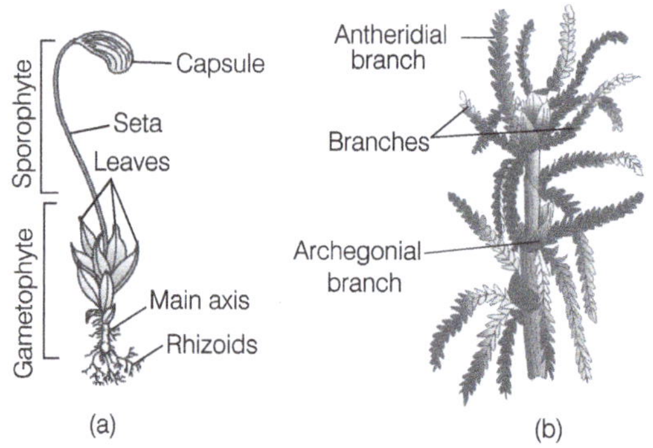


Fig. 3.6 Mosses : (a) *Funaria: gametophyte and sporophyte*, (b) *Sphagnum:* gametophyte

## Economic Importance of Bryophytes

Bryophytes are generally of little economic importance. However, several species have some uses, which are listed below.

- Some mosses provide food for herbaceous mammals, birds and other animals.
- Species of *Sphagnum* (a moss), provides peat that have long been used as fuel. It has the capacity to hold water and hence, is also used as **packing material** for trans-shipment of living material.
- Mosses along with lichens are the first organisms to colonise rocks. Hence, these help in plant **succession on bare rocks**. They decompose rocks making the substrate suitable for the growth of higher plants.
- Mosses form dense mats on the soil. Thus, they reduce the impact of falling raindrops and thus **prevent soil erosion**.

## Quick Test 3

1. Name the stage in the life cycle of bryophytes that is haploid, photosynthetic, and independent.
2. **State True or False.**
   The antheridium produces antherozoids, each with a single flagellum, which swim towards the archegonium to fertilise a single egg cell.
3. In a damp environment, which reproductive structure allows liverworts to rapidly colonise new areas without the need for sexual reproduction?
4. Give two examples of bryophytes whose gametophytic stage consists of two phases, the protonema stage and the leafy stage.
5. Which bryophyte is used in ecological studies and soil conservation efforts due to its ability to retain moisture?

# 3.4 Pteridophytes

These are the first land plants to possess vascular tissues, i.e. xylem and phloem. They are commonly grown as ornamental plants. They are also used for medicinal purposes and as soil binders. Pteridophytes include horsetail and ferns.

## General Characteristics

Some general characteristics of pteridophytes are as follows

- **Habitat** The pteridophytes are found in **cool, damp shady** places though some may flourish well in sandy-soil conditions.
- Their distribution is generally limited and restricted to narrow geographical area due to their dependence on water for fertilisation.
- **Plant Body** The main plant body is a **sporophyte** (dominant phase). It possesses well-differentiated vascular tissues.
  - The plant body is differentiated into true root, stem and leaves.
  - The leaves are **small (microphylls)** as in *Selaginella* or **large (macrophylls)** as in ferns.
  - The sporophytes bear sporangia that are subtended by leaf like appendages called **sporophylls**.
  - In some cases, sporophylls may form distinct compact structures called **strobili** or **cones** (*Selaginella* and *Equisetum*).
  - The sporangia produce spores by meiosis in spore mother cells.
- **Spores** They germinate to give rise to inconspicuous, small but multicellular, free-living, mostly photosynthetic thalloid gametophytes called **prothallus**.
  - In majority of the pteridophytes, all the spores are of similar kinds, such plants are called **homosporous**.
  - Genera like *Selaginella* and *Salvinia* produce two kinds of spores, macro (large) and micro (small) spores, thus are called **heterosporous**.
- **Gametophyte** The thalloid gametophyte or prothallus requires cool, damp, shady places to grow.
  - The megaspores and microspores germinate and give rise to female and male gametophytes, respectively.
  - The female gametophyte in these plants is retained on the parent sporophytes for variable periods.
  - The gametophytes bear male sex organs called **antheridia** and female sex organs called **archegonia**.

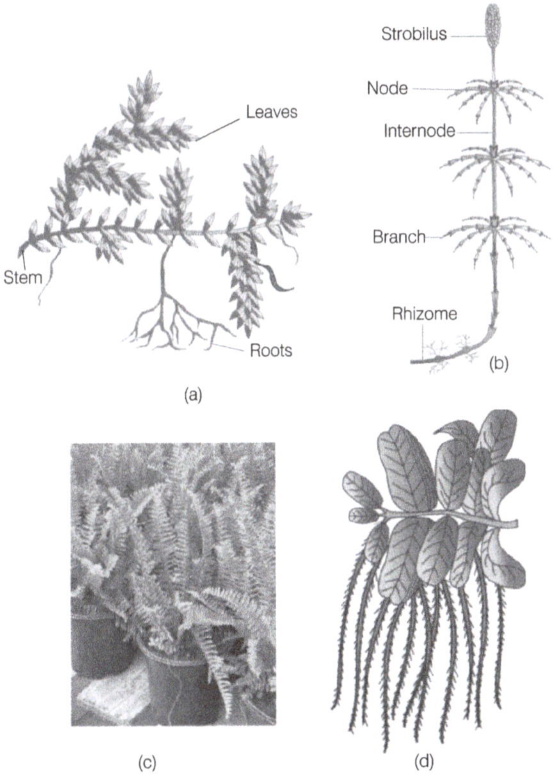


Fig. 3.7 Pteridophytes; (a) *Selaginella*, (b) *Equisetum*, (c) Fern, (d) *Salvinia*

- **Reproduction** The sexual reproduction occurs by fusion of male gamete with the egg present in the archegonium.
  - During fertilisation, **water is required** for the transfer of male gametes. These are released from the antheridia and reach to the mouth of archegonium through a film of water only.
  - Fusion of male gamete with the egg results in the formation of zygote.
  - Zygote develops into multicellular, well-differentiated sporophyte (2*n*) which is the dominant phase of the pteridophytes.
  - The development of zygote into young embryo takes place within the female gametophyte. This event is a precursor of the **seed habit** and is considered as an important step in evolution.

## Classification of Pteridophytes

The pteridophytes are further classified into four classes.

- **Psilopsida** (*Psilotum*)
- **Lycopsida** (*Selaginella* and *Lycopodium*)
- **Sphenopsida** (*Equisetum*)
- **Pteropsida** (*Dryopteris, Pteris* and *Adiantum*)

### Quick Test 4

1. Give examples of pteridophytes that possess microphylls and macrophylls, respectively.
2. **State True or False.**
   In *Psilotum*, the sporophyte bears sporangia that are subtended by a leaf like appendages known as strobili.
3. State one point of difference between the *Equisetum* and *Salvinia*, on the basis of spore production.
4. Plants like *Selaginella* are unable to grow in the arid region. Why?
5. Name any two pteridophytes that belongs to the class-Pteropsida.

# 3.5 Gymnosperms

- These are a group of **naked seeded plants** in which the ovules are not enclosed by any ovary wall and remain exposed, both before and after fertilisation.
- These are small groups of seed plants in which, the male and the female gametophytes do not have an independent **free-living existence.**
- They remain within the sporangia retained on the sporophytes.

## General Characteristics

Some general characteristics of gymnosperms are as follows.

### Morphology

- Gymnosperms include medium-sized trees or the tall trees and shrubs.
- The giant redwood tree *Sequoia* is one of the tallest tree species.

### Plant Body

- The main plant body is sporophytic and is well-differentiated into root, stem and leaves.

#### Root

- The roots are generally **tap roots** that serve the function of proper anchorage of plant to the soil.
- In some genera, roots have fungal association in the form of **mycorrhiza** (*Pinus*), while in some others (*Cycas*) small specialised roots called **coralloid roots** are associated with $N_2$-fixing cyanobacteria.

#### Stem

- It may be branched (*Pinus, Cedrus*) or unbranched (*Cycas*).

#### Leaves

- They may be **simple** or **compound.** In *Cycas*, the pinnate leaves persist for few years.
- The leaves in gymnosperms are well-adapted to withstand extremes of temperature, humidity and wind.
- In conifers, the needle-like leaves reduce the surface area to withstand the extremes of cold temperatures and snowfall. Their thick cuticle and sunken stomata also help to reduce water loss.

### Reproduction

- Plant body of gymnosperms is sporophyte but it reproduces by sexual methods.
- All gymnosperms are **heterosporous**, i.e. they produce haploid microspores and megaspores. These aid in reproduction.
- The two kinds of spores are produced within sporangia that are born on **sporophylls,** which are

arranged spirally along an axis to form lax or compact strobili or **cones**.

- The strobili bearing microsporangia and microsporophylls are called microsporangiate or male **strobili** and the cones bearing megasporophylls with ovules or megasporangia are called macrosporangiate or **female strobili**.
- The plant may be **monoecious** in *Pinus* (i.e. male and female cones or strobili may be borne on same tree) or may be **dioecious** in *Cycas* (i.e. they are borne on different tree).
- The microspores develop into a male gametophytic generation, which is highly reduced and is confined only to a limited number of cells. This reduced gametophyte is known as **pollen grain**. The development of pollen grains occurs within the microsporangia.
- The megaspore mother cell is differentiated from one of the cells of the nucellus, which is protected by envelopes and the composite structure is called an **ovule**.
- The ovules are borne on the **megasporophylls** which may be clustered together forming female cones.
- The megaspore mother cell, thus undergoes meiotic division forming four megaspores. Out of which one megaspore enclosed within the megasporangium develops into a multicellular female gametophyte, bearing two or more **archegonia** or female sex organs. The multicellular female gametophyte is also retained within megasporangium.
- The pollen grain is released from the microsporangium and is carried in air current. It come in contact with the opening of the ovules on megasporophylls.

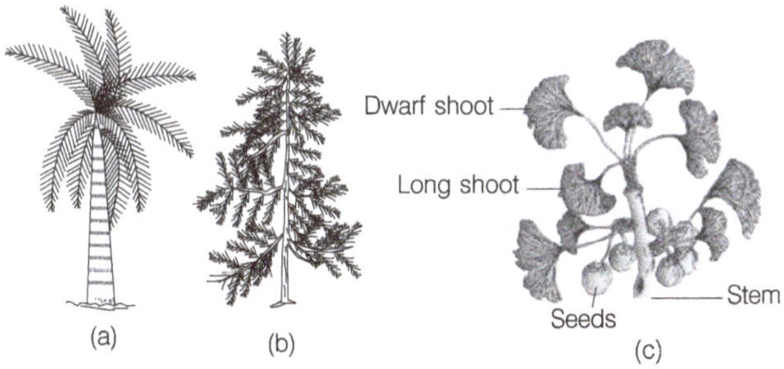


Fig. 3.8 Gymnosperms; (a) *Cycas*, (b) *Pinus*, (c) *Ginkgo*

- The male gamete inside the pollen grain is carried to the ovule by means of a tube called pollen tube which discharges its contents near the mouth of the archegonia.
- After fertilisation, zygote develops into an embryo and the ovules into seeds. The seeds are naked or exposed.

**TEACHER'S TIP**

Gymnosperms have also been classified into four classes, i.e. Cycadopsida, Coniferopsida Ginkgopsida and Gnetopsida.

## 3.6 Angiosperms

- These are also known as flowering plants.
- This group of plants is exceptionally large and found in a wide range of habitats.
- They vary in size from the smallest *Wolffia* to the tallest *Eucalyptus* trees, which can exceed 100 meters.
- Angiosperms develop their pollen grains and ovules within specialised structures called flowers.
- Their seeds are enclosed in fruits, which makes them distinct from gymnosperms.
- They provide us with food, fodder, fuel, medicines and several other commercially important products.
- They are classified into two classes, i.e. **dicotyledons** and **monocotyledons**.

### Quick Test 5

1. Name the dominant generation in the life cycle of *Pinus*.
2. The roots of gymnospermic plant '*A*' form a fungal association to enhance nutrient absorption capacity of the plant. Identify '*X*'.
3. Name one gymnosperm in which male and female cones are borne on
   (a) different plants
   (b) same plants
4. Give the location of seeds in the *Pinus* plant.
5. **Stare Truc or False.**
   Angiosperms are the most advanced group of plants in the classification system but are present in very few habitats.

# Mind Map

## Plant Kingdom

### System of Classification

**Artificial system** Used only gross superficial morphological characters (e.g. leaf shape).

**Natural system** Based on natural relationships (external and internal features).

**Phylogenetic system** Based on evolutionary relationships.

**Types of Taxonomy**

- **Numerical taxonomy** Based on shared characteristics.
- **Cytotaxonomy** Based on chromosome number, structure and behaviour.
- **Chemotaxonomy** Utilise chemical constituents for classification.

### Algae

- Simple, non-vascular thallus body structure.
- Reproduce sexually and asexually (e.g. binary fission, spore formation).
- They are classified into three classes: Chlorophyceae, Phaeophyceae and Rhodophyceae.

| Classes | Common name | Major pigments | Stored food | Cell wall | Flagellar number and position of insertions | Habitat |
|---|---|---|---|---|---|---|
| Chlorophyceae | Green algae | Chlorophyll-*a*, *b* | Starch | Cellulose | 2-8 equal, apical | Freshwater, brackish water, salt water |
| Phaeophyceae | Brown algae | Chlorophyll-*a*, *c*, fucoxanthin | Mannitol, laminarin | Cellulose and algin | 2 unequal, lateral | Freshwater (rare), brackish water, salt water |
| Rhodophyceae | Red algae | Chlorophyll-*a*, *d*, phycoerythrin | Floridean starch | Cellulose, pectin and poly sulphate esters | Absent | Freshwater (some), brackish water, salt water (most) |

### Pteridophytes

- Vascular, seedless plants with true roots, stems and leaves.
- Reproduce *via* spores.
- They possess vascular tissue.
- **Examples** ferns, horsetails and club mosses.
- They aid in soil stabilisation and are used in horticulture and traditional medicine.
- They are classified into four classes : Psilopsida, Lycopsida, Sphenopsida and Pteropsida.

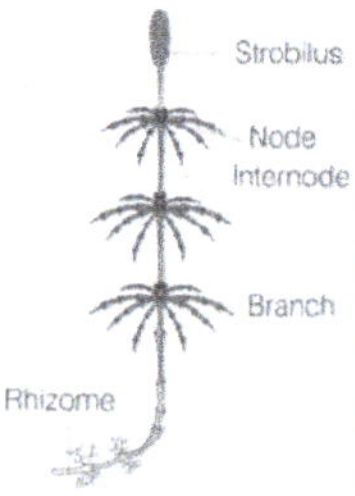

*Equisetum*

### Gymnosperms

- Seed-producing, vascular plants with naked seeds (not enclosed in fruits).
- They have a dominant sporophyte generation and reproduce through cones (strobili).
- They possess well-developed vascular tissues nutrient transport.
- Their seeds are adapted for dispersal by wind.
- Gymnosperms include conifers, cycads.

### Bryophytes

- Amphibians of plant kingdom.
- Non-vascular plants with conducting tissues.
- Reproduction occurs through vegetative or sexual methods.
- They have antheridium (male) and archegonium (female) for gamete production.
- It is divided into two main classes.

#### Liverworts

- Reproduce through spores.
- Tend to prefer damp and shady environment.

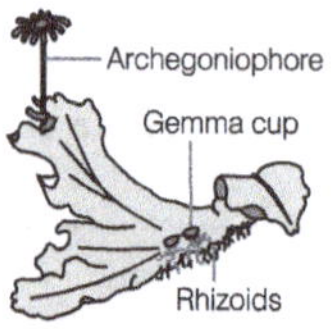


#### Mosses

- Reproduce through spores.
- Can thrive in various habitats, including dry areas.

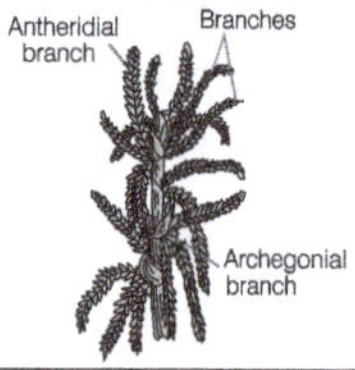


### Angiosperms

- Flowering plants have pollen grains and ovules in flowers.
- Their seeds are enclosed in fruits.
- They vary in size from smallest *Wolffia* to tallest *Eucalyptus* trees.
- They are classified into two groups: Dicotyledons and monocotyledons.

# Exam Pattern Questions

## Objective Type Questions

### Multiple Choice Questions

**1. Which of the following is discussed under phylogenetic system of classification?**

(a) Evolutionary relationship of organism
(b) Cytotaxonomy
(c) Cytological information
(d) Structural embryology

**Ans.** *(a)*

**2. Select the incorrect pair.**

(a) Numerical taxonomy — All observable characteristics
(b) Cytotaxonomy — Cytological information
(c) Chemotaxonomy — Chromosome number and structure
(d) Natural system of classification — Bentham and Hooker

**Ans.** *(c)*

**3. Fusion of two gametes which are dissimilar in size is termed** DIKSHA

(a) oogamy (b) isogamy
(c) anisogamy (d) zoogamy

**Ans.** *(c)*

**4. Identify the given figures of algae and select the correct option.** Competency Based Que.

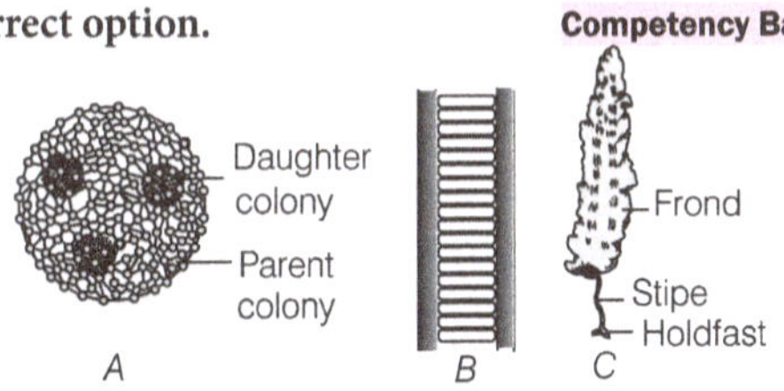


(a) *A–Chlamydomonas, B–Chara, C–Volvox*
(b) *A–Volvox, B–Ulothrix, C–Laminaria*
(c) *A–Chara, B–Laminaria, C–Volvox*
(d) *A–Porphyra, B–Polysiphonia, C–Fucus*

**Ans.** *(b)*

**5. *Volvox, Chlamydomonas, Chara, Ulothrix* are the examples of**

(a) Class–Chlorophyceae (green algae)
(b) Class–Rhodophyceae (red algae) and Chlorophyceae
(c) Class–Phaeophyceae (brown algae)
(d) Class–Cyanophyceae (blue-green algae)

**Ans.** *(a)*

**6. Holdfast, stipe and frond constitute the plant body in case of** NCERT Exemplar

(a) Rhodophyceae (b) Chlorophyceae
(c) Phaeophyceae (d) All of these

**Ans.** *(c)* In the members of class– Phaeophyceae, the plant body is usually attached to the substratum by a holdfast and has a stalk called stipe and a leaf like photosynthetic organ called frond.

**7. Stored food material in class– Phaeophyceae is**

(a) mannitol and laminarin (b) floridean starch
(c) pyrenoids (d) starch and oil

**Ans.** *(a)*

**8. How many of the following characteristics are related to *Fucus*?** Competency Based Que.

I. Class- Rhodophyceae
II. Major pigment- Fucoxanthin
III. Stored food- Floridean starch
IV. Flagella- 2, unequal, lateral

**Choose the correct option**

(a) 3 (b) 2
(c) 1 (d) 4

**Ans.** *(b)*

**9. Cell wall of *Porphyra* (red algae) contains**

(a) cellulose (b) pectins
(c) polysulphate esters (d) All of the above

**Ans.** *(d)*

**10. Consider the following statements.** Competency Based Que.

I. Large amounts of hydrocolloids are produced by certain marine red and brown algae.

II. Algin and carrageenan are commercially used as water holding materials.

**Choose the correct option.**

(a) Statement I is correct, but II is incorrect
(b) Statement I is incorrect, but II is correct
(c) Both statements I and II are correct
(d) Both statements I and II are incorrect

Ans. (c)

**11. The main plant body of bryophyte is ... *A*... . It produces ... *B*... , hence is called as ... *C*.... .**

**Fill in the blanks with respect to *A*, *B* and *C* and choose the correct option.**

(a) *A*–diploid, *B*–endospores, *C*–sporophyte
(b) *A*–haploid, *B*–conidia, *C*–gametophyte
(c) *A*–diploid, *B*–spores, *C*–sporophyte
(d) *A*–haploid, *B*–gametes, *C*–gametophyte

Ans. (d)

**12. A plant shows thallus level of organisation. It shows rhizoids and is haploid. It needs water to complete its life cycle because the male gametes are motile. Identify the group to which it belongs to** NCERT Exemplar

(a) pteridophytes
(b) gymnosperms
(c) monocots
(d) bryophytes

Ans. (d) Bryophyta is a group of plants which have gametophytic haploid thalloid body. The motile male gamete are produced in special male reproductive structure called antheridia.

**13. The unique feature of bryophytes in comparison to other green plant groups is that**

(a) they produce spores
(b) they lack vascular tissue
(c) they lack roots
(d) their sporophyte is attached to the gametophyte

Ans. (d)

**14. Protonema is** NCERT Exemplar, DIKSHA

(a) haploid and is found in mosses
(b) diploid and is found in liverworts
(c) diploid and is found in pteridophytes
(d) haploid and is found in pteridophytes

Ans. (a)

**15. In given figure, *A*, *B*, *C* and *D* represent**

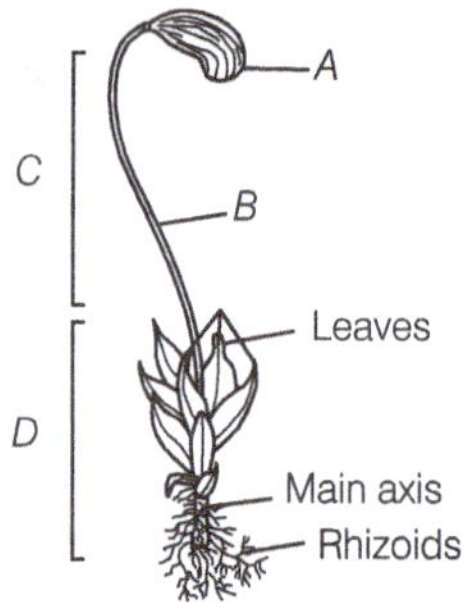


(a) *A*–Apophysis, *B*–Capsule, *C*–Sporophyte, *D*–Gametophyte
(b) *A*–Capsule, *B*–Seta, *C*–Sporophyte, *D*–Gametophyte
(c) *A*–Apophysis, *B*–Seta, *C*–Gametophyte, *D*–Sporophyte
(d) *A*–Capsule, *B*–Seta, *C*–Gametophyte, *D*–Sporophyte

Ans. (b)

**16. In pteridophyte, the sporophyte consists of leaf-like appendages called**

(a) megaphylls (b) sporophylls
(c) thalli (d) sporangia

Ans. (b)

**17. A prothallus is** NCERT Exemplar

(a) a structure in pteridophyte formed before the thallus develops
(b) a sporophytic free-living structure formed in pteridophyte
(c) a gametophytic free-living structure formed in pteridophytes
(d) a primitive structure formed after fertilisation in pteridophyte

Ans. (c) In pteridophytes the sporangia produce spores by meiosis in spore mother cells. These spores germinate to give rise to incospicous, small but muticellular free-living photosynthetic thalloid gametophyte called prothallus.

**18. From evolutionary point of view, retention of the female gametophyte with developing young embryo on the parent sporophyte for some time, is first observed in**

(a) mosses (b) pteridophytes
(c) gymnosperms (d) liverworts

Ans. (b)

**19. Which plant group has vascular tissue, produces spores, but does not have seeds?**

(a) Bryophyta (b) Pteridophyta
(c) Gymnosperms (d) Angiosperms

Ans. (b)

**20.** **Identify the given figure of a pteridophyte species and answer the questions that follows.**

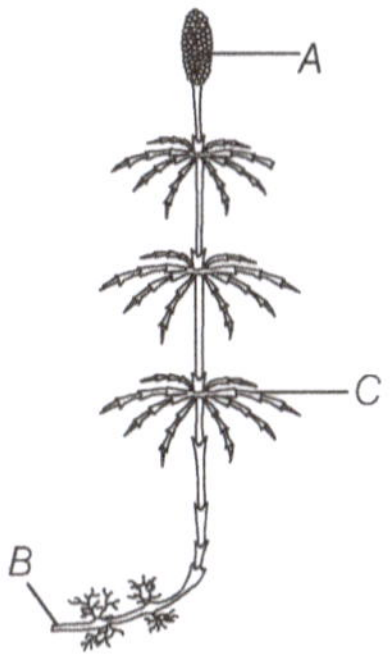


**Choose the correct option for the match about the labels *A, B* and *C* in the above given figure.**

(a) *A*— Strobilus (b) *B*—Internode
(c) *C*—Roots (d) All of the abvoe

**Ans.** (*a*)

**21.** ***Selaginella*** **and** ***Salvinia*** **are considered representing a significant step towards evolution of seed habit because** **Competency Based Que.**

(a) female gametophyte is free and gets dispersed like seeds
(b) female gametophyte lacks archegonia
(c) megaspores possess endosperm and embryo surrounded by seed coat
(d) embryo develops in female gametophyte which is retained on parent sporophyte

**Ans.** (*d*)

**22.** **Match the following columns.** **Competency Based Que.**

| | Column I (Products) | | Column II (Gymnosperm) |
|---|---|---|---|
| A. | Psilopsida | 1. | *Equisetum* |
| B. | Lycopsida | 2. | *Selaginella* |
| C. | Sphenophida | 3. | *Psilotum* |
| D. | Pteropsida | 4. | *Adiantum* |

**Codes**

| | A | B | C | D | | A | B | C | D |
|---|---|---|---|---|---|---|---|---|---|
| (a) | 4 | 2 | 1 | 3 | (b) | 3 | 2 | 1 | 4 |
| (c) | 3 | 4 | 1 | 2 | (d) | 2 | 3 | 1 | 4 |

**Ans.** (*b*)

**23.** **The giant redwood tree (*Sequoia sempervirens*) is a/an** **NCERT Exemplar**

(a) angiosperm (b) free fern
(c) pteridophyte (d) gymnosperm

**Ans.** (*d*) *Sequoia sempervirens* is a gymnospermic plant. It is a group of plants having thick, woody, branched stems. These plants also have some xeric adaptations which help them survive in adverse climatic conditions.

**24.** **Which of the following gymnosperm has coralloid roots associated with $N_2$ -fixing cyanobacteria?**

(a) *Pinus* (b) *Cycas*
(c) *Cedrus* (d) *Ginkgo*

**Ans.** (*b*)

**25.** **Which one of the following is not the feature of *Cycas*?**

(a) Presence of unbranched stem
(b) Presence of pinnate leaves
(c) Male and female cones are borne on the same trees.
(d) Presence of coralloid roots.

**Ans.** (*c*)

**26.** **Conifers are adapted to tolerate extreme environmental conditions because of** **DIKSHA**

(a) thick cuticle
(b) presence of vessels
(c) broad hard leaves
(d) superficial stomata

**Ans.** (*a*)

**27.** **A plant producing seeds but lacking flowers is** **DIKSHA**

(a) gymnosperm (b) pteridophyte
(c) angiosperm (d) bryophyte

**Ans.** (*a*)

**28.** **Select the incorrect statement w.r.t. angiosperms.** **NCERT Exemplar**

(a) They develop pollens and ovules within flowers.
(b) They are classified into dicots and monocots
(c) These are group of naked seeded plants
(d) These are large group of plants occuring in a wide range of habitats.

**Ans.** (*c*)

## Assertion-Reason Questions

**Direction** (Q. Nos. 1-9) *In each of the following questions, a statement of Assertion (A) is given followed by corresponding statement of Reason (R). Of the statements, mark the correct answer as*

(a) Both A and R are true and R is the correct explanation of the A.
(b) Both A and R are true, but R is not the correct explanation of the A.
(c) A is true, but R is false.
(d) A is false, but R is true.

1. **Assertion** (A) Artificial system of classification separated closely related species.

   **Reason** (R) Artificial system gave equal weightage to vegetative and sexual characteristics.

**Ans.** (*a*)

2. **Assertion** (A) The members of Chlorophyceae are usually grass-green.

   **Reason** (R) They have chlorophyll-*a* and *b* in abundance

**Ans.** (*a*)

3. **Assertion** (A) Algae are the primary producers of many food cycles.

   **Reason** (R) Half of the total carbon dioxide-fixation on earth is carried out by algae.

**Ans.** (*b*)

4. **Assertion** (A) Bryophytes is a division of under kingdom–Plantae.

   **Reason** (R) Algae, fungi, lichens and mosses are included in bryophytes.

**Ans.** (*c*) A is true, but R is false. It can be corrected as

Algae, fungi and lichens are not included in bryophytes. Only mosses and liverworts are included in bryophytes.

5. **Assertion** (A) Pteridophytes are the amphibians of plant kingdom.

   **Reason** (R) Pteridophytes are found in cool, damp and shady places.

**Ans.** (*d*) A is false, but R is true. A can be corrected as

Bryophytes are the amphibians of plant kingdom.

6. **Assertion** (A) *Lycopodium* and *Selaginella* are heterosporous.

   **Reason** (R) In heterosporous condition, two kinds of spores are produced by the plant.

**Ans.** (*d*) A is false, but R is true A can be corrected as

*Salvinia* and *Selaginella* are heterosporous.

7. **Assertion** (A) Production of two types of spores is a pre-requisite of seed habit.

   **Reason** (R) In pteridophytes, *Lycopodium* is precursor of seed habit.

**Ans.** (*c*)

8. **Assertion** (A) The leaves in gymnosperms are well-adapted to withstand extremes of temperature, humidity and wind.

   **Reason** (R) Unlike bryophytes and pteridophytes, in gymnosperms, the male and female gametophytes do not have an independent free-living existence.

   **Competency Based Que.**

**Ans.** (*b*)

9. **Assertion** (A) In gymnosperms, the female gametophyte is entirely dependent on the sporophyte.

   **Reason** (R) Their ovules are not enclosed by an ovary wall.

**Ans.** (*b*)

# Subjective Questions

## Very Short Answer Type Questions

**1. Mention different types of system of classification of plants.**

**Ans.** Artificial, natural and phylogenetic system of classification.

**2. Are the main food reserves in algae different for different species? Give two examples.**

**Ans.** Yes, reserved food for algae are different for different species, e.g. starch (Chlorophyceae) and laminarin (Phaeophyceae). (½ + ½)

**3. Write one characteristic feature of the diagram given below.**

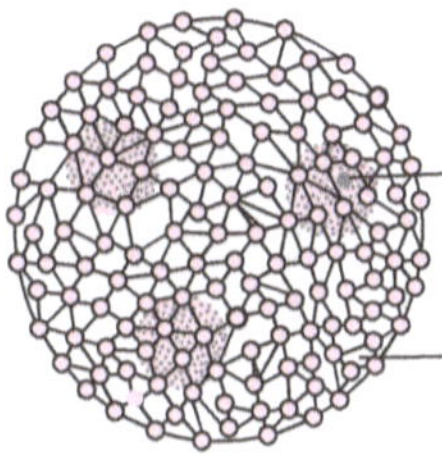


**Ans.** The diagram provided depicts *Volvox*, which exists in a colonial form.

**4. Food is stored as floridean starch in Rhodophyceae. Mannitol is the reserve food material of which group of algae?** **NCERT Exempler**

**Ans.** The members of Phaeophyceae (brown algae) store mannitol as a reserve food material.

**5. Which green algae is used by space travellers as protein rich food?**

**Ans.** *Chlorella*

**6. Which plants are called amphibians?**

**Ans.** Bryophytes

**7. Where do mosses grow?**

**Ans.** Mosses grow in moist, shaded areas in hills.

**8. Arrange the given plant species into mosses and liverworts.**

***Funaria, sphagnum, Riccia, Marchantia, Polytrichum*** **Competency Based Que.**

**Ans.** (a) **Mosses** *Funaria, Polytrichum, Sphagnum*

(b) **Liverworts** *Riccia, Marchantia* (½ + ½)

**9. How are mosses considered ecologically important?**

**Ans.** Mosses, along with lichens are the first organism to colonise rocks, hence are ecologically important to develop an ecosystem in bare places.

**10. Give two examples of heterosporous ferns.**

**Ans.** *Selaginella, Salvinia* (½ + ½)

**11. In which plant coralloid roots are present?**

**Ans.** *Cycas* have coralloid root in which nitrogen fixing cyanobacteria is present.

**12. Match the following (Column I with Column II).** **NCERT**

| | Column I | | Column II |
|---|---|---|---|
| (a) | *Chlamydomonas* | (i) | Moss |
| (b) | *Cycas* | (ii) | Pteridophyte |
| (c) | *Selaginella* | (iii) | Algae |
| (d) | *Sphagnum* | (iv) | Gymnosperm |

**Ans.** (a)-(iii), (b)-(iv), (c)-(ii), (d)-(i) (1)

**13. Mention tallest gymnosperm and smallest angiosperm.**

**Ans.** *Sequoia* sp. is the tallest gynmnosperm and *Wolffia* is the smallest angiosperm.

## Short Answer Type Questions

**1. Artificial system of classification compares certain superficial morphological characters. List the disadvantages of such a system of classification.**

**Ans.** Refer to text on page no. 43.

**2. Schemes like artificial classification is easy to deveolop, it still possesses drawback. List out the drawback of artificial system of classification.**

**Ans.** The artificial system of classification was mainly based on vegetative characters or on the androecium structure (system given by Linnaeus).

Such system separated the closely related species, since they were based on a few characteristics. The artificial system gives equal weightage to vegetative and sexual characteristics. This is not convincing because the vegetative characters are more easily affected by the environment.

**3. On which criteria is chemotaxonomy based? How it be used for classification?**

**Ans.** Chemotaxonomy is based on the protein analysis and on the chemical constituents of the organisms. This type of taxonomy is particularly utilised in the classification of plants, as chemical constituents of plant species are stable and do not change easily. (1+1)

**4. What is the basis of classification of algae?** NCERT

**Ans.** The basis of classification of algae are as follows.

(i) The type of photosynthetic pigments.
(ii) Nature of reserve food materials.
(iii) Cell wall composition
(iv) Presence and absence of flagella as well as position of flagella. (½ × 4)

**5. Give one example each of the three main classes of algae.**

**Ans.** The three main classes of algae with their examples are

(i) Chlorophyceae, e.g. *Spirogyra*
(ii) Phaeophyceae, e.g. *Sargassum* and
(iii) Rhodophyceae, e.g. *Porphyra*. (1 × 3)

**6. Give one word answer for the following.**

**(i) In brown algae, what is the function of frond present?**
**(ii) Name the constituents of cell wall in green algae.**

**Ans.** (i) Frond is a leaf-like organ meant for performing photosynthesis process. (1)
(ii) The cell wall in green algae is made up of cellulose (inner layer) and pectose (outer layer). (1)

**7. What are the two features of brown algae? Give two examples.**

**Ans.** The two main features of brown algae are

(i) They are multicellular eukaryotic algae. (1)
(ii) They contain chlorophyll-*a* and *c* along with fucoxanthin, which gives them their characteristic brown colour. e.g. *Laminaria and Fucus*. (1)

**8. Compare green algae with red algae.**

**Ans.** Differences between red algae and green algae are

| Green Algae | Red Algae |
|---|---|
| Chlorophyll- *a* and *b* are present. | *r*-phycoerythrin, chlorophyll-*a* and *d* are present. |
| Reserve food is in the form of pyrenoids and oil droplets. | Reserve food materials are in the form of floridean starch. |
| Cell wall is made up of cellulose and pectose. | Cell wall is made up of cellulose and algin. |
| They live in moderate depths. | They live in very deep water. |

(½ × 4)

**9. Write a note on economic importance of algae.**

**Ans.** Refer to text on page no. 46.

**10. Write a brief account of reproduction in bryophytes.**

**Ans.** Refer to text on page no. 47.

**11. Name the group in which bryophytes are classified and give an example for each.**

**Ans.** Bryophytes are classified into two groups these are liverworts, mosses for example, *Marchantia* and *Funaria*, respectively.

**12. Give a brief account of the plant having foot, seta and capsule.**

**Ans.** Mosses are the plants having their sporophyte usually differentiated into foot, seta and capsule. The gametophytic plant body is with leafy axis and shows a radial symmetry. The rhizoid are multicellular and branched. Sex organs, i.e. antheridia and archegonia are usually borne in groups at the apices of reproductive branches.

**13. Identify *A*, *B*, *C*, and *D* in the given diagram and describe the features of *D*.** Competency Based Que.

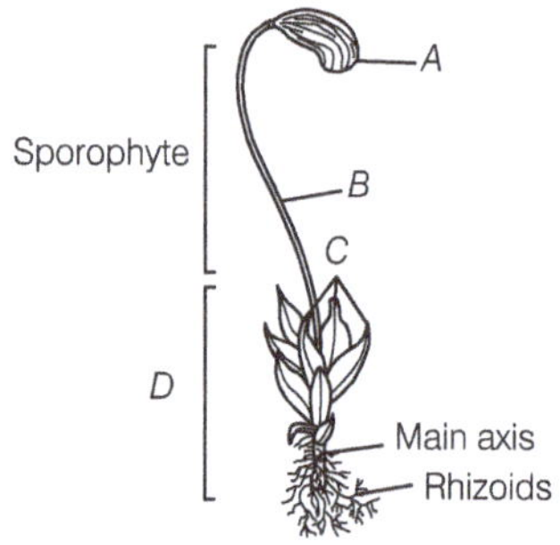


**Ans.** In the given diagram, *A*, *B*, *C*, and *D* represent the capsule, seta, leaves, and gametophyte, respectively. (1)

In bryophytes, the gametophyte is the dominant and long-living phase of the life cycle. It is the haploid (*n*) generation that develops from a spore and gives rise to reproductive organs (antheridia and archegonia) where gametes (sperm and eggs) are produced. (1)

**14. Differentiate between the following**

**(i) red algae and brown algae**

**(ii) liverworts and moss**

**Ans.** (i) Refer to the table on page no. 46.

(ii) Differences between liverworts and mosses are as follows

| Liverworts | Mosses |
|---|---|
| They have unicellular rhizoids. | They have multicellular rhizoids. |
| The sporophyte is not differentiated into foot, seta and capsule. | The sporophyte is more elaborate and differentiated into foot, seta and capsule. |
| Some common members are *Riccia*, *Marchantia* | Some common members are *Funaria*, *Polytrichum* and *Sphagnum*. |

(1½ × 2)

**15. Explain the nature of sporophylls in pteridophytes.**

**Ans.** The sporophytes bear sporangia that are substended by leaf-like appendages called sporophylls. In some cases, sporophylls may form distinct compact structure called strobili or cones (e.g. *Selaginella* and *Equisetum*). The sporangia produce spores by meiosis in spore mother cells.

**16. Differentiate between homosporous and heterosporous pteridophytes.** NCERT

**Ans.** Differences between homosporous and heterosporous pteridophytes are given below

| Homosporous Pteridophytes | Heterosporous Pteridophytes |
|---|---|
| These pteridophyte produce only one kind of spores. | These pteridophytes produce microspores and megaspores. [1] |
| Each spore germinates into a monoecious prothallus, that bears both antheridia and archegonia, e.g. *Dryopteris*. | Microspores germinate into male gametophyte and megaspores germinate into female gamete, e.g. *Selaginella*, *Salvinia*. [1] |

**17. What is heterospory? Briefly comment on its significance. Give two examples.** NCERT

**Ans.** Heterospory is the phenomenon in which a plant produces two types of spores, namely microspores and megaspores.

Heterospory is significant in the following ways

(i) Microspores give rise to male gametophyte and megaspores give rise to female gametophyte.

(ii) Female gametophyte is retained on the parent plant. The development of zygote takes place within the female gametophyte.

(iii) This leads to evolution of seed habit.

For example *Selaginella* and *Salvinia* are heterosporous pteridophytes. (1+2)

**18. Which event in pteridophytes is considered an important step in evolution of seed habit in plants?** Competency Based Que.

**Ans.** The development of heterospory in pteridophytes, which involves the production of two types of spores, i.e. microspores and megaspores and is considered an important step in the evolution of seed habit in plants. Additionally, the development of the zygote into a young embryo within the female gametophyte is also a crucial event, as it serves as a precursor to the seed habit and marks a significant advancement in plant evolution.

**19. Mention the different classes of pteriodphytes along with examples.**

**Ans.** Refer to text on page. no 50.

(½ × 4 = 2)

**20. Describe the important characteristics of gymnosperms.** NCERT

**Ans.** Characteristics of gymnosperms are as follows (any six)

(i) These are naked-seeded plants, i.e. their ovules are exposed and not enclosed in ovaries. Hence, the seeds are naked without fruits.

(ii) Tap root system is present. They show symbiotic association with fungi to form mycorrhizae or with $N_2$-fixing cyanobacteria to form coralloid roots as in *Cycas*.

(iii) Leaves are large and needle-shaped.

(iv) Vascular tissues are well-developed.

(v) Gymnosperms are heterosporous.

(vi) Pollination occurs by wind.

(vii) Fertilisation occurs in archegonia.

(viii) Retention of female gametophyte inside the ovule and the ovules on the sporophytic plant for complete development is responsible for the development of seed habit. (½ × 6)

**21. In which plant will you look for mycorrhiza and coralloid roots? Also explain what these terms mean** NCERT Exemplar

**Ans.** Mycorrhiza and coralloid roots can be found in *Pinus* and *Cycas* respectively. Mycorrhiza refers to a symbiotic association between fungi and plant roots whereas, coralloid roots are irregular, dichotomously branched coral like roots which do not possess root hair and root cap.

**22. Each plant or group of plants have some phylogenetic significance in relation to evolution.**
***Cycas*, one of the few living members of gymnosperms and is called as 'relic of the past". Can you establish a phylogenetic relationship of *Cycas* with any other group of plants that justifies the above statement.** Competency Based Que., NCERT Exemplar

**Ans.** *Cycas* is called 'The relic of past' since it is one of the oldest surviving plant genera. It shows phylogenetic relationship with pteridophytes due to the following features-

- Presence of flagellated antherozoids
- Presence of leaf-like structure of megaspores
- Presence of archegonia

**23. Mention the ploidy of the following**

**Protonemal cell of a moss, primary endosperm nucleus in dicot, leaf cell of a moss, prothallus of a fern, gemma cell in *Marchantia*, meristem cell of monocot, ovum of a liverwort and zygote of a fern.** NCERT

**Ans.** Protonemal cell of moss — haploid Competency Based Que.

- Primary endosperm nucleus in dicots— triploid
- Leaf cell of moss— haploid
- Prothallus cell of ferns— haploid

- Gemma cell in *Marchantia*— haploid
- Meristem cell of monocots— diploid
- Ovum of liverworts— haploid
- Zygote of ferns— diploid

**24. Both gymnosperms and angiosperms bear seeds, then why are they classified separately?** NCERT

**Ans.** Both gymnosperms and angiosperms bear seeds, but they are classified separately because, in gymnosperms, the seeds are naked, i.e. they are not produced inside a fruit. In contrast, angiosperms have seeds that are enclosed within a fruit.

## Long Answer Type Questions

**1. How is natural system different from artificial system of classification? List some features.**

**Ans.** Differences between natural and artificial systems are

| Natural System | Artificial System |
|---|---|
| It is based on large number of characters. | It is based on only one or a few characters. |
| The studied characters are stable. | The studied characters are liable to change with change in environment. |
| It is based on morphology, anatomy, cytology, embryology, molecular biology and genetics. | It is based on morphological or reproductive traits. Others are not used. |
| Natural system brings out homology. | Artificial system does not study homology. |
| It explains natural and some phylogenetic relationships. | It does not give any idea about natural and phylogenetic relationships. |

(1 × 5)

**2. Lichen is usually cited as an example of 'symbiosis' in plants where an algal and a fungal species live together for their mutual benefit. Which of the following will happen if algal and fungal partners are separated from each other?** Competency Based Que., NCERT Exemplar

(a) Both will survive and grow normally and independent from each other.

(b) Both will die

(c) Algal component will survive, while the fungal component will die.

(d) Fungal component will survive, while algal partner will die.

**Based on your answer how do you justify this association as symbiosis?**

**Ans.** (b) Option (b) is correct,

Lichen is a symbiotic association between an alga and a fungi, which live together for their mutual benefit. If both are separated from each other then they will die. The fungus holds water, provides protection and ideal housing to the alga.

The alga in turn supplies carbohydrate food for the fungus. If the alga is capable of fixing nitrogen (*e.g.*, *Nostoc*), it supplies fixed nitrogen to the fungus.The kind of mutual inter-dependence helps lichens to grow on dry, barren rocks, where the other plants fail to exist. Morever, the algae or the fungi alone cannot grow in such places. Thus, both the partners cannot survive without each other. (1 + 4)

**3. Gametophyte is a dominant phase in the life cycle of a bryophyte. Explain.**

**Ans.** Gametophyte is a haploid' multicellular structure in a bryophyte's life cycle. It bears male reproductive structure (antheridia) and female reproductive structure called archegonia, and thus produce haploid gametes antherozoids (male gamete) and egg cell (female gamete) respectively.

The antherozoids are released into water where they come in contact with archegonium and fuses with egg to form zygote. The zygote develops into the sporophyte which is attached to the photosynthetic gametophyte and derives its nourishment from it. Some cells of sporophyte undergo reduction division to produce haploid spores which germinates to produce gametophyte. Hence, gametophyte is a dominant phase in the life cycle of a bryophyte.

**4. Describe the plant body of a moss with the help of a well-labelled diagram.**

**Ans.** Refer to text on page no. 48.

**5. Distinguish between bryophytes and pteridophytes.**

**Ans.** Differences between bryophytes and pteridophytes (any five)

| Bryophytes | Pteridophytes |
|---|---|
| The main plant body is gametophyte. | The main plant body is sporophyte. |
| These are non-vascular plants. | These are vascular plants. |
| Sporophyte is parasitic over gametophyte. | Sporophyte is independent of gametophyte. |
| Plant body can be thallus or foliose. | It is differentiated into stems, leaves and roots. |
| True stems and leaves are not present. | It has true stems and leaves. |
| Roots are absent, rhizoids are present. | Roots are present. |
| Sex organs are stalked. | Sex organs are sessile. (1 × 5) |

**6. Name three groups of plants that bear archegonia. Briefly describe the life cycle of any one of them.** NCERT

**Ans.** Archegonia are the female sex organs that produce the female gamete or egg. It is present in bryophytes, pteridophytes and gymnosperms. (1)

Life cycle of a pteridophyte is as follows

- The main plant body of pteridophyte is a sporophyte that is differentiated into true roots, stem, and leaves. Sporangia bearing leaves, i.e sporophylls are present either singly or condensed in some species to form a compact structure known as strobili or cones.
- Diploid spore mother cells are present in these sporangia. They undergo meiosis one time to produce four haploid spores.
- The haploid spores are released from the sporangium and dispersed by wind currents to a new substratum.
- After falling on suitable soil, the germination of spores produces a green, thalloid, and free- living gametophyte known as prothallus. It represents the gametophyte stage in its life cycle.
- The prothallus bears both the type of sex organs, i.e antheridium or male sex organ and archegonia or female sex organ. Antheridium produces motile sperms that require water to make its way to the mouth of archegonia.
- Their fusion produces a diploid zygote that divides repeatedly and forms an embryo. This marks the beginning of an independent sporophyte stage. (4)

**7. Write a note on economic importance of algae and gymnosperms.** **NCERT**

**Ans.** The economic importance of algae is as follows

(i) They are responsible for carrying out about a half of the total carbon dioxide fixation on earth by the process of photosynthesis. They increase the level of dissolved oxygen in their immediate environment.

(ii) They are of paramount importance as primary producers of energy-rich compounds which form the basis of food cycles of all aquatic animals.

(iii) About 70 species of marine algae are used as food, e.g. *Porphyra, Laminaria* and *Sargassum.*

(iv) Some forms of marine brown and red algae produce large amounts of hydrocolloids (water holding substance), e.g. are **algin** (brown algae) and **carrageenan** (red algae), which have many commercial uses.

(v) The algae *Gelidium* and *Gracilaria* are used to produce **agar**, which is used to grow microbes and in preparation of ice creams and jellies.

(vi) Some protein rich unicellular algae, like *Chlorella* are used as food supplements by space travellers.

(vii) About 70 species of marine algae are used as food, e.g. *Porphyra, Laminaria* and *Sargassum.* (3)

The economic importance of gymnosperms is as follows

(i) Many members of gymnosperms like coniferous trees, such as pine, deodar, etc., are used in the purposes of construction.

(ii) The seeds of the tree *Pinus gerardiana* which is popularly known as chilgoza are a popular eatery.

(iii) A lot of gymnosperm plants have medicinal values. Taxus tree produces taxol, which is used as an anti-cancerous agent. Ephedrine is obtained from several species of *Ephedra*. Ephedrine is used in the treatment of asthma and bronchitis. (2)

**8. How are the male and female gametophytes of pteridophytes and gymnosperms different from each other?** **NCERT Exemplar**

**Ans.** The male and female gametophytes of pteridophytes and gymnosperms different from each other are

| Male Gametophyte of Pteridophyte | Male Gametophyte of Gymnosperm |
|---|---|
| A distinct male gametophyte may not be present. | A male gametophyte is always present. |
| It contains an antheridium. | An antheridium is not found. |
| Male gametes are flagellated. | Male gametes may or may not be flagellated. |
| Male gametes reach the female gamete by swimming in a film of water. | Male gametes reach the female gamete through a pollen tube. Water is not required. |

(2½)

| Female Gametophyte of Pteridophyte | Female Gametophyte of Gymnosperm |
|---|---|
| A distinct female gametophyte may or may not be present. | A distinct gametophyte is always present. |
| It is largely independent. | Female gametophyte does not leave the parent plant. |
| It is not enclosed is an ovule. | It is enclosed inside an ovule. |

(2½)

**9. Explain briefly the following terms with suitable examples:** **NCERT**

(i) protonema (ii) antheridium
(iii) archegonium (iv) diplontic
(v) sporophyll (vi) isogamy

**Ans.** (i) **Protonema:** It forms the first stage in the life cycle of a moss which develops directly from the spore. It consists of creeping, green, branched, and often filamentous structures.

(ii) **Antheridium** It is the male sex organ present in bryophytes and pteridophytes which give rise to the male gametes.

(iii) **Archegonium** It is the female sex organ present in bryophytes, pteridophytes, and gymnosperms. In bryophytes and pteridophytes, it is multicellular and generally has a swollen venter and a tubular neck, where neck consists of neck canal cells and venter contains venter canal cells and egg.

(iv) **Diplontic** It is the term used for life cycles of seed-bearing plants (gymnosperms and angiosperms). In these plants, the diploid sporophyte is dominant, photosynthetic, and independent. The gametophyte is represented by a single-celled (or a few-celled) structure.

(v) **Sporophyll** It bears sporangia in pteridophytes. These sporangia are subtended by leaf-like appendages known as sporophyll. In gymnosperms, microsporophyll and megasporophyll are found. These bear microspores and megaspores respectively.

(vi) **Isogamy** It is a type of sexual reproduction involving the fusion of morphologically similar gametes. This means that the gametes are of the same size but perform different functions. This type of reproduction is commonly observed in *Spirogyra*.

**10. When and where does reduction division take place in the life cycle of a liverwort, a moss, a fern, a gymnosperm and an angiosperm?** **NCERT**

**Ans.** Reduction divisions in the life cycle of a liverwort, a moss, a fern and a gymnosperm take place during the production of spores from spore mother cells. (1)

**Liverwort** In liverworts, many haploid spores are produced as a result of the reduction division taking place inside the capsule.

**Moss** In mosses many spores are formed as a result of the reduction division taking place in the capsule of the sporophyte.

**Fern** In ferns, the main plant body is sporophytic. Its leaves are known as sporophylls and these bear the sporangia. Reduction division takes place in these sporangia, thereby producing many spores.

**Gymnosperm** In gymnosperms, the main plant-body is sporophytic. They bear two types of leaves – microsporophylls and megasporophylls. Reduction division takes place in the microsporangia present on the microsporophylls (producing pollen grains) and on the megasporangia present on the megasporophylls (producing megaspores).

**Angiosperm** In angiosperms, the main plant body is sporophytic and bears flowers. The male sex organ in the flower is the stamen, while the female sex organ is the pistil. Reduction division takes place in the anthers of the stamen (producing haploid pollen grains) and in the ovary of the pistil (producing eggs). (4)

## Source Based/Case Based/Passage Based Questions

**1. *Sphagnum* is a genus of mosses, often referred to as peat moss, with over 300 species. This moss thrives in wetlands, including bogs and fens, preferring acidic and waterlogged conditions. The graph below shows the use of *Sphagnum* in recent years as packing material for the trans-shipment of living materials. Analyse the graph and answer the questions that follow.**

**Competency Based Que.**

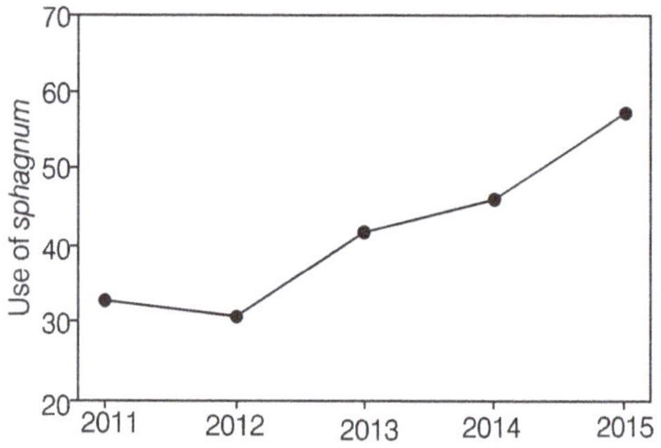


(i) What property of *Sphagnum* leads to such an increase in its use?

(ii) State one use of *Sphagnum* apart from the one mentioned above.

(iii) How does reproduction take place in the mentioned species?

(iv) How does this group differ from liverworts?

**Ans.** (i) The property of *Sphagnum* that leads to such an increase in its use is its ability to retain water. This characteristic makes it an ideal packing material for the trans-shipment of living materials. (1)

(ii) Besides its use as packing material, *Sphagnum* can produce peat, which has long been utilised as a fuel source. (1)

(iii) *Sphagnum* reproduces both sexually and asexually. Vegetative reproduction (asexual) occurs through fragmentation and budding in the secondary protonema, whereas sexual reproduction involves the production of sex organs. (1)

(iv) *Sphagnum* is classified as a moss which is characterised by upright, slender stems with spirally arranged leaves. In contrast, liverworts have a thalloid structure that is dorsiventral and closely appressed to the substrate. (1)

**2. Recognise the figure of the given pteridophyte species and answer the questions that follows.**

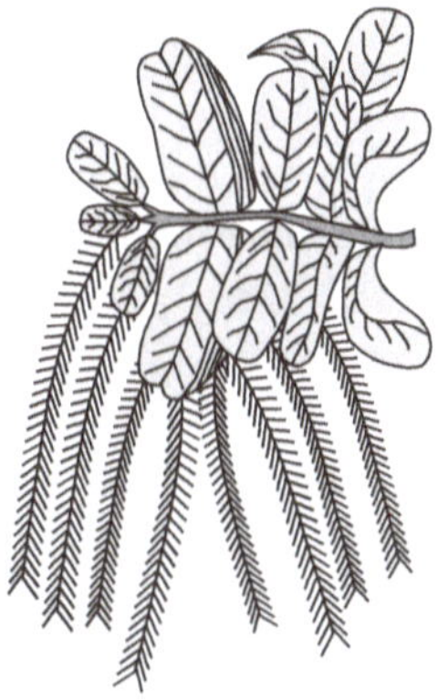

(i) Identify the pteridophyte and name the kind of spores formed in them.

(ii) What do you call the leaf-like appendages in the sporophyte of this plant that bear sporangia?

(iii) The given pteridophyte show characteristics that are considered as precursor to seed habit. Comment.

*Or*

(iii) Comment upon the fertilisation pattern of pteridophytes.

**Ans.** (i) The given plant is *Salvinia* in which two kinds of spores, macro (large) and micro (small) spores, are formed. Thus, it is known as a heterosporous plant. (1)

(ii) The sporophytes bear sporangia that are subtended by leaf-like appendages called sporophylls in pteridophytes. (1)

(iii) The phenomenon of heterospory, i.e. production of two types of spores–micro and megaspore, leads to the reduction of gametophyte, germination of spores and retention of megagametophyte in the megasporangium. This finally leads to seed development. (2)

*Or*

(iii) Antherozoids (male gametes) are released by the antheridia. These can get transferred to the archegonia, the female sex organs. This occurs only in the presence of water. Fusion of gametes takes place resulting in the formation of zygote. This zygote after division, produces sporophyte. (2)

**3. Rama conducted an experiment on two types of gymnosperm species, species A and species B. She removed both species from their original habitats and placed them in a nitrogen-deficient environment. After a period of one month, she made the following observations:**

**Species A developed specialised roots near the soil surface and flourished in the new environment.**

**Species B exhibited no such adaptations and showed signs of stress and struggles to survive.**

**Competency Based Que.**

**Based on the given information, answer the following questions.**

(i) Why was species A able to survive in the nitrogen-deficient environment?

(ii) State one characteristic of gymnosperms that distinguishes them from other plant groups.

(iii) What is the term for these specialised roots? Also, give an example of a gymnosperm that possesses such roots.

*Or*

(iii) What are the roots developed in species A called? What is special about them?

**Ans.** (i) Species A was able to survive in the nitrogen- deficient environment because it developed specialised roots near the soil surface. This adaptation allowed it to better access available nitrogen and nutrients, enabling it to thrive despite the nutrient scarcity. (2)

(ii) One characteristic that sets gymnosperms apart is that their male and female gametophytes do not exist independently; instead, they are retained within the sporangia of the sporophyte. (1)

(iii) The specialised roots are called coralloid roots. An example of a gymnosperm that possesses such roots is *Cycas*. (1)

*Or*

(iii) The roots developed in species A are known as coralloid roots. These are associated with $N_2$- fixing cyanobacteria. (1)

# SELF ASSESSMENT TEST

## Multiple Choice Questions

1. Classification done on the basis of information such as chromosome number structure, and behaviour is known as
   (a) chemotaxonomy
   (b) numerical taxonomy
   (c) cytotaxonomy
   (d) molecular taxonomy
2. Laminarin is a reserved food material found in all of the following except
   (a) *Ectocarpus* and *Dictyota*
   (b) *Gracilaria* and *Gelidium*
   (c) *Laminaria* and *Sargassum*
   (d) *Fucus* and *Dictyota*
3. Which of the following is not matched correctly?
   (a) Algin- *Laminaria*
   (b) Carrageen- *Ulothrix*
   (c) Agar- *Gelidium*
   (d) Food supplement- *Chlorella*
4. Why are bryophytes referred to as the amphibians of the plant kingdom?
   (a) They can only survive in moist environments
   (b) They live on land but requires water for fertilisation
   (c) They require water for spore formation
   (d) They can live in both aquatic and terrestrial habitats
5. Which of the following is incorrect regarding *Selaginella*?
   (a) The main plant body is gametophyte
   (b) It is a heterosporous fern
   (c) It is a vascular plant
   (d) The plant body is differentiated into root, stem and leaves
6. Which of the following features of gymnosperms does not help them to withstand extreme temperatures, humidity and wind?
   (a) Presence of thick cuticle
   (b) Presence of sunken stomata
   (c) Presence of needle like leaves
   (d) Presence of coralloid roots
7. Which of the following plant species bear covered seeds, enclosed in a fruit?
   (a) *Cedrus, Adiantum*
   (b) *Wolffia, Eucalyptus*
   (c) *Lycopodium, Psilotum*
   (d) *Polytrichum, Sphagnum*

## Assertion-Reason Questions

**Direction** (Q. Nos. 8-11) *In each of the following questions, a statement of Assertion (A) is given followed by corresponding statement of Reason (R). Of the statements, mark the correct answer*

(a) Both A and R are true and R is the correct explanation of the A.
(b) Both A and R are true, but R is not the correct explanation of the A.
(c) A is true, but R is false.
(d) A is false, but R is true.

8. **Assertion** (A) Members of Rhodophyceae are commonly called red algae.

   **Reason** (R) Rhodophyceae possess chlorophyll-*a, d,* fucoxanthin and phycoerythrin.
9. **Assertion** (A) Species of *Sphagnum* are used as a packing material for trans -shipment of living material.

   **Reason** (R) *Sphagnum* have the ability to hold water.

10. **Assertion** (A) The spread of living pteridophyte is limited and restricted to narrow geographical area.

**Reason** (R) The sporophyte of pteridophytes require cool, damp and shady places to grow.

11. **Assertion** (A) Gymnosperms are called naked seeded plants.

**Reason** (R) In gymnosperms, ovules are not enclosed by any ovary wall.

## Very Short Answer Type Questions

12. Who proposed the natural system of classification for flowering plants?
13. Mention the characters considered in cytotaxonomic studies.
14. Mention the name and location of the storage bodies located in green algae.
15. Give an example of homosporous and heterosporous pteridophyte.

## Short Answer Type Questions

16. Differentiate between oogamy and anisogamy.
17. Describe the process of sexual reproduction in *Funaria*.
18. Why are gymnosperms and angiosperms classified into different groups, even though they both bear seeds?

## Long Answer Type Questions

19. Differentiate between Chlorophyceae and Rhodophyceae.
20. Mention the economic importance of algae and bryophytes.
21. Discuss some general characteristics of pteridophytes.

## Case Based Question

22. In a high school biology class, the teacher is teaching students about different types of algae and their characteristics. To engage students in critical thinking and observation, the teacher presents two different algae spots, labelled as Spot *A* and Spot *B*.

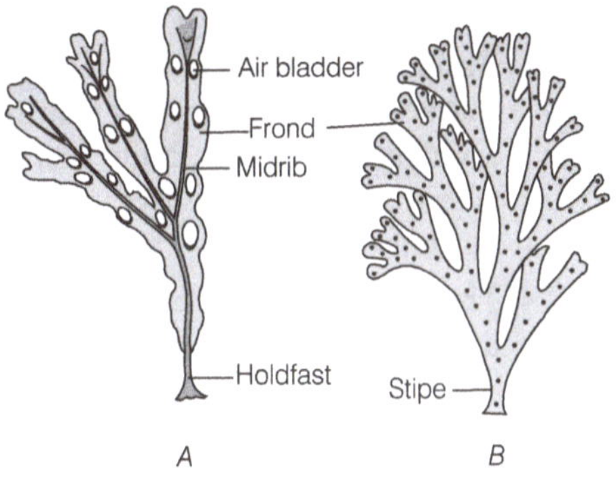


(a) Identify the two algae *A* and *B* and name the class, which they both belong to.

(b) Name the pigment which gives them the characteristic colour.

(c) Mention the characteristics of their gametes with reference to
(i) shape and (ii) flagellation.

# Answers

| | | | | | | |
|---|---|---|---|---|---|---|
| 1. (c) | 2. (b) | 3. (b) | 4. (b) | 5. (a) | 6. (d) | 7. (b) |
| 8. (c) | 9. (a) | 10. (c) | 11. (a) | | | |

04

CHAPTER

Biologist have described and named over a millions living organisms present on earth. Out of these, approximately 1 million are animals. These animals share similarities and differences with each other on their basis of body features which helps to classify or group them.

### YOUR STUDY GOALS



### YOUR PRACTICE GOAL

- Objective Type Questions (51 Qs ; MCQs, A-R) Case Based Questions (6)
- Subjective Type Questions
- (24 VSAs, 26 SAs, 13 LAs)

# Animal Kingdom

## 4.1 Basis of Classification

- The classification helps in easy identification and also in assigning a systematic position to newly discovered species.
- Animals exhibit a variety of structures and forms, yet they share several fundamental features. These include the arrangement of cells, body symmetry, types of coelom, and patterns in their digestive, circulatory, and reproductive systems.
- These shared characteristics form the basis for classifying different animal groups, some of them are discussed below.

### Level of Organisation

- All members of kingdom– **Animalia** are multicellular, yet all of them do not exhibit the same pattern of cellular organisation.
- The animal body shows four basic plan of structural organisation as given below:

#### 1. Cellular Level

- The body consists of many cells arranged as loose cell aggregates.
- These cells show a certain degree of **division of labour**, e.g. sponges (Porifera).

## 2. Tissue Level

- Several cells combine together to perform a same function, i.e. arranged into tissues.
- Here, the complexity of cellular arrangement increase, e.g. coelenterates.

## 3. Organ Level

- The tissues are grouped together to form organs, each organ is specialised for a particular function, e.g. Platyhelminthes and other higher phyla.

## 4. Organ System Level

- The organs are associated to form functional systems, each system concerned with a specific physiological function, e.g. annelids, arthropods, molluscs, echinoderms and chordates.
- Organ systems in different groups of animals exhibit various patterns of complexities. For example,
  - **Digestive System** Animals show two different patterns in digestive system, i.e.
    - **Incomplete digestive system**, present in Platyhelminthes, has a single opening to the outside of the body that serve as both mouth and anus.
    - **Complete digestive system**, present in annelids and arthropods, has two openings, mouth and anus.
  - **Circulatory System** Animals show two types of circulatory systems, i.e.
    - **Open type** in which the blood is pumped out of the heart; the cells and tissues are directly bathed in it.
    - **Closed type** in which the blood is circulated through a series of vessels of varying diameters (arteries, veins and capillaries).

# Symmetry

- The symmetry refers to the arrangement of parts on the opposite sides of the central axis of a three dimensional animal.
- Animals can be categorised, based on their symmetry, into the following types.

## 1. Asymmetrical

Animals in which, any plane passes through the centre does not divide them into equal halves such animals are called **asymmetrical**, e.g. sponges.

## 2. Symmetrical

The body of some animals can be divided into two similar equal halves by one or more planes. Such animals are called **symmetrical**. The symmetry can be further divided as

- **Radial Symmetry** In some animals body can be divided into two identical halves by any plane passing through the central axis of the body, e.g. coelenterates, ctenophores and echinoderms.

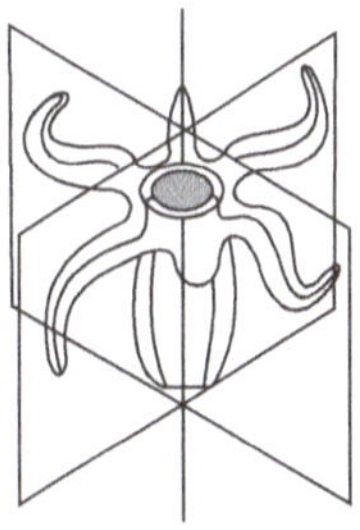

Fig 4.1 Radial symmetry

- **Bilateral Symmetry** In some animals, body can be divided into identical left and right halves in only one plane, e.g. annelids, arthropods, etc.

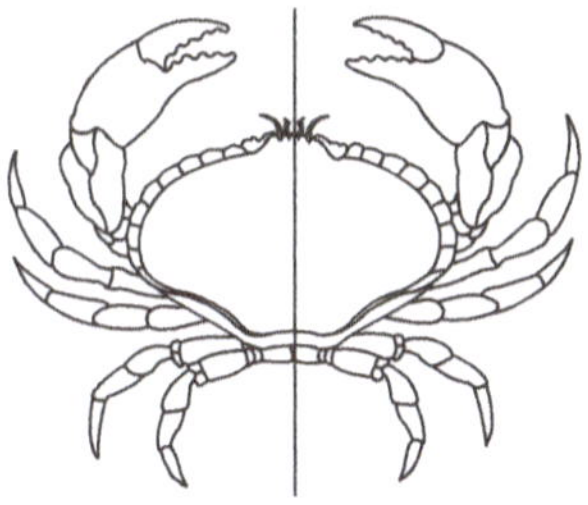

Fig 4.2 Bilateral symmetry

# Diploblastic and Triploblastic Organisation

- **Germ layers** are group of cells behaving as a unit during early stages of embryonic development.
- These germ layers differentiate to give rise to all the tissues/organs of the fully formed body of individuals.
- On the basis of arrangement of germ layers, the animals are classified into following types

## 1. Diploblastic

- Animals in which the cells are arranged in two embryonic layers—an **external ectoderm** and an **internal endoderm** are called **diploblastic** animals.
- In addition, an undifferentiated layer, **mesoglea** is present in between the ectoderm and the endoderm, e.g. coelenterates.

### 2. Triploblastic

- Animals in which the developing embryo has a third germinal layer **mesoderm**, in between the ectoderm and endoderm are called **triploblastic** animals, e.g. all animals from phylum-Platyhelminthes to phylum-Chordata.

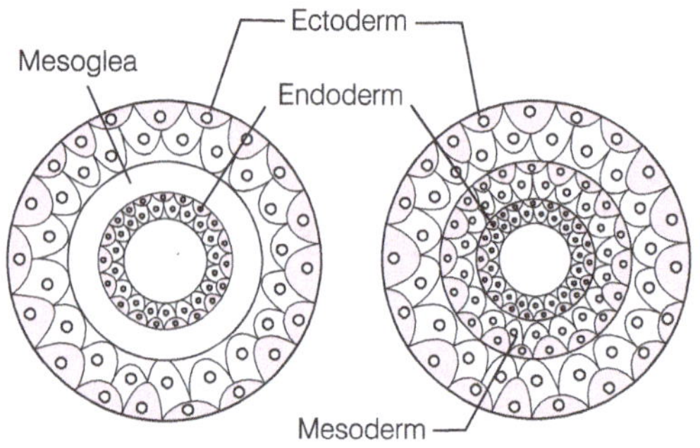


Fig 4.3 Showing germinal layers : (a) Diploblastic, (b) Triploblastic

## Coelom

- The body cavity (between the body wall and gut wall) which is lined by mesoderm is called **coelom**.
- The presence or absence of coelom is very important in classification.
- On the basis of coelom, animals can be classified into three different groups

### 1. Coelomates

- The animals in which coelom is present are called **coelomate**, e.g. Annelida, Arthropoda, Mollusca, Echinodermata, Hemichordata and Chordata.

### 2. Pseudocoelomates

- The animals in which the body cavity is not lined by mesoderm.
- Instead, the mesoderm is present as scattered pouches in between the ectoderm and endoderm. Such a body cavity is called **pseudocoelom** and the animals possessing them are called **pseudocoelomates**, e.g. Aschelminthes.

### 3. Acoelomates

The animals in which the body cavity is absent are called acoelomate, e.g. Platyhelminthes.

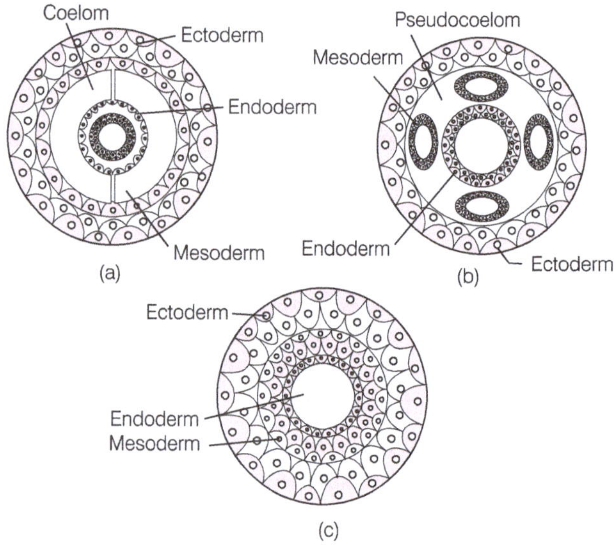


Fig 4.4 Sectional view of (a) Coelomates, (b) Pseudocoelomate, (c) Acoelomates

## Segmentation

- In some animals, the body is divided into segments both externally and internally, displaying a repeated arrangement of some organs.
- For example, in earthworms, the body show **metameric segmentation**, and the phenomenon is known as **metamerism**.

## Notochord

It is a mesodermally derived rod-like structure formed on the dorsal side during embryonic development in some animals. Based upon its presence or absence animals are classified into two categories.

- **Chordates** Animals with notochord are chordates and these animals belong to phylum-Chordata.
- **Non-chordates** These are animals which lack notochord. All animals belonging to Porifera upto Echinodermata are non-chordates.

## 4.2 Classification of Animals

An overview of the broad classification of the Kingdom–Animalia based on common fundamental features is given below:

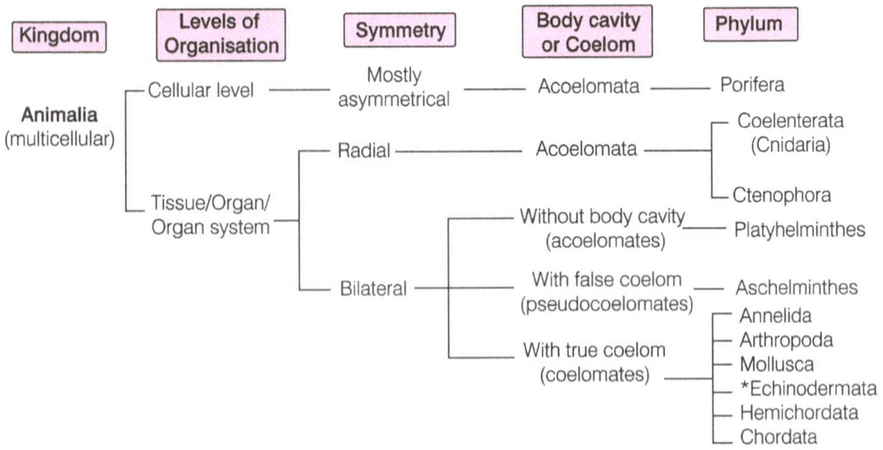


*Echinodermata exhibits radial or bilateral symmetry depending on the stage.

### Quick Test 1

1. Given an example of phylum that has tissue-level organisation.
2. The body of an animal can be divided into two halves in only one plane. Identify the type of symmetry.
3. **State True or False.**
   In terms of body plan complexity, triploblastic organisms are more advanced than diploblastic organisms due to the presence of three germ layers.
4. **State True or False.**
   Acoelomates lack a body cavity, which limits the development of complex organs and efficient organ function.
5. The structure *X* is a mesodermally derived rod-like structure that is found in animals belonging to phylum–Chordata. Identify *X*.

## 4.3 Non-chordates

Animals that do not possess a notochord at any stage of their life cycle are called as non-chordates.

The non-chordates includes the following phyla.

### Phylum–Porifera

The phylum-Porifera (*Porous* - pore; *ferre* - to bear) includes the first and the most primitive group of multicellular animals, referred to as **poriferans**, i.e. pore bearing animals.

The members of this phyla are also known as **sponges**. Some general features of phylum–Porifera are discussed below

- **Habitat** These are marine animals.
- **Symmetry** They show irregular shape and have no symmetry (asymmetrical)
- **Body Organisation** These are diploblastic organisms with cellular level of organisation.
- **Canal System** They possess a water transport or canal system, which is helpful in food gathering, respiratory exchange and removal of waste. Water flows in through tiny pores **(ostia)** in the body wall into a central cavity called the **spongocoel**, and then it exits through the **osculum**.
- **Body wall** It contain **choanocytes**, also known as collar cells, lining the **spongocoel** and the canals of the sponge.
- **Digestion** The animals of this phylum show intracellular (inside collar cells) digestion.

- **Skeletal system** Skeleton is internal and made up of inorganic **spicules** or organic **spongin fibres.**
- **Sex organs** All sponges are **hermaphrodite**, meaning a single individual produces both eggs and sperms.
- **Reproduction** Sponges reproduce both asexually and sexually. The asexual reproduction takes place by **fragmentation** on the other hand sexual reproduction takes place by formation of **gametes.**
- **Fertilisation and Development** Fertilisation is internal and development is indirect having a larval stage which is morphologically distinct from the adult.
- **Example** *Sycon* (Scypha), *Spongilla* (Fresh water sponges) and *Euspongia* (Bath sponge).

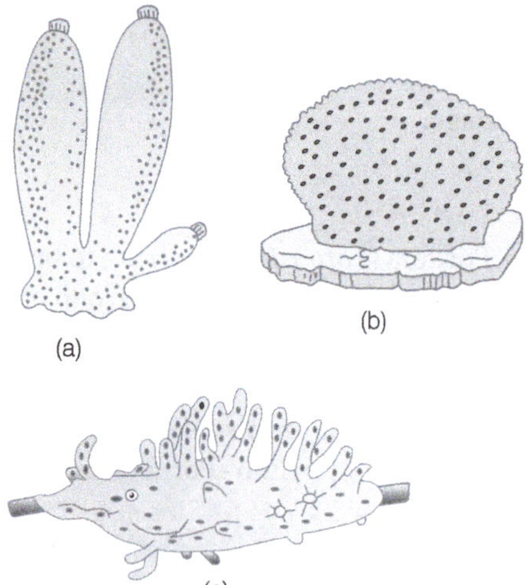


Fig 4.5 Examples of Porifera : (a) *Sycon*, (b) *Euspongia*, (c) *Spongilla*

**TEACHER'S TIP**

**Intracellular digestion** occurs within cells, where food is engulfed and broken down in vacuoles or lysosomes. Whereas, the **extracellular digestion** happens outside cells in a digestive system, where enzymes breakdown the food for absorption.

## Phylum–Coelenterata (Cnidaria)

The name Cnidaria (*Knide* - nettle or sting cells) is derived from the **cnidoblasts** or **cnidocytes** (which contain the stinging capsule or nematocysts) present on the tentacles and body of these animals.

Some important general features of phylum–Coelenterata are discussed below.

- **Habitat** These are aquatic, mostly marine and sessile or free-swimming animals.
- **Symmetry** They show radial symmetry.
- **Body Organisation and Body wall** They have tissue level of organisation and are diploblastic organisms. The body wall contain cnidoblast cells, which are used for anchorage, defense and for the capture of prey.

Fig 4.6 Diagrammatic view of cnidoblast

- **Body Cavity** A central gastrovascular cavity with a single opening, mouth on hypostome is present.
- **Digestion** Both intracellular as well as extracellular digestion takes place.
- **Skeletal System** Some of the cnidarians, e.g. **corals** have a skeleton composed of **calcium carbonate.**
- **Polymorphism** Cnidarians body exist in two forms, i.e. **polyp** (cup-shaped) and **medusa** (umbrella-shaped).
- Polyp is sessile, cylindrical form with mouth and tentacles facing upwards, e.g. *Hydra, Adamsia*, etc.
- Medusa is free-swimming form with mouth and tentacles facing downwards, e.g. *Aurelia* (jelly fish).
- **Alternation of Generation** The cnidarians which exist in both forms exhibit **alternation of generation (metagenesis)**, i.e. medusae may form polyps after sexual reproduction while polyps form medusae through asexual reproduction (e.g. *Obelia*).
- **Reproduction** Coelenterates reproduce both by asexual and sexual method.

- **Example** *Physalia* (Portuguese man-of-war), *Adamsia* (Sea anemone), *Pennatula* (Sea-pen), *Gorgonia* (Sea-fan) and *Meandrina* (Brain coral)

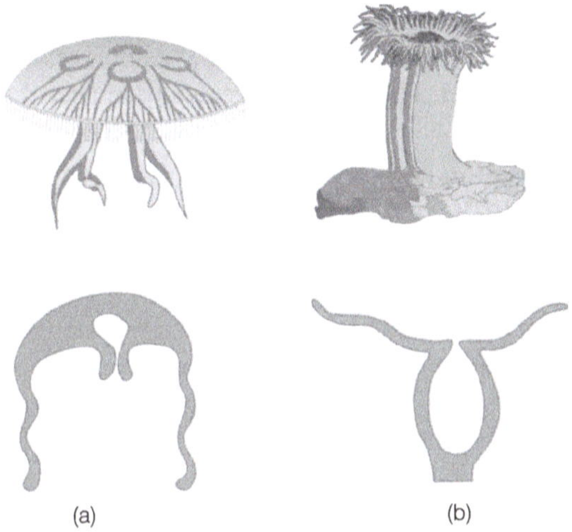


Fig 4.7 Some examples of coelenterates indicating outline of their body form : (a) *Aurelia* (medusa), (b) *Adamsia* (polyp)

## Phylum–Ctenophora

Members of phylum-Ctenophora (*cteno*-comb; *phora*-bearing) are commonly known as **comb jellies** or **sea walnuts**.

Some important general features of phylum–Ctenophora are discussed below

- **Habitat** These are exclusively marine animals.
- **Symmetry** They are radially symmetrical.
- **Body Cavity** These are acoelomate animals.
- **Body Organisation** Ctenophores are diploblastic organisms with tissue level of organisation.
- **Locomotion** The body bears eight external rows of ciliated **comb plates** that aid in locomotion.
- **Digestion** Show both extracellular and intracellular digestion.
- **Bioluminescence** The property of a living organism to emit light is called **bioluminescence**, which is well-marked in ctenophores.
- **Sex Organs** They are hermaphrodite or monoecious.
- **Reproduction** These animals show only sexual method of reproduction.
- **Fertilisation and Development** Fertilisation is generally external. Development is indirect.
- **Example** *Pleurobrachia* and *Ctenoplana.*

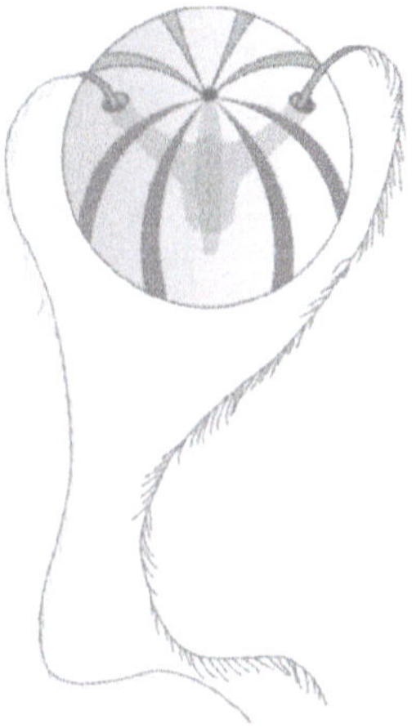

Fig 4.8 Example of Ctenophora (*Pleurobrachia*)

## Phylum– Platyhelminthes

The members of Phylum-Platyhelminthes (*Platy* - flat; *helminth* -worm) are called **flatworms** as they have dorso-ventrally flattened body. Some important general features of phylum–Platyhelminthes are discussed below

- **Habitat** They primarily exist as endoparasites in various animals, including humans and possess hooks and suckers as adhesive organs.
- **Symmetry** These are bilaterally symmetrical animals.
- **Body Cavity** These are acoelomate animals.
- **Body Organisation** Flatworms are triploblastic animals with an organ system level of organisation.
- **Digestive System** They have incomplete digestive system. Some parasites absorb nutrients from the host directly through their body surface.
- **Excretion** Flatworms have **flame cells** that help in osmoregulation and excretion.
- **Sex Organs** These are hermaphrodite, monoecious or bisexual organisms, having both male and female reproductive system.
- **Fertilisation and Development** Fertilisation is internal and development often includes one or more larval stages. Some members like *Planaria* show high regeneration capacity.

- **Example** *Taenia* (Tapeworm) and *Fasciola* (Liver fluke).

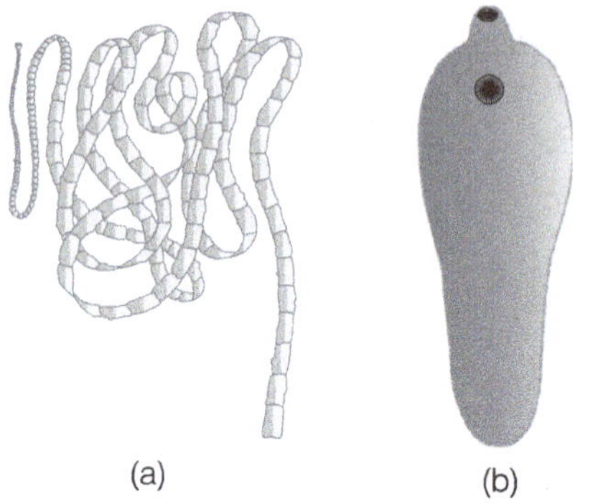

Fig 4.9 Examples of Platyhelminthes : (a) Tapeworm (*Taenia solium*) (b) Liver fluke (*Fasciola hepatica*)

## Quick Test 2

1. Identify the phylum that is characterised by the presence of choanocytes.
2. Name the free swimming organism with a downward facing mouth and tentacles.
3. **State True or False.**
   (a) Polyps form medusae through sexual reproduction.
   (b) Ctenophores are dioecious organisms.
4. Mention an animal that exhibits the property of bioluminescence.
5. *X* is the structure which helps in osmoregulation and excretion in *Fasciola*. Identify *X*.

## Phylum–Aschelminthes

The phylum-Aschelminthes or Nemathelminthes (*Nema* - thread; *helminth* - worms) includes **roundworms** that have cylindrical body. Some important general features of phylum– Aschelminthes are discussed below.

- **Habitat** They are mostly free-living and may occur in water or within the soil. There are several parasitic species that live within the body of animals or plants.
- **Symmetry** These are bilaterally symmetrical.
- **Body Cavity** The body cavity present between the body wall and gut is not lined by mesoderm. Therefore, they are pseudocoelomate animals.
- **Body Organisation** Roundworms are triploblastic animals with organ-system level of body organisation.
- **Digestion** Digestive system consists of a complete alimentary canal and a well-developed **muscular pharynx.**
- **Excretion** Excretory system consists of a pair of excretory tubes.
  - These tubes remove waste from the body cavity through excretory pore.
- **Sex Organs** Sexes are separate and exhibit **sexual dimorphism.** The males are generally smaller than the females.
- **Fertilisation and Development** Fertilisation is internal. The fertilised eggs develop directly or indirectly through larvae that undergo moulting and finally grow into adults.
- **Example** *Ascaris* (Roundworm), *Wuchereria* (Filaria worm) and *Ancylostoma* (Hookworm).

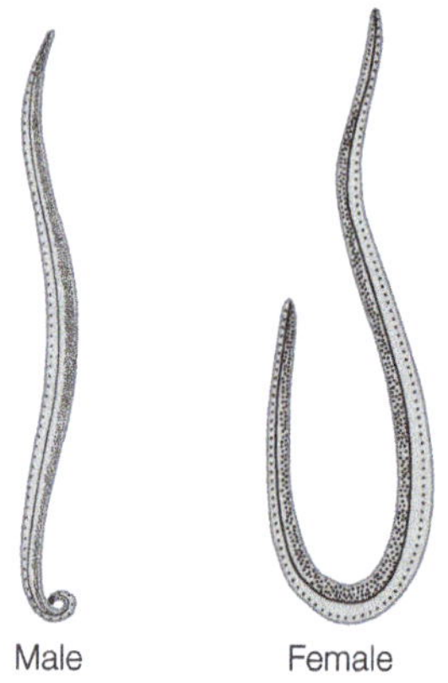

Fig 4.10 Example of Aschelminthes : Roundworm

## Phylum–Annelida

The members of phylum-Annelida (*Annulus* - ring; *lidos* - form) are called **segmented worms** as they bear metameric segmentation.

Some important general features of phylum–Annelida are discussed below.

- **Habitat** These animals may be aquatic, terrestrial and free-living or parasitic.
- **Symmetry** They show bilateral symmetry.
- **Body Cavity** These are coelomate animals, i.e. body cavity is lined by mesoderm.
- **Body Organisation** These are triploblastic animals that show organ system level of body organisation.
- **Segmentation** The body shows metameric segmentation, which means surface is distinctly marked out into **segments** or **metameres.**
- **Locomotion** It is supported by circular and longitudinal muscles.

- Aquatic annelids like *Nereis* possess lateral appendages, **parapodia**, which help in swimming.

- **Circulatory System** Annelids are among the earliest animals that have developed a closed circulatory system.
- **Excretion** The excretory organs called **nephridia** are present in each segment, which helps in excretion and osmoregulation.
- **Neural System** It consists of paired ganglia and a double ventral nerve cord, which are connected by lateral nerves.
- **Reproduction** Annelids reproduce sexually.
- They can be unisexual, e.g. *Nereis*, an aquatic form, or bisexual (hermaphrodite), e.g. leech, earthworm.
- **Example** *Nereis*, *Pheretima* (Earthworm) and *Hirudinaria* (Blood sucking leech).

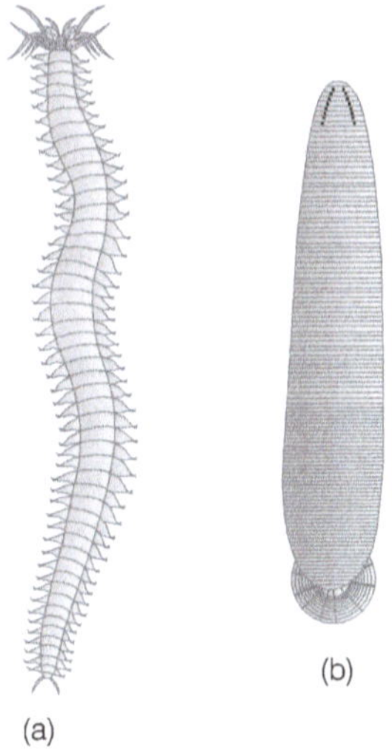


Fig 4.11 Examples of Annelida : (a) *Nereis*, (b) *Hirudinaria*

## Phylum–Arthropoda

The phylum-Arthropoda (*Arthros* - jointed; *poda* - appendages) is the **largest group of animal kingdom,** representing about two-third of total known animal species.

Some important general features of phylum–Arthropoda are discussed below:

- **Habitat** They may be aquatic or terrestrial. They may occur as free-living or parasitic forms.
- **Symmetry** They show bilateral symmetry.
- **Body Cavity** Arthropods are coelomate animals, i.e. body cavity is lined by mesoderm.
- **Body Organisation** They are triploblastic animals and have organ system level of body organisation.
- **Body Form** The body shows external segmentation, featuring a distinct **head, thorax**, and **abdomen**, and is covered by a **chitinous exoskeleton.**
- **Appendages** These animals are characterised by the presence of **jointed appendages**.
- **Respiration** It occurs through general body surface, gills, book lungs, tracheal system and book gills.
- **Circulatory System** The circulatory system is open type, i.e. blood flows in the body cavity instead of blood vessels.
- **Sense Organs** These animals have antennae and eyes (simple and compound).
- Aquatic forms have **statocysts** for balancing.
- **Excretion** The excretory organs are **Malpighian tubules.**
- **Sex Organs** They are mostly dioecious and reproduce by sexual methods.
- **Fertilisation and Development** Fertilisation is usually internal. Most arthropods are oviparous though a few are viviparous.
- Development may be direct or indirect involving **metamorphosis.**
- **Example**
  - **Economically important insects** – *Apis* (Honeybee), *Bombyx* (Silkworm), *Laccifer* (Lac insect).
  - **Vectors** – *Anopheles, Culex* and *Aedes* (Mosquitoes)
  - **Gregarious pest** – *Locusta* (Locust)
  - **Living fossil** – *Limulus* (King crab).

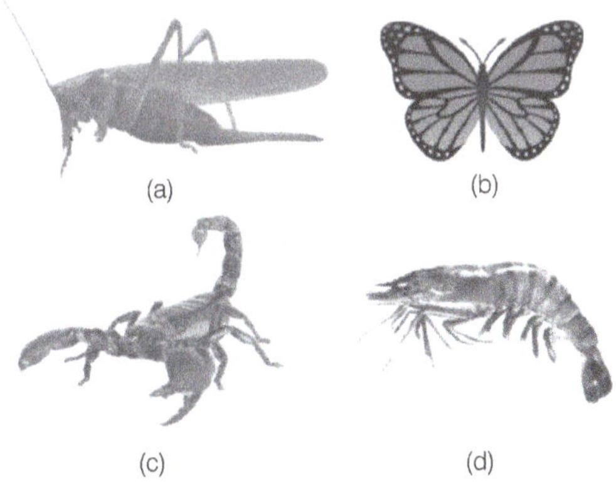


Fig 4.12 Examples of Arthropoda: (a) Locust, (b) Butterfly, (c) Scorpion, (d) Prawn

## Phylum–Mollusca

The phylum-Mollusca constitute the **second largest phylum** of the animal kingdom.

Some important general features of phylum–Mollusca are discussed below.

- **Habitat** Molluscs are found in terrestrial or aquatic (marine or freshwater) habitats.
- **Symmetry** They show bilateral symmetry.
- **Body Cavity** Molluscs are coelomate animals, i.e. body cavity is lined by mesoderm.
- **Body Organisation** They are triploblastic animals, having organ system level of body organisation.
- **Body Form** They have unsegmented, soft body, covered by a calcareous shell, which is differentiated into **head, muscular foot** and **visceral hump**.
- A soft, spongy thick fold of skin called **mantle** is present over the visceral hump.
- The space between the hump and the mantle is called the **mantle cavity** in which feather-like gills are present. They have excretory and respiratory functions.
- **Digestive System** The digestive tract is complete. The mouth contains a file-like rasping organ for feeding, called **radula**.
- **Sense organs** The anterior head region has sensory tentacles.
- **Reproduction** They are usually dioecious and oviparous animals with indirect development.
- **Example** *Pila* (Apple snail), *Pinctada* (Pearl oyster), *Sepia* (Cuttlefish), *Loligo* (Squid), *Octopus* (Devil fish), *Aplysia* (Sea-hare), *Dentalium* (Tusk shell) and *Chaetopleura* (Chiton).

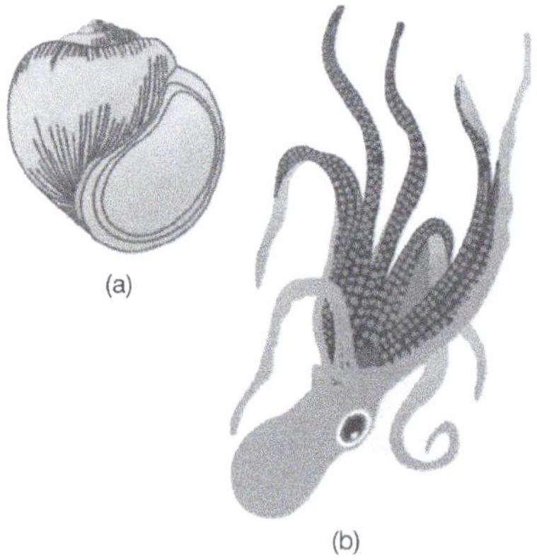


Fig 4.13 Examples of Mollusca : (a) *Pila*, (b) *Octopus*

## Phylum–Echinodermata

The phylum-Echinodermata (*Echinos*-spines; *derma*-skin) is characterised by the presence of spiny bodied animals, which are **exclusively marine**.

Some important general features of phylum–Echinodermata are discussed below.

- **Habitat** These are exclusively marine and are generally bottom dwellers.
- **Symmetry** The adults show radial (pentamerous) symmetry, but the larval forms show bilateral symmetry.
- **Body Cavity** These are coelomate animals.
- **Body Organisation** They are triploblastic animals, having organ system level of body organisation
- **Digestion** The digestive system is simple and complete. The mouth is present on the ventral (lower) side and the anus is on the dorsal (upper) side.
- The most distinguishing feature of echinoderms is the presence of **water vascular system** which helps in locomotion, food capture, transport as well as in respiration.
- **Endoskeleton** These animals contains numerous calcareous plates called **ossicles** beneath the skin.
- **Excretion** The excretory organs are absent.
- **Reproduction** These are dioecious and sexually reproducing animals.
- **Fertilisation and Development** Fertilisation is external and development is indirect with free swimming larva.
- **Example** *Asterias* (Star fish), *Echinus* (Sea urchin), *Antedon* (Sea lily), *Cucumaria* (Sea cucumber) and *Ophiura* (Brittle star).

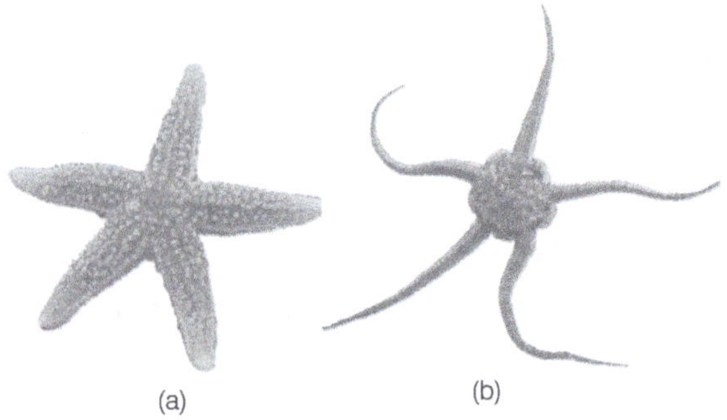


Fig 4.14 Examples of Echinodermata : (a) *Asterias*, (b) *Ophiura*

## Phylum–Hemichordata

Hemichordata (*Hemi* - half; *chordata* - notochord) was earlier placed as a sub-phylum under phylum–Chordata. But, now it is considered as a separate phylum under non-chordata. It includes small **worm-like** marine animals.

Some important general features of phylum–Hemichordata are discussed below.

- **Habitat** They are exclusively marine and mostly live in **burrows.**
- **Symmetry** Bilateral symmetry is found in hemichordates.
- **Body Cavity** They are coelomate animals.
- **Body Organisation** These are triploblastic animals and have organ system level of body organisation.
- **Body Form** They have cylindrical body, divisible into anterior **proboscis**, a **collar** and long **trunk**. Presence of **stomochord** (rudimentary structure similar to notochord) in the collar region.
- **Digestion** Digestive system is complete.
- **Circulation** Circulatory system is of open type.
- **Respiration** Respiration occurs through several pairs of gills.
- **Excretion** Excretory organ is **proboscis gland.**
- **Reproduction** Sexes are separate. Fertilisation is external and development is direct.
- **Examples** *Balanoglossus* and *Saccoglossus.*

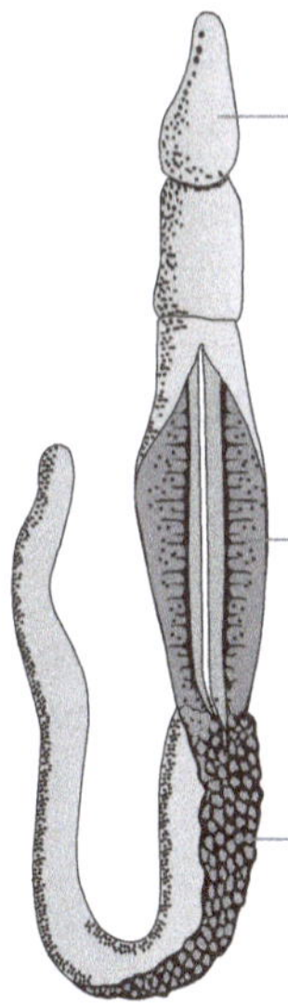


Fig 4.15 *Balanoglossus*

### Quick Test 3

1. Give an example of organism that is characterised by a muscular pharynx and a pair of excretory tubes.
2. Aquatic arthropods have a structure X for balancing. Identify X.
3. Name the rasping organ which is present in molluscs for feeding.
4. **State True or False**

   *Echinus* and *Asterias* have an incomplete digestive system.
5. Identify the structure found in hemichordates that is similar to notochord.

## 4.4 Chordates

- Animals belonging to phylum-Chordata are fundamentally characterised by the presence of following features:
  - **Notochord**
  - **Dorsal hollow nerve cord**
  - **Paired pharyngeal gill slits**
- These are bilaterally symmetrical, triploblastic, coelomate animals with organ system level of organisation.
- They possess a post-anal tail and a closed circulatory system.

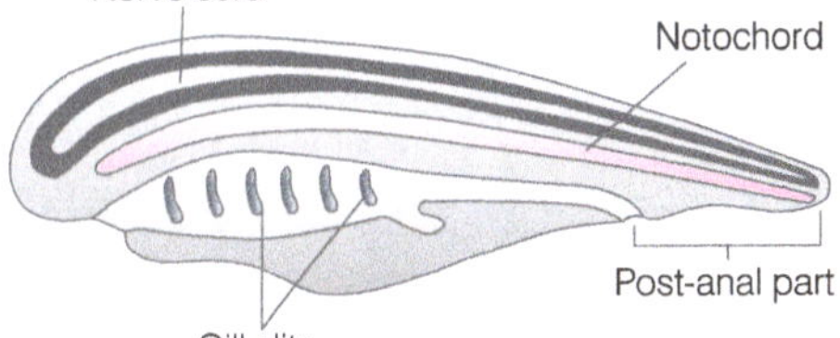


Fig 4.16 Chordata characteristics

**Differences between Chordates and Non-Chordates**

| Chordates | Non-Chordates |
|---|---|
| Notochord is present. | Notochord is absent. |
| Central nervous system is dorsal, hollow and single. | Central nervous system is ventral, solid and double. |
| Pharynx is perforated by gill slits. | Gill slits are absent. |
| Heart is ventral. | Heart is dorsal (if present). |
| Post- anal part (tail) is present. | Post-anal tail is absent. |

## Classification of Phylum–Chordata

- The phylum–Chordata is divided into three sub-phyla, i.e.,
  - **Urochordata (Tunicata)**
  - **Cephalochordata**
  - **Vertebrata**
- Urochordata and Cephalochordata are often referred to as **protochordates** and are exclusively **marine**.

Details of each subphyla and its numerous classes are given below.

## Subphylum–Urochordata

These are sessile, filter feeding invertebrates.

Some important general features of subphylum-Urochordata are discussed below:

- The body is covered by a test (tunic) composed largely of **tunicin**. So, they are commonly called **tunicates**.
- These animals lack body cavity (coelom).
- The notochord is present only in the tail of the larva and disappears in the adult.
- **Example** *Ascidia*, *Salpa* and *Doliolum*.

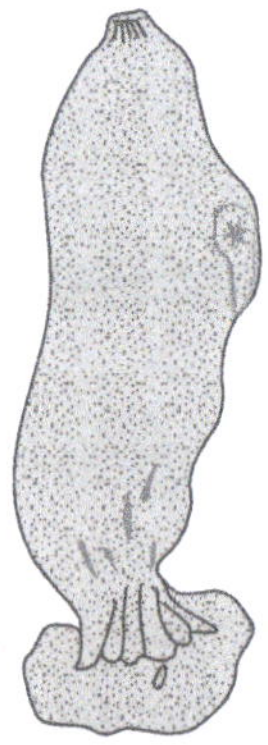

Fig 4.17 *Ascidia*

## Subphylum – Cephalochordata

These are also marine, filter feeding, invertebrates.

Some important general features of subphylum-Cephalochordata are discussed below.

- The notochord extends the entire length of the body and passes a head of the nerve cord in front.
- Notochord persists throughout the life.
- **Example** *Branchiostoma* (Amphioxus or Lancelet).

## Subphylum –Vertebrata

The subphylum-Vertebrata represents advanced or higher chordates which include vertebrates.

Some important general features of subphylum-Vertebrata are discussed below.

- **Notochord** is present only in the embryonic stage.
- In adults, it is replaced by a **cartilaginous** or **bony vertebral column**.
- Thus, all vertebrates are chordates but all chordates are not vertebrates.
- Vertebrates have a **closed circulatory system** with ventrally situated heart (two, three or four-chambered).
- They possess a **pair of kidneys** for osmoregulation and excretion.
- They have **paired appendages** for locomotion, which maybe fins or limbs.
- Some major classes of subphylum- Vertebrata are given below.

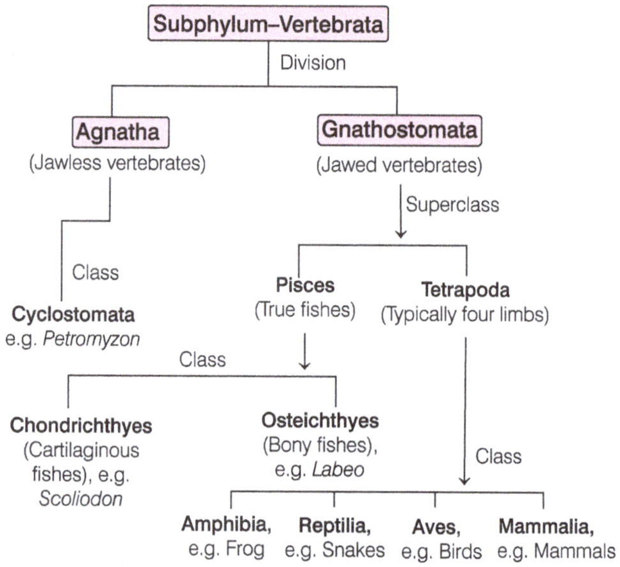


### Agnatha

The members of division Agnatha possess **jawless mouths**. These jawless vertebrates have been placed under a single class-Cyclostomata.

## Class–Cyclostomata

The class-Cyclostomata (*Cyklos* - circular; stoma - mouth) includes vertebrates having circular mouth.

Some important general features of class-Cyclostomata are discussed below.

- All living members of the class–Cyclostomata are **ectoparasites** on some fishes.
- They are **marine**, but migrate to freshwater for spawning. The adult die within few days after spawning but their larvae after **metamorphosis** return to the ocean.
- The body of cyclostomes is elongated and is devoid of scales and paired fins.
- They have sucking and circular mouth without jaws.
- They have 6-15 pairs of gill slits for respiration.
- The cranium and vertebral column are cartilaginous. Circulation is of closed type.
- **Example** *Petromyzon* (Lamprey) and *Myxine* (Hagfish).

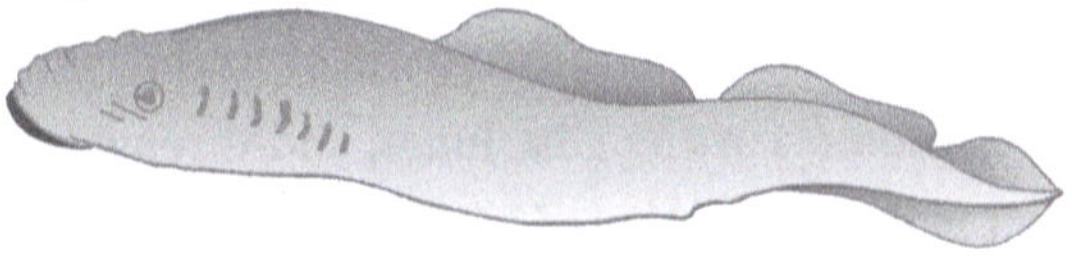

Fig 4.18 Examples of Cyclostomata-*Petromyzon*,

## Gnathostomata

It includes a group of vertebrates that have jaws. This section includes two superclass-**pisces** and **tetrapoda**.

## Superclass– Pisces

- The members of superclass–Pisces are considered as true fishes.
- Pisces includes two main classes, i.e. Chondrichthyes and Osteichthyes.

### Class–Chondrichthyes

The members of class-Chondrichthyes (*Chondros*-cartilage; *ichthys*-fish) are called **cartilaginous fishes** due to the presence of cartilaginous endoskeleton.

The common features of Chondrichthyes are as follows.

- They are mostly **marine** animals with streamlined body.
- **Notochord** is **persistent** throughout the life.
- **Mouth** is ventral in position, skin is tough containing minute **placoid scales** and teeth are also modified **placoid scales**, which are directed backwardly.
- They have strong jaw and are predaceous by nature.
- Gill slits are separate and **operculum** (gill cover) is absent.
- **Heart** is two-chambered with one auricle and one ventricle.
- **Air bladders** are absent, so they swim constantly to avoid sinking.
- Some of them possess **electric organs** (e.g. *Torpedo*) and some possess **poison sting** (e.g. *Trygon*).
- They are **cold-blooded (poikilothermous)** animals, i.e. they lack the capacity to regulate their body temperature.
- **Sexes** are separate and fertilisation is **internal**.
- Males usually have **claspers** on pelvic fins.
- They can be **oviparous** or **viviparous**.
- **Example:** *Scoliodon* (dog fish), *Carcharodon* (great white shark), *Pristis* (saw fish), *Trygon* (sting ray).

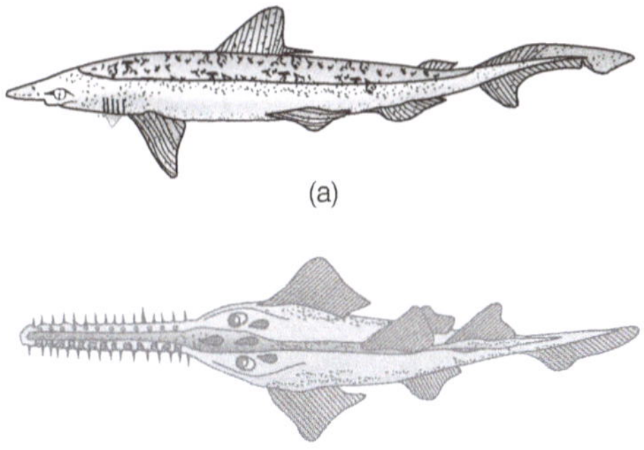

(a)

(b)

Fig 4.19 Examples of cartilaginous fishes : (a) *Scoliodon*, (b) *Pristis*

### Class-Osteichthyes

The class-Osteichthyes (*Osteon* - bone; *ichthys* - fish) includes bony fishes such as carps, catfishes, sardines, mackerels, seahorse, etc.

The common features of Osteichthyes are as follows.

- They are found in **marine water** as well as in **freshwater**.
- They are cold-blooded animals.
- Their body is **streamlined** and mouth is mostly terminal.
- **Exoskeleton** contains **cycloid** or **ctenoid** scales.

- **Gills** are generally four paired and covered with an operculum (gill cover).
- **Air bladder** is present which regulates buoyancy.
- **Heart** is two-chambered with one auricle and one ventricle.
- **Sexes** are separate. Fertilisation is usually **external**, mostly oviparous and development is **direct**.
- **Example**
  - **Marine** – *Exocoetus* (Flying fish), *Hippocampus* (Sea horse)
  - **Freshwater** – *Labeo* (Rohu), *Catla* (Katla), *Clarias* (Magur)
  - **Aquarium** – *Betta* (Fighting fish), *Pterophyllum* (Angel fish).

Fig 4.20 Some bony fishes: (a) *Hippocampus* (seahorse), (b) *Catla*

## Quick Test 4

1. A marine animal has notochord in its larval stage, but it disappears in adulthood. To which class in phylum–Chordata does this animal most likely belong?
2. A vertebrate is characterised by a circular mouth without jaws. Give an example of such organism.
3. In Chondrichthyes, which types of scales are modified into teeth?
4. **State True or False.**
   (a) Gills in most bony fishes are generally covered with an operculum.
   (b) In bony fishes cartilaginous exoskeleton is present.
5. An organism of class – Chondrichthyes, possesses a poisonous sting. Identify the organism.

## Superclass–Tetrapoda

- The members of superclass- Tertrapoda are four-limbed vertebrate animals.
- Tetrapoda is sub-divided into four main classes, i.e. Amphibia, Reptilia, Aves and Mammalia. Which are explained below

### Class-Amphibia

The class-Amphibia (*Amphi*-double; *bios*-life) includes animals like frogs, toads and salamanders that can live in aquatic as well as terrestrial habitats.

The common features of amphibians are as follows

- **Body** is differentiated into head and trunk.
- **A tympanum** represents the ear.
- A pair of eyes with movable eyelids are present.
- **Skin** is mostly smooth, moist and rich in gland. Scales are generally absent and tail may be present in some.
- Amphibians mostly have **two pairs of limbs.**
- **Respiration** occurs by gills, lungs, and through skin.
- **Heart** is **three-chambered**, with two auricles and one ventricle. These are **cold-blooded** animals.
- Alimentary canal, urinary and reproductive tracts open into a common chamber called **cloaca**, which opens to exterior.
- **Sexes** are separate and fertilisation is **external.**
- They are oviparous animals. Development is **indirect.**
- **Example** *Bufo* (Toad), *Rana* (Frog), *Hyla* (Tree frog), *Salamandra* (Salamander), *Ichthyophis* (Limbless amphibia).

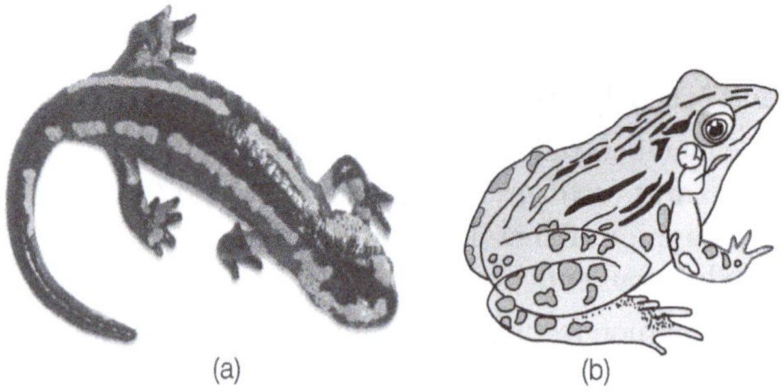


Fig 4.21 Some examples of amphibians: (a) *Salamandra*, (b) *Rana* ( frog)

## Class-Reptilia

The class-Reptilia (*repere* or *reptum* - to creep or crawl) include animals like lizards, snakes, turtles, tortoises, crocodiles, etc.

Reptiles are the first fully adapted terrestrial animals. The common features of reptiles are as follows:

- These animals show **creeping** or **crawling** mode of locomotion.
- They are mostly terrestrial, but a few of them live in water.
- They have dry, rough and cornified skin, provided with epidermal **scales** or **scutes**.
- They lack external ear openings and it is represented by **tympanum**.
- They have two pairs of limbs (absent in snakes).
- **Heart** is usually **three-chambered** with two auricles and one ventricle. The heart is **four-chambered** in crocodiles.
- Reptiles are **cold-blooded** (poikilothermic) animals. They hibernate in winter.
- Snakes and lizards shed their scales as skin cast.
- These are unisexual and show sexual dimorphism. Fertilisation is **internal** with **direct development**.
- These are egg laying animals.
- **Example** *Calotes* (Garden lizard), *Chelone* (Turtle), *Testudo* (Tortoise), *Chameleon* (Tree lizard), *Hemidactylus* (Wall lizard), *Crocodilus* (Crocodile), *Alligator* (Alligator).
  **Poisnous snakes** - *Naja* (Cobra), *Bangarus* (Krait), *Vipera* (Viper).

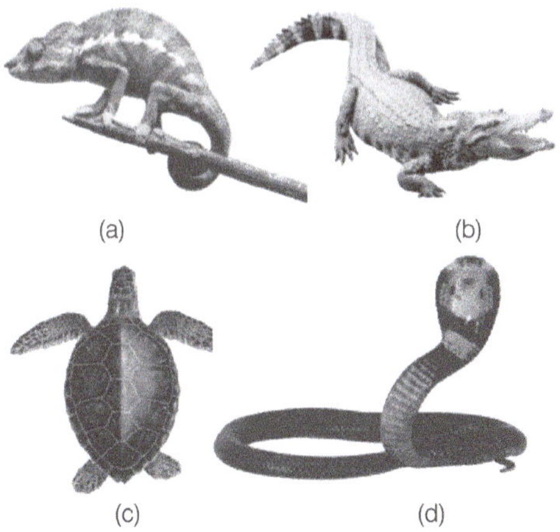


Fig 4.22 Examples of Reptilia : (a) *Chameleon* (tree lizard), (b) *Crocodilus*, (c) *Chelone*, (d) *Naja*

## Class-Aves

The class-Aves include flying vertebrates, such as parrots, pigeons, crows, etc.
The members of class–Aves are characterised by the presence of **feathers on the body**.
The common features of class-Aves are as follows

- Most of them can fly except the flightless birds (e.g. ostrich).
- The skin is dry without glands except the oil gland at the base of the tail.
- **Mouth** is extended into beak.
- **Endoskeleton** is fully ossified (i.e. bony) and the long bones are hollow with **air cavities** (pneumatic).
- **Locomotion** occurs through **wings**, which are modified forelimbs.
- Hind limbs generally have scales and are modified for walking, swimming or clasping the tree branches.
- **Lungs** are respiratory organs, which are spongy, inelastic and are connected to large air sacs.
- The **digestive system** of birds has additional chambers, the crop and gizzard.
- **Heart** is **four-chambered** with two auricles and two ventricles. Only right aortic arch persists.
- Birds are **warm-blooded** or **homoiothermous** animals, i.e. they maintain the constant body temperature.
- **Sexes** are separate with sexual dimorphism. Fertilisation is **internal** and development is **direct**.
- Birds are oviparous.
- **Example**
  - **Flight birds**- *Corvus* (crow), *Columba* (pigeon), *Psittacula* (parrot), *Pavo* (peacock), *Milvus* (kite), *Neophron* (vulture), etc.
  - **Flightless**- *Struthio* (ostrich), *Aptenodytes* (penguin), etc.

Fig 4.23 Some birds : (a) *Neophron*, (b) *Struthio*, (c) *Psittacula*

## Class-Mammalia

The members of class–Mammalia (Mamma - breast) are characterised by the presence of **mammary glands** to nourish young ones.

The common features of class- Mammalia are as follows

- Mammals are found in a variety of habitats, such as forests, grasslands, mountains, deserts, polar ice caps, caves, etc.
- Some of them have adapted to fly or live in water.
- **Skin** in mammals is unique in possessing hair.
- External ear called **pinnae** are present.
- Two pairs of pentadactyl limbs are present for walking, running, climbing, burrowing, flying and swimming.
- Different types of teeth are present in the jaw.
- **Heart** is **four-chambered** with two auricles and two ventricles.
- **Respiration** takes place through lungs.
- They are **warm-blooded** or **homoiothermous** animals.
- Mammals are unisexual and show prominent sexual dimorphism.
- Fertilisation is **internal**. Development is direct.
- They are generally viviparous. Exception is *Ornithorhynchus* (platypus), which is oviparous.
- **Example** *Macropus* (kangaroo), *Pteropus* (flying fox), *Camelus* (camel), *Macaca* (monkey), *Rattus* (rat), *Canis* (dog), *Felis* (cat), *Elephas* (elephant), *Equus* (horse), *Delphinus* (common dolphin). *Balaenoptera* (blue whale), *Panthera tigris* (tiger), *Panthera leo* (lion).

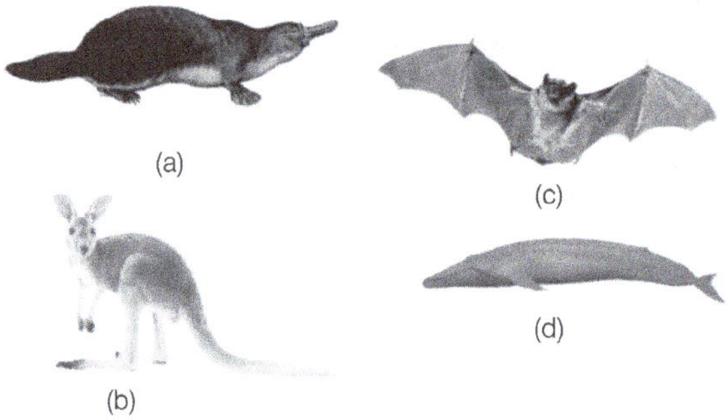


Fig 4.24 Some mammals : (a) *Ornithorhynchus*, (b) *Macropus*, (c) *Pteropus*, (d) *Balaenoptera*

**Salient Features of Different Phyla in the Animal Kingdom**

| Phylum | Level of Organisation | Symmetry | Coelom | Segmentation | Digestive System | Circulatory System | Respiratory System | Distinctive Features |
|---|---|---|---|---|---|---|---|---|
| Porifera | Cellular | Various | Absent | Absent | Absent | Absent | Absent | Body with pores and canals in walls. |
| Coelenterata (Cnidaria) | Tissue | Radial | Absent | Absent | Incomplete | Absent | Absent | Cnidoblasts present. |
| Ctenophora | Tissue | Radial | Absent | Absent | Incomplete | Absent | Absent | Comb plates for locomotion. |
| Platyhelminthes | Organ and organ system | Bilateral | Absent | Absent | Incomplete | Absent | Absent | Flat body, suckers. |
| Aschelminthes | Organ system | Bilateral | Pseudo-coelomate | Absent | Complete | Absent | Absent | Often worm-shaped, elongated. |
| Annelida | Organ system | Bilateral | Coelomate | Present | Complete | Present | Absent | Body segmentation like rings. |
| Arthropoda | Organ system | Bilateral | Coelomate | Present | Complete | Present | Present | Exoskeleton of cuticle, jointed appendages. |
| Mollusca | Organ system | Bilateral | Coelomate | Absent | Complete | Present | Present | External skeleton of shell is usually present. |

| Phylum | Level of Organisation | Symmetry | Coelom | Segmentation | Digestive System | Circulatory System | Respiratory System | Distinctive Features |
|---|---|---|---|---|---|---|---|---|
| Echinodermata | Organ system | Radial | Coelomate | Absent | Complete | Present | Present | Water vascular system, radial symmetry. |
| Hemichordata | Organ system | Bilateral | Coelomate | Absent | Complete | Present | Present | Worm-like with proboscis, collar and trunk. |
| Chordata | Organ system | Bilateral | Coelomate | Present | Complete | Present | Present | Notochord, dorsal hollow nerve cord, gill slits with limbs or fins. |

## Quick Test 5

1. Name the structure which represents the ear in amphibians.
2. **State True or False.**
   Reptiles possess desiccated, rough, and cornified skin with epidermal scales or scutes.
3. State one common feature between the members of the classes Reptilia and Aves.
4. Name the spongy and inelastic structure present in birds that is connected to air sacs.
5. Some organisms are capable of maintaining a stable internal body temperature despite changes in the external environment. Mention the term which is used to described such organisms.

# Mind Map

## Animal Kingdom

### Basis of Classification

| Kingdom | Levels of organisation | Symmetry | Body cavity or Coelom | Phylum |
|---|---|---|---|---|
| Animalia (multicellular) | Cellular level | Mostly asymmetrical | Acoelomata | Porifera |
| | Tissue/Organ/Organ system | Radial | Acoelomata | Coelenterata (Cnidaria) |
| | | | | Ctenophora |
| | | Bilateral | Without body cavity (acoelomates) | Platyhelminthes |
| | | | With false coelom (pseudocoelomates) | Aschelminthes |
| | | | With true coelom (coelomates) | Annelida |
| | | | | Arthropoda |
| | | | | Mollusca |
| | | | | *Echinodermata |
| | | | | Hemichordata |
| | | | | Chordata |

### Classification of Animals

Animals are classified into two phylum : Non-chordata and Chordata.

### Non-chordata

Animals without notochord.

#### Phylum-Porifera

- Skeleton is made up of spicules.
- Canal system is lined by choanocytes.

#### Phylum-Coelenterata

- Presence of cnidoblasts.
- A central gastrovascular cavity on hypostome.
- Metagenesis between polymorphic forms.

#### Phylum-Ctenophora

- Body bears ciliated comb plates.
- Shows biolumniscence.

#### Phylum-Platyhelminthes

- Flat body, presence of hooks and suckers.
- Flame cells are present.

#### Phylum-Aschelminthes

- Often elongated in shape.
- Pseudocoelomate, with females longer than males.
- Well-developed alimentary canal.

#### Phylum-Annelida

- Segmented body.
- Presence of parapodia in aquatic annelids.
- Neural system with paired ganglia.

#### Phylum-Arthropoda

- Chitinous exoskeleton.
- Presence of jointed appendages.
- Excretion by Malpighian tubules.

#### Phylum-Mollusca

- External skeleton is made up of calcareous shell.
- Body is distinct into head, muscular foot and visceral hump.
- Presence of radula for feeding.

#### Phylum-Echinodermata

- Presence of water vascular system.
- Bilateral symmetry in larval stage and radial in adults.

#### Phylum-Hemichordata

- Worms with probosics, collar and trunk.
- Presence of stomochord in collar region.

### Chordata

Animals with notochord, dorsal hollow nerve cord and paired pharyngeal gill slits.

#### Sub-phylum-Cephalochordata

They are marine animals with a segmented, elongated body and a notochord extending from head to tail.

#### Sub-phylum-Urochordata

Notochord is found only in larval tail.

#### Sub-phylum-Vertebrata

It is divided into two divisions ; Agnatha and Gnathostomata

#### Division-Gnathostomata

Animals possess jaw.

#### Division–Agnatha

Jawless animals. 6-15 pairs of gill slits.

#### Superclass-Pisces

**Class–Chondrichthyes**
- Skin has placoid scales.
- Gill slits are without an operculum.

**Class–Osteichthyes**
- Streamlined body with gills covered by an operculum.
- Have cycloid/ctenoid scales and an air bladder.

#### Superclass-Tetrapoda

**Class–Amphibia**
- Terrestrial with two pairs of limbs and a 3-chambered heart.
- Body is divided into head and trunk, with a tympanum for hearing.

**Class–Reptillia**
- Dry, cornified skin with scales or scutes.
- 3-chambered heart (4 in crocodiles).

**Class–Aves**
- Feathers, wings, and warm-blooded with air cavities.
- Digestive tract includes a crop and gizzard, 4-chambered heart.

**Class–Mammalia**
- Mammary glands and hair, external ears (pinnae).
- 4-chambered heart.

# EXAM PATTERN QUESTIONS

## Objective Type Questions

### Multiple Choice Questions

**1.** Some characteristics of animal having cellular level of organisation are given below.

I. Seen in sponges.
II. Cells shows division of labour.
III. Cells are arranged in loose cell aggregates.
IV. Arrangement of cells is complex .

How many statements are correct?

(a) 2 (b) 4
(c) 3 (d) 1

**Ans.** (*c*)

**2.** Choose the correct type of symmetry for the animals, *A* and *B*. **NCERT Exemplar**

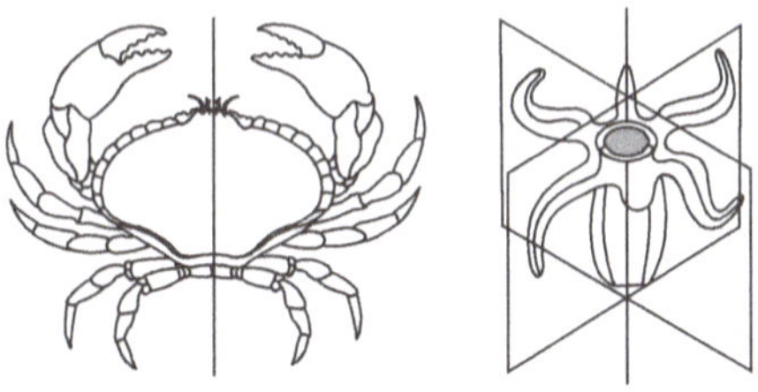


(a) Bilateral, Asymmetrical, respectively
(b) Bilateral, Radial, respectively
(c) Radial, Bilateral, respectively
(d) Radial, Radial, respectively

**Ans.** (*b*)

**3.** Choose the correct option with respect to 'A', 'B' and 'C' respectively. **Competency Based Que.**

(a) Acoelomate, coelomate and pseudocoelomate
(b) Pseudocoelomate, coelomate and acoelomate
(c) Pseudocoelomate, acoelomate and pseudocoelomate
(d) Coelomate, pseudocoelomate and acoelomate

**Ans.** (*d*)

**4.** Body cavity is the cavity present between body wall and gut wall. In some animals the body cavity is not lined by mesoderm. Such animals are called **NCERT Exemplar**

(a) acoelomate (b) pseudocoelomate
(c) coelomate (d) haemocoelomate

**Ans.** (*b*)

**5.** In some animal groups, the body is found divided into compartments with at least some organs. This characteristic feature is called **NCERT Exemplar**

(a) segmentation (b) metamerism
(c) metagenesis (d) metamorphosis

**Ans.** (*b*)

**6.** Which of the following organisms exhibit cellular level of organisation

(a) *Sycon* (b) *Hydra*
(c) *Obelia* (d) *Gonyaulax*

**Ans.** (*a*)

**7.** In most simple type of canal system of Porifera, water flows through which one of the following way?

(a) Ostia → Spongocoel → Osculum → Exterior
(b) Spongocoel → Ostia → Osculum → Exterior
(c) Osculum → Spongocoel → Ostia → Exterior
(d) Osculum → Ostia → Spongocoel → Exterior

**Ans.** (*a*)

**8.** Which of the following is not true regarding phylum–Coelenterata?

(a) They are diploblastic animals
(b) They have cellular level of organisation
(c) They have nematocyte cells present on the tentacles
(d) The gastrovascular opening is called the hypostome

**Ans.** (*b*)

**9.** Choose the correct option for the following diagram. **Competency Based Que.**

(a) It represents choanocyte in Porifera
(b) It represents cnidoblasts in Platyhelminthes
(c) It represents cnidoblast in Coelenterata
(d) It represents choanocyte in Coelenterata

**Ans.** (*c*)

**10. The body of *Ctenoplana* bears eight external rows of ciliated comb plates. What is the role of these plates in body?**

(a) Defence (b) Locomotion
(c) Capturing their prey (d) Achorage

**Ans.** (*b*)

**11. Given below are three statements regarding Platyhelminthes.**

I. They have dorso - ventrally flattened body.
II. Most of them are endoparasites that possess hooks and suckers.
III. Pseudocoelomate animals with organ level of organisation.

**Select the options that has the correct statements.**

(a) I and III (b) II and III (c) I and II (d) I and III

**Ans.** (*c*)

**12. Identify the incorrect option with respect to liver fluke.**

(a) Flame cells help in osmoregulation and excretion.
(b) Alimentary canal is complete with a well-developed muscular pharynx.
(c) Presence of dorso-ventrally flattened body.
(d) Hooks and suckers are present.

**Ans.** (*b*)Liver fluke (*Fasciola*) belongs to phylum-Platyhelminthes and members of this phylum has incomplete digestive system.

**13. Identify the given diagram of the animal and select the correct option which includes the correct features of that animal.** **Competency Based Que.**

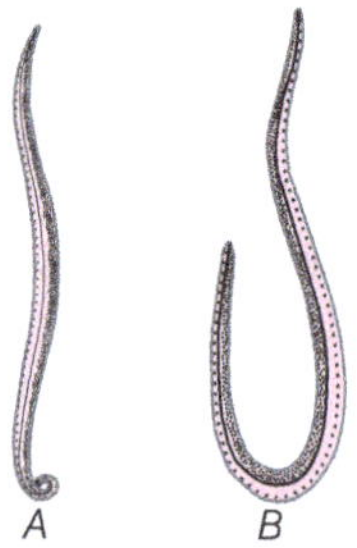


(a) *A* is ♀ *Ascaris* and *B* is ♂ *Ascaris*. Male *Ascaris* is smaller than female *Ascaris*
(b) *A* is ♂ *Ascaris* and *B* is ♀ *Ascaris*. Posterior terminal of male is curved, while in ♀ *Ascaris*, it is straight
(c) *A* is ♂ *Ascaris* and *B* is ♀ *Ascaris*. Male *Ascaris* is more longer than female *Ascaris*
(d) *A* is ♀ *Ascaris* and *B* is ♂ *Ascaris*. ♀ *Ascaris* has curved posterior end, while in ♂ *Ascaris*, it is straight

**Ans.** (*b*) In *Ascaris*, the females (♀) are longer than males (♂). In male *Ascaris*, the posterior portion is curved, while in female *Ascaris*, it is straight.

**14. Segmentation in the body is first observed in which of the following?** **NCERT**

(a) Platyhelminthes (b) Aschelminthes
(c) Annelida (d) Arthropoda

**Ans.** (*c*)

**15. Members of phylum–Annelida have**

(a) nephridia – Excretion
(b) parapodia – Swimming
(c) double ventral nerve cord – Neural system
(d) All of the above

**Ans.** (*d*)

**16. Match the following list of animals with their level of organisation.** **NCERT Exemplar**

| | Division of Labour | | Animal |
|---|---|---|---|
| (i) | Organ level | A. | *Pheretima* |
| (ii) | Cellular aggregate level | B. | *Fasciola* |
| (iii) | Tissue level | C. | *Spongilla* |
| (iv) | Organ system level | D. | *Obelia* |

**Choose the correct match showing division of labour with animal example.**

(a) (i)-B, (ii)-C, (iii)-D and (iv)-A
(b) (i)-B, (ii)-D, (iii)-C and (iv)-A
(c) (i)-D, (ii)-A, (iii)-B and (iv)-C
(d) (i)-A, (ii)-D, (iii)-C and (v)-B

**Ans.** (*a*)

**17. The option that is not the respiratory organ of phylum–Arthropoda is**

(a) tracheal system (b) gills
(c) water vascular system (d) book lungs

**Ans.** (*c*)

**18. Malpighian tubules are**

(a) excretory organs of insects
(b) excretory organs of frog
(c) respiratory organs of insects
(d) endocrine glands of insects

**Ans.** (*a*)

**19. The organ that enables feeding in phylum–Mollusca is**

(a) ctenidia (b) undulating membrane
(c) ganglia (d) radula

**Ans.** (*d*)

**20. Identify the incorrect match-pair.**

(a) *Spongilla* – Fresh water sponge
(b) *Physalia* – Sea pen
(c) *Ancylostoma* – Hookworm
(d) *Octopus* – Devil fish

**Ans.** (*b*)The match pair given in option (b) is incorrect. It can be corrected as:

The common name of *Physalia* is Portuguese man-of-war, while sea pen is common name of *Pennatula*.

**21. Which of the following features is commonly found in animals belonging to the phylum–Mollusca?**

(a) Jointed appendages
(b) Exoskeleton made of chitin
(c) Soft body with a muscular foot and mantle
(d) Segmented body plan

**Ans.** (*c*)

**22. Match the following columns.**

| | Column I (Parts) | | Column II (Description) |
|---|---|---|---|
| A. | Hypostome | 1. | The oral tip surrounded by tentacles in *Hydra* |
| B. | Muscular pharynx | 2. | Present in Aschelminthes to ingested food. |
| C. | Radula | 3. | Rasping organ for feeding in *Pinctada* |
| D. | Malpighian tubules | 4. | Excretory organ in cockroach |

**Codes**

| | A | B | C | D | | A | B | C | D |
|---|---|---|---|---|---|---|---|---|---|
| (a) | 1 | 2 | 3 | 4 | (b) | 4 | 3 | 2 | 1 |
| (c) | 2 | 1 | 4 | 3 | (d) | 3 | 4 | 2 | 1 |

**Ans.** (*a*)

**23. The name Echinodermata is given to the group of organisms because** **DIKSHA**

(a) they have spiny skin
(b) due to water vascular system
(c) having tube feet
(d) dorsoventrally compressed body

**Ans.** (*a*)

**24. Water vascular system is the characteristic of which group of the following?** **NCERT**

(a) Porifera (b) Ctenophora
(c) Echinodermata (d) Chordata

**Ans.** (*c*)

**25. Which one of the following statements is incorrect?**

(a) Mesoglea is present in between ectoderm and endoderm in *Obelia*
(b) Radial symmetry is found is *Asterias*
(c) *Fasciola* is a pseudocoelomate animal
(d) *Taenia* is triploblastic animal

**Ans.** (*c*)

**26. Match the Column I with Column II and choose the correct option.** **NCERT Exemplar**

| | Column I | | Column II |
|---|---|---|---|
| A. | Porifera | 1. | Canal system |
| B. | Aschelminthes | 2. | Water vascular system |
| C. | Annelida | 3. | Muscular pharynx |
| D. | Arthropoda | 4. | Jointed appendages |
| E. | Echinodermata | 5. | Metameres |

**Codes**

| | A | B | C | D | E |
|---|---|---|---|---|---|
| (a) | 2 | 3 | 5 | 4 | 1 |
| (b) | 2 | 5 | 3 | 4 | 1 |
| (c) | 1 | 3 | 5 | 4 | 2 |
| (d) | 1 | 5 | 3 | 4 | 2 |

**Ans.** (*c*)

**27. The body of *Balanoglossus* is divided into**

(a) head and trunk
(b) head, neck and abdomen
(c) proboscis, collar and trunk
(d) prosoma, mesosoma and metasoma

**Ans.** (*c*)

**28. Animals belonging to phylum–Chordata are fundamentally characterised by the presence of structure noted as *A, B, C* and *D*. Identify *A, B, C* and *D*.** **Competency Based Que.**

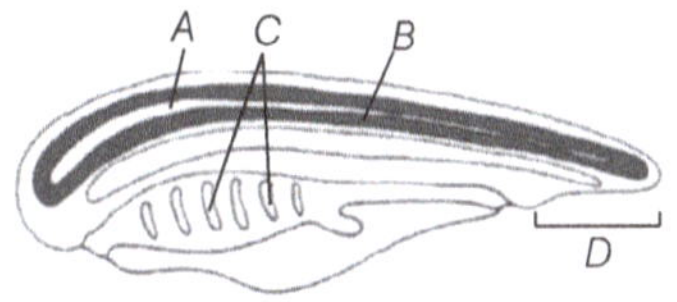


(a) *A*–Notochord, *B*–Nerve cord, *C*–Gill slits, *D*–Post-anal part
(b) *A*–Nerve cord, *B*–Notochord, *C*–Gill slits, *D*–Post-anal part
(c) *A*–Nerve cord, *B*–Notochord, *C*–Post-anal part, *D*–Gill slits
(d) *A*–Nerve cord, *B*–Gill slits, *C*–Notochord, *D*–Post-anal part

**Ans.** (*b*)

**29.** Select the correct difference between the notochord in the following.

| | Urochordata | Cephalochordata |
|---|---|---|
| (a) | Present only in larval tail | Extend from head to tail throughout life |
| (b) | Present only in adult | Present only in larval tail |
| (c) | Persistent throughout their life | Present only in adult |
| (d) | Extend from head to tail throughout life | Present only in larval tail |

**Ans.** (*a*)

**30.** **The correct classification of the animal is**

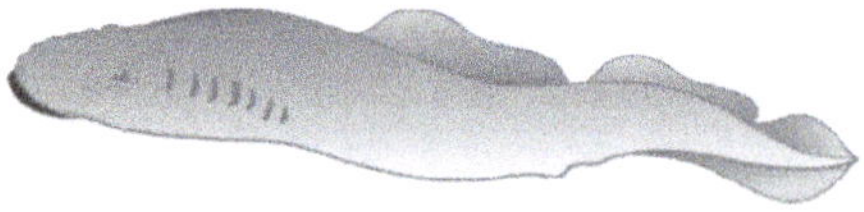

(a) Class - Osteichthyes
(b) Phylum – Cephalochordata
(c) Class – Cyclostomata
(d) Subphylum – Chondrichthyes.

**Ans.** (*c*)

**31.** **Which statement is incorrect about class–Chondrichthyes?**

(a) Presence of placoid scales
(b) Absence of air bladder
(c) Presence of cartilaginous endoskeleton
(d) Notochord is persistent only at larval stage, after that it disappears

**Ans.** (*d*)

**32.** **What are the characteristic features of the skin of the members belonging to class–Amphibia?**

(a) Skin is dry cornified and have scales
(b) The skin is dry without scales
(c) Skin is moist and is without scales
(d) The skin is with scales but moist

**Ans.** (*c*)

**33.** **Which one of the following is not a poisonous snake?** NCERT Exemplar

(a) Cobra (b) Viper
(c) Python (d) Krait

**Ans.** (*c*) **Except Python,** all other snakes are highly poisonous in nature. Python is large in size and kills its prey by constriction of their body.

**34.** **Which of the following pairs of animals has non-glandular skin?** NCERT Exemplar

(a) Snake and frog
(b) *Chameleon* and turtle
(c) Frog and pigeon
(d) Crocodile and tiger

**Ans.** (*b*) Chameleon and turtle belong to class–Reptilia and possess dry and non-glandular skin with scales, frog, pigeon and tiger possess modifications in their skin according to adaptations in their respective habitats.

**35.** **Which one of the following sets of animals share a four-chambered heart?** NCERT Exemplar

(a) Amphibian, reptiles, birds
(b) Crocodiles, birds, mammals
(c) Crocodiles, lizards, turtles
(d) Lizards, mammals, birds

**Ans.** (*b*)

**36.** **Birds and mammals share one of the following characteristics as a common feature.** NCERT Exemplar

(a) Pigmented skin (b) Pneumatic bones
(c) Viviparity (d) Warm blooded body

**Ans.** (*d*)

**37.** **Which one of the following sets of animals belong to a single taxonomic group?** NCERT Exemplar

(a) Cuttlefish, jellyfish, silverfish, dogfish, starfish
(b) Bat, pigeon, butterfly
(c) Monkey, chimpanzee, man
(d) Silkworm, tapeworm, earthworm

**Ans.** (*c*)

**38.** **Organisms having monoecious bodies are**

(a) earthworm, tapeworm (b) earthoworm, crab
(c) cockroach, mosquito (d) cow, hen

**Ans.** (*a*)

**39.** **Which one of the following is oviparous?** NCERT Exemplar

(a) Platypus (b) Flying fox (bat)
(c) Elephant (d) Whale

**Ans.** (*a*) Platypus is a primitive mammal which shows many characters of their reptilian descent, such as ovaparity, i.e., these lay eggs.

Rest all three animals, i.e., flying fox, elephant and whale are viviparous mammals and giving birth to young ones.

## Assertion–Reason Questions

**Direction** (Q. Nos. 1-12) *In each of the following questions, a statement of Assertion (A) is given followed by corresponding statement of Reason (R). Of the statements, mark the correct answer as*

(a) Both A and R are true and R is the correct explanation of A
(b) Both A and R are true, but R is not the correct explanation of A
(c) A is true, but R is false
(d) A is false, but R is true

**1.** Given below is the diagrammatic sectional view of a cavity between the body wall and the gut wall which is very important in classification. Study the animal and comment upon the appropriateness of the Assertion and the Reason. Competency Based Que.

**Assertion** (A) It is a sectional view of pseudocoelom.

**Reason** (R) It has the body cavity not lined by mesoderm, instead, the mesoderm is present as scattered pouches in between the ectoderm and endoderm.

**Ans.** (*a*)

2. **Assertion** (A) Polyp produce medusa asexually.

   **Reason** (R) Medusa produce polyp sexually.

**Ans.** (*b*)

3. **Assertion** (A) Digested and semi-digested food is absorbed by body surface in tapeworms.

   **Reason** (R) Digestive organs are absent in tapeworms.

**Ans.** (*a*)

4. **Assertion** (A) Aschelminthes are called as pseudocoelomates.

   **Reason** (R) In Aschelminthes, mesoderm is present as scattered pouches in between ectoderm and endoderm

**Ans.** (*a*)

5. **Assertion** (A) Arthropods are able to survive in adverse conditions.

   **Reason** (R) They have well-developed sense organs, compound eyes and taste receptors. **Competency Based Que.**

**Ans.** (*b*) Arthropods survive adverse conditions due to their protective exoskeleton, diverse adaptations, physiological flexibility, rapid reproductive strategies, and ability to thrive in varied habitats.

6. **Given below is the representative animal of phylum having an endoskeleton of calcareous ossicles. Study the animal and comment upon the appropriateness of the Assertion and the Reason.** **Competency Based Que.**

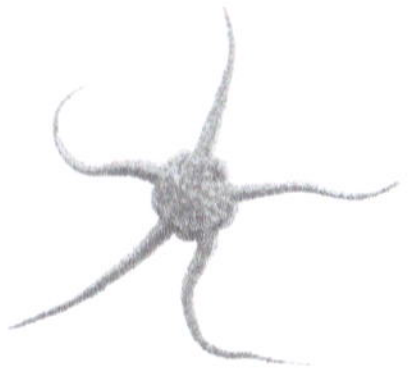

   **Assertion** (A) Presence of water vascular system is the characteristic of this animal.

   **Reason** (R) Main function of water vascular system is locomotion.

**Ans.** (*b*)

7. **Assertion** (A) All vertebrates are chordates, but all chordates are not vertebrates.

   **Reason** (R) Notochord is replaced by vertebral column in the adult vertebrae.

**Ans.** (*b*)

8. **Assertion** (A) Sting ray and saw fish swim constantly to avoid sinking.

   **Reason** (R) They lack air bladder which is used to maintain buoyancy.

**Ans.** (*a*)

9. **Assertion** (A) Amphibians are capable of livng in both aquatic and terrestrial environment.

   **Reason** (R) Body of amphibians is covered by epidermal scales.

**Ans.** (*c*) The body of amphibians is covered with moist, permeable skin that often contains mucus glands.

10. **Assertion** (A) Air sacs are connected to lungs in class–Aves.

    **Reason** (R) Air sacs supplement respiration in birds.

**Ans.** (*a*)

11. **Assertion** (A) Avian bones are pneumatic.

    **Reason** (R) Pneumatic bones contain air spaces that reduce weight, aiding in flight.

**Ans.** (*a*)

12. **Assertion** (A) Duck-bill platypus is not a mammal.

    **Reason** (R) Mammals are generally viviparous, while platypus lays eggs.

**Ans.** (*d*)

# Subjective Questions

## Very Short Answer Type Questions

**1. Which animals have tissue level of organisation?**

**Ans.** Members of Cnidaria and Ctenophora have tissue level of organisation.

**2. What is the bilateral symmetry?**

**Ans.** In bilateral symmetry, the body can be divided into identical left and right halves in only one plane.

**3. Diagrammatically show the types of symmetry in animals.**

**Ans.** Refer to fig. 4.1 and 4.2 on page no. 67.

**4. In some animals, the body cavity is not lined by mesoderm. What are these animals called?**

**Ans.** Pseudacoelomates

**5. Name the phylum in which pseudocoelom is present.**

**Ans.** Aschelminthes

**6. In some animal groups, the body is found to be divided into compartments with repetition of some organs. Name this characteristic feature.**

**Ans.** It is the segmentation that simultaneously divides body both externally and internally and is also called metamerism.

**7. Name an animal having canal system and spicules.**

**Ans.** *Scypha (Sycon)/Leucosolenia.*

**8. Name the cells that line the spongocoel in *Sycon*.**

**Ans.** Choanocytes (collar cells).

**9. What is the name give to the cellulosic fibre forming the skeleton of poriferans?**

**Ans.** Spongin fibres.

**10. Coelenterata is called Cnidaria. Give reason.** **Competency Based Que.**

**Ans.** Coelenterata is called Cnidaria because of the presence of stinging cells called cnidoblasts or nematoblasts.

**11. Write the scientific name of roundworm.** **NCERT Exemplar**

**Ans.** *Ascaris lumbricoides.*

**12. Provide an appropriate technical term for lateral appendages in aquatic annelids.**

**Ans.** Parapodia are lateral, unjointed and paired appendages present in aquatic annelids like *Nereis.*

**13. Which organ helps in excretion in**

**(i) arthophods**

**(ii) hemichordates**

**Ans.** (i) Malphigian tubules (½)

(ii) Proboscis gland (½)

**14. Write the name of structure *A* and *B* in the diagram given below.**

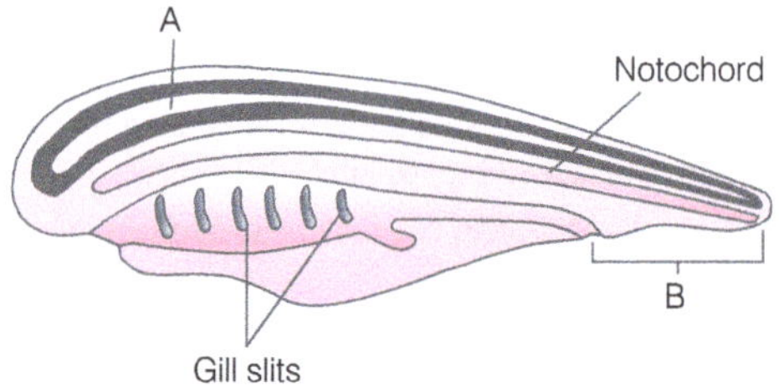


**Ans.** (A) Nerve cord

(B) Post-anal part (½ + ½)

**15. In phylum *X* the body of an organism is covered with tunic. Give an example of members belonging to this phylum.**

**Ans.** *Salpa, Doliolum, Ascidia,* etc.

**16. Which structure replaces notochord in vertebrates?**

**Ans.** Vertebral column.

**17. All vertebrates are chordates, but all chordates are not vertebrates. Justify the statement.** **Competency Based Que.**

**Ans.** All chordates have a notochord, but only in vertebrate the vertebral column develops from notochord, so all chordates are not vertebrates. All vertebrates are chordates as they have notochord in embryonic stage.

**18. Give one example each for an animal possessing placoid scales and that with cycloid scales.** **NCERT Exemplar**

**Ans.** Placoid scales-*Scoliodon* (dog fish), cycloid scales-*Labeo* (rohu)

**19. What kind of body scales are present in bony fishes?**

**Ans.** Ctenoid or cycloid scales

**20. How important is the presence of air bladder in Pisces?** **NCERT, Competency Based Que.**

**Ans.** In fishes, air bladder regulates buoyancy and helps them to floating in water. If it is absent, animals need to swim constantly to avoid sinking.

**21. Identify the class of Tetrapoda which is characterised by scaly bodies rather than hair or feathers.**

**Ans.** Class-Reptilia

**22. What is the importance of pneumatic bones and air sacs in Aves?**

**Ans.** (i) Pneumatic bones are light but strong, this feature helps birds in flight. (½)

(ii) Air sacs increase the efficiency of respiration in the animal. (½)

**23. Name the following. (i) Limbless animal (ii) Dry cornified skin**

**Ans.**

| | | |
|---|---|---|
| (i) | Limbless animal | Snake (reptile), *Ichthyophis* (amphibian) |
| (ii) | Dry cornified skin | *Chameleon* |

**24. Match the following.** **NCERT**

| | | | |
|---|---|---|---|
| A. | Operculum | 1. | Ctenophora |
| B. | Parapodia | 2. | Mollusca |
| C. | Scales | 3. | Porifera |
| D. | Comb plates | 4. | Reptilia |
| E. | Radula | 5. | Annelida |
| F. | Hairs | 6. | Cyclostomata and Chondrichthyes |
| G. | Choanocytes | 7. | Mammalia |
| H. | Gill slits | 8. | Osteichthyes |

**Ans.** A-8, B-5, C-4, D-1, E-2, F-7, G-3, H-6.

## Short Answer Type Questions

**1. What are the difficulties that you would face in classification of animals, if common fundamental features are not taken into account?** **NCERT**

**Ans.** The difficulties that will be faced if common fundamental features are not taken into account are as follows

(i) There are numerous animal species which show great variations. The various common fundamental characters are taken into account for the classification of these animals. If this has not been done then the classification of animals separately at individual level would be difficult. (1)

(ii) The inter-relationship among different animals cannot be traced. (1)

**2. Organ system in different groups of animals exhibit various patterns of complexities. Explain.** **Competency Based Que.**

**Ans.** In animals like annelids, arthropods, molluscs, echinoderms and chordates, organs have associated to form functional systems, where each system is concerned with a specific physiological function. This pattern is called organ system level of organisation. Organ systems in different groups of animals exhibit various patterns of complexities.

For example, the digestive system in Platyhelminthes has only a single opening to the outside of the body that serves as both mouth and anus and is hence called incomplete. A complete digestive system has two separate openings, mouth and anus.

**3. How useful is the study of the nature of body cavity and coelom in the classification of animals?** **NCERT**

**Ans.** Presence or absence of a cavity between the body wall and the gut wall is very important in classification. The body cavity which is lined by mesoderm is called coelom.

(i) Animals possessing coelom are called coelomate, e.g. annelids, molluscs, arthropods, echinoderms, hemichordates and chordates.

(ii) In some animals, the body cavity is not lined by mesoderm, instead the mesoderm is present as scattered pouches in between the ectoderm and endoderm. Such a body cavity is called pseudocoelom and the animals possessing them are called pseudocoelomates, e.g. Aschelminthes.

(iii) The animals in which the body cavity is absent are known as acoelomates, e.g. Platyhelminthes.
This helps in assigning the exact taxonomic position of the animal on the basis of its presence or absence in the animal's body.

**4. Draw the sectional view of coelomate, pseudocoelomate and acoelomate.**

**Ans.** Refer to fig. no. 4.4. on page no. 68.

**5. Write about the mesodermally derived rod-like structure in higher animals.**

**Ans.** Notochord is a flexible rod-like structure, present on dorsal side in some animals during embryonic development. It is derived from mesoderm.

Notochord is found in chordates (atleast in some stages of their life cycle, e.g. vertebrates).

**6. If you are given a specimen, what are the steps that you would follow to classify it?** **NCERT**

**Ans.** One has to follow the following steps to classify a specimen

(i) Level of organisation. (ii) Body symmetry.

(iii) Segmentation pattern.

(iv) Presence or absence of vertebral column.

(v) Locomotory organelles limbs/fins/wings.

(vi) Presence of organ systems like digestive, circulatory or reproductive systems. (3)

**7. What is the difference between direct and indirect development?** **NCERT**

**Ans.** Differences between direct and indirect development are as follows

(i) **Direct Development** In case of direct development, the life cycle of an adult individual lacks any larval stage in its life cycle. The adults give rise to young ones which directly develop into the adult, e.g. mammals. (1)

(ii) **Indirect Development** It is present mostly in case of lower animals, the adult individual gives rise to eggs which develop into the adult after being passing through several larval stages, e.g. echinoderms, *Ascaris*, cockroach have prolonged larval stages in their life cycle. (1)

**8. Could the number of eggs or young ones produced by an oviparous and viviparous mother be equal? Why?** NCERT

**Ans.** An oviparous animal always produces more number of eggs than the young ones produced by a viviparous animal. This is because their eggs are exposed to external environment and predators. Also they have to pass through a large number of developmental stages before becoming an adult. Hence, they face less chances of survival than the foetus developing inside the mother's body. The large number of eggs compensates the inevitable loss and ensures the continuation of race. (2)

**9. Distinguish between intracellular and extracellular digestion.** NCERT

**Ans.** Differences between intracellular and extracellular digestion are

(i) **Intracellular digestion** occurs inside the living cells with the help of lysosomal enzymes. Food particle is taken in through endocytosis. It forms a phagosome, which fuses with a lysosome.
The digested material passes into the cytoplasm. The undigested matter is thrown out by exocytosis. It occurs in *Amoeba, Paramecium,* etc. (1)

(ii) **Extracellular digestion** In case of coelenterates, digestion occurs in gastrovascular cavity. This cavity has gland cells which secrete digestive enzymes over the food. The partially digested fragmented food particles are ingested by nutritive cells. It occurs in *Hydra, Aurelia* and higher animals, etc. (1)

**10. Write an account on skeleton of sponges.**

**Ans.** The body of sponges contains a supporting exoskeleton. It is made up of either spicules or spongin fibres. Spongin fibres are protein fibres. They are either highly branched or unbranched. Spicules are calcareous or siliceous hard spine-like structures.

**11. What do you understand by alternation of generation in cnidarians?**

**Ans.** The cnidarians complete their life cycle through two phases, i.e. asexually reproducing polyp phase and sexually reproducing medusa phase. Those cnidarians which exist in both forms exhibit alternation of generation (metagenesis).

**12. Differentiate between polyp and medusa.** NCERT Exemplar

**Ans.** Differences between polyp and medusa are

| Polyp | Medusa |
|---|---|
| It is a sessile. | It is free-swimming. |
| It reproduces asexually. | It reproduces sexually. |
| It is cylindrical in outline. | Medusa is umbrella-shaped. |
| Mouth is terminal . | Mouth, lies at the lower end of hanging manubrium. |

**13. What are the peculiar features that you find in parasitic helminthes?** NCERT

**Ans.** Parasitic Platyhelminthes have a thick cuticle which protects them from the action of digestive juices of the host. . They lack alimentary canal and absorb the nutrients directly through their body surface. Some parasites are also provided with hooks and suckers.

**14. Describe the type of excretory and circulatory system in Annelida.**

**Ans.** Annelids have closed circulatory system and excretory organs are nephridia. Nephridia are present in each segment and also help in osmoregulation. (1+1)

**15. What are the reasons that you could think for the arthropods to constitute the largest group of animal kingdom?** Competency Based Que., NCERT

**Ans.** Arthropods constitute the largest group of animal kingdom due to following reasons

(i) Arthropods have a chitinous exoskeleton, that gives protection. (1)

(ii) The presence of jointed appendages allow variety of movements. (1)

**16. Which animals have compound eyes? What other sense organs are present in these animals?**

**Ans.** Arthropods have compund eyes. Aquatic forms of arthropods also have statocysts for balancing. (1+1)

**17. Write the name of one animal which show these kind of respiration.**

**(i) Tracheal respiration**

**(ii) Cutaneous respiration**

**Ans.** (i) Insects

(ii) Frog (1+1)

**18. Correctly match the Column I and II. Also give the correct reason.**

| Column I | | Column II | |
|---|---|---|---|
| A. | Parapodia | 1. | Porifera |
| B. | Choanocytes | 2. | Mollusca |
| | | 3. | Annelida |

**Ans.** A–3, B–1.

Choanocytes or collar cells are characteristic features of Porifera. They take part in ingestion of food, formation and differentiation of sex cells, while parapodia in annelids are used for locomotion.

**19. Distinguish between Urochordata and Cephalochordata.**

**Ans.** In Urochordata, notochord is present only in larval tail, while in Cephalochordata, it extends from head to tail region and is persistent throughout their life.

**20. List out any five general features of cartilaginous fishes.**

**Ans.** Features of cartilaginous fishes are as follows.

(i) Cartilaginous endoskeleton is present.
(ii) These are mostly marine, poikilothermic animals.
(iii) Notochord is persistent throughout the life.
(iv) Placoid scales are present.
(v) Heart is two-chambered having one auricle and one ventricle.

**21. Given below is the representative animal of phylum having bony endoskeleton. Study the animal and answer the following question.** **Competency Based Que.**

**(i) Identify the class of the given organism.**

**(ii) Write any two features of organisms belonging to this class.**

**Ans.** (i) The given organism belongs to class-osteichthyes.
(ii) Two features are as follows
(a) Presence of air bladder which regulates buoyancy. (1)
(b) Presence of four pairs of gills. (1)

**22. Identify the important characters *a, b, c, d, e* and f of the organisms mentioned in the following grid.** **DIKSHA**

| | |
|---|---|
| Cyclostomes | *a* |
| *b* | Chondrichthyes |
| *c* | Osteichthyes |
| Amphibian | *d* |
| *e* | Cephalochordate |
| Vertebrate | *f* |

**Ans.** (a) Circular mouth
(b) Have cartilaginous endoskeleton
(c) Have bony endoskeleton
(d) Exhibits cutaneous respiration/metamorphic life cycle/three-chambered heart
(e) Having notochord that extends from head to tail
(f) Notochord replaced by vertebral column (½ × 6)

**23. How do the appendages support the bird's body?** **Competency Based Que.**

**Ans.** Birds have two pairs of limbs, forelimbs are modified into wings for flight. The wings are powered by the flight muscles attached to the large sternum (breast bone). Hindlimbs support the body and used for grasping, perching, wading and swimming.

**24. What flight adaptations are present in birds?**

*Or*

**What are the modifications observed in birds that help them to fly?** **NCERT**

**Ans.** Flight adaptations found in birds are as follows.

(i) Body is streamlined to reduce air resistance during flight.
(ii) Forelimbs are modified into wings.
(iii) Wings have long quill feathers to increase the efficiency of beating of wings.
(iv) Pneumatic bones are present to reduce the body weight.
(v) High metabolic rate to provide energy for flight.
(vi) Air sacs present in lungs help in double respiration.

(½ × 6)

**25. Mention two similarities between**

**(i) Aves and mammals**
**(ii) A frog and crocodile**
**(iii) A turtle and *Pila***

**Ans.** (i) Aves and mammals are homeothermic animals and have four chambered heart. (1)
(ii) Frog and crocodile are cold-blooded and are tetrapods. (1)
(iii) A turtle and *Pila* have hard covering over the body and are cold-blooded animals. (1)

**26. There has been an increase in the number of chambers in heart during evolution of vertebrates. Give the name of the class of vertebrates having two, three or four-chambered heart.** **NCERT Exemplar**

**Ans.** (i) **Two-chambered heart**—Pisces
(ii) **Three-chambered heart**—Amphibians and reptiles except crocodiles.
(iii) **Four-chambered heart**—Crocodiles, Aves and Mammalia. (1 × 3)

## Long Answer Type Questions

**1. Describe the different levels of organisation of body of animals, with an example of each.**

**Ans.** Refer to text on page no. 66-67.

**2. What is the relationship between germinal layers and the formation of body cavity in case of coelomate, acoelomates and pseudocoelomates?** **NCERT Exemplar**

**Ans.** Refer to text on page no. 68.

**3. Differentiate between**

**(a) Acoelomate and pseudocoelomate**
**(b) Notochord and nerve cord**
**(c) Polyp and medusa**

**Ans.**

| (a) Acoelomate | Pseudocoelomate |
|---|---|
| The animals without coelom are called as acoelomates.<br>e.g., sponges, cnidarians, ctenophores and flatworms. | The animals in which body cavity is derived from the blastocoel of the embryo but is not lined with mesoderm are called pseudocoelomates.<br>e.g., roundworms. (2) |

| (b) Notochord | Nerve Cord |
|---|---|
| Notochord is the skeletal rod which lies lengthwise between the central nervous system and the alimentary canal or the gut.<br>Vertebrates possess it at the young stage of development.<br>In adults vertebrates, notocord is replaced by vertebral column. | Nerve cord is the solid strand of nervous tissue forming a part of central nervous system, especially in invertebrates. (1) |

| (c) Polyp | Medusa |
|---|---|
| Polyp is sessile and cylindrical form e.g. *Aurelia*.<br>Polyp produces medusa asexually. | Medusa is umbrella-shaped and free swimming form e.g. *Aurelia*.<br>Medusa forms polyp sexually. |

Polyp in *Adamsia*

Medusa in *Aurelia* (2)

**4. What are the general features of members of Ctenophora?**

**Ans.** Refer to text on page no. 71.

**5. Write an account of general features of roundworms.**

**Ans.** General features of roundworms are as follows:

(i) The body is cylindrical and tapering at both ends.
(ii) No segmentation.
(iii) Bilateral symmetry.
(iv) They have organ system level of organisation.
(v) There are no locomotory appendages in roundworms.
(vi) The body wall consists of firm, thick, resistant cuticle, epidermis and muscle layer.
(vii) These are pseudocoelomates.
(viii) Digestive system is complete. Respiration occurs by body surface.
(ix) Circulatory system is not well developed. Excretion occurs through excretory tubes.
(x) Sexes are separate. Sexual dimorphism is present. Fertilisation is internal. There is no asexual reproduction.
(xi) Development is direct or indirect.

**6. *Pheretima* belongs to which phylum? Write characteristics of the same.**

**Ans.** *Pheretima* belongs to phylum—Annelida. For important characteristics of Annelida phylum refer to text on page no. 72-73.

**7. Distinguish between chordates and non-chordates.**

**Ans.** Differences between chordates and non-chordates are given below

| Chordates | Non-Chordates |
|---|---|
| Notochord is present atleast in some stages of development. | Notochord is absent. |
| Central nervous system is dorsal, hollow, single and non-ganglionated. | Central nervous system is ventral, solid, double and gangliolated. |
| Gill slits present on lateral side of pharynx in some stages or throughout the life. | Gill slits are absent. |
| Heart is ventral. | Heart is dorsal. |
| Haemoglobin is present in RBCs. | Haemoglobin is either absent or present in plasma. |

**8. List any six features of cartilaginous fishes.**

**Ans.** (i) They are mostly marine and are called poikilothermic animals (i.e. they donot have the capacity to regulate their body temperature).
(ii) The body is laterally compressed and streamlined.
(iii) **Notochord** is persistent throughout the life.
(iv) Mouth is ventral in position, skin is tough containing minute placoid scales and teeth are also modified placoid scales. They have strong jaw and are predaceous by nature.
(v) Gill slits are generally five pairs and gill cover (operculum) are absent.
(vi) Heart is two-chambered with one auricle and one ventricle.

**9. Give the characteristic features of the following citing one example of each** **NCERT Exemplar**

**(i) Chondrichthyes and Osteichthyes**

**(ii) Urochordata and Cephalochordata**

**Ans.** (i) Refer to text on page no. 77-78.
(ii) Refer to text on page no. 76.

**10. How are Pisces different from Tetrapoda?** **Competency Based Que.**

**Ans.** Differences between Pisces and Tetrapoda are given below

| Pisces | Tetrapoda |
|---|---|
| They have two-chambered heart (1 auricle, 1 ventricle) in most cases. | They have three or four-chambered heart (2 auricles, 1 or 2 ventricles). |
| Pisces breathe through gills. | They breathe through lungs except some amphibians. |

| Pisces | Tetrapoda |
|---|---|
| They are aquatic. | They are terrestrial, some have secondarily became aquatic. |
| They are poikilothermic. | Some are poikilothermic and some are homeothermic. |
| They have 10 pairs of cranial nerves. | They have 10-12 pairs of cranial nerves. |

**11. Comment upon the habitats and external features of animals belonging to class–Amphibia and Reptilia.** **NCERT Exemplar**

**Ans.** Refer to text on page no. 78-79.

**12. Which features make mammals as most successful and dominant animals?** **Competency Based Que.**

**Ans.** Features which make mammals as dominant and successful animals are

(i) The presence of an insulating and protective hairy epidermis.
(ii) They are warm-blooded so have high rate of metabolism.
(iii) They are viviparous animals and show placentation and intra-uterine development which increases the chances for survival of young ones.
(iv) They show high degree of parental care.
(v) They have more developed hearing efficiency due to the presence of pinna, three ear-ossicles and coiled cochlea in the ear.
(vi) They have good power of learning due to the presence of more developed brain.

**13. Give an example for each of the following.**

**(i) A viviparous animal**
**(ii) A fish possessing a poison sting**
**(iii) A fish possessing an electric organ**
**(iv) An organ which regulates buoyancy**
**(v) Animal, which exhibits alternation of generation**
**(vi) Oviparous animal with mammary gland** **NCERT Exemplar**

**Ans.** (i) A viviparous animal is the one in which development of young ones is direct, later they provides nutrition to their offspring. It includes all mammals, except platypus. (1)

(ii) A fish possessing a poison sting is *Trygon* (sting-ray). It is found on its tail. The poison released is strong enough to stun an animal. (½)

(iii) A fish possessing an electric organ *Torpedo* (electric ray). Large *Torpedo* can generate a fish killing current of up to 200 volts. (½)

(iv) An organ, which regulates buoyancy is air bladder present in class–Osteichthyes. (e.g., *Exocoetus, Catla*). (1)

(v) Animal exhibiting alteration of generation *Obelia* of phylum–Cnidaria. It has two basic body forms called polyp and medusa. Polyp is sessile and cylindrical whereas medusa is umbrella shaped and free swimming form. Polyp produces medusa asexually and medusa forms polyps sexually. (1)

(vi) Oviparous animal with mammary gland is *Ornithorhynchus* (duck-billed platypus). Duck-bill platypus is the only mammal which lays egg and also bears mammary gland, which is a characteristic feature of mammals. (1)

## Source Based/Case Based/Passage Based Questions

**1.** ***Read the following passage and answer the questions that follows***

**Coelenterates are aquatic, mostly marine organisms exhibiting tissue level of organisation. Their body is characterised by tentacles, stinging cells and horny or calcareous exoskeleton. They possess well-defined gastrovascular cavity having single opening, polymorphism is one of the major characteristic of coelenterates.**

**In this, the organism exists in different forms out of which one is sessile, while the other is free-swimming. These forms exhibit division of labour and alternation of generation. Major representative animals of this group are *Adamsia, Physalia, etc.***

**(i) Name a freshwater coelenterate.**
**(ii) What is the exoskeleton of corals composed of**
**(iii) In which coelenterates medusae form is seen?**
**(iv) What is the common name of *Adamsia*?**

***Or***

**(iv) What is the special character of Coelenterata?**

**Ans.** (i) *Hydra* is a freshwater coelenterate. (1)

(ii) The exoskeleteon of corals is formed of calcium carbonate. (1)

(iii) Medusa or free-swimming form is seen in *Aurelia*. (1)

(iv) The common name of *Adamsia* is sea anemone. (1)

*Or*

(iv) The nematocysts are special characteristics of coelenterates. It is an organ of offence and defence in coelenterates.
It also helps in food capture, locomotion and anchorage. (1)

**2.** ***Read the following passage and answer the questions that follows***

**Prakhar, a class XI student went out after rains in the garden. He saw earthworms on the ground and wondered how they are able to move, eat and perform various function of life. Next day, he went to his biology teacher and asked her about the same. Her biology teacher politely explained him about how**

different animals have various levels of organisation of cells. She also told her that except sponges and coelenterates, all the animals of the kingdom–Animalia have either organ level or organ- system level of organisation.

(i) What kind of body organisation are present in sponges and coelenterates?

(ii) In which phylums organ system level organisation is found?

(iii) Why does the digestive system of Platyhelminthes is called incomplete?

(iv) What the type of body organisation seen in starfish and jelly fish?

**Ans.** (i) In sponges, cellular level organisation and in coelenterates, tissue level organisation is present. (1)

(ii) Organ system level organisation is found in Platyhelminthes, Aschelminthes, Annelida, Arthropoda, Mollusca, Echinodermata and Hemichordata. (1)

(iii) The digestive system of Platyhelminthes has only a single opening to the outside of the body that serves as both mouth and anus and hence is called incomplete. (1)

(iv) Star fish is an echinoderm thus has organ system level of body organisation. Jellyfish (*Aurelia*) is a cnidarian. Thus, has tissue level of body organisation. (1)

**3.** Dr. Gupta is investigating three distinct animal species, each exhibiting unique adaptations to their environments. Species A, with its hard, segmented exoskeleton and jointed appendages, demonstrates high ecological adaptability and complex moulting. Meanwhile, species B possesses a calcareous endoskeleton and a water vascular system, allowing for locomotion and notable regenerative abilities in marine habitats. This study aims to explore how these morphological traits influence their survival strategies, ecological roles, and interactions within their ecosystems. **Competency Based Que.**

(i). What excretory structures are likely present in species A?

(ii) Name two examples of species B.

(iii) Comment on digestive and excretory system in species B.

(iv) Species A belong to which phylum. Write some basic characteristics of the same.

**Ans.** (i) Species A likely possesses Malpighian tubules for excretion. (1)

(ii) *Asterias* (Sea star) and *Echinus* (Sea urchin). (1)

(iii) The digestive system is complete with mouth on ventral side and anus on the dorsal side. Excretory system is absent in these animals. (1)

(iv) Species A belong to phylum–Arthropoda. The basic characteristics of phylum–Arthropoda are as follows:

- These are triploblastic animals with organ-system level of body organisation. (1)
- The body consists of head, thorax and abdomen.
- Circulatory system is open type.

**4.** *Read the following passage and answer the questions that follows*

In a fishery lecture, Amar was stunned to learn about the variety of fishes across world. Upon further investigation, Amar found that these fishes belongs to three major classes, *viz.*, Cyclostomata, Chondrichthyes and Osteichthyes.

(i) Mention any two characteristic features of cyclostomes.

(ii) Give two examples of class-Cyclostomata.

(iii) What type of scales are found in Chondrichthyes and Osteichthyes?

(iv) In which class would you find operculum and air bladder?

*Or*

(iv) Give scientific names of saw fish, sting ray, flying fish and angel fish.

**Ans.** (i) Cyclostomes have sucking and circular mouth without jaws. They bear 6-15 pairs of gill slits but lack paired fins and scales. (1)

(ii) *Petromyzon* (Lamprey) and *Myxine* (Hagfish) (1)

(iii) Chondrichthyes contain placoid scales whereas Osteichthyes possess cycloid or ctenoid scales. (1)

(iv) Operculum and air bladder are found in bony fishes of class-Osteichthyes. (1)

*Or*

(iv) Saw fish – *Pristis*

Sting ray – *Trygon*

Flying fish – *Exocoetus*

Angel fish – *Pterophyllum* (1)

**5.** Case : A group of children is exploring a vibrant tropical habitat during the rainy season, where heavy rains create temporary pools and lush vegetation. As they wander near the edges of a pond, they hear the distinctive calls of a familiar creature that can live both on land and in water. This animal is recognised for its smooth, moist skin and striking colours. It relies on its skin for moisture retention and gas exchange, thriving in the humid environment. **Competency Based Que.**

(i) To which phylum does this animal belong to?

(ii) Provide more examples of animals that belong to the same class as the animal mentioned above.

(iii) What excretory structures are likely found in this animal?

(iv) Compare the circulatory system of the observed animal with that of mammals in terms of structure and function.

**Ans.** (i) This animal belongs to the phylum–Chordata. (1)

(ii) *Salamandra* and *Ichthyophis* (1)

(iii) This creature likely possesses kidneys that filter waste from the bloodstream, excreting it as urine through a common chamber known as the cloaca. (1)

(iv) The observed animal typically has a three-chambered heart, consisting of two atria and one ventricle, which allows for some mixing of oxygenated and deoxygenated blood. In contrast, mammals possess a four-chambered heart with two atria and two ventricles, ensuring complete separation of oxygenated and deoxygenated blood for efficient circulation. (1)

**6. Study the chart of evolutionary classification of vertebrates given below and answer the questions that follow.** **Competency Based Que.**

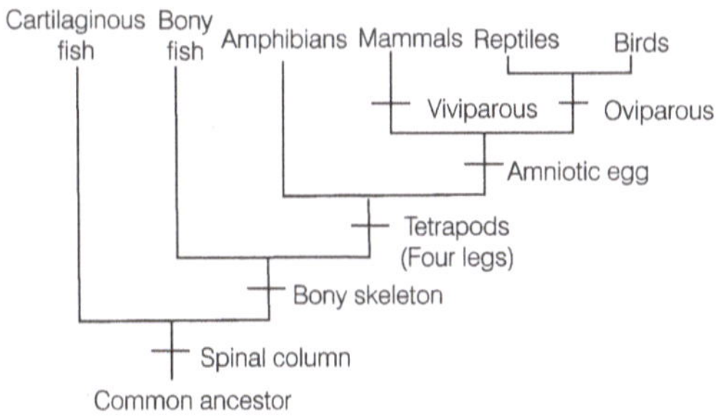


**(i) On the basis of the classification pattern exhibited in this chart, why are mammals- viviparous and reptiles-oviparous?**

**(ii) There has been an increase in the number of chambers in heart during evolution of vertebrates. Give the names of the class of vertebrates having two, three or four-chambered heart.**

**(iii) To which class cartilaginous and bony fishes belong.**

**(iv) Write one feature common to all vertebrates.**

**Ans.** (i) Mammals are viviparous because they give birth to offspring, whereas reptiles are oviparous because they lay eggs. (1)

(ii) Vertebrates have evolved a muscular heart to pump blood to body parts. Fishes have two-chambered heart. Birds and mammals have four-chambered heart having two auricles and two ventricles. Reptiles, except crocodile have three-chambered heart. (1)

(iii) Cartilaginous fishes belongs to class-Chondrichthyes and bony fishes belongs to class-Osteichthyes. (1)

(iv) The members of subphylum–Vertebrata possess notochord during the embryonic period. The notochord is replaced by a cartilaginous or bony vertebral column in the adult. (1)

# SELF ASSESSMENT TEST

## Multiple Choice Questions

1. Which of the following examples correctly represents the type of symmetry illustrated in figures *A* and *B* ?
   (a) Ctenophora and Arthropoda respectively
   (b) Annelida and Mollusca respectively
   (c) Echinodermata and Cnidaria respectively
   (d) Annelida and Hemichordata respectively

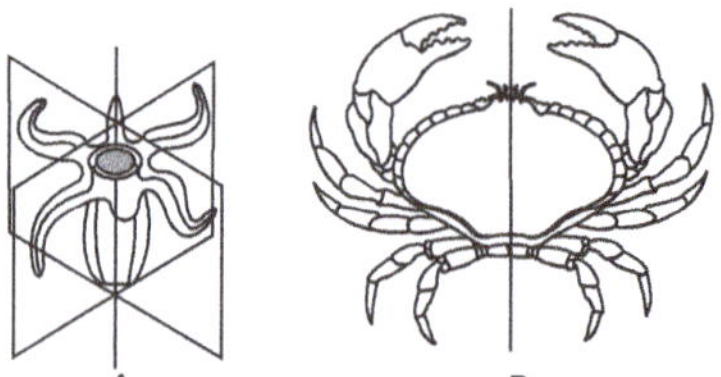

A B

2. Some characteristics of animals having cellular level of body organisation are given below.
   I. Skeleton is made up of spicules or spongin fibres.
   II. Incomplete digestive system is present.
   III. Water vascular system help in respiration and excretion.
   IV. Show both sexual and asexual type of reproduction.

   How many of the given statements are correct.
   (a) 4 (b) 3 (c) 2 (d) 1

3. Identify the animals that belong to phylum – Mollusca.
   (a) *Chaetopleura, Ophiura* and *Loligo* (b) *Antedon, Hirudinaria* and *Sepia*
   (c) *Echinus, Pila* and *Octopus* (d) *Dentalium, Pinctada* and *Aplysia*

4. Water vascular system is the characteristic feature of
   (a) star fish and brittle star (b) sea cucumber and devil fish
   (c) cuttlefish and sea lily (d) sea urchin and sea-hare

5. Identify the class of fishes given in figure '*A*' and '*B*' respectively.
   (a) '*A*' belongs to class–Cyclostomata and '*B*' belong to class–Chondrichthyes.
   (b) Both '*A*' and '*B*' belong to class–Osteichthyes.
   (c) '*A*' belongs to class–Osteichthyes and '*B*' belong to class–Chondrichthyes.
   (d) Both '*A*' and '*B*' belong to class–Chondrichthyes.

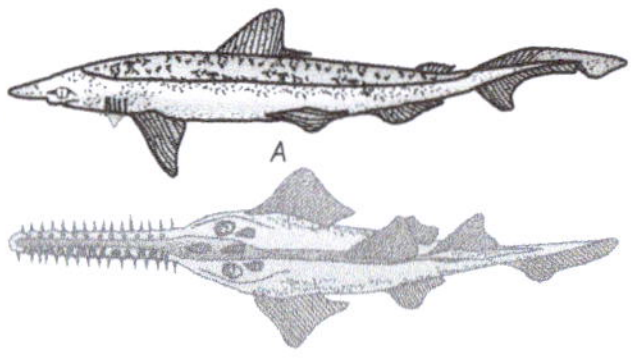


6. Identify the incorrect match-pair.
   (a) *Aptenodytes* – Ostrich (b) *Pteropus* – Flying fox
   (c) *Hemidactylus* – Wall lizard (d) *Neophron* – Vulture

7. How many of the given animals are oviparous.
   *Columba, Ornithorhynchus, Balaenoptera, Pavo,*
   *Macaca, Macropus, Equus, Elephas, Psittacula, Struthio*
   (a) 7 (b) 5 (c) 3 (d) 6

## Assertion-Reason Questions

**Direction** (Q. Nos. 8-10) *In each of the following questions, a statement of Assertion (A) is given followed by corresponding statement of Reason (R). Of the statements, mark the correct answer as*

(a) If both A and R are true and R is the correct explanation of A
(b) If both A and R are true, but R is not the correct explanation of A
(c) If A is true, but R is false
(d) If A is false, but R is true

8. **Assertion** (A) Ctenophores are also known as comb jellies.
   **Reason** (R) The body of ctenophores bear eight external rows of ciliated comb plates.

9. **Assertion** (A) Members of class–Cyclostomata show migration from marine to fresh water bodies.
**Reason** (R) Cyclostomes migrate to marine water body for spawning.

10. **Assertion** (A) Members of class-Chondrichthyes need to swim constantly to avoid sinking.
**Reason** (R) Air bladder is absent in cartilaginous fishes.

## Very Short Answer Type Questions

11. Define the role of radula in molluscs.
12. Give an example of the following:
    (i) Fish possessing poisonous sting.
    (ii) Reptile with four-chambered heart
13. What is the role of pneumatic bones in birds?

## Short Answer Type Questions

14. Differentiate between:
    (i) Polyp and Medusa
    (ii) Chondrichthyes and Osteichthyes
15. Write any four characteristics of phylum–Chordata.
16. Why hemichordata was earlier placed as a sub-phylum under Chordata.

## Long Answer Type Questions

17. Explain five features that are used as the basis of animal classification.
18. Describe the characteristic features of largest and second largest phylum of animal kingdom.
19. Differentiate between the four different classes of super class-Tetrapoda.

## Case Based Question

20. Study the graph of hagfish species in freshwater given below and answer the questions that follows

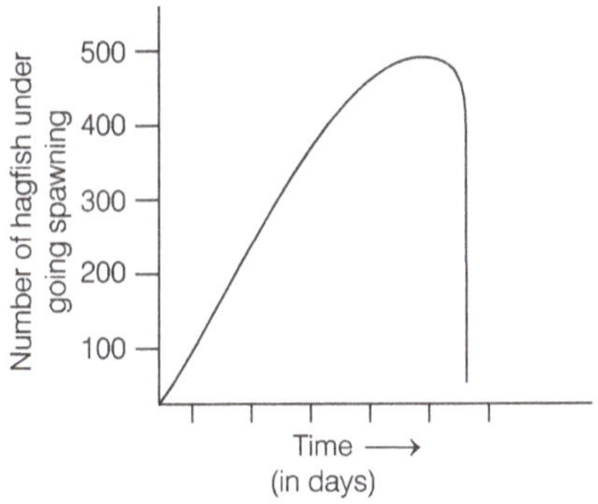


(i) With reference to the above graph explain why there is seen sudden decline in hagfish population in freshwater?
(ii) To which animal class does hagfish belong?
(iii) What happens to the larval population of hagfish after metamorphosis ?
(iv) Given one difference between hagfish and flying fish.

# Answers

1. (a) 2. (c) 3. (d) 4. (a) 5. (d) 6. (a) 7. (b) 8. (a)
9. (c) 10. (a)

# 05

CHAPTER

# Morphology of Flowering Plants

Angiosperms or flowering plants, are the most diverse and widespread group among all plant groups. They are seed bearing plants having seeds enclosed in an ovary.

▼ **YOUR STUDY GOALS**

5.1 Flowering Plants
5.2 The Root
5.3 The Stem
5.4 The Leaf
5.5 Flower
5.6 The Inflorescence
5.7 The Fruit
5.8 The Seed
5.9 Semi-Technical Description of a Typical Flowering Plant

▼ **YOUR PRACTICE GOAL**

- Objective Type Questions (34 Qs ; MCQs, A-R) Case Based Questions (3)
- Subjective Type Questions
- (14 VSAs, 31 SAs, 11 LAs)

- Angiosperms are identified and classified on the basis of their external as well as internal structure. The branch of biology that deals with the study of physical form and external structure of the plants is termed as **morphology**.
- Knowledge of morphology helps us to know other aspects of plants like plant habit and habitat, crop production, etc.
- Even though angiosperms show such a large diversity in their morphology, they all are characterised by the presence of roots, stems, leaves, flowers and fruits.
- In this chapter, we will study the morphology of different parts of flowering plants along with their semi-technical description in detail.

## 5.1 Flowering Plants

The plant body of flowering plants consists of a main axis, which may be branched or unbranched, bearing lateral appendages. The main axis is divided into two parts.

### 1. Root System

It is the underground part of the plant that develops from the radicle of embryo. It helps in fixation of the plant as well as absorption of water and minerals.

## 2. Shoot System

- It is the aerial system that develops from the plumule of embryo. It contains stem, leaves as **vegetative parts** and flowers, fruits and seeds as **reproductive parts.**
- The **vegetative parts** are involved in various vegetative functions like structural organisation, fixation, absorption, nourishment, growth and maintenance of various components.
- On the other hand, **reproductive parts** are involved in sexual reproduction and germination of seeds to form new plants.

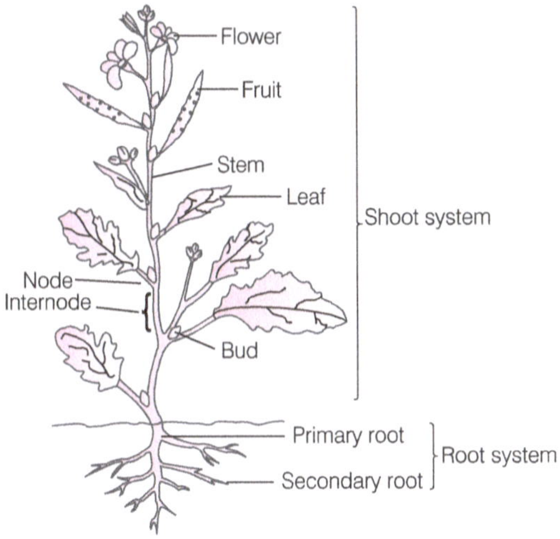

Fig. 5.1 Parts of a flowering plant

Let's discuss each part of the flowering plant in detail.

# 5.2 The Root

- It is the non-green (due to the absence of chlorophyll), cylindrical and descending part that normally grows downwards into the soil.
- The root of a plant is typically divided into various regions, each of which plays a crucial role in its growth and function.

## Region of the Root

A typical root contains four regions. However, there is no clear line of distinction between them. These regions are described below.

### 1. Root Cap

- The root is covered at the apex by a thimble or cap-like structure called the **root cap.**
- It protects the tender apex of the root as it makes its way through the soil.

### 2. Region of Meristematic Activity

- This region lies few millimetres above the root cap.
- The cells of this region are **very small, thin-walled** and have **dense protoplasm**.
- These cells divide repeatedly.

### 3. Region of Elongation

- It is situated above the meristematic region.
- The cells of this region undergo rapid elongation and enlargement and are responsible for the growth of the root in length.

### 4. Region of Maturation

- This region lies proximal to the region of elongation.
- The cells in this region are differentiated and mature.
- Some epidermal cells of this region form very fine and delicate, thread-like structures called **root hairs**.
- These root hairs absorb water and minerals from the soil.

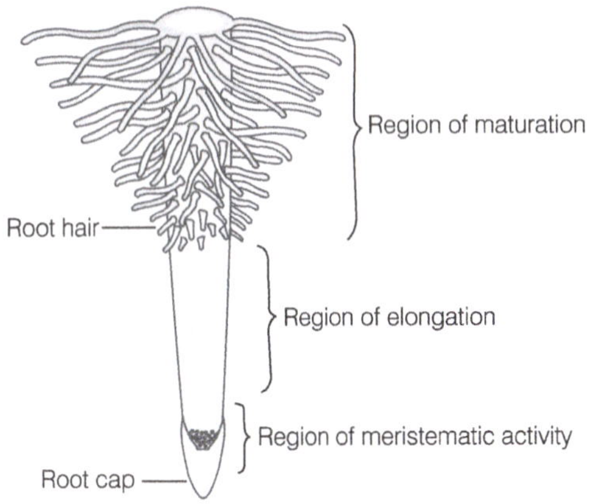

Fig. 5.2 The region of the root tip

## Types of Root System

There are two major types of root systems in plants which are described below.

### 1. Tap Root System

- The tap root develops from the radicle of embryo of a seed.
- In majority of the dicotyledonous plants, the direct elongation of the radicle results in the formation of a **primary root** that grows into the soil.

- It continuously grows and produces lateral roots called **secondary roots**.
- The further branches of the secondary roots are called **tertiary roots** and so on.
- This root system is present in dicots, e.g. mustard.

## 2. Adventitious Root System

- The roots developing from any part of the plant other than the radicle are known as adventitious roots, e.g. grasses, *Monstera*, banyan tree, etc.
- On the basis of the nature of development of adventitious roots, fibrous roots can also be classified as adventitious roots.

### Fibrous Roots

- In some plants, the primary root is short lived and is replaced by a large number of roots. These roots originate from the base of the stem and constitute the fibrous root system.
- These roots are present in monocots, e.g. wheat.

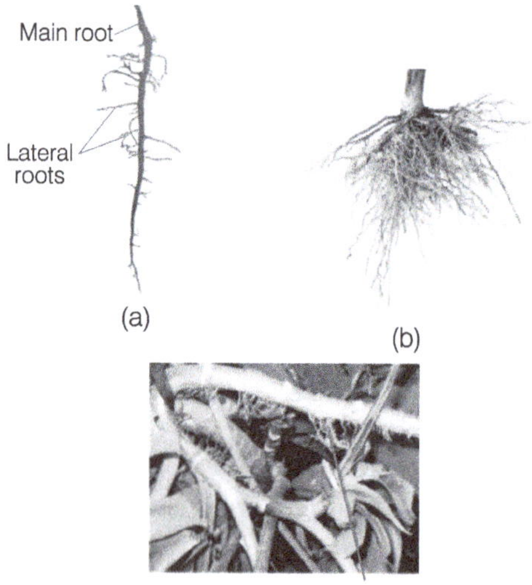


**Fig. 5.3** Different types of roots : (a) tap, (b) fibrous, (c) adventitious

## Functions of the Roots

The major functions of the roots are as follows.

- **Anchorage** Roots provide proper anchorage to the plants with soil.
- **Absorption** Roots absorb water and minerals from the soil.
- **Storage** Roots of many plants store reserve food material for future use.
- **Plant growth regulators** Roots are also responsible for the synthesis of plant growth regulators.

### Quick Test 1

1. Name the region of the root which protects the tender apex of the root.
2. A structure *X* is derived from the epidermal cells of the maturation region. State the function of *X*.
3. **State True or False.**
   The region of maturation lies proximal to the region of the elongation.
4. Mention the root system which is found in the mustard plant.
5. Give an example of the plant in which roots arises from any part of the plant, other than radicle.

# 5.3 The Stem

- It is the ascending part of the axis bearing branches, leaves, flowers and fruits.
- It develops from the **plumule of the embryo** of a germinating seed.
- It shows distinction into **nodes** and **internodes**, where node is the region from where leaves are borne and internodes are the region between two nodes.
- The stem bears **bud**, which may be **terminal** or **axillary**.
- A bud can be defined as a condensed embryonic shoot that has a growing point surrounded by closely packed immature leaves.
- When the bud grows, the internodes become longer, and the leaves spread out, resulting in the formation of a young shoot.
- The stem is generally green when young and later often become woody and dark brown.

## Functions of Stem

The stem performs various primary and secondary functions which are discussed below.

### 1. Primary Functions

- It spreads out branches that bears leaves, fruits, flowers and seeds.
- It **conducts** water, minerals and photosynthates throughout the plant body.

### 2. Secondary Functions

- Many stems **store food** as reserve food materials.
- Some stems also help provide support, protection and aids in **vegetative propagation**.

## 5.4 The Leaf

- It is a lateral, generally flattened structure borne on the stem.
- It develops at the **node** and **bears a bud** in its axil.
- The **axillary bud** later develops into a branch.
- Leaves originate from shoot apical meristems and are arranged in an acropetal order.
- They are the most important vegetative organs for **photosynthesis.**

### Parts of a Leaf

A typical leaf has three main parts which are as follows.

#### 1. Leaf Base

- The leaf is attached to the stem by the leaf base.
- It may bear two lateral small leaf like structures called **stipules**.
- Leaves with stipules are called **stipulate** and those without them are termed as **exstipulate.**
- In monocots, the leaf base expands into a sheath that partially or completely surrounds the stem.
- In some leguminous plants, the leaf base may become swollen and is called the **pulvinus.**

#### 2. Petiole

- It is the stalk of a leaf that helps to hold the leaf blade towards light.
- Long thin flexible petioles allow leaf blades to flutter in wind, thereby cooling the leaf and bringing fresh air to leaf surface.

#### 3. Lamina (leaf blade)

- It is the green, expanded part of the leaf with **veins** and **veinlets.**
- It has a prominent median vein called the **midrib.**
- Veins provide rigidity to the leaf blade and act as channels of transport for water, minerals and food materials.
- The lamina is the site of photosynthesis, gaseous exchange, transpiration and other metabolic activities.
- The shape, margin, apex, surface and extent of incision of lamina varies in different leaves.

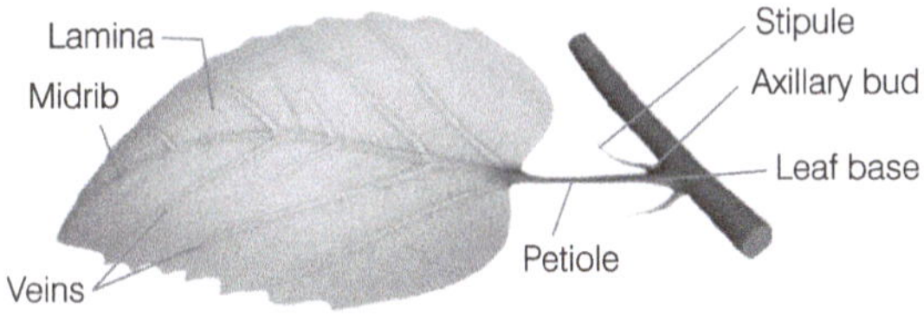


Fig. 5.4 Parts of a leaf

### Venation

The arrangement of veins and veinlets in the lamina of leaf is called **venation**. Leaves have mainly two types of venations which are as follows.

#### 1. Reticulate Venation

- When the veinlets form a network, the venation is called **reticulate**.
- It is generally found in dicot leaves, e.g. gram, pea, etc.

#### 2. Parallel Venation

- When the veins run parallel to each other within the lamina, the venation is termed as **parallel**.
- It is generally found in monocot leaves, e.g. *Zea mays* (maize), grass, etc.

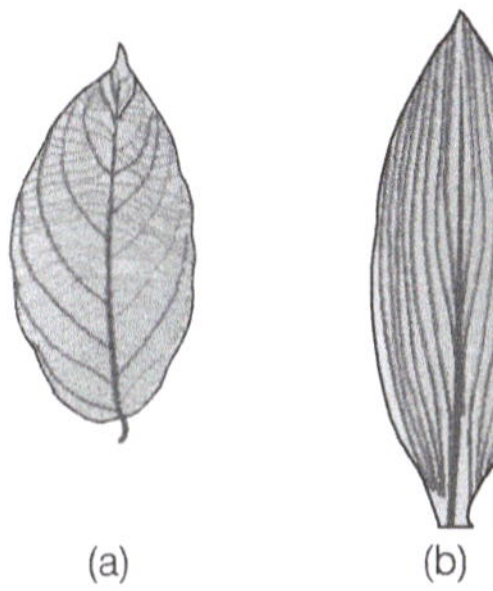


Fig. 5.5 Venation : (a) Reticulate venation, (b) Parallel venation

### Types of Leaves

Depending on the incision of the lamina, there are two types of leaves, which are described as follows.

#### 1. Simple Leaf

- A leaf having a single or undivided lamina is called simple leaf.

- The lamina of a simple leaf may be incised, but the incisions do not touch the midrib.
- An axillary bud is always present in the axil of leaf petiole and stem.

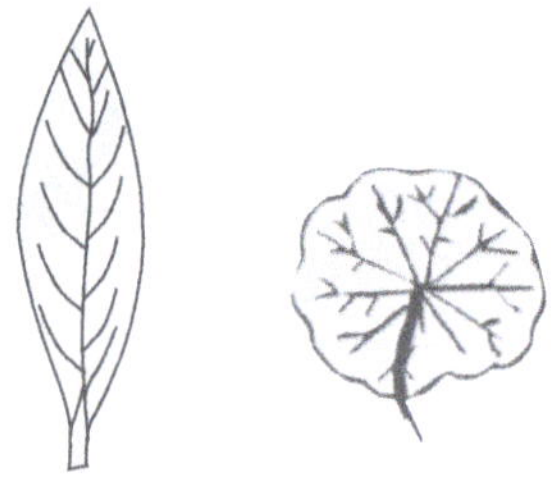

Fig. 5.6 Types of simple leaves

## 2. Compound Leaf

- A leaf is called compound when the incision of the leaf blade reaches up to the midrib (rachis) so that the leaf is broken up into a number of segments called **leaflets**.
- A bud is present in the axil of petiole in compound leaves, but not in the axil of leaflets of the compound leaf.
- A compound leaf can be of following two types.
  - **Pinnately Compound Leaves** In these leaves the incision of lamina is directed towards the midrib, which is known as **rachis**.

    Leaflets are arranged on both side of the rachis, e.g. neem, rose, etc.
  - **Palmately Compound Leaves** In these leaves, the leaflets are attached at a common point, i.e. at the tip of petiole, e.g. silk cotton.

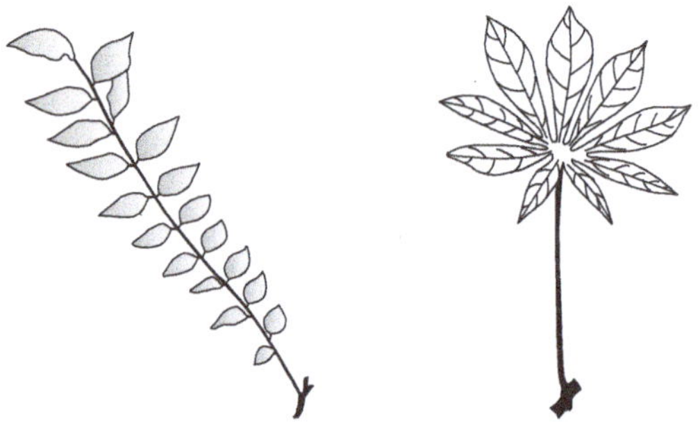


Fig. 5.7 (a) Pinnately compound leaf, (b) Palmately compound leaf

## Phyllotaxy

The pattern of arrangement of leaves on the stem or branch is called **phyllotaxy**.

It is usually of three types which are described below.

- **Alternate Phyllotaxy** In this type, a single leaf arises at each node in alternate manner, e.g. China rose, mustard and sunflower plants.
- **Opposite Phyllotaxy** In this type, a pair of leaves arise at each node and lie opposite to each other, e.g. *Calotropis* and guava plants.
- **Whorled Phyllotaxy** In this type, more than two leaves arise at a node and form a whorl, e.g. *Alstonia*.

Fig. 5.8 Different types of phyllotaxy : (a) Alternate, (b) Opposite, (c) Whorled

## Functions of Leaves

The leaves perform many functions which are listed below.

- They carry out **photosynthesis** with the help of sunlight and carbon dioxide.
- They contain stomata through which **gaseous exchange** occurs.
- They are the site of **transpiration.**
- They protect axillary and terminal bud from **mechanical injury**.

### Quick Test 2

1. Stem is the ascending part of the axis that bears flowers, branches, leaves, fruits, etc. Which part of the germinating seed, gives rise to the stem?
2. A structure '*X*' later develops into the branch. Identify '*X*'.
3. State one function of the stem, other than the conduction of water and minerals.
4. **State True or False.**

   The base of stem becomes swollen and is known as pulvinus.
5. Name the kind of phyllotaxy present in China rose and *Calotropis*.

## 5.5 Flower

- A flower is a characteristic feature of angiosperms that is responsible for sexual reproduction in plants.
- These flowers are generally arranged on the shoot axis in the form of inflorescences.
- Upon maturity, the flower develops into fruits and seeds, which play crucial roles in the plant's life cycle.
- Morphologically, it is considered as a shoot bearing nodes and modified floral leaves.

### Structure of a Flower

- A flower arises at the axil of a leaf-like structure called **bract**.
- Bract is reduced leaf found at the base of pedicel.
- Flowers with bracts are called **bracteate** and those without bracts are called **ebracteate**.
- The terminal and swollen part of the axis of the flower is the **receptacle** or **thalamus**.
- The receptacle contains four different types of whorls arranged in successive manner. These whorls consist of the **calyx, corolla, androecium,** and **gynoecium**.
- In some flowers like lily, the calyx and corolla are not distinct and are termed as **perianth**.

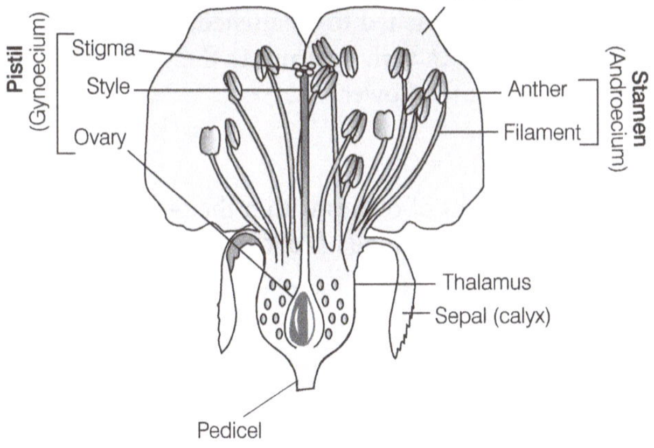


Fig. 5.9 Structure of a typical flower

- When a flower has both androecium and gynoecium, it is known as **bisexual**. However, if it has only one of the reproductive whorls, it is known as **unisexual**.
- A flower may be **trimerous, tetramerous** or **pentamerous** when the floral appendages are in multiple of 3, 4 or 5, respectively.

### Parts of a Flower

- A typical flower consists of four distinct parts the **calyx**, the **corolla**, the **androecium** and the **gynoecium**.
- The calyx and corolla are **accessory organs**, while androecium and gynoecium are **reproductive organs.**
- The different whorls of the flower are described below.

#### 1. Calyx

- It is the outermost whorl of a flower.
- It is made up of units called **sepals.**
- The sepals are generally green, leaf-like and protect the flower in the bud stage.
- The calyx may be **gamosepalous** (sepals united) or **polysepalous** (sepals free).

#### 2. Corolla

- It is composed of **petal** and lies inner to calyx.
- Petals are usually brightly coloured to attract insects for pollination.
- The corolla may be **gamopetalous** (petals united) or **polypetalous** (petals free).
- The shape and colour of corolla may vary greatly in shape.
- Corolla may be tubular, bell-shaped, funnel-shaped or wheel-shaped.

Both calyx and corolla determine the aestivation of a flower.

#### Aestivation

The mode of arrangement of sepals or petals in floral bud with respect to the other members of the same whorl is known as aestivation.

It is important in classification of plants. It is of following types.

- **Valvate** The margins of adjacent sepals or petals in a whorl just touch one another, without overlapping, e.g. *Calotropis*.
- **Twisted** The margin of one sepal or petal overlaps with the margin of next petal and so on, e.g. China rose, lady's finger and cotton.
- **Imbricate** The margins of sepals or petals overlap one another but not in any particular direction, e.g. *Cassia* and gulmohar.

- **Vexillary** In this aestivation, the largest petal (standard) overlaps the two lateral petals (wings) which in turn overlap the two smallest anterior petals (keel). This type of aestivation is also known as papilionaceous, e.g. pea and bean.

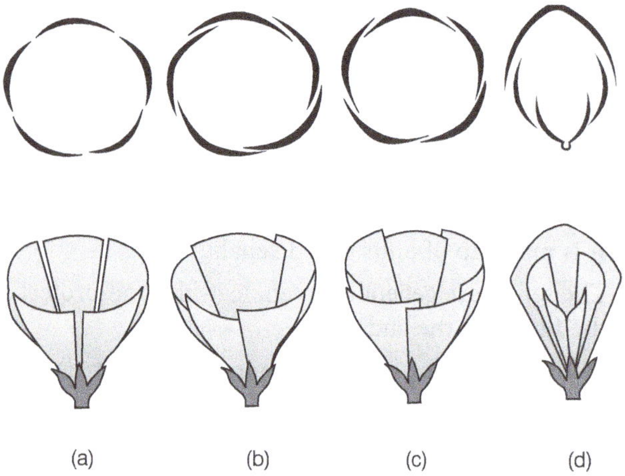


**Fig. 5.10** Types of aestivation in corolla : (a) Valvate, (b) Twisted, (c) Imbricate, (d) Vexillary

## 3. Androecium

- It is the third whorl of flower composed of **stamens**.
- Each stamen, which represents the male reproductive organ consists of a stalk or a **filament** and an **anther**.
- Each anther is usually bilobed and each lobe has two chambers, the pollen sacs.
- The pollen grains are produced in **pollen sacs**.
- A sterile stamen is called **staminode** (without anther).
- Stamens can be of different types depending on their union with other members such as petals or among themselves such as,
  - When stamens are attached to the petals, they are **epipetalous**, e.g. brinjal.
  - When stamens are attached to the perianth, the condition is called **epiphyllous**, e.g. lily.
- The stamens in a flower may either remain free, i.e. **polyandrous** or may be united in varying degrees such as,
  - When the stamens may be united into one bunch or one bundle, they are called **monoadelphous** as in China rose.
  - When they may be grouped into two bundles, they are called **diadelphous** as in pea.
  - When they can be grouped into more than two bundles, they are called **polyadelphous** as in citrus.
- There may be a variation in the length of filament as in *Salvia* and mustard.

## 4. Gynoecium

- It is the female reproductive part of the flower.
- Gynoecium is made up of one or more carpels.
- Depending on whether the carpels are fused or separate, gynoecium can be of following types.
  - **Apocarpous** When more than one carpel is present, they may be free and are called **apocarpous**, e.g. lotus and rose.
  - **Syncarpous** When carpels are fused together, the gynoecium is called **syncarpous**, e.g. mustard and tomato.
- A carpel (or pistil) consists of three parts, i.e. **stigma, style** and **ovary**.
- The stigma is usually present at the tip of the style and is the receptive surface for pollen grains.
- Style is a stalk-like structure that connects ovary to the stigma.
- Ovary is the enlarged basal part. Each ovary bears one or more ovules attached to a flattened, cushion-like **placenta**, which in turn determines the type of placentation in the flower.

### Placentation

- The arrangement of ovules within the ovary is known as placentation. It can be of following types.
  - **Marginal** In this type, the placenta forms a ridge along the ventral suture of the ovary and the ovules are borne on this ridge forming two rows, e.g. pea.
  - **Axile** When the placenta is axial and the ovules are attached to it in a multilocular ovary, the placentation is called axile, e.g. China rose, tomato and lemon.
  - **Parietal** In this type, the ovules develop on the inner wall of the ovary or on peripheral part. The ovary is one-chambered, but it becomes two-chambered due to the formation of false septum, e.g. mustard and *Argemone*.

- **Free central** In this type, the ovules are borne on central axis and septa are absent, e.g. *Dianthus* and primrose.
- **Basal** In this type, the placenta develops at the base of ovary and a single ovule is attached to it, as in sunflower, marigold.

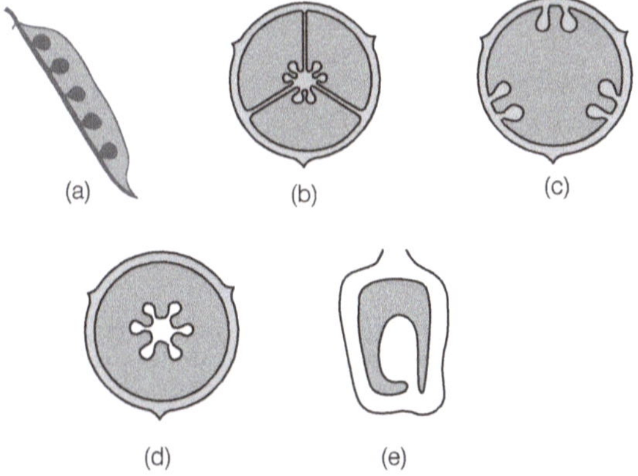


Fig. 5.11 Types of placentation : (a) Marginal, (b) Axile, (c) Parietal, (d) Free central, (e) Basal

**TEACHER'S TIP**

The cavity enclosed by the ovary wall is called **locule**. The number of locules in the ovary correspond to the number of carpels in the gynoecium. Based on this, ovary may be **unilocular** (one locule), **bilocular** (two locules), **trilocular** (three locules) or **multilocular** (many locules) .

## Symmetry of a Flower

- The symmetry of a flower depends upon the shape, size and arrangement of floral parts, e.g. calyx, corolla, androecium and gynoecium.
- The symmetry of a flower is of following types.

### 1. Actinomorphic

- In this type, a flower can be divided into exactly equal halves by any radial plane passing through the centre of a flower.
- Therefore, it has radial symmetry, e.g. mustard, *Datura*, chilli.

### 2. Zygomorphic

- In this type, flower can be divided into two identical halves through only one particular vertical plane.
- Therefore, it has bilateral symmetry, e.g. pea, gulmohar, bean, *Cassia*.

### 3. Asymmetric

When a flower cannot be divided into two similar halves by any vertical plane passing through the centre, it is asymmetrical (irregular), e.g. *Canna*

## Position of Floral Parts on Thalamus

- The positions of different floral whorls is influenced by the position of ovary in the flower.
- Based on the position of calyx, corolla and androecium in respect of the ovary on thalamus, the flowers are of following types.

### 1. Hypogynous Flower

- The gynoecium occupies the highest position, while the other parts are situated below it.
- The ovary in such flowers is said to be **superior**, e.g. mustard, China rose and brinjal.

### 2. Perigynous Flower

- The gynoecium is situated in the centre and other parts of the flower are located on the rim of the thalamus almost at the same level.
- The ovary here is said to be **half inferior**, e.g., plum, rose, peach.

### 3. Epigynous Flower

- In such flowers, the margin of thalamus grows upward enclosing the ovary completely and getting fused with it.
- The other parts of flower arise above the ovary.
- The ovary is said to be **inferior**, e.g., guava and cucumber, and the ray florets of sunflower.

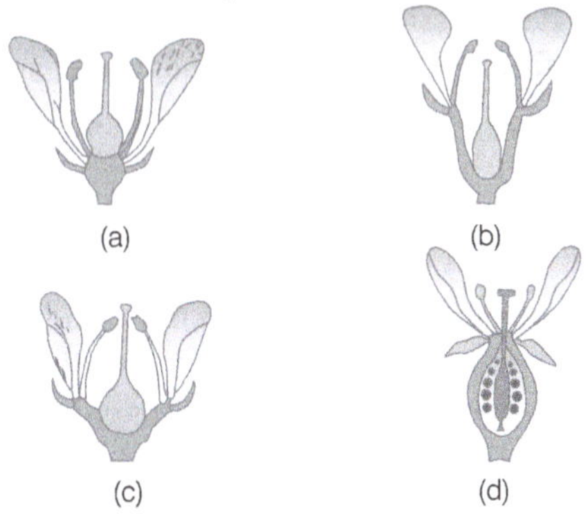


Fig. 5.12 Position of floral parts on thalamus : (a) Hypogynous, (b) and (c) Perigynous, (d) Epigynous

## Quick Test 3

1. Mention the scientific term for the terminal and swollen part of the flower axis.
2. 'X' is the female reproductive part of the flower, which consist of three parts *A*, *B* and *C*. '*A*' is the swollen bottom part and *C* is the sticky part. Name *X* and *C*.
3. State the term for the brightly coloured part of the flower that attracts insects for pollination.
4. **State True or False.**
   In the flower of the bean plant, the largest petals overlap the two lateral petals which in turn overlaps two smallest anterior petals.
5. Give the example of two plants in which ovules are borne on the central axis and septa are absent.
6. Name any two plants in which ovary is half inferior in the position.

## 5.6 The Inflorescence

- The arrangement of flowers on the floral axis is called inflorescence. A flower is a modified shoot wherein the shoot apical meristem changes to floral meristem.
- The shoot apex produces different kinds of floral appendages laterally at successive nodes instead of leaves. When a shoot tip transforms into a flower, it is always solitary.
- Depending on whether the apex gets develops into a flower or continues to grow, there are two types of inflorescences, which are described below.

### 1. Racemose Inflorescence

- In this type of inflorescence, the main axis continues to grow and the flowers are borne laterally in an **acropetal succession** (the older flowers are found towards the base and younger ones at the apex).
- In this inflorescence the growth of main axis is **indefinite**.

### 2. Cymose Inflorescence

- In this type of inflorescence, the tip of the main axis terminates in a flower and further growth continues by one or more lateral branches. These branches also behave like the main axis.
- The flowers are borne in **basipetal succession** (younger flowers occupy basal position, while older flowers are towards the apex).
- In this inflorescence, the growth of main axis is limited.

(a) (b)

Fig. 5.13 Inflorescence : (a) Racemose, (b) Cymose

**TEACHER'S TIP**

The main portion of the branch that bears the cluster of flowers is called **peduncle**, whereas, the stalk of an individual flower is called **pedicel**.

## 5.7. The Fruit

- The characteristic feature of flowering plants is fruit.
- It is a mature or ripened ovary, developed after fertilisation.
- When a fruit is formed without fertilisation, it is called **parthenocarpic fruit**.
- During fertilisation, some important changes take place in the ovary. These changes are
  - The ovules present in it develops into **seeds**.
  - The wall of the ovary thickens and ripens into **pericarp** (fruit wall).
- The pericarp may be dry or fleshy.
- When pericarp is thick and fleshy, it is differentiated into outer **epicarp**, the middle **mesocarp** and the inner **endocarp**.
- In mango and coconut, the fruit is known as a **drupe**.
- The drupe develops from monocarpellary superior ovary and is one seeded.
- In mango the pericarp is well differentiated into an outer thin **epicarp**, a middle fleshy edible **mesocarp** and an inner stony hard **endocarp**.

- In coconut which is also a drupe, the mesocarp is fibrous.

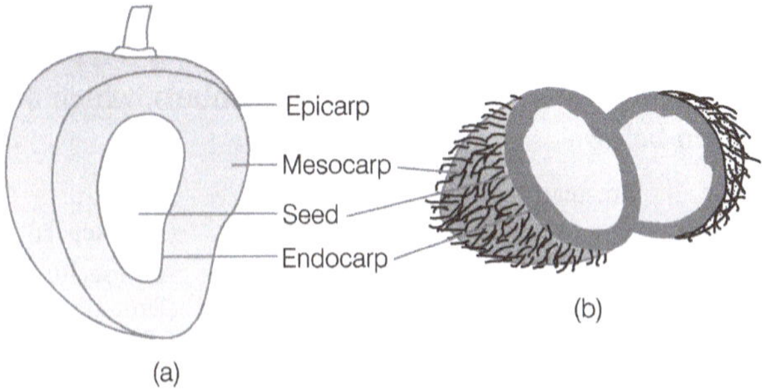


Fig. 5.14 Parts of fruits : (a) Mango, (b) Coconut

## 5.8 The Seed

- A ripened ovule which contains an embryo or tiny plant with sufficient reserve food for the development of embryo is known as seed.
- It is made up of seed coat and an embryo.
- The embryo is made up of a radicle, an embryonal axis and one or two cotyledons.
- In some seeds such as castor the endosperm is formed as a result of double fertilisation and is a food storing tissue. Such seeds are called **endospermic seeds**.
- In plants such as bean, gram and pea, the endosperm is not present in mature seeds and such seeds are called **non-endospermic seeds**.

### Types of Seeds

Based on the number of cotyledons the seeds are of following types.

#### 1. Dicotyledonous Seed

These seeds possess two cotyledons. e.g., gram and pea.

Endosperm is generally absent in a dicot seed.

#### Structure of Dicotyledonous Seed

- The outermost covering of a seed is the **seed coat**.
- The seed coat has two layers, the outer **testa** and the inner **tegmen**.
- A small scar called **hilum** is present on the seed coat through which developing seeds were attached to the fruit.
- A small pore called **micropyle** is present above the hilum.

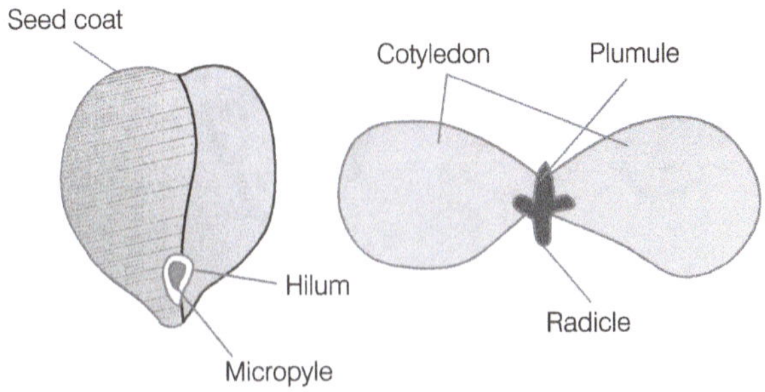


Fig. 5.15 Structure of dicotyledonous seed

- The seed coat encloses the embryo, consisting of an embryonal axis and two cotyledons.
- The cotyledons are often fleshy and full of reserve food materials.
- At the two ends of the embryonal axis are present the radicle and the plumule.

#### 2. Monocotyledonous Seed

- These seeds possess one cotyledon. e.g., maize and wheat.
- The monocotyledonous seeds are endospermic, but some as in orchids are non-endospermic.

#### Structure of Monocotyledonous Seed (Maize)

- The seed coat is membranous and generally fused with the fruit wall.
- The aleurone layer is a distinct proteinous layer that separates the embryo from the endosperm.
- The endosperm is bulky and stores food.
- The embryo is small and situated in a groove at one end of the endosperm.
- It consists of one large shield-shaped cotyledon known as **scutellum** and a short axis with a **plumule** and a **radicle**.

- The plumule and radicle are enclosed in sheaths which are called **coleoptile** and **coleorhiza**, respectively.

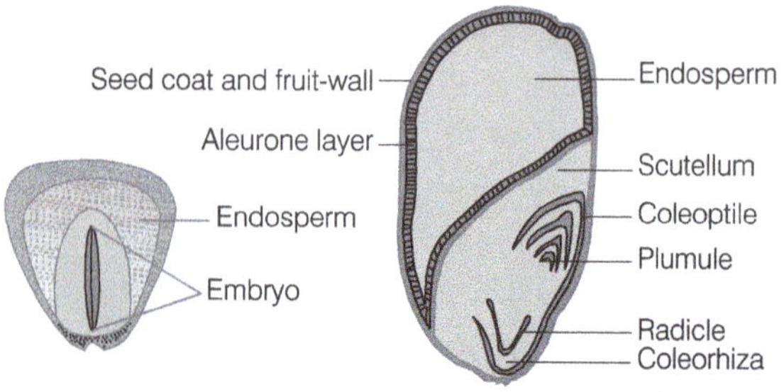


Fig. 5.16 Structure of a monocotyledonous seed

**Quick Test 4**

1. Mention the scientific term for the arrangement of the flowers on the floral axis.
2. A plant bears flowers that grow along a central axis and continue to bloom in a sequence from bottom to top. Identify the type of inflorescence in such plant.
3. Mention the term used to describe fruits that are formed without fertilisation.
4. Mango and coconut are drupe type of fruits. In mango, fleshy mesocarp is edible. What is the edible part of coconut? What does milk of tender coconut represent? *NCERT Exemplar*
5. **State True or False.**
   The monocotyledons seeds are generally non-endospermic, but some as in orchids are endospermic.

## 5.9 Semi-Technical Description of a Typical Flowering Plant

- Various morphological features are used to describe a flowering plant.
- The description of a flowering plant should be brief, sequential and in a simple and scientific language.
- This is required to designate a plant in its appropriate taxonomic position.
- The plant is described beginning with its habit, vegetative characters – roots, stem and leaves and then floral characters - inflorescence and flower parts.
- After describing various parts of plant, a floral diagram and a floral formula are presented.

## Floral Formula

- The symbolic representation of floral characters of a flower is called **floral formula**.
- It is represented by some specific symbols, which are given below.

| | | | | | |
|---|---|---|---|---|---|
| Br | – | Bracteate | P | – | Perianth (Unit-tepals) |
| Ebr | – | Ebracteate | A | – | Androecium (Unit-stamens) |
| $\oplus$ | – | Actinomorphic flower | G | – | Gynoecium (Unit-carpels) |
| % | – | Zygomorphic flower | $\underline{G}$ | – | Superior ovary |
| ⚥ | – | Bisexual flower | $\overline{G}$ | – | Inferior ovary |
| ♀ | – | Female flower | 1, 2, 3, 4, ... ∞ | – | Number of units |
| ♂ | – | Male flower | () | – | Fused |
| K | – | Calyx (Unit-sepals) | | | |
| C | – | Corolla (Unit-petals) | $\overset{\frown}{C\ A}$ | – | Epipetalous condition |

- The floral formula of *Brassica* (mustard) represented as given

$$\oplus ⚥ K_{2+2}\ C_4 A_{2+4} \underline{G}_{(2)}$$

- **Description of this floral formula** This flower is actinomorphic and bisexual. The calyx consists of four polysepalous sepals arranged in two whorls of two each. The corolla has four polypetalous, cruciform petals. The androecium consists of six stamens, arranged in two whorls and is polyandrous. The gynoecium is bicarpellary, syncarpous, and superior.

## Floral Diagram

- It provides information about the number of parts of a flower, their arrangement and the relation they have with one another.
- The various symbols used in the floral diagram along with their description is given below.

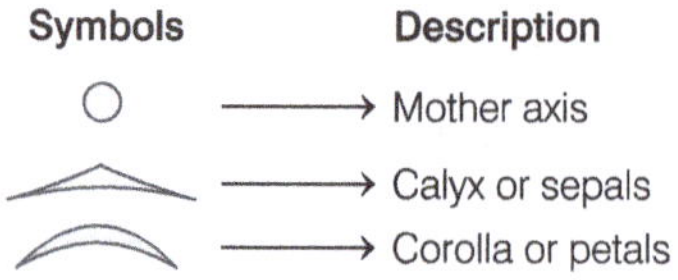


- In the floral diagram, the position of the mother axis with respect to the flower is represented by a dot on the top of the floral diagram.

- Calyx, corolla, androecium and gynoecium are drawn in successive whorls, calyx being the outermost and the gynoecium being in the centre.
- Floral formula also shows cohesion and adhesion within parts of whorls and between whorls.

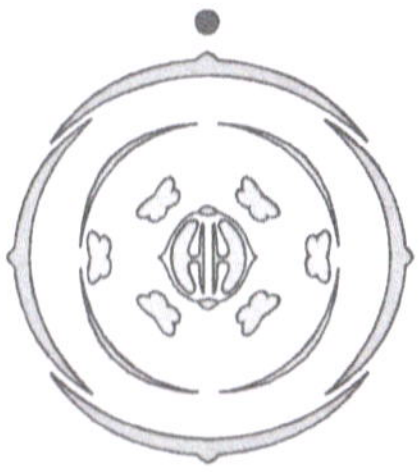

**Fig. 5.17** Floral diagram of mustard (family–Brassicaceae)

## Description of Family–Solanaceae

Solanaceae is a large family, commonly called as the 'potato family'. It is widely distributed in tropics, sub-tropics and even in temperate zones. The plants are mostly herbs, shrubs and rarely small trees.

The comparative account of the Solanaceae family is discussed below.

### 1. Vegetative Characters

- **Stem** Herbaceous rarely woody, aerial; erect, cylindrical, branched, solid or hollow, hairy or glabrous, underground stem in potato (*Solanum tuberosum*).
- **Leaves** Alternate, simple, rarely pinnately compound, exstipulate; venation reticulate.

### 2. Floral Characters

- **Inflorescence** Solitary, axillary or cymose as in *Solanum*.
- **Flower** Bisexual, actinomorphic, pedicellate, pentamerous and hypogynous.
- **Calyx** Sepals 5, united, valvate aestivation, usually persistent.
- **Corolla** Petals 5, united, valvate aestivation.
- **Androecium** Stamens 5, epipetalous.
- **Gynoecium** Bicarpellary obligately placed, syncarpous; ovary superior, bilocular, placenta swollen with many ovules, axile.
- **Fruits** Berry or capsule.
- **Seeds** Many, endospermous.

### 3. Floral Formula

$$\oplus\ ⚥\ K_{(5)}\ \overset{\frown}{C_{(5)}\ A_5}\ \underline{G}_{(2)}$$

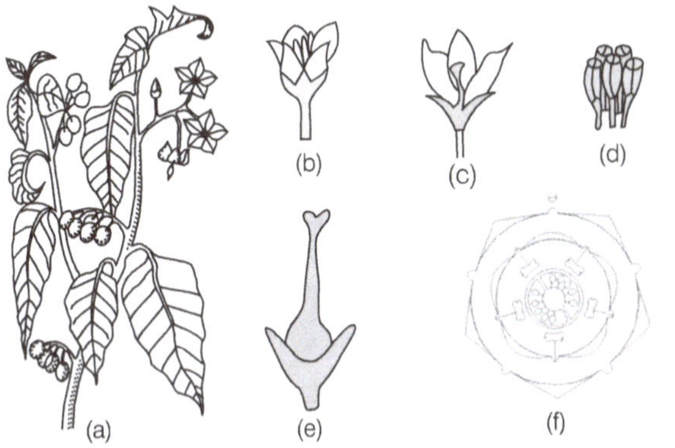


**Fig. 5.18** *Solanum nigrum* (makoi) plant : (a) Flowering twig, (b) Flower, (c) LS of flower, (d) Stamens, (e) Carpel, (f) Floral diagram

### Economic Characters

Plants belonging to the family–Solanaceae have their importance in the following fields.

- **Food** The family–Solanaceae includes a number of vegetables and spice yielding plants, e.g., potato (*Solanum tuberosum*), brinjal (*Solanum melongena*), tomato, chillies, etc.
- **Fumigatory** *Nicotiana tobacum* (tobacco) is used for chewing, smoking and sniffing.
- **Medicines** Belladonna and ashwagandha are used to obtain medicines.
- **Ornamentals** *Petunia* is the commonly used ornamental plant.

## Quick Test 5

1. A floral formula is a symbolic representation of floral characters of a flowers. What do the symbols ⊕ and % indicate in a floral formula?
2. Write the floral formula of an actinomorphic, bisexual, hypogynous flower with five united sepals, five free petals, five free stamens and two united carpels with superior ovary and axile placentation.
3. Mention the type of inflorescence that is found in Solanaceae family.
4. Given below is floral formula of some well-known plants. Identify the family to which this plant belongs.

   $\oplus\ ⚥\ K_{(5)}\ \overset{\frown}{C_{(5)}\ A_5}\ \underline{G}_{(2)}$
5. Name a plant from family–Solanaceae which yield the ornamental value.

# Mind Map

## Morphology of Flowering Plants

### Root

- Part of plant that lies below the surface of soil.

**Types of Root**
- → Tap root (e.g. mustard)
- → Fibrous root (e.g. wheat)
- → Adventitious roo (e.g. *Monestra*)

**Regions of Root**

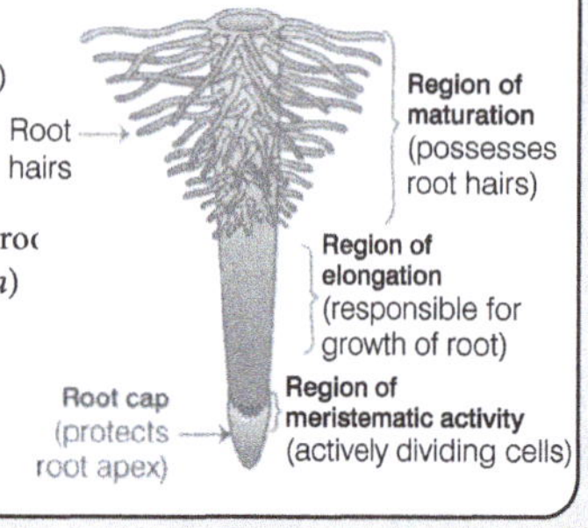


### Leaf

- Borne on the stem at node and bearing a branch in its axil.

**Types of Leaves**
- → Simple (e.g. peepal tree)
- → Pinnately compound (e.g. neem)
- → Palmately compund (e.g. silk cotton)

**Phyllotaxy**
- → Alternate (e.g. China rose)
- → Opposite (e.g. *Calotropis*)
- → Whorled (e.g. *Alstonia*)

**Types of Venation**
- → Reticulate (in dicots)
- → Parallel (in monocots)

### Fruit

- Fruit is the ripened or mature ovary.
- Composed of fruit wall, pericarp and seeds.
- Mesocarp is fibrous in coconut, while fleshy edible in mango.

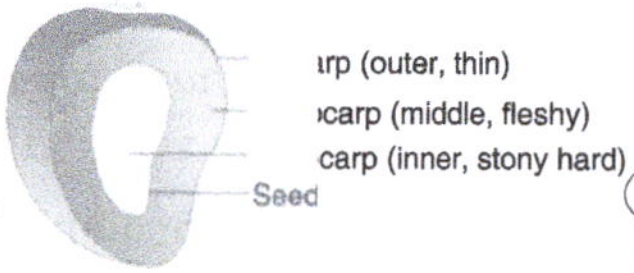

Sectional view of mango fruit

### Seed

Seed coat has two layers - Outer testa and inner tegmen.

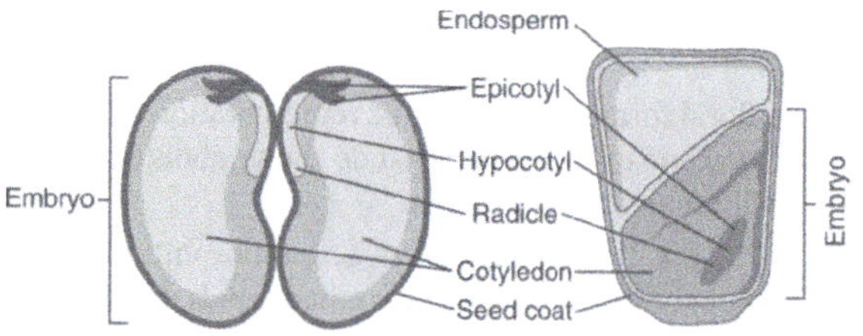


**Dicot seeds** (generally non-endospermic /non-albuminous), two cotyledons, e.g. beans.

**Monocot seeds** (generally, endospermic/ albuminous), one cotyledons, e.g. wheat.

### Floral Features of Solanaceae

- Solitary, axillary or cymose inflorescence.
- Persistent calyx.
- Gamopetalous, epipetalous stamen.

$\oplus ⚥ K_{(5)} \overset{\frown}{C_{(5)} A_5} \underline{G}_{(2)}$

- e.g. *Withania, Solanum.*

Floral diagram of Solanaceae

### Stem

- Ascending part of plant axis bearing nodes and internodes. Contains flower, leaves, etc.

### Flower

- Reproductive unit in angiosperms. Generally, flower has four whorls, i.e. calyx, corolla, androecium and gynoecium.

### Types of Flower

- Based on the presence of sex organs.
  - **Unisexual** (both androecium and gynoecium)
  - **Bisexual** (only androecium or only gynoecium)
- Based on symmetry
  - Actinomorphic (e.g. mustard), zygomorphic (e.g. *Cassia*), asymmetric (e.g. *Canna*)
- Based on the position of ovary with respect to other parts.

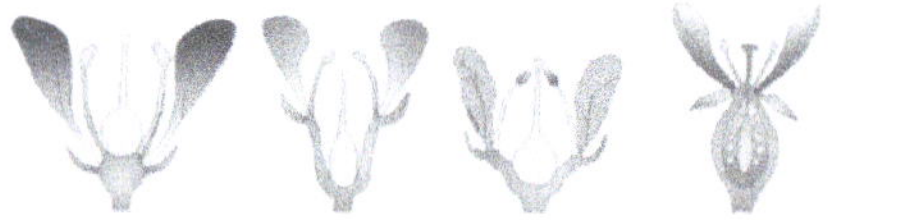

**Hypogynous** superior ovary (e.g. mustard) | **Perigynous** half inferior ovary (e.g. rose) | **Epigynous** inferior ovary (e.g. ray florets of sunflower)

### Aestivation

The mode of arrangement of sepals or petals in floral bud with respect to the other members of the same whorl is known as aestivation. It is of following types

**Valvate** e.g. *Calotropis.* | **Twisted** e.g. China rose, lady's finger and cotton. | **Imbricate** e.g. *Cassia* and gulmohur. | **Vexillary or Papilionaceous** e.g. pea and bean flowers.

### Placentation

It is the arrangement of ovules within the ovary. It is of following types

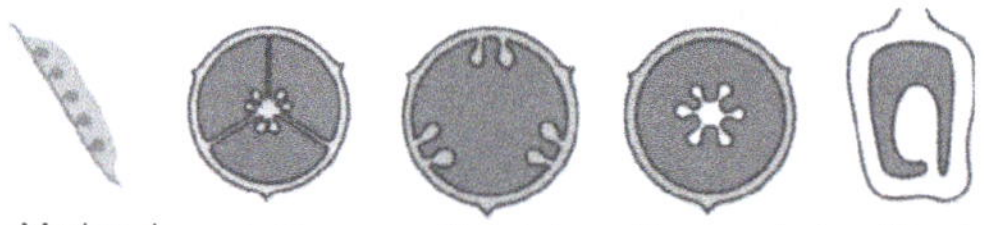

Marignal | Axile | Parietal | Free central | Basal

### Inflorescence

- Arrangement of flowers on floral axis (peduncle).

**Racemose**
- Unlimited growth of main axis.
- Flowers borne acropetally, e.g. mustard.

**Cymose**
- Limited growth of main axis.
- Flowers borne basipetally, e.g. *Solanum.*

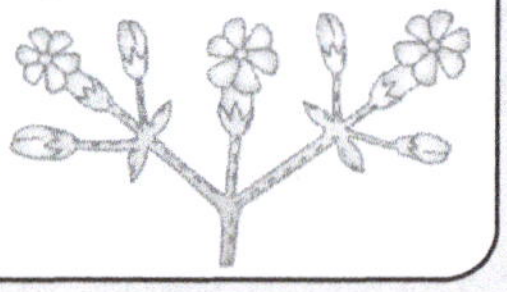

# EXAM PATTERN QUESTIONS

## Objective Type Questions

### Multiple Choice Questions

**1.** The cells of this region in a root are small, thin walled and have dense protoplasm, identify the region. **DIKSHA**

(a) Region of maturation
(b) Region of root hair
(c) Region of elongation
(d) Region of meristematic activity

**Ans.** (*d*)

**2.** Rearrange the following zones as seen in the root in vertical section and choose the correct option. **NCERT Exemplar, Competency Based Que.**

A. Root hair zone
B. Zone of meristems
C. Root cap zone
D. Zone of maturation
E. Zone of elongation

Codes

(a) C, B, E, A, D
(b) A, B, C, D, E
(c) D, E, A, C, B
(d) E, D, C, B, A

**Ans.** (*a*)

**3.** Roots developed from parts of the plant other than radicle are called **NCERT Exemplar**

(a) tap roots
(b) fibrous roots
(c) adventitious roots
(d) nodular roots

**Ans.** (*c*)

**4.** Nodes are the region of stem where

(a) food is stored by plant
(b) leaves are borne
(c) xylem and phloem are present
(d) internodes buds develop

**Ans.** (*b*)

**5.** Which of the following options represents the function of stem in plants?

(a) To bear leaves and branches
(b) Conduction of water and minerals
(c) Storage of food, protection and vegetative propagations
(d) All of the above

**Ans.** (*d*)

**6.** Veins of the leaves are useful for

(a) mechanical support
(b) transport of water and minerals
(c) transport of organic nutrients
(d) All of the above

**Ans.** (*d*)

**7.** Venation is a term used to describe the pattern of arrangement of **NCERT Exemplar**

(a) floral organs
(b) flower in inflorescence
(c) veins and veinlets in a lamina
(d) all of them

**Ans.** (*c*)

**8.** Monocot can be distinguished from dicot by

(a) aestivation
(b) venation
(c) Both (a) and (b)
(d) None of the above

**Ans.** (*b*)

**9.** Which group of plants given below, show pinnately compound leaves?

(a) Silk cotton, maple
(b) Tulip, neem
(c) Maple, *Acacia*
(d) Neem, rose

**Ans.** (*d*)

**10.** Arrangement of leaves on a stem or branch is called

(a) phyllotaxy
(b) venation
(c) inflorescence
(d) vernation

**Ans.** (*a*)

**11.** Perianth is the condition in which

(a) calyx and corolla are not distinct
(b) calyx is present, but corolla is absent
(c) corolla is present, but calyx is absent
(d) calyx and corolla are not present

**Ans.** (*a*)

**12.** Trimerous, tetramerous and pentamerous are terms related to

(a) placentation
(b) position of ovary
(c) number of floral appendages
(d) number of stamens

**Ans.** (*c*)

**13.** **Arrange in correct order according to the given figures.** Competency Based Que.

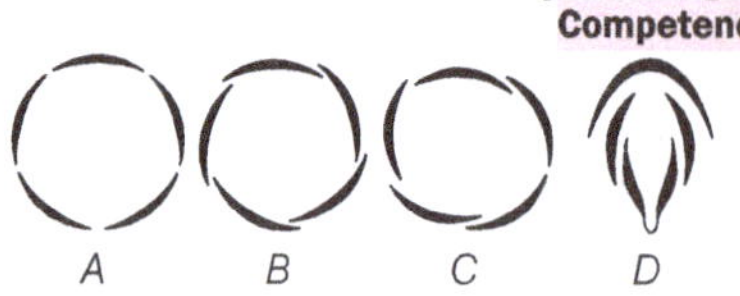


(a) *A* – Imbricate, *B* – Vexillary, *C* – Valvate, *D* – Twisted
(b) *A* – Vexillary, *B* – Valvate, *C* – Twisted, *D* – Imbricate
(c) *A* – Valvate, *B* – Twisted, *C* – Vexillary *D* – Imbricate
(d) *A* – Valvate, *B* – Twisted, *C* – Imbricate, *D* – Vexillary

**Ans.** (*d*)

**14.** **Stamens attached to the petals are called** DIKSHA

(a) epipetalous (b) epiphyllous
(c) staminode (d) perianth

**Ans.** (*a*)

**15.** **Syncarpous gynoecium has two or more**

(a) free carpel (b) fused carpel
(c) free ovaries (d) All of the above

**Ans.** (*b*)

**16.** **Select the incorrect pair.**

(a) Marginal placentation - Pea, beans
(b) Axile placentation - Tomato, lemon
(c) Parietal placental - Mustard, *Argemone*
(d) Free central - Sunflower, marigold

**Ans.** (*d*) The match pair given in option (d) is incorrect. It can be corrected as
Free central - *Dianthus*, primrose

**17.** **Radial symmetry is found in the flowers of**

(a) *Cassia* (b) *Canna*
(c) *Pisum* (d) *Brassica*

**Ans.** (*d*)

**18.** **Inflorescence is the arrangement of**

(a) leaves on the floral axis
(b) buds on the floral axis
(c) flowers on the floral axis
(d) petioles on the floral axis

**Ans.** (*c*)

**19.** **Depending on whether, the apex gets converted into a flower or continues to grow, how many major types of inflorescences are defined?**

(a) Two (b) Three
(c) Four (d) Five

**Ans.** (*a*)

**20.** **In an inflorescence where flowers are borne laterally in an acropetal succession, the position of the youngest floral bud shall be** Competency Based Que., NCERT Exemplar

(a) proximal (b) distal
(c) intercalary (d) any where

**Ans.** (*b*) In racemose inflorescence younger flowers are born at the apex or distal end while older flowers are at the base, this type of succession is acropetal succession.

**21.** **The flowers are arranged in which order in cymose inflorescence** DIKSHA

(a) acropetal (b) axipetal (c) basipetal (d) tapetal

**Ans.** (*c*)

**22.** **The placenta is attached to the developing seed near the** NCERT Exemplar

(a) testa (b) hilum
(c) micropyle (d) chalaza

**Ans.** (*b*) The placenta is attached to the developing seed near hilum. It is the scar located on the seed coat through which developing seeds were attached to the fruit.

**23.** **The mature seeds of plants such as gram and peas possess no endosperm, because** NCERT Exemplar

(a) these plants are not angiosperms
(b) there is no double fertilisation in them
(c) endosperm is not formed in them
(d) endosperm gets used up by the developing embryo during seed development

**Ans.** (*d*)

**24.** **Match the Column I with Column II and choose the right answer from the options given below.** Competency Based Que.

| Column I (Symbols of floral formula) | | Column II (Description) | |
|---|---|---|---|
| A. | ⊕ | 1. | Zygomorphic |
| B. | % | 2. | Actinomorphic |
| C. | K | 3. | Calyx |
| D. | C | 4. | Corolla |

**Codes**

| | A | B | C | D | | A | B | C | D |
|---|---|---|---|---|---|---|---|---|---|
| (a) | 4 | 3 | 2 | 1 | (b) | 2 | 1 | 3 | 4 |
| (c) | 3 | 4 | 2 | 1 | (d) | 1 | 2 | 3 | 4 |

**Ans.** (*b*)

**25.** **Which of the following statement is incorrect regarding Solanaceae?**

(a) The flower is unisexual and zygomorphic
(b) Gynoecium is bicarpellary and syncarpous
(c) The leaves are arranged in an alternate manner and has reticulate venation
(d) Calyx is usually persistent and has valvate aestivation.

**Ans.** (*a*) The plants belonging to family–Solanaceae have bisexual and actinomorphic flower.

## Assertion-Reason Questions

**Direction** (Q. Nos. 1-9) *In each of the following questions, a statement of Assertion (A) is given followed by corresponding statement of Reason (R). Of the statements, mark the correct answer as*

(a) Both A and R are true and R is the correct explanation of the A.
(b) Both A and R are true, but R is not the correct explanation of the A.
(c) A is true, but R is false.
(d) A is false, but R is true.

**1. Assertion** (A) Root hairs are not present on whole root surface.

**Reason** (R) Root hairs absorb water.

**Ans.** (*b*) Both Assertion and Reason are true, but Reason is not the correct explanation of Assertion. It can be explained as

Root hairs specifically arise from the epidermal cells of the maturation regions, where they can absorb water and minerals from the soil.

**2. Assertion** (A) Adventitious roots develop from any part of plant except radicle.

**Reason** (R) Adventitious roots are found in both monocot and dicot pants. **Competency Based Que.**

**Ans.** (*b*)

**3. Assertion** (A) Stem develops from hypocotyl of embryo.

**Reason** (R) Nodes bear axillary buds.

**Ans.** (*d*) Assertion is false, but reason is true.
It can be corrected as
Stem develops from the plumule of the embryo of a germinating seed.

**4. Assertion** (A) In some flowers like lily, perianth is a term used when calyx and corolla are not distinct.

**Reason** (R) Calyx and corolla are the reproductive organs.

**Ans.** (*c*) Assertion is true, but reason is false. It can be corrected as

Calyx and corolla are the accessory organs.

**5. Assertion** (A) Monoadelphous stamens are found in China rose.

**Reason** (R) When the stamens are united into one bunch or bundle, the condition is said to be monoadelphous. **Competency Based Que.**

**Ans.** (*a*)

**6. Assertion** (A) In racemose type of inflorescence, the main axis grows indefinitely.

**Reason** (R) Main axis is not terminated by flower.

**Ans.** (*a*)

**7. Assertion** (A) In cymose inflorescence, growth of terminal bud stops after sometime.

**Reason** (R) The growth of the main axis is definite.

**Ans.** (*b*)

**8. Assertion** (A) In maize, the seeds are endospermous. **Competency Based Que.**

**Reason** (R) In some seeds endosperm is formed as a result of double fertilisation and is a food storing tissue.

**Ans.** (*b*)

**9. Assertion** (A) $\underline{G}$ is the symbol for inferior ovary.

**Reason** (R) Fusion is indicated by enclosing the figure within bracket.

**Ans.** (*d*) Assertion is false, but Reason is true. It can be corrected as
$\underline{G}$ is the symbol for superior ovary.

# Subjective Questions

## Very Short Answer Type Questions

**1. Roots help in absorption of water. What other function does it perform?**

**Ans.** Root anchors the plants in the soil.

**2. List out any two functions of a stem.**

**Ans.** Refer to text on page no. 100, 101. (½ × 2)

**3. State the difference between gamosepalous and polysepalous.** **DIKSHA**

**Ans.** Gamosepalous refers to flowers having fused sepals, while polysepalous refers to those having separate sepals. (1)

**4. Which is the technical term used for the androecium in a flower of China rose?**

**Ans.** Monoadelphous

**5. Name the type of placentation shown in the given figures (*a*) and (*b*).**

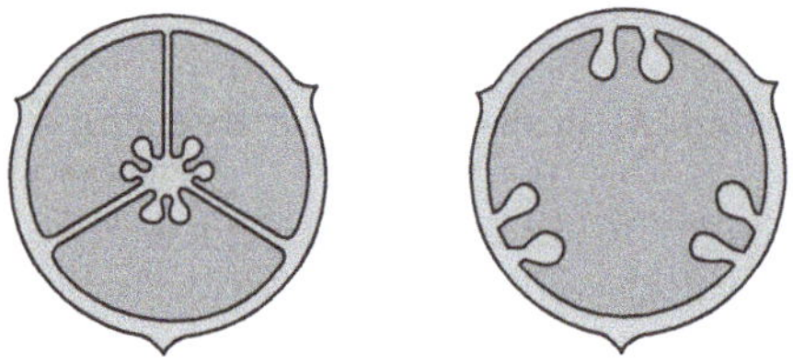

(a) (b)

**Ans.** The type of placentation given in the figure (*a*) and (*b*) is axile and parietal, respectively. (½ × 2)

**6. Differentiate between pedicel and peduncle.** **NCERT Exemplar**

**Ans.** Differences between pedicel and peduncle are

| Pedicel | Peduncle |
|---|---|
| It is a stalk of the flower. | It is the axis of inflorescence. |
| Pedicel bears a single flower. | It generally bears a number of flowers. |

(½ × ½)

**7. What are the two layers of seed coat?**

**Ans.** Testa is the outer hard layer of seed coat, while tegmen is inner thin layer of seed coat. (½ + ½)

**8. What is the name given to the cotyledon in case of monocot?**

**Ans.** Scutellum

**9. The scutellum observed in a grain of wheat or maize is comparable to which part of the seed in other monocots?** **Competency Based Que.**

**Ans.** Cotyledons

**10. Write floral formula for a flower which is bisexual, actinomorphic, petamerous sepal, petals, stamens free with ovary, syncarpous, superior, trilocular with axile placentation.** **NCERT Exemplar**

**Ans.** Floral formula would be $\oplus$ ⚥ $K_5\ C_5\ A_6\ \underline{G}_{(3)}$

**11. Where is mother axis drawn in a floral diagram.**

**Ans.** Mother axis is drawn at the top of floral diagram.

**12. Write the floral formula of family–Solanaceae and give its two examples.**

**Ans.** Floral formula- $\oplus$ ⚥ $K_{(5)}\ \overset{\frown}{C_{(5)}\ A_{(5)}}\ \underline{G}_{(2)}$.

Examples are *Capsicum annuum* (chillies) and *Solanum lycopersicum* (tomato).

**13. Name the family in which ovary of the flower is obliquely placed.**

**Ans.** Solanaceae

**14. Name the ornamental plants of potato family.**

**Ans.** *Petunia*, *Lycianthes*, etc. are some ornamental plants of potato family.

## Short Answer Type Questions

**1. Root hair zone is the most important part of the root for absorption of water. How do these hair maximise the water absorption?** **Competency Based Que.**

**Ans.** Root hair zone is the most important part of the root. As the root hairs present in this zone, increase the surface area of the root for the absorption of water. Thus, increasing or maximising the water absorption.

**2. Write a short note on two main types of roots.**

**Ans.** Two main type of roots are tap root and adventitious root. Tap root develops from the radicle of the embryo, e.g. pea, gram, etc. Adventitious root develops from any part of the plant other than the radicle, e.g. wheat, rice, etc. (1+1)

**3. How is primary root different from secondary root?**

**Ans.** Primary root, also known as main root, develops from the radicle of the germinating seed. While, secondary root, also known as lateral root emerges from the primary root.

**4. Differentiate between fibrous roots and adventitious roots.**

**Ans.** Differences between fibrous and adventitious roots are

| Fibrous Roots | Adventitious Roots |
|---|---|
| They arise from the radicle. | These develop from any part of the plant other than radicle. |
| They help in anchorage and absorption. | They help in different functions like storage, climbing, respiration, etc. |
| They are found in grasses. | They are found in a variety of plants. |
| They are usually below the soil. | They may be underground or aerial. |

**5. What is pulvinus? Given two example of a plant that has pulvinus.**

**Ans.** Pulvinus is the swollen leaf base. It is found in some plants belonging to Leguminosae e.g. pea, bean, etc.

**6. Differentiate between pulvinus and petiole.**

**Ans.** Pulvinus is the swollen leaf base base whereas petiole is the stalk of the leaf that holds the leaf blade towards the light.

**7. Differentiate between reticulate venation and parallel venation.**

**Ans.** Differences between reticulate and parallel venation are

| Reticulate Venation | Parallel Venation |
|---|---|
| Veins are not oriented parallel to one another. | Veins are oriented parallel to one another. |
| Smaller veins produce a network or reticulum. | A reticulum is absent. |
| It is the characteristic feature of dicotyledons. | It is the characteristic feature of monocotyledons. |

(1 × 3)

**8. Venation is the network of veins on the lamina of a leaf.**

**(i) What is its use?**

**(ii) Name its types**

**Ans.** (i) The use of network of veins on lamina is to conduct water, mineral salts and food as they contain vascular tissues.

(ii) Venation is of two types, reticulate venation and parallel venation. (1 × 2)

**9. How is pinnately compound leaf different from a palmately compound leaf?** NCERT

**Ans.** Differences between pinnately and palmately compound leaf are

| Pinnately Compound Leaf | Palmately Compound Leaf |
|---|---|
| The leaflets arise lateral to the rachis all along its length. | Leaflets arise from the tip of the petiole like the fingers of a palm. |
| The rachis is present | The rachis is absent |
| e.g. rose, neem. | e.g. silk cotton. |

(1 × 3)

**10. Explain and draw the structure of flower.**

**Ans.** Refer to text on page no. 103 and fig. no. 5.9.

**11. A typical angiospermic flower consists of four floral parts. Give the names of the floral parts and their arrangement sequentially.** NCERT Exemplar

**Ans.** The four floral parts of typical angiospermic flower are

(i) **Calyx** It is the outermost whorl of the flower and its members are called sepals. These are usually green and are protective in function (in bud stage).

(ii) **Corolla** It is composed of petals, usually bright coloured to attract insects for pollination.

(iii) **Androecium** It is composed of stamens, the male reproductive organ. Each stamen has stalk or filament and anther (containing pollen sac and pollen grains).

(iv) **Gynoecium** It is the female reproductive part and made up of one or more carpels. Each carpel has stigma, style and ovary. (½ × 4)

**12. Flower is a reproductive unit of a plant.**

**(i) It is called modified shoot. Explain.**

**(ii) On which part, floral whorls are arranged?**

Competency Based Que.

**Ans.** (i) Flower is the reproductive unit of plant. It is called modified shoot. It has closely spaced nodes and condensed internodes, similar to a vegetative shoot. The various floral appendages such as petals and sepals arise from the nodes. (1)

(ii) Floral whorls are arranged on the thalamus, swollen end of the the stalk. (1)

**13. Define aestivation. Which type of aestivation is found in China rose, *Calotropis*, Gulmohar and Pea?**

**Ans.** The mode of arrangement of sepals and petals in a floral bud is known as aestivation. The type of aestivation found in the given plants are as follows.

- China rose - Twisted
- Gulmohar - Imbricate
- Calotropis - Valvate
- Pea - Vexillary (1+1)

**14. Distinguish between stamen and staminoide.** NCERT Exemplar

**Ans.** Differences between stamen and staminoide are

| Stamen | Staminoide |
|---|---|
| It is a complete functional male reproductive part of a flower. | It is rudimentary, sterile or non-functional male reproductive part of a flower. |
| It produces pollen grains. | It does not produce pollen grains. |

(1 × 2)

**15. Differentiate between apocarpous and syncarpous ovary.** NCERT

**Ans.** Difference between apocarpous and syncarpous ovary is

| Apocarpous Ovary | Syncarpous Ovary |
|---|---|
| It has more than one and free carpels. | It has more than one and fused carpels. |
| e.g. lotus, rose | e.g. tomato, mustard |

(1 × 2)

**16. Write the name of units of these flower parts.**

(i) Calyx (ii) Corolla
(iii) Androecium (iv) Gynoecium

**Ans.** (i) Calyx–Sepals
(ii) Corolla–Petals
(iii) Androecium–Stamens
(iv) Gynoecium–Carpels (½ × 4)

**17. Which structures forms the gynoecium? How is placenta related to gynoecium? What are its types?** Competency Based Que.

**Ans.** Gynoecium is the female reproductive whorl of the flower. It is composed of one or more carpels. Each carpel is differentiated into three parts, i.e. the ovary, style and stigma. (1)

Placenta is the tissue on which ovules develops in the ovary. The placentation in the ovary can be

(i) marginal (ii) axile
(iii) parietal (iv) basal
(v) free-central (2)

**18. How can you differentiate between free central and axile placentation?** NCERT Exemplar

**Ans.** **Placentation** is the arrangement of ovules within ovary with the help of special kind of tissue called placenta. Plants show different types of placentation, free-central and axile are among them. (1)

They have the following differences

| Free-central Placentation | Axile Placentation |
|---|---|
| Ovary is unilocular | Ovary is multilocular |
| The ovules are borne on the central axis and lies free inside the ovary. The septa are absent. | Placenta arise from the central axis where the septa fuse to form axile column to which ovules are attached. |

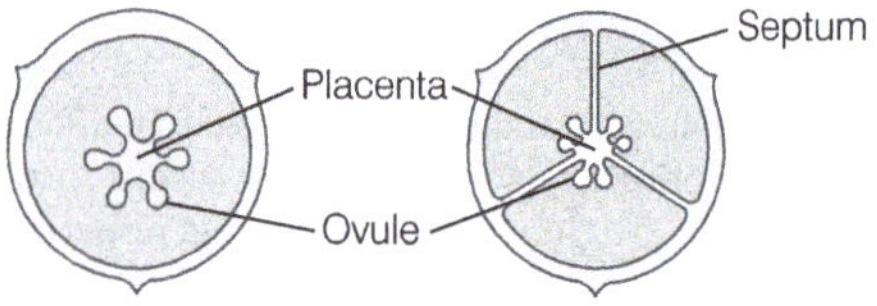


*e.g., Dianthus*, primrose, etc, *e.g., Citrus*, tomato, etc. (2)

**19. Draw the diagram of different types of arrangement of floral leaves on thalamus**

**Ans.** Refer to fig 5.12 on page no. 105.

**20. Define the term inflorescence. Explain the basis for the different types of inflorescence in flowering plants.** NCERT

**Ans.** Inflorescence is the arrangement and distribution of flowers on the floral axis.

Based on whether the floral axis continues to grow or ends in a flower, the inflorescence is classified into racemose and cymose. (1 × 2)

**21. Differentiate between racemose inflorescence and cymose inflorescence.** NCERT

**Ans.** Difference between racemose and cymose inflorescence are

| Racemose Inflorescence | Cymose Inflorescence |
|---|---|
| Flowers are borne in an acropetal succession. | Flowers are borne in the basipetal succession. |
| The growth of main axis is unlimited. | The growth of main axis is limited. |

(1 × 3)

**22. Describe the structure of a fruit with the help of a diagram.**

**Ans.** The fruit is a mature ovary that develops after fertilisation. Fruit consists of a wall named pericarp and seeds. Sometimes pericarp is fleshy and differentiated into outer epicarp, middle mesocarp and inner endocarp. (1½)

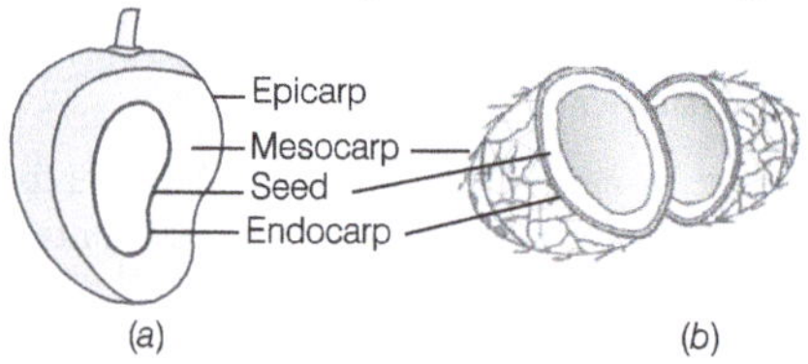


(a) (b) (1½)

**23. Distinguish between endospermic and non-endospermic seeds.**

**Ans.** Seeds that have endosperm as a food reserve are called endospermic seeds, e.g. castor, tomato, etc. while, seeds that lack endosperm on maturity are called non-endospermic seeds, e.g. pea, beans, etc.

**24. A maize grain is not a seed. Explain.**

**Ans.** A maize grain is a single-seeded fruit called caryopsis or grain, in which the pericarp (fruit wall) is inseparably fused with testa.

**25. (i) Why should plants be described morphologically?**

**(ii) What precautions should be taken while describing the features of plants?**

**(iii) Name some taxonomic characters to be described.**

**Ans.** (i) The description of morphological features helps in identifying and assigning a plant with its appropriate position in a taxonomic group.

(ii) While describing a plant, one should keep in mind that the description should be brief, in a simple and scientific language and presented in definite sequence.

(iii) The taxonomic characters to be described are habitat, habit, root, stem, leaves, flowers, inflorescence, calyx, corolla, androecium, gynoecium, fruits and seeds.

(1 × 3)

**26. How superior and inferior ovaries are indicated by symbol? How are the two different?**

**Ans.** Superior ovary, is represented by $\underline{G}$. Inferior ovary is represented by $\overline{G}$.

The ovary is superior when it is present at the upper position on thalamus as compared to other whorls as seen in China rose. On the other hand, it is inferior when the margin of thalamus grows inward and encloses the ovary completely, while the other parts rise above the ovary. It is seen in guava or cucumber.

**27. Draw or write the symbols for following.**

**(i) Hermaphrodite (bisexual)**
**(ii) Pistillate**
**(iii) Perianth**
**(iv) Staminate**
**(v) Inferior ovary**
**(vi) Ebracteate**

**Ans.** (i) ⚥ (ii) ♀
(iii) P (iv) ♂
(v) $\overline{G}$ (vi) Ebr (½ × 6)

**28. Explain the following floral diagram.**

**Competency Based Que.**

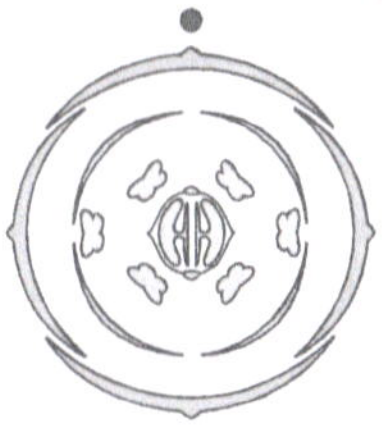

**Ans.** The floral formula of the given floral diagram is

Ebr ⊕ ⚥ $K_{2+2}$ $C_4$ $A_{2+4}$ $G_{(2)}$ belongs to mustard (*Brassica*). It represents ebracteate, actinomorphic, bisexual flower; calyx-4, polysepalous, in two whorls of two each; corolla 4, polypetalous, androecium-6, polyandrous, tetradynamous in two whorls, gynoecium-bicarpellary, syncarpous and superior. (1+2)

**29. Describe the vegetative characteristics of family–Solanaceae.**

**Ans.** Refer to text on page no. 109.

**30. List out any five diagnostic features of family–Solanaceae.**

**Ans.** Diagnostic features of Solanaceae family are as follows

(i) Annual or perennial herbs.
(ii) Flowers are actinomorphic, hypogynous and pentamerous.
(iii) Corolla has 5, united sepals having valvate aestivation.
(iv) Stamens are five having epipetalous condition.
(v) Gynoecium is bicarpellary, syncarpous having bilocular ovary with swollen placenta and many ovules.

**31. Describe the economic importance of family-Solanaceae.**

**Ans.** Refer to text on page no. 109.

## Long Answer Type Questions

**1. Describe the different regions of root and draw a well-labelled diagram.**

**Ans.** Refer to text on page no. 99 and fig. no. 5.2.

**2. Explain with suitable examples the different types of phyllotaxy.** **NCERT**

**Ans.** The mode of arrangement of leaves on the stem and its branches is called phyllotaxy (*Phyllon*–leaf; *taxis*–arrangement). Leaves are arranged systematically, so as to get proper sunlight and avoid overcrowding. (2)

Phyllotaxy in leaves is of following three types

(i) **Alternate** A single leaf arises at a node in alternate manner, e.g. China rose, mustard, sunflower, etc.

(ii) **Opposite** Two leaves arise at a node, opposite to each other, e.g. guava, *Calotropis*, etc.

(iii) **Whorled** More than two leaves arise at each node forming a circle or whorl, e.g. *Alstonia* , etc. (3)

**3. What is flower? Describe the parts of a typical angiospermic flower.** NCERT

**Ans.** A flower is a modified, condensed shoot specialised to carry out sexual reproduction in higher plants. A typical flower has a stalk, called pedicel and four different whorls arranged in a ring and fixed on a swollen structure called thalamus. (2)

A typical angiospermic flower consists of following four parts

(i) **Calyx** It is the outermost whorl of flower. Its individual units are sepals.

(ii) **Corolla** It is the inner whorl of flower next to calyx. The individual units are petals. They are brightly coloured.

(iii) **Androecium** It is the third whorl of flower whose individual units are stamens.

(iv) **Gynoecium or Pistil** It is the fourth and the inner most whorl. The individual units are carpels. (3)

**4. The mode of arrangement of sepals or petals in the floral bud is known as aestivation. Draw the various types of aestivation possible for a typical pentamerous flower.** NCERT Exemplar

**Ans.** Refer to fig. no. 5.10 on page no. 104.

**5. Describe the various types of placentations found in flowering plants.** NCERT

**Ans.** The arrangement of ovules within the ovary is called placentation.

It is of following types

(i) **Marginal** The placenta forms a ridge along the ventral suture and ovules are borne on the ridge, e.g. pea, bean, etc.

(ii) **Axile** The margins of the carpels fuse to form a central axis on which the ovules are attached, e.g. *Hibiscus, Citrus,* etc.

(iii) **Parietal** The placenta develops on the ovary wall, e.g. *Argemone.*

(iv) **Basal** The placenta arises from the base of the unilocular ovary and bears a single ovule, e.g. sunflower.

(v) **Free-Central** The ovules are borne on central axis and septa are absent, e.g. primrose. $(1 \times 5)$

**6. The arrangement of ovules within the ovary is known as placentation. What does the term placenta refer to? Name and draw various types of placentations in the flower as seen in TS or VS.** NCERT Exemplar

**Ans.** Refer to text on page no. 104 and 105. For diagram refer to fig. 5.11 on page no. 105.

**7. Define the following terms.**

(i) Aestivation

(ii) Placentation

(iii) Actinomorphic

(iv) Zygomorphic

(v) Superior ovary

(vi) Perigynous ovary

(vii) Epipetalous stamen NCERT

**Ans.** (i) **Aestivation** The mode of arrangement of sepals or petals in relation to one another in a flower bud is called aestivation.

(ii) **Placentation** The pattern by which the ovules are arranged in an ovary is called placentation.

(iii) **Actinomorphic** A flower having radial symmetry is said to be actinomorphic. The parts of each whorl are similar in size and shape. The flower can be divided in two equal halves along more than one median longitudinal plane.

(iv) **Zygomorphic** A flower having bilateral symmetry is termed as **zygomorphic**. The parts of one or more whorls are dissimilar. The flower can be divided into two equal halves in only one vertical plane.

(v) **Superior ovary** The ovary is called superior when it occupies the highest position and the other parts are situated below it.

(vi) **Perigynous ovary** It is the condition in which gynoecium of a flower is situated in the centre and other parts of the flower are located on the rim of the thalamus almost at the same level.

(vii) **Epipetalous stamen** Stamens that are connected to the petals by their filaments, are said to be epipetalous. [5]

**8. Describe the arrangement of floral members in relation to their insertion on thalamus.** NCERT

**Ans.** Refer to text on page no. 105.

**9. Sunflower is not a flower. Explain.** NCERT Exemplar

**Ans.** Sunflower is not a flower, but it is a kind of inflorescence called capitulum in which the receptacle is flattened. It bears numerous sessile and small florets. The youngest floret is in the centre and oldest lies at the periphery. Whole cluster of florets gets surrounded by bracts, known as involucre. (2½)

Two kinds of florets are recognised in sunflower

(i) **Ray Florets** Arranged on the rim of receptacle having distinct yellow and strap-shaped petals. These florets are female, sterile and are always zygomorphic and may be arranged in one or more whorls.

(ii) **Disc Florets** Grouped in the centre, bisexual and actinomorphic. (2½)

**10. Draw the labelled diagram of the following.** **NCERT**

**(i) Gram seed**

**(ii) VS of maize seed**

**Ans.** (i)

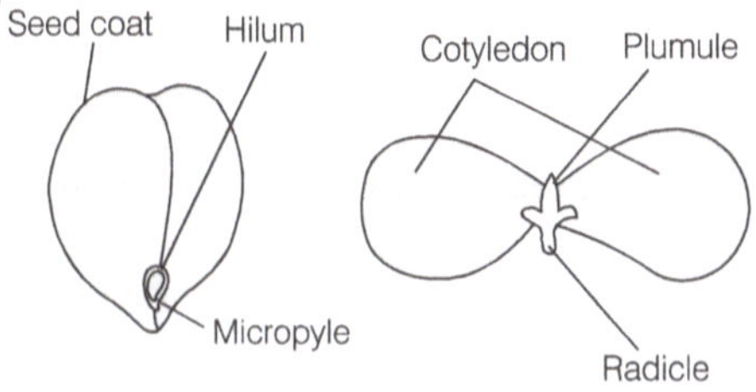


Structure of gram seed (2½)

(ii)

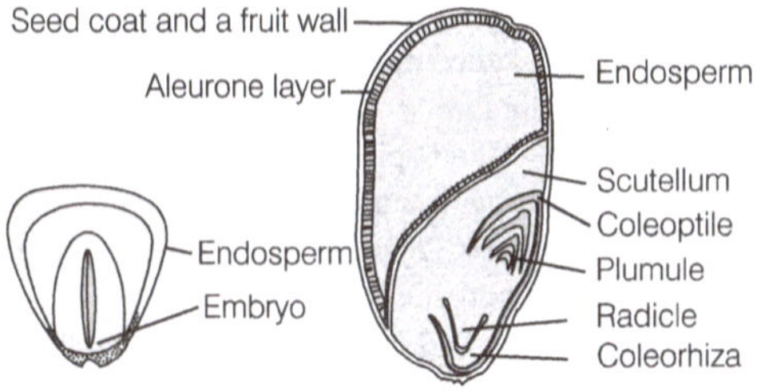


VS of maize seed (2½)

**11. Take one flower of the family–Solanaceae and write its semi-technical description. Also draw their floral diagram.** **NCERT**

**Ans.** *Solanum tuberosum* (potato) flower of family–Solanaceae.

- **Vegetative characters** Plants mostly herbs, shrubs and rarely small trees
- **Stem** Herbaceous, aerial; erect, cylindrical, branched, solid
- **Leaves** Alternate, simple, venation reticulate
- **Floral Characters**
- **Inflorescence** Solitary and axillary
- **Flower** Bisexual, actinomorphic
- **Calyx** Sepals five united valvate aestivation
- **Corolla** Petals five united valvate aestivation
- **Androecium** Stamens five, epipetalous
- **Gynoecium** Bicarpellary obligately placed, syncarpous, ovary superior, bilocular, placenta swollen with many ovules, axile
- **Fruits** berry or capsule
- **Seeds** many, endospermous
- **Floral Formula** $\oplus$ ⚥ $K_{(5)}\,\widehat{C_{(5)}\,A_5}\,\underline{G}_{(2)}$ (3)

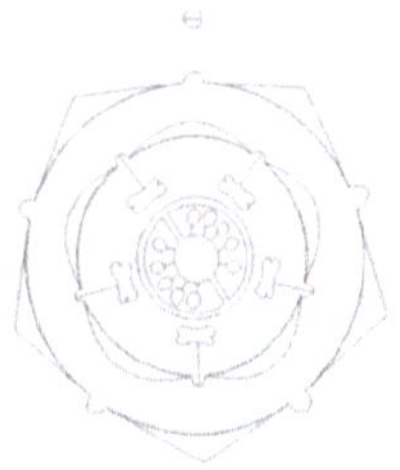

Floral diagram of *Solanum*

## Source Based/Case Based/Passage Based Questions

**1. Read the following passage and answer the questions that follows**

**During the field trip to a botanical garden, Raju observed different patterns of leaves arranged on the stem/branch of different plants. He collected three samples, given below as *A*, *B* and *C*. Study the figure and answer the following question.** **Competecny Based Que.**

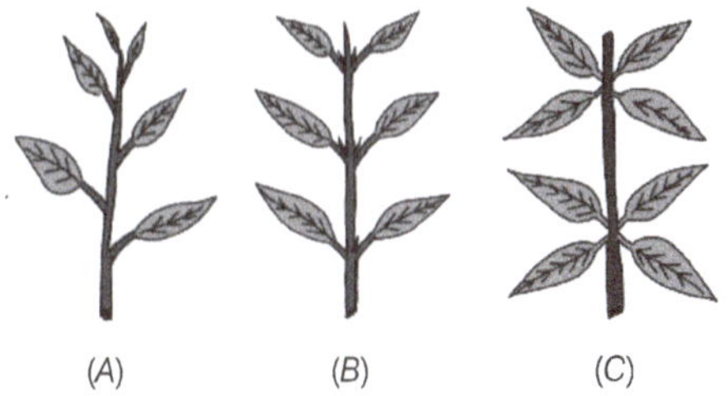


**(i) What term is used for this arrangement in the samples?**

**(ii) Identify the type of arrangement in *B*.**

**(iii) Describe the type of leaf arrangement as observed in *C*. Give an example of a plant with this arrangement.**

*Or*

**(iii) Which of the given plant denotes alternate phyllotaxy? Give two examples of plants with this arrangement.**

**Ans.** (i) Phyllotaxy (1)

(ii) Opposite phyllotaxy (1)

(iii) *C* denotes whorled phyllotaxy. In this more than two leaves arise at a node, forming whorl, e.g *Alstonia*. (2)

*Or*

(iii) Plant *A* represents alternate phyllotaxy. In this, a single leaf arises at each node in alternate manner, e.g. in China rose, mustard. (2)

**2.** **Ramesh visited the botanical garden during the spring season and observed various plants with colourful inflorescences. He noticed two major types of inflorescences (*A* and *B*) shown below. Study the figures and answer the questions that follows.**

A

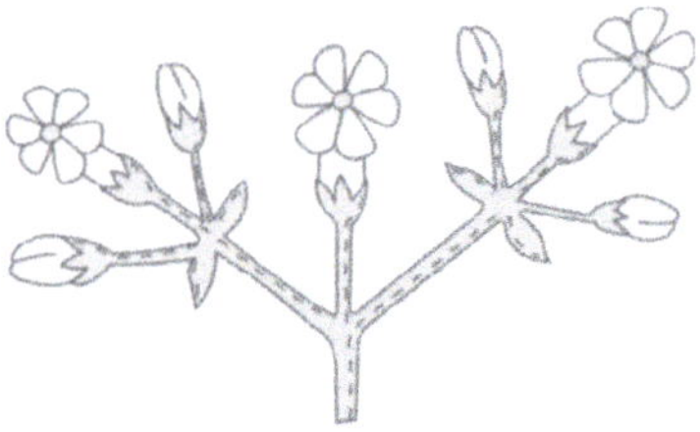

B

**(i) Identify the type of inflorescence, *A* and *B* shown above.**

**(ii) What forms the basis for this classification?**

**(iii) How are the flowers borne in *A* different from those borne in *B*?**

**(iv) Which of the following, *A* or *B*, has the definite growth, and why?**

**Ans.** (i) A represents racemose inflorescence, while *B* represents cymose inflorescence. (1)

(ii) They are both classified based on whether the apex develops into a flower or continues to grow. (1)

(iii) In inflorescence *A*, the flowers are borne in acropetal succession, whereas in *B*, they are borne in basipetal succession. (1)

(iv) Inflorescence *B* has a definite axis because the growth of main axis is terminated by a flower. (1)

**3.** **Read the given passage and answer the questions that follows.**

**Ramesh's mother planted various plants in her garden, and he observed that all the plants exhibited cymose inflorescence with pentamerous, bisexual, and actinomorphic flowers. He further noted that each plant had five sepals and petals, both of which were united. Moreover, the sexual organs, i.e., the gynoecium, were bicarpellary, syncarpous, and had a superior ovary, while the androecium was comprised of five stamens, having a polyandrous and epipetalous condition.**

**(i) Based on the given information, write the floral formula of the plants.**

**(ii) What type of placentation will be present in these plants?**

**(iii) Write any two economic importance of the plant family discussed above.**

**Ans.** (i) $\oplus ⚥ K_{(5)} \overset{\frown}{C_{(5)} A_5} \underline{G}_{(2)}$ (1)

(ii) Axile placentation (1)

(iii) Plants belonging to the family–Solanaceae have their importance in the following fields (any two)

- **Food** The family–Solanaceae includes a number of vegetables and spice yielding plants, e.g., potato, brinjal, tomato, chillies etc.
- **Fumigatory** Tobacco is used for chewing, smoking and snuff.
- **Medicines** *Belladonna* and ashwagandha are used to obtain medicines.
- **Ornamentals** *Petunia* is the commonly used ornamental plant. (2)

# SELF ASSESSMENT TEST

## Multiple Choice Questions

1. Which of the following functions is not associated with roots?
   (a) Synthesis of plant growth regulators
   (b) Storage of reserve food material
   (c) Conduction of water, mineral and photosynthates
   (d) Absorption of water and minerals

2. Which of the following is not matched correctly?
   (a) Alternate phyllotaxy- China rose, mustard
   (b) Pinnately compound leaves- Neem, rose
   (c) Palmately compound leaves- Silk, cotton
   (d) Opposite phyllotaxy- *Alstonia* and guava

3. Which of the following statement is correct for perianth?
   (a) Calyx and corolla are not distinct
   (b) Calyx is present, corolla is absent
   (c) Calyx is absent, corolla is present
   (d) Calyx and corolla are absent

4. The following diagrams represent the types of aestivation in corolla. Identify the correct combination of labeling.

   (a) *A*- Twisted, *B*- Vexillary
   (b) *A*-Vexillary, *B*- Twisted
   (c) *A*-Imbricate, *B*-Twisted
   (d) *A*-Twisted, *B*-Imbricate

5. In China rose, the stamens are united to form a single bundle. The plant is said to be
   (a) monadelphous (b) diadelphous (c) polyadelphous (d) apocarpous

6. If the gynoecium is situated in the centre and other parts of the flower are located on the rim of the thalamus almost at the same level, then the flower is referred to as
   (a) hypogynous, having inferior ovary
   (b) perigynous, having superior ovary
   (c) epigynous, having inferior ovary
   (d) perigynous, having half inferior ovary

7. Mango and coconut have fruits called drupes. Identify the correct statement regarding the fruit.
   (a) It develops from monocarpellary superior ovary and is one seeded
   (b) It develops from bicarpellary superior ovary and is many seeded
   (c) It develops from monocarpellary inferior ovary and is one seeded
   (d) It develops from bicarpellary inferior ovary and is many seeded

8. Which of the following features are related to gynoecium of Solanaceae family?
   (a) Bicarpellary, apocarpous, axile placentation
   (b) Monocarpellary, apocarpous, basal placentation
   (c) Bicarpellary, syncarpous, axile placentation
   (d) Bicarpellary, syncarpous, axile placentation

## Assertion-Reason Questions

**Direction** (Q. Nos. 9-12) *In each of the following questions, a statement of Assertion (A) is given followed by corresponding statement of Reason (R). Of the statements, mark the correct answer as*

(a) If both A and R are true and R is the correct explanation of A.
(b) If both A and R are true, but R is not the correct explanation of A.
(c) If A is true, but R is false.
(d) If A is false, but R is true.

9. **Assertion** (A) The root is the non -green, and descending part of the plant.

   **Reason** (R) The chlorophyll is absent in the roots and they grows downward due to influence of gravity.

10. **Assertion** (A) In reticulate venation, the veins run parallel to each other within the lamina.
**Reason** (R) Reticulate venation is generally absent in monocot leaves.

11. **Assertion** (A) Corolla lies inner to the calyx and is generally composed of brightly coloured petals.
**Reason** (R) Petals attract insects for pollination.

12. **Assertion** (A) In the floral diagram, there is a dot on the top of the floral diagram.
**Reason** (R) The dot represents the position of the mother axis with respect to the flower.

## Very Short Answer Type Questions

13. Give any two examples of plants having syncarpous ovary.
14. Name the type of placentation found in *Agremone*.
15. Distinguish between testa and tegmen.
16. How is mother axis represented in the floral diagram?

## Short Answer Type Questions

17. What are root hairs? Also, mention their function.
18. List the important functions performed by the stem.
19. How valvate aestivation is different from twisted aestivation?

## Long Answer Type Questions

20. Differentiate between the following
(i) Region of elongation and region of maturation
(ii) Gynoecium and androecium
21. Describe the structure of the maize grain with the help of well-labelled diagram.
22. Give a comparative account of family–Solanaceae.

## Case Based Question

23. A group of students went on a field trip to explore the natural environment around them. As part of their activity, they collected samples of leaves from various plants in their area. They managed to collect three distinct types of leaves, each with unique characteristics, which are given below as *A*, *B* and *C*. Study the figure and answer the following questions.

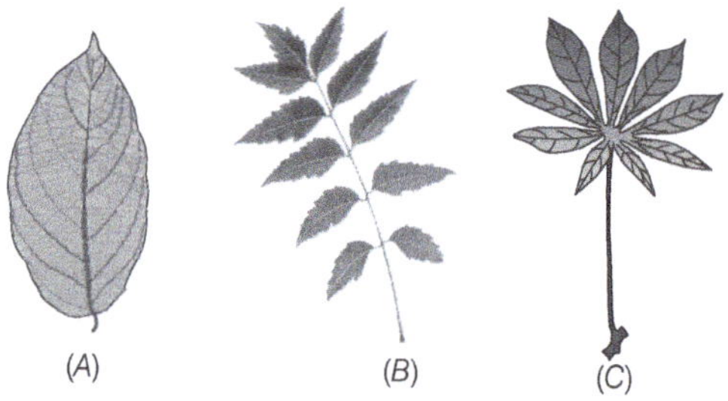

(A) (B) (C)

(i) Identify the type of leaves shown in the *A*, *B* and *C*.
(ii) Give the example of the plants that have *B* and *C* types of leaves.
(iii) Write two point of difference between *B* and *C*.

# Answers

| | | | | | | |
|---|---|---|---|---|---|---|
| 1. (c) | 2. (d) | 3. (a) | 4. (d) | 5. (a) | 6. (d) | 7. (a) |
| 8. (c) | 9. (a) | 10. (d) | 11. (a) | 12. (a) | | |

06

CHAPTER

# Anatomy of Flowering Plants

The study of internal structure of plant is called **plant anatomy.**
Plants consists of cells as the basic unit of life. These cells are organised into tissues, which are further organised into organs. Different plant organs display variations in their internal structure.
These variations in internal structure also provides information about the structural adaptations of plants to diverse environments.

### YOUR STUDY GOALS

6.1 Tissue System
6.2 Anatomy of Dicotyledonous and Monocotyledonous Plants

### YOUR PRACTICE GOAL

- Objective Type Questions (24 Qs ; MCQs, A-R) Case Based Questions (3)
- Subjective Type Questions
- (11 VSAs, 17 SAs, 10 LAs)

In this chapter, we will study different plant tissue systems and internal structure of dicot and monocot plants.

## 6.1 Tissue System

- It refers to a group of tissues that work together to perform a specific functions in the plant body.
- The structure and function of tissues depend on their location in the plant body.
- Thus, on the basis of their structure and location, there are three different types of tissue system, i.e. epidermal tissue system, ground or fundamental tissue system and vascular or conducting tissue system.
- Let us study each of them in detail given below.

### I. Epidermal Tissue System

- It forms the outermost covering of the whole plant body.
- It consists of **epidermis, stomata** and the **epidermal appendages,** (i.e. trichomes and hairs).

- These are discussed in detail below.

## 1. Epidermis

- The epidermis (Gk. *Epi*–upon; *derma* –skin) is the **outermost protective layer** of the primary plant body.
- The epidermal cells are elongated and compactly arranged to form a continuous layer.
- It is usually **single-layered.**
- The epidermal cells are **parenchymatous** and **living.** These cells possess a large vacuole and a small amount of cytoplasm lining the cell wall.
- The outside of the epidermis is covered with a thick waxy layer called **cuticle,** which prevents the loss of water.
- The cuticle is absent in roots.

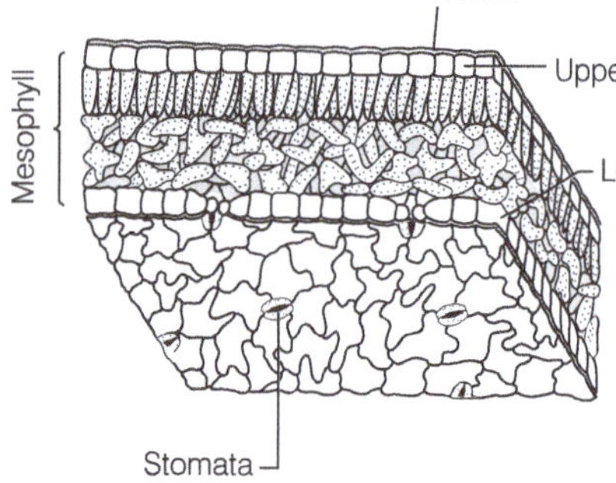


Fig. 6.1 Epidermis with a layer of cuticle

## 2. Stomata

- The stomata (Sing. stoma) are the openings found in the epidermis of most of the aerial parts of the plants, especially the leaves.
- They regulates the process of transpiration and gaseous exchange.
- Each stoma is composed of two bean-shaped cells called **guard cells,** which enclose stomatal pore.
- In grasses, the guard cells are **dumb-bell shaped.**
- The **outer walls** of guard cells (away from the stomatal pore) are thin and the **inner walls** (towards the stomatal pore) are highly thickened.
- The guard cells possess **chloroplasts** and regulate the opening and closing of stomata.
- Sometimes, a few epidermal cells, in the vicinity of the guard cells became specialised in their shape and size and are known as **subsidiary cells.**
- The stomatal aperture, guard cells and the surrounding subsidiary cells are together called **stomatal apparatus.**

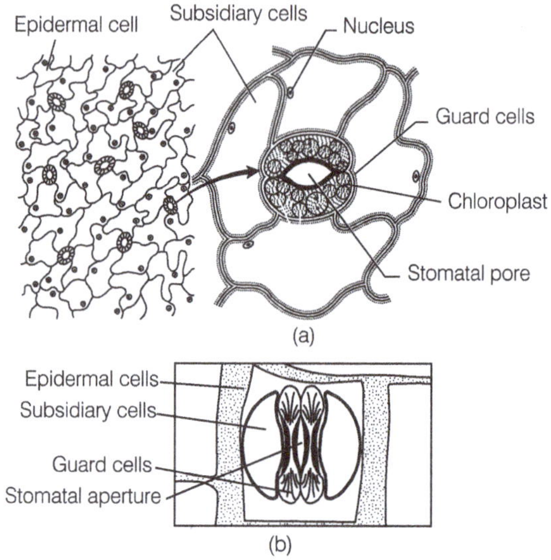


Fig. 6.2 Structure of stomata, (a) in dicot plant (Bean-shaped) (b) in monocot plant (Dumb-bell shaped)

## 3. Epidermal Appendages (Outgrowths)

The epidermis of most plants often bears an outgrowth known as epidermal appendages or epidermal outgrowths. They are of following two main types

- **Trichomes** The epidermal hairs present on the stem are called trichomes.
  - They are usually multicellular which can be branched or unbranched and soft or stiff.
  - They may even be secretory in nature.
  - They also help in checking the rate of transpiration from aerial plant surfaces.
- **Root hairs** They are unicellular elongations of the epidermal cells. They help to absorb water and minerals from the soil.

## Functions of Epidermal Tissue System

Epidermal tissue system serves the following important functions.

- It provides a **protective covering** all over the plant parts.
- It helps in **gas exchange** through the stomata.
- The presence of cuticle helps in the **reduction of evaporation** of water.
- The glandular trichomes excrete various **useful plant products** for the plant function.

## II. Ground Tissue System

- All tissues, except epidermis and vascular bundles constitutes the ground tissue.
- It consists of a simple tissues, such as parenchyma, collenchyma and sclerenchyma.
- Parenchymatous cells are commonly located in the cortex, pericycle, pith and medullary rays in the primary stem and roots.
- In leaves, the ground tissue consists of thin-walled chloroplast containing cells is called **mesophyll**.

## III. Vascular Tissue System

- A vascular bundle is a strand of conducting tissue, which is generally composed of complex tissues, the xylem and phloem.
- In dicots, a meristematic tissue called **cambium** is present between xylem and phloem.
- The arrangement of xylem and phloem is the characteristic to particular plant organs.
- Thus, on the basis of arrangement of xylem and phloem in the vascular bundles, there are two types of bundles, i.e. **radial** and **conjoint**.

### 1. Radial

- The xylem and phloem within a vascular bundle alternate with each other along the different radii.
- It is found mainly in roots.

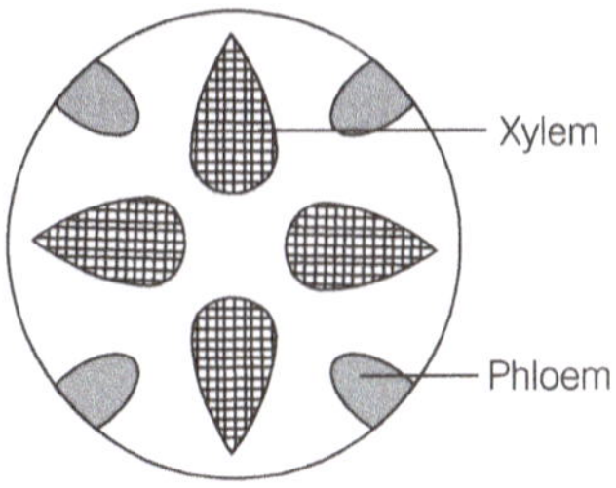

Fig. 6.3 Radial vascular bundle

### 2. Conjoint

- The xylem and phloem are present together in the same bundle on the same radius.
- It is mainly found in stem and leaves.
- They usually have phloem located only on the outer side of xylem.
- Conjoint vascular bundles are of two types

#### Conjoint Open

- **In dicot stem**, the cambium is found to be present in between the xylem and phloem. (vascular bundle).
- Such vascular bundles possess the ability to form secondary xylem and phloem tissues and hence, are called **open vascular bundles**.

#### Conjoint Closed

- **In monocots**, the cambium is absent in between the vascular bundle. Hence, since they do not form secondary tissues they are referred to as a **closed vascular bundle**.

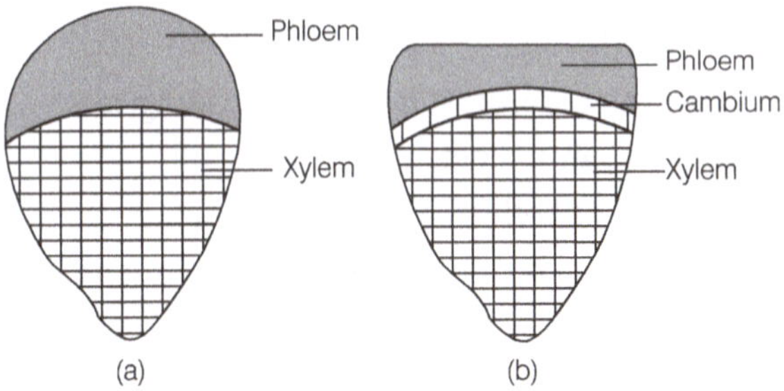

Fig. 6.4 Conjoint vascular bundle : (a) Closed, (b) Open

**TEACHER'S TIP**

On the basis of size and development, xylem is classified into two types: protoxylem and metaxylem. **Protoxylem** consists of smaller cells that are formed first during the plant's development, whereas **metaxylem** consists of larger cells that are formed after protoxylem.

**Quick Test 1**

1. Mention different type of tissue system on the basis of structure and location.
2. A separate layer of cuticle covers the epidermis. Give its one use.
3. Which tissue of the leaves contains chloroplasts?
4. A plant part, 'X' has unicellular outgrowth and lacks the waxy layer called cuticle. Identify 'X'.
5. Name the type of vascular bundles in case of
   (a) root
   (b) stems and leaves
6. Name the term used to describe the vascular bundles in which cambium is present between xylem and phloem.

## 6.2 Anatomy of Dicotyledonous and Monocotyledonous Plants

The tissue organisation of roots, stems and leaves can be studied better and conveniently by the **transverse sections** of the mature zones of the following mentioned plant parts.

### Dicotyledonous Root

- The internal structure of dicot root can be studied from the transverse section (TS) of a young root of sunflower, pea or gram.
- The following structures can be seen from periphery towards the centre.

#### 1. Epiblema

- It forms the **outermost layer** in the young root.
- It is equivalent to epidermis of stem.
- It is devoid of both stomata and cuticle.
- Some of the epiblema cells protude to form unicellular structures called **root hairs.**

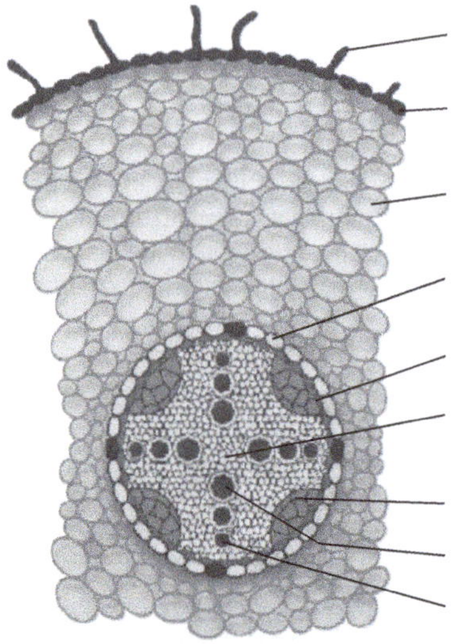


Fig. 6.5 TS of a dicot root (primary)

#### 2. Cortex

- It lies beneath the epiblema.
- It consists of several layers of thin-walled parenchymatous cells with conspicuous intercellular spaces.

#### 3. Endodermis

- The **innermost layer** of the cortex is endodermis.
- It comprises of a single layer of barrel-shaped cells without any intercellular spaces.
- They have characteristic bands of thickenings along their radial and tangential walls. These are called **Casparian strips.**
- The Casparian strips are made up of water impermeable, waxy material called suberin.

#### 4. Stele

All tissues on the innerside of the endodermis such as pericycle, vascular bundle and pith constitute the stele. These are described below.

- **Pericycle** It is a layer of thick-walled parenchymatous cells that lies next to endodermis.

  The initiation of lateral roots and vascular cambium during the secondary growth takes place in these cells.
- **Vascular Bundles** It consists of separate bundles of xylem and phloem arranged alternately inner to the pericycle.
  - There are usually two to four xylem and phloem patches.
  - The phloem and xylem bundles are separated from each other by parenchymatous cells called **conjunctive tissue.**
  - Later, it becomes meristematic and forms a vascular cambium between xylem and phloem.
  - Secondary growth occurs in dicot roots.
- **Pith** It is generally small or inconspicuous in dicot roots.

### Monocotyledonous Root

- The anatomy of the monocot root is similar to the dicot root in many aspects.
- It has epidermis, cortex, endodermis, pericycle, vascular bundles and pith.
- In contrast to dicot roots, which have fewer xylem bundles, monocot roots usually have more than six (polyarch) xylem bundles.
- Pith is large and well-developed.

- Monocotyledonous roots do not undergo any secondary growth.

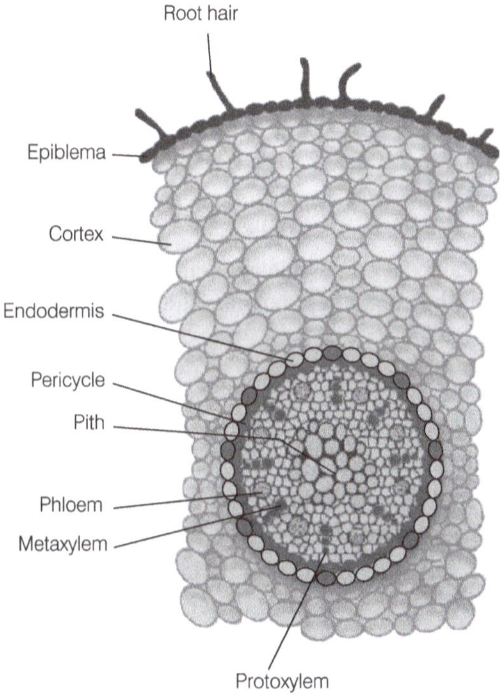


**Fig. 6.6** TS of monocot root

## Dicotyledonous Stem

The transverse section (TS) of a typical young dicotyledonous stem shows the following areas.

### 1. Epidermis

- It is the outermost protective layer of the stem.
- It is covered with a thin-layer of cuticle and may bear **trichomes** and a few **stomata**.

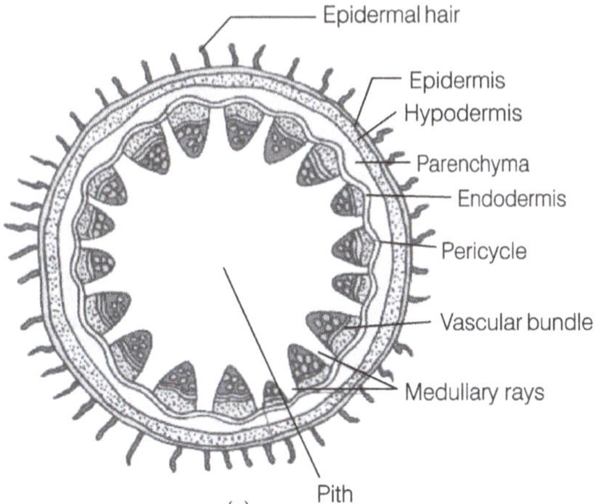


(a)

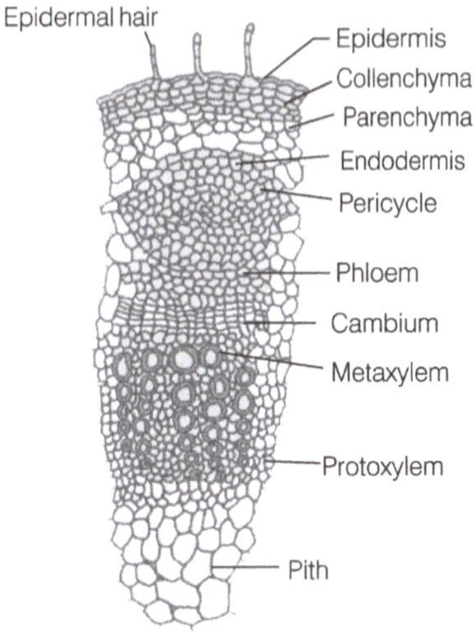


(b)

**Fig. 6.7** (a) and (b) TS of a dicot stem

### 2. Cortex

This layer lies just below the epidermis and extends till pericycle. The cells in this layer are arranged in multiple layers. It consists of three sub-zones, i.e. hypodermis, cortical layer and endodermis. These are described below.

- **Hypodermis** It is found just below the epidermis consisting of few layers **collenchymatous cells**. It provides **mechanical strength** to the young stem.
- **Cortical layer** It is located just below the hypodermis and consists of a few layers of parenchymatous cells. These cells are round, thin-walled with conspicuous intercellular spaces.
- **Endodermis** It is the innermost layer of cortex. The endodermal cells are abundant in starch grains and thus, this layer is also known as **starch sheath.**

### 3. Pericycle

- It is present on the inner side of the endodermis and above the phloem in the form of semi-lunar patches of sclerechyma.

### 4. Vascular bundles

- They are arranged in the form of a ring which is a characteristic feature of dicot stem.
- Each vascular bundle consists of **phloem** (on the outside), **xylem** (towards the inner side) with a strip of **cambium**, in between the two.
- The vascular bundles are thus, **conjoint**, **open** and with **endarch protoxylem** (protoxylem is situated closer to the centre of the vascular bundle).

### 5. Medullary

These are non-vascular areas present in between the vascular bundles. It consists of few layers of radially placed parenchymatous cells.

### 6. Pith

- It occupies the central part of the stem.
- It consists of rounded, parenchymatous cells with large intercellular spaces.

## Monocotyledonous Stem

- It has a sclerenchymatous hypodermis, a large number of scattered vascular bundles and a large, conspicuous parenchymatous ground tissue.
- Vascular bundles are conjoint and closed.
- Each vascular bundle is surrounded by a sclerenchymatous bundle sheath.
- Peripheral vascular bundles are generally smaller than the centrally located ones.
- The phloem parenchyma is absent, and water-containing cavities are present within the vascular bundles.

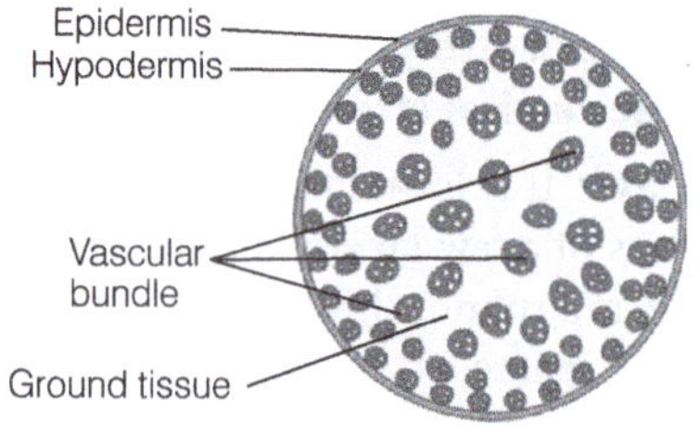


(a)

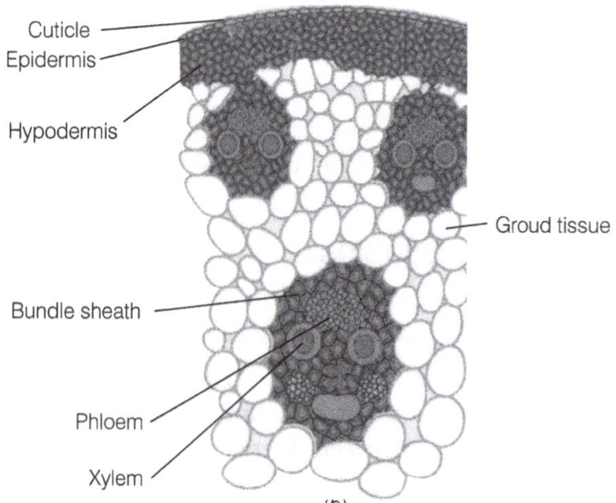


(b)

Fig. 6.8 (a) and (b) TS of monocot stem

## Dicotyledonous (Dorsiventral) Leaf

The vertical section of a dorsiventral leaf through the lamina shows the following main parts.

### 1. Epidermis

- It covers both the upper (adaxial) and the lower (abaxial) surfaces of the leaf.
- Both the surfaces are characterised by the presence of a conspicuous cuticle.
- The abaxial epidermis generally has more stomata than the adaxial epidermis. The later may even lack stomata.

### 2. Mesophyll

- It is the tissue present between the upper and the lower epidermis.
- Mesophyll, which possesses chloroplast and carry out photosynthesis is made up of parenchyma.
- It is differentiated in two parts in dorsiventral leaves, i.e. **upper palisade** and **lower spongy parenchyma**.
- The adaxially placed palisade parenchyma is made up of elongated cells, which are arranged vertically and parallel to each other.
- The oval or round and loosely arranged spongy parenchyma lies below the palisade parenchyma and extends to the lower epidermis.
- There are numerous large spaces and air cavities between these cells.

### 3. Vascular System

- It includes vascular bundles, which can be seen in the veins and the midrib.
- The vascular bundles are conjoint and closed.

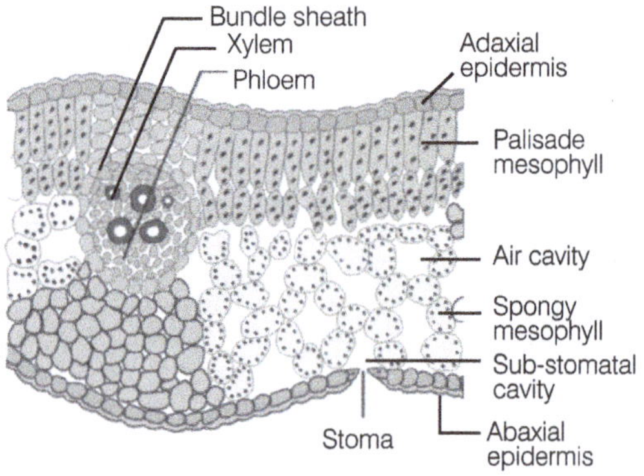


Fig. 6.9 TS of dicot leaf

- Each vascular bundle is surrounded by a layer of thick-walled cells known as **bundle sheath cells.**

- The size of vascular bundles varies according to the size of the veins.
- The veins vary in thickness in the reticulate venation of the dicot leaves.

## Monocotyledonous (Isobilateral) Leaf

The anatomy of isobilateral leaf is similar to that of the dorsiventral leaf in many ways. It shows the following characteristic differences.

- The stomata are present on both the surfaces of the epidermis.
- The mesophyll is not differentiated into palisade and spongy parenchyma.
- In grasses, certain adaxial epidermal cells along the veins modify themselves into large, empty, colourless cells. These are called **bulliform cells**.

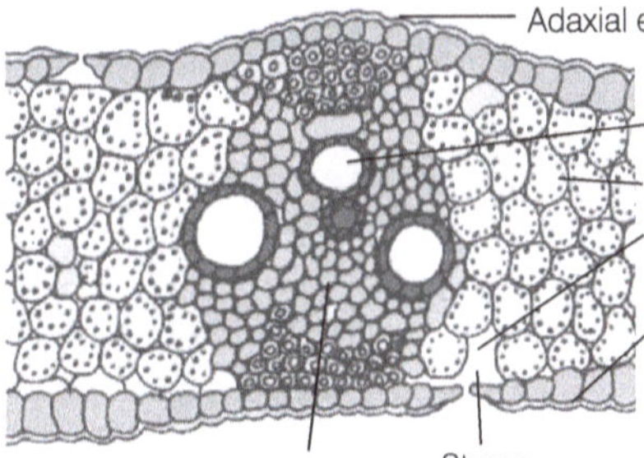


Fig. 6.10 TS of a monocot leaf

- When the bulliform cells in the leaves have absorbed water and are turgid, the leaf surface is exposed. When they are flaccid due to water stress, they make the leaves curl inwards to minimise water loss.
- The parallel venation in monocot leaves is reflected in the near similar sizes of vascular bundles (except in main veins) as seen in vertical sections of the leaves.

### Quick Test 2

1. The cross-section of a plant material showed the following features when viewed under the microscope.
   (a) Vascular bundles were radially arranged
   (b) Four xylem strands with exarch condition of protoxylem. To which organ should it be assigned? *NCERT Exemplar*
2. Name the tissue that lies between epidermis and pericycle.
3. What is present on the surface of the leaves, which helps the plan to prevent loss of water, but is absent in roots? *NCERT Exemplar*
4. **State True or False.**
   In monocot leaves, the size of vascular bundles is dependent on the size of veins.
5. Certain adaxial epidermal cells in grasses, along the veins modify themselves to large, empty, colourless cells. Name these cells.

# Mind Map

## Anatomy of Flowering Plants

### Tissue System

**Tissue System**

**Epidermal**
- **Cuticle** (waxy thick layer)
- **Epidermis** (outermost layer)
- **Epidermal appendages** — Epidermal hair; Trichome
- **Stomata** (transpiration and gaseous exchange)

**Ground tissue**
- **Hypodermis**
- **Cortex**
- **Endodermis, pericycle**
- **Medullary rays and pith**

**Vascular tissue**
- **Xylem**
- **Phloem**

**Types of Vascular Bundle**

**Radial bundles**
(Xylem and phloem occur on different radii)

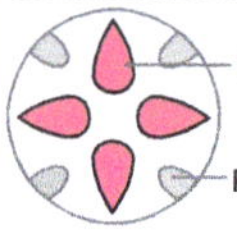


**Conjoint bundles**
(Xylem and phloem are situated at the same radius of vascular bundle)

**Open**

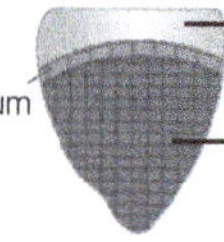


**Closed**

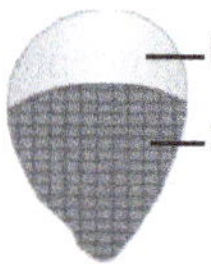


### Anatomy of Dicot and Monocot Roots

**Dicot Root**
- Cortex is comparatively narrower
- Endoderm is less thickened with more prominent Casparian strips
- 2-5 xylem and phloem bundles.
- Pith is small or inconspicuous or absent.
- Secondary growth takes place with the help of vascular cambium and cork cambium.
- Conjunctive tissue-parenchymatous.

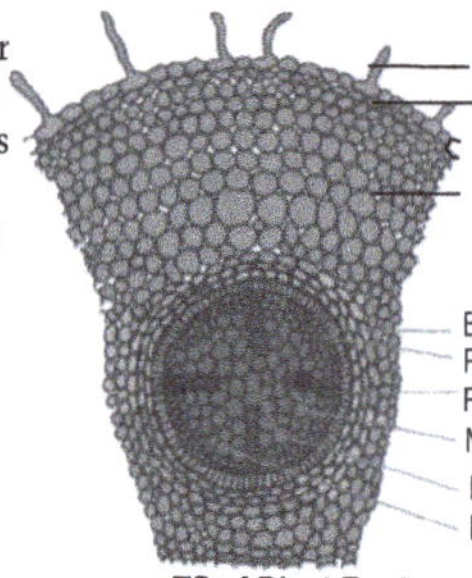


TS of Dicot Root

**Monocot Root**
- Cortex is wide.
- Endodermis with highly thickened Casparian strips (only visible in young roots).
- Xylem and phloem are more than 6 (polyarch).
- Pith is well-developed and large.
- Secondary growth is absent due to the absence of cambium.
- Conjunctive tissue-sclerenchymatous.

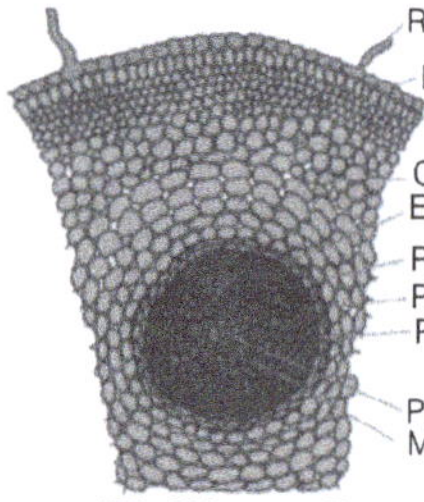


TS of Monocot Root

### Anatomy of Dicot and Monocot Stems

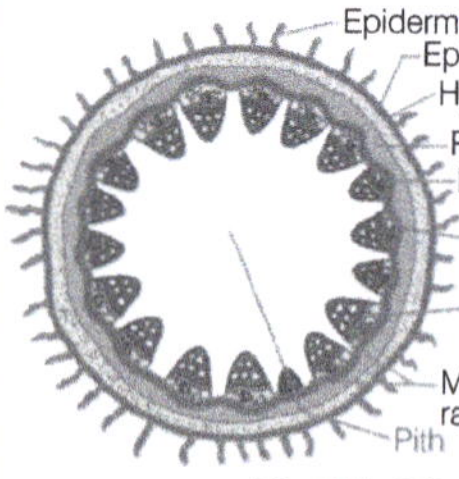


TS of Dicot Stem

**Dicot Stem**
- Vascular bundles are almost uniform size and are arranged in a ring.
- Vascular bundles are open.
- Presence of secondary growth (presence of cambium within phloem).
- Pith is well-developed.
- Presence of endodermis and pericycle.

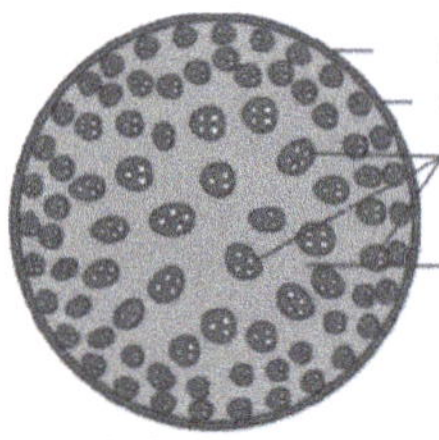


TS of Monocot Stem

**Monocot Stem**
- Vascular bundles are numerous and are scattered throughout the ground tissues.
- Vascular bundles are closed.
- Absence of secondary growth (on cambium).
- Pith is not well-developed or absent, endodermis and pericycle are absent.

### Anatomy of Dorsiventral (Dicot) and Isobilateral (Monocot) Leaf

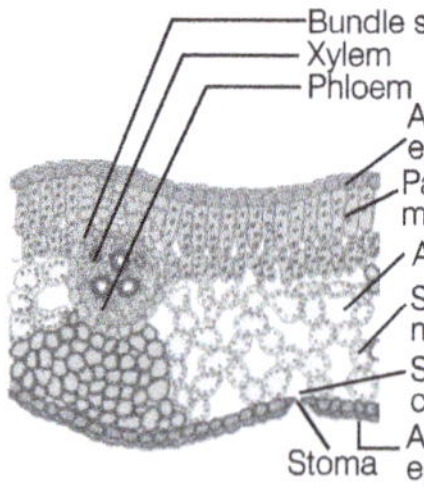


LS of Dicot Leaf

**Dicot Leaf**
- Stomata absent or less abundant on upper side.
- Mesophyll differentiated into palisade, parenchyma and spongy parenchyma.
- Bundle sheath layer is single layered.
- Kidney shaped guard cells.
- Absence of bulliform cells.

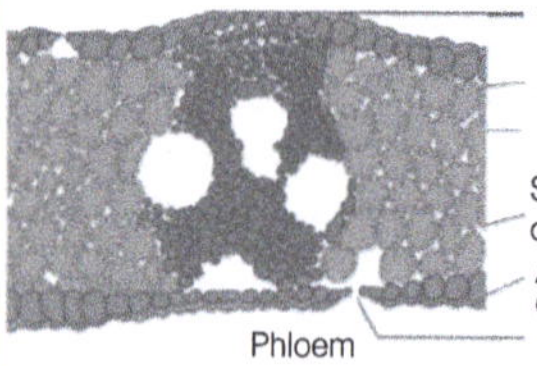


LS of Monocot Leaf

**Monocot Leaf**
- Stomata are equally distributed on both sides.
- Undifferentiated mesophyll.
- One or two layered bundle sheath.
- Dumb-bell shaped guard cells.
- Presence of bulliform cells.

# EXAM PATTERN QUESTIONS

## Objective Type Questions

### Multiple Choice Questions

**1. Read the given statements about epidermal tissue system and identify the incorrect statement.** **DIKSHA**

(a) Epidermal tissues are made up of elongated, compactly arranged cells, which form a continuous layer
(b) Epidermal hairs on the stem are called trichomes
(c) Stomata are present in the epidermis of leaves
(d) Epidermal tissue system consists of xylem and phloem

**Ans.** (*d*)

**2. Match the following columns.** **Competency Based Que.**

| | Column I | | Column II |
|---|---|---|---|
| A. | Bean-shaped guard cell | 1. | Dicot stem |
| B. | Dumb-bell shaped guard cell | 2. | Monocot leaf |
| C. | Trichome | 3. | Dicot leaf |
| D. | Mesophyll | 4. | Ground tissue system |

Codes

| | A | B | C | D | | A | B | C | D |
|---|---|---|---|---|---|---|---|---|---|
| (a) | 2 | 3 | 1 | 4 | (b) | 3 | 2 | 1 | 4 |
| (c) | 4 | 3 | 1 | 2 | (d) | 3 | 4 | 2 | 1 |

**Ans.** (*b*)

**3. Vascular bundle is considered open vascular bundle, when** **DIKSHA**

(a) cambium is present on the terminal side of xylem
(b) cambium is present between xylem and phloem
(c) no cambium present between xylem and phloem
(d) cambium is present on the terminal side of phloem

**Ans.** (*b*)

**4. A vascular bundle is a strand of conducting tissue which is generally composed of complex tissues-the xylem and phloem. Which out of the following type of vascular bundles is incorrect match?** **Competency Based Que.**

| | Diagram | Vascular bundle |
|---|---|---|
| (a) |  | Closed vascular bundle |
| (b) | 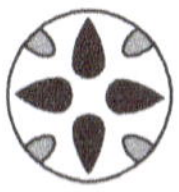 | Radial vascular bundle |
| (c) | 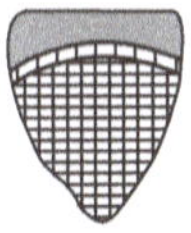 | Open vascular bundle |
| (d) |  | Conjoint open vascular bundle |

**Ans.** (*d*)

**5. Epiblema of roots is equivalent to** **NCERT Exemplar**

(a) pericycle
(b) endodermis
(c) epidermis
(d) stele

**Ans.** (*c*) Epidermis is usually a single layered structure, present all over the body surface of the plant. In case of root, it is called epiblema instead of epidermis.

**6. Water impermeable, waxy material secreted by endodermal cells in the form of Casparian strip is**

(a) lignin
(b) suberin
(c) conjunctive tissue
(d) pectin

**Ans.** (*b*)

**7. The central part of root occupied by parenchymatous (thin or thick-walled) cells is called**

(a) pith (b) pericycle
(c) endodermis (d) meristem

**Ans.** (*a*)

**8. Choose the correct option for monocotyledonous root.**

(a) Pith is large and well-developed
(b) No secondary growth
(c) Polyarch condition
(d) All of the above

**Ans.** (*d*)

**9.** A conjoint and open vascular bundle will be observed in the transverse section of **NCERT Exemplar**

(a) monocot root (b) monocot stem
(c) dicot root (d) dicot stem

**Ans.** (*d*)

**10.** Protoxylem is the first formed xylem. If the protoxylem lies closer to the centre of the vascular bundle. What kind of arrangement of xylem would you call it? **Competency Based Que.**

(a) Exarch (b) Endarch
(c) Mesarch (d) Centrarch

**Ans.** (*b*)

**11.** Vascular bundle is enclosed within a well-developed sclerenchymatous sheath in

(a) monocot stem (b) dicot stem
(c) monocot root (d) dicot root

**Ans.** (*a*)

**12.** Which of the following is characterised by the presence of water filled cavities within the vascular bundle?

(a) Monocotyledonous stem
(b) Dicotyledonous root
(c) Monocotyledonous root
(d) Dicotyledonous stem

**Ans.** (*a*)

**13.** Identify the false statement.

(a) Most of the dicotyledonous leaves are dorsiventral
(b) Stomata are aerating pores in the bark of plants
(c) The medullary rays are present in dicot stem
(d) Dicot stem has collenchymatous hypodermis

**Ans.** (*b*)

**14.** The vertical section of a dorsiventral leaf through the lamina shows three main parts namely, epidermis, ...*A*... and vascular system. The epidermis, which covers the upper surface is ...*B*... and lower surface is covered by ...*C*... of the leaf.

Choose the correct option to replace *A*, *B* and *C*.

(a) *A*–mesophyll, *B*–adaxial epidermis, *C*–abaxial epidermis
(b) *A*–endodermis, *B*–adaxial epidermis, *C*–abaxial epidermis
(c) *A*–endodermis, *B*–abaxial epidermis, *C*–adaxial epidermis
(d) *A*–mesophyll, *B*–abaxial epidermis, *C*–adaxial epidermis

**Ans.** (*a*)

**15.** Bulliform cells are present **DIKSHA**

(a) in some abaxial epidermal cells of monocots
(b) in both abaxial and adaxial epidermal cells of dicot leaves
(c) in some adaxial epidermal cells of grasses
(d) in adaxial epidermal cells of dicot leaves

**Ans.** (*c*)

**16.** Match the following columns. **Competency Based Que., NCERT Exemplar**

| | Column I | | Column II |
|---|---|---|---|
| A. | Cuticle | 1. | Guard cells |
| B. | Bulliform cells | 2. | Single layer |
| C. | Stomata | 3. | Waxy layer |
| D. | Epidermis | 4. | Empty colourless cell |

**Codes**

| | A | B | C | D | | A | B | C | D |
|---|---|---|---|---|---|---|---|---|---|
| (a) | 3 | 4 | 1 | 2 | (b) | 1 | 2 | 3 | 4 |
| (c) | 3 | 2 | 4 | 1 | (d) | 3 | 2 | 1 | 4 |

**Ans.** (*a*)

**17.** Choose the incorrect pair.

(a) Isobilateral leaf – Stomata are present on both surfaces
(b) Bulliform cells – Modified adaxial epidermal cells
(c) Monocot stem – Sclerenchymatous hypodermis
(d) Dicot root – Pith is large and well-developed

**Ans.** (*d*) The pair in option (d) is incorrect. It can be corrected as Monocot root- Pith is large and well-developed.

## Assertion-Reason Questions

**Direction** (Q. Nos. 1-7) *In each of the following questions, a statement of Assertion (A) is given followed by corresponding statement of Reason (R). Of the statements, mark the correct answer as*

(a) Both A and R are true and R is the correct explanation of the A.
(b) Both A and R are true, but R is not the correct explanation of the A.
(c) A is true, but R is false.
(d) A is false, but R is true.

**1. Assertion** (A) Root hairs are unicellular and trichomes are usually multicellular.

**Reason** (R) Root hairs are found in root epidermis and trichomes are found in stem epidermis.

**Ans.** (*b*)

2. **Assertion** (A) Vascular bundles are conjoint and closed in monocot stem.

 **Reason** (R) Vascular bundles are conjoint and open in dicot stem.

Ans. (*b*)

3. **Assertion** (A) The endodermal cells of dicot root do not contain Casparian strips thickening on their tangential walls.

 **Reason** (R) Casparian strips are made up of suberin that is impervious to water.

Ans. (*d*) A is false, but R is correct. It can be corrected as

The endodermal cells of dicot root contain Casparian strips thickening on their radial and transverse walls.

4. **Assertion** (A) Monocotyledonous roots do not undergo any secondary growth.

 **Reason** (R) Monocotyledonous roots have polyarch xylem bundles.

Ans. (*b*) Both A and R are true, but R is not the correct explanation of A

Monocotyledonous roots do not undergo any secondary growth due to the absence of cambium in their vascular tissues.

5. **Assertion** (A) Vascular bundles in monocots are considered closed.

 **Reason** (R) A bundle sheath surrounds each vascular bundle in monocot stem.

Ans. (*b*)

6. **Assertion** (A) Mesophyll consists of two types of cells palisade and spongy parenchyma.

 **Reason** (R) Mesophyll tissue is rich in chlorophyll and carries out photosynthesis.

Ans. (*b*)

7. **Assertion** (A) In dicot leaf, mesophyll is absent in the region of midrib and other larger veins, where vascular tissue are present.

 **Reason** (R) The size of vascular bundles varies according to the size of the veins.

Ans. (*b*) **Competency Based Que.**

# Subjective Questions

## Very Short Answer Type Questions

**1. Identify the structure *A* and *B*.**

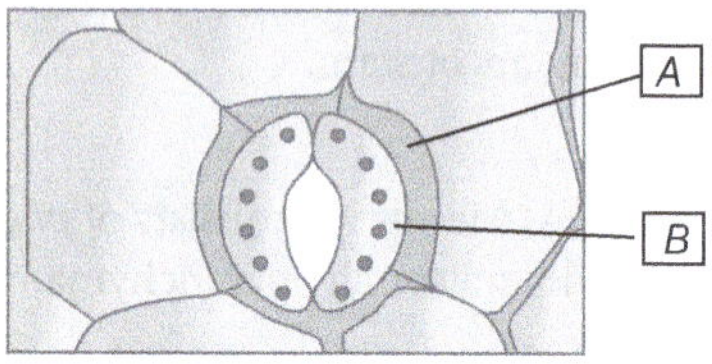


**Ans.** In the given figure *A* represents the subsidiary cells and *B* represents guard cells. (½ + ½)

**2. List two types of epidermal appendages found in epidermal tissue system.**

**Ans.** The two main types of epidermal appendages are
(i) Trichomes (ii) Root hairs (½ + ½)

**3. Why the endodermis of dicot stem is called the starch sheath?**

**Ans.** The endodermis of dicot stem is called the starch sheath as it contains cells that are rich in starch grains.

**4. (i) Which kind of cells form pericycle?**

**(ii) What is its function?**

**Ans.** (i) Pericycle is formed of parenchymatous cells.
(ii) It gives rise to lateral roots. (½ × 2)

**5. The transverse section of a plant material shows the following anatomical features**

**(i) the vascular bundles are conjoint, scattered and surrounded by a sclerenchymatous bundle sheaths.**

**(ii) phloem parenchyma is absent. What will you identify it as?** **Competency Based Que., NCERT**

**Ans.** The transverse section is of monocot stem as vascular bundles are scattered and phloem parenchyma is absent.

**6. Name the epidermis which covers both the upper surface and lower surface of the leaf.**

**Ans.** **Upper surface** is covered by adaxial epidermis.

**Lower surface** is covered by abaxial epidermis. (½ × 2)

**7. Write one difference between mesophyll of dicot leaf and a monocot leaf.**

**Ans.** In dicot leaves, mesophyll is differentiated into palisade and spongy parenchyma. In case of monocot leaves, mesophyll is not differentiated and all cells are like spongy parenchyma. (1)

**8. What part of the plant would show the following?**

**(i) Medullary rays**

**(ii) Differentiated palisade and spongy parenchyma.**

**Ans.** (i) Dicot stem (ii) Dicot leaves. (½ × 2)

**9. The bulliform cells present in the epidermis help grasses. What is it significance?**

**Ans.** The bulliform cells present in the epidermis of grasses help in folding of leaves during hot summer day and prevent transpiration.

**10. What are the cells that make the leaves curl in plants during water stress?**

**Ans.** Bulliform or motor cells.

**11. What is the epidermal cell modification in plants which prevents water loss?** **NCERT Exemplar**

**Ans.** Bulliform cells are the epidermal cell modification in plants which prevents the water loss.

## Short Answer Type Questions

**1. How is the study of anatomy is useful to us?** **NCERT**

**Ans.** The study of anatomy is useful to us in
(i) solving taxonomic problems.
(ii) understanding the structural adaptations of plants to diverse environments.
(iii) extraction of compounds for use as medicine.
(iv) differentiation of inferior quality wood from the superior quality. (½ × 4)

**2. The stomatal pore is guarded by two kidney-shaped guard cells. Name the epidermal cells surrounding the guard cells. How does a guard cell differ from an epidermal cell? Use a diagram to illustrate your answer.** **NCERT Exemplar**

**Ans.** The epidermal cells surrounding the guard cells of stomata are called subsidiary cells. Differences between guard cells and epidermal cells are

| Guard Cells | Epidermal Cells |
|---|---|
| They are bean or kidney- shaped. | They are barrel-shaped. |
| They possess chloroplasts. | They lack chloroplasts. |
| They are smaller. | They are bigger. |
| The inner walls of guard cells are thick, while the outer walls are thick | Epidermal cells are uniformly thin. |

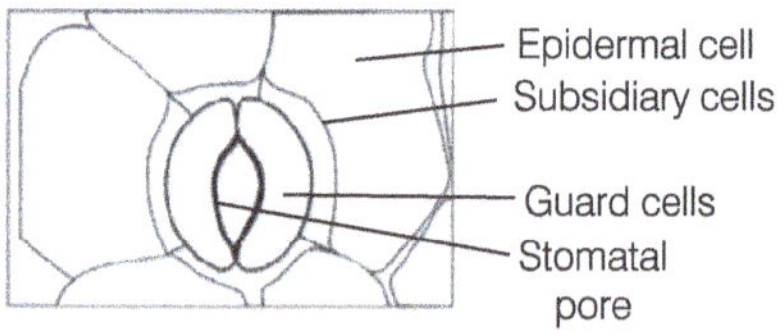


Diagrammatic representation of stomata with bean-shaped guard cells

**3. Epidermal cells are often modified to perform specialised functions in plants. Name some of them and function they perform.** NCERT Exemplar

**Ans.** Epidermal cells are modified to form various structures such as root hairs and trichomes.

**Root Hairs** They are unicellular extensions of the epidermal cells of roots. They increases the surface area for absorption of water and minerals. (1)

**Trichomes** They are multicellular extensions of the epidermal cells of stem.

They produce some glandular secretions and also help in checking the rate of transpiration. (1)

**4. List the functions of ground tissue system.**

**Ans.** Functions of ground tissue systems are

(i) It provides mechanical strength to the plant.
(ii) It has spaces to allow gaseous exchange between cortex and atmosphere.
(iii) It carries out photosynthesis in leaves.
(iv) It forms the bulk of the plant body. (½ × 4)

**5. How open vascular bundles differ from closed vascular bundles?**

**Ans.** The differences between open and closed vascular bundles are as follows.

| Open Vascular Bundles | Closed Vascular Bundles |
|---|---|
| It contains cambium in between phloem and xylem | It does not contain cambium between xylem and phloem |
| These are found in dicot stem | These are found in leaves and monocot stem. |

(1 × 2)

**6. Why are secondary xylem and phloem generally formed in dicots?** Competency Based Que.

**Ans.** Secondary xylem and phloem are generally formed in dicots due to the presence of cambium between the xylem and phloem in the vascular bundles.

**7. Describe the cortex region of dicot root.**

**Ans.** The cortex consists of several layers of thin-walled parenchyma cells. Intercellular spaces are small but abundant. The cortical cells can be rounded, oval or angular. They store food. The major function of the cortex in the root hair zone is conduction of water and minerals from epiblema to the interior of the root.

**8. Answer the following questions with reference to anatomy of dicot root.**

**(i) What are Casparian strips and where they present?**
**(ii) Type of cells present in cortex.**
**(iii) Name the innermost layer of the cortex.**

**Ans.** (i) Casparian strips are the depositions of the waxy material, suberin which is impermeable to water. It is present on the tangential and radial walls of endodermal cells.
(ii) Thin walled parenchymatous cells with intercellular spaces are present in the cortex.
(iii) Endodermis (1 × 3)

**9. What are the identifying features of dicotyledonous roots?**

**Ans.** Dicotyledonous root can be easily identified with the following features

- Endodermis with Casparian strips.
- Presence of small or inconspicuous pith.
- Radial bundles less than six.

**10. Differentiate between pith in dicot root and monocot root.**

**Ans.** Differences in pith in monocot and dicot root are as follows

| Pith in Monocot Root | Pith in Dicot Root |
|---|---|
| The centre of root is occupied by the pith. | It is often absent. When present, it is very small. |
| Intercellular spaces are present in between pith cells. | Intercellular spaces are absent. |

(1 × 2)

**11. Describe the features of pith in dicot stems.**

**Ans.** The pith consists of a large number of rounded, parenchymatous cells with big intercellular spaces. It occupies the central portion of the stem.

**12. Write the identifying features of dicotyledonous stem.**

**Ans.** Dicotyledonous stem can be easily identified with the following features

- Occurrence of multicellular hair over epidermis.
- Collenchymatous hypodermis.
- Presence of sclerenchymatous pericycle over vascular bundles. (1 × 3)

**13. What is the difference between hypodermis of dicot and monocot stems?**

**Ans.** In dicot stems, hypodermis consists of a few layers of collenchyma cells, whereas, in case of monocot stems, hypodermis consists of sclerenchyma cells.

**14. Cut a transverse section of young stem of a plant from your school garden and observe it under the microscope. How would you as certain whether, it is a monocot stem or a dicot stem? Give reasons.** NCERT

**Ans.** If the section has several scattered, vascular bundles with sclerenchymatous bundle sheath, undifferentiated ground tissue and no pith, then it is the transverse section is of a monocot stem.

If the section has vascular bundles arranged in a ring, differentiated ground tissue into cortex, endodermis, pericycle and pith, then the section is of dicot stem.

**15. Which part of the plant would show the following?** NCERT Exemplar

(i) Radial vascular bundle

(ii) Polyarch xylem

(iii) Well-developed pith

**Ans.** (i) Root (ii) Monocot root (iii) Monocot root (1 × 3)

**16. Point out the differences in the anatomy of leaf of peepal (*Ficus religiosa*) and maize (*Zea mays*).** NCERT Exemplar

**Ans.** Differences between peepal (dicot leaves) and maize (monocot leaves) are

| Dicot Leaves (Peepal) | Monocot Leaves (Maize) |
|---|---|
| The leaf is dorsiventral. | The leaf is isobilateral. |
| Mesophyll is differentiated into palisade and spongy parenchyma. | There is no differentiation of mesophyll cells. |
| Bulliform cells are absent | Bulliform cells are present |

(1 × 3)

**17. Refer to the given figures and answer the following questions.**

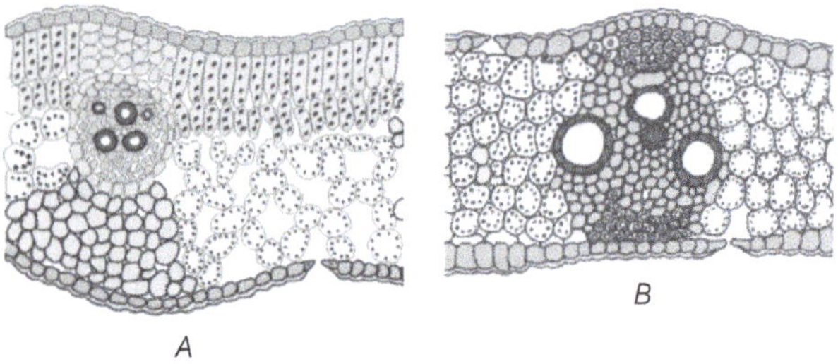


(i) Identify *A* and *B*.

(ii) Write any one difference between *A* and *B*.

**Ans.** (i) A represents the TS of dicot leaf and *B* represents the TS of monocot leaf.

(ii) In a dicot leaf, mesophyll is differentiated into palisade and spongy layers whereas in a monocot leaf, mesophyll is undifferentiated with no clear distinction between the layers. (1 + 1)

## Long Answer Type Questions

**1. Name the three basic tissue systems in the flowering plants. Give the tissue names under each system.** NCERT

**Ans.** Refer to text on page no. 123-125.

**2. What is stomatal apparatus? Explain the structure of stomata with a labelled diagram.** NCERT

**Ans.** Stomata are structures present in the epidermis of leaves. Each stoma is composed of two bean-shaped cells called guard cells, which enclose stomatal pore. In grasses, guard cells are dumb-bell-shaped. The guard cells possess chloroplasts and regulate the opening and closing of stomata. Sometimes, a few epidermal cells in the vicinity of the guard cells become specialised in their shape and size known as subsidiary cells. The stomatal aperture, guard cells and the surrounding subsidiary cells are together called stomatal apparatus. (3)

**For diagram** Refer to fig. no. 6.2 on page no. 124. (2)

**3. (i) How will you classify vascular bundles in different types?**

**(ii) Describe the open and closed type of conjoint vascular bundles.**

**Ans.** (i) According to the arrangement of xylem and phloem in the vascular bundles, there are two types of bundles. These are radial and conjoint. (2)

(ii) Refer to text on page no. 125. (3)

**4. In the following figure showing vascular bundles.**

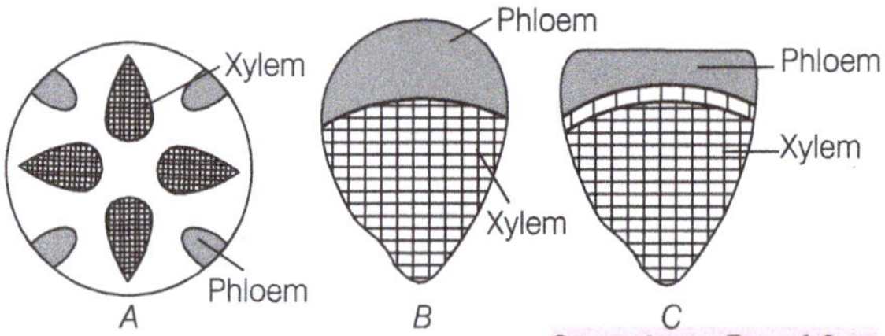


Competency Based Que.

(i) Identify the type *A*, *B* and *C*.

(ii) Name the type of plant and the plant part in which the above are found.

(iii) Which one of them can carry out secondary growth?

**Ans.** (i) *A*- Radial vascular bundle

*B* - Conjoint closed vascular bundle

*C* - Conjoint open vascular bundle (2)

(ii) • Radial vascular bundle present in roots

• Conjoint closed vascular bundle present in monocot stem and leaves.

• Conjoint open vascular bundle present in dicot stem. (2)

(iii) Conjoint open vascular bundle, i.e. '*C*' can carry out the secondary growth. (1)

**5. Distinguish between following.**

(i) Stele and vascular bundles

(ii) Protoxylem and metaxylem

(iii) Open and closed vascular bundles

(iv) Stem hairs and root hairs NCERT Exemplar

**Ans.** (i) Stele is the central part of the root or stem that consists of vascular tissues along with pericycle and ground tissue whereas vascular bundle is a group of xylem and phloem.

(ii) Protoxylem is an early formed xylem and metaxylem is lately formed xylem.

(iii) Open vascular bundles have cambium and show secondary growth. Closed vascular bundles do not have cambium.

(iv) Stem hairs are multicellular, whereas root hairs are unicellular.

**6. (i) How the arrangement of cambium in the vascular bundles of monocots differs from dicots?**

**(ii) Describe the stele in dicot root.**

**Ans.** (i) In dicots, cambium is present between phloem and xylem. These type of vascular bundles are capable to form secondary xylem and phloem tissues. These are known as open vascular bundles. In monocots, vascular bundle have no cambium, hence they do not form secondary tissues. These are known as closed vascular tissues. (2)

(ii) Refer to text on page no. 126 (3)

**7. Explain the anatomy of a monocot root with the help of well labelled diagram.**

**Ans.** Refer to text on page no. 126-127.

**8. Draw illustrations to bring out the anatomical difference between** **NCERT**

**(i) Monocot root and dicot root**

**(ii) Monocot stem and dicot stem**

**Ans.** (i) For diagram, refer to fig. no. 6.6 and 6.5

(ii) Refer to fig no 6.8 and 6.7 (2.5 × 2)

**9. Describe the internal structure of a dorsiventral leaf with the help of labelled diagram.** **NCERT**

**Ans.** The adaxial (upper) epidermis and abaxial (lower) epidermis, both have a layer of conspicuous cuticle. The abaxial epidermis generally bears more stomata than the adaxial epidermis. The latter may even lack stomata. The tissue between the upper and lower epidermis is called mesophyll. It contains palisade and spongy parenchyma. The vascular bundles are present in the midrib and veins. They are surrounded by a layer of thin-walled bundle sheath cells.

**For diagram** Refer to fig. no. 6.9. page no. 128.

**10. Write the significance of bulliform cells.**

**Describe features for identification of monocot leaf.**

**Ans.** Refer to text on page no. 129. (2 + 3)

Monocotyledonous leaf can be easily identified with the following features.

- Undifferentiated mesophyll
- Xylem vessels are rounded
- Presence of few large sized bulliform cells on upper surface (adaxial).

## Source Based/Case Based/Passage Based Questions

**1. A student observed a slide of root under microscope. He saw four xylem and phloem patches in radial arrangement in the root. He also observed thick-walled cells of endodermis. He discussed about the anatomy of the given root with his teacher.**

**(i) Identify the root and give one example.**

**(ii) What is Casparian strip?**

**(iii) Write the features of pith of this root.**

**(iv) What is epiblema?**

*Or*

**(iv) Write characteristic features of the cells which give rise to lateral roots.**

**Ans.** (i) These are dicotyledonous roots, e.g. sunflower, pea, etc. (1)

(ii) The radial and transverse walls of the endodermal cells contain a thickening of suberin known as the Casparian strips. (1)

(iii) Pith is usually absent in dicotyledonous root and if present it is small or inconspicuous. (1)

(iv) The outermost layer of the dicot root is known as epiblema. Many of the cells of epiblema protrude in the form of unicellular root hairs. (1)

*Or*

(iv) Lateral roots originate from pericycle. The pericycle is composed of thick-walled parenchymatous cells. (1)

**2. During the biology practical examination, the teacher provided two slides labelled *A* and *B* for identification. After placing the slides under the microscope, the Transverse Sections (TS) shown below were observed. Carefully observe the image and answer the questions that follows.** **Competency Based Que.**

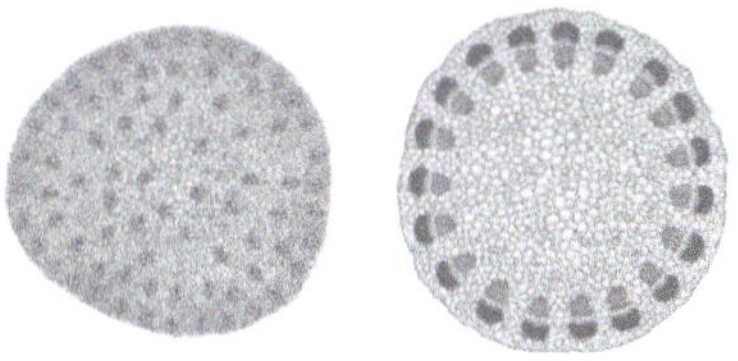

A B

**(i) Identify whether the given slides are of root or stem. Also, provide a reason for your answer.**

**(ii) Identify the slide *A* and *B*.**

(iii) **Which of the two slides *A* or *B*, is characterised by the presence of water containing cavities within the vascular bundles?**

**Ans.** (i) The given slides are of stem because both the transverse sections have conjoint vascular bundles, which are a characteristic feature of stem. (2)

(ii) Slide *A* is of monocot stem and slide *B* is of dicot stem. (1)

(iii) Slide *A* is characterised by the presence of water containing cavities within the vascular bundles. (1)

**3.** **In a botanical research lab, two unknown types of flowering plants were being studied and were named *A* and B. The researchers noticed significant differences in the arrangement of vascular bundles in the stems, leaves, and roots of both plants. The plant *A* had vascular bundles arranged in a ring in the stem, with a well-developed cortex and a central pith. In contrast, the plant *B* had scattered vascular bundles in the stem, with no distinct cortex or pith structure.**

(i) **Write the type of venation that can be seen in the leaves of the plant *A*?**

(ii) **Give two examples of each plant that belong to the categories of plant *A* and plant *B*.**

(iii) **Write one point of difference in the anatomy of plant *A* and plant *B* with respect to root.**

**Ans.** (i) Since plant A has vascular bundles arranged in a ring in the stem, it is likely a dicot. Dicot plants typically have reticulate venation in their leaves, where the veins form a branching or net-like pattern. (1)

(ii) Examples of plants that belong to plant *A* (dicots):

1. Sunflower 2. Bean

Examples of plants that belong to plant B (monocots):

3. Maize

4. Wheat ($\frac{1}{2} \times 4$)

(iii) A significant anatomical difference between plant A (dicot) and plant B (monocot) roots is the presence of a vascular cambium.

In dicot roots, a vascular cambium is typically present between the xylem and phloem, which allows for secondary growth (thickening of the root) in older plants.

In monocot roots, there is no vascular cambium, meaning monocots do not undergo secondary growth, and their roots typically do not increase in girth after they mature. (1)

# SELF ASSESSMENT TEST

## Multiple Choice Questions

1. Which of the following tissue system is responsible for providing protective covering to the plant body?
   (a) Ground tissue system
   (b) Epidermal tissue system
   (c) Conducting tissue system
   (d) Fundamental tissue system
2. Choose the incorrect match pair from the given options.
   (a) Trichomes- Multicellular structures
   (b) Guard cells- Bean-shaped cells
   (c) Root hair- Branched or unbranched structures
   (d) Stomata- Transpiration
3. Choose the incorrect statement with respect to conjoint vascular tissue.
   (a) It is generally found in the roots.
   (b) It is present in both stem and leaves.
   (c) The xylem and phloem are present together on the same radius.
   (d) The phloem is usually located only on the outer side of the xylem.
4. The conjunctive tissue found in the root, is made up of
   (a) thick-walled parenchymatous cells
   (b) thick-walled sclerenchymatous cells
   (c) thin-walled parenchymatous cells
   (d) thin-walled collenchymatous cells
5. The water containing cavities within the vascular bundles are found in
   (a) isobilateral leaf
   (b) monocotyledonous stem
   (c) dorsiventral leaf
   (d) dicotyledonous stem
6. Choose the incorrect pair from the following with respect to dorsiventral leaf.
   (a) Palisade parenchyma- Arranged vertically towards the adaxial surface
   (b) Mesophyll- Possesses chloroplast and carry out photosynthesis
   (c) Stomata - Present equally on both the surfaces of epidermis
   (d) Spongy parenchyma- Arranged loosely below the palisade cells
7. What leads to the inward curling of grass leaves during periods of water stress?
   (a) Turgidity in bulliform cells
   (b) Flaccidity in bulliform cells
   (c) Shrinkage of air spaces in spongy mesophyll
   (d) Closure of stomata

## Assertion-Reason Questions

**Direction** (Q. Nos. 8-10) *In each of the following questions, a statement of Assertion (A) is given followed by corresponding statement of Reason (R). Of the statements, mark the correct answer as*

(a) Both A and R are true and R is the correct explanation of the A.
(b) Both A and R are true, but R is not the correct explanation of the A.
(c) A is true, but R is false.
(d) A is false, but R is true.

8. **Assertion** (A) Cuticle is the waxy layer formed over the epidermis of stem and leaves.
**Reason** (R) Cuticle prevents the loss of water from the plant body.

9. **Assertion** (A) The endodermal layer of dicotyledonous stem is also known as starch sheath.
**Reason** (R) The endodermal cells are abundant in starch grains.

10. **Assertion** (A) The adaxial surface of monocot leaf has more stomata as compared to the abaxial surface.
**Reason** (R) The stomata in monocots are usually dumb-bell shaped.

## Very Short Answer Type Questions

11. Mention the ground tissue system found in leaves.
12. What is conjunctive tissue? Where they are located?
13. Name the epidermis that covers the upper surface of the leaf.
14. Mention any one identifying feature of monocot leaf.

## Short Answer Type Questions

15. List the functions of the epidermal tissue system.
16. Differentiate between radial and conjoint vascular bundle.
17. Write a brief description about the arrangement of vascular bundle in a dicot stem.

## Long Answer Type Questions

18. Write a note on the epidermal tissue system.
19. Explain the anatomy of dicot stem in brief.
20. Draw an outline diagram of TS of monocot leaf and label the following:
    (i) Adaxial surface (ii) Abaxial surface
    (iii) Mesophyll (iv) Stoma
    (v) Sub-stomatal cavity

## Case Based Question

21. During a biology practical class, while preparing for a lesson on plant anatomy, the teacher discovers an unlabelled slide in the slide box. The slide is not marked, and there are no superficial identifying features to suggest whether it is a dicot or monocot cross-section. The teacher needs to identify the slide based on the anatomical features observed under the microscope.

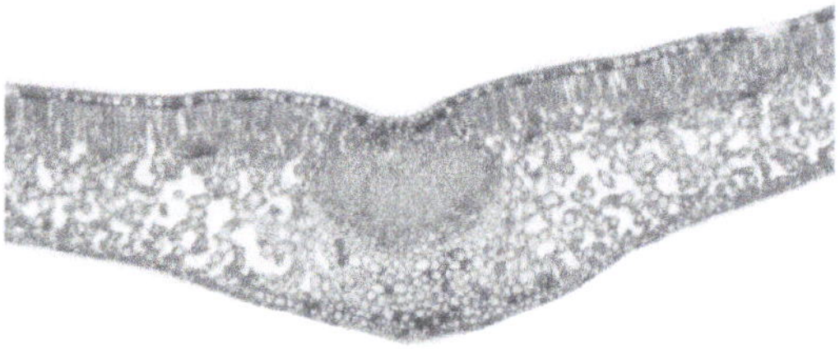

(i) Identify the slide.
(ii) Write any two characteristic feature of this slide.
(iii) Give any two examples of plants in which this structure can be observed.

# Answers

| | | | | | | |
|---|---|---|---|---|---|---|
| 1. (b) | 2. (c) | 3. (a) | 4. (c) | 5. (b) | 6. (c) | 7. (b) |
| 8. (a) | 9. (a) | 10. (d) | | | | |

07

CHAPTER

# Structural Organisation in Animals

In this chapter, we will briefly discuss the organ and organ system along with morphology and anatomy of frog to show their structural body organisation and functioning.

**YOUR STUDY GOALS**

7.1 Organ and Organ System

7.2 Frog

**YOUR PRACTICE GOAL**

- Objective Type Questions (16 Qs ; MCQs, A-R) Case Based Questions (2)
- Subjective Type Questions
- (14 VSAs, 18 SAs, 7 LAs)

- In **unicellular organisms**, all vital cellular functions like digestion, respiration, excretion, etc., are performed by a single cell.
- While, in the complex body of **multicellular animals**, the same basic functions are carried out by different groups of cells in a well organised manner.
- For example, the body of a simple organism like *Hydra* is made up of different types of cells and the number of cells in each type can be in thousands.
- Similarly, in the human body, there are billions of cells that perform various functions in a coordinated manner.
- In all multicellular organisms, a group of similar cells having the same origin and performing a specific function form an organisation called **tissue**.
- There are four basic types of tissues that organise to form organs which in turn associate to form organ systems in multicellular organisms.
- Cells, tissues, organs and organ systems split up the work in a way that exhibits division of labour and contribute to the survival of the body as a whole.

## 7.1 Organ and Organ System

- All complex animals consist of only four basic types of tissues such as **epithelial**, **connective**, **muscular** and **neural**.
- These tissues are organised in specific proportion and pattern to form an organ like stomach, lung, heart and kidney.
- When two or more organs perform a common function by their physical and/or chemical interaction, they together form organ system, e.g., digestive system, respiratory system, etc.

## 7.2 Frog

- The frog is an **amphibious animal** as it can live both on land and in water.
- It belongs to class-Amphibia of phylum-Chordata.
- The most common species of frog found in India is *Rana tigrina.*
- Frog is a **cold-blooded** or **poikilothermic animal** as its body temperature fluctuates according to its surrounding temperature.
- It can also darken or lighten its body shade to blend with the background and thus, prevent easy detection by its enemies (camouflage). This protective colouration is called **mimicry**.
- To avoid the adverse conditions of environment, frog burrows inside the soil and lies in a state of rest or sleep during summer and winter.
- The resting condition in winter is called **hibernation** or **winter sleep** and the condition of rest in summer is called **aestivation** or **summer sleep**.

### Morphology

- The term 'morphology' refers to the study of form or externally visible features.
- In case of animals, it refers to the external appearance of the organs or parts of the body.
- The description of frog's morphology is discussed below.
  - Frog is generally **olive green** in colour with dark irregular spots on the dorsal side, while in the ventral side it is **pale yellow** in colour.
  - The skin of frog is smooth, moist and slippery due to the presence of mucus.
  - Frog never drinks water, but absorbs it through the skin.
  - It lacks neck and tail, as found in majority of vertebrates.
  - The body of frog is divisible into **head** and **trunk**.

### 1. Head

It is triangular in shape with a blunt snout. It bears mouth, a pair of nostrils, eyes and ear drums.

- **Mouth** It is a wide transverse opening that opens only during feeding.
- **External Nostrils** Above the mouth, the head bears two small apertures called **nostrils**.
- **Eyes** Two large bulging eyes are present on the head. They are covered by **nictitating membrane** that protects the eyes when the frog is in water.
- **Eardrums** On either side of eyes, a membranous **tympanum** (ear) is present. It receives sound waves.

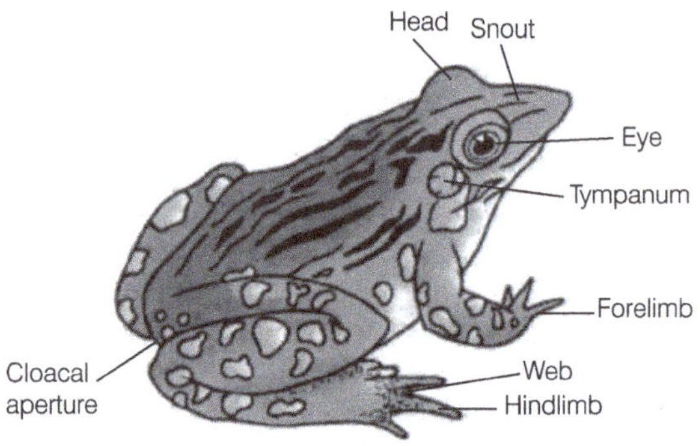


Fig 7.1 External features of frog

### 2. Trunk

- A pair of forelimbs and hindlimbs is attached to the trunk. They help in swimming, walking, leaping and burrowing.
- **Hindlimb** It ends in five digits and is larger and muscular than the fore limbs.
- Feet have **webbed digits** that help in swimming.
- **Forelimbs** Each forelimb ends in four digits.

## Frogs Exhibit Sexual Dimorphism

- Male frogs can be distinguished by the presence of sound producing vocal sacs and also a copulatory pad on the first digit of the forelimbs which are absent in female frogs.

## Anatomy

- The term 'anatomy' conventionally is used for the study of morphology of internal organs in animals.
- The body cavity of frogs accommodate different organ systems such as digestive, circulatory, respiratory, nervous, excretory and reproductive systems with well-developed structures and functions.
- These systems are described below.

## Digestive System

- The digestive system of frog consists of alimentary canal and associated digestive glands.

### 1. Alimentary Canal

- The alimentary canal of frog is short because frogs are carnivores and hence, the length of intestine is reduced.
- It contains mouth, buccal cavity, oesophagus, stomach, small intestine, rectum and cloaca.
- **Mouth** As soon as the food is captured by bilobed tongue, it enters the mouth. The mouth opens into the buccal cavity that leads to oesophagus through pharynx.
- **Oesophagus** It is a narrow, short tube, which continues in large and distended stomach.
- **Stomach** It helps in converting the food into **chyme** and secretes gastric juice and HCl.
- **Intestine** It is a coiled structure continued with the stomach.
    - The intestinal wall has several finger-like folds called **villi** and **microvilli**, which enhance the surface area for absorption of digested food.
    - The first part of small intestine lying parallel to the stomach is called **duodenum**.
    - The duodenum is followed by **ileum.**
    - Small intestine continues into a wider **rectum** which opens into a **cloaca** through an aperture called **anus.**

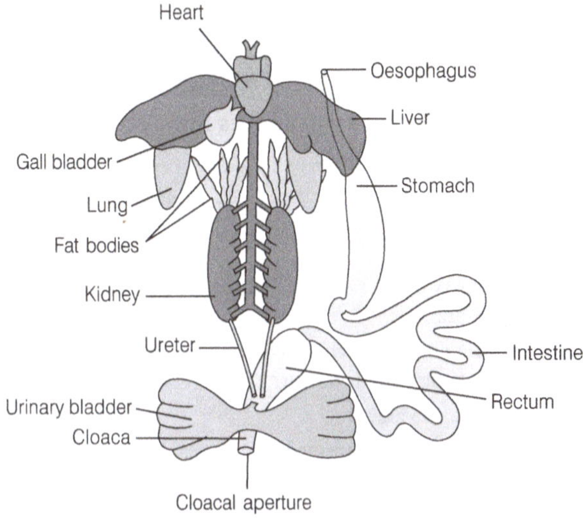


Fig 7.2 Diagrammatic representation of internal organs of frog showing complete digestive system

### 2. Digestive Glands

These glands include gastric glands, intestinal glands, liver and pancreas.

- **The gastric glands** secrete **gastric juice.**
- The **intestinal glands** secrete **intestinal juice**, which contains a number of digestive enzymes.
- The **liver** produces bile which is temporarily stored in the gall bladder before being released into duodenum.
- **Pancreas** produces pancreatic juice containing several digestive enzymes.

### Digestion of Food

- The digestion of food takes place by the action of **HCl** and **gastric juices** secreted from the walls of stomach.
- The partially digested food called **chyme** is passed from stomach to the first part of the intestine, the **duodenum.**
- The duodenum receives bile from gall bladder and pancreatic juice from the pancreas through a common bile duct.
- Bile emulsifies fat and pancreatic juices digest carbohydrates and proteins.
- Final digestion occurs in the intestine.

- Digested food is absorbed by the numerous finger-like folds in the inner wall of intestine called **villi** and **microvilli**.
- The digested food is distributed to different body tissues and cell through blood to release energy.
- The undigested solid waste moves into rectum and passes out through cloaca.

## Quick Test 1

1. Name any two types of tissue which are present in all complex animals.
2. What role does the nictitating membrane play for frogs in their aquatic environment?
3. State True or False.
   (a) Unicellular organisms have tissues that perform specific functions like digestion and respiration.
   (b) Frogs enter a dormant state during extreme temperatures, called aestivation in summer and hibernation in winter.
4. Name the structure which helps the frog in swimming.
5. Bile emulsifies fat, name the organ which produces bile .

## Respiratory System

Frogs respire on land and in water by two different modes of respiration.

### Cutaneous Respiration

- It occurs through moist skin of the frog.
- Frogs respire only by the skin when under water or deep under the mud.
- Dissolved oxygen in water is exchanged through the skin by diffusion.
- During aestivation and hibernation gaseous exchange also occurs through skin.

### Pulmonary Respiration

- It occurs by the lungs.
- It occurs on land.
- The lungs are a pair of elongated, pink coloured sac-like structures present in the upper part of the trunk region (thorax).
- Air enters through the nostrils into the buccal cavity and then to the lungs.

Apart from the lungs, the buccal cavity and skin also functions as respiratory organs on land.

## Circulatory System (Vascular system)

- The circulatory system of frog is well-developed and is of **closed type**.
- It also has a **lymphatic system**.
- The blood vascular system includes the heart, blood and blood vessels.

### 1. Heart

- The circulation of blood is achieved by the pumping action of heart.
- Heart is a muscular structure situated in the upper part of the body cavity.
- It has three chambers, i.e. two atria (sing. atrium) and one ventricle.
- The heart is covered by a membrane called **pericardium.**
- A triangular accessory chamber called **sinus venosus** is present on the dorsal side of the frog's heart.
- It receives blood through the major veins called **vena cava** and opens into right auricle.
- The auricles send their blood into ventricle where the blood gets mixed up.
- The ventricle opens into a sac-like **conus arteriosus** on the ventral side of the heart.

### 2. Blood

- The blood is composed of **plasma** and **blood cells**.
- The blood cells are RBCs (Red Blood Cells) or erythrocytes, WBCs (White Blood Cells) or leucocytes and platelets.
- RBCs are nucleated and contain red coloured pigment namely **haemoglobin**.
- The blood carries nutrients, gases and water to the respective sites during circulation.

### 3. Blood Vessels

- The major blood vessels found in frogs are **arteries** and **veins**.
- **Arteries** carry blood from the heart to different body parts and forms the arterial system.
- **Veins** bring blood from different body parts to the heart.
- Special venous connection between liver and intestine as well as the kidney and lower parts of the body are present in frogs.

- The former is called **hepatic portal system** and the latter is called **renal portal system.**

## Lymphatic System

- The lymphatic system comprises of lymph, lymphatic channels and lymph nodes.
- **Lymph** is a mobile connective tissue that lacks few proteins and red blood cells.

## Excretory System

- The elimination of nitrogenous wastes is carried out by a well-developed excretory system.
- It consists of a pair of kidneys, ureters, cloaca and urinary bladder.
- The kidneys are compact, dark red and bean-like structures, situated slightly little posterior in the body cavity on both sides of the vertebral column.
- Each kidney is composed of several structural and functional units called **uriniferous tubules** or **nephrons**.
- **In male frogs**, two ureters emerge from the kidney which act as urinogenital ducts and opens into the cloaca.
- **In females**, the ureters and oviduct open separately into the cloaca.
- The thin-walled urinary bladder is present ventral to the rectum which also opens in the cloaca.
- The frog excretes urea and thus is a **ureotelic animal**.
- The excretory wastes are carried by blood into the kidney where these are separated and excreted.

## Nervous System

- The system for control and coordination is highly evolved in the frog.
- It includes both **nervous system** and **endocrine system**.
- The nervous system of frogs consists of a central nervous system, a peripheral nervous system and an autonomic nervous system.

### Central Nervous System

- It includes **brain** and **spinal cord**.
- The brain is enclosed in a bony structure called **cranium** or **brain box** and the spinal cord lies inside the vertebral column.
- The brain is divided into **forebrain**, **midbrain** and **hindbrain**.
  - The **forebrain** consists of olfactory lobes, paired cerebral hemispheres and unpaired diencephalon.
  - The **midbrain** comprises paired optic lobes.
  - The **hindbrain** comprises cerebellum and medulla oblongata.
- The medulla oblongata thus, passes out through the **foramen magnum** and continues into spinal cord present in the vertebral column.

### Peripheral Nervous System

- It contains cranial and spinal nerves, arising from the central nervous system.
- Ten pairs of **cranial nerves** arise from the brain.

### Autonomic Nervous System

- It consists of **sympathetic nervous system** and **parasympathetic nervous system**.
- The autonomic nervous system controls the functions of organs that are not under the voluntary control.

## Endocrine System

- The chemical coordination of various organs of the body is carried out by **hormones,** which are secreted by the endocrine glands.
- The prominent endocrine glands found in the frog are pituitary, thyroid, parathyroid, thymus, pineal body, pancreatic islets, adrenals and gonads.

## Sensory System

- Frog has different types of sensory organs for different functions
  - **Sensory papillae** organs for touch.
  - **Taste buds** for taste.
  - **Nasal epithelium** for smell.
  - **Eyes** for vision.
- There are two large simple eyes (possessing only one unit) in frog.
- Each eyeball is spherical in structure and lodged inside the orbit of skull.
- **Tympanum** with internal ears for hearing and balancing (equilibrium).
- External ears are absent in frogs.
- Out of these, eyes and internal ears are well organised structures and the rest are cellular aggregations around the nerve endings.

## Reproductive System

Frogs have well-organised male and female reproductive system. It shows **sexual dimorphism.**

### Male Reproductive System

It consists of testes, vasa efferentia, urinogenital duct and cloaca.

- **Testes** A pair of yellowish, ovoid **testes**, are found adhered to the upper part of the kidneys by a double fold of peritoneum called **mesorchium.**
- **Vasa Efferentia** These are 10-12 in numbers and arise from testes.
- They enter the kidneys on their side and open into **Bidder's canal.**
- **Urinogenital Duct** It comes out of the kidneys and opens into the **cloaca.**
- **The cloaca** is a small, median chamber that is used to pass faecal matter, urine and sperm to the exterior.

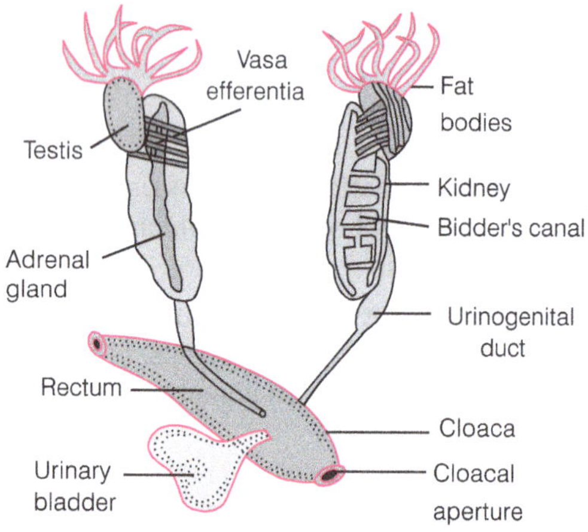

Fig 7.3 Reproductive system of male frog

**TEACHER'S TIP**
In male frog, ureter serves as urinary duct as well as vas deference to transfer urine and sperms. Hence, it is called a **urinogenital duct**.

### Female Reproductive System

It consists of a pair of ovaries and a pair of oviducts.

- **Ovaries** They are situated near the kidneys and there is no functional connection with kidneys.
- **Oviducts** A pair of long **oviducts** from ovaries opens into the cloaca. A mature female frog can release about 2500-3000 eggs at a time.

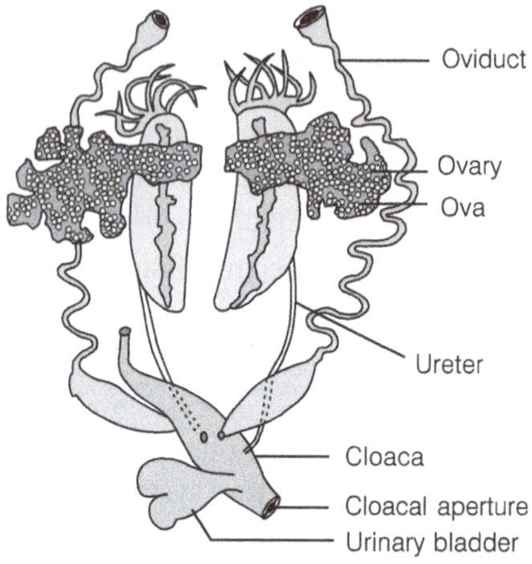

Fig 7.4 Reproductive system of female frog

### Fertilisation

- In frogs, the fertilisation is **external** and takes place in water.
- Development involves a larval stage called **tadpole.**
- The tadpole undergoes **metamorphosis** to form an adult.

## Economic Importance of Frogs

Frog is a useful animal for humans in the following ways

- It feeds on insects which destroy crops and eat up mosquitoes, which are the carriers of various diseases.
- They help to maintain **ecological balance** by forming an important part of food chain and food web.
- The muscles of legs of frogs are used as food in some countries.

## Quick Test 2

1. Frogs have a pair of elongated, pink-coloured sac like structure present in the thorax region, identify the structure.
2. *X* is the major vein through which heart receives blood. Identify the *X*.
3. Olfactory lobes are found in which part of frog's brain?
4. State an important role of the kidneys in the excretory system of frogs.
5. **State True or False.**
   (a) Male frogs have a direct connection between their testes and kidneys for the passage of sperm.
   (b) The ovaries of female frogs are functionally connected to the kidneys.

# Mind Map

## Structural Organisation in Animals

### Organ and Organ System

Epithelial, connective, muscular and neural are four types of tissues present in multicellular organisms. These four types of basic tissues organise to form organs and then organs associate to form organ system. For example, the human heart consists of all four types of tissues.

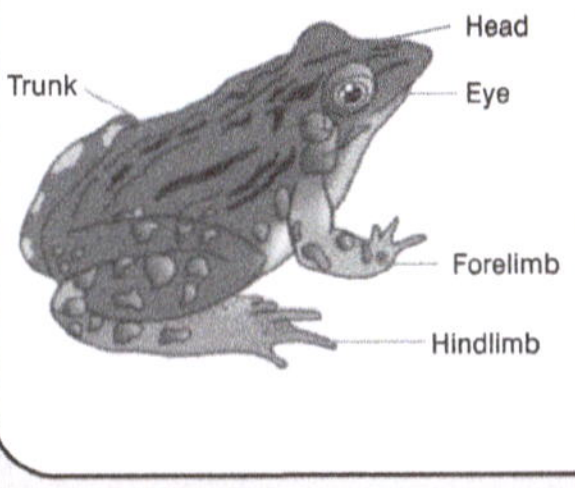


- Sexual dimorphism (vocal sacs and copulatory pads only in males).
- Body-Head (mouth, external nostrils, bulged eyes, tympanum) and trunk (forelimbs, hindlimbs, webbed feet).

### Digestive System

**Digestive System**

- **Alimentary Canal**
  Mouth→Buccal cavity →
  Pharynx→ Oesophagus →
  Stomach→ Intestine →
  Rectum → Cloaca

**Digestive Glands**

- **Liver** (secretes bile juice)
- **Pancreas** (secretes enzymes to digest carbohydrates, proteins, fats)

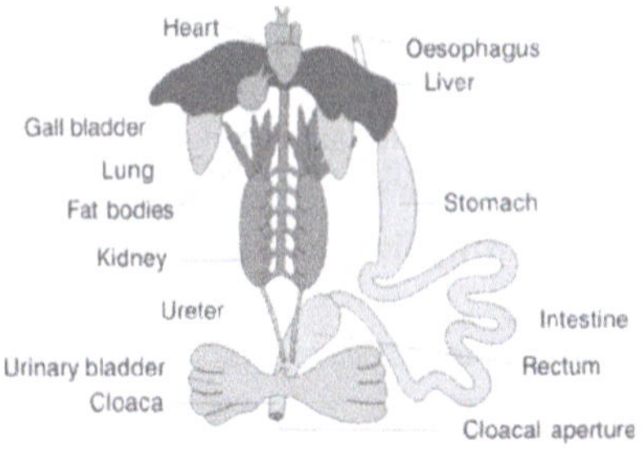


**Alimentary canal of frog**

### Respiratory System

**Respiratory System**

- **On Land**
  - Buccal cavity
  - Skin
  - Lungs (pulmonary)
- **In Water**
  - Skin (cutaneous)
- **During Hibernation and Aestivation**
  - Skin

### Circulatory System

- Closed type; 3-chambered heart (two atria and one ventricle).
- Myogenic heart which is self-contractile or auto-excitable.
- Two portal systems
  - Venous connection between liver and intestine called **hepatic portal system.**
  - Venous connection between kidney and lower parts of the body called **renal portal system.**
- Blood cells= RBCs (with nucleus), WBCs and platelets.
- Lymphatic system is also present.

### Reproductive System

**Male Reproductive System**

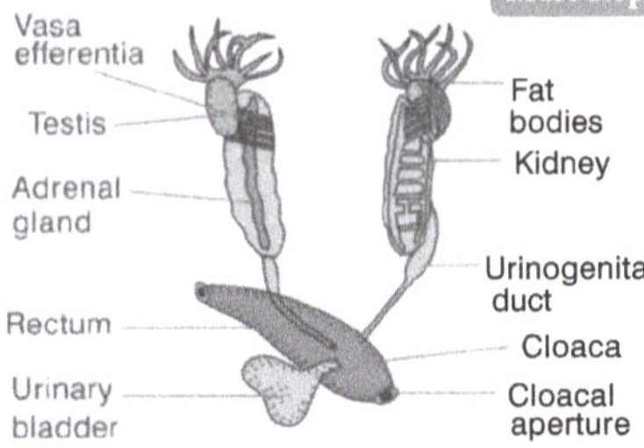


Male : A pair of yellowish ovoid testes → vasa efferentia (10–12) → enters into kidneys on their side → open into Bidder's canal → urinogenital duct → Cloaca.

**Female Reproductive System**

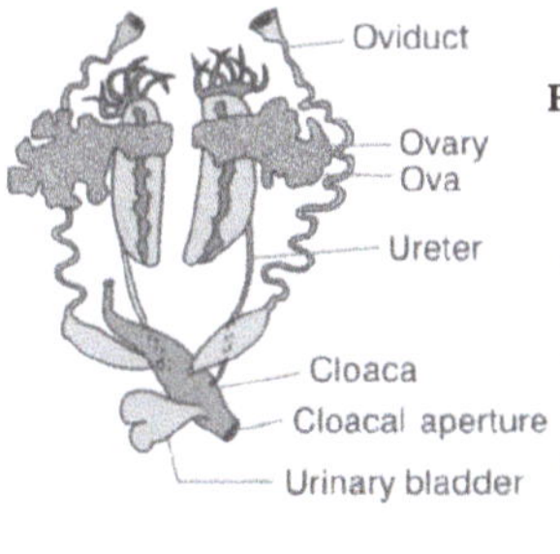


**Female :** A pair of ovaries → A pair of oviduct → Cloaca

**Life Cycle**

- A mature female can lay 2500 to 3000 ova (eggs) at a time.
- Fertilisation is external and takes place in water.
- Development involves larval stage called **tadpole**, which undergoes metamorphosis to form the adult.

### Excretory System

- Ureotelic animals.
- Consists of a pair of kidneys, ureters, cloaca and urinary bladder.

### Chemical Coordination

By endocrine glands - pituitary, thyroid, parathyroid, thymus, pineal body, pancreatic islets, adrenals and gonads.

### Nervous System

**Nervous System**

- **Central Nervous System** (brain and spinal cord)
- **Peripheral Nervous System** (cranial and spinal nerves)
- **Autonomous Nervous System**

### Sensory Organs

Sense organs for touch (sensory papillae), taste (taste buds), smell (nasal epithelium), vision (eye) and hearing (tympanum) are present.

# EXAM PATTERN QUESTIONS

## Objective Type Questions

### Multiple Choice Questions

**1.** What is the correct order of organisation in complex animals?

(a) Cells → Tissue → Organ → Organ system
(b) Cells → Organ system → Organ → Tissue
(c) Tissue → Organ → Organ system → Cells
(d) Tissue → Organ → Cells → Organ system

**Ans.** (*a*)

**2.** Which of the following statements are correct with reference to the frog? **Competency Based Que.**

I. Eyes are bulged and covered by nictitating membrane.
II. Membranous tympanum receives the sound signal.
III. The frog never drinks water.
IV. A pair of nostrils is present above the mouth.

Codes

(a) I and II (b) III and IV
(c) I and IV (d) I, II, III and IV

**Ans.** (*d*)

**3.** Read the following statements for frog and answer accordingly.

I. Duodenum receives bile and pancreatic juice through a common bile duct.
II. Salivary glands are absent in frog, so digestion starts in stomach.

(a) Both the statements I and II are correct and II is the correct explanation of I
(b) Both the statements I and II are correct, but II is not the correct explanation of I
(c) Statement I is correct, but II is incorrect
(d) Statement I is incorrect and II are correct

**Ans.** (*b*)

**4.** Which of the following statements are correct about the respiration in frog? **Competency Based Que.**

I. In frog, cutaneous and pulmonary respirations are found.
II. A pair of elongated pink hollow lungs are found in thorax.
III. During aestivation and hibernation, gaseous exchange takes place through skin.

Codes

(a) I, II and III (b) I and II
(c) II and III (d) I and II

**Ans.** (*a*)

**5.** Which of the following statement is incorrect about circulatory system of frog?

(a) It is well-developed and of closed type
(b) The heart has three chambers, i.e. two atria and one ventricle
(c) The blood vascular system comprises of heart, blood vessels and blood
(d) A triangular structure called conus arterious is present on the dorsal side of frog's heart

**Ans.** (*d*) The statement in option (d) is incorrect. It can be corrected as

A triangular structure called sinus venosus is present on the dorsal side of frog's heart.

**6.** Which of the following statement is incorrect regarding frog?

(a) Renal portal vein in frog carries blood from lower part of the body to kidney.
(b) Arterial system of frog carries blood from the heart to different parts of the body.
(c) External ears are absent and only tympanum can be seen.
(d) Lymphatic system consists of lymph and lymph nodes only.

**Ans.** (*d*) The statement in option (d) is incorrect. It can be corrected as

Lymphatic system of frog consist of lymph, lymphatic channels and lymph nodes.

**7.** Match the following columns.

| | Column I | | Column II |
|---|---|---|---|
| A. | Forebrain | 1. | A pair of optic lobes |
| B. | Midbrain | 2. | Cerebellum and medulla oblongata |
| C. | Hindbrain | 3. | Olfactory lobe, paired cerebral hemispheres, unpaired diencephalon |

Codes

| | A | B | C | | A | B | C |
|---|---|---|---|---|---|---|---|
| (a) | 1 | 3 | 2 | (b) | 2 | 1 | 3 |
| (c) | 3 | 1 | 2 | (d) | 1 | 2 | 3 |

**Ans.** (*c*)

**8.** **Which of the following is not the part of frog's sensory system?**

(a) Uriniferous tubule (b) Tympanum
(c) Nasal epithelium (d) Sensory papillae

**Ans.** (*a*) Uriniferous tubule is the structural and functional unit of kidney and is the part of frog's excretory system.

**9.** **Select the correct route for the passage of sperms in male frog.**

(a) Testes → Bidder's canal → Kidney → Vasa efferentia → Urinogenital duct → Cloaca
(b) Testes → Vasa efferentia → Kidney → Seminal vesicle → Urinogenital duct → Cloaca
(c) Testes → Vasa efferentia → Bidder's canal → → Ureter → Cloaca
(d) Testes → Vasa efferentia → Kidney → Bidder's canal → Urinogenital duct → Cloaca

**Ans.** (*d*)

**10.** **Observe the following figure indicating the male reproductive system of frog.**

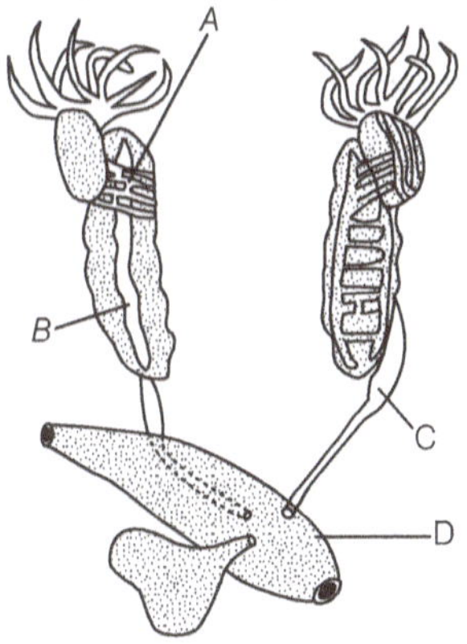


**Which of the labelling (*A*, *B*, *C*, *D*) is representing urinogenital duct.**

(a) *A* (b) *C*
(c) *B* (d) *D*

**Ans.** (*b*)

**11.** **Consider the following statements.**

I. **In female frog, there is no functional connection of ovaries with the kidneys.**
II. **A mature female frog releases about 2500-3000 eggs at a time.**

(a) Both the statements I and II are correct and II is the correct explanation of I
(b) Both the statements I and II are correct, but II is the correct explanation of I
(c) Statement I is correct, but II is incorrect
(d) Statements I incorrect and II are correct

**Ans.** (*b*)

**12.** **Consider the following four statements (I-IV) related to the common frog *Rana tigrina* and select the correct option stating which ones are True (T) and which ones are False (F).**

I. **In some countries, the muscular legs of frogs are used as food by man.**
II. **It has four-chambered heart.**
III. **On dry land, it turns ammonotelic from ureotelic.**
IV. **Fertilisation is carried out in pond water.**

**Codes**

| | I | II | III | IV | | I | II | III | IV |
|---|---|---|---|---|---|---|---|---|---|
| (a) | F | F | T | T | (b) | F | T | T | F |
| (c) | T | F | F | T | (d) | T | T | F | F |

**Ans.** (*c*)

## Assertion-Reason Questions

**Direction** (Q. Nos. 1-4) *In each of the following questions, a statement of Assertion (A) is given followed by corresponding statement of Reason (R). Of the statements, mark the correct answer as*

(a) Both A and R are true and R is the correct explanation of the A.
(b) Both A and R are true, but R is not the correct explanation of the A.
(c) A is true, but R is false.
(d) A is false, but R is true.

**1.** **Assertion** (A) Frog exhibits sexual dimorphism.

**Reason** (R) Male frogs can be distinguished from female frogs by the presence of sound producing vocal sacs.

**Ans.** (*a*)

**2.** **Assertion** (A) The alimentary canal of the frog is short.

**Reason** (R) Frogs are carnivores.

**Ans.** (*a*)

**3.** **Assertion** (A) In frog's vascular system, the composition of lymph is same as that of blood.

**Reason** (R) In frog, lymph lacks RBCs and few proteins.

**Ans.** (*d*) A is false, but R is true. A can be corrected as

In frog's vascular system, the composition of lymph is not same as that of blood.

**4.** **Assertion** (A) In male frogs, urine and sperm are transferred to the exterior through different aperture.

**Reason** (R) In female frog, ureters and oviduct open separately into cloaca.

**Ans.** (*d*) A is false, but R is true. A can be corrected as

In male frogs, urine and sperms are transferred to the exterior through same aperture called cloaca.

# Subjective Questions

## Very Short Answer Type Questions

**1. Name the types of tissue present in the heart.**

**Ans.** The heart consists of four types of tissues, i.e. epithelial, connective, muscular and neural.

**2. Name the phylum and class to which frog belongs.**

**Ans.** Phylum - Chordata (½)

Class - Amphibia (½)

**3. State the appearance of dorsal side of frog's body.**

**Ans.** Dorsal side of frog's body is generally olive green with dark irregular spots.

**4. In frog the two bulging eyes are covered by which membrane? Mention its function.**

**Ans.** The two large bulging eyes are covered by nictitating membrane. This membrane protects the eye when frog is in water or under the mud. (½ + ½)

**5. State the significance of webbed digits in frogs.**

**Ans.** The webbed digits help in swimming.

**6. Identify the sex of a frog in which sound producing vocal sacs are present.** NCERT Exemplar

**Ans.** Sound producing vocal sacs are present in male frogs.

**7. Which digit of the male frog develops into copulatory pad?**

**Ans.** The first digit of male frog develop into copulatory pad.

**8. Give two identifying features of an adult male frog.** NCERT Exemplar

**Ans.** The two identifying features of an adult male frog are as follows

(i) **Vocal Sacs** These are loose skin folds on throat of male frogs for producing louder sounds. (½)

(ii) **Copulatory Pad** It is present on the first digit of the forelimb of male frog and helps in closing female during amplexus. (½)

**9. The digestive system of frog is made of the following parts. Arrange them in an order beginning from mouth.**
**Mouth, Oesophagus, Buccal cavity, Stomach, Intestine, Cloaca, Rectum, Cloacal aperture.** NCERT Exemplar

**Ans.** The correct arrangement of the parts of digestive system in frog is as follows

Mouth $\rightarrow$ Buccal cavity $\rightarrow$ Oesophagus $\rightarrow$ Stomach $\rightarrow$ Intestine $\rightarrow$ Rectum $\rightarrow$ Cloaca $\rightarrow$ Cloacal aperture.

**10. Where is bile stored in the body of frog?**

**Ans.** The liver produces bile which is temporarily stored in the gall bladder before being released into duodenum.

**11. Special venous connection between liver and intestine and between kidney and intestine is found in frog, what are they called?** Competency Based Que., NCERT Exemplar

**Ans.** Special venous connection between liver and intestine is called hepatic portal system and venus connection between the kidney and the lower parts of the frog is called renal portal system.

**12. Name the process by which a tadpole develops into an adult frog.** NCERT Exemplar

**Ans.** Tadpole undergoes metamorphosis to form an adult.

**13. Write the correct route for the passage of sperms in male frog.**

**Ans.** The correct route for the passage of sperms in male frog is Testes $\rightarrow$ Vasa efferentia $\rightarrow$ Kidney $\rightarrow$ Bidder's canal $\rightarrow$ Urinogenital tract $\rightarrow$ Cloaca.

**14. Write the name of the structure *X* and *Y* from the diagram given below.**

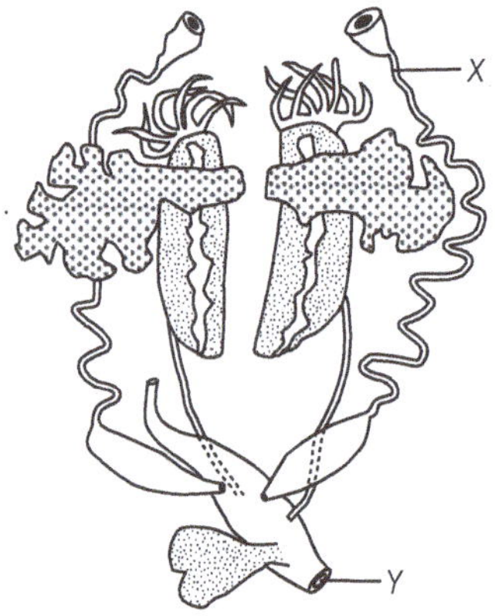


**Ans.** In the given diagram *X* represents oviduct and *Y* represents cloacal aperture. (½ + ½)

## Short Answer Type Questions

**1. Write a brief note on organ and organ system.**

**Ans.** Refer to text on page. no 142.

**2. Frog is a poikilotherm, exhibits camouflage and undergoes aestivation and hibernation, how are all these beneficial to it?** NCERT Exemplar

**Ans.** Frog is a poikilotherm (cold blooded) animal, *i.e.*, it regulates its body temperature according to its environment. (1)

For withstanding very cold temperatures, it undergoes winter sleep (hibernation) and summer sleep in hot temperatures (aestivation). During this period, it lives in a dormant stage with very minimal vital body activities. (1)

Also, frog is capable of changing its body colour, though gradually, with the change in its surrounding and climatic conditions. This capability in frog is called as camouflage which helps the frog to escape it from the predators. (1)

**3. Why the alimentary canal of frog is short? Write its various parts.** **Competency Based Que.**

**Ans.** The alimentary canal of frog is short because it is a carnivorous animal. The various parts of alimentary canal includes mouth, buccal cavity, oesophagus, stomach, small intestine, rectum and cloaca. (1 + 1)

**4. Draw a neat diagram of digestive system of frog.** **NCERT**

**Ans.** Refer to text on page. no 143.

**5. Write the steps involved in the process of digestion of frog.**

**Ans.** Refer to text on page no. 143 and 144.

**6. What are the reasons that makes frog suitable in both land and water ?** **Competency Based Que.**

**Ans.** Frog are well suited for both land and water due to their ability to respire in both habitats. In water, frogs can respire by their skin (cutaneous respiration). Whereas, on land, skin, buccal cavity and lungs function as respiratory organs.

**7. Identify the organ *A* and *B* in the diagram given below and state their function also.**

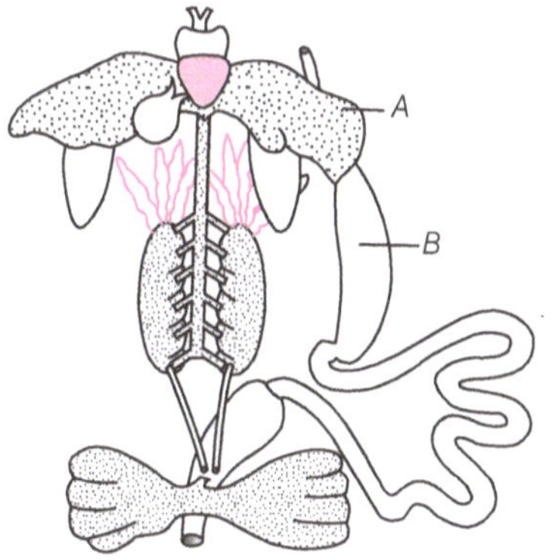


**Ans.** In the given diagram *A* represents stomach and *B* represents liver. (1)

Stomach helps in converting the food into chyme and secretes gastric juice and HCL. Liver produces bile which is temporarily stored in the gall bladder before being released into the duodenum. (1)

**8. What is the difference between cutaneous and pulmonary respiration?** **NCERT Exemplar**

**Ans.** Cutaneous respiration refers to the exchange of gases through skin whereas pulmonary respiration refers to the exchange of gases through lungs.

**9. Write a note on cutaneous respiration.**

**Ans.** Refer to text on page. no 144.

**10. In frog, there are special venous connection between some parts of the body. Comment.**

**Ans.** Special venous connection between liver and intestine as well as the kidney and lower parts of the body are present in frogs. The former is called hepatic portal system and latter is renal portal system.

**11. How the central nervous system differ from peripheral nervous system in frog ?**

**Ans.** Refer to the text on page no. 145.

**12. Write a short note on sensory system of frog.**

**Ans.** Refer to text on page. no 145.

**13. State the significance of cloaca aperture in frogs.**

**Ans.** Cloaca is the chamber which is used to pass urine, sperms and faecal matter outside the body. Hence, it is a common chamber for urinary tract, reproductive tract and alimentary canal.

**14. Mention the function of the ureter in frog.** **NCERT**

**Ans.** In male frogs, ureter function as a urinogenital duct and used for transport of urine as well as sperms. (1)

In female frogs, ureter transport urine from kidney to cloaca. (1)

**15. Where is the Bidder's canal located and how is it useful in frog?**

**Ans.** Bidder's canal is present in the kidney of frog. (1)

It communicates with the ureter, which leaves the kidney near its end and opens into the cloaca. (1)

**16. Which structure in male frog act as urinogenital tract mention its function?**

**Ans.** In male frogs, the ureter function as urinogenital duct that opens into cloaca. It helps in passing the urine as well as sperm outside the body.

**17. Draw a neat and well-labelled diagram of male reproductive system of a frog.** **NCERT Exemplar**

**Ans.** Refer to text on page. no 146.

**18. Frogs are beneficial to mankind, comment on this statement.**

**Ans.** Refer to text on page. no 146.

## Long Answer Type Questions

**1. Describe the external characters of frog.**

**Ans.** Refer to the text on page no. 142.

**2. Describe the respiratory system of frog.**

**Ans.** Refer to text on page no 144.

**3. Write the function of the following in case of frog.**

(i) Tongue (ii) Nictitating membrane
(iii) Vocal sacs (iv) Sinus venosus
(v) Tympanic membrane

**Ans.** (i) Tongue is used to capture the prey. (1)

(ii) Nictitating membrane protects the eyes of the frog, when it is in the water. (1)

(iii) Vocal sacs raise pitch on the sound during croaking. (1)

(iv) Sinus venosus is present of the dorsal side of the frog's heart. It receives blood through vena cava and opens into right auricle. (1)

(v) Tympanic membrane serves to receive the sound waves. (1)

**4. Describe the circulatory system of frog.**

**Ans.** Refer to text on page no. 144-145.

**5. Give an account of nervous system of frog.**

**Ans.** Refer to text on page. no 145.

**6. Describe the male reproductive organs of frog.**

**Ans.** Refer to text on page. no 146.

**7. Distinguish between male frog and female frog.**

**Ans.** Differences between male and female frog are as follows

| Male frog | Female frog |
|---|---|
| Vocal cords are present on ventrolateral side of throat. | Vocal sacs are absent. |
| Croaking is more louder. | Croaking is less louder. |
| Forelimbs are stouter and more muscular. | Forelimbs are less muscular. |
| Copulatory pads are present on ventral side of index fingers. | Copulatory pads are absent. |
| During breeding season, abdomen does not change much. | Abdomen gets swollen during breeding season as it is full of ova released from mature ovaries. |

## Source Based/Case Based/Passage Based Questions

**1. The graph below indicates the population of frogs in a pond over a one-year period. Observe it carefully and answer the following questions.** **Competency Based Que.**

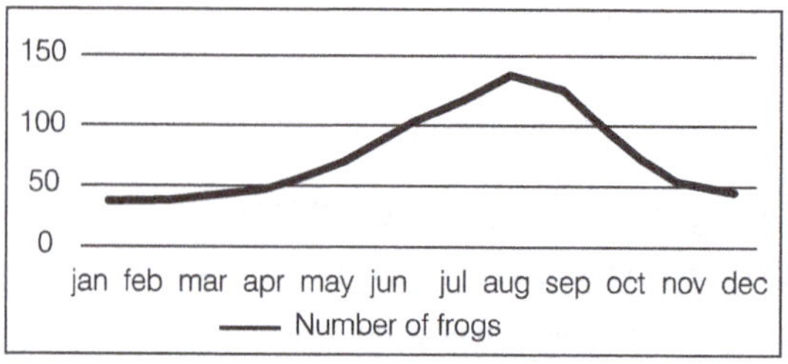


**(i) Why does there is a change in the population of frog during July and August?**

**(ii) Which month has the constant population of frogs? Give reason.**

**(iii) What type of fertilisation is found in the frog?**

**(iv) Is there a link between the increasing population of frogs and mosquitoes? Explain.**

**Ans.** (i) July and August are the monsoon months, which provide suitable conditions for reproduction and thereby increase in their population. (1)

(ii) January and February have a constant population of frogs. This is because during these months, the weather is extremely cold, and frogs undergo hibernation. (1)

(iii) External fertlisation is found in the frogs. (1)

(iv) Yes, there is a link between the increasing population of frogs and mosquitoes. Frogs primarily feed on insects, so an increase in the frog population often leads to a decrease in mosquito numbers. (1)

**2. A teacher assigns a specific spot within an anatomy diagram to the entire class, instructing each student to observe it carefully. The teacher encourages students to consider nearby structures, the spot's shape, and its possible function within the body.** **Competency Based Que.**

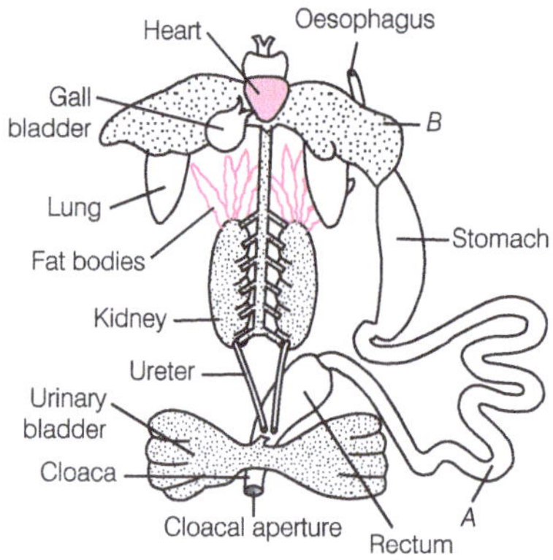


**(i) Identify the given spot. What does structure *A* and *B* represents?**

**(ii) What is the function of structure A in the given diagram?**

**(iii) What is the function of structure B in the given diagram?**

**Ans.** (i) The given spot is represents the digestive system of frog.
In the diagram structure A represents small intestine and structure B represents liver. (1)

(ii) The **small intestine** in frog digests food and absorbs nutrients. Digestive enzymes break down food, and the inner walls, lined with villi, increase surface area to absorb nutrients like proteins, fats, and carbohydrates into the bloodstream. (2)

(iii) The **liver** in frogs produces bile, which helps in the digestion and breakdown of fats. It also stores nutrients and detoxifies harmful substances. (1)

# SELF ASSESSMENT TEST

## Multiple Choice Questions

1. Which of the following best describes the role of tissues in multicellular organisms?
   (a) Tissues consist of one type of cell and can perform various functions.
   (b) Tissues consist of similar cells that work together to perform specific functions
   (c) Tissues are the smallest functional unit of life that perform specific functions
   (d) Tissues forms organ system and serve to connect different organs.
2. *Rana tigrina* belongs to the phylum
   (a) Chordata (b) Amphibia
   (c) Arthropoda (d) Mollusca
3. Which of the following is the most distinguishing sexual characteristic of male frog?
   (a) Presence of copulatory pads on the first digits of forelimbs
   (b) Presence of membranous tympanum
   (c) Presence of a well- developed lymphatic system
   (d) Presence of nictitating membrane
4. The cloaca in male frog is a common chamber for the urinary tract, reproductive tract and .............. .
   (a) lymphatic system (b) digestive tract
   (c) respiratory tract (d) sensory system
5. Identify the incorrect statement regarding the blood vascular system of frog.
   (a) It consists of heart, blood and blood vessels
   (b) A special venous connection called hepatic portal system is present between liver and intestine
   (c) The heart consists of three chambers, i.e. one atrium and two ventricles
   (d) The blood carries nutrients, gases and water to all parts of the body
6. The system for control and coordination in frogs is
   (a) highly evolved and consists of nervous system only
   (b) less developed and includes endocrine system only
   (c) highly evolved and includes both nervous and endocrine system
   (d) composed of highly evolved nervous system and less developed endocrine system
7. Select the correct match pair with respect to nervous system of frog.
   (a) Forebrain- Olfactory lobes
   (b) Midbrain- Paired cerebral hemisphere
   (c) Hindbrain- Paired optic nerves
   (d) Peripheral nervous system- Unpaired diencephalon

## Assertion-Reason Questions

**Direction** (Q. Nos. 8-11) *In each of the following questions, a statement of Assertion (A) is given followed by corresponding statement of Reason (R). Of the statements, mark the correct answer as*

(a) Both A and R are true and R is the correct explanation of the A.
(b) Both A and R are true, but R is not the correct explanation of the A.
(c) A is true, but R is false.
(d) A is false, but R is true.

8. **Assertion** (A) The large intestine in frogs plays a crucial role in water absorption.
   **Reason** (R) The large intestine helps in the digestion of proteins from the undigested food.

9. **Assertion** (A) Frog heart pumps mixed blood to different part of the body.

**Reason** (R) In frogs, the oxygenated and deoxygenated blood gets mixed in the ventricle of heart.

10. **Assertion** (A) The mature female frog's ovaries release 2500-3000 eggs at a time.

**Reason** (R) The eggs are released in the water and the fertilisation is external.

11. **Assertion** (A) Frogs are beneficial for mankind.

**Reason** (R) Frogs help in maintaining the ecological balance by forming an important part of food chain.

## Very Short Answer Type Questions

12. Identify the term for protective colouration in frogs.
13. Where does final digestion take place in a frog?
14. Mention the structural and functional unit of kidney in frog.
15. How do frogs help maintain balance in the ecosystem?

## Short Answer Type Questions

16. Why are frogs not seen during peak summer and winters?
17. What do you understand by camouflage and mimicry? How are they beneficial for frogs?
18. Describe the mode of respiration preferred by the frog when it is inside the water.

## Long Answer Type Questions

19. Write a short note on
    (i) Digestive glands of frog
    (ii) Central nervous system of frogs
20. Give an account on the excretory system of *Rana tigrina*.
21. Give a breif account on female reproductive system of frog.

## Case Based Question

22. The graph given below indicates the population of frogs in different areas. Observe the graph carefully and answer the following question.

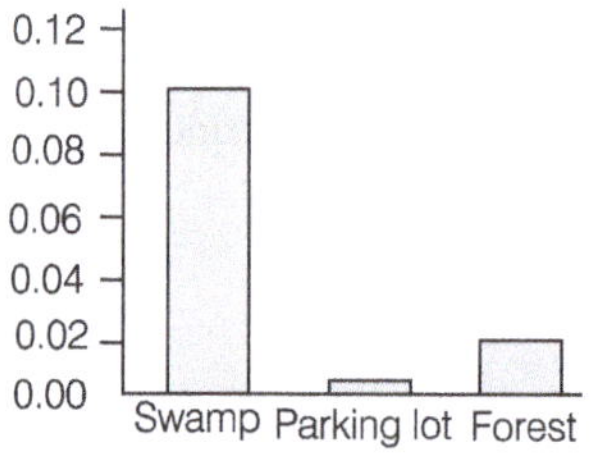


(i) In which area the populaiton of frog is higher and why?
(ii) Frogs show sexual dimorphism, how can a male frog be distinguished from a female frog?
(iii) On the basis of the above graph in which area the population fo tadpole is higher?
(iv) Name the process by which a tadpole converts into an adult.

# Answers

| | | | | | | |
|---|---|---|---|---|---|---|
| 1. (b) | 2. (a) | 3. (a) | 4. (b) | 5. (c) | 6. (c) | 7. (a) |
| 8. (c) | 9. (a) | 10. (b) | 11. (a) | | | |

08

CHAPTER

# Cell : The Unit of Life

Cell is said to be the fundamental structural and functional unit of all living organisms. Anything less than a complete structure of a cell does not ensure independent living. All living organisms, whether plants or animals are made up of either single cell or many cells.

▼ **YOUR STUDY GOALS**



▼ **YOUR PRACTICE GOAL**

- Objective Type Questions
  (47 Qs ; MCQs, A-R)
  Case Based Questions (2)
- Subjective Type Questions
- (16 VSAs, 38 SAs, 9 LAs)

- **Anton von Leeuwenhoek** first saw and described a living cell. Later, **Robert Brown** discovered the nucleus within the cell.
- This discovery was made possible by the invention of the microscope.
- Further improvements in the microscope led to the development of the electron microscope, which revealed all the structural details of the cell.
- In this chapter, we will discuss cell theory, the different types of cells, and the various cellular organelles in detail.

## 8.1 Cell : An Overview

- An organism consists of one or more cells, accordingly there are two types of organisms, i.e. **unicellular** (composed of single cell) and **multicellular** (composed of many cells).
- Unicellular organisms are capable of independent existence and can perform all the essential functions of life.

### Cell Theory

- The cell theory was formulated by two scientists, **Matthias Schleiden** and **Theodore Schwann** independently.
- **Schleiden** (1838) was a **German botanist** who examined a large variety of plants. He observed that all plants are

composed of different kinds of cells which form the tissues of the plant.

- At about the same time, **Schwann** (1839), a **British zoologist**, closely studied different types of animal cells and found that the animal cell had a very thin outer layer known as **plasma membrane**.
- From his studies, he also concluded that the presence of a cell wall is a unique characteristic of plant cells.
- On the basis of this, Schwann proposed the hypothesis that the bodies of animals and plants are composed of cells and products of cells.
- Discoveries of Schleiden and Schwann lead to the formulation of cell theory.

## Objections to Cell Theory

- Cell theory failed to explain how new cells were formed.
- **Rudolf Virchow** in 1855 modified the hypothesis of Schleiden and Schwann. He explained that cells divide and new cells are formed from pre-existing cells, i.e. *Omnis cellula-e-cellula.*
- This finding gave cell theory its final shape. Cell theory as understood today is
  - all living organisms are composed of cells and their products.
  - all cells arise from pre-existing cells.

## Structural Outline of a Cell

The basic structural organisation of a typical cell is as follows

### 1. Nucleus

- It is the central part of the cell, which is spherical in shape.
- It is denser than the surrounding cytoplasm.
- It contains chromosomes which in turn contain the genetic material, i.e. DNA.
- Cells that have membrane bound nuclei are called **eukaryotes**, whereas cells that lack membrane bound nucleus are called **prokaryotes**.

### 2. Cytoplasm

- It is the semi-fluid matrix that occupies the volume of both prokaryotic and eukaryotic cell.
- It is the main arena of cellular activities in both plant and animal cells.
- Various chemical reactions occur inside the cytoplasm to keep the cell in the living state.

### 3. Cell Organelles

- Eukaryotic cells contain membrane bound distinct structures called **cell organelles**, like mitochondria, microbodies, vacuoles, Endoplasmic Reticulum (ER), Golgi complex and lysosomes.
- The prokaryotic cells lack all these **membrane bound organelles**.

### 4. Ribosomes

- They are non-membrane bound organelles found in both prokaryotic and eukaryotic cells.
- They are also found within the two organelles, i.e. chloroplasts (in plants) and mitochondria and on rough ER.

### 5. Centrosome

- Animal cells contain another non-membrane bound organelle called **centrosome**, which helps in cell division.

### 6. Outer Membrane

- It is the boundary of the cell, which provides protection to the cell and controls the exchange of ions, molecules and other components in and out of the cell.
- The outer membrane of a cell contains **cell wall** (only in plant cells) and **plasma membrane** (in both plant and animal cell).

## Size of a Cell

- The cells exhibit an endless variation in size, shape and activities of the cell.
- For example, mycoplasma (**smallest cell**) is only 0.3 μm in length, while bacteria measures approx. 3-5 μm in length.

- The **largest isolated single cell** is the egg of the ostrich.
- In human beings, Red Blood Cells (RBCs) are about 7 μm in diameter and the nerve cells are some of the **longest cell**.

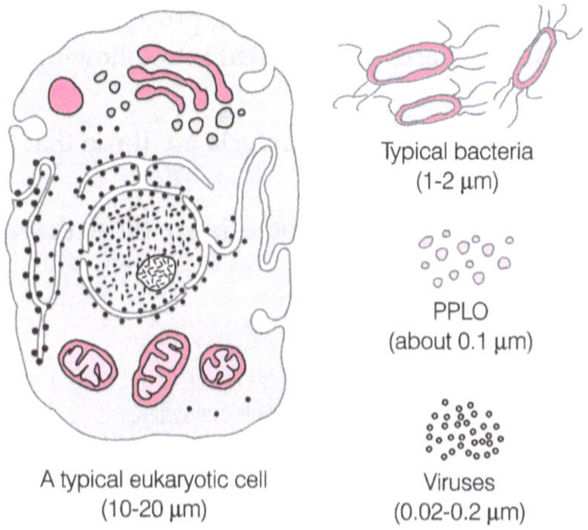


Fig. 8.1 Diagram showing comparison of eukaryotic cell with other organisms

## Shape of a Cell

- The cells also vary greatly in their shapes.
- They may be polygonal, columnar, disc-like amoeboid, thread-like, cuboid or irregular.
- The shape of the cell may vary with the function they perform.

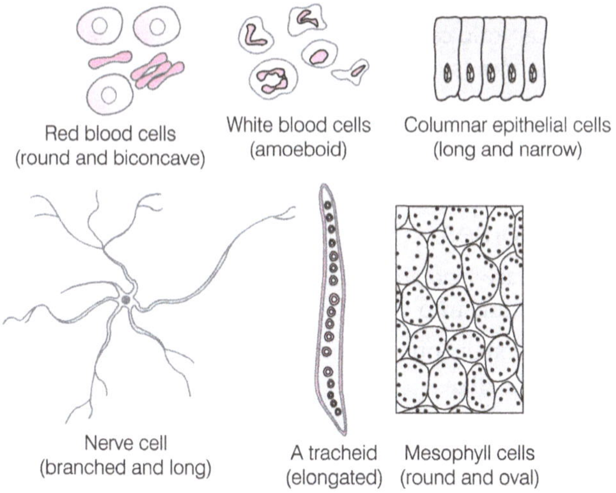


Fig. 8.2 Diagram showing different shapes of the cells

## Types of Cells

On the basis of the organisation of DNA, complexity and variety, the cells can be grouped into two types, i.e. prokaryotic cells and eukaryotic cells.

### Quick Test 1

1. Name the German botanist who observed that all plants are composed of cells.
2. **State True or False.**
   According to the cell theory, cells are the smallest living units but are not responsible for the reproduction of organisms.
3. Name the type of the cell which has a membrane around its nucleus.
4. *X* is the longest, branched cell, present in all higher vertebrates. Identify *X*.
5. Name the cell organelle found within chloroplast and mitochondria.

# 8.2 Prokaryotic Cell

- Cell, which does not have a nuclear membrane and other membrane bound organelles, is called prokaryotic cell.
- These cells are represented by bacteria, cyanobacteria (blue-green algae), mycoplasma or PPLO (Pleuro Pneumonia Like Organism).

## Shape and size

- Prokaryotic cells may vary greatly in shape and size.
- They are generally smaller and multiply more rapidly than the eukaryotic cell.
- There are four basic shapes of bacteria, i.e. bacillus (rod-like), coccus (spherical), vibrio (comma-shaped) and spirillum (spiral).

## Components of a Prokaryotic Cell (Bacteria)

- All prokaryotic cells are similar in their organisation, although they exhibit a wide variety of shapes and functions.

- A bacterial cell is composed of various components i.e, cell envelope, genetic material, membranous structures like mesosomes and chromatophores, flagella, pili, fimbriae, inclusion bodies, ribosomes, etc., which are discussed below

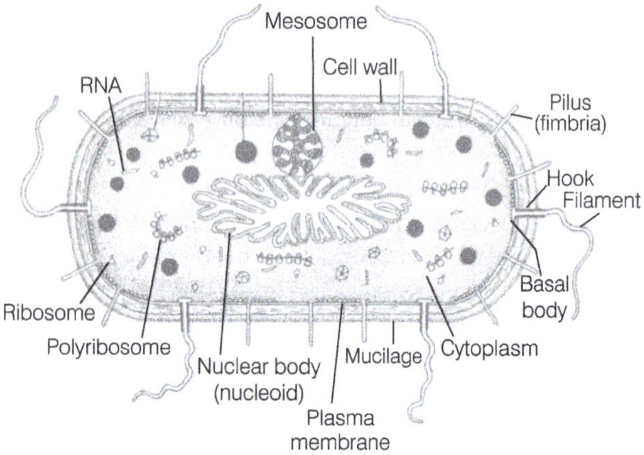


**Fig. 8.3** Diagrammatic representation of a typical bacterial cell

## Cell Envelope

- Cell envelope is the outermost covering of protoplasm of the bacterial cell.
- It is known to protect the cell from mechanical shocks and injuries.
- It consists of a tightly bound three layered structure, with each layer performing specialised functions that are discussed below.

### 1. Glycocalyx

- It is the **outermost layer** of the cell envelope.
- It differs in composition and thickness among different bacteria.
- The glycocalyx could be in the form of loose sheath called the **slime layer** or thick and tough covering called the **capsule**.

### 2. Cell Wall

- It is present just below the **glycocalyx**.
- It determines the shape of the cell and provides strong structural support to prevent the bacterium from bursting or collapsing.
- All prokaryotes have a cell wall surrounding the cell membrane except in mycoplasma.

### 3. Plasma Membrane

- It is the **innermost layer** of the cell envelope.
- This membrane is similar structurally to that of the eukaryotes.
- On the basis of the differences in the cell envelope and the response to the staining procedure developed by Gram, bacteria are classified into following two types.
  - **Gram positive** (+ve) **bacteria** are those that take up the Gram stain.
  - **Gram negative** (-ve) **bacteria** are those that do not take up the Gram stain.

**TEACHER'S TIP**

Gram positive bacteria stain violet due to the presence of a thick layer of peptidoglycan in their cell walls.

## Genetic Material

- There is no well-defined nucleus and the genetic material is **naked**, i.e., not enclosed by a nuclear membrane.
- Many bacteria contain a small circular DNA known as **plasmid** other than the chromosomal or genomic DNA.
- These plasmids confer certain unique characters to the bacteria like antibiotic resistance, etc.

## Membranous Structures

- Prokaryotic cells lack the complex membrane bound organelles (such as chloroplast, mitochondria, etc).
- However, some other special membranous structures like **mesosomes** and **chromatophores** are found in them.

### Mesosomes

- These are formed by the extensions of the plasma membrane into the cell.
- These extensions are in the form of **vesicles, tubules** and **lamellae**.
- Mesosomes perform the following functions in the bacterium.
  - They help in increasing the enzymatic content and surface area of the plasma membrane.
  - They help in the formation of cell wall.

- They help in the replication of DNA and distribution of genetic material to daughter cells during fission.
- They also help in respiration, cellular secretion, etc.

## Chromatophores

- They are another membranous structure present in some prokaryotes like cyanobacteria, etc.
- They are internal membrane systems of photosynthetic forms, which possess photosynthetic pigments.

## Flagella

- Flagella (sing flagellum) are present in some bacteria.
- On the basis of the presence or absence of flagella, bacteria may be motile or non-motile in nature.
- The motile bacteria possess one or more filamentous extension from their cell wall called flagella.
- They help in locomotion, i.e. movement from one place to another.
- Bacteria also show range in the number and arrangement of flagellum.
- The bacterial flagellum is differentiated into the following three parts.
  - **Filament** It is the longest portion, extending from the cell surface to the outside.
  - **Hook** It is the curved and tubular structure that connects the filament with the basal body.
  - **Basal Body** It is inserted in the cell envelope.

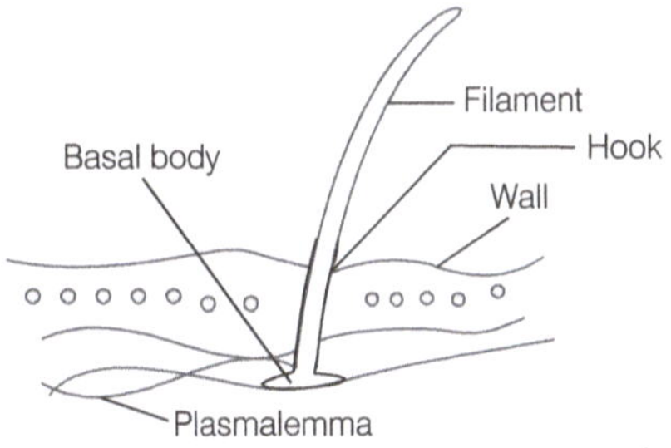


Fig. 8.4 Bacterial flagellum showing different parts

## Pili and Fimbriae

- These are also the surface structures, but do not play any role in locomotion of bacteria.
- The pili are the elongated, tubular structures made up of a special protein.
- While, fimbriae are the small **bristle like fibres** sprouting out of the cell.
- In some bacteria, they are known to help attach the bacteria to rocks in streams and also to the host tissues.

## Ribosomes and Inclusion Bodies

Cytoplasm in prokaryotes appears granular, due to the presence of following structures.

### 1. Ribosomes

- Like eukaryotes, ribosomes are also found in prokaryotes and serve a common function, i.e. acts as a site of protein synthesis.
- They are about 15-20 nm in size.
- In prokaryotes, ribosomes are found in association with the plasma membrane of the cell (as it lacks the endoplasmic reticulum) in the cytoplasmic matrix.
- The prokaryotic ribosomes are of 70S type. It has following two subunits
  - **Smaller subunit** (30S)
  - **Larger subunit** (50S)
- Ribosomes may attach to a single strand of mRNA and form a chain called **polyribosomes** or **polysomes**.
- The ribosomes of a polysome help in the process of **translation** (mechanisms to synthesise several copies of the same protein) of *m*RNA into protein.

### 2. Inclusion Bodies

- The **reserve material** in the prokaryotic cells are stored in the form of inclusion bodies.
- These are not bounded by any membrane system.
- They lie free in the cytoplasm (e.g. cyanophycean granules, glycogen granules and phosphate granules).
- Another type of inclusion body called **gas vacuoles** are also found in blue-green and purple and green photosynthetic bacteria.

## Quick Test 2

1. Name the structure which lies between the glycocalyx and plasma membrane of bacteria.
2. A bacteria *X* does not contain cell wall. Identify the organism.
3. **State True or False.**
   Many bacteria contain small linear DNA known as plasmid.
4. Name the structure which are the extension of plasma membrane into the cell.
5. In cyanobacteria, name the structure which possess pigment for photosynthesis.

## 8.3 Eukaryotic Cell

- Cell which has a well-organised nucleus, with a nuclear envelope and several membrane bound cell organelles is called **eukaryotic cell**.
- Internal organisation of eukaryotic cells is more advanced and elaborate, than the prokaryotic cells.
- Eukaryotic organisation is seen in all the protists, plants, fungi and animals.

### Structure of Eukaryotic cell

- An extensive compartmentalisation of cytoplasm is seen through the presence of membrane bound organelles.
- Eukaryotic cells also possess a variety of **locomotory** and **cytoskeletal** structures.
- Their genetic material is organised into chromosomes.
- All eukaryotic cells are not identical, instead they differ from each other on the basis of structure and function.
- For instance, both plant and animal cells are eukaryotic, however, there are differences in their structures, which are tabulated below

**Differences Between Plant and Animal Cells**

| Characters | Animal Cells | Plant Cells |
|---|---|---|
| **Cell wall** | Absent | Present (formed of cellulose). |
| **Shape** | Round (irregular shape) | Rectangular (fixed shape). |
| **Centrioles** | Present in all animal cells | Absent |
| **Vacuole** | One or more small vacuoles (much smaller than plant cells) | One, large central vacuole taking up 90% of cell volume. |
| **Cytoplasm** | Present | Present |
| **Ribosomes** | Present | Present |
| **Plastids** | Absent | Present |
| **Cell membrane** | Present | Present |
| **Golgi apparatus** | Present | Present |
| **Mitochondria** | Present | Present |
| **Endoplasmic reticulum** (smooth and rough) | Present | Present |
| **Chloroplast** | Animal cells do not have chloroplasts because they do not have the ability to prepare their food. | Plant cells have chloroplasts because they make their own food (autotrophs). |
| **Flagella** | May be found in some cells | May be found in some cells. |
| **Microtubules** | Present | Present |
| **Microfilaments** | Present | Present |
| **Cilia** | Present | Absent |
| **Lysosomes** | Lysosomes occur in cytoplasm. | Lysosomes are usually not evident. |
| **Nucleus** | Present | Present |

| Characters | Animal Cells | Plant Cells |
|---|---|---|

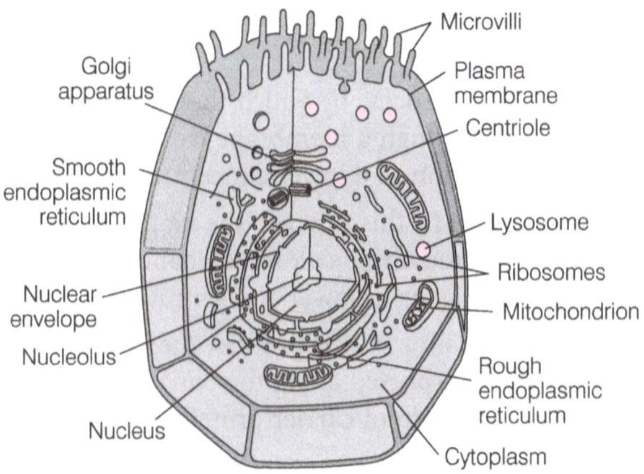


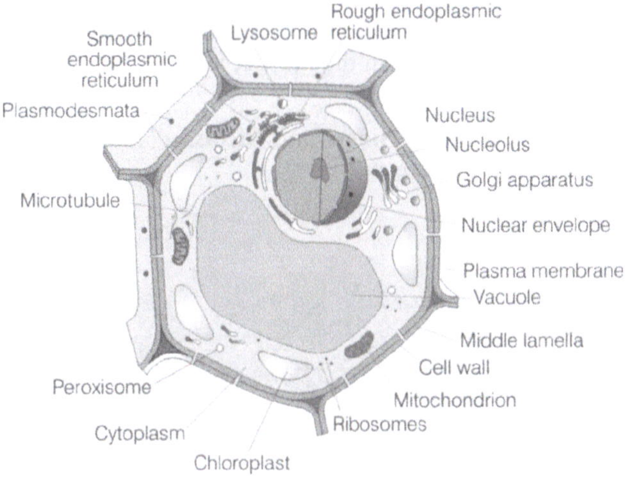


## Components of a Eukaryotic Cell

- A eukaryotic cell is composed of various cell components such as cell membrane, cell wall (only in plants), mitochondria, chloroplast, Golgi bodies, ribosomes, centrioles (only in animals), etc.
- All these components are described below in detail.

## Cell Membrane

- Every living cell is covered by a thin and semi-permeable membrane called **cell membrane**.
- It is also called **plasma membrane**.
- The plasma membrane separates the internal environment of the cell from the external environment.
- The detailed structure of the membrane was studied in 1950s with the advancement of electron microscope.
- Chemical studies on cell membrane structure, i.e. especially on the human Red Blood Cells (RBCs), enabled the scientists to deduce its possible structure.

### Structure of Cell Membrane

- Studies on human RBCs concluded that the cell membrane is composed of lipid which forms a bilayer, with protein molecules embedded in it at various places.
- Later, it was revealed that the cell membrane also possesses protein and carbohydrates.
- The ratio of protein and lipid varies considerably in different cell types.
- In human beings, the membrane of the erythrocytes (RBCs) has approximately **52% protein** and **40% lipid**.

#### Lipid

- The major lipids are **phospholipids** that are arranged in a bilayer.
- Also, the lipids are arranged within the membrane with the polar head or the **hydrophilic part** towards the outer sides and the **hydrophobic tails** towards the inner part.
- This arrangement ensures that the non-polar tail of saturated hydrocarbons is protected from the aqueous environment.
- In addition to phospholipids, membrane also contains **cholesterol**.

#### Proteins

Depending upon the ease of extraction, the membrane proteins can be classified as

- **Integral Proteins** These proteins are buried partially or totally in the phospholipid bilayer.
- **Peripheral Proteins** These proteins lie on the surface of membrane.

## Fluid Mosaic Model

- To understand the structure of plasma membrane, various models have been put forward by different scientists out of which the most accepted model is **Fluid Mosaic Model**.
- It was proposed by **Singer** and **Nicolson** (1972).

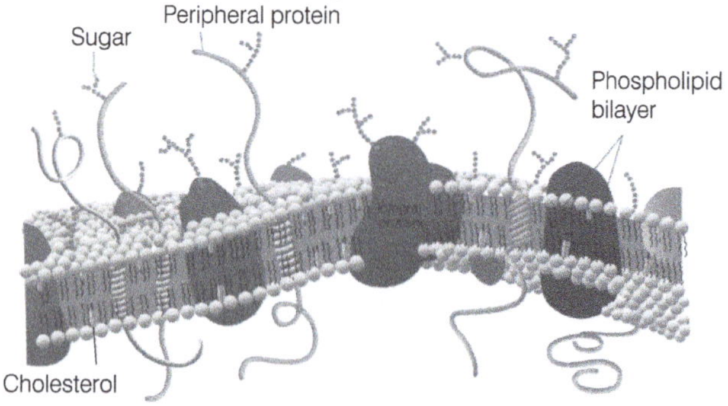


Fig. 8.5 Fluid mosaic model of plasma membrane

- According to this model, the lipid bilayer and integral proteins appear like a mosaic arrangement and the quasi-fluid nature of lipid enables the lateral movement of the proteins within the overall bilayer.
- This ability of proteins to move within the membrane indicates the fluidity of the lipid part.
- The fluid nature of the membrane is important as it support many important functions like formation of intercellular junctions, cell growth, secretion, endocytosis, cell division, etc.

## Functions of Cell Membrane

- One of the most important functions of the plasma membrane is the **transport of the molecules across it**.
- The membrane is selectively permeable to some molecules present on either side of it.
- Passage of substances across the membrane occurs mainly by two methods.

### 1. Active Transport

- It is the movement of the molecules across the membrane **against their concentration gradient,** i.e. from lower to the higher concentration.
- It is an energy dependent process, in which ATP is utilised.
- It occurs in few ions and molecules, e.g. $Na^+/K^+$ pump.

### 2. Passive Transport

It is the movement of molecules or substances across the membrane **without any requirement of energy**. It can be further of following three types

- **Osmosis** It is the process by which the water molecules pass through a membrane from a region of higher concentration to a lower concentration.
- **Simple Diffusion** In this process, the neutral solutes move across the membrane along the concentration gradient (from higher to lower concentration).
- **Facilitated Diffusion** In this process, the polar molecules are transported along the concentration gradient with the help of carrier proteins.

  Polar molecules require a carrier protein to facilitate their transport across the membrane because they cannot pass through the non-polar lipid bilayer.

# Cell Wall

- It is the rigid, protective and non-living structure which forms an outer covering of the plasma membrane in **plants** and **fungi**.
- It is **absent in animal cells.**
- Algae have cell wall, made of cellulose, galactans, mannans and minerals like calcium carbonate, while in other plants it consists of cellulose, hemicellulose, pectins and proteins.

## Structure of Cell Wall

On the basis of the structure, cell wall is differentiated into the following three parts

- **Middle Lamella** It is the layer mainly made up of **calcium pectate.**
  - It cements the cell walls of two adjoining cells together.
  - The middle lamella along with a cell wall is transversed by **plasmodesmata** which connects cytoplasm of neighbouring cells.
- **Primary Cell Wall** It is produced inner to the middle lamella in a young and growing cell.
  - It is capable of growth and extension.
  - It tends to diminish gradually as the cell attains maturity.
- **Secondary Cell Wall** It is formed inner towards membrane to the primary wall.

## Functions of Cell Wall

Cell wall performs the number of functions as given below.

- It helps in providing a definite shape to the cell.
- It protects protoplasm against any mechanical injury, i.e. damage and infection.
- It helps in cell-to-cell interaction.
- It provides barrier to undesirable macromolecules.

### Quick Test 3

1. Name the structural component that makes the cell membrane flexible.
2. Identify the part of a plant cell which acts as a protective barrier and helps to maintain its shape.
3. Name the main molecule that gives plant cell walls their strength and structure.
4. **State True or False.**
   (a) The cell wall is present in both plant and animal cells.
   (b) The cell membrane is selectively permeable, controlling what enters and exits the cell.
5. Name the proteins which are buried partially or totally in the phospholipid bilayer.

## Endomembrane System

- It consists of Endoplasmic Reticulum (ER), Golgi complex, lysosomes and vacuoles.
- These are considered together as an **endomembrane system** because their functions are coordinated with each other, despite each membranous organelle being distinct in terms of structure and function.
- Since the functions of the mitochondria, chloroplast and peroxisomes are not coordinated with the above components, these are not considered as part of the endomembrane system.

## 1. Endoplasmic Reticulum (ER)

- The electron microscopic studies of eukaryotic cells reveals that there is presence of a network or reticulum of tiny tubular structures that are being scattered in the cytoplasm that is called **endoplasmic reticulum**.
- Endoplasmic reticulum divides the intracellular space into two main compartments as given below.
  - **Luminal** (inside ER) **compartment**
  - **Extra luminal** (cytoplasm) **compartment**

### Types of Endoplasmic Reticulum

Depending upon the nature of its membranes endoplasmic reticulum are of two main types,

#### Smooth Endoplasmic Reticulum (SER)

- These are smooth because they do not bear ribosomes, in the form of granules, on their surfaces.
- They act as a major site for the synthesis of lipid and also help in synthesis of steroidal hormone in animal cells.

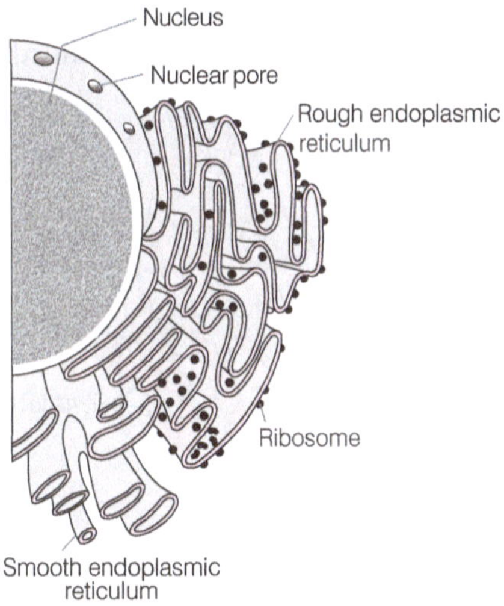


Fig. 8.6 Structure of an endoplasmic reticulum

#### Rough Endoplasmic Reticulum (RER)

- They are found extensively and in continuation with outer membrane of nucleus.
- These have rough membrane because a number of ribosomes are attached to their outer surfaces.
- They are actively seen in the cells which are involved in the synthesis and secretion of proteins.

## 2. Golgi Apparatus

- It was first discovered by **Camillo Golgi** (1898) as the densely stained reticular structures present near the nucleus of the cell.

- These structures were named Golgi bodies after his discovery.
- Golgi complex or Golgi apparatus is made up of many smooth, flat, disc-shaped **sacs** or **cisternae** (0.5-1.0 μm in diameter).
- These cisternae are stacked parallel to each other.
- The number of cisternae in a Golgi complex may vary in different cells.
- They are concentrically arranged near the nucleus with two distinct faces.
  - ***Cis* Face** (forming face) This is convex in shape and is responsible for receiving vesicles, containing enzyme or protein from the ER.
  - ***Trans* Face** (maturing face) This is concave in shape and is responsible for releasing the material, which is being received by *cis* face and modified in the cisternae.

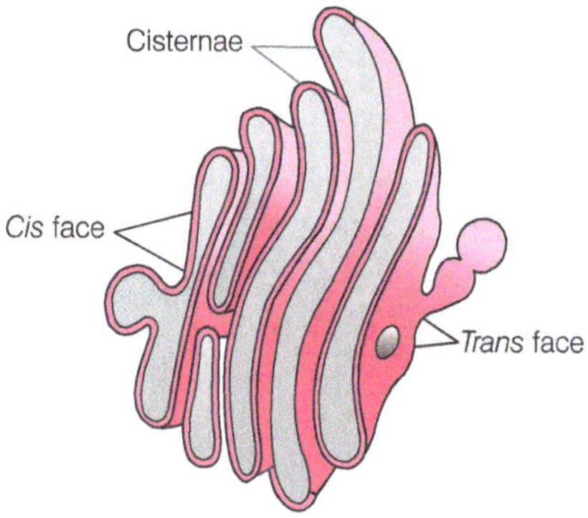


Fig. 8.7 Golgi apparatus

- Materials to be packaged in the form of vesicles from the ER fuse with the *cis* face of the Golgi apparatus and moves towards the maturing face.
- This explains the close association of Golgi apparatus with endoplasmic reticulum.

### Functions

Golgi apparatus performs the following functions.

- It modifies proteins, synthesised by ribosomes on the endoplasmic reticulum, in its cisternae before releasing them from its *trans* face.
- It acts as a site where the material to be released is being packaged in the form of vesicles delivered either to the intracellular targets or secreted outside the cell.
- Golgi apparatus is involved in the **formation of lysosomes**.
- It performs the function of **packaging material**.
- It acts as an important site for the **formation of glycoproteins** and **glycolipids**.

## 3. Lysosomes

- These are membrane bounded vesicles that are produced by the process of packaging in the **Golgi apparatus**.
- They are rich in several **hydrolytic digestive enzymes** (hydrolases, lipases, proteases, carbohydrases, etc).
- These are optimally active at the acidic pH (less than 7).
- They are capable of digesting macromolecules like carbohydrates, lipids and nucleic acids. Hence, they are also called the **suicidal bags of the cell**.

## 4. Vacuoles

- These are a large membrane-bound sac found in the cytoplasm.
- They contain water, sap, excretory product and other materials that are not essentially useful for the cell.
- In plants, vacuoles can occupy upto 90% of the volume of the cell.
- The vacuole is bounded by a single membrane structure known as **tonoplast**, which in plant cells facilitates the transport of materials and some ions against the concentration gradient into the vacuole.
- Thus, the concentration of substances tends to be the higher in vacuole than in the cytoplasm.
- Depending upon the contents and function, following types of vacuoles are being found in different organisms.

- **Contractile Vacuole** They plays an important role in osmoregulation and excretion in *Amoeba*, etc.
- **Food Vacuole** It occurs in the cells of protists. It is formed by engulfing the food particles.

## Mitochondria

- Mitochondria (sing. mitochondrion) are membrane bound cell organelles mainly found in aerobic eukaryotes as it is essential for **aerobic respiration**.
- They are not easily visible under the microscope, unless they are specifically stained.
- These are also known as **powerhouse of the cell** because they produce cellular energy in the form of ATP.

### Shape and Size

- Mitochondria vary considerably in terms of shape and size.
- Typically, these are sausage-shaped or cylindrical having a diameter of 0.2-1.0 μm (average 0.5 μm) and length 1.0-4.1 μm.

### Ultrastructure

- Each mitochondrion is a **double membrane bound** structure having an outer and an inner membrane.
- The **outer membrane** is smooth and forms the continuous boundary of the organelle.
- The **inner membrane** is infolded into the matrix as incomplete partitions called cristae (sing: crista).
- The cristae increase the surface area of the membrane for chemical reactions.
- The area between the inner and outer membranes is called **inter-membrane space**.
- The outer and the inner membranes divide its lumen into two aqueous compartments separately, i.e. the **outer** and the **inner compartments**.
- Inner compartment is filled with dense homogenous substance called **matrix**, which forms the inner core of the mitochondrion.
- The matrix possesses single circular DNA molecule, a few RNA molecules, ribosomes (70S) and the components required for the synthesis of proteins.
- The mitochondria divide by the method of fission.
- The two membranes of mitochondria have their own specific enzymes associated with mitochondrial function.

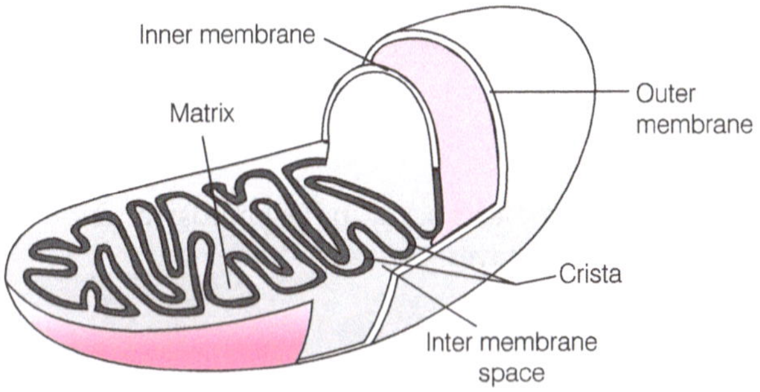


Fig. 8.8 Structure of mitochondria (Longitudinal section)

## Plastids

- They are found in all plant cells and euglenoids.
- Due to their large size, they are easily seen under the microscope.
- They bear some specific pigments, thus imparting specific colours to the plants.

## Types

Based on the type of pigments found in them, plastids are of three different types.

### 1. Chloroplasts

- These are green **colour plastids** containing **chlorophyll** and **carotenoids**.
- These pigments are responsible for trapping the light energy, essential for the photosynthesis, i.e. synthesis of organic food from inorganic materials in the presence of sunlight.

### 2. Leucoplasts

- These are the **colourless plastids** of varied shapes and sizes that stored nutrients in the form of carbohydrates, lipids and proteins.
- These are further divided into three main types.
  - **Amyloplasts** are the carbohydrates (starch) containing leucoplast, e.g. present in potato.
  - **Elaioplasts** are the leucoplast which stores oils and fats, e.g., endosperm of castor seeds.
  - **Aleuroplasts** are the protein storing leucoplast, e.g., maize (aleurone layer).

### 3. Chromoplasts

- In these plastids, fat soluble carotenoid pigments like carotene, xanthophylls and others are present.
- These pigments give the part of the plant a yellow, orange or red colour.

## Chloroplasts

Majority of chloroplasts occur in the photosynthetic mesophyll cells of leaves.

### Shape and Size

- They may be lens-shaped, oval, spherical, discoid or even ribbon-like organelles.
- They also have variable length (5-10 μm) and width (2-4 μm).

### Number

- Different species of a genus may have different number of chloroplasts.
- Their number also varies from 1 per cell of the *Chlamydomonas* (a green alga) to 20-40 per cell in the mesophyll.

### Ultrastructure

- The chloroplast is also bounded by double membrane envelope, just like mitochondria.
- The space between the two layers in a chloroplast is called inter-membrane space.
- The inner membrane of chloroplast is less permeable than the outer one.
- The space limited by the inner membrane of chloroplast is known as **stroma**.
- Stroma contains enzymes which are essential for the synthesis of carbohydrates and proteins.
- It also contains small, double-stranded circular DNA molecules and ribosomes.
- The ribosomes of chloroplasts are smaller (70S) than the ribosomes of cytoplasm (80S).
- A number of organised flattened membranous sacs called **thylakoids** are present in the stroma.
- The thylakoids contain chlorophyll pigments, thus are the sites of photosynthesis.
- These are arranged in the stack (like the piles of coins), called **grana** (sing. granum) or the **intergranal thylakoids**.
- Many flat membranous tubules that interconnect the thylakoids of different grana. These tubules are known as **stroma lamellae**.
- The membrane of the thylakoids encloses a space called a lumen.

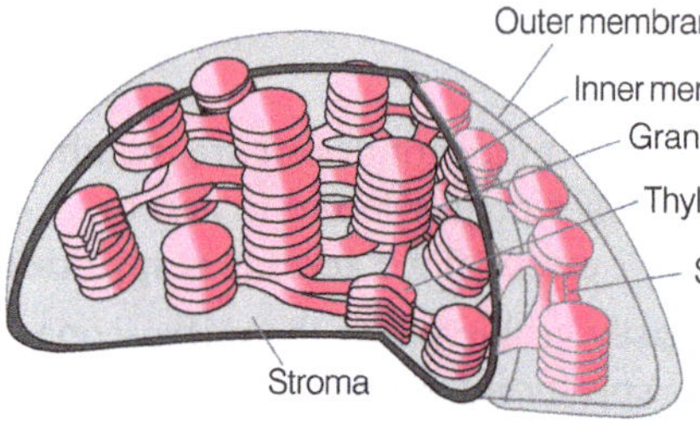


Fig. 8.9 Sectional view of chloroplast

> **Quick Test 4**
>
> 1. Name the organelle which modifies, sorts, and packages proteins and lipids for transport.
> 2. *Y* is the structure of golgi body which is convex in shape and is responsible for receiving vesicles, containing enzyme or protein from the ER. Identify *Y*.
> 3. Identify the cell organelle in which aerobic respiration occurs.
> 4. Name of the membrane-bound compartments inside a chloroplast where photosynthesis occurs.
> 5. **State True or False.**
>    (a) Chloroplasts are primarily involved in cellular respiration.
>    (b) Chloroplasts convert sunlight into chemical energy through photosynthesis.

## Ribosomes

- These are the small granular structures, not bounded by any membrane.
- Ribosomes were first observed by **George Palade** (1953), as the dense particles under the electron microscope.
- Ribosomes are mainly composed of **ribonucleoproteins** (i.e. RNA + proteins).
- They are also known as **protein factories**, as they are primarily involved in the synthesis of proteins or polypeptides.
- As studied earlier, the prokaryotic ribosomes are 70S type, while the eukaryotic ribosomes are 80S type.
- Here, 'S' (Svedberg's unit) stands for **sedimentation coefficient** (indirect measure of density and size).

- Both 70S and 80S ribosomes contain two subunits, i.e. the smaller and the larger subunit.

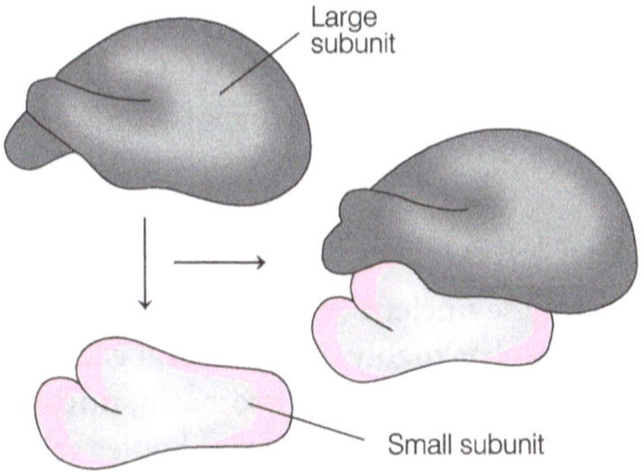

Fig. 8.10 Ribosomes

**Differences between 70S and 80S Ribosomes**

| 70S Ribosomes | 80S Ribosomes |
|---|---|
| They are found in prokaryotes (bacteria and cyanobacteria). | They are found in eukaryotes (algae, fungi, higher plants and animals). |
| Larger subunit (50S). | Larger subunit (60S). |
| Smaller subunit (30S). | Smaller subunit (40S). |
| Comparatively smaller | Larger than 70S. |

## Cytoskeleton

The network of interconnected proteinaceous structure consisting of microtubules, microfilaments and intermediate filaments present in the cytoplasm is collectively referred to as the **cytoskeleton**.

### Functions

Cytoskeleton performs the following functions.

- The cytoskeletal structure maintains the shape of the cell.
- It is also involved in many other functions in a cell as providing mechanical support, motility, etc.

## Cilia and Flagella

- These are **hair-like projections** of cell membrane.
- Both cilia and flagella are almost identical in structure, but differ somewhat in length.
- Cilia are small structures that function like oars, causing the movement of either the cell or the surrounding fluid.
- Flagella are comparatively longer in size than cilia and are responsible for the movement of cell.
- The prokaryotic bacteria also possess flagella but these are structurally different from that of eukaryotic flagella.

### Ultrastructure

- According to the electron microscopic studies, the cilium or the flagellum are covered with **plasma membrane**.

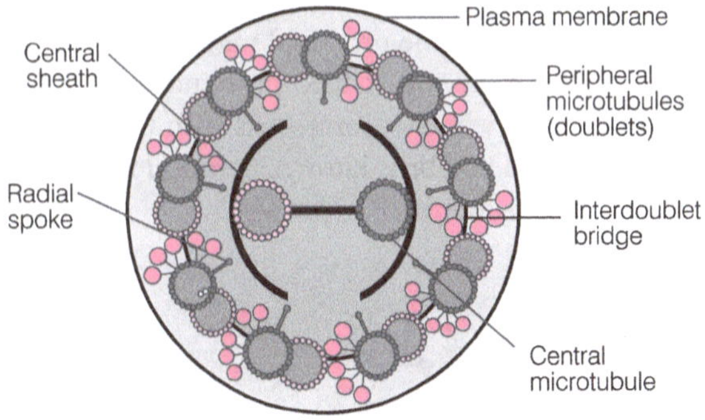

Fig. 8.11 Diagrammatic representation of internal structure of cilia/flagella

- Their core called the **axoneme**, contains a number of microtubules, running parallel to the long axis.
- Usually, the axoneme has nine doublets of peripheral microtubules that are radially arranged and a pair of centrally located microtubules.
- This arrangement of axonemal microtubules is referred to as the **(9+2) array**.
- The central tubules are connected by bridges and is also enclosed by a central sheath, which is connected to one of the tubules of each peripheral doublets by a **radial spoke**.
- Thus, it has been estimated that there are nine radial spokes.
- The peripheral doublets are also interconnected by linkers.
- Both the cilium and flagellum emerge from centriole-like structure called the **basal bodies**.

**Differences between Cilia and Flagella**

| Cilia | Flagella |
|---|---|
| Cilia are short, hair-like organelles, 2-20 μm in length. | Flagella are long, whip-like organelles that may be 10-200 μm long. |
| They occur relatively in large numbers per cell. | They are usually fewer per cell. |

## Centrosomes and Centrioles

- Centrosome is an organelle that generally have two cylindrical structures known as **centrioles.**
- They are surrounded by an amorphous pericentriolar materials.
- Both the centrioles in a centrosome lie perpendicular to each other in which each has an organisation like the cart-wheel.
- They are usually made up of nine evenly spaced peripheral fibrils (triplet in nature) of tubulin protein.
- The central part of the proximal region of the centriole possesses rod-shaped proteinaceous mass known as **hub,** which is connected with tubules of the peripheral triplets fibrils known as **radial spokes** (made up of protein).

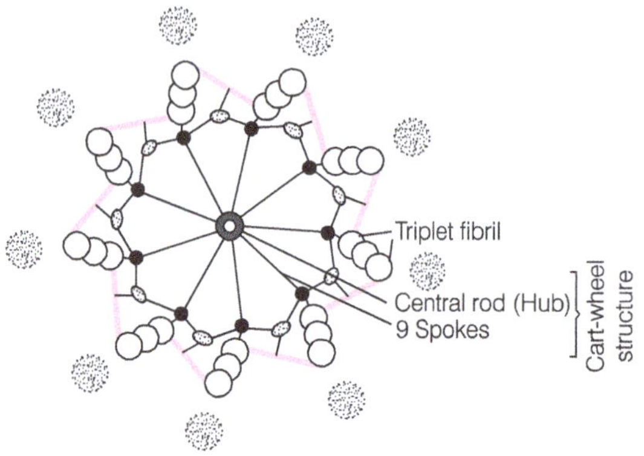


Fig. 8.12 Ultrastructure of centriole as seen in TS

### Functions

Centrosomes and centrioles perform the following functions

- These structures form the spindle fibres and move to the poles, at the time of cell division, which thus, help in the movement of chromatids in daughter cells.
- They form the basal body of cilia and flagella.

## Nucleus

- It is the specialised and principal organelle of the cell, which contains all the genetic information for controlling essential processes related to metabolism and hereditary transmission.
- Nucleus as a cell organelle was first described by **Robert Brown** as early as 1831.
- Later the name **chromatin** was given by **Flemming** when the material of the nucleus was stained by the basic dyes.

### Occurrence

- A nucleus is known to be present in all eukaryotic cells except a few cell types such as RBCs of humans, sieve tube cells of vascular plants, etc.
- Prokaryotic cell lacks a well-organised nucleus, instead they have a nucleoid.

### Ultrastructure

- The interphase nucleus (nucleus of a cell when it is not dividing) has highly extended and elaborate nucleoprotein fibres called **chromatin, nuclear matrix** and one or more spherical bodies called **nucleoli** (sing. nucleolus).
- Nuclear envelope is found on the outside of the nucleus.
- The nuclear envelope consists of two parallel membranes which are separated by a space called the **perinuclear space** (the space 10 to 50 nm in width) that forms a barrier between the materials present inside the nucleus and that of the cytoplasm.

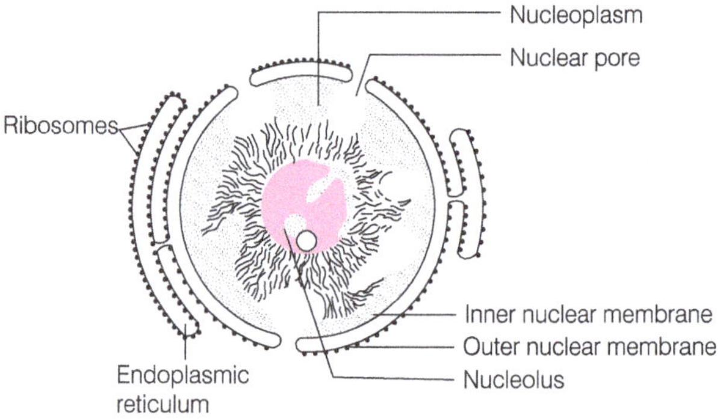


Fig. 8.13 Ultrastructure of interphase nucleus

- The outer membrane is connected with the endoplasmic reticulum and also bears ribosomes on it.
- The nuclear envelope contains a large number of minute pores called **nuclear pores** which are formed by the fusion of its two membranes.
- These pores control the passage of substances, e.g. RNA, protein.
- The nucleoplasm (also called nuclear matrix) is a semi-fluid and colloidal substance that fills the nucleus.
- The nucleoplasm contains nucleolus and chromatin.
- The nucleoli are naked, spherical structures present in the nucleoplasm.

- The content of nucleolus is in direct contact with the nucleoplasm because a covering membrane is absent around nucleolus.
- It is the principal site for the active ribosomal RNA synthesis.
- Larger and more numerous nucleoli are present in cells actively carrying out protein synthesis.

## Chromosomes

The chromosomes are rod-shaped or thread like deeply stainable condensed chromatin fibres that are the hereditary vehicles as they store and transmit hereditary information.

- The nucleus in the interphase has a loose and indistinct network of nucleoprotein fibres called **chromatin**.
- But during different stages of cell division, cells show structured **chromosomes** in place of the nucleus.
- The chromosomes are meant for the equal distribution of genetic material from parents to next generations.
- The number of chromosomes is fixed and is same in all individuals of a species. For example, a single human cell has approximately two meters long thread of DNA distributed among its (23 pairs) chromosomes.
- Chromatin is composed of DNA and some basic proteins called **histones**.
- Some non-histone proteins and RNA are also present in the chromatin.

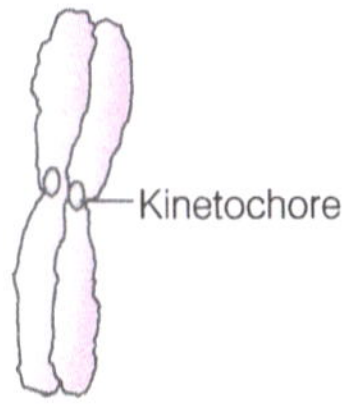


Fig. 8.14 Chromosome with kinetochore

- Every chromosome has a primary constriction or the **centromere** on the sides of which the disc-shaped structures known as kinetochores are present.
- Centromere holds two chromatids of a chromosome.

## Types

On the basis of the position of the centromere, the chromosomes can be classified into four following types.

- **Metacentric Chromosome** has two equal arms and centromere lies in the centre.
- **Sub-metacentric Chromosome** has one shorter arm and one longer arm with centromere slightly away from the middle of the chromosome.
- **Acrocentric Chromosome** has one extremely short and one very long arm and centromere is located near the end of the chromosome.
- **Telocentric Chromosome** has the terminal centromere, i.e. centromere is placed at an extreme end.

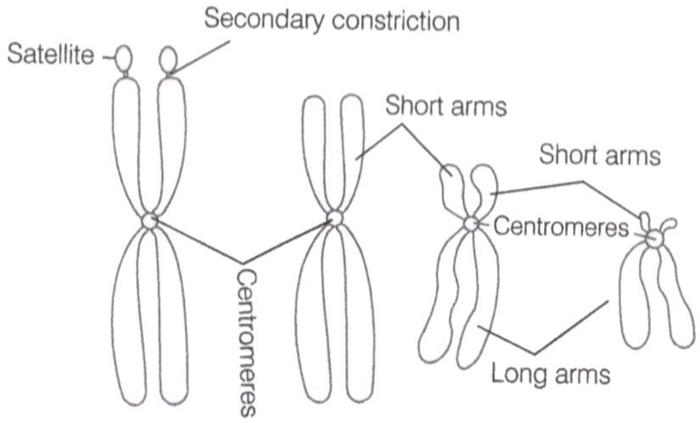


Fig. 8.15 Types of chromosomes based on the position of centromere

- Few chromosomes have non-staining secondary constrictions at a constant location. This gives the appearance of a small fragment known as **satellite**.

## Microbodies

- These are the membrane bound cytoplasmic elements that are composed of enzymes and other substances.
- These are minute vesicles found in both plant cells and animal cells.

### Quick Test 5

1. Name the component of the cytoskeleton which is responsible for maintaining cell shape and aiding in cell division.
2. Identify the whip like, long structure, found in cytoskeleton.
3. **State True or False.**
   (a) Ribosomes are responsible for producing ATP in the cell.
   (b) Centrosomes play a key role in organizing microtubules during cell division.
4. Identify the structure within the nucleus which is responsible for producing ribosomal RNA.
5. Name the type of chromosome which has centromere at terminal position.

# Mind Map

## Cell : The Unit of Life

### Eukaryotic Cell

- Contain membrane bound organelles.

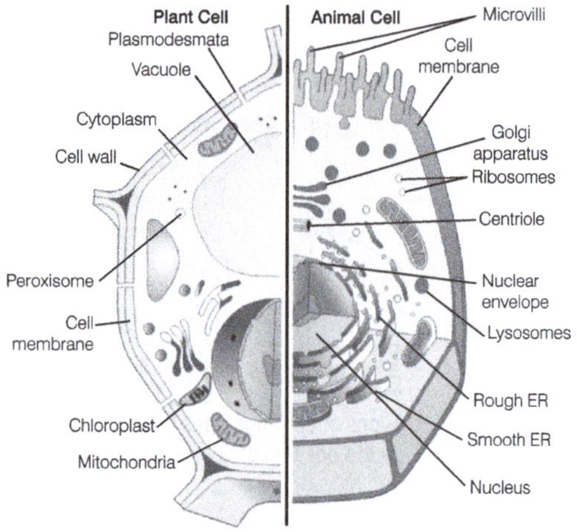


### Prokaryotic Cell

- Cell that does not have a nuclear membrane and the nucleoid represents the genetic material.
- Lack membrane bound organelles.
- Most prokaryotic cells, majorly the bacterial cell have cell envelope that consists of an outer glycocalyx, followed by peptidoglycan cell wall and cell membrane.

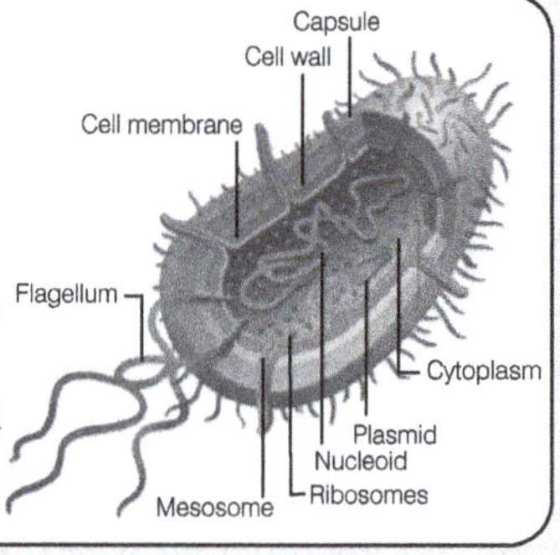


### Cell Wall

Present in plant, bacterial and fungal cells. It consists of three layers ; middle lamella, primary cell wall, secondary cell wall.

### Cell Membrane

- The membrane is composed of phospholipids, proteins and carbohydrates.
- It allows only selected substances into the cell, maintains cell shape, plays role in cell-cell recognition, and controls and regulates, reaction sequences.

### Vacuoles

- These are single membrane (tonoplast) bound structures found in the cytoplasm.
- It contains water, sap, excretory products and other products that are not useful for the cell.
- Presence of contractile vacuole in *Amoeba* and food vacuoles in protists.

### Mitochondria

- Double membrane bound structure with the outer membrane and the inner membrane having specific enzymes.
- It is the site of aerobic respiration. So, they are termed as powerhouses of the cell.

### Ribosomes

- They synthesise proteins.
- Ribosomes are of two types, i.e. 70S in prokaryotes and 80S in eukaryotes.

### Plastids

- These are double membrane bound and semi-autonomous organelles found in plants.
- Based on pigment, they are of three types
(a) **Chromoplasts,** (b) **Leucoplasts,** (c) **Chloroplasts**

### Nucleus

- A double membrane bound cell organelle.
- Controls the heredity characters of an organisms.

### Endoplasmic Reticulum

- Membrane bound channels seen in the form of network of delicate strands and vesicles in cytoplasm.
- It is of two types, i.e. smooth ER and rough ER.
- RER is involved in protein synthesis and secretion.
- SER is the major site for lipid synthesis.

### Golgi Apparatus

- Composed of flattened stacks (cisternae) which receive protein from ER.
- Golgi packages materials, to be delivered either to the intracellular targets or secreted outside the cell.
- It is involved in the formation of lysosomes vesicles, glycoproteins and glycolipids.

### Lysosomes

- Also known as **suicidal bags** of the cell.
- These are single membrane bound structures, containing hydrolytic enzymes in them.

### Centrosome and Centriole

- Centrosome contains two cylindrical structures known as centrioles.
- Centrioles form the basal body of cilia or flagella and spindle fibres that given rise to spindle apparatus during cell division in animal cells.

# EXAM PATTERN QUESTIONS

## Objective Type Questions

### Multiple Choice Questions

**1. Which of the following is not correct?** **NCERT**

(a) Robert Brown discovered the cell
(b) Schleiden and Schwann formulated the cell theory
(c) Virchow explained that cells are formed from pre-existing cells
(d) A unicellular organism carries out its life activities within a single cell

**Ans.** (*a*)

**2. Who reported that cells had a thin outer layer which is today known as the plasma membrane?** **DIKSHA**

(a) Robert Hooke (b) Robert Brown
(c) Schleiden (d) T Schwann

**Ans.** (*d*)

**3. The cell theory, jointly given by Schleiden and Schwann did not explain**

(a) all living organisms are composed of cells and their products
(b) cell is the structural and functional unit of living organisms
(c) formation of new cells
(d) None of the above

**Ans.** (*c*)

**4. New cells arise from** **NCERT**

(a) bacterial fermentation (b) regeneration of old cells
(c) pre-existing cells (d) abiotic materials

**Ans.** (*c*)

**5. Which of the following is correct?** **NCERT**

(a) Cells of all living organisms have a nucleus
(b) Both animal and plant cells have a well-defined cell wall
(c) In prokaryotes, there are no membrane bound organelles
(d) Cells are formed *de novo* from abiotic materials

**Ans.** (*c*)

**6. Different cells have different sizes. Arrange the following cells in an ascending order of their size. Choose the correct option among the followings.**

**I. Mycoplasma** **Competency Based Que., NCERT Exemplar**
**II. Ostrich eggs III. Human RBC IV. Bacteria**

(a) I, IV, III, II (b) I, II, III, IV
(c) II, I, III, IV (d) III, II, I, IV

**Ans.** (*a*) Option (a) Represents the correct ascending order of cell's size.
Cells in organism vary greatly in their size, shapes and activities.

I. Mycoplasmas are the smallest cell with size only 0.3 μm.
II. Bacterial cell are of size 1 – 2 μm.
III. In human red blood cells are of about 7.0 μm in diameter.
IV. Ostrich eggs are among the largest cells with size $(15 \times 13)$ cm.

**7. The cell envelope of bacteria is composed of**

(a) outermost cell wall followed by glycocalyx and plasma membrane
(b) plasma membrane and cell wall
(c) outermost glycocalyx followed by cell wall and plasma membrane
(d) plasma membrane

**Ans.** (*c*)

**8. Mesosomes are the infoldings of cell membrane, which**

**I. are in the form of vesicles tubules and lamellae.**
**II. increase the surface area of plasma membrane.**
**III. are present in both prokaryotic and eukaryotic cells.**

**Which of the following option is most appropriate?** **Competency Based Que.**

(a) II and III (b) I and II (c) I and III (d) I, II and III

**Ans.** (*b*)

**9. Choose the incorrect pair.**

(a) Gram-positive bacteria–Take up the Gram stain
(b) Cell wall–Prevents bacterium from collapsing
(c) Capsule–Thick and tough glycocalyx
(d) Pili– Locomotory structure in bacteria

**Ans.** (*d*)

**10. Select the incorrect statement about prokaryotic ribosomes.**

(a) 50S and 30S subunits unites to form 70S ribosomes
(b) Polysome consists of many ribosomes attached to *t*RNA
(c) Ribosome is the site of protein synthesis
(d) Polysomes indicate the synthesis of identical polypeptides in multiple copies

**Ans.** (*b*)

**11.** **Which of the following statements is incorrect for prokaryotic inclusion bodies?**

(a) These are storage granules in the cytoplasm
(b) They are membrane bound structures
(c) Phosphate granules, cyanophycean granules and glycogen granules are the examples of cell inclusions
(d) Gas vacuole is found in BGA and purple and green photosynthetic bacteria

**Ans.** (*b*)

**12.** **Which of the following features is common to prokaryotes and many eukaryotes?** NCERT Exemplar

(a) Chromatin material present
(b) Cell wall present
(c) Nuclear membrane present
(d) Membrane bound sub-cellular organelles present

**Ans.** (*b*)

**13.** **Which one of the following differentiates plant cells from animal cells?**

(a) Large vacuole, plastid and cell wall
(b) Cell wall, plastid and centriole
(c) Cell wall, plastid and mitochondria
(d) Cell membrane, plastid and cell wall

**Ans.** (*a*)

**14.** **Which of the following is not true of a eukaryotic cell?** NCERT Exemplar

(a) Cell wall is made up of peptidoglycans
(b) It has 80S type of ribosome present in the cytoplasm
(c) Mitochondria contain circular DNA
(d) Membrane bound organelles are present

**Ans.** (*a*) A cell wall made up of peptidoglycan is found in bacteria and not in eukaryotes. Eukaryotic cell wall is made up of cellulose, hemicellulose, pectin, chitin, etc. Thus, is not true for eukaryotic cell.

The other options stands true for eukaryotic cell.

**15.** **Which of the following statement is not true for plasma membrane?**

(a) It is present in both plant and animal cell
(b) Lipid is present as a bilayer in it
(c) Proteins are present integrated as well as loosely associated with the lipid bilayer
(d) Carbohydrate is never found in it

**Ans.** (*d*) Statement given in option (d) is false.

The biochemical investigation done on cell membrane clearly demonstrate that the cell membrane possess protein and carbohydrates as biochemical components.

The other options stand true for plasma membrane.

**16.** **Why tails of lipids in the membrane are towards inner part?**

(a) The tail is non-polar hydrocarbon and so protected with an aqueous environment
(b) The tail is polar hydrocarbon and so is protected from aqueous environment
(c) The non-polar or hydrophobic hydrocarbon tails of lipid, being on innerside ensure their protection from aqueous environment
(d) The tail is hydrophilic, so it tends to be located in the aqueous innerside of membrane

**Ans.** (*c*)

**17.** **Who proposed the fluid mosaic model of plasma membrane?**

(a) Camillo Golgi
(b) Schleiden and Schwann
(c) Singer and Nicolson
(d) Robert Brown

**Ans.** (*c*)

**18.** **The main difference between active and passive transport across the cell membrane is**

(a) passive transport is non-selective whereas active transport is selective
(b) passive transport requires a concentration gradient across a biological membrane whereas active transport requires energy to move solutes
(c) passive transport is confined to anionic carrier proteins whereas active transport is confined to cationic channel proteins
(d) active transport occurs more rapidly than passive transport

**Ans.** (*b*)

**19.** **The layer of cell wall common to two adjacent cell walls in plants is called**

(a) middle lamella
(b) middle layer
(c) common lamella
(d) common layer

**Ans.** (*a*)

**20.** **Observe the diagram given below and answer the questions that follows.**

**Identify the labels *A*, *B* and *C* shown in the above diagram.**

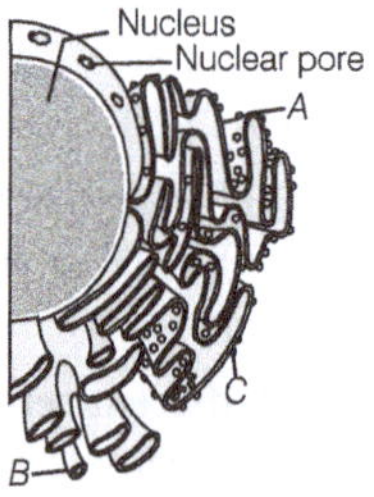


| | *A* | *B* | *C* |
|---|---|---|---|
| (a) | Ribosomes | SER | RER |
| (b) | RER | SER | Ribosomes |
| (c) | SER | Ribosomes | RER |
| (d) | RER | Ribosomes | SER |

Competency Based Que.

**Ans.** (*b*)

**21.** **Consider the figure given below.**

**How many of the following statement(s) is/are true regarding the figure above?**

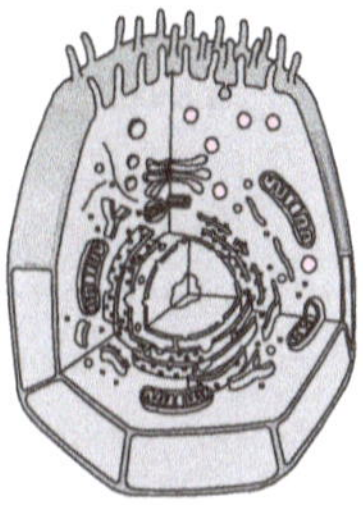

**I. Vacuole in case of cell shown above is small in size.**

**II. Presence of genetic material is seen inside a membrane bound nucleus.**

**III. Cell shows higher complexity along with complex organs and a distinct cell wall.**

**IV. Ribosomes act as protein factories in the cell.**

**Codes** **Competency Based Que.**

(a) Three (b) Four (c) One (d) Two

**Ans.** (*a*)

**22.** **Difference between rough and smooth endoplasmic reticulum is that**

(a) rough ER has ribosomes
(b) smooth ER has ribosomes
(c) smooth ER takes part in protein synthesis
(d) Both have $F_1$-particles

**Ans.** (*a*)

**23.** **Which one of the following is the incorrect feature of given structure?**

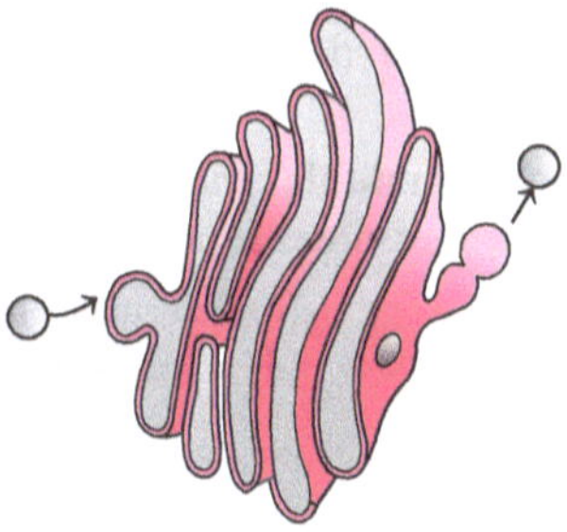

(a) The structure was named after Camillo Golgi who first observed them near nucleus
(b) These structures are stacked parallel to each other
(c) Varied number of cristae are present in Golgi complex
(d) These consist of many flat, disc shaped sacs

**Ans.** (*c*)

**24.** **Which of the following statement is not correct?**

(a) Lysosomes have numerous hydrolytic enzymes
(b) The hydrolytic enzymes of lysosomes are active under acidic pH
(c) Lysosomes are membrane bound structures
(d) Lysosomes are formed by the process of packaging in the endoplasmic reticulum

**Ans.** (*d*)

**25.** **Given below is the list of different cell organelles and their function. Select the correct match.**

| | Cell Organelle | | Function |
|---|---|---|---|
| A. | Endoplasmic Reticulum | (i) | Have digestive enzymes in them |
| B. | Ribosomes | (ii) | Packaging of products |
| C. | Golgi complex | (iii) | Means of quick intracellular transport |
| D. | Lysosomes | (iv) | Protein factories |

(a) A - (ii), B - (i), C - (iii), D - (iv)
(b) A - (iii), B - (iv), C - (ii), D - (i)
(c) A - (iv), B - (ii), C - (iii), D - (i)
(d) A - (i), B - (ii), C - (iii), D - (iv)

**Ans.** (*b*)

**26.** **Match the Column I with Column II and choose the right option given below.** **Competency Based Que.**

| | Column I (Cell organelles) | | Column II (Functions) |
|---|---|---|---|
| A. | RER | 1. | Intracellular and extracellular digestion. |
| B. | SER | 2. | Lipid synthesis. |
| C. | Golgi complex | 3. | Protein synthesis and secretion. |
| D. | Lysosomes | 4. | Moves materials out of the cells. |

**Codes**

| | A | B | C | D | | A | B | C | D |
|---|---|---|---|---|---|---|---|---|---|
| (a) | 3 | 2 | 4 | 1 | (b) | 2 | 3 | 4 | 1 |
| (c) | 1 | 3 | 2 | 4 | (d) | 4 | 2 | 3 | 1 |

**Ans.** (*a*)

**27.** **What is a tonoplast?** **NCERT Exemplar**

(a) Outer membrane of mitochondria
(b) Inner membrane of chloroplast
(c) Membrane boundary of the vacuole of plant cells
(d) Cell membrane of a plant cell

**Ans.** (*c*)

**28.** **The cristae in mitochondria is important because**

(a) increases surface area
(b) decreases surface area
(c) have fluid in it
(d) it increases intensity by which stain is absorbed

**Ans.** (*a*)

**29.** **Plastid differs from mitochondria on the basis of one of the following features. Mark the right answer.**

(a) Presence of two layers of membrane
(b) Presence of ribosome
(c) Presence of thylakoids
(d) Presence of DNA

**Ans.** (*c*)

**30.** **Plastids are found in all plant cells and in euglenoid. They bear some specific pigments, thus imparting specific colours to the plants. On the basis of the type of pigments, plastids can be classified into many different types. Identify the plastid and the correct role it plays.** **Competency Based Que.**

| | Plastids | Role |
|---|---|---|
| (a) | Leucoplast | Trap light energy |
| (b) | Chloroplast | Stores proteins |
| (c) | Amyloplast | Store carbohydrates |
| (d) | Chromoplast | Store oils and fats |

**Ans.** (*c*)

**31.** **Identify *A* to *F* in the sectional view of a chloroplast showing the different parts.**

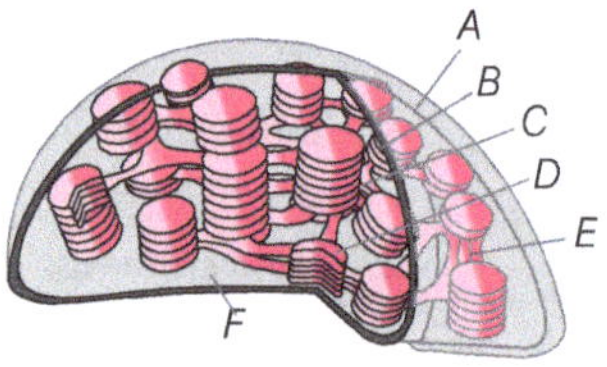


(a) *A*–Inner membrane, *B*–Granum, *C*–Outer membrane, *D*–Stroma lamella, *E*–Stroma, *F*–Thylakoid
(b) *A*–Outer membrane, *B*–Inner membrane, *C*–Granum, *D*–Thylakoid, *E*–Stroma lamella, *F*–Stroma
(c) *A*–Thylakoid, *B*–Outer membrane, *C*–Stroma, *D*–Stroma lamella, *E*–Granum, *F*–Inner membrane
(d) *A*–Outer membrane, *B*–Stroma, *C*–Inner membrane, *D*–Granum, *E*–Thylakoid, *F*–Stroma lamella

**Ans.** (*b*)

**32.** **Ribosomes are**

I. non-membrane bound.
II. absent in plastids and mitochondria.
III. present in the cytoplasm and RER.

**Choose the correct option.**

(a) Only II (b) I and II
(c) I, II and III (d) I and III

**Ans.** (*d*)

**33.** **Select one which is not true for ribosome.** **NCERT Exemplar**

(a) Made up of two subunits
(b) Form polysome
(c) May attach to *m*RNA
(d) Have no role in protein synthesis

**Ans.** (*d*) Ribosomes are truly called as **protein factory** as they play a vital role in protein synthesis. Thus, the statement that ribosomes have no role in protein synthesis is not true.

Other statements are true for ribosome.

**34.** **Which of the following is not a function of cytoskeleton in a cell?** **NCERT Exemplar**

(a) Intracellular transport
(b) Maintenance of cell shape and structure
(c) Support of the organelle
(d) Cell motility

**Ans.** (*a*)

**35.** **Choose the incorrect statement.**

(a) Centrosome is cytoplasmic structure of animal cells
(b) Centrioles form spindle poles
(c) Centriole is membrane less, but surrounded by amorphous pericentriolar bodies
(d) Centrosome occurs in all eukaryotic cells

**Ans.** (*b*)

**36.** **A common characteristic feature of plant sieve tube cells and most of mammalian erythrocytes is**

(a) absence of mitochondria
(b) presence of cell wall
(c) presence of haemoglobin
(d) absence of nucleus

**Ans.** (*d*) The common characteristic feature of plant sieve tube and mammalian erythrocyte is the absence of nucleus. Sieve tubes are the component of phloem and do not contain nucleus. Similarly, erythrocytes in mammalian cell also do not posses nucleus. Erythrocytes are the RBCs which helps in gaseous exchange.

**37.** **Chromosome has middle centromere forming two equal arms of the chromosomes is called** **DIKSHA**

(a) metacentric (b) sub-metacentric
(c) telocentric (d) acrocentric

**Ans.** (*a*)

## Assertion-Reason Questions

**Direction** (Q. Nos. 1-10) *In each of the following questions, a statement of Assertion (A) is given followed by corresponding statement of Reason (R). Of the statements, mark the correct answer.*

(a) Both A and R are true and R is the correct explanation of A.
(b) Both A and R are true, but R is not the correct explanation of A.
(c) A is true, but R is false.
(d) A is false, but R is true.

**1.** **Assertion** (A) Cell is the structural and functional unit of life.

**Reason** (R) Unicellular organisms are capable of independent existence and can perform all essential all functions of life.

**Ans.** (*b*)

**2.** **Assertion** (A) Mesosomes are equal to mitochondria in eukaryotes.

**Reason** (R) These structures participate in aerobic cellular respiration in prokaryotes.

**Ans.** (*a*)

**3.** **Assertion** (A) The cisternae in Golgi complex have *cis* face and *trans* face.

**Reason** (R) The *cis* face is also called forming face and *trans* face is also called maturing face.

**Ans.** (*b*)

**4.** **Assertion** (A) The vacuole is bounded by a single membrane structure known as tonoplast.

**Reason** (R) In plants, vacuole facilitates the transport of materials against the concentration gradient inside the vacuole.

**Ans.** (*b*)

**5.** Given below is the structure of a mitochondria found in the cytoplasm of every cell. It is often known as the powerhouse of the cell. Study its internal structure and comment upon the appropriateness of the Assertion and the Reason. **Competency Based Que.**

**Assertion** (A) The inner membrane forms the number of infolding called the cristae.

**Reason** (R) The matrix of the mitochondria increase the surface area.

**Ans.** (*c*) A is true, but R is false. R can be corrected as

The cristae of mitochondria increase the surtace area of the membrane.

**6.** **Assertion** (A) Chloroplast is a cell organelle.

**Reason** (R) An organelle is a distinct part of cell which has a particular structure and function.

**Ans.** (*a*)

**7.** **Assertion** (A) The chromoplasts contain fat soluble carotenoid pigments.

**Reason** (R) These pigments provide colour to plant parts other than green.

**Ans.** (*b*)

**8.** **Assertion** (A) Plastids can impart specific colour to the plant.

**Reason** (R) Plastids are pigment bearing cell organelle

**Ans.** (*a*)

**9.** **Assertion** (A) The prokaryotic ribosomes are 70S, while the eukaryotic ribosomes are 80S.

**Reason** (R) Here 'S' stands for the sedimentation coefficient which is indirectly measure of density and size.

**Ans.** (*b*)

**10.** **Assertion** (A) The content of nucleolus are in direct contact with the nucleoplasm.

**Reason** (R) A covering membrane is absent around nucleolus.

**Ans.** (*a*)

# Subjective Questions

## Very Short Answer Type Questions

**1. Give one difference between the characteristic feature of Gram positive and Gram negative bacteria.**

**Ans.** Gram positive bacteria retain the gram stain while Gram negative bacteria loose the gram stain on washing.

**2. Many bacteria contain circular DNA '*X*' other than the chromosomal or genomic DNA. Identify the '*X*' and write its unique characters.** **Competency Based Que.**

**Ans.** '*X*' is plasmid. These plasmids confer certain unique characters to the bacteria like antibiotic resistance.

**3. Is cell membrane permeable, semipermeable or impermeable?**

**Ans.** Cell membrane is semi-permeable.

**4. Which layer is referred to as the cementing layer and why?**

**Ans.** Middle lamella is referred to as the cementing layer because it holds the primary cell wall of adjacent cells together.

**5. ER divides the intracellular space of the cell into two distinct compartments. Name them.**

**Ans.** Luminal compartment and extraluminal compartment.

**6. Which type of endoplasmic reticulum has its main functioning in the synthesis of lipid?**

**Ans.** Smooth Endoplasmic Reticulum (SER) helps in the synthesis of lipid.

**7. Mention a single membrane bound organelle which is rich in hydrolytic enzymes.** **NCERT Exemplar**

**Ans.** Lysosome is the single membrane bound organelle which is rich in all types of hydrolytic enzymes, i.e. hydrolase, lipases, proteases and carbohydrases.

**8. What is the significance of vacuole in a plant cell?** NCERT Exemplar

**Ans.** The vacuole in plant cell helps to maintain osmotic pressure for turgidity and osmosis. It also stores useful as well as waste substances.

**9. Why are the mitochondria and plastids called semiautonomous particles?**

**Ans.** These are called so, because they contain their own DNA and ribosomes, allowing them to synthesise some of their own proteins.

**10. Give the term used for the stacks of thylakoids.**

**Ans.** Grana or intergranal thylakoids.

**11. What does 'S' refer in a 70S and 80S ribosome?** NCERT Exemplar

**Ans.** The 'S' refers to (Svedberg units) sedimentation coefficient, is a measure of the speed of the sedimentation for a particular cell organelle in ultracentrifuge.

**12. Animal cells contain non-membrane bound organelle. Identify the cell organelle and write its function.**

**Ans.** Centriole is the non- membrane bound organelle present in the animal cells. It helps in cell division.

**13. What technical term is given to the type of chromosomes that has** Competency Based Que.

(i) two equal arms

(ii) one arm much longer than the other.

**Ans.** (i) Metacentric chromosomes (½)

(ii) Acrocentric chromosomes (½)

**14. What is the feature of a metacentric chromosome?**

**Ans.** In metacentric chromosome centromere is median, i.e. centromere lie in the middle portion. Thus, forming two equal arms of chromosome.

**15. Identify the following structure.** Competency Based Que.

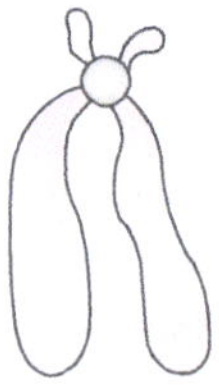

**Ans.** Telocentric chromosome.

**16. What is referred to as satellite chromosome?** NCERT Exemplar

**Ans.** Few chromosomes have additional constriction or secondary constriction at distal part of the arm formed by chromatin thread are known satellite chromosome. These constriction gives appearance of an outgrowth or small fragment.

## Short Answer Type Questions

**1. Multicellular organisms have division of labour. Explain.** NCERT

**Ans.** Multicellular organisms are made up of millions and trillions of cells. All these cells perform specific functions. All the cells specialised for performing similar functions are grouped together as tissues in the body. Hence, a particular function is carried out by a group of cells at a definite place in the body. Similarly, different functions are carried out by different groups of cells in an organism. This is known as the division of labour in multicellular organisms.

**2. Cell is the basic unit of life'. Discuss in brief.** NCERT

**Ans.** All organisms begin their life as a single cell. Some organisms are unicellular, consisting of only one cell. In contrast, multicellular organisms develop from a single cell that undergoes divisions to form a complex body. All the cells in an organism carry the same genetic material, originating from pre-existing cells, and contain various organelles to perform essential life activities. Therefore, cells are considered the basic unit of life.

**3. Briefly give the contributions of the following scientists in formulating the cell theory**

**(i) Rudolf Virchow**

**(ii) Schleiden and Schwann** NCERT Exemplar

**Ans.** (i) Rudolf Virchow (1855) first explained that the cells divide and new cells are formed from the pre-existing cells. (1)

(ii) Schleiden and Schwann observed the cells and cell membranes for the first time. They proposed the cell theory which explains that the animal and plant cells are composed of cells and product of cells. (1)

**4. Write the name of four prokaryotic cells. Write the name of two types of bacterial cells on the basis of its cell envelope.** DIKSHA

**Ans.** The four prokaryotic cells are
Bacteria, blue-green algae, mycoplasma (the smallest cell), PPLO (Pleuro Pneumonial Like Organisms). (1)

Gram positive and Gram negative are two types of bacterial cells on the basis of its cell envelope. (1)

**5. What are the characteristics of prokaryotic cells?** NCERT

**Ans.** Characteristics of prokaryotic cells are as follows

- The prokaryotic cell is essentially a single–envelope system.
- Prokaryotes lack membrane bound cell organelles.
- Prokaryotes have 70S ribosomes.
- DNA is naked and lies coiled in cytoplasm. Nucleus is not covered by nuclear membrane and is termed as nucleoid.
- Nuclear components, like, nucleolus, nucleoplasm are absent.

- Cell wall is present in bacteria and cyanobacteria, but absent in mycoplasma.

**6. What are plasmids? Describe their role in bacteria.**

**Ans.** A plasmid is usually a circular (sometimes linear) piece of double-stranded DNA found in bacteria that is different from bacterium's chromosome. It carries non-essential genes that can facilitate a bacterium's ability to survive in certain circumstances.

For example, plasmids carry genes that enable a bacterium to metabolise a certain type of nutrient otherwise it cannot enable to conjugate. Plasmids are used for a vast variety of experiments from expressing human genes in bacterial cells to DNA sequencing. (1+1)

**7. What is a mesosome in a prokaryotic cell? Mention the functions that it performs.** NCERT

**Ans.** Mesosome is a special membrane structure, formed by the extension of the plasma membrane into the cell in a prokaryotic cell.

It helps in cell wall formation, DNA replication and its distribution to daughter cells. It also helps in respiration, secretion process, to increase the surface area of the plasma membrane and enzymatic content. (1+1)

**8. Match the items listed in Column I with the appropriate items from Column II.**

| Column I | Column II |
|---|---|
| A. Spherical bacteria | 1. Contractile vacuole |
| B. A double membrane system | 2. 70S ribosomes |
| C. Rod-shaped bacteria | 3. Cocci |
| D. Mesosomes | 4. Prokaryotic cell |
| E. *Amoeba* | 5. Bacilli |
| F. Prokaryotic cell | 6. Eukaryotic cell |

**Ans.** A–3, B–6, C–5, D–4, E–1, F–2

**9. (i) Name two surface extensions that are not concerned with motility in bacterial cells.**

**(ii) Give the name of the structure that helps in motility of bacterial cells.**

**Ans.** (i) Pili and fimbriae are the two surface extensions that are not concerned with motility. (1)

(ii) Structure that helps in motility of bacterial cell is flagella. (1)

**10. (i) Do bacterial cells have nucleus like eukaryotic cell? Explain.** Competency Based Que.

**(ii) Are there any form of bacteria present that are made up of more than one cell?**

**Ans.** (i) No, bacterial cells do not have well-defined nucleus instead, their genetic material is dispersed in the cytoplasm. Also, there is no internal membrane that delimits a nucleus. (1)

(ii) No, there is no multicellular bacteria, i.e. made up of more than one cell. All bacterial cells are unicellular. (1)

**11. Differentiate between animal cell and plant cell.**

**Ans.** Differences between animal cell and plants cell are as follows.

| Animal Cell | Plant Cell |
|---|---|
| Cell wall absent | Cell wall present |
| Chloroplast absent | Chloroplast present in green parts |
| Centriole present | Centriole absent |
| Vacuoles are smaller | Comparatively vacuoles are larger |

**12. In the figure below the fluid mosaic model of plasma membrane is given. Study the model and answer the questions that follows.** Competency Based Que.

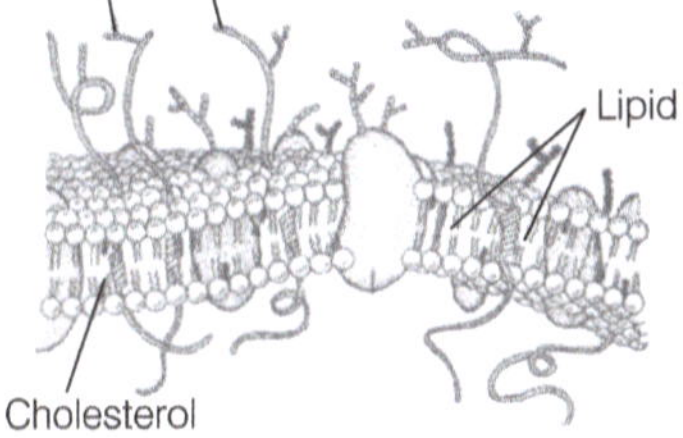


**(i) What does the term fluidity in this model signifies?**

**(ii) How does the passages of substances across the membrane occurs? Describe any one method.**

**Ans.** (i) Fluidity is defined as the ability of proteins to move within the membrane. The fluid nature of the membrane is important as it allows the interaction of molecules within the membrane and support many other functions. (1)

(ii) The passage of substances across the membrane occurs mainly through either of the two methods

(a) Active transport, (b) Passive transport (1)

**Active Transport** It is the movement of the molecules across the membrane against their concentration gradient or electrochemical gradient, i.e. from lower to the higher concentration. It is an energy dependent process, in which ATP is utilised. It occurs in few ions and molecules, e.g. $Na^+/K^+$pump. (1)

**13. Give the biochemical composition of plasma membrane. How are lipid molecules arranged in the membrane?** NCERT Exemplar

**Ans.** Chemically, the plasma membrane consists of proteins , lipids, carbohydrates and water. The lipids present in the plasma membrane are phospholipids, glycolipids (sugar lipids) and sterols. (1)

Each lipid molecule consists of a three carbon glycerol poles (head) which are hydrophilic (water loving) in nature and two long tails of fatty acids which are hydrophobic (water-fearing) in nature.

The hydrophilic glycerol poles of lipid are located towards the outer side of the lipid bilayer whereas, the hydrophobic fatty acid tails are repelled by water and face towards the inner side of the membrane. The hydrophilic and hydrophobic forces in lipid molecules cause the membrane to become a bilayer. (2)

**14. Differentiate between active and passive transport.**

**Ans.** Refer to text on page no. 162.

**15. How do neutral solutes move across the plasma membrane? Can the polar molecules also move across in it the same way? If not, then how are these transported across the membrane?** **Competency Based Que., NCERT**

**Ans.** Neutral solutes may move across the membrane by the process of simple diffusion along the concentration gradient. The polar molecules cannot pass through the non-polar lipid bilayer, they require a carrier protein to facilitate their transport across the membrane.

A few ions or molecules are transported across the membrane against their concentration gradient, i.e., from lower to the higher concentration. Such transport is an energy dependent process in which ATP is utilised and is called active transport, e.g. $Na^+/K^+$ pump.

**16. Differentiate between primary cell wall and secondary cell wall.**

**Ans.** The difference between primary cell wall and secondary cell wall are as follows.

| Primary Cell Wall | Secondary Cell Wall |
|---|---|
| It is arranged inner to the middle lamella | It is arranged inner to the primary wall |
| It is produced in young growing cell | It is produced after development of primary cell wall |

(1 + 1)

**17. The lysosomal enzyme does not destroy the cell's own cytoplasm. Why?** **Competency Based Que.**

**Ans.** The lysosomal enzyme does not destroy its own cytoplasm, because of the following reasons

(i) The enzymes are separated from the cytoplasm by the lysosomal membrane. (1)

(ii) The enzymes have the capability of recognising and digest only foreign matter. (1)

(iii) The lysosomal enzymes usually work in acidic medium of pH less than 7 and the cytoplasmic medium is more than 7, i.e. around 7.4 or more. (1)

**18. Both lysosomes and vacuoles are endomembrane 'structures, yet they differ in terms of their functions. Comment.** **Competency Based Que., NCERT**

**Ans.** Organelles of endomembrane system such as lysosomes and vacuoles function in close coordination with one another but are specialised to perform different functions. Lysosomes breakdown the ageing and dead cells as wall as help in digestion of food as they contain hydrolytic digestive enzymes.

Vacuoles on other hand, help in excretion and osmoregulation in *Amoeba* (contractile vacuole) or provides buoyancy, mechanical strength in prokaryotes (air vacuoles).

**19. What are the major functions of plant cell vacuoles? What is the covering membrane of the vacuoles called?**

**Ans.** Vacuole in a plant cell primarily serves to store substances such as water, nutrients and waste. It also help to maintain turgor pressure for structural support. Tonoplast is the covering membrane of the vacuoles. (1 × 2)

**20. What are mitochondria? What is the basic morphology of these organelles and in which cell can they be found?**

**Ans.** Mitochondria are the organelles in which the most important part of the cellular respiration, i.e. the ATP production occurs. (1)

These organelles are bounded by two lipid membranes. The inner membrane infolded to the interior of the organelle forming cristae that defines the internal space known as mitochondrial matrix and where the mitochondrial DNA (*mt*DNA), mitochondrial RNA (*mt*RNA), mitochondrial ribosomes and respiratory enzymes can be found. Mitochondria are found in eukaryotic cells in high number and are also more abundant in those cells that use more energy, like muscle cells. (2)

**21. Justify the statement, 'mitochondria are the powerhouse of the cell.'** **NCERT Exemplar**

**Ans.** Mitochondria are known as powerhouse of the cell because they generate ATP, the energy currency of the cell. ATP synthesised inside mitochondria provides energy for all cellular activities.

**22. Why mitochondrion and chloroplast are not considered a part of endomembrane system?**

**Ans.** Mitochondrion and chloroplast are not considered a part of endomembrane system as their functions are not coordinated by other component of the cells as ER, lysosomes, Golgi complex, etc.

**23. Are the different types of plastids interchangeable? If yes, give examples where they are getting converted from one type to another.** **Competency Based Que., NCERT Exemplar**

**Ans.** The different types of plastids such as leucoplasts (colourless), chromoplasts (coloured), chloroplasts (green coloured) are interchangeable.

The transformation from chloroplasts is observed during ripening of fruits (e.g. tomato, chilli) when they change their colour from green to reddish orange.

It takes place through loss of chlorophylls and degeneration of lamellae. Carrot root develops its characteristic colour because of the conversion of leucoplasts into chromoplasts. It is rich in carotene.

**24. Distinguish between chloroplast and chromoplast (any three).**

**Ans.** Differences between chloroplast and chromoplast are as follows

| Chloroplasts | Chromoplasts |
|---|---|
| They contain mainly chlorophylls and carotenoids | They contain mainly carotene and xanthophyll. |
| They are present in the mesophyll of leaves. | They are present in the petals of flowers, skin of fruits, etc. |
| Their main role is to prepare food by the process of photosynthesis. | Their main role is to impart colouration to plants. |

(1 × 3)

**25. Is extragenomic DNA present in prokaryotes and eukaryotes? If yes, locate their position in both types of organisms.** **NCERT Exemplar**

**Ans.** Yes, extragenomic DNA is present in both prokaryotes and eukaryotes. (1)

In case of eukaryotes, extragenomic DNA is present in two organelles, e.g. plastids and mitochondria. Both these organelles with the help of their own DNA, synthesise some of their proteins. Thus, these organelles are known as semiautonomous organelles. (1)

In case of prokaryotic cells, the extragenomic DNA is present in the form of plasmids. The plasmids are circular DNA molecules, which confer certain unique phenotypic characters to such bacteria. One such character is resistance to bacteria. This plasmid DNA is also used to monitor bacteria transformation with foreign DNA. (1)

**26. In what respect the mitochondria and plastids resemble the bacteria.** **Competency Based Que.**

**Ans.** Mitochondria and plastids are known as semiautonomous organelles. They have their own genetic material, i.e. DNA. They both have matrix containing 70S type of ribosomes, which are found in prokaryotes. That is why they resemble the bacteria.

**27. Name the non-membrane bound organelle found in both prokaryotic and eukaryotic cells. Differentiate between the two.**

**Ans.** The non-membrane bound organelle found in both prokaryotic and eukaryotic cell is ribosomes. (1)

In prokaryote, the ribosomes found are 70S type, while in eukaryotes they are 80S type. (1)

**28. Which four different sites in plant cells have ribosomes?**

**Ans.** Ribosomes are found in plant cell at following different sites

(i) Freely in the cytoplasm. (½)

(ii) Attached to ER in the cytoplasm. (½)

(iii) Inside mitochondria. (½)

(iv) Inside plastids (chloroplasts). (½)

**29. How do the ribosomes of prokaryotic cells differ from the ribosomes of eukaryotic cells? Also tell what is similar about them?**

**Ans.** Ribosomes in the cytoplasm of prokaryotic and eukaryotic cells differ slightly. Prokaryotes have 70S ribosomes, each consisting of a 30S (small) and a 50S (large) subunit whereas, eukaryotes have 80S ribosomes, each consisting of (small) 40S and a bound (large) 60S subunit. (1)

Both prokaryotic and eukaryotic ribosomes are composed of ribosomal RNA and ribosomal proteins. Their basic functioning is protein synthesis. (1)

**30. Describe the differences between cilia and flagella.**

**Ans.** Refer to text on page no. 167.

**31. What do you mean by (9 + 2) array? Describe it with reference to cilia and flagella.**

**Ans.** Refer to text on page no. 167.

**32. Describe the ultrastructure of cilia and flagella diagrammatically.**

**Ans.** Refer to fig. no. 8.11 on page no. 167. (2)

**33. The genomic content of the nucleus is constant for a given species whereas, the extrachromosomal DNA is found to be variable among the members of a population. Explain.** **Competency Based Que., NCERT Exemplar**

**Ans.** The DNA content of the nucleus is constant for a given species. The haploid organisms have half the content of DNA than that of their diploid parents. The amount of DNA remains constant in all the members of a given species. On the other hand, the extrachromosomal DNA which occur either in the mitochondria or in chloroplast is found to be variable among the members of a population.

This is because the extra-chromosomal DNA can be transferred between organisms through processes like conjugation, transformation and transduction. This genetic transfer introduces diverse traits, such as antibiotic resistance, within the population. (2)

**34. What are nuclear pores? State their function.** **NCERT**

**Ans.** Nuclear envelope bounds the nucleus from outside and separates it from cytoplasm. It consists of two membranes, with outer membrane continuous with endoplasmic reticulum. The nuclear envelope is interrupted by minute nuclear pores, at a number of places, which are produced by the fusion of its two membranes. These nuclear pores are the passages through which movement of RNA and protein molecules takes place in both directions between the nucleus and the cytoplasm. (2)

**35.** Given below is the structure of a chromosome that are meant for the equal distribution of the genetic material from one generation to another. Study the figure and answer the question that follows **Competency Based Que.**

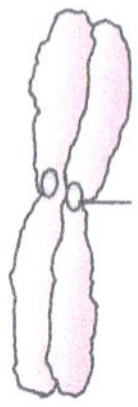


(i) Describe the types of chromosome based on the given structure.

(ii) What are the other different types of chromosomes found on the basis of the position of the centromere.

**Ans.** (i) The given structure of chromosomes is a metacentric chromosome.

It has two equal chromosomes arms called **chromatids.** The two chromatids are attached to each other by a narrow area called **centromere** or **primary constriction.** (1)

(ii) Refer to text on page no. 169. (1)

**36.** What are histones? What are their functions? **Competency Based Que., NCERT Exemplar**

**Ans.** Histones are basic proteins which are soluble in water or dilute acids but are insoluble in dilute ammonia ($NH_3$). They are rich in basic amino acids like histidine and arginine. Histones play an important role in organisation and packaging of DNA inside the nucleus. (2)

**37.** Match the following. **NCERT**

| | Column I | | Column II |
|---|---|---|---|
| (a) | Cristae | (i) | Flat membranous sacs in stroma |
| (b) | Cisternae | (ii) | Infoldings in mitochondria |
| (c) | Thylakoids | (iii) | Disc-shaped sacs in Golgi apparatus |

**Ans.** (a)–ii, (b)–iii, (c)–i. (2)

**38.** Eukaryotic cells have organelles which may **NCERT Exemplar**

(i) not bounded by a membrane.

(ii) bounded by a single membrane.

(iii) bounded by a double membrane.

Group the various sub-cellular organelles into these categories.

**Ans.** (i) Ribosomes are membraneless organelle. (1)

(ii) Lysosomes are single membrane bounded organelle. Microbodies are also with single membranes. (1)

(iii) Mitochondria and plastids are double membrane bounded organelles. (1)

## Long Answer Type Questions

**1.** Discuss the basic structural organisation of a typical cell.

**Ans.** Refer to text on page. no. 156-157.

**2.** Discuss in detail about the outermost covering of the bacterial cell and its three layers.

**Ans.** Refer to the text on page no. 158. (5)

**3.** After studying the detailed structure of cell membrane and after the discovery of electrons microscope. It was revealed from chemical studies that cell membrane is a lipid bilayer structure with integral and peripheral proteins. After that it was also concluded that cell membrane also contain some amount of carbohydrate unit. **Competency Based Que.**

(i) What do you mean by the bilayer of cell membrane made up of lipids?

(ii) What are peripheral and integral proteins?

**Ans.** (i) Refer to text on page no. 161. (2½)

(ii) Refer to text on page no. 161. (2½)

**4.** (i) Discuss the structure of cell wall in plant with all three layers.

(ii) List any few important functions of a cell wall.

**Ans.** (i) Refer to text on page no. 162. (2½)

(ii) Refer to text on page no. 163. (2½)

**5.** Name two cell organelles that are double membrane bound. What are the characteristics of these two organelles? State their functions and draw labelled diagrams of both. **NCERT**

**Ans.** Refer to the text on page no. 165-166.

**6.** Is there a species or region specific type of plastids? How does distinguish one plastid from the other? **NCERT Exemplar**

**Ans.** Plastids are both species or region specific. They are found in all plant cells and euglenoids. (1)

Plastids can be distinguished from one another on the basis of pigments present in them. They are classified into following three types.

(i) **Leucoplasts** These are colourless plastids that occur in non-green plant cells, commonly near the nucleus. They are as follows

(a) **Amyloplasts** These leucoplasts store starch, e.g. tuber of potato, grain of rice and wheat.

(b) **Elaioplasts** These store fats.

(c) **Aleuroplasts** They are protein storing plastids, e.g. maize. (2)

(ii) **Chromoplasts** These are non-photosynthetic coloured plastids which synthesise and store carotenoid pigments. They appear, orange, red or yellow in colour. (1)

(iii) **Chloroplasts** These are photosynthetic plastids, which are green in colour and found in the leaves of all green plants. (1)

**7. Describe the structure of the following with the help of labelled diagram** **NCERT**

**(i) Nucleus** **(ii) Centrosome**

**Ans.** (i) Refer to text on page no. 168. (2½)

(ii) Refer to text on page no. 168. (2½)

**8. Write the functions of the following** **NCERT Exemplar**

**(i) Centromere** **(ii) Cell wall** **(iii) Smooth ER**

**(iv) Golgi apparatus** **(v) Centrioles**

**Ans.** (i) **Centromere** It is required for proper chromosome segregation. The centromere connect the two sister chromatids. It is the point where chromosome attaches to the spindle apparatus during mitosis and meiosis. (1)

(ii) **Cell Wall** It gives a definite shape to the cell and protects the cell from mechanical injury and infections. It also helps in cell to cell interaction and act as a barrier for undesirable macromolecules. (1)

(iii) **Smooth ER** It helps in synthesis of lipids, metabolism of carbohydrates, regulation of calcium concentration, drug detoxification and attachment of receptor on cell membrane proteins. (1)

(iv) **Golgi Apparatus** It is the important site for the formation of glycoproteins and glycolipids. It is involved in the synthesis of cell wall materials and also play an important role in formation of cell plate during cell division. (1)

(v) **Centrioles** They form the base body of cilia and flagella. They also help in cell division in animal cell. (1)

**9. What is a centromere? How does the position of centromere form the basis of classification of chromosomes. Support your answer with a diagram showing the position of centromere on different types of chromosomes.** **NCERT**

**Ans.** Refer to text on page no. 169.

## Source Based/Case Based/Passage Based Questions

**1. Read the following passage and answer the questions that follows.**

**Manish, while performing a practical in laboratory on Gram stain observed that one type of bacteria stained dark blue or purple in colour, while the other type of bacteria did not retain the crystal violet dye even after staining again and again. Instead it keeps on loosing the dye on washing. He rushed to his teacher for showing the specimen.**
**His teacher explained that there is nothing to get worried about. As different kinds of bacteria are found.**

**(i) Name the instrument that allows us to study the unicellular organism.**

**(ii) What is the basis of classifying bacteria?**

**(iii) Name the type of bacteria observed by him that does not retain the dye.**

**(iv) What is the basic difference between Gram positive and Gram negative bacteria?**

**Ans.** (i) Microscope (1)

(ii) Bacteria are classified into two groups on the basis of the differences in the cell envelopes and the manner in which they respond to Gram stain. Staining of bacteria with Gram stain revealed the basis to differentiate bacteria into two categories, i.e. Gram positive and Gram negative bacteria. (1)

(iii) Gram negative bacteria (1)

(iv) The basic difference between the two types of bacteria lies in their cell wall. The Gram positive bacteria contain peptidoglycan and teichoic acid in their cell wall while, the cell wall of Gram negative bacteria is not composed of peptidoglycan (in high amount), instead they have an outer layer made up of lipids. They also do not contain teichoic acid. (1)

**2. Sunil found two unlabelled permanent slides in the laboratory. He observed the slides under a microscope and noted the following features**

**Slide *A* Contains round, irregularly shaped cells with a centrally placed nucleus and a continuous cell membrane.**

**Slide *B* Contains rectangular cells with a large central vacuole and double layered outer walls.**

**Based on these observations, please answer the following questions:**

**(i) Identify slide *A* and slide *B*.**

**(ii) Write two common characteristics between the two slides.**

**(iii) Name two cell organelles that are present in the cells of slide *A*, but absent in slide *B*.**

**(iv) How is the presence of a double outer layer in the cells of slide *B* beneficial?** **Competency Based Que.**

**Ans.** (i) Based on the given features, slide *A* is of animal cell and slide *B* is of plant cell. (1)

(ii) Both slide *A* and *B* consists of eukaryotic cells. They have both have nucleus with a well-defined nuclear membrane and membrane bound organelles. (1)

(iii) Two organelles that are present in the cells of slide *A*, but absent in slide *B* are centriole and lysosomes. (1)

(iv) The presence of double outer layer in the cells of slide *B* are beneficial in the following ways.

(a) They provide definite shape to the cell (½)

(b) They protect the protoplasm from mechanical injury. (½)

# SELF ASSESSMENT TEST

## Multiple Choice Questions

1. Schleiden and Schwann's cell theory could not explain
   (a) how new cells were formed
   (b) the organisation of living body
   (c) body of organism is composed of cells
   (d) plant cell is surrounded by plasma membrane
2. Select the incorrect match pair.
   (a) Robert Brown- Discovered the nucleus
   (b) Anton von Leeuwenhoek- First saw and described live cells
   (c) Rudolf Virchow- *Omnis cellula-e-cellula*
   (d) Theodore Schwann- Plant cell is surrounded by a plasma membrane
3. Plasmid of bacterial cells possess all the following characteristics except
   (a) these are extra chromosomal DNA
   (b) these are used in genetic engineering
   (c) these help in replication of nucleoid
   (d) these confer some phenotypic resistance to some bacteria
4. Which of the following is not true regarding prokaryotic cell?
   (a) They are smaller than eukaryotic cells
   (b) They have well-defined nucleus
   (c) They have specialised differentiated form of cell membrane
   (d) They have cell wall surrounding the plasma membrane
5. Why endoplasmic reticulum, Golgi complex, lysosomes and vacuoles are components of endomembranous system?
   (a) Their structures are different
   (b) Their functions are coordinated
   (c) Their functions are similar
   (d) They are present within the eukaryotic cell
6. Two cell organelles in plant cell having their own genetic material are
   (a) mitochondria and Golgi bodies
   (b) chloroplast and Golgi bodies
   (c) mitochondria and chloroplast
   (d) Golgi bodies and lysosomes
7. Which of the following is not the component of cytoskeleton?
   (a) Microtubules
   (b) Microfilaments
   (c) Intermediate filaments
   (d) Axoneme filaments
8. Match the columns.

| | Column I | | Column II |
|---|---|---|---|
| I. | Cytoskeleton | A. | Hair-like outgrowth |
| II. | Flagella | B. | Proximal region of centriole |
| III. | Hub | C. | Work like oars |
| IV. | Cilia | D. | Filamentous protein structure |

   Choose the correct option.
   (a) I-D, II-A, III-B, IV-C
   (b) I-D, II-C, III-B, IV-A
   (c) I-B, II-D, III-A, IV-C
   (d) I-D, II-A, III-C, IV-B

## Assertion-Reason Questions

**Direction** (Q. Nos. 9-12) *In each of the following questions, a statement of Assertion (A) is given followed by corresponding statement of Reason (R). Of the statements, mark the correct answer if*

(a) Both A and R are true and R is the correct explanation of the A.
(b) Both A and R are true, but R is not the correct explanation of the A.
(c) A is true, but R is false.
(d) A is false, but R is true.

9. **Assertion** (A) Endoplasmic reticulum is the important site of formation of glycoprotein and glycolipids.
   **Reason** (R) Endoplasmic reticulum divides the intracellular space into luminal and extra-luminal compartment.
10. **Assertion** (A) Prokaryotic cells lack well-defined nucleus and membrane bound organelles.
    **Reason** (R) Ribosomes are non-membrane bound organelles found in the prokaryotic cells only.
11. **Assertion** (A) Lysosomes are called the suicidal bags of cells.
    **Reason** (R) Lysosomes contain digestive enzymes that can breakdown the cell's biomolecules.
12. **Assertion** (A) The nucleoplasm contains nucleolus and chromatin.
    **Reason** (R) Nucleolus is the site for active ribosomal RNA synthesis.

## Very Short Answer Type Questions

13. Name the site of synthesis of lipid-like steroidal hormones in animal cells.
14. Mention the functions of contractile vacuole in *Amoeba*?
15. What type of molecules move out of the nucleus through nuclear pores?
16. Name two membrane bound organelle found in both plant and animal cells.

## Short Answer Type Questions

17. Mention any two similarities between mitochondria and chloroplast.
18. Differentiate between cilia and flagella.
19. Write the functions of the following.
    (i) Cell wall (ii) Smooth ER

## Long Answer Type Questions

20. Briefly describe the cell theory.
21. With the help of well-labelled diagram, describe the fluid mosaic model of plasma membrane.
22. Describe the structure and functions of powerhouse of the cell.

## Case Based Question

24. In a laboratory, Priya is examining a slide under a microscope. She observes two structures in which structure *A* is a round-shaped structure and upon closer inspection, she identifies the structure *B* which is a thread-like structure not appear to be loosely arranged.
    On the basis of following observations, answer the following questions
    (i) Identify the structure *A* and *B*.
    (ii) Are these structures found in both prokaryotic and eukaryotic cells, explain?
    (iii) What are the functions of these two structures?

## Answers

| | | | | | | | |
|---|---|---|---|---|---|---|---|
| 1. (a) | 2. (d) | 3. (c) | 4. (b) | 5. (b) | 6. (c) | 7. (d) | 8. (a) |
| 9. (d) | 10. (c) | 11. (a) | 12. (b) | | | | |

# 09

# CHAPTER

# Biomolecules

A cell is composed of variety of elements (like carbon, hydrogen, oxygen) which are also the components of many **biologically** important molecules.
These elements combine in different ways in order to form various biomolecules, which play a vital role in the maintenance of metabolic processes.
The elemental analysis shows that all the elements present in earth's crust are similar to the elements present in living tissues, but living organisms have proportionally more carbon and hydrogen compared to earth's crust.

### YOUR STUDY GOALS



### YOUR PRACTICE GOAL

- Objective Type Questions (40 Qs ; MCQs, A-R) Case Based Questions (3)
- Subjective Type Questions
- (35 VSAs, 31 SAs, 11 LAs)

- In this chapter, we will discuss about the analysis of different biomolecules, their structure and functions along with properties of enzymes.

## 9.1 How to Analyse Chemical Composition?

- To analyse the chemical composition of any organic compound of a living organism, the chemical analysis of living tissue is done.
- As organic compounds play a major role, it is essential to have knowledge of their molecular formula and structure.
- This can be easily done by performing following steps
  - Weight of a living tissue (like a piece of a liver, fruit, vegetable or any other body tissue) is taken.
  - The tissue is then grinded in a solvent called **trichloroacetic acid** ($Cl_3CCOOH$) with the help of mortar and pestle.
  - The thick slurry obtained is then filtered through a cheese-cloth or cotton. This will generate two fractions of solution as given below

(a) **Filtrate** or the **acid-soluble fraction**.

(b) **Retentate** or the **acid-insoluble fraction**.

- The acid-soluble pool contains numerous organics compounds as identified by the scientists.
- By using different separation techniques, each compound can be isolated and purified.
- Analytical techniques are used to obtain the molecular formula and probable structure of the compound.
- All the carbon compounds that were obtained from living tissues are called **biomolecules**.

## Ash Analysis for Inorganic Compound and Elements

- After the analysis of chemical composition of organic compounds in a tissue, it is necessary to do the analysis of inorganic elements and compounds.
- It can be done easily by performing a destructive experiment that separate inorganic compounds from organic compounds in the form of **ash** (i.e. contains inorganic compounds and elements).
- Ash is the remaining part of any living tissue, which remains after burning of all organic compound.
- Ash analysis is done in order to analyse the chemical composition of different inorganic compounds and elements present in the organic materials after burning.
- It is done in the following way
  - For analysis, weigh a small amount of a living tissue (gives wet weight) and dry it till all the water evaporates.
  - The remaining material gives the dry weight.
  - Now, if tissue is fully burnt, all the carbon compounds are oxidised to gaseous form (i.e. $CO_2$, water vapour) and are removed. This will result in the formation of **ash**.
- This, ash contains inorganic elements like potassium, sodium, calcium, magnesium, etc.
- Inorganic compounds like sulphate, phosphate, etc., are also seen in the acid-soluble fraction.
- Therefore, analysis for compound gives an idea of the kind of organic and inorganic constituents present in living tissue.
- While, the elemental analysis gives elemental composition of living tissues in the form of hydrogen, oxygen, chlorine, carbon, etc.
- The table given below compares the human body composition and the earth's crust.

**A Comparison of Elements Present in Non-living and Living Matter***

| Elements | % Weight of Earth's Crust | % Weight of Human Body |
|---|---|---|
| Hydrogen (H) | 0.14 | 0.5 |
| Carbon (C) | 0.03 | 18.5 |
| Oxygen (O) | 46.6 | 65.0 |
| Nitrogen (N) | Very little | 3.3 |
| Sulphur (S) | 0.03 | 0.3 |
| Sodium (Na) | 2.8 | 0.2 |
| Calcium (Ca) | 3.6 | 1.5 |
| Magnesium (Mg) | 2.1 | 0.1 |
| Silicon (Si) | 27.7 | negligible |

**Adapted from CNR Rao, Understanding Chemistry, Universities Press, Hyderabad.*

- The table given below lists out the inorganic constituents occurring in the form of salts and ions.

**List of Few Main Representative Inorganic Constituents of Living Tissues**

| Components | Formula |
|---|---|
| Sodium | $Na^+$ |
| Potassium | $K^+$ |
| Calcium | $Ca^{2+}$ |
| Magnesium | $Mg^{2+}$ |
| Water | $H_2O$ |
| Compounds | $NaCl, CaCO_3, PO_4^{3-}, SO_4^{2-}$ |

## Quick Test 1

1. Mention the elements which are found in higher concentrations in living organisms than in the earth's crust.
2. Name the term used for carbon compounds obtained from living tissues.
3. After filtering the slurry through cheese cloth or cotton, *X* and *Y* fractions are obtained, identify *X* and *Y*.
4. Name the compounds found in the acid-soluble fraction of ash.
5. **State True or False.**
   (a) The analysis of living tissues for elemental composition reveals the presence of elements such as hydrogen, oxygen, carbon and chlorine.
   (b) After burning living tissue, the remaining material is called 'ash,' which contains both organic and inorganic elements.

# 9.2 Biomicromolecules

- These molecules are small in size, with low molecular weight (18-800 Da), highly soluble (if polar) and have simple molecular conformation.
- Micromolecules can be inorganic such as water, mineral salts, gases or organic compounds such as sugars, amino acids, nucleotides, etc.
- Various micromolecules in detail are as follows

## 1. Carbohydrates

- These are the organic compounds mainly made up of C, H and O.
- Carbohydrates are also known as saccharides because their major constituents are **sugars**.
- These are divided into following types.

### Monosaccharides

- These are simplest carbohydrate monomers which cannot be hydrolysed further into smaller components.

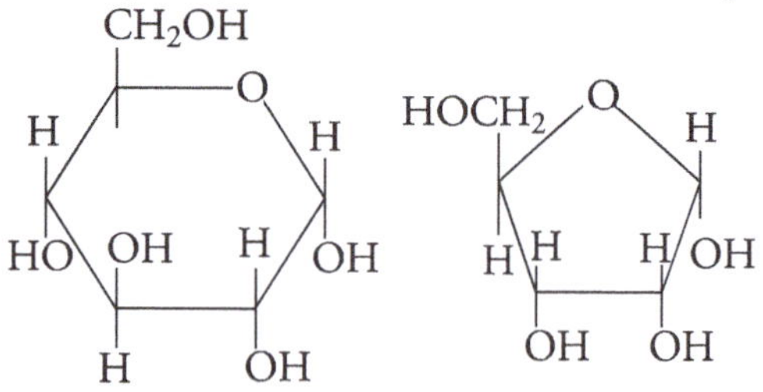


$C_6H_{12}O_6$ (glucose) $C_5H_{10}O_5$ (ribose)

Fig. 9.1 Sugars (carbohydrates)

### Oligosaccharides

- These are small carbohydrates formed by the condensation of 2-9 monosaccharide molecules. Hence, belongs to the category of compound carbohydrates.

## 2. Amino Acids

- These are organic compounds containing an amino group (—NH2) and an acidic group (—COOH) as substituent on the same carbon, i.e. the **α-carbon** (i.e. carbon next to the carboxylic group). Hence, they are called **α-amino acids.**
- These are substituted methanes.
- There are four substituent groups present on α-carbon, which occupy the four different valency position. These are **hydrogen, carboxyl group, amino group** and ***R* group** (variable group).
- Based on the nature of *R* group, there are many amino acids. However, those which occur in proteins are only of twenty types.
- General formula of α-amino acid is given below as

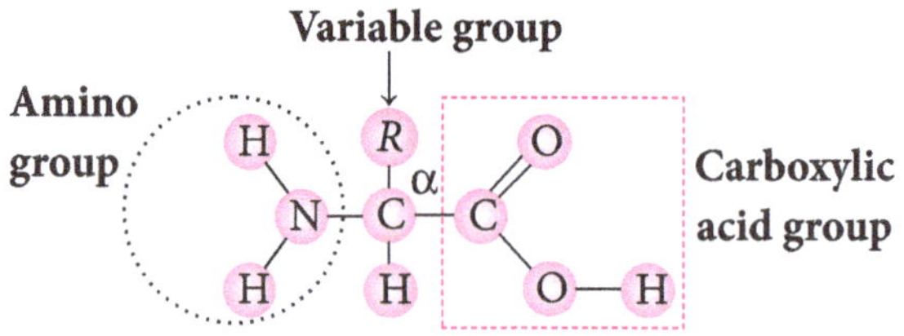


where, $R$ = side chain of amino acids

- The *R* group in these proteinaceous amino acids could be a hydrogen (glycine), a methyl group (alanine), hydroxyl methyl (serine), etc.
- The diagrammatic representation of some amino acids are given below.

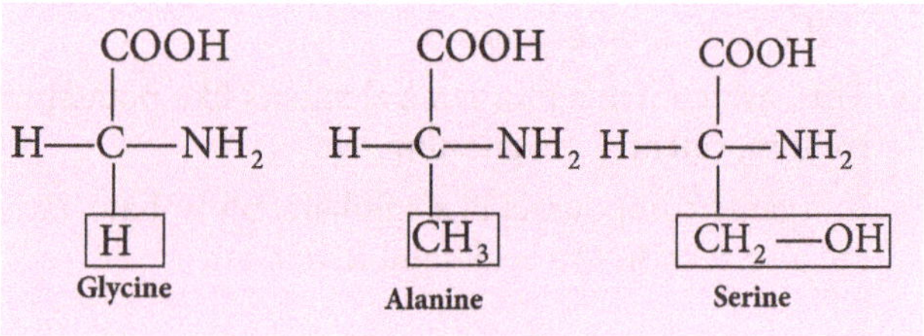


Amino acids

- The chemical and physical properties of amino acids are essentially due to the amino, carboxyl and *R*-functional groups present.

## Classification of Amino Acids

Based on the number of amino and carboxyl group present, amino acids are categorised into following types

- **Acidic Amino Acids** These contain one amino group and two carboxyl group per molecule, e.g. glutamic acid.
- **Basic Amino Acids** These contain two amino groups and one carboxyl group per molecule, e.g. lysine.
- **Neutral Amino Acids** These contain one amino group and one carboxyl group per molecule, e.g. valine.
- **Aromatic Amino Acids** These contain aromatic rings in their side chain, e.g. phenylalanine, tyrosine and tryptophan.

### Zwitter Ion

The formation of zwitter ion is another particular property of amino acid. It is a neutral molecule (with positive and negative charge) having $—NH_2$ and —COOH which are ionisable in nature. Hence, in solutions of different pH, the structure of amino acid changes variably.

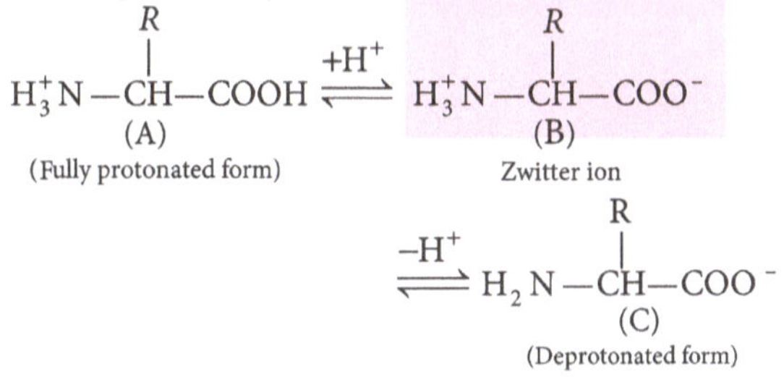

Representations of a zwitter ion formation

## 3. Lipids

- They are the esters of **fatty acids** and **alcohol**.
- These are generally insoluble in water, but can dissolved in a number of non-polar organic solvents such as ether, benzene, chloroform, acetone, etc.
- They could be simply fatty acids.
- Lipids are mainly made up of carbon, hydrogen and sometimes oxygen in which the content of oxygen is lesser as compared to carbon and hydrogen.

### Fatty Acids

- These are the organic acids having hydrocarbon chains that end in a carboxylic group (— COOH).
- The carboxylic group is attached to an *R* group that could be a methyl ($—CH_3$) or ethyl ($—C_2H_5$) or higher number of ($—CH_2$) groups (1 carbon to 19 carbons), for example
  - **Palmitic acid** has 16 carbons including carboxyl carbon.
  - **Arachidonic acid** has 20 carbon atoms including the carboxyl carbon.
- Depending upon the types of bonds present, fatty acids are of following two types
  - **Saturated Fatty Acids** These do not have any double bond, (C—C), e.g. palmitic acid.

$$CH_3—(CH_2)_{14}—COOH$$

**Palmitic acid**

  - **Unsaturated Fatty Acids** This type of fatty acid contain one or more than one double bond (C=C), e.g. oleic acid.

$$CH_3(CH_2)_7\ CH=CH\ (CH_2)_7\ COOH$$

**Oleic acid**

## Classification of Lipids

Lipids are classified into the following sub-groups

### Simple Lipids

- Glycerol, which is trihydroxy propane is an example of simple lipid.
- Many lipids have both **glycerol** and **fatty acids**.
- The fatty acids are found esterified with glycerol.
- Lipids can be monoglycerides, diglycerides and triglycerides.

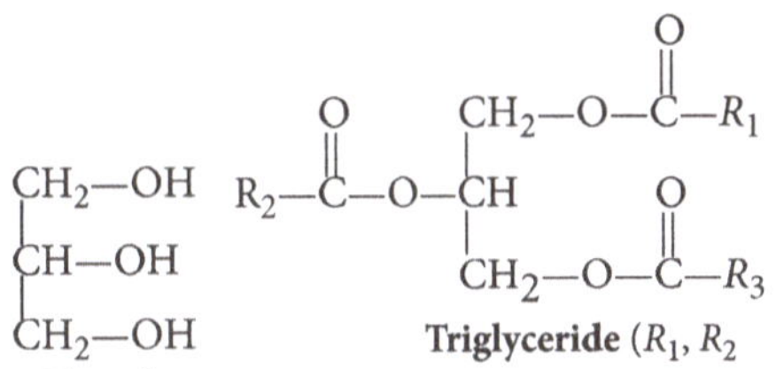

**Glycerol**

**Triglyceride** ($R_1$, $R_2$ and $R_3$ are fatty acids)

- Simple lipids are also differentiated into two main types on the basis of their melting points.
- These are as follows
  - **Fats** are solids at room temperature.
  - **Oils** are usually liquid at room temperature because they have low melting point, hence remain oil in winters, e.g. gingelly oil.

## Compound or Conjugated Lipids

- These are the esters of fatty acids and alcohol, which also contain other chemical groups, e.g. phospholipids, glycolipids, etc.
- **Phospholipids** have phosphorus and phosphorylated organic compound in them. They are found in cell membrane.
- One of the common example of phospholipid is **lecithin.**
- Some tissues, i.e. neural tissues have lipids with complex structure.

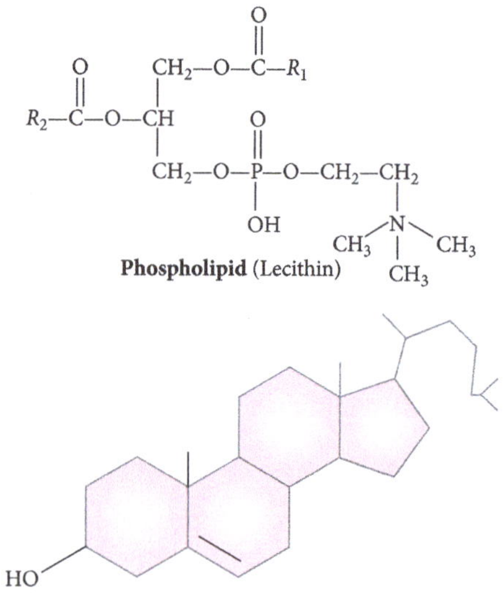


Fig. 9.2 Compound lipids

## 4. Nucleotides

- These are the monomers of nucleic acids.
- The nucleotides are made up of three molecules, i.e. **a pentose sugar, a cyclic nitrogenous base** and **a phosphate group**, e.g. adenylic acid, thymidylic acid, guanylic acid, uridylic acid and cytidylic acid.

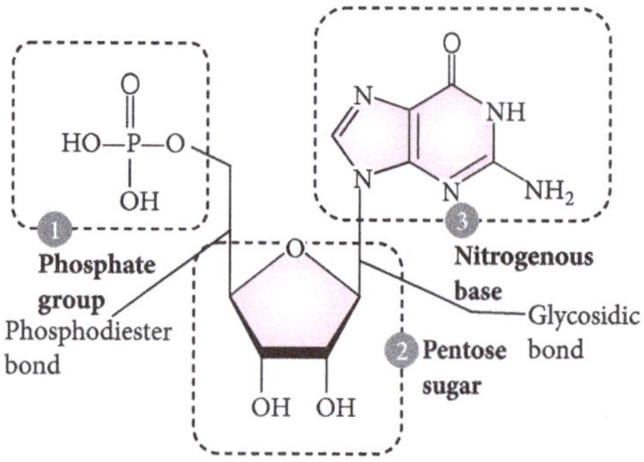


Fig. 9.3 Nucleotide (adenylic acid)

- The units of a nucleotides are as follows
  - **Pentose Sugar** It exist in pentagon form with four carbon and one oxygen forming a ring.
  - It is present in the form of ribose or deoxyribose sugar in RNA and DNA, respectively.
  - **Nitrogenous Bases** These are the flat heterocyclic compounds having nitrogen and carbon in a ring structure. These are basically of two types

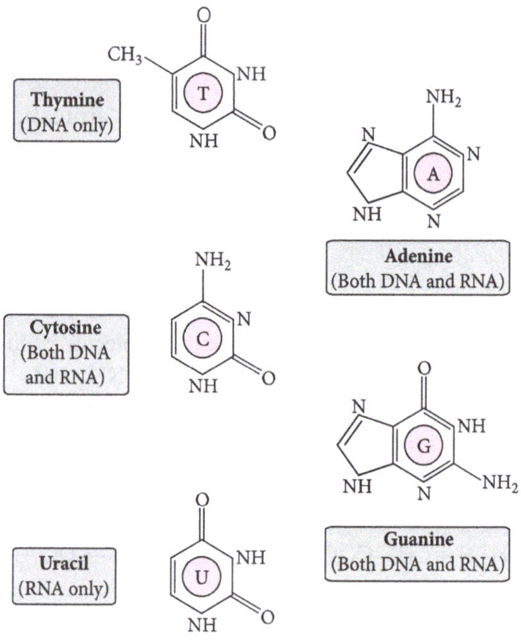


Fig. 9.4 Nitrogen bases

    - **Purines** It is larger and composed of two rings. They are of further two types, i.e. **Adenine** (A) and **Guanine** (G).
    - **Pyrimidines** It is smaller and composed of single ring. They are of further three types, i.e. **Cytosine** (C), **Thymine** (T) and **Uracil** (U).
  - **Phosphoric Acid** (Phosphate Group) A nucleotide may have 1, 2 or 3 phosphate groups. It gives acidic nature to the nucleotide.

## Nucleoside

- If a pentose sugar is attached to a nitrogen base by a glycosidic bond, it is called **nucleoside**.
  e.g. adenine + ribose $\rightarrow$ adenosine.
- Likewise guanosine, thymidine, uridine and cytidine are the examples of nucleoside.

- The nucleoside combines with a phosphate group at 5-position by an ester bond to form a nucleotide.

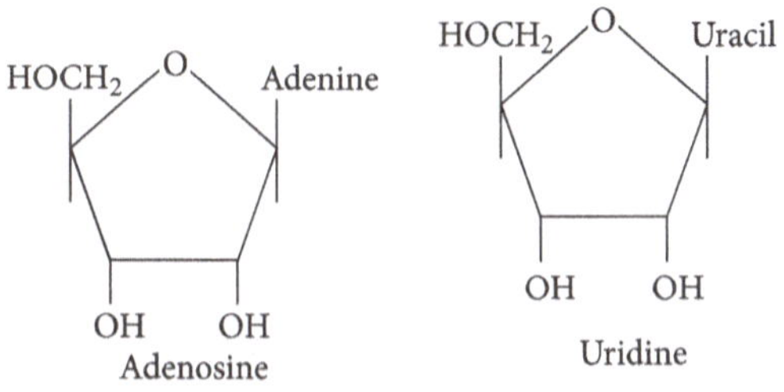


Fig. 9.5 Nucleosides

**Differences between Nucleoside and Nucleotide**

| Nucleoside | Nucleotide |
|---|---|
| It is a compound formed by the combination of a nitrogen base with a pentose sugar. | It is a compound formed by the combination of a nitrogen base, pentose sugar and a phosphate group. |
| It is a component of nucleotide. | It is a component of nucleic acids (formed by phosphorylation of a nucleoside). |
| Slightly basic in nature. | Acidic in nature. |
| e.g. guanosine, adenosine, etc. | e.g. guanylic acid, adenylic acid, etc. |

## 9.3 Primary and Secondary Metabolites

- A large number of organic biomolecules are present in the cells which are used in various metabolic reactions of cell. Hence, these compounds are called **metabolites**.
- These are divided into two types

### 1. Primary Metabolites

- These metabolites are found in all living organisms.
- Their functions are easily indentifiable.
- They play specific known roles in the normal physiological processes, e.g. amino acids, carbohydrates, proteins, nitrogen bases, nucleic acids, etc.

### 2. Secondary Metabolites

- These metabolites are generally found in plant, fungal and microbial cells.
- Their functions are not identifiable in host organism and are not yet understood.
- These are the derivatives of primary metabolites, e.g. alkaloids, flavonoids, rubber, essential oils, antibiotics, coloured pigments, scents, gums, spices.
- Many of them are used for welfare of human beings, e.g. rubber, drugs, spices, scents, pigments.
- Some secondary metabolites also have ecological importance.

**Some Secondary Metabolites**

| | |
|---|---|
| Pigments | Carotenoids, Anthocyanins, etc. |
| Alkaloids | Morphine, codeine, etc. |
| Terpenoides | Monoterpenes, diterpenes, etc. |
| Essential oils | Lemon grass oil, etc. |
| Toxins | Abrin and ricin |
| Lectins | Concanavalin-A |
| Drugs | Vinblastin, curcumin, etc. |
| Polymeric substances | Rubber, gums and cellulose |

### Quick Test 2

1. The different types of carbohydrates, classified based on their structure, include which categories?
2. Name the amino acids containing an amino group and an carboxylic group on the same carbon.
3. Name the form of amino acids with both a positive and a negative charge.
4. **State True or False.**
   (a) Lipids are primarily composed of fatty acids and glycerol and are mainly used for energy storage and insulation.
   (b) Nucleotides are the building blocks of nucleic acids and consist of a sugar, a phosphate group, and a nitrogenous base.
5. *X* is an alkaloid substance that is used as a painkiller. What is *X* ?

## 9.4 Biomacromolecules

- The molecules which are found in living organisms are divided into two main types, i.e. **biomicromolecules** (already been described in detail in this chapter) and **biomacromolecules**.
- The biomacromolecules are larger in size with higher molecular weight ranging from **10,000 Dalton** (Da) and above (except lipids).
- These compounds are found in the acid insoluble pool. There are four major types of biomacromolecules, i.e. **proteins**, **polysaccharides**, **nucleic acids** and **lipids**.
- The molecules in the acid insoluble fraction are polymeric substances except lipids.
- Although lipids have their molecular weight below 800 Da, but they comes under acid insoluble fraction (i.e. biomacromolecular category).
- This happens because these are compounds with small molecular weight and are present not only as such, but are also arranged in structures like cell membranes and other membranes.
- When we grind a tissue, **the cell structure, cell membrane** and **other membranes** are broken down into pieces and form vesicles that are not water soluble.
- Therefore, these are separated along with acid insoluble pool and are placed in macromolecule pool. Hence, lipids are not strictly biomacromolecule.
- Along with lipids, the macromolecules from cytoplasm and organelles forms acid-inoluble fraction.
- On the other hand the acid-soluble pool represents roughly the cytoplasmic composition.
- Together they represent the entire chemical composition of living tissues or organisms.
- If representation of the chemical composition of living tissue is done from abundance point of view and arranged class wise, it is observed that water is the most abundant chemical found in living organisms.

**Average Composition of Cells**

| Components | % of the Total Cellular Mass |
|---|---|
| Water | 70-90 |
| Proteins | 10-15 |
| Carbohydrates | 3 |
| Lipids | 2 |
| Nucleic acids | 5-7 |
| Ions | 1 |

- All the macromolecules are actually polymers of their biomicromolecules commonly known as **monomers**, e.g. polysaccharides are **polymers** of monosaccharides, **proteins** are polymers of amino acids and **nucleic acids** are polymers of nucleotides.
- Hence, on the basis of the number and types of monomer present, polymers are of following two types
  - **Homopolymers** are the type of polymers, which have only one type of monomer. These monomers can be repeated '*n*' number of times in a chain, e.g. starch, insulin, etc.
  - **Heteropolymers** are the type of polymers, which have two or more than two types of monomers, e.g. proteins.
- Various biomacromolecules and their major roles are described as follows

### Proteins

- These are one of the most important and abundant intracellular organic biomolecules.
- The proteins are large sized heteropolymeric macromolecules having one or more polypeptides (i.e chains of amino acids).
- The amino acids in a polypeptide chain are arranged linearly and are linked by the type of bond called **peptide bond**.
- Thus, each protein is a polymer of amino acids (as studied earlier in the chapter).
- The sequence of amino acids present in a polypeptide is specific for a particular protein.
- There are 20 types of amino acids (e.g. alanine, valine, arginine, leucine, histidine, etc.), that are used in the synthesis of all types of proteins.
- This is the reason proteins are considered as heteropolymer not homopolymer.
- These amino acids are divided into two main types, on the basis of their utility
  - **Essential Amino Acids** These are the type of amino acids that are essential for health so, are needed to be supplied through our diet. The

dietary proteins are the source of essential amino acids, e.g. leucine, isoleucine, etc.

- **Non-Essential Amino Acids** These are the amino acids that are synthesised by the body, e.g. proline, serine.

> **Collagen** is the most abundant protein of animal world and Ribulose Bisphosphate Carboxylase Oxygenase (RuBisCO) is the most abundant protein in plants and in the whole of the biosphere.

## Structure of Proteins

- Every protein molecule has a three-dimensional structure that corresponds to its function.
- Biologists described the protein structure at four different levels, i.e. primary, secondary, tertiary and quaternary.
- These are as follows

### 1. Primary Structure

- It is the basic structure of a protein in which the amino acids are arranged in linear sequence of a polypeptide chain.
- The left end of the polypeptide chain is represented by the first amino acid, also called as the **N-terminal amino acid** and the right end is represented by the last amino acid called the **C-terminal amino acid**.
- A protein thread does not exist throughout as an extended rigid rod.

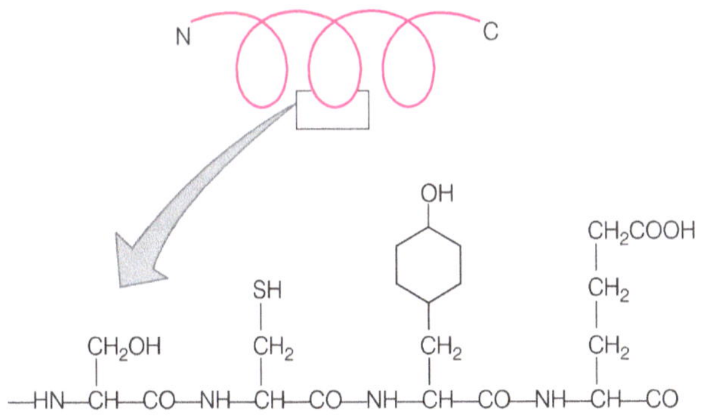


Fig. 9.6 Primary structure of a protein. N and C represent its first and last termini.

### 2. Secondary Structure

- It is developed by the interactions of amino acids present in the linear sequence inside the polypeptide.
- There are mainly two types of secondary structure, i.e. α- helix and β-pleated structure.
  - **α- helix** In α- helix, the thread of the primary protein is coiled spirally, generally in right-handed manner.
  - **β -pleated Structure** In β-pleated secondary structure, two or more polypeptide chains get interconnected by hydrogen bonds.

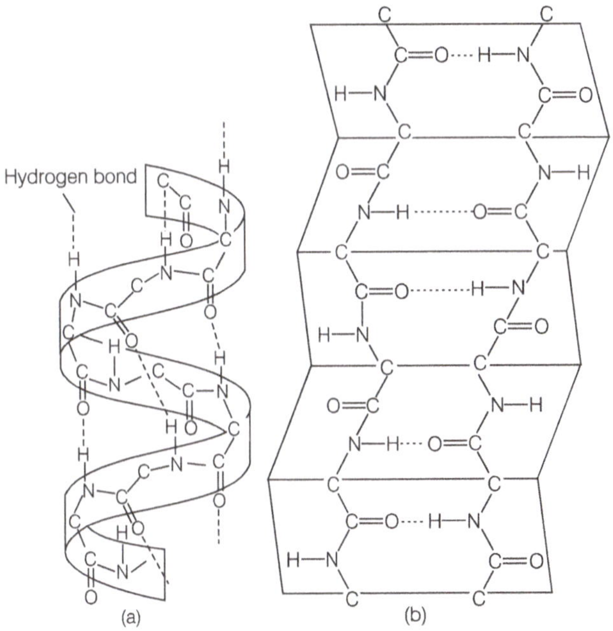


Fig. 9.7 Secondary structure of protein : (a) α-helix (b) β-pleated structure

**Differences between α-Helix and β-Pleated Structures of Proteins**

| α-Helix Structure | β-Pleated Structure |
|---|---|
| The polypeptide chain curls longitudinally by the action of hydrogen bonds forming a spiral or helix. | The protein is more extended and the hydrogen bond forms a *zig-zag* shaped protein structure called β-strand (which combines and forms β-sheet). |
| It is highly compact and rigid. | It is less compact and rigid. |

### 3. Tertiary Structure

- The bending and folding of polypeptides driven by various interactions including hydrogen and disulphide band, results in tertiary structure (hollow wollen ball-like structure).
- It gives a three-dimensional (3-D) configuration of the protein molecule.

- Tertiary structure is absolutely necessary for many biological activities of proteins.

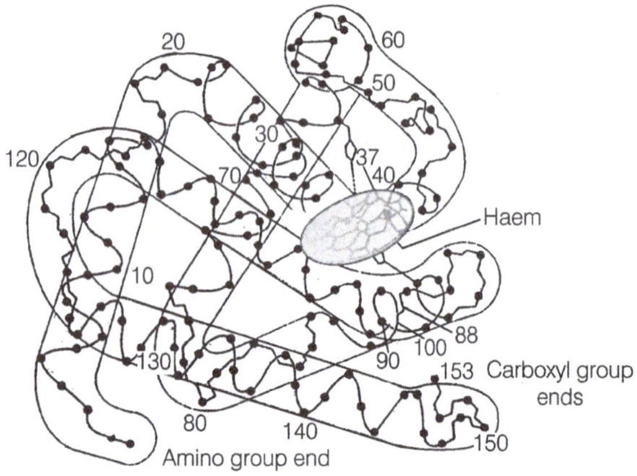


Fig. 9.8 A tertiary structure of protein

### 4. Quaternary Structure

- Certain proteins consist of an assembly of more than one polypeptide or subunits.
- The manner in which these individual folded polypeptides are arranged with respect to each other (e.g. linear string of spheres, spheres arranged one upon each other in the form of a cube or plate, etc.) is the architecture of a protein otherwise called the **quaternary structure** of a protein.
- Adult human haemoglobin consists of 4 subunits. Two of these are identical to each other.
- Hence, two subunits of $\alpha$-type and two subunits of $\beta$-type together constitute the human haemoglobin (Hb).

**TEACHER'S TIP**
Based on their shape and structural organisation, proteins are divided into **fibrous** and **globular proteins.** The fibrous proteins (e.g., collagen) have long, elongated structures with repetitive amino acid sequences, whereas the globular proteins (e.g., enzymes) have a compact, spherical-shape with diverse folding patterns.

## Functions of Proteins

The various basic functions of protein in living organism are given below

- Helps in transportation of nutrients across the cell membrane by acting as protein transporter.
- Helps in fighting with infectious organisms.
- Helps at the time of injury in blood clotting and also acts as antibodies and provide immunity.
- Helps in growth and repair of body tissues.
- Some proteins function as hormones and some functions as enzymes and catalyse the reactions.

**Some Proteins and their Functions**

| Protein | Functions |
|---|---|
| Collagen | Intercellular ground substance |
| Trypsin | Enzyme |
| Insulin | Hormone |
| Antibody | Fight infectious agents |
| Receptor | Sensory reception (smell, taste, etc.) |
| GLUT-4 | Enables glucose transport into cells |

## Polysaccharides

- These are another class of macromolecules that are present in the acid insoluble fraction.
- Polysaccharides are long chains of sugars.
- They are threads containing different monosaccharides as building blocks.
- A polysaccharide chain (like glycogen) is made up of two ends, the right end is called **reducing end** and the other left end is called **non-reducing end**.

## Types of Polysaccharides

Polysaccharides are of two types as given below

### 1. Homopolysaccharides

- These are the complex carbohydrates which are formed by polymerisation of only one type of monosaccharide as building block, e.g. starch, glycogen and cellulose (composed of single type of monosaccharide unit namely glucose).
- Some of them are as follows
  - **Cellulose** It is a polymer of glucose and is known to be a rigid and insoluble polysaccharide found in **cell wall** of most plants.
  - The paper made from pulp of plant and cotton fibres are cellulosic.
  - As cellulose is not composed of complex helices so, it cannot hold iodine ($I_2$) and import any colour with iodine solution.
  - **Starch** It is a storage polysaccharide because it helps in storing energy in plant tissues.
  - Starch forms helical secondary structures. Thus, it can hold iodine ($I_2$) molecules in it's helical portions.

Therefore, gives blue colour with iodine solution.

- **Inulin** Polymer of fructose.
- **Glycogen** It is also storage polysaccharide found in animals only (in liver cells and muscles).

## 2. Heteropolysaccharides

These are complex carbohydrates formed by the polymerisation of two or more than two types of monosaccharide units, e.g. chitin, pectin, peptidoglycans (murein), hyaluronic acid.

One of them is explained in detail below

### Chitin

- It is the second most abundant natural polymer, found in exoskeleton of arthropods (e.g. prawns, crabs, etc.)
- It has building blocks of amino-sugars and chemically modified sugar, e.g. glucosamine and N-acetyl galactosamine.

## Functions of Polysaccharide

Polysaccharides play multiple functions as described below

- Acts as structural component in the cell wall of plants, certain fungi and protists, e.g. cellulose, chitin.
- Acts as a reserve food material in plants, e.g. starch.
- Helps in anticoagulation and prevents blood clotting inside the vessels, e.g. heparin.

## Nucleic Acids

- The other type of macromolecule found as a part of acid insoluble fraction of any living tissue is the nucleic acids.
- These are polymeric compounds of nucleotides, therefore are called polynucleotides.
- A nucleotide (as discussed previously in the chapter) is composed of three chemically distinct components
  - **Heterocyclic compound-nitrogen base** (adenine, guanine, uracil, cytosine and thymine). The skeletal heterocyclic ring of DNA/RNA is called as **purine** and **pyrimidines**.
  - Adenine and guanine are purines, while uracil (only in RNA), thymine (only in DNA) and cytosine are pyrimidines.
  - **Monosaccharide** (ribose or deoxyribose).
  - **Phosphoric acid** or **phosphate** group.
- A nucleic acid which contains deoxyribose sugar is called **Deoxyribonucleic Acid** (DNA), while that which contains ribose sugar is **Ribonucleic Acid** (RNA).

## Functions of Nucleic Acids

Nucleic acids play multiple role in living organism, these are given as follows

- Acts as a genetic material, i.e. transfer hereditary information from one generation to the next.
- It enables cell to grow, maintain and divide by directing the synthesis of structural proteins.

**Differences between DNA and RNA**

| **Deoxyribonucleic Acid** (DNA) | **Ribonucleic Acid** (RNA) |
|---|---|
| Found in nucleus in the form of chromosomes. | Found in the cytoplasm, in nucleolus, nucleoplasm and associated with chromosomes. |
| Double-stranded structure; two strands coiled spirally in opposite direction. | Single-stranded polynucleotide chains. |
| The sugar is deoxyribose. | The sugar is ribose. |
| Four nitrogenous bases in it are<br>(i) Adenine, (ii) Guanine } **Purine**<br>(iii) Cytosine, (iv) Thymine } **Pyrimidine** | Four nitrogenous bases in it are<br>(i) Adenine, (ii) Guanine } **Purine**<br>(iii) Cytosine, (iv) Uracil } **Pyrimidine**<br>i.e. in RNA, thymine is replaced by uracil. |
| Purines and pyrimidines occur in equal proportion. | Do not occur in equal proportion/ratio. |
| DNA is the hereditary material in all prokaryotic and eukaryotic cells. | It is heredity material only in few viruses. |
| Controls structure, metabolism, differentiation and inheritance. | Helps in protein synthesis; function as a messenger . |
| Long molecule with high molecular weight. | Relatively short molecule with low molecular weight. |
| It does not occur in different types. | It occurs in three different types (i) *m*RNA (ii) *t*RNA (iii) *r*RNA |

## Quick Test 3

1. Mention the name of a protein that facilitates the transport of glucose into cells.
2. Name the term used to denote the left end of a polysaccharide chain.
3. Name the molecule which is a polymeric polysaccharide and do not contain complex helices.
4. Name the sugar found in DNA and RNA.
5. **State True or False.**
   (a) Cellulose is a polysaccharide that provides structural support in plant cell walls.
   (b) Glycogen is primarily stored in plant seeds for energy production.
   (c) The nitrogenous bases in nucleic acids are important for encoding genetic information.

## 9.5 Enzymes

- The enzymes are colloidal organic macromolecules, which are mostly proteinaceous in nature.
- Some nucleic acids also behave like enzymes and these are called ribozymes.
- An enzyme like any protein has primary (i.e. amino acid sequence of protein), secondary and tertiary structures.
- The tertiary structure has the backbone of the protein chain folded upon itself, the chain criss-crosses itself and hence, many cervices or pocket are made. One such pocket is the active site.
- An active site is a crevice or pocket of an enzyme into which a particular substrate fits.
- Thus, the enzymes through their active site, catalyse reactions at high rate.
- Enzymes, due to their protein structure, require specific conditions for activity, unlike inorganic catalysts that can operate under a broader range.
- But the enzymes, isolated from the organisms, who normally live under extremely high temperatures, e.g. hot thermal vents, under sea water and sulphur springs are stable and retain their catalytic power even at high temperature (upto 80°–90°).

**Differences between Enzyme Catalysts and Inorganic Catalysts**

| Enzyme Catalysts | Inorganic Catalysts |
|---|---|
| These get damaged at high temperature and pressure (above 40°C). | These do not get affected by high temperature and pressure. |
| Catalyses only specific reactions. | Can catalyse a number of reactions. |
| Sensitive to changes of the medium like pH, etc. | Do not have any effect of the changes in pH, etc. |

### Classification and Nomenclature of Enzymes

- The enzymes have been classified into six different categories on the basis of the type of reaction they catalyse.
- The six main classes of enzymes are further sub-divided into 4-13 sub-classes and are named accordingly by a four-digit number.

**International System of Enzyme Classification**

| Enzymes | Types of Reaction Catalysed and Examples |
|---|---|
| **Oxidoreductases/ Dehydrogenase** | Enzyme which catalyse oxidoreduction between two substrates S and S' e.g. S reduced + S' oxidised → S oxidised + S' reduced. |
| **Transferases** | Enzyme catalysing a transfer of a group G (other than hydrogen) between a pair of substrate S and S' e.g. $S{-}G + S' \rightarrow S + S' - G$ |
| **Hydrolases** | Enzyme catalysing hydrolysis of ester, ether, peptide, glycosidic, C–C, C-halide or P— N bonds |
| **Lyases** | Enzymes that catalyse removal of groups from substrates by mechanisms other than hydrolysis leaving double bonds. $\underset{\text{C—C}}{\overset{X\quad Y}{\mid\quad\mid}} \longrightarrow X - Y + C{=}C$ |
| **Isomerases** | Includes all enzymes catalysing inter-conversion of optical, geometric or positional isomers. |
| **Ligases** | Enzymes catalysing the linking together of 2 compounds, e.g. enzymes which catalyse joining of C –O, C –S, C — N, P — O, etc bonds. |

## Properties of Enzymes

Enzymes show the various important properties. These are as follows

- They enhance the rate of a chemical reaction without themselves being changed or used.
- The efficiency of an enzyme mainly depends upon the number of active sites present over an enzyme (i.e. more active site, the more efficient an enzyme).
- Being protein in nature, the enzymes are the giant molecules with high molecular weight.
- Enzymes are highly efficient, required in only small amount to catalyse large quantities of reaction.
- Enzymes are generally globular proteins. They may have additional inorganic or organic substances for their activity.
- Enzymes are highly specific, as each of them catalyses only a specific reaction, e.g. maltase acts only on maltose.
- Enzymes can be denatured by heat (thermolabile or heat sensitive). Human enzymes are active at 35-40°C, denature at 50-55°C. The enzymes of bacteria living in hot springs have optimal temperature of 70°C.

## Chemical Reactions

- For understanding enzymes, it is important to have knowledge about the chemical reactions that occurs between the compounds.
- Chemical compounds undergo following two types of changes.

### Physical Changes

These are those changes in which the shape of a molecule or a substance change without breaking of bonds or change in state of matter, e.g. melting of ice in water, etc.

### Chemical Changes

- These are those changes in which the bonds are broken and new bonds are formed during transformation, e.g.
  - $Ba(OH)_2 + H_2SO_4 \longrightarrow BaSO_4 + 2H_2O$
    (Inorganic chemical reaction)
  - Hydrolysis of starch into glucose
    (Organic chemical reaction)

- The rate of a physical or a chemical process refers to the amount of product formed in per unit time.

  Thus, $$\text{Rate} = \frac{\delta P}{\delta t}$$

- The rate can also be called **velocity** if the direction is specified.
- The rate of physical and chemical processes are influenced by different factors like **temperature**.
- A general thumb rule states that the rate gets doubled or decreased by half for every 10°C change in either direction.
- It is believed that the reaction that are catalysed by enzymes take place at higher rates than that of the uncatalysed ones, e.g.

$$\underset{\text{(Carbon dioxide)}}{CO_2} + \underset{\text{(Water)}}{H_2O} \underset{\text{anhydrase}}{\overset{\text{Carbonic}}{\rightleftharpoons}} \underset{\text{(Carbonic acid)}}{H_2CO_3}$$

- Hence, in the absence of any enzyme, the rate of reaction is very low, e.g. the reaction produces around 200 molecules of **carbonic acid** in an hour without enzyme, but when catalysed by an enzyme (carbonic anhydrase, present in cytoplasm) the reaction rate speeds up dramatically with about 6,00,000 molecules being formed every second.
- The rate is accelerated by about 10 million times.

## Metabolic Pathway

- It is a multistep chemical reaction in which each step is catalysed by the same enzyme complex or different enzymes, e.g.

$$\text{Glucose} \longrightarrow 2 \text{ pyruvic acid}$$
$$C_6H_{12}O_6 + O_2 \longrightarrow 2C_3H_4O_3 + 2H_2O$$

- During the above reaction, i.e. glycolysis (a metabolic pathway), one molecule of glucose gets converted to 2 molecules of pyruvic acid through 10 different enzymes catalysed metabolic reactions.
- The same pathway also gives rise to a variety of different metabolic end products, with one or two additional reactions, e.g.
  - Under anaerobic conditions, in skeletal muscles, lactic acid is produced, whereas under normal aerobic conditions pyruvic acid is produced (as explained above).
  - The same pathway during fermentation in yeast leads to the production of ethanol (ethyl alcohol).

## How do Enzymes bring About such High Rate of Chemical Conversion?

- For a chemical reaction to proceed, the **Substrate** (S) must bind to the enzyme at the active site.
- The substrate has to diffuse towards active site.
- During conversion of substrate into a **Product** (P), formation of an **Enzyme-Substrate** (ES) **Complex** takes place.

$$\text{E (enzyme)} + \text{S (substrate)} \longrightarrow \text{ES complex}$$

- This complex formation is a **transient phenomenon**. Thus, during the state, when substrate is bound to the enzyme active site, a new structure of the substrate, called **transition state structure** is formed.
- After the expected reaction of breaking and making of bond is completed, the product is released from the active site and the substrate gets transformed into the structure of product.
- The pathway of this transformation must go through the transition state structure.
- There are many altered structural states found between the stable substrate and product stability is related to the energy status of the molecule or the structure.

### Concept of Activation Energy

- Activation energy is pictorially represented through a graph as given below.
- In the graph *Y*-axis represents the potential energy content and the *X*-axis represents the progression of the structural transformation (states through the transition state).

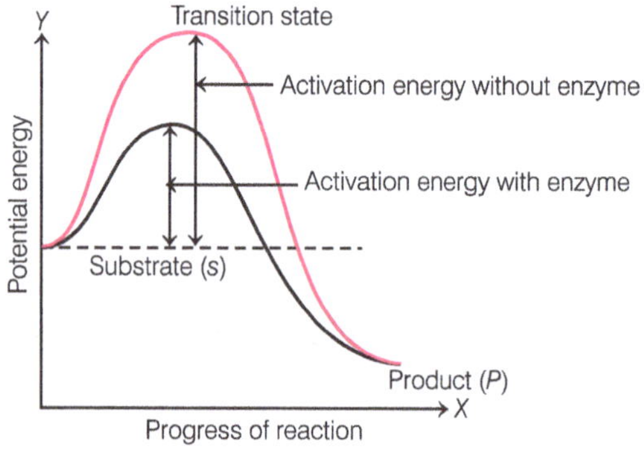


**Fig. 9.9** Concept of activation energy

- Following levels are noticed between the energy levels of S and P
  - When P is at a lower level than S, reaction is **exothermic** or **spontaneous**, (i.e. no need for external supply of energy).
  - When P is at higher level than S, reaction is **endothermic** or **energy requiring reaction,** (i.e. external supply of energy is needed).
- It proves that whether it is an exothermic or an endothermic reaction, the 'S' has to go through a much higher energy state (transition state).
- This difference between the average energy content of S from that of its transition state is called **activation energy.**

## Quick Test 4

1. Name the enzyme which is made up of nucleic acid.
2. Name the pocket or crevice present in an enzyme where the substrate fits to catalyse a reaction.
3. Which enzyme is involved in removing functional groups from substrates by mechanisms other than hydrolysis?
4. Name the enzyme present within the cytoplasm that speeds up the formation of $H_2CO_3$.
5. **State True or False.**
   (a) In the enzyme-substrate complex, the substrate undergoes a conformational change to fit perfectly into the enzyme's active site.
   (b) Enzymes remain unchanged after the formation of the enzyme-substrate complex and can participate in multiple reaction cycles.

## Nature of Enzyme Action

- Each **Enzyme** (E) has a **Substrate** (S) binding site in its molecule in order to form a highly reactive **Enzyme-Substrate** (ES) **complex.**
- This complex is short-lived and dissociates into its **Product** (P) and unchanged enzyme with an intermediate formation of the **Enzyme-Product** (EP) **complex.**
- The formation of the ES complex is essential for catalysis.

$$\underset{\text{Enzyme}}{\text{E}} + \underset{\text{Substrate}}{\text{S}} \rightleftharpoons \underset{\text{Enzyme - Substrate complex}}{\text{ES}} \longrightarrow \underset{\text{Enzyme - Product complex}}{\text{EP}} \longrightarrow \underset{\text{Enzyme}}{\text{E}} + \underset{\text{Product}}{\text{P}}$$

- The catalytic cycle of an enzyme action can be described in the following steps

- Initially, the substrate binds to the active site of the enzyme, fitting into the active site.
- The binding of the substrate induces the enzyme to alter its shape, so that it can fit more tightly around the substrate.
- The active site of the enzyme now in close proximity of the substrate breaks the chemical bonds of the substrate, due to which the new enzyme product complex is formed.
- The enzyme releases the products of the reaction and the free enzyme is ready to bind to another molecule of the substrate, so that it can run through the catalytic cycle once again.

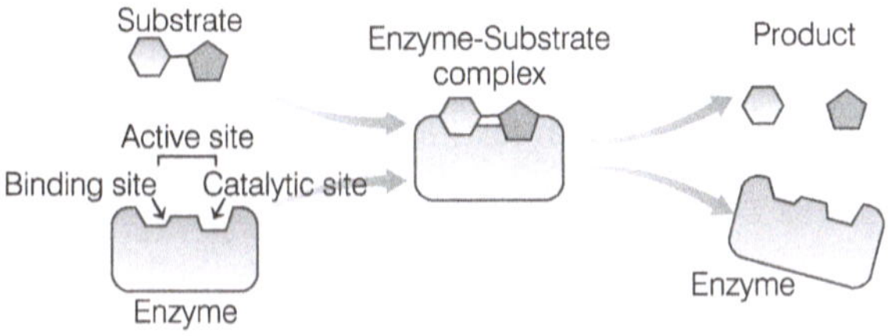


Fig. 9.10 Mechanism of enzyme reaction through enzyme substrate complex formation

## Factors Affecting Enzyme Activity

Enzyme activity is altered or affected by the change in the conditions that can alter the tertiary structure of the protein.

- The factors include temperature, pH, change in substrate concentration or binding of specific chemicals that regulate its activity.
- Some of the factors responsible for such are described in detail below

### 1. Temperature and pH

- Enzymes generally work at narrow range of temperature and pH.
- Each enzyme shows highest activity at a specific temperature and pH known as **optimum temperature** and **optimum pH**.
- Activity declines both below and above the optimum value.
- During low temperature, the enzyme is preserved temporarily in an inactive state, whereas at high temperature its activity gets destroyed (because proteins are denatured at high temperature).
- Change in pH of the medium also alters the physical structure of the enzyme molecule (or denaturation) and decreases enzyme activity.
- The peaks in the graphs (9.11) show maximum (optimum) enzymatic activity.

### 2. Concentration of Substrate

- With the increase in the concentration of substrate, the velocity of the enzymatic reaction rises at first.
- Thus, the reaction finally reaches a maximum velocity, i.e. $V_{max}$ which is not exceeded by any further rise in concentration of the substrate.
- This is because at this stage, the enzyme molecules (fewer than substrate molecules) become fully saturated and no more free enzyme molecules are left free to bind to additional substrate molecules.

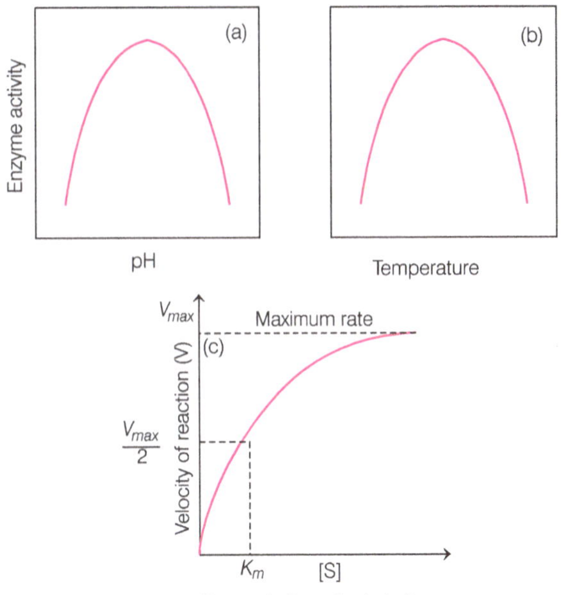


Fig. 9.11 Effect of change in (a) pH (b) Temperature (c) Concentration of substrate on enzyme activity

### 3. Enzyme Inhibitor

- The enzyme activity is also sensitive to the presence of specific chemicals that shuts off the enzyme activity the moment they binds to the enzyme.
- This process is known as **inhibition** and the chemical responsible is known as **inhibitor**.

### Competitive Inhibitor

- When the inhibitor closely resembles the molecular structure of the substrate and inhibits the activity of the enzyme, it is known as **competitive inhibitor.**
- The inhibitor competes with the substrate for binding to the enzyme (active site).
- Consequently, the substrate is unable to bind, while the inhibitor binds to it.
- Thus, the overall activity of the enzyme declines, e.g. inhibition of **succinic dehydrogenase** by malonate which closely resembles the substrate succinate in structure.
- These type of competitive inhibitors are used in controlling bacterial pathogens.

## Co-factors

- Enzyme are composed of one or several polypeptide chains.
- However, there are a number of cases in which non-protein constituents called **co-factors** bound to the enzyme in order to make it catalytically active.
- The protein portion of the enzyme is called the **apoenzyme.**
- Catalytic activity is lost when the co-factor is removed from the enzyme which testifies that they play a crucial role in the catalytic activity of the enzyme.
- The co-factors are following three types

**Co-factors**

**Prosthetic Groups**
- Organic compounds
- They are tightly bound to the apoenzyme.
- e.g. in **peroxidase** and **catalase**, which catalyse the breakdown of hydrogen peroxide to water and oxygen, **haem** is the prosthetic group and it is a part of the active site of the enzyme.

**Co-enzyme**
- Organic compounds
- Association with apoenzyme is only transient.
- Essential chemical component of many coenzymes are vitamins.
- e.g. Nicotinamide Adenine Dinucleotide (NAD) and NADP (contain vitamin niacin).

**Metal Ions**
- They forms coordination bonds with side chains at the active site and at the same time form one or more coordination bonds with substrate.
- e.g. zinc is a co-factor for the proteolytic enzyme carboxypeptidase.

## Quick Test 5

1. Name the chemical that is converted into a product in a reaction.
2. Name the process by which high temperature destroys the enzymatic activity by altering protein structure.
3. Name the inhibitor that resembles the substrate succinate and inhibits succinic dehydrogenase.
4. **State True or False.**
   (a) Co–factors are non-protein chemical compounds that are required for an enzyme's biological activity.
   (b) Some enzymes can function without any co-factor, relying solely on their protein structure.
5. Name the enzyme that catalyses the breakdown of hydrogen peroxide.

# Mind Map

## Nucleotides

- Composed of pentose sugar, nitrogen base and phosphate group.
- Nitrogen base.

**Purines**
- Adenine (A)
- Guanine (G)

**Pyrimidine**
- Cytosine (C)
- Thymine (T)
- Uracil (U)

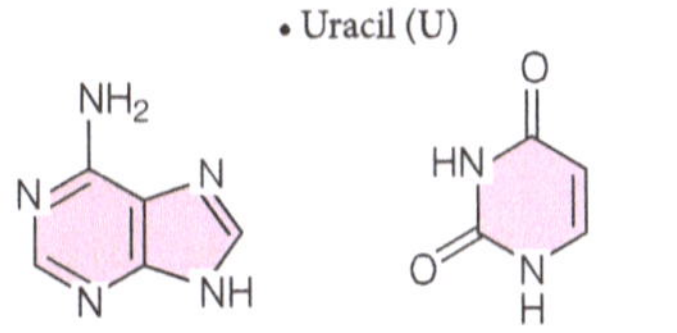


Adenine (Purine) Uracil (Pyrimidine)

## Amino Acids

These are organic compounds containing an amino group and an acidic group.

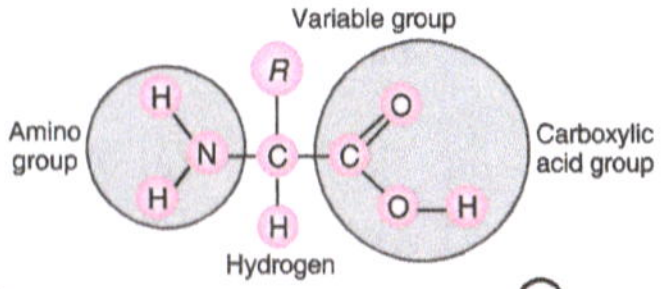


## Carbohydrates

Organic compounds, mainly made up of C, H and O.

- Monosaccharides
- Oligosaccharides

## Lipids

These are water insoluble esters of fatty acids and alcohol, containing C, H, O.

**Types of Lipids**

- **Simple lipids**
- **Compound lipids**
- **Derived lipids**
  - Fatty acid
  - Glycerol
  - Estars of fatty acid and glycerol

## Biomicromolecules

- Small, low molecular weight (18-800 Da) biomolecules like monosaccharides, amino acids, nucleotides and lipids.

# Biomolecules

## Biomacromolecules

Large, complex, high molecular weight (10,000 Da or more) molecules such as protein, nucleic acid, polysaccharide and nucleic acid.

## Nucleic Acids

- Heteropolymers of nucleotides with a monosaccharide, phosphate group and nitrogenous base can be DNA (with 2-deoxyribose sugar) or RNA (with ribose sugar).
- Pairing of nitrogenous bases in nucleic acids
  A = T (DNA)/ U (RNA); G≡C

## Protein

Heteropolymers of amino acids and are polypeptides linked by peptide bond.

**Primary structure of protein**
- linear sequence of amino acids

→ **Secondary structure of protein**
- folding of polypeptide chains, e.g. keratin.

→ **Tertiary structure of protein**
- 3-D ball like structure, e.g. myoglobin.

→ **Quartenary structure of protein**
- e.g. haemoglobin ($2\alpha$ and $2\beta$ subunits)

## Polysaccharides

Long chain polymers of monosaccharides (sugars) bound with glycosidic bonds.

(i) **Starch** (polymer of glucose; forms helical secondary structure, can hold $I_2$ to give blue colour, storage polysaccharide in plants)
(ii) **Cellulose** (homopolymer of glucose; no complex helices).
(iii) **Glycogen** (branched homopolymer; storage polysaccharide in animals).
(iv) **Inulin** (polymer of fructose).
(v) **Chitin** (homopolymer of N-acetyl glucosamine; exoskeleton of arthropods).

## Enzymes

- Biocatalyst influencing speed of biochemical reactions without taking part in it.
- Almost all enzymes are proteins (e.g. ribozyme is a RNA molecule).

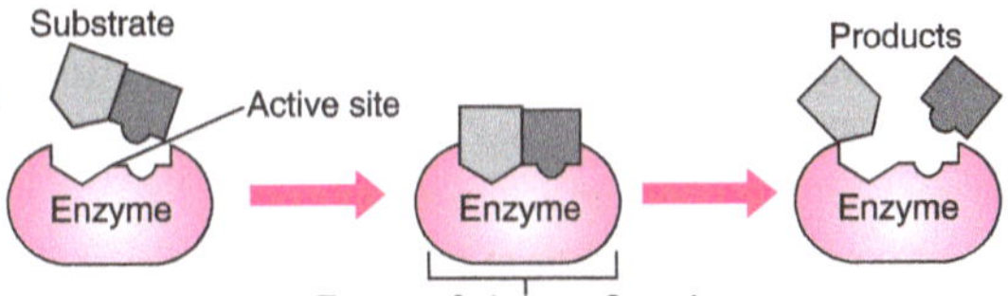


Enzyme-Substrate Complex
**Lock and key model of enzyme**

**Classes of Enzymes**
- Oxidoreductases/ Dehydrogenases
- Transferases
- Lyases
- Hydrolases
- Isomerases
- Ligases

## Types of Enzyme Inhibition

(a) **Competitive Inhibition** Inhibitor binds at active site; ↓ the reaction rate.
(b) **Non-competitive Inhibition** Inhibitor binds at sites other than active sites.
(c) **Allosteric Modulation (feedback inhibition)** Inhibitor binds to enzyme at specific site other than active site, but change the structure of active site to affect substrate binding.

## Factors Affection Enzyme Action

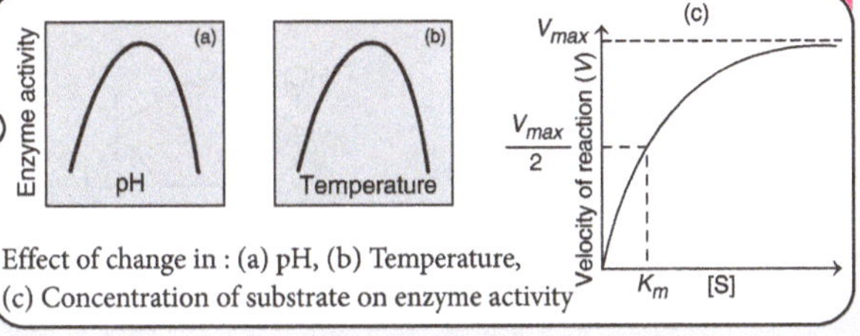


Effect of change in : (a) pH, (b) Temperature, (c) Concentration of substrate on enzyme activity

# EXAM PATTERN QUESTIONS

## Objective Type Questions

### Multiple Choice Questions

**1. It is said that elemental composition of living organisms and that of inanimate objects (like earth's crust) are similar in the sense that all the major elements are present in both.**
**Then what would be the difference between these two groups? Choose a correct answer from among the following.** **Competency Based Que., NCERT Exemplar**

(a) Living organisms have more gold in them than inanimate objects
(b) Living organisms have more water in their body than inanimate objects
(c) Living organisms have more carbon, oxygen and hydrogen per unit mass than inanimate objects
(d) Living organisms have more calcium in them than inanimate objects

**Ans.** (*c*)

**2. After doing the chemical analysis of organic compounds found in living organisms, two fractions were observed namely**

(a) acid-soluble pool and acid insoluble pool
(b) carbon pool and hydrogen pool
(c) inorganic pool and organic pool
(d) aqueous pool and non-aqueous pool

**Ans.** (*a*)

**3. Identify the term 'ash' in terms of living tissue sample analysis from the statements given below.**

(a) Organic compounds oxidised to gaseous form ($CO_2$ and water vapour) after burning of the tissue
(b) The material left after burning the tissue, which contains inorganic elements such as calcium, magnesium, etc.
(c) Compounds removed in the form of gases
(d) Compounds which may be soluble in intracellular fluid

**Ans.** (*b*)

**3. Identify the given structures and name the compound.**

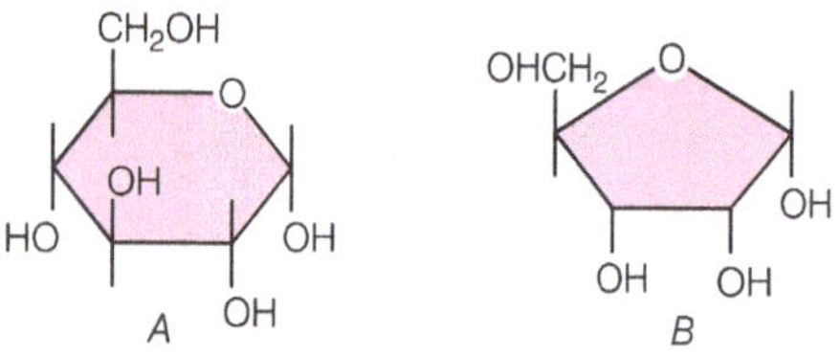


(a) *A*-Ribose, *B*-Glucose (b) *A*-Deoxyribose, *B*-Ribose
(c) *A*-Glucose, *B*-Ribose (d) *A*-Ribose, *B*-Deoxyribose

**Ans.** (*c*)

**5. Amino acids have both an amino group and a carboxyl group in their structure. Which amongst the following is an amino acid?** **NCERT Exemplar**

(a) Formic acid (b) Glycerol (c) Glycolic acid (d) Glycine

**Ans.** (*d*) Glycine is the **simplest amino acid** with an amino group and a carboxyl group. Whereas formic acid is the simplest carboxylic acid, glycerol is a fatty acid and glycolic acid is carboxylic acid substituted with hydroxyl group.

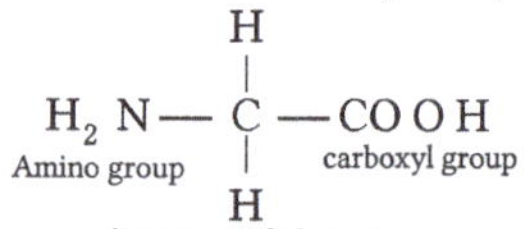


(Structure of glycine)

**6. An amino acid under certain conditions have both positive and negative charges simultaneously in the same molecule. Such a form of amino acid is called**

(a) acidic form (b) basic form **NCERT Exemplar**
(c) aromatic form (d) zwitter ionic form

**Ans.** (*d*) A zwitter ion is a neutral molecule having both the cationic and anionic charges on the same molecule. Amino acids are the best known examples of zwitter ion.

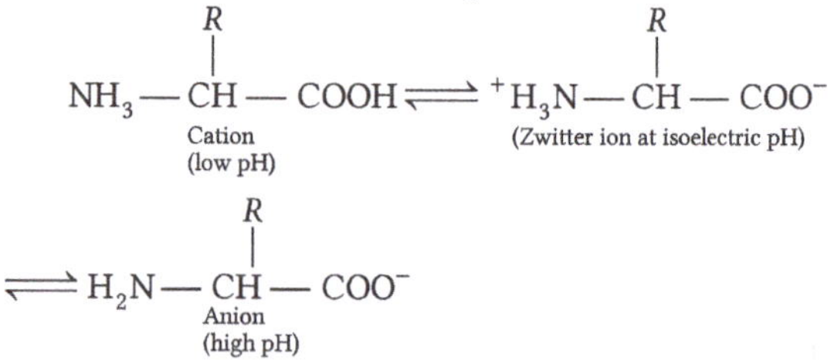


**7. Identify the zwitter ionic form in the given reversible reaction.** **Competency Based Que.**

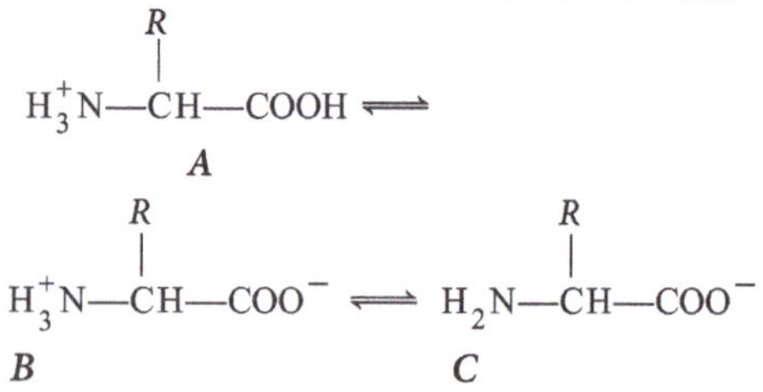


**Choose the correct option.**

(a) *A* (b) *C* (c) *B* (d) None of these

**Ans.** (*c*)

**8. The variety of amino acids are formed on the basis of**

(a) position of hydroxyl group
(b) position of carboxyl group
(c) position of hydrogen
(d) types of *R* group

**Ans.** (*d*) The variety of amino acids are determined by the different *R* groups (side chains) attached to the central carbon, which vary in size, charge and polarity, influencing their chemical properties and functions in proteins.

**9. A peptide bond is formed between**

(a) an aldehyde group and an amino group
(b) an aldehyde group and a carboxyl group
(c) an aldehyde group and an ester group
(d) a carboxyl group and an amino group

**Ans.** (*d*) A peptide bond is formed between the carboxyl group of one amino acid and the amino group of another, resulting in the release of a water molecule during a dehydration reaction. This bond links amino acids together to form polypeptides and proteins.

**10. Which of the following organic compounds is the main constituent of lecithin?**

(a) Arachidonic acid (b) Phospholipid
(c) Cholesterol (d) Phosphoprotein

**Ans.** (*b*)

**11. Choose the correct option for the molecule given below.** **Competency Based Que.**

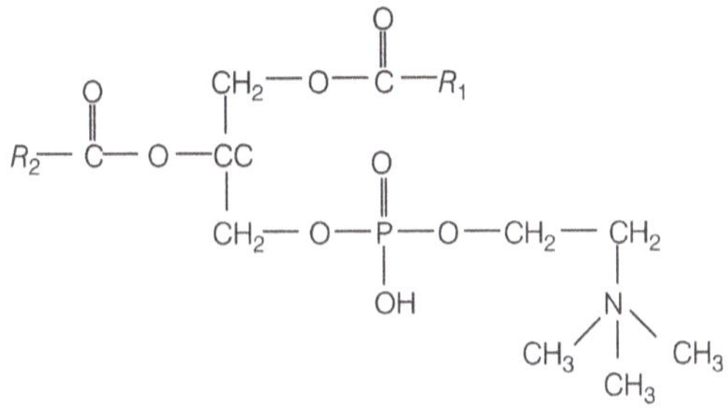

(a) Cholesterol – A component of animal cell membrane
(b) Lecithin – A component of cell membrane
(c) Triglyceride – An energy source
(d) Adenosine – A component of nucleic acids

**Ans.** (*b*)

**12. Identify three structural formula *A*, *B* and *C* given below and choose the correct option.** **Competency Based Que.**

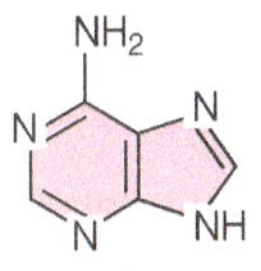

*A*

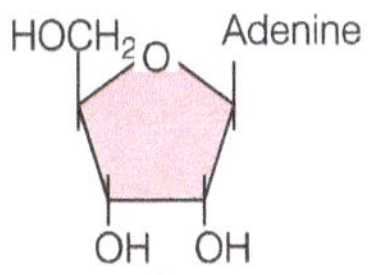

*B*

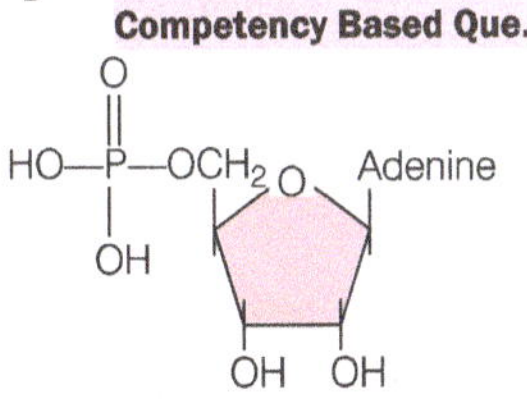

*C*

| | *A* | *B* | *C* |
|---|---|---|---|
| (a) | Adenine (N-base) | Adenosine (Nucleotide) | Adenylic acid (Nucleoside) |
| (b) | Adenine (N-base) | Adenosine (Nucleoside) | Adenylic acid (Nucleotide) |
| (c) | Adenosine (Nucleoside) | Adenylic acid (Nucleotide) | Deoxyadenylic acid |
| (d) | Adenosine (Nucleoside) | Adenine (N-base) | Adenylic acid (Nucleotide) |

**Ans.** (*b*)

**13. Name the heterocyclic compounds, which are known as nitrogenous bases.** **Competency Based Que.**

**Choose the most appropriate option.**

(a) Adenine, guanine, uracil, cytosine and thymine
(b) Adenine, guanine, uracil and thymine
(c) Adenine, guanine, cytosine, uracil
(d) None of the above

**Ans.** (*a*)

**14. Secondary metabolites can be observed in**

(a) plant cells (b) fungal cells
(c) microbial cells (d) All of these

**Ans.** (*d*)

**15. Identify the secondary metabolites from the following option.**

(a) Amino acid (b) Codeine (c) Collagen (d) Trypsin

**Ans.** (*b*)

**16. Given below are the category of substances or compounds and their examples.**
**Choose the correct option out of these.**

| | Compounds | | Examples |
|---|---|---|---|
| (a) | Pigments | — | Carotenoids, anthocyanins |
| (b) | Alkaloids | — | Monoterpenes |
| (c) | Toxins | — | Morphine |
| (d) | Polymeric substances | — | Ricin |

**Ans.** (*a*)

**17. Given below are the secondary metabolites and the category to which they belong. Choose the correct match.**

| | Category | | Secondary Metabolite |
|---|---|---|---|
| A. | Alkaloids | 1. | Lemon grass oil |
| B. | Essential oils | 2. | Morphine |
| C. | Toxins | 3. | Concanavalin-A |
| D. | Lectins | 4. | Abrin |

**Codes**

| | A | B | C | D | | A | B | C | D |
|---|---|---|---|---|---|---|---|---|---|
| (a) | 2 | 1 | 3 | 4 | (b) | 1 | 2 | 3 | 4 |
| (c) | 2 | 1 | 4 | 3 | (d) | 4 | 2 | 3 | 1 |

**Ans.** (*c*)

**18.** **The term cellular pool means** DIKSHA

(a) some total of different types of biomolecules and other compounds that are present in a cell
(b) different chemical compounds and metabolites
(c) inorganic molecules and elements present in the cell
(d) minerals and organic materials present in the cell.

**Ans.** (*a*)

**19.** **The area rich in A-T base pairs can undergo easy denaturation whereas area rich in G-C base pairs is**

(a) A-T base pairs has only two hydrogen bonds and G-C base pair has three hydrogen bonds DIKSHA
(b) A-T base pair has weak hydrogen bonds whereas G-C base pair has strong hydrogen bond
(c) it is difficult to break bond between G-C base pairs as compared to break bonds between A-T base pairs.
(d) A-T base pairs has four hydrogen bods and G-C base pair has three hydrogen bonds

**Ans.** (*a*)

**20.** **Which structure of the protein molecule will be most affected, when a hydrophilic amino acid is replaced by neutral one?** Competency Based Que.

(a) Only primary (b) Only secondary
(c) Tertiary and secondary (d) Primary and secondary

**Ans.** (*c*) Replacing a hydrophilic amino acid with a neutral amino acid can disrupt both secondary and tertiary structures by affecting hydrogen bonding and hydrophobic interactions, potentially altering the protein's folding and function.

**21.** **Proteins perform many physiological functions. For example, some functions as enzymes. Which of the following represents an additional function that some proteins discharge?** NCERT Exemplar

(a) Antibiotics
(b) Pigment conferring colour to skin
(c) Pigments making colours of flowers
(d) Hormones

**Ans.** (*d*)

**22.** **A homopolymer has only one type of building block called monomer repeated '*n*' number of times. A heteropolymer has more than one type of monomer. Proteins are heteropolymers usually made of** Competency Based Que., NCERT Exemplar

(a) 20 types of monomers (b) 40 types of monomers
(c) 30 types of monomers (d) only one type of monomer

**Ans.** (*a*) Proteins are heteropolymers made of about **20 different kinds of monomers, i.e., amino acids.** Each of these amino acids is made up of carbon, amino group, carboxyl group, hydrogen and a *R*—functional group. This variable *R*—group is what that makes each monomer different from one another.

**23.** **In a polysaccharide, the individual monosaccharides are linked by a**

(a) glycosidic bond
(b) peptide bond
(c) ester bond
(d) phosphodiester bond

**Ans.** (*a*) In a polysaccharide, individual monosaccharides are linked together by glycosidic bonds, which form through a dehydration reaction between the hydroxyl groups of the monosaccharides.

**24.** **The number of 'ends' in a glycogen molecule would be** NCERT Exemplar

(a) equal to the number of branches plus one
(b) equal to the number of branch points
(c) one
(d) two, one on the left side and another on the right side

**Ans.** (*a*)

**25.** **Which of the following reactions is not enzyme mediated in biological system?** NCERT Exemplar

(a) Dissolving $CO_2$ in water
(b) Unwinding the two strands of DNA
(c) Hydrolysis of sucrose
(d) Formation of peptide bond

**Ans.** (*a*)

**26.** **Which of the following option correctly express the rate of chemical reaction?** Competency Based Que.

(a) Rate $\frac{\delta P}{\delta t}$ (b) Rate $\frac{\delta S}{\delta P}$

(c) Rate $\frac{\delta S}{\delta t}$ (d) Rate $\frac{\delta S + \delta P}{\delta t}$

**Ans.** (*a*)

**27.** **Identify the correct graph displaying the effect of pH on the velocity of a typical enzymatic reaction (*V*).** Competency Based Que.

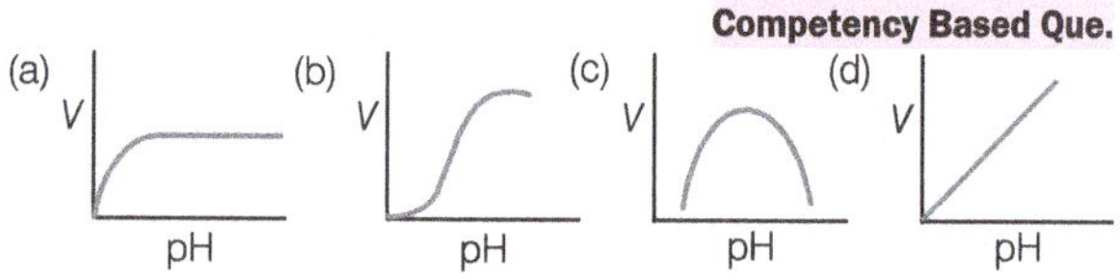


**Ans.** (*c*)

**28.** **Match the following columns.**

| Column I | | Column II | |
|---|---|---|---|
| A. | Dehydrogenases | 1. | Interconversion of optical, geometrical or positional isomers |
| B. | Ligases | 2. | Oxidoreduction between two substances |
| C. | Isomerases | 3. | Linking together of two bonds |
| D. | Hydrolases | 4. | Hydrolysis of bonds |

Codes

| | A | B | C | D | | A | B | C | D |
|---|---|---|---|---|---|---|---|---|---|
| (a) | 2 | 3 | 1 | 4 | (b) | 3 | 2 | 4 | 1 |
| (c) | 4 | 1 | 2 | 3 | (d) | 1 | 4 | 3 | 2 |

**Ans.** (*a*)

**29. Which enzymes catalyse the breakdown of hydrogen peroxide to water and oxygen?**
(a) A carbonic anhydrase and catalase
(b) Hydrolyase and oxidase
(c) Peroxidase and catalase
(d) Hydrolase and oxidase

**Ans.** (*c*)

**30. The co-factors that associate with the apoenzyme only during course of catalysis are called**
(a) co-factors
(b) co-enzymes
(c) metal ion
(d) prosthetic group

**Ans.** (*b*)

## Assertion-Reason Questions

**Direction** (Q. Nos. 1-10) *In each of the following questions, a statement of Assertion (A) is given followed by corresponding statement of Reason (R). Of the statements, mark the correct answer*

(a) Both A and R are true and R is the correct explanation of A.
(b) Both A and R are true, but R is not the correct explanation of A.
(c) A is true, but R is false.
(d) A is false, but R is true.

**1. Assertion** (A) In the solutions of different pH, structure of amino acids changes.

**Reason** (R) It is because of the ionisable nature of $—NH_2$ and —COOH groups.

**Ans.** (*a*)

**2. Assertion** (A) Nine amino acids are referred to as essential amino acids for humans.
**Reason** (R) These are synthesised in the human body.

**Ans.** (*c*) A is true, but R is false. R can be corrected as

The essential amino acids cannot be synthesised by the human body and must be obtained from dietary sources.

**3. Given below is the structure of an animal steroid. Which is insoluble in water and chemically unreactive. Study the structure and comment upon the appropriateness of Assertion and the Reason.**

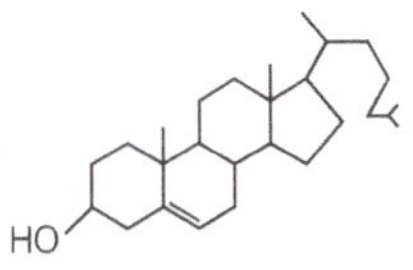


**Competency Based Que.**

**Assertion** (A) It is an important component of the membranes of cells, providing stability.
**Reason** (R) Phospholipid consists of a hydrophilic head containing a phosphate group and two hydrophobic fatty acid tails.

**Ans.** (*b*)

**4. Assertion** (A) Secondary metabolites are produced in small quantities and their extraction from the plant is difficult and expensive.

**Reason** (R) Secondary metabolites are essential for the growth and development of the plant.

**Ans.** (*c*) A is true, but R is false. R can be corrected as

Secondary metabolites are not essential for the growth and development of the plant; instead, they serve roles in defence, signalling, and interaction with the environment.

**5. Assertion** (A) Starch is a polymer of glucose.

**Reason** (R) Starch is made of several glucose units.

**Ans.** (*a*)

**6. Assertion** (A) Enzymes are not divided into different classes.
**Reason** (R) All enzymes catalyse the different reactions.

**Ans.** (*d*)

**7. Assertion** (A) Enzymes lower down the activation energy of the reactant molecule to make its transition into product easier.

**Reason** (R) Enzyme are highly substrate specific catalysts.

**Ans.** (*b*)

**8. Assertion** (A) Co-enzyme is a non-protein group without which certain enzymes are inactive or incomplete.

**Reason** (R) Co-enzymes not only provide a point of attachment to the chemical group being transformed, but also influence the properties of the group.

**Ans.** (*a*)

**9. Assertion** (A) An example of non-competitive inhibitor is cyanide.
**Reason** (R) Cyanide kills animals by inhibiting cytochrome oxidase.

**Ans.** (*b*) Both A and R are true, but R is not the correct explanation of A. A can be explained as

Cyanide is a non-competitive inhibitor that binds to an enzyme regardless the presence substrate and reducues the enzyme's activity by altering its shape.

**10. Assertion** (A) Zinc is an apoenzyme for carboxypeptidase.
**Reason** (R) A complete catalytically active enzyme together with its bound prosthetic group is called holo-enzyme.

**Ans.** (*d*)

# Subjective Questions

## Very Short Answer Type Questions

**1. Mention four essential major elements of life.**

**Ans.** Oxygen, carbon, hydrogen and nitrogen are the four basic essential elements of life.

**2. A chemical is used for grinding the animal tissue for chemical analysis of organic compounds. Can you name it?** **Competency Based Que.**

**Ans.** Trichloroacetic acid is used for grinding the animal tissue for chemical analysis of organic compounds.

**3. Give the cyclic structural formula of any two monosaccharides.**

**Ans.** Refer to fig. no. 9.1 on page no 186.

**4. In the figure below, the structure of a carbohydrate is given. Study the same and identify to which category does this belong?** **Competency Based Que.**

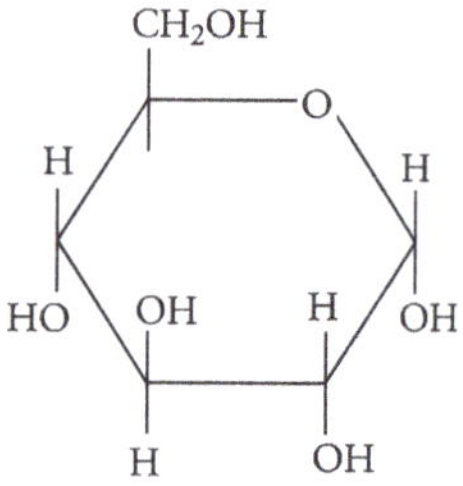


**Ans.** The given structure is of glucose. It is a monosaccharide.

**5. Draw the structure of amino acid alanine.** **NCERT**

**Ans.** Refer to fig. on page no 186. (1)

**6. Attempt titrating an amino acid against a weak base and discover the number of dissociating (ionisable) functional groups in the amino acid.**

**Ans.** When an amino acid is titrated against a weak base, it dissociates and gives two functional groups

(i) —COOH group (carboxylic group) (½)

(ii) Amino group (—$NH_2$). (½)

**7. Give one example each of**

**(i) an acidic amino acid**

**(ii) a basic amino acid**

**Ans.** (i) An acidic amino acid–Aspartic acid. (½)

(ii) A basic amino acid–Arginine. (½)

**8. Name any two amino acids containing aromatic ring.**

**Ans.** Tyrosine and tryptophan are the two aromatic amino acids. (½ + ½)

**9. Different forms of the amino acids also have acidic amino acids. Write about it. Also, give structure of any one acidic amino acid.** **Competency Based Que.**

**Ans.** Acidic amino acids are those which contain one amino group and two carboxylic groups, e.g.

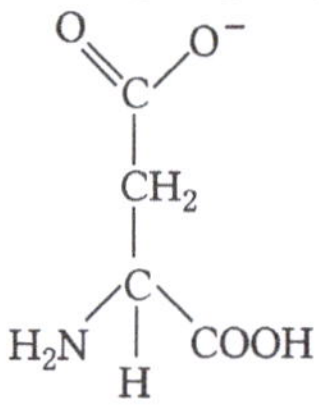


Aspartic acid (½ + ½)

**10. Write the name of any one amino acid, nucleotide and fatty acid.**

**Ans.** Alanine is an amino acid, adenylic acid is a nucleotide and linolenic acid is a fatty acid.

**11. What is trihydroxy propane commonly called? Write its structural formula.**

**Ans.** Trihydroxy propane is commonly known as glycerol. Its general formula is $CH_2OH$ $CH(OH)$ $CH_2OH$. (½ + ½)

**12. Explain the composition of triglyceride.** **NCERT**

**Ans.** Triglycerides consist of one glycerol molecule and three fatty acids, which can be saturated or unsaturated, determining their physical properties.

**13. Nucleotides are phosphorylated nucleosides. Justify.** **Competency Based Que.**

**Ans.** A nucleoside consists of a nitrogen base and a pentose sugar, but when a phosphate group is added to the nucleoside, it is called nucleotide, hence a nucleotide is a phosphorylated nucleoside.

**14. Is rubber a primary metabolite or a secondary metabolite?**

**Ans.** Natural rubber (*cis*-1, 4-polyisoprene) is a secondary metabolite.

**15. Secondary metabolites are considered to be the end products of primary metabolites. Justify.**

**Ans.** Secondary metabolites are considered to be the end products of primary metabolites because they are derived by the pathways in which the primary metabolite are involved e.g. antibiotics, pheromones, etc.

**16. Name the protein that is most abundant in the**

**(i) animal world** **(ii) plant world**

**Ans.** (i) Collagen. (ii) Ribulose bisphosphate carboxylase oxygenase. (½ + ½)

**17. Name one element invariably found in proteins, but not in all carbohydrates and lipids.**

**Ans.** Nitrogen is found invaribly in proteins, but not in all carbohydrates and lipids.

**18. What is the role of haemoglobin?**

**Ans.** Haemoglobin is a heme containing globulin proteins, which carries oxygen in the blood.

**19. What is the name given to a polysaccharide composed of two different monomers? Also give example for this.**

**Ans.** The name given is heteropolysaccharide to the type of polysaccharide, which is composed of different types of monomers, e.g. pectin. (½ × 2)

**20. Why does starch turn blue-black with iodine solution?**

**Ans.** Starch turns blue-black with iodine solution because iodine molecules fit into the helical structure of starch, forming a complex that results in a colour change.

**21. Name one homopolysaccharide and one heteropolysaccharide.**

**Ans.** Homopolysaccharide – Starch
Heteropolysaccharide – Chitin (¼ + ½)

**22. Starch is regarded as a homopolysaccharide. Explain.**

**Ans.** Starch consists of two components, i.e. unbranched spirally coiled amylose molecules and branched amylopectin molecules. Both are glucose polymers, hence it is called as homopolysaccharide.

**23. Why is cellulose considered as a homopolymer?**

**Ans.** Cellulose is considered a homopolymer because it is composed entirely of repeating units of the same monosaccharide, specifically glucose.

**24. The macromolecules that form the hereditary determinants of the living organism. Name it.**

**Ans.** Nucleic acid

**25. The backbone of DNA molecule is formed of two different molecules. Name them.**

**Ans.** Backbone of DNA molecule is formed of sugar and phosphates.

**26. Mention the chemical nature of enzymes.**

**Ans.** Enzymes are proteinaceous in nature.

**27. What is the term given to ribonucleic acid with catalytic power?**

**Ans.** Ribozymes are ribonucleic acid enzyme that catalyse a chemical reaction.

**28. What does the part of the enzyme called where catalytic activity is carried out?**

**Ans.** Active or catalytic site is that part of an enzyme where catalytic activity is carried out.

**29. According to the classification of enzymes ligases are one of the important class of enzymes. Explain it by giving example.**

**Ans.** Ligases are the class of enzymes that function in the formation of bond with ATP cleavage, e.g. DNA ligases play an essential role is maintaining genomic integrity by joining breaks in the phosphodiester backbone of DNA.

**30. Bring out the difference between the enzymes ligases and lyases.**

**Ans.** Difference between ligases and lyases is as follows

| Ligases | Lyases |
|---|---|
| These are the enzymes which catalyse the covalent bonding between two substrates to form a large molecule. | These are the enzymes which catalyse the cleavage of specific covalent bonds in a large molecule to form smaller molecules without the addition of water. |

**31. Give the basic representation of the rate of a chemical reaction. Also define the same.**

**Ans.** Rate of a chemical reaction refers to the amount of product formed per unit time. (½)

It is represented as Rate $= \frac{dP}{dt}$ (½)

**32. Reaction given below is catalysed by oxidoreductase between two substrates *A* and *A'*. Complete the reaction.**
***A* reduced + *A'* oxidised** **NCERT Exemplar**

**Ans.** $A$ reduced $+ A'$ oxidised $\rightarrow A$ oxidised $+ A'$ reduced

**33. The enzymes activity gets destroyed on increasing high temperature. What happens during that state that enzyme loses its activity?** **Competency Based Que.**

**Ans.** The enzyme becomes inactive on increasing temperature because the proteins denature at high temperature due to disruption in tertiary structure.

**34. Name two physical factors which can affect the enzyme activity.**

**Ans.** Temperature and pH are the two physical factors that affects activity of an enzyme.

**35. The efficiency of an enzyme mainly depends upon the number of active site present over an enzyme. Justify.** **Competency Based Que.**

**Ans.** The efficiency of an enzyme depends on the number of active sites because each active site facilitates the binding of a substrate, allowing the enzyme to catalyse more reactions simultaneously.

## Short Answer Type Questions

**1. Define monosaccharides. Give any two examples.**

**Ans.** Monosaccharides are the simplest groups of carbohydrates and are often referred to as simple sugars. (1)

Glucose and ribose are the examples of monosaccharides. (1)

**2. What are gums made of? Is fevicol different?** **NCERT**

**Ans.** Gums are sticky metabolic products of plant cell walls consisting of polysaccharides and pectins which exude from the wounds in the bark. They are generally water soluble. (1)

Fevicol is a synthetic resin-based sticky substance. Resins are insoluble in water. (1)

**3. Amino acids are substituted methane, Justify. Why are they called α-amino acids?** **Competency Based Que.**

**Ans.** Amino acids are substituted methane because they contain four substituent groups, hydrogen, carboxyl group, amino group and a variable group (*R*). As these substituents are present on the α-carbon and hence are called α-amino acids.

**4. Glycine and alanine are different with respect to one substituent on the α-carbon. What are the other common substituent groups?** **Competency Based Que.**

**Ans.** There are four substituent groups occupying the four valency positions in an amino acid. These are hydrogen, carboxyl group, amino group and a variable group designated as *R* group. The *R* group in amino acid glycine is hydrogen and it is methyl group in case of alanine. The other common substituent between these two are $NH_2$, COOH and H.

**5. Do amino acids exist as zwitter ion. Give its structure. Why is it formed?**

**Ans.** Yes, amino acids exist as zwitter ion. Refer to text on page no. 187. (1+1)

**6. Oil does not dissolve in water. Give scientific explanation.**

**Ans.** Oil does not dissolve in water, i.e. it is immiscible in water. Oils molecules are not polar, while water is a polar solvent. Non-polar substances do not dissolve in polar solvents and *vice versa*.

**7. Differentiate between nucleosides and nucleotides. Give one example for each.**

**Ans.** Refer to text on page no. 189.

**8. What are macromolecules? Give examples.** **NCERT**

**Ans.** Macromolecules are large, complex molecules essential for life, typically consisting of thousands of atoms. (1)

Examples include proteins, nucleic acids (like DNA and RNA), carbohydrates (such as starch), and lipids (like fats and oils). (1)

**9. Proteins have been called 'biological polymers'. Explain.**

**Ans.** All the cells are basically made up of proteins (polymer of amino acids). Enzymes which carry out biological reactions are also proteinaceous in nature.

Antibodies, haemoglobin and even adrenaline receptors all are proteins. Therefore, they are called as biological polymers.

**10. Peptide bonds are formed between two groups. Name them.**

**Ans.** Peptide bond is formed between the carboxyl group (-COOH) of one amino acid and amino group (-$NH_2$) of the next amino acid with elimination of water.

**11. How does the secondary structure of protein is formed? Give its types.**

**Ans.** Secondary structure of protein is formed when the linear thread of the primary protein is folded in a *zig-zag* shaped structure by the help of hydrogen bonds. The two types of secondary structure of proteins are α-Helix and β-pleated structure. (2)

**12. What is meant by tertiary structure of proteins?** **NCERT**

**Ans.** The tertiary structure of proteins refers to the overall three-dimensional structure formed by the folding and interactions of a protein's polypeptide chains. This structure is stabilised by various interactions, including hydrogen bonds, ionic bonds, hydrophobic interactions and disulphide bridges and is crucial for the protein's functionality.

**13. How do proteins act as carrier proteins?**

**Ans.** Proteins acts as a carrier in the following ways

(i) Some proteins act as carrier which bind and transport specific molecules across a membrane or in a body fluid. (½)

(ii) Haemoglobin of RBCs transports oxygen in the body. (½)

(iii) Myoglobin of muscles store and transport oxygen. (½)

(iv) Serum albumin carries fatty acids and lipids in the blood. (½)

**14. Find out and make a list of proteins used as therapeutic agents. Find other applications of proteins (e.g. cosmetics, etc.)** **NCERT**

**Ans.** Some proteins and their therapeutic functions are as follows

| Proteins | Functions |
|---|---|
| Insulin | It maintains blood glucose (½) |
| Antibody | Fights infectious agents (½) |

Some proteins and their use in cosmetics are as follows

(i) **Calcium Caseinate** It is used in hair conditioning agent. (½)

(ii) **Collagen** It maintains the younger-looking skin. (½)

**15. Both starch and cellulose are polymers of glucose, but starch gives blue-black colour with iodine whereas no such colour is obtained with cellulose.** **DIKSHA**

**Ans.** Starch forms helical secondary structure and holds iodine molecules in the helical portion which imparts blue-black colour.

Cellulose is made up of unbranched chains of glucose molecule which are arranged parallel to each other and can not hold iodine molecules. Hence no colour is imparted to cellulose by iodine. (2)

**16. Distinguish between purine and pyrimidine.**

**Ans.** Differences between purine and pyrimidine are given below

| Purine | Pyrimidine |
|---|---|
| These are large sized nitrogen containing biomolecules. | These are smaller sized nitrogen containing biomolecules. |
| It is nine membered and has a double ring. A purine contains four nitrogen atoms at 1′, 3′, 7′ and 9′. | It is six membered and has a single ring. A pyrimidine has nitrogen atoms at two places 1′ and 3′. |
| e.g. adenine and guanine. | e.g. cytosine, thymine and uracil. |

(1½)

**17. Differentiate between homopolysaccharide and heteropolysaccharide.**

**Ans.** Differences between homopolysaccharide and heteropolysaccharide are given below

| Homopolysaccharide | Heteropolysaccharide |
|---|---|
| They are the complex carbohydrates formed by the polymerisation of one type of monosaccharide units. e.g. starch, glycogen and cellulose. | They are the complex carbohydrates formed by the polymerisation of more than one type of monosaccharide units. e.g. chitin and agar. |

**18. Schematically represent primary and secondary structures of a protein.**

**Ans.** Refer to text on page no. 191.

**19. Proteins have primary structure. If you are given a method to know which amino acid is at either of the two termini (ends) of a protein, can you connect this information to purity or homogeneity of a protein?** **Competency Based Que.**

**Ans.** Yes, knowing the amino acids at the termini of a protein can provide insights into its purity or homogeneity. If a protein is pure and homogeneous, the termini should consistently display the same amino acids across multiple samples. Variations in the terminal amino acids might indicate the presence of different isoforms, impurities, or incomplete protein synthesis, suggesting that the sample is not homogeneous. Thus, terminal analysis can be a useful tool in assessing protein quality and consistency.

**20. Find out how much cellulose is made by all the plants in the biosphere and compare it with how much of paper is manufactured by man and hence, what is the consumption of plant material by man annually? What is a loss of vegetation?** **NCERT**

**Ans.** Most paper is formed from wood pulp. The main component of wood pulp is cellulose. Almost 100 billion tonnes of cellulose is produced by all the plants in the biosphere. About 400 million tonnes of paper is produced by man in a year. This means about 0.4% of cellulose produced by plant of is used to manufacture paper. The vincrease in consumption of plant materials leads to loss of vegetation and we need to use the sources wisely.

**21. All enzymes are globular proteins but all proteins are not enzymes. Justify.** **Competency Based Que.**

**Ans.** Enzymes are proteins that helps in lowering the activation energy of the reaction. Only few proteins have the capability to bind the substrate with the help of their active sites in such a manner that allows the reaction to take place. Hence, all enzymes are proteins, but all proteins are not enzymes.

**22. Describe the important properties of enzymes.** **NCERT**

**Ans.** Refer to text on page no. 195.

**23. Which two changes does a chemical compound undergo? Explain each with example.**

**Ans.** Chemical compounds undergo following two types of changes

(i) **Physical changes** are those in which shape of a molecule or a substance change without breaking of bonds, e.g. melting of ice in water.

(ii) **Chemical changes** are those changes in which the bonds are broken and new bonds are formed, e.g.

(a) $Ba(OH)_2 + H_2SO_4 \rightarrow BaSO_4 + 2H_2O$ (inorganic chemical reaction).

(b) Hydrolysis of starch into glucose (organic chemical reaction).

**24. Observe the given figure related to enzyme action and answer the following questions.** **Competency Based Que.**

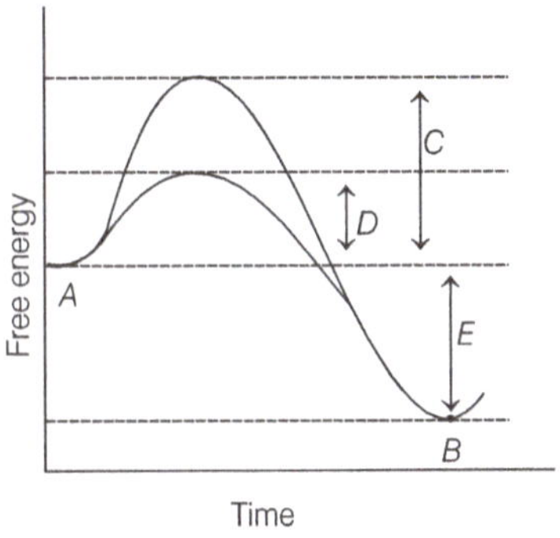


**(i) What is the figure showing?**

**(ii) Name the substances marked as *A* and *B*.**

**(iii) What does the arrows marked *C* to *D* indicate?**

**Ans.** (i) Figure is showing the activation energy requirement for non-catalysed and enzyme catalysed reactions. (1)

(ii) Substances marked on arrows *A* and *B* are substrate and end products respectively. (1)

(iii) Arrows marked shows

*C*–Energy of activaton without enzymes.

*D*–Energy of activation with enzymes. (1)

**25.** **Use the following images as a guide to answer the questions listed below.** **Competency Based Que.**

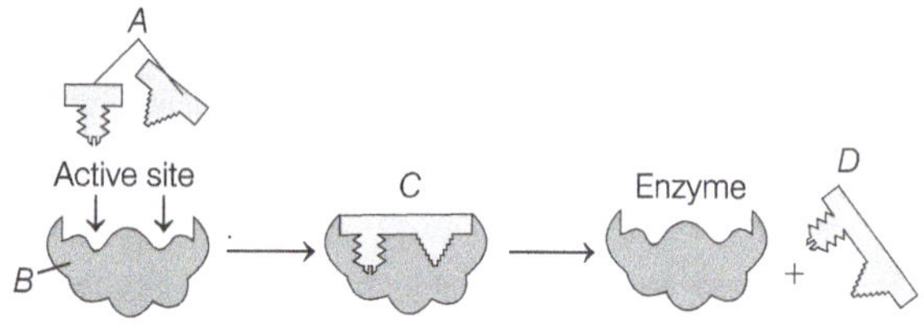


**(i) Label the parts marked as *A*-*D* in an enzyme catalysed reaction.**

**(ii) How formation of enzyme-substrate complex is a transient phenomenon.**

**Ans.** (i) Part *A*-Substrate ; *B* - Enzyme
*C* - Enzyme-substrate complex; *D* - Product (1)

(ii) During the conversion of substrate into a product formation of an enzyme-substrate complex takes place.
i.e. $E + S \rightarrow ES$
The formation of this complex is transient because it involves a temporary binding between the enzyme and substrate. Once the substrate binds to the enzyme's active site, the enzyme catalyses the reaction, converting the substrate into products. (2)

**26.** **Describe the influence of temperature on enzyme action.**

**Ans.** Enzymes generally function at a narrow range of temperature. The temperature at which the enzyme shows its maximum activity is called its optimum temperature. The enzyme activity decreases at temperature below and above the optimum temperature. At low temperatures, the enzyme is inactive, while at high temperature, the enzyme is denatured and so it loses its activity.

**27.** **Draw graphs for the following.**

**(i) Effect of change in pH** (1)

**(ii) Effect of change in temperature** (1)

**Ans.** Refer to text on page no. 197.

**28.** **The velocity of the enzymatic reaction increases with the increase of substrate concentration initially but after some time it gets constant. Explain.**

**Ans.** The increase in substrate concentration leads to the rise in velocity of the enzymatic reaction at first. The reaction ultimately reaches a maximum velocity ($V_{max}$) which is not exceeded by any further rise in concentration of the substrate molecules. This is because, there are no free enzyme molecules to bind with the additional substrate molecule.

**29.** **Discuss about competitive inhibition of enzymes. How is it different from non-competitive inhibition?**

**Ans.** When the enzyme inhibitor closely resembles the molecular structure of the substrate, they acquire active site and the enzyme action is inhibited. This is called competitive inhibition. When the site other than active site is blocked by the inhibitor, the inhibition is said to be non-competitive and no enzyme substrate complex is formed. (1+2)

**30.** **Succinic dehydrogenase is an enzyme that causes the substrate, succinate, to breakdown into fumarate. Malonate is a substance that resembles succinate and inhibits the activity of succinic dehydrogenase.** **Competency Based Que.**

**Study the above passage and answer the following questions.**

**(i) State the type of inhibition of succinic dehydrogenase by malonate.**

**(ii) Explain how this type of inhibition affects the activity of the enzyme.**

**Ans.** (i) The type of inhibition of succinic dehydrogenase by malonate is competitive inhibition. (1)

(ii) The inhibitor competes with the substrate for the active sites of enzyme molecules as it has structure similar to the substrate. It allows the inhibitor to combine with the active site, preventing any substrate molecule from occupying that site. This reduces the rate of the reaction since, the substrate can only use the enzyme molecules that are not occupied by the inhibitor, resulting in the same quantity of product being formed at a slower rate. (2)

**31.** **How are prosthetic groups different from co-factors?**

**Ans.** Differences between prosthetic groups and co-factors are as follows

| Prosthetic Groups | Co-factors |
|---|---|
| It is the non-protein part or the group which gets permanently attached to the enzyme. | It is the non-protein substance or group which gets attached to the enzyme, temporarily. |
| Prosthetic groups are organic factors, but some are metallic also like iron, porphyrin of the cytochromes. | These can be organic, inorganic or metallic factors. |

## Long Answer Type Questions

**1.** **Find out a qualitative test for proteins, fats and oils, amino acids and test any fruit juice, saliva, sweat and urine for them.** **NCERT**

**Ans.** (i) **Proteins** The biuret test is used to detect proteins; when biuret reagent is added to a sample, a colour change to violet indicates the presence of proteins. (1½)

(ii) **Fats and Oils** The grease spot test is used to check fats and oils. It include applying a sample to brown paper and allowing it to dry, a translucent spot remaining indicates the presence of fats or oils. (1½)

(iii) **Amino Acids** The ninhydrin test identifies amino acids, adding ninhydrin to a sample and heating it will result in a colour change (usually purple or blue) if amino acids are present. (1)

You can test fruit juice, saliva, sweat and urine for proteins, fats, oils and amino acids using these tests. (1)

**2. Find and write down structures of 10 interesting small molecular weight biomolecules. Find if there is any industry which manufactures the compounds by isolation. Find out who are the buyers.** NCERT

**Ans.** For the structure of **10 interesting small molecular weight biomolecules** refer to page no 186-188. (3)

Various industries manufacture these compounds by isolation, e.g. glucose is been manufactured by health and energy drink producing companies, likewise fatty acids by companies that produce cooking oils, etc. The buyers are drug and pharmaceutical companies. These products are consumed directly by common man as well. (2)

**3. What are the different levels of organisation in proteins? Explain diagrammatically.**

**Ans.** Refer to text on page no.191 and 192.

**4. What are the different types of proteins and write their functions?**

**Ans.** Refer to text on page no. 191-192.

**5. Explain briefly the types of polysaccharides.**

**Ans.** Refer to text on page no. 192 and 193.

**6. What are the functions of polysaccharides?**

**Ans.** The functions of polysaccharides are as follows

(i) Starch and glycogen are the major storage molecules in plants and animals, respectively. (1)

(ii) On hydrolysis, stored carbohydrates provide both energy and carbon skeleton. (1)

(iii) Chitin is the structural carbohydrate of fungal walls and exoskeleton of arthropods (insects). (1)

(iv) Cellulose is the structural substance of cell walls in most of the plants. (1)

(v) Cellulose is economically important in the production of furniture, shelter, fuel, paper, textiles, ropes, rayon, cellophane, plastics, etc (1)

**7. Differentiate between DNA and RNA.**

**Ans.** Refer to text on page no. 193.

**8. Explain different classes of enzymes. Explain any two with the type of reaction they catalyse.**

**Ans.** Refer to text on page no. 194.

**9. Formation of Enzyme-Substrate (ES) complex is the first step in catalysed reactions. Describe the other steps till the formation of product.**

**Ans.** Refer to text on page no. 196.

**10. What are factors which affect action of enzyme?**

**Ans.** Refer to text on page no. 197-198.

**11. Discuss the types of enzyme co-factors that are required for the efficient activity of enzymes.**

**Ans.** Refer to text on page no. 198.

## Source Based/Case Based/Passage Based Questions

**1. Study the diagram given below and answer the questions that follows.**

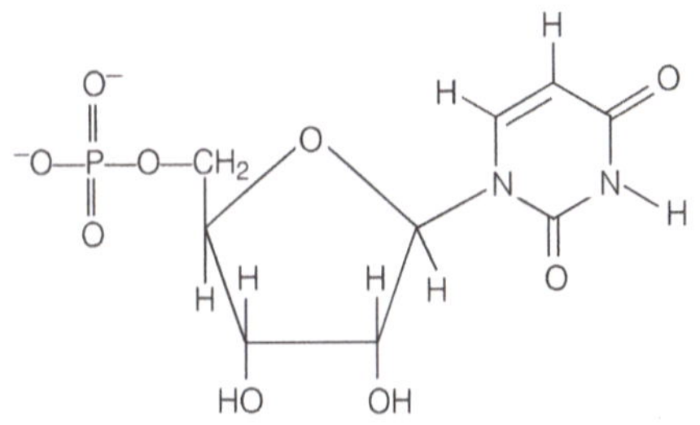

**(i) What does the image represent, and what is the overall function of this molecule in biological systems?**

**(ii) What nitrogenous base is present in the nucleotide shown in the image, and how does it compare to the nitrogenous bases found in DNA?**

**(iii) To which category does the given nitrogen base belong, and what are the characteristics of this category?**

**(iv) Explain two other components of a nucleotide.**

**Ans.** (i) The image represents a nucleotide, which serves as a building block for RNA and plays essential roles in cellular processes, including protein synthesis and energy transfer. (1)

(ii) The nitrogenous base present is uracil. Unlike DNA, which contains thymine, RNA contains uracil, which pairs with adenine during base pairing. (1)

(iii) Uracil belongs to the category of pyrimidines, which are characterised by a single six-membered ring structure and include other bases like cytosine and thymine. (1)

(iv) Refer to text on page. no. 188. (1)

**2. Observe the given graph showing a chemical reaction taking place in the presence and absence of an enzyme.** **Competency Based Que.**

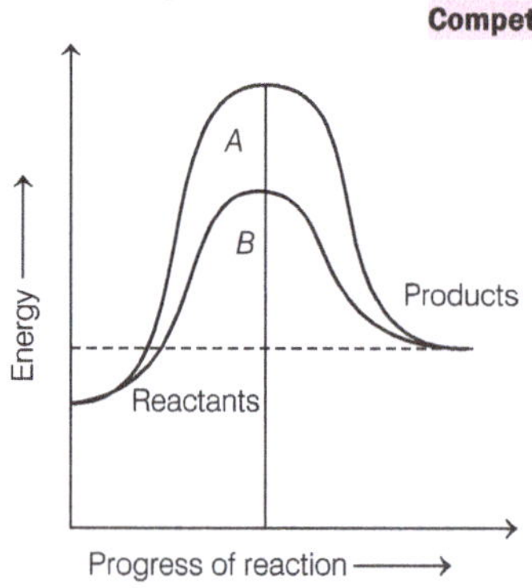


**(i) Based on the energy level difference between the substrate and products identify the type of reaction.**

**(ii) Which of the two curves depicts the reaction catalysed by enzyme? Give reason.**

**(iii) If a chemical closely resembling the substrate is added to the reaction, which of the curves in the graph will be affected and why ?**

**Ans.** (i) It is an endothermic reaction because the energy level of product is higher than the substrate. (1)

(ii) Curve *B* represents the enzyme catalysed reaction. Since, the transition state energy or energy requires to overcome the energy barrier is much lower in *B* in comparison to *A*. (2)

(iii) In curve *B*, chemical will act as a competitive inhibitor. It will bind to the active site of enzyme and affect conversion of substrate to product. (1)

**3. The following graph shows the relationship between the enzyme activity and temperature for two different enzymes use the graph and answer the questions that follows.** **Competency Based Que.**

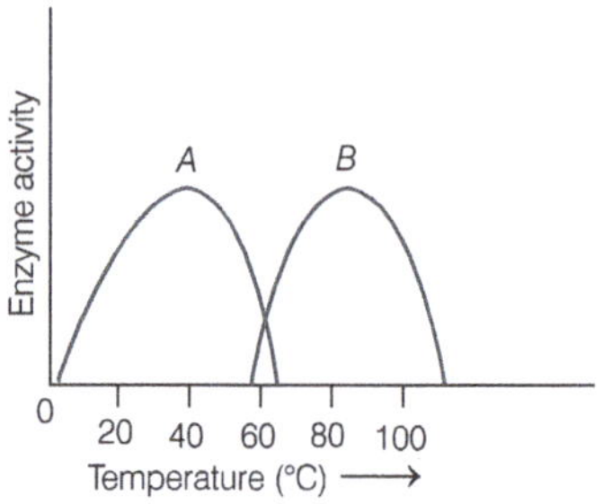


**(i) What is the optimum temperature for enzyme *B*?**

**(ii) At what temperature is the enzyme *A* denatured?**

**(iii) What happens to the enzyme at low temperature?**

**(iv) Does enzyme *B* show activity at temperature 60°C?**

**Ans.** (i) The optimum temperature for enzyme *B* in 80°C. (1)

(ii) The enzyme *A* will be denatured at about 60°C. (1)

(iii) At low temperature the enzyme is preserved temporarily in an active state. (1)

(iv) No, enzyme *B* will not show activity at temperature 60°C because, its optimum temperature range between 70°C to 80°C. (1)

# SELF ASSESSMENT TEST

## Multiple Choice Questions

1. Choose the pair which correctly depicts the aromatic amino acids.
   (a) Alanine, glutamic acid and glycine
   (b) Valine, glutamine and tyrosine
   (c) Glycine, methionine and serine
   (d) Tyrosine, tryptophan and phenylalanine

2. Identify the amino acids given below.

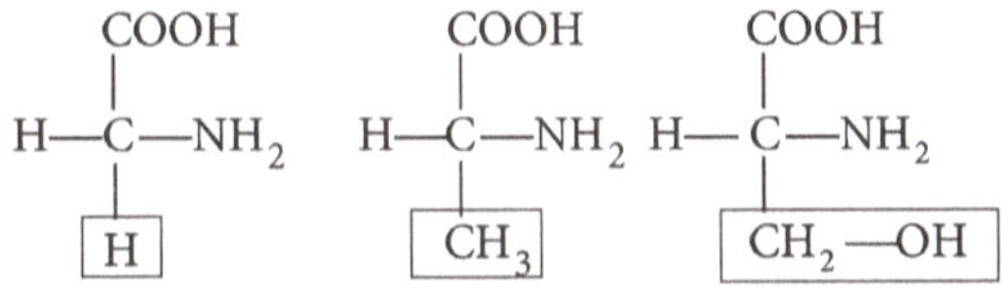

   (a) Glycine, alanine and serine respectively
   (b) Alanine, valine and glycine respectively
   (c) Serine, glycine and alanine respectively
   (d) Tyrosine, valine and glycine respectively

3. Which of the following nitrogenous bases are classified as purines?
   (a) Cytosine and thymine
   (b) Adenine and guanine
   (c) Uracil and thymine
   (d) Cytosine and adenine

4. How many of the following are secondary metabolites?
   Rubber, Adenine, Ricin, Galactose, Morphine, Diterpenes, Vinblastin, Cellulose
   (a) Eight (b) Seven (c) Six (d) Five

5. Choose the incorrect match pair.
   (a) Insulin – Hormone
   (b) Collagen – Intercellular ground substance
   (c) GLUT-4 – Enables glucose transport outside the cell
   (d) Receptor – Secondary reception

6. Identify *A*, *B*, and *C* in the graph given below.

| | *A* | *B* | *C* |
|---|---|---|---|
| (a) | $K_m$ | $V_{max}$ | $V_{max}/2$ |
| (b) | $V_{max}$ | $V_{max}/2$ | $K_m$ |
| (c) | $V_{max}/2$ | $K_m$ | $V_{max}$ |
| (d) | $K_m$ | $V_{max}/2$ | $V_{max}$ |

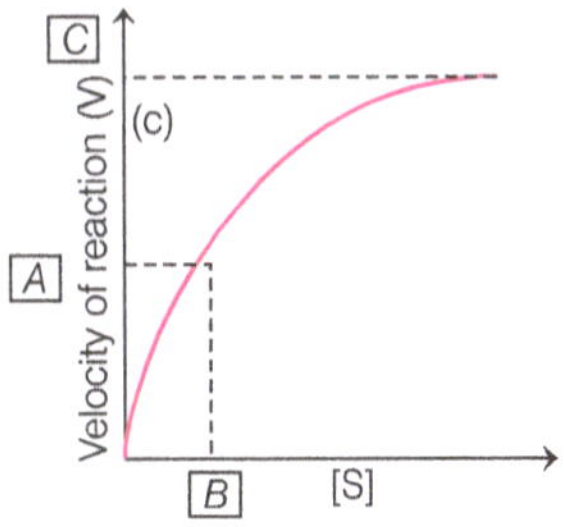


7. Which of the following statement correctly depicts the prosthetic group?
   (a) They tightly bound to apoenzyme
   (b) These are inorganic compounds
   (c) Vitamins are essential components of many prosthetic group.
   (d) They form coordination bond with side chains at the active site.

## Assertion-Reason Questions

**Direction** (Q. Nos. 8-11) *In each of the following questions, a statement of Assertion (A) is given followed by corresponding statement of Reason (R). Of the statements, mark the correct answer*

(a) Both A and R are true and R is the correct explanation of A.
(b) Both A and R are true, but R is not the correct explanation of A.
(c) A is true, but R is false.
(d) A is false, but R is true.

8. **Assertion** (A) Amino acids can exist in charged forms depending on the pH of their environment.
   **Reason** (R) The overall charge of an amino acid is determined by the ionisation of its amino and carboxyl groups.

9. **Assertion** (A) Proteins can exhibit diverse biological functions due to their unique three-dimensional structures.

**Reason** (R) The specific sequence of amino acids determines the protein's folding patterns, which ultimately dictate its shape and function.

10. **Assertion** (A) Enzymes are effective catalysts that significantly increase the rate of biochemical reactions.

**Reason** (R) Enzymes can bind to multiple types of substrates due to a flexible active site, allowing them to catalyse various reactions.

11. **Assertion** (A) Polysaccharides are composed of long chains of monosaccharide units linked by glycosidic bonds.

**Reason** (R) The structure of polysaccharides allows them to serve as energy storage molecules and structural components in cells.

## Very Short Answer Type Questions

12. Why enzymes are called bio-catalysts?
13. Glycine and alanine are different with respect to one subsequent on the $\alpha$-carbon. Explain.
14. What is glycosidic bond?
15. The protein portion of an enzyme, which requires co-factors for activity, is called?
16. Write three functions of polysaccharides.

## Short Answer Type Questions

17. Differentiate between homopolysaccharide and heteropolysaccharide.
18. Differentiate between $\alpha$-helix and $\beta$-pleated structure of protein.
19. How are prosthetic groups different from co-factors?

## Long Answer Type Questions

20. Explain briefly the structural level of proteins.
21. List the six classes of enzyme and explain any three in detail.
22. Write a short note on

(a) Non-essential amino acids (b) Pentose sugar (c) Competitive inhibitor

## Case Based Question

23. Study the diagram given below and answer the following questions.

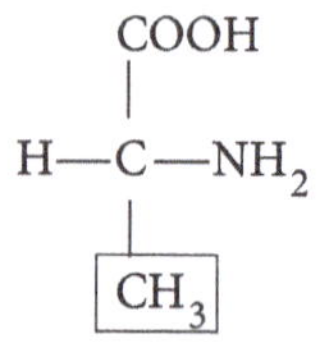


(i) What is the name of the amino acid shown in the structure?

(ii) Name the functional groups present in this amino acid.

(iii) What are the functions of amino acids in biological system?

(iv) Which type of *R* group present in this structure?

# Answers

1. (d) 2. (a) 3. (b) 4. (c) 5. (c) 6. (c) 7. (a) 8. (b)
9. (b) 10. (c) 11. (b)

# 10

CHAPTER

# Cell Cycle and Cell Division

Growth and reproduction are the most vital characteristics of all living beings. Reproduction result in production of new individual which eventually grows into an adult. Thus, both these processes go hand in hand and involve the process of cell division.

**YOUR STUDY GOALS**

10.1 Cell Cycle
10.2 Mitosis
10.3 Meiosis

**YOUR PRACTICE GOAL**

- Objective Type Questions (40 Qs ; MCQs, A-R)
  Case Based Questions (3)
- Subjective Type Questions
- (21 VSAs, 43 SAs, 9 LAs)

## 10.1 Cell Cycle

- Cell division is an essential process in all living organisms.
- During the division of a cell, the processes like DNA replication and cell growth must take place in a sequential and coordinated manner to ensure the correct division and formation of progeny cells with intact genomes.
- The sequence of events or set of stages by which a cell duplicates its genome, synthesises the other constituents and eventually divides into two daughter cells is called **cell cycle**.
- In the cell cycle, cell growth (in terms of cytoplasmic increase) is a continuous process, while DNA synthesis occurs during a specific stage only.
- The replicated DNA (chromosomes) are further distributed to daughter nuclei by a series of events during cell division.
- The duration of cell cycle can vary from one organism to other and also from one cell type to another, e.g. **yeast cell** progresses through the cell cycle and divides in only about **90 min**, whereas a typical **eukaryotic cell** (human cell) divides once in every **24 hours**.
- All these events are well-coordinated and are under genetic control.

## Phases of Cell Cycle

The cell cycle is divided into two phases.

I. **Interphase** Long, non-dividing growth phase.

II. **M-phase** Short, dividing or mitotic phase.

## I. Interphase

- It is the period between the end of one cell division and the beginning of the next, i.e. between two successive M-phase.
- During this phase, cell prepares itself for division by undergoing both cell growth and DNA replication in an orderly manner.
- So, it is also known as **resting phase** or **preparatory phase**.
- It lasts more than 95% of the total duration of cell cycle.
- In a human cell, out of 24 hours duration of one cell cycle, only about one hour is taken by the dividing phase and rest is taken by preparatory phase.
- Interphase is further divided into following three phases

### 1. $G_1$(Gap-1)-Phase

- It corresponds to the duration between the mitosis (M-phase) and initiation of DNA replication.
- The cell becomes metabolically very active during this period. It grows continuously and prepares itself for DNA replication.

### 2. S (Synthesis)-Phase

- It represents the phase in which synthesis or replication of DNA takes place.
- During this phase, the overall amount of DNA doubles per cell. If the initial amount of DNA is 2C, it will become 4C.
- However, the number of chromosomes remains the same. If the cell had $2n$ number of chromosome at $G_1$, it will remain $2n$ even after S-phase.
- In case of animal cell, during S-phase DNA replication begins inside the **nucleus**, while the duplication of centrioles takes place in the **cytoplasm**.

### 3. $G_2$ (Gap-2)-Phase

This phase is also called **post-synthetic** or **pre-mitotic phase**. During this phase, the proteins required for mitosis are being synthesised, while the growth of cell continues.

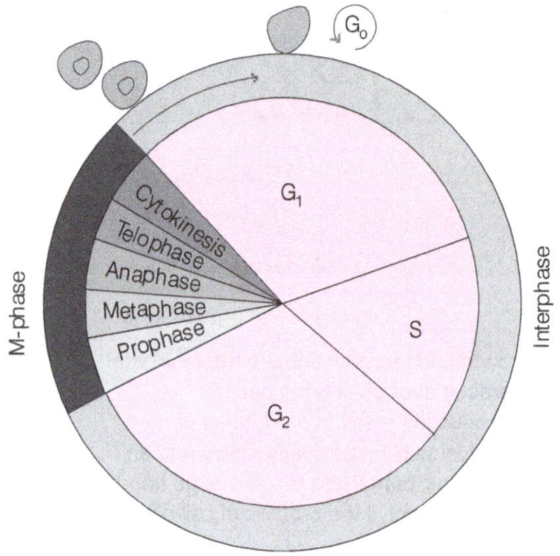


Fig. 10.1 A diagrammatic view of cell cycle indicating formation of two cells from one cell

### $G_0$-phase (Quiescent Stage)

- In adult animals, some cells like heart cells or nerve cells do not undergo division and many other cells divide only occasionally, to replace cells that have been lost (because of some injury or cell death).
- The cells that do not divide further exit $G_1$-phase to enter on inactive stage called **quiescent stage** ($G_0$) rather than S-phase of the cell cycle.
- Cells in $G_0$-phase remain metabolically active, but do not proliferate. This means that these cells do not grow or differentiate till the time they do not get instruction to do so, depending upon the requirement of an organism.

## II. M-phase

Following the interphase, the cell enters into **M-phase** or **mitotic phase**.

**Quick Test 1**

1. An organism, $X$ has a cell cycle duration of 90 minutes, identify the organism.
2. Identify the given statement is correct or incorrect.
   The duration of the cell cycle is believed to vary, depending on the type of cell.
3. In which phase of the cell cycle is the genome replicated to ensure accurate genetic transmission?
4. What happens to the chromosome number after DNA replication in S-phase?
5. **State True or False.**
   Cells that enter the $G_0$-phase exit the cell cycle permanently and lose all metabolic activity until reactivated.

## 10.2 Mitosis

- In this type of division, the chromosomes get equally distributed into daughter nuclei, i.e. the chromosome number in the parental and progeny cell (diploid) remains the same. Therefore, it is also known as **equational division**.
- This cell division is usually seen in the **diploid somatic cells** in animals. However, there are few exceptions to this where haploid cells divide by mitosis, e.g. male honeybee.
- In plants, mitotic division is seen in **both haploid** and **diploid cells**.

**TEACHER'S TIP**
The cell division does not always ensure equal distribution of the genetic material; some divisions, such as **amitosis**, result in unequal distribution of the genetic material. Amitosis is a simple form of cell division where the nucleus divides directly without the typical stages of mitosis. It involves the constriction or fragmentation of the nucleus, resulting in two daughter nuclei.

- Mitosis is known to be the **phase of actual cell division**, which starts with nuclear division, corresponding to the separation of daughter chromosomes, i.e. **karyokinesis** and terminates with the cytoplasmic division, i.e. **cytokinesis**.

### Karyokinesis

It is further divided into four main stages, i.e., prophase, metaphase, anaphase and telophase.

### Prophase

- It is the first stage of karyokinesis and follows the S and $G_2$-phases of interphase.
- In the S and $G_2$-phase the newly formed DNA molecules are not distinct but interwined
- This phase is marked by **condensation of chromosomal material**. The chromosomal material becomes untangled during the process of chromatin condensation.

#### Characteristic Features of Prophase

Following changes are observed during prophase

- During this phase, chromosomal material condenses to form compact mitotic chromosomes, composed of two **chromatids**.
- These chromatids are attached together at the **centromere**.
- The already duplicated centrosome begin to move towards the opposite poles of the animal cells.
- These centrosomes, radiates out microtubules called **asters**. The asters together with spindle fibres form mitotic apparatus.
- At the end of the prophase, i.e. during late prophase the Golgi complex, endoplasmic reticulum and nucleolus disintegrate gradually and the nuclear envelope disappears. This disappearance marks the end of the prophase.

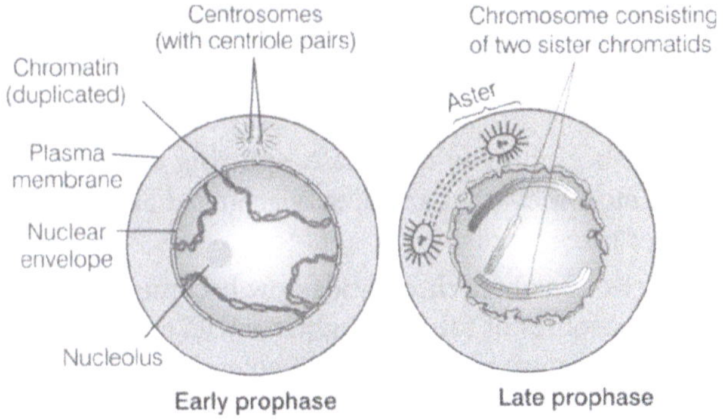


Fig. 10.2 Prophase

### Metaphase

- This phase starts after the **complete disintegration of nuclear envelope**. As a result, the chromosomes spread-out through the cytoplasm of the cell.
- The condensation of chromosome is completed and they can be easily observed under the microscope.

This is the stage at which the morphology of chromosome is most easily studied.

- Each chromosome at this stage is made up of two longitudinal threads (**sister chromatids**) and are held together by the centromere in the centre.
- At the surface of each centromere, disc-shaped structures called **kinetochores** are present, which help in the attachment of spindle fibres to the chromosomes.
- The chromosomes finally arrange themselves at the equator in one equatorial plate known as **metaphase plate**.

### Characteristic Features of Metaphase

Following changes are observed during metaphase.

- Attachment of spindle fibres to kinetochores of chromosomes.
- Movement of chromosomes to spindle equator and their alignment along the metaphase plate through spindle fibres, to both poles.

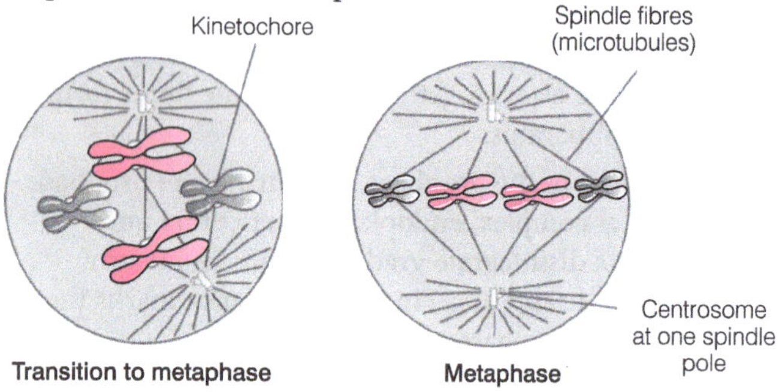


Fig. 10.3 Metaphase

## Anaphase

- At the beginning of this phase, **splitting of chromosomes** (that are already arranged at metaphase plate) takes place.
- The two daughter chromatids now become the chromosomes of future daughter nuclei and start migrating towards the opposite poles.
- As each chromosome moves away from the equatorial plate, the centromere of each chromosome remains attached at the pole and hence, the arms of the chromosome trail behind at the leading edge.

### Characteristic Features of Anaphase

Following changes are observed during anaphase

- Splitting of centromeres and separation of chromatids.
- Movement of chromatids towards the opposite poles.

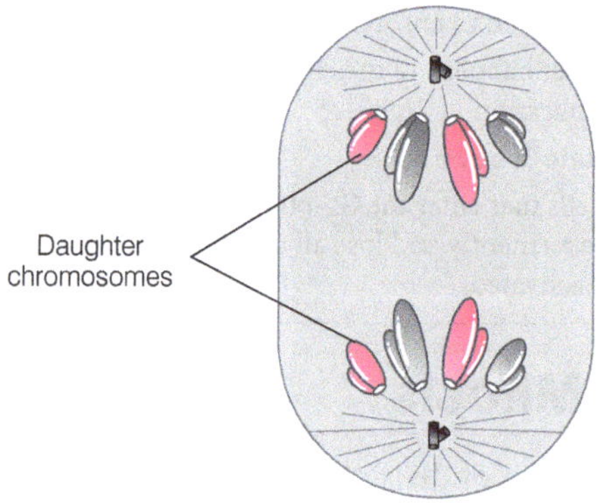


Fig. 10.4 Anaphase

## Telophase

- It is the final stage of karyokinesis. At the onset of this stage, the spindle fibres disappear.
- The chromosomes decondense and further lose their individuality after reaching their respective poles.
- Thus, the individual chromosome can no longer be seen and the chromatin material gets collected in the form of mass at opposite poles.
- In general terms, the events of prophase occur just in reverse sequence during this phase.

### Characteristic Features of Telophase

Following changes are observed during telophase

- The chromosomes gradually uncoil and cluster at opposite spindle poles. Thus, their individual identity as discrete elements is lost.
- Nuclear envelope slowly reforms around the chromosomes clusters, at each pole forming two daughter nuclei.

- Reappearance of nucleolus, Golgi complex and ER also takes place.

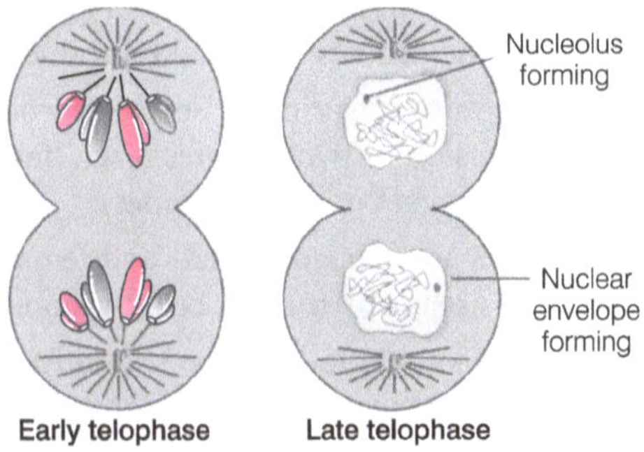


Fig. 10.5 Telophase

# Cytokinesis

Mitosis is not only the segregation of nucleus into two daughter nuclei, but the cell itself divides into two daughter cells by the process of cytokinesis.

## Cytokinesis in Animal Cells

- Animal cells typically divide by the appearance of furrow in the plasma membrane.
- The furrow starts deepening gradually during telophase and finally joins in the centre, dividing the cytoplasm into two.

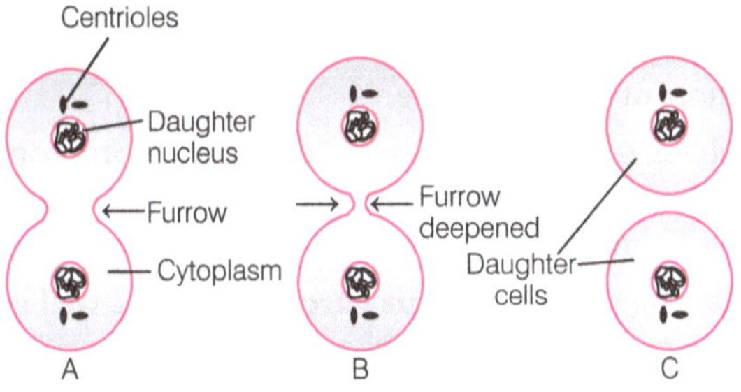


Fig. 10.6 Cytokinesis in animal cells

## Cytokinesis in Plant Cells

- The division of cytoplasm in plant cells is different from that in the animal cells.
- This is due to the presence of a solid, rigid and inextensible cell wall on the outside of the plasma membrane.
- The plant cell cannot undergo cytokinesis by furrowing method therefore, it divides by the **cell-plate method**.
- The formation of a new wall in plant cells starts in the centre of the cell and grows outward towards the opposite sides in order to reach the already existing lateral walls (centrifugal duration).
- The formation of new cell wall begins with the formation of simple precursor, called **cell plate**.

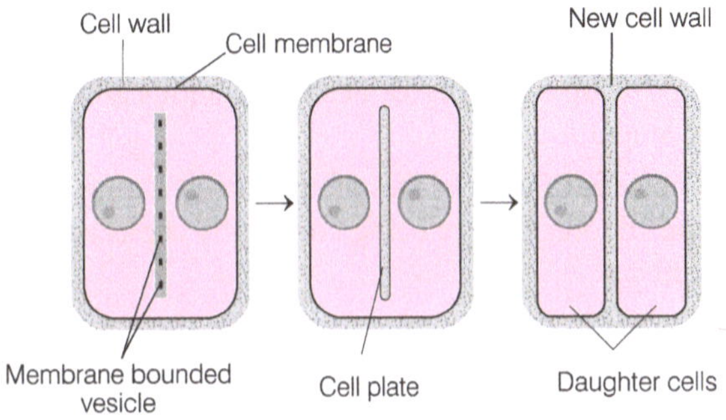


Fig. 10.7 Cytokinesis in plant cells

- The cell plate represents the middle lamella between the walls of two adjacent cells.
- Once cell plate has divided the cell into two cells. The cell organelles (like mitochondria and plastids) are also distributed among two daughter cells.

**Differences between Karyokinesis and Cytokinesis**

| Karyokinesis | Cytokinesis |
|---|---|
| It is the division of nucleus. | It is the division of cytoplasm. |
| The nucleus gets divided into two daughter nuclei. | The cytoplasm, cell organelles and nuclei divides equally and passed to daughter cells. |
| It can occur without being followed by cytokinesis. | It cannot occur without karyokinesis. |

# Syncytium Cells

In some organisms, karyokinesis is not followed by cytokinesis.

As a result, multinucleated condition arises leading to the formation of syncytium, e.g., liquid endosperm in coconut.

# Significance of Mitosis

Mitosis has the following significances

- It helps in the production of diploid daughter cells with equal and identical genetic composition.
- The growth of multicellular organism is due to mitosis.

- A cell cannot grow in size beyond a certain limit without disturbing the ratio between the nucleus and the cytoplasm. Thus, after reaching the particular size, the cell divides in order to restore the **nucleo-cytoplasmic ratio**.
- It is helpful in cell repair mechanism, as well as producing new cells for healing wounds and for regeneration.
- The cells of upper layer of epidermis, lining of the gut and blood cells are being constantly replaced by mitosis.
- Mitosis in meristematic tissues like the apical and the lateral cambium plays an important role in continuous growth of plants throughout their life.

**Differences between Mitosis in Animal and Plant Cells**

| Animal Cells | Plant Cells |
|---|---|
| Centrioles are present at spindle poles. | Centrioles are absent at spindle poles. |
| Cytokinesis occur by furrowing of cytoplasm. | Cytokinesis occur mostly by cell plate formation. |
| Furrow extends centripetally. | Cell plate grows centrifugally. |
| Occurs nearly in all tissues. | Occurs mainly at meristems. |

## Quick Test 2

1. How does the chromosomal material change as the cell transitions from the interphase to prophase?
2. While studying a slide under the microscope at which stage of mitosis would Riya observe the most distinct morphology of chromosomes?
3. Which phase of mitosis is responsible for the separation of sister chromatids?
4. In which phase of cell cycle, does formation of furrow taken place?
5. **State True or False.**
   (a) In metaphase, chromosomes align the metaphase plate due to the attachment of spindle fibres to the centromeres.
   (b) An imbalance between the nucleus and cytoplasm due to cell growth might not necessitate division to restore the nucleo-cytoplasmic ratio.

# 10.3 Meiosis

- The phenomenon of meiosis occurs in any life cycle that involves the process of sexual reproduction.
- The production of offspring by sexual reproduction involves the fusion of two gametes (each having a complete haploid set of chromosomes).
- These gametes are formed in male and female reproductive organs by meiotic cell division.
- The meiosis is known to be a specialised form of cell division which reduces the chromosome number by half.
- The reduction occurs in such a way that each daughter nuclei receives only one of chromosome. Thus, it is also known as the **reductional division**.
- Meiosis ensure the production of haploid phase in the life cycle of sexually reproducing organisms whereas fertilisation restores the diploid phase.

## Characteristic Features of Meiosis

The essential features of meiosis are as follows

- Meiosis undergoes two successive cycles of nuclear and cytoplasm division, i.e. meiosis-I and II. But the replication of chromosome takes place only once during the cycle.
- Meiosis-I and II occur one after another with a very short or no interphase.
- Meiosis-I initiates after the parental chromosomes have replicated to create identical sister chromatids at the S-phase.
- Pairing of **homologous chromosomes** as well as **recombination** between non-sister chromatids of homologous chromosomes takes place during meiosis.
- Finally, after the second meiotic division four haploid cells are formed.

## Meiosis-I

- During this division, the homologous chromosomes of each pair separate from each other and the number of chromosomes reduces from diploid to haploid, i.e. from $2n$ to $n$.
- Meiosis-I is further divided into four phases, i.e. prophase-I, metaphase-I, anaphase-I and telophase-I.

## Prophase-I

- It is considered to be **more complicated** and **prolonged phase** as compared to the similar stage in mitosis.
- This stage is further subdivided into five phases on the basis of chromosomal behaviour, i.e. leptotene, zygotene, pachytene, diplotene and diakinesis.

### 1. Leptotene

- It is known to be the very first stage of meiotic division following the interphase. Following features are seen during this stage.
- Chromosomes become gradually visible under light microscope.
- Compaction of chromosomes continues throughout leptotene.

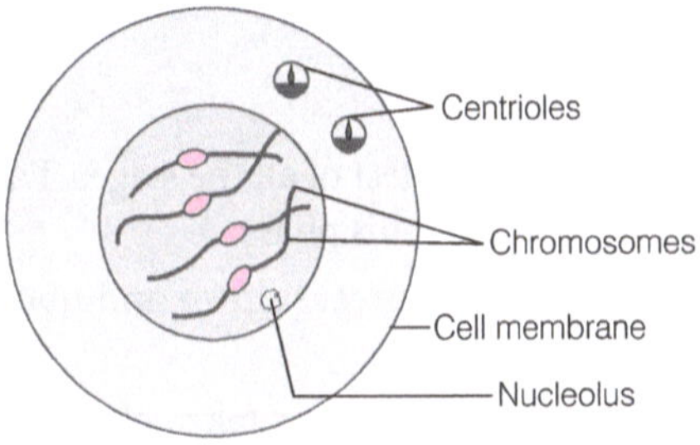


Fig. 10.8 Leptotene

### 2. Zygotene

- This is also a short lived stage like leptotene. Following changes are seen during this stage.
- **Homologous chromosomes** pair up and this process of association is known as **synapsis.**
- It is revealed from the electron micrographic studies that chromosome synapsis is accompanied by the formation of complex structure called **synaptonemal complex**.
- The complex so formed, on account of synapsis is called a **bivalent** or a **tetrad**.

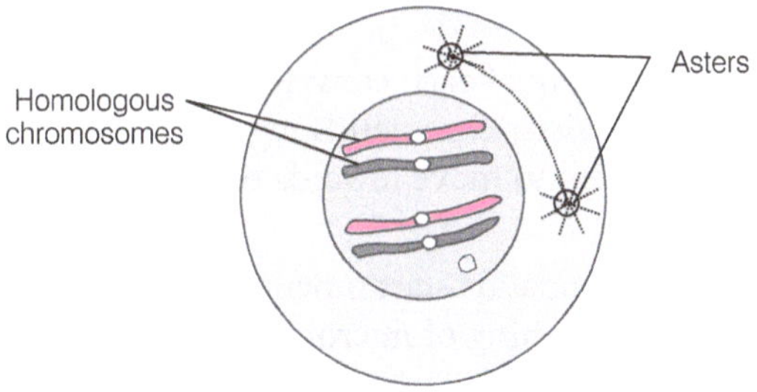


Fig. 10.9 Zygotene

### 3. Pachytene

This is the stage which immediately follows zygotene. Following changes are seen during this stage

- Four chromatids of each bivalent chromosomes are clearly seen as tetrads.
- In this stage, recombination of genetic material or **crossing over**, between the two non-sister chromatids of homologous chromosomes occurs at the points called **recombination nodules.**
- Crossing-over is an enzyme mediated process and the enzyme involved is called **recombinase.**
- By the end of pachytene, recombination gets completed leaving the chromosomes linked at the sites of crossing over.

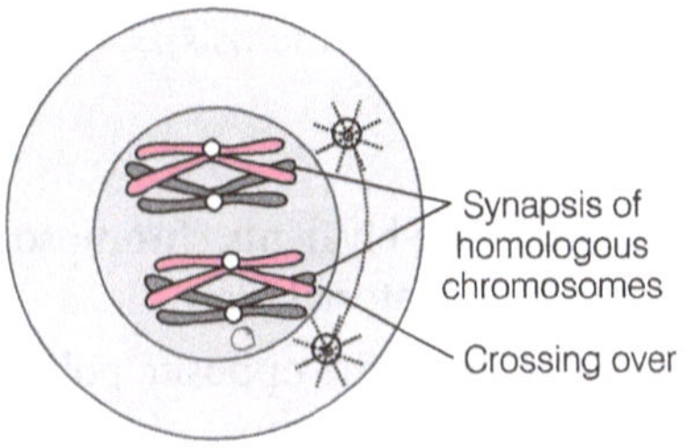


Fig. 10.10 Pachytene

### 4. Diplotene

- It is the longest stage of all the phases of meiosis. In oocytes of some vertebrates diplotene can last for months or years. Following changes are observed during this stage
- In this stage, the dissolution of synaptonemal complex takes place.
- The recombined homologous chromosomes of the bivalents get separated except at crossover sites, where chromosomes remain attached and form chiasmata (**X-shaped structures**).

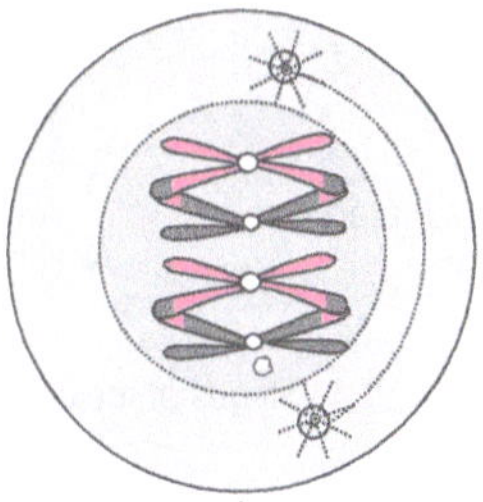

Fig. 10.11 Diplotene

One of the most important aspects of diplotene is that it marks a prolonged arrest of oocyte, lasting years before ovulation.

### 5. Diakinesis

This is known to be the final stage of meiotic prophase-I. Following changes are observed during this stage.

- This stage is marked by the **terminalisation of chiasmata**.
- Chromosomes become fully condensed.
- Nucleolus degenerates and nuclear envelope also breaks down.

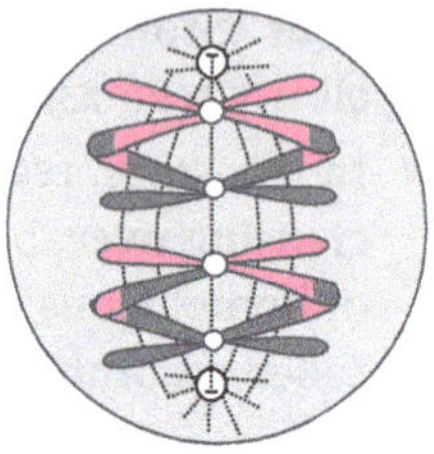

Fig. 10.12 Diakinesis

- Formation of meiotic spindle (as in mitosis) in order to prepare the homologous chromosomes for separation also occurs.
- Diakinesis stage represents the transition from prophase to metaphase of meiosis-I.

### Metaphase-I

- During this phase, the bivalents chromosomes arrange themselves on the equatorial plate.
- The microtubules from the opposite poles of the spindle attach to the kinetochore of homologous chromosomes.

### Anaphase-I

The homologous chromosomes separate, while sister chromatids remain associated at their centromere.

### Telophase-I

This is the last stage of meiosis-I in which the reappearance of nuclear membrane and nucleolus takes place.

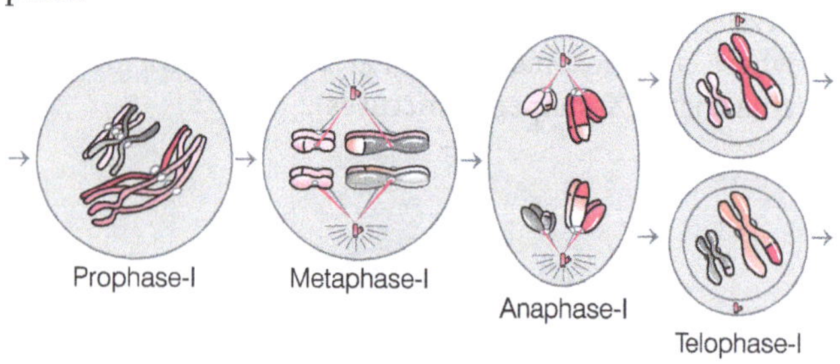


Fig. 10.13 Stages of meiosis-I

### Cytokinesis

It is the stage during which the cytoplasm and other organelles divide into two equal halves and dyad of cells is formed.

### Interkinesis

- This is the stage between the two meiotic divisions, i.e. the meiosis-I and II. It is generally **short lived.**
- During this process, no replication of DNA occurs.
- Interkinesis is followed by prophase-II, which is a much simpler prophase than prophase-I.

## Meiosis-II

- In this division, chromosome number remains same as produced in meiosis-I. Thus, it is also known as **equational division**.
- It is initiated immediately after cytokinesis, even before the chromosomes have fully elongated.
- Meiosis-II is further divided into prophase-II metaphase-II, anaphase-II and telophase-II which are discussed as follows.

### Prophase-II

This is known to be shortest of all the stages. Following changes are seen during this phase

- The nuclear envelope breaks down and nucleoli disappears.
- Compaction of chromosomes takes place.

### Metaphase-II

This is the next phase followed immediately after prophase-II. Following changes are seen during this stage.

- The chromosomes align at the equator or the metaphase plate, in the similar way as in mitosis.
- The microtubules from opposite poles of the spindle get attached to the kinetochore of sister chromatids.

### Anaphase-II

This is the phase followed immediately after metaphase-II. Following changes are seen during this stage

- The centromere of each chromosome (that was holding the sister chromatids together) splits, allowing them to move towards opposite poles of the cell.
- The two chromatids start moving away from each other by shortening of microtubules attached to kinetochores.

## Telophase-II

- This is known to be the last stage of second meiotic division. It shows changes equally opposite to that of the prophase-II.
- Meiosis ends up with the progress ion of this particular stage, i.e. telophase-II. Following changes are seen during this stage
- Formation of a nuclear envelope around each set of chromosomes.
- Nucleoli reappears in telophase-II as the nuclear envelope reforms and chromosomes decondense into chromatin.

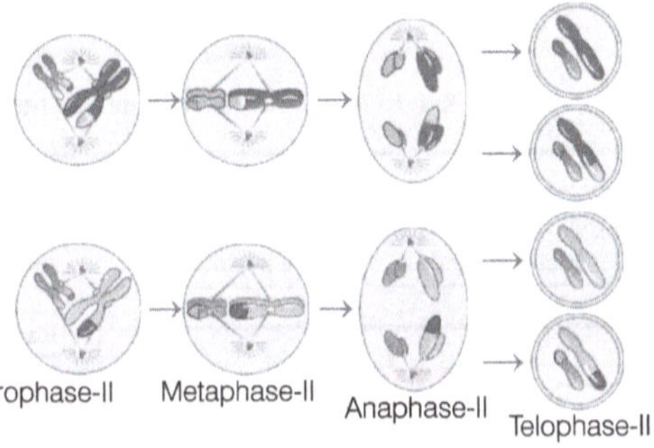


Fig. 10.14 Stages of meiosis-II

## Cytokinesis

- This occurs after every nuclear division.
- It includes separation of cytoplasm and organelles in the two halves of the cell.
- The dyad of cells produced during meiosis-I, undergo divisions and give rise to **four cells.**

## Significance of Meiosis

The meiotic division has the following significances

- It maintains the same chromosome number in the sexually reproducing organisms.
- From a diploid cell, haploid gametes are produced due to the reduction in number of chromosomes to half.
- These haploid gametes then fuse to form a diploid cell during fertilisation.
- Maternal and paternal genes get exchanged during crossing over. It results in variations among the offspring.
- It increase genetic variability in the population of organisms from one generation to other. Variations help in the process of evolution.

Major differences between mitosis and meiosis can be understand by following flow chart

Cell Division

| Mitosis | Properties | Meiosis |
|---|---|---|
| Occurs during interphase before mitosis begins. | DNA replication | Occurs during interphase before meiosis begins. |
| One | No. of division | Two |
| Two diploid ($2n$) daughter cells that are genetically identical to the parent cell. | No. of daughter cells and genetic composition | 4 haploid ($n$) daughter cells, each containing half as many chromosomes as the parent cell. Daughter cells are genetically different from parent cell and each other. |
| Does not occur | Synapsis of homologous chromosomes | Occur along with crossing over between non-sister chromatids of homologous chromosomes in prophase-I. |
| Produce cells for growth and repairs. It occurs in somatic cells. | Role in the organism's body | Produces gametes and assures genetic diversity in sexual reproduction. It occurs in reproductive cells. |

### Quick Test 3

1. In $X$ phase, chromosomes gradually become visible, and their compaction continues. Identify $X$.
2. Identify the point in the meiosis where chromosomes begin pairing and the synaptonemal complex forms.
3. **State True or False.**
   (a) In diplotene, homologous chromosomes remain tightly paired without any separation.
   (b) Diakinesis is characterised by the complete condensation of chromosomes and disintegration of the nucleolus, marking the transition to metaphase.
4. During which stage of prophase-I, do homologous chromosomes pair to form tetrads?
5. In an organism with a diploid chromosome number of 16($2n$=16). Mention the number of chromosomes and chromatids present during metaphase-II.

# Mind Map

# Cell Cycle and Cell Division

## Interphase

Time during which cell prepares for division by undergoing both cell growth and DNA replication.

- $G_1$-phase (Gap 1)
- S-phase (Synthetic)
- $G_2$-phase (Gap 2)

Some cells exits to enter the inactive stage called **quiescent stage ($G_0$-phase).**

## M-phase

Starts with the nuclear division, corresponding to the separation of daughter chromosomes (karyokinesis) and usually ends with division of cytoplasm (cytokinesis).

## Mitosis

### Karyokinesis

**Prophase**

Chromosomal material condenses, centriole moves towards opposite poles, ER, nuclear membrane, Golgi complex disappears.

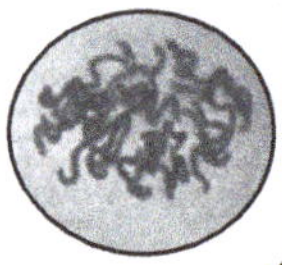

**Metaphase**

- Condensation of chromosomal material completes.
- Chromosomes get arranged at metaphase plate.

**Anaphase**

Splitting of chromosome into two sister chromatids and they starts to move towards opposite poles.

**Telophase**

- Chromosomes loses its identity as discrete unit.
- Nuclear membrane, nucleolus, ER and Golgi complex reappears.

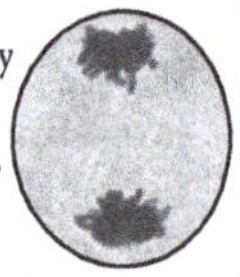

### Cytokinesis

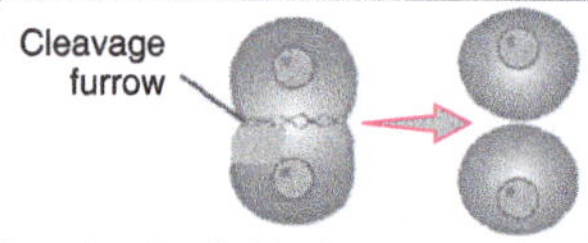


**In animal cell:** By deepening of **cell furrow.**

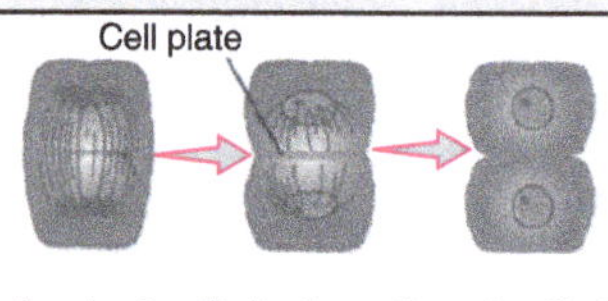


**In plant cell:** By formation of **cell plate.**

## Meiosis

**Results in four haploid unique daughter cells.**

- **Meiosis-I** → **Cytokinesis-I** (Results in dyad of cells)
- **Interkinesis** (Short lived: between meiosis-I and II)
- **Meiosis-II** (Resembles normal mitosis) → **Cytokinesis-II** (Results in formation of 4 haploid cells)

### Karyokinesis-I

**Prophase-I**

Longer ; five phases

**Leptotene**

- Chromosomes become distinct.
- Compaction continues.

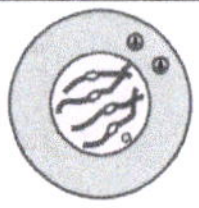

**Zygotene**

- Synapsis between homologous chromosome.
- Synaptonemal complex called **tetrad** or **bivalent.**

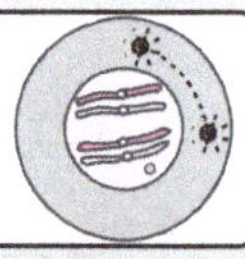

**Pachytene**

Recombination between non-sister chromatids of homologous chromosomes (enzyme recombinase).

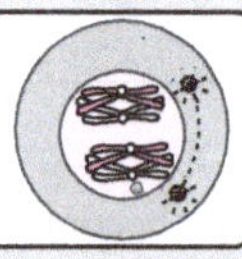

**Diplotene**

- Dissolution of synaptonemal complex.
- Formation of chiasmata.

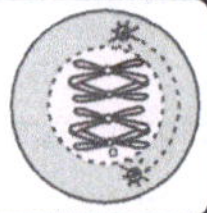

**Diakinesis**

- Terminalisation of chiasmata.
- Nuclear membrane breaks and nucleolus disappears.

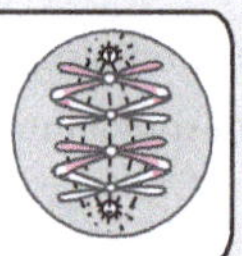

**Metaphase-I**

Bivalent chromosomes align on equatorial plate.

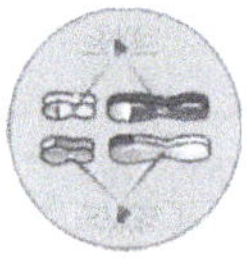

**Anaphase-I**

Homologous chromosomes separate, but sister chromatids remain attached at centromere.

**Telophase-I**

Nuclear membrane and nucleolus reappears.

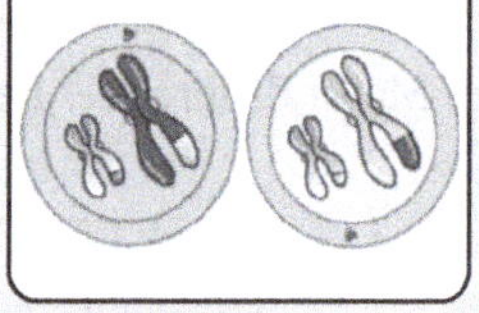

### Karyokinesis-II

**Prophase-II**

- Nuclear membrane disappears.
- Chromosomes again become compact.

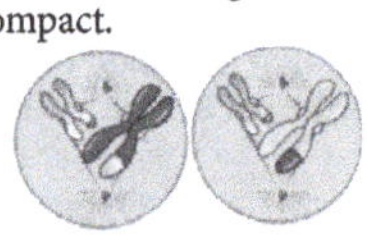

**Metaphase-II**

Chromosomes align at equator.

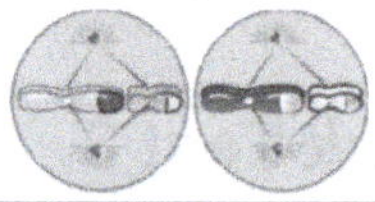

**Anaphase-II**

Starts with splitting of centromere of each chromosome to move towards opposite poles.

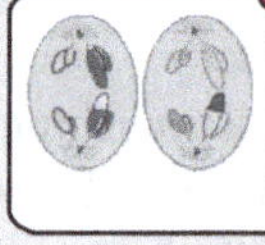

**Telophase-II**

Two group of chromosomes get enclosed by nuclear membrane.

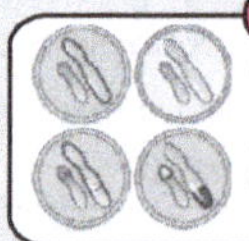

# EXAM PATTERN QUESTIONS

## Objective Type Questions

### Multiple Choice Questions

**1. Which of the following matched pair is correct?**

(a) Cell duplication – sequence of events by which cell constituents divide

(b) Cell cycle - process by which cell duplicates its genome and eventually divides into daughter cells

(c) Cell growth -distribution of chromosomes by a sequential series of division

(d) Cell division - constricted growth of cytoplasm content of a cell

Ans. (*b*)

**2. Two basic stages of cell cycle are**

(a) interphase and M-phase /divisional phase

(b) karyokinesis and cytokinesis

(c) prophase, metaphase, anaphase and telophase

(d) $G_1$, S and $G_2$-phases

Ans. (*a*)

**3. In which phase of cell cycle, DNA content gets doubled?**

(a) Interphase (b) Anaphase (c) Prophase (d) Telophase

Ans. (*a*)

**4. During the $G_1$ -phase of cell division**

(a) RNA and proteins are synthesised for cell growth and subsequent DNA replication

(b) DNA and proteins are synthesised

(c) centriole duplicates in the cytoplasm

(d) cell undergoes duplication

Ans. (*a*)

**5. Select the correct statement about $G_1$ -phase.** NCERT Exemplar

(a) Cell is metabolically inactive

(b) DNA in the cell does not replicate

(c) It is not a phase of synthesis of macromolecules

(d) Cell stops growing

Ans. (*b*)

**6. Given below are few statements respect to $G_1$ -phase of cell cycle.** NCERT Exemplar

**I. It is the last substage of interphase.**

**II. Cell organelles do not increase in number.**

**III. Both cell and nucleus grow in size.**

**IV. Synthesis of RNA, proteins and other biochemicals for cell growth, takes place.**

**Choose the correct option.**

(a) I and II (b) II and IV

(c) I and III (d) II and III

Ans. (*b*)

**7. An onion root tip has 14 chromosomes in each cell. How many chromosomes the cell would have at $G_1$-phase?** Competency Based Que.

(a) 28 (b) 14

(c) 62 (d) 7

Ans. (*b*) The onion root tip will have 14 chromosomes as $G_1$ is the stage right after mitosis and before DNA replication, the number of chromosomes will remains the same.

**8. The phase of cell cycle in which the centriole duplicates in the cytoplasm is**

(a) S-phase (b) $G_1$-phase (c) $G_2$-phase (d) $G_0$-phase

Ans. (*a*) The DNA content doubles during the S-phase (synthesis phase) of the interphase. During this phase, each chromosome is replicated, resulting in two sister chromatids for each chromosome, effectively doubling the DNA content in preparation for cell division.

**9. In the diagrammatic view of cell cycle, the $G_0$ -phase is represented as** Competency Based Que.

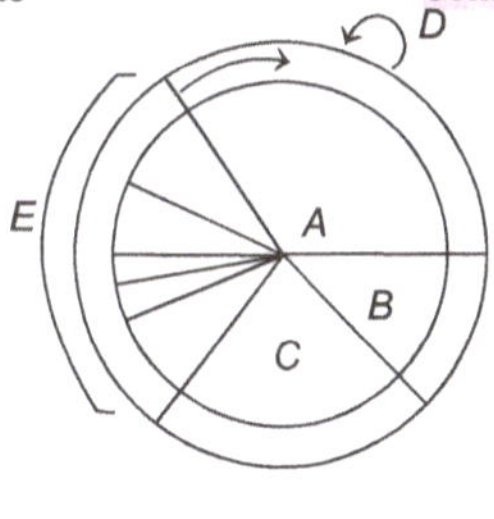


(a) *A* (b) *B*

(c) *C* (d) *D*

Ans. (*d*)

**10. Cells which are not dividing are likely to be at** NCERT Exemplar

(a) $G_1$-phase (b) $G_2$-phase

(c) $G_0$-phase (d) S-phase

Ans. (*c*)

**11. Select the incorrect statement for prophase.**

(a) Chromosomal material condenses to form compact mitotic chromosomes
(b) They assembly of mitotic spindle is initiated by the microtubules
(c) Cells at the end of prophase contain membrane bound organelles when viewed under the prophase
(d) The nucleolus or nucleoli deforms completely

Ans. (c)

**12. Which of cell division is best for counting the number of chromosomes?**

(a) Interphase (b) Anaphase (c) Metaphase (d) Telophase

Ans. (c)

**13. At which stage of mitosis, the two daughter chromatids separate from each other, migrate towards the opposite poles and are now referred to as chromosomes of the future daughter nuclei?** Competency Based Que.

(a) Prophase (b) Metaphase
(c) Anaphase (d) Telophase

Ans. (c)

**14. Phases of mitosis which are opposite to each other are**

(a) anaphase and telophase
(b)telophase and prophase
(c) metaphase and anaphase
(d) prophase and metaphase

Ans. (b)

**15. See the diagrams carefully and identify the different stages of mitosis (*A-B*) by choosing appropriate option given below.** Competency Based Que.

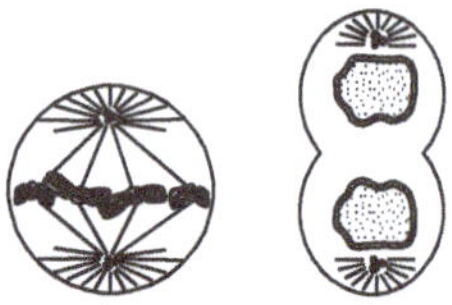


(a) *A*–Metaphase, *B*–Telophase
(b) *A*–Telophase, *B*–Metaphase
(c) *A*–Anaphase, *B*–Telophase
(d) *A*–Telophase, *B*–Anaphase

Ans. (a)

**16. Which of the events listed below is not observed during mitosis?** NCERT Exemplar

(a) Chromatin condensation
(b) Movement of centrioles to opposite poles
(c) Appearance of chromosomes with two chromosome joined together at the centromere
(d) Crossing over

Ans. (d)

**17. When karyokinesis is not followed by cytokinesis, it results in the formation of**

(a) uninucleate cells
(b) multinucleate cells
(c) undifferentiated cells
(d) diploid cells

Ans. (*b*) When karyokinesis is not followed by cytokinesis, it results in multinucleation, where a single cell contains multiple nuclei. This can disrupt normal cellular function and is often observed in certain pathological conditions.

**18. Which of the following is not a significance of mitosis?**

(a) Production of progeny having identical genetic complement
(b) Restoration of nucleo-cytoplasmic ratio
(c) Replacement of dead tissue
(d) Contributes to evolution

Ans. (d)

**19. Match the words listed in Column I with suitable words from the Column II.**

| | Column I | | Column II |
|---|---|---|---|
| A. | Karyokinesis | 1. | Reductional division |
| B. | Cytokinesis | 2. | Plant cells |
| C. | Meiosis | 3. | Nuclear division |
| D. | Cell plate | 4. | Cytoplasmic division |

Codes

| | A | B | C | D | | A | B | C | D |
|---|---|---|---|---|---|---|---|---|---|
| (a) | 1 | 3 | 2 | 4 | (b) | 3 | 4 | 1 | 2 |
| (c) | 1 | 4 | 3 | 2 | (d) | 4 | 3 | 2 | 1 |

Ans. (b)

**20. Meiosis occurs in organisms during** NCERT Exemplar

(a) sexual reproduction (b) vegetative reproduction
(c) Both (a) and (b) (d) None of these

Ans. (a)

**21. Meiosis in diploid organisms results in** NCERT Exemplar

(a) production of gametes
(b) reduction in the number of chromosomes
(c) introduction of variation
(d) All of the above

Ans. (d)

**22. A bivalent of meiosis-I consists of** NCERT Exemplar

(a) two chromatids and one centromere
(b) two chromatids and two centromeres
(c) four chromatids and two centromeres
(d) four chromatids and four centromeres

Ans. (*c*) The complex formed by a pair of synapsed homologous chromosome is called bivalent or a tetrad. It has two centromeres and four chromatids.

**23.** **When paternal and maternal chromosomes exchange their genetic material with each other in cell division, this event is called**

(a) bivalent forming (b) crossing over
(c) synapsis (d) dyad forming

**Ans.** (*b*)

**24.** **Select the incorrectly matched pair.**

(a) **Resting phase** – **Interphase**
(b) **Reductional division** – **Meiosis-I**
(c) **Equational division** – **Meiosis-II**
(d) **Crossing over** – **Non -homologous chromosomes**

**Ans.** (*d*)

**25.** **During anaphase-I of meiosis** NCERT Exemplar

(a) homologous chromosomes separate
(b) non-homologous autosomes separate
(c) sister chromatids separate
(d) non-sister chromatids separate

**Ans.** (*a*) During anaphase-I, homologous chromosomes separate, while sister chromatids remain associated at their centromere.

**26.** **At which stage of meiosis does the genetic constitution of gametes is finally decided** NCERT Exemplar

(a) metaphase-I
(b) anaphase-II
(c) metaphase-II
(d) anaphase-I

**Ans.** (*d*)

**27.** **Choose the correct option with respect to the figure given below.** Competency Based Que.

| | No. of Homologous Chromosomes | Phase of Cell Division |
|---|---|---|
| (a) | 2 | Telophase -II |
| (b) | 4 | Telophase-II |
| (c) | 2 | Telophase-1 |
| (d) | 4 | Telophase |

**Ans.** (*c*)

**28.** **Splitting of centromere and hence separation of chromatids occur during**

(a) prophase - II (b) anaphase -I
(c) anaphase -II (d) metaphase-II

**Ans.** (*c*)

**29.** **Identify the wrong statement about meiosis.** NCERT Exemplar

(a) Pairing of homologous chromosomes
(b) Four haploid cells are formed
(c) At the end of meiosis the number of chromosomes are reduced to half
(d) Two cycle of DNA replication occurs

**Ans.** (*d*)

## Assertion-Reason Questions

**Direction** (Q. Nos. 1-11) *In each of the following questions, a statement of Assertion (A) is given followed by corresponding statement of Reason (R). Of the statements, mark the correct answer*

(a) Both A and R are true and R is the correct explanation of A.
(b) Both A and R are true, but R is not the correct explanation of A.
(c) A is true, but R is false.
(d) A is false, but R is true.

**1.** **Assertion** (A) Cell normally proceeds to mitosis without interruption, once it enters the $G_1$-phase.

**Reason** (R) Replicated chromosomes (DNA) are distributed to daughter nuclei by a complex series of events under genetic control.

**Ans.** (*d*)

**2.** **Assertion** (A) Some cells enter $G_0$-phase leading to inactivation of cell cycle.

**Reason** (R) Cells at $G_0$ stage remain metabolically active, but no longer proliferate.

**Ans.** (*b*) Both A and R are true, but R is not the correct explanation of A. The A can be explained as:

Cells enter the $G_0$ -phase due to a lack of growth signals or nutrient scarcity leading to a temporary or permanent halt in the cell cycle. This inactivation allows cells to conserve resources and maintain their functions without actively dividing.

**3.** **Assertion** (A) Mitosis restores the nucleo-cytoplasmic ratio.

**Reason** (R) Equational division is significant in the life of an organism, especially in the growth of multicellular organism.

**Ans.** (*b*) Both A and R are true, but R is not the correct explanation of A. The A can be explained as:

Mitosis restores the nucleocytoplasmic ratio by evenly distributing the replicated DNA into two daughter cells, ensuring each cell has the correct amount of nuclear material.

**4.** **Assertion** (A) Apical and lateral meristems are responsible for growth of plants.

**Reason** (R) Mitosis occurs in apical meristems and lateral meristems.

**Ans.** (*a*)

**5.** **Assertion** (A) In mitosis, two identical cells are produced from a single cell and karyokinesis is followed by cytokinesis.

**Reason** (R) Cytokinesis occurs by two different methods, i.e. by cell-furrow method and cell-plate method.

**Ans.** (*b*)

**6.** **Assertion** (A) Small disc-shaped structures at the surface of the centromeres are called kinetochores .

**Reason** (R) Kinetochores are proteinaceous structures.

**Ans.** (*b*) Both A and R are true, but R is not the correct explanation of A. The A can be explained as:

Kinetochores are small disc-shaped structures located at the surface of the centromere, serving as attachment points for spindle fibres during cell division.

They play a crucial role in the proper segregation of chromosomes by facilitating the movement of chromatids to opposite poles during mitosis and meiosis.

**7.** **Assertion** (A) In animal cells, cytokinesis is achieved by the appearance of a furrow in plasma membrane.

**Reason** (R) In plant cells, the formation of the new cell wall begins with the formation of simple precursor called cell-plate.

**Ans.** (*b*)

**8.** The following graph shows the total amount of DNA present in a cell during various stages of the cell cycle.
**Competency Based Que.**

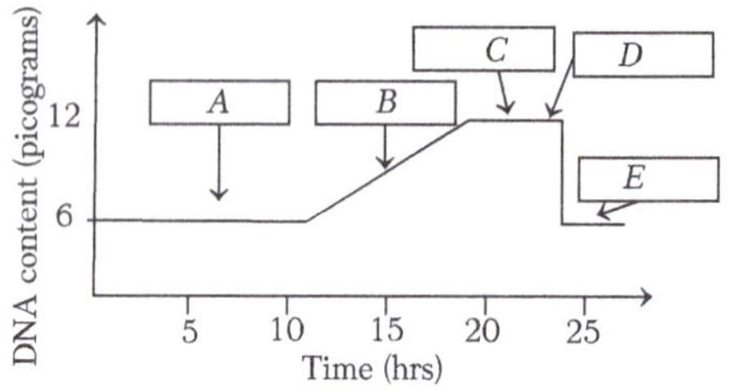


**Assertion** (A) The stage *E* in the above graph is showing the division of protoplast.

**Reason** (R) Cytokinesis is the physical splitting of parent cell into two identical daughter cells.

**Ans.** (*b*)

**9.** **Assertion** (A) Gametes formed as a result of meiosis are haploid in nature.

**Reason** (R) Meiotic division occurs in reproductive cells.

**Ans.** (*b*) Both A and R are true, but R is not the correct explanation of A. The A can be explained as:

Gametes formed as a result of meiosis are haploid because meiosis reduces the chromosome number by half, ensuring that each gamete contains only one set of chromosome. This reduction is crucial for maintaining the diploid chromosome number in the resulting zygote upon fertilisation.

**10.** **Assertion** (A) Diakinesis is the final stage of prophase-I.

**Reason** (R) Terminalisation of chiasmata occurs in diakinesis.

**Ans.** (*b*)

**11.** **Assertion** (A) In anaphase-II, chromosomes align at the equator.

**Reason** (R) During anaphase, the centromere of each chromosome splits and chromatids separate.

**Ans.** (*d*) A is false, but R is true. The A can be correct as:

During metaphase-II, chromosomes align at the equator, while during anaphase-II, the sister chromatids are pulled apart and move towards opposite poles of the cell.

# Subjective Questions

## Very Short Answer Type Questions

**1. What is the average cell cycle span for a mammalian cell?** NCERT

**Ans.** Average cell cycle span of a mammalian cell is 24 hours.

**2. Give the name of the phase between the two successive mitotic divisions.**

**Ans.** Interphase is the period between the two successive mitotic cell divisions. (1)

**3. It is said that the one cycle of cell division in human cells (eukaryotic cells) takes 24 hours. Which phase of the cycle, do you think occupies the maximum part of cell cycle?** Competency Based Que., NCERT Exemplar

**Ans.** If a cell takes 24 hours to divide, it will spent 18- 20 hours on interphase stage to prepare itself to undergo cell division.

**4. During which part of interphase does overall amount of DNA in a cell doubles.**

**Ans.** Duplication of DNA occurs in S-phase.

**5. Cell cycle is divided into two basic phases. At which stage of cell cycle the grown up cell divides?**

**Ans.** Cell divides in M-phase of cell cycle.

**6. Which part of the human body should one use to demonstrate stages in mitosis?** NCERT Exemplar

**Ans.** All the cells in the human body are somatic cells except germinal cells in the male and female reproductive organs. The somatic cells divide by mitotic cell division for growth and regeneration.These can be used to demonstrate mitosis. (1)

**7. Why do the chromosomes become short and thick in prophase?**

**Ans.** It happens so because it is physically easier for short and compact chromosomes to move through the cytoplasm than the very long and twisted interphase chromosomes. (1)

**8. The shortest phase of mitosis is anaphase. State whether this statement is true or false. Does this phase relate to separation of chromatids?** Competency Based Que.

**Ans.** True, anaphase is the shortest phase of mitosis. Yes anaphase is related to splitting of centromere and separation of chromatids. (½ + ½)

**9. The following statements describe the four main stages in the process of mitosis.** Competency Based Que.

**I. The spindle fibres breakdown and the nuclear membrane forms.**

**II. The chromosomes arrange themselves on the equator of the cell.**

**III. The spindle forms and the nuclear membrane disintegrates.**

**IV. The centromere splits and the sister chromatids migrate to the opposite poles of the cell.**

**Write the correct sequence of the stages in mitosis and also name the each stage.**

**Ans.** III (prophase) → II (metaphase) → IV (anaphase) → I (telophase)

**10. Cell 'X' contains 24 chromosomes. It is divided by mitosis to produce cells 'Y' and 'Z'.**

**Deduce how many chromosomes cell Z will contain after division.** Competency Based Que.

**Ans.** The cell Z will also contain 24 chromosomes after mitotic division. Because mitosis is a copying process in which daughter cells have same number of chromosomes as the parent cell.

**11. If a tissue has 1024 cells at a given time, how many cycles of mitosis had the original parental single cell undergone?** NCERT Exemplar

**Ans.** Each cycle produces 2 daughter cells. $2^n$ = no. of daughter cells $2^{10} = 1024$.

$\therefore$ 10 cycles are required to produce 1024 daughter cells. (1)

**12. Meiosis occurs in plant and animal cells in similar locations. Comment.**

**Ans.** Meiosis occurs in sex cells of plants and in germ cells of animals.

**13. Identify the phase which is considered as the most complicated and prolonged phase. Mention the substages of this phase.**

**Ans.** Prophase-I is considered as the most complicated and the most prolonged phase.The various substages of prophase that occur in meiosis are leptotene, zygotene, pachytene, diplotene and diakinesis. (½ + ½)

**14. These are a pair of chromosomes one from each parent, which are similar in length, gene position and also location of a centromere. Identify the type of chromosomes.**

**Ans.** Homologous chromosomes.

**15. What indicates the beginning of diplotene stage of prophase-I?**

**Ans.** On the beginning of diplotene stage, synaptonemal complex dissolutes and homologous chromosomes separate from each other (except at crossing over sites).

**16. Meiosis consists of four substages. In which stage of prophase-I of meiosis, homologous chromosomes lie side by side in pairs?**

**Ans.** Homologous chromosomes lie side by side in zygotene.

**17. What attributes does a chromatid require to be classified as a chromosome?** **NCERT Exemplar**

**Ans.** To be classified as a chromosome, there should be two identical sister chromatids attached at the centre by centromere.

**18. Find examples where the four daughter cells from meiosis are equal in size and where they are found unequal in size.** **NCERT**

**Ans.** During formation of male gametes (spermatozoa) in a typical mammal, the four daughter cells formed from meiosis are equal in size. Whereas, during formation of female gamete (ovum), the four daughter cells are unequal in size. (1)

**19. An anther has 1200 pollen grains. How many pollen mother cells must have been there to produce them?** **Competency Based Que., NCERT Exemplar**

**Ans.** Three hundred pollen mother cells have to be there to produce 1200 pollen grains. Because one pollen mother cell will produce four pollen grains.

**20. How many chromosomes in daughter cells are formed by mitosis from diploid parent cells? And what is the chromosome number in daughter cells formed by meiosis from diploid parent cells?**

**Ans.** In mitosis, daughter cells have the same chromosome number as diploid parent ($2n$), while in meiosis, daughter cells have half the chromosome number ($n$). (½ + ½)

**21. The diagram given below represents different stages of cell division. Identify the diagrams.**

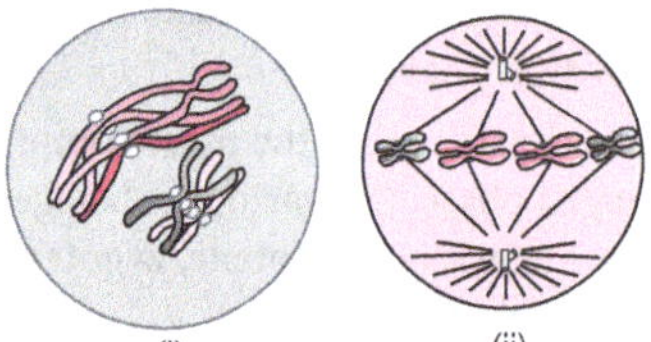

(i) (ii)

**Ans.** (i) Prophase-I (½)

(ii) Metaphase (½)

## Short Answer Type Questions

**1. Describe cell division. List various types of cell division. Also mention about the need of cell division.**

**Ans.** Cell division or cell multiplication is the process of formation of new daughter cells from the pre-existing cell or parent cell. (1)

It is of three types

(i) Amitosis (ii) Mitosis (iii) Meiosis. (½)

Cell division is essential for growth and development of multicellular organisms. It is also involved in reproduction in case of unicellular organisms. (½)

**2. Describe the events taking place during interphase.** **NCERT**

**Ans.** Three main events that occur in interphase are $G_1$-phase (post-mitotic or pre-synthetic phase), S-phase (synthesising phase) and $G_2$-phase (post-synthetic or pre-mitotic phase).

Major events of each phase are as follows

(i) **$G_1$-phase** It is the longest phase during which cell growth takes place. (1)

(ii) **S-phase** It is the phase during which chromosomes replicates in nucleus and centrioles duplicate in cytoplasm. (1)

(iii) **$G_2$-phase** It is the phase in which synthesis of DNA gets stopped. However, formation of proteins and RNA takes place. (1)

**3. Differentiate between S-phase and $G_2$-phase.**

**Ans.** Differences between S-phase and $G_2$- phase are as follows

| S-phase | $G_2$-phase |
|---|---|
| It is called synthesis phase. | It is called pre-mitotic phase. |
| Replication of DNA occurs. | RNA of all three types and proteins are synthesised in it. |
| It lasts for 6-8 hours in a 24 hour cycle. | It lasts for 2-5 hours in a 24 hour cycle. (1 × 3) |

**4. What is $G_0$ (quiescent phase) of cell cycle?** **NCERT**

**Ans.** The $G_0$ (quiescent phase) is a resting state of the cell cycle where cells are not actively dividing but remain metabolically active. Cells can exit this phase in response to a stimuli, allowing them to re-enter the cell cycle, when necessary, contributing to tissue maintenance and repair. (2)

**5. Can there be mitosis without DNA replication in S-phase?** **NCERT**

**Ans.** Mitosis cannot occur without DNA replication in S-phase because the trigger for mitosis takes place due to the disturbance in nucleocytoplasmic ratio caused by DNA replication in S-phase. (2)

**6. Can there be DNA replication without cell division?** **Competency Based Que., NCERT**

**Ans.** Yes, DNA replication takes place during the synthetic stage of interphase in the cell cycle. It is totally independent of cell division. After $G_2$-phase a cell may or may not enter into the M-phase. (2)

**7. Distinguish cytokinesis from karyokinesis.** **NCERT**

**Ans.** The differences between cytokinesis and karyokinesis are as follows.

| Cytokinesis | Karyokinesis |
|---|---|
| It is the process of cytoplasmic division that follows karyokinesis, resulting in the separation of the cytoplasm and formation of two distinct daughter cells. | It is the process of nuclear division where nucleus divides, resulting in the separation of duplicated chromosomes into two daughter nuclei. |
| It occurs at the end of M - Phase. | It occurs during M-phase. |

(2)

**8. (i) During cell division in apical meristem, the nuclear membrane appears in which phase?**

**(ii) At which point the sister chromatids appear to be attached?**

Ans. (i) The nuclear membrane appears in telophase stage of mitosis. (1)

(ii) The point at which the sister chramatids appear to be attached is centromere. (1)

**9. Both unicellular and multicellular organisms undergo mitosis. What are the differences observed in the process between the two?** NCERT Exemplar

Ans. Cell division is the first stage of growth in living organisms whereby cells divide to form new cells.

(i) In unicellular organisms, cell division is a process of asexual reproduction. It leads to an increase in the total number of individuals. (1)

(ii) In multicellular organisms, the division of all cells, other than the reproductive cells occurs through mitosis. It is a process of cell division related to growth and is accompanied by the cellular enlargement and differentiation. (1)

**10. Analyse the events during every stage of cell cycle and notice how the following two parameters change?**

**(i) Number of chromosomes (*n*) per cell.**

**(ii) Amount of DNA content (*c*) per cell.** NCERT

Ans. (i) During the complete cell cycle, the number of chromosomes (*n*) per cell remains same. It does not show any changes if the division is of mitosis type. In case of meiosis cell division, the number of chromosomes reduced to half. (1)

(ii) The overall DNA content will remain same however it becomes doubled during the S-phase and afterwards becomes half during the dividing phase. (1)

**11. Describe the prophase and metaphase of mitosis with neat and labelled diagrams.**

Ans. Refer to text on page no. 215-216.

**12. What are kinetochores? Give their function.**

Ans. Refer to text on page no. 216.

**13. State the role of centrioles in cell division.**

Ans. Centrioles play an important role in the formation of spindle fibres during cell division. They organise the mitotic spindle and thus, help in the separation of chromosomes.

**14. Give the sequence of events occurring during anaphase of mitosis, diagrammatically.**

Ans. Refer to text on page no. 216.

**15. Comment on the statement 'telophase is reverse of prophase'.** NCERT Exemplar

Ans. In prophase, the chromatin network begins to condense and appears as long thread-like structures called chromosomes. The nucleolus disappear and nuclear membrane also breakdown in late prophase. (1)

In telophase, the chromosomes lose their identity and nuclear membrane is again formed around the daughter nuclei. Nucleolus also reappears. So, it is reverse of prophase. (1)

**16. The following events occur during the various phases of the cell cycle. Name the phase against each of the events.**

**(i) Disintegration of nuclear membrane .............. .**

**(ii) Appearance of nucleolus ................ .**

**(iii) Division of centromere ................ .**

**(iv) Replication of DNA ............... .** NCERT Exemplar

Ans. (i) prophase (ii) telophase

(iii) anaphase (iv) S-phase ($\frac{1}{2} \times 4$)

**17. Discuss with your teacher about** NCERT

**(i) haploid insects and lower plants where cell division occurs, and**

**(ii) some haploid cell in higher plants where cell division does not occur.** Competency Based Que.

Ans. (i) Haploid insects where cell division occurs is drones of honeybee and lower plants are *Spirogyra* and *Chlamydomonas*. (1)

(ii) Pollen grains and egg cells of higher plants do not undergo cell division. (1)

**18. (i) Why is mitosis also known as an equational division?**

**(ii) How can you determine whether a dividing cell is an animal cell or a plant cell?**

Ans. (i) Mitosis is the process of cell division in which the chromosomes replicate and divide equally into two daughter cells. The chromosome number in each daughter cell is equal to that in the parent cell (2*n*). Thus, the process is known as equational division. (1)

(ii) Cytokinesis is different in plant cells and animal cells. Animal cell divides by cell furrow method, while plant cell divides by cell plate method. (1)

**19. Why is mitosis called equational division?** NCERT

**Ans.** Mitosis is called an equational division because it divides the mother cell into two daughter cells, which are identical to the original mother cell in every aspect. In mitosis, the chromosomes of the mother cell are duplicated and distributed equally to the two daughter cells and daughter cells have same number of chromosome as mother cell has.

**20. While examining the mitotic stage in a tissue, one finds some cells with 16 chromosomes and some with 32 chromosomes. What possible reasons could you assign to this difference in chromosome number?** Competency Based Que.

**Ans.** The difference in chromosome number (16 *vs* 32) in mitotic cells is due to different stages of the cell cycle. Cells with 32 chromosomes are likely in the S-phase or mitotic stages like metaphase or anaphase, where DNA has replicated but sister chromatids are still attached. In contrast, cells with 16 chromosomes are likely in the $G_1$ phase or after cytokinesis, where the chromosome number is restored to the normal diploid state.

**21. How does cytokinesis in plant cells differ from that in animal cells?** NCERT

**Ans.** Refer to text on page no. 217.

**22. (i) How many divisions take place in meiosis? How many times, the chromosomes replicate during meiotic cell division?**

**(ii) How many daughter cells are produced during mitotic cell division and a meiotic cell division?**

**(iii) What is the status of chromosomes and DNA content in each daughter cell?**

**Ans.** (i) Two divisions take place in meiosis, i.e. meiosis-I and meiosis-II. During meiotic division, chromosomes replicate one time in meiosis-I. (1)

(ii) 2 daughter cells are produced in mitotic division and 4 daughter cells are produced in meiotic division. (1)

(iii) During mitosis, DNA and chromosomes remain same in daughter cells as in parent cell, while DNA and chromosome number reduces to half in meiosis in daughter cells. (1)

**23. The diagram given below represents the changes in the number of chromosomes during several processes that occur in an animal cell.** Competency Based Que.

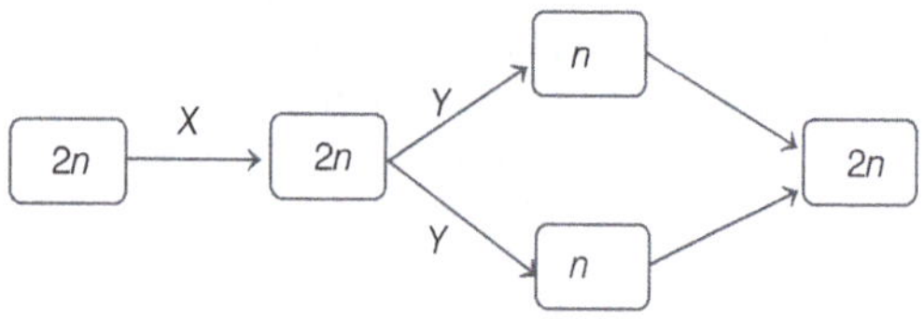


**(i) Name the process of cell division occurring at *X* and *Y*.**

**(ii) State two differences in the behaviour of chromosomes between *X* and *Y*.**

**Ans.** (i) *X*–Mitosis, *Y*–Meiosis (1)

(ii) (a) In *X*, there is no association of homologous chromosomes, but in *Y* homologous chromosomes pair up together to form bivalents during prophase-I. (1)

(b) In *X*, there is no crossing over as there is no formation of chiasmata, but in *Y*, crossing over occurs at the chiasmata whereby some genes are swapped between homologous chromosomes. (1)

**24. Complete the following sentences with suitable words.**

**(i) Chromosome condensation occurs during…… .**

**(ii) ….is marked by the alignment of chromosomes at the equatorial plate.**

**(iii) ….is the equational division in which the chromosome number of the parent is conserved in the daughter cell.**

**(iv) Each parent cell has pairs of….chromosomes, one from the father and one from the mother.**

**Ans.** (i) Prophase (ii) Metaphase

(iii) Mitosis (iv) homologous. (½ × 4)

**25. Discuss about the synaptonemal complex.**

**Ans.** It is a protein complex, visible with the electron microscope and is the physical basis of the pairing of homologous chromosomes (synapsis) during meiosis. It is assembled during zygotene stage of meiosis-I, as homologous chromosomes pair up.

**26. Differentiate pachytene and diakinesis. Also support your answer with suitable diagram.**

**Ans.** Refer to text on page no. 219 and 220 and fig. 10.10 and 10.12.

**27. Describe the following in brief.**

**(i) Leptotene**

**(ii) Zygotene**

**(iii) Diakinesis**

**(iv) Metaphase-I**

**Ans.** Refer to text on page no. 219-220.

**28. Name a cell that is found arrested in diplotene stage for months and years.**

**Ans.** The cells found arrested in diplotene stage for months and years are oocytes of vertebrates such as tailed and tailless amphibians, birds and mammals.

**29. What is chiasmata? Mention its significance also.**

**Ans.** Chiasmata is the point where homologous chromosomes exchange genetic material during meiosis, specially during prophase-I.

This occurs as a result of crossing over, where segments of DNA are swapped between non-sister chromatids. Chiasmata are crucial for genetic diversity and accurate chromosome segregation during meiosis, ensuring proper formation of gametes. (1 + 2)

**30.** **Name the stage of cell cycle at which one of the following events occur?** NCERT

(i) **Chromosomes move to spindle equator.**
(ii) **Centromere splits and chromatids separate.**
(iii) **Pairing between homologous chromosomes takes place.**
(iv) **Crossing over between homologous chromosomes takes place.**

**Ans.** (i) Metaphase
(ii) Anaphase
(iii) Zygotene stage of meiosis-I
(iv) Pachytene stage (½ × 4)

**31.** **Answer the following questions based upon the given figure.**

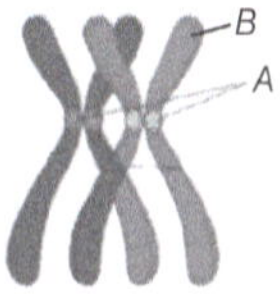


(i) **Identify the type of cell division. (Whether meiotic or/and mitotic stage).**
(ii) **What is *A* and *B*?** Competency Based Que.

**Ans.** (i) It is a meiotic division showing synapsis and it is in the zygotene stage of prophase-I of meiosis-I. (1)
(ii) *A*–Centromere, *B*–Chromatid. (1)

**32.** **Write brief note on the following.**

(i) **Synaptonemal complex**
(ii) **Metaphase plate**

**Ans.** (i) **Synaptonemal complex** It is formed, when homologous chromosome becomes closely associated. The process of pairing is known as synapsis. (1)
(ii) **Metaphase plate** The bivalent arrange themselves on the equator in one equatorial plate, known as metaphase plate. (1)

**33.** **List the differences between metaphase of mitosis and metaphase-I of meiosis.**

**Ans.** Differences between metaphase of mitosis and metaphase-I of meiosis are

| Mitotic Metaphase | Meiotic Metaphase-I |
|---|---|
| The chromosomes in metaphase are arranged in such a way that the centromeres lie at the metaphase plate and the arms of chromosomes are free. | The chromosomes at the metaphase (meiosis-I) are arranged in such a way that the centromeres of homologous chromosomes lie on either side of the metaphase plate, pointing towards the opposite poles. (1) |
| A chromosome is connected to both the spindle poles due to the presence of two tractile fibrils. | In metaphase-I, a chromosome is connected to only one spindle pole of its side due to the presence of a single tractile fibril. (1) |

**34.** (i) **Name the stages and type of cell division represented in *A* and *B*, respectively.**

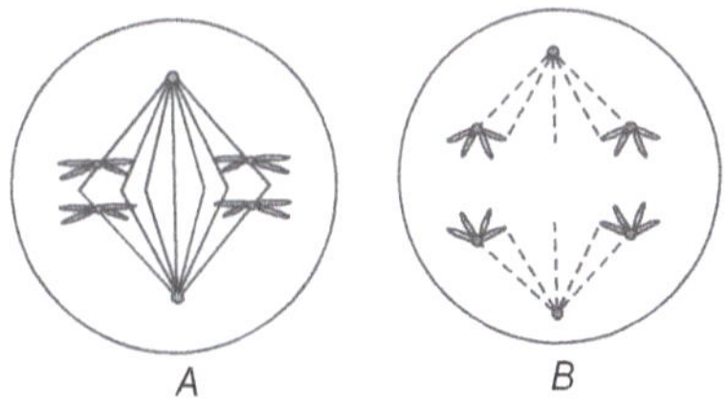


(ii) **Also explain any one of them.**

**Ans.** (i) Stages and type of cell division are
(*A*) Metaphase-I and meiosis (B) Anaphase-I and meiosis (1)
(ii) **For metaphase-I** and **anaphase-I** refer to text on page no. 220. (1)

**35.** **Distinguish between anaphase of mitosis and anaphase-I of meiosis.** NCERT

**Ans.** Differences between anaphase of mitosis and anaphase-I of meiosis are

| Anaphase of Mitosis | Anaphase-I of Meiosis |
|---|---|
| Each chromosome arranged at the metaphase plate, splits simultaneously and the two daughter chromatids migrate towards the two opposite poles. | The spindle fibres contract and pull the centromeres of homologous chromosomes towards the opposite poles. So, each chromosome goes to opposite pole. |
| The centromere of each chromosome is towards the pole with arms of chromosome trailing behind. | The centromere is not divided, so half set of the chromosomes of parent nucleus go to one pole and the remaining half set in the opposite pole. |

(1 × 3)

**36.** **The second meiotic division is similar to mitosis as it results in the separation of the sister chromatids. However, it also differs from mitosis. Explain how?** Competency Based Que.

**Ans.** The main reason for the difference between the two is that the separating sister chromatids during the meiosis-II differ genetically due to crossing over that had occurred during prophase-I.

**37.** **Draw a neat and labelled diagram of the following.**

(i) **Metaphase-I** (ii) **Prophase-II**
(iii) **Telophase-II**

**Ans.** Refer to fig. no. 10.13 and 10.14 on page no. 220 and 221.

**38.** **In which phase of meiosis are the following formed? Choose the answer from hint points given below.** NCERT Exemplar

(i) **Synaptonemal complex....**
(ii) **Recombination nodules....**

(iii) Appearance/activation of enzyme recombinase...
(iv) Termination of chiasmata....
(v) Interkinesis
(vi) Formation of dyad of cells....

**Ans.** (i) Synaptonemal complex–Zygotene.
(ii) Recombination nodules–Pachytene.
(iii) Appearance/activation of enzyme recombinase–Pachytene.
(iv) Termination of chiasmata–Diakinesis.
(v) Interkinesis–After telophase-I/before meiosis-II.
(vi) Formation of dyad of cells–Telophase-I. (½ × 6)

**39. Label the following structures of plant cell labelled as *A-E* in the diagram.**

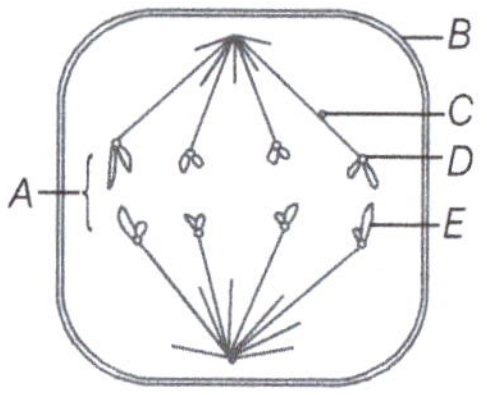


**Ans.** *A* – Chromosomes *B* – Cell wall
*C* – Spindle fibres *D* – Centromere
*E* – Chromatid (½ × 6)

**40. What is the significance of meiosis?** **NCERT**

**Ans.** Meiosis is the mechanism by which conservation of specific chromosome number of each species is achieved across generations in sexually reproducing organisms.

It also increases the genetic variability in the population of sexually reproducing organisms from one generation to the next. Variations are very important for the process of evolution.

**41. List the main differences between mitosis and meiosis.**

**Ans.** Refer to text on page no. 221. **NCERT**

**42. How meiosis leads to variation in the daughter cells genetically?**

**Ans.** Meiosis occurs in the germ cells of the sexually reproducing organisms. This process is responsible for reducing the ploidy level of gametes from diploid to haploid.

During the pachytene stage of meiosis-I, exchange of genetic material takes place between the non-sister chromatids. This further leads to recombination of genetic material thereby leading to variations.

**43. Meiosis is advantageous than mitosis as it produces variations. So it plays important role in evolution. What are the stages during which chances of recombination of genes are increased during meiosis? Explain these events.**

**Ans.** Stages during which recombination of genes occurs in meiosis are

(i) Crossing over between the non-sister chromatids of homologous chromosomes. It occurs at recombination nodules during pachytene stage of prophase-I of meiosis-I and is regulated by recombinase enzyme. (1)
(ii) Arrangement of bivalents at the equator of the spindle during metaphase-I of meiosis. (1)

## Long Answer Type Questions

**1. What is cell cycle? Explain cell cycle and interphase in detail.**

**Ans.** Refer to text on page no. 213- 214.

**2. Briefly describe the significance of cell division.**

**Ans.** Cell division is significant in the following ways

(i) **Cell Multiplication** Cell division is a means of cell multiplication or formation of new cells from pre-existing cells. (1)
(ii) **Continuity** It maintains continuity of living matter generation after generation. (1)
(iii) **Multicellular Organisms** The body of a multicellular organism is formed of innumerable cells. They are formed by repeated divisions of a single cell or zygote. As the number of cells increases, many of them begin to differentiate to form tissues and organisms. (1)
(iv) **Cell Size** Cell division helps in maintenance of a particular cell size which is essential for efficiency and control of cell activities. (1)
(v) **Genetic Similarity** The common type of cell division or mitosis maintains genetic similarity of all the cells in an individual. (1)

**3. Describe the process of mitosis and give a short account of its various stages.**

**Ans.** Refer to text on page no. 215-216.

**4. Describe briefly the phases prophase -I of meiotic cell division.**

**Ans.** Refer to text on page no. 219-220.

**5. Why does a multicellular organism require two types of cell division? Which of the two produces the greater number of cells? Describe prophase-I stage.**

**Ans.** A multicellular organism requires two types of cell division, i.e. mitosis for growth, while meiosis for reproduction. (1)

Meiosis produces greater number of cells, i.e. 4 daughter cells per division. (1)

Refer to text on page no. 219-220. (3)

**6. What are homologous chromosomes? What happens to homologous chromosomes during meiosis?**

**Ans.** Homologous chromosomes are pairs of chromosomes that have the same structure and size and carry genes for the same traits at corresponding positions, known as loci. One chromosome in the pair is inherited from the mother (maternal) and the other from the father (paternal).

During meiosis, homologous chromosomes go through the following key steps:

- Homologous chromosomes pair up (synapsis) and exchange genetic material (crossing over) during prophase I.
- They align randomly at the cell's equator during Metaphase-I and are pulled to opposite poles during Anaphase-I.

**7. Describe the following words.**

**(i) Synapsis** **(ii) Bivalent**

**(iii) Chiasmata**

**Draw a diagram to illustrate your answer.** **NCERT**

**Ans.** (i) **Synapsis** During meiosis-I, the process of pairing of two homologous chromosomes is known as synapsis. (1)

(ii) **Bivalent** The complex formed by a pair of synapsed homologous chromosomes is called a bivalent or a tetrad. It consists of four chromatids. (1)

(iii) **Chiasmata** The chiasmata formation is the indication of completion of crossing over and beginning of separation of homologous chromosomes. The chiasmata is formed, when the chromosomal parts begin to repel each other except in the region where these are in contact. Thus, chiasmata formation is necessary for the separation of homologous chromosomes. (1)

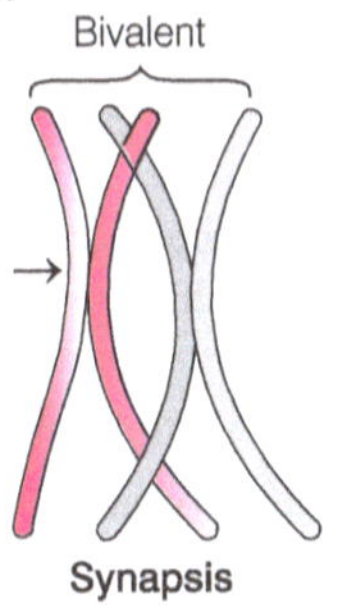


Bivalent and synapsis

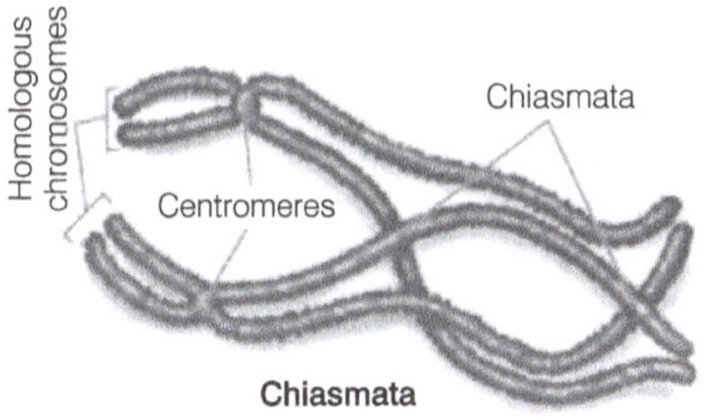


(2)

**8. Explain why a pair of homologous chromosomes is genetically different, but a pair of sister chromatids is genetically identical before crossing over in meiosis.**

**Ans.** A pair of homologous chromosomes is genetically different because in a set of homologous chromosomes, one of the chromosome belongs to the male parent and the other comes from the female parent.

Therefore, one out of a pair will contain paternal genes and the other will contain maternal genes. (2½)

However, a pair of sister chromatids is genetically identical before crossing over as the chromatids are formed from the replication of DNA during the 'S'-phase of interphase. DNA replication ensures that the DNA content is doubled with identical genes being copied from the original DNA. Therefore, there is no genetic variation because there is no exchange of genetic material between sister chromatids. (2½)

If crossing over occurs, then it would be possible for some genes to be exchanged between the chromatids of homologous chromosomes that have chiasmata, thus leading to genetic variation.

**9. Explain meiosis-II in an animal cell.**

**Ans.** Following events take place in the two haploid nuclei simultaneously.

(i) **Prophase-II** Takes short time as compared to prophase-I, spindle formation begins and the chromosomes become short. Two chromatids are joined to a single centromere. Nuclear membrane and nucleolus disintegrate. (1)

(ii) **Metaphase-II** The chromosomes align at the equator and spindle is formed. The centromere of every chromosome is joined to the spindle fibre. (1)

(iii) **Anaphase-II** The centromere divide and daughter chromosomes are formed. Chromatids move towards their poles with the spindle fibres. (1)

(iv) **Telophase-II** Chromosomes reach the poles of the cell. Again nuclear membrane is constructed. Nucleolus now becomes clearly visible. (1)

**Cytokinesis** It result in formation of four haploid ($n$) daughter cells. (1)

## Source Based/Case Based/Passage Based Questions

**1. The figure given below depicts 'X' stage of mitosis.**

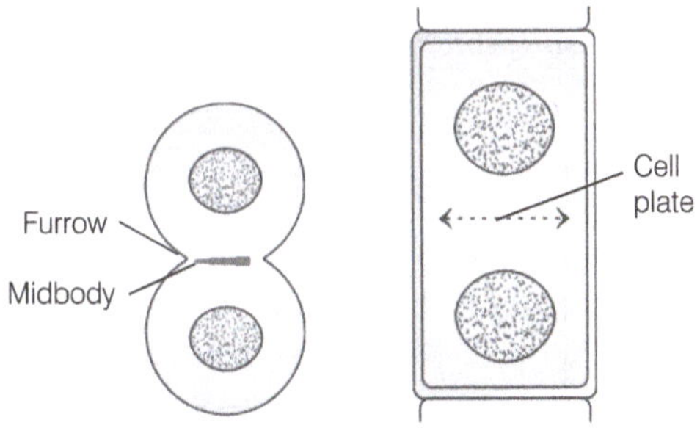


**Answer the questions given below.**

**(i) Identify 'X'.**

**(ii) State the stage of mitosis at which the 'X' begins in the plant cells.**

**(iii) Can a cell undergo 'X' before it has divided its nuclear content?**

**(iv) In which type of cell, karyokinesis is not followed by 'X'?**

**Ans.** (i) The 'X' represents cytokinesis stage of mitosis cell division. (1)

(ii) In plant cells, cytokinesis starts at telophase cells typically divide by cell plate formation. (1)

(iii) No, cytokinesis occurs after karyokinesis, i.e. after the parent cell has doubled up its nuclear content for its distribution into daughter cells. (1)

(iv) In a syncytium (multiple nucleus in a cell), karyokinesis is not followed by cytokinesis. (1)

**2. The graph below shows the two cycles of mitotic cell division. Read it carefully and answer the questions given below.** **Competency Based Que.**

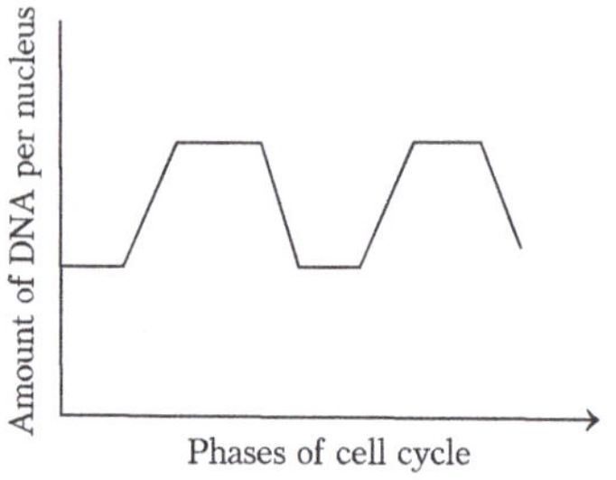


**(i) Label $G_1$, $G_2$ and S-phase on this graph.**

**(ii) At which phase of mitosis DNA is most difficult to visualise?**

**(iii) If you started with one cell at the beginning (left) how much total DNA would you have at the end of each phases?**

*Or*

**(iii) Consider a somatic cell having 38 chromosomes fill in the table below.**

| Per Cell | $G_1$-Phase | $G_2$-Phase |
|---|---|---|
| No. of chromosomes | | |
| No. of sister chromatids | | |

**Ans.** (i)

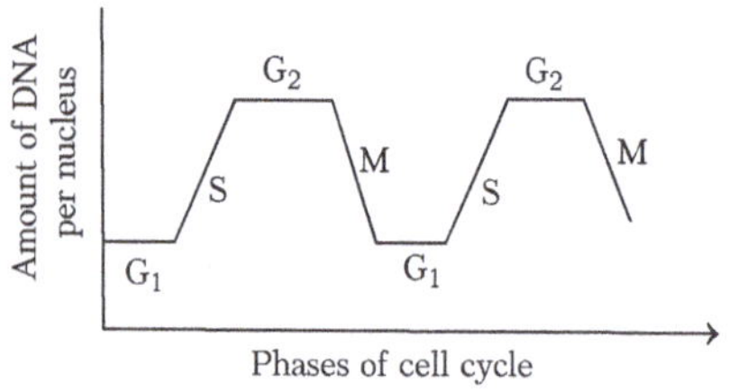


(1)

(ii) DNA is most difficult to visualise at prophase stage of mitosis. (1)

(iii) Consider the amount of DNA $= x$

| Phase | DNA Content |
|---|---|
| $G_1$ | $x$ |
| S | $2x$ |
| $G_2$ | $2x$ |
| M-phase or mitotic phase | $x$ |

($\frac{1}{2} \times 4$)

*Or*

| Per Cell | $G_1$-Phase | $G_2$-Phase |
|---|---|---|
| No of chromosomes | 38 | 38 |
| No. of sister chromatids | 38 | 76 |

(2)

**3. Consider the given graph, showing a type of division at a point X. Observe the graph carefully and answer the questions that follows.** **Competency Based Que.**

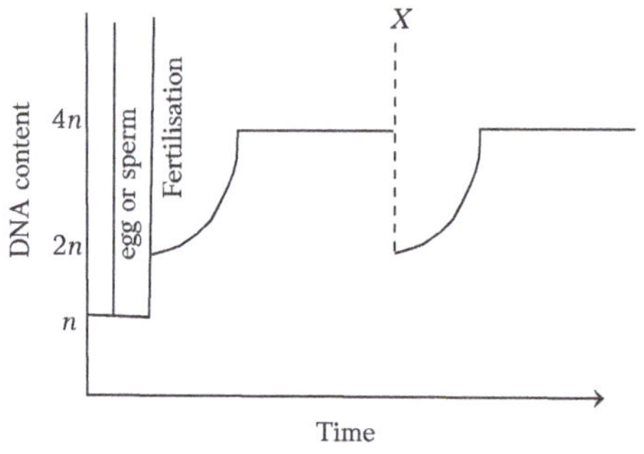


**(i) On the basis of the above graph, what conclusion do you draw about the chromosome numbers in daughter cells ?**

**(ii) What would happen if the division X does not happen ?**

**(iii) Give some real-life advantages of the cell division X.**

*Or*

**(iii) How does the role of the above division in gamete production differ between organisms with diploid dominant life cycle?**

**Ans.** (i) By the end of meiosis the resulting reproductive cells or gametes have '$n$' chromosomes. The overall process of meiosis produce four daughter cells from single parent. Each daughter cell is haploid as it has half the number of chromosomes to the original parent cell. (1)

(ii) If meiotic division does not take place, the number of chromosomes will not remain constant in a species across generations and will be duplicated everytime after sexual reproduction. (1)

(iii) Refer to the text on page no. 221. (2)

*Or* (iii) The above shown division is meiosis. In the organisms showing diploid dominant life cycle, the germ cells, undergo meiosis to produce haploid gametes. After fertilisation, they restore the diploid state. (2)

# SELF ASSESSMENT TEST

## Multiple Choice Questions

1. In which of the following phase the amount of DNA present in a cell doubles its initial amount?

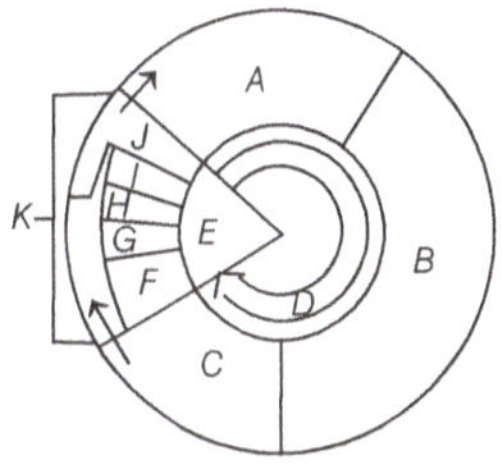


(a) *K*
(b) *A*
(c) *H*
(d) *B*

2. Choose the correct option with respect to cytokinesis in plant cell.

I. Cell plate formation II. Furrow formation III. Centripetal IV. Centrifugal

(a) I and III (b) I and IV (c) II and III (d) II and IV

3. During which phase(s) of the cell cycle does the amount of DNA in a cell remain at the 4C level, assuming the initial amount is denoted as 2C?

I. $G_1$-phase II. S-phase III. $G_2$-phase IV. M-phase

Choose the correct answer.

(a) I and II (b) I and III (c) II and III (d) III and IV

4. Choose the incorrect match pair.

(a) Leptotene – Formation of synapsis
(b) Zygotene – Formation of tetrad
(c) Pachytene – Appearance of recombination nodule
(d) Diplotene – Formation of chiasmata

5. Choose the correct option with respect to the diagram given below.

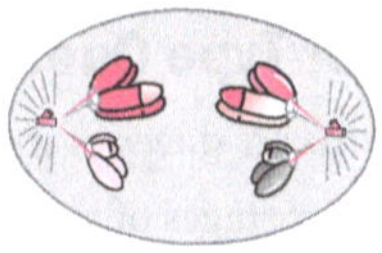

(a) The given image represents anaphase of mitosis.
(b) The given image represents anaphase of meiosis-I.
(c) The given image represents anaphase of meiosis-II.
(d) The given image represents telophase of mitosis.

6. How many of the following terms given in box are associated with zygotene stage of meiosis-I.

Synapsis, Homologous chromosomes, Tetrad, Chiasmata, Bivalent, Crossing over, Recombinase.

(a) Four
(b) Five
(c) Six
(d) Seven

7. Which of the following features is not associated with anaphase during cell division?

I. Separation of sister chromatids
II. Movement of chromosomes toward opposite poles
III. Replication of DNA
IV. Shortening of spindle fibres

Choose the correct option.

(a) II and IV
(b) Only III
(c) I and IV
(d) II and III

## Assertion-Reason Questions

**Direction** (Q. Nos. 8-11) *In each of the following questions, a statement of Assertion (A) is given followed by corresponding statement of Reason (R). Of the statements, mark the correct answer*

(a) Both A and R are true and R is the correct explanation of A.
(b) Both A and R are true, but R is not the correct explanation of A.
(c) A is true, but R is false.
(d) A is false, but R is true.

8. **Assertion** (A) Meiotic division occur in reproductive cells.

**Reason** (R) Meiosis produce haploid gametes, ensuring genetic variation and the maintenance of the species chromosome number during sexual reproduction.

9. **Assertion** (A) Cells remain metabolically active during the $G_1$-phase of the cell cycle.

**Reason** (R) The $G_1$-phase of the cell cycle is primarily focused on cell growth and DNA replication.

10. **Assertion** (A) In animal cells, cytokinesis is achieved by the appearance of a furrow in plasma membrane.

**Reason** (R) The cleavage furrow forms due to the presence of a rigid cell wall that pushes the membrane inward.

11. **Assertion** (A) Crossing over occurs during meiosis-I.

**Reason** (R) Crossing over facilitates the exchange of genetic material between homologous chromosomes, increasing genetic variation.

## Very Short Answer Type Questions

12. Where does mitosis takes place in plant and animal cell?
13. During which phase of the cell cycle does DNA synthesis occur?
14. What process involves the pairing of homologous chromosomes during cell division?
15. At which phase of the cell cycle does the nuclear membrane breakdown?

## Short Answer Type Questions

16. Differentiate between anaphase of meiosis-I and meiosis-II.
17. Define crossing over and state its significance.
18. Differentiate between chromatin and chromatid.

## Long Answer Type Questions

19. Give an account on stages of mitosis. Why is it called equational division?
20. Explain different stages of prophase-I with diagrams.
21. Write a brief note on

(a) Metaphase plate (b) Recombinase (c) Chiasmata

## Case Based Question

22. Observe the figure given below which represents a certain event at a particular stage of cell division. Answer the following questions.

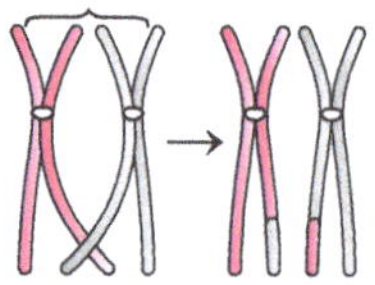


(i) Identify the event represented by the figure.

(ii) This event is the characteristic of which stage and type of cell division?

(iii) State the advantage of this process in sexually reproducing organisms.

(iv) At which stage (*A* or *B*) these chromosomes are called bivalents?

# Answers

| | | | | | | | |
|---|---|---|---|---|---|---|---|
| 1. (d) | 2. (b) | 3. (c) | 4. (a) | 5. (b) | 6. (a) | 7. (b) | 8. (a) |
| 9. (c) | 10. (c) | 11. (b) | | | | | |

# 11

CHAPTER

# Photosynthesis in Higher Plants

All animals including human beings depend on plants for their requirement of food. Green plants can synthesise their own food by the process called **photosynthesis.** Photosynthesis (*Photos*-light, *synthesis*-putting together) is an enzyme regulated anabolic process for the manufacture of organic compounds. It occurs inside a **chlorophyll** containing cells using carbon dioxide and water with sunlight as a source of energy.

**YOUR STUDY GOALS**



**YOUR PRACTICE GOAL**

- Objective Type Questions (40 Qs ; MCQs, A-R) Case Based Questions (3)
- Subjective Type Questions
- (25 VSAs, 48 SAs, 5 LAs)

This chapter focuses on the structure of photosynthetic machinery and the various reactions that transform light energy into chemical energy.

## 11.1 Introduction to Photosynthesis

- The energy required by all living organisms comes directly or indirectly from the sunlight.
- Sunlight plays an important role in the fixation of $CO_2$ through which conversion of solar energy into chemical energy takes place.
- Water also plays a significant role during this process.
- Hence, photosynthesis is the only process by which all green plants, some bacteria and some protists (*Euglena*) manufacture their organic food (sugar) from inorganic raw materials with the help of solar energy.
- The sugar produced through photosynthesis liberate ATP *via* cellular respiration the fuel used by all living organisms.
- Photosynthesis is an important phenomenon due to the following two reasons
  - It is the primary source of all food on the earth.
  - It is also responsible for the release of oxygen into the atmosphere by green plants.

## 11.2 Early Experiments

- Study of photosynthesis started about hundreds of years ago.
- Prior to that, researchers used to believe that plants get all of their nourishment from soil only by the means of roots.
- Thus, several simple experiments led to the development of understanding of the process involved.
- Some early experiments performed by different scholars proved the following facts regarding photosynthesis.

### Joseph Priestley

- **Joseph Priestley** (1733-1804) performed a series of experiments in 1770s that revealed about the **essentiality of air** in the growth of green plants.
- He observed that a burning candle or a respiring mouse in a closed space, (i.e. bell jar) soon gets extinguished and died due to suffocation, respectively.
- He concluded that a burning candle or an animal that breathe the air both somehow, damage the air.
- But when he placed a mint plant in the same bell jar along with the burning candle and mouse, he observed that the mouse stayed alive and also the candle continued to burn for a longer time.

Fig. 11.1 Priestley's experiment; (a), (b) Mouse dies in foul air and (c), (d) Mouse survives in air purified by mint plant

- **Conclusion** He hypothesised that the foul air produced by the burning of candle and the breathing of mouse could be restored into pure air by plant (mint plant in this case).

### Jan Ingenhousz

- In this experiment with an aquatic plant, **Jan Ingenhousz** (1730-1799) showed that in bright sunlight, formation of small bubbles takes place around the green parts, while in the dark, formation of those bubbles did not take place.
- **Conclusion** He concluded that the bubbles he observed were of oxygen and showed that only green parts of plants could release oxygen.

### Julius Von Sachs

- **Julius von Sachs** with his experiments in 1854 provided evidence that glucose is produced when plants grow, which is usually stored as starch.
- He later showed that a green substance, i.e. chlorophyll is found to be located in special bodies called **chloroplast** in plant cells.
- **Conclusion** He came to the conclusion that green parts are the sites in the plants where **production of glucose** takes place and the same gets converted in the form of starch for storage.

### TW Engelmann

- **TW Engelmann** (1843-1909) performed an interesting experiment with green alga, *Cladophora*.
- He splitted light into its **spectral components** by using prism and then illuminated the alga placed in a suspension of aerobic bacteria.
- He noticed that the accumulation of bacteria was mainly in the region of the blue and red light of the split spectrum.

#### Conclusion

- Through his work, the first action spectrum of photosynthesis was described, which roughly resembles the **absorption spectra** of chlorophyll-*a* and *b*. The key features of the process of photosynthesis were known by the middle of the nineteenth century, which detailed that plants utilise light energy harvested from sunlight for the formation of carbohydrates (food) from $CO_2$ and water.
- The empirical equation, represents the total process of photosynthesis for organisms that evolves oxygen is understood as

$$nCO_2 + nH_2O \xrightarrow{\text{Light}} [CH_2O]_n + O_2$$

$[CH_2O]_n$ is a carbohydrate here, like glucose (six carbon sugar).

### Cornelius van Neil

- **Cornelius van Neil** (1897-1985) was a microbiologist, who made a significant contribution on the basis of his studies of **purple** and **green** sulphur bacteria (photosynthetic bacteria) in understanding the photosynthesis.

- He demonstrated that during the process of photosynthesis, the hydrogen from a suitable oxidisable compound reduces carbon dioxide to carbohydrates in the presence of sunlight.
- This can be expressed by

$$2H_2A + CO_2 \xrightarrow{\text{Light}} 2A + CH_2O + H_2O$$

- With the help of this, he concluded that photosynthesis is a **light dependent** phenomenon.
- Further, he states that in **photosynthetic bacteria** $H_2S$ acts as a **hydrogen donor,** which gets oxidised to sulphur or sulphate depending on the organism. So, this bacterium does not evolve $O_2$ during the process of photosynthesis.
- While in case of green plants, $H_2O$ acts as a hydrogen donor, which evolves $O_2$ as a product.
- Thus, he inferred that $O_2$, which is evolved by the green plants comes from the water ($H_2O$) not from the $CO_2$ (later proved by the use of radioisotopic techniques).
- Thus, the overall reaction of photosynthesis is represented as

$$6CO_2 + 12H_2O \xrightarrow{\text{Light}} C_6H_{12}O_6 + 6H_2O + 6O_2$$

**Conclusion** He concluded that the light is necessary to oxidise the photosynthetic substrate ($H_2S$ in photosynthetic bacteria and $H_2O$ in green plants) and release byproducts sulphur and $O_2$ in bacteria and green plants, respectively.

- In the absence of sunlight, this process does not occur.

## Quick Test 1

1. In Priestley's experiment, which factor was essential for keeping a flame burning in a closed container?
2. Julius von Sachs found *X* part of the plant to be responsible for starch production during photosynthesis. Name *X*.
3. Mention the part of the light spectrum that Engelmann found to be most effective for photosynthesis.
4. In Engelmann's experiment, the presence of which type of bacteria near the algae indicated high photosynthetic activity?
5. Name the compound that split during photosynthesis in purple sulphur bacteria as suggested by van Neil.

## 11.3 Chloroplast : The Site of Photosynthesis

- These are the green plastids that function as the site of photosynthesis in eukaryotic organisms, i.e. help in the synthesis of organic food.
- The process of photosynthesis takes place in the green leaves of the plants, but it also occurs in other green parts of plants.
- As chloroplasts are abundantly present in the mesophyll cell of the leaves they are placed along the walls of mesophyll cells, for easy diffusion of gases and receiving optimum quantity of incident light.

**TEACHER'S TIP**

Chloroplasts align themselves with their flat surfaces parallel to the walls of the mesophyll cells under optimum light intensities and they would be perpendicular to the walls of the mesophyll cells when the intensity goes very high, just to prevent photo-oxidation of chlorophyll-*a*.

- Chloroplast is a double membrane bound, DNA and ribosome containing semi-autonomous cell organelle.
- Within the chloroplast there is a membranous system consisting of **grana**, the **stroma lamellae** and the **matrix stroma.**
- The fluid stroma contains DNA, RNA, ribosomes, enzymes for $CO_2$ assimilation.
- At some places, the thylakoid gets aggregated to form stacks of discs, called **grana.**
- A grana may have 20-50 thylakoids discs.

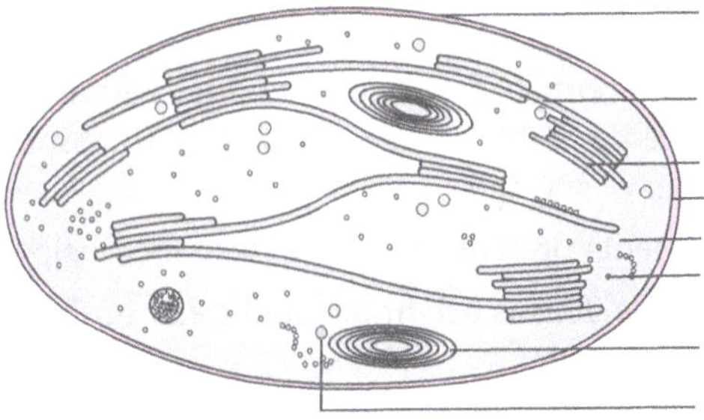


Fig. 11.2 Diagrammatic representation of an electron micrograph of a section of chloroplast

- There is a clear **division of labour** occurs within the chloroplasts, i.e. the membrane system is responsible for trapping of solar energy and for the synthesis of ATP and NADPH.

- Whereas the stroma has enzymes, which are responsible for the reduction of carbon dioxide into carbohydrates and formation of sugars.
- These sugars in turn form starch.
- As the former set of reactions is dependent on light so they are called **light reactions** (photochemical reactions).
- While the latter is dependent on the products of light reactions, i.e. ATP and NADPH (and independent from direct sunlight), thus are called **dark reactions** (carbon reactions). However, it never means that they occur in darkness.

## 11. 4 Pigments Involved in Photosynthesis

- The pigments are substances which have an ability to absorb light of specific wavelength.
- The pigments involved in the process of photosynthesis are called **photosynthetic pigments**.
- These pigments provide different shades of green in the leaves in different plants or in the leaves of same plant.
- On the basis of their significance, the photosynthetic pigments are of two types
  - **Primary Pigments** The pigment forms the main molecule of photosystem, e.g. chlorophyll- *a*, *b*.
  - **Accessory Pigments** These support the function of primary pigments, e.g. xanthophylls and carotenoids.
- A chromatographic separation of the leaf pigments shows that it is not only the single pigment, which is responsible for the colour in the leaves.
- Instead, the different shades in leaf are due to four different pigments that have different ability to absorb light at specific wavelength.
- Different pigments present in leaf are described below
  - **Chlorophyll-*a*** This is bright or blue-green in the chromatogram.
  - **Chlorophyll-*b*** This is yellow-green in colour.
  - **Xanthophylls** This is yellow in colour.
  - **Carotenoids** This is yellow to yellow-orange in colour.

Chlorophyll is the most abundant plant pigment found in the world. It contains magnesium ($Mg^{2+}$) metal as its constituent.

### Absorption Spectrum

- It is the curve that shows the amount of energy of different wavelength of lights absorbed by a substance (photosynthetic pigment).
- The graph given below shows the ability of different pigments to absorb lights of different wavelengths.

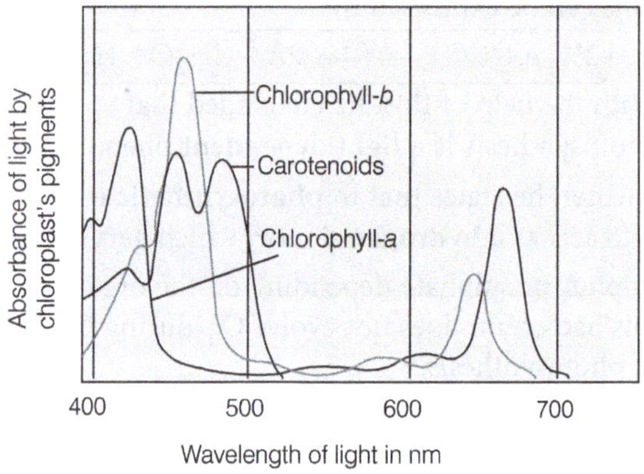


Fig. 11.3 Graph showing the absorption spectrum of chlorophyll-*a*, *b* and the carotenoids

- Chlorophyll-*a* shows the maximum absorption peak at 450 nm and also shows another peak at 650 nm.
- The absorption spectrum is composed of pigments that absorbs light in the violet (400-450 nm), blue (450-495 nm) and red (600-700 nm) ranges.

### Action Spectrum

- The curve that depicts the relative rates of photosynthesis at different wavelengths of light is called the **action spectrum**.
- The graph given below, shows that the maximum photosynthesis occurs at blue and red wavelength in a plant (the wavelengths at which there is maximum absorption shown by chlorophyll-*a*).

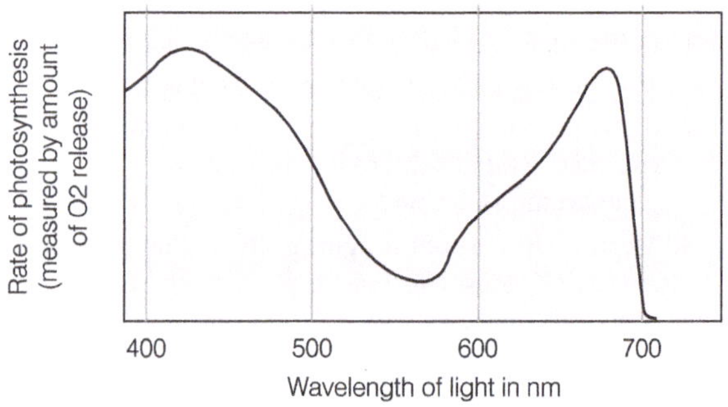


Fig. 11.4 Graph showing action specturm of photosynthesis

- Hence, this concludes that chlorophyll-*a* is the chief pigment, which is majorly responsible for the process of photosynthesis.
- Another graph given below shows the action spectrum of photosynthesis, which coincide closely to the absorption spectrum of chlorophyll-'a'.

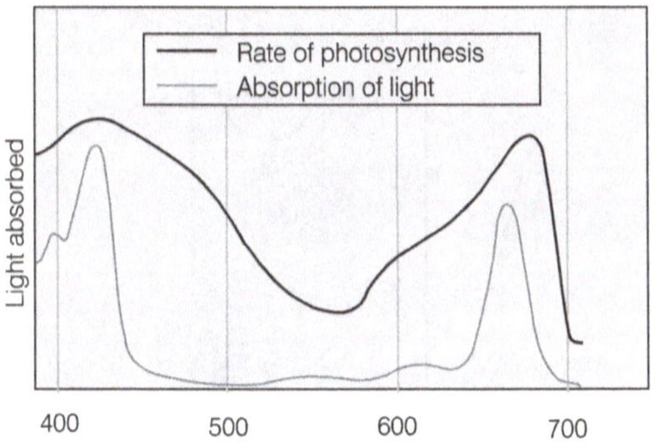


Fig. 11.5 Graph showing action spectrum of photosynthesis superimposed on absorption spectrum of chlorophyll-*a*

- Hence, all three graphs together show that the major part of the photosynthesis takes place in the blue and red regions, while some of the photosynthesis takes place at other wavelengths of the visible spectrum.
- Apart from chlorophyll-*a* (the major pigment) which is mainly responsible for trapping of light, other thylakoid pigments such as chlorophyll-*b*, xanthophylls and carotenoids also absorb light, transferring energy to chlorophyll-*a*.
- These pigments enable a wider range of wavelength of incoming light to be utilised for photosynthesis and also provide protection to chlorophyll-*a* from photo-oxidation.

### Quick Test 2

1. Name any two pigments that form the main molecule of photosystem.
2. A pigment *X* appears yellow to yellow-orange in the chromatogram. Identify *X*.
3. A pigment shows maximum absorption peaks at the 450 nm and 650 nm. Identify this pigment.
4. Which light wavelength, as per the action spectrum, shows minimal photosynthetic activity?
5. Apart from the chlorophyll-*a*, name the pigment that is responsible for absorption of light.

## 11. 5 Mechanism of Photosynthesis

The process of photosynthesis takes place in following two steps

### Light Reaction (The Photochemical Phase)

- It includes the following steps, i.e. absorption of light, splitting of water, release of oxygen and finally the formation of high energy chemical intermediates, i.e. ATP and NADPH.
- During the course of light reaction, light is trapped by photosynthetic pigments present in the thylakoids.

### Photosystems

- The photosynthetic pigments are organised into two discrete photochemical **Light Harvesting Complexes** (LHCs) within the **Photosystem-I** (PS-I) and **Photosystem-II** (PS-II).
- The light harvesting complexes or are made up of hundreds of pigment molecules bounded by proteins.
- Each photosystem has a photocentre or reaction centre, where actual reaction takes place.
- This reaction centre contains a special chlorophyll-*a* molecule.

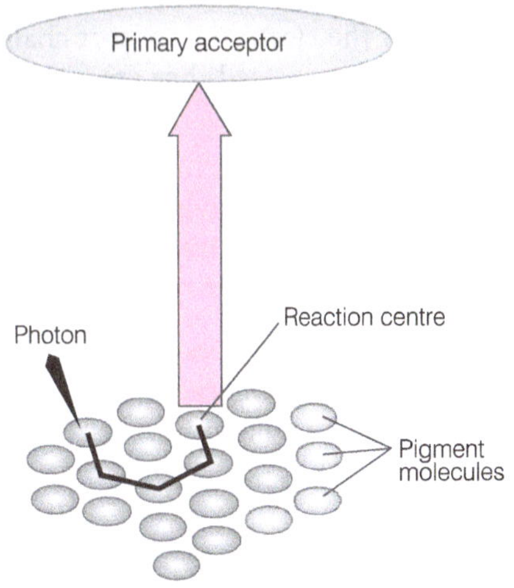


Fig. 11.6 The light harvesting complex

- Each photosystem consist of hundred other pigment (except chlorophyll-*a*) molecules and it forms the light harvesting system called **antennae**.

These antennae molecule absorb light of different wavelength, to make photosynthesis more efficient.

- The reaction centre is different in both the photosystems as given below
  - In PS-I, the reaction centre or chlorophyll-*a* has peak of absorption at 700 nm, known as **P700**.
  - In PS-II, the reaction centre has absorption peak at 680 nm, hence called **P680**.

These photosystems are named according to the sequence of their discoveries and not in the sequence in which they function during the light reaction.

## The Electron Transport

- The photosynthetic electron transport chain initiates with the absorption of light energy by the photosystem-II.
- The light of wavelength 680 nm is absorbed by the reaction centre of photosystem-II, which causes the electrons to becomes excited and jump into an orbit away from the atomic nucleus.
- These electrons are then picked up by an **electron acceptor**, which passes them further to an **electron transport system consisting of cytochromes**.
- This movement of electrons is **downhill** according to the **redox potential scale** (oxidation-reduction scale).
- The electrons of the electron transport chain are not used up in the chain instead they are further passed on to the pigments of PS-I.
- Simultaneously the electrons in the reaction centre of PS-I also get excited on receiving red light of wavelength 700 nm and get transferred to the another electron acceptor with higher redox potential.
- But this time the electron does not move to a reaction centre or chlorophyll-*a*. Instead, it moves to a molecule that is rich in energy, i.e. $NADP^+$.
- On addition of these electrons the $NADP^+$ gets reduced to $NADPH + H^+$.
- This whole scheme of electron transfer initiating from PS-II, uphill to the acceptor molecule, down the electron transport chain to PS-I, excitation of electrons and then their transfer to another acceptor and finally downhill to $NADP^+$ in order to get reduced to NADPH and $H^+$ is called **Z-scheme** due to its characteristic shape.
- This shape is formed when all the carriers are placed in a sequence on a redox potential scale.

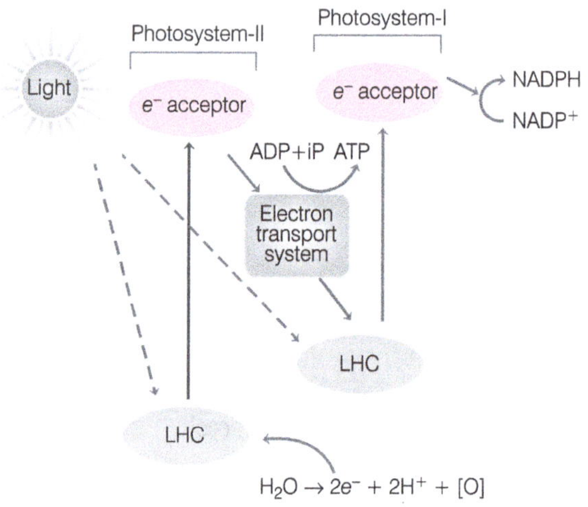


**Fig. 11.7** Z-scheme of light reaction

## Splitting of Water

- It is a crucial process in photosynthesis that occurs during the light-dependent reactions.
- The electrons that were removed from photosystem-II must be replaced.
- To ensure a continuous supply of electrons, water molecules are split into oxygen, protons, and electrons.
- The complex of water splitting is associated with the photosystem-II that is located on the inner side of the thylakoid membrane.

$$2H_2O \rightarrow 4H^+ + O_2\uparrow + 4e^-$$

- While the electrons of photosystem-I are provided by photosystem-II.

**TEACHER'S TIP**
All the electrons formed are replaced and protons get accumulated in the lumen of the thylakoid and the oxygen is evolved into the atmosphere.

## Photophosphorylation

- Phosphorylation is the process through which, ATP is synthesised from ADP and inorganic phosphate (Pi) by the cell organelles (like mitochondria and chloroplasts).

- When this process occurs in the presence of sunlight in chloroplast, it is called photophosphorylation.
- The process of photophosphorylation is of two types, these are as follows

## 1. Non-cyclic Photophosphorylation

- In this a type of photophosphorylation, both the photosystems (PS-I and PS-II) cooperate in light driven synthesis of ATP.
- During this cycle, the electron released from the PS-II does not return back to it, hence it is known as non-cyclic photophosphorylation.
- Both NADPH and ATP are formed during this reaction.

## 2. Cyclic Photophosphorylation

- It is the type of photophosphorylation in which only PS-I takes part.
- It occur only when light of wavelengths beyond 680 nm are available for excitation.
- During this cycle the electron released from the reaction centre PS-I returns back to it after passing through a series of carrier, i.e. circulation takes within the photosystem and the phosphorylation occurs due to cyclic flow of electrons.

When non-cyclic form of photophosphorylation gets stopped under certain conditions, the cyclic photophosphorylation keeps operating and photosynthesis continues for sometime.

- The cyclic photophosphorylation takes place in the **stromal lamellae** of the chloroplast under the condition of low light intensities.
- This happens because the stroma lamellae does not possess enzyme NADP reductase (essential for reducing $NADP^+$ to NADPH) and PS-II.
- Thus, the excited electrons in the cyclic photophosphorylation does not pass on to $NADP^+$ instead it gets cycled back to the PS-I complex through electron transport chain.
- Hence, in this type of photophosphorylation, only the synthesis of ATP takes place.

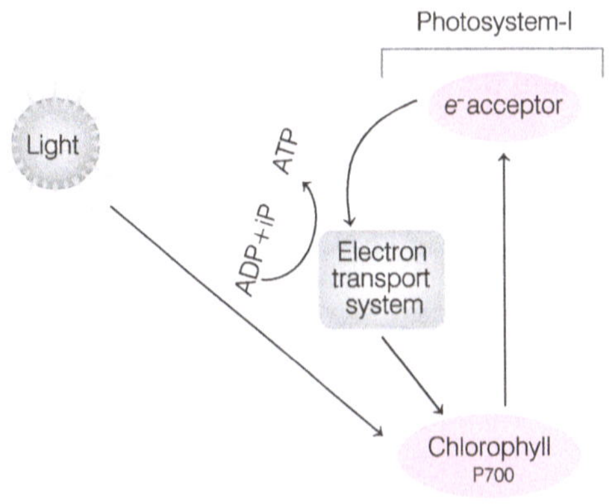


**Fig. 11.8** Cyclic photophosphorylation

## Chemiosmotic Hypothesis

- This hypothesis was given by **Peter Mitchell** (1961) in order to explain the ATP synthesis in photosynthesis (also in respiration).
- The synthesis of ATP is directly linked to the development of a proton gradient across the thylakoid membranes of a chloroplast.

> - The main difference that lies between the ATP synthesis in the photosynthesis and respiration is the location, where the accumulation of protons takes place.
> - In photosynthesis accumulation of protons occurs in the thylakoid lumen of chloroplast, while in respiration it occurs in intermembrane space of the mitochondria.

- The development of proton gradient results due to the reasons given below
  - As the water molecule splits into the inner side of the membrane, the protons or hydrogen ions that are produced by the water splitting, get accumulated in the lumen of thylakoids.
  - Transportation of protons takes place across the membrane when the electron moves through the photosystems.
  - This happens because the primary acceptor of electron is located towards the outer side of the membrane, which transfers electron to the proton ($H^+$) carrier and not to the electron carrier.

So, this molecule, while transporting an electron removes a proton from the stroma, thus release of proton takes place into the inner side of thylakoid, i.e. on the lumen side of the membrane.

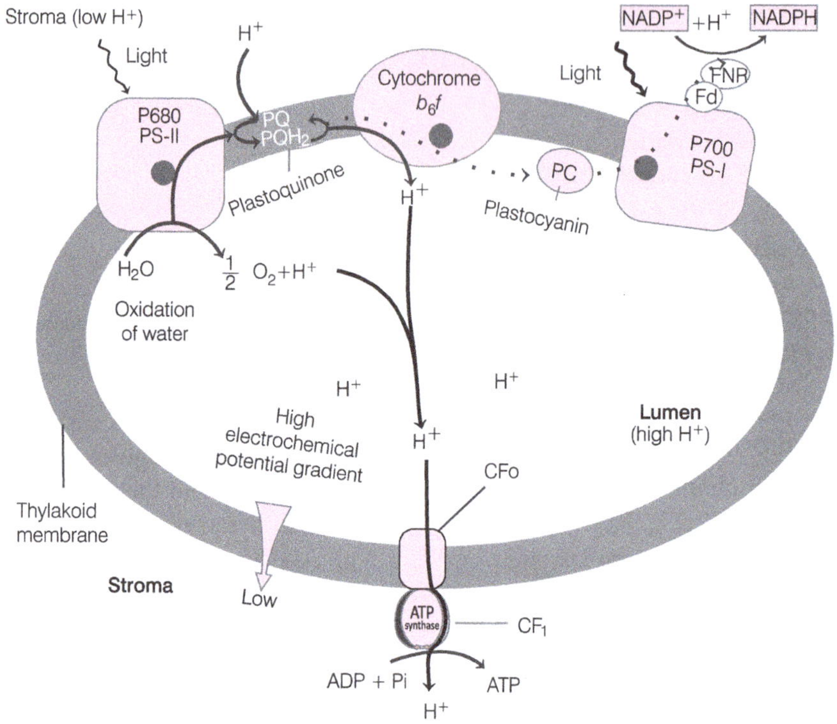


Fig. 11.9 ATP synthesis through chemiosmosis

- The enzyme NADP reductase is present on the stromal side of the membrane. Thus, along with the electrons that comes from the acceptor of electrons of PS-I, protons are also necessary to reduce $NADP^+$ to $NADPH+H^+$.
- Hence, protons in the stroma within the chloroplasts decrease in number, while their accumulation takes place in the lumen.
- Due to which the proton gradient is created across thylakoid membrane as well as measurable decrease in the pH at the side of lumen.
- This gradient is broken down due to the movement of protons across the membrane to the stroma through the transmembrane channel of the $CF_0$ portion of the ATP synthase.
- Therefore, the proton gradient is important as it is the gradient whose breakdown leads to the release of energy (ATP).
- The enzyme ATP synthase consists of the following two parts
  - **$CF_0$-particle** This portion remains embedded in the thylakoid membrane and forms a transmembrane channel, which carries out facilitated diffusion of protons ($H^+$) across the membrane.
  - **$CF_1$-particle** This portion protrudes towards the outer surface of the thylakoid membrane, which faces the stroma.
- Conformational change occurs in $CF_1$-particle of **ATP synthase,** which are caused due to the breakdown of the gradient. This allows the enzyme ATP synthase to synthesise several molecules of ATP from ADP and inorganic phosphate.
- Thus, the chemiosmosis, for its functioning, requires a membrane, a proton pump, a proton gradient and ATP synthase.
- Energy is utilised to transport protons across a membrane, generating a gradient with a high concentration of protons in the thylakoid lumen.
- ATP synthase has a channel that permits protons to diffuse back across the membrane, releasing sufficient energy to activate the ATP synthase enzyme, which catalyses the production of ATP.
- Together with the NADPH generated from electron movement, this ATP will be immediately used in the

biosynthetic reactions occurring in the stroma, which are responsible for fixing $CO_2$ and synthesising sugars.

**Quick Test 3**

1. Name the structure within the photosystem that is responsible for the absorption of light energy.
2. State the photosystems that are associated with the absorption peak at 680 nm and 700 nm, respectively.
3. **State True or False.**
   The half number of electrons in the electron transport chain are used up in the chain and half of them are passed on to the pigments of PS-I.
4. According to the chemiosmotic hypothesis, what is the driving force for the production of ATP in photosynthesis?
5. Name the protein complex that helps in electron transport between photosystems.

## Dark Reaction (Biosynthetic Phase)

- This phase does not require direct sunlight, but it depends on the products of the light reaction, i.e. **ATP** and **NADPH** (produced during photochemical phase) beside $CO_2$ and water that drive the processes leading to the synthesis of food, more accurately, the sugars (glucose is the first product of photosynthesis).
- As soon as the light becomes unavailable, the biosynthetic process continues for some time and then eventually stops and starts again if the light is made available. This proves that it is dependent on the products of light reaction.
- These processes are sensitive to temperature change, but are independent of light, hence called **dark reaction**. This takes place in the stroma of chloroplast.
- The fixation of $CO_2$ during photosynthesis is of two main types, i.e. $C_3$-pathway and $C_4$-pathway.

## Calvin Cycle ($C_3$-Pathway)

- The Calvin cycle was discovered by **Calvin**, **Benson** and their colleagues in California, USA.
- Melvin Calvin used radioactive $^{14}C$ in algal photosynthesis which led to the discovery, that the first $CO_2$ fixation product was a 3-carbon organic compound.
- This pathway is followed by the plants when the first product of $CO_2$-fixation is a $C_3$ acid, i.e. 3-Phosphoglyceric Acid (PGA).
- The Calvin cycle occurs in all photosynthetic plants (whether they have $C_3$ or $C_4$-pathways).
- It takes place inside the stroma of the chloroplast.
- This is a cycle of biochemical pathway of reduction of $CO_2$.
- After a long research and conducting many experiments it was concluded by the scientists that in $C_3$ pathway, the primary acceptor molecule is a 5-carbon ketose sugar, i.e. **Ribulose 1, 5-Bisphosphate** (5 RuBP).
- The Calvin cycle is divided into following three phases that are as carboxylation, reduction and regeneration.

### 1. Carboxylation

- It is the process of fixation of $CO_2$ into stable organic intermediate.
- The photosynthetic carboxylation requires Ribulose 1, 5-bisphosphate or RuBP as acceptor of $CO_2$.
- It is the most crucial step of the Calvin cycle.
- This reaction is catalysed by the enzyme RuBP carboxylase, which results in the formation of two molecules of 3-Phosphoglyceric Acid (3PGA).

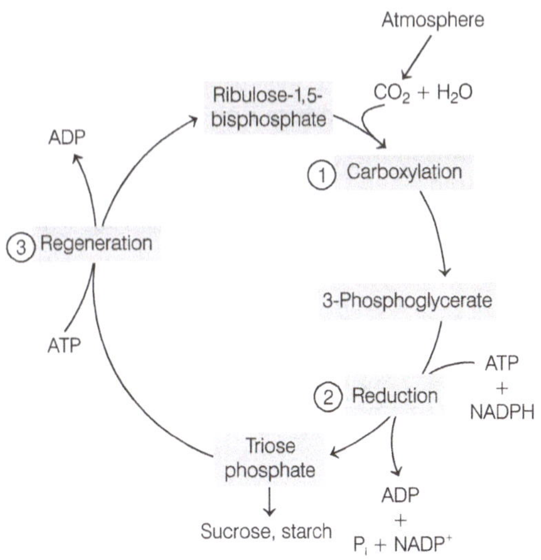


Fig. 11.10 Calvin cycle ($C_3$-pathway)

- The RuBP carboxylase enzyme also has an activity of oxygenation, so it is more commonly known as **RuBP carboxylase-oxygenase** or **RuBisCO**.

$$CO_2 + RuBP + H_2O \xrightarrow[Mg^{2+}]{RuBisCO} 2\,(3\text{-PGA})$$

## 2. Reduction

- After the carboxylation reaction, reduction of PGA takes place through a series of reactions leading to the formation of glucose.
- In this step, the ATP (as energy source) and NADPH (hydrogen atom carrier) are utilised.
- It is to be noted that 2 molecules of ATP and 2 molecules of NADPH are utilised in this step for phosphorylation and for the reduction of $CO_2$, respectively.
  Hence, for the fixation of 6 molecules of $CO_2$, 6 turns of the cycle are required in order to release one molecule of glucose from the pathway.

## 3. Regeneration

- For the continuous and uninterrupted functioning of the Calvin cycle, there must be a regular supply of ATP, NADPH along with sufficient amount of RuBP.
- The regeneration of RuBP ($CO_2$ acceptor) is a complex process and involves many types of sugar starting from triose (3C).
- The regeneration step requires one ATP molecule for phosphorylation.
- Hence, for every $CO_2$ molecule that enters the Calvin cycle, requires 3 molecules of ATP and 2 molecules of NADPH.
- Thus, in order to produce one molecule of glucose through the Calvin pathway, 18 ATPs and 12 NADPHs are required.
  This can be easily understood by the following table given below

| In | Out |
|---|---|
| 6 $CO_2$ | 1 glucose |
| 18 ATP | 18 ADP |
| 12 NADPH | 12 NADP |

## $C_4$-Pathway

- This pathway is followed or shown by the plants in which first product of $CO_2$-fixation is a $C_4$ acid, i.e. **Oxaloacetic Acid** (OAA).
- It was worked out by the two Australian scientists **Hatch** and **Slack** (1966). Thus, this is also known as **Hatch** and **Slack pathway.**
- Inspite of having Oxaloacetic Acid (OAA) as their first $CO_2$-fixation product, they use $C_3$-pathway or the Calvin cycle as the main biosynthetic pathway.
- This cycle occurs mostly in $C_4$ plants like monocots as maize and *Sorghum*, etc.
- $C_4$ plants have a special type of leaf anatomy that can tolerate high temperatures and show a response to high light intensities.
- They have large cells around the vascular bundles and these large cells are known as **bundle sheath cells.**
- The leaves which have such anatomy are said to have **'Kranz anatomy'** ('Kranz' means 'wreath' and is a reflection of the arrangement of cells).
- The bundle sheath cells tend to form several layers around the vascular bundles.
- They possess several special features such as
  - Have large number of chloroplast.
  - Thick walls which are impervious to gaseous exchange.
  - There are no intercellular spaces.
- The Hatch and Slack pathway is also a cyclic process, which occurs in the following steps

**Step I** In $C_4$ plants, the initial fixation of $CO_2$ occurs in mesophyll cells because the primary acceptor of $CO_2$ is a 3-carbon molecule, i.e. **Phosphoenol Pyruvate** (PEP) which is present in these cells.

**Step II** It combines with $CO_2$ in the presence of an enzyme **Phosphoenol Pyruvate Carboxylase** or **PEP Carboxylase** (PEPcase) to form the first stable (or a 4 carbon organic acid) product of $C_4$ pathway, i.e. the **Oxaloacetic Acid** (OAA).

**Step III** The compound OAA is formed in the mesophyll cells and changes to other 4-carbon compounds like malic acid or aspartic acid in these cells itself which are then transported bundle sheath cells where it is broken down, releasing $CO_2$ and a 3-carbon molecule.

**Step IV** The 3-carbon compound is again transported back to the mesophyll cells where regeneration of PEP takes place, thus completing the cycle.

**Step V** The $CO_2$ thus released in the bundle sheath cells enters the $C_3$ or the Calvin cycle (common pathway to all plants).

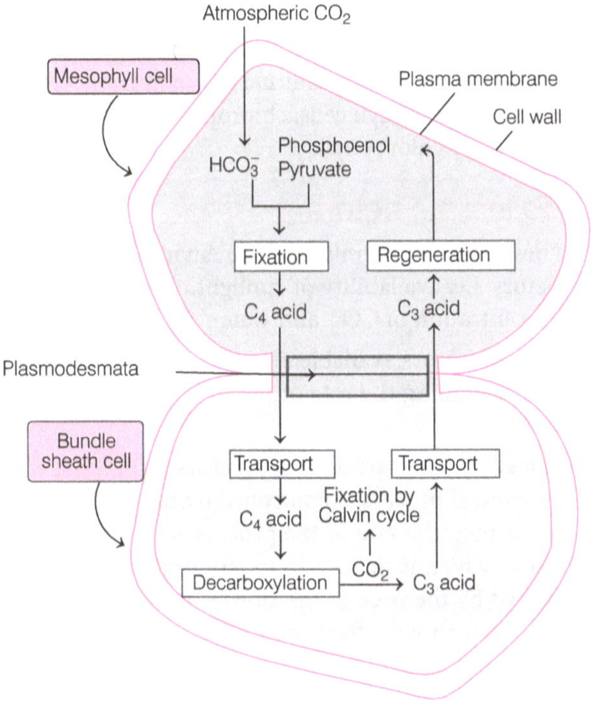


Fig. 11.11 Diagrammatic representation of Hatch and Slack pathway

**Note** The mesophyll cells lack RuBisCO enzyme, while the bundle sheath cell are rich in enzyme RuBisCO, but lack PEPCase.

## Quick Test 4

1. Name the phase of Calvin cycle that involves the production of triosphosphate from the 3-phosphoglycerate.
2. **State True or False.**
   The regeneration phase of the Calvin cycle requires one ATP and one NADPH for the phosphorylation.
3. State the type of leaf arrangement that is commonly seen in $C_4$ plants to support efficient gas exchange.
4. Name the molecule that is transported from the mesophyll cells to the bundle sheath cells in $C_4$ plants.
5. Name the structure in $C_4$ plants that is involved in the transport of four-carbon compounds between mesophyll and bundle sheath cells.

## 11. 6 Photorespiration

- It is light dependent cyclic process of oxygenation of RuBP and release of carbon dioxide by the photosynthetic organs of a plant.
- Normally, photosynthetic organs do the reverse in the light, i.e. uptake of $CO_2$ and release of $O_2$.
- The RuBP carboxylase oxygenase is the main enzyme of dark reaction.
- It has active site for both, i.e. $CO_2$ and $O_2$. The relative concentration of $CO_2$ and $O_2$ determines which of the two will bind to the enzyme.
- Under the conditions, when $O_2$ concentration is more in atmosphere than $CO_2$, then in $C_3$-plants, RuBisCO act as oxygenase enzyme and $CO_2$-fixation does not lead to PGA formation.
- Instead phosphoglycerate and phosphoglycolate (2C) are formed and photorespiration occurs.
- Thus, the photorespiratory pathway is called a **wasteful process** due to following two reasons
  - There is no synthesis of sugar and ATP or NADPH.
  - The $CO_2$ is released with the utilisation of ATP.

The process of photorespiration generally occurs in temperate plants such as beet, bean, cotton, rice, wheat, barley, etc., while the tropical grasses such as maize, sugarcane, *Sorghum*, etc., lacks this process.

- On the other side, the process of photorespiration does not take place in $C_4$ plants, because through a certain mechanism the $CO_2$ concentration increases at the enzyme site.
- This happens when the $C_4$ acid, i.e. OAA from the mesophyll cells is broken down in the bundle sheath cells releasing $CO_2$ thereby, increasing the intracellular concentration of $CO_2$.
- Hence, in $C_4$-plants the RuBisCO enzyme functions more as carboxylase while minimising the role of oxygenase.
- As $C_4$-plants lack the process of photorespiration the productivity and yields in these plants are better than those in $C_3$-plants.

**Differences between $C_3$ and $C_4$ Plants**

| Characteristics | $C_3$ Plants | $C_4$ Plants |
|---|---|---|
| Cell type in which the Calvin cycle takes place | Mesophyll | Bundle sheath |
| Cell type in which initial carboxylation takes place | Mesophyll | Mesophyll |
| How many types of cells does the leaf have that fix $CO_2$ | 1; mesophyll | 2; mesophyll and bundle sheath |
| Number of carbons in primary $CO_2$ acceptor | 5 | 3 |
| Primary $CO_2$-fixation product | 3 Phosphoglyceric Acid (PGA) | Oxaloacetic Acid (OAA) |
| Numbers of carbons in primary $CO_2$-fixation product | 3 | 4 |
| Presence of RuBisCO | Yes | Yes |
| Presence of PEPCase | No | Yes |
| Cells having RuBisCO | Mesophyll | Bundle sheath |
| $CO_2$-fixation rate under high light conditions | Medium | High |
| Presence of photorespiration at low light intensities | No | No |
| Presence of photorespiration at high light intensities | Yes | No |
| Presence of photorespiration at low $CO_2$ concentration | Yes | No |
| Presence of photorespiration at high $CO_2$ concentration | No | No |
| Optimum temperature | 20-25° C | 30-40 ° C |
| Geographical location of plants | Present everywhere | In tropical climate |
| Examples | Mango and guava | Maize and sugarcane |

## 11.7 Factors Affecting Photosynthesis

- The rate of photosynthesis is essential in determining the plants yield including the crop plants.
- It is generally influenced by the number of factors including both **external**, i.e. environmental and **internal** (plant) **factors**.
- These are as follows

### 1. Internal Factors

- The internal or plant factors greatly depend on the **genetic predisposition** and basically the growth of the plant.
- These factors include the number, size, age and orientation of leaves, internal concentration of $CO_2$, mesophyll cells, chloroplasts and the amount of chlorophyll.

### 2. External Factors

- These factors generally include environmental factors, i.e. availability of sunlight, temperature, concentration of $CO_2$ and water.
- Hence, factors available at sub-optimal levels help in determining the rate of photosynthesis at any point.
- **Blackman's law of limiting factors** stated that when a chemical process is controlled by more than one factor then the rate of the process is limited by the factor, which is nearest to its **minimal value** (is limited by the pace of the slowest factor), i.e. it is the factor which will affect the rate if its quantity will changed.
- For example, despite the presence of a green leaf and optimal light and $CO_2$ conditions, the plant may not photosynthesise if the temperature is very low. But if the optimal temperature is provided again to the plant, it will surely start photosynthesising.

Some of the factors that affect the photosynthetic rate are discussed ahead in detail.

### Light

- The light provides the energy for photosynthesis. Thus, it is one of the major factors, which affect the rate of photosynthesis.
- Three characteristics of light, i.e. the intensity, quality and duration of exposure generally influence the rate.
- While discussing the light as a factor that affects photosynthesis, two conditions are observed.
  - At **low light intensities**, there is a the linear relationship between incident light and rate of $CO_2$ fixation.
  - While at **higher intensity of light**, the rate fails to show further increase as the other factors become limiting. (saturation point).

- But, if an increase of light beyond a certain limit or point occurs it causes the breakdown of chlorophyll and decrease in the rate of photosynthesis.
- At 10% of full sunlight, the saturation of light occurs. Thus, except for plants in shade or in the dense forests, the light is rarely a limiting factor in nature.

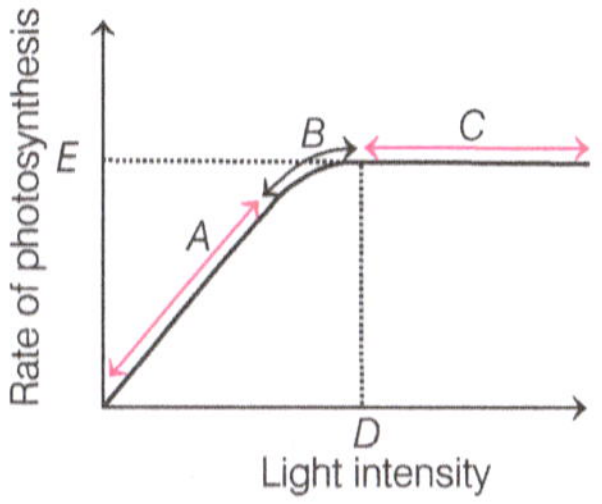


**Fig. 11.12** Graph of light intensity on the rate of photosynthesis

## Carbon Dioxide Concentration

- Carbon dioxide is the major limiting factor for photosynthesis.
- The concentration of $CO_2$ is very low in the atmosphere (between 0.03 and 0.04 per cent). Therefore, increase in the concentration upto 0.05 per cent can cause an increase in $CO_2$ fixation rates.
- Although $CO_2$ concentration beyond this level can become damaging over longer periods.
- The $C_3$ and $C_4$ plants responds differently to $CO_2$ concentrations.
- In $C_4$ plants, the photosynthesis increases as the $CO_2$ concentration increases, but at much lower concentration of $CO_2$, these plants tend to attain saturation (around 360 $\mu L^{-1}$).
- While the $C_3$ plant become saturated at much higher $CO_2$ level (around 450 $\mu L^{-1}$).
- Thus, the current availability of $CO_2$ levels is a limiting factor to the $C_3$ plants.
- The $C_3$ plants respond to higher $CO_2$ concentration by showing increased rates of photosynthesis leading to higher productivity.
- Thus, in order to obtain higher yield some greenhouse crops like tomatoes, bell pepper, etc., are allowed to grow in atmosphere enriched with carbon dioxide.

If low light conditions are prevail, both $C_3$ and $C_4$ plants fail to respond to high $CO_2$ conditions, while at high light intensities, both show increase in the photosynthetic rates, but upto a certain limits.

## Temperature

- The enzyme controlled dark reactions are affected by change in temperature.
- Though the light reactions are also temperature sensitive, they are affected to much lesser extent.
- Photosynthesis occurs in a very wide range of temperature.
- The $C_4$ plants respond to a higher temperature showing higher rate of photosynthesis, on the other hand, the $C_3$ plants have much lower optimum temperature range.
- Different plants have different optimum temperature range for photosynthesis. It depends on their habitat they are adapted to.
- The tropical plants have higher temperature range for photosynthesis than the temperate plants.

## Water

- The effect of water as a factor is more on the plant as a whole, rather than directly on photosynthesis.
- In water stress conditions, the **stomata** become closed which reduces the availability of $CO_2$ to plants, thereby causing reduction in the rate of photosynthesis.
- Besides this, the decrease in water availability causes leaves to **wilt**, thus reducing the surface area of the leaves ultimately reducing their **metabolic activity.**

### Quick Test 5

1. Name the process in plants that involves the consumption of oxygen and the release of carbon dioxide.
2. **State True or False.**
   At low intensity of the light there is a linear relationship between the incident light and the rate of $CO_2$ fixation.
3. Give example of any two plants that shows increased rate of photosynthesis in the high carbon dioxide concentration.
4. **State True or False.**
   The $C_4$ plants respond to a higher temperature showing higher rate of photosynthesis in comparison to the $C_3$ plants.
5. When water availability is low, what common stress response occurs in plants, affecting photosynthesis?

# Mind Map

## Photosynthesis in Higher Plants

### Photosynthetic Pigments

- Involves pigments like chlorophyll-*a*, chlorophyll-*b*, xanthophylls and caroteniods, with chlorophyll-*a* being the primary pigment absorbing blue and red light.
- Accessory pigments like chlorophyll-*b* and carotenoids expand the light absorption range, supporting higher photosynthetic efficiency.

### Light Harvesting Complex (LHC)

- **PS-I-700** nm and **PS-II-680 nm.**
- Each photosystem has a **reaction centre** (chlorophyll-*a*) and **antennae** (other pigments except chlorophyll-*a*)

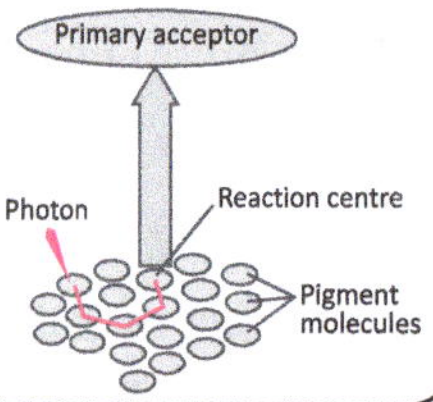


### Photorespiration

- A process in which oxidation of organic compounds occur in plants by the enzyme RuBP carboxylase and $O_2$ in the presence of sunlight.
- This is a **wasteful process**. Neither there is synthesis of sugar nor of ATP. Rather, results in release of $CO_2$ with utilisation of ATP.
- It requires three organelles-chloroplasts, peroxisome and mitochondria.

### Factors Affecting Photosynthesis

- Photosynthesis is influenced by internal factors such as leaf characteristics, mesophyll cells, chloroplasts, $CO_2$ concentration and chlorophyll, which depend on the plant's genetics and growth, as well as on external factors like light, temperature, $CO_2$ concentration, and water.

### Dark Reaction

**$C_3$-pathway**

- Involves carbon reduction and fixation cycle (Calvin cycle)

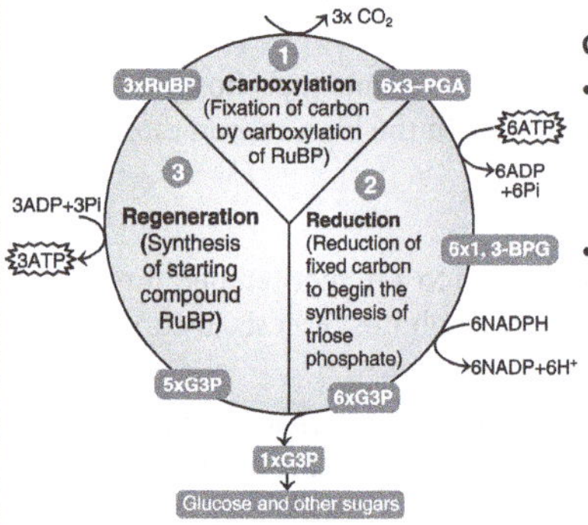


**$C_4$-pathway** (Hatch-Slack Cycle)

- Here, initial acceptor is PEP in mesophyll cells and first stable product is 4C compound oxaloacetic acid.
- $C_4$ plants have **Kranz anatomy** and are more efficient than $C_3$-plants.

### Phases of Photosynthesis

- Photosynthesis consists of two main phases, i.e. the light reaction and the dark reaction.
- The light reaction occurs in the thylakoid membranes, whereas the dark reaction, takes place in the stroma and utilises ATP and NADPH from the light reaction to fix carbon dioxide into glucose.

### Light Reaction

**Cyclic Phosphorylation**

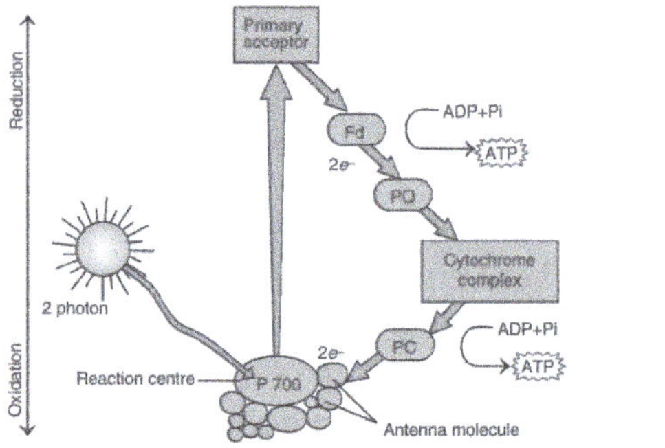


**Non-cyclic Phosphorylation**

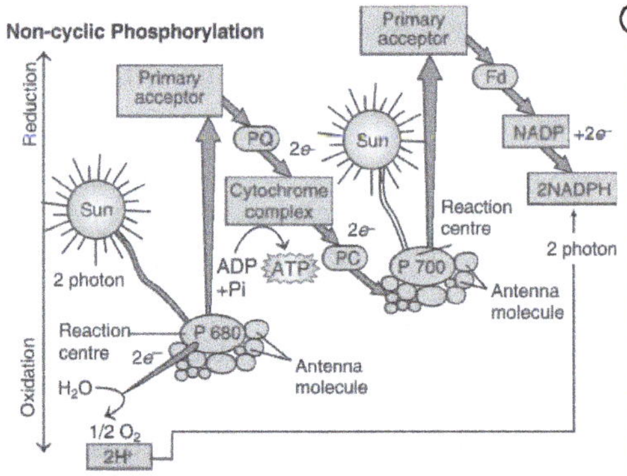


**Chemiosmotic Hypothesis**

It explains ATP production in the light reaction of photosynthesis through a proton gradient created by the electron transport chain, driving ATP synthase.

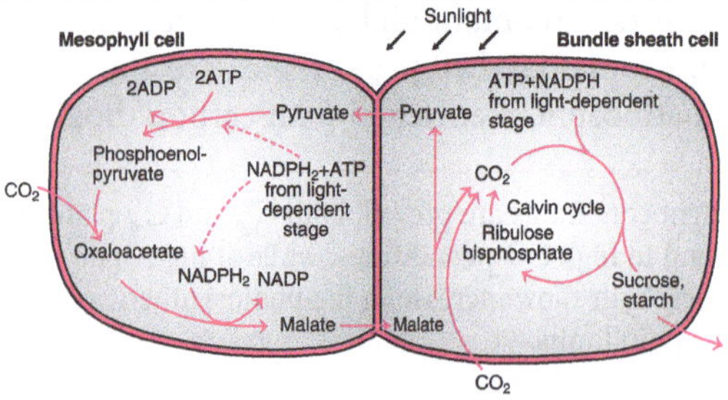


An outline of the photosynthetic metabolism in $C_4$ plants

# EXAM PATTERN QUESTIONS

## Objective Type Questions

### Multiple Choice Questions

**1. Photosynthesis is an essential process for life on earth because**

(a) it is the primary source of all food on earth
(b) it is responsible for the release of the oxygen
(c) it is the only natural process responsible for the utilisation of sunlight
(d) All of the above

**Ans.** (*d*)

**2. Select the correct match.**

| | Column I | | Column II |
|---|---|---|---|
| A. | Joseph Priestley | 1. | Necessity of light |
| B. | Julius von Sachs | 2. | Splitted light using prism |
| C. | TW Engelmann | 3. | Essentiality of air |
| D. | van Neil | 4. | Specialised bodies in the plant cells |

**Codes**

| | A | B | C | D |
|---|---|---|---|---|
| (a) | 1 | 2 | 3 | 4 |
| (b) | 3 | 4 | 2 | 1 |
| (c) | 4 | 3 | 1 | 2 |
| (d) | 3 | 4 | 1 | 2 |

**Ans.** (*b*)

**3. Identify *A*, *B* and *C* in given figure.**

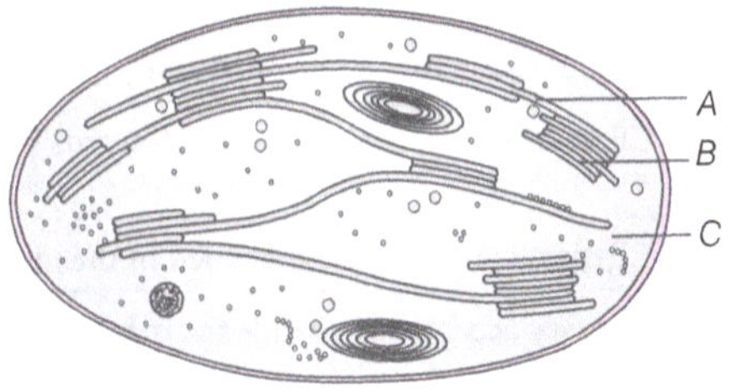


(a) *A*–Stroma wall, *B*–Granum, *C*–Stroma
(b) *A*–Stroma lamella, *B*–Granum, *C*–Stroma
(c) *A*–Stroma lamella, *B*–Stroma, *C*–Granum
(d) *A*–Stroma wall, *B*–Stroma, *C*–Granum

**Ans.** (*b*)

**4. Which pigment acts directly to convert light energy to chemical energy?** **NCERT Exemplar**

(a) Chlorophyll-*a*
(b) Chlorophyll-*b*
(c) Xanthophyll
(d) Carotenoid

**Ans.** (*a*) Chlorophyll-*a* acts directly to convert light energy to chemical energy. The other pigments chlorophyll-*b*, xanthophyll and carotenoids are accessory pigments associated with the main pigment, i.e. chlorophyll-*a* to harvest the light energy.

**5. Match the following columns.**

| | Column I | | Column II |
|---|---|---|---|
| A. | Chlorophyll-*a* | 1. | Yellow |
| B. | Chlorophyll-*b* | 2. | Bright or blue-green |
| C. | Xanthophyll | 3. | Yellow or yellow-orange |
| D. | Carotenoids | 4. | Yellow-green |

**Codes**

| | A | B | C | D | | A | B | C | D |
|---|---|---|---|---|---|---|---|---|---|
| (a) | 2 | 4 | 1 | 3 | (b) | 3 | 4 | 2 | 1 |
| (c) | 4 | 3 | 2 | 1 | (d) | 4 | 2 | 1 | 3 |

**Ans.** (*a*)

**6. The absorption spectrum of chlorophyll-*a* and the action spectrum of photosynthesis does not exactly overlap. This is because**

(a) chlorophyll-*a* absorbs the maximum light
(b) chlorophyll-*b* absorbs the minimum light
(c) other pigments of thylakoids also absorb light
(d) action spectrum of photosynthesis has two main peaks

**Ans.** (*c*)

**7. Light Harvesting Complexes (LHCs) are**

(a) present within PS-I and PS-II
(b) composed of only chlorophyll-*a*
(c) made up of hundred of pigment molecules bound to proteins
(d) Both (a) and (c)

**Ans.** (*d*)

**8. Which of the following is correctly labelled for the given figure?** **Competency Based Que.**

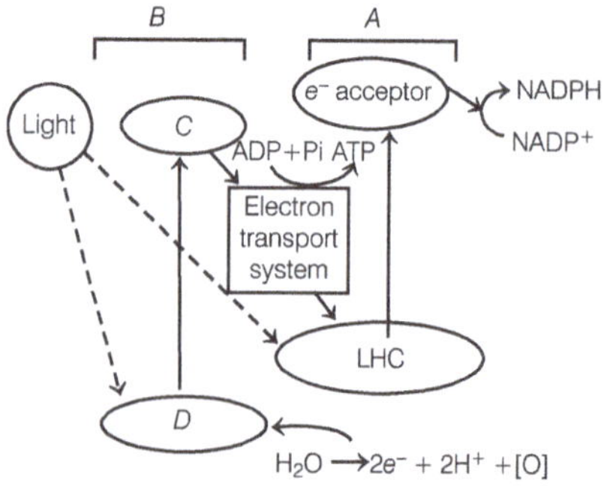


(a) *A*–PS-II, *B*–PS-I, *C*– $e^-$ acceptor, *D*–LHC
(b) *A*–LHC, *B*– $e^-$ acceptor, *C*–PS-I, *D*–PS-II
(c) *A*–PS-I, *B*–PS-II, *C*– $e^-$ acceptor, *D*–LHC
(d) *A*– $e^-$ acceptor, *B*–LHC, *C*–PS-II, *D*–PS-I

**Ans.** (*c*)

**9. During light reaction in photosynthesis the following are formed** **NCERT Exemplar**

(a) ATP and sugar
(b) hydrogen, $O_2$ and sugar
(c) ATP, hydrogen donor and $O_2$
(d) ATP, hydrogen and $O_2$ donor

**Ans.** (*c*) Light dependent reaction uses solar power to generate ATP and $NADPH_2$ which provide chemical and reducing power respectively to sugar synthesising reaction of the Calvin cycle, while the $O_2$ in released as a byproduct of light dependent reaction.

**10. PS-I functions when** **NCERT Exemplar**

(a) wavelength of light is around 700 nm
(b) NADPH accumulates in the stroma
(c) wavelength of light is lower than 680 nm
(d) ATP synthesis is inhibited

**Ans.** (*a*)

**11. The first acceptors of electrons from an excited chlorophyll molecule of photosystem-II is**

(a) quinone
(b) iron-sulphur protein
(c) ferredoxin
(d) cytochrome

**Ans.** (*a*)

**12. The correct sequence of flow of electrons in the light reaction is** **NCERT Exemplar**

(a) PS-II, plastoquinone, cytochromes, PS-I, ferredoxin
(b) PS-I, plastoquinone, cytochromes, PS-II, ferredoxin
(c) PS-I, ferredoxin, PS-II
(d) PS-I, plastoquinone, cytochromes, PS-II, ferredoxin

**Ans.** (*a*)

**13. Splitting of water is associated with** **NCERT Exemplar**

(a) photosystem-I
(b) lumen of thylakoid
(c) both photosystems-I and II
(d) inner surface of thylakoid membrane

**Ans.** (*d*) The thylakoid is a photosynthetic unit in the chloroplast. It is a membrane bound structure. The membrane has photosystems-I and II embedded in it, as protein-pigment complex. Splitting of water is associated with PS-II, which occurs in the presence of $Mn^{2+}$ and $Cl^-$ ions on the inner surface of thylakoid membrane.

**14. The water splitting complex is associated with**

(a) PS-I
(b) PS-II
(c) carotenoid
(d) xanthophyll

**Ans.** (*b*)

**15. In a chloroplast, the highest number of protons are found in**

(a) lumen of thylakoids
(b) stroma
(c) inner membrane space
(d) antennae complex

**Ans.** (*a*)

**16. ATP synthesis in chloroplast according to chemiosomotic hypothesis is based on** **DIKSHA**

(a) osmotic pressure
(b) proton gradient
(c) movement of $K^+$ ions
(d) potential difference in membranes

**Ans.** (*b*)

**17. Chemiosmotic hypothesis is used to explain the synthesis of ATP in photosynthesis. The ATP synthesis is directly linked to the development of a proton gradient across the thylakoid membrane of a chloroplast. Identify the correct match related to the chemiosmosis.** **Competency Based Que.**

| | Components | Functions |
|---|---|---|
| (a) | NADP reductase | Stromal side |
| (b) | $CF_0$-particle | Protrudes towards the other surface |
| (c) | $CF_1$-particle | Embedded in the membrane |
| (d) | Primary acceptor | Inside the matrix |

**Ans.** (*a*)

**18. Consider the following statements.**

**I. During chemiosmotic synthesis of ATP, one ATP molecule is formed when $4H^+$ pass through ATPase.**

**II. Light reaction of photosynthesis involves photochemical reactions.**

III. Dark reaction of photosynthesis involves carbon fixation.

IV. Splitting of water takes place on the inner surface of the thylakoid membrane. **Competency Based Que.**

Choose the option containing correct statements.

(a) I, III and IV (b) I, II and IV
(c) I, II, III and IV (d) I, II and III

**Ans.** (*c*)

**19.** Dark reaction in photosynthesis is called so because **NCERT Exemplar**

(a) it can occur in dark also
(b) it does not depend on light energy
(c) it cannot occur during day light
(d) it occurs more rapidly at night

**Ans.** (*b*)

**20.** PGA as the first $CO_2$ - fixation product was discovered in the photosynthesis of

(a) algae (b) bryophytes
(c) angiosperm (d) gymnosperm

**Ans.** (*a*)

**21.** The reaction that is responsible for the primary fixation of $CO_2$ is catalysed by **NCERT Exemplar**

(a) RuBP carboxylase
(b) PEP carboxylase
(c) RuBP carboxylase and PEP carboxylase
(d) PGA synthase

**Ans.** (*c*)

**22.** The enzyme that is not found in a $C_3$ plant is **NCERT Exemplar**

(a) RuBP carboxylase (b) PEP carboxylase
(c) NADP reductase (d) ATP synthase

**Ans.** (*b*)

**23.** In $C_4$ plants Kranz anatomy refers to arrangement of **DIKSHA**

(a) bundle sheath cells around vascular bundles
(b) vascular bundles scattered in mesophyll
(c) spongy parenchyma loosely held
(d) sunken stomata in epidermis

**Ans.** (*a*)

**24.** Plant in a garden avoids photorespiratory losses, has improved water use, shows high rates of photosynthesis at high temperatures and has improved efficiency of nitrogen utilisation.

In which of the following physiological groups would you assign this plant? **Competency Based Que.**

(a) $C_3$ (b) CAM
(c) $C_4$ (d) Nitrogen fixer

**Ans.** (*c*)

**25.** PEP is primary $CO_2$ acceptor in **NCERT Exemplar**

(a) $C_4$ plants
(b) $C_3$ plants
(c) $C_2$ plants
(d) Both $C_3$ and $C_4$ plants

**Ans.** (*a*)

**26.** When $CO_2$ is added to PEP, the first stable product synthesised is **NCERT Exemplar**

(a) pyruvate
(b) glyceraldehyde-3-phosphate
(c) phosphoglycerate
(d) oxaloacetate

**Ans.** (*d*)

**27.** Which of the following characteristics is true for $C_3$ and $C_4$ plants? **Competency Based Que.**

| | Characteristics | $C_3$ plants | $C_4$ plants |
|---|---|---|---|
| (a) | Types of cells present in the leaf to fix $CO_2$ | 1, bundle sheath cell | 1, mesophyll cell |
| (b) | Presence of photo-respiration at high light intensitites | No | Yes |
| (c) | Optimum temperature | 10-15°C | 20°–25°C |
| (d) | Geographical location plants | Present everywhere | In tropical climate |

**Ans.** (*d*)

**28.** Which of the following statement(s) regarding photorespiration is/are true?

(a) It is a metabolically expensive pathway
(b) It is avoided when $CO_2$ is abundant
(c) It results in a loss of usable carbon dioxide
(d) All of the above

**Ans.** (*d*)

**29.** The process of breakdown of water molecule in photosynthesis is known as

(a) CAM
(b) carbon assimilation
(c) photolysis
(d) photorespiration

**Ans.** (*c*)

**30.** Which of the following is not included in the list of internal factor influencing photosynthesis?

(a) Orientation of leaves
(b) Amount of chlorophyll
(c) Internal concentration of $CO_2$
(d) Internal $O_2$ concentration

**Ans.** (*a*)

## Assertion-Reason Questions

**Direction** (Q. Nos. 1-10) *In each of the following questions, a statement of Assertion (A) is given followed by corresponding statement of Reason (R). Of the statements, mark the correct answer as*

(a) Both A and R are true and R is the correct explanation of A.
(b) Both A and R are true, but R is not the correct explanation of A.
(c) A is true, but R is false.
(d) A is false, but R is true.

**1. Assertion** (A) During photosynthesis, glucose is formed, but it is stored in the form of starch.

**Reason** (R) Glucose is osmotically active, while starch is inactive.

**Ans.** (*a*)

**2.** Given below is the graph showing the absorption spectrum of chlorophyll-*a* and *b*. Comment upon the appropriateness of both Assertion and Reason. **Competency Based Que.**

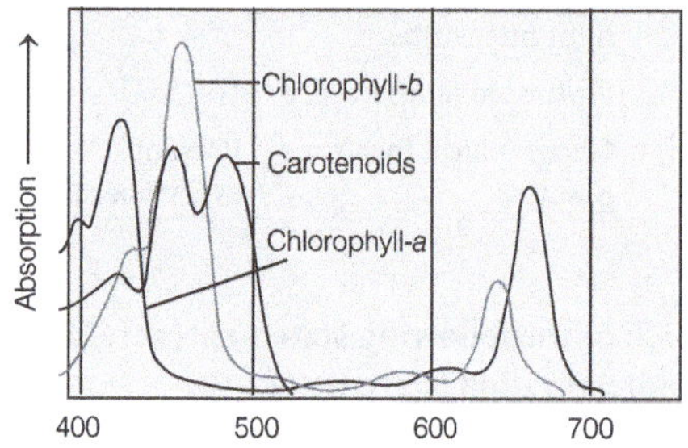


**Assertion** (A) Chlorophyll-*a* shows the maximum absorption peak at 450 nm and also shows another peak at 650 nm.

**Reason** (R) Absorption spectrum is constituted by the pigments like violet, blue, orange and red.

**Ans.** (*b*)

**3. Assertion** (A) Chlorophyll is the primary pigment involved in photosynthesis.

**Reason** (R) Chlorophyll reflects green light and absorbs blue and red light, which is necessary for energy capture.

**Ans.** (*b*)

**4. Assertion** (A) In thylakoid, Light Harvesting Complex (LHC) broadens the range of light absorption.

**Reason** (R) LHC transfer electrons to reaction centre.

**Ans.** (*b*)

**5. Assertion** (A) PS-I and PS-II names are given on the basis of activity in the photosynthesis.

**Reason** (R) During non-cyclic photophosphorylation, PS-II works first and then PS-I.

**Ans.** (*d*) A is false, but R is true. A can be corrected as PS-I and PS-II names are given on the basis of their discoveries.

**6. Assertion** (A) Assimilatory power in photosynthesis is generated in ETS occurring in thylakoid membrane.

**Reason** (R) They are required for $CO_2$ reduction.

**Ans.** (*a*)

**7. Assertion** (A) In photosynthesis, dark reactions are temperature controlled processes.

**Reason** (R) In biosynthetic pathway, most of the reaction are enzymatic in nature.

**Ans.** (*a*)

**8. Assertion** (A) The Calvin cycle does not require light to occur.

**Reason** (R) The Calvin cycle uses ATP and NADPH produced during the light reactions to fix carbon dioxide into organic compounds.

**Ans.** (*a*)

**9. Assertion** (A) In $C_4$ plants, initial fixation of $CO_2$ occurs in the bundle sheath cells.

**Reason** (R) The bundle sheath cells are mainly meant to carryout $C_4$ cycle.

**Ans.** (*d*) A is false, but R is true. A can be corrected as In $C_4$ plants, initial fixation of $CO_2$ occurs in the mesophyll cells.

**10. Assertion** (A) Photorespiration is a waste process.

**Reason** (R) During photorespiration, neither ATP nor NADPH is formed.

**Ans.** (*a*)

# Subjective Questions

## Very Short Answer Type Questions

**1. Why photosynthesis is an oxidation-reduction process?**

**Ans.** Photosynthesis is an oxidation-reduction process because water is oxidised to release oxygen and carbon dioxide is reduced to produce carbohydrate (glucose).

**2. Purple and green sulphur bacteria are photosynthetic, but they do not use $H_2O$ as raw material. Justify.** **Competency Based Que.**

**Ans.** The purple and green sulphur bacteria are photosynthetic. They utilise $H_2S$ as photosynthetic substrate and release sulphur as byproduct.

**3. Write the simplified equation of photosynthesis given by van Neil.**

**Ans.** $2H_2A + CO_2 \xrightarrow{\text{Light}} 2A + CH_2O + H_2O$.

**4. Oxygen evolved during photosynthesis comes from $H_2O$ or $CO_2$.**

**Ans.** Oxygen evolved in photosynthesis comes from $H_2O$ (i.e. by splitting of water) during light reaction.

**5. Photosynthetic pigments are located in which part of the chloroplast?**

**Ans.** Photosynthetic pigments are located in the thylakoid membrane of the chloroplast.

**6. Enumerate the type of chlorophyll known as universal photosynthetic pigment.**

**Ans.** Chlorophyll-a is known as the universal photosynthetic pigment present in almost all photosynthetic organisms.

**7. Which two photosynthetic pigments belong to carotenoids?**

**Ans.** The two photosynthetic pigments belongs to carotenoids are carotenes and xanthophylls. (½ + ½)

**8. Differentiate between stroma and grana of chloroplasts.**

**Ans.** Differences between stroma and grana of chloroplasts are as follows

| Stroma | Grana |
|---|---|
| It is the jelly-like matrix of the chloroplast. | These are formed of stacks of thylakoids. |
| Dark reaction takes place here. | Light reaction takes place here. |

(½ + ½)

**9. Which mechanism of photosynthesis is responsible for trapping of light energy, splitting of water, oxygen release and formation of ATP and NADPH?** **Comptency Based Que.**

**Ans.** Light reaction is responsible for trapping of light energy, splitting of water, oxygen release and formation of ATP and NADPH.

**10. Which photosystem will work, if only longer wavelengths of light are given to a plant?**

**Ans.** At longer wavelength of light, photosystem-I, i.e. P700 will work.

**11. Where do the electrons move from the electron acceptor of PS-II in the Z-scheme?**

**Ans.** The electrons move to PS-I from the electron acceptor of the PS-II in the Z-scheme.

**12. In which photosystem, you find $O_2$ evolving complex?**

**Ans.** Oxygen evolving complex is observed associated with PS-II.

**13. Mention the source of electrons for non-cyclic photophosphorylation.**

**Ans.** Photolysis of water molecule acts as a source of electrons for non-cyclic photophosphorylation.

**14.** $2H_2O \longrightarrow 4H^+ + 4e^- + O_2 \uparrow$

**Based on the above equation, answer the following questions.**

**(i) Where does this reaction take place in plants?**

**(ii) What is the significance of this reaction?**

**Ans.** (i) Inner side of the membrane of the thylakoids.

(ii) $O_2$ is evolved during this reaction, moreover electrons are made available to PS-II continuously. (½ × 2)

**15. Name the final electron acceptor in photosynthesis.**

**Ans.** The $NADP^+$ acts as the final electron acceptor in the photosystem.

**16. Mention the possible location in the chloroplast, where cyclic flow of electrons (cyclic photo phosphorylation) occurs.**

**Ans.** Cyclic flow of electrons occur in the stroma lamellae of chloroplast.

**17. In the diagram shown below, label *A*, *B* and *C*.**

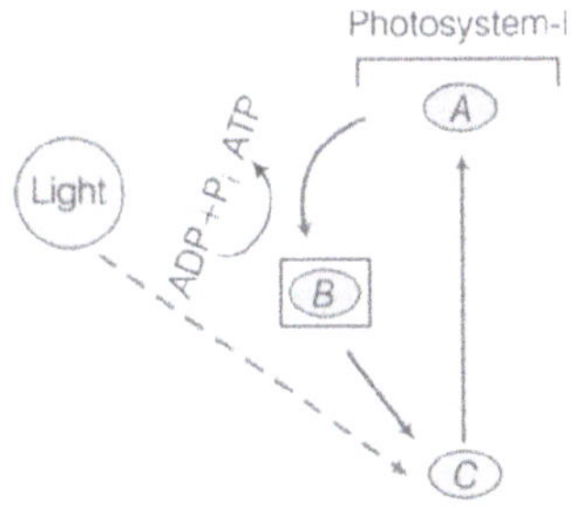


**Ans.** Here, *A* is electron acceptor, *B* is electron transport system and *C* is photosystem-I P700.

**18. Mention the any two basic requirements for chemiosmosis to occur.**

**Ans.** Four basic requirements are as follows (any two)

(i) A unit membrane. (ii) A proton pump.

(iii) A proton gradient. (iv) ATP synthase enzyme. (½ × 2)

**19. Why is proton gradient important in photosynthesis?** **Competency Based Que.**

**Ans.** Proton gradient is important as it leads to the formation of ATP.

**20. Identify *A* and *B* from the following.**

**(i) NADP reductase enzyme is located on *A*.**

**(ii) Breakdown of proton gradient leads to release of *B*.**

**Ans.** (i) *A*-Stroma side of the thylakoid membrane.

(ii) *B*-Energy in the form of ATP. (½ × 2)

**21. During dark phase of photosynthesis, which is oxidised and which is reduced?** **Competency Based Que.**

**Ans.** The NADPH is oxidised to $NADP^+$ and $CO_2$ is reduced to glucose during dark phase of photosynthesis.

**22. List the main steps of the Calvin cycle.**

**Ans.** The main steps of Calvin cycle are carboxylation, reduction and regeneration.

**23. How many molecules of carbon dioxide, ATP and NADPH are required to make one molecule of glucose?**

**Ans.** 6 molecules of carbon dioxide, 18 molecules of ATP and 12 molecules of NADPH are required to make 1 glucose molecule.

**24. Name the enzyme, which is not found in $C_3$ plants.**

**Ans.** PEP carboxylase enzyme is not found in $C_3$ plants.

**25. Which range of wavelength (in nm) is called Photosynthetically Active Radiation (PAR)?** **NCERT Exemplar**

**Ans.** The light range between 400-700 nm of wavelength is called PAR.

## Short Answer Type Questions

**1. Mention any two reasons, which prove that photosynthesis is essential for sustaining life on the earth.**

**Ans.** Two reasons are as follows

(i) It is the process by which food is manufactured for all living organisms.

(ii) It is the only natural process by which oxygen is liberated into the atmosphere. This $O_2$ is used by all living organisms respiring aerobically. (1 × 2)

**2. Describe how Engelmann arrived at the first action spectrum of photosynthesis.**

**Ans.** Refer to text on page no. 238.

**3. If a green plant is kept in dark with proper ventilation, can this plant carryout photosynthesis?**

**Can anything be given as supplement to maintain its growth or survival?** **NCERT Exemplar**

**Ans.** Plants need sunlight for photosynthesis. The sun is among the essential raw material that help plants to make their own food. Due to the absence of sunlight, this plant cannot carry out photosynthesis. To maintain survival, the plant can be supplied proper amount of water. But the plant would eventually die because of lack of nutrients. (1 × 2)

**4. Cyanobacteria and some other photosynthetic bacteria do not have chloroplasts. How do they conduct photosynthesis?** **NCERT Exemplar**

**Ans.** Cyanobacteria and some other photosynthetic bacteria have photosynthetic lamellae (membranes) suspended freely in the cytoplasm. These photosynthetic lamellae possess bacteriochlorophyll to conduct photosynthesis.

**5. Is it correct to say that photosynthesis occurs only in leaves of a plant? Besides leaves, what are the other parts that may be capable of carrying out photosynthesis? Justify.** **Competency Based Que.**

**Ans.** No, it is correct to say that photosynthesis only occurs in the leaves of a plant. Photosynthesis can also occur in other green parts of the plant, such as stems, branches, flowers, fruits, and seeds. (1 + 2)

**6. (i) Identify the parts *A* and *C* in the diagram given below.**

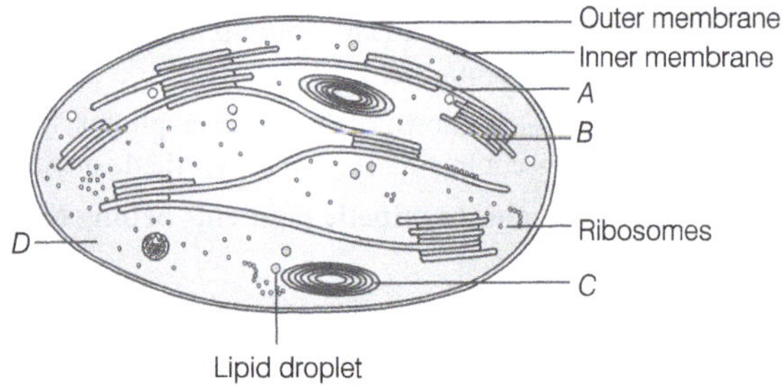


**(ii) Mention the role played by stroma.**

**(iii) What is the role played by membrane system of the chloroplast?**

**Ans.** (i) Parts labelled as *A* and *C* are

*A* - Stromal lamellae; *C* - Starch granule (½ × 2)

(ii) Internally, a chloroplast contains two structures, a proteinaceous matrix or fluid called stroma and the membrane system called lamellae or thylakoids. The stroma has enzymes, which are responsible for the reduction of $CO_2$ into carbohydrates and formation of sugars. (1)

(iii) The membrane system is responsible for trapping the light energy and also for the synthesis of ATP and NADPH. (1)

**7. Mention the name and characteristics of various classes of pigments used in photosynthesis?**

**Ans.** Refer to text on page no. 240.

**8. Why is the colour of a leaf kept in the dark frequently becomes yellow or pale green? Which pigment do you think is more stable?** **NCERT**

**Ans.** The colour of leaf kept in the dark frequently becomes yellow or pale green due to disintegration of chlorophyll pigment in continuous absence of light and xanthophylls and carotenoids become more prominent. (2)

Carotene pigment is more stable as they do not get affected by the absence of light. (1)

**9. Suppose there were plants that had a high concentration of chlorophyll-*b*, but lacked chlorophyll-*a*, would it carry out photosynthesis? Also mention why do plants have chlorophyll-*b* and other accessory pigments?** **NCERT**

**Ans.** Chlorophyll-*a* is the major pigment responsible for trapping light. Photosynthetic pigments like chlorophyll-*b*, xanthophylls and carotenoids are called accessory pigments and absorb light of different energy wavelengths and transfer their energy to chlorophyll-*a*. Therefore if any plant lack chlorophyll-*a* and contain high concentration of *b*, then that plant would not carry out photosynthesis. (1½ × 2)

**10. What can we conclude from the statement that the action and absorption spectra of photosynthesis overlap? At which wavelength, do they show peaks?** **NCERT Exemplar**

**Ans.** The absorption spectrum is the graph, plotted with the amount of light absorbed *vs* function of wavelength. The action spectrum is the graph plotted with the rate of photosynthesis *vs* function of wavelength. Since, the amount of light absorbed and the rate of photosynthesis have a direct relationship, the two curves overlap.

They show peaks around wavelengths 450 nm (blue region) and 650-680 nm (red region). (2 + 1)

**11. Two groups (*A* and *B*) of bean plants of similar size and same leaf area were placed in identical conditions. Group *A* was exposed to light of wavelength 400-450 nm and group *B* to the light of wavelength of 500-550 nm. Compare the photosynthetic rate of the two groups by giving reason.** **Competency Based Que.**

**Ans.** Group *A* will show more photosynthesis. Chlorophyll absorbs maximum light in the blue region of the spectrum, i.e. 400-450 nm and hence photosynthetic rate will also be high. Group *B* will show negligible amount of photosynthesis or no photosynthesis. As chlorophyll does not absorb any light in the green region, i.e. 500-550 nm, but reflects green, so plants appear green.

**12. Name the end products of light reaction of photosynthesis. Mention the fate of each of them.**

**Ans.** ATP, NADPH and oxygen are the end products of light reaction. ATP and NADPH are used in the reduction step of biosynthetic phase of photosynthesis. Oxygen is liberated into the atmosphere. (1 + 1)

**13. What are the roles played by antenna complex and photosystems in the process of photosynthesis?**

**Ans.** Refer to text on page no. 241-242.

**14. Mention any two conditions for under which PS-I functions.**

**Ans.** Necessary conditions required for PS-I to functions are

(i) When the wavelength of light is longer than 680 nm.

(ii) When NADPH accumulates cyclic phosphorylation is triggered to generate ATP without producing NADPH. (1 × 2)

**15. Where is NADP reductase enzyme located in the chloroplasts? What is the role of this enzyme in proton gradient development?** **NCERT Exemplar**

**Ans.** NADP reductase enzyme is located on the outer/stroma side of the thylakoid membrane.

Along with the electrons from the primary acceptor of PS-I, it uses the protons of stroma for the reduction of $NADP^+$ to NADPH; this removal of protons from the stroma causes a proton gradient between the lumen of thylakoids and the stroma. (1 + 2)

**16. Given below is a *Z*-scheme of a light reaction. Study the same and answer the questions that follows.**

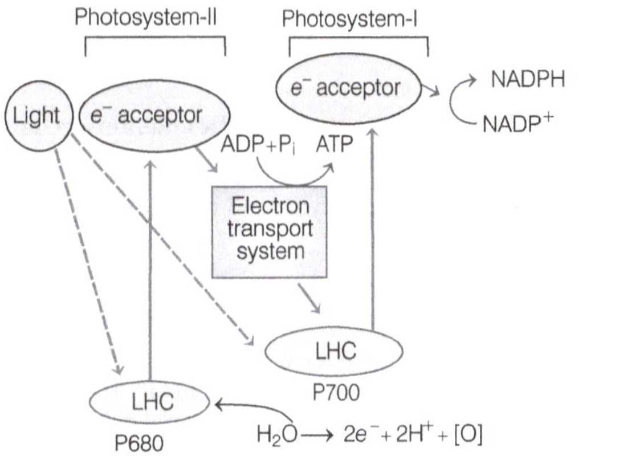


**(i) How does the photosynthetic electron transport chain initiates ?**

**(ii) What happens to the electrons in the reaction centre of PS-I?**

**Ans.** (i) The photosynthetic electron transport chain initiates with the absorption of light energy by the photosystem-II. (1)

(ii) Like PS-II, the electrons in the reaction centre of PS-I also gets excited on receiving the red light of wavelength 700 nm and gets transferred to the another electron acceptor with higher redox potential. (2)

**17. What is the advantage of having more than one pigment molecule in photosystem?**

**Ans.** The advantage of having more than one pigment molecule in the photosystem is that it allows the plant to

(i) Absorb a wider range of light wavelengths.
(ii) Increase the overall light-harvesting efficiency.
(iii) Provide protection against excess light energy (photo protection).
(iv) Optimise photosynthesis under varying light conditions. (½ × 4)

**18 Photosynthetic organisms occur at different depths in the ocean. Do they receive the light? How do they adapt to carry out photosynthesis under these conditions?** **NCERT Exemplar**

**Ans.** Photosynthetic organisms present at different depths in the ocean do not receive the same light qualitatively and quantitatively. The plants growing at the banks of water bodies get good quality of light. Algae which can tolerate more dilutions of light penetrate deeper inside water. Green algae remain in the shore line, brown algae descend to intermediate depths, while red algae form the limit below where no other autotrophic plants can grow. (1 + 2)

**19. Cyclic photophosphorylation results in the production of ATPs and not NADPH. Give reasons.** **Competency Based Que.**

**Ans.** Cyclic photophosphorylation occurs when only 700 nm light is available and PS-I is functional. It occurs in the stroma lamellae where enzyme NADP reductase is absent and PS-II is also absent. Hence, electrons are passed on back to PS-I and not to $NADP^+$ . So, the cyclic flow results in the formation of ATP, but not NADPH.

**20. Give comparison between cyclic and non-cyclic photophosphorylations.** **NCERT**

**Ans.** Comparison between cyclic and non-cyclic photophosphorylation

| Cyclic Photophosphorylation | Non-cyclic Photophosphorylation |
|---|---|
| It occurs in photosystem-I in stromal or intergranal lamellae. | It is carried out by both PS-I and PS-II in the granal thylakoids. |
| It is not connected to photolysis of water, so no oxygen is evolved. | It is connected with photolysis of water, so oxygen is evolved in it. |
| It is activated by light of 700 nm wavelength. | It occurs in 680 nm as well as 700 nm wavelength. |
| It generates ATP only, there is no formation of $NADPH_2$. | It produces both ATP as well as $NADPH_2$. |

(½ × 4)

**21. The entire process of photosynthesis consists of a number of reactions. Name the part of the cell where following reactions take place.**

**(i) Synthesis of ATP and NADPH ................ .**
**(ii) Photolysis of water .................. .**
**(iii) Fixation of $CO_2$ .................. .**

**Ans.** (i) Synthesis of ATP and NADPH takes place in thylakoids.
(ii) Photolysis of water occurs in inner side of thylakoid membrane in PS-II (680 nm).
(iii) Fixation of $CO_2$ occurs in stroma of chloroplast.

**22. What are the two components of ATPase complex? Where are these located and what are their functions?**

**Ans.** Refer to text chemiosmosis hypothesis on page no. 244.

**23. Answer the following questions.**

**(i) How many molecules of ATP and NADPH are required to fix one molecule of $CO_2$ ?**
**(ii) Where in the chloroplast does this process occur?**

**Ans.** (i) 3 molecules of ATP and 2 molecules of NADPH are required to fix one molecule of $CO_2$.
(ii) It occurs in the stroma of chloroplast. (1 × 2)

**24. Why is the lumen of thylakoids is acidic, while the stroma is alkaline in nature?** **Competency Based Que.**

**Ans.** The acidic nature of lumen of thylakoids is due to the accumulation of protons by the photolysis of water. The same reaction does not occur in stroma, so it is alkaline in nature.

**25. ATPase enzyme consists of two parts. What are those parts? How are they arranged in the thylakoid membrane?**

**The conformational changes occur in which part of the enzyme?** **Competency Based Que.**

**Ans.** ATPase enzyme consists of two parts, i.e. a stalk ($CF_0$) and a head piece ($CF_1$).

These two parts are located completely across the membrane of thylakoid membrane.

The conformational changes occur in the head piece ( $CF_1$) of this enzyme. (1 × 3)

**26. Dark reactions are dependent on light reaction yet are called dark reactions. Justify.**

**Ans.** Dark reactions are dependent on the products of light reaction that are ATP and NADPH to carryout reduction of $CO_2$ to form glucose. This does not need light so they are called dark reactions.

**27. The diagram given below shows stages in the light-independent reactions of photosynthesis. Answer the following.** **Competency Based Que.**

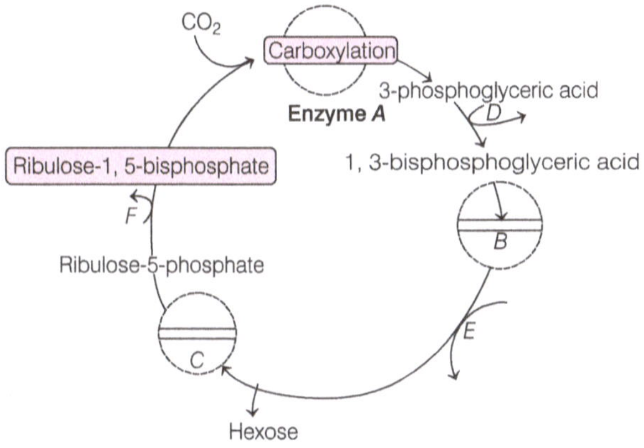


**(i) At which stage, NADPH is oxidised?**
**(ii) What are *A*, *B* and *C*?**
**(iii) At which stages, ATP is converted into ADP?**

**Ans.** (i) NADPH is oxidised at stage *E*.
(ii) *A*—RuBP Carboxylase Oxygenase (RuBisCO), *B*—Reduction, *C*—Regeneration
(iii) ATP is converted to ADP at stages *E* and *F*. (1 × 3)

**28. Six turns of Calvin cycle are required to generate one mole of glucose. Explain.**

**Ans.** Calvin cycle is a series of reactions that leads to the formation of glucose. For every $CO_2$ molecule fixation 3 molecules of ATP and 2 molecules of NADPH are required. Since, glucose is a six carbon compound the fixation of six molecules of $CO_2$ and six turns of the cycle are required for the synthesis of one molecule of glucose through these reactions.

**29. Why is RuBisCO enzyme, the most abundant enzyme in the world?** **Competency Based Que.**

**Ans.** The enzyme Ribulose-1 , 5-bisphosphate carboxylase oxygenase, most commonly known by the shorter name RuBisCO is used in the Calvin cycle of photosynthesis to catalyse the first major step of carbon fixation. RuBisCO is thought to be the most abundant protein in the world, since it is present in every plant that performs photosynthesis and makes about 20-25% of the soluble protein in the leaves.

**30. RuBisCO is an enzyme that acts both as a carboxylase and oxygenase. Why do you think RuBisCO carries out more carboxylation in $C_4$ plants?** **NCERT**

**Ans.** RuBisCO carries out more carboxylation in $C_4$ plants due to several key adaptations. First, $C_4$ plants utilise spatial separation, where carbon dioxide is initially fixed by PEP carboxylase in mesophyll cells, forming a four-carbon compound that is then transported to bundle sheath cells. This environment has a higher concentration of $CO_2$, which favours carboxylation over oxygenation.

Additionally, the structure of $C_4$ plants limits RuBisCO's exposure to oxygen, reducing the likelihood of photorespiration. These factors enhance the efficiency of carbon fixation in $C_4$ plants, especially under high light and temperature conditions.

**31. What is the advantage we find in $C_4$ plant with respect to high temperature?**

**Ans.** Refer to text on page no. 246.

**32. Fill in the blanks at *A*, *B*, *C*, *D*, *E* and *F* and complete the $C_4$-pathway/Hatch-Slack pathway.**

Atmospheric $CO_2$ enters *A*
↓
$CO_2$ is accepted by *B* and forms four carbon acid compound *C*
↓
$C_4$ acid enters into *D* and splits into $CO_2$ and *E*
↓
$CO_2$ enters Calvin cycle and 3C acid *F* is formed

**Ans.** *A*–Mesophyll cell, *B*–Phosphoenol Pyruvate (PEP), *C*–Oxaloacetic Acid (OAA), *D*–Bundle sheath cells, *E*–Pyruvate, *F*–Phosphoglyceric Acid (PGA). (½ × 6)

**33. In high oxygen concentration, $C_3$-plant shows low $CO_2$-fixation. Explain.**

**Ans.** In high oxygen concentration, oxygen binds to RuBisCO instead of carbon dioxide through the process of photorespiration. Hence, $CO_2$ fixation reduces.

**34. RuBisCO is an enzyme that acts both as a carboxylase and oxygenase. Why do you think RuBisCO carries out more carboxylation in $C_4$-plants?** **NCERT**

**Ans.** RuBisCO has a much greater affinity for $CO_2$ than $O_2$ under normal conditions. It is the relative concentration of $O_2$ and $CO_2$ that determines which of the two will bind to the enzyme. (1)

In $C_4$ plants RuBisCO carries out more carboxylation because they have a mechanism that increases the concentration of $CO_2$ at the enzyme site.

This occur when the $C_4$ acid from the mesophyll is broken down in the bundle cells to release $CO_2$, which results in increasing the intracellular concentration of $CO_2$. In turn, this ensures that the RuBisCO functions as a carboxylase minimising the oxygenase activity.

**35. What conditions enable RuBisCO to function as an oxygenase? Explain the ensuring process.**

**Ans.** The oxygenase activity of RuBisCO activated when $CO_2$ concentration in the atmosphere decreases and oxygen concentration exceeds. They undergo the pathway known as photorespiration.

**36. Give the comparison between the $C_3$ and $C_4$-pathway.** NCERT

**Ans.** Comparison $C_3$ and $C_4$ pathway are as follows.

| $C_3$-Pathway | $C_4$-Pathway |
|---|---|
| In the $C_3$-pathway, $CO_2$ is fixed by the enzyme RuBisCO, forming two molecules of 3-phosphoglycerate (3-PGA). | In the $C_3$-pathway, $CO_2$ is first fixed by the enzyme PEP carboxylase into oxaloacetate, which is converted to malate. |
| The Calvin cycle occurs in the mesophyll cells of $C_3$ plants. | In $C_4$ plants, the Calvin cycle occurs in the bundle cells, while the initial $CO_2$ fixation occurs in the mesophyll cells. |
| Photorespiration is high in the $C_3$-pathway, which decreases the efficiency of photosynthesis. | Photorespiration is low in the $C_4$-pathway, as $CO_2$ is concentrated in the bundle sheath cells, reducing the competition between $CO_2$ and oxygen. |

(1 × 3)

**37. A type of anatomy of leaves possessed by $C_4$ plants is different from those of $C_3$ plants. Explain.**

**Ans.** $C_4$ plants possess a special anatomy of leaves called Kranz anatomy, which means the presence of two types of chloroplasts, agranal in bundle sheath cells and granal in mesophyll cells.

Kranz means wreath and is a reflection of the arrangement of cells. The bundle sheath cells may form several layers around the vascular bundles; they are characterised by having a large number of chloroplasts, thick walls impervious to gaseous exchange and no intercellular spaces. (2)

**38. Give comparison between the $C_3$ leaf anatomy and $C_4$ leaf anatomy.** NCERT

**Ans.** Comparisons between anatomy of leaf in $C_3$ and $C_4$ plants are as follows

| $C_3$ Leaf Anatomy | $C_4$ Leaf Anatomy |
|---|---|
| Only one type of chloroplast is present. | Kranz anatomy, i.e. presence of two types of cell, each with its own type of chloroplast, is present. |
| Less efficient in photosynthesis than $C_4$ leaves. | More efficient in photosynthesis than $C_3$ leaves. |
| Only mesophyll cells carryout photosynthesis. | Both mesophyll cells and bundle sheath cells carryout photosynthesis. |

(1 × 3)

**39. What is the basis for designating $C_3$ and $C_4$-pathways of photosynthesis?**

**Ans.** In Calvin cycle, carbon is fixed into a 3-carbon compound, i.e. 3-PGA. On the other hand in $C_4$ cycle, oxaloacetic acid (4C) is the first $CO_2$ -fixation product. Thus, the number of carbon in first $CO_2$ -fixation product is the basis of $C_3$ and $C_4$ designation.

**40. Name the two important enzymes of $C_3$ and $C_4$ pathways, respectively. What important role do they play in fixing $CO_2$ ?**

**Ans.** The important enzymes of $C_3$-cycle is RuBisCO and that of $C_4$-pathway is PEP carboxylase. They help in the fixation of $CO_2$ . In $C_3$ -cycle, the $CO_2$ acceptor is Ribulose-1, 5 Bisphosphate (RuBP) and the first stable product is Phosphoglyceric Acid (PGA). In $C_4$-cycle, the $CO_2$ acceptor is PEP carboxylase and the first stable product is Oxaloacetic Acid (OAA). (1+2)

**41. By looking at a plant externally can you tell whether a plant is $C_3$ or $C_4$? Why and how?** NCERT

**Ans.** To distinguish between $C_3$ and $C_4$ plants based on external traits, we have to observe their leaf structure, colour, and growth form. $C_3$ plants typically have broad, flat leaves with simpler vascular arrangements, while $C_4$ plants often exhibit thicker leaves with Kranz anatomy, where bundle sheath cells surround the vascular bundles. Additionally, $C_4$ plants may appear more robust and waxy, indicating adaptations to drought. They are usually found in warmer, arid environments, often as grasses.

**42. By looking at which internal structure of a plant can you tell whether a plant is $C_3$ or $C_4$? Explain** NCERT

**Ans.** To identify whether a plant is $C_3$ or $C_4$ based on internal structures, examine the leaf anatomy and chloroplast distribution. $C_4$ plants exhibit Kranz anatomy, where vascular bundles are surrounded by a layer of bundle sheath cells packed with chloroplasts, facilitating efficient carbon fixation. In contrast, $C_3$ plants have a more scattered arrangement of vascular bundles and chloroplasts primarily in mesophyll cells. Additionally, $C_4$ plants often have lower stomatal density, adapted for water conservation in hotter environments. These features can be observed under a microscope to distinguish between the two types.

**43. Does moonlight support photosynthesis? Find out.** NCERT Exemplar

**Ans.** The intensity of moonlight is several thousands times less than that of direct sunlight, which is insufficient for the light-dependent phase of photosynthesis. So, photosynthesis does not occur in moonlight.

**44. In tropical rainforests, the canopy is thick and shorter plants growing below it receive filtered light. How are they able to carry out photosynthesis?**

**Ans.** The light transmitted through the tree canopy is of low intensity. Therefore, plants growing under the thick canopy of tree have adapted themselves to carry out photosynthesis in low light intensities. (1)

The quality and intensity of light affect only the rate of photosynthesis. (1)

**45. The current availability of $CO_2$ levels is a limiting factor to the $C_3$ plants. Justify.**

**Ans.** Refer to text on page no. 249.

**46. What would happen to the rate of photosynthesis in $C_3$ plants, if $CO_2$ concentration level almost doubles from its present level in the atmosphere?** **Competency Based Que.**

**Ans.** If the $CO_2$ concentration in $C_3$ plants almost get doubles from its present level in the atmosphere, plants will grow much faster and lead to the higher productivity due to higher rate of photosynthesis. However, this increase in photosynthesis would not continue indefinitely. After a certain threshold, other factors such as light intensity, temperature and nutrient availability would become limiting, preventing further increase in photosynthetic rate.

**47. How does water stress affect/decrease the rate of photosynthesis?**

**Ans.** Water stress causes closure of stomata and decreases the availability of $CO_2$ for photosynthesis. Water stress also causes wilting of leaves, thus reducing the surface area of leaves and metabolic functions as well. (2)

**48. Look at leaves of the same plant on the shady side and compare it with the leaves on the sunny side.**

*Or*

**Compare the potted plants kept in the sunlight with those in the shade. Which of them has leaves that are darker green? Why?** **NCERT**

**Ans.** Leaves in the shade are typically darker green because they have a higher concentration of chlorophyll to capture more light for photosynthesis. In contrast, leaves in direct sunlight have less chlorophyll because they do not need as much to absorb light, often resulting in a lighter green colour. The increased chlorophyll in shaded leaves helps them to optimise photosynthesis in lower light conditions.

## Long Answer Type Questions

**1. Explain the structure of chloroplast. Why is the spatial separation of photosynthesis within the chloroplast important?**

**Ans.** Refer to text on page no. 239.

**2. What is photophosphorylation? Where does non-cyclic photophosphorylation take place? Describe this process. Why is this process called so?**

**Ans.** Refer to text on page no. 242-243.

**3. Even though a very few cells in a $C_4$-plant carry out the biosynthetic -Calvin pathway, yet they are highly productive. Can you discuss why?** **NCERT**

**Ans.** $C_4$ plants are highly productive despite having only a few cells that carry out the Calvin cycle due to their unique anatomical and biochemical adaptations. Here are some key reasons (1)

(i) **$C_4$ Photosynthesis Mechanism** $C_4$ plants utilise a two-step process for photosynthesis. In the mesophyll cells, they initially fix carbon dioxide into a four-carbon compound (oxaloacetate) using the enzyme PEP carboxylase.

(ii) **Bundle Sheath Cells** The four-carbon compounds are then transported to bundle sheath cells, where they release $CO_2$ for the Calvin cycle. This spatial separation reduces photorespiration, which is a wasteful process that occurs in $C_3$ plants, especially under stressful conditions. By concentrating $CO_2$ around the RuBisCO enzyme in the bundle sheath cells, $C_4$ plants minimise oxygen interference, enhancing the efficiency of photosynthesis.

(iii) **High Light Utilisation** $C_4$ plants are often adapted to high light environments, allowing them to maximise light capture and energy conversion, further increasing their productivity.

(iv) **Enhanced Growth Rates** The efficiency of carbon fixation and reduced photorespiration allows $C_4$ plants to grow faster and produce more biomass, contributing to their overall productivity. These adaptations enable $C_4$ plants to thrive in a variety of environments, making them some of the most productive plants on earth, despite the fact that only a small fraction of their cells are directly involved in the Calvin cycle. $(1 \times 4)$

**4. RuBisCO carries a dual role as carboxylase as well as oxygenase. Explain both the reactions. Under what conditions does this shift from one to other take place?**

**Ans.** Refer to text on page no. 245 and 247.

**5. Give reasons for the following.**

**(i) Plants are the lungs of nature.**

**(ii) Chlorophyll-*b* and other accessory pigments are necessary for photosynthesis.**

**(iii) In the high light intensities, the chlorophyll-*a* gets damaged.** **Competency Based Que.**

**Ans.** (i) Plants are also called lungs of the nature because they perform the exact function as lungs do in mammals. They provide oxygen, which is necessary for all forms of life. So, in essence since our lungs keep us alive, in the same way, the trees also keep our nature alive by providing oxygen rich air. (2)

(ii) Chlorophyll-*b* and other accessory pigments are necessary as these are light absorbing compounds found in photosynthetic organisms. These pigments enable a wider range of wavelength of incoming light to be utilised for photosynthesis. (2)

(iii) Chlorophyll-*a* structure is such that it gets damaged by bright/high light due to photooxidation. (1)

## Source Based/Case Based/Passage Based Questions

**1. In the figure given below, the black line (upper) indicates action spectrum for photosynthesis and the lighter line (lower) indicates the absorption spectrum of chlorophyll-*a*, answer the following.**

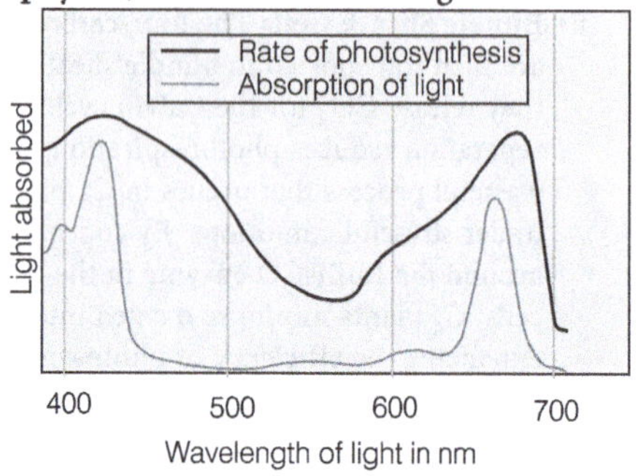


**(i) What does the given graph indicate?**

**(ii) How can we derive an absorption spectrum for any substance?**

**(iii) If chlorophyll-*a* is responsible for light reaction of photosynthesis, why do the action spectrum and absorption spectrum not overlap?** **NCERT Exemplar**

**Ans.** (i) It is the relative rates of photosynthesis at different wavelengths of light. For details refer to text on page no. 241. (1)

(ii) Absorption of different wavelengths of light by a particular pigment is plotted and the graph is called the absorption spectrum of that pigment. (1)

(iii) Chlorophyll-*a* is responsible for light reaction of photosynthesis, but the action spectrum and absorption spectrum do not overlap because though chlorophyll is the main pigment responsible for absorption of light, other thylakoid pigments like chlorophyll-*b*, xanthophylls and carotenoids, which are called accessory pigments, also absorb and transfer the energy to chlorophyll-*a*. Indeed they not only enable a wider range of wavelength of incoming light to be utilised for photosynthesis, but also protect chlorophyll-*a* from photo-oxidation. (2)

**2. The graph below shows the absorption spectra of three photosynthetic pigments.** **Competency Based Que.**

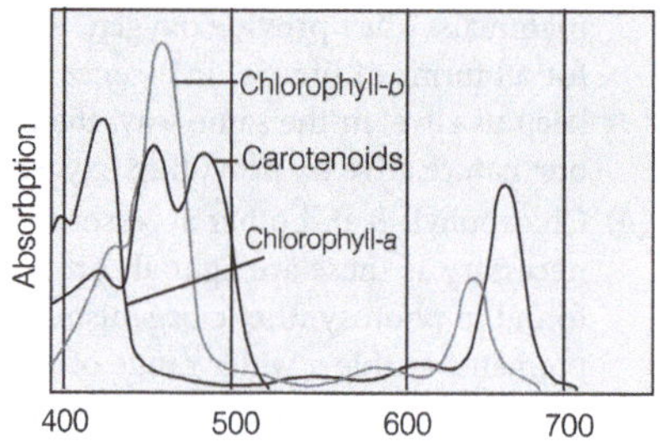


**(i) Which out of the three are the main photosynthetic pigment?**

**(ii) Name the instrument used to study the phenomenon of absorption spectrum.**

**(iii) What does the absorption spectra of chlorophyll-*a* and *b* shows ?**

*Or*

**(iii) How does the pigment are often known ?**

**Ans.** (i) The major photosynthetic pigments are chlorophyll-*a* and *b*. (1)

(ii) The instrument is spectrophotometer. (1)

(iii) The absorption spectra of chlorophyll-*a* and *b* shows that they absorb maximum light in the blue-violet and red wavelength. (2)

*Or*

(iii) The pigments are often known after the wavelength which is absorbed to the maximum. For example, chlorophyll-*a* and *b* absorbs light mainly in red and blue regions. (2)

**3. The following figure shows the effect of light on the rate of photosynthesis. Based on the graph, answer the following questions.** **NCERT**

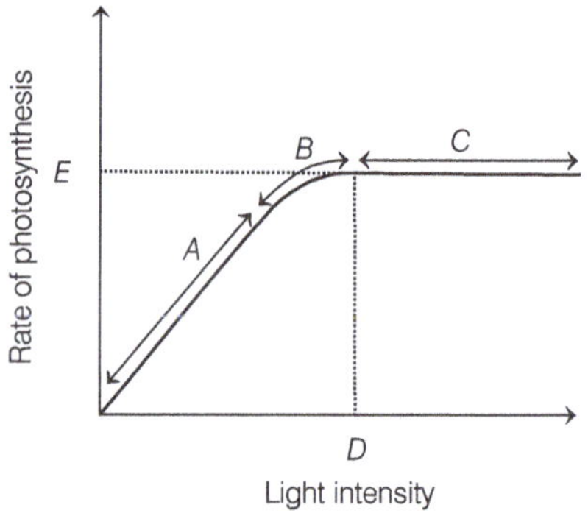


**(i) At which point(s) (*A*, *B* or *C*) in the curve, light acts as a limiting factor?**

**(ii) What could be the limiting factor(s) in region *A*?**

**(iii) What do *C* and *D* represent on the curve?**

**Ans.** (i) In the given graph, light is a limiting factor at the point *A*. Here, the rate by photosynthesis is slow. (1)

(ii) Light is a limiting factor in region *A*. Water, temperature and the $CO_2$ concentration could also be limiting factors in this region. (1)

(iii) Point *D* represents the optimum point and gives the light intensity at which the maximum photosynthesis is recorded. The rate of photosynthesis remains constant after this point, even though the intensity of light increases in region *C*. Point *C* represents the region of saturation. (2)

# SELF ASSESSMENT TEST

## Multiple Choice Questions

1. The photosystem-I and photosystem-II are named
   (a) in the sequence they work in light reaction
   (b) according to their molecular weight
   (c) in sequence of their discovery
   (d) in sequence of their constituents

2. Identify the correct description about given diagram.

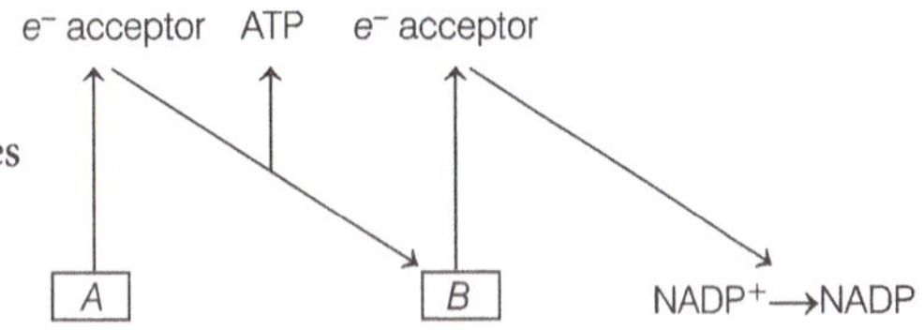


   I. *A* and *B* represent P700 and P680, respectively.
   II. The given process depicts oxidation/reduction changes during the light reaction of photosynthesis.
   III. The given process was discovered by Bendall and Hill in 1960.

   Choose the correct option.
   (a) I, II and III
   (b) I and II
   (c) II and III
   (d) I and III

3. The products of light-dependent reactions are
   (a) $CO_2$ and ATP
   (b) NADPH, ATP and $CO_2$
   (c) $O_2$ , ATP and NADPH
   (d) $O_2$ and $FADH_2$

4. Which molecule is split during the light reactions and what is the significance of this process?
   (a) Glucose; it releases energy for the Calvin cycle.
   (b) Water; it provides electrons and releases oxygen as a byproduct.
   (c) Carbon dioxide; it is converted into organic compounds.
   (d) $NADP^+$ it becomes reduced to NADPH.

5. Which of the following statement about the Calvin cycle is false?
   (a) It occurs in the stroma of chloroplasts.
   (b) It requires ATP and NADPH produced in the light reactions.
   (c) It directly produces glucose as a final product.
   (d) It utilises carbon dioxide to synthesise organic compounds.

6. Which of the following statement correctly describes the impact of photorespiration on a plant's carbon balance and overall metabolism?
   (a) Photorespiration increases the amount of glucose produced, enhancing the plant's energy reserves during periods of high light intensity.
   (b) By converting ribulose bisphosphate to 2-phosphoglycolate, photorespiration decreases the efficiency of carbon fixation, leading to potential carbon loss under certain conditions.
   (c) The products of photorespiration are recycled to produce more chlorophyll, thereby improving light absorption and photosynthetic rates.
   (d) Photorespiration only occurs in $C_4$ plants, providing a mechanism to reduce, water loss while maximising carbon gain.

## Assertion-Reason Questions

**Direction** (Q. Nos. 7-10) *In each of the following questions, a statement of Assertion (A) is given followed by corresponding statement of Reason (R). Of the statements, mark the correct answer as*

(a) Both A and R are true and R is the correct explanation of A.
(b) Both A and R are true, but R is not the correct explanation of A.
(c) A is true, but R is false.
(d) A is false, but R is true.

7. **Assertion** (A) Photosynthesis consists of two main stages, i.e. the light reactions and the Calvin cycle.

   **Reason** (R) The light reactions capture sunlight to produce glucose, while the Calvin cycle converts light energy into chemical energy.

8. **Assertion** (A) The Calvin cycle takes place in the thylakoid membranes of the chloroplasts.

   **Reason** (R) The Calvin cycle uses ATP and NADPH produced during the light reactions to convert carbon dioxide into glucose.

9. **Assertion** (A) $C_4$ plants are more efficient in photosynthesis than $C_3$ plants under high temperature conditions.

   **Reason** (R) $C_4$ plants utilise a different pathway that minimises photorespiration by fixing carbon dioxide into a four-carbon compound.

10. **Assertion** (A) Oxygen released during photosynthesis comes from the splitting of water molecules.

    **Reason** (R) This process occurs during the Calvin cycle when carbon dioxide is incorporated into glucose.

## Very Short Answer Type Questions

11. What is produced as a byproduct of the light reactions?
12. What role do carotenoids play in photosynthesis?
13. What are the three main phases of the Calvin cycle?
14. What is the significance of the proton gradient in the light reactions?

## Short Answer Type Questions

15. Describe the process of photolysis and its importance in photosynthesis.
16. Draw and label the $C_4$ cycle, illustrating the key steps and the enzymes involved in carbon fixation.
17. What is photorespiration? Explain.

## Long Answer Type Questions

18. Explain the role of pigments in photosynthesis and their significance in capturing light energy.
19. Answer the following questions.
    (i) Compare and contrast $C_3$ and $C_4$ photosynthesis in terms of their processes.
    (ii) Explain the advantages of $C_4$ photosynthesis in hot environments.
20. At high oxygen concentrations, RUBP combines with oxygen, producing one molecule of phosphoglycerate and one molecule of phosphoglycolate.
    (i) What is this process called?
    (ii) Explain briefly how some plants ensure that the RuBisCO functions as a carboxylase, minimizing the oxygenase activity.

## Case Based Question

21. In the figure below, parts *A* and *B* shows the portion of the light harvesting complex. Study the figure and answer the questions that follows.

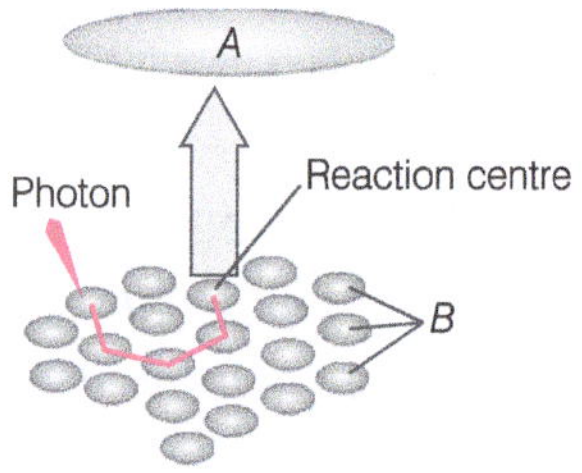


    (i) Label the parts marked as *A* and *B* in the figure. Which type of chlorophyll pigment molecule is found in the reaction centre? Name it.
    (ii) How does the both photosystems differentiates from each other in terms of a reaction centre?

# Answers

| | | | | | | | |
|---|---|---|---|---|---|---|---|
| 1. (c) | 2. (c) | 3. (c) | 4. (b) | 5. (c) | 6. (b) | 7. (c) | 8. (d) |
| 9. (b) | 10. (c) | | | | | | |

# 12 CHAPTER

All living organisms require a continuous supply of energy for their survival. This energy is used to carry out various functions such as uptake of nutrients, absorption, growth, development, movement, reproduction and even breathing.
Thus, the energy needed by cells is obtained from food, which is released through the breakdown of food material in a process called **cellular respiration**.

## YOUR STUDY GOALS



## YOUR PRACTICE GOAL

- Objective Type Questions (41 Qs ; MCQs, A-R)
- Case Based Questions (3)
- Subjective Type Questions (15 VSAs, 36 SAs, 8 LAs)

# Respiration in Plants

- About 50% of the energy produced by the cell is utilised by cellular activities and rest of it is changed into heat and is lost into the environment.
- This chapter deals with the basic concepts of energy producing biological process called **cellular respiration**.

## 12.1 Respiration : The Basics

- We eat food in order to obtain energy.
- The **macromolecules** present in our food are oxidised to fulfill the energy requirement of our body for carrying out all the basic life processes.

### Photosynthesis : Essential for Respiration

- Only green plants and cyanobacteria can prepare their own food by the process called **photosynthesis**.
- They obtain their food by converting light energy into chemical energy, which thereby gets stored into the bonds of carbohydrate molecules such as glucose, sucrose, starch, etc.
- But not all the cells, tissues and organs in plants can photosynthesise instead, only the cells that contain **chloroplasts**, that are most often located in the superficial layers, carry out photosynthesis.

- Hence, even in the plants, all other non-green parts of plant need food for oxidation to get energy.
- Thus, food has to be translocated from the green parts to the non-green parts for the oxidation processes to generate energy.
- Animals are **heterotrophic** in nature, i.e. they either obtain their food directly from the plants (herbivores) or indirectly dependent on herbivores for their food (carnivores) or dependent on dead and decaying matter for their food (saprophytes), e.g. fungi, some bacteria.
- Thus, it can be concluded that all the food that is respired for life processes ultimately comes from photosynthesis. Hence, photosynthesis is the biggest life process of biological world.

## Cellular Respiration

- It is the process of breaking of the C-C bonds of complex compounds through oxidation within the cells, leading to release of considerable amount of energy in the form of ATP.
- It is to be noted that the site of breaking down of complex molecules to yield energy is **cytoplasm** and **mitochondria** (only in eukaryotes) of the living cell.
- Plant cells also carry out cellular respiration to get energy.
- Like respiration, combustion also involves the release of energy from chemical reactions, but there are some differences between the two processes, which are discussed below.

**Differences between Respiration and Combustion**

| Respiration | Combustion |
|---|---|
| It is the breakdown of complex compounds through oxidation within the cells, leading to release of considerable amount of energy. | Combustion is the complete burning of organic compounds which produces $CO_2$ and $H_2O$ and yield energy in the form of heat and light. |
| It is a controlled stepwise biochemical process. | It is an uncontrolled physico-chemical process. |
| Many chemical bonds break simultaneously releasing large amount of energy. | Chemical bonds break one after another to release energy. |
| Enzymes are involved. | Enzymes are not involved. |
| A number of intermediates are formed for the synthesis of different organic compounds. | No intermediate products are produced during combustion. |

## Respiratory Substrates

- The compounds that are oxidised during the process of respiration are called **respiratory substrates.**
- Carbohydrates are used as major respiratory substrates by most of the organisms to get energy.
- However, under some conditions proteins, fats and organic acids are also used as respiratory substrates in some plants.

## ATP : Energy Currency of the Cell

- During the process of oxidation of food within a cell, all the energy contained in the respiratory substrates is not released free into the cell, or in a single step.
- Instead, it is released in a series of slow **step-wise reactions** controlled by enzymes and is trapped as chemical energy in the form of **ATP**.
- Hence, the energy released in respiration by the process of oxidation is not used directly but is used in synthesising ATP (which is utilised whenever energy is needed).
- Thus, it is said that ATP acts as the **energy currency of the cell**.
- The energy trapped in ATP is used in many energy requiring processes of the organisms, and the carbon skeleton produced during respiration is used as precursors for the biosynthesis of other molecules in a cell.

## Do Plants Breathe?

- For the process of respiration, plant takes $O_2$ and releases $CO_2$.
- Instead of specialised organs that are present in animals, plants have **stomata** and **lenticels** for gaseous exchange.
- Following are the reasons which show, how plants can get along without respiratory organs
  - Every part of the plant has the ability to take care of its own needs of gaseous exchange. There is very little transport of gases that occur from one part of the plant to another.
  - Plants do not present great demands for gas exchange.
    - Roots, stems and leaves respire at rates far lower than animals do.
    - Only during the process of photosynthesis, large volumes of gases are exchanged and each

leaf of the plant has the ability to take care of its own needs during these periods.

- Thus, when cells photosynthesise, availability of $O_2$ is not a problem in these cells due to a continuous release of $O_2$ that takes place within the cell.

- Gases easily diffuse in large, bulky plants as distance for diffusion is not great in these plants. This is because living cells in a plant are located quite close to the surface of the plant.
  - In case of stems, which are thick and woody in nature, the organisation of living cells is in the form of thin layers, which are found inside and beneath the bark.
  - Like leaves which have **stomata** for gaseous exchange, these stems also have openings called **lenticels.**
  - Internal cells of lenticels are dead and provide only mechanical support to the plant.
  - This depicts that most cells of the plant have atleast a part of their surface in contact with the air.
  - The loose packing of **parenchyma cells** in leaves, stems and roots provides an interconnected network of air spaces, which help in facilitating this process.
  - The process of gaseous exchange is very much connected to the process of respiration.

## 12.2 Types of Respiration

Cellular respiration may be classified into two types as given below

### 1. Aerobic Respiration

- This is the type of respiration that takes place in the presence of oxygen. It involves complete oxidation of organic food into $CO_2$, water and energy.
- It starts in cytoplasm and get completed inside the **mitochondria.**

The complete oxidation of glucose can be summarised as

$$C_6H_{12}O_6 + 6O_2 \xrightarrow{\text{Enzymes}} 6CO_2 + 6H_2O + \text{Energy (ATP)}$$

> Aerobic respiration yields more energy as the respiratory substrate is completely oxidised in the presence of $O_2$.

### 2. Anaerobic Respiration

- In this type of respiration, organic food is oxidised incompletely in the absence of oxygen.
- It occurs in **cytoplasm** and releases small amount of energy.

The common products of anaerobic respiration are $CO_2$, ethyl alcohol or lactic acid.

$$C_6H_{12}O_6 \xrightarrow{\text{Enzymes}} 2CO_2 + \underset{\text{Ethyl alcohol}}{2C_2H_5OH} + \text{Energy}$$

$$C_6H_{12}O_6 \xrightarrow{\text{Enzymes}} \underset{\text{Lactic acid}}{2C_3H_6O_3} + \text{Energy}$$

- It is believed that the first cells on this planet lived in a reducing environment when $O_2$ was not present in the atmosphere, i.e. they were **anaerobes.**
- Even among present day living organisms, many of them are adapted to anaerobic conditions.
- Some of them are **facultative anaerobes** (organisms that have the capability of switching from aerobic to anaerobic conditions according to the availability of oxygen) while others are **obligate anaerobes** (organisms that are not able to survive under normal atmospheric concentration of oxygen).
- In any case, all living organisms retain the enzymatic machinery for partial oxidation of glucose in the absence of oxygen. This breakdown of glucose into pyruvic acid is called **glycolysis.**

### Quick Test 1

1. All living organisms need '*A*' for carrying out daily life activities and is obtained by '*B*' of macromolecules. Identify *A* and *B* in the above statement.
2. The process of breaking of the '*A*' bonds of complex compounds through '*B*' within the cells, leading to release of considerable amount of energy in the form of ATP.
   Identify '*A*' and '*B*' in the above statement and name the process.
3. **State True or False.**
   During the oxidation of food within a cell, energy is absorbed in rapid single step reactions.
4. Name two openings in plants through which exchange of gases take place.
5. Respiration requires $O_2$. How did the first cells on earth manage to survive in an atmosphere with no oxygen present at that time?

## 12.3 Cellular Respiration : The Process

- Cellular respiration occurs in all living cells and proceeds with the help of enzymes.
- The first step in respiration is the **glycolysis** (glucose is oxidised to pyruvic acid).
- After which the pyruvic acid may enter the **Krebs' cycle** (aerobic respiration) or undergoes **fermentation** (anaerobic respiration).

### Glycolysis

- Glycolysis (Gk. *Glycos*–sugar; *lysis*–splitting), is a stepwise process by which one molecule of glucose (6C) breaks down into two molecules of pyruvic acid (3C).
- The scheme of glycolysis was given by **Gustav Embden, Otto Meyerhof** and **J Parnas** and is often referred to as the **EMP pathway**.
- It is a common pathway in both aerobic and anaerobic modes of respiration. But in case of anaerobic organisms, it is the only process in respiration.
- Glycolysis occurs in the **cytoplasm** of the cell and is present in all living organisms.
- During this process glucose gets partially oxidised to form two molecules of pyruvic acid.
- In plants, this glucose is derived from sucrose (end product of photosynthesis) or from stored carbohydrates.
- During the course of process in plant, this sucrose is first converted into glucose and fructose by the action of **invertase** enzyme, after this, these two monosaccharides enter the glycolytic pathway.

### Steps Involved in Glycolysis

In glycolysis, a chain of 10 reactions occur under the control of different enzymes.

It involves the following steps

**Step ❶ Phosphorylation of glucose** occurs by the action of an **enzyme hexokinase** that gives rise to **glucose-6-phosphate** by the utilisation of ATP.

**Step ❷ Isomerisation** of glucose-6-phosphate takes place to form **fructose-6-phosphate** with the help of an enzyme **phosphohexose isomerase**.

**Step ❸** This fructose-6-phosphate is again phosphorylated by ATP in order to form **fructose 1, 6-bisphosphate** in the presence of an enzyme **phosphofructokinase**.

**Step ❹** Splitting of fructose 1, 6-bisphosphate takes place into two triose phosphate molecules, i.e. **dihydroxyacetone phosphate** and **3-phosphoglyceraldehyde** (i.e. PGAL). This reaction is catalysed by an enzyme **aldolase**.

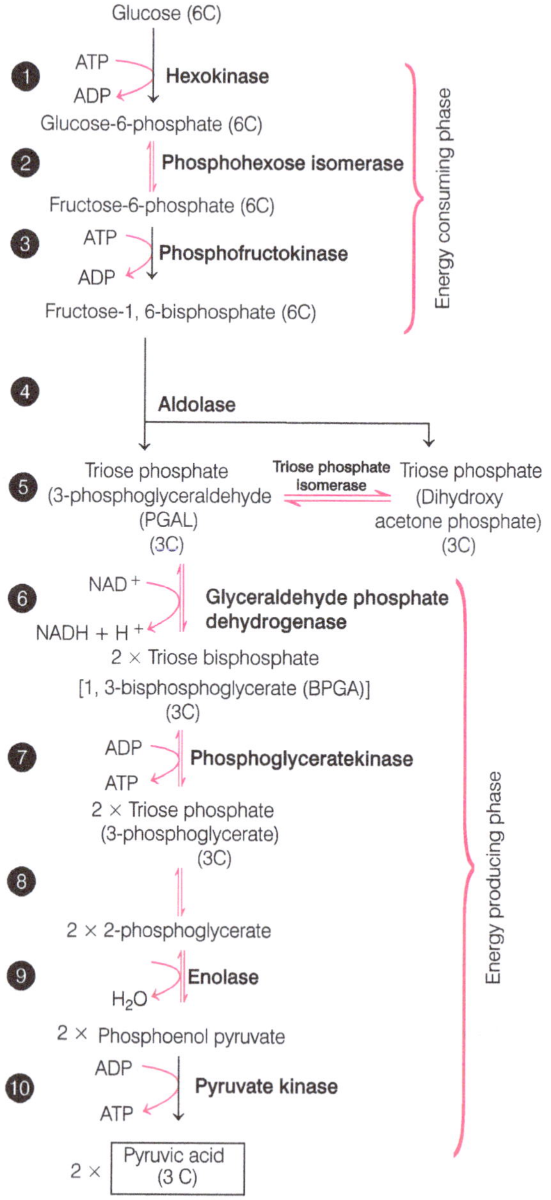


Fig 12.1 Steps of glycolysis

**Step 5** The **dihydroxyacetone phosphate** isomerises to yield **3-phosphoglyceraldehyde** (i.e. PGAL) in the presence of **triose phosphate isomerase**.

Now, there are 2 molecules of 3-PGAL which participates in further reaction.

**Step 6** Each molecule of PGAL removes two redox equivalents in the form of hydrogen atom and transfer them to a molecule of $NAD^+$ (i.e. the $NAD^+$ forms $NADH + H^+$) and accepts inorganic phosphate (Pi) from phosphoric acid.

This reaction in turn leads to the conversion to PGAL (which gets oxidised) to **1, 3-bisphosphoglycerate** (BPGA) (reversible reaction).

**Step 7** 1, 3-bisphosphoglycerate is converted to **3-phosphoglycerate** with the formation of ATP. This reaction is catalysed by an enzyme **phosphoglycerate kinase**. It is also known as energy yielding process. The formation of ATP directly from metabolites constitutes **substrate level phosphorylation**.

**Step 8** In this step, 3-phosphoglycerate is subsequently isomerised to form **2-phosphoglycerate**.

**Step 9** In the presence of enzyme **enolase**, with the loss of a water molecule, 2-phosphoglycerate is converted to **Phosphoenol Pyruvate** (PEP).

**Step 10** High energy phosphate group from Phosphoenol Pyruvate (PEP) is transferred to a molecule of ADP, by the action of enzyme **pyruvate kinase**. This in turn produces two molecules of **pyruvic acid** (pyruvate) and a molecule of ATP by substrate level phosphorylation. The pyruvic acid thus, produced is the key product of glycolysis.

Glycolysis has two phases, i.e. **preparatory** (glucose is broken down to glyceraldehyde-3-phosphate) and **pay off phase** (the glyceraldehyde-3-phosphate is changed into pyruvate producing NADH and ATP).

## Energy Yield in Glycolysis

The overall reaction of glycolysis can be depicted as

- Glucose + 2Pi + 2ADP + $2NAD^+ \rightarrow$ 2 Pyruvate + 2ATP + 2NADH + $2H^+$
- From the above equation, it can be concluded that there is net gain of 2 ATP and 2 molecules of NADH.
- Each NADH is equivalent to 3 ATP, therefore the net gain of ATP in glycolytic pathway is 8 ATP.

## Metabolic Fate of Pyruvate

- The fate of pyruvate depends upon the cellular need.
- In the presence of oxygen, pyruvic acid will enter the mitochondrion and undergo complete oxidation to yield $CO_2$ and $H_2O$ in **aerobic respiration** (Krebs' cycle and ETC).
- On the other hand in the absence of oxygen, the pyruvic acid will undergo anaerobic respiration (lactic acid fermentation or alcoholic fermentation).

## Fermentation

- Various microorganisms, bacteria, animals and plants are known to catabolise pyruvic acid anaerobically into various organic compounds depending upon the specific enzymes they possess. This process is known as fermentation.
- Some of its types are as follows

### 1. Alcoholic Fermentation

- In fungi (e.g. **yeast**), the incomplete oxidation of glucose is achieved under anaerobic condition by a series of reactions in which pyruvic acid is converted to $CO_2$ and ethanol.
- It is done under two steps
  - **Pyruvic acid** is first decarboxylated to acetaldehyde in the presence of enzyme pyruvic acid decarboxylase.
  - This acetaldehyde is further reduced to **ethyl alcohol** or **ethanol** in the presence of enzyme, i.e. alcohol dehydrogenase.

### 2. Lactic Acid Fermentation

- It occurs in organisms like bacteria, etc.

- In them lactic acid is produced as an end product of fermentation.
- Likewise, in case of animal cells also (such as muscles) during exercise, when there is inadequate amount of oxygen for cellular respiration, pyruvic acid is reduced to lactic acid in the presence of enzyme **lactate dehydrogenase** and NADH + $H^+$ gets reoxidised to $NAD^+$ and there is no production of $CO_2$.

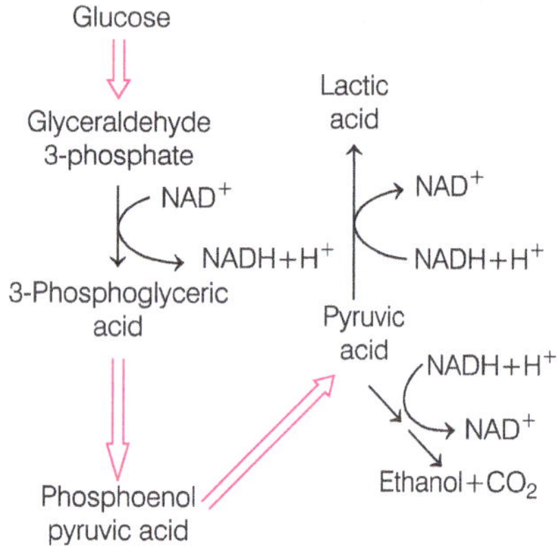


**Fig 12.2** Major pathways of anaerobic respiration

## Energy Yield in Fermentation

- In both alcoholic and lactic acid fermentation, the energy released is very less, i.e. less than 7% of the energy is released from glucose and not all of it is trapped as high energy bonds of ATP.
- The net gain of ATP from anaerobic respiration (fermentation) is 2 ATP molecules per glucose molecule.
- Also, the fermentation processes are proved to be hazardous in nature because either acid or alcohol is produced on oxidation.
- Apart from this, yeasts may also poison themselves to death if the concentration of alcohol reaches about 13%.

**TEACHER'S TIP**
The maximum concentration of alcohol in naturally fermented beverages is usually around 12-13%. In order to obtain alcoholic beverages with higher alcohol concentration, the process of distillation is utilised.

**Differences between Glycolysis and Fermentation**

| Glycolysis | Fermentation |
|---|---|
| It is the first step of respiration which occurs without requirement of oxygen and is common to both aerobic and anaerobic mode of respiration. | It is anaerobic respiration which does not require oxygen. |
| It produces pyruvic acid. | Fermentation produces different products. The common ones are ethanol (and $CO_2$) and lactic acid. |
| It produces two molecules of NADH per glucose molecule. | It generally utilises NADH produced during glycolysis. |
| Glycolysis forms 2ATP molecules per glucose molecule. | It does not produce ATP. |

### Quick Test 2

1. In plants, sucrose is first converted into glucose and fructose by the action of which enzyme?
2. Pyruvic acid, the key end product of glycolysis has many metabolic fates. What does it form under aerobic condition?
3. Name the end products of alcoholic fermentation.
4. Name the conditions under which fermentation occurs in yeast cells.
5. **State True or False.**
   During anaerobic respiration, yeast can poison themselves, if the concentration of alcohol reaches upto 5%.

## Aerobic Respiration

- It is the next step (after glycolysis) that leads to complete oxidation of organic substances.
- It occurs in the presence of oxygen.
- The final product of glycolysis, i.e. pyruvic acid is transported from the cytoplasm into the mitochondria and thus the second phase of respiration is initiated.
- The process of aerobic respiration involves two crucial events, which are as follows
  - The complete oxidation of pyruvate occurs by the stepwise removal of all the hydrogen atoms, thereby leaving three molecules of $CO_2$. This occurs in the **matrix of mitochondria**.

- The electrons removed as a part of the hydrogen atoms are then passed on to molecular $O_2$ with the simultaneous synthesis of ATP. This process takes place on the **inner membrane** of the **mitochondria**.

- Aerobic respiration comprises of following interdependent major processes.

## Oxidative Decarboxylation of Pyruvic Acid

- In mitochondria, pyruvic acid (formed by the glycolytic catabolism of carbohydrates in the cytosol) undergoes oxidative decarboxylation (i.e. removal of $CO_2$ in aerobic conditions).
- It results in the formation of key compound, i.e. **acetyl Co-A** by the action of pyruvic acid dehydrogenase (in mitochondrial matrix) through a series of reactions.
- The reactions catalysed by pyruvic dehydrogenase require the participation of several coenzymes, including $NAD^+$ and Coenzyme-A.
- Pyruvic acid + Co-A + $NAD^+$ $\xrightarrow[\text{Pyruvate dehydrogenase}]{Mg^{2+}}$ Acetyl Co-A + $CO_2$ + NADH + $H^+$
- During this process, two molecules of NADH are produced from the metobolism of two molecules of pyruvic acid (produced from one glucose molecule during glycolysis).
- Thus, acetyl Co-A acts as a connecting link between glycolysis and tricarboxylic acid cycle.

## Tricarboxylic Acid (TCA) Cycle

- The acetyl Co-A enters a cyclic pathway, Krebs' cycle or Tricarboxylic Acid Cycle (TCA) in mitochondrial matrix.
- It was first elucidated by **Sir Hans Kreb**, a British Biochemist.
- Following are the steps of Krebs' cycle
  - **Condensation** The Krebs' cycle starts with the condensation of acetyl group with oxaloacetic acid and water to yield citric acid, a 6C compound.
    - This is the first stable product of the cycle.
    - This step is catalysed by an enzyme citrate synthetase.
    - A molecule of Co-A is liberated during this reaction.
  - **Isomerisation** Citric acid then undergoes isomerisation to form isocitrate.
  - **Oxidative Decarboxylation** Isocitrate undergoes two successive steps of oxidative decarboxylation, that leads to the formation of α-ketoglutaric acid, (a 5C compound) and then succinyl Co-A.
    - The succinyl Co-A then splits into a 4C compound succinic acid and CoA with the addition of water. During this conversion, a molecule of GTP (guanosine triphosphate) is synthesised.
    - This is a **substrate level phosphorylation.**
    - In a coupled reaction GTP is converted to GDP with the simultaneous synthesis of ATP from ADP.

GTP is also an energy carrier like ATP. Thus, this is the only high energy phosphate produced in the Krebs' cycle.

- In the remaining steps of Krebs' cycle, succinyl Co-A is oxidised to oxaloacetic acid, a 4C compound following the formation of fumaric acid and malic acid.

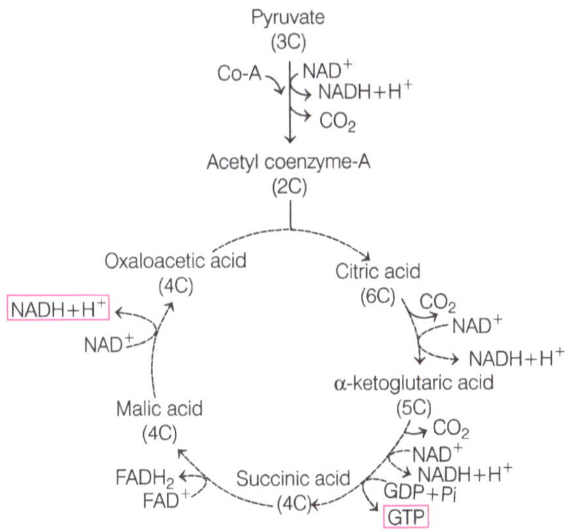


**Fig 12.3** The citric acid cycle or Krebs' cycle or tricarboxylic acid cycle

### Output of Tricarboxylic Acid Cycle

- During Krebs' cycle, 3 molecules of $NAD^+$ are reduced to NADH + $H^+$, and one molecule of $FAD^+$ is reduced to $FADH_2$.

- Also one molecule of ATP is produced directly from GTP (by substrate level phosphorylation).
- For continuous oxidation of acetyl Co-A, *via* the TCA cycle, the continued replenishment of oxaloacetic acid (the first member of the cycle) is necessary.
- In addition to this, regeneration of $NAD^+$ and $FAD^+$ from NADH and $FADH_2$, respectively are also required.
- The summary equation for this phase of respiration is as follows

$$\text{Pyruvic acid} + 4NAD^+ + FAD^+ + 2H_2O + ADP + Pi \xrightarrow{\text{Mitochondrial matrix}} 3CO_2 + 4NADH + 4H^+ + FADH_2 + ATP$$

- Till now, glucose has been broken down to release $CO_2$ gas, 8 molecules of $NADH+H^+$, two molecules of $FADH_2$ and 2 molecules of ATP.

## Importance of Tricarboxylic Acid Cycle

The citric acid cycle is important in the following ways

- This is the major pathway for the formation of ATP molecules.
- Many intermediate compounds of this cycle are used in the synthesis of other biomolecules.

**Differences between Glycolysis and Krebs' cycle**

| Glycolysis | Krebs' Cycle |
|---|---|
| It takes place in the cytoplasm. | It takes place in the matrix of mitochondria. |
| It is a linear pathway. | It is a cyclic pathway. |
| It occurs in aerobic as well as anaerobic respiration. | It occurs in aerobic respiration only. |
| It consumes 2 ATP molecules. | It does not consume ATP. |
| It yields 2 NADH per glucose molecule. | It yields 6 NADH molecules and 2 $FADH_2$ molecules from 2 acetyl coenzyme-A molecules. |
| It generates 2 ATP molecules net from 1 glucose molecule. | It generates 2 GTP/ATP molecules from 2 acetyl coenzyme-A molecules. |
| It oxidises glucose partly, producing pyruvate. | It completely oxidises acetyl coenzyme-A. |
| It does not produce $CO_2$. | It produces $CO_2$. |

### Quick Test 3

1. For aerobic reaction to takes place, the product of glycolysis is transported from *A* to *B*. Identify *A* and *B*.
2. Name the compound that acts as a connecting link between the glycolysis and tricarboxylic acid cycle.
3. The Krebs' cycle starts with the condensation of acetyl group with *X* to yield citric acid. Identify *X*.
4. Which amongst the following are 3 and 6 carbon compound?

   Oxaloacetate, Phophoglyceraldehyde, Isocitrate, α-ketoglutarate.
5. **State True or False.**

   Krebs' cycle results in the formation of 2 molecules of NADH and 3 molecules of $FADH_2$ from one acetyl co-enzyme-A .

## 12.4 Electron Transport System (ETS)

- At the end of Krebs' cycle, the oxidation of glucose is completed to give out $6CO_2$ molecules. But the energy obtained till now is very less (i.e. 2ATPs in each glycolysis and Krebs' cycle).
- Thus, the full amount of energy is yet to be obtained from the substrate, i.e. glucose.
- This occurs through the following steps in the respiratory process and utilises the energy stored in the $NADH + H^+$ and $FADH_2$.
- Electron Transport System (ETS) is the metabolic pathway through which the electron passes from one carrier to another.
- It occurs in the inner mitochondrial membrane.
- The electron transport system consists of four enzyme complexes, which are arranged in a series on the inner membrane of the mitochondria.
  - Electrons from NADH produced in the mitochondrial matrix during citric acid cycle are oxidised by NADH dehydrogenase (**complex I**) and are transferred to ubiquinone located within the inner membrane of the mitochondria.
  - Reducing equivalents are also received by ubiquinone *via* $FADH_2$ (**complex II**), generated during the oxidation of succinate in the citric acid cycle.

- **This reduced ubiquinone** (ubiquinol) is then oxidised with the transfer of electron to cytochrome-*c* (small protein attached to the outer surface of the inner membrane) *via* cytochrome-$bc_1$ complex (**complex III**).
- Cytochrome-*c*, acts as a mobile carrier for transfer of electrons between complex III and IV.

- **Complex IV** known as **cytochrome-*c* oxidase complex** contains cytochromes *a*, $a_3$ and two copper centres.

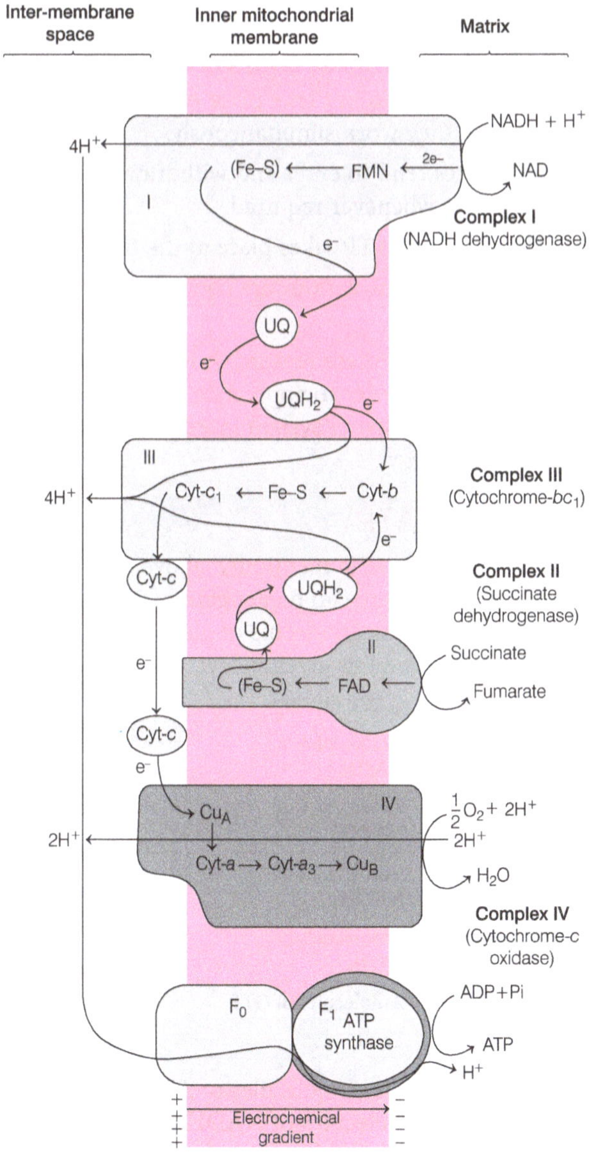


Fig. 12.4 Electron Transport System (ETS)

- During the course of transfer, when electrons pass from one carrier molecule to another (*via* complex I to IV) in the electron transport chain, they are coupled to ATP synthase (i.e. complex V) for the production of ATP from ADP and inorganic phosphate.
- The number of ATP molecules synthesised depends on the nature of the electron donor.
- One molecule of NADH on oxidation provides 3 molecules of ATP while one molecule of $FADH_2$ produces 2 molecules of ATP.

## Final Hydrogen Acceptor

- The electrons are finally accepted by **oxygen** having the highest redox potential in the series which along with $H^+$ ions forms water.
- Although, aerobic process of respiration takes place only in the presence of $O_2$, the role of $O_2$ is limited to the terminal stage of the process.
- Yet, the presence of oxygen is vital because it drives the whole process by removing hydrogen from the system.
- Oxygen acts as the final hydrogen acceptor.
- Unlike photophosphorylation where it is the light energy that is utilised for the production of proton gradient for phosphorylation, in respiration it is the energy of oxidation-reduction utilised for phosphorylation.

## Oxidative Phosphorylation

- It is the synthesis of energy rich ATP molecules by chemiosmotic hypothesis with the help of energy liberated by oxidation of reduced coenzymes ($NADH+FADH_2$) produced during respiration.
- Oxidative phosphorylation in mitochondria is catalysed by a multicomponent enzymatic complex called **ATP synthase**, (**complex V**) or **coupling factor.**
- The ATP synthase complex consists of two major components
  - **$F_1$-particle** The $F_1$ head piece is a peripheral membrane protein complex and contains the site for ATP synthesis from ADP and inorganic phosphate.
  - **$F_0$-particle** It is an integral membrane protein complex that forms the channel through which protons cross the inner membrane.

- The passage of protons through the channel is coupled to the catalytic site of the $F_1$-component for the production of ATP.
- For every $4H^+$ that passes through $F_0$ from the intermembrane space to the matrix (down the electrochemical proton gradient), one ATP molecule is produced.

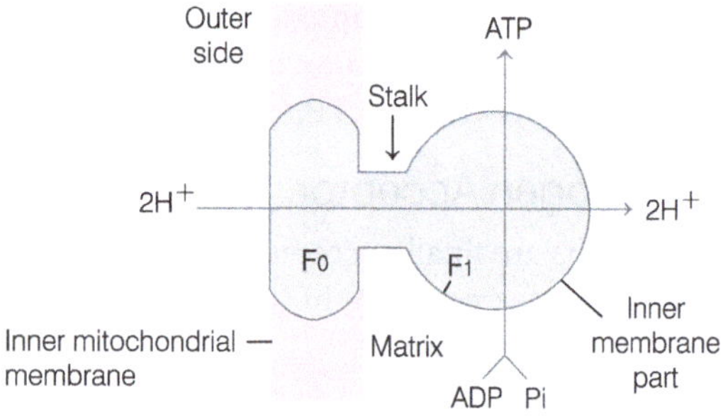


Fig. 12.5 Diagrammatic representation of ATP synthesis in mitochondria

### Quick Test 4

1. Name the mobile carrier present in electron transport chain.
2. FMN, a derivative of riboflavin (vitamin-$B_2$), plays a role in electron transfer reactions. Name the complex that contains FMN as a cofactor.
3. Oxidative phosphorylation occurs in the mitochondria and is responsible for producing ATP. Name the components of complex that takes part in oxidative phosphorylation.
4. **State True or False.**
   ATP synthase is one of the complex, that participates in the electron transport system.
5. Mention the number of protons that passes through complex V for the synthesis of 2 molecules of ATP.

## 12.5 The Respiratory Balance Sheet

- The complete aerobic breakdown of one molecule of glucose results in the release of 2 molecules of NADH from glycolysis. And 8 molecules of NADH and 2 molecules of $FADH_2$ within the mitochondrial matrix.
- The calculation of the net gain of ATP for every glucose molecule oxidised can be made only on following certain assumptions
  - All pathways function in an orderly sequential manner with one substrate forming the next and with glycolysis, TCA cycle and ETS pathway following one after another.
  - The NADH synthesised during glycolysis is transferred into the mitochondria for oxidative phosphorylation.
  - None of the intermediates in the pathway are utilised to synthesise any other compound.
  - Only glucose is being respired, no other alternative substrates are entering in the pathway at any of the intermediary stages.
- But this kind of assumptions are not exactly valid in a living system due to the following reasons
  - All pathways do not take place one after another instead, they work simultaneously.
  - Substrates tend to enter and withdraw from the pathways whenever required.
  - Utilisation of ATP takes place at the time of need.
  - Rates of enzyme actions are controlled by multiple means.
- Yet, inspite of all these reasons, it is necessary to do this exercise in order to appreciate the beauty and efficiency of the living system in extracting and storing of energy.

### Net Gain of ATP

- Due to all the criteria mentioned above, it is predicted that there can be net gain of 38 ATP molecules from one molecule of glucose during aerobic respiration as given below

| | | | |
|---|---|---|---|
| **Glycolysis** | 2 ATP directly | = | 2 ATP |
| | 2 molecules of NADH | = | 6 ATP |
| **Pyruvic acid to acetyl Co-A** | 2 molecules of NADH | = | 6 ATP |
| **Citric acid cycle** | 6 molecules of NADH | = | 18 ATP |
| | 2 molecules of FADH | = | 4 ATP |
| | 2 molecules of GTP | = | 2 ATP |
| | Total | = | 38 ATP |

- In eukaryotic cells, 2 molecules of ATP are spent for transporting 2 molecules of NADH formed during glycolysis (in the cytoplasm) to the mitochondria, hence the net gain is 36 molecules of ATP.

**Comparison between Fermentation and Aerobic Respiration**

| Fermentation | Aerobic Respiration |
|---|---|
| It accounts for only a partial breakdown of glucose. | It accounts for complete degradation of glucose to $CO_2$ and $H_2O$. |
| There is a net gain of only two molecules of ATP for each molecule of glucose degraded to pyruvic acid. | In this, many more molecules of ATP are generated (i.e. 38). |
| Electron transport is absent in this. | It involves electron transport system. |
| NADH is slowly oxidised to $NAD^+$. | The reaction is very vigorous. |

## 12.6 Amphibolic Pathway

- The term amphibolic is used to denote a biochemical pathway involving both catabolism and anabolism.
- Usually, glucose is the primary or favoured substrate for respiration for most of the organisms.
- All carbohydrates are first converted into glucose before they are used for respiration.
- Different substrates like fats and proteins can also be respired, but they do not enter the respiratory pathway at the very first step.
- If fats have to enter the pathway, they first have to be converted into fatty acids and glycerol. Fatty acids are then degraded into acetyl Co-A, which enters the citric acid cycle.
- Glycerol is first converted to 3-phosphoglyceraldehyde (PGAL), before entering the pathway.
- Likewise, the proteins (if acts as respiratory substrates) are degraded by **proteases** into individual amino acids which after deamination (removal of amine group from a molecule), depending on their structure would enters the Krebs' cycle either as pyruvate or acetyl Co-A.
- Since, respiration involves breakdown of substrates (i.e. organic compounds), it has been considered as a catabolic process and the respiratory pathway is thus called **catabolic pathway**.
- But at the same time certain intermediates of respiratory pathway are also withdrawn in order to synthesise other compounds, e.g. fatty acids would be broken down to acetyl Co-A, but when organisms need to synthesise fatty acids, acetyl Co-A would be withdrawn from respiratory pathway.
- Hence, respiratory pathway comes into picture both during breakdown and synthesis of compounds.
- Thus, it would be better to consider the respiratory pathway as an amphibolic pathway rather than as a catabolic one.

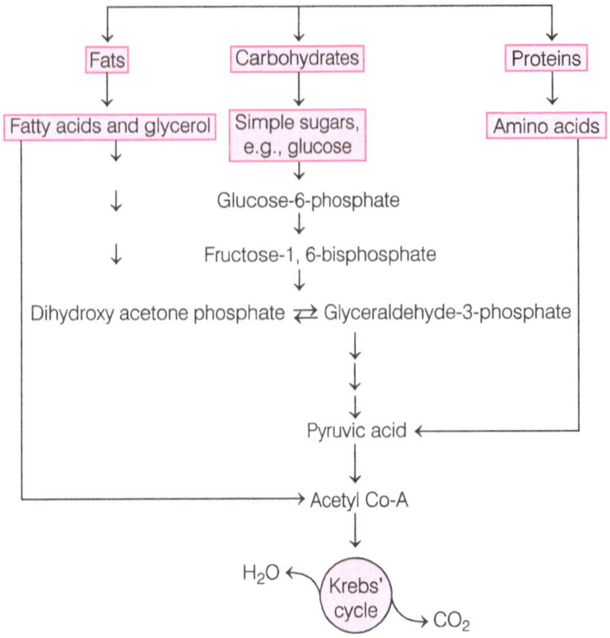


Fig. 12.6 Interrelationship among metabolic pathway showing respiration mediated breakdown of different organic molecules to $CO_2$ and $H_2O$

## 12.7 Respiratory Quotient (RQ)

- It is the ratio of the volume of $CO_2$ evolved to the volume of $O_2$ consumed during respiration.
- It is also known as **respiratory ratio.**

$$RQ = \frac{\text{Volume of } CO_2 \text{ evolved}}{\text{Volume of } O_2 \text{ consumed}}$$

- The respiratory quotient tend to vary with respiratory substrate used during respiration.

This can be understood from following

## 1. Respiratory Quotient of Carbohydrates

- When carbohydrates are used as substrate and are completely oxidised, the RQ is always 1 because amount of $CO_2$ evolved is always equal to the amount of $O_2$ consumed.

$$C_6H_{12}O_6 + 6O_2 \longrightarrow 6CO_2 + 6H_2O + \text{Energy}$$

$$RQ = \frac{6CO_2}{6O_2} = 1.0$$

## 2. Respiratory Quotient of Fats

- If the respiratory substrate is fat, then RQ of the respiring cells will be less than 1, because the volume of $CO_2$ evolved is quite less in comparison to the volume of $O_2$ being consumed.
- Calculations for a fatty acid, tripalmitin, if used as a substrate is shown below

$$\underset{\text{Tripalmitin}}{2(C_{51}H_{98}O_6)} + 145\,O_2 \longrightarrow$$

$$102\,CO_2 + 98\,H_2O + \text{Energy}$$

$$RQ = \frac{102CO_2}{145O_2} = 0.7$$

- Fats always require more amount of $O_2$ for their oxidation as compared to other substrates.

## 3. Respiratory Quotient of Proteins

- If the respiratory substrate is protein then the RQ is would be about 0.9.
- It is important to recognise that in living organisms respiratory substrates are often more than one.
- Also, pure proteins or fats are never used as respiratory substrates.

## Quick Test 5

1. All carbohydrates are first converted into *X* before being used for respiration. Identify '*X*'.
2. Name the process that is concerned with the removal of amine group from the molecule.
3. **State True or False.**
   Respiration involves both the formation and breakdown of substances.
4. Fatty acids undergo beta-oxidation to be converted into a molecule that enters the Krebs' cycle. Name this compound.
5. **State True or False.**
   Fats always require more amount of $O_2$ for their oxidation as compared to carbohydrates and proteins.

# Mind Map

## Respiration in Plants

### Respiration

- Liberation of energy from food by chemical breakdown.
- **Cellular respiration** is the chemical breakdown of food substrate mediated by several enzymes to release energy stored in chemical bonds.
- Respiratory pathway is an amphibolic pathway.
- **Types of Cellular Respiration**

**Anaerobic respiration** (in absence of $O_2$)

**Aerobic respiration** (in presence of $O_2$)

### Glycolysis

- It is first step of respiration.
- Occurs in **cytosol**.
- Common to both aerobic and anaerobic respiration.
- Given by three scientists Embden, Meyerhof and Parnas, thus called **EMP pathway**.
- Series of biochemical reactions in which glucose is broken down to pyruvate with release of usable energy in the form of ATP.
- Net output→2 Pyruvate + 2ATP + 2NADH

### Respiratory Balance Sheet

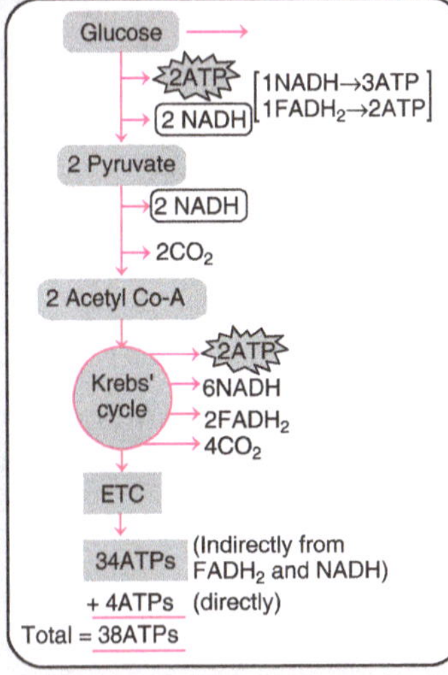


### Respiratory Quotient (RQ)

- It is the ratio of volume of $CO_2$ produced to the volume of oxygen consumed.

$$RQ = \frac{\text{Volume of } CO_2 \text{ produced}}{\text{Volume of } O_2 \text{ consumed}}$$

- RQ can be unity, more than one, less than one, zero and infinity.
- RQ for different respiratory substrates
  - Proteins =0.9
  - Fats ⇒ < 1 (e.g. tripalmitin = 0.7)
  - Organic acid ⇒ > 1
  - Carbohydrates = 1
  - Anaerobic respiration = ∞

### Fermentation (Anaerobic)

- Occurs in cytosol.
- Conversion of pyruvate to alcohol and organic acids in the absence of oxygen.
- Depending upon its product, it can be

| Alcoholic Fermentation | Lactic Acid Fermentation |
|---|---|
| Ethanol and $CO_2$ are produced.<br>Pyruvate → (Decarboxylase/ Alcohol dehydrogenase; 2 NADH → 2 $NAD^+$, $+H^+$) → Ethanol + $CO_2$<br>• e.g. yeast. | Lactic acid is produced without evolution of $CO_2$.<br>Pyruvate → (Lactic dehydrogenase; 2 NADH → 2 $NAD^+$) → Lactic acid<br>• e.g. muscles during vigorous exercise. |

### Krebs' Cycle

- Also known as Tricarboxylic Acid (TCA)/Citric acid cycle
- Occurs in mitochondrial matrix.

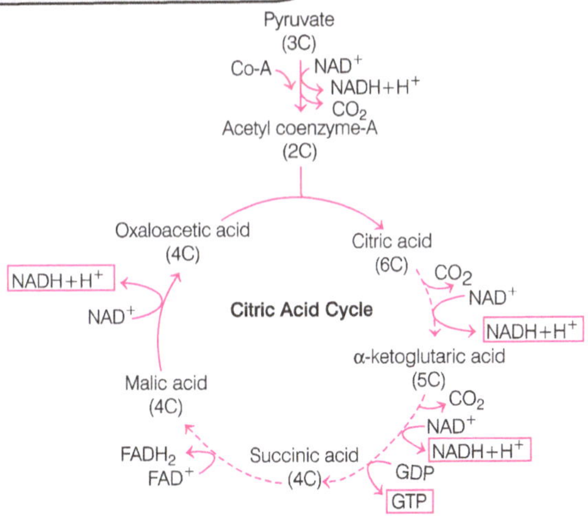


- There are three steps in the cycle where $NAD^+$ is reduced to $NADH^+$ and $FAD^+$ is reduced to $FADH_2$.
- Products of TCA cycle → 3 NADH + 1 $FADH_2$ + 1 ATP + 2 $CO_2$
- Respiratory pathway or TCA cycle is an amphibolic pathway as it involves both anabolism and catabolism.
- All enzymes of TCA cycle are located in the mitochondrial matrix except succinate dehydrogenase, i.e. located in inner membrane in eukaryotes.

### Pyruvate Oxidation/Oxidative Decarboxylation

- Occurs in mitochondria.
- It involves conversion of glycolysis product pyruvate into acetyl Co-A that enters into next step, i.e. Krebs' cycle. It is also called **link reaction** as it links glycolysis with Krebs'
- Pyruvate +Co-A $\xrightarrow[Mg^{2+},\ NAD^+ \to NADH+H^+]{\text{Pyruvate dehydrogenase complex}}$ Acetyl Co-A + $CO_2$ (enters Krebs' cycle)

### Electron Transport Chain

- Occurs in the inner mitochondrial membrane.
- Involves the oxidation of NADH and $FADH_2$ to release energy. Electrons from NADH and $FADH_2$ are passed through complexes I-IV, ultimately reducing oxygen to form water.
- This process is coupled with ATP synthesis *via* ATP synthase (complex-V). As protons move through the $F_0$ component of ATP synthase, ATP is synthesised from ADP and inorganic phosphate. Oxygen acts as the final electron acceptor, driving the process, which is known as **oxidative phosphorylation**.
- For every NADH molecule, 3 ATP are produced and for $FADH_2$, 2 ATP are produced.

# EXAM PATTERN QUESTIONS

## Objective Type Questions

### Multiple Choice Questions

**1.** The complete combustion of glucose in respiration is represented by

(a) $C_6H_{12}O_6 + 6O_2 \rightarrow 6CO_2 + 6H_2O + \text{Energy}$
(b) $C_6H_{12}O_6 + 6CO_2 \rightarrow 6O_2 + 6H_2O + \text{Energy}$
(c) $C_6H_{12}O_6 + 6O_2 + 6CO_2 \rightarrow + 6CO_2 + 6H_2O + \text{Energy}$
(d) $C_6H_{12}O_6 + 6O_2 + 6CO_2 + ATP \rightarrow 6CO_2 + 6H_2O + 6O_2 + \text{Energy}$

**Ans.** (*a*)

**2.** Steps of respiration are controlled by

(a) substrates (b) enzymes
(c) hormone (d) bile juice

**Ans.** (*b*)

**3.** The released energy obtained by oxidation is stored as

(a) a concentration gradient across a membrane
(b) ADP
(c) ATP
(d) $NAD^+$

**Ans.** (*c*)

**4.** Consider the given features possessed by plants.

I. Maximum transport of gases from one part to another.
II. Low demands for gaseous exchange
III. Roots, stems and leaves respire at lower rates.
IV. Most cells have complete surfaces dose to air.

How many of these features allow plant to get along without respiratory organs?

(a) 2 (b) 4
(c) 1 (d) 3

**Ans.** (*d*)

**5.** Select the correct order of reactions in glycolysis.

I. Conversion of 3-phosphoglyceraldehyde to 1, 3-bisphosphoglycerate
II. Conversion of 3-phosphoglyceric acid to 2-phosphoglycerate
III. Conversion of BPGA to 3-phosphoglyceric acid
IV. Splitting of fructose 1, 6-bisphosphate into dihydroxyacetone phosphate and 3-phosphoglyceraldehyde **Competency Based Que.**

Codes

(a) IV, III, I, II (b) II, III, I, IV
(c) II, IV, I, III (d) IV, I, III, II

**Ans.** (*d*)

**6.** In which of the following reaction of glycolysis, reduction of $NAD^+$ takes place?

(a) Glucose-6-$PO_4$ to fructose-6-$PO_4$
(b) Glyceraldehyde-3-phosphate to 1, 3-bisphosphoglycerate
(c) 1, 3-diphosphoglycerate to 3-phosphoglycerate
(d) 2-phosphoglycerate to phosphoglycerate

**Ans.** (*b*)

**7.** Phosphorylation of glucose during glycolysis is catalysed by **NCERT Exemplar**

(a) phosphoglucomutase
(b) phosphoglucoisomerase
(c) hexokinase
(d) phosphorylase

**Ans.** (*c*)

**8.** Pyruvic acid, the key product of glycolysis can have many metabolic fates. Under aerobic condition it forms **NCERT Exemplar**

(a) lactic acid (b) $CO_2 + H_2O$
(c) acetyl Co - A + $CO_2$ (d) ethanol + $CO_2$

**Ans.** (*b*)

**9.** Which of the following statement regarding fermentation is incorrect?

(a) It occurs in the absence of oxygen
(b) It generates significantly more ATP than aerobic respiration
(c) Ethanol and carbon dioxide are common products of alcoholic fermentation
(d) It can occur in both prokaryotic and eukaryotic organisms

**Ans.** (*b*)

**10. Which of the following describes the metabolic fate of pyruvate under aerobic conditions?**

(a) Pyruvate is converted to acetyl Co-A, which enters the Krebs' cycle

(b) Pyruvate is converted to oxaloacetic acid, which enters the Krebs' cycle

(c) Pyruvate is converted to lactic acid when oxygen is limited

(d) Pyruvate is converted to ethanol through alcoholic fermentation

**Ans.** (*a*)

**11. Connecting link between glycolysis and Krebs' cycle is**

(a) acetyl Co-A

(b) pyruvic acid

(c) $CO_2$

(d) None of the above

**Ans.** (*a*)

**12. The reaction that is called link reaction between glycolysis and Krebs' cycle** **DIKSHA**

(a) conversion of pyruvate to acetyl Co-A

(b) conversion of acetyl Co-A to citric acid

(c) conversion of oxaloacetate to citrate

(d) oxidation of malate to oxaloacetate

**Ans.** (*a*)

**13. TCA cycle enzymes are present in**

(a) cytoplasm

(b) intermembrane space of mitochondria

(c) mitochondrial matrix

(d) inner membrane of mitochondria

**Ans.** (*c*)

**14. α-ketoglutarate acid, an intermediary compound of Krebs' cycle is a**

(a) 5 carbon compound (b) 6 carbon compound

(c) 4 carbon compound (d) 3 carbon compound

**Ans.** (*a*)

**15. In which of the following, reduction of NAD does not takes place?**

(a) Isocitric acid $\rightarrow$ α- ketoglutaric acid

(b) Malic acid $\rightarrow$ Oxaloacetic acid

(c) Pyruvic acid $\rightarrow$ Acetyl Co-A

(d) Succinic acid $\rightarrow$ Fumaric acid

**Ans.** (*d*)

**16. How many NADH + $H^+$ molecules are released from a single pyruvate in Krebs' cycle?**

(a) 4 (b) 6

(c) 12 (d) 8

**Ans.** (*a*)

**17. Match the following columns about ETS.**

| | Column I (ETS Complexes) | | Column II (Names) |
|---|---|---|---|
| A. | Complex-I | 1. | NADH dehydrogenase |
| B. | Complex-II | 2. | Succinate dehydrogenase |
| C. | Complex-III | 3. | Cytochrome-$bc_1$ complex |
| D. | Complex-IV | 4. | Cytochrome-*c* oxidase complex |

**Codes**

| | A | B | C | D |
|---|---|---|---|---|
| (a) | 1 | 4 | 3 | 2 |
| (b) | 1 | 2 | 3 | 4 |
| (c) | 2 | 3 | 1 | 4 |
| (d) | 3 | 4 | 1 | 2 |

**Ans.** (*b*)

**18. The last or terminal cytochrome in respiratory chain is**

(a) cytochrome-*a*

(b) cytochrome-$a_3$

(c) cytochrome-*c*

(d) cytochrome-*f*

**Ans.** (*b*)

**19. The main purpose of electron transport chain is to**

(a) release the energy stored in NADH +$H^+$ and $FADH_2$

(b) use the intermediate from TCA cycle

(c) breakdown pyruvic acid

(d) to produce NADH + $H^+$

**Ans.** (*a*)

**20. Which of the following statement is incorrect?** **DIKSHA**

(a) ETS operates in the inner mitochondrial membrane

(b) NADPH yields 3 ATP

(c) glycolysis operates in the cytoplasm

(d) First product of Krebs' cycle is succinate

**Ans.** (*d*)

**21. The ultimate electron acceptor of respiration in an aerobic organism is** **NCERT Exemplar**

(a) cytochrome (b) oxygen

(c) hydrogen (d) glucose

**Ans.** (*b*) Oxygen is the ultimate hydrogen acceptor in aerobic respiration because at the end of electron transport chain it accepts a pair of electron and combines with hydrogen atom to form water molecule.

**22. The end product of oxidative phosphorylation is** **NCERT Exemplar**

(a) NADH (b) oxygen

(c) ADP (d) ATP + $H_2O$

**Ans.** (*d*)

**23.** Match the following columns. **NCERT Exemplar**

| | Column I | | Column II |
|---|---|---|---|
| A. | Molecular oxygen | 1. | α- ketoglutaric acid |
| B. | Electron acceptor | 2. | Hydrogen acceptor |
| C. | Pyruvate dehydrogenase | 3. | Cytochrome- *c* |
| D. | Decarboxylation | 4. | Acetyl Co-A |

Codes

| | A | B | C | D |
|---|---|---|---|---|
| (a) | 2 | 3 | 4 | 1 |
| (b) | 3 | 4 | 2 | 1 |
| (c) | 2 | 1 | 3 | 4 |
| (d) | 4 | 3 | 1 | 2 |

**Ans.** (*a*)

**24.** Select the incorrect match pair.

(a) Glycolysis–Breakdown glucose to pyruvic acid
(b) Krebs' cycle–Generates GTP *via* substrate level phosphorylation
(c) ETS –Located in the inner mitochondrial membrane of eukaryotic cells
(d) Fermentation –Produces large amounts of ATP

**Ans.** (*d*)

**25.** In the terminal oxidation, ATP synthase is considered as

(a) a proton pump that actively transports protons in the mitochondrial matrix
(b) an enzyme that catalyses the conversion of ADP and Pi to ATP *via* proton gradient
(c) a component of Krebs' cycle that directly produces ATP
(d) a receptor that initiates electron transport chain

**Ans.** (*b*)

**26.** Mitochondria are called powerhouses of the cell. Which of the following observations support this statement? **NCERT Exemplar**

(a) Mitochondria synthesise ATP
(b) Mitochondria have a double membrane
(c) The enzymes of the Krebs' cycle and the cytochromes are found in mitochondria
(d) Mitochondria are found in almost all plant and animal cells

**Ans.** (*a*) Mitochondria are the site of ATP production which is the energy currency of the cell.

The rest of the statements, though are correct but, does not verify and support the fact that mitochondria are the powerhouses of the cell.

**27.** Which one of the following substances is the starting point of various respiratory pathway? **DIKSHA**

(a) Acetyl Co-A
(b) Pyruvic acid
(c) Glucose
(d) Glucose-6-Phosphate

**Ans.** (*a*)

**28.** Glycerol is a product of fat breakdown. It sometimes enters the respiratory pathway after being converted to

(a) Fatty acids
(b) PEP
(c) PGAL
(d) None of these

**Ans.** (*c*)

**29.** The Respiratory Quotient (RQ) or respiratory ratio is

(a) $RQ = \dfrac{\text{Volume of } O_2 \text{ evolved}}{\text{Volume of } CO_2 \text{ consumed}}$

(b) $RQ = \dfrac{\text{Volume of } O_2 \text{ consumed}}{\text{Volume of } CO_2 \text{ evolved}}$

(c) $RQ = \dfrac{\text{Volume of } CO_2 \text{ consumed}}{\text{Volume of } O_2 \text{ evolved}}$

(d) $RQ = \dfrac{\text{Volume of } CO_2 \text{ evolved}}{\text{Volume of } O_2 \text{ consumed}}$

**Ans.** (*d*)

## Assertion-Reason Questions

**Direction** (Q. Nos. 1-12) *In each of the following questions, a statement of Assertion (A) is given followed by corresponding statement of Reason (R). Of the statements, mark the correct answer as*

(a) Both A and R are true and R is the correct explanation of A
(b) Both A and R are true, but R is not the correct explanation of A
(c) A is true, but R is false
(d) A is false, but R is true

**1. Assertion** (A) Aerobic respiration is bioenergetically more efficient than anaerobic glycolysis.

**Reason** (R) Aerobic respiration occurs in the presence of oxygen, while fermentation occurs in the absence of oxygen.

**Ans.** (*b*)

**2. Assertion** (A) Glycolysis occurs in the cell's cytoplasm.

**Reason** (R) Enzymes for glycolysis are found in the cytoplasm.

**Ans.** (*a*)

**3. Assertion** (A) The conversion of glyceraldehyde-3-phosphate into 1,3- bisphosphoglycerate is an oxidation reaction.

**Reason** (R) The reaction in which 1, 3-bisphosphoglycerate is formed from glyceraldehyde-3-phosphate utilises $NAD^+$.

**Ans.** (*a*)

**4. Assertion** (A) Glycolysis produces a net gain of 2ATP molecules of glucose.

**Reason** (R) In glycolysis, 4ATP molecules are produced, but 2 ATP molecules are consumed during the initial steps.

**Ans.** (*a*)

**5. Assertion** (A) Yeast cells show alcoholic fermentation.

**Reason** (R) Fermentation is an aerobic process.

**Ans.** (*c*) A is true, but R is false. R can be corrected as Fermentation is an anaerobic process.

**6. Given below is the metabolic breakdown of respiratory substrate under anaerobic condition in living organisms. Study this reaction and comment upon the appropriateness of the Assertion and the Reason.** **Competency Based Que.**

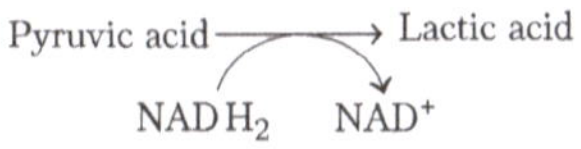


**Assertion** (A) The above reaction occurs when there is lack of oxygen in muscles leading to muscle cramps.

**Reason** (R) Accumulation of lactic acid from anaerobic respiration causes cramping in muscles.

**Ans.** (*a*)

**7. Assertion** (A) GTP is also an energy carrier like ATP.

**Reason** (R) GTP is the high energy phosphate produced in the Krebs' cycle.

**Ans.** (*b*)

**8. Assertion** (A) For every $4H^+$ that passes through $F_0$ from the intermembrane space to the matrix, one ATP molecule is produced.

**Reason** (R) The ATP synthase complex consists of $F_0$ and $F_1$ -particles.

**Ans.** (*b*)

**9. Assertion** (A) The calculation of net ATP gain during cellular respiration can vary significantly in different cells.

**Reason** (R) Factors like different respiratory substrate and variation in metabolic pathway can influence ATP production.

**Ans.** (*a*)

**10. Given below is the complex-V of ETS, which is the actual site of ATP synthesis in mitochondria. Study the given diagrammatic representation and comment upon the appropriateness of the Assertion and the Reason.** **Competency Based Que.**

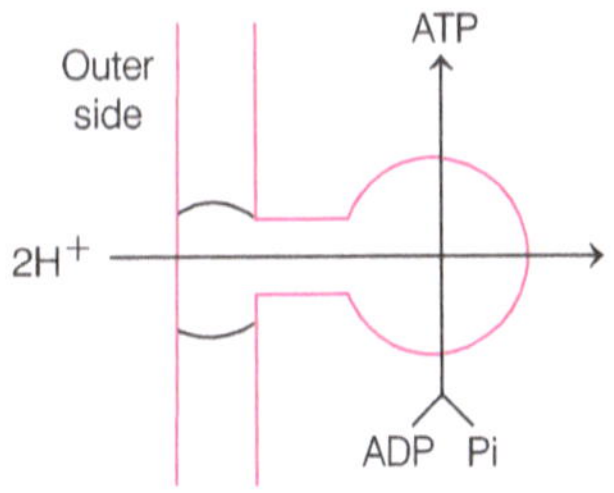


**Assertion** (A) It is ATP synthase having two parts; one called the $F_1$ is embedded in the mitochondrial membrane and the other portion is called $F_0$ that protrudes from the mitochondrial membrane towards the matrix.

**Reason** (R) The passage of protons through the channel $F_0$ is coupled to the catalytic site of $F_1$ component for the production of ATP.

**Ans.** (*d*) A is false, but R is true. A can be correcteed as It is ATP synthase having two parts; one called the $F_0$ is embedded in the mitochondrial membrane and the other portion is $F_1$ that protrudes from the mitochondrial membrane towards the matrix.

**11. Assertion** (A) Carbohydrates are used first by most cells in respiration.

**Reason** (R) Fats are never used in respiration.

**Ans.** (*c*)

**12. Assertion** (A) Respiratory pathway is considered as an amphibolic pathway.

**Reason** (R) Respiratory pathway involves both anabolic and catabolic pathway.

**Ans.** (*a*)

# Subjective Questions

## Very Short Answer Type Questions

**1. Why plant does not need specialised respiratory system?**

**Ans.** Plants can get along without respiratory organ because various plant parts take care of their own gas exchange needs.

**2. Complete the overall equation of respiration.**

$$C_6H_{12}O_6 + x \longrightarrow 6CO_2 + y + ATP$$

**Ans.** $C_6H_{12}O_6 + 6O_2 \rightarrow 6CO_2 + 6H_2O + ATP$

$x - 6O_2$, $y - 6H_2O$ (½ × 2)

**3. What are the products formed by the splitting of fructose-1, 6-bisphosphate?**

**Ans.** Glyceraldehyde-3-phosphate and dihydroxy acetone phosphate. (1)

**4. Write two energy yielding reactions of glycolysis.**

**Ans.** (i) Conversion of BPGA to 3-Phosphoglyceric Acid (PGA).
(ii) Conversion of PEP to pyruvic acid. (½ × 2)

**5. Where does the formation of acetyl Co-A take place in a cell?**

**Ans.** Acetyl Co-A synthesis takes place in the mitochondrial matrix. (1)

**6. Why their is no distinction made between ATP and GTP in calculating energy yield in cellular respiration?** Competency Based Que.

**Ans.** The energy produced from the breaking of high energy bonds of both GTP and ATP are of same amount. (1)

**7. Study the following figure and label *A* and *B* pathway of anaerobic respiration in yeast.**

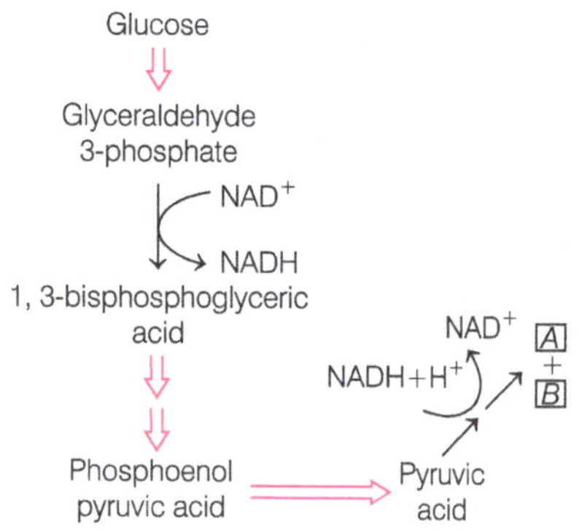


**Ans.** *A* – Ethyl alcohol, *B* – $CO_2$ (½ × 2)

**8. Do you know any step in the TCA cycle, where there is substrate level phosphorylation? Which one?** NCERT Exemplar

**Ans.** In TCA cycle, during the conversion of succinyl Co-A to succinic acid, a molecule of GTP is synthesised. This is substrate level phosphorylation.

**9. (i) Where is the respiratory electron transport system located in a cell?**

**(ii) What compound is the terminal electron acceptor in aerobic respiration?**

**Ans.** (i) Mitochondrial membrane.
(ii) Oxygen. (½ × 2)

**10. How many $NADH_2$ molecules are produced from one molecule of acetyl Co-A in TCA cycle?**

**Ans.** $3NADH_2$ molecules are produced from one molecule of acetyl Co-A in TCA cycle.

**11. For what purpose is the energy from electron transfer is used in electron transport chain** Competency Based Que.

**Ans.** The energy carried by electrons is used for synthesis of ATP from ADP and Pi in the ETS.

**12. Give names of any two energy carriers present in the cell, other than ATP.**

**Ans.** The other energy carriers present in a cell are GTP and NADH. (½ × 2)

**13. Why oxygen is an ultimate acceptor of electrons in ETS?** Competency Based Que.

**Ans.** Oxygen is the ultimate acceptor of electrons in ETS because it is highly reactive and combines with protons to form metabolic water.

**14. What is oxidative phosphorylation?** NCERT

**Ans.** Synthesis of ATP is known as phosphorylation. If ATP synthesis utilises energy obtained through oxidation of molecules. It is oxidative phosphorylation.

**15. If a person is feeling dizzy, glucose or fruit juice is given immediately, but not a chese sandwich, which might have more energy. Explain.** NCERT Exemplar

**Ans.** If a person is feeling dizzy, glucose or fruit juice is given immediately because it is readily oxidised and oxidation of 1 g of glucose yields more energy than a cheese sandwich. (1)

## Short Answer Type Questions

**1. In what way green plants and cyanobacteria have synthesised all the food on the earth? Comment.** Competency Based Que.

**Ans.** The green plants and cyanobacteria has chloroplast bearing chlorophyll pigment that has the ability to trap sunlight and produce carbohydrate by using raw materials from the environment. Thus, can be said to have synthesised all the food on the earth.

**2. Differentiate between respiration and combustion.**

**Ans.** Refer to text on page no. 266. NCERT

**3. What are respiratory substrates? Name the most common respiratory substrate.** NCERT

**Ans.** The organic substances which are catabolised in the living cells to release energy are called as respiratory substrates. Though any food component, i.e. carbohydrate, fat or protein may act as a respiratory substrate, the common respiratory substrate is glucose. (1 + 1)

**4. What is the significance of stepwise release of energy in respiration?** NCERT

**Ans.** The stepwise release of energy is advantageous for the cell. Because if all the energy from the glucose would be released at once then most of it would be lost in the form of heat. (1)

The energy released in stepwise manner is thus trapped in ATP, to be utilised in various energy requiring processes of the organisms and for the synthesis of other biomolecules in the cell. (1)

**5. Respiration is an energy releasing and enzymatically controlled catabolic process, which involves a stepwise oxidative breakdown of organic substances inside living cells. In this statement about respiration explain the meaning of**

**(i) stepwise oxidative breakdown**

**(ii) organic substances (used as substrates).**

Competency Based Que., NCERT Exemplar

**Ans.** (i) **Stepwise Oxidative Breakdown** The series of reactions transform the energy of glucose to ATP.

(ii) **Organic Substances** (used as substrates) The organic substances, which are catabolised in the living cells to release energy are called as respiratory substrates. Though any food stuff, carbohydrate, fat or protein may act as a respiratory substrate, the common respiratory substrate is glucose because it can be oxidised easily and is present abundantly. (1+2)

**6. What are the two types of respiration? Differentiate between the two.**

**Ans.** Refer to text on page no. 267.

**7. Respiration requires $O_2$. How did the first cells on the earth manage to survive in an atmosphere that lacked $O_2$?** NCERT Exemplar

**Ans.** Respiration always does not require $O_2$. There are organisms which respire even in the absence of $O_2$ through anaerobic respiration. (1)

The first cells of earth, i.e. chemosynthetic bacteria are the primitive organisms of early life on earth. They obtained energy by breaking down inorganic molecules like $H_2S$, $NO_2^-$, etc. (1)

**8. Why most of the living cells cannot survive without oxygen?** Competency Based Que.

**Ans.** All living cells need energy for their functioning. The easiest way to obtain this energy is by the oxidation of food materials during respiration. In the absence of oxygen, organic food is oxidised incompletely and produce less amount of energy. It is called anaerobic respiration.

But this type of respiration cannot continue for a long time in higher organisms. This is because of the toxic effect of the end product formed, i.e. lactic acid, ethanol, etc. Hence, most of the cells need oxygen for the breakdown of food and release of sufficient energy by the process called aerobic respiration.

**9. When does anaerobic respiration occur in human and yeast?**

**Ans.** Anaerobic respiration occurs in human muscles at the time of excessive exercising, when blood supply does not meet the oxygen demand of the exercising body. At that time in muscle, lactic acid is produced as a result of anaerobic respiration. In yeast also, anaerobic respiration occurs in the condition of absence of oxygen. (1 × 2)

**10. What is fermentation? Name any two organic compounds produced in the process.**

**Ans.** Fermentation is an anaerobic process that involves oxidation of glucose in the absence of oxygen. Organic compounds produced in the process are

(i) Ethyl alcohol in yeast cell.

(ii) Lactic acid in muscles. (1 × 2)

**11. List two instances where lactic acid is formed by fermentation.**

**Ans.** Instances where lactic acid is formed by fermentation are

(i) During fermentation in lactic acid bacteria.

(ii) During strenuous exercise in the striated muscles of humans. (1 × 2)

**12. Anaerobic respiration cannot continue for long in higher organisms. Why?**

**Ans.** Anaerobic respiration cannot continue for long in higher organisms because of

(i) low yield of energy.

(ii) decomposition of large amount of substrates, so that little is left for growth and repairs.

(iii) toxic effect of end products (like lactic acid) in higher concentration.

(iv) inhibition of a number of physiological process linked with aerobic respiration. (½ × 4)

**13. The energy yield in terms of ATP is higher in aerobic respiration than during anaerobic respiration.**

**Why is there anaerobic respiration even in organisms that live in aerobic condition like human beings and angiosperms?** **NCERT Exemplar**

**Ans.** The anaerobic respiration occurs even in organisms that live in aerobic condition like human beings and angiosperms under conditions of oxygen scarcity that happens in the muscle tissue (in humans). Under intense use, muscles demand too much energy (ATP) and consume much more oxygen to produce that energy.

This high consumption leads to oxygen scarcity and the muscle cells begin to make lactic acid by anaerobic respiration trying to fulfill their energetic needs. Similarly, yeast cells under deficient conditions carry out anaerobic respiration.

**14. Name the site (*s*) of pyruvate synthesis. Also, write the chemical reaction, wherein pyruvic acid dehydrogenase acts as a catalyst.**

**Ans.** Pyruvate synthesis takes place in cytoplasm by the process of glycolysis.

The chemical reaction, wherein pyruvic acid dehydrogenase acts as a catalyst is as follows

$$\text{Pyruvic acid} + \text{Co-A} + NAD^+ \xrightarrow[\text{Pyruvate dehydrogenase}]{Mg^{2+}} \text{Acetyl Co-A} + CO_2 + NADH + H^+$$

(1 + 1)

**15. Complete the following equation of conversion of pyruvic acid into acetyl coenzyme-A. Where does this process occur inside the cell?**

$$\textbf{Pyruvic acid + Co-A + ...} \xrightarrow[\text{Pyruvate dehydrogenate}]{Mg^{2+}} \textbf{Acetyl Co-A + ... + ...}$$

**Ans.** $$\text{Pyruvic acid} + \text{Co-A} + NAD^+ \xrightarrow[\text{Pyruvate dehydrogenate}]{Mg^{2+}} \text{Acetyl Co-A} + CO_2 + NADH + H^+$$

The pyruvic acid produced in the cytosol by the process of EMP pathway, enters into mitochondria where it is converted into acetyl Co-A inside the matrix. (1 × 2)

**16. Aerobic respiration occurs inside the mitochondria in the presence of molecular oxygen. Glycolysis is also called EMP pathway. In glycolysis, net gain is 2 ATP molecules, 2 pyruvate and 2 $NADH_2$.**

**(i) Name two phases of glycolysis. Which of these two phases produce energy?**

**(ii) What is the fate of pyruvate after glycolysis?**

**Ans.** Refer to text on page no. 269.

**17. Write the reaction where substrate level phosphorylation takes place in glycolysis.**

**Ans.** Substrate level phosphorylation takes place during the following steps of glycolysis

(i) When 1, 3-bisphosphoglycerate is converted into 3-phosphoglycerate.

(ii) When phosphoenol pyruvate is converted into pyruvic acid. (1 × 2)

**18. What is meant by the statement 'aerobic respiration is more efficient'?** **NCERT Exemplar**

**Ans.** The aerobic respiration is a high energy yielding process. During the process of aerobic respiration as many as 38 molecules of ATP are produced for every molecule of glucose that is utilised.

This shows that aerobic respiration produces much more energy than anaerobic respiration, which produces only 2 ATP molecules. (2)

**19. Name the end products of aerobic and anaerobic fate of glycolysis. List two ways by which molecules of ATP are produced in glycolysis during aerobic respiration in a cell.**

**Ans.** End product of aerobic glycolysis is pyruvic acid . (1)

The end product of anaerobic glycolysis are $CO_2$ and ethanol or lactic acid. (1)

Molecules of ATP are produced in two ways in glycolysis by

(i) direct transfer of phosphate to ADP.

(ii) oxidation of NADH produced during glycolysis to $NAD^+$. (1)

**20. Does pyruvic acid enter the Krebs' cycle directly?** **Competency Based Que.**

**Ans.** No, pyruvic acid does not enter Krebs' cycle directly. The pyruvic acid is first decarboxylated, and then oxidised by the enzyme pyruvate dehydrogenase to form acetyl Co-A. This molecule further participates in the Krebs' cycle. This is the connecting link between glycolysis and Krebs' cycle.

**21. Differentiate between** **NCERT**

**(i) Glycolysis and Krebs' cycle**

**(ii) Glycolysis and fermentation**

**Ans.** (i) Refer to text on page no. 272.

(ii) Refer to text on page no. 270.

**22. Comment on the statement, 'respiration is an energy producing process, but ATP is being used in some steps of the process'.** **Competency Based Que.**

**Ans.** Respiration is a complex oxidative process in which there is formation of several intermediate molecules. Although ATP molecules are consumed in the glycolysis and Krebs' cycle, there is also production of more molecules of ATP, thus a positive balance of ATP molecules is obtained.

**23. Energy is released during the oxidation of compounds in respiration. How is this energy stored and released as and when it is needed?**

**Ans.** Energy is stored in the cell in the form of ATP, NADH and $FADH_2$. When energy is needed, ATP is broken down to release energy. Additionally, the energy stored in NADH and $FADH_2$ is used to produce more ATP during cellular respiration.

This process ensures that the cell always has a ready supply of energy for various functions.

**24. Where is cytochrome-c located? What is its function?**

**Ans.** Cytochrome-*c* is attached to the outer surface of the inner membrane of mitochondria. It acts as a mobile carrier for the transfer of electrons between complex III and complex IV. (1 × 2)

**25. Mention the significance of $F_0$-$F_1$ combination in mitochondria.**

**Ans.** It helps in maintaining proton gradient on the two sides of the mitochondrial membrane. It also helps in the synthesis of ATP molecule.

**26. Oxygen is critical for aerobic respiration. Explain its role with respect to ETS.**

**Ans.** Oxygen is critical for aerobic respiration due to the following reasons

(i) It acts as the terminal acceptor of hydrogen.

(ii) It drives the whole process by removing hydrogen from the system. (1 × 2)

**27. Given below is a diagram showing ATP synthesis during aerobic respiration, replace the symbols *A, B, C, D* and *E* by appropriate terms as given below.**

**$F_1$- particle, formation of Pi, $2H^+$, inner mitochondrial membrane, ATP, $F_0$-particle, ADP.** **NCERT Exemplar**

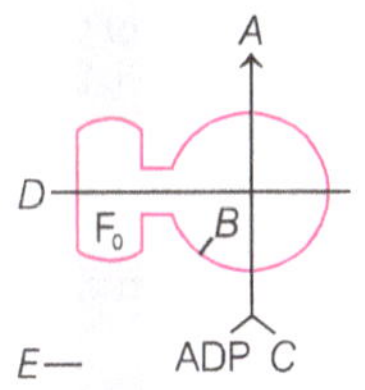


**Ans.** Symbol *A, B, C, D* and *E* in the diagram represents

*A* – ATP

*B* – $F_1$-particle

*C* – Pi

*D* – $2H^+$

*E* – Inner mitochondrial membrane. (½ × 4)

**28. What are the main steps in aerobic respiration? Where does it take place?** **NCERT**

**Ans.** There are four main steps in aerobic respiration, which along with their site of occurrence are given below.

(i) Glycolysis – It takes place in the cytoplasm.

(ii) Krebs' cycle – It takes place in mitochondrial matrix.

(iii) ETS – It takes place in inner mitochondrial membrane.

(iv) Oxidative phosphorylation – It occurs in the $F_0$–$F_1$ particles in the inner mitochondrial membrane. (½ × 4)

**29. What are the assumptions made during the calculation of net gain of ATP?** **NCERT**

**Ans.** Refer to text on page no. 274.

**30. Discuss 'the respiratory pathway is an amphibolic pathway.'** **NCERT**

**Ans.** Refer to text on page no. 275.

**31. A process is occurring throughout the day in '*X*' organism. Cells are participating in this process. During this process, ATP, $CO_2$ and water are formed. It is not a light dependent process.**

**(i) Name the process.**

**(ii) It is a catabolic or an anabolic process.**

**(iii) What could be the raw material of this process?**

**Competency Based Que., NCERT Exemplar**

**Ans.** (i) Cellular respiration. (1 × 3)

(ii) It is a catabolic process, in which one molecule of glucose produces ATP, $CO_2$ and water.

(iii) Carbohydrates, proteins, fats and organic acids can be the raw material of this process. (1 × 3)

**32. RuBP carboxylase, PEP carboxylase, pyruvate dehydrogenase, ATPase, cytochrome oxidase, hexokinase, lactate dehydrogenase.**
**Select the enzymes from the list above which are involved in**

**(i) photosynthesis (ii)respiration.** **NCERT Exemplar**

**Ans.** (i) **Photosynthesis** RuBP carboxylase, PEP carboxylase.

(ii) **Respiration** Pyruvate dehydrogenase, hexokinase, ATPase, lactate dehydrogenase and cytochrome oxidase.

**33. What is the respiratory quotient when fats are used in respiration?**

**Ans.** If the respiratory substrate is fat, then RQ of the respiring cells will be less than one because the volume of $CO_2$ evolved is quite less in comparison to the volume of $O_2$ being consumed.

**34. What would be the RQ value of yeast if it were to respire glucose anaerobically?**

**Ans.** The RQ will be infinity (∞) during anaerobic respiration. In anaerobic respiration, $CO_2$ is evolved, but oxygen is not used.

Therefore, RQ in such a case, will be infinite.

e.g. $C_6H_{12}O_6 \rightarrow 2C_2H_5OH + 2CO_2$ + Energy

$$RQ = \frac{2CO_2 \text{ (2 molecules)}}{O_2 \text{(zero molecules)}} = \text{Infinity.}$$

**35. Different substrates get oxidised during respiration. How does Respiratory Quotient (RQ) indicate which type of substrate, i.e. carbohydrate, fat or protein is getting oxidised?**

$$RQ = \frac{A}{B}$$

**What do $A$ and $B$ stand for?**
**What type of substrates have RQ of 1, < 1 or > 1?** **NCERT Exemplar**

**Ans.** The ratio of $CO_2$ evolved and consumption of $O_2$ in respiration is called the **Respiratory Quotient** (RQ) or respiratory ratio.

$$RQ = \frac{A}{B} = \frac{\text{Volume of } CO_2 \text{ evolved}}{\text{Volume of } O_2 \text{ consumed}}$$ (1)

Substrates like carbohydrates have RQ =1 during aerobic respiration.

Proteins and fats have RQ of < 1 and it occurs during germination of seeds.

Substrates like organic acids have RQ of > 1 under aerobic conditions. (1)

**36. Define respiratory quotient. What is its value for fats?**

**Ans.** Refer to text on page no. 275-276. **NCERT**

## Long Answer Type Questions

**1. (i) Define the following**
**(a) Respiration (b) Respiratory substrate**
**(ii) What are the facultative anaerobes?**
**(iii) Which is the most important energy carrier? Is this compound mobile?**
**(iv) Name the major respiratory substrates used by most organisms. If unavailable at time, what other substances can be used for respiration?**

**Ans.** (i) (a) The enzymes controlled process of biological oxidation of various organic food materials in a living cell, producing $CO_2$ and $H_2O$, and releasing energy in the form of ATP, is called respiration.

(b) The organic compounds catabolised in the living cells to release energy are called respiratory substrates. (2)

(ii) These are organisms which have the capability of switching from aerobic to anaerobic conditions as per oxygen availability. (1)

(iii) The most important energy carrier is ATP. This energy rich compound is mobile, but cannot pass from one cell to another. (1)

(iv) Carbohydrates are used as a respiratory substrate by most organisms. In condition of its unavailability, proteins, fats and organic acids can be used. (1)

**2. Give the schematic representation of glycolysis.** **NCERT**

**Ans.** Refer to text on page no. 268.

**3. Trace the fate of the products formed during glycolysis.**

**Ans.** Refer to text on page no. 269.

**4. Give the schematic representation of an overall view of Krebs' cycle.** **NCERT**

**Ans.** Refer to text on page no. 271.

**5. Explain the major steps of Krebs' cycle. Where does this process occur in a cell ?**

**Ans.** Refer to text on page no. 271.

**6. Describe output of TCA cycle in terms of its end products. Also, discuss its importance in the metabolism of living cell.**

**Ans.** Refer to text on page no. 271-272.

**7. Differentiate between** **NCERT**
**(i) Aerobic and anaerobic**
**(ii) Glycolysis and fermentation**
**(iii) Glycolysis and citric acid cycle.**

**Ans.** (i) Difference between aerobic and anaerobic respiration are as follows

| Aerobic Respiration | Anaerobic Respiration |
|---|---|
| It occurs in the presence of oxygen. | It occurs in the absence of oxygen. |
| It occurs in the cytoplasm and mitochondria. | It occurs in the cytoplasm. |
| End products are $CO_2$ and $H_2O$. | End products are ethyl alcohol and carbon dioxide (in yeast). |
| Complete oxidation of the respiratory substrate takes place. | Incomplete oxidation of the respiratory substrate takes place. |

(1½)

(ii) Differences between glycolysis and fermentation are as follows

| Glycolysis | Fermentation |
|---|---|
| It is the first step of respiration which occurs without requirement of oxygen and is common to both aerobic and anaerobic mode of respiration. | It is anaerobic respiration which does not require oxygen. |
| It produces pyruvic acid. | Fermentation produces different products. The common ones are ethanol (and $CO_2$) and lactic acid. |

| Glycolysis | Fermentation |
|---|---|
| It produces two molecules of NADH per glucose molecule. | It generally utilises NADH produced during glycolysis. |
| Glycolysis forms 2ATP molecules per glucose molecule. | It does not produce ATP. (1½) |

(iii) Differences between glycolysis and citric acid cycle are as follows

| Glycolysis | Citric Acid Cycle |
|---|---|
| It takes place in the cytoplasm. | It takes place in the matrix of mitochondria. |
| It is a linear pathway. | It is a cyclic pathway. |
| It occurs in aerobic as well as anaerobic respiration. | It occurs in aerobic respiration only. |
| It consumes 2 ATP molecules. | It does not consume ATP. |
| It yields 2 NADH per glucose molecule. | It yields 6 NADH molecules and 2 $FADH_2$ molecules from 2 acetyl coenzyme-A molecules. |
| It generates 2 ATP molecules net from 1 glucose molecule. | It generates 2 GTP/ATP molecules from 2 acetyl coenzyme-A molecules. |
| It oxidises glucose partly, producing pyruvate. | It completely oxidises acetyl coenzyme-A. |
| It does not produce $CO_2$. | It produces $CO_2$. |

(2)

**8. It is necessary to calculate and study the respiratory balance sheet occurring during respiration. Why? What are the factors taken into account for this study?**

**Ans.** Refer to text on page no. 274.

## Source Based/Case Based/Passage Based Questions

**1. The flowchart given below depicts the major pathway of anaerobic respiration. Based on the figure answer the following questions.**

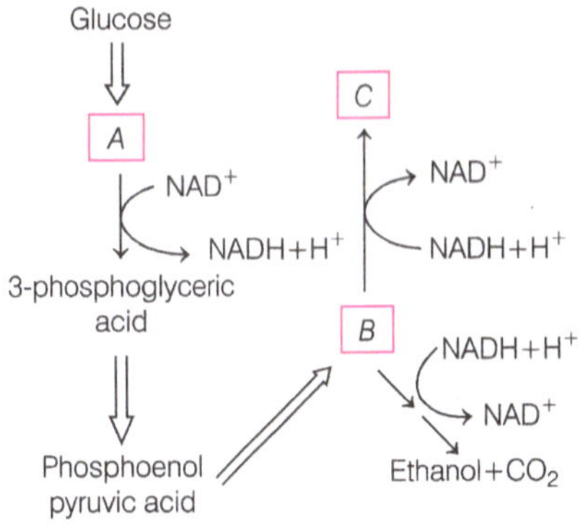


**(i) Identify the *A* and *C* in the figure given above.**

**(ii) In the production of ethanol, pyruvic acid is first converted to acetaldehyde by which enzyme?**

**(iii) In yeast during anaerobic respiration, how many glucose molecules are required for the production of 38 ATP molecules?**

**(iv) Which products are produced by bacteria in anaerobic respiration?**

**Ans.** (i) In the given figure,
*A* is glyceraldehyde-3-phosphate
*C* is lactic acid (½ × 2)

(ii) In the production of ethanol, pyruvic acid is first converted to acetaldehyde by enzyme pyruvate decarboxylase. (1)

(iii) During anaerobic respiration of yeast, two ATP produced from a single glucose molecule. Hence,
38 ATP will be produced from 19 glucose molecules. (1)

(iv) In anaerobic respiration, some bacteria produce lactic acid from pyruvic acid. (1)

**2. The data given below shows the effect of exercise intensity on carbohydrate consumption (and lactate production).** **Competency Based Que.**

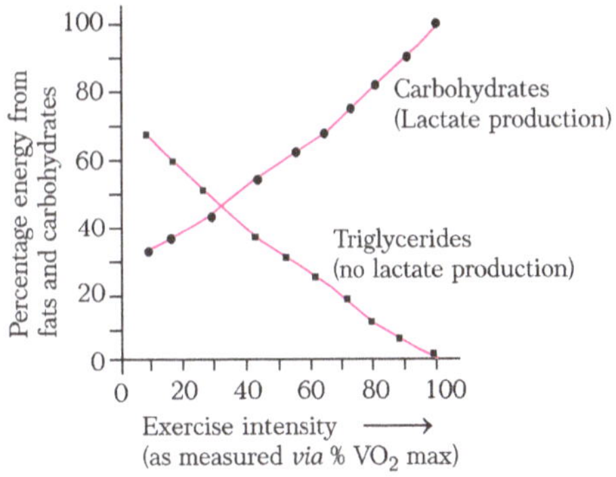

(i) **With reference to the above graph what trend is seen for change in cellular respiration with increasing energy demand?**

(ii) **In our skeletal muscle undergoing anaerobic respiration, lactic acid is formed. What is formed in our muscles under normal aerobic conditions?**

(iii) **How are lactic acid fermentation and alcoholic fermentation similar? How are they different?**

(iv) **Name the enzyme involved in lactic acid fermentation.**

**Ans.** (i) At high energy demand, the aerobic consumption of fats is decreased, while the anaerobic consumption of sugars/carbohydrates increases. (1)

(ii) Pyruvic acid is formed under aerobic conditions. (1)

(iii) The similarity is that they both happen under anaerobic conditions and produce a little amount of ATP.

The difference is that alcoholic fermentation gives $CO_2$ while lactic acid does not. (½ × 2)

(iv) Lactate dehydrogenase. (1)

**3.** **Study the diagram given below and answer the questions that follows.** **Competency Based Que.**

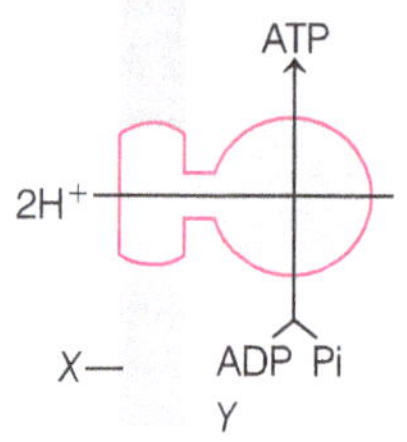


(i) **Identify *X* and *Y* in the given diagram.**

(ii) **Describe the structure of the given diagram.**

(iii) **List the function of the given structure.**

**Ans.** (i) In the given diagram *X* is inner mitochondrial membrane and *Y* is mitochondrial matrix. (½ × 2)

(ii) The given diagram is of ATP synthase. It contain $F_1$-particle and $F_0$-particle. The $F_1$ head piece is a peripheral membrane protein complex and $F_0$ is an integral membrane protein complex. (2)

(iii) The function of ATP synthase is to synthesise ATP from ADP and inorganic phosphate due to electrochemical proton gradient. (1)

# SELF ASSESSMENT TEST

## Multiple Choice Questions

1. Plants can get along without respiratory organs because of the following except
   (a) each plant part takes care of its own gas exchange needs
   (b) plants do not present great demands for gas exchange
   (c) gas diffusion in plants occurs easily over long distances
   (d) each living cell in a plant is located quite close to the surface of the plant
2. In the absence of oxygen, the primary purpose of fermentation is to
   (a) produce amino acids for protein synthesis
   (b) generate a proton gradient for ATP synthesis
   (c) oxidise glucose to generate reduce electron carriers
   (d) regenerate $NAD^+$ from NADH allowing glycolysis to continue
3. Which of the following statement is not true for glycolysis?
   (a) It occurs in the mitochondria of the cell.
   (b) It occurs in both aerobic and anaerobic respiration.
   (c) It involves a series of 10 enzyme-catalysed reactions.
   (d) ATP is generated through substrate-level phosphorylation during glycolysis.
4. Which of the following step during glycolysis is associated with utilisation of ATP?
   (a) Glucose-6-phosphate to fructose-6-phosphate (b) Fructose-6-phosphate to fructose-1, 6-bisphosphate
   (c) Phosphoenolpyruvate to pyruvic acid (d) 3-phosphoglycerate to 2-phosphoglycerate
5. Which of the following enzymes are necessary for the given reaction?
   Pyruvate $\longrightarrow$ Ethyl alcohol + $CO_2$
   (a) Pyruvate decarboxylase and alcohol dehydrogenase (b) Pyruvate decarboxylase and lactate dehydrogenase
   (c) Cytochrome-*c* oxidase and ATP synthase (d) Pyruvate carboxylase and alcohol dehydrogenase
6. In the electron transport system present in the inner mitochondrial membrane, complex- II and complex-III are respectively known as
   (a) NADH dehydrogenase and cytochrome-*c* oxidase
   (b) succinate dehydrogenase and cytochrome-$bc_1$ complex
   (c) cytochrome-*c* oxidase and ATP synthase
   (d) cytochrome-*c* oxidase and ATP synthase
7. How many ATPs are released respectively when NADH and $FADH_2$ molecules gets oxidised?
   (a) 3 ATP, 2 ATP (b) 4 ATP, 3ATP (c) 2 ATP, 3 ATP (d) 3 ATP, 4 ATP
8. Which of the following pairs of respiratory substrates will have unity respiratory quotient?
   (a) Glucose, fats (b) Glucose, fructose (c) Oils, palmitic acid (d) Sucrose, oxalate

## Assertion-Reason Questions

**Direction** (Q. Nos. 9-12) *In each of the following questions, a statement of Assertion (A) is given followed by corresponding statement of Reason (R). Of the statements, mark the correct answer as*

(a) Both A and R are true and R is the correct explanation of A.
(b) Both A and R are true, but R is not the correct explanation of A.
(c) A is true, but R is false.
(d) A is false, but R is true.

9. **Assertion** (A) Only green plants and cyanobacteria can prepare their own food by the process of photosynthesis.

**Reason** (R) They trap light energy and convert it into chemical energy that is stored in the bonds of carbohydrates like glucose, sucrose and starch.

10. **Assertion** (A) Plants do not have specialised respiratory organs like animals.

**Reason** (R) Roots, stems and leaves respire at rates far lower than animals do.

11. **Assertion** (A) The breaking of the C- C bonds of complex compound through oxidation within the cells and release of large amount of energy is respiration.

**Reason** (R) During respiration, the compounds that are oxidised are called respiratory substrates.

12. **Assertion** (A) Both aerobic and anaerobic respiration accounts for only a partial breakdown of glucose.

**Reason** (R) All carbohydrates are usually first converted into glucose before they are used for respiration.

## Very Short Answer Type Questions

13. Name the cell organelle where aerobic respiration takes place.
14. Write the end products of a glucose molecule when it is completely oxidised.
15. Mention the first 5C compound formed during the TCA cycle.
16. A substrate '*X*' has less than 1 respiratory quotient. Identify *X*.

## Short Answer Type Questions

17. What is the function of hexokinase during glycolysis?
18. Write two energy yielding reactions of glycolysis.
19. Write any three similarities between aerobic and anaerobic respiration.
20. Define RQ. Write its value for tripalmitin.

## Long Answer Type Questions

21. What is cellular respiration? How it is different from combustion?
22. Give an account on glycolysis. Mention the end products of glycolysis. Trace the fate of these products in both aerobic and anaerobic condition.
23. Define fermentation. Explain the two types of fermentation with the help of chemical equation.

## Case Based Question

24. The flowchart given below represents the steps involved in aerobic respiration. Observe it carefully and answer the questions that follows.

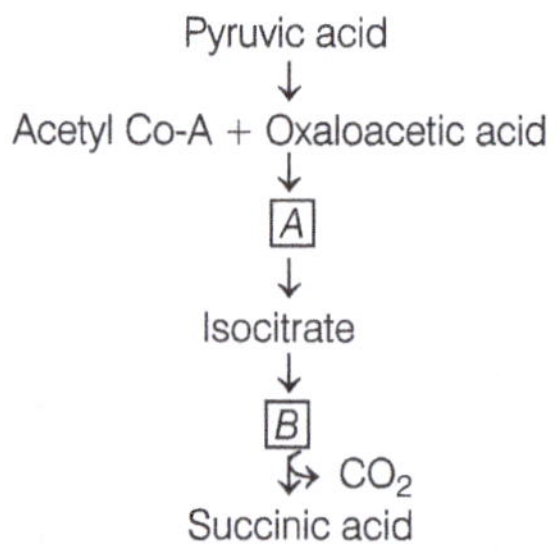


(i) Identify *A* and *B* from the given flowchart.

(ii) What are the number of carbons in *A* and *B*.

(iii) Identify the pathway shown.

(iv) Where does this pathway takes place?

## Answers

| | | | | | | | |
|---|---|---|---|---|---|---|---|
| 1. (c) | 2. (d) | 3. (a) | 4. (b) | 5. (a) | 6. (b) | 7. (a) | 8. (b) |
| 9. (a) | 10. (a) | 11. (b) | 12. (d) | | | | |

# 13

CHAPTER

# Plant Growth and Development

Development is the sum total of two processes-growth and differentiation. The development of a plant follows a very precise and orderly growth pattern.
During this period, differentiation results in the formation of roots, leaves, branches, flowers, fruits, seeds, before the plant completes its life cycle and ultimately dies.

## YOUR STUDY GOALS

13.1 Growth
13.2 Differentiation, Dedifferentiation and Redifferentiation
13.3 Development
13.4 Plasticity
13.5 Plant Growth Regulators (PGRs)

## YOUR PRACTICE GOAL

- Objective Type Questions (41 Qs ; MCQs, A-R)
  Case Based Questions (3)
- Subjective Type Questions (13 VSAs, 32 SAs, 18 LAs)

- The life of a plant initiates from a single cell called **zygote**. (fertilised egg).
- All the structures of plants such as roots, stems, leaves, flowers, fruits and seeds arise from seed on its germination.
- The first step in the process of plant growth is **seed germination**.
- The seed germinates when favourable conditions for growth exist in the environment.
- Under unfavourable conditions, the seeds do not germinate and undergo a period of suspended growth or rest.

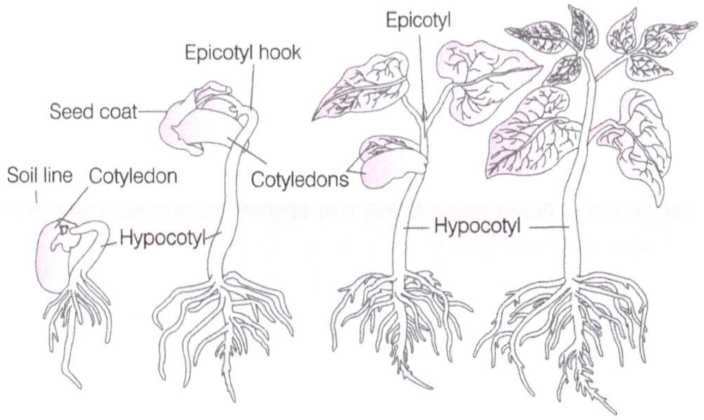


Fig. 13.1 Germination and seedling development in bean

- Once the favourable condition return, the seeds resume metabolic activity and growth takes place.
- They germinate by absorbing water through micropyle.
- The radicle grows first, followed by growth of either epicotyl or hypocotyl (depending on the plant type) and then plumule grows.
- **Factors that affect seed germination** are divided into two main categories
  - **Internal Factors** These include seed viability, seed dormancy, enzymes, maturity of embryo, etc.
  - **External Factors** These include water, light, oxygen and temperature.

## 13.1 Growth

- It is regarded as an essential, fundamental and one of the most conspicuous characteristics of a living being.
- Growth can be defined as a dynamic, irreversible permanent increase in size of an organ, its parts or even an individual cell.
- The growth is generally accompanied by the metabolic processes, i.e. anabolic and catabolic reactions, occurring in an organism at the expense of energy.
- Thus, growth in living organism is an intrinsic phenomenon (unlike, non-living organisms in which growth is extrinsic).

### Plant Growth is Generally Indeterminate

- Growth of plant is unique as plants retain the capacity for unlimited growth throughout their life.
- In plants, the growth is generally confined only to the meristematic tissues present at definite locations in the their body.
- Meristematic tissue have certain cells that have the capacity of dividing and self-perpetuation.
- The new cells produced by the division of meristematic cells, soon loose the ability to divide and make up the plant body.
- The form of growth in which newly produced cells are always being added to the body of the plant by the activity of meristems is called the **open form of growth**.

### Regions of Growth

- Apical, lateral and intercalary are the special regions, where growth is localised in plants.
- The meristem present at the apex of every **root** and **shoot** is responsible for the elongation of plant along their axis. This is known as **primary growth of the plant.**

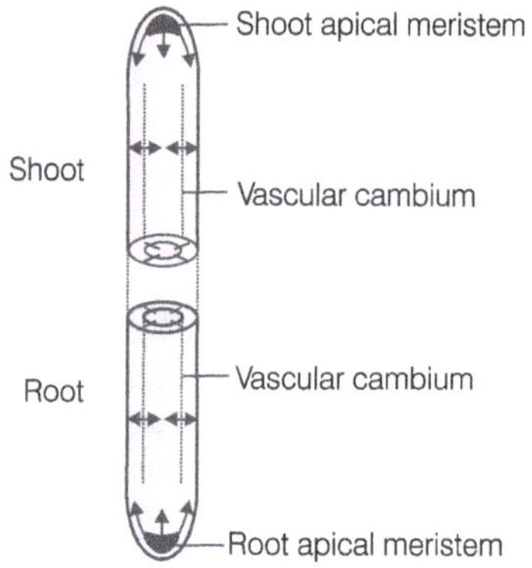


Fig. 13.2 Diagrammatic representation of locations of root apical meristem, shoot apical meristem and vascular cambium. Arrows exhibit the direction of growth of cells and organ

- The lateral meristems, vascular cambium and cork cambium appear later in life in dicotyledonous plants and gymnosperms.
- They are responsible for the increase in the girth of the organ in which they are active. This increase in girth is known as **secondary growth of the plant**.

### Growth is Measurable

- It is stated that at cellular level, growth is mainly the consequence of increase in the amount of protoplasm.
- It is difficult to measure the increase in the protoplasm directly.
- Thus, growth can generally be measured by measuring some quantity which is more or less proportional to it.
- Hence, growth can be easily measured by a variety of parameters such as – increase in dry weight, increase in fresh weight, length, area, volume and cell number.
- In conclusion,
  - Growth can be expressed in terms of increase **in the cell number**, e.g. single root apical meristem in maize gives rise to more than 17,500 new cells per hour.

- It can also be expressed as an increase in the **size of the cell**, e.g. cells in watermelon increases about 3,50,000 times in size.
- Growth can be measured in terms of **length** of plant parts, e.g. pollen tube.
- It can also be measured in terms of **surface area**, e.g. increase in surface area of dorsiventral leaf.

**Quick Test 1**

1. Mention the first step in the process of plant growth.
2. State any two internal factors that affect the seed germination.
3. In a root, growth is localised to the three special regions. Name them.
4. Name the tissue that is responsible for increase in the girth of the plant.
5. **State True or False.**
   Growth can be measured in terms of the length of plant parts, but it cannot be measured in terms of surface area.

## Phases of Growth

- Under favourable conditions, growth of plant shows a characteristic course.
- The period of growth is generally divided into three phases as discussed below

### 1. Meristematic Phase

- The cells that are constantly dividing, i.e. both at the apex of the root and the shoot represent the meristematic phase of growth.
- Features shown by the cells of this phase are as follows.
  - Rich protoplasmic content.
  - Large conspicuous nuclei.
  - Cell walls are primary in nature (thin and cellulosic).
  - Abundant plasmodesmatal connections.

### 2. Elongation Phase

- This phase is proximal to the growing parts, i.e. behind the meristematic zones, away from the growing tip.
- Features shown by the cells of this phase are as follows.
  - Increased vacuolation.
  - Enlargement of cell.
  - Deposition of new cell wall.

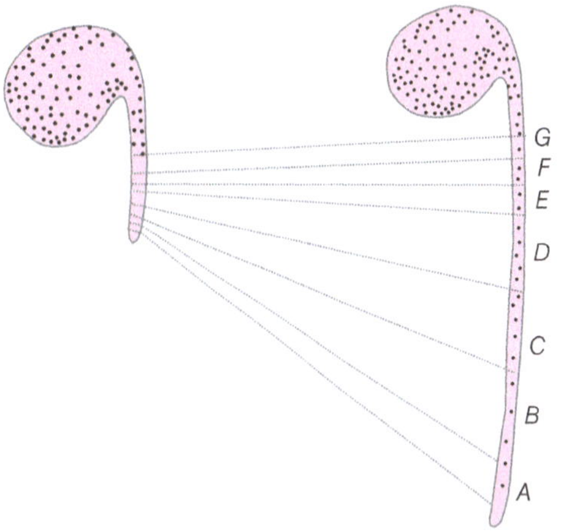


Fig. 13.3 Detection of zones of elongation by the parallel line technique. Zones *A, B, C and D* immediately behind the apex have elongated most

### 3. Maturation Phase

- It occurs further away from the apex, i.e. more proximal to the elongation phase.
- Features shown by this phase are as follows.
  - Cells attain maximum thickening of their walls.
  - Protoplasmic modifications are maximum as per need of the cells.

## Growth Rate

- The growth rate is defined as the increased growth per unit time.
- Rate of growth can be expressed mathematically.
- It shows an increase that may be arithmetic or geometric in nature.

### 1. Arithmetic Growth

- This type of growth, occurs by **mitotic cell division.**
- Somatic cells increase in number due to mitosis.
- In this type of growth, only one daughter cell continues to divide, while others differentiates and attain maturity.

- Expression of arithmetic growth can be exemplified by a root elongating at a constant rate.

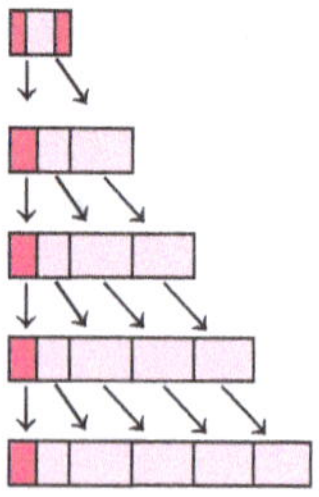

Fig. 13.4 Diagrammatic representation of arithmetic growth

- A linear curve is obtained by plotting the length of organ (e.g. root) against time.

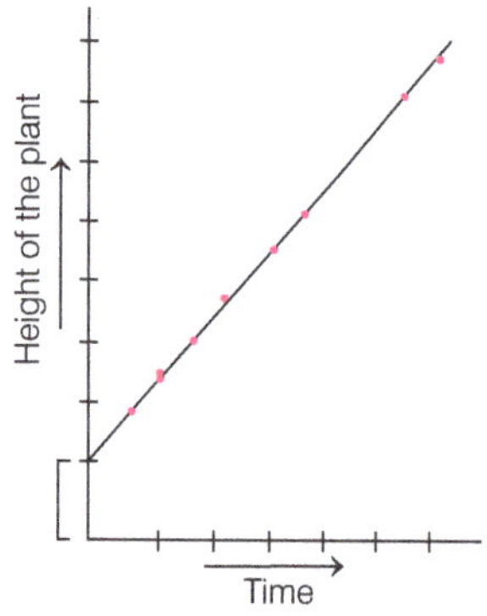


Fig. 13.5 Constant linear growth: a plot of length ($L$) againsts time ($t$)

- Mathematical expression of this growth is given as

$$L_t = L_0 + rt$$

where $L_t$ = Length at time '$t$',

$L_0$ = Length at time 'zero'

$r$ = Growth rate/elongation per unit time.

## 2. Geometric Growth

In living organisms, geometric type of growth follows three important phases

- **Lag Phase** (Initial or the Beginning Phase) It is mainly characterised by very slow growth.
- **Log Phase** (Exponential Phase) It is the middle phase of the system and is characterised by rapid growth of the plant body.
  - After initiation of growth, the number of cells increases rapidly at an exponential rate.
  - During this phase, both progeny cells following mitotic cell division retain the ability to divide and continue to divide till the next phase appears or the time nutrient supply is appropriate.
- **Stationary Phase** (Steady Phase) This phase occurs when either the plant reaches maturity or the supply of nutrients becomes limited.
- Due to the above mentioned factors, the growth of the plant slows down and comes to a halt.

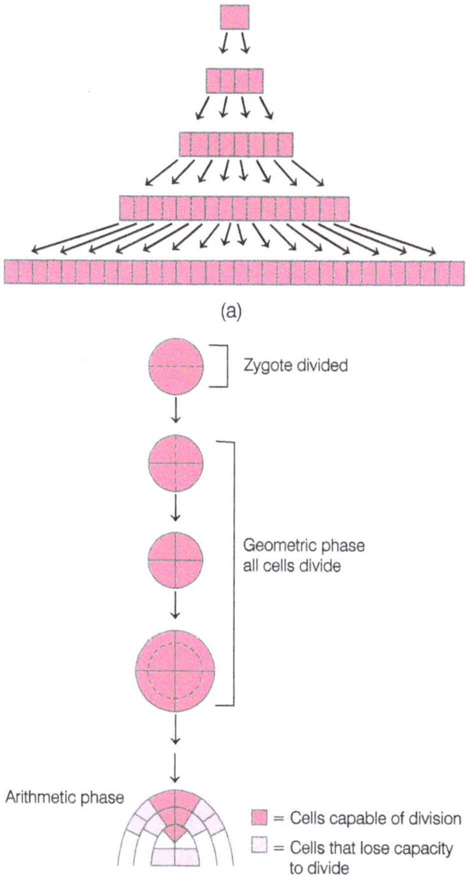


Fig. 13.6 Diagrammatic representation of (a) Geometric growth and (b) Stages during embryo development showing geometric and arithmetic phases

- Under favourable conditions, the characteristic course of growth is observed.
- Thus, if we plot the parameter of growth against time, a typical **sigmoid curve** or S-curve is observed.
- It is a characteristic feature of living organisms growing in a natural environment.

- This curve is typical for all cells, tissues and organs of a plant.

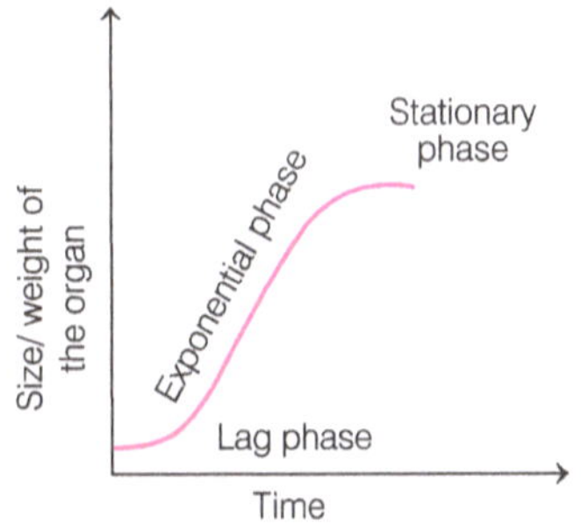


Fig. 13.7 An idealised sigmoid growth curve typical of cells in culture and many higher plants and plant organs

- The exponential growth can be expressed as

$$W_1 = W_0 e^{rt}$$

where, $W_1$ = Final size (weight, height, number, etc.)
$W_0$ = Initial size at the beginning of the period
$r$ = Growth rate
$t$ = Time of growth
$e$ = Base of natural logarithms

- Here, $r$ is the relative growth rate, that measures the ability of the plant to produce new plant material, known as **efficiency index**.
- Hence, the final size of $W_1$ depends on the initial size, $W_0$.

## Quantitative Comparisons of Growth Rate

- The quantitative comparisons between the growth of living systems is done in following two ways
  - **Absolute Growth Rate** It is the measurement and comparison of total growth per unit time.
  - **Relative Growth Rate** It is the growth of the given system per unit time expressed on a common basis, e.g. per unit initial parameter.
  - Relative growth rate $= \dfrac{\text{Growth per unit time}}{\text{Initial parameter (e.g. size)}}$
- Leaves $A$ and $B$ shown in the figure have grown 5 $cm^2$ in one day. Although their sizes are different, i.e. 5 $cm^2$ and 50 $cm^2$, respectively but both of them show same absolute increase in area in the given time to give leaves $A^1$ and $B^1$, i.e. 5 $cm^2$.
- Out of these two, the relative growth rate is higher or faster in leaf $A$.

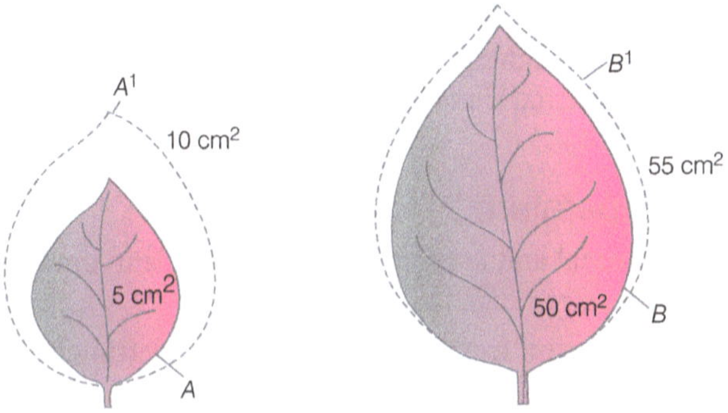


Fig. 13.8 Diagrammatic comparison of absolute and relative growth rate. Both leaves $A'$ and $B'$ have increased their area by 5 $cm^2$ in a given time to produce $A^1$, $B^1$ leaves.

## Conditions or Factors for Growth

- The growth of plant involves synthesis of protoplasm, cell division, cell enlargement and cell differentiation.
- The growth of a plant is influenced by a variety of external and internal factors.
- Some of these are mentioned below

### 1. Water

- It is the first and the foremost requirement of the plants aiding in cell enlargement and maintaining turgidity that helps in extension growth.
- Water also acts as a medium for many enzymatic activities needed for growth.
- In water stress conditions, growth of the plants seems to get retarded.

### 2. Oxygen

It helps in releasing metabolic energy essential for growth activities.

### 3. Nutrients

- Both macro and micro nutrients act as raw materials for synthesis of protoplasm and also as sources of energy.
- Under nutrient deficient conditions, the growth of the plant is negatively affected.

### 4. Light and Gravity

- Light helps in synthesis of food. It also determines the root and shoot growth.
- Along with light, gravity also serves as an environmental signal that affects certain phases/stages of growth.

### 5. Temperature

- For normal and appropriate growth of plant, optimum temperature range is also necessary.
- Any deviation from this range could be detrimental to its survival.

**Quick Test 2**

1. During the meristematic phase, the cells are constantly dividing. Give any one characteristic feature of the cells of this phase.
2. In plants, name the phase that lies proximal to the growing part.
3. State the mathematical expression showing the linear growth in the plants.
4. **State True or False.**
   Relative growth rate is the measurement and comparison of total growth per unit time.
5. Name any two factors that influences the growth of the plant.

## 13.2 Differentiation, Dedifferentiation and Redifferentiation

### Differentiation

- During growth, meristematic cell divides by mitotic division to form daughter cells.
- The cells derived from root and shoot apical meristem and cambium differentiate and mature to perform specific functions.
- This act of differentiation of which leads to maturation of cells and organs to perform specific function is called **differentiation**.
- During differentiation, cells undergo few to major structural changes in their cell walls and protoplasm.
- For example, cells tend to loose their protoplasm, in order to form tracheary element.
- These cells also develop a very strong, elastic, lignocellulosic secondary cell wall in order to carry water to long distance even under extreme conditions.

### Dedifferentiation

- The living differentiated cells also show another interesting phenomenon of dedifferentiation.
- During this, these cells regain the capacity to divide mitotically under certain conditions.
- The dedifferentiated cell can act as a meristem, e.g. **interfasicular cambium** and **cork cambium** from fully differentiated parenchyma cells.
- Parenchyma cells that are made to divide to form callus under controlled laboratory conditions are examples of dedifferentiated tissue.

### Redifferentiation

- The products of dedifferentiated cells or tissue lose the capacity to divide and mature to perform specific functions. This phenomenon is known as redifferentiation, e.g. **secondary cortex** and **cork**.
- From the above discussion, it is very much clear that growth in plants is open inspite of differentiation shown by them.
- It is so because cells/tissues that arise out of the single or same meristem have different structures after attaining maturity.
- The final structure at maturity of a cell/tissue arising from the same tissue is also determined by the location of the cells.
- For example, cells positioned away from the root apical meristems differentiate as root cap cells, while those which are pushed to the periphery develop and mature as epidermis.

## 13.3 Development

- It is the process that includes a series of changes that an organism goes through during its life cycle, i.e. from germination of the seed till senescence.
- In broad terms, development is the sum total of both growth and differentiation in plants.

- Thus, growth, differentiation and development are closely related events in the life of a plant.

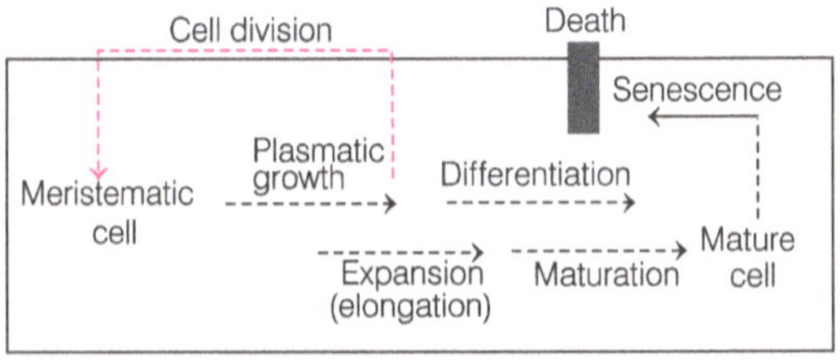


Fig. 13.9 Sequence of the developmental process in a plant cell

- The developmental process of growth and differentiation is controlled by several intrinsic and extrinsic factors.
  - **Intrinsic factors** includes both intracellular (genetic) or intercellular factors (chemicals such as plant growth regulators).
  - **Extrinsic factors** includes light, temperature, water, oxygen, nutrition, etc.

## 13.4 Plasticity

- It refers to the ability of plants to follow different pathways in response to environment or different phases of life forming different kinds of structures.
- The phenomenon of **heterophylly** is an example of plasticity.
- Heterophylly is the phenomenon in plants in which more than one types of leaves occur on the same plant.
- It is common in cotton, coriander and larkspur.
- The environmental plasticity is best seen in emergent hydrophytes, e.g. buttercup.
- In this, the submerged leaves are highly dissected, while emerged leaves are broad and lobed.

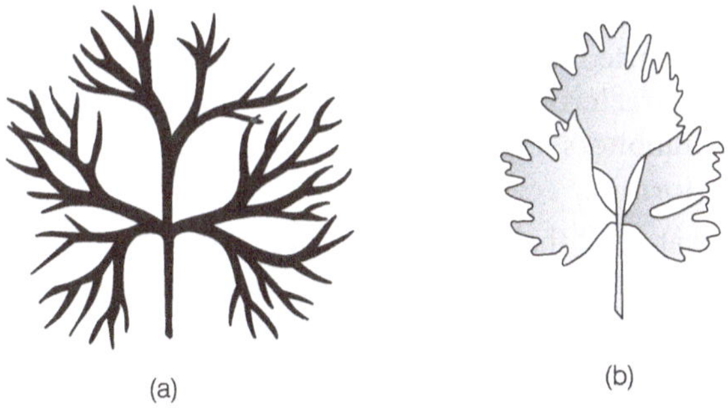


Fig. 13.10 Heterophylly in buttercup : (a) Water habitat, (b)Terrestrial habitat

- Similarly in larkspur the juvenile leaves are different from the mature leaves.

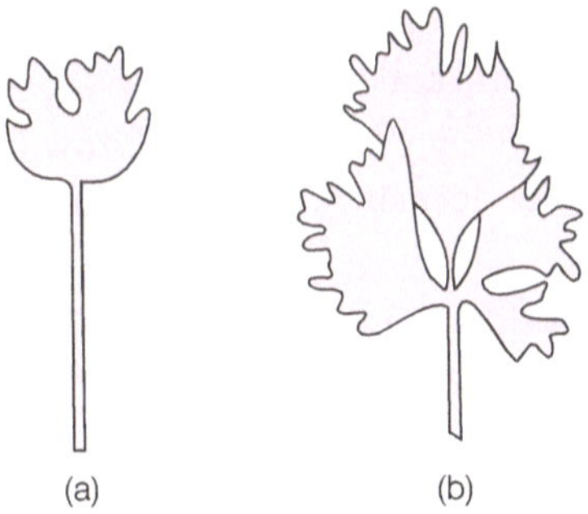


Fig. 13.11 Heterophylly in larkspur: (a) Juvenile leaf, (b) Adult leaf

## 13.5 Plant Growth Regulators (PGRs)

- It has been suggested from sufficient evidences that the plants have certain chemical substances, which help to control the mechanism of growth.
- These are known as **plant growth regulators** or **plant hormones** or simply **phytohormones**.
- PGRs are the small, simple organic molecules of diverse chemical composition.
- They are produced naturally in higher plants that control the growth and other physiological functions.

### Classification of Plant Growth Regulators

- The plant growth regulators fall under the following categories of chemical groups.
  - **Indole Compounds,** e.g. Indole-3-Acetic Acid (IAA).
  - **Adenine Derivatives**, e.g. $N^6$-furfuryl amino purine, kinetin.
  - **Carotenoid Derivatives,** e.g. Abscisic Acid (ABA)
  - **Terpenes,** e.g. Gibberellic Acid (mainly $GA_3$)
  - **Gases,** e.g. Ethylene ($C_2H_4$).
- On the basis of functions they perform in a living plant body, PGRs are divided into two groups

### 1. Plant Growth Promoters

PGRs that exhibit growth promoting activities such as cell division, cell enlargement, tropic growth, pattern formation, flowering, fruiting, seed formation, etc., are called **plant growth promoters**, e.g. auxins, gibberellins and cytokinins.

## 2. Plant Growth Inhibitors

- These primarily function in responses to wounds and stresses of biotic and abiotic origin.
- These are also involved in various growth inhibiting processes like dormancy and abscission, e.g. abscisic acid.
- The gaseous form of PGR (ethylene), may function both as promoter and inhibitor. But largely it functions as an inhibitor of growth activities.

## Discovery of Plant Growth Regulators

- It is interesting to know that the discovery of all five major groups of plant growth regulators has been done accidentally.
- All these help in understanding the phenomenon of development and abnormal behaviour in plants.

### 1. Discovery of Auxin

- This is the **first growth hormone** to be discovered.
- The knowledge of this hormone came into existence through the observation of **Charles Darwin** and his son **Francis Darwin.**
- They observed that the coleoptiles of canary grass responded to unilateral source of light (phenomenon known as phototropism) by growing towards it.
- After performing a series of experiments they came to the conclusion that **coleoptile tip** was the site of transmittable influence that caused bending of entire coleoptile.
- Auxin was isolated by **FW Went** from coleoptile tip of oat seedlings.

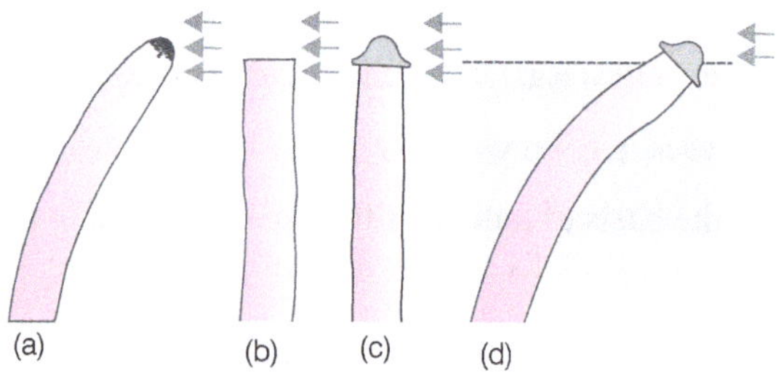


Fig. 13.12 Experiment used to demonstrate that tip of the coleoptile is the source of auxin. Arrows indicate the direction of light

### 2. Discovery of Gibberellins

- In early part of the 20th century the **bakanae** (foolish seedlings) disease of rice, was reported to be caused by a fungal pathogen *Gibberella fujikuroi.*
- The Japanese plant pathologist **E Kurosawa** (1926), reported the appearance of symptoms of the disease in rice seedlings when they were treated with **sterile filtrate** of the fungus.
- It was later identified that the active substance involved here was gibberellic acid.

### 3. Discovery of Cytokinins

- **F Skoog** and his coworkers, studied the nutritional requirements of tissue culture.
- They made nutrient medium for the internodal segments of tobacco stems.
- They observed that from the internodal segments of tobacco stem, the **callus** (i.e. a mass of undifferentiated cells) proliferated, only when the nutrient medium containing auxin was supplemented with the extract of vascular tissues or yeast extract or DNA or coconut milk (liquid endosperm of coconut).
- **Miller *et al.*** (1955), later identified and crystallised the cytokinesis promoting active substance that they termed **kinetin.**

### 4. Discovery of Ethylene

- **HH Cousins** (1910), confirmed the release of a volatile substance from ripened oranges that hastened the ripening of stored unripened bananas.
- This volatile substance was later identified to be a gaseous plant growth regulator, i.e. ethylene.

### 5. Discovery of Abscisic Acid

- During mid-1960s, three independent researchers reported the purification and chemical characterisation of three different kinds of inhibitors, i.e. **inhibitor-B, abscission-II** and **dormin.**
- Later, all the three were proved to be chemically identical in nature and were named as Abscisic Acid (ABA).

## Quick Test 3

1. Given any two examples of dedifferentiated tissue.
2. The developmental process of growth and differentiation is controlled by several intrinsic and extrinsic factors. Name any two extrinsic factors.
3. Name the type of heterophylly shown by buttercup.
4. Which plant growth regulator is known as carotenoids derivatives?
5. Mention the name of the growth regulator which was first to be discovered.

# Physiological Effects of Plant Growth Regulators

- All five categories of plant growth regulators discussed earlier, have various physiological effects on the growth of the plant.
- These are discussed below

## 1. Auxins

- This plant growth hormone (Gk. *auxein*–to grow) was initially isolated from the urine of human, but later on, its presence was also found in plants.
- The plant auxin is chemically known as **Indole -3-Acetic Acid** (IAA).
- The term auxin is also applied to other natural and synthetic compounds having various growth regulating properties.
- Production of auxin generally takes place in the region of **growing apices** of the stems and roots, from where they migrate to the site of their action.

### Types of Auxins

- There are generally two basic categories in which auxins are divided
  - **Natural Auxins** These occur naturally in plants, e.g. Indole Acetic Acid (IAA) and Indole Butyric Acid (IBA).
  - **Synthetic Auxins** These are prepared from synthetic compounds that cause several responses in plants, e.g. Naphthalene Acetic Acid (NAA) and 2, 4-dichlorophenoxyacetic acid (2,4-D).
- All these types of auxins are extensively been used in agricultural and horticultural practices.

**TEACHER'S TIP**

The compounds, which can be converted into auxins, are called **auxin precursors.** e.g. IAA is synthesised from amino acid tryptophan.

### Functions of Auxins

Auxins perform several functions, these are as follows.

- **Apical Dominance** Presence of auxin in higher concentration (in higher plants) in shoot apex, promotes apical dominance.
  - In most higher plants, that presence of apical buds does not allow the lateral (axillary) buds to grow. This phenomenon is called apical dominance.
  - Removal of shoot tip (decapitation) usually results in the growth of lateral buds.
  - This process is widely applied in tea plantation and hedge making.

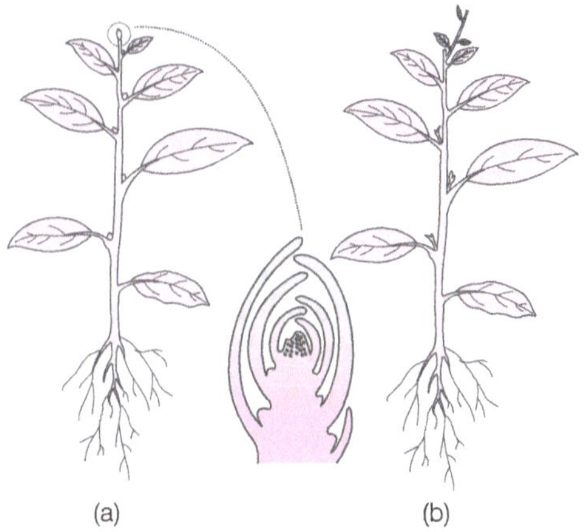


Fig. 13.13 Apical dominance in plants: (a) A plant with apical bud intact, (b) A plant with apical bud removed

- **Initiation of Roots** Higher concentration of auxin initiates rooting in stem cuttings. This property is widely used for plant propagation.
- **Abscission** Natural auxins delay abscission of young fruits and leaves and also used to control pre-harvest fruit drop. However, they promotes the abscission of order mature leaves and fruits.
- **Promotes Flowering** Auxin helps in promoting flowering in some plants, e.g. pineapple.
- **Parthenocarpy** Auxins are used to induce parthenocarpy, e.g. in tomatoes. It refers to the development of fruits without fertilisation.

### Applications of Auxins

- As stated, use of synthetic auxins is widely accepted in various agricultural and horticultural practices.
- Following are the applications of auxins
  - **Eradication of Weeds** Auxins are used as weedicides and herbicides.
    - Application of 2, 4-dichlorophenoxyacetic acid (2, 4-D) is widely used in order to kill dicotyledonous weeds.
    - However, it does not affect mature, monocotyledonous plants.
    - It is used to prepare weed-free lawns by gardners.
  - **Helps in Cell Division** Besides cell elongation, auxin also plays an important role in cell division.
  - **Controls Xylem Differentiation** Auxin controls differentiation of xylem in stems and roots.

## 2. Gibberellins

- These are another group of plant growth regulators, which are known to be acidic in nature. Thus, they are termed as **gibberellic acids**.
- There are more than 100 different types of gibberellins reported from widely different organisms like fungi and higher plants, thus named as $GA_1$ , $GA_2$, $GA_3$ and so on.
- $GA_3$ is the most important gibberellic acid as it was first to be discovered and the most extensively studied amongst all gibberellins.

### Functions of Gibberellins

Following are the various important physiological effects of gibberellins on the plants.

- **Elongation of Internodes** They help in elongation of the internodes, so as to increase the height of the plant. They cause an increase in length of axis and are also used in increasing length of grapes stalks.
- **Elongation of Fruits** They cause fruits to elongate and improve their shape, e.g. in apple.
- **Bolting** The gibberellins help in promoting bolting (internode elongation) just prior to their reproductive phase or flowering.

  When gibberellin is sprayed on rosette plants like beet, cabbage, etc. These plants show extensive internodal growth.

### Applications of Gibberellins

Apart from showing varied physiological effects gibberellins also have numerous applications. These are as follows

- **Delay Senescence** Gibberellins can delay the senescence and ripening of fruits.
- Thus, the fruits can be left on the tree longer, so as to extend the market period.
- They can also be used for safe and prolonged storage of the fruits.
- **Malting Process** The process of malting in brewing industry can be speed up by the use of $GA_3$.
- **Sugar Yield** Carbohydrate is stored in the form of sugar in the stems of sugarcane.
  - Spraying the sugarcane crop with gibberellins, results in increased internodal length of the stem.
  - This enhances the increase in the yield of sugarcane as much as 20 tonnes per acre.
- **Early Seed Production** Gibberellic acid, when sprayed on juvenile conifers, hastens their maturity period leading to early seed production.

## 3. Cytokinins

- These plant growth promoters have specific effects on cytokinesis (division of cytoplasm).
- They were discovered as kinetin (a modified form of adenine, a purine) from the autoclaved herring sperm DNA.
- Kinetin does not occur naturally in plants.
- The search for a natural substance with cytokinin-like activity leads to isolation of zeatin from corn kernels and coconut milk.
- Presently, several naturally occurring cytokinins and some synthetic compounds having cell division promoting activities have been identified after the discovery of zeatin.
- Natural cytokinins are known to be synthesised in the regions where rapid cell division takes place, e.g. root apex, developing shoot buds, young fruits, etc.

### Functions of Cytokinins

Cytokinins have following remarkable physiological effects on the plants.

- **Promotes Cell Division** They promote rapid cell division or cytokinesis in plant's roots and shoots.
- **Reduces Apical Dominance** They promote the growth of lateral buds and help to overcome apical dominance.
- **Delay Senescence** These also help in delaying senescence (ageing) of leaves and other organs by promoting mobilisation of resources or nutrients.
- **Chloroplast Development and Chlorophyll Synthesis** Cytokinins enhance the development of chloroplasts and synthesis of chlorophyll.
- **Other Functions** This hormone is also known to produce new leaves and help in adventitious shoot formation.

## 4. Ethylene

- It is a simple gaseous plant growth regulator.
- This hormone is synthesised in large amounts by tissues that undergo senescence and ripening of fruits.

### Functions of Ethylene

Ethylene shows various important physiological effects which are as follows.

- **Horizontal Growth of Seedling** In dicot seedlings, ethylene influences the horizontal growth of seedling, swelling of the axis and formation of apical hook.
- **Senescence** It promotes senescence and abscission of plants organs especially leaves and flowers.
- **Fruit Ripening** It is highly effective in fruit ripening. It stimulates ripening of fruits like lemons, oranges, etc. Thus, it is called fruit ripening hormone.
- **Enhances Rate of Respiration** It increases the rate of respiration during ripening of fruits. This rise in the respiration rate is called **respiratory climactic**.
- **Breaks Dormancy** Ethylene helps in breaking seed and bud dormancy.
- **Initiate Germination** Ethylene initiates germination in peanut seeds. Sprouting of potato tubers is also due to the production of ethylene in plants.
- **Internode Elongation** In deep water rice plants, ethylene promotes rapid **internode** and **petiole elongation**. It helps leaves or upper parts of the shoots to remain above water.
- **Promotes Growth of Root and Root Hairs** It proves to be helpful in increasing the surface area for absorption of water and minerals by promoting growth of root and formation of root hairs.
- **Initiate Flowering** It stimulates flowering in plants like pineapple, mango etc. It is also used for synchronising fruit-set in pineapples.

### Applications of Ethylene

- This gaseous hormone helps in regulating many physiological processes in plants. Thus, it is the most widely used PGR in agricultural field.
- The most widely used compound as a source of ethylene is **ethephon**.
- Ethephon tends to be readily absorbed in an aqueous solution and is easily transported within the plant. It then slowly releases ethylene.
- Following functions are performed by ethephon
  - **Fruit Ripening** It is known to hasten fruit ripening (in tomatoes and apples).
  - **Abscission** It also helps in accelerating abscission in flowers and fruits (causes thinning of fruits like cotton, cherry, walnut, etc).
  - **Increases Yield** It helps in promoting formation of female flowers, thus enhancing the yield of the fruits, e.g. cucumber.

## 5. Abscisic Acid (ABA)

- It is a slightly acidic growth hormone that functions as a **growth inhibitor**.
- As its production is stimulated under stress (unfavourable conditions such as drought, water lodging, excessive temperature, etc.) so, it is known as **stress hormone**.
- It acts antagonist to gibberellic acid.

### Functions of Abscisic Acid

Various important physiological effects of abscisic acid are as follows.

- **Induces Dormancy** It has a primary role in regulating abscission and dormancy of buds and seeds. By inducing dormancy it helps the seeds to withstand the dessication and other factors related to unfavourable growth.

- **Inhibits Metabolism** It acts as a general plant growth inhibitor and also inhibits metabolism of plants.
- **Inhibits Seed Germination** It has its role in inhibition of seed germination.
- **Seed Development** ABA plays an important role in seed development and maturation.
- **Stomatal Closure** Abscisic acid stimulates the closure of stomata and increases tolerance of plants to various other kinds of stresses.

## Interaction between Growth Regulators

- For the regulation of every phase of growth, i.e. for differentiation and developmental processes in plants two or more phytohormones are intimately related to each other.
- These can either act **synergistically** (individualistic) or **antagonistically** (complimentary).
- Thus, every PGR has one or the other role to play.
- There are number of events in the life of a plant where more than one PGR is involved to affect that particular event. For example. Dormancy of seeds and buds is mostly due to abscisic acid, while it is broken down by gibberellins.
- Auxins and cytokinins act antagonistically in controlling apical dominance, i.e. auxins cause apical dominance, while cytokinins help to overcome them.
- Senescence is prevented by both auxins and cytokinins, while its stimulation is done by abscisic acid.
- Auxins and cytokinins act synergistically in promoting cell division.
- The role of PGR is of only one kind of intrinsic control. Along with genomic control and extrinsic factors, they play an important role in plant growth and development.
- Many of the extrinsic factors such as temperature and light, control plant growth and development *via* PGR.
- Some of such events could be vernalisation, flowering, dormancy, seed germination, plant movements, etc.

### Quick Test 4

1. In most plants, the terminal bud suppresses the development of lateral buds into branches. What is this phenomenon called?
2. A farmer is using a substance called 2, 4-D in his field to grow wheat crop. Mention the purpose of using this substance in the field.
3. Name a plant hormone which causes internodal elongation in plants.
4. A student culture a callus from the tobacco pith in a sterilised nutritive medium, but adds more cytokinins, than auxin. What would develop first from the callus, the shoots or the roots?
5. State one antagonistic effect of cytokinins and auxins.

# Mind Map

## Plant Growth and Development

### Growth

- **Growth *Vs* Development**
  - Growth is defined as an irreversible increase in size of an organ or its parts even of an individual cell.
  - Development is the sum of two processes- growth and differentiation.
- **Plant growth generally is indeterminate.**
  - It means that plant growth continues throughout life.
- **Growth is measurable.**
  - At cellular level, measured as increase in amount of protoplasm.
  - Growth can be in term of increase in cell number and increase in size.
- **Phases of Growth**
  - **Meristematic Phase** Constant division of cells in shoot and roots.
  - **Elongation Phase** Cell enlargement, increased vacuole formation and new cell wall deposition.
  - **Maturation Phase** Protoplasm and cell wall thickening has attained maximum growth.

### Growth Rate

- Increase in growth per unit time.
- It can be arithmetic or geometrical.

**Arithmetic**

- The rate of growth is constant and increase in growth occurs in arithmetic progression.

$1 \xrightarrow{+1} 2 \xrightarrow{+1} 3 \xrightarrow{+1} 4 \xrightarrow{+1} 5 \xrightarrow{+1} 6$

- Found in root and shoot elongation.

$L_t = L_o + r_t$

Length after time = Length at beginning + Growth

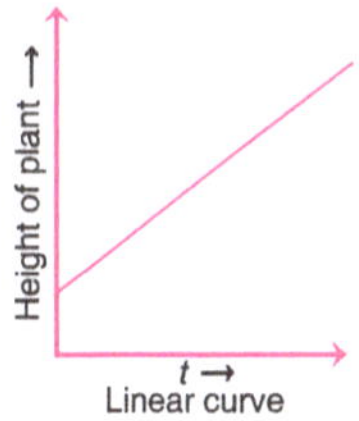

Linear curve

**Geometric**

- The initial growth is slow but increase rapidly thereafter. Here, exponential growth occurs.

$1 \xrightarrow{x2} 2 \xrightarrow{x2} 4 \xrightarrow{x2} 8 \xrightarrow{x2} 16 \xrightarrow{x2} 32$

- Common in unicellular organisms growing under nutrient rich medium.

$W_1 = W_0 e^{rt}$

Final size = Initial size × (Base of natural logarithms) Growth rate × Time

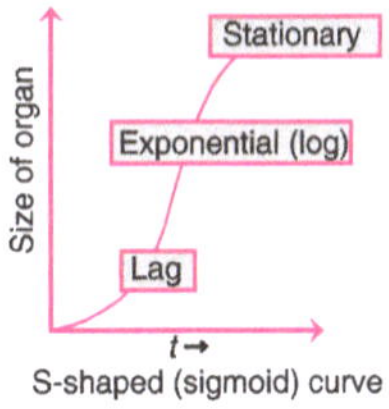

S-shaped (sigmoid) curve

**Absolute Growth Rate** Measurement and comparison of total growth per unit time.

**Relative Growth Rate** Growth of given system per unit time expressed on common basis.

### Conditions of Growth

- **Water** Cell enlargement; turgidity, etc.
- **Essential Nutrients** Protoplast synthesis and source of energy
- **Oxygen** Metabolic activities
- **Environmental Signals** Light and gravity
- **Optimum Temperature** Suitable for growth

### Differentiation, Dedifferentiation and Redifferentiation

- Cells produced by apical meristems become specialised to perform specific function. This act of maturation is called **differentiation**.
- The living differentiated cells that have lost ability of division can regain the capacity of division. This phenomenon is called **dedifferentiation**, e.g. interfascicular cambium and cork cambium.
- Dedifferentiated cells mature and lose the capacity of cell division again to perform specific functions. This process is called **redifferentiation**.

### Development in Plants

- Development is a term that includes all changes that an organism goes through during its life cycle from germination of the seed to senescence.
- Sequence of development in higher plants is as follows

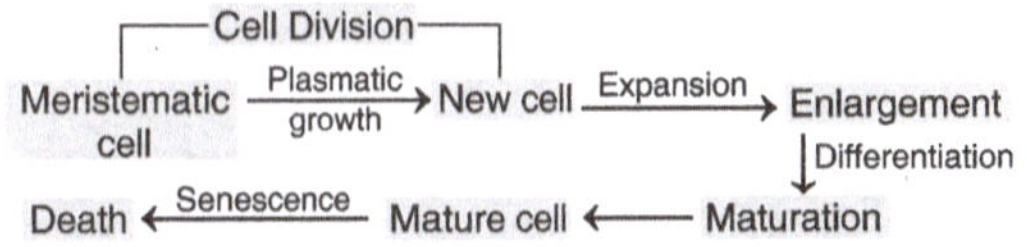


- **Plasticity** Ability of a plant to follow different pathways and produce different structures in response to environment, e.g. heterophylly.
- **Heterophylly** Phenomenon of appearance of different forms of leaves on the same plant, e.g. butter cup (due to different environment).

### Plant Growth Regulators (PGRs)

**Types of PGRs**

**Plant Growth Promoters**

**Auxins (IAA)**

- F W Went

**Physiological Effects**

- Cell enlargement
- Apical dominance
- Cell division
- Inhibition of abscission
- Induce parthenocarpy

**Gibberellins (GA)**

- E Kurosawa

**Physiological Effects**

- Cell elongation
- Breaking dormancy
- Early maturity
- Seed germination

**Cytokinins (Kinetin, Zeatin)**

- Skoog and Miller

**Physiological Effects**

- Cell division and cell differentiation
- Essential for tissue culture
- Overcome apical dominance
- Promote nutrient metabolism

**Plant Growth Inhibitors**

**Abscisic Acid (Stress Hormone)**

- HH Cousins

**Physiological Effects**

- Bud dormancy
- Leaf senescence
- Induce parthenocarpy
- Seed development and maturation

**Ethylene (Gaseous)**

**Physiological Effects**

- Inhibition of longitudinal growth
- Fruit ripening and senescence
- Promote apical dominance
- It has both promoting and inhibitory functions.

# EXAM PATTERN QUESTIONS

## Objective Type Questions

### Multiple Choice Questions

**1.** **Identify *A*, *B*, *C* and *D* in the given figure and choose the correct option.**

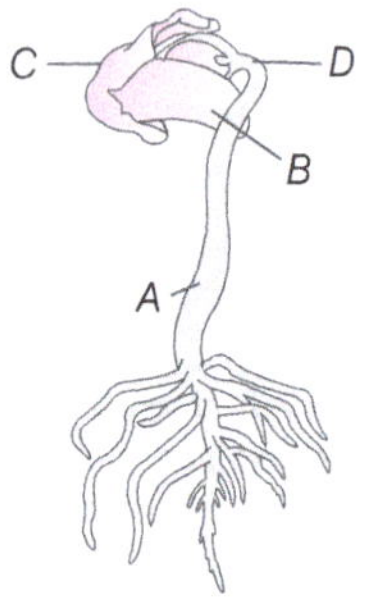


(a) *A*–Hypocotyl, *B*–Cotyledon, *C*–Seed coat, *D*–Epicotyl
(b) *A*–Epicotyl, *B*–Cotyledon, *C*–Hypocotyl, *D*–Seed coat
(c) *A*–Epicotyl, *B*–Seed coat, *C*–Hypocotyl, *D*–Cotyledon
(d) *A*–Hypocotyl, *B*–Seed coat, *C*–Epicotyl, *D*–Cotyledon

**Ans.** (*a*)

**2.** **Identify *A* and *B* in the given figure and choose the correct option.**

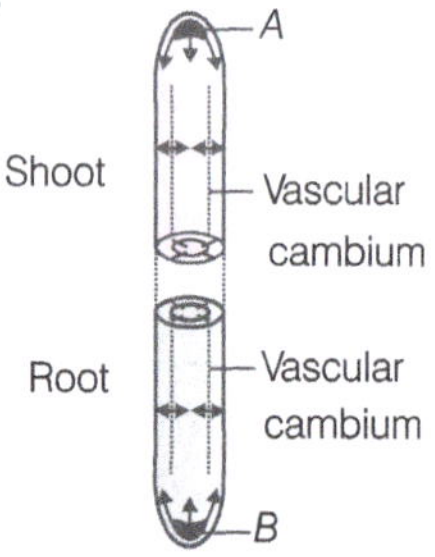


(a) *A*–Root apical meristem; *B*–Shoot apical meristem
(b) *A*–Shoot apical meristem; *B*–Root apical meristem
(c) *A*–Permanent tissue; *B*–Radicle tissue
(d) *A*–Radicle tissue; *B*–Apical tissue

**Ans.** (*b*)

**3.** **Growth can be measured in various ways. Which of these can be used as parameters to measure growth?**

(a) Increase in cell number **NCERT Exemplar**
(b) Increase in cell size
(c) Increase in length and weight
(d) All of the above

**Ans.** (*d*)

**4.** **The cells in the root and shoot apex have all features, except that they**

(a) are rich in protoplasm
(b) have conspicuous nuclei
(c) have cell walls which are primary in nature, thin and cellulosic with abundant plasmodesmatal connections
(d) have cell wall which is secondary in nature initially, but becomes primary

**Ans.** (*d*)

**5.** **Type of growth in which only one daughter cell divides while the other differentiates is called** **DIKSHA**

(a) geometric growth
(b) logarithmic growth
(c) arithmetic growth
(d) relative growth

**Ans.** (*c*)

**6.** **Arithmetic growth is linear because**

(a) one daughter cell remains meristematic and other differentiates and mature
(b) both daughter cells remain meristematic
(c) both daughter cells get matured
(d) All of the above

**Ans.** (*a*)

**7.** **Growth rate is slow but not constant in**

(a) stationary phase (b) log phase
(c) lag phase (d) exponential phase

**Ans.** (*c*)

**8.** **In geometrical growth, exponential phase is represented by**

(a) rapid consumption of nutrients
(b) rapid increase in cell number
(c) highest growth rate
(d) All of the above

**Ans.** (*d*)

**9.** **Consider the following factors.**

I. Temperature and light availability
II. Water and oxygen
III. Nutrients
IV. Gravity
V. Bacterial association

How many of the above given factors are essential for growth of all plants?

(a) 4 (b) 3
(c) 5 (d) 2

**Ans.** (*a*)

**10.** **Which one of the following is not performed by a differentiated cell?** **DIKSHA**

(a) Cell division (b) Photosynthesis
(c) Conduction of sap (d) Mechanical strength

**Ans.** (*a*)

**11.** **The tissue responsible for secondary growth in plants are**

(a) vascular cambium (b) cork cambium
(c) root and shoot apical meristem (d) Both (a) and (b)

**Ans.** (*d*)

**12.** **Identify the correct sequence from the following events of developmental process in a plant cell. Choose the correct option.**

**I. Plasmatic growth** **II. Differentiation**
**III. Maturation** **IV. Senescence**

(a) I → II → III → IV (b) I→ II → IV → III
(c) IV → III → II → I (d) IV → I → II → III

**Ans.** (*a*)

**13.** **Plasticity in plant growth means that** **NCERT Exemplar**

(a) plant roots are extensible
(b) plant development is dependent on the environment
(c) stems can extend
(d) None of the above

**Ans.** (*b*) The plants have the ability to change its phenotype according to the changes in environment. So, the plant growth show plasticity (ability to change/adapt according to environment).

**14.** **The ability of plants to follow different pathways to form different structures in response to environment is called**

(a) plasticity (b) elasticity
(c) growth (d) development

**Ans.** (*a*)

**15.** **One group of PGRs involved in growth promoting activities are called growth promoters. Which one the following includes growth promoters?** **Competency Based Que.**

(a) Auxin, cytokinin, ABA (b) GAs, cytokinin, $C_2H_4$
(c) $C_2H_2$, ABA (d) Auxin, cytokinin, $GA_3$

**Ans.** (*d*)

**16.** **The first hormone to be isolated from human urine was**

(a) auxin (b) ABA (c) ethylene (d) gibberellic acid

**Ans.** (*a*)

**17.** **Which of the following is not an influence of auxin?**

(a) Apical dominance (b) Parthenocarpy
(c) Initiation of roots (d) Bolting

**Ans.** (*d*)

**18.** **Which of the following effects of auxins on plants is the basis for their commercial application?**

(a) Callus formation
(b) Curvature of stem
(c) Eradication of weeds
(d) Induction of shoot formation

**Ans.** (*c*)

**19.** **To increase sugar production in sugarcanes, they are sprayed with** **NCERT Exemplar**

(a) IAA (b) cytokinin
(c) gibberellin (d) ethylene

**Ans.** (*c*) Gibberellin spray on sugarcane induces the growth in the internodal area of the sugarcane plant. Larger is the area larger will the sugar content, as sucrose is the main constituent in the sap of sugarcane stem.

**20.** **Apple's elongation and improvement of its shape is brought about by**

(a) auxin (b) ethylene
(c) $C_2H_4$ (d) GAs

**Ans.** (*d*)

**21.** **Application of gibberellin can induce which one of the following?**

(a) Leaf fall (b) Promote senescence
(c) Elongation of shoot system (d) Diversed root system

**Ans.** (*c*)

**22.** **Fruits can be left on the tree for longer time, so as to increase the market period. This is due to the function of**

(a) delayed senescence by auxin
(b) delayed senescence by $CH_2—CH_2$
(c) delayed senescence by cytokinin
(d) delayed senescence by GAs

**Ans.** (*d*)

**23.** **Difference between the kinetin and zeatin is that**

(a) kinetin is active, zeatin is non-active
(b) zeatin is synthetic, kinetin is natural
(c) zeatin is active, kinetin is non-active
(d) zeatin is natural, kinetin is synthetic

**Ans.** (*d*)

**24.** **A hormone used for promoting cell division in plant tissue culture is**

(a) ABA (b) $GA_3$
(c) cytokinins (d) ethylene

**Ans.** (*c*)

**25.** The affect of apical dominance can be overcome by which of the following hormone? **NCERT Exemplar**

(a) IAA (b) Ethylene
(c) Gibberellin (d) Cytokinin

**Ans.** (*d*) Cytokinin is antagonistic to the action of auxin and thus overcome the phenomenon of apical dominance.

**26.** Which hormone helps in increasing the surface area of roots by promoting root growth and root hair formation?

(a) Cytokinin (b) Kinetin
(c) Ethylene (d) ABA

**Ans.** (*c*)

**27.** ABA acts as antagonistic to **NCERT Exemplar**

(a) ethylene (b) cytokinin
(c) gibberellic acid (d) IAA

**Ans.** (*c*)

**28.** Which of the following functions is not performed by ABA ?

(a) Stomatal closure
(b) Promote seed germination
(c) Induce dormancy
(d) Inhibit plant metabolism

**Ans.** (*b*)

**29.** Consider the following functions.

I. Induce seed dormancy.
II. Inhibits seed germination.
III. Prepares plants to cope with stress.
IV. Stimulates stomatal closure. **Competency Based Que.**

Which hormone performs the above functions?

(a) Kinetin (b) Stress hormone (c) $GA_3$ (d) IBA

**Ans.** (*b*)

**30.** Match the following columns and choose the correct option from the codes given below. **Competency Based Que.**

| | Column I | | Column II |
|---|---|---|---|
| A. | IAA | 1. | Gaseous |
| B. | Kinetin | 2 | Bolting |
| C. | ABA | 3. | Dormin |
| D. | $GA_3$ | 4. | Modified form of adenine |
| E. | $C_2H_4$ | 5. | Indole compounds |

**Codes**

| | A | B | C | D | E |
|---|---|---|---|---|---|
| (a) | 1 | 2 | 3 | 4 | 5 |
| (b) | 5 | 4 | 3 | 2 | 1 |
| (c) | 5 | 4 | 1 | 2 | 3 |
| (d) | 4 | 5 | 1 | 2 | 3 |

**Ans.** (*b*)

**31.** Match the following. **NCERT Exemplar**

| | Column I | | Column II |
|---|---|---|---|
| A. | IAA | 1 | Herring sperm DNA |
| B. | ABA | 2 | Bolting |
| C. | Ethylene | 3. | Stomatal closure |
| D. | GA | 4. | Weed-free lawns |
| E. | Cytokinins | 5. | Ripening of fruits |

**Codes**

| | A | B | C | D | E |
|---|---|---|---|---|---|
| (a) | 4 | 3 | 5 | 2 | 1 |
| (b) | 5 | 3 | 4 | 2 | 1 |
| (c) | 4 | 1 | 4 | 3 | 2 |
| (d) | 5 | 3 | 2 | 1 | 4 |

**Ans.** (*a*)

**32.** The term synergistic action of hormones refers to **NCERT Exemplar**

(a) when two hormones act together, but bring about opposite effects
(b) when two hormones act together and contribute to the same function
(c) when one hormone affects more than one function
(d) when many hormones bring about any one function

**Ans.** (*b*) Synergistic effect means when two hormones work together, they increase the effect or functioning of each other, so there will be enhanced effect of both the hormones.

## Assertion-Reason Questions

**Direction** (Q. Nos. 1-9) *In each of the following questions, a statement of Assertion (A) is given followed by corresponding statement of Reason (R). Of the statements, mark the correct answer as*

(a) Both A and R are true and R is the correct explanation of A
(b) Both A and R are true, but R is not the correct explanation of A
(c) A is true, but R is false
(d) A is false, but R is true

**1. Assertion** (A) Growth in plants is indeterminate.

**Reason** (R) Plant cells can divide and enlarge continuously for life time.

**Ans.** (*a*)

**2. Assertion** (A) The cells that are constantly dividing represents the meristematic phase of growth.

**Reason** (R) These cells attain maximum thickening of their walls. **Competency Based Que.**

**Ans.** (*c*) A is true, but R is false. R can be corrected as
The cells of meristematic region have thin and cellulosic cell wall.

**3. Assertion** (A) Sigmoid growth curve consists of three parts.
**Reason** (R) Log phase is also known as declining phase of growth.

**Ans.** (*c*) A is true, but R is false. R can be corrected as
Log phase is also known as exponential phase of growth.

**4. Assertion** (A) Hormones are also called growth regulators.
**Reason** (R) These promote or inhibit plant growth.

**Ans.** (*a*)

**5. Assertion** (A) Plants have hormones called phytohormones.
**Reason** (R) PGRs are the small simple organic molecules of diverse chemical composition.

**Ans.** (*b*)

**6. Assertion** (A) Removal of shoot tip increases apical dominance.
**Reason** (R) Decapitation is widely applied in tea plantation and hedge making .

**Ans.** (*d*) A is false, but R is true. A can be corrected as
Removal of shoot tip decreases apical dominance.

**7. Assertion** (A) Gibberellin is useful in early seed production in conifers.
**Reason** (R) Ethephon is responsible for early ripening in tomato and apple.

**Ans.** (*b*)

**8. Assertion** (A) Ethylene freely diffuses across the membrane of plant cells.
**Reason** (R) It causes climacteric ripening of fruit.

**Ans.** (*b*)

**9. Assertion** (A) ABA acts as anti-transpirant.
**Reason** (R) It promotes closing of stomata.

**Ans.** (*a*)

# Subjective Questions

## Very Short Answer Type Questions

**1. Growth is a permanent process that cannot be reversed. Do you agree ?** **Competency Based Que.**

**Ans.** Yes, growth is considered as a permanent and irreversible process because all living organisms grow from a single cell to an adult, bearing billions of cells. However, the reverse is not possible.

**2. Explain whether the growth in plants is definite or indefinite.**

**Ans.** Growth in plants is indefinite because they have the capacity for unlimited growth throughout their life. This ability of the plants is due to the presence of meristems at certain locations.

**3. In the figure of sigmoid growth curve below label segments *A*, *B* and *C*.**

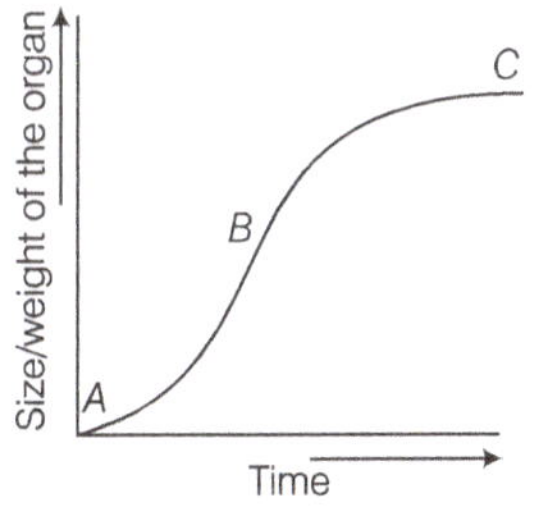


**Ans.** *A*–Lag phase, *B*–Log phase and *C*–Steady phase.

**4. Throughout their life, plants undergo distinct changes in order to seek development. Write the correct chronological sequence of developmental stages in plants.**

**Ans.** The correct chronological sequence of developmental stages in plants is

Germination → Vegetative growth → Flowering → Fruiting

**5. Mention the name of the internal factors that control development in plants.**

**Ans.** Internal factors that control development in plants are
(i) Genetic factors (intracellular).
(ii) Plant growth regulators (intercellular). (½ × 2)

**6. Define plasticity. Give one example.**

**Ans.** Refer to text on page no. 297.

**7. Name the plant that shows heterophylly in two different habitat.** **NCERT Exemplar**

**Ans.** Buttercup shows heterophylly in two different habitat.

**8. What conditions can induce the phenomenon of bolting artificially?**

**Ans.** Bolting can be induced artificially by the application of gibberellins.

**9. Name the groups of growth regulating plant hormones, which stimulate the following.**
**(i) Cell division even in non-meristematic tissues.**
**(ii) Elongation of stem and expansion of leaves.** **Competency Based Que.**

**Ans.** (i) Cytokinin (ii) $GA_3$ (½ × 2)

**10. Give the scientific terms for the following.**
**A growth promoting substance first isolated from maize kernels.**

**Ans.** Zeatin

**11. Why do cut leaves dipped in cytokinins stay green for longer duration?** **Competency Based Que.**

**Ans.** Cut leaves in cytokinins stay green for longer duration because cytokinins retard ageing of plant organs by promoting protein synthesis and mobilisation of nutrient resources.

**12. Release of which plant hormone from over-ripened apple, can affect other apples in the basket?**

**Ans.** Presence of ethylene hormone can affect other apples in the basket.

**13. Explain inhibitory effect of ethylene with the help of one example.**

**Ans.** Ethylene is a gaseous PGR that can have inhibitory effect on plant. For instance, it promotes senescence and abscission of plant organs especially leaves and flowers.

## Short Answer Type Questions

**1. Justify the statement. Growth of plant is unique.** **Competency Based Que.**

**Ans.** Plant growth is unique, as plants retain the capacity to grow throughout their life. This ability is due to the presence of meristems. The cells of meristematic tissue have the capacity to divide and self-perpetuate.

**2. Why is not only one parameter good enough to demonstrate growth throughout the life of a flowering plant?** **NCERT**

**Ans.** Any one parameter is not good enough to demonstrate growth throughout the life of a flowering plant because the plants exhibit different types of growth during different stages of their life cycle. (1)

In the seedling stage, they are in state of active mitotic cell division, then they undergo active cell enlargement stage during growing stage. After the formation of various organs, they undergo cell differentiation or get matured. Finally, in the reproductive or flowering stage of their life cycle, they exhibit reductional division. (1)

**3. What happens if the meristematic cells ever cease to divide?**

**Ans.** If meristematic cells cease to divide, Plant growth would be severely affected, leading to stunted development and a lack of new tissues such as leaves, stems and roots. This would also impair the plant's ability to heal from injuries and negatively impact reproductive processes, such as flower and seed formation. Overall, the plant's survival would be threatened due to it's inability to grow, repair and reproduce effectively.

**4. Identify the actively dividing cells in plants.**

**Ans.** Meristems are the actively dividing cells present in the higher plants like gymnosperms and angiosperms.

These are found in actively growing regions (like root and shoot of the plant) and are responsible for horizontal and vertical growth of the plant.

**5. Does the growth pattern in plants differ from that in animals? Do all the parts of plant grow indefinitely? If not, name the regions of plant, which can grow indefinitely.** **NCERT Exemplar**

**Ans.** **Growth in plants** is of indeterminate type, i.e. plant grow through out their life because of the presence of meristematic tissues present in specific parts of plant i.e. apical, intercalary and lateral. These tissue has ability to divide continuously and contribute to localised plant growth.

**Growth in animals** They have limited growth period after which further growth of their body stops. (2)

All the parts of the plant do not grow indefinitely. The root apex and shoot apex having apical meristematic tissues keep growing, thus contributing to the elongation of plant axis-(height). (1)

**6. Both animals and plants grow. Why do we say that growth and differentiation in plants is open and not so in animals? Does this statement hold true for sponges also?** **NCERT Exemplar**

**Ans.** Plant growth is a unique phenomenon because plants retain the capacity for unlimited growth throughout their life. This ability of the plants is due to the presence of meristems at certain locations in their body. The cells of meristems have the capacity to divide and self- perpetuate.
The cells thus produced, however soon lose the capacity to divide and such cells make up the plant body. This form of growth wherein new cells are always being added to the plant body by the activity of the meristem is called the open form of growth. Yes, this statement holds true for sponges also.

**7. Growth is one of the fundamental characteristics of all living organisms. Do unicellular organisms also grow? If so, what are the parameters?** **NCERT Exemplar**

**Ans.** Yes, growth is one of fundamental characteristic of all living organism. All living organism grow in number and then accumulate biomass and grow in size as well. In unicellular organisms, the growth is synchronous with reproduction. Their cells accumulate (synthesise) protoplasm and increase in size but upto a certain limit and then divide to form two cells.

**8. What are the structural characteristics of** NCERT Exemplar

**(i) Meristematic cells near root tip?**

**(ii) The cells in the elongation zone of the root?**

**Ans.** (i) **Meristematic Cells Near Root Tip** The cells of this region are called Root Apical Meristems (RAMs) and are in active state of division, thus their number increases continuously. The cells of this region are thin walled with dense cytoplasm and large nucleus. They have the ability to divide and self perpetuate.

(ii) **The Cells in the Elongation Zone of the Root** This region is situated just above the meristematic zone. In the cells of this zone, a large number of small vacuoles develop and later these vacuoles fuse to form one large central vacuole filled with cell sap. The cells of this region are elongated having new cell wall deposition. (1½ × 2)

**9. In a slide showing different types of cells, can you identify which type of the cell may be meristematic and the one which is incapable of dividing. How?** NCERT Exemplar

**Ans.** Meristematic cells are actively dividing cells which show mitotic divisions, i.e. each chromosome is split lengthwise into two homologous chromatids, which pass equally into daughter cells. These possess thin cell wall and a dense cytoplasm.

Mature cells are incapable of divisions because in these cells differentiation has taken place. Also mature cells do not possess thin cell wall in and a dense cytoplasm.

**10. In which type of growth, all daughter cells produced after mitotic cell division, grow and divide? Is the growth pattern ideal?**

**Ans.** In geometric growth, all daughter cells produced after mitotic cell division undergo cell division. (1)

No, the growth is not ideal since a condition of limited nutrient supply, occurs that affects the growth of organism. (1)

**11. The diagram given below shows the comparison of absolute and relative growth rates.** Competency Based Que.

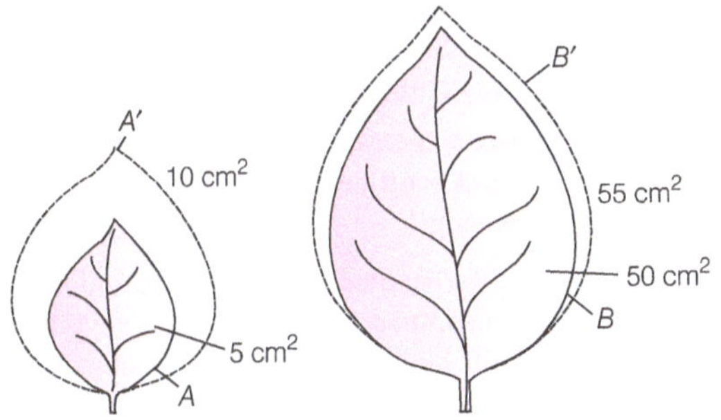


**Which of them shows higher relative growth rate? Justify.**

**Ans.** Relative growth rate of $A = \frac{(10-5)}{x \times 5} = \frac{5}{5x} cm^2$

Relative growth rate of $B = \frac{(55-50)}{x \times 50}$

$= \frac{5}{50x} cm^2$

Thus, $A$ shows higher relative growth rate.

**12. Both growth and differentiation in higher plants are open. Comment.** NCERT

**Ans.** The higher plants retain the capacity for growth throughout their life. This ability of plants is due to the presence of meristems at certain locations in the body. The cells of such meristems have the capacity to divide and self-perpetuate. Thus, growth in higher plants are open. Also some of these cells undergo differentiation after some rounds of cell division. Hence, the differentiation is also open.

**13. In which region of the plant, production of auxin is abundant. Name one natural and synthetic auxin each.**

**Ans.** The production of auxins is abundant in the meristematic region of shoot and root. One natural auxin is Indole-3-Acetic Acid (IAA) and one synthetic auxin is 2,4-dichlorophenoxy acetic acid (2,4-D)

**14. Auxins are growth hormones capable of promoting cell elongation. They have been used in horticulture to promote growth, flowering and rooting. Write a line to explain the meaning of the following terms related to auxins.** NCERT Exemplar

**(i) Auxins precursors** **(ii) Anti-auxins**

**(iii) Synthetic auxins**

**Ans.** Auxin is an important plant phytohormone required for the growth and development of every plant in its life cycle.

(i) **Auxin precursors** are raw materials required to initials synthesis of auxins. IAA is synthesised from tryptophan. (1)

(ii) **Anti-auxins** are compounds that inhibit action of auxins. (1)

(iii) **Synthetic auxin** are synthesised not by plants but artificially by man, e.g. 2, 4 D (weedicide) and NAA are synthetic auxin. (1)

**15. To get a carpet-like grass lawns are mowed regularly. Is there any scientific explanation for this?** NCERT Exemplar

**Ans.** Regular mowing (cutting at apex) of lawn grass removes the apical portion of the plant which causes the lateral branches to grow faster. As the apical buds inhibits growth of lateral buds by releasing auxin, the phenomenon called apical dominance.

So, as to make evenness of the grass (carpet-like) in the lawn this practice is followed regularly to overcome the problem of apical dominance.

**16. In botanical gardens and tea gardens, gardeners trim the plants regularly so that they remain bushy. Does this practice have any scientific explanation?** **NCERT Exemplar**

**Ans.** The apical buds present in tea and other plants prevents the growth of lateral buds in them, by releasing auxin hormone. This phenomenon is called apical dominance. Trimming of tea garden and botanical garden removes the apical bud and allowing the lateral buds to grow laterally and give plants a dense bushy appearance.

The scientific explanation for this trimming method is that apical bud is removed thus results in the removal of auxin and phenomenon an of apical dominance is overcomed.

**17. What is the mechanism underlying the phenomenon by which the terminal/ apical bud suppresses the growth of lateral buds? Suggest measures to overcome this phenomenon.** **NCERT Exemplar**

**Ans.** This phenomenon is known as apical dominance. It refers to the suppression of lateral bud growth due to the growth of terminal bud, which is influenced by the high auxin concentration. (1)

Removal of apical bud causes the sprouting of lateral buds and the phenomenon of apical dominance is overcomed. (1)

**18. How are IBA and 2, 4-D used in agriculture?**

**Ans.** IBA is used to induce rooting in plant cuttings. It helps to stimulate root growth and is widely used in plant propagation especially in horticulture. 2, 4-D can be used as a weedicide in order to prevent damage to plants due to weeds. (1 × 2)

**19. Gibberellins were first discovered in Japan when rice plants were suffering from bakane (the foolish seedling disease) caused by a fungus *Gibberella fujikuroi*.** **NCERT Exemplar**

**(i) Give two functions of this phytohormone.**

**(ii) Which property of gibberellin caused foolish seedling disease in rice?**

**Ans.** (i) The two functions of the gibberellins are as follows

(a) Produce the phenomenon of bolting, i.e. the growth of the internodal region of stem in plants with rosette habit.

(b) Delay senescence and ripening of fruits. (½ × 2)

(ii) The rice seedling/plant show excessive growth in their internodal region when get infected with fungus *Gibberella fujikuroi*.

This fungus produces excessive amount of plant hormone GA which makes the plants taller than the normal plant foolishly and many result into death of the plant. (2)

**20. How are gibberellins useful in agriculture to improve productivity? Give any three points in support of your answer.** **Competency Based Que.**

**Ans.** Gibberellins are useful in agriculture in the following ways

(i) Application of gibberellins increases the length of the stem and increases the yield of sugar in sugarcane.

(ii) Gibberellin is used to speed up the malting process in brewing industry.

(iii) It can cause fruits like apple to elongate and improve in shape. (1 × 3)

**21. Which plant hormone can transform genetically dwarf plants into tall plants ? State the mechanism involved with suitable example.** **Competency Based Que.**

**Ans.** Cabbage and beet plants have rosette habit of leaves. The leaves in these plants are condensed because of shortening of internodal area of the stem. It is a genetic character.

When we spray $GA_3$ solution on these plants, these become abnormally tall. It happens because of increase in internodal area. Thus, such genetically dwarf plant is made tall by $GA_3$. (1 + 2)

**22. The rice seedlings infected with fungus *Gibberella fujikuroi* are called foolish seedlings? What was the reason behind it?** **NCERT Exemplar**

**Ans.** The rice seedlings infected with fungus *Gibberella fujikuroi* are called foolish seedlings because these seedlings grow foolishly tall as compared to the normal ones, i.e. there is abnormal increase in internodal area of rice and ultimately, fall on ground resulting into death of plants.

**23. How does spraying of sugarcane plants with gibberellins increase the yield of sugar?** **Competency Based Que.**

**Ans.** Spraying of sugar cane plants with gibberellins increase the length of internodes and increased or lengthy internodes will produce more sugar. Thus, gibberellins can increase sugar yield.

**24. (i) Which hormones are considered more efficient to produce parthenocarpic fruits?**

**(ii) Which hormone breaks seed dormancy? State the mechanism involved.**

**Ans.** (i) Auxins are considered more efficient to produce parthenocarpic fruits.

(ii) Gibberellin breaks seed dormancy. It mobilises the enzyme to hydrolyse stored food present in seed at the time of seed germination. (1 × 2)

**25. In an experiment, the callus produced from internodal segments did not proliferate until coconut water was added. Give reason.** **Competency Based Que.**

**Ans.** Callus (i.e. undifferentiated mass of cells) proliferates only when nutrient medium containing auxin is supplemented with coconut milk because the latter contains kinetin (a cytokinin) which stimulates growth of plant tissues.

**26. Where are the following hormones synthesised in plants?** **NCERT Exemplar**

**(i) IAA (ii) Gibberellins (iii) Cytokinins**

**Ans.** (i) **IAA** (Indole Acetic Acid) is synthesised at the growing apices of the plant, e.g. shoot tip, leaf primordia etc.
(ii) **Gibberellins** is synthesised in the apical shoot buds, young leaves, root tips and developing seeds.
(iii) **Cytokinins** are synthesised mainly in roots meristematic regions. (1 × 3)

**27. What would be expected to happen if**
(i) **$GA_3$ is applied to rice seedlings?**
(ii) **dividing cells stop differentiating?**
(iii) **a rotten fruit gets mixed with unripe fruits?**
(iv) **you forget to add cytokinin to the culture medium?**
**Competency Based Que., NCERT**

**Ans.** . (i) Rice seedlings will grow extremely tall.
(ii) An undifferentiated mass of cells is formed.
(iii) The unripe fruits will ripen quickly.
(iv) The callus will not develop shoot buds. [½ × 4]

**28. A farmer grows cucumber plants in his field. He wants to increase the number of female flowers in them. Which plant growth regulator can be applied to achieve this?** **NCERT Exemplar**

**Ans.** Ethylene is associated with the promotions of femaleness in plants, thus the farmer must spray ethylene hormone on the cucumber crop to produce female flowers and to increase the yield (number of fruits produced).

**29. Why is abscisic acid also known as stress hormone?** **NCERT**

**Ans.** Abscisic acid stimulates the closure of stomata in the epidermis and increase the tolerance of plants to various kinds of stresses. Hence, it is also called the stress hormone.

**30. Name the categories of plant hormones concerned with each of the following and describe one other function of each of the three categories of plant hormones.**
(i) **Inhibition of seed germination.**
(ii) **Promote flowering.**
(iii) **Cell division promoting activity.**

**Ans.**

| | PGR | Function |
|---|---|---|
| (i) | **Abscisic acid** | Gives signals for closure of stomata in plants to prevent water loss during water stress. |
| (ii) | **Auxin** | Controls cell division and xylem differentiation. |
| (iii) | **Cytokinin** | Helps in the growth of lateral buds and overcome apical dominance. (1 × 3) |

**31. Plant Growth Substances (PGSs) have innumerable practical applications. Name the PGR you should used to** **NCERT Exemplar**
(i) **increase yield of sugarcane.**
(ii) **promote lateral shoot growth.**
(iii) **cause sprouting of potato tuber.**
(iv) **inhibit seed germination.**

**Ans.** (i) Gibberellin
(ii) Cytokinins
(iii) Ethylene
(iv) Abscisic acid (½ × 4)

**32. Which one of the plant growth regulators would you use if you are asked to** **NCERT**
(i) **induce rooting in a twig?**
(ii) **quickly ripen a fruit?**
(iii) **delay leaf senescence?**
(iv) **induce growth in axillary buds?**
(v) **bolt a rosette plant?**
(vi) **induce immediate stomatal closure in leaves?**

**Ans.** (i) Auxins like Indole Butyric Acid (IBA)
(ii) Ethylene
(iii) Cytokinin
(iv) Cytokinin
(v) Gibberellin
(vi) Abscisic acid (½ × 6)

## Long Answer Type Questions

**1. Mention the phenomenon of growth in plants. Explain the regions of growth in detail.**

**Ans.** Refer to text on page no. 292.

**2. What are meristems? How does the primary growth differ from secondary growth?**

**Ans.** Meristems are the tissues present in the growing regions of plants. (1)

Primary growth refers to the elongation (growth in length) of stems and roots. All plants exhibit primary growth. Root apical meristem and shoot apical meristem are responsible for the primary growth of the plants and principally contribute to the elongation of the plants along their axis. (2)

The growth that makes plants thicker (growth in diameter) is called secondary growth.

For example, in dicotyledonous plants and gymnosperms, the lateral meristems, vascular cambium and cork cambium appear later in life. These are the secondary meristems. Their activity in plant helps these plants to grow in girth (diameter). (2)

**3. Describe briefly.** **NCERT**
(i) **Arithmetic growth**
(ii) **Geometric growth**
(iii) **Sigmoid growth curve**
(iv) **Absolute and relative growth rates**

**Ans.** Refer to text on page no. 293-295.

**4. Describe the necessary conditions for the occurrence of growth in detail.**

**Ans.** Refer to text on page no. 295-296.

**5. Define differentiation. Also give details about how can you distinguish between dedifferentiation and redifferentiation?**

**Ans.** The cells which are derived from root apical meristem and shoot apical meristem and other meristems undergo certain changes to attain maturity to perform specific functions. This process which leads to maturation of cells is termed as differentiation. During this, the cells undergo a few major structural changes both in their cell walls and protoplasm to perform some specific functions throughout their life. (1)

(i) In plants, some living differentiated cells, e.g. parenchyma can regain the capacity to divide mitotically under certain conditions. A dedifferentiated tissue can act as meristem, e.g. interfascicular vascular cambium and cork cambium. (2)

(ii) The product of dedifferentiated cells or tissues which lose the ability to divide is called redifferentiated cells and the process is known as redifferentiation. Secondary xylem and secondary phloem from interfascicular vascular cambium, secondary cortex and cork are the examples of redifferentiated tissues. (2)

**6. Define growth, differentiation, development, dedifferentiation, redifferentiation, determinate growth, meristem and growth rate.** NCERT

**Ans.** Determinate growth refers to a type of growth pattern in which an organism or its part grows to a specific shape and size and then stops growing.

For other terms

Refer to text on page no. 292, 295-296.

**7. (i) Explain the factors that controls the growth and development.**

**(ii) Describe the mechanism of plasticity in plants with suitable examples.**

**Ans.** Refer to text on page no. 295, 297.

**8. What are plant growth regulators? Name four different chemical types of them with one example of each.**

**Ans.** Plant growth regulators are small, simple molecules secreted in minute quantities that influence various physiological functions in plants. These are of diverse chemical composition. (1)

(i) Indole compounds [such as- Indole-3- Acetic Acid (IAA)].

(ii) Adenine derivatives [such as kinetin, $N^6$-furfuryl amino purine].

(iii) Derivatives of carotenoids [such as Abscisic Acid (ABA)].

(iv) Terpenes [such as gibberellic acids] (1 × 4)

**9. (i) Define plant growth regulators. Name two growth inhibitors.**

**(ii) What is the meaning of bakanae?**

**(iii) Name the microorganism which yields gibberellins. State one application of gibberellins in agricultures.**

**Ans.** (i) Refer to text on page no. 297, 298. (2)

(ii) Refer to text on page no. 298. (1)

(iii) Refer to text on page no. 298, 300. (2)

**10. List five main natural plant growth regulators. Write a note on discovery, physiological functions and agricultural /horticultural applications of any one of them.** NCERT

**Ans.** Five main natural plant growth regulators are auxins, gibberellins, ethylene, cytokinins and ABA. (1)

**Auxins**

(i) **Discovery** Auxins was first isolated from human urine. They are generally produced by the growing apices of the stems and roots of plants. Auxins like IAA and IBA have been isolated from plants. NAA (Naphthalene Acetic Acid) and 2, 4-D (2, 4-dichlorophenoxyacetic acid) are synthetic auxins.

(ii) **Physiological Functions** They help to initiate rooting in stem cuttings, an application widely used for plant propagation. Auxins promote flowering, i.e. in pineapples.
They help to prevent fruit and leaf drop at early stages, but promote the abscission of older mature leaves and fruits.

(iii) **Agricultural/Horticultural Applications** Auxins also induce parthenocarpy, (e.g. in tomatoes). They are widely used as herbicides (e.g. 2, 4-D) and are used to kill dicotyledonous weeds.
They do not affect mature monocotyledonous plants, instead are used to prepare weed-free lawns by gardeners. Auxins also control xylem differentiation and help in cell division. (4)

**11. Which parts of the plants produce gibberellins? State two functions of this hormone and mention why it was named gibberellin.**

**Ans.** The major sites of gibberellin production in plants are embryos, roots and young leaves near the shoot tip. (1)

**For two functions of gibberellins** Refer to text on page no. 300.

It was named after the fungus, which is the source of it, i.e. *Gibberella fujikuroi*. (4)

**12. (i) Name the cytokinin like substance isolated from corn kernels and coconut milk.**

**(ii) Write a short note on functions of cytokinins.**

**Ans.** (i) Refer to text on page no. 300.

(ii) Refer to text on page no. 301.

**13.** **Name the only gaseous natural plant growth regulator. Mention any four of its effects on plants in detail.**

**Ans.** Refer to text on page no. 301.

**14.** **Write in detail about abscisic acid.**

**Ans.** Refer to text on page no. 301-302.

**15.** **Give one antagonistic function of each of the following hormone pairs.**

(i) Gibberellins — Abscisic acid
(ii) Cytokinin — Auxins
(iii) ABA — Auxin

**Ans.** Refer to interactions between growth regulators on page no. 302.

**16.** **The role of ethylene and abscisic acid is both positive and negative. Justify the statement.**

**Competency Based Que., NCERT Exemplar**

**Ans.** The role of ethylene and abscisic acid is both positive and negative. Ethylene is a simple gaseous PGR. It is synthesised in large amount by tissues undergoing senescence and ripening. It also promotes senescence and abscission of plant organs especially of leaves and flowers. This is its negative effect.

As it's positive effect, ethylene breaks seed and bud dormancy, initiates germination in peanut seeds, sprouting of potato tubers. It promotes internode/petiole elongation in deep water rice plants. It helps leaves/ inner parts of the shoot to remain above water. (1½ × 2)

Abscisic Acid (ABA) is a stress hormone released only during unfavourable conditions of drought heat stress, etc. It has both positive and negative roles to play during the growth of a plant.

It shows a positive effect by aiding in seed development and maturation. During stressful conditions such as drought and salinity, ABA brings about stomatal closure which further reduces the rate of water loss during transpiration. This prevents the plant from wilting. On the other hand, ABA is general plant growth inhibitor.

It inhibits seed germination and other plant metabolism. Thus, the role of both ethylene and ABA is both positive and negative effect.

**17.** **While experimentation, why do you think it is difficult to assign any effect observed to a single hormone?** **Competency Based Que.**

**Ans.** Most of the hormones are synergistic to each other in their mode of functions. Thus, during experimentation, we cannot judge whether, a particular effect is produced by a single hormone or is an additive effect of many hormones. (1)

For example,

(i) Auxins help to initiate rooting in stem cuttings (an application widely used for plant propagation). Cytokinins also show the similar function of root formation. Auxins promote flowering, e.g. in pineapples. They also induce parthenocarpy, e.g. in tomatoes.

(ii) Ethylene act synergistic to auxin in initiating flowering and for synchronising fruit set in pineapples.

(iii) Cytokinins and gibberellins help overcome the apical dominance and delay the process of leaf senescence respectively. On the other hand, ethylene promotes senescence and abscission of plant organs especially of leaves and flowers.

(iv) This shows that all hormones are synergistic or antagonistic to each other in their mode of action in plants. (1 × 4)

Hence, it is difficult to assign any effect to any single hormone.

**18.** **Mention the factors which prove that phytohormones act synergistically or antagonistically.**

**Ans.** The factors which prove that phytohormones act synergistically or antagonistically are

(i) Cell division is promoted by both auxins and cytokinins acting synergistically.

(ii) Auxins and cytokinins interact to control morphogenetic differentiation of shoot and root. When auxin is in excess, roots differentiate on the callus, while excess of cytokinins promotes shoot bud formation.

(iii) Auxins and cytokinins act antagonistically in controlling apical dominance. Auxins cause apical dominance, while cytokinins overcome the same.

(iv) Senescence of leaves is delayed by auxins and cytokinins, while it is stimulated by abscisic acid.

(v) The dormancy of seeds and buds is mostly due to abscisic acid and the same is broken by gibberellins.

(vi) Cytokinins cause opening of stomata, while abscisic acid results in their closure.

## Source Based/Case Based/Passage Based Questions

**1.** **Plant growth regulators are the chemicals that controls the growth and development of the plants. Two graphs given below represent two conditions (i) Before and (ii) After the application of a hormone 'X'.**

**Competency Based Que.**

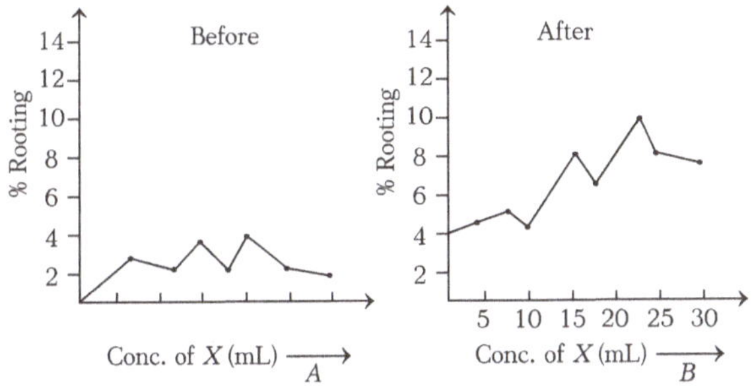


**(i) Which hormone is referred to here as 'X' ?**

**(ii) Why is there a difference in the percentage of rooting as visible from the graphs above?**

**(iii) Can the same hormone also be used to induce parthenocarpy?**

**(iv) State two functions of the hormone identified in (i) above.**

**Ans.** (i) Auxin that acts as a plant growth regulator is referred to here as *X*. (1)

(ii) Differences in the percentage of rooting are seen due to the addition of auxin or its forms like IAA, IBA in case B.

These forms tend to initiate rooting in the stem cuttings. Thus, making extensive use in agricultural and horticultural practices. (1)

(iii) Yes, the same hormone is also used to induce parthenocarpy which is development of fruit without fertilisation. (1)

(iv) Two functions of auxin are

- These promote flowering in pineapples.
- These prevent fruit and leaf drop at early stages. (1)

**2. The graph given below depicts the length of sugarcane before and after the application of Gibberellic Acid ($GA_3$) in the sugarcane field.** **Competency Based Que.**

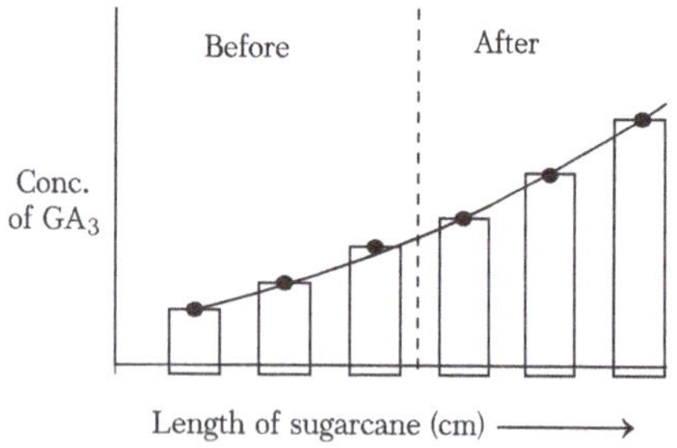


**Consider the graph given above and answer the following questions.**

**(i) What conclusion can be drawn from the above graph ?**

**(ii) Application of gibberellins in the sugarcane field, tend to increase sugarcane yield upto 20 tonnes/acre. How?**

**(iii) Gibberellins can be used to store fruits for a long time. Why ? Give two other applications of gibberellins.**

**Ans.** (i) The above graph shows the increase in length of sugarcane after the application of gibberellins. (1)

(ii) Spraying of sugarcane crop with gibberellins increases the length of stem. Thus, increasing the yield of sugarcane to as much as 20 tonnes/acre. (1)

(iii) Gibberellins help in delaying the ripening of fruits like apples, citrus fruits, etc. Thus, fruits can be stored for a longer time.

Two other applications of gibberellins includes

- They speed up process of malting in brewing industry.
- They break seed and bud dormancy. (2)

**3. Read the following passage and answer the questions that follows.**

**Arun visited his village in vacations to see his grandfather. He went to the field one day along with his grandfather where he observe that the mangoes faced significant challenges in the ripening timing. He discussed the issue and the reason behind this, with his grandfather. His grandfather asked him to suggest some methods in order to solve this issue.**

**(i) Name the synthetic plant growth regulator that Arun can suggest to his grandfather.**

**(ii) List any two functions performed by the hormone as stated in (i)**

**(iii) Describe the mechanism of this plant growth regulator.**

**Ans.** (i) Arun can suggest the use of 'ethephon' to his grandfather in order to resolve the issue. (1)

(ii) Following functions are performed by ethephon.

- It helps in accelerating abscission in flowers and fruits.
- It helps in promoting formation of female flowers, thus enhancing the yield. (2)

(iii) Ethephon tends to be readily absorbed in an aqueous solution and is easily transported within the plant. It then slowly releases ethylene. (1)

# SELF ASSESSMENT TEST

## Multiple Choice Questions

1. Growth is regarded as one of the most fundamental characteristics of living being. Which of the following option does not define growth?
   (a) Expansion of leaf
   (b) Increase in length of pollen tube
   (c) Photosynthesis in leaves
   (d) Formation of roots
2. The type of growth where new cells are always being added to the plant body by the activity of the meristem is called
   (a) continuous type of growth
   (b) open form of growth
   (c) diffused form of growth
   (d) closed form of growth
3. Which of the following is not a characteristic of cells present in the meristematic phase of growth?
   (a) Presence of large conspicuous nuclei
   (b) Presence of thin and cellulosic cell wall
   (c) Abundant plasmodesmatal connections
   (d) Increased vacuolation
4. Formation of interfascicular cambium and cork cambium from parenchyma cells is an example of
   (a) differentiation (b) dedifferentiation (c) redifferentiation (d) development
5. Identify the correct sequence of the events of the developmental process in a plant cell.
   I. Plasmatic growth II. Differentiation III. Maturation IV. Senescence
   Choose the correct option.
   (a) I-II-III-IV (b) I-III-II-IV (c) IV-III-II-I (d) IV-II-III-I
6. Select the pair that contains plant growth promoter.
   (a) Auxins and cytokinins
   (b) Abscisic acid and gibberellins
   (c) Ethylene and abscisic acid
   (d) Abscisic acid and auxins
7. Which of the following is not true regarding cytokinins?
   (a) They increases the rate of chlorophyll synthesis
   (b) They helps in adventitious shoot formation
   (c) They promote rapid cell division
   (d) They are plant growth inhibitors
8. Match the following.

| | Column I | | Column II |
|---|---|---|---|
| A. | Gaseous PGR | 1 | Promotes cell division |
| B. | NAA | 2 | Antagonist to GA |
| C. | Stress hormone | 3. | Fruit ripening hormone |
| D. | Zeatin | 4. | Synthetic auxin |

**Codes**

| | A | B | C | D | | A | B | C | D |
|---|---|---|---|---|---|---|---|---|---|
| (a) | 3 | 2 | 4 | 1 | (b) | 4 | 1 | 3 | 2 |
| (c) | 3 | 4 | 2 | 1 | (d) | 3 | 4 | 1 | 2 |

## Assertion-Reason Questions

**Direction** (Q. Nos. 9-12) *In each of the following questions, a statement of Assertion (A) is given followed by corresponding statement of Reason (R). Of the statements, mark the correct answer as*

(a) Both A and R are true and R is the correct explanation of A.
(b) Both A and R are true, but R is not the correct explanation of A.
(c) A is true, but R is false.
(d) A is false, but R is true.

9. **Assertion** (A) Parenchyma cells can be made to divide to form callus under controlled conditions.

**Reason** (R) The differentiated cells can regain their capacity to divide under certain conditions.

10. **Assertion** (A) Ethylene is a simple gaseous plant growth regulator.

**Reason** (R) Ethylene is synthesised in large amounts by tissues that undergo senescence and ripening of fruits.

11. **Assertion** (A) ABA is also known as stress hormone.

**Reason** (R) ABA is stimulated under unfavourable conditions such as drought, water lodging, excessive temperature, etc.

12. **Assertion** (A) During differentiation, tracheary elements lose their protoplasm and develop lignocellulosic secondary cell walls.

**Reason** (R) Strong, elastic secondary cell walls in tracheary elements enable the conduction of water over long distances under extreme tension.

## Very Short Answer Type Questions

13. Name the two processes that forms the basis of development.
14. List the three phases of growth in a plant.
15. Mention any two intrinsic and extrinsic factors that regulate development.
16. Name the hormones which

(i) is used for killing weed (ii) induces seed dormancy

## Short Answer Type Questions

17. Differentiate between dedifferentiation and redifferentiation.
18. Define parthenocarpy. Name any two plant hormones that are used to induce parthenocarpy.
19. (i) Write the full form of NAA and IAA. (ii) Write the horticulture application of auxin.

## Long Answer Type Questions

20. Describe the three phases of growth.
21. Write a note on the discovery, structure and function of gibberellin.
22. Describe briefly

(i) Plasticity (ii) Applications of ethephon

## Case Based Question

23. The diagram given below represents the chemical structure of a PGR. Observe the diagram and answer the following questions.

(i) In which part of the plant this hormone is synthesised?

(ii) What is the effect of using this hormone along with cytokinin in tissue culture?

(iii) Write any two applications of this hormone.

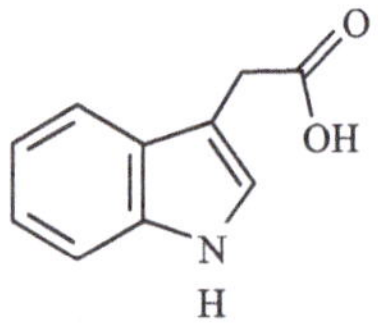


# Answers

| | | | | | | |
|---|---|---|---|---|---|---|
| 1. (c) | 2. (b) | 3. (d) | 4. (b) | 5. (a) | 6. (a) | 7. (d) |
| 8. (c) | 9. (a) | 10. (b) | 11. (a) | 12. (a) | | |

# 14 CHAPTER

# Breathing and Exchange of Gases

All living organisms require energy for carrying out various cellular activities. They obtain this energy from oxidation of food material at cellular level.
This breakdown process is called **respiration** and is usually occurs in the presence of oxygen.

### YOUR STUDY GOALS

14.1 Respiratory Organs in Animals
14.2 Human Respiratory System
14.3 Mechanism of Breathing
14.4 Respiratory Volumes and Capacities
14.5 Exchange of Gases
14.6 Transport of Gases
14.7 Regulation of Respiration
14.8 Disorders of the Respiratory System

### YOUR PRACTICE GOAL

- Objective Type Questions (37 Qs ; MCQs, A-R) Case Based Questions (4)
- Subjective Type Questions
- (19 VSAs, 30 SAs, 9 LAs)

- **Breathing** is the first step of respiration and involves the movement of air in and out from the respiratory tract.
- There is a continuous need of intake of oxygen, from the atmosphere and removal of carbon dioxide during the process of respiration, thus making breathing a vital process.
- In this chapter, we will study about the respiratory organ and mechanism of breathing in human beings in detail.

## 14.1 Respiratory Organs in Animals

Various kinds of structures called respiratory organs are found in different animals which facilitate the exchange of gases between the body and the environment.

Different animal groups have evolved different modes of respiration for the exchange of gases. Some of them are mentioned below.

- **Lower invertebrates** like sponges, cnidarians, platyhelminths and free-living roundworms exchange $O_2$ with $CO_2$ by simple diffusion through body surface.
- **Annelids** like earthworms respire through moist cuticle.
- **Insects** have a network of tubes (**tracheal tubes**) to transport atmospheric air within the body (**tracheal respiration**).
- Special vascularised structures called **gills** (branchial respiration) are used by most of the **aquatic arthropods**, **molluscs** and **fishes**.

- The highly vascularised bags called **lungs** (**pulmonary respiration**) are used by the terrestrial forms for the exchange of gases, e.g. reptiles, birds and mammals.
- Amphibians like frog can respire through their moist skin (**cutaneous respiration**) as well as lungs.

## 14.2 Human Respiratory System

The human respiratory system may be divided into two major components

### I. Conducting Part

- This part act as passage for the air, comprising of structures starting from external nares upto terminal bronchiole.
- It transports the atmospheric air to the lung alveoli and return it from the lungs to the exterior. This part clears the air by removing foreign particles, humidifies it and also brings it to the body temperature.
- In conducting part, gaseous exchange does not take place. The various structure of conducting part are as follows

#### 1. External Nares (Nostrils)

These are the paired openings present at the lower end of the nose, which opens into the nasal chamber through the nasal passage.

#### 2. Nasal Chambers

- These are the pair of cavities located at the back of nostrils just above the mouth cavity.
- **Nasal septum** is a median partition that separates these two chambers.

#### 3. Pharynx

The nasal chambers open into pharynx, a portion of which is the common passage for both food and air.

#### 4. Larynx

- It is a cartilaginous box which helps in sound production and hence called the **sound box**.
- The pharynx opens through the **glottis** of the larynx into the trachea.
- Glottis is a slit-like aperture that remains open except during swallowing.
- The glottis bears a thin elastic cartilaginous flap, called **epiglottis**. It closes the glottis to prevent the entry of food into the larynx during swallowing.

#### 5. Trachea

- It is a straight thin-walled tube that extends upto the mid-thoracic cavity.

#### 6. Bronchi

- At the level of 5th thoracic vertebra, the trachea divides into two tubes, right and left **primary bronchi**.
- Each bronchi further divides into **secondary bronchi**. The secondary bronchi subdivides into smaller **tertiary bronchi**, which is further divided into smaller **bronchioles**.
- The small terminal bronchioles give rise to a number of thin, irregular walled, one cell thick, vascular bag-like structure called **lung alveoli**.
- The trachea, primary, secondary and tertiary bronchi along with initial bronchioles are supported by incomplete **cartilaginous rings** which prevent them from collapsing during inspiration.

### II. Respiratory Part (Exchange Part)

- The alveoli and their ducts form this part of the respiratory system.
- It is the site of actual diffusion of $O_2$ and $CO_2$ between blood and atmospheric air.
- The branching network of bronchi, bronchioles and alveoli comprise the lungs, which provide the surface for exchange of gases in humans.

### Lungs

- It lies in the thoracic cavity on the sides of the heart.
- Thoracic cavity is an anatomically air tight chamber.
- It is enclosed dorsally by **thoracic vertebrae**, laterally by the **ribs**, ventrally by the **sternum** and closed below by a dome-shaped **diaphragm**.
- The arrangement of lungs in thorax is such that any change in the volume of thoracic cavity will be manifested in the pulmonary (lung) cavity.

- This arrangement is necessary for breathing as the pulmonary volume cannot be altered directly.

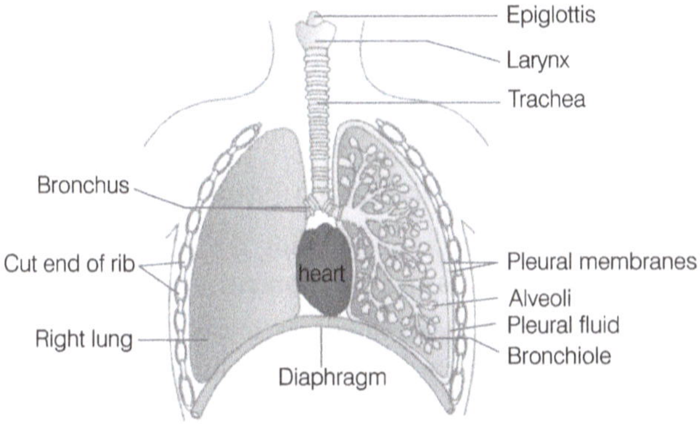


Fig. 14.1 Diagrammatic view of human respiratory system (sectional view of the left lung is also shown)

### Protective Coverings of Lungs

- Each lung is enclosed by two layered membrane called the **pleura**.
- The inner membrane is firmly bound to the surface of lung. Whereas the outer membrane is held close to the thoracic wall.
- **Pleural cavity** is a very narrow space that exists between the two pleura.
- It contains the **pleural fluid** secreted by the pleura, for reducing friction on the lung surface.

## Steps Involved in the Process of Respiration

Respiration is an important process that allow living things to survive by taking in oxygen, releasing carbon dioxide and producing energy.

The main mechanism of respiration involves the following steps.

- **Pulmonary ventilation or breathing** by which atmospheric air is drawn in and $CO_2$ rich alveolar air is released out.
- **Diffusion of gases** ($O_2$ and $CO_2$) across alveolar membrane.
- **Transport of gases** by the blood to every tissues in body.
- **Diffusion of $O_2$ and $CO_2$** between blood and tissues.
- **Utilisation of $O_2$** by the cells for catabolic reactions and resultant release of $CO_2$ and energy.

### Quick Test 1

1. Name the process used by sponges and Platyhelminthes for gaseous exchange.
2. A structure *X* checks the entry of food during swallowing. Identify *X*.
3. **State True or False.**
   The incomplete cartilaginous rings of the trachea are responsible for gas exchange during respiration.
4. Give the name of the site where actual diffusion of $O_2$ and $CO_2$ occurs in humans.
5. A fluid filled membranous layer surrounds the lungs. Name it. *(NCERT Exemplar)*

## 14.3 Mechanism of Breathing

- Breathing is an extracellular, energy consuming and physical process.
- It involves movement of thorax, inflation (expansion) and deflation of lungs and flow of air into and out from the lungs by creating a pressure gradient between the lungs and the atmosphere.
- The movement of diaphragm and a specialised set of **muscles** (i.e. **external** and **internal intercostals** between the ribs) help in generation of such pressure gradients between lungs and the atmosphere.
- Humans also have the ability to increase the strength of breathing with the help of additional muscles present in abdomen.
- Breathing mainly involves the following two steps

### 1. Inspiration

- It is an active process by which fresh air enters the lungs.
- Inspiration can occur if the pressure within the lungs (intra-pulmonary pressure) is less than the atmospheric pressure, i.e. there is a negative pressure in lungs with respect to atmospheric pressure.
- Following muscles play an important role in the process of inspiration

#### (i) Diaphragm

It moves downward due to the contraction of muscle fibres attached to it and becomes flat. This causes an increase in the volume of thoracic chamber in the antero-posterior axis.

### (ii) External Intercostal Muscles

- These muscles are present between the ribs.
- The external intercostal muscles contract and pull the **ribs** and the **sternum** upward and outward, thus increasing the volume of thoracic chamber in dorso–ventral axis.
- Thus, the overall increase in the volume of thoracic cavity causes an increase in pulmonary volume.
- An increase in pulmonary volume decreases the intra-pulmonary pressure to less than atmospheric pressure which forces the air from outside to move into the lungs.

## 2. Expiration

- It is a passive process by which $CO_2$ is expelled out from the lungs.
- It takes place when the intra-pulmonary pressure is higher than the atmospheric pressure.

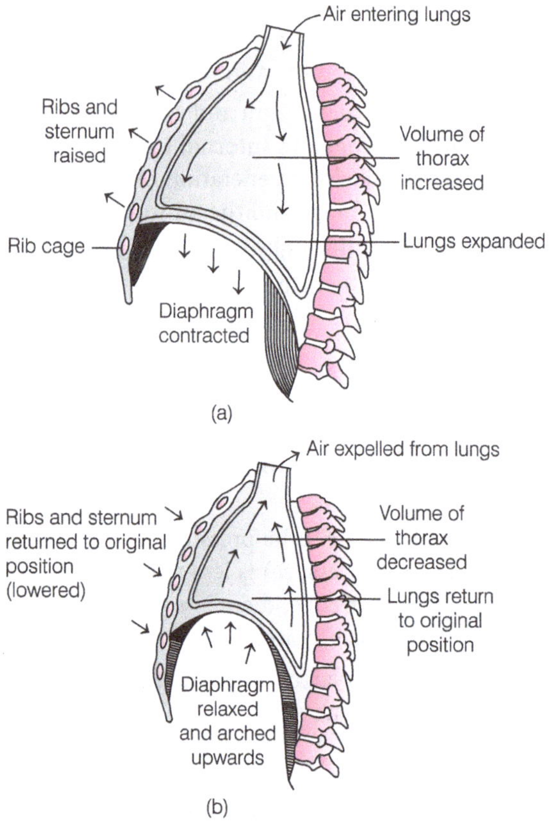


Fig. 14.2 Mechanism of breathing showing (a) Inspiration, (b) Expiration

- The movements of muscles involved in the expiration are as follows

### (i) Diaphragm

The muscle fibres of the diaphragm relax making it convex, decreasing volume of the thoracic cavity.

### (ii) External Intercostal Muscles

- These muscles relax thus, pulling the ribs downward and inward, decreasing the thoracic volume.
- The overall volume of the thoracic cavity decreases, thereby reducing the pulmonary volume.
- As a result, the intra-pulmonary pressure increases slightly above the atmospheric pressure.
- This inturn causes the expulsion of air from the lungs. The process of expiration is simpler than inspiration.

**TEACHER'S TIP**

The internal intercostal muscles are located between the ribs and primarily aid in forced expiration by pulling the ribs downward and inward, reducing the volume of the thoracic cavity and pushing air out of the lungs. These muscles are most active during activities that require increased respiratory effort, such as exercise or coughing.

## 14.4 Respiratory Volumes and Capacities

- On an average, a healthy human adult breathes about 12-16 times/minute.
- The volume of air involved in breathing movements can be estimated by using an instrument known as **spirometer**. This instrument helps in clinical assessment of pulmonary functions.
- The quantity of air, the lungs can receive, hold or expel under different conditions are called **pulmonary volumes.**
- Combination of two or more pulmonary volumes are called **pulmonary capacities.**
- The different respiratory (pulmonary) volumes and capacities are as follows
  - **Tidal Volume** (TV) It is the volume of air inspired or expired during normal breathing in relaxed or resting position. It is about 500 mL. A

healthy man can inspire or expire approximately 6000-8000 mL of air per minute.

- **Inspiratory Reserve Volume** (IRV) It is the additional amount of air that can be inspired forcibly after a normal inspiration. It is about 2500-3000 mL of air.
- **Expiratory Reserve Volume** (ERV) It is the additional volume of air that can be expired forcibly after a normal expiration. It is about 1000-1100 mL.
- **Residual Volume** (RV) It is the volume of air remaining in the lungs even after a forcible expiration. It is about 1100-1200 mL. It cannot be measured by spirometer.

- Various **pulmonary capacities** are derived from the combination of above mentioned volumes. These help in the clinical diagnosis of functioning of lungs. These are as follows.
  - **Inspiratory Capacity** (IC) It is the total volume of air a person can inspire after a normal expiration. It is about 3000-3500 mL. It includes tidal volume and inspiratory reserve volume.

$$IC = TV + IRV$$

  - **Expiratory Capacity** (EC) It is the total volume of air a person can expire after a normal inspiration. It includes tidal volume and expiratory reserve volume.

$$EC = TV + ERV$$

  - **Functional Residual Capacity** (FRC) It is the volume of air that will remain in the lungs after a normal expiration. It includes residual volume and expiratory reserve volume.

$$FRC = RV + ERV$$

  - **Vital Capacity** (VC) It is the maximum volume of air a person can breathe in after a forced expiration or the maximum volume of air a person can breathe out after a forced inspiration.
This includes tidal volume, inspiratory reserve volume and expiratory reserve volume.

$$VC = TV + IRV + ERV.$$

It varies from 3400-4800 mL depending upon age, sex and height of an individual.

  - **Total Lung Capacity** (TLC) It is the total volume of air present in the lungs after a forced (maximum) inspiration. It includes reserve volume, expiratory reserve volume, tidal volume and inspiratory reserve volume.

$$TLC = RV + ERV + TV + IRV \text{ or } (VC+RV)$$

## Quick Test 2

1. Can impaired diaphragm movement lead to breathing difficulties?
2. Name the muscles involved when a person exhales forcefully during breathing exercises.
3. An instrument *X* helps in the clinical assessment of pulmonary function. Identify *X*.
4. A child is running a marathon. Mention the volume of air inspired forcefully during running.
5. **State True or False.**
   Total lung capacity is the sum of vital capacity and residual volume.

## 14.5 Exchange of Gases

- Alveoli are the primary sites of exchange of gases. This gaseous exchange also occurs between blood and tissues.
- Gases are exchanged in these sites by **simple diffusion** which mainly based on the pressure/concentration gradient.
- The **factors that affect rate of diffusion** are
  - Thickness of the membrane.
  - Surface area of the membrane.
  - Permeability of the membrane.
  - Solubility of the gases.
  - Partial pressure gradient (difference) of gases on the two sides of the diffusing surfaces.

### 1. Exchange of Gases between Alveoli and Blood

- The exchange of gases between lung alveoli and pulmonary capillaries is called **external respiration**.
- The alveolar wall is very thin with a rich network of blood capillaries. It is also called as **diffusion membrane** (alveolar-capillary membrane).
- The diffusion membrane is made up of
  - Thin squamous epithelium of alveoli
  - Basement substance
  - Endothelium of alveolar capillaries.

- The basement substance is composed of a thin basement membrane supporting the squamous epithelium and the basement membrane surrounding the single layer endothelial cells of capillaries.
- All these form a membrane with thickness of less than a millimetre.
- The volume of gas that diffuses through this membrane each minute for a pressure gradient of 1mm Hg is called **diffusing capacity.**

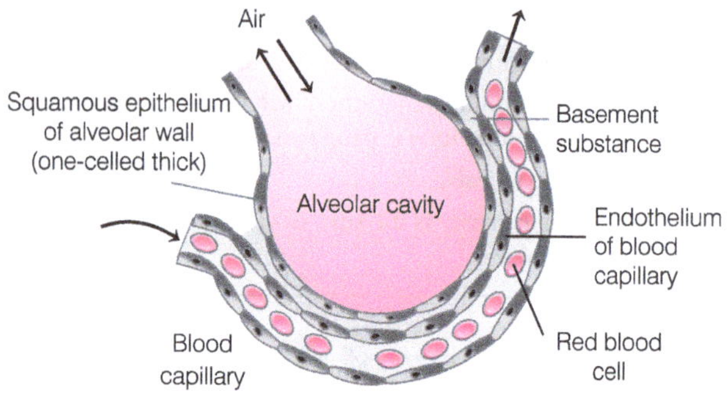


Fig. 14.3 A diagram of a section of an alveolus with a pulmonary capillary

- At a particular pressure difference, the diffusing capacity of $CO_2$ is 20-25 times faster than oxygen because of its solubilty.
- Thus, the amount of $CO_2$ that can diffuse through the diffusion membrane per unit difference in partial pressure is much higher as compared to oxygen.
- Pressure contributed by an individual gas in a mixture of gases is called **partial pressure** and is represented as $pO_2$ for oxygen and $pCO_2$ for carbon dioxide.
- Partial pressure (in mm Hg) of oxygen and carbon dioxide at different parts involved in diffusion in comparison to those in atmosphere are as follows

| Respiratory Gas | $O_2$ | $CO_2$ |
|---|---|---|
| Atmospheric Air | 159 | 0.3 |
| Alveoli | 104 | 40 |
| Blood (Deoxygenated) | 40 | 45 |
| Blood (Oxygenated) | 95 | 40 |
| Tissues | 40 | 45 |

- As seen in the above table, $pO_2$ in the alveoli (104 mm Hg) is higher than that in the deoxygenated blood in the capillaries of pulmonary arteries (40 mm Hg). So, there is diffusion of $O_2$ from alveoli to the blood capillary.
- Also, $pCO_2$ is higher in deoxygenated blood (45 mm Hg) than in alveoli (40 mm Hg), therefore, $CO_2$ diffuses from blood to the alveoli.

## 2. Exchange of Gases between Blood and Tissue Cells

- The exchange of gases between tissue blood capillaries and tissue cells is called **internal respiration.**
- $pO_2$ in oxygenated blood (95 mm Hg) is higher than $pO_2$ in tissues (40 mm Hg) and $pCO_2$ in oxygenated blood (40 mm Hg) is lower than $pCO_2$ in tissues (45 mm Hg).
- Due to this partial pressure differences, oxygen diffuses from the capillary blood to the tissues and $CO_2$ diffuses from the tissues to the capillary blood *via* tissue fluid.
- Now, the blood becomes deoxygenated. It is further carried to the heart by veins and finally goes to lungs for purification.

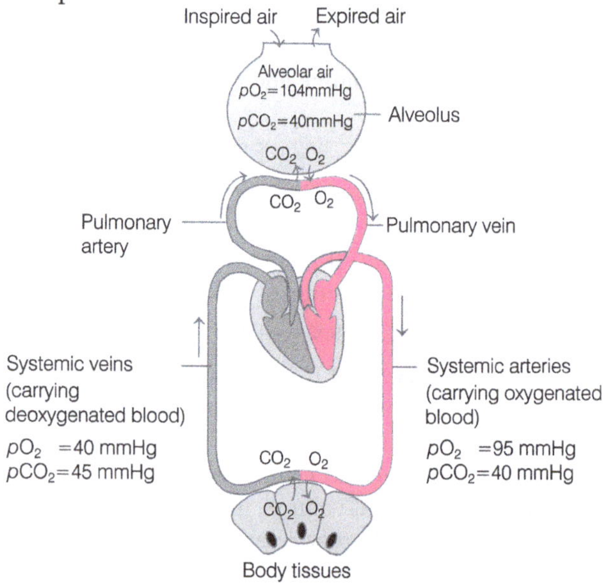


Fig. 14.4 Diagrammatic representation of exchange of gases at the alveolus and the body tissues with blood and transport of oxygen and carbon dioxide.

## 14.6 Transport of Gases

- Blood carries oxygen from the lungs to tissues for oxidation and carbon dioxide from the tissues to the respiratory surface for elimination.
- Transport of oxygen and carbon dioxide in detail is discussed below

### Transport of Oxygen

- Oxygen is transported from alveoli to the cells in two forms.
  - **As Dissolved Gas** About **3% of oxygen** is carried in a dissolved state through the plasma.
  - **As Oxyhaemoglobin** About **97% of oxygen** is carried in combination with haemoglobin present in the blood.
- **Haemoglobin** (Hb) is a red coloured iron containing pigment, present in RBCs, to which $O_2$ can bind in a reversible manner to form **oxyhaemoglobin.**
- Four molecules of oxygen bind with one molecule of haemoglobin.

$$\underset{\text{Haemoglobin}}{Hb} + \underset{\text{Oxygen}}{O_2} \underset{\text{In tissues}}{\overset{\text{In lungs}}{\rightleftharpoons}} \underset{\text{Oxyhaemoglobin}}{HbO_2}$$

- Factors affecting the binding of oxygen with haemoglobin are
  - Partial pressure of oxygen
  - Partial pressure of carbon dioxide
  - Hydrogen ion concentration
  - Temperature

### Oxygen Dissociation Curve

- It is the **sigmoid curve** (S-shaped) obtained on plotting percentage saturation of Hb with $O_2$ against $pO_2$.
- This curve is useful in studying the effect of factors like $pCO_2$, $H^+$ concentration and temperature, etc., on binding of $O_2$ with Hb.
- The oxygen haemoglobin dissociation curve can be shifted either to left or right by various factors.
  - **Shift to left** indicates association of $O_2$ with Hb.
    It occurs in the alveoli where there is low $pCO_2$, high $pO_2$, lesser $H^+$ concentration and low temperature.
  - **Shift to right** indicates dissociation of $O_2$ from Hb. It occurs in the tissues where there is low $pO_2$, high $pCO_2$, high $H^+$ concentration and higher temperature.

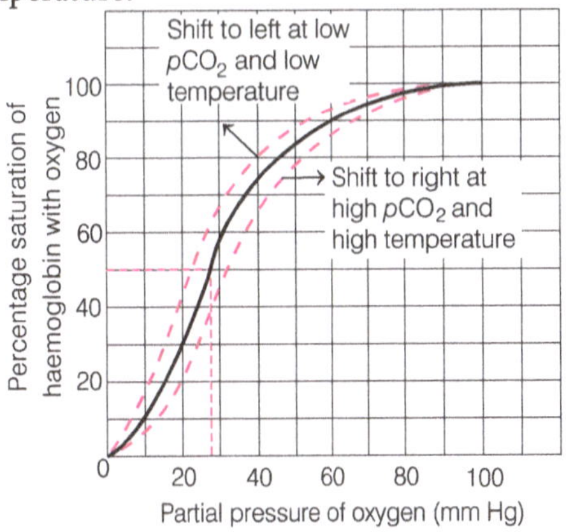


Fig. 14.5 Oxygen dissociation curve

- This clearly indicates that $O_2$ gets bound to Hb on the lung surface and gets dissociated at the tissue level.
- Every 100 mL of oxygenated blood can deliver around 5 mL of $O_2$ to the tissues under normal physiological conditions.
- People experience difficulty in breathing at high altitudes because the air pressure decreases, leading to lower oxygen availability. So, less oxygen is diffused to the blood vessels of lungs.

### Transport of Carbon Dioxide

$CO_2$ in gaseous form diffuses out of the cells into the capillaries, where it is transported in following ways

#### 1. As Dissolved Gas

About **7% $CO_2$** is carried in dissolved form through the plasma because of its high solubility.

#### 2. As Bicarbonate

- The largest fraction **(about 70%)** is carried in plasma as bicarbonate ions ($HCO_3^-$).
- At the tissues site, where $pCO_2$ is high due to catabolism, $CO_2$ diffuses into the blood (RBCs and plasma) and forms $HCO_3^-$ and $H^+$.
- This reaction is catalysed by an enzyme, **carbonic anhydrase**, which is present in very high concentration in RBCs and minute concentration in plasma.
- The enzyme facilitates the following reaction in both directions.

$$\underset{\text{Carbon dioxide}}{CO_2 + H_2O} \underset{\text{anhydrase}}{\overset{\text{Carbonic}}{\rightleftharpoons}} \underset{\text{Carbonic acid}}{H_2CO_3} \underset{\text{anhydrase}}{\overset{\text{Carbonic}}{\rightleftharpoons}} \underset{\text{Bicarbonate ion}}{HCO_3^-} + \underset{\text{Hydrogen ion}}{H^+}$$

- At the alveolar site, where $pCO_2$ is low, the reaction proceeds in opposite direction forming $CO_2$ and $H_2O$.

- Thus, $CO_2$ is trapped as bicarbonate at tissue level and is transported to alveoli where it is released as $CO_2$.

### 3. As Carbamino-haemoglobin

- Nearly **20-25% $CO_2$** is carried by haemoglobin as carbamino-haemoglobin.
- $CO_2$ entering the blood combines with the $NH_2$ group of the haemoglobin.

$$\underset{\text{Carbon dioxide}}{CO_2} + \underset{\text{Haemoglobin}}{Hb} \rightleftharpoons \underset{\text{(Carbaminohaemoglobin)}}{HbCO_2}$$

- Factors affecting the binding of $CO_2$ and Hb are
  - Partial pressure of $CO_2$.
  - Partial pressure of $O_2$ (major factor).
- In tissues, $pCO_2$ is high and $pO_2$ is low, thus more binding of $CO_2$ occurs at tissues, while in the alveoli, $pCO_2$ is low and $pO_2$ is high, thus dissociation of $CO_2$ from $HbCO_2$ takes place, i.e. $CO_2$, which is bound to Hb from the tissues is delivered at the alveoli.
- Every 100 mL of deoxygenated blood delivers approximately 4 mL of $CO_2$ to the alveoli.

### Quick Test 3

1. A person experiences swelling in the alveolar walls due to certain lung diseases. Will the rate of gaseous exchange increase or decrease?
2. If the partial pressure of oxygen in the alveoli changes from 104 mm Hg to 75 mm Hg, will there be any diffusion of oxygen from the alveoli to the capillaries?
3. Name the molecule that is primarily responsible for transporting the majority of oxygen in the blood.
4. In which direction will the oxygen dissociation curve shift if oxygen dissociates from haemoglobin?
5. **State True or False.**
   Carbamino-haemoglobin is formed when carbon dioxide binds to haemoglobin in the blood.

## 14.7 Regulation of Respiration

- The respiratory rhythm can be maintained and moderated by human beings to suit the demands of the body tissues.
- This is done by the neural system.
- The complex interaction of respiratory parts, control centres and receptors regulates respiration, which are discussed below.

### 1. Control Centres

- **Respiratory Rhythm Centre** It is a specialised centre of neurons located in the medulla oblongata and is primarily responsible for maintaining respiratory rhythm.
- **Pneumotaxic Centre** The pneumotaxic centre is present in the pons region of the brain. It can regulate the functions of respiratory rhythm centre.
- Neural signal stimulated from pneumotaxic centres reduces the duration of inspiration and alter the respiratory rate.

### 2. Receptors

- A chemosensitive area is located adjacent to rhythm centre that is highly sensitive to $CO_2$ and hydrogen ions.
- Increase in these substances can activate this centre which inturn signals the respiratory centre to make necessary changes in order to eliminate these substances.
- Receptors associated with aortic arch and carotid artery can also recognise changes in $CO_2$ and $H^+$ concentration and send necessary signals to the rhythm centre for remedial actions.
- The role of oxygen in the regulation of respiratory rhythm is quite insignificant.

## 14.8 Disorders of the Respiratory System

The respiratory system can be affected by a number of disorders as given in table below

**Disorders of Respiratory System**

| Disorders | Causes | Symptoms | Preventions |
|---|---|---|---|
| **Asthma** (difficulty in breathing) | Inflammation of bronchi and bronchioles. | Coughing, wheezing, excess amount of mucus clog the bronchi and bronchioles. | By avoiding exposure to allergens. |
| **Emphysema** (inflation or distension of bronchioles or alveolar sacs) | Cigarette smoking and inhalation of other smoke or toxic substances over a period of time leads to damage of alveolar walls. | Due to collapse of alveolar septa, surface area for gaseous exchange is reduced, lungs gets inflated, exhalation becomes difficult. | Cigarette smoking and exposure to air pollutants must be avoided. |
| **Occupational respiratory disorders** (it occurs in individuals working in grinding or stone breaking industry) | Occur due to chronic exposure to harmful substances as silica, asbestos, etc., the defence mechanism of body fails to cope with the situation. | Proliferation of fibrous connective tissue (fibrosis) of upper part of lung causing inflammation. | Use of protective masks and clothing at work place. Regular health check up of workers. |

### Quick Test 4

1. Mention the part of the brain that is responsible for maintaining the respiratory rhythm.
2. **State True or False.**
   The detection of changes in oxygen and carbon dioxide levels in the blood is primarily carried out by receptors in the respiratory system.
3. Name the disorder associated with inflammation of bronchi and bronchioles.
4. Mention the respiratory disorder that is likely to occur due to exposure to pollutants or in areas with a high air quality index.
5. Workers in grinding and stone breaking industries are recommended to wear masks. What is the primary reason for this precaution?

# Mind Map

## Breathing and Exchange of Gases

### Respiration

It is the process by which nutrients oxidising to release energy, which is used in varions bodily functions.

### Human Respiratory System

A system that enables the transport and exchange of gases ($O_2$ and $CO_2$) in the body.

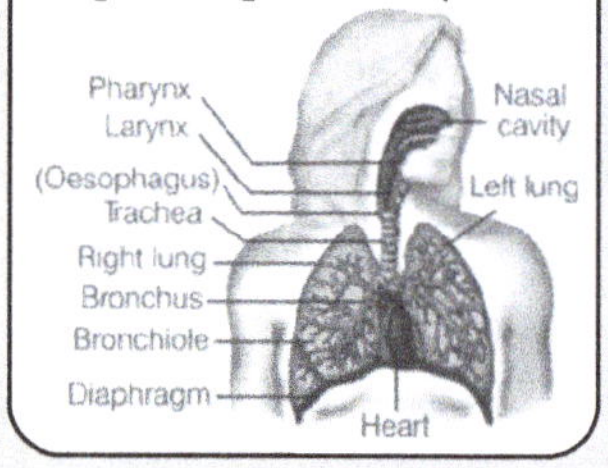


### Respiratory Tract

The pathway through which air travel through breathing.
Nose → Nasal cavities → Pharynx → Larynx → Trachea → Bronchi → Alveoli

### Breathing

The process of exchange of $O_2$ from the atmosphere with $CO_2$ produced by the cells.

### Mechanism of Breathing

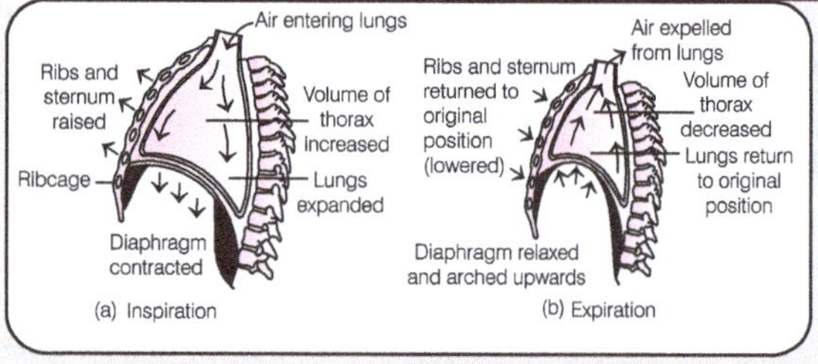


### Exchange of Gases

Exchange of respiratory gases at alveoli and tissue occur simultaneously due to differential partial pressure of $CO_2$ and $O_2$.

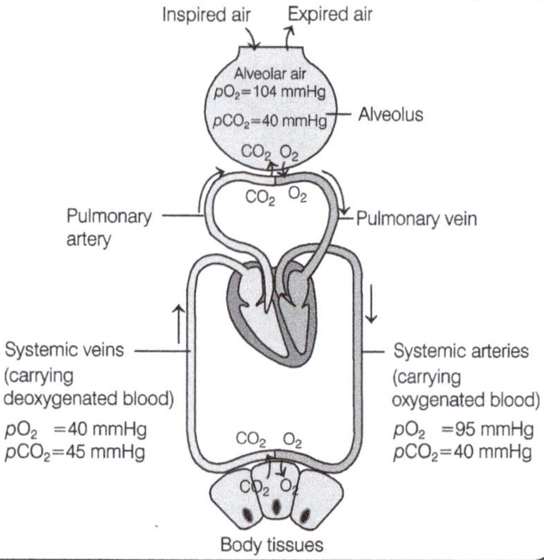


### Respiratory Organs in Animals

- Sponges and coelenterates — Simple diffusion over body surface.
- Earthworm — Cutaneous or by skin
- Insects — Tracheal system
- Aquatic arthropods and molluscs — Gills
- Terrestrial forms — Lungs

### Respiratory Volumes and Capacities

Respiratory volumes are the different amounts of air the lung can hold during various phases of breathing such as TV, IRC, ERV and RV.
Respiratory capacities are combination of these volumes such as
VC = IRV+ TV + ERV,
IC = IRV + TV,
FRC = ERV + RV and TLC = IRV + TV + ERV + RV

### Regulation of Respiration

- Respiratory rhythm centre in medulla of brain is primary responsible for this regulation.
- Pneumotaxic centre in pons region moderates function of respiratory rhythm centre.
- Chemosensitive area adjacent to rhythm centre is highly sensitive to $CO_2$ and $H^+$ ions.
- Chemoreceptors associated with aortic arch and carotid artery also can recognise changes in $CO_2$ and $H^+$ concentration and send

### Respiratory Disorders

- **Asthma** Difficulty in breathing.
- **Emphysema** Irreversible distension of alveolar walls.
- **Occupational** Inflammation and fibrosis of lungs.

### Transport of Gases

**Transport of Gases**

- $O_2$
  - 97% by RBCs (as oxyhaemoglobin)
  - 3% by plasma
- $CO_2$
  - 20-25% by RBCs (as carbaminohaemoglobin)
  - 70% as bicarbonate
  - 7% through plasma

**Oxygen Dissociation Curve**

A sigmoid-shaped graph showing the relationship between the partial pressure of oxygen ($pO_2$) and haemoglobin's oxygen saturation.

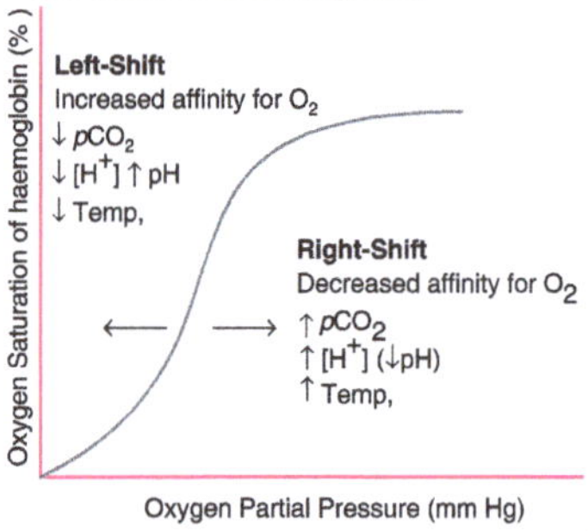

# EXAM PATTERN QUESTIONS

## Objective Type Questions

### Multiple Choice Questions

**1.** Respiration in insects is called direct because **NCERT Exemplar**

(a) the cells exchange $O_2/CO_2$ directly with the air in the tubes
(b) the tissues exchange $O_2/CO_2$ directly with coelomic fluid
(c) the tissues exchange $O_2/CO_2$ directly with the air outside through body surface
(d) tracheal tubes exchange $O_2/CO_2$ directly with the haemocoel which then exchange with tissues

**Ans.** (*a*) Insects have a network of tubes (tracheal tubes) that transport atmospheric air into the body. These tubes open through spiracles present on insects body lead to trachea. Gas exchange $O_2/CO_2$ occurs directly between the cells and the air with in the tracheal tubes.

**2.** **Match the following columns.**

| | Column I | | Coulmn II |
|---|---|---|---|
| A. | Earthworm | 1. | Moist cuticle |
| B. | Insects | 2. | Gills |
| C. | Fishes | 3. | Lungs |
| D. | Birds/Reptiles | 4. | Trachea |

**NCERT Exemplar**

**Codes**

| | A | B | C | D | | A | B | C | D |
|---|---|---|---|---|---|---|---|---|---|
| (a) | 2 | 1 | 4 | 3 | (b) | 1 | 4 | 2 | 3 |
| (c) | 1 | 3 | 2 | 4 | (d) | 1 | 2 | 4 | 3 |

**Ans.** (*b*)

**3.** **Which of the following statement is correct about respiratory organs of different animals?**

(a) The exchange of $O_2$ and $CO_2$ *via* simple diffusion across body surface occurs in aquatic arthropods
(b) A complex system of air tubes called trachea is present in earthworm for respiration
(c) Fishes have lungs for respiration
(d) Cutaneous respiration occurs in amphibians

**Ans.** (*d*)

**4.** What is not the role of conducting part of human respiratory system? **DIKSHA**

(a) Clears air from foreign particles
(b) Humidifier air
(c) Allows diffusion of oxygen and carbon dioxide
(d) Brings air to body temperature

**Ans.** (*c*) The exchange of gases takes place in the respiratory part of the respiratory system.

**5.** **In the figure given below, which of the following changes had occurred in the diaphragm and intercostal muscles when the movement of air takes place as shown.** **Competency Based Que.**

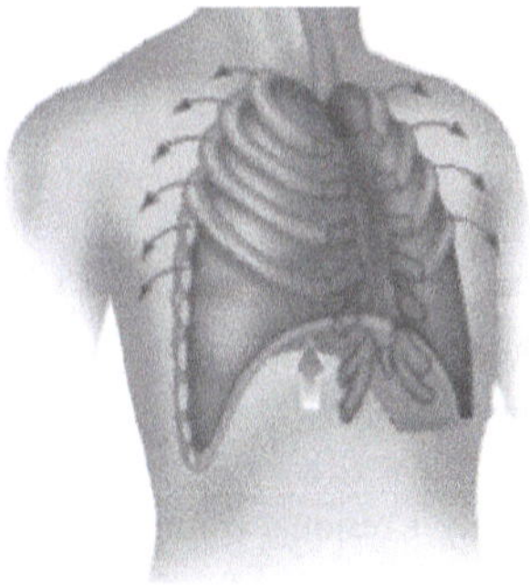

(a) External intercostal muscles relax and diaphragm contracts
(b) External intercostal muscles contract and diaphragm relaxes
(c) External intercostal muscles and diaphragm relax
(d) External intercostal muscles and diaphragm contract

**Ans.** (*c*)

**6.** **Mark the true statement among the following with reference to normal breathing.** **NCERT Exemplar**

(a) Inspiration is a passive process whereas expiration is active
(b) Inspiration is a active process whereas expiration is passive
(c) Inspiration and expiration are active processes
(d) Inspiration and expiration are passive processes

**Ans.** (*b*)

7. Match the items given in Column I with those in Column II and select the correct option given below.

| Column I (Lung Volume) | Column II (Value) |
|---|---|
| A. Tidal volume | 1. 2500-3000 mL |
| B. Inspiratory reserve volume | 2. 1100-1200 mL |
| C. Expiratory reserve volume | 3. 500 mL |
| D. Residual volume | 4. 1000-1100 mL |

Codes

| | A | B | C | D |
|---|---|---|---|---|
| (a) | 1 | 4 | 2 | 3 |
| (b) | 3 | 1 | 4 | 2 |
| (c) | 3 | 2 | 1 | 4 |
| (d) | 4 | 3 | 2 | 1 |

**Ans.** (*b*)

8. Lungs are made up of air-filled sacs, called alveoli. They do not collapse even after forceful expiration, because of **Competency Based Que.**

(a) inspiratory reserve volume
(b) residual volume
(c) expiratory reserve volume
(d) tidal volume

**Ans.** (*b*)

9. Total lung capacity is

(a) total volume of air accomodated in lungs at the end of a forced inspiration
(b) RV + ERV + TV + IRV
(c) vital capacity + residual volume
(d) All of the above

**Ans.** (*d*)

10. From the following relationships between respiratory volume and capacities, mark the correct option. **NCERT Exemplar**

(i) Inspiratory Capacity (IC) = Tidal Volume (TV) + Residual Volume (RV)
(ii) Vital Capacity (VC) = Tidal Volume (TV) + Inspiratory Reserve Volume (IRV) + Expiratory Reserve Volume (ERV).
(iii) Residual Volume (RV) = Vital Capacity (VC) – Inspiratory Reserve Volume (IRV)
(iv) Tidal Volume (TV) = Inspiratory Capacity (IC) – Inspiratory Reserve Volume (IRV)

Codes

(a) (i) Incorrect, (ii) Incorrect, (iii) Incorrect, (iv) Correct
(b) (i) Incorrect, (ii) Correct, (iii) Incorrect, (iv) Correct
(c) (i) Correct, (ii) Correct, (iii) Incorrect, (iv) Correct
(d) (i) Correct, (ii) Incorrect, (iii) Correct, (iv) Incorrect

**Ans.** (*b*)

11. The partial pressure of oxygen in the alveoli of the lungs is

(a) equal to that in the blood
(b) more than that in the blood
(c) less than that in the blood
(d) less than that of carbon dioxide

**Ans.** (*b*)

12. Almost same $pO_2$ in humans is found in

(a) alveoli and tissues
(b) oxygenated blood and deoxygenated blood
(c) alveoli and oxygenated blood
(d) tissues and deoxygenated blood

**Ans.** (*d*)

13. What will be the $pO_2$ and $pCO_2$ in the atmospheric air compared to that in the alveolar air? **NCERT**

(a) $pO_2$ lesser and $pCO_2$ higher
(b) $pO_2$ higher and $pCO_2$ lesser
(c) $pO_2$ higher and $pCO_2$ higher
(d) $pO_2$ lesser and $pCO_2$ lesser

**Ans.** (*b*)

14. After oxygen diffuses into pulmonary capillaries, it

| | Diffuses into | Bind with |
|---|---|---|
| (a) | Interstitial fluid | Red blood cells |
| (b) | Interstitial fluid | Carbon dioxide |
| (c) | Red blood cells | Haemoglobin |
| (d) | Red blood cells | Carbon dioxide |

**Ans.** (*c*)

15. Consider the following statements.

I. The percentage of haemoglobin that is bound with oxygen is called per cent saturation of haemoglobin.
II. Every 100 mL of oxygenated blood can deliver 60 mL $O_2$ to the tissues under normal conditions.
III. $P_{50}$ value is the value of $O_2$ at which Hb is 50% saturated with oxygen.
IV. $pO_2$ and $pCO_2$ of inhaled air is 159 mm Hg and 40 mm Hg, respectively.

Choose the option containing incorrect statements. **Competency Based Que.**

(a) I and III (b) II and IV (c) III and IV (d) I and II

**Ans.** (*b*)

16. It is known that exposure to carbon monoxide is harmful to animals because **NCERT Exemplar**

(a) it reduces $CO_2$ transport
(b) it reduces $O_2$ transport
(c) it increases $CO_2$ transport
(d) it increases $O_2$ transport

**Ans.** (*b*) The complex formed by the reaction of carbon mono oxide and haemoglobin is incredibly strong

As a result of this complex, the haemoglobin looses its affinity to oxygen, thus may lead to choking or even death.

**17. One haemoglobin molecule carries**

(a) 2 oxygen molecules
(b) 3 oxygen molecules
(c) 4 oxygen molecules
(d) 1 oxygen molecule

**Ans.** (*c*)

**18. Mark the incorrect option in context to $O_2$ binding to Hb.** **NCERT Exemplar**

(a) Higher pH (b) Lower temperature
(c) Lower $pCO_2$ (d) Higher $pO_2$

**Ans.** (*a*)

**19. Which of the following statement is incorrect about the given graph?** **Competency Based Que.**

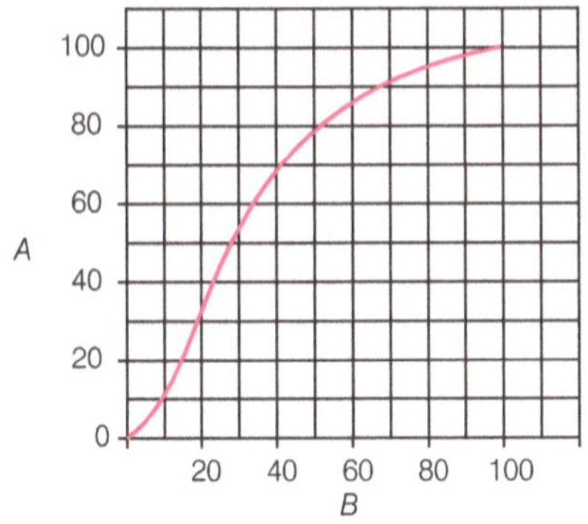


(a) The curve is called oxygen dissociation curve
(b) The part *A* represents percentage saturation of haemoglobin with oxygen
(c) The part *B* represents partial pressure of carbon dioxide
(d) This curve is highly useful in studying the effect of factors like $pCO_2$, $H^+$ concentration, etc on binding of $O_2$ with haemoglobin.

**Ans.** (*c*)

**20. Oxyhaemoglobin dissociation at tissues occurs under**

(a) low $pO_2$ and low $pCO_2$
(b) low $pO_2$, high $pCO_2$ and high $H^+$
(c) low $pO_2$, low $H^+$ and low $pCO_2$
(d) low $pO_2$, low $H^+$ and high $pCO_2$

**Ans.** (*b*)

**21. $CO_2$ dissociates from carbaminohaemoglobin when** **NCERT Exemplar**

(a) $pCO_2$ is high and $pO_2$ is low
(b) $pO_2$ is high and $pCO_2$ is low
(c) $pCO_2$ and $pO_2$ are equal
(d) None of the above

**Ans.** (*b*)

**22. When you hold your breathe, which of the following gas changes in blood would first lead to the urge to breathe?** **Competency Based Que.**

(a) Falling $CO_2$ concentration (b) Rising $O_2$ concentration
(c) Falling $O_2$ concentration (d) Rising $CO_2$ Concentration

**Ans.** (*d*) An increase in carbon dioxide ($CO_2$) levels in the blood leads to a decrease in pH (increased acidity).
Chemoreceptors detect this change and send signal to the brain's respiratory centres. This stimulates the urge to breathe, typically occurring before oxygen levels drop significantly.

**23. Pneumotaxic centre of the brain, i.e. pons region can**

(a) moderate the function of respiratory system
(b) decrease the heart rate
(c) increase the heart rate
(d) increase the flow of blood

**Ans.** (*a*)

**24. Respiratory process is regulated by certain specialised centres in the brain. One of the following listed centres can reduce the inspiratory duration upon stimulation.**

(a) Medullary inspiratory centre **NCERT Exemplar**
(b) Pneumotaxic centre
(c) Apneustic centre
(d) Chemosensitive centre

**Ans.** (*b*)

**25. Receptors in aortic arch and carotid arch recognise the changes in the concentration of**

(a) $OH^-$ and $H^+$ (b) $O_2$ and $CO_2$
(c) $CO_2$ and $H^+$ (d) blood circulation

**Ans.** (*c*)

**26. Due to increasing airborne allergens and pollutants, many people in urban areas are suffering from respiratory disorder causing wheezing due to** **Competency Based Que.**

(a) inflammation of bronchi and bronchioles
(b) proliferation of fibrous tissues and damage of alveolar walls
(c) reduction in secretion of surfactants by pneumocytes
(d) benign growth on mucus lining of nasal cavity

**Ans.** (*a*)

**27. What is incorrect in case of emphysema?** **DIKSHA**

(a) Is a chronic disorder
(b) Respiratory surface is increased
(c) Alveolar walls are damaged
(d) Caused due to cigarette smoking

**Ans.** (*b*) Option (b) is incorrect with respect to emphysema. It can be corrected as

Emphysema is a respiratory disorder that is associated with decrease in surface area for gaseous exchange.

## Assertion-Reason Questions

**Direction** (Q. Nos. 1-10) *In each of the following questions, a statement of Assertion (A) is given followed by corresponding statement of Reason (R). Of the statements, mark the correct answer.*

(a) Both A and R are true and R is the correct explanation of A.
(b) Both A and R are true, but R is not the correct explanation of A.
(c) A is true, but R is false.
(d) A is false, but R is true.

**1. Assertion** (A) Humans can swim and breathe inside water.

**Reason** (R) Respiratory organ in humans are lungs.

**Ans.** (*d*) A is false, but R is true. A can be corrected as

Humans cannot breathe underwater because they lack gills, which are necessary for extracting oxygen from water. While they can swim and hold their breath for a limited duration, they eventually need to resurface to take in air.

**2. Assertion** (A) Trachea and primary bronchi are supported by cartilaginous ring.

**Reason** (R) Trachea can collapse during expiration.

**Ans.** (*c*) A is true, but R is false. R can be corrected as

The trachea usually remains open during expiration due to the support provided by its cartilaginous rings. While it can collapse under specific conditions, it does not collapse during normal expiration.

**3. Assertion** (A) In normal breathing, inspiration is an active process.

**Reason** (R) Inspiration is facilitated by contraction of diaphragm and external intercostal muscles.

**Ans.** (*a*)

**4. Assertion** (A) Expiration is a passive process.

**Reason** (R) It occurs when the intra-pulmonary pressure is higher than the atmospheric pressure.

**Ans.** (*b*) Both A and R are true, but R is not the correct explanation of A. The A can be explained as

Expiration is a passive process because it depends on the elastic recoil of the lungs and thoracic cavity. When the diaphragm and intercostal muscles relax, air is pushed out without needing active muscle contraction.

**5. Assertion** (A) The amount of $CO_2$ that can diffuse through diffusion membrane per unit difference in partial pressure is much higher as compared to $O_2$.

**Reason** (R) Solubility of $CO_2$ is 20-25 times higher than that of $O_2$.

**Ans.** (*a*)

**6. Assertion** (A) $pO_2$ is the highest in alveoli.

**Reason** (R) Partial pressure of a gas is the pressure contributed by individual gas in a mixture.

**Ans.** (*b*)

**7.** The pie chart given below shows the amount of different gases present in the inhaled and exhaled air. Read the chart carefully and answer according to the appropriateness of the Assertion and Reason given below.

**Competency Based Que.**

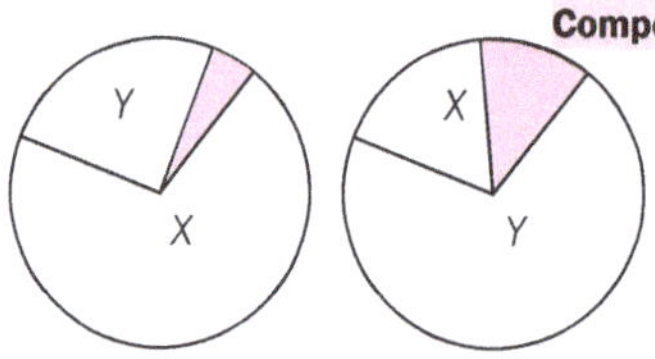


**Assertion** (A) The 97% of gas *X* is carried by RBC's in the blood as oxyhaemoglobin.

**Reason** (R) *X* gets bound to Hb on the lung surface and gets dissociated at the tissue level.

**Ans.** (*b*)

**8. Assertion** (A) $CO_2$ transport occurs very fast through RBCs.

**Reason** (R) Enzyme carbonic anhydrase is absent in the blood plasma.

**Ans.** (*c*)

**9. Assertion** (A) Oxygen present in blood does not have significant effect on the respiratory centre of brain.

**Reason** (R) Increased $pCO_2$ and $H^+$ levels detected by chemoreceptors activate the respiratory centres to mediate the necessary adjustments. **Competency Based Que.**

**Ans.** (b)

**10. Assertion** (A) Receptors of aortic arch and carotid artery recognise change in $CO_2$ and $H^+$ concentration.

**Reason** (R) These receptors send signal to respiratory rhythm centre for remedial actions.

**Ans.** (*b*)

# Subjective Questions

## Very Short Answer Type Questions

**1. Why do cells need a constant supply of oxygen?**

**Ans.** Cells need a constant supply of oxygen to perform the metabolic reactions that releases energy from the molecules. This energy is used by cells for various functions of body.

**2. How is respiration carried out in earthworm?**

**Ans.** Earthworm respires through moist cuticle. It is called cutaneous respiration.

**3. What is the site of gaseous exchange in an insect?** **NCERT**

**Ans.** The actual site of gaseous exchange in an insect is trachea.

**4. Give the name of the organ that produces sound.**

**Ans.** The sound producing organ is larynx.

**5. Observe the diagram carefully and identify the structure marked as *A* and *B*.** **Competency Based Que.**

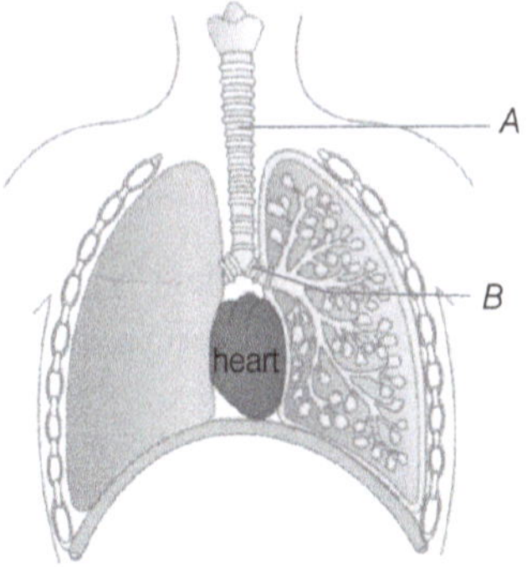


**Ans.** In the given figure, *A* represents trachea and *B* represents bronchus.

**6. Name the double-walled sac, which covers the lung in mammals.**

**Ans.** It is called pleura.

**7. Name the important parts involved in creating a pressure gradient between lungs and the atmosphere during normal respiration.** **NCERT Exemplar**

**Ans.** The diaphragm and intercostals muscles between the ribs, help in the generation of pressure gradient during normal respiration.

**8. How is clinical assessment of pulmonary function done?**

**Ans.** It is done with a special instrument called spirometer.

**9. What do you understand by expiratory reserve volume?**

**Ans.** It is the additional volume of air that can be expired forcibly after normal expiration. It is about 1000-1100 mL.

**10. Arrange the following terms based on their volumes in an ascending order.** **Competency Based Que.**

(i) Tidal Volume (TV) (ii) Residual Volume (RV)
(iii) Inspiratory Reserve Volume (IRV)
(iv) Expiratory Capacity (EC)

**Ans.** Tidal volume $\rightarrow$ Expiratory reserve capacity
(500 mL) (1000-1100 mL)
$\rightarrow$ Residual volume $\rightarrow$ Inspiratory reserve volume
(1100-1200 mL) (2500-3000 mL)

**11. A major percentage (97%) of $O_2$ is transported by RBCs in the blood. How does the remaining percentage (3%) of $O_2$ transported?** **Competency Based Que.**

**Ans.** About 97% of $O_2$ is transported by RBCs in the blood. The remaining 3% of $O_2$ is carried in a dissolved state through the plasma.

**12. What is the role of oxyhaemoglobin after releasing molecular oxygen in the tissues?**

**Ans.** Amino group of reduced haemoglobin combines with $CO_2$, forming carbamino-haemoglobin to transport $CO_2$.

**13. What is the effect of $pCO_2$ on oxygen transport?** **NCERT**

**Ans.** The partial pressure of $CO_2$ ($pCO_2$) influences oxygen binding to haemoglobin.

(i) In the alveoli (high $pO_2$, low $pCO_2$, low $H^+$ and low temperature), oxyhoemoglobin is formed.
(ii) In tissue (high $pCO_2$, low $pO_2$, high $H^+$ and high temperature) low is favourable for dissociation of oxygen from oxyhaemoglobin.

**14. What is the amount of $O_2$ supplied to tissues through every 100 mL of oxygenated blood under normal physiological conditions?** **NCERT Exemplar**

**Ans.** Every 100 mL of oxygenated blood can deliver around 5 mL of $O_2$ to the tissue under normal physiological conditions.

**15. Write the reaction involved in transport of major fraction of $CO_2$ in the body?**

**Ans.** Refer to text on page no. 323.

**16. Give one main factor which affect the binding of $CO_2$ and Hb ?**

**Ans.** Partial pressure of $O_2$.

**17. Where is the fastest enzyme responsible for $CO_2$ transport found in human body?**

**Ans.** Carbonic anhydrase is the fastest enzyme known so far. It is found in RBC.

**18. Where is the pneumotaxic centre located ?**

**Ans.** The pneumotaxic centre is present in the pons region of the brain.

**19. Which condition is characterised by excess mucus production that clogs the bronchi and bronchioles, causing difficulty in breathing?**

**Ans.** Asthma

## Short Answer Type Questions

**1. Give the name of the organs of respiration in the following organisms.**

**(i) Flatworm** **(ii) Birds**

**(iii) Frog** **(iv) Cockroach**

**NCERT Exemplar**

**Ans.** (i) Body surface (ii) Lungs

(iii) Skin and lungs (iv) Tracheal tubes. (½ × 4)

**2. Give two examples of each of the following**

**(i) Animal groups showing tracheal respiration.**

**(ii) Animal groups having gills**

**Ans.** (i) Insects, centipedes and millipedes, etc. (1)

(ii) Molluscs and fishes (1)

**3. Name the cartilage box present above the trachea. Also, mention its function.**

**Ans.** The cartilage box is known as larynx. It helps in sound production. (1+1)

**4. State the route of foul air from the lungs to outside.**

**Ans.** The foul air follows the route given below

Alveoli → Alveolar ducts → Bronchioles → Bronchi → Trachea → Larynx → Glottis → Pharynx → Internal nares → Nasal chambers → External nares → Atmosphere.

**5. (i) What prevents the trachea and the bronchi from collapsing?**

**(ii) Give the name of the site of actual diffusion of $O_2$ and $CO_2$.**

**Ans.** (i) Cartilaginous rings present in the walls of the trachea and bronchi prevent them from collapsing.

(ii) Alveoli and their ducts. (1 + 1)

**6. Mention the boundaries of the thoracic cavity.**

**Ans.** Refer to text on page no. 318.

**7. For completion of respiration process, write the given steps in sequential manner**

**(i) diffusion of gases ($O_2$ and $CO_2$) across alveolar membrane.**

**(ii) transport of gases by blood.**

**(iii) utilisation of $O_2$ by the cells for catabolic reactions and resultant release of $CO_2$.**

**(iv) pulmonary ventilation by which atmospheric air is drawn in and $CO_2$ rich alveolar air is released out.**

**(v) diffusion of $O_2$ and $CO_2$ between blood and tissues.**

**NCERT Exemplar**

**Ans.** Steps in the process of respiration

(i) Pulmonary ventilation by which atmospheric air is drawn in and $CO_2$ rich alveolar air is released out.

(ii) Diffusion of gases ($O_2$ and $CO_2$) across alveolar membrane.

(iii) Transport of gases by blood every tissues of the body.

(iv) Diffusion of $O_2$ and $CO_2$ between blood and tissues.

(v) Utilisation of $O_2$ by the cells for catabolic reaction and resultant release of $CO_2$ and energy.

**8. Write the role of diaphragm and intercostal muscles in the inspiratory process.**

**Ans.** The diaphragm and intercostal muscles (external and internal), present between the ribs, help in generation of a pressure gradient between the lungs and the atmosphere. During inspiration, diaphragm is lowered by contraction of its muscle fibres and becomes flat.

The external intercostal muscles contract pulling the ribs and sternum upward and outward. This increases the volume of thoracic cavity and thus, decrease the intra-pulmonary pressure. The greater atmospheric pressure outside the body now causes the air to flow rapidly into external nares, which sequentially leads to alveoli. Thus, causing inspiration. (3)

**9. Give the condition of the following muscles during expiration.**

**(i) Diaphragm muscles**

**(ii) External intercostal muscles**

**Ans.** (i) The muscles of the diaphragm are in a relaxed position, making it convex. (1)

(ii) The external intercostal muscles are in relaxed state thus pulling the ribs downward and inward. (1)

**10. In normal breathing, which is the active process inspiration or expiration? Explain.**

**Ans.** In normal breathing, inspiration is an active process as it is brought about by the contraction of diaphragm and external intercostal muscles, while expiration is a passive process as it simply involves relaxation of inspiratory muscles.

**11. A person dies in an accident in which his chest cavity was punctured, but no lung damage was found. Point out the cause of death.** **Competency Based Que.**

**Ans.** The movement of air into and out of the lungs is carried out by creating a pressure gradient between the lungs and the atmosphere.

The pressure within the lungs is less than the atmospheric pressure, so there is a negative pressure in the lungs with respect to atmospheric pressure.

The puncture in the chest affects this pressure gradient maintained by the lungs and thus may cause cessation of breathing.

**12. What is tidal volume? Find out the tidal volume for a healthy human in an hour time.** NCERT

**Ans.** Tidal volume is the volume of air inspired or expired during normal breathing in relaxed or resting position. Its volume is about 500 mL. (1)

Amount of Tidal Volume (TV) in an hour

$= \text{Respiratory rate} \times \text{TV} \times 60\,\text{min}$

$= (12-16 \text{ breaths per minute}) \times 500 \text{ mL} \times 60$

$= 6-8 \text{ L} \times 60$

$\text{TV} = 360-480 \text{ L}$ (2)

**13. Distinguish between**

**(i) IRV and ERV**

**(ii) Inspiratory capacity and expiratory capacity**

**(iii) Vital capacity and total lung capacity**

**Ans.** (i) Refer to text on page no. 321. (1)

(ii) Refer to text on page no. 321. (1)

(iii) Refer to text on page no. 321. (1)

**14. State the volume of air remaining in the lungs after a normal breathing.** NCERT

**Ans.** The volume of air that will remain in the lungs after a normal expiration is called functional residual volume. It is the sum of residual volume (1100 to 1200mL) and expiratory reserve volume (1000 to 1100mL). So, the functional residual volume is about 2100 to 2300mL.

**15. Define vital capacity. What is its significance?** NCERT

**Ans.** The maximum volume of air a person can breathe in after a forced expiration or the maximum volume of air a person can breathe out after a forced inspiration. It is significant because it reflects lung health and capacity, helping diagnose and manage respiratory disorders. (1 + 1)

**16. Name the factors that affect the rate of diffusion of gases in the lungs.**

**Ans.** Refer to text on page no. 321.

**17. Give the name of the three major layers of diffusion membrane.**

**Ans.** (i) Thin squamous epithelium of alveoli.

(ii) Endothelium of alveolar capillaries.

(iii) Basement substance in between. (1 × 3)

**18. Diffusion of gases occurs in the alveolar region only and not in other parts of the respiratory system. Why?** NCERT

**Ans.** For efficient exchange of gases, respiratory surface must have certain characteristics such as

(i) It must be thin, moist and permeable to respiratory gases.

(ii) It must have large surface area.

(iii) It must be highly vascular.

Only alveolar region have these characteristics. Thus, diffusion of gases occurs in this region only. (1 × 3)

**19. What are the values of $pO_2$ and $pCO_2$ of the following:** DIKSHA

**(i) Alveolar air** **(ii) Systemic arteries**

**(iii) Systemic veins**

**Ans.** (i) Alveolar air

$pO_2 = 104$ mm Hg

$pCO_2 = 40$ mm Hg (1)

(ii) Systemic arteries

$pO_2 = 95$ mm Hg

$pCO_2 = 40$ mm Hg (1)

(iii) Systemic veins

$pO_2 = 40$ mm Hg

$pCO_2 = 45$ mm Hg (1)

**20. What happens to the respiratory process when a man going up to hill?** NCERT

**Ans.** At hills, the pressure of air falls and the person cannot get enough oxygen in the lungs for diffusion into the blood. Due to the deficiency of oxygen, the person feels breathlessness, headache, dizziness, nausea, mental fatigue and a bluish colour on the skin, nails and lips.

**21. How does haemoglobin help in the transport of oxygen from lungs to tissues?**

**Ans.** Haemoglobin combines with $O_2$ in a reversible manner to form oxyhaemoglobin. This oxygenated blood circulates in the body. When, it reaches the tissues having low $pO_2$, the oxygen is released into the tissues.

**22. State the factors affecting the oxygen haemoglobin binding.**

**Ans.** Refer to text on page no. 323.

**23. What does the oxygen-haemoglobin dissociation curve indicate?**

**Ans.** The oxygen-haemoglobin dissociation curve indicates that haemoglobin's ability to bind and release oxygen varies with oxygen levels, pH, temperature and carbon dioxide concentration. It shows that haemoglobin binds to oxygen more readily in the lungs and release it more actively in tissue.

**24. Study the diagram carefully and answer the questions that follows.** Competency Based Que.

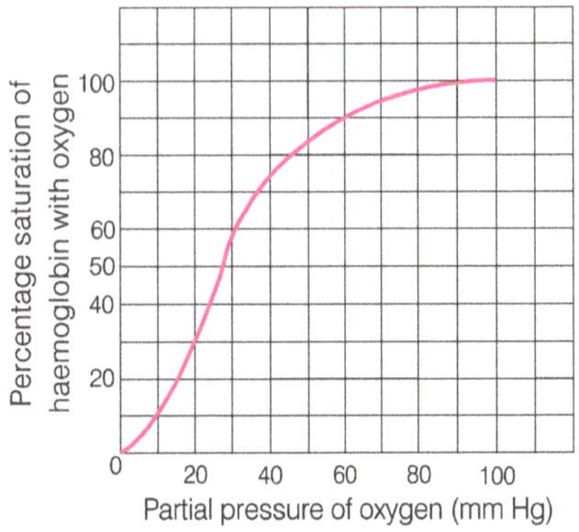


**(i) Identify the graph shown above and what is its shape?**

(ii) **List the factors that will shift the graph towards the right.**

**Ans.** (i) The graph represents the oxygen dissociation curve. It has sigmoid curve.

(ii) Several factors such as low $pO_2$, high $CO_2$, high $H^+$ concentration will shift the graph towards the right. (1 × 2)

**25. Give differences between oxyhaemoglobin and carbaminohaemoglobin.**

**Ans.** Differences between oxyhaemoglobin and carbaminohaemoglobin are as follows

| Oxyhaemoglobin | Carbaminohaemoglobin |
|---|---|
| It is formed by the combination of oxygen with the $Fe^{2+}$ part of haemoglobin. | It is formed by the combination of $CO_2$ with the amino group of haemoglobin. |
| Its formation occurs on the alveolar surface. | Its formation occurs in the tissues. (1×2) |

**26. How is respiration regulated?** NCERT

**Ans.** A specialised centre present in the medulla region of the brain called respiratory rhythm centre is primarily responsible for the regulation of respiration. Another centre present in the pons region of the brain called pneumotaxic centre can moderate the functions of the respiratory rhythm centre. Neural signal from this centre can reduce the duration of inspiration and thereby, alter the respiratory rate.

**27. Which of the regulatory centre of respiration can reduce the inspiratory duration when it is stimulated?**

**Ans.** Respiratory process is regulated by certain specialised centres present in hindbrain. Amongst them, pneumotaxic centre, located in the dorsal part of pons, of the brain, can reduce the duration of inspiration and thus alter the respiratory rate.

**28. Cigarette smoking causes emphysema. Give reason.** NCERT Exemplar

**Ans.** Cigarette smoking causes damage to the alveolar walls and reduces elasticity of the lungs, which leads to decreased respiratory surface for exchange of gases. Thus, causing emphysema.

**29. Write the causes and prevention of emphysema.**

**Ans.** Refer to table on page no. 325.

**30. Have you heard about hypoxia? Try to gather information about it and discuss with your friends.** NCERT

**Ans.** Hypoxia is characterised by insufficient supply of oxygen to the body's tissues, caused by factors like high altitude, respiratory issues, anaemia or carbon monoxide exposure. Symptoms include shortness of breath, confusion and a bluish tint to the skin. Awareness of hypoxia helps in recognising its causes and preventing complications.

## Long Answer Type Questions

**1. Explain human respiratory system with a labelled diagram.**

**Ans.** Refer to text on page no. 318 and 319 and refer to the fig. no. 14.1.

**2. Explain the process of inspiration under normal conditions.** NCERT

**Ans.** Refer to text on page no. 319 and 320.

**3. Explain the mechanism of expiration in humans. Also, give diagrams for the process of breathing.**

**Ans.** Refer to text on page no. 320 and fig no. 14.2.

**4. Give diagrammatic representation of exchange of gases at the alveolus and the body tissues with transport of $O_2$ and $CO_2$. Also, explain how does exchange of gases occur between blood and tissue cells.**

**Ans.** Refer to text on page no. 321 and 322 and fig no. 14.4.

**5. How do gases ($O_2$ and $CO_2$) are transported in blood?**

**Ans.** Refer to text on page no. 323 and324.

**6. Define oxygen dissociation curve. Can you suggest any reason for its sigmoidal pattern?** NCERT, Competency Based Que.

**Ans.** Refer to text on page no. 323.

The sigmoid curve represents the gradual increase in oxygen binding at low oxygen partial pressure, followed by a steep rise as haemoglobin's affinity increases, and then a leveling off when haemoglobin is fully saturated. This allows for efficient oxygen uptake in the lungs and release in tissues.

**7. What are the major transport mechanisms for $CO_2$? Explain.** NCERT

**Ans.** Refer to text on page no. 323-324.

**8. Explain the role of neural system in regulation of respiration.**

**Ans.** Refer to text on page no. 324.

**9. Give cause and symptoms of the following disorders.**

(i) **Asthma**

(ii) **Emphysema**

(iii) **Occupational respiratory disorder**

**Ans.** Refer to text on page no. 325.

## Source Based/Case Based/Passage Based Questions

**1. The first graph below (*A*) shows a normal spirometry pattern. The second graph (*B*) shows the results in a patient with respiratory disorder. Observe both graphs (*A* and *B*) carefully and answer the questions that follows.** **Competency Based Que.**

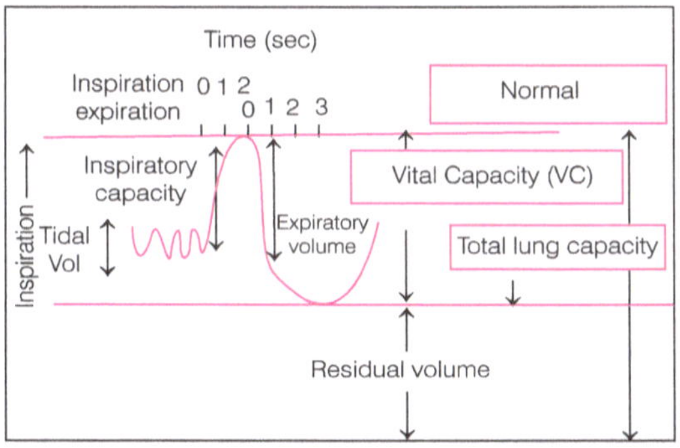


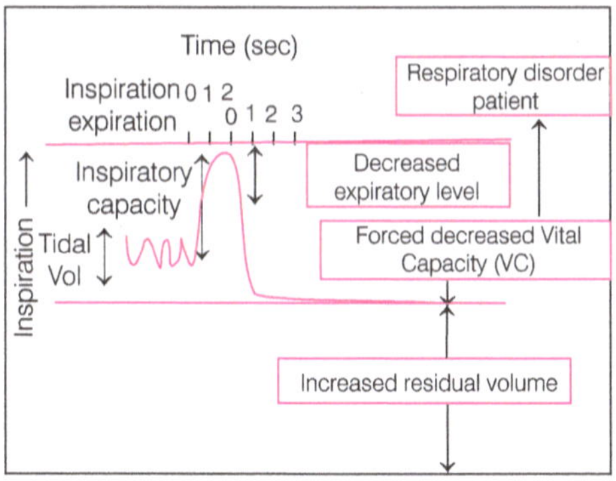


**(i) Refer to the graph above and examine the vital capacity to identify the possible disease that may occurs.**

**(ii) Explain why respiratory disorder of the patient in (i) affects his vital capacity ?**

**(iii) Mention the causes of the disease.**

**(iv) Name other respiratory disorders and their causes.**

**Ans.** (i) The decreased vital capacity range indicates the patient is suffering from emphysema. (1)

(ii) Due to damaged alveolar walls in patient having emphysema in which he/she experience difficulty in expiration, thereby decreasing VC. (1)

(iii) Emphysema is caused by cigarette smoking and inhalation of other toxic substances. (1)

(iv) Refer to the table on page no. 325. (1)

**2. Observe the diagram given below and answer the questions that follows.**

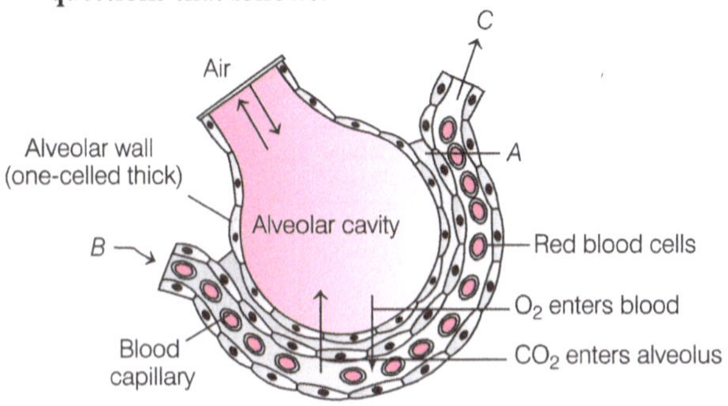


**(i) What is being represented in the above diagram?**

**(ii) Identify *A* and write its feature.**

**(iii) The vein labelled as *C* carries which type of blood in the body.**

**(iv) How is oxygen carried from alveoli into the blood in pulmonary capillaries?**

**(v) Which factors affect the rate of diffusion?**

**Ans.** (i) The given diagram represents a section of an alveolus with pulmonary capillary, showing gaseous exchange. (1)

(ii) *A* is basement substance, which plays a crucial role in forming alveolar capillary membrane that allows gaseous exchange between blood and alveolar air. (1)

(iii) The vein labelled as '*C*' represent pulmonary vein, which is the only vein in the body that carries oxygenated blood, from the lungs to the left auricle and thereafter, it gets distributed to all parts of the body. (1)

(iv) Movement of oxygen from alveoli into the blood in pulmonary capillaries occurs by the process of simple diffusion. (1)

(v) Concentration/.pressure gradient, solubility of gases and the thickness of the membranes involved in diffusion are some important factors which affect the rate of diffusion. (1)

**3. The figure given below represents the exchange of $CO_2$ and $O_2$ at the alveolus and the body tissues. Observe the figure and answer the questions that follows.** **Competency Based Que.**

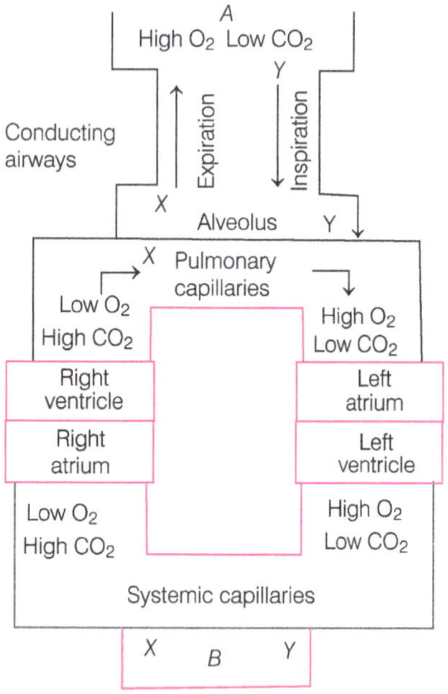


**(i) At a particular pressure difference, among *X* and *Y*, which gas can diffuse faster.**

**(ii) With reference to the above figure, mention the partial pressure of gases *X* and *Y* at location *A* and *B*.**

**(iii) How will the decreased partial pressure of *X* affect the oxygen dissociation curve ?**

**(iv) How does the transport of *Y* takes place ?**

**Ans.** (i) In the above figure, *X* is $CO_2$and *Y* is $O_2$. Among $CO_2$ and $O_2$ at a particular partial pressure, the diffusion of $CO_2$ is 20-25 times faster than oxygen.

(ii)

| | Location *A* | Location *B* |
|---|---|---|
| *X* | 0.3 | 45 |
| *Y* | 159 | 40 |

(iii) Low $pCO_2$ along with lesser $H^+$concentration and low temperature indicates the association of $O_2$with Hb. It will shift the oxygen dissociation curve to left.

(iv) Transport of oxygen (*Y*) takes place by the following process

(i) As dissolved gas

(ii) As oxyhaemoglobin (1 × 4)

**4. Ram joined a coal mine as manager in Jharkhand. He found that the working condition there (in the factory) was not suitable. The workers were often unwell, some were even suffering from respiratory disorders that hindered their income as well as the work of the coal mine. Ram took the matter to the higher authorities and suggested some preventive measures regarding health of the workers. The measures proved to be helpful. Soon, the worker's performance and their attendance improved.**

**(i) What are these respiratory disorders called?**

**(ii) What are the preventive measures?**

**(iii) Give the symptoms and cause of these disorders.**

**(iv) Is there a permanent cure to above disorders?**

**Ans.** Refer the disorders of respiratory system on page no. 325. for (i) (ii) and (iii).

(iv) No, there is no permanent cure for occupational respiratory disorders. The patient is given antibiotics and bronchodilators for secondary infection. (1 × 4)

# SELF ASSESSMENT TEST

## Multiple Choice Questions

1. Which of the following option is correct with respect to the sequence of the air passage in the humans?
   (a) Nose, pharynx, larynx, bronchioles and trachea
   (b) External nostrils, pharynx, larynx, trachea and bronchioles
   (c) Nose, larynx, pharynx, bronchioles and trachea
   (d) External nostrils, trachea, larynx, pharynx and bronchioles
2. Select the incorrect match-pair.
   (a) IC=TV+IRV (b) EC=TV+ERV (c) FRC=RV+IRV (d) TLC=VC+RV
3. How many factors affect the exchange of gases in alveoli?
   I. Surface area of the diffusion membrane
   II. Concentration of $OH^-$ ions
   III. Permeability of the diffusion membrane
   IV. Polarity of the gases
   V. Temperature of tissue
   VI. Partial pressure gradient of gases.
   Choose the correct option.
   (a) 3 (b) 5 (c) 2 (d) 4
4. Choose the correct option with respect to 'A' as marked in the given diagram.

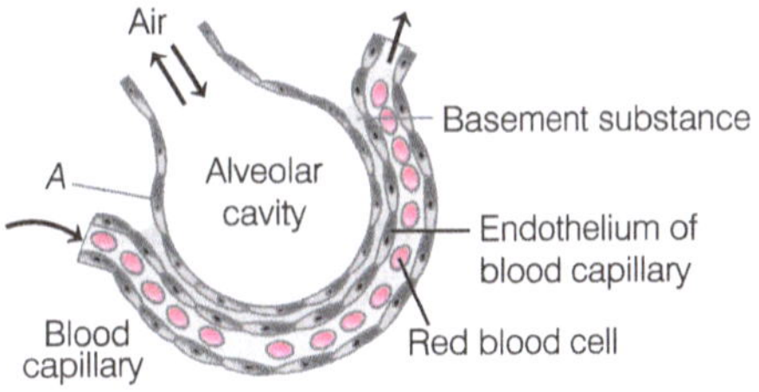


   (a) 'A' represent squamous epithelium of alveolar wall
   (b) 'A' represent squamous epithelium of a blood capillary.
   (c) 'A' represent columnar epithelium of alveolar wall.
   (d) 'A' represent columnar epithelium of blood capillary
5. Which of the following option correctly mentions the partial pressure of carbon dioxide at *A*, *B* and *C* respectively.

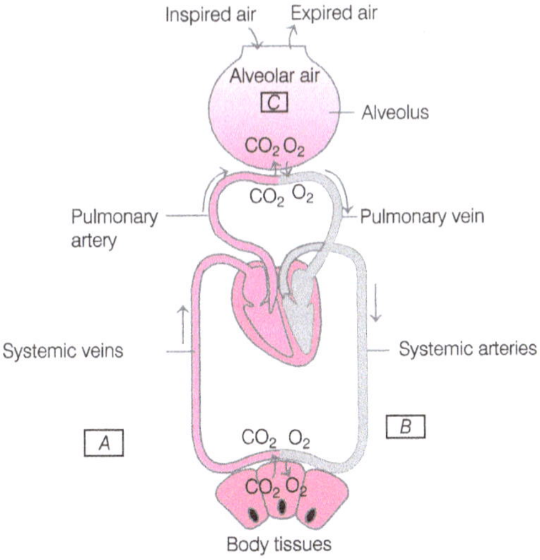


   (a) 45 mm Hg, 40 mm Hg and 40 mm Hg (b) 40 mm Hg, 45 mm Hg and 40 mm Hg
   (c) 45 mm Hg, 45 mm Hg and 40 mm Hg (d) 40 mm Hg, 40 mm Hg and 45 mm Hg

## Assertion-Reason Questions

**Direction** (Q. Nos. 6-9) *In each of the following questions, a statement of Assertion (A) is given followed by corresponding statement of Reason (R). Of the statements, mark the correct answer*

(a) Both A and R are true and R is the correct explanation of A.

(b) Both A and R are true, but R is not the correct explanation of A.

(c) A is true, but R is false.

(d) A is false, but R is true.

6. **Assertion** (A) Most fishes, when out of water die of suffocation.

   **Reason** (R) Atmospheric air contain far less oxygen then the dissolved oxygen in water.

7. **Assertion** (A) During inspiration, pressure of air falls in the thorax.

   **Reason** (R) There is a rise in the volume of the thorax during inspiration.

8. **Assertion** (A) Symptoms of emphysema develops when a person living on planes ascends and stays on mountain.

   **Reason** (R) Partial pressure of oxygen decrease with increase in altitude.

9. **Assertion** (A) People suffering from asthma face difficulty in breathing.

   **Reason** (R) In asthma, the bronchial wall secrete excess of mucus that clog the bronchi and bronchioles.

## Very Short Answer Type Questions

10. How entry of food is prevented in respiratory system?
11. Mention the factors that affect rate of diffusion in alveoli.
12. Give the significance of carbonic anhydrase.
13. Name the chronic disorder in which walls of alveoli are damaged and also mention its causes.

## Short Answer Type Questions

14. With the help of flow chart, give the pathway of air flow from nose to the alveoli of lungs.
15. Differentiate between external and internal intercostal muscles.
16. Write a short note on the control centres that regulate the rate of respiration.

## Long Answer Type Questions

17. Briefly describe the various parts of human respiratory system.
18. Explain the transport of $CO_2$ and $O_2$ from lungs to tissues.
19. Describe the various factors affecting the oxygen dissociation curve.

## Case Based Question

20. The two stages in the breathing process are shown in the diagram. Observe the diagram and answer the questions that follow.

    (i) Identify the two stages (*A* and *B* of breathing).

    (ii) Mention the condition and the position of diaphragm in *A* and *B*, respectively.

    (iii) Compare the intra-pulmonary air pressure in the stages *A* and *B*.

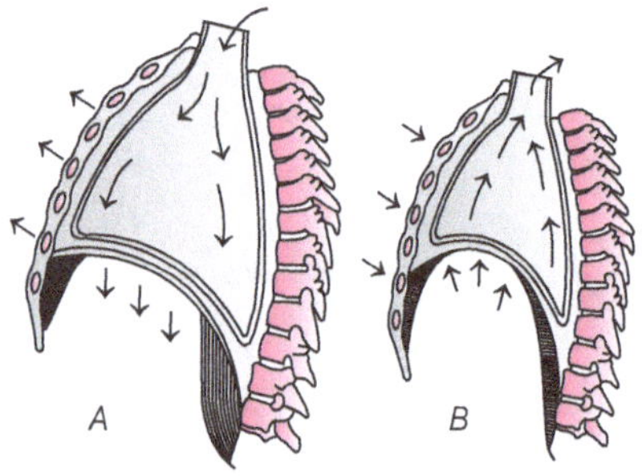


## Answers

| | | | | | | |
|---|---|---|---|---|---|---|
| 1. (b) | 2. (c) | 3. (a) | 4. (a) | 5. (a) | 6. (c) | 7. (a) |
| 8. (d) | 9. (a) | | | | | |

# 15 CHAPTER

# Body Fluids and Circulation

All living cells require nutrients, oxygen and other essential substances for survival. Similarly, the harmful or waste substances, produced by cells, are to be removed from the body for its efficient functioning. In order to fulfill these requirement a well developed **transport system** is present in different living organism.

### YOUR STUDY GOALS



### YOUR PRACTICE GOAL

- Objective Type Questions (41 Qs ; MCQs, A-R) Case Based Questions (3)
- Subjective Type Questions
- (32 VSAs, 28 SAs, 12 LAs)

- Different groups of animals have evolved different methods for the transport of essential and non-essential substances.
- **Simple organisms** such as **sponges** and **coelenterates** circulate water from their surroundings through their body cavities. This facilitates the cells to exchange gases and excretory substances with immediate surroundings.
- In more **complex organisms**, special body fluids, (i.e. Blood and Lymph) are used to transport these substances within the body.
- In this chapter, we will discuss about the composition and properties of these body fluids as well as their mechanism of circulation in detail.

## 15.1 Body Fluids

- These are the medium of transportation within the body.
- Blood and lymph are the two types of fluids that act as a carrier in the body.

### Blood

- It is a **special connective tissue** comprising of a fluid matrix, plasma and formed elements.
- The constituents are described below

## Plasma

- It is a straw coloured, viscous fluid that constitute about **55%** of the blood.
- Plasma forms the fluid medium in which the blood cells (corpuscles) float and carry out different important functions.

### Composition of Plasma

- It is composed of many **organic** and **inorganic substances**.
- It contains **90-92% water** and **6-8%** of proteins.
- The solutes found in plasma are various ions (like $Na^+$, $Mg^{2+}$, $Ca^{2+}$, $HCO_3^-$, $Cl^-$, etc.), along with glucose, amino acids, hormones, lipids, urea and other organic wastes.
- Factors for clotting or coagulation of blood are also present in the plasma in an inactive form.
- Plasma without the blood clotting factors is called **serum**.

### Plasma Proteins

- The major proteins found in plasma are **fibrinogen**, **globulins** and **albumins**.
- The various functions of plasma proteins are as follows
  - **Fibrinogen** helps in blood clotting.
  - **Globulins** are involved in defence mechanisms of the body.
  - **Albumins** help in maintaining osmotic balance.

## Formed Elements

- The formed elements constitute about 45% of the blood.
- These include **erythrocytes**, **leucocytes** and **platelets**, which are explained below.

### 1. Erythrocytes (Red Blood Cells)

- These are the most abundant of all the cells found in the blood.
- They are red in colour due to the presence of a iron containing pigment called **haemoglobin**, which acts as an oxygen carrier.
- A healthy individual has about 12-16 gm of haemoglobin in every 100 mL of blood.
- The formation of RBCs takes place in the **red bone marrow** in adults.
- RBCs are biconcave, disc-shaped cells that lack nucleus in most mammals.
- In men, the average number of RBC is about 5-5.5 million per cubic millimeter ($mm^{-3}$) of blood.
- Total lifespan of RBC is **120 days**.
- After this duration, RBCs become non-functional and get destroyed in spleen. So, spleen is called **graveyard of RBCs**.

### 2. Leucocytes (White Blood Cells)

- They are **colourless** in nature as they do not possess the red colour pigment (haemoglobin).
- Leucocytes are nucleated and are generally short-lived cells.
- The number of WBCs is relatively lesser (about 6000-8000 $mm^{-3}$ of blood).
- Leucocytes or white blood corpuscles are differentiated into two main categories such as

#### Granulocytes

They contain small granules in the cytoplasm and have lobed nucleus. The granulocytes are further subdivided into three main types

- **Neutrophils** These are the most abundant cells (about 60-65%) of the total WBCs. They are phagocytic in nature.
- **Eosinophils** They constitute about 2-3% of total WBCs. They resist infections and are also associated with all allergic reactions. During allergic conditions, the number of eosinophils increases in the body.
- **Basophils** They are found least abundant (0.5-1.0%) among WBCs. They secrete histamine, serotonin, heparin, etc., and are involved in **inflammatory reactions**.

#### Agranulocytes

They lack granules in their cytoplasm and have rounded or oval nucleus. Agranulocytes are also further subdivided into two main types

- **Lymphocytes** These cover 20-25% of the total WBCs. Lymphocytes are of further two types, i.e. **B-cells** and **T-cells**. Both of these (i.e. B and T-cells) are responsible for **immune responses** of the body.

- **Monocytes** These constitute 6-8% of the total WBCs. They help to kill foreign particles and are **phagocytic in nature**.

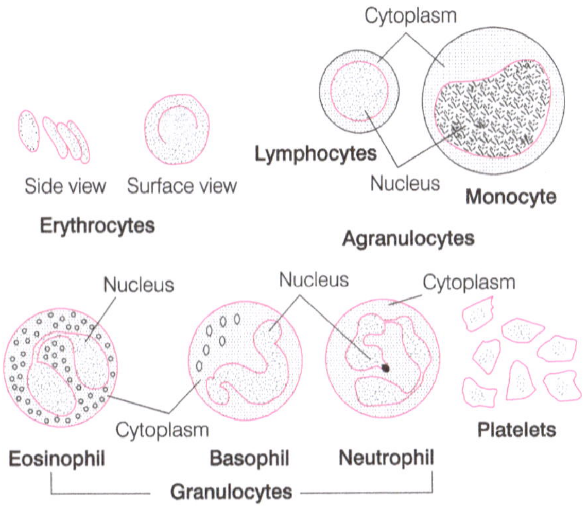


Fig. 15.1 Diagrammatic representation of formed elements in blood

## 3. Blood Platelets (Thrombocytes)

- These are cell fragments produced from **megakaryocytes** (special cells found in the red bone marrow).
- Blood normally contains 1,50,000-3,50,000 platelets per cubic milli meter ($mm^{-3}$).
- Their main function in the body is to release variety of factors most of which are involved in **coagulation** or **clotting of blood**.
- A reduction in their number can lead to clotting disorders which will lead to excessive blood loss from the body, if someone get injured.

**Differences between Red Blood Cells and White Blood Cells**

| Red Blood Cells | White Blood Cells |
|---|---|
| These are smaller in size and more numerous in number, i.e. number of RBCs per cubic millimeter of blood is 5.5 million. | These are larger in size and fewer in number, i.e. number of WBCs per cubic millimeter of blood is only 6000-8000. |
| These are non-nucleated, biconcave or disc-like cells. | WBCs are nucleated and amoeboid cells. |
| RBCs contain haemoglobin (respiratory pigment). | WBCs do not contain haemoglobin. |
| RBCs help in gaseous transport. | WBCs help in killing bacteria and foreign particles. |

## Blood Groups

- The plasma membrane of RBCs contain certain glycoprotein molecules known as **antigens**, which vary among individuals.
- Depending upon the nature of antigens, two important types of blood grouping found in human beings, that are discussed below

### 1. ABO Grouping

- This grouping is based on the presence or absence of **antigen-A** or **antigen-B** on the surface of RBCs.
- Similarly the plasma of different individuals also contains two natural antibodies (proteins produced as response to antigens).
- Based on this, people have different types of blood groups, given as below
  - People with blood group A have the antigen-A on the surface of their RBCs and have antibodies against antigen-B in their plasma.
  - People with blood group B have the antigen-B on the surface of their RBCs and have antibodies against antigen-A in their plasma.
  - People with blood group AB have both antigen-A and B on their RBCs surface and no antibodies, for either of the antigens, in their plasma.
  - In people with blood group O, both antigen-A and B are absent on the RBCs, but antibodies against both the antigens are present in the plasma.
- This distribution of antigens and antibodies result in the four blood groups (A, B, AB and O).
- These can be well-explained through the table given below

**Blood Groups and Donor Compatibility**

| Blood Group | Antigens on RBCs | Antibodies in Plasma | Donor's Group |
|---|---|---|---|
| A | A | Anti-B | A, O |
| B | B | Anti-A | B, O |
| AB | A, B | Nil | AB, A, B, O |
| O | Nil | Anti-A, B | O |

### Blood Reactions

- In humans, during transfusion of blood any blood group cannot be used. The blood of a donor has to be carefully matched with the blood of the recipient before transfusing, so as to avoid the problem of **clumping** (destruction of RBC).
- A person with blood group O can donate blood to persons with any of the other blood group (i.e. either A, B, AB and O). Hence, is called **universal donor**.
- Whereas, the person with blood group AB can accept blood from any blood group (i.e. AB as well as A, B, and O). Hence, is called **universal recipients**.

## 2. Rh Grouping

- Apart from the antigens discussed in the previous section, another antigen, known as **Rh antigen** (similar to the one present in **Rhesus monkey**) is also found on the surface of RBCs in majority of humans (nearly about 80%).
- Individuals having Rh antigen are called **Rh positive** ($Rh^+$) and those without the Rh antigen are called **Rh negative** ($Rh^-$).
- Rh group should to be matched before blood transfusions.
- An $Rh^-$ person if gets exposed to $Rh^+$ blood, he/she will form specific antibodies against the Rh antigens.
- A special case of **mismatching** of Rh group or **Rh incompatibility** has been discussed below.

### Rh Incompatibility During Pregnancy

- This is observed between the $Rh^-$ blood of a pregnant mother and $Rh^+$ blood of the foetus (the foetus of $Rh^-$ woman and a $Rh^+$ man).
- The Rh antigens of the foetus do not get exposed to the $Rh^-$ blood of the mother in case of first pregnancy (because two blood remain well separated by placenta).
- However, during delivery of the first child, there is a possibility that maternal blood may get exposed to small amounts of $Rh^+$ blood from the foetus.
- In such a case, mother start preparing antibodies against Rh antigen in her blood.
- Thus, in case of subsequent pregnancies, these antibodies can leak into the blood of the foetus ($Rh^+$) and destroy foetal RBCs.
- This could be fatal to the developing foetus and could cause severe **anaemia** and **jaundice** to the developing baby. This is known as **erythroblastosis foetalis** or **haemolytic disease of newborn.**

**Ist Pregnancy**

- Rh+ve (Father)
- Rh–ve (Mother)
- Rh+ve (Foetus)

No mixing of two bloods during pregnancy due to placenta → Foetal and maternal blood mixes during delivery

- First newborn Rh+ve (Safe)
- But Rh–ve mother prepares antibodies against Rh factor

**2nd Pregnancy**

- Rh+ve (Father)
- Rh–ve (Mother)
- Rh+ve (Foetus)

Maternal antibodies leak into the blood of foetus →

- Destroy foetal RBCs,
- Leads to erythroblastosis foetalis

### Precautions

This condition can be avoided by administering anti-Rh antibodies to the mother immediately after the delivery of the first child.

### Quick Test 1

1. X is a protein present in blood and helps in maintaining the osmotic balance. Identify the X.
2. In adults, which anatomical site is responsible for erythropoiesis (production of RBCs)?
3. Name the WBCs involved in inflammatory reactions.
4. Name the disease that occurs due to Rh incompatibility, when an Rh-negative mother carrying a Rh-positive child.
5. **State True or False.**
   (a) The presence of the Rh factor in blood makes someone a universal plasma donor.
   (b) Type O positive blood can receive blood from any Rh-positive blood group.
   (c) Neutrophils play a primary role in the humoral immune response.

## Coagulation or Clotting of Blood

- When an injury is caused, the wound normally does not continue to bleed for a long time, but eventually stops flowing after sometime.
- Coagulation or clotting is the natural property exhibited by the blood to prevent the excessive loss of blood from an injury or trauma.
- Clotting of blood is a complex process that involves various enzymatically controlled steps for its completion.

## Formation of a Clot

- An injury or trauma causes stimulation of platelets cells to release certain platelet factors.
- This inturn activates the mechanism of coagulation or clotting of blood at the site of injury.
- It occurs in following three steps
  - **Thrombokinase,** converts the inactive plasma protein, i.e. **prothrombin** into its active form **thrombin**. The **thrombokinase,** is an enzyme complex, which is formed by a series of linked enzymatic reactions (with cascade effects) which involves a number of factors present in the plasma in their inactive state.
  - Thrombin thus, acts as a **proteolytic enzyme** to convert **fibrinogen** molecule to form insoluble **fibrin**. Both the changes mentioned above require $Ca^{2+}$ ions for their reaction.
    The fibrin threads form a fine network of threads in which dead and damaged formed elements of blood are trapped.
- This finally leads to the formation of a **clot** or **coagulum,** which is a dark reddish brown **scum** formed over the surface of injury.

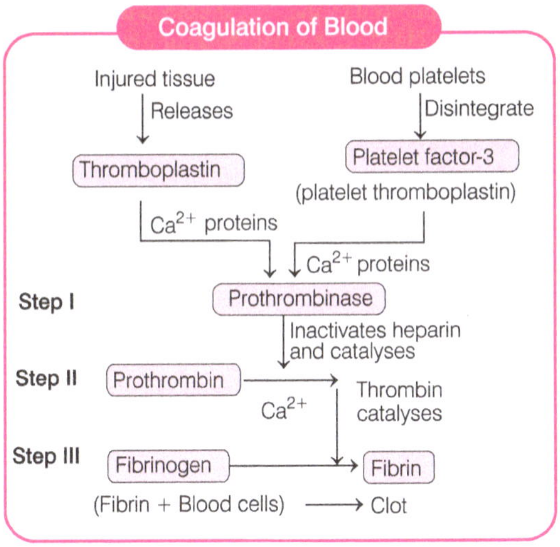


## Functions of Blood

Various functions performed by blood are as follows

- Helps in transportation of respiratory gases (i.e. $O_2$, $CO_2$, etc).
- Helps in healing of wounds.
- Maintains body pH as well as water and ionic balance.
- Fight against infections by providing immunity to the body.
- Helps in transportation of hormones from endocrine glands to target organs.
- Helps in transportation of body wastes from different body parts to kidneys.
- Maintains normal body temperature.

## Lymph (Tissue Fluid)

- It is an another fluid connective tissue that flows inside the specialised vessels known as **lymph vessels**.

### Formation of Lymph

- As the blood passes through the capillaries in the tissues, some water along with many water soluble substances come out in the spaces between the cells of tissues.
- Only a very small amount of proteins come out from the capillary with the plasma (leaving the larger proteins and most of the formed elements in the blood vessel).
- The fluid thus, released out is called **interstitial fluid** (tissue fluid) or **Extracellular Fluid** (ECF).
- After entering the lymph vessel, the ECF becomes lymph.

### Composition

- It is a colourless fluid containing high concentration of WBCs (specialised lymphocytes).
- The overall composition of lymph is similar to blood with the exception of absence of RBCs, platelets and some plasma proteins.

### Lymphatic System

It is an elaborate network of vessels, which collects the **interstitial fluid** (tissue fluid), along with some protein molecules and drains it back into the major veins.

### Functions of Lymph

- Exchange of gases, nutrients, etc., between the blood and the cells always occur through it.
- Lymph contain specialised lymphocytes which are responsible for the immune responses of the body.

- It is an important carrier for nutrients, hormones, etc.
- Fats are absorbed through lymph in the lacteals present in the intestinal villi.

**Differences Between Blood and Lymph**

| Blood | Lymph |
|---|---|
| It is red in colour due to the presence of haemoglobin in red blood cells. | It is colourless as red blood cells are absent. |
| It consists of plasma, RBC, WBC and platelets. | It consists of plasma and WBC. |
| It transports materials from one organ to other. | It transports materials from cells into the blood. |
| Its plasma has more proteins, calcium and phosphorus. | Its plasma has less protein, calcium and phosphorus. |
| It flows bidirectionally, i.e. both away and towards the heart. | It moves in one direction, i.e. from tissues towards heart. |

### Quick Test 2

1. The enzyme complex required for the conversion of prothrombin into thrombin is known as?
2. The element involved in creating the fibrinous framework that constitutes a blood clot is?
3. The fluid responsible for transporting immune cells in the body is?
4. Lymph is involved in absorption of fat in which part of body?
5. **State True or False.**
   Thrombokinase is essential for converting prothrombin into thrombin during blood clotting.

## 15.2 Circulatory Pathways

- Blood and lymph are the important fluids that act as a carrier in transporting nutrients, hormones, and various other materials, even to the farthest tissue in the body.
- The circulation of blood throughout the body is made possible by a muscular pump known as **heart.**
- Depending upon the circulatory patterns in higher organisms, the circulatory system is of following two types

### 1. Open Circulatory System

- It is the type of circulatory system in which blood pumped by the heart passes through large vessels into the spaces or body cavities known as **sinuses.**
- From there, the blood is collected by large veins, which open into the heart.
- This type of system is found in **arthropods** and **molluscs.**

### 2. Closed Circulatory System

- In this type of circulatory system, the blood pumped by the heart is always circulated inside the vessels (i.e. it is never present in large spaces or sinuses).
- This pattern is considered to be more advantageous as the flow of blood can be precisely regulated.
- It is found in **annelids** and **chordates.**
- It relies on heart to efficiently pump blood through vessels ensuring rapid transport of nutrients and oxygen.

**Differences between Open and Closed Circulatory System**

| Open Circulatory System | Closed Circulatory System |
|---|---|
| The blood is pumped by the heart into the blood vessels that open into blood spaces (sinuses). | The blood is pumped by the heart into closed blood vessels. |
| Blood is in direct contact with the tissue cells. | Blood does not come in direct contact with the tissue cells. |
| Exchange of respiratory gases, nutrients and waste products occurs directly between blood and tissues. | Exchange of respiratory gases, nutrients and waste products between tissues and blood occurs *via* tissue fluid. |

## Heart (The Pumping Organ in Vertebrates)

- All vertebrates possess a muscular chambered heart.
- Heart is of following three types

### 1. Two Chambered Heart

- This is found mostly in **fishes**. It is comprised of an atrium and a ventricle.
- During circulation of blood, the heart pumps out **deoxygenated** blood.

- This blood gets **oxygenated** by the gills and is then supplied to the body parts from where the deoxygenated blood is returned to the heart.
- Hence, the type of circulation is called **single circulation.**

## 2. Three Chambered Heart

- **Amphibians** and **reptiles** (except crocodiles) possess a three-chambered heart, which comprises of two atria and a single ventricle.
- During the circulation of blood, the left atrium receives the oxygenated blood from the gills/lungs/skin.
- The right atrium receives the deoxygenated blood from the other body parts.
- However, the blood gets mixed up in the single ventricle which further pumps out the mixed blood.
- This type of circulation is called **incomplete double circulation**.

## 3. Four Chambered Heart

- **Crocodiles, birds** and **mammals** possess this type of heart.
- It comprises of two atria and two ventricles.
- During the course of circulation, the oxygenated and deoxygenated blood are received by the left and the right atria, respectively.
- The blood from each atria is passed on to the ventricles of the same sides (i.e. left and right ventricles).
- There is no mixing of oxygenated and deoxygenated blood as both flow simultaneously but separately, in heart chambers so it is called **double circulation**.

# 15.3 Human Circulatory System

- Circulatory system in humans is also known as **blood vascular system.**
- It consists of a muscular chambered heart, a network of closed branching blood vessels and the fluid which is circulated, i.e. blood.

## Heart

- Heart is a **mesodermally derived organ**, situated in the thoracic cavity, in between the two lungs.
- It appears to be slightly tilted towards the left side.
- It has a size of a clenched fist.
- Structure of human heart can be studied under two heads for easy understanding, i.e. external and internal structure.

### External Structure

- The heart is protected by a double-walled membranous sac or bag called **pericardium**.
- The fluid present between two membranes is called **pericardial fluid.**
- This fluid helps in keeping the surface of the heart moist and also protects it from **shock** and **mechanical injuries**.

### Internal Structure

- Internally, the human heart is composed of four chambers, i.e. two relatively small upper chambers called **auricles** (atrium, sing. atria) and two larger lower chambers called **ventricles**.
- These are separated by different **septa** and **valves**.
- The chambers of heart as well as septa and valves present between them are discussed below

### Auricles (Atria)

- These are the upper two thin-walled and smaller chambers.
- They serve to receive the blood, therefore are called **receiving chambers** (right atrium and left atrium).
- Both the right and the left atria are separated by a thin, muscular wall known as **inter-atrial septum.**
- The brief description of both the chambers is given below
  - **Right Atrium** This right chamber deals with only **impure** (deoxygenated) blood. It receives impure blood from various parts of the body, through two vena cava. The right atrium is slightly larger than the left atrium.

- **Left Atrium** This chamber is meant to deal with only **pure** (oxygenated) blood. It receives blood (pure) from lungs through two **pulmonary veins** (i.e. one from each lung).

## Ventricles

- These are lower two chambers of the heart, that pump the blood away from the heart.
- Since, the ventricular walls are thicker than that of the atria, these function as **pumping chambers.**
- Both the right and the left ventricles are separated by the **inter-ventricular septum.**
- The atrium and the ventricle of the same side are also separated by another septum, a thick fibrous tissue called **atrio-ventricular septum** (i.e. AV septum).
- Each atrio-ventricular septum is provided with an opening through which the two chambers of the same side are connected.

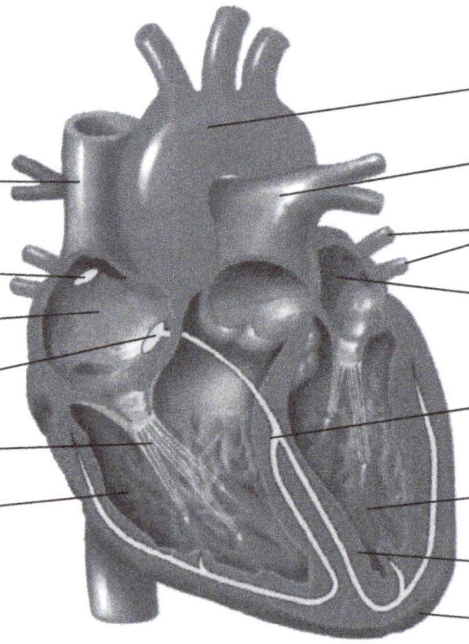


Fig. 15.2 Section of a human heart

- The brief description of both the chambers is given below
  - **Right Ventricle** It receives impure blood from right atrium and pumps it into **pulmonary artery**, which further takes this blood to lungs for oxygenation.
  - **Left Ventricle** It receives pure (oxygenated) blood from left atrium and pumps it to **aorta** (largest artery in the pathway), which inturn takes this blood to whole body.

**TEACHER'S TIP**
The left ventricle has thicker walls than the right ventricle because it needs to generate higher pressure to pump oxygenated blood throughout the entire body, while the right ventricle pumps blood to the lungs at a lower pressure.

## Cardiac Valves

- These valves act as door-like structures in the heart that serve to maintain the **unidirectional flow** of blood.
- Different valves present in the heart are given below
  - **Tricuspid Valve** It is formed by **three muscular flaps** or **cusps** and guard the opening between the right atrium and the right ventricle.
  - **Bicuspid Valve** (Mitral valve) It is formed by two muscular flaps and guards the opening between the left atrium and the left ventricle.

- **Semilunar Valve** The opening of the right and the left ventricles into the pulmonary artery and the aorta, respectively are provided with the semilunar valves.

## Functions of Cardiac Valves

The valves in the heart allow the flow of blood only in **one direction**, i.e. from the atria to ventricles and from the ventricles to the pulmonary artery or aorta. They **prevent any backward flow** of blood into the heart.

## Conducting System of Heart

- The heart is made up of cardiac muscles.
- The rhythmic movement of heart is maintained by a highly specialised cardiac musculature called the **nodal tissue** distributed evenly in the heart muscles. It consists of the following parts.

### 1. The Sinoatrial Node or SA Node (SAN)

- It is a small flattened patch of the specialised tissue present in the right upper corner of the right atrium.
- The impulse generated by this node spreads in all directions of the heart (i.e. go to both auricles and causes their relaxation and contraction).

### 2. The Atrioventricular Node or AV Node (AVN)

Another mass of tissue is seen in the lower left corner of the right atrium close to the **atrio-ventricular septum** (i.e. at the junction of ventricles and atrium) is known as AV node.

### 3. Bundle of His

- A bundle of **nodal fibres**, i.e. Atrio-ventricular bundle (AV bundle) continues from the AV node, which passes through the atrioventricular septum to emerge on the top of the interventricular septum immediately dividing into a right and left bundle.
- This bundle gives rise to a network of minute fibres (which are myocardial in origin) throughout the ventricular musculature of the respective side. These fibres are known as **Purkinje fibres**.
- These fibres along with the right and left bundles are called **bundle of His**.
- The Purkinje fibres conduct impulses to all portions of ventricular walls of the heart.

**Differences between SA Node and AV Node**

| SA Node | AV Node |
|---|---|
| It is located at the upper lateral wall of right auricle. | It is situated at the base of right auricle, near atrio-ventricular junction. |
| It generates impulses to initiate heartbeat. | Normally it does not generate impulse, but strengthen them. |
| It is not associated with bundle of His and Purkinje fibres. | It is associated with bundle of His and Purkinje fibres. |

## Working of Nodal Tissue

- The nodal musculature possesses the ability of generating action potentials without any external stimuli, i.e. it is **autoexcitable.**
- However, the number of action potentials that could be generated in a minute vary at different parts of the nodal system.
- The SAN can generate the maximum number of action potentials, i.e. 70-75 $min^{-1}$.
- It is also responsible for initiation and maintenance of the **rhythmic contractile activity** of the heart.
- Therefore, the SAN (i.e. SA Node) is also called **pacemaker.**
- Our heart normally beats 70-75 times in a minute (i.e. average 72 beats/min).

**Quick Test 3**

1. Name the circulatory system, where blood flows through large vessels into sinuses, in arthropods and molluscs.
2. In fishes, the oxygenation of deoxygenated blood, pumped by the heart, occurs through X organs, Identify X.
3. Name the natural substances that shield the heart from physical trauma or mechanical shock.
4. The nodal structure responsible for relaying electrical impulses between the atria and ventricles is called?
5. **State True or False.**
   (a) The inter-ventricular septum serves as the structural partition between the left and right atria.
   (b) SA node is present in the right upper corner of the right atrium.

## Blood Vessels

- As humans have closed type of circulatory system, the blood strictly flows in a fixed route through blood vessels.
- This maintains a continuous flow throughout the body, inside the closed tubes or blood vessels.
- These tubes or vessels are of mainly two types.

### Arteries

- These blood vessels carry blood away from the heart to different body parts.
- All arteries carry pure or oxygenated blood, with the exception of **pulmonary artery** that carries the impure or deoxygenated blood (i.e. from heart to the lungs for purification).
- Arteries are divided into fine branches, known as **arterioles,** which are further divided to form finer branches, called **capillaries.**

### Veins

- These are the another type of blood vessels that bring blood from different body parts to the heart, i.e. carry blood towards the heart.
- All veins are meant to carry impure blood except the **pulmonary vein** that carries pure blood. (i.e. from lungs to the heart).

**Differences between Arteries and Veins**

| Arteries | Veins |
|---|---|
| Arteries carry blood from the heart to the different parts of the body. | Veins bring blood back from different parts of the body to the heart. |
| Tunica media is thick. | Tunica media is comparatively thinner than arteries. |
| Except the pulmonary arteries, all the arteries carry oxygenated blood. | Except pulmonary veins all the veins carry deoxygenated blood. |

Each artery and vein is made up of three layers as given below

- **Tunica intima** Inner lining of squamous endothelium.
- **Tunica media** Middle layer of smooth muscle and elastic fibres.
- **Tunica externa** External layer of fibrous connective tissue with collagen fibres.

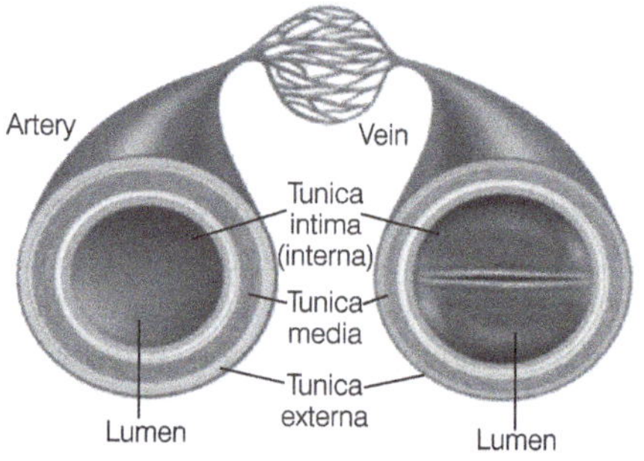


Fig. 15.3 Coverings of the blood vessels

## Cardiac Cycle

- The heart pumps blood to all parts of the body.
- The changes that take place in heart during one heartbeat, together constitute **cardiac cycle.**
- During a heartbeat, the contraction and relaxation of atria and ventricles take place.
- The phase of contraction is known as **systole,** while the relaxation phase is called the **diastole.**
- Thus, a single heartbeat consists of a systole and diastole of both the atria and the ventricles.
- To begin with the cardiac cycle, initially all four chambers of the heart are in a relaxed state, i.e. they are in **joint diastole.**
- The semilunar valves are closed at this stage.
- During this, the blood flows from the **pulmonary veins** and **vena cava** into the atria and from there to the respective ventricles through **atrio-ventricular valves.**
- The complete cardiac cycle is comprised of the following events that take place in a sequential manner.

### Atrial Systole

- The SA node generates action potential which leads to the simultaneous contraction of both the atria.
- This increases the flow of blood into the ventricles by about 30% as 70% filling of ventricles occurs passively during relaxation of ventricles, before the atrial contraction.

### Ventricular Systole

- After atrial systole, this step involves the **simultaneous relaxation** of atria (atrial diastole) and contraction of ventricles (ventricular systole).
- Ventricular systole occur due to contraction of muscle fibres, initiated by an action potential.
- The conduction of action potential to the ventricular side occurs by the AV node and AV bundle.
- The **bundle of His** then, transmits it through the entire ventricular musculature causing the ventricular muscles to contract (ventricular systole).
- The contraction of ventricles thereby, increases the ventricular pressure causing the closure of the tricuspid and bicuspid valves due to attempted backflow of blood into the atria.
- As ventricle pressure further increases, the semilunar valves guarding the pulmonary artery (right side) and the aorta (left side) are forced open and blood in the ventricle enters through these arteries into circulatory pathway.
- When ventricles relax (ventricular diastole), the ventricular pressure falls which causes the closure of semilunar valves.
- This prevents the backflow of blood into the ventricles.
- A further decline in the ventricular pressure, opens the tricuspid and bicuspid valves by the pressure in the atria exerted by the blood which was being emptied into them by the veins.
- This allows the blood to move freely to the ventricles once again.
- The ventricles and atria are now again in a **relaxed state** (joint diastole) as earlier.
- Soon, the SAN generates a new action potential and the events described above are sequentially repeated to continue the process (next cardiac cycle).

### Heart Rate and Cardiac Output

- In humans, the heart beats for about 72 times per minute (on an average).
- The duration of a each cardiac cycle is **0.8 s.**
- This concludes that in a single minute, many cardiac cycles are performed.
- During a cardiac cycle (i.e. in one beat) each ventricle pumps out about 70 mL of blood. This is known as **stroke volume**.
- The volume of blood pumped out by each ventricle in one minute is called **cardiac output**.
- Thus,

Cardiac output = Stroke volume × Number of beats /min.

- In one minute heart beats for 72 times. Thus, cardiac output will be 5040 mL or approx. 5L in a normal individual.
- The body has the ability to alter stroke volume as well as the heart rate and thereby, the cardiac output.
- Concludingly, an athlete has much higher cardiac output than the normal man.

## Heart Sounds

- During each cardiac cycle, two prominent sounds are produced which can be easily heard by a **stethoscope** (an instrument used for the amplification of sound).
- The basic reason for the production of these sounds is the **closure of various valves.**
- The sounds produced during each heartbeat are as follows
  - **Lub** It is the first sound, being produced when atrio-ventricular valves (tricuspid and bicuspid valve) are closed.
  - **Dup** It is the second sound, being produced when semilunar valves (of aorta and pulmonary artery) get closed. These sounds are of clinical diagnostic significance.

## Electrocardiograph (ECG)

- The electrical activity of the heart during a single cardiac cycle is obtained in the form of a graphical representation. This representation is known as **electrocardiogram**.
- It is obtained by a machine known as electrocardiograph.

- To obtain an ECG, a patient is connected to the machine with **three electrical leads** (i.e. one to each wrist and one to the left ankle) monitoring the activity of heart continuously.
- For detailed assesment of the heart's activity, multiple leads are attached to the chest region.

## Reading an ECG

- An ECG consists of different waves, identified with the letter from P to T that corresponds to a specific electrical conductivity of the heart.
- These waves are explained as follows

### 1. P-Wave

- It represents the **electrical excitation** or **depolarisation of the atria** which leads to contraction of both the atria.

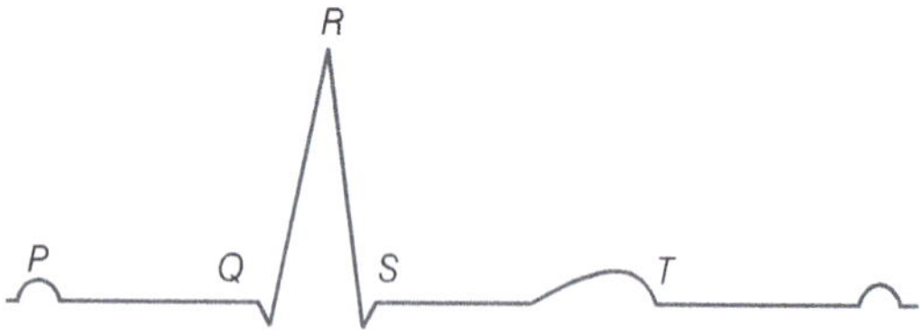


Fig. 15.4 Diagrammatic representation of a standard ECG

### 2. QRS-Wave or Complex

- The Q, R and S wave together form the *QRS* complex. This represents the **depolarisation of the ventricles**, which represent the ventricular contraction.
- The contraction starts shortly after Q and marks the beginning of the systole.

### 3. T-Wave

- It is a broad and smoothly rounded deflection, which represents the return of the ventricles from excited to normal state (repolarisation).
- The end of T-wave marks the end of systole.
- By counting the number of *QRS* complex, that occur in a given time period, one can easily determine the rate of heartbeat of an individual.
- The deviation in the ECG of any person from the normal shaped ECG, indicates a possible abnormality or a disease.

### Quick Test 4

1. Name the layer of blood vessel that is primarily made of fibrous connective tissue and collagen fibres.
2. In which phase of cardiac cycle, does the closure of semilunar valve occurs, due to the fall in ventricular pressure?
3. The volume of blood pumped by each ventricle with every contraction is referred to as?
4. Name the wave which is associated with the electrical excitation of the atria in an ECG.
5. **State True or False.**
   (a) The AVN and AV bundle transmit the action potential to the ventricular side.
   (b) ECGs from different individuals will always show significantly different shapes for the same lead configuration.

## 15.4 Double Circulation

- The mammalian heart is four-chambered, undergoing the process of complete double circulation.
- This means that blood passes twice through the heart to supply the blood to the body.
- The double circulation consist of following processes.

### 1. Pulmonary Circulation

- In this system, blood completes its circulation from right ventricle to the left atria through the lungs.
- Here, the deoxygenated blood pumped by the right ventricle enters the **pulmonary artery,** which passed it on to the lungs for oxygenation.
- The oxygenated blood is then carried out by the **pulmonary veins** into the left atrium of the heart.

### 2. Systemic Circulation

- In this system, the pure (oxygenated) blood is supplied to all parts of the body.
- During this transport, the oxygenated (pure) blood enters the aorta is carried by a network of **arteries, arterioles** and **capillaries** to the tissues.
- Deoxygenated (impure) blood from there, is collected by a system of **venules, veins** and **vena cava,** thus, emptying it into the right atrium.

- This system provides nutrients, $O_2$ and other essential substances to all the tissues of the body and eventually takes $CO_2$ and other harmful substances away from the tissues for their elimination from the body.

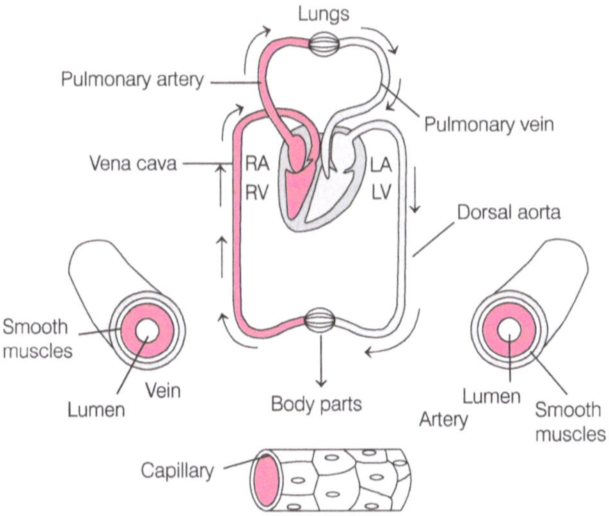


Fig. 15.5 Schematic plan of bood circulation in human

**Differences between Pulmonary Circulation and Systemic Circulation**

| Pulmonary Circulation | Systemic Circulation |
|---|---|
| It is a smaller circuit, which carries blood to the lungs and back to the heart. | It is a larger circuit, which supplies blood to the various parts of the body and back to the heart. |
| It carries deoxygenated blood to the lungs for oxygenation. | It supplies oxygenated blood to all parts of the body. |
| The blood is pumped by right ventricle and received by the left atrium. | The blood is pumped by left ventricle and received by the right atrium. |

## Circulation through Special Regions

Apart from the pulmonary or systemic circulation body possess some special circulations.

Two of them are discussed below

### Coronary Circulation

- A coronary system supply oxygen and nutrients to the muscles of the heart.
- The **right** and **left coronary arteries** arise from the ascending aorta which supply oxygenated blood to the heart muscles.
- The coronary veins bring deoxygenated blood to coronary sinus which then carries it to the right atrium.

### Hepatic Portal Circulation

- A specialised vascular arrangement in which blood from the capillaries of one organ is transported to the capillaries of another organ is called **portal system**.
- The portal system exists between the digestive tract and liver is called **hepatic portal system**.
- A vein called **hepatic portal vein**, carries blood from intestine to the liver (hepatic gland) before delivering it to the systemic circulation.

## 15.5 Regulation of Cardiac Activity

- The normal activities of the heart are intrinsically regulated, i.e. autoregulated by the specialised muscles, (nodal tissue). Thus, the heart is known as **myogenic.**
- The cardiac activity in humans is regulated in the following manner

### 1. Neural Regulation

- In medulla oblongata, a special neural centre is present, which can moderate, the cardiac function through the **Autonomic Nervous System** (ANS).
- The neural signals through the **sympathetic nerves** (part of ANS) can increase the rate of heartbeat, the strength of ventricular contraction and thereby, the cardiac output.
- On the contrary, the neural signal through **parasympathetic nerves** (another component of ANS) can decrease the rate of heartbeat by inhibiting the SA, speed of conduction of action potential, thereby decreasing the cardiac output.

### 2. Hormonal Regulation

Hormones secreted by the medulla region of adrenal gland have significant role in regulating heartbeat and thus, increasing the cardiac output.

## 15.6 Disorders of Circulatory System

Many diseases may affect the blood vessels and thereby the normal functioning of the heart.
Some of the common disorders are as follows

### 1. High Blood Pressure (Hypertension)

- The pressure exerted by the flow of blood on the **elastic walls** of the arteries is known as **blood pressure**.
- **Hypertension** is the term used for blood pressure higher than the normal.
- The normal blood pressure in humans is measured as **120/80 mm Hg** (millimetres of mercury pressure), in which 120 mm Hg is the **systolic pressure** (pumping pressure), while, the 80 mm Hg is the **diastolic pressure** (or resting pressure).
- Persistent increase in blood pressure above 140 mm Hg (systolic) and 90 mm Hg (diastolic) is termed as **hypertension**.

#### Consequences of Hypertension

It may lead to many heart diseases and also affects vital organs of the body, like the brain and kidney.

### 2. Coronary Artery Disease (CAD)

- It is often referred to as **atherosclerosis**.
- This mainly affects the vessels, that are responsible for supplying blood to the heart muscle.
- It seems to occur due to deposition of calcium, fat cholesterol and fibrous tissues, making the lumen of arteries narrower.

### 3. Angina (Angina Pectoris)

- This tends to occur when enough oxygen does not reach the heart muscles.
- It occurs both in men and women of any age but seems to be more common among the middle-aged and elderly individuals.
- A symptom of **acute chest pain** occurs in individual suffering from angina.

### 4. Heart Failure

- It is the condition of the heart when it fails to pump blood effectively to meet the needs of the body.
- The heart failure is sometimes called the **congestive heart failure**, as its main symptom is **congestion of lungs.**
- However, heart failure is not the same as **cardiac arrest** (when the heart stops beating) and **heart attack** (damaged heart muscle due to inadequate blood supply).

## Quick Test 5

1. Identify the vessels that facilitate the transport of deoxygenated blood from the tissues to the right atrium.
2. Name the specialised muscle tissue responsible for the intrinsic regulation of the heart.
3. A person experiencing acute chest pain due to insufficient oxygen reaching the heart muscle is most likely suffering from?
4. Raman visited a doctor for a regular health checkup and was found to have increased diastolic pressure. What condition might he be suffering from?
5. **State True or False.**
   (a) The condition in which the heart muscles are damaged due to inadequate blood supply is known as congestive heart failure.
   (b) The normal blood pressure in humans is 120/80mm Hg in which 120mm Hg is diastolic pressure and 80mm Hg is systolic pressure.

# Mind Map

## Body Fluids and Circulation

### Body Fluids
Essential substances in the body that facilitate communication, transport nutrients, remove waste and maintain homeostasis.

### Lymph
Colourless fluid that circulates through the lymphatic system, carrying WBCs, especially lymphocytes and aiding in immune response.

### Blood
- Blood
  - Plasma
  - Formed elements
    - Blood corpuscles
      - Red blood cells
      - White blood cells
        - Granulocyte
          - Neutrophil
          - Basophil
          - Eosinophil
        - Agranulocyte
          - Lymphocyte
          - Monocyte
    - Platelets

### ABO Blood Grouping
Classified blood into four (A, B, AB and O) types based on the presence or absence of A and B antigens on RBCs.

### RH Blood Grouping
Based on the presence or absence of the Rh factor on the surface of RBCs, blood is classified into $Rh^+$ and $Rh^-$

### Disorders of Respiratory System
- **Hypertension** Consistently high blood pressure (above 140/90mm Hg) increasing heart, brain and kidney risks.
- **Coronary Artery Disease (CAD)** Narrowed heart arteries due to plaque buildup.
- **Angina** Chest pain from reduced oxygen to the heart.
- **Heart Failure** Heart's inability to pump blood effectively, causing lung congestion and fatigue.

### Regulation of Cardiac Activity
The heart's activity is regulated by the autonomic nervous system and adrenal hormones, where sympathetic stimulation enhances heart rate and output, while parasympathetic stimulation reduces them.

### Circulatory Pathways
- Fishes-2-chambered heart
- Amphibians/reptiles-3-chambered heart
- Birds/mammals-4-chambered

Circulatory Pathways
- Open (arthropods/molluscs)
- Closed (annelids/chordates)

### Human Circulatory System
Consists of a muscular heart, a network of blood vessels and blood. The heart is located between the lungs, has septa and valves ensuring one- way blood flow. The ventricles have thicker walls, and nodal tissue, including pacemaker, (SAN) present at right atrium, which regulates the heart's rhythm at 70-75 beats per minute.

### Heart and Circulation of Blood
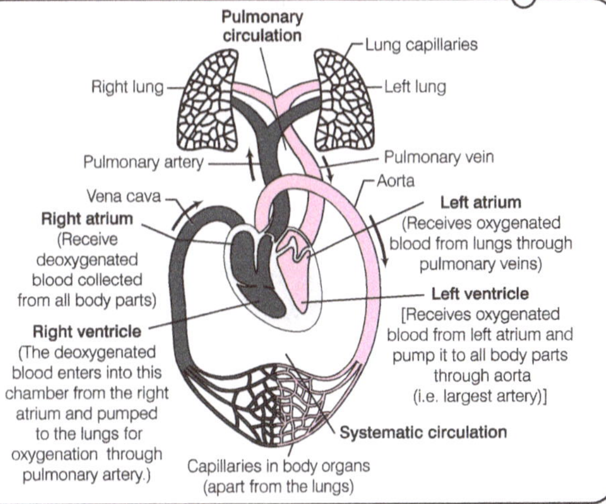


### Cardiac Cycle
It involves a heartbeat or one cycle of contraction and relaxation of cardiac muscles.

Cardiac output = Stroke volume × Heart rate

### ECG
It is a graphic record of the electric current produced by the excitation of cardiac muscles. A normal ECG is composed of
- **P-wave** depolarisation of atria.
- **QRS**- complex depolarisation of ventricle.
- **T-wave** repolarisation of ventricles.

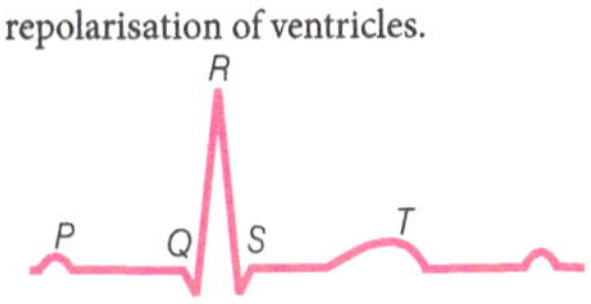

# EXAM PATTERN QUESTIONS

## Objective Type Questions

### Multiple Choice Questions

**1.** **The percentage of water and protein in a straw coloured viscous fluid, i.e. plasma is**

(a) 92% and 8% (b) 50% each
(c) 60% and 40% (d) 32% and 68%

Ans. (*a*)

**2.** **Your friend has gone for blood test and his haemoglobin count is 17 gm per 100 mL.**
**What should he do?** **Competency Based Que.**

(a) No need to worry
(b) Take rest
(c) Take rest and prescribed medicines
(d) Take rest and lots of leafy vegetables

Ans. (*a*)

**3.** **Identify the following types of blood cells and mark the correct option.**

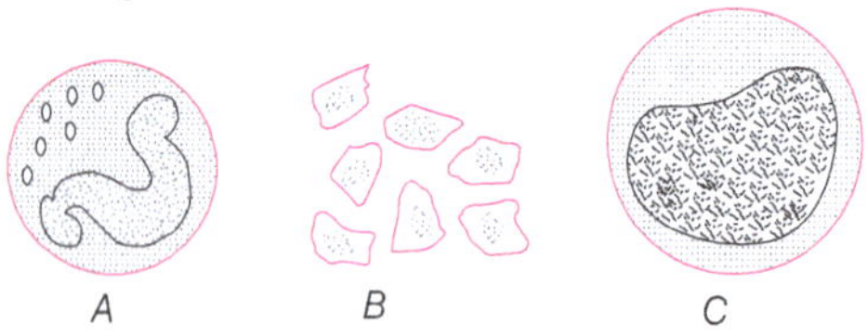


| | *A* | *B* | *C* |
|---|---|---|---|
| (a) | Monocyte | Eosinophil | Neutrophil |
| (b) | Monocyte | Basophil | Neutrophil |
| (c) | Basophil | Blood platelets | Monocyte |
| (d) | Basophil | Blood platelets | Eosinophil |

Ans. (*c*)

**4.** **Which of the following cells do not exhibit phagocytotic activity?** **NCERT Exemplar**

(a) Monocytes (b) Neutrophil (c) Basophil (d) Macrophage

Ans. (*c*)

**5.** **Which one of the following blood cells is involved in antibody production.** **NCERT Exemplar**

(a) B-lymphocytes
(b) T-lymphocytes
(c) RBC
(d) Neutrophils

Ans. (*a*) The principal function of B-lymphocytes is to make antibodies against antigens that are important in regulating humoral immunity.

**6.** **Which of the following statements is incorrect?** **NCERT Exemplar**

(a) A person of 'O' blood group has anti-'A' and anti-'B' antibodies in his blood plasma.
(b) A person of 'B' blood group cannot donate blood to a person of 'A' blood group.
(c) Blood group is designated on the basis of the presence of antibodies in the blood plasma.
(d) A person of AB blood group is universal recipient.

Ans. (*c*)

**7.** **If husband is $Rh^+$ and wife is $Rh^-$ then** **Competency Based Que.**

(a) there will be no problem with first child
(b) second child would have anaemia (erythroblastosis foetalis)
(c) second child would be normal
(d) Both (a) and (b)

Ans. (*d*)

**8.** **Given below is a flowchart showing the formation of blood clot.**

Thrombokinase
↓ $Ca^{2+}$
Prothrombin ⟶ Thrombin
↓
Ⓧ ⟶ Ⓨ

**Choose the correct option.**

| | *X* | *Y* |
|---|---|---|
| (a) | Fibrinogen | Insoluble fibrin |
| (b) | Fibrinogen | Soluble fibrinogen |
| (c) | Soluble fibrin | Fibrinogen |
| (d) | Soluble fibrin | Soluble fibrin |

Ans. (*a*) Thrombin is responsible for converting fibrinogen into insoluble fibrin.

The fibrin form a fine network of threads in which dead and damaged formed elements of blood are trapped.

**9. Mark the pair of substances among the following which is essential for coagulation of blood.** NCERT Exemplar

(a) Heparin and calcium ions
(b) Calcium ions and platlet factors
(c) Oxalates and citrates
(d) Platelet factors and heparin

Ans. (*b*)

**10. Which of the following representation holds true for lymph?**

(a) Serum + WBCs
(b) Blood – RBCs and proteins
(c) RBCs + WBCs + plasma
(d) RBCs + proteins + platelets

Ans. (*b*)

**11. The number of chambers in the muscular heart of fishes, amphibians and birds is**

(a) 2, 2, 4 (b) 2, 3, 4 (c) 2, 4, 4 (d) 3, 3, 4

Ans. (*b*)

**12. Which of the following chambers of the heart has the thickest muscular wall?**

(a) Left atrium (b) Right atrium
(c) Right ventricle (d) Left ventricle

Ans. (*d*)

**13. Which of the following is correct about human heart?**

(a) The volume of both atria is more than the volume of both ventricles
(b) The volume of both ventricles is more than the volume of both atria
(c) The volume of both atria is equal to the volume of both ventricles
(d) Ventricles are upper chambers and atria are lower chambers

Ans. (*b*)

**14. SA node is called the pacemaker of heart because**

(a) it can change the contractile activity generated by AV node
(b) it delays the transmission of impulse between the atria and ventricles
(c) it gets stimulated when it receives neural signals
(d) it initiates and maintains the rhythmic contractile activity of the heart

Ans. (*d*)

**15. The correct route through which pulse making impulse travels in the heart is** Competency Based Que.

(a) SA node → Purkinje fibres → Bundle of His → AV node → Heart muscles
(b) SA node → AV node → Bundle of His → Purkinje fibres → Heart muscles
(c) AV node → Bundle of His → SA node → Purkinje fibres → Heart muscles
(d) AV node → SA node → Purkinje fibres → Bundle of His → Heart muscles

Ans. (*b*) In myogenic heart the contraction is initiated by SA node. The wave of contraction reaches AV node which is stimulated to emit an impulse of contraction spreading to the ventricular muscle *via* the atrio-ventricular bundle. The bundle of His conducts electrical impulse then to the Purkinje fibres, which stimulating heartbeat.

**16. Which among the following is correct during each cardiac cycle?** NCERT Exemplar

(a) The volume of blood pumped out by the Rt and Lt ventricles is same
(b) The volume of blood pumped out by the Rt and Lt ventricles is different
(c) The volume of blood received by each atrium is different
(d) The volume of blood received by the aorta and pulmonary artery is different

Ans. (*a*)

**17. What would be the cardiac output of a person having 72 heart beats per minute and a stroke volume of 50 mL?** Competency Based Que., NCERT Exemplar

(a) 360 mL (b) 3600 mL
(c) 7200 mL (d) 5000 mL

Ans. (*b*) Cardiac output is determined by multiplying the heart rate with the volume of blood ejected by each ventricle during each beat, which is called as stroke volume.

Cardiac output = Heart rate × Stroke volume

= 72 beats/min × 50 mL = 3600 mL

**18. The second heart sound (dub) is associated with the closure of** NCERT Exemplar

(a) tricuspid valve (b) semilunar valve
(c) bicuspid valve (d) tricuspid and bicuspid valve

Ans. (*b*)

**19. ECG depicts the depolarisation and repolarisation processes during the cardiac cycle. In the ECG of a normal healthy individual one of the following waves is not represented.** NCERT Exemplar

(a) Depolarisation of atria
(b) Repolarisation of atria
(c) Depolarisation of ventricles
(d) Repolarisation of ventricles

Ans. (*b*) A normal ECG represents, P-wave (atrial depolarisation), QRS complex (ventricular depolarisation), T-wave (ventricular repolarisation). Therefore, atrial repolarisation is not represented in an Electrocardiogram (ECG).

**20.** Given below is the diagrammatic representation of standard Electrocardiogram (ECG). Identify the figure which is the correct one. **Competency Based Que.**

(a) 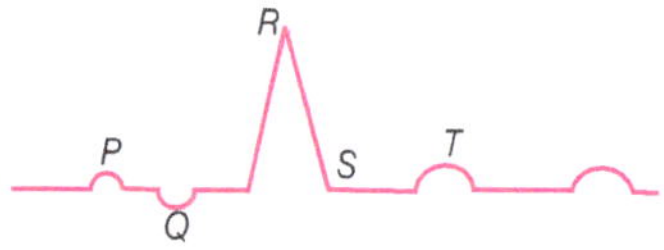


(b) 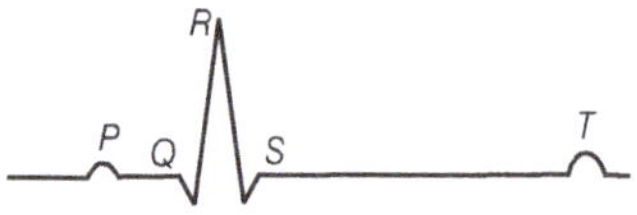


(c) 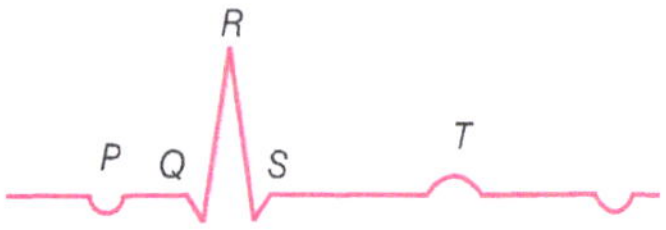


(d) 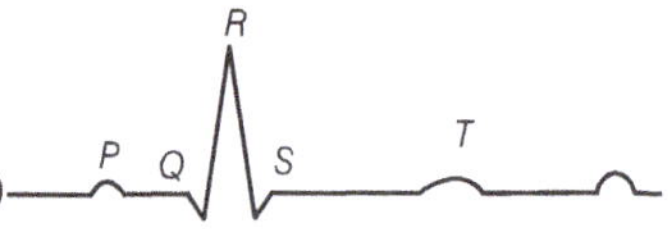


Ans. (*d*)

**21.** Match the following columns. **Competency Based Que.**

| Column I (ECG Wave) | | Column II (Features) | |
|---|---|---|---|
| A. | P-wave | 1. | Depolarisation of ventricles |
| B. | QRS complex | 2. | Repolarisation of ventricles |
| C. | T-wave | 3. | Depolarisation of inter ventricular septum |
| D. | Q-wave | 4. | Depolarisation of atria |

**Codes**

| | A | B | C | D | | A | B | C | D |
|---|---|---|---|---|---|---|---|---|---|
| (a) | 4 | 1 | 3 | 2 | (b) | 2 | 3 | 1 | 4 |
| (c) | 2 | 1 | 3 | 4 | (d) | 4 | 1 | 2 | 3 |

Ans. (*d*)

**22.** Which of the following correctly explains a phase/event in cardiac cycle in a standard electrocardiogram? **NCERT Exemplar**

(a) QRS complex indicates atrial contraction
(b) QRS complex indicates ventricular contraction
(c) Time between S and T represents atrial systole
(d) P-wave indicates beginning of ventricular contraction

Ans. (*b*)

**23.** The systemic circulation

(a) provides nutrients to tissues
(b) takes out $CO_2$ from tissues
(c) provides $O_2$ to tissues
(d) All of the above

Ans. (*d*)

**24.** The figure given below represents the condition of double circulation found in humans. Choose the correct option that matches perfectly with the identification and function of the part labelled as *A*, *B*, *C* and *D*.

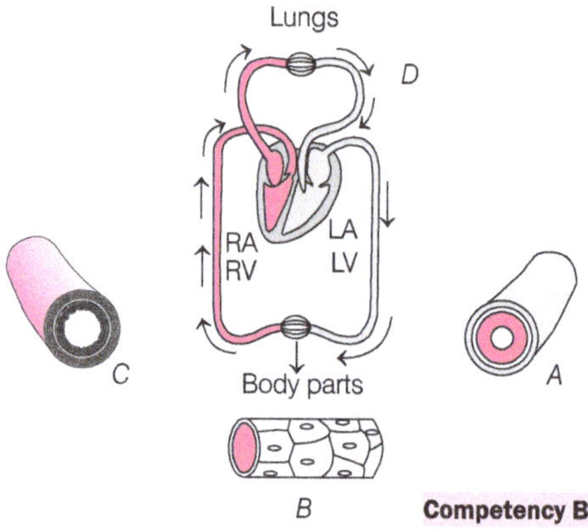


**Competency Based Que.**

(a) *B*- Capillary-thin, with two cell thick wall
(b) *D*- Pulmonary vein-takes oxygenated blood to heart
(c) *C*- Vein-thin walled with blood flowing in jerks
(d) *A*- Artery-thick walled with blood flowing slowly

Ans. (*b*)

**25.** Match the following columns. **NCERT Exemplar**

| Column I | | Column II | |
|---|---|---|---|
| A. | Lymphatic system | 1. | Carries oxygenated blood |
| B. | Pulmonary vein | 2. | Immune response |
| C. | Thrombocytes | 3. | To drain back the tissue fluid to the circulatory system |
| D. | Lymphocytes | 4. | Coagulation of blood |

**Codes**

| | A | B | C | D | | A | B | C | D |
|---|---|---|---|---|---|---|---|---|---|
| (a) | 2 | 1 | 3 | 4 | (b) | 3 | 1 | 4 | 2 |
| (c) | 3 | 1 | 2 | 4 | (d) | 2 | 1 | 3 | 4 |

Ans. (*b*)

**26.** Heart is termed as myogenic because

(a) normal activities of the heart are extrinsically controlled
(b) normal activities are intrinsically controlled
(c) normal activities are self-regulated
(d) Both (b) and (c)

Ans. (*d*)

**27.** Cardiac activity could be moderated by the autonomous neural system. Tick the correct answer. **NCERT Exemplar**

(a) The parasympathetic system stimulates heart rate and stroke volume
(b) The sympathetic system stimulates heart rate and stroke volume

(c) The parasympathetic system decreases the heart rate but increase stroke volume

(d) The sympathetic system decreases the heart rate but increase stroke volume

Ans. (*b*)

**28. Which is not the property of autonomic nervous system.** DIKSHA

(a) Increase the rate of heartbeat

(b) Decrease the speed of conduction of action potential

(c) Increase the strength of ventricular contraction

(d) increase the cardiac ouput

Ans. (*b*)

**29. Neural signal through the sympathetic nerves (part of ANS) can increase the rate of heartbeat by**

(a) decreasing speed of action potential

(b) increasing the contraction of atrium

(c) Increasing the stroke volume

(d) Increasing the strength of contraction of ventricle

Ans. (*d*)

**30. Systolic or pumping pressure in a normal human is**

(a) 120 mm of Hg (b) 80 mm of Hg

(c) 70 mm of Hg (d) 90 mm of Hg

Ans. (*a*)

**31. Atherosclerosis is caused by the deposition of**

(a) calcium (b) fat and cholesterol

(c) fibrous tissue (d) All of the above

Ans. (*d*)

## Assertion-Reason Questions

**Direction** (Q. Nos. 1-10) *In each of the following questions, a statement of Assertion (A) is given followed by corresponding statement of Reason (R). Of the statements, mark the correct answer if*

(a) Both A and R are true and R is the correct explanation of A

(b) Both A and R are true, but R is not the correct explanation of A

(c) A is true, but R is false

(d) A is false, but R is true

**1. Assertion** (A) A person with blood group O is considered to be universal recipient.

**Reason** (R) O blood group has no antigens, but have anti-A and anti-B antibodies.

Ans. (*d*) A is false, but R is true. A can be corrected as
A person with blood group O is considered a universal donor becasue its blood lacks A and B antigens, making it safe for recipients of any blood type.

**2. Assertion** (A) Reduction in number of platelets can lead to excessive loss of blood from the body in case of injury.

**Reason** (R) Platelets help in the coagulation of blood.

Ans. (*a*)

**3. Assertion** (A) Thrombin is essential for blood clotting.

**Reason** (R) $Ca^{2+}$ plays an important role in blood clotting.

Ans. (*b*) Both A and R are true, but R is not the correct explanation of A. The A can be explained as

Thrombin convert fibrinogen, a protein in the blood into fibrin, strands that stick together to form a mesh. This mesh creates a solid structure that helps to stop bleeding and supports healing.

**4. Assertion** (A) In amphibians and reptiles, the double circulation is incomplete.

**Reason** (R) In amphibians and reptiles, the left atrium receives oxygenated blood and right atrium receives deoxygenated blood. Competency Based Que.

Ans. (*c*)

**5. Assertion** (A) The SA node acts as pacemaker.

**Reason** (R) The SA node is located in the wall of the right atrium near the inter-atrial septum.

Ans. (*c*) A is true, but R is false. R can be corrected as
SA node is located at the right upper corner of the right atrium.

**6. Assertion** (A) Bundle of His is a part of autoexcitable tissue

**Reason** (R) Bundle of His comprises of cardiac tissue that can generate impulse on its own at a frequency less than SA node.

Ans. (*a*)

**7. Assertion** (A) The end of T-wave marks the end of ventricular systole.

**Reason** (R) T-wave represents the return of ventricles from excited to normal state which is repolarisation.

Ans. (*a*)

**8. Assertion** (A) Human heart is termed as myogenic.

**Reason** (R) Impulse of contraction originates intrinsically within the heart.

Ans. (*a*)

**9. Assertion** (A) Atherosclerosis affects the blood vessels which supply blood to the heart.

**Reason** (R) Atherosclerosis is caused by the deposition of fats, calcium, cholesterol and fibrous tissue which makes the lumen narrower.

Ans. (*a*)

**10. Assertion** (A) Heart fails to pump blood effectively in case of heart failure.

**Reason (R)** Heart attack is synonymous to heart failure.

Ans. (*c*)

# Subjective Questions

## Very Short Answer Type Questions

**1. List three things found in blood plasma.**

**Ans.** Plasma contains proteins, clotting factors and small amount of minerals.

**2. Total life span of RBCs is 120 days. What is the fate of RBCs after this?**

**Ans.** RBCs have a lifespan of about 120 days or 4 months. After this, they become non-functional and are destroyed in spleen.

**3. Write the function of lymphocytes.**

**Ans.** Refer to text on page no. 340.

**4. Mention the function of neutrophils.**

**Ans.** Refer to text on page no. 340.

**5. What will happen if total leucocyte count in humans falls below the normal range?** Competency Based Que.

**Ans.** A lower count of total leucocytes indicates a higher risk for infections.

**6. A person suffering from allergy visits a pathology lab for a blood test. His medical blood test report concludes a specific type of blood cell in increased numbers. Which of the formed cells are these?** Competency Based Que.

**Ans.** The formed cells are eosinophils, a type of white blood cells. During allergic reactions, their number increases in the body.

**7. A person has a blood group AB positive. What does it mean?**

**Ans.** AB positive means that a person has both A and B antigens as well as also has Rh factor on his/her RBCs.

**8. A person with blood group O can receive which type of blood?**

**Ans.** Refer to text on page no. 341. (1)

**9. Sneha is having blood group A-ve, while her husband's blood group is O+ve. Their first child is A +ve, but her second child was born with severe anaemia and jaundice. What could be the condition ?** Competency Based Que.

**Ans.** Erythroblastosis foetalis.

**10. What will happen to the clotting process if thrombin is absent ?** Competency Based Que.

**Ans.** Fibrinogen will not be able to convert into fibrin. Thus, no clot formation will occur.

**11. How is lymph different from the blood ?**

**Ans.** Lymph has all the elements of blood except RBCs and platelets.

**12. Give examples of the organisms in which the blood gets mixed in a single ventricle, that pumps the mixed blood ?**

**Ans.** Amphibians and reptiles

**13. Name the following.**

**(i) the receiving chambers and**

**(ii) the pumping chambers of the heart.**

**Ans.** (i) The blood receiving chambers of the heart are left and right atrium. (½)

(ii) The blood pumping chambers of the heart are left and right ventricles. (½)

**14. Due to developmental abnormality, the wall of the left ventricle of an infant's heart is as thin as that of right ventricle. What would be its specific effect in circulation of blood?** Competency Based Que.

**Ans.** If the wall of left ventricle is as thin as that of right ventricle. It may not be able to develop sufficient pressure to pump blood to all distant parts of the body.

**15. When the right ventricle contracts, blood flows from it to which part of the heart?**

**Ans.** When the right ventricle contracts, the blood flows from to the lungs *via* pulmonary artery in order to get oxygenated. From there, blood reaches the left atrium of the heart.

**16. Give the location of atrio-ventricular septa in the heart.**

**Ans.** The atrio-ventricular septa is present between atria and ventricles of both sides.

**17. Name the vessels that enter and leave the heart.**

**Ans.** Superior and inferior vena cava enter the heart whereas aorta leaves the heart.

**18. List the location of each of the valves of the heart.**

**Ans.** The tricuspid valves are present between the right atrium and right ventricle. Bicuspid valves are present between left atrium and left ventricle.

The semilunar valves are present in the inner wall of aorta and pulmonary artery.

**19. Sinoatrial node is called the pacemaker of our heart. Why?** NCERT

**Ans.** Sinoatrial node is responsible for initiating and maintaining the rhythmic activity, therefore it is known as pacemaker of the heart.

**20. Veins are situated superficially under the skin. Why are these provided with valves along their length?**

**Ans.** Veins have valves to prevent the backflow of blood, ensuring that it flows towards the heart.

**21. Mention the stages of cardiac cycle.**

Ans. Stages of cardiac cycle are

Joint diastole → atrial systole → ventricular systole.

**22. What does the T-wave in a normal electrocardiogram indicate?**

Ans. It indicates the return of ventricles from excited to normal state (repolarisation).

**23. With the help of ECG, how can you determine the heartbeat of an individual?**

Ans. Heartbeat of an individual can be determined by counting the QRS complexes.

**24. Given below is the diagrammatic representation of a standard ECG. Label its different peaks.** **NCERT Exemplar**

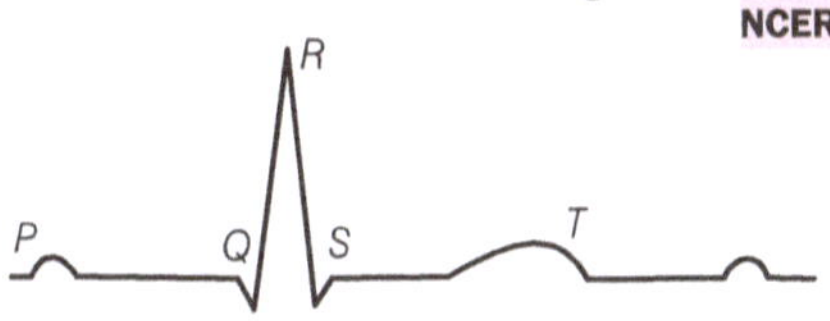


Ans.

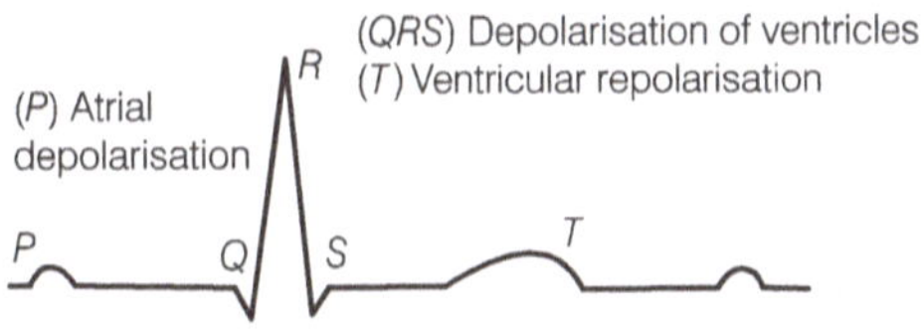


(1)

**25. Give the path of pulmonary circulation.**

Ans. The pulmonary circulation include circulation of blood from right ventricle to the left atria through the lungs. The pathway followed is

Right ventricle → Pulmonary artery → Lungs → Pulmonary vein → Left atria.

**26. Why do we call our heart myogenic?** **NCERT**

Ans. Refer to text on page no. 351.

**27. What factors are responsible for increasing the cardiac output?**

Ans. Hormones and autonomic innervations (sympathetic system), can increase cardiac output.

**28. What will happen to the cardiac activity if sympathetic nerves are stimulated?**

Ans. If the sympathetic nerves get stimulated, the heartbeat, strength of ventricular contraction and cardiac output increases.

**29. Hormones play an important role in the regulation of heartbeat. Comment.** **Competency Based Que.**

Ans. Hormones like adrenaline and nor-adrenaline, secreted by the medulla region of adrenal gland, play a significant role in regulating heart beat and thus, increasing cardiac output.

**30. Which coronary artery disease is caused due to narrowing of the lumen of arteries?** **NCERT Exemplar**

Ans. Atherosclerosis affects the vessels that supply blood to the heart muscle. It is caused by the deposits of calcium, fat, cholesterol and fibrous tissues, which makes the lumen of arteries narrower.

**31. Given below are the abnormal conditions related to blood circulation. Name the disorders.**

**(i) Acute chest pain due to failure of oxygen supply to heart muscles.**

**(ii) Increased systolic pressure.** **NCERT Exemplar**

Ans. (i) Angina

(ii) High blood pressure (½ + ½)

**32. Heart failure is called congestive heart failure. Why?**

Ans. The congestion of lungs is a symptom of heart failure. Thus, it is also called congestive heart failure.

## Short Answer Type Questions

**1. Why do we consider blood as a connective tissue?** **NCERT**

Ans. Blood is a mobile connective tissue derived from mesoderm. It consists of fibre-free fluid matrix, plasma and other cells. It is called so, as it regularly circulates in the body and takes part in transport of various materials like hormones, gases, etc.

**2. What is the importance of plasma proteins?** **NCERT**

Ans. Fibrinogen, globulins and albumins are the major plasma proteins. Fibrinogens (present in insoluble form) are needed for clotting or coagulation of blood. Globulins are primarily involved in defence mechanisms of the body and the albumins help in osmotic balance.

**3. Name the components of the formed elements in the blood and mention one major function of each of them.** **NCERT**

Ans. Refer to text on page no. 340-341.

**4. State the functions of the following in blood.**

**(i) Fibrinogen** **(ii) Globulin**

**(iii) Neutrophils** **(iv) Lymphocytes**

**NCERT Exemplar**

Ans. Functions of the following in blood are

(i) Fibrinogens are needed for clotting or coagulation of blood at the site of injury to stop bleeding.

(ii) Globulins are primarily involved in immunity, i.e. defence mechanisms of the body (to fight infections).

(iii) Neutrophils and monocytes are phagocytic cells which destroy foreign organisms entering the body.

(iv) Lymphocytes provide immunity to the body. (½ × 4)

**5. One of the ABO blood groups is sometimes called the universal donor. Which group do you think it is and why?**

Ans. Individuals with blood group O are called universal donors. These individuals do not have A and B antigens on the surface of their RBCs, but their blood serum contains antibodies against both A and B antigens. (1)

Therefore, a person with blood group 'O' can only receive blood from a group O individual, but they can donate blood to individuals of any blood group (i.e. A, B, O or AB). (1)

**6. An $Rh^-$ woman is carrying an $Rh^+$ foetus for the second time. Describe the consequences of $Rh^-$ incompatibility in this case?** Competency Based Que.

*Or*

**Why is it necessary to check the Rh factor of the blood in a pregnant woman?**

*Or*

**What physiological circumstances lead to erythroblastosis foetalis?** NCERT Exemplar

Ans. Rh-antigen is present on the surface of erythrocytes in about 80-85% of the human beings. The individuals, who possess this antigen are called $Rh^+$(Rh positive) and those, who do not have it are called $Rh^-$(Rh negative). A person when exposed to $Rh^+$ blood, develops anti Rh-antibodies.

A pregnant woman who is $Rh^-$, if bears an $Rh^+$ foetus, will develop anti-Rh-antibodies during the first delivery, when the foetal blood comes in contact with her blood. These antibodies remains in the blood for sufficiently longer periods.

If she carries a second foetus, that is $Rh^+$, the anti-Rh-antibodies in her blood enter the foetal circulation and cause damage to the foetal RBCs, which could become fatal. This condition is called erythroblastosis foetalis.

**7. Explain the chemical events that take place to form a blood clot to seal the wound.**

Ans. Chemical events that take place to form a blood clot are as follows

(i) When blood comes out of a blood vessel in case of injury the platelets clump together, break and release platelet factors, thrombokinase.

(ii) The enzyme thrombokinase initiates the conversion of prothrombin into thrombin.

(iii) Thrombin thus, catalyses the conversion of fibrinogen into fibrin which forms a mesh/network in which blood cells get entangled, leading to formation of scum at the site of injury. (1 × 3)

**8. Explain how the heart functions as a pump and keeps blood flowing only in one direction?**

Ans. Refer to text cardiac cycle on page no. 348-349.

**9. Why lymph is known as interstitial fluid?**

Ans. Refer to text on page no. 343.

**10. Describe the evolutionary change in the pattern of heart among the vertebrates.** NCERT

Ans. The evolutionary changes in heart structure among vertebrates reflect adaptations to different lifestyles and environments. Vertebrate hearts have evolved from the two-chambered heart of fish to a more complex three-chambered heart in amphibians and some reptiles, allowing for improved separation of oxygenated and deoxygenated blood. Birds and mammals have further advanced to a four-chambered heart, supporting higher metabolic rates and greater activity levels.

**11. Explain the advantage of the complete partition of ventricle among birds and mammals and hence, leading to double circulation.**

Ans. The birds and mammals have evolutionary advancement as far as structure of heart is concerned. They need more oxygen to live in terrestrial habitat.

In these animals, the blood received by left and right auricles is oxygenated and deoxygenated, respectively.

It passes towards the left and right ventricles and thus, no oxygenated and deoxygenated blood is mixed. The ventricles pump oxygenated and deoxygenated blood without mixing.

Thus, two separate circulatory pathways are found and this type of blood circulation is called double circulation, which includes systemic and pulmonary circulation.

**12. Differentiate between right ventricle and left ventricle.**

Ans. Differences between right ventricle and left ventricle are as follows

| Right Ventricle | Left Ventricle |
|---|---|
| Right ventricle is smaller than the left ventricle. | Left ventricle is comparatively larger than right ventricle. |
| Receives and pushes deoxygenated blood. | Receives and pumps oxygenated blood. |
| The wall of right ventricle is thinner than left ventricle. | The wall of it is thicker than right ventricle. |

(1 × 3)

**13. Answer the following**

**(i) Name the major site where RBCs are formed.**

**(ii) Which valve guard the opening between right atrium and right ventricle?**

(iii) **Which part of the heart is responsible for initiating and maintaining its rhythmic activity?**

Ans. (i) Bone marrow.
(ii) Tricuspid valve.
(iii) Sinoatrial node (SA node). (1 × 3)

**14. What is the significance of atrioventricular node and atrioventricular bundle in the functioning of heart?** **NCERT**

Ans. Refer to text on conducting system of heart on page 347.

**15. How can we say that artificial pacemaker is a life saving instrument?** **Competency Based Que.**

Ans. The artificial pacemaker is called a life-saving instrument because, it stimulates the heart electrically at regular intervals to maintain its beats. Thus, it replaces the SA node as the originator of the cardiac impulse. It is to be noted that some pacemakers stimulate the heart at a fixed rate, others sense when the natural heart rate falls below a predetermined value and then stimulates the heart.

**16. What is the significance of time gap in the passage of action potential from sinoatrial node to the ventricle?**

Ans. The time gap in the passage of action potential from sinoatrial node to the ventricles allows ventricles to relax. The ventricular pressure falls, causing the closure of semilunar valves, which prevent the backflow of blood into the ventricles.

**17. What happens to the mitral valve and the related blood flow during ventricular systole?**

Ans. At the start of the ventricular systole, the mitral valve closes to prevent the back flow of blood into the atrium. As systole continues, blood from the right ventricle enters the pulmonary artery and blood from the left ventricle enters the aorta.

**18. Define cardiac cycle and cardiac output.** **NCERT**

Ans. Refer to text on page no. 348 and 349.

**19. What are the two heart sounds heard through stethoscope? How is each of these produced?**

*Or* **What are two heart sounds? When and how are these sounds produced?**

*Or* **Explain heart sounds.** **NCERT**

Ans. The stethoscope is used to hear the two main heart sounds (i.e. lub and dup), which repeat rhythmically. These sounds result from the closure of the heart valves. The first sound (lub), is created by the closure of the atrio-ventricular valves immediately after the start of the ventricular systole.

The second heart sound (dupp) is created by the closure of the semilunar valve at the end of the ventricular systole.

**20. What is meant by P – Q interval and S-T interval in electrocardiography?**

Ans. In electrocardiography, *P-Q* interval (also called *PR* interval) is the time taken by the impulse to travel through atria, AV node and the rest of the conducting tissues, to ventricles. The *S-T* interval is the representation of time between the end of the spread of impulse through ventricles and its repolarisation.

**21. What is meant by double circulation? What is its significance?** **NCERT**

Ans. Refer to text on page no. 350 and 351.

The closed circulatory system ensures efficient and regulated blood flow allowing for better nutrient gas and waste exchange while maintaining higher pressure.

**22. Schematically represent double circulation.**

Ans. Flowchart of double circulation is as follows

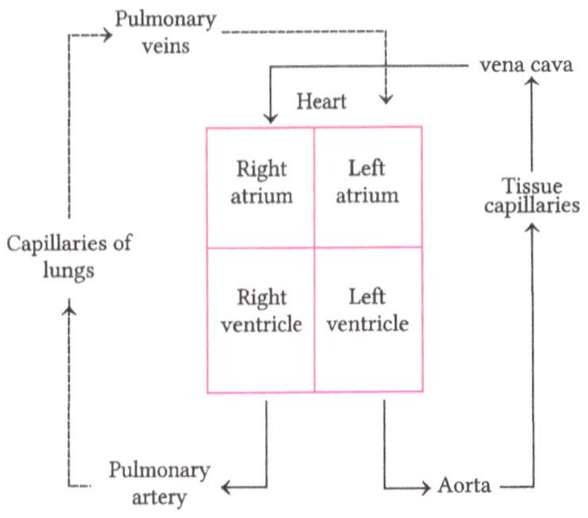


**23. Differentiate between pulmonary and systemic circulation.**

Ans. Refer to text on page no. 350-351.

**24. Describe coronary circulation.**

Ans. Refer to text on page no. 351.

**25. Define portal system. Explain the function of hepatic portal veins in the digestive system.**

Ans. Refer to text on page no. 351.

**26. What is the significance of hepatic portal system in the circulatory system?** **NCERT Exemplar**

Ans. A unique vascular connection exists between the digestive tract and liver called hepatic portal system. The hepatic portal vein carries blood from intestine to the liver before it is delivered to the systemic circulation.

This ensures that the liver, which has the metabolic versatility to interconvert various organic molecules has first access to nutrients after the food is digested.

**27. How is the flow of blood to the organs regulated?**

Ans. Refer to text neural and hormonal regulation on page no. 351.

**28.** (i) To which tissue, does the coronary arteries carry blood in human body?

(ii) Apart from adrenaline and nor-adrenaline, which other hormones are involved in regulation of cardiac activity?

**Ans.** (i) Refer to text on page no. 351.

(ii) Refer to text on regulation of cardiac activity on page no. 351. (2 × 1)

## Long Answer Type Questions

**1.** Explain different types of blood groups and donor compatibility making a table. **NCERT Exemplar**

**Ans.** Refer to text on page no. 341-342.

**2.** Thrombocytes are essential for coagulation of blood. Comment. **NCERT Exemplar**

**Ans.** Refer to text on page no. 341.

**3.** Explain the process of blood clotting in detail.

**Ans.** Refer to text formation of clot on page no. 342-343.

**4.** Describe briefly the external structure of human heart with neat and labelled diagram.

**Ans.** Refer to text on page no. 345. Refer to the fig no. 15.2.

**5.** Give details of human heart covering internal structure, from conducting system and working of nodal tissue.

**Ans.** Refer to text on page no. 345 and 347.

**6.** With reference to human heart, answer the following:

(i) What are SA and AV nodes? Where they located?

(ii) How heart sounds are produced? Name the two heart sounds? **Competency Based Que.**

**Ans.** (i) A specialised cardiac musculature called nodal tissue, distributed in the heart. These nodal tissues include SA (sinoatrial) and AV (atrio-ventricular) nodes.

A patch of tissue is called SA node, which is nodel tissues located in the right upper corner of the right atrium.

Another mass of nodal tissue located in the lower left corner of the right atrium close to the atrioventricular septum called AV node (Atrioventricular node). (3)

(ii) **Heart sounds**

First heart sound (lub) is associated with the closure of the tricuspid and bicuspid valves.

Whereas the second heart sound (dup) is associated with the closure of semilunar valves. (2)

**7.** Explain how the difference in the pressure of the blood in the pulmonary artery and in the aorta is related to

(i) the structure of the ventricles and

(ii) where the blood is going?

**Ans.** The left ventricle, which pumps blood into the aorta, has a thicker, more muscular wall compared to the right ventricle. This is because the left ventricle needs to generate higher pressure to pump blood through the entire systemic circulation, which delivers oxygen and nutrients to all parts of the body. In contrast, the right ventricle, which pumps blood into the pulmonary artery, has a thinner wall, as it only needs to pump blood to the lungs a much shorter distance that requires lower pressure.

Blood in the aorta is pumped to the entire body (systemic circulation), which requires high pressure to ensure oxygen and nutrients are effectively delivered to tissues and organs. In contrast, blood in the pulmonary artery is pumped to the lungs (pulmonary circulation) for gas exchange. This process requires lower pressure to prevent damage to the delicate capillaries in the lungs and to facilitate the efficient exchange of oxygen and carbon dioxide.

**8.** (i) What is cardiac output and how it is calculated?

(ii) Why is the left ventricular wall thicker than the right ventricular wall in the human heart?

(iii) Explain cardiac cycle in brief.

**Ans.** (i) Refer to text on page no. 349. (1)

(ii) This is because the left ventricle is required to pump oxygenated blood all over the body, while the right ventricle needs to pump deoxygenated blood to the nearby lungs only. (1)

(iii) Refer to text on page no. 348-349. (3)

**9.** Write the differences between:

(i) Blood and lymph

(ii) Open and closed circulatory system

(iii) Systole and diastole

(iv) P-wave and T-wave **NCERT**

**Ans.** (i) Refer to the text on page no. 344. (1)

(ii) Refer to the text on page no. 344. (1)

(iii) The differences between systole and diastole are as follows

| Systole | Diastole |
|---|---|
| It represent the phase of contraction in cardiac cycle. | It represent the phase of relaxation in cardiac cycle. |
| During systole, blood pressure is increased inside the heart. | During relaxation, blood pressure is decreased inside the heart. |

(½ × 2)

(iv) Difference between P-wave and T-wave is as follows

| P-wave | T-wave |
|---|---|
| This wave represents the electrical excitation (or depolarisation) of the atria, which leads to the contraction of both the atria. | This wave represents the return of the ventricles from excited to normal state (repolarisation). The end of the T-wave marks the end of systole. |

(1)

**10. Draw a standard ECG and explain the different waves in it.** **NCERT**

Ans. Refer to text on page no. 349 and 350.

**11. Describe in detail the neural and hormonal regulation of heart functioning.**

Ans. Refer to text on page no. 351.

**12. Briefly describe the followings (any two).**

**(i) Angina pectoris**

**(ii) Atherosclerosis**

**(iii) Hypertension**

**(iv) Heart failure** **NCERT Exemplar**

Ans. Refer to text on page no. 352.

## Source Based/Case Based/Passage Based Questions

**1. Given below is a graphical representation of the two processes, which constitute the double circulation. Consider the graph and answer the following questions.**

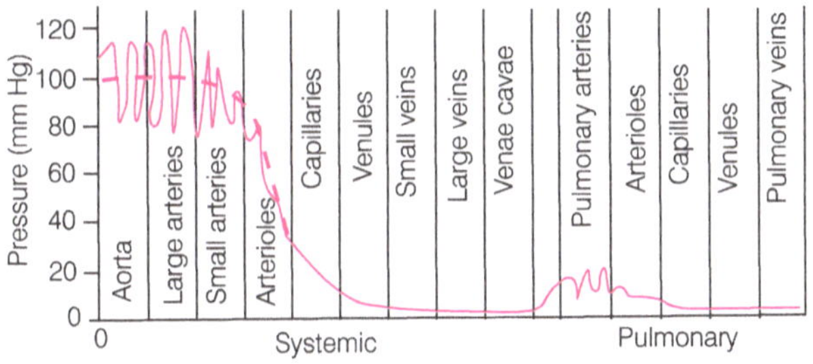


**(i) On the basis of the blood pressure pattern in the above graph, what conclusion can you draw about the pressure difference in systemic and pulmonary circulation?**

**(ii) What will happen to the double circulation, if valves are absent in the circulatory system?**

**(iii) Why aorta has the highest blood pressure ? What will happen if its pressure increases?**

***Or***

**(iii) How does the lumen of arteries turn out to be narrower than normal?** **Competency Based Que.**

Ans. (i) Pressure difference is usually observed when both pulmonary and systemic circulation are taken into consideration. This is because blood has to be transported initially *via* aorta (with highest pressure). As the aorta branches off, pressure inside the vessels tend to decrease (until vena cava).

Similarly, pressure is highest in pulmonary artery as it carries blood from heart (right ventricle) to the lungs. This pressure decreases subsequently and is least in pulmonary vein. (2)

(ii) Valves present in the heart permits the unidirectional flow of blood from atria to ventricles and then to aorta. These valves keep a check on the backflow of blood. Thus, if they are absent, a proper circulation of blood will be disturbed. (1)

(iii) Blood pressure is the highest in arteries like aorta since, they are directly connected to the ventricles. An increasing blood pressure in the aorta would definitely result in an increased risk of hypertension. (1)

*Or*

(iii) Lumen of arteries becomes narrower than normal due to the deposition of calcium, fat, cholesterol and fibrous tissue. (1)

**2. The graph below shows the events occurring in a cardiac cycle. Observe the graph carefully and answer the questions that follows.** **Competency Based Que.**

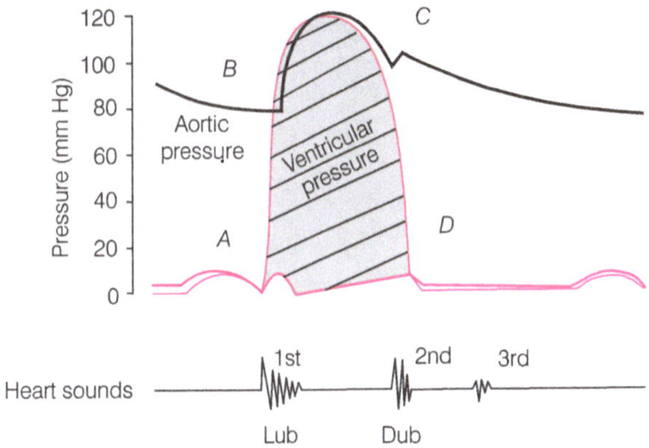


**(i) Give the labelling of *A*, *B*, *C* and *D* with respect to the opening and closure of the valve.**

(ii) **Comment upon the event occurring in the shaded area of the above graph.**

(iii) **What will happen if the valve *A* and *B* get damaged?**

*Or*

(iii) **The beating of heart produces sounds that are heard by phonocardiogram. According to you in the above graph at which points the 1st and 2nd sound will be produced ?**

Ans. (i) *A*- AV valve close. *B*- Semilunar valve open. *C*- Semilunar valve close. *D*- AV valve open. (2)

(ii) Shaded area in the above given graph represent ventricular contraction. (1)

(iii) The main function of valves in the overall circulatory process is to prevent the backflow of blood.
Thus, in case bi or tricuspid and semilunar valves (*A* and *B* respectively) get damaged, it will leads to a condition of backflow of blood into the left or right atrium as well as to the right ventricle. (1)

*Or*

(iii) First heart sound (lubb) is produced on the closure of AV valve (at the starting of ventricular systole) (*A*).
Second heart sound (dupp) is produced when semilunar valves get closed (*C*). (1)

**3.** **Emily Johnson, a 28-year-old pregnant woman, is in her third trimester and has blood type A. During a routine check-up, it's discovered that she has developed Rh incompatibility.**

**The healthcare team discusses the implications of her blood type and the potential need for a blood transfusion during delivery.**

(i) **How does Rh incompatibility affect Emily?**

(ii) **If a blood transfusion were necessary, which blood types would be considered safe for Emily?**

(iii) **How might blood type affect the baby during pregnancy and delivery?**

*Or*

(iii) **What significance does being Rh-negative hold in the context of blood transfusions?**

Ans. (i) Rh incompatibility can lead to the mother's immune system producing antibodies against Rh-positive blood cells, which may harm the baby if he or she inherits the Rh-positive factor, potentially causing haemolytic disease of the newborn. (2)

(ii) A- individuals can safely receive A- and O- blood types. (1)

(iii) If the baby is Rh-positive, maternal antibodies could attack the baby's blood cells, leading to complications like anaemia, jaundice or other serious health issues. (1)

*Or*

(iii) Being Rh-negative means that caution is required when receiving blood. Rh-negative individuals should avoid Rh-positive blood to prevent an immune response. (1)

# SELF ASSESSMENT TEST

## Multiple Choice Questions

1. Identify the correct match pair.
   (a) Neutrophils -65-70%
   (b) Lymphocytes-10-15%
   (c) Basophils-0.5-1%
   (d) Eosinophils -5-7%

2. An individual with AB blood group cannot donate blood to patients with B blood group. Which of the following statements correctly justifies this?
   (a) AB blood type contains A and B antigens, which can trigger an immune response in B blood type recipients.
   (b) B blood type lacks antigens, making it compatible with all blood types
   (c) AB blood type contains only A antigen, which is universally accepted by all blood types
   (d) B blood type can receive blood from any donor, including AB

3. What can occur if an Rh-negative ($Rh^-$) person is exposed to Rh-positive ($Rh^+$) blood?
   (a) The $Rh^-$ person will have no reaction as they can accept any blood type
   (b) The $Rh^-$ person may develop antibodies against the Rh factor, potentially leading to haemolytic reactions
   (c) The $Rh^-$ person will produce more red blood cells to compensate for the exposure
   (d) The $Rh^-$ person's blood will immediatedly become $Rh^+$ after exposure to $Rh^+$ blood

4. Which of the following best describes the role of thrombokinase in the coagulation cascade?
   (a) It converts fibrin to fibnrinogen to regulate clot size
   (b) It triggers the release of calcium ions necessary for clotting
   (c) It activates prothrombin leading to thrombin formation
   (d) It directly forms the fibrin mesh that stabilises clots

5. Which of the following statements correctly describes both Atrioventricular (AV) valves and the interventricular septum?
   (a) The AV valves prevent backflow of blood, while the interventricular septum separates the right and left atria.
   (b) The AV valves are responsible for blood flow regulation, while the interventricular septum anchors the heart valves.
   (c) The AV valves prevent backflow of blood, while the interventricular septum separates the right and left ventricles
   (d) Both the AV valves and the interventricular septum are made of muscular tissue

6. With human heart, the AV node is located at
   (a) lower left corner of right atrium
   (b) upper right corner of right ventricle
   (c) lower left corner of left ventricle
   (d) upper right corner of left ventricle

7. Identify *A*, *B*, *C* and *D* in the given diagram of human heart.

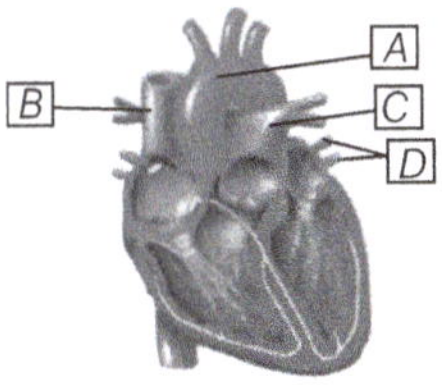


   (a) Aorta, vena cava, pulmonary artery and pulmonary vein respectively
   (b) Pulmonary artery, pulmonary vein, aorta and vena cava respectively
   (c) Pulmonary vein, aorta, vena cava and pulmonary artery respectively
   (d) Vena cava, pulmonary vein, pulmonary artery and aorta respectively

8. Which of the following correctly describes the sequence of blood flow through the heart during one complete cardiac cycle?
   (a) Right atrium → Right ventricle → Lungs → Left atrium → Left ventricle
   (b) Left atrium → Left ventricle → Aorta → Body → Right atrium
   (c) Right atrium → Right ventricle → Lungs → Left atrium → Aorta
   (d) Left ventricle → Aorta → Body → Right ventricle → Right atrium

## Assertion Reason Questions

**Direction** (Q. Nos. 9-11) *In each of the following questions, a statement of Assertion (A) is given followed by corresponding statement of Reason (R). Of the statements, mark the correct answer.*

(a) Both A and R are true and R is the correct explanation of A.
(b) Both A and R are true, but R is not the correct explanation of A.
(c) A is true, but R is false.
(d) A is false, but R is true.

9. **Assertion** (A) Rh incompatibility can cause haemolytic disease of the newborn (HDN).
**Reason** (R) If a Rh-negative mother is carrying a Rh-positive baby, her immune system may attack the baby's red blood cells, leading to HDN.
10. **Assertion** (A) Left atrium possess thickest muscles in all four chambers of the heart.
**Reason** (R) Left atrium receives blood from the lungs.
11. **Assertion** (A) Malfunctioning of SA node can result in disturbance of heart rate.
**Reason** (R) The SA node is responsible for generating electrical impulses that initiate the heartbeat and regulate the heart's rhythm.

## Very Short Answer Type Questions

12. Name the vascular connection that exists between the digestive tract and liver. **NCERT Exemplar**
13. Describe the composition of lymph.
14. Explain the consequences of a situation in which blood does not coagulate. **NCERT Exemplar**
15. What does T-wave in a normal electrocardiogram indicate?

## Short Answer Type Questions

16. Differentiate between cardiac arrest, heart attack and heart failure.
17. Mention functions of blood.
18. Write a short note on- (i) Heart valves (ii) Cardiac output

## Long Answer Type Questions

19. Neena is having blood group A-ve while her husbands blood group is O + ve. Their first child is having blood group A + ve. Her second child was born with severe anaemia and jaundice. What could be the reason? How this situation could have been avoided?
20. Explain different types of blood group and donor compatibility by making a table. **NCERT Exemplar**
21. Explain the concept of double circulation in mammals and its significance in maintaining efficient oxygen supply to the body. **NCERT Exemplar**

## Case Based Question

22. 17-year-old boy comes to the clinic for a physical examination. During the ECG a doctor notices a prolonged QRS complex of 0.12 seconds. The patient reports no symptoms but mentions occasional fatigue during intense workouts. He is otherwise healthy and has no significant medical history.
(i) What does the abnormal QRS complex indicate?
(ii) How might the abnormal QRS complex affect cardiac output?
(iii) Does the condition mentioned above can affect the conduction of blood throughout the body?
(iv) How does impaired ventricular contraction affect overall blood pressure?

## Answers

1. (c) 2. (a) 3. (b) 4. (c) 5. (c) 6. (a) 7. (a) 8. (a) 9. (a) 10. (d) 11. (a)

# 16
CHAPTER

# Excretory Products and their Elimination

Excretion is the process of elimination of **nitrogenous waste** products and other metabolites from the body of animals to regulate the composition of the body fluids and tissues.
**Ammonia**, **urea** and **uric acid** are the major forms of nitrogenous wastes excreted by different animals. These are eliminated by different organisms based on the availability of water.

### YOUR STUDY GOALS



### YOUR PRACTICE GOAL

- Objective Type Questions
  (48 Qs ; MCQs, A-R)
  Case Based Questions (4)
- Subjective Type Questions
- (23 VSAs, 28 SAs, 8 LAs)

In this chapter, we will learn about the mechanism of elimination of the nitrogenous substances in different animals as well as a detailed explanation of the human excretory system.

## 16.1 Forms of Nitrogen Excretion

Depending upon the nature of the excretory product, animals exhibit different processes of nitrogenous excretion. These are described as follows

### 1. Ammonotelism

- Ammonia is the most toxic form of nitrogenous waste. It requires a large amount of water for its elimination.
- The organisms that excrete ammonia are called **ammonotelic** and the process of eliminating ammonia is known as **ammonotelism**.
- Examples of ammonotelic animals are **bony fishes**, **aquatic amphibians** and **aquatic insects**.
- Ammonia, as it is readily soluble in water, is generally excreted by diffusion across body surfaces or through **gill surfaces** (in fish) as ammonium ions. So, ammonotelism is found in aquatic animals.

- Terrestrial adaptation necessitated the production of lesser toxic nitrogenous wastes like urea and uric acid for the conservation of water.

## 2. Ureotelism

- The process of excreting urea is called **ureotelism** and the animals that excrete urea are called **ureotelic**.
- Urea is less toxic and thus requires less water for excretion.
- Examples of ureotelic animals are **mammals, many terrestrial amphibians** and **marine fishes**.
- In these animals, ammonia produced by metabolism is converted into urea (in the liver) and released into the blood, which is filtered and excreted out as urine by the kidney.
- Some amount of urea may be retained in the kidney matrix of some of these animals to maintain a desired **osmolarity**.

## 3. Uricotelism

- The process of excreting uric acid is called **uricotelism** and the animals that excrete uric acid are called **uricotelic**.
- Uric acid, being the least toxic nitrogenous waste can be removed with a minimum loss of water from the animal body. Thus, it is excreted in the form of a pellet or paste (i.e. semisolid form).
- Normally, the animals that live in the desert exhibit uricotelism. Examples of uricotelic animals are **reptiles, birds, land snails** and **insects**.

## Excretory Organs

- Different animal groups have a variety of excretory structures (organs) to perform the process of excretion.
- In most of the invertebrates, these structures are simple tubular form, whereas vertebrates have complex structured organs called **kidneys**.

Some of these structures are mentioned below in the given table

| Excretory Organs | Examples |
|---|---|
| **Protonephridia or flame cells** (primarily concerned with osmoregulation, i.e. ionic and fluid volume regulation). | Platyhelminthes (flatworms, e.g. *Planaria*), rotifers, cephalochordates (e.g. *Amphioxus*) and some annelids. |
| **Nephridia** (tubular excretory structures which remove nitrogenous waste and maintains a fluid and ionic balance) | Earthworm and other annelids. |
| **Malpighian tubules** (helps in removal of nitrogenous waste and osmoregulation) | Insects, e.g. cockroach. |
| **Antennal or green glands** (eliminate ammonium waste from the body) | Crustaceans, e.g. prawns. |

### Quick Test 1

1. Ammonotelism is primarily seen in which group of organisms?
2. In which form does the ammonia is diffused through the gill surface of fish?
3. The excretion of urea in humans suggests a high degree of water conservation. Name the excretory process?
4. In earthworms, excretion and osmoregulation occur through a specialised tube-like structures. Name it.
5. **State True or False.**
   (a) Terrestrial molluscs excrete a paste-like substance to minimise water loss.
   (b) The green glands in molluscs perform functions other than excretion and osmoregulation.

# 16.2 Human Excretory System

The human excretory system consists of a pair of kidneys, a pair of ureters, a urinary bladder and a urethra. These structures are described below in detail

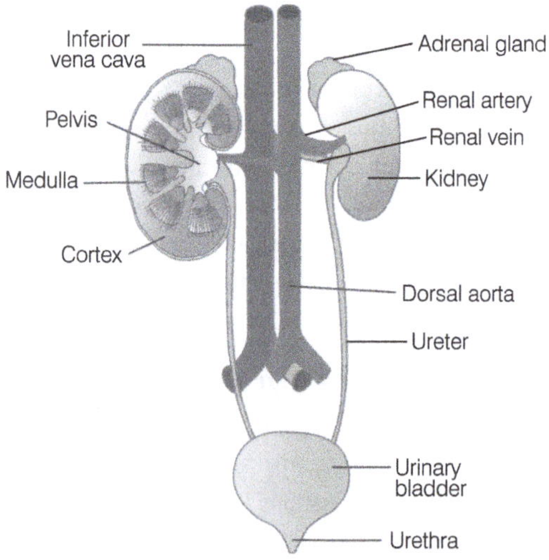


Fig. 16.1 Human excretory system

## 1. Kidneys

- These are reddish brown, bean-shaped structures situated between the levels of **last thoracic** and **third lumbar vertebra**.
- These are situated close to the dorsal inner wall of the abdominal cavity.
- Each kidney of an adult human measures, 10-12 cm in length, 5-7 cm in width and 2-3 cm in thickness with an average weight of 120-170 gm.
- Kidneys are **mesodermal in origin**.

## Structure of Kidney

The structure of the kidney can be studied well under two headings, i.e. external as well as internal structures. These are described below as

### External Structure

- The outer surface of each kidney is convex.
- Towards the center of the inner concave surface of the kidney is a notch called the **hilum**.
- The supply of blood occurs through the hilum, i.e. renal artery and renal vein, pass in and out of the kidneys along with the ureter and the nerve supply of the kidney.
- The outer layer of kidney is tough capsule.

### Internal Structure

- The LS of a mammalian kidney shows an **outer cortex** and **inner medulla**.
- Inner to the hilum, is a broad a funnel-shaped cavity called **renal pelvis**.
- The free end of pelvis has number of cup-like cavities, called **calyces** (sing. calyx).
- The medulla projects into conical processes, called **renal pyramids** or **medullary pyramids**. The tips of pyramids are called **renal papillae**.
- The cortex spreads in between medullary pyramids as renal columns called **columns of Bertini**.
- Each kidney is composed of numerous (nearly one million) complex tubular structures called **nephrons**. These are the functional units of the kidney.

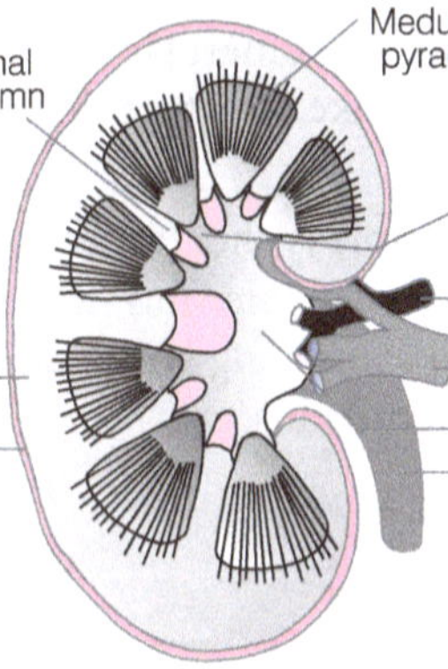


Fig. 16.2 Longitudinal section of kidney

## Functions of Kidney

The following functions are served by the kidney

- Regulation of arterial pressure.
- Excretion of metabolic waste and foreign chemicals.
- Secretion of hormones like renin.
- Regulation of water and electrolyte balance.

> **Osmoregulation**
>
> Osmoregulation is the process by which organisms control the balance of water and solutes in their bodies to maintain proper cellular function. For example, freshwater animals excrete excess water, while marine animals manage salt levels by drinking seawater and excreting excess salts. Terrestrial animals conserve water through concentrated urine and behavioural adaptations, enabling survival in varying environments.

## Structure of Nephron or Uriniferous Tubule

Each nephron consists of two parts, i.e. the **Malpighian body** or **renal corpuscle** and the **renal tubule**.

### I. Malpighian Body or Renal Corpuscle

- **Glomerulus** along with **Bowman's capsule** is called the Malpighian body or renal corpuscle which filtres out large solutes from the blood and delivers small solutes to the renal tubule
- Glomerulus is a tuft of thin-walled capillaries formed by the branching of afferent arteriole (a fine branch of renal artery).

- **Bowman's Capsule** (Glomerular capsule) is a double-walled, cup-like structure that surrounds the glomerulus.
- The **afferent arteriole** is short and wide vessel that supplies blood to the glomerulus, while the **efferent arteriole** is narrow and long vessel carrying blood away from the glomerulus.

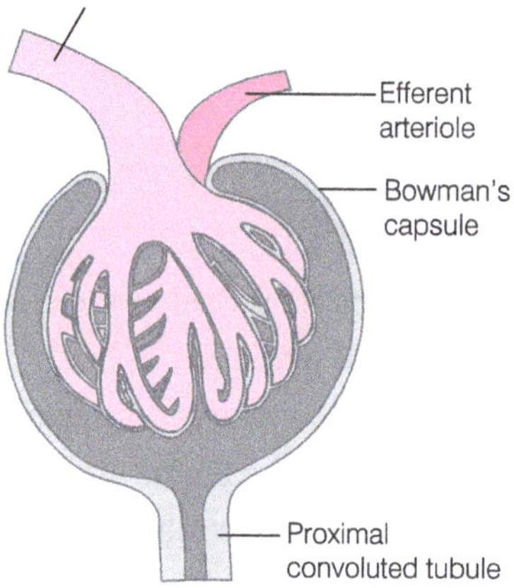


Fig. 16.3 Malpighian body (renal corpuscle)

**Differences between Afferent Arteriole and Efferent Arteriole**

| Afferent Arteriole | Efferent Arteriole |
|---|---|
| These are the fine branches of renal artery which arise from dorsal aorta and enter in each kidney | These are the fine branches of renal vein which leave the kidney and joins with inferior vena cava. |
| They bring arterial blood to the renal corpuscles. | They carry venous blood away from the renal corpuscles. |
| The blood flowing in it is rich in waste products. | The blood flowing in it is poor in waste products. |

## II. Renal Tubules

- The lumen of Bowman's capsule is continuous with the narrow lumen of the renal tubule. It is a long, thin tubule with three distinct regions.
- These regions are described as follows
  - **Proximal Convoluted Tubule** (PCT) Highly coiled region immediately after Bowman's capsule. It is restricted to the cortical region of the kidney.
  - **Henle's Loop** U-shaped (or hair pin-shaped) structure having a descending limb that extends into the medulla and an ascending limb that extends back from the medulla into the cortex.

**Differences between Descending Limb and Ascending Limb of Henle's Loop**

| Descending Limb | Ascending Limb |
|---|---|
| It is very thin. | It is thick. |
| Direction of fluid flow is downward. | Direction of fluid flow is upward. |
| Permeable to water. | Impermeable to water. |

**TEACHER'S TIP**

The primary function of Henle's loop is to conserve water; in animals with longer loops, greater water reabsorption occurs, resulting in the production of more concentrated urine.

  - **Distal Convoluted Tubule** (DCT) Thicker and highly coiled structure situated after the Henle's loop. It is also situated in the cortex like the proximal tubule.
  - **Collecting Duct** Straight tube that extends from DCT and opens into the renal pelvis through medullary pyramids in the calyces.

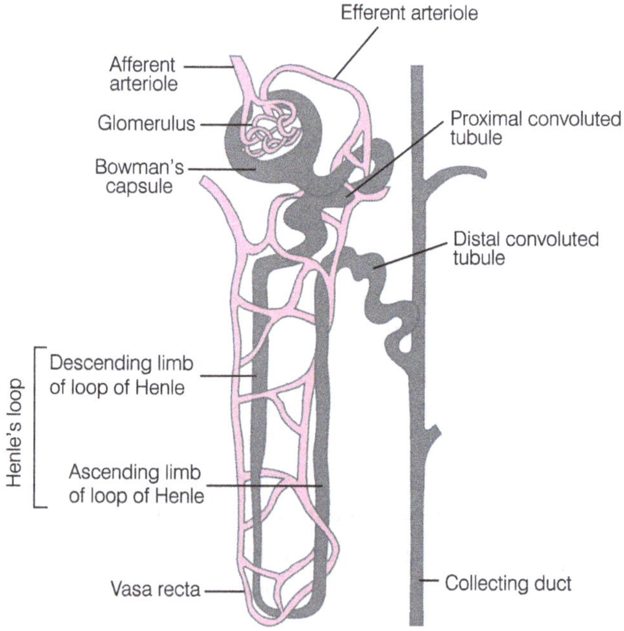


Fig. 16.4 A diagrammatic representation of a nephron showing blood vessels, duct and tubule

- The efferent arteriole emerging from glomerulus divides to form a network of peritubular capillaries around the proximal and distal convoluted tubules of the nephrons.
- From the peritubular capillary network arise the capillaries of the **vasa recta**, which extend parallel to the loops of Henle and the collecting ducts in the medulla.

## Types of Nephrons

Based on the location in the kidney, nephrons are of the following two types

### I. Cortical Nephrons

- In the majority of nephrons, the loop of Henle is too short and extends only very little into the medulla, i.e. lying in the renal cortex. Such nephrons are called **cortical nephrons**.
- **Vasa recta** is absent or highly reduced in cortical nephrons.

### II. Juxtamedullary Nephrons

In some of the nephrons, the loop of Henle is very long and runs deep into the medulla. These nephrons are called juxta medullary nephrons.

## 2. Ureters

- The pelvis of each kidney is continues as a ureter and emerges out at the hilum.
- It is a long and muscular tube.
- The ureters of both sides extend posteriorly and open into the urinary bladder.

## 3. Urinary Bladder

- It is a thin-walled, pear-shaped, muscular sac present in the pelvic cavity.
- The urinary bladder temporarily stores the **urine**.

## 4. Urethra

- It is a membranous tube, which conducts urine to the exterior of the body.
- The **urethral sphincters** keep the urethra closed except during voiding of urine.

### Quick Test 2

1. Identify the structure in the kidney through which the ureter, blood vessels, and nerves enter or exit.
2. *X* is the structure that supplies blood to the glomerulus. Identify *X*.
3. Structure *X* functions as the basic functional unit of the kidney. Identify *X*.
4. **State True or False.**
   (a) The medulla projects into the calyces as conical processes, called renal papillae.
   (b) The LS of a mammalian kidney shows an outer medulla and inner coretx.
5. The pelvis of each kidney is continued as a long and muscular tube like structure. Identify the structure.

# 16.3 Urine Formation

- The formation of urine is the result of processes like glomerular filtration, reabsorption and secretion.
- These processes occur in different parts of nephrons.
- Details of these processes are as follows

## 1. Glomerular Filtration

- The first step of urine formation is the filtration of blood.
- It is carried out by the glomerulus. Hence, this step is called **glomerular filtration**.
- On an average, the kidneys filtre about 1100-1200 mL of blood per minute, which constitutes roughly 1/5th of the blood pumped out by each ventricle of the heart in a minute.
- The glomerular capillary blood pressure causes filtration of blood through three layers, i.e.
  - The **endothelium** of glomerular blood vessels.
  - The **epithelium** of Bowman's capsule.
  - A **basement membrane** (present between the above-mentioned two layers).
- The epithelial cells of Bowman's capsule called **podocytes**, are arranged in such an intricate manner so that some minute spaces called **filtration slits** or **slit pores** are present between them.
- Blood is filtered so finely through these membranes, that almost all the constituents of the plasma except the proteins pass onto the lumen of Bowman's capsule.

- Therefore, it is considered as the process of ultra-filtration and the filtrate is called **glomerular filtrate**.
- The amount of the filtrate formed by the kidneys per minute is called **Glomerular Filtration Rate** (GFR).
- In a healthy person it was found approximately 125 mL /min, i.e. **180 L/day**.
- GFR is regulated by one of the efficient mechanisms carried out by **Juxta Glomerular Apparatus** (JGA).
- JGA is a special sensitive region formed by cellular modifications in the distal convoluted tubule and the afferent arteriole at the location of their contact.
- A fall in GFR can activate the JG cells to release renin, which can stimulate the glomerular blood flow and thereby, the GFR back to normal.

## 2. Selective Reabsorption

- This is the second step in the formation of urine.
- The urine released is 1.5 L as compared to the volume of the filtrate formed per day (180 L). This suggests that as much as 99% of the material in the filtrate is reabsorbed by the renal tubules. Thus, this process is called **reabsorption**.
- Depending upon the types of molecules being reabsorbed, in different segments of nephron occur either by passive transport or active transport.
- These are described as follows
  - Water and urea are reabsorbed by passive transport (i.e. water is reabsorbed by osmosis and urea by simple diffusion).
  - Glucose, amino acids and $Na^+$ are reabsorbed by active transport.

## 3. Tubular Secretion

- It is also an important step in urine formation.
- Certain chemicals in the blood that are not removed by filtration from the glomerular capillaries are removed by the process of tubular secretion.
- It helps in the maintenance of ionic and acid-base balance of body fluids by removing substances like foreign bodies, ions ($K^+$, $H^+$, $NH_4^+$) and molecules (medicines), etc., that are toxic at elevated levels.

**Differences between Tubular Reabsorption and Tubular Secretion**

| Tubular Reabsorption | Tubular Secretion |
|---|---|
| It involves the absorption of water and useful solutes from the glomerular filtrate into the blood. | It refers to the moving of waste materials from blood into the filtrate or nephrons. |

# 16.4 Functions of the Tubules

When the glomerular filtrate/primary urine passes through renal tubule, water and different molecules get reabsorb at various places. These are given below in the following manner

## 1. Proximal Convoluted Tubule (PCT)

- The epithelial cells of the PCT have numerous **microvilli** (simple cuboidal brush-border epithelium) which increase the surface area available for reabsorption.
- The process of reabsorption mostly takes place within PCT (i.e. nearly all of the essential nutrients, 70-80% of electrolytes and water).
- PCT also helps in the absorption of $HCO_3^-$ from the filtrate.
- Selective secretion of hydrogen ions and ammonia takes place here to maintain the pH and ionic balance of the body fluids. The filtrate is considered isotonic to blood plasma.

## 2. Henle's Loop

- Reabsorption in ascending limb Henle's loop is minimum; besides this, it plays an important role in maintaining the high osmolarity of medullary interstitial fluid.
- Two portions of Henle's loop, play different role in osmoregulation. These are as follows
  - **Descending Limb of Loop of Henle** Water is reabsorbed here due to increasing osmolarity of interstitial fluid, while sodium and other electrolytes are not reabsorbed. This concentrates the filtrate as it moves down.

- **Ascending Limb of Loop of Henle** This segment is impermeable to water, but permeable to $K^+$, $Cl^-$ and $Na^+$. Thus, in the ascending limb of the loop of Henle $Na^+$, $K^+$, $Mg^{2+}$ and $Cl^-$ are reabsorbed. Therefore, as the concentrated filtrate pass upward, it gets diluted due to the passing out of electrolytes to the medullary fluid of kidney.

## 3. Distal Convoluted Tubule (DCT)

- Conditional reabsorption of sodium ions and water from the filtrate takes place in this segment.
- $HCO_3^-$ is also reabsorbed here, with associated secretion of potassium ($K^+$), hydrogen ($H^+$) ions and $NH_3$, which is necessary to maintain the pH and sodium-potassium balance in blood.

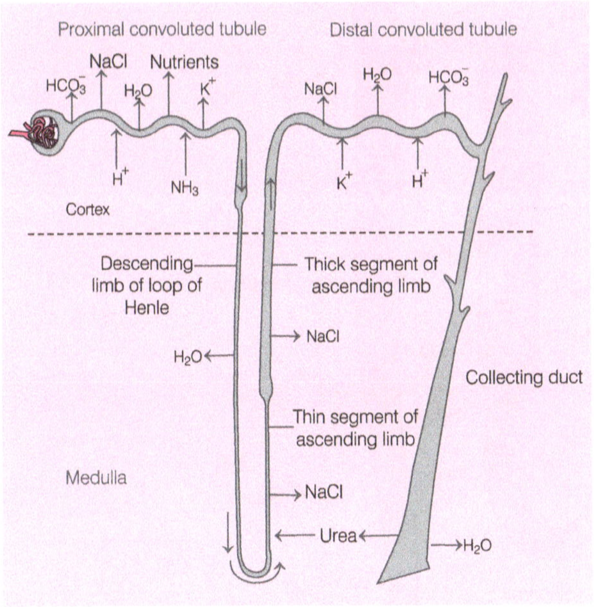


Fig. 16.5 Reabsorption and secretion of major substances at different parts of the nephron (Arrows indicate the direction of movement of materials)

## 4. Collecting Duct

- This duct extends from the cortex of the kidney to the inner parts of the medulla and is highly permeable to water.
- Thus, a considerable amount of water is reabsorbed here to produce concentrated filtrate.
- This segment allows passage of small amounts of urea into the medullary interstitial tissue to maintain the osmolarity.
- It also plays an important role in the maintenance of pH and ionic balance of the blood by the selective secretion of $H^+$ and $K^+$ ions.
- Therefore, the filtrate produced now is called urine.

### Quick Test 3

1. Name the structure in the nephron where filtration of blood takes place.
2. Identify the structure of the nephron which is responsible for reabsorbing water and solutes back into the blood.
3. **State True or False.**
   (a) The amount of the filtrate formed by the kidneys per minute is called glomerular filtration rate.
   (b) In a healthy person GFR is found approximately 125 litre per day.
4. Give the name of the layers through which the glomerular capillary blood pressure causes filtration?
5. The process by which excess substances are added to the filtrate from the blood is known as?

## 16.5 Counter-Current Mechanism

The counter-current mechanism is a physiological process where fluids flow in opposite directions to maximise exchange efficiency, such as in the gills of fish or the nephron in kidneys.

The mechanism of counter-current is as follows

- Henle's loop and vasa recta (capillary loop) play an important role in this mechanism.
- The flow of filtrate in the limbs of Henle's loop is in opposite direction and thus forms a counter-current.
- The flow of blood within the two limbs of vasa recta also occur in the counter-current pattern.
- The proximity between the Henle's loop and vasa recta, as well as the counter-current in them help in maintaining an increasing osmolarity towards the **inner medullary interstitium,** i.e. from 300 $mOsmolL^{-1}$ in the cortex to about 1200 $mOsmolL^{-1}$ in the inner medulla.

- This gradient is mainly caused by the movements of NaCl and urea.
- NaCl is transported by the ascending limb of Henle's loop which is exchanged with the descending limb of vasa recta.
- NaCl is returned to the interstitium by the ascending portion of vasa recta. Similarly, small amounts of urea enter the thin segment of the ascending limb of Henle's loop which is transported back to the interstitium by the collecting tubule.
- This transport of substances facilitated by the special arrangement of Henle's loop and vasa recta is called the **counter-current mechanism**. It helps to maintain a concentration gradient in the medullary interstitium.
- The presence of such interstitial gradient helps in an easy passage of water from the collecting tubule thereby concentrating the filtrate (urine).
- The human kidneys can produce urine nearly four times concentrated than the initial filtrate formed.

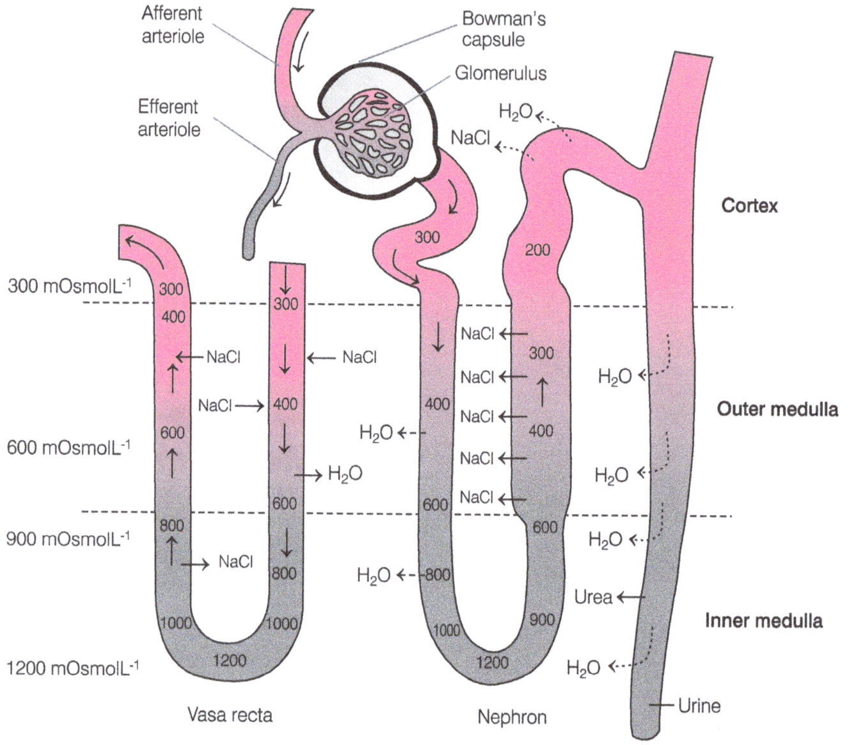


Fig. 16.6 Diagrammatic representation of a nephron and vasa recta showing counter-current mechanism

## 16.6 Regulation of Kidney Functions

- The homeostasis of the body fluids, i.e. the regulation of water and solute contents is maintained by the kidneys. The vertebrate kidney is very flexible in its functioning.
- It excretes larger quantities of dilute urine when water is abundant in the body tissues and small amounts of concentrated urine when there is shortage of water.
- Hormones act as an important signaling molecule in controlling the regulation of water content in blood along with kidneys.
- The functioning of the kidneys is efficiently monitored and regulated by hormonal feedback mechanism involving hypothalamus, JGA (Juxta Glomerular Apparatus) and to a certain extent, the heart.
- Regulation of the functioning of kidneys can be discussed under the following headings

## 1. Regulation by the Hypothalamus

- Osmoreceptors in the body are activated by changes in blood volume, body fluid and ionic concentration.
- Excessive loss of fluid from the body activates osmoreceptors present in hypothalamus, thus stimulating it to release **Antidiuretic Hormone** (ADH) or **vasopressin** from the neurohypophysis.
- ADH increases water reabsorption from DCT, thereby preventing diuresis.
- An increase in body fluid volume switches off the osmoreceptors and suppresses the ADH release to complete the feedback.
- ADH also causes constrictory effects on blood vessels of glomerulus, thus increasing blood pressure.
- An increase in blood pressure can increase the glomerular blood flow and thereby GFR.
- A reduction in ADH secretion can lead to the development of diabetes insipidus, a condition characterised by excessive thirst and urination.

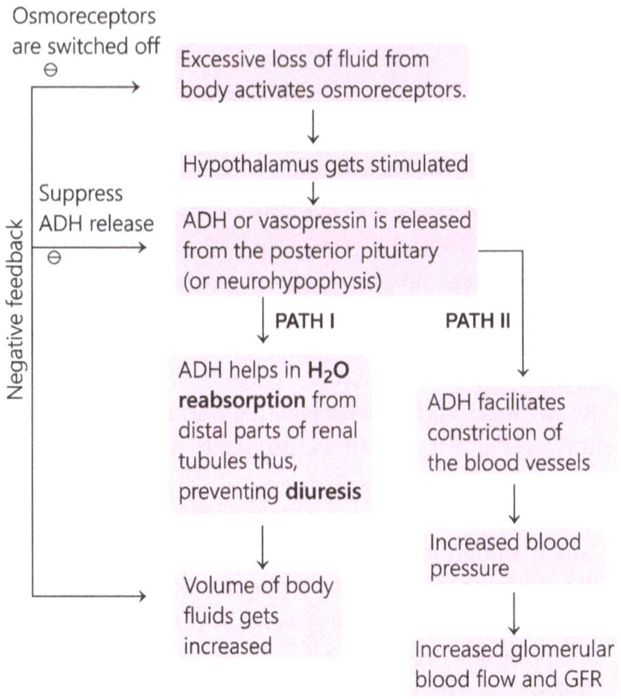


## 2. Regulation by the Juxtaglomerular Apparatus (JGA)

- As blood pressure/glomerular blood flow /GFR decreases, the cells of the JGA release the enzyme renin.
- Renin converts angiotensinogen in blood to angiotensin-I and further angiotensin-II (active form).
- This mechanism is generally known as the **renin-angiotensin mechanism**.
- Angiotensin has following effects
  - Raises blood pressure by constricting blood vessels (being a powerful vasoconstrictor) and thereby GFR.
  - Activates the adrenal cortex to release aldosterone, which causes reabsorption of $Na^+$ and water from the distal parts of the tubule. This also leads to an increase in blood pressure and GFR.

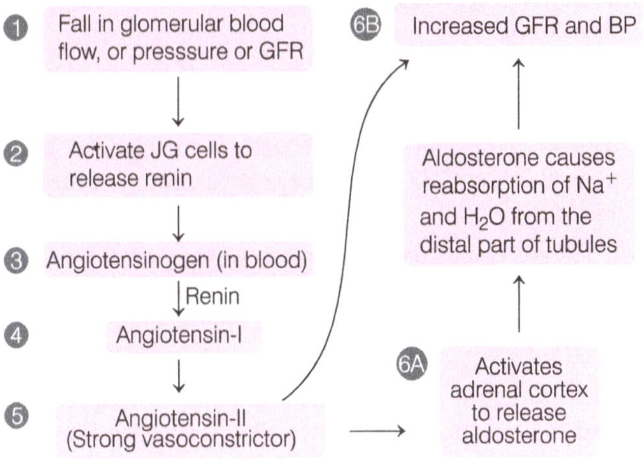


## 3. Regulation by the Heart

- Atrial Natriuretic Factor (ANF) is produced by the atria of heart on detecting an increase in blood flow. ANF causes vasodilation (dilation of blood vessels) and thereby decreases the blood pressure. ANF mechanism, therefore acts as a check on the renin-angiotensin mechanism.

**Quick Test 4**

1. Name the process in which the filtrate flow in opposite direction to maximise exchange efficiency.
2. The process by which the body maintains a stable internal environment is known as?
3. *X* is the hormone responsible for regulating water balance, by promoting water reabsorption in the kidneys. Identify the *X*.
4. **State True or False.**
   Angiotensin activates the adrenal cortex to release aldosterone, which causes reabsorption of $Ca^+$.
5. Name the factor that cause vasodilation.

## 16.7 Micturition

- Urine is produced and drained continuously by the nephrons into the renal pelvis, from here it is carried down to the ureters and then into the urinary bladder.
- The bladder serves to store the urine temporarily till a voluntary signal is given by the **Central Nervous System** (CNS).
- As urine collects, the muscular walls of the bladder distend to accommodate it.
- The stretch receptors on the walls of the bladder send signals to the CNS, by sensory nerve ending in the bladder.
- The CNS passes on motor message to initiate the contraction of smooth muscles of the bladder and simultaneously relaxation of the internal and external urethral sphincters causing release of urine.
- The process of release of urine is called **micturition** and the neural mechanism causing it is called the **micturition reflex**.

### Urine

- An adult man normally passes about 1-1.5 L of urine per day.
- **Colour** Pale yellow, due to pigment urochrome.
- **pH** Ranges from 4.5-8.2, average pH 6.0 (i.e. slightly acidic).
- **Odour** Unpleasant, if allowed to stand imparts strong smell like, ammonia.
- On an average, 25-30 g of urea is excreted out per day.
- Various conditions can affect the characteristics of urine.
- Analysis of urine helps in clinical diagnosis of many metabolic disorders as well as malfunctioning of the kidney.
- For example, presence of glucose (Glycosuria) and ketone bodies (Ketonuria) in urine are indicative of diabetes mellitus.

## 16.8 Role of Other Organs in Excretion

Other than the kidneys, there are some accessory excretory organs that also help in the elimination of excretory wastes. These are described as follows

### 1. Lungs

- Carbon dioxide and water are the waste products formed in respiration.
- About 200 mL/min of $CO_2$ and significant amount of water per day are eliminated by human lungs.

### 2. Liver

- It changes the decomposed haemoglobin of the worn-out red blood corpuscles into bile pigments, i.e. bilirubin and biliverdin.
- The liver also excretes cholesterol, steroid hormones, certain vitamins and drugs *via* bile.
- Most of these substances ultimately pass out along with digestive waste.

### 3. Skin

The sweat glands and sebaceous glands in the skin can eliminate certain substances through their secretions.

- **Sweat Glands** The secretion of sweat glands (sweat) is an aqueous fluid containing NaCl, lactic acid, small amounts of urea, amino acids and glucose. Though the main function of sweat is to facilitate a cooling effect on the body surface, it also help in removal of waste material from the body.
- **Sebaceous Glands** Sebum from sebaceous glands eliminates sterols, waxes and hydrocarbons. This secretion is mainly meant for protective oily covering of the skin.

## 16.9 Disorders of the Excretory System

Malfunctioning of kidneys can lead to several disorders of the excretory system.

Some of these are as follows

### 1. Uremia

- It is the presence of an excessive amount of urea in the blood.
- Urea is highly harmful as it poisons the cells at high concentration and may lead to kidney failure.
- In such patients, urea can be removed by haemodialysis.

### 2. Kidney Failure (renal failure)

- Partial or total inability of kidneys to carry on excretory and salt-water regulatory functions is called **renal** or kidney failure.
- Kidney transplantation is the ultimate method in correction of acute renal failure.

### 3. Renal Calculi

It is the formation of stone or insoluble mass of crystallised salts (calcium, magnesium, phosphates and oxalates, etc.), within the kidney.

### 4. Glomerulonephritis

It is the inflammation of glomeruli of kidney.

### Artificial Kidney (Haemodialyser)

- It is a machine that is used to filtre the blood (to remove urea and other nitrogenous wastes) of a person, whose kidneys are damaged.
- The process is called **haemodialysis**, which is considered a boon for thousands of uremic patients all over the world.

The outline details of apparatus and the process are as follows

- It works on the principle of dialysis i.e. diffusion of small solute molecules through a semipermeable membrane (cellophane).
- Blood of the patient is pumped from one of the arteries into the dialysing unit (haemodialyser) after adding an anticoagulant (heparin).
- Haemodialyser contain coiled cellophane tube suspended in a dialysing fluid (salt-water solution) having same composition as that of plasma except the nitrogenous wastes (urea).
- Pores of the cellophane tube allow the passage of molecules based on concentration gradient. As nitrogenous wastes are absent in the dialysing fluid, these substances can easily get diffuse from the blood into the surrounding solution. Thus, the blood is cleared of nitrogenous waste products, without loosing plasma proteins.
- Now, the anti-heparin is added to the blood, to restore its normal clotting power and then pumped back to the body of patient.

### Renal (Kidney)Transplantation

- Grafting a kidney from a compatible donor to restore kidney functions in a recipient, suffering from kidney failure, is called renal or kidney transplantation.
- It is an ultimate method in the correction of acute renal failures.
- A living donor can be used in a kidney transplant. It may be an identical twin, a sibling or a close relative to minimise the chances of rejection by the immune system of the host.
- To prevent the rejection of transplanted kidney, special drugs are also used, which suppress the recipients immune system.
- Modern clinical procedures have increased the success rate of such a complicated technique.

### Quick Test 5

1. The neural mechanism which is used in micturition is known as?
2. The colour of urine is pale yellow due the presence of X pigment, identify the pigment.
3. **State True or False.**
   (a) Sebum is the protective oily covering of the skin.
   (b) Bile contains certain vitamins and cholesterol.
4. Identify the condition in which an excessive amount of urea is present in the blood.
5. Name the substance used in hemodialysis to prevent blood clotting.

# Mind Map

## Excretory Products and their Elimination

### Excretion

- Elimination of metabolic waste like ammonia, urea, uric acid, etc., from the tissues.
- **Mode of excretion** (On the basis of types of excretory end products)
- **Ammonotelism** Excretion of ammonia, e.g. bony fishes, aquatic insects, etc.
- **Ureotelism** Excretion of urea, e.g. mammals, marine fishes, etc.
- **Uricotelism** Excretion of uric acid, e.g. snails, birds, etc.

### Human Excretory System

Consists of main organs like kidney and accessory organs like skin (sweat gland), lungs (expel $CO_2$) and liver (detoxifies and produce urea).

### Kidney

- Reddish-brown bean-shaped structure situated between last thoracic and third lumbar vertebrae.
- Each kidney of an adult human measures, 10-12 cm in length, 5-7 cm in width and 2-3 cm in thickness with an average weight of 120-170 gm.

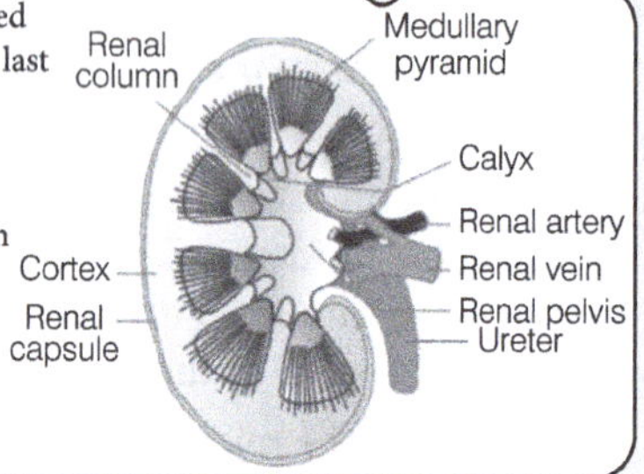


### Nephron

- Structural and functional unit of kidney.
- Divided into two parts, i.e. Malpighian body and renal tubule.

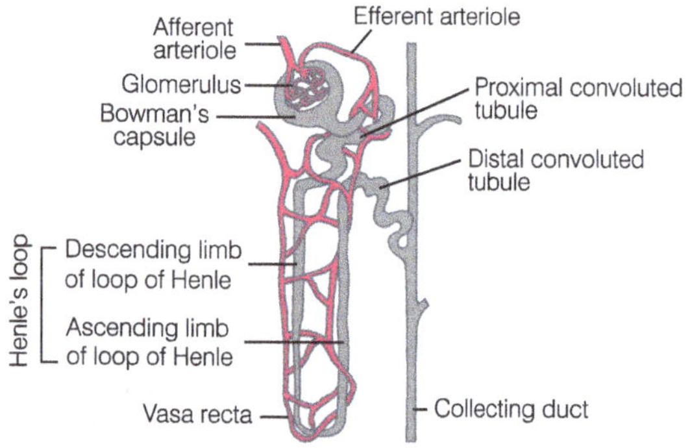


### Urine Formation

- **Glomerular Filtration** Filtration of blood in glomerular forming filtrate.
- **Tubular Reabsorption** Reabsorption of useful substances like water, glucose and ions into blood strseam.
- **Tubular Secretion** Secretion of waste products and ions into filtrate.

### Disorders of Excretory System

- **Uremia** Accumulation of urea in blood due to kidney malfunction.
- **Renal Calculi** Formation of insoluble mass of crystallised salts.
- **Glomerulonephritis** Inflammation of glomeruli of kidney.
- **Renal Failure** Partial or total inability of kidney to carry out

### Regulation of Kidney Function

- **Control by ADH** (Anti-Diuretic Hormone) (e.g. Vasopressin)

**Decrease in body fluid volume**
↓ Activation of osmoreceptors
↓ Stimulation of hypothalamus
↓ Release of ADH (from posterior pituitary gland)
↓ Facilitates water reabsorption from DCT
↓ Prevents diuresis

**Increase in body fluid volume**
↓ Switch off the osmoreceptors
↓ Signal to hypothalamus
↓ Suppress the ADH release
↓ Reduce water reabsorption
↓ Excessive loss of water from body.

**Control by ANF** (Atrial Natriuretic Factor)

Increase in blood flow to atria of heart release ANF.
↓ Causes vasodilation and thus decrease blood pressure.
↓ ANF acts as a check on renin-angiotensin mechanism.

**Control by Renin Angiotensin Aldosterone System** (RAAS)

Fall in GFR —(Renin from)→ Angiotensinogen ⟶ Angiotensin-I

Reabsorption of $Na^+$ and water from DCT → Increase in GFR

Secrete aldosterone ⟵ Adrenal cortex ⟵(Acts on) Angiotensin-II

### Mechanism of Concentration of Urine

- It occurs by **counter-current mechanism**.
- The flow of filtrate in the limbs of Henle's loop and the flow of blood in the two limbs of vasa recta is in opposite direction, thus forming a counter-current.
- It maintains the gradient of increasing osmolarity of medullary interstitium. This gradient is mainly caused by NaCl and urea, where reabsorption of ions and water in long loop of juxta-medullary nephron and recycling of salts and urea in vasa recta occurs.

# EXAM PATTERN QUESTIONS

## Objective Type Questions

### Multiple Choice Questions

**1.** Which of the following pair is wrong? **NCERT Exemplar, Competency Based Que.**

(a) Uricotelic ……… Birds
(b) Ureotelic ……… Insects
(c) Ammonotelic ……… Tadpole
(d) Ureotelic ……… Elephant

**Ans.** (*b*)

**2.** Which of the following structures help in the removal of nitrogenous waste as well as concerned with osmoregulation?

(a) Protonephridia
(b) Nephridia
(c) Malpighian tubules
(d) All of the above

**Ans.** (*d*)

**3.** Which one of the following statement is incorrect? **NCERT Exemplar**

(a) Birds and land snails are uricotelic animals
(b) Mammals and frogs are ureotelic animals
(c) Aquatic amphibians and aquatic insects are ammonotelic animals
(d) Birds and reptiles are ureotelic

**Ans.** (*d*)Birds and reptiles are uricotelic (not ureotelic) as they excrete uric acid (nitrogenous waste) in the form of pellet or paste with a minimum loss of water.

**4.** Different types of excretory structures and animals are given below. Match them appropriately and mark the correct answer from among those given below **NCERT Exemplar**

| | Excretory Structure/Organ | | Animals |
|---|---|---|---|
| A. | Protonephridia | 1. | Prawn |
| B. | Nephridia | 2. | Cockroach |
| C. | Malpighian tubules | 3. | Earthworm |
| D. | Green gland or antennal gland | 4. | Flatworms |

**Codes**

| | A | B | C | D | | A | B | C | D |
|---|---|---|---|---|---|---|---|---|---|
| (a) | 4 | 3 | 2 | 1 | (b) | 2 | 3 | 1 | 2 |
| (c) | 4 | 3 | 1 | 2 | (d) | 2 | 3 | 2 | 4 |

**Ans.** (*a*)

**5** Choose the correct match for the measurement of an adult human kidney.

(a) Length – 7 to 8cm; thickness – 3 to 4 cm
(b) Length – 7 to 10 cm; thickness – 2 to 4 cm
(c) Length – 6 to 8 cm; thickness – 2 to 4 cm
(d) Length – 10 to 12 cm; thickness – 2 to 3 cm

**Ans.** (*d*)

**6.** The part of the kidney through which the ureter, blood vessels and nerves enter, it is known as

(a) renal cortex
(b) renal medulla
(c) hilum
(d) urethra

**Ans.** (*c*)

**7.** Which one of the following statement is incorrect? **Competency Based Que., NCERT Exemplar**

(a) The medullary zone of kidney is divided into a few conical masses called medullary pyramids projecting into the calyces
(b) Inside the kidney the cortical region extends in between the medullary pyramids as renal pelvis
(c) Glomerulus along with Bowman's capsule is called the renal corpuscle
(d) Renal corpuscle, Proximal Convoluted Tubule (PCT) and Distal Convoluted Tubule (DCT) of the nephron are situated in the cortical region of kidney

**Ans.** (*b*)

**8.** Figure shows human urinary system with structures labelled *A-D*. Select option, which correctly identifies them and gives their characteristics and functions? **Competency Based Que.**

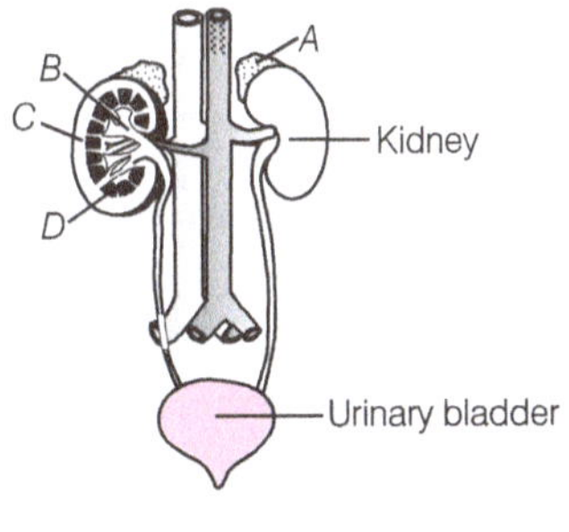

(a) A–Adrenal gland–located at the posterior part of kidney, secretes catecholamines, which stimulate glycogen breakdown
(b) B–Pelvis–broad funnel-shaped space inner to hilum, directly connected to loop of Henle
(c) C–Medulla–inner zone of kidney and contains complete nephrons
(d) D–Cortex–outer part of kidney and does not contain any part of nephrons

**Ans.** (b)

**9. Identify A-D in the given diagram of LS of kidney and choose the correct option.** **Competency Based Que.**

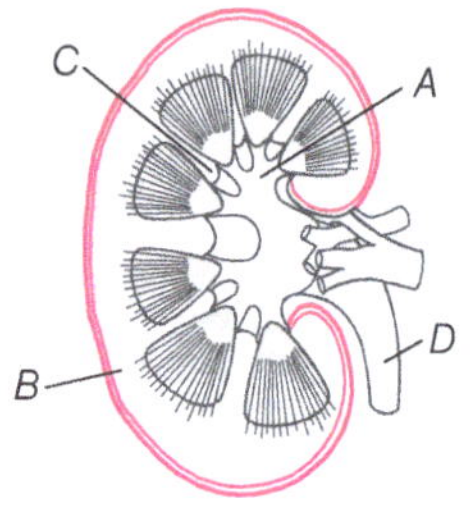


(a) A–Calyx, B–Cortex, C–Renal column, D–Ureter
(b) A–Calyx, B–Cortex, C–Renal column, D–Urethra
(c) A–Urethra, B–Cortex, C–Renal column, D–Calyx
(d) A–Urethra, B–Calyx, C–Renal column, D–Cortex

**Ans.** (a)

**10. Study the given structure of a nephron and match A, B, C, D, E, F and G with correct option.** **Competency Based Que.**

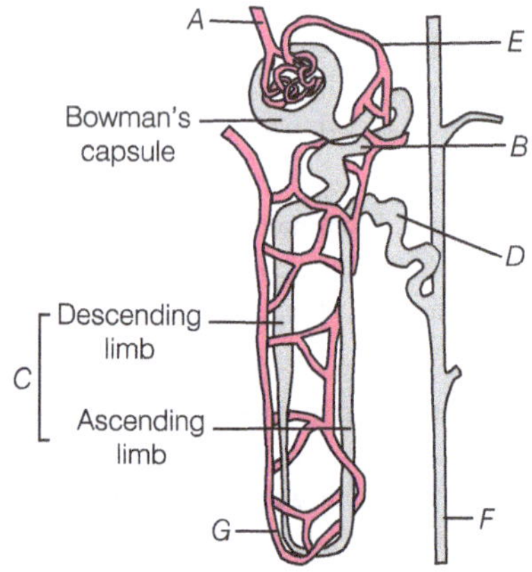


(a) A–Afferent arteriole, B–Proximal convoluted tubule, C–Henle's loop, D–Distal convoluted tubule, E–Efferent arteriole, F– Collecting duct, G–Vasa recta
(b) A–Efferent arteriole, B–PCT, C–Henle's loop, D–DCT, E–Peritubular capillaries, F– Collecting duct, G–Vasa recta
(c) A–Afferent arteriole, B–Peritubular capillaries, C–Henle's loop, D–DCT, E–PCT, F–Collecting duct, G–Vasa recta
(d) A–Afferent arteriole, B–Henle's loop, C– Collecting duct, D–PCT, E–DCT, F–Peritubular capillaries, G–Vasa recta

**Ans.** (a)

**11. Identify A-D in the diagram of Malpighian body (renal corpuscle) and choose the correct option for A, B, C and D.** **Competency Based Que.**

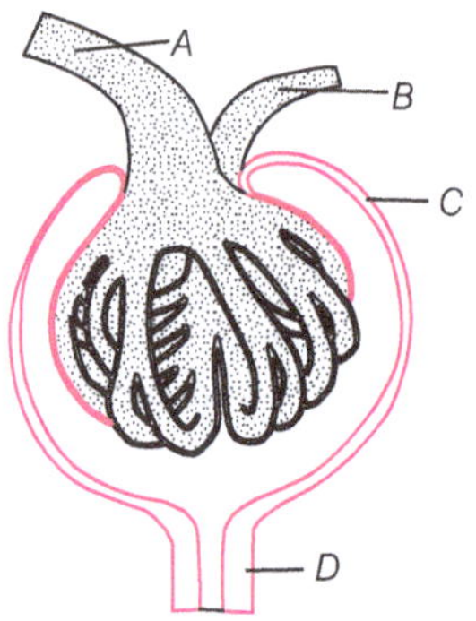


(a) A–Afferent arteriole, B–Efferent arteriole, C–Bowman's capsule, D–Proximal convoluted tubule
(b) A–Efferent arteriole, B–Afferent arteriole, C–Bowman's capsule, D–Distal convoluted tubule
(c) A–Afferent arteriole, B–Efferent arteriole, C–Bowman's capsule, D–Distal convoluted tubule
(d) A–Efferent arteriole, B–Afferent arteriole, C–Bowman's capsule, D–Distal convoluted tubule

**Ans.** (a)

**12. Which of the following structure extends into the medullary pyramid?**
(a) Proximal convoluted tubule
(b) Distal convoluted tubule
(c) Malpighian corpuscle
(d) Loop of Henle

**Ans.** (d)

**13 Which of the following option is correct w.r.t. juxta medullary nephron?**
(a) Loop of Henle runs deep into the vasa recta
(b) PCT extends up to medulla
(c) Loop of Henle is very long
(d) Vasa recta is not prominent

**Ans.** (c)

**14. Choose the incorrect option for the layers present between the glomerulus and Bowman's capsule.**
(a) Epithelium is the layer of glomerular blood vessels
(b) Basement membrane is present between the endothelium and epithelium
(c) Endothelium is the layer of Bowman's capsule
(d) Both (a) and (c)

**Ans.** (d)

**15.** **Filtration of the blood takes place at** NCERT Exemplar

(a) PCT (b) DCT

(c) Collecting ducts (d) Malpighian body

**Ans.** (*d*) Filtration of blood takes place at Malpighian body, which comprises of glomerulus and Bowman's capsule. Filtration of blood takes place in glomerulus through glomerular filtration.

**16.** **The podocytes are**

(a) endothelial cells of the glomerulus

(b) endothelial cells of the Bowman's capsule

(c) epithelial cells of the Bowman's capsule

(d) epithelial cells of the glomerulus

**Ans.** (*c*)

**17.** **Ultrafiltrate formed by the glomerulus contains all the constituents of the blood plasma except**

(a) protein (b) minerals

(c) urea (d) All of these

**Ans.** (*a*)

**18.** **Juxta Glomerular Apparatus (JGA) which regulates the glomerular filtration rate is formed at the point of contact of** Competency Based Que.

(a) DCT and PCT

(b) DCT and efferent arteriole

(c) DCT and afferent arteriole

(d) loop of Henle and DCT

**Ans.** (*c*)

**19.** **Match the following parts of a nephron with their functions.**

| Column I (Parts of Nephron) | | Column II (Functions) | |
|---|---|---|---|
| A. | Descending limb of Henle's loop | 1. | Reabsorption of salts only |
| B. | Proximal convoluted tubule | 2. | Reabsorption of water only |
| C. | Ascending limb of Henle's loop | 3. | Conditional reabsorption of sodium ion and water |
| D. | Distal convoluted tubule | 4. | Reabsorption of ion, water and organic nutrients |

**Codes**

| | A | B | C | D |
|---|---|---|---|---|
| (a) | 1 | 3 | 2 | 4 |
| (b) | 2 | 4 | 1 | 3 |
| (c) | 1 | 4 | 2 | 3 |
| (d) | 4 | 1 | 3 | 2 |

**Ans.** (*b*)

**20.** **Part of nephron involved in active reabsorption of sodium is**

(a) Proximal convoluted tubule

(b) Distal convoluted tubule

(c) Descending limb of loop of Henle

(d) Bowman's capsule

**Ans.** (*b*)

**21.** **Pick the correct statement.** Competency Based Que.

(a) Ascending limb of loop of Henle is impermeable to water

(b) Descending limb of loop of Henle is impermeable to water

(c) Ascending limb of loop of Henle is impermeable to electrolytes

(d) Descending limb of loop of Henle is permeable to electrolytes.

**Ans.** (*a*)

**22.** **The main function of Distal Convoluted Tubule (DCT) of nephron is to maintain the**

(a) pH in blood (b) Na-K balance of blood

(c) temperature of blood (d) Both (a) and (b)

**Ans.** (*d*)

**23.** **Choose the mismatched part of nephron with its function.**

(a) Bowman's capsule–Glomerular filtration

(b) PCT–Reabsorption of $Na^+$ and $K^+$

(c) DCT–Reabsorption of glucose

(d) Loop of Henle–Urine concentration

**Ans.** (*c*)The match pair given in option (c) is incorrect and it can be corrected as

The Distal Convoluted Tubule (DCT) is involved in the reabsorption of sodium and bicarbonate ions.

**24.** **We can produce a concentrated/dilute urine. This is facilitated by a special mechanism. Identify the mechanism.** NCERT Exemplar

(a) Reabsorption from PCT

(b) Reabsorption from collecting duct

(c) Reabsorption/Secretion in DCT

(d) Counter-current mechanism in Henle's loop/vasa recta

**Ans.** (*d*)

**25.** **Counter-current mechanism helps to maintain a concentration gradient. This gradient helps in**

(a) easy passage of water from medulla to collecting tubule and thereby concentrating urine

(b) easy passage of water from collecting tubule to interstitial fluid and thereby concentrating urine

(c) easy passage of water from medullary interstitial fluid to collecting tubule and thereby diluting urine
(d) inhibition of passage of water between the collecting tubule and medulla and so isotonic urine is formed

**Ans.** (*b*)

**26.** **Which of the following factor is responsible for the formation of concentrated urine?** **Competency Based Que.**

(a) Maintaining hyperosmolarity towards inner medullary interstitium in the kidneys
(b) Secretion of erythropoietin by juxtaglomerular complex
(c) Hydrostatic pressure during glomerular filtration
(d) Low levels of antidiuretic hormone

**Ans.** (*a*)

**27.** **Regulation of GFR does not occur *via***

(a) vasopressin
(b) renin-angiotensin mechanism
(c) juxtamedullary apparatus
(d) blood glucose

**Ans.** (*d*)

**28.** **Which of the following statement is correct?** **NCERT Exemplar**

(a) ADH prevents conversion of angiotensinogen in blood to angiotensin
(b) Aldosterone facilitates water reabsorption
(c) ANF enhances sodium reabsorption
(d) Renin causes vasodilation

**Ans.** (*b*)

**29.** **Which one of the following is also known as antidiuretic hormone?** **NCERT Exemplar**

(a) Oxytocin (b) Vasopressin
(c) Adrenaline (d) Calcitonin

**Ans.** (*b*)Vasopressin is also known as Antidiuretic Hormone (ADH). It is secreted from the neurohypophysis of pituitary and facilitates water reabsorption from latter parts of the tubule, thereby preventing diuresis.

**30.** **Osmoreceptors activated in response to excessive loss of fluid from body stimulate the release of**

(a) ADH from neurohypophysis
(b) Renin from JG cells
(c) ADH from adenohypophysis
(d) ANF from anterior pituitary

**Ans.** (*a*)

**31.** **The human urine is usually acidic because**

(a) the sodium transporter exchanges one hydrogen ion for each sodium ion in peritubular capillaries
(b) excreted plasma proteins are acidic
(c) potassium and sodium exchange generates acidity
(d) hydrogen ions are actively secreted into the filtrate

**Ans.** (*d*)

**32.** **A large quantity of one of the following is removed from our body by lungs.** **NCERT Exemplar**

(a) $CO_2$ (b) $H_2O$
(c) $CO_2$ and $H_2O$ (d) Ammonia

**Ans.** (*c*)

**33.** **Which among the following functions are performed by accessory excretory organs in human body?**

(a) Elimination of sterols, hydrocarbons, waxes through sebum by sebaceous glands
(b) Secretion of oil by sebaceous glands which provide oily protective covering of skin
(c) Small amount of nitrogenous waste elimination through saliva
(d) All of the above

**Ans.** (*d*)

**34.** **The condition of accumulation of urea in the blood is termed as** **NCERT Exemplar**

(a) renal calculi (b) glomerulonephritis
(c) uremia (d) ketonuria

**Ans.** (*c*)Uremia is accumulation of urea in blood. It occurs due to malfunctioning of kidney.

**35.** **Match the following columns.**

| | Column I | | Column II |
|---|---|---|---|
| A. | Glycosurea | 1. | Accumulation of uric acid in joints |
| B. | Renal calculi | 2. | Inflammation in glomeruli |
| C. | Glomerular nephritis | 3. | Mass of crystallised salts within the kidney |
| D. | Gout | 4. | Presence of glucose in urine |

**Codes** **NCERT Exemplar**

| | A | B | C | D | | A | B | C | D |
|---|---|---|---|---|---|---|---|---|---|
| (a) | 1 | 3 | 2 | 4 | (b) | 3 | 2 | 4 | 1 |
| (c) | 4 | 3 | 2 | 1 | (d) | 4 | 2 | 3 | 1 |

**Ans.** (*c*)

**36.** **Which one of the following are components of the dialysing unit used to carry out haemodialysis in uremic patients?** **Competency Based Que.**

**I. Urea** **II. Heparin**
**III. Anti-heparin** **IV. Coiled cellophane tube**
**V. Dialysing fluid**

(a) I, II, III and IV (b) II, III, IV and V
(c) III, IV, V and I (d) None of these

**Ans.** (*b*)

**37. Dialysing unit (artificial kidney) contains a fluid which is almost same as plasma except that it has** NCERT Exemplar

(a) high glucose (b) high urea
(c) no urea (d) high uric acid

Ans. (*c*)

## Assertion-Reason Questions

**Direction** (Q. Nos. 1-11) *In each of the following questions, a statement of Assertion (A) is given followed by corresponding statement of Reason (R). Of the statements, mark the correct answer*

(a) Both A and R are true and R is the correct explanation of the A.
(b) Both A and R are true, but R is not the correct explanation of the A.
(c) A is true, but R is false.
(d) A is false, but R is true.

**1. Assertion** (A) Some ureotelic organisms retain some amount of urea in their kidney matrix.

**Reason** (R) The ureotelic organisms maintain desired osmolarity by retaining some urea.

Ans. (*a*)

**2. Assertion** (A) Malpighian tubules are excretory organs in most of the insects.

**Reason** (R) Malpighian tubules help in excretion of urea and creatinine.

Ans. (*c*) A is true, but R is false. R can be corrected as Malpighian tubules help in the excretion of nitrogenous wastes, primarily uric acid.

**3. Assertion** (A) Members of class–Aves are uricotelic.

**Reason** (R) Birds excrete nitrogenous waste as uric acid.

Ans. (*a*)

**4. Assertion** (A) Protonephridia or flame cells in flatworms help in osmoregulation.

**Reason** (R) Flame cells are excretory organs.

Ans. (b)

**5. Assertion** (A) Hilum is a part of human excretory system.

**Reason** (R) Hilum is helpful in collection of urine.

Ans. (*c*) A is true, but R is false. R can be corrected as

Hilum is a notch like structure in kidney through which ureter, blood vessels and nerves enter the kidney.

**6. Assertion** (A) Conditional reabsorption of $Na^+$ and water takes place in Distal Convoluted Tubule (DCT).

**Reason** (R) The DCT allows passive absorption of $Na^+$ and active absorption of $Cl^-$ along with water.

Ans. (*c*)

**7. Assertion** (A) The vasa recta forms the capillary networks that supply blood to the medulla.

**Reason** (R) Vasa recta plays a very important role in concentrating the urine.

Ans. (*b*) Both A and R are true, but R is not the correct explanation of A. A can be explained as

The vasa recta forms the capillary networks that supply blood to the medulla because they are specialised for maintaining the osmotic gradient in the renal medulla, which is essential for the concentration of urine.

**8. Assertion** (A) During urination, the backflow of urine into the ureters is prevented.

**Reason** (R) Urethral sphincters relax during urination.

Ans. (*b*) Both A and R are true, but R is not the correct explanation of A. A can be explained as

During urination, the backflow of urine into the ureters is prevented by the pressure from the full bladder and the oblique entry of ureters into the bladder wall, which acts as a functional valve.

**9.** Given below is the diagrammatic representation of a nephron. Comment upon the appropriateness of both Assertion and Reason. **Competency Based Que.**

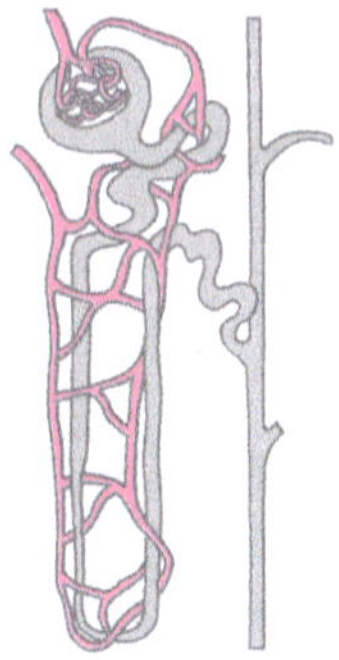

**Assertion** (A) Tubular secretion is an important step in urine formation which occurs in nephron.

**Reason** (R) Tubular secretion helps in the maintenance of ionic and acid-base balance of body fluids.

Ans. (*a*)

**10. Assertion** (A) Haemodialysis is used to clean the excretory products generated from the blood.

**Reason** (R) Dialysing fluid has same composition as that of plasma except, nitrogenous wastes.

Ans. (*b*)

**11. Assertion** (A) Dialytic fluid/solution is iso-osmotic to blood plasma.

**Reason** (R) The fluid used during dialysis procedure contain glucose and ions.

Ans. (*d*) A is false, but R is true. A can be corrected as

Fluid used in dialysis has similar composition to blood plasma except for the presence of proteins and urea.

# Subjective Questions

## Very Short Answer Type Questions

**1. What is the excretory product from the kidney of reptiles?** **NCERT Exemplar**

**Ans.** Reptiles excrete nitrogenous wastes such as uric acid in the form of a pellet.

**2. Give the name of the three common nitrogenous waste materials in vertebrates. Which of these is most toxic and which one is least toxic?**

**Ans.** The three common nitrogenous waste materials are ammonia, urea and uric acid. Ammonia is most toxic, while uric acid is least toxic. (½ × ½)

**3. Give the name of the nitrogenous waste which is produced in birds. What is the advantage of this type of excretion?**

**Ans.** Birds excrete uric acid in the form of pellet or paste (semi-solid form). It helps in conservation of water. (½ × ½)

**4. Observe the given diagram and identify the structure *A* and *B*.** **Competency Based Que.**

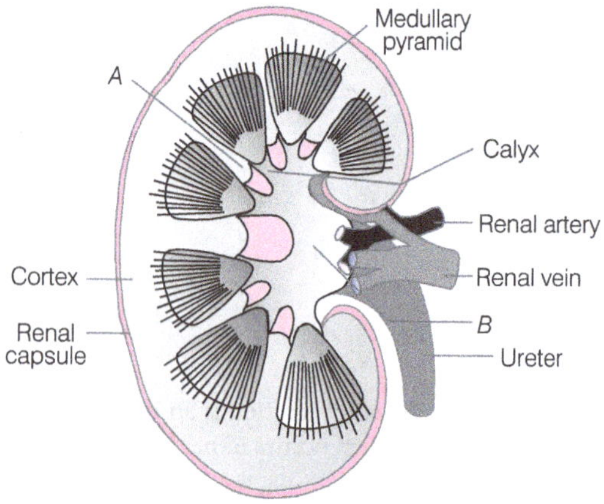


**Ans.** *A* – Renal column, *B* – Renal pelvis. (½ × 2)

**5. Give the name of vessel of peritubular capillaries that runs parallel to the loop of Henle.**

**Ans.** Vasa recta.

**6. Give the name of the reservoir of urine in the body.**

**Ans.** Urinary bladder.

**7. Name the two components of nephron that together form Malpighian body or renal corpuscle.**

**Ans.** Glomerulus and Bowman's capsule. (½ × 2)

**8. Define Glomerular Filtration Rate (GFR).** **NCERT**

**Ans.** Glomerular Filtration Rate (GFR) is the amount of the filtrate formed by the kidneys per minute. GFR in a healthy individual is approximately 125 mL/min, i.e. 180 L/day.

**9. What is meant by the term osmoregulation?** **NCERT**

**Ans.** Osmoregulation is the phenomenon of regulation of change in the concentration of body fluids according to the concentration of external environment. It can be clearly seen in most marine invertebrates, some freshwater invertebrates, hagfish, etc., but it is found in all animals.

**10. What are the two main types of nephrons?**

**Ans.** Cortical nephrons and juxtamedullary nephrons. (½ × 2)

**11. What is the ratio of the concentrated filtrate to that of the initial filtrate?**

**Ans.** The concentrated urine (filtrate) is nearly four times concentrated than the initial filtrate formed.

**12. Give the name of the two actively transported substances in glomerular filtrate.** **NCERT Exemplar**

**Ans.** Glucose and amino acids are actively transported substances in glomerular filtrate. (½ × 2)

**13. What is the function of vasa recta?**

**Ans.** The vasa recta help in reabsorption of important nutrients from medullary interstitial tissues.

**14. What difference is observed in the ascending and the descending limbs of Henle's loop regarding permeability to $H_2O$?** **Competency Based Que.**

**Ans.** The descending limb is permeable to water, while ascending limb is impermeable to water. (½ × 2)

**15. What are the two substances responsible for causing the gradient for increasing hyperosmolarity of medullary interstitium?**

**Ans.** NaCl and urea (½ × 2)

**16. Give the name of the main components that play an important role in the counter-current mechanism.**

**Ans.** Henle's loop and vasa recta.

**17. Explain micturition.** **NCERT**

**Ans.** Micturition is the expulsion of urine from the urinary bladder through the urethra, regulated by neural signals and sphincter control.

**18. What is the pH of urine?** **NCERT Exemplar**

**Ans.** It ranges from 4.5-8.2, average pH is 6.0.

**19. What is the composition of sweat produced by sweat gland?**

**Ans.** The sweat is released by sweat glands present in skin. It contains certain ions, little urea and lactic acid. It is acidic in nature.

**20. How do lungs help in excretion?**

**Ans.** Carbon dioxide and water are the waste products removed by the lungs in the expired air.

**21. Match the items of Column I with those of Column II.** NCERT

| Column I | | Column II | |
|---|---|---|---|
| (a) | Ammonotelism | (i) | Birds |
| (b) | Bowman's capsule | (ii) | Water reabsorption |
| (c) | Micturtion | (iii) | Bony fish |
| (d) | Uricotelism | (iv) | Urinary bladder |
| (e) | ADH | (v) | Renal tubule |

**Ans.** (a) – iii, (b) – v, (c) – iv, (d) – i, (e) - ii

**22. What will be the effect on the amount of urine released when water is abundant in the body tissues in case of vertebrates?** Competency Based Que.

**Ans.** Vertebrates excrete large quantities of dilute urine when water is abundant in the body tissues and *vice-versa.*

**23. What is the principle on which dialysis work?**

**Ans.** The diffusion of small solute molecule through a semi-permeable membrane (cellophane).

## Short Answer Type Questions

**1. What is ureotelism? Describe the process of formation of urea.**

**Ans.** The process of excreting urea is called ureotelism. Animals, which live in habitats with abundance of water convert toxic ammonia produced in the body into urea by the liver and then release it into the blood. This in turn is filtered and excreted out by the kidneys. (1 × 2)

**2. Give the name of the excretory organ present in the following animals.**

(i) Rotifers (ii) Cockroaches
(iii) Lancelets

**Ans.** (i) Rotifers — Flame cells
(ii) Cockroaches — Malpighian tubules
(iii) Lancelets — Protonephridia (1 × 3)

**3. Explain ammonotelic animals.**

**Ans.** Refer to text on page no. 367.

**4. Terrestrial animals are generally either ureotelic or uricotelic, not ammonotelic, why?** Competency Based Que., NCERT

**Ans.** Terrestrial adaptation requires the production of less toxic nitrogenous wastes like urea and uric acid for the conservation of water. Aquatic animals excrete ammonia which requires large amount of water to dissolve.

The huge quantity of water is easily available to such animals from surroundings. However, for terrestrial animals, such a huge quantity of water is not available, hence they modify $NH_3$ to comparatively less toxic products like urea and uric acid which require less amount of water for their excretion.

**5. Draw a simple diagram of a human kidney. Label any six parts.**

**Ans.** Refer to text on page no. 369.

**6. Show the structure of a renal corpuscle with the help of a diagram.** NCERT Exemplar

**Ans.** Glomerulus along with Bowman's capsule is called the Malpighian body or renal corpuscle.

For diagram refer to fig. on page no. 370 fig. 16.3.

**7. Explain the structure of renal tubules.**

**Ans.** Refer to text on page no. 370.

**8. Name the following.**

(i) A chordate animal having flame cells as excretory structures.
(ii) Cortical portions projecting between the medullary pyramids in the human kidney.
(iii) A loop of capillary running parallel to the Henle's loop. NCERT

**Ans.** (i) Cephalochordate - Amphioxus
(ii) Columns of Bertini
(iii) Vasa recta (1 × 3)

**9. Where does the urine formation take place? Name three steps of urine formation.**

**Ans.** Urine formation occurs in the kidneys. It involves three steps (½)
(i) Glomerular filtration
(ii) Selective reabsorption
(iii) Tubular secretion (1 × 3)

**10. Explain the process of ultrafiltration occur in a nephron.** (½ × 3)

**Ans.** Refer to text on page no. 371-372.

**11. Where do ultrafiltration, reabsorption and secretion occur in a nephron?**

**Ans.** (i) Ultrafiltration occurs in Bowman's capsule.
(ii) Reabsorption occurs in PCT, loop of Henle, DCT and collecting ducts.
(iii) Secretion occurs in PCT, loop of Henle and DCT. (1 × 3)

**12. Explain mechanism by which nephron adds some materials to the filtrate.**

**Ans.** Refer to text on page no. 372.

**13. The longer loop of Henle produces more hypertonic urine. Is this statement true or false? Explain it correctly.**

**Ans.** The principle function of the loop of Henle is the recovery of water and sodium chloride from the urine. This allows production of urine that is far more concentrated than blood, limiting the amount of water needed as intake. For survival, longer the loop of Henle, greater is its ability to concentrate urine, resulting in more hypertonic urine. So, the statement is true.

**14. How does the loop of Henle help in concentrating the urine in mammals of terrestrial adaptation?**

**Ans.** Refer to text on page no. 373-374.

**15. How is glomerular filtrate become hypertonic and hypotonic in descending and ascending limb of loop of Henle, respectively?** **Competency Based Que.**

**Ans.** Counter-current system is found in two limbs of loop of Henle. The ascending limb transports $Na^+$ and some urea into surrounding medullary tissue. It is impermeable to water. So, it makes urine diluted or hypotonic. The walls of descending limbs are permeable to water and salt, so $Na^+$ and water from surrounding fluid are absorbed. So, the content of urine becomes hypertonic.

**16. Examine the given diagram and answer the following questions.** **Competency Based Que.**

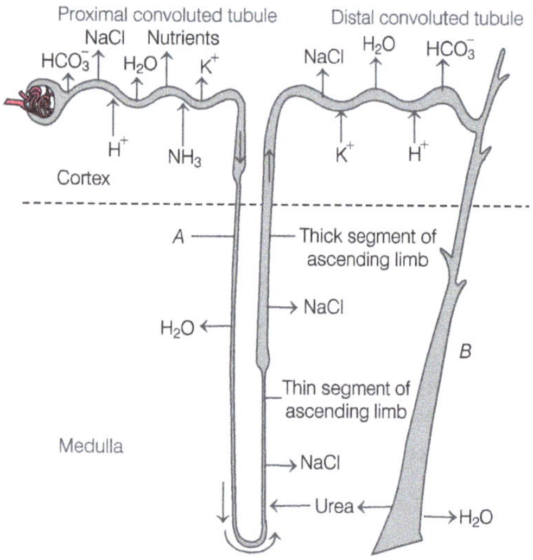


(i) **Identify the process it represents.**

(ii) **Name parts *A* and *B*.**

**Ans.** (i) The given diagram represents reabsorption of major substances at different parts fo nephron. (1)

(ii) *A*–Descending limb of loop of Henle.

*B* – Collecting duct. (½ × 2)

**17. State the importance of counter-current systems in renal functioning.**

**Ans.** The counter-current mechanism has been evolved in higher vertebrates (birds and mammals, including man) to excrete hypertonic urine (urine is more concentrated than blood) for conserving body water which is necessary for terrestrial life.

**18. What is the effect of ADH on collecting tubules?**

**Ans.** ADH (Antidiuretic Hormone) is secreted when the osmotic pressure of blood increases due to excess loss of water from the body. The hormone renders the walls of distal convoluted tubule and collecting duct of a nephron which is permeable to water and increases the reabsorption of water from the surrounding tissues. The urine becomes hyperosmotic and less in volume and water is conserved in the body.

**19. Describe the role of alcohol and caffeine in the concentration of urine.**

**Ans.** Both alcohol and caffiene increase urine production by reducing water reabsorption in the kidneys. Alcohol inhibits the release of ADH, reducing kidney's ability to retain water, while caffeine blocks sodium reabsorption and mildly suppress ADH.

**20. What is the significance of Juxtaglomerular apparatus in kidney function?** **NCERT**

**Ans.** The Juxtaglomerular Apparatus (JGA) plays an important role in monitoring and regulation of kidney functioning by hormonal feedback mechanism. It involves hypothalamus and upto a certain extent, the heart also.

**21. How does ADH regulate body fluid volume? Explain.**

**Ans.** The excessive loss of fluid from the body activates osmoreceptors, which stimulate the hypothalamus to release ADH from the neurohypophysis. ADH facilitates water reabsorption from posterior parts of tubule. This decreases osmolarity of blood. An increase in body fluid volume can switch off the osmoreceptors and suppress the ADH release to complete the feedback. ADH also shows constrictory effects on blood vessels.

**22. Briefly describe the hormonal regulation of kidney function.**

**Ans.** Refer to text on page no. 375.

**23. Explain the autoregulatory mechanism of GFR.** **NCERT**

**Ans.** Refer to text on page no. 375.

**24. Give full form of ANF. Name the organ that secretes it. Under what condition of the body is it released? What is its role in regulating kidney function?**

**Ans.** ANF is commonly known as Atrial Natriuretic Factor. Atrial Natriuretic Factor (ANF) is a hormone produced by the walls of the atria of the heart in response to an increase in blood volume and pressure. It increases sodium excretion and decreases blood pressure.

**Function** ANF inhibits release of renin from Juxta-Glomerular Apparatus (JGA) and thereby inhibits NaCl reabsorption by the collecting duct and reduces aldosterone release from the adrenal gland. (½ × 4)

**25. What changes occur in blood pressure when vasopressin is released by pituitary into the blood stream?**

**Ans.** Refer to text under heading regulation of kidney functions on page no. 375.

**26. Describe the disorders of excretory system.**

**Ans.** Refer to text on page no. 377.

**27. What is an artificial kidney?**

**Ans.** Refer to text on page no. 377.

**28.** Indicate whether the following statements are true or false.
(i) Micturition is carried out by a reflex.
(ii) ADH helps in water elimination making the urine hypotonic.
(iii) Protein-free fluid is filtered from blood plasma into the Bowman's capsule.
(iv) Henle's loop plays an important role in concentrating the urine.
(v) Glucose is actively reabsorbed in the proximal convoluted tubule. **NCERT**

**Ans.** (i) True (ii) False
(iii) True (iv) True
(v) True

## Long Answer Type Questions

**1.** Sketch and label the excretory system of human. Also give a brief account on the functions of kidney.

**Ans.** Refer to fig. on page no. 368 and text function of kidney on page no. 369. (5)

**2.** (i) Study the given structure carefully and label the parts given as *A*, *B*, *C*, *D* and *E*.
(ii) Give one major function of each of these. **Competency Based Que.**

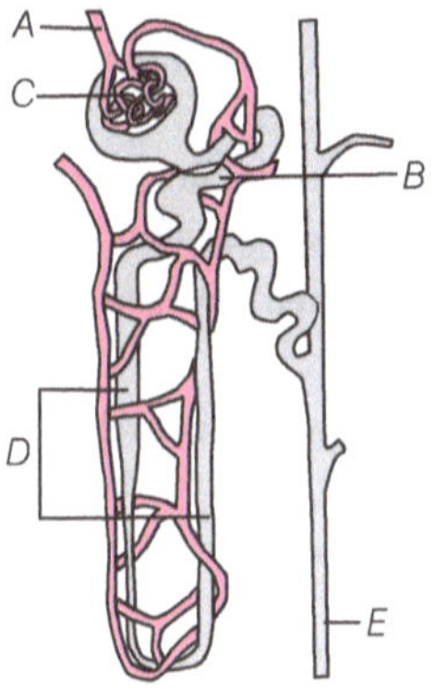


**Ans.** (i) *A*– Afferent arteriole, *B*– Proximal convoluted tubule, *C*– Glomerulus, *D*– Loop of Henle, *E*– Collecting duct. (2½)

(ii) Following are the functions of each above mentioned part
*A*– Carry blood to glomerulus for ultrafiltration.
*B*– Selective reabsorption of useful substances.
*C*– Ultrafiltration of blood.
*D*– Maintenance of the high osmolarity of medullary interstitial fluid.
*E*– Reabsorption of water to form hypertonic urine. (2½)

**3.** What is the selective reabsorption process? Differentiate between tubular reabsorption and tubular secretion.

**Ans.** Refer to text on page no. 372.

**4.** Describe the process of urine formation in the nephron through filtration, reabsorption and secretion.

**Ans.** Refer to text on page no. 371-372.

**5.** The glomerular filtrate in the loop of Henle gets concentrated in the descending and then gets diluted in the ascending limbs. Explain. **NCERT Exemplar**

**Ans.** Refer to text on page no. 372-373.

**6.** Give a brief account of the counter-current mechanism.

**Ans.** Refer to text on page no. 373-374. **NCERT**

**7.** Describe the role of liver, lungs and skin in excretion.

**Ans.** Refer to table on page no. 376. **NCERT**

**8.** Define haemodialyser. Describe the process of kidney transplantation.

**Ans.** Refer to text on page no. 377.

## Source Based/Case Based/Passage Based Questions

**1.** Observe the given diagram and answer the questions that follows

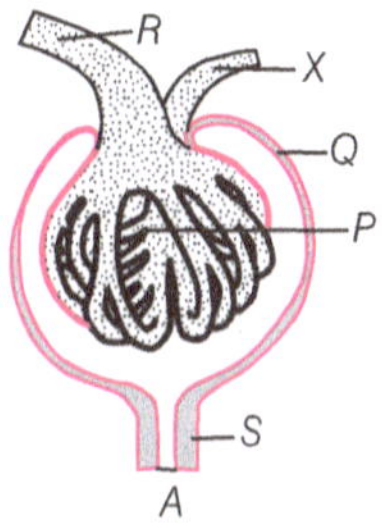


(i) What is the role of structure *A* shown above?
(ii) Give one point of differentiation between labels *R* and *X*.
(iii) Identify *X* and write any one of its feature.
(iv) Define podocytes.
*Or* (iv) Where do we find label *S* in the kidney?

**Ans.** (i) Glomerulus along with Bowman's capsule is called Malpighian body or renal corpuscle. It filtres out large solutes from blood and delivers the blood to renal tubule for modification. (1)
(ii) One point of differentiation in that the blood flowing in *R* is rich in waste products, whereas the blood flowing in *X* contains less quantity of waste product. (1)
(iii) *X* is efferent arteriole. It carries venous blood away from renal corpuscle. (1)
(iv) The outer parietal wall of glomerulus is composed of flattened (squamous) cells and the inner visceral wall is made up of a special type of less flattened cell called podocytes. (1)
*Or* (iv) Label *S* is Proximal Convoluted Tubule (PCT), which is restricted to the cortical region of the kidney. (1)

**2.** **A 60-year-old patient is suffering from kidney failure, which results in the accumulation of waste products and excess fluids in the body. To manage this condition, the patient is undergoing a medical treatment in which blood is pumped through an artificial kidney, which is a rectangular or cylindrical device that contains a semipermeable membrane and is connected to the patient *via* tubes.** **Competency Based Que.**

(i) **What is the process the patient is undergoing?**

(ii) **What property does the mentioned process rely on to function effectively?**

(iii) **What is the role of the tubes connected to the patient during this treatment?**

(iv) **Why is blood anticoagulated with heparin during the process?**

**Ans.** (i) The patient is undergoing haemodialysis, a treatment that filtres waste products and excess fluids from the blood. (1)

(ii) The dialysis process relies on the property of diffusion, specifically the movement of small solute molecules across a semipermeable membrane based on concentration gradients. (1)

(iii) The tubes connected to the patient facilitate the withdrawal of unfiltered blood to the dialyser for purification and the return of the cleaned blood back into the patient's circulation. This continuous flow ensures effective removal of waste products and excess fluids during treatment. (1)

(iv) Blood is anticoagulated with heparin to prevent clotting within the dialyser, ensuring continuous blood flow and effective filtration during the treatment. (1)

**3.** **Study the given figure and answer the following questions.** **Competency Based Que.**

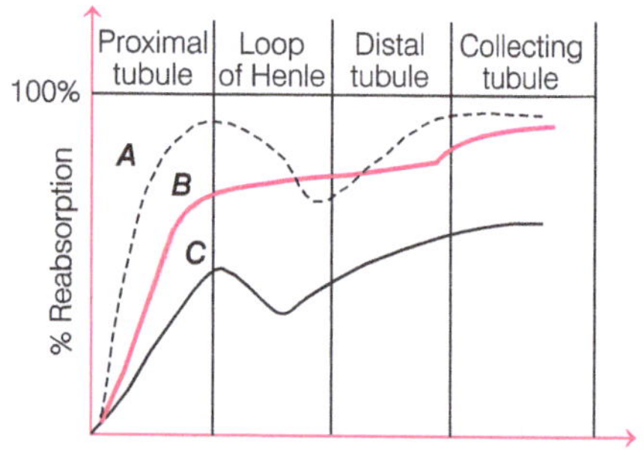


(i) **Identify *A* and *B* from the graph.**

(ii) **Reabsorption of *A* takes place by which type of transport mechanism?**

(iii) **Describe permeability of *B* in ascending and descending limbs of loop of Henle.**

(iv) **Explain how PCT helps to maintain pH and ionic balance of the body fluids.**

**Ans.** (i) In the given graph, *A* represents $Na^+$ ions and *B* represents water. (1)

(ii) The reabsorption of $Na^+$ takes place by active transport in which molecules move across a membrane against their concentration gradient, requiring energy in the form of ATP. (1)

(iii) In the descending limb of the loop of Henle, water is reabsorbed, making it permeable to water but not solutes. In the ascending limb, water is not reabsorbed, as it is impermeable to water and actively transports ions out, diluting the tubular fluid. (1)

(iv) PCT helps to maintain the pH and ionic balance of the body fluids by selective secretion of hydrogen ions and ammonia into the filtrate and by absorption of $HCO_3^-$ from it. (1)

**4.** **Read the following passage and answer the questions that follows.**

**Human kidneys possess the ability to produce concentrated or diluted urine, depending on how hydrated a person is. No wonder this process is controlled by hormonal feedback mechanisms. But, after the consumption of alcohol, person feel dehydrated and the urine production increases.**

(i) **Which hormone is produced by hypothalamus due to the excessive loss of fluids from the body?**

(ii) **Name the gland which release the hormone mentioned in (i). What function is performed by this hormone?**

(iii) **Why the urine production does not stop even after the person feel dehydrated after alcohol consumption?**

(iv) **What happen when a person do not drink sufficient water?**

*Or* (iv) **When does aldosterone is released from the adrenal cortex and how it affect kidney functions?**

**Ans.** (i) Antidiuretic Hormone (ADH) or vasopressin is produced by hypothalamus due to the excessive loss of fluids from the body. (1)

(ii) ADH is released from the posterior pituitary or neurohypophysis. It helps in water reabsorption from latter parts of nephron and thus prevents diuresis. (1)

(iii) Alcohol inhibits the release of ADH and thus diuresis could not be prevented after alcohol consumption. (1)

(iv) Due to insufficient water intake, blood volume decreases and ADH is released. It constricts blood vessels which in turn increases glomerulus filtration rate. It helps to conserve water in body. (1)

*Or*

(iv) Aldosterone is released in response to low glomerular blood pressure. It increases reabsorption of $Na^+$ and water from distal parts of nephron and thus increases blood pressure and GFR. (1)

# SELF ASSESSMENT TEST

## Multiple Choice Questions

1. What is the correct order of urine formation processes?
   (a) Filtration → Reabsorption → Secretion
   (b) Secretion → Filtration → Reabsorption
   (c) Reabsorption → Excretion → Filtration
   (d) Excretion → Reabsorption → Filtration

2. The glomerular filtration rate would be decreased by
   (a) constriction of the afferent arteriole
   (b) an increase in afferent arteriolar
   (c) compression in the renal capsule
   (d) an increase in renal blood flow

3. Maximum amount of electrolytes and water, about 70 - 80%, from the glomerular filtrate is reabsorbed in which part of nephron?
   (a) Distal convoluted tubule
   (b) Proximal convoluted tubule
   (c) Ascending limb of loop of Henle
   (d) Descending limb of loop of Henle

4. Juxtaglomerular cells secrete $X$ when there is a fall in $Y$ ion concentration.
   (a) $X$ – vasopressin; $Y$ – chloride
   (b) $X$ – renin; $Y$ – sodium
   (c) $X$ – angiotensinogen; $Y$ – chloride
   (d) $X$ – ANF; $Y$ – sodium

5. Refer to the given flowchart and identify $A$, $B$ and $C$.

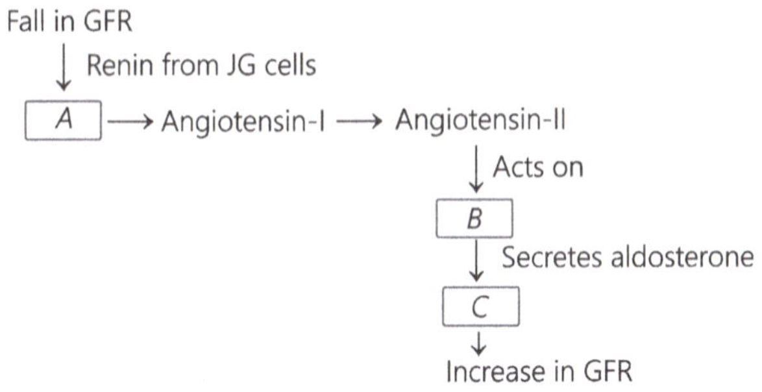


   (a) A – Angiotensin; B – Adrenal medulla; C – Secretion of water
   (b) A – Angiotensinogen; B – Adrenal cortex; C – Reabsorption of $Na^+$ ions
   (c) A – Angiotensin; B – Adrenal cortex; C – Reabsorption of water from DCT
   (d) A – Angiotensinogen; B – Adrenal medulla; C – Secretion of $Na^+$ ions

6. Which of the following option correctly represents a vasoconstrictor and a vasodilator respectively?
   (a) ANF and ADH
   (b) Renin and ADH
   (c) Angiotensinogen-II and ANF
   (d) ADH and angiotensinogen

7. Among the given substances, how many are excreted through sweat?
   I. Lactic acid    II. Sterols    III. Waxes
   IV. Small amount of urea    V. Hydrocarbons    VI. NaCl
   Choose the correct option.
   (a) Four    (b) Six    (c) Five    (d) Three

## Assertion-Reason Questions

**Direction** (Q. Nos. 8-11) *In each of the following questions, a statement of Assertion (A) is given followed by corresponding statement of Reason (R). Of the statements, mark the correct answer*

(a) Both A and R are true and R is the correct explanation of A.
(b) Both A and R are true, but R is not the correct explanation of A.
(c) A is true, but R is false.
(d) A is false, but R is true.

8. **Assertion** (A) In cortical nephrons, vasa recta is absent or highly reduced.

**Reason** (R) Cortical nephrons are mainly concerned with concentration of urine.

9. **Assertion** (A) Nephridia in earthworms are considered to be a form of metanephridia.

**Reason** (R) Metanephridia are more advanced excretory organs that function by filtering coelomic fluid and reabsorbing useful substances before excreting waste.

10. **Assertion** (A) Vasopressin increases the water permeability of the DCT.

**Reason** (R) In the absence of ADH, water reabsorption is considerably reduced.

11. **Assertion** (A) Glomerular filtration requires expenditure of energy by kidney.

**Reason** (R) Glomerular filtration occurs because pressure in the glomerular capillaries is higher than the pressure in Bowman's capsule.

## Very Short Answer Type Questions

12. The mechanism of concentration of filtrate is also known as counter-current mechanism. Justify the statement.
13. Name two actively transported substances in glomerular filtrate. **NCERT Exemplar**
14. Blood plasma contains protein, but glomerular filtrate does not. Why?
15. State the function of atrial natriuretic factor.

## Short Answer Type Questions

16. Describe the structure of Bowman's capsule.
17. Explain why a haemodialysing unit is called artificial kidney. **NCERT Exemplar**
18. Write a short note on

(i) Uremia (ii) Sebaceous gland

## Long Answer Type Questions

19. Draw a labelled diagram of human urinary system and write one function of each adrenal gland, ureter, urinary bladder, kidney and urethra.
20. How does tubular secretion contribute to the regulation of ionic and acid-base balance in body fluids?
21. Explain the role of organs other than kidney in excretion.

## Case Based Question

22. Study the given figure and answer the following questions.

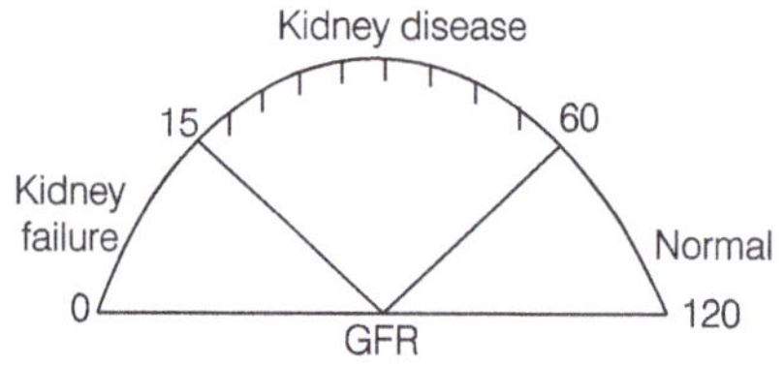


**(i) How does a GFR of 0-15 impact the choice of treatment options compared to a GFR of 15-60?**

**(ii) What is the potential significance of a GFR fluctuating between 40 and 50 over time?**

**(iii) What is the use of GFR test?**

**(iv) In what ways can regular monitoring of GFR help prevent progression to kidney failure?**

## Answers

| | | | | | | | |
|---|---|---|---|---|---|---|---|
| 1. (a) | 2. (b) | 3. (b) | 4. (b) | 5. (b) | 6. (c) | 7. (d) | 8. (c) |
| 9. (a) | 10. (b) | 11. (d) | | | | | |

# 17 CHAPTER

One of the distinctive character that separates living from non-living is that they can change their position or orientation. This is required for various purposes such as search of food, shelter, preying, mating, etc. When organism does not change its position and just orient from one side to other, it is called as **movement**. Some of the movements result in a change of place or location. Such voluntary movements are called **locomotion**.

**YOUR STUDY GOALS**

17.1 Movements and Locomotion in Organisms
17.2 Muscles
17.3 Skeletal System
17.4 Joints
17.5 Disorders of Muscular and Skeletal System

**YOUR PRACTICE GOAL**

- Objective Type Questions (42 Qs ; MCQs, A-R) Case Based Questions (3)
- Subjective Type Questions
- (23 VSAs, 33 SAs, 8 LAs)

# Locomotion and Movement

- In humans and other higher vertebrates, muscles plays a vital role in locomotion and movement.
- In this chapter, you will learn about the types of muscles, their structure, mechanism of muscle contraction and human skeletal system.

## 17.1 Movements and Locomotion in Organisms

### Movement

- It is one of the most important characteristics of living organisms.
- Both animals and plants exhibit wide range of movements.
- For example, movement of cilia, flagella and tentacles shown by many organisms and movement of limbs, jaws, eyelids, tongue, etc., in human beings.

## Types of Movement

Four main types of movement are exhibited by the cells of the human body. These are as follows

### 1. Amoeboid (Pseudopodial) Movement

- The movement facilitated by finger-shaped protoplasmic extensions (i.e. pseudopodia or false feet as seen in *Amoeba*) is called **amoeboid movement**.
- These types of movements are also exhibitted by leucocytes and macrophages of blood. When they move out of the blood into tissues.
- Cytoskeletal elements, like microfilaments are also involved in this type of movement.

### 2. Ciliary Movement

- The movement in the cells or organs with the help of cilia is called **ciliary movement**.
- Cilia are short, fine, hair-like structures present all over the body surface in large numbers. They beat in in **coordinated manner** to help in movements.
- Removal of dust particles and foreign substances in the trachea, passage of ova through female reproductive tract occurs through cilia.
- This type of movement occurs in most of the internal tubular organs that are lined by ciliated epithelium.

### 3. Flagellar Movement

- This type of movement occurs in protozoans like *Trypanosoma*, *Euglena*, etc., along with sponges.
- In protozoans, flagella help in locomotion, while in sponges, it maintain a regular current of water through the canal system.
- In case of human beings, the sperms swim in water or in female genital tract with the help of flagellar movement only.

### 4. Muscular Movement

- Movement with the help of muscles is called **muscular movement**.
- The alternate contraction and relaxation property of muscles is used effectively to bring the movement.
- This type of movement is found in majority of multicellular animals including humans.

## Locomotion

- It is the movement of an animal as a whole from one place to another.
- It requires a perfect coordinated activity of **muscular**, **skeletal** and **neural system**.
- Locomotion takes several, forms such as walking, running, flying and swimming, etc.

## Advantages of Locomotion

It helps the animal in search of food, shelter, mate, to escape from enemies/predators, to locate suitable areas for breeding or to disperse to new locations. Methods of locomotion in animals vary with their habitats and the demand of situation.

**Locomotion *vs* Movement**

- It is very difficult to separate movement from locomotion because an animal cannot change its place (locomotion) without movement, e.g. in *Paramecium* **cilia** helps in movement of food through the cytopharynx and in locomotion. **Tentacles** in *Hydra* are used for capturing prey and in locomotion.
- Limbs are used for change of body postures as well as for locomotion in humans and other animals.
- This suggests that movements and locomotion are interlinked thus, stating that all locomotions are movements, but all movements are not locomotions.

# 17.2 Muscles

- They arise from the embryonic mesoderm.
- It makes about 40-50% of a human body weight.
- These are made up of highly specialised thin and elongated cells called **muscle fibres**.

## Special Properties of Muscles

Muscles exhibit various special properties, some of them are given below

- **Contractility** The ability of muscle fibres to shorten and generate force, allowing for movement and posture.
- **Excitability** The capacity of muscle cells to respond to stimuli, such as nerve impulses, triggering contraction.

- **Extensibility** The ability of muscle tissue to stretch without damage, enabling normal movement and flexibility.
- **Elasticity** The capacity of muscles to return to their original shape and length after being stretched or contracted, ensuring functional integrity.

## Types of Muscles

Muscles have been classified using different criteria, i.e. location, appearance and nature of regulation of their activities. Based on their location, the muscles are of three types, i.e. **skeletal, visceral** and **cardiac**.

### 1. Skeletal or Striated Muscles

- These muscles are found in the limbs, body wall, tongue, pharynx and beginning of oesophagus.
- These muscles function in association with the skeleton of an organism.
- Under the microscope, they show a striped appearance and hence, are called **striated muscles**.
- They are also known as **voluntary muscles** as their activities are under the voluntary control of the central nervous system.
- They are primarily involved in locomotory actions and change of body postures.

### 2. Visceral or Smooth Muscles

- They are found in the inner walls of hollow visceral (internal) organs of body like alimentary canal, reproductive tract, etc.
- They do not exhibit any striation and are smooth in appearance and hence, are called **smooth muscles** (non-striated muscle).
- They are also known as **involuntary muscles** as they are not under the voluntary or direct control of the nervous system.
- They assist in the transportation of materials, e.g. movement of food through the digestive tract and gametes through the genital tract.

### 3. Cardiac Muscles

- These muscles are present in the wall of the heart.
- These are striated and involuntary in nature.
- Many cardiac muscle cells assemble in a branching pattern to form a cardiac muscle.

> **Quick Test 1**
>
> 1. What type of movement is facilitated by protoplasmic extensions?
> 2. Which type of movement is found in majority of multicellular animals?
> 3. *X* organ in *Hydra* is used for locomotion. Identify the organ *X*.
> 4. Which type of cell in humans shows amoeboid movement?
> 5. **State True or False.**
>    (a) Voluntary muscles show striated appearance under the microscope.
>    (b) Smooth muscles are found in the hollow visceral organ.

## Detailed Structure of a Skeletal Muscle

- Skeletal muscle is made up of a number of **muscle bundles** or **fascicles** held together by **fascia** (common collagenous connective tissue layer).
- Each fascicle contains a number of muscle fibres (muscle cells).

### Detailed structure of Muscle Fibre

- Each muscle fibre is lined by **sarcolemma** (plasma membrane) and contains well-developed sarcoplasmic reticulum (endoplasmic reticulum), specialised for calcium storage, in its sarcoplasm (cytoplasm).

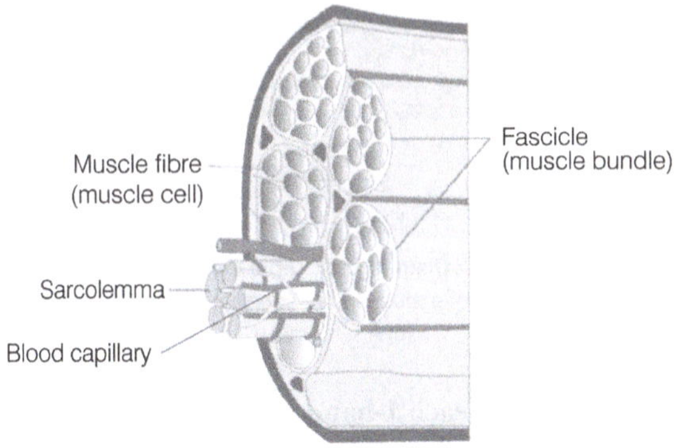


Fig. 17.1 Diagrammatic cross sectional view of a muscle showing muscle bundles and muscle fibres

- Muscle fibre is a **syncytium** as its sarcoplasm contains many nuclei.
- A characteristic feature of muscle fibre in the presence of large number of parallelly arranged filaments called **myofilaments** or **myofibrils** (characteristic feature of muscle fibre).

## Detailed Structure of a Myofibril

- A myofibril has alternate dark and light bands (stripped appearance) due to the distribution pattern of two important proteins- **actin** and **myosin**.
- The dark bands are also called **anisotropic band** or **A-band**, which contains myosin protein.
- The light bands are called **isotropic band** or **I-band**, which contain actin protein.
- Both these proteins are arranged as rod-like structures, parallel to each other and also to the longitudinal axis of myofibrils.
- Actin filaments are thinner than myosin filaments.
- Hence are commonly called as thin and thick filaments, respectively.

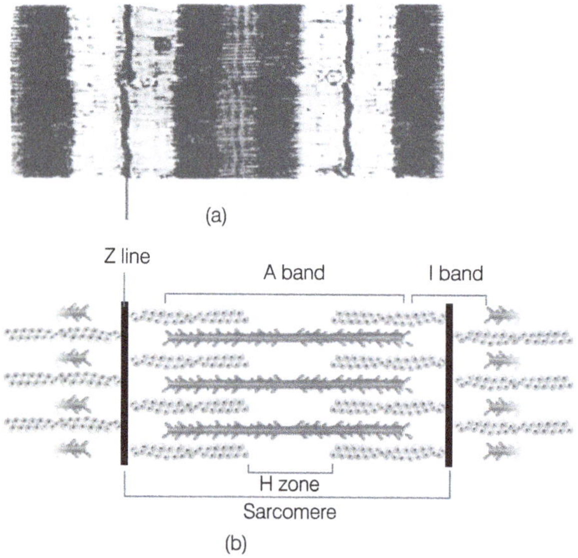


**Fig. 17.2** Diagrammatic representation of (a) Anatomy of a muscle fibre showing a sarcomere (b) A sarcomere

- In the centre of each **I-band** is an elastic fibre called **Z-line** (an elastic fibre) which bisects it.
- The thin filaments are attached to the Z-lines.
- The thick filament in the **A-band** are also held together in the middle of this band by a thin fibrous membrane called **M-line**.
- The A and I-bands are arranged alternately throughout the length of myofibril.
- The part of the myofibril between two successive Z-lines is called a **sarcomere** (functional unit of muscle contraction).
- Infact each sarcomere is a bundle of actin (thin) filaments and myosin (thick) filaments.
- In resting state, the edges of thin filaments on either side of thick filaments partially overlap free ends of thick filaments leaving H-zone in the centre of thick filaments.
- The central part of thick filament, not overlapped by thin filaments is called the **H-zone**.

## Structure of Contractile Proteins

The thick myofilaments are formed by **myosin protein** and the thin myofilaments are formed by three types of proteins called **actin, tropomyosin** and **troponin**. These three proteins are collectively known as **contractile proteins.**

### Thick Myofilament

- It mainly consists of myosin protein. Each myosin filament is a polymerised protein made up of many monomeric proteins called **meromyosins.**
- Each meromyosin has two important parts which are as follows
  - **Globular Head** The head together with a short arm constitute called **Heavy Meromyosin** (HMM).
    - The HMM components project outwards at regular distance and angle from each other, from surface of a polymerised myosin filament and is known as **cross arm.**

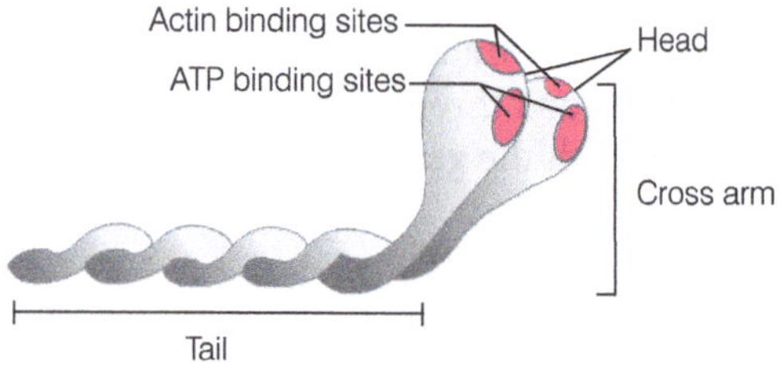


**Fig. 17.3** Myosin monomer (meromyosin)

- The globular head is an active ATPase enzyme, and has binding sites for ATP and active sites for actin.
- **Tail** is called the **Light Meromyosin** (LMM

### Thin Myofilament or Secondary Myofilament

It is composed of following proteins

- **Actin** It is a globular protein with low molecular weight. This is made up of two 'F' (filamentous) actin helically wound to each other. Each F actin is a polymer of monomeric '**G**' (globular) actins.
- **Tropomyosin** It is a double-stranded helical rod. Tropomyosin is a fibrous molecule that runs close to 'F' actin throughout its length.
- **Troponin** It is a complex protein of three globular peptides. It is distributed at regular intervals on the tropomyosin.
- In the resting state a subunit of troponin masks the active binding sites for myosin on the actin filaments.

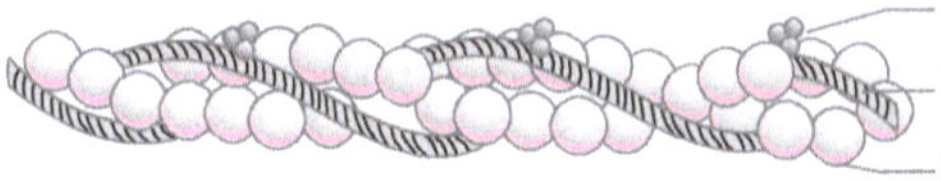


Fig. 17.4 An actin (thin) filament

## Mechanism of Muscle Contraction

The contraction of muscle is best explained by the **sliding filament theory**. It states that contraction of muscles takes place by the sliding of thin over thick filaments with the help of **cross-bridge.** It reduces the length of the sarcomere.

### 1. Depolarisation and Calcium ion Release

- The sequence of events leading to contraction is initiated by a signal in the Central Nervous System (CNS), either from the **brain** (voluntary activity) or from the **spinal cord** (reflex activity) *via* a motor neuron.
- A **motor neuron** along with the muscle fibres connected to it, forms a motor unit.
- The junction between a motor neuron and the sarcolemma of the muscle fibre is called the **neuromuscular junction** or **motor-end-plate.**
- A neural signal reaching this junction releases a **neurotransmitter** (**Acetylcholine**) which generates an action potential in the sarcolemma.
- This spreads through the muscle and causes the release of calcium ions into the sarcoplasm.
- Calcium plays a key regulatory role in muscle contraction.
- Increase in calcium ions level leads to binding of $Ca^{2+}$ ions with a troponin subunit on actin filament.
- This removes the masking of active sites for myosin.

### 2. Formation of Cross-Bridge

- An ATP molecule joins the active site on head of myosin myofilament.
- These heads contain an enzyme, **myosin ATPase** that catalyses the breakdown of ATP.
- The energy is transferred to myosin head, which then binds to the exposed active sites on actin to form a **cross-bridge.**

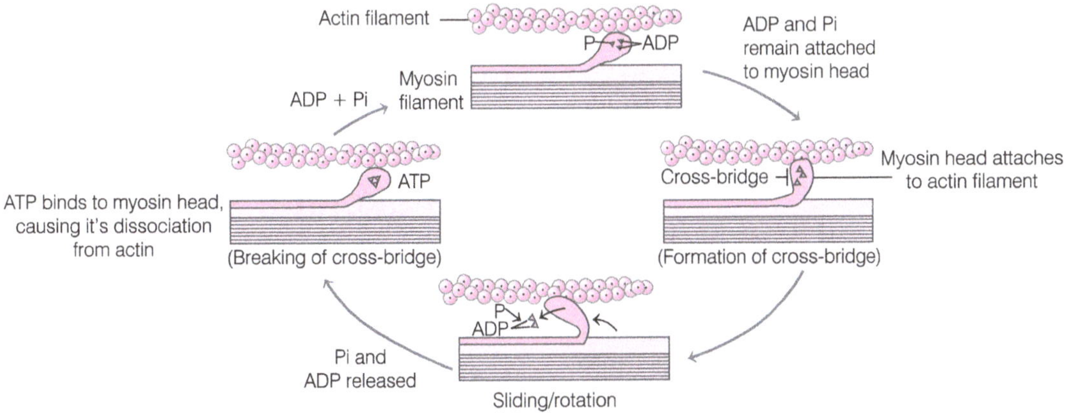


Fig. 17.5 Stages in cross-bridge formation, rotation of head and breaking of cross-bridge

- The energised cross-bridges move, causing the attached actin filaments to move towards the centre of A-band.
- The Z-line is also pulled inwards causing shortening of sarcomere, i.e. contraction.
- It is clear from the above explanation that during contraction, A-bands retain its length, while I-bands get reduced.
- The myosin head releases ADP and Pi and then relaxes to its low-energy state.
- The head detaches from actin myofilaments when new ATP bind to it (cross-bridge broken).
- In repeating cycle, the free myosin head cleaves the new ATP.
- The cycles of cross-bridge formation and breakage is repeated causing further sliding.

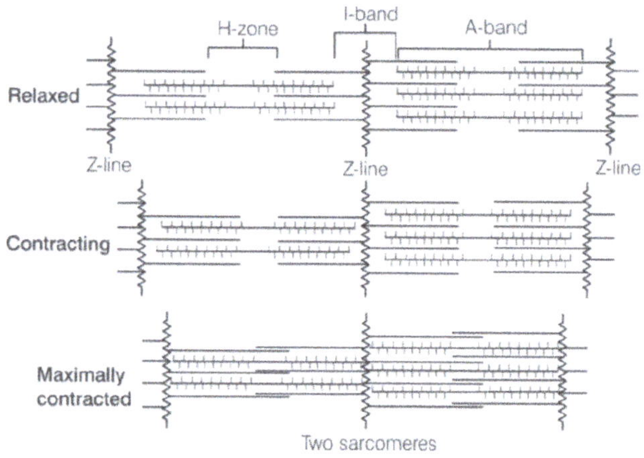


Fig. 17.6 Sliding filament theory of muscle contraction (movement of the thin filaments and the relative size of the I-band and H-zones)

## 3. Muscle Relaxation

- After contraction, the calcium ions are pumped back to the sarcoplasmic cisternae, masking the active sites present on actin myofilaments.
- The Z-line returns to original position, i.e. relaxation of muscle fibre takes place.
- The reaction time of the fibres can vary in different muscles.

**TEACHER'S TIP**
In the absence of ATP, myosin heads remain attached to actin filaments, preventing muscle relaxation. This constant binding leads to sustained muscle tension and rigidity, as observed in post-mortem conditions. As a result, the muscles become stiff and immobile.

## Muscle Fatigue

Repeated activation of the muscles can lead to the accumulation of lactic acid due to anaerobic breakdown of glycogen in them, causing fatigue.

## Red and White Muscle Fibres

Birds and mammals have two kinds of striated muscle fibres, in their skeletal muscles, i.e. red (or slow) and white (or fast) muscle fibres.

**Differences between Red and White Muscle Fibres**

| Red Muscle Fibres | White Muscle Fibres |
|---|---|
| They are dark red in appearance due to the presence of abundant myoglobin in them. | They are pale or whitish as they have less myoglobin. |
| Mitochondria are more in number, but they have less sarcoplasmic reticulum. | Mitochondria are few in number, but amount of sarcoplasmic reticulum is high. |
| They depend on aerobic process for energy. | They depend on anaerobic process for energy. |
| They contract at slow rate for long periods. | They contract at fast rate for short periods. |
| e.g. extensor muscle of the human back. | e.g. eyeball muscles. |

### Quick Test 2

1. Name the condition in which many nuclei are present in sarcoplasm.
2. State True or False.
   The part between two successive Z-lines is called sarcoplasm.
3. Muscles contain two types of bands. Name the band which contain actin.
4. A neurotransmitter *X* generates an action potential in sarcolemma. Identify *X*.
5. Which muscle fibre is characterised by a high content of myoglobin?

## 17.3 Skeletal System

- The framework of bones and few cartilages constitute the skeletal system or skeleton.
- It is present inside the human body so it is called **endoskeleton**.
- **Bone** and **cartilage** both are specialised connective tissues.

- Bone has a very hard matrix due to calcium salts, while cartilage has slightly pliable matrix due to chondroitin salts.
- Skeleton serves to perform following functions
  - **Support** It gives support to softer body parts.
  - **Protection** It protects the delicate internal organs like brain, heart, lungs, etc.
  - **Muscle attachment** provide surface for attachment of muscles.
  - **Movement** Bones help in bringing about movements also.
  - **Blood Cell Formation** It helps to manufacture blood corpuscles in bone marrow.
- The skeleton in human body is made up of **206 bones** and few cartilages. It is grouped into two principal divisions.

## 1. Axial Skeleton

- It lies along the main axis of the body. It comprises of 80 bones, which include skull, vertebral column, ribs and sternum.
- The details of axial skeleton system are as follows

### Skull

- It is the bony framework of the head. It is composed of two sets of bones, i.e. cranial and facial skull that form total of **22 bones**.

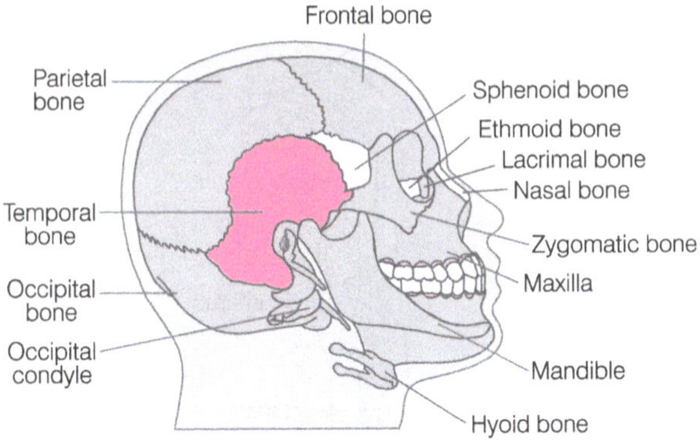


Fig. 17.7 Diagrammatic view of human skull

- Bones of skull are as follows
  - **Cranium (8)** includes frontal (1), parietal (2), temporal (2), occipital (1), sphenoid (1), ethmoid (1). They form the hard protective outer covering (cranium) for the brain.
  - **Facial bones (14)** include maxillae (2), palatine (2) mandible (1), vomer (1), nasal (2), zygomatic (2), lacrimal (2), inferior turbinate (2). They form the front part of the skull.
  - **Ear ossicles (6)** includes 2 malleus, 2 incus, 2 stapes. These three tiny bones belong to the middle ear.
  - **Hyoid** A U-shaped bone, present at the base of buccal cavity.
- Human skull is dicondylic, i.e. the skull region articulates with vertebral column with the help of two occipital condyles.

### Vertebral Column

- It is also called **backbone** or **spine**.
- Vertebral column is dorsally placed, extending from the base of the skull and constitutes the main framework of the trunk.
- Each vertebra has a central hollow portion (neural canal) through which the spinal cord passes.
- The vertebral column is made up of 26 serially arranged units called **vertebrae**.
- There are 7 cervical, 12 thoracic, 5 lumbar, sacral (1 fused) and coccygeal (1 fused).
- The vertebral formula for humans is $C_7$, $T_{12}$, $L_5$, $S_{(5)}$, $C_{(4)}$.
- The number of cervical vertebrae are seven in almost all mammals including human beings.

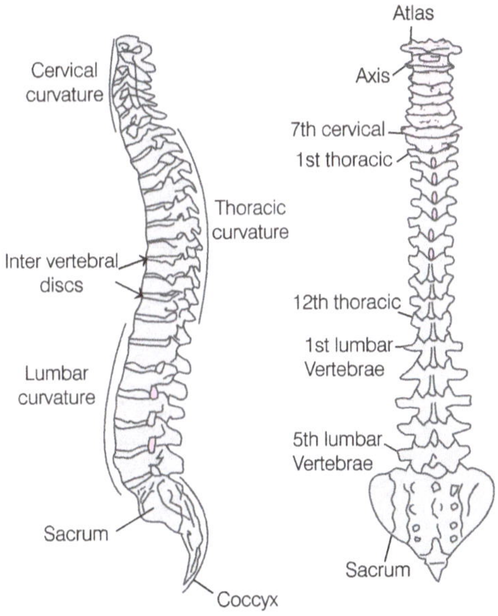


Fig. 17.8 Vertebral column (human)

### Functions of Vertebral Column

Vertebral column performed following functions

- Provides protection to the spinal cord.
- Supports the head.
- Allows flexion and bending of the back and body.
- Also serves as point of attachment for the ribs and musculature of the back.

## Sternum

It is a flat dagger-shaped bone located on the ventral midline of thorax.

### Functions of Sternum

- It protects the internal organs in the thoracic region.
- It also provides the surface for muscle attachment.
- The sternum helps in the respiratory mechanism.

## Ribs

- These are the thin, flat curved bones that form a protective cage around the organs of upper body.
- The ribs are composed of **24 bones** arranged in **12 pairs**, connected dorsally to thoracic vertebrae and ventrally to the sternum.
- It has two articulation surfaces on its dorsal end and hence called **bicephalic**.
- Ribs are mainly categorised into following types
  - **True Ribs** The first seven ribs are called true ribs. Dorsally, they are attached to the thoracic vertebrae and ventrally connected to the sternum with the help of hyaline cartilage.
  - **False Ribs** The 8th, 9th and 10th pairs of ribs join the seventh rib with the help of hyaline cartilage. They do not articulate directly with sternum. Hence, are called vertebrochondral (false) ribs.
  - **Floating Ribs** The last two (11th and 12th) pairs of ribs remain free and are called floating ribs.

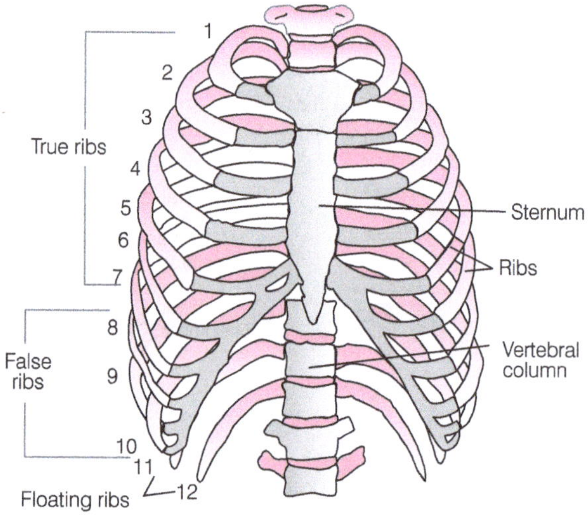


Fig. 17.9 Ribs and rib cage

### Functions of Ribs

Ribs serve following functions

- They protect the heart, large blood vessels and lungs.
- Support respiratory muscles.
- The lower two pairs of ribs also protect the organs of abdominal cavity.
- Ribs along with sternum and thoracic vertebrae form the rib cage.

# 2. Appendicular Skeleton

- It lies along the transverse (side) axis. It comprises of **126 bones**, which include pectoral and pelvic girdles and limb bones, i.e. bones of arms and legs.
- The details of appendicular skeleton are as follows

## Limbs

Each limb is made up of **30 bones**.

### Forelimb

- The bones of the hand (forelimb) constitute humerus (1), radius (1), ulna (1), carpals/wrist bones (8), metacarpals/palm bones (5) and phalanges/digits (14).

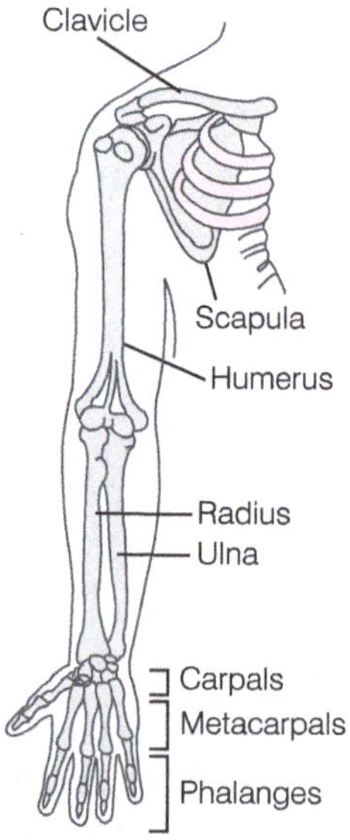


Fig. 17.10 Right pectoral girdle and upper arm (frontal view)

## Hindlimb

- The bones of the leg (hindlimb) constitute femur (1), tibia (1), fibula (1), tarsals (7), metatarsals (5) and phalanges (14). A cup-shaped bone called **patella** covers knee ventrally.
- Tarsals form the ankle, metatarsals form the sole and phalanges form the **digits** of the foot.

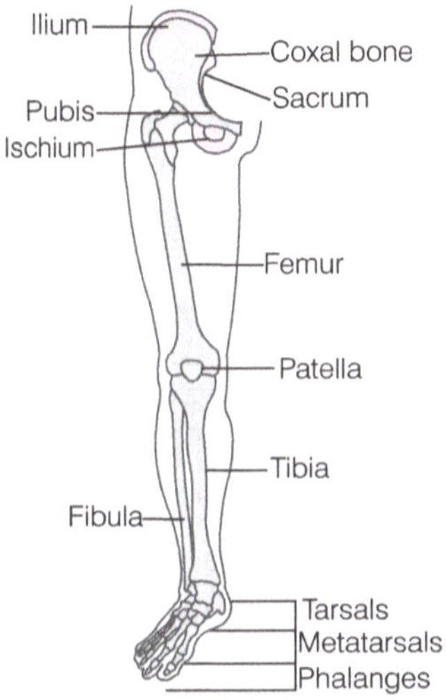


Fig. 17.11 Right pelvic girdle and lower limb bones (frontal view)

## Pectoral (Shoulder) Girdle

It consists of following two bones, i.e. scapula and clavicle.

### (i) Scapula (Shoulder blade)

- Scapula is a large triangular bone situated in the dorsal part of the thorax between the second and the seventh ribs.
- It consists of a sharp ridge- the **spine** and a **triangular bone**.
- The end of spine projects as a flattened and expanded portion called **acromion**.
- This articulates with the clavicle.

### (ii) Clavicle (Collar bone)

- Each clavicle is a long slender bone with two curvatures. The clavicle helps in articulation of the upper limb with axial skeleton.
- **Glenoid cavity** is a depression below the acromion to which head of humerus articulates, forming shoulder joint.

### Function of Pectoral Girdle

It provides an attachment point for numerous muscles that allows shoulder and elbow joints to move.

## Pelvic (Hip) Girdle

- It is located in the lower part of the trunk. It consists of **two coxal** (hip) bones. Each coxal bone is formed by fusion of the following three bones
  - **Upper ilium**
  - **Lower ischium**
  - **Inner pubis**
- At the point of fusion of these three bones, a deep, cup-shaped cavity called **acetabulum**, where head of femur (thigh bone) articulates.
- The two halves of the pelvic girdle meet ventrally to form **pubic symphysis** containing fibrous cartilage.

### Functions of Pelvic Girdle

It provides articulation to the bones of the leg, supports and protects abdominal viscera. It also provides attachment to certain leg muscles.

### Quick Test 3

1. Name the U-shaped structure found at the base of the buccal cavity.
2. Identify the structure that provides the point of attachment for the ribs.
3. **State True or False.**
   (a) In humans, the skull region articulates with nerves with the help of two occipital condyles.
   (b) There are 14 facial bones in a skull and among them there are 2 inferior turbinate bones.
4. Name the bone which is long and slender with two curvatures and helps in the articulation of upper limb.
5. Name the bones that fuses to form a coxal bone?

## 17.4 Joints

- The place of articulation between two or more bones or between a bone and a cartilage is called a **joint**.
- Force generated by the muscles is used to carry out movement through joints,where the joints act as a **fulcrum**.

- According to the mobility, joints are classified as fibrous, cartilaginous and synovial. The description of these joints are as follows

## 1. Fibrous (Immovable Joints)

- The bones are held firmly by bundles of dense fibrous connective tissue.
- These joints do not allow any movement of bones.
- **Example** this type of joint is present between the flat skull bones which fuse end-to-end with the help of dense fibrous connective tissues in the form of sutures, to form the cranium.

## 2. Cartilaginous (Slightly Movable Joints)

- In this type of joint the bones are joined together by cartilage.
- These joints allow for slight movement of bones.
- **Example** the joints between the adjacent vertebrae in the vertebral column and between pubic bones in pelvic girdle.

## 3. Synovial (Freely Movable Joints)

- This joint allows a considerable amount of movement.
- It is because of the presence of fluid-filled synovial cavity between articulating surface of bones.
- These joints help in locomotion and many other movements.

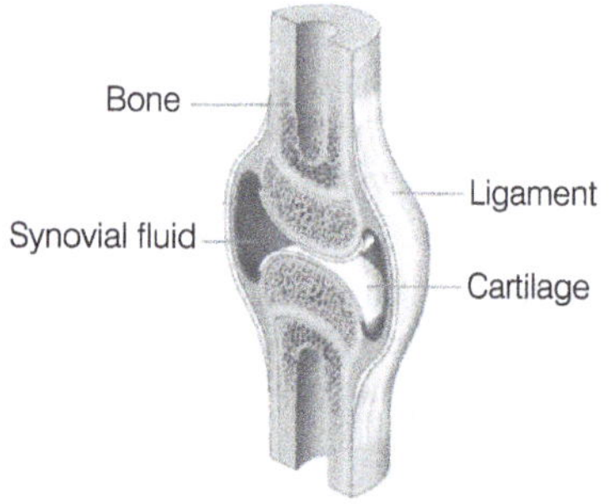


Fig. 17.12 Synovial joint

### Types of Synovial Joints

According to shape of bones and types of movement, the synovial joints are of following six types

- **Ball and Socket Joint** In this type of joint, a ball-like structure of one bone fits into a socket-like structure of another bone, e.g., shoulder joint (between pectoral girdle and head of humerus) and hip joint (between acetabulum and head of the femur).

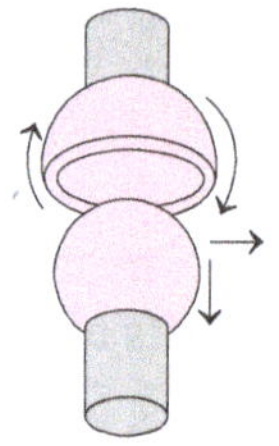

- **Hinge (Knee) Joint** This joint allows the movement in one plane only, e.g. elbow, knee, ankle and interphalangeal joints.

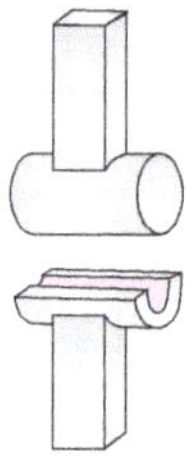

- **Pivot Joint** This joint is responsible for providing movement in one plane, e.g. joint between atlas and axis and radioulnar joint (between radius and ulna).

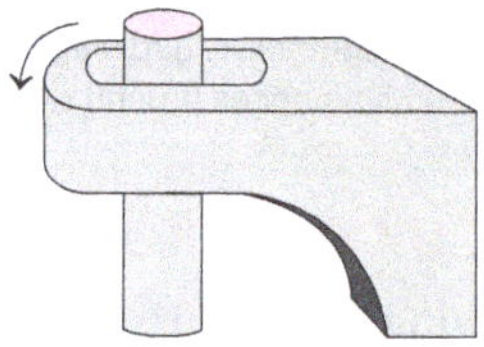

- **Gliding Joint** This joint allows two or more bones to move freely against each other without rubbing or crushing. e.g. joints between the carpal bones and between the tarsal bones.

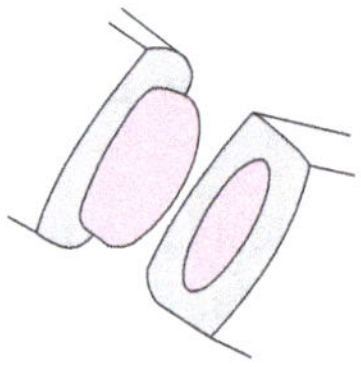

- **Saddle Joint** This type of joint is like ball and socket joint, but not fully developed, e.g. joint between carpal of hand and metacarpal of thumb.

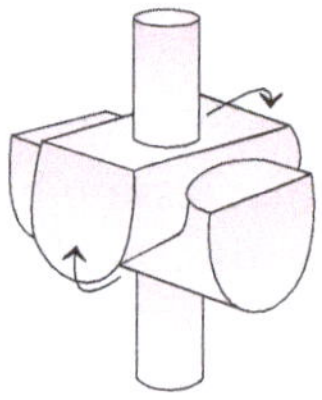

### Functions of Joints

Joints serve following functions in human body

- These are essential for all types of movement.
- The joints make body flexible.

## 17.5 Disorders of Muscular and Skeletal System

Some disorders of muscular and skeletal system are as follows

1. **Myasthenia Gravis** It is a chronic, autoimmune, neuromuscular disease characterised by varying degrees of weakness in the skeletal muscles of body.
   It leads to fatigue and ultimately to paralysis of skeletal muscles.
2. **Muscular Dystrophy** It is an inborn (genetic) disorder of muscles, associated with progressive degeneration of skeletal muscles.
3. **Tetany** It is an abnormal condition characterised by periodic painful muscular spasms (wild contractions).
   Tetany is caused by low calcium levels in body fluid.
4. **Arthritis** Causes inflammation of the **joints**.
5. **Osteoporosis** In this, a reduction in bone tissue mass occurs, which results in weakness of skeletal muscles.
   - It is an age-related disorder that is more common in women than in men.
   - The decreased level of oestrogen is a common cause for this disease.
   - It leads to increased chances of fractures.
6. **Gout** Inflammation of joints due to accumulation of uric acid crystals.

### Quick Test 4

**1.** *X* joint is present between two bones which are fuse end to end with the help of dense fibrous connective tissues. Identify *X*.

**2.** Which type of joint allows considerable movement between the articulating bones?

**3.** Name the joint that allows movement in two planes, providing flexibility for thumb motion.

**4.** **State Ture or False.**

(a) Pivot joint is responsible for providing movement in one plane.

(b) In gout, the inflammation of joints occurs due to the accumulation of calcium ions.

**5.** Name the condition which involves the progressive degeneration of skeletal muscles due to a genetic disorder.

# Mind Map

## Locomotion and Movement

### Types of Movement

**Types of Movement**

- **Amoeboid**: Movement with the help of pseudopodia formed by cytoplasmic streaming.
- **Ciliary**: Occurs in internal organs lined by ciliary epithelium.
- **Muscular**: Occurs due to contraction and relaxation of muscles.

**Muscles**

- **Skeletal**
  - Striated
  - Voluntary
- **Cardiac**
  - Striated
  - Involuntary
- **Visceral**
  - Smooth
  - Involuntary

### Structure of Myofibril

- Consists of alternate light and dark bands.
- Dark band contain myosin protein (A-band)
- Light band contain actin protein (I-band)

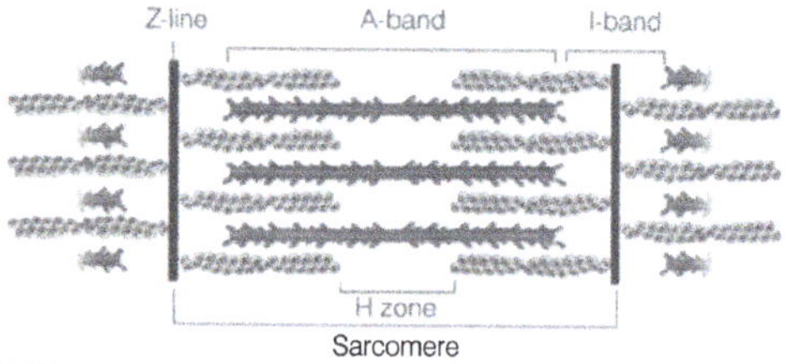


### Mechanism of Muscle Contraction

- Contraction of muscle fibres takes place by sliding of actin and myosin.
- During contraction, the sarcomere shortens, I-band get reduced and A-band retains the length.

### Joints

Structure where two bones articulate; acts as fulcrum.

**Types of Joints**

- **Synovial joint**
- **Cartilaginous joint**
- **Fibrous joint**

- **Ball and socket joints** e.g. between humerus and pectoral girdle, between femur and pelvic girdle.
- **Hinge joints** e.g. knee joint elbow joint
- **Pivot joint** e.g. atlas and axis
- **Gliding joint** e.g. between carpals
- **Saddle joint** e.g. between carpals and metacarpals of thumb

### Human Skeletal System

Consists of 206 bones, divided into the **axial skeleton** (skull, spine, ribs) and the **appendicular skeleton** (limbs, girdles), providing structure, protection and facilitating movement.

### Axial Skeleton (80 Bones)

**Skull** (29 bones)-Cranial bone-8, Facial bone-14, Ear ossicle-6, Hyoid-1

**Vertebral Column**
26 serially arranged units called **vertebrae**.

**Sternum** (1) Flat dagger-shaped bone; provides a surface to attach muscle and helps in respiratory mechanism.

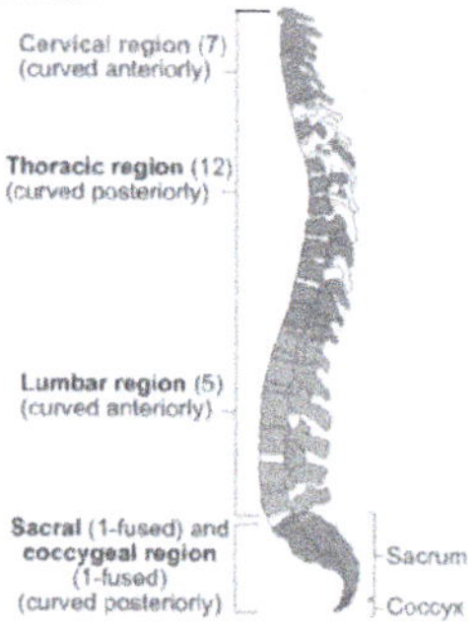


Vertebral Column (26 bones)

### Appendicular Skeleton (126 Bones)

**Girdles** (6 bones)

**Limbs** (120 bones)

Pectoral

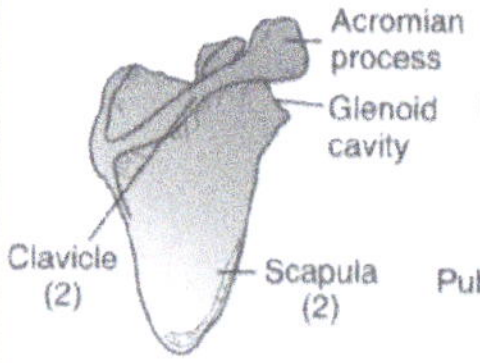


Pelvic

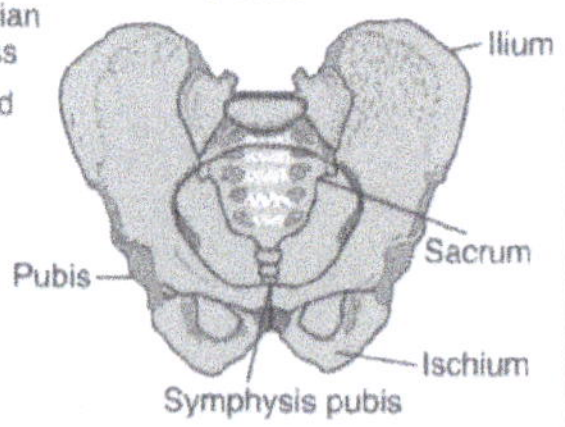


**Forelimb** (60 bones)

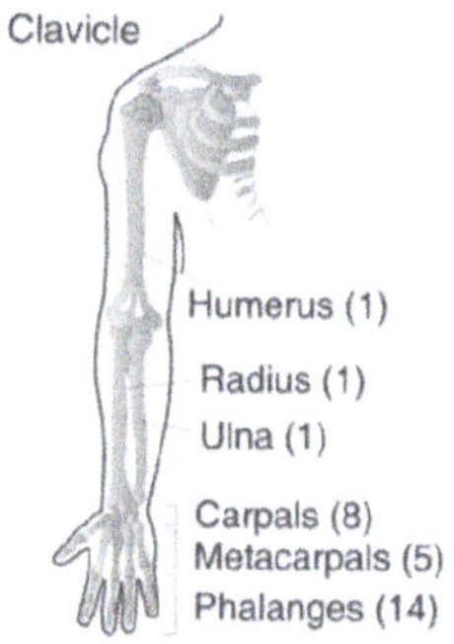


**Hindlimb** (60 bones)

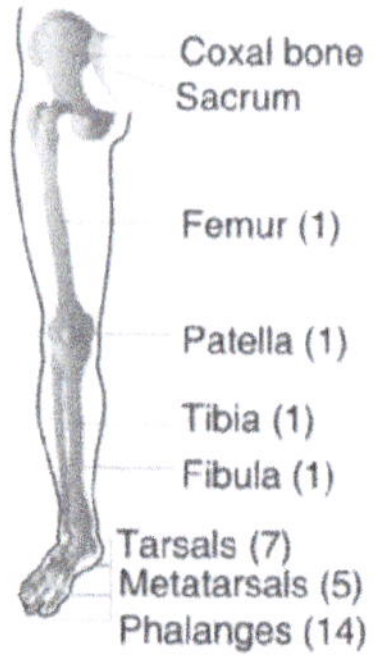

# EXAM PATTERN QUESTIONS

## Objective Type Questions

### Multiple Choice Questions

**1. Macrophages and leucocytes exhibit** NCERT Exemplar

(a) ciliary movement (b) flagellar movement
(c) amoeboid movement (d) gliding movement

Ans. (*c*)

**2. Ciliary movement within human body can be observed in**

(a) trachea (b) lungs
(c) stomach (d) gall bladder

Ans. (*a*)

**3. Movements of limbs, jaws tongue, etc. requires**

(a) ciliary movement
(b) amoeboid movement
(c) muscular movement
(d) flagellar movement

Ans. (*c*)

**4. Which one of the following statement is incorrect?** NCERT Exemplar

(a) Heart muscles are striated and involuntary
(b) The muscles of hands and legs are striated and voluntary
(c) The muscles located in the inner walls of alimentary canal are striated and involuntary
(d) Muscles located in the reproductive tracts are unstriated and involuntary

Ans. (*c*) Smooth muscles are involuntary and non-striated muscles found in inner wall of alimentary canal. These muscles of cannot be controlled directly, unlike skeletal muscles which are voluntary, controlled and possess striations.

**5. Muscles with characteristic striations and involuntary are** NCERT Exemplar

(a) muscles in the wall of alimentary canal
(b) muscles of the heart
(c) muscles assisting locomotion
(d) muscles of the eyelids

Ans. (*b*)

**6. The muscle bundles, fascicles are held together by the collagenous connective tissue called**

(a) intercalated disc (b) myofibril
(c) fascia (d) All of these

Ans. (*c*)

**7. In the centre of each I-band, there is an elastic fibre called**

(a) I-line (b) Z-line
(c) A-line (d) H-zone

Ans. (*b*)

**8. What is a sarcomere?**

(a) It is the functional unit of contraction
(b) It is the portion of myofibril present in between two M-lines
(c) It is the complete bundle of muscles
(d) It is the portion of myofibril present in between two A-bands

Ans. (*a*)

**9. Choose the incorrect match pair.** NCERT Exemplar

| | | | |
|---|---|---|---|
| (a) | Globular head of meromyosin | – | Active ATPase enzyme |
| (b) | Thin fibrous membrane holding thick filaments in A-band | – | M-line |
| (c) | Dark bands | – | Isotropic band |
| (d) | Motor end plate | – | Junction between motor neuron and muscle fibres |

Ans. (*c*)

**10. Cross arms of the myosin monomer consist of**

(a) outward projection of G-actin filament
(b) outward projection of the head region of meromyosin
(c) outward projection of the tail region of meromyosin
(d) Both (b) and (c)

Ans. (*b*)

**11.** **Identify the correct match which correctly states the labelled part and their function.** **Competency Based Que.**

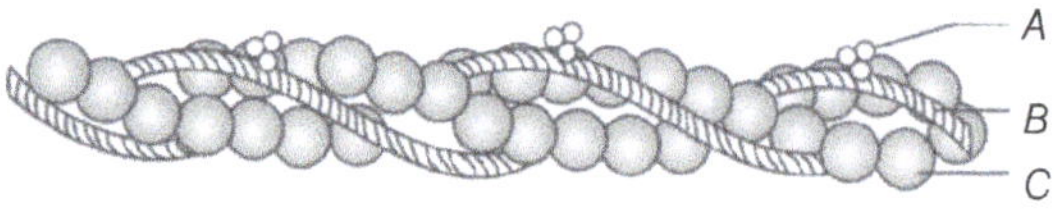


(a) *A*–Troponin, masks the active binding sites for myosin on the actin filaments.
(b) *B*–Thick filament, it initiates the contraction process
(c) *A*–Troponin, initiate the contraction process
(d) *C*–Tropomyosin, it is a polymer of monomeric actins.

**Ans.** (*a*)

**12.** **During muscle contraction which of the following events takes place.** **Competency Based Que.**

I. **I-band decreased in width**
II. **H-zone disappear**
III. **A-band widens**
IV. **M-line and Z-line come closer**

(a) I, II and III
(b) I, II and IV
(c) II and IV
(d) II, III and IV

**Ans.** (*b*) During muscle contraction, the A-band remains of the same length. This is because the A-band contains thick myosin filaments, which do not shorten; instead, the thin actin filaments slide past the thick filaments, causing the sarcomere to shorten.

**13.** **For how long, contraction of the muscles continues in sliding filament theory?**

(a) Till ATP binds to myosin head
(b) Till ADP binds to myosin head
(c) Till $Ca^{2+}$ present in sarcoplasm
(d) Till polymerisation of myosin head is going on

**Ans.** (*c*) Muscle contraction continues as long as calcium ions remain in the cytoplasm, allowing the binding sites on actin filaments to stay exposed for interaction with myosin.

**14.** **Muscle contains a red coloured oxygen containing pigment called**

(a) rhodopsin (b) myoglobin
(c) haemocyanin (d) Both (a) and (b)

**Ans.** (*b*)

**15.** **Aerobic muscles and anaerobic muscles are called**

(a) red fibres; white fibres, respectively
(b) white fibres; red fibres, respectively
(c) white fibres; yellow fibres, respectively
(d) red fibres; yellow fibres, respectively

**Ans.** (*a*) Aerobic muscles, which are rich in myoglobin and have a sufficient blood supply, are referred to as red fibres, while anaerobic muscles, which are less vascularised and contain less myoglobin, are called white fibres.

**16.** **Match the following columns.**

| | Column I | | Column II |
|---|---|---|---|
| A. | White muscle fibres | 1. | Myoglobin |
| B. | Red muscle fibres | 2. | Sarcoplasmic reticulum |
| C. | Actin filament | 3. | Contractile unit |
| D. | Sarcomere | 4. | I-band |

**Codes**

| | A | B | C | D |
|---|---|---|---|---|
| (a) | 1 | 2 | 4 | 3 |
| (b) | 2 | 1 | 3 | 4 |
| (c) | 2 | 1 | 4 | 3 |
| (d) | 3 | 2 | 4 | 1 |

**Ans.** (*c*)

**17.** **Which of the following are associated with skeletal system?**

I. **Frame of cartilages and bones**
II. **Movement of cilia in tubles**
III. **Cycloskeletal movement**
IV. **Chewing food with jaws**
V. **Walking action**

(a) II, III and V
(b) Only III
(c) I, IV and V
(d) III, IV and V

**Ans.** (*c*)

**18.** **The human cranium is made up of ............ bones.**

(a) 5 (b) 6
(c) 7 (d) 8

**Ans.** (*d*)

**19.** **Identify *A*, *B*, *C* and *D* in the diagram given below.** **Competency Based Que.**

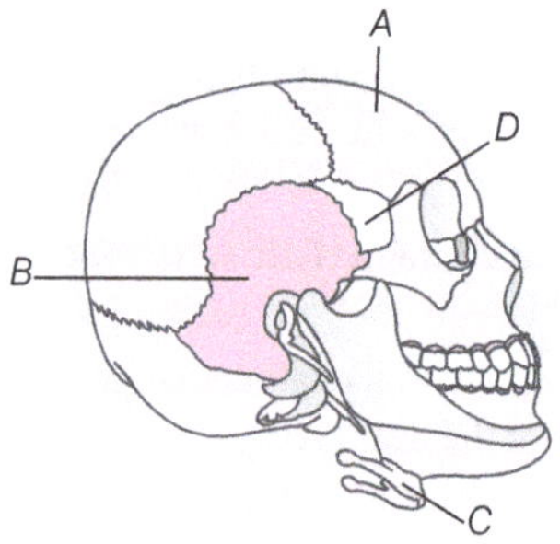


(a) Frontal, temporal, hyoid and sphenoid
(b) Parietal, occipital, mandible and ethmoid
(c) Occipital, sphenoid, mandible and ethmoid
(d) Parietal, temporal, hyoid and ethmoid

**Ans.** (*a*)

**20.** **All mammals (except few) have ..........cervical vertebrae.**

(a) 7 (b) 8
(c) 9 (d) 6

**Ans.** (*a*)

**21.** **Which one of the following is showing the correct sequential order of vertebrae in the vertebral column of human beings?** **NCERT Exemplar**

(a) Cervical — Lumbar — Thoracic — Sacral — Coccygeal
(b) Cervical — Thoracic — Sacral — Lumbar — Coccygeal
(c) Cervical — Sacral — Thoracic — Lumbar — Coccygeal
(d) Cervical — Thoracic — Lumbar — Sacral — Coccygeal

**Ans.** (*d*)

**22.** **............. and ............ pairs of ribs are called floating ribs.**

(a) 10th and 11th
(b) 11th and 12th
(c) 5th and 6th
(d) None of these

**Ans.** (*b*)

**23.** **The number of phalanges in each limb of human is**

(a) fourteen (b) fifteen
(c) twelve (d) ten

**Ans.** (*a*)

**24.** **Number of tarsals, metatarsals and phalanges in human skeleton is**

(a) 7, 5, 14 (b) 8, 5, 14
(c) 9, 5, 14 (d) 5, 6, 7

**Ans.** (*a*)

**25.** **Which one of the following statement is true?** **NCERT Exemplar**

(a) Head of humerus bone articulates with acetabulum of pectoral girdle.
(b) Head of humerus bone articulates with glenoid cavity of pectoral girdle.
(c) Head of humerus bone articulates with a cavity called acetabulum of pelvic girdle.
(d) Head of humerus bone articulates with a glenoid cavity of pelvic girdle.

**Ans.** (*b*)

**26.** **A cup-shaped cavity called acetabulum is formed by the fusion of**

(a) ilium and incus
(b) ilium and ischium
(c) incus and ischium
(d) ilium, ischium and pubis

**Ans.** (*d*)

**27.** **Which one of the following pair is incorrect?** **NCERT exemplar**

(a) Hinge joint – Between humerus and pectoral girdle
(b) Pivot joint – Between and atlas, axis
(c) Gliding joint – Between the carpals
(d) Saddle joint – Between carpals and metacarpals of thumb

**Ans.** (*a*)

**28.** **Where is saddle joint present?** **DIKSHA**

(a) Between carpal and metacarpal of thumb
(b) Between atlas and axis
(c) Between humerus and pectoral girdle
(d) Between the carpals

**Ans.** (*a*)

**29.** **Match the following columns.** **NCERT Exemplar**

| Column I | | Column II | |
|---|---|---|---|
| A. | Sternum | 1. | Synovial fluid |
| B. | Glenoid cavity | 2. | Vertebrae |
| C. | Freely movable joint | 3. | Pectoral girdle |
| D. | Cartilagenous joint | 4. | Flat bones |

**Codes**

| | A | B | C | D | | A | B | C | D |
|---|---|---|---|---|---|---|---|---|---|
| (a) | 2 | 1 | 3 | 4 | (b) | 4 | 3 | 1 | 2 |
| (c) | 2 | 1 | 4 | 3 | (d) | 3 | 1 | 2 | 4 |

**Ans.** (*b*)

**30.** **Choose the incorrect match pair.**

(a) Myasthenia gravis – Paralysis of skeletal muscle
(b) Tetany – Low calcium level in body fluids
(c) Gout – Accumulation of urea in joints
(d) Muscular dystrophy – Degeneration of skeletal muscles

**Ans.** (*c*) The match-pair given in option (c) is incorrect. It can be corrected as

Gout refers to inflammation of joints due to accumulation of uric acid crystals.

## Assertion-Reason Questions

**Direction** (Q. Nos. 1-12) *In each of the following questions, a statement of Assertion (A) is given followed by corresponding statement of Reason (R). Of the statements, mark the correct answer.*

(a) Both A and R are true and R is the correct explanation of A
(b) Both A and R are true, but R is not the correct explanation of A
(c) A is true, but R is false
(d) A is false, but R is true

**1. Assertion** (A) Muscle fibre is syncytium.

**Reason** (R) The sarcoplasm of muscle fibre contains numerous nuclei.

**Ans.** (*a*)

**2. Assertion** (A) Calcium is required for skeletal muscle contraction.

**Reason** (R) Calcium binds with tropomyosin of the thin filament.

**Ans.** (*c*)

**3. Assertion** (A) On stimulation, a muscle cell releases calcium ions ($Ca^{2+}$) from sarcoplasmic reticulum.

**Reason** (R) By reacting with a protein complex, $Ca^{2+}$ uncover active sites on the actin filaments.

**Ans.** (*b*)

**4. Assertion** (A) The myosin rich zone, called A-band, maintains its length during sarcomere contraction.

**Reason** (R) The length of I-band remains the same during muscle contraction.

**Ans.** (*c*) A is true, but R is false. R can be corrected as

The length of the I-band decreases during muscle contraction as the thin filaments slide over the thick filaments.

**5. Assertion** (A) The contraction of muscle is best explained by the sliding filament theory.

**Reason** (R) It states that contraction of muscles take place by the sliding of thin and thick filaments with the help of cross-bridge.

**Ans.** (*a*)

**6. Assertion** (A) Energy from ATP hydrolysis moves the myosin-actin cross-bridges.

**Reason** (R) Movement of cross-bridge cause thick myofilaments to slide along the thin myofilament.

**Ans.** (*b*)

**7. Assertion** (A) Red muscle fibres depend on anaerobic process for energy.

**Reason** (R) Red muscle fibres have more number of mitochondria in them.

**Ans.** (*d*)

**8. Assertion** (A) The cranium and carpals are the part of axial skeleton.

**Reason** (R) Both carpals and cranium have 8 bones each.

**Ans.** (*d*) A is false, but R is true. A can be corrected as

The cranium is part of the axial skeleton, but the carpals are part of the appendicular skeleton.

**9. Assertion** (A) Human skull is dicondylic.

**Reason** (R) It is attached to vertebral column through two occipital condyles.

**Ans.** (*a*)

**10. Assertion** (A) The most abundant joints in human body are synovial joints.

**Reason** (R) Gliding joints offer limited movement in all the three planes/axis.

**Ans.** (*b*)

**11. Consider the given diagram of a joint. Comment upon the appropriateness of Assertion and Reason.**

**Competency Based Que.**

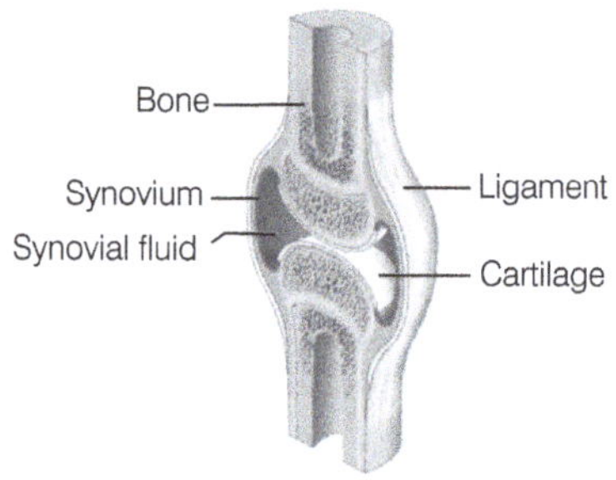


**Assertion** (A) The joint allows considerable movement.

**Reason** (R) A space filled with synovial fluid is found in the joints.

**Ans.** (*a*)

**12. Assertion** (A) Knee joint is the hinge type of joint.

**Reason** (R) Femur and humerus are associated with the knee joint.

**Ans.** (*c*) A is true, but R is false. R can be corrected as

The femur is associated with the knee joint, but the humerus is associated with the shoulder joint.

# Subjective Questions

## Very Short Answer Type Questions

**1. Give reason for variation in methods of locomotion.**

**Ans.** Methods of locomotion vary with animal's habitat and demand of situation.

**2. Give the name of the cells/tissues in human body which exhibit ciliary movement.** NCERT Exemplar

**Ans.** Ciliated epithelium of trachea.

**3. Name the two important parts of meromyosin.**

**Ans.** The two important parts of meromyosin are

(i) Globular head with short arm, called Heavy Meromyosin (HMM).

(ii) Tail, called the Light Meromyosin (LMM). (½ × 2)

**4. Label the different components of actin filament in the diagram given below.**

Competency Based Que., NCERT Exemplar

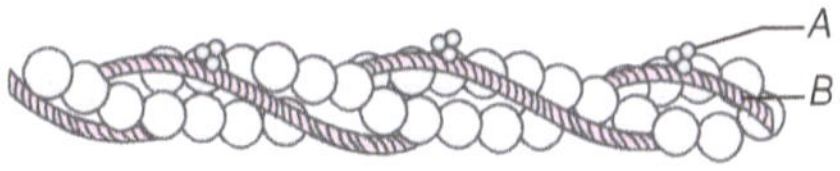


**Ans.** *A*–Troponin complex

*B*–Tropomyosin (½ × 2)

**5. Define sliding filament theory of muscle contraction.**

**Ans.** The sliding filament theory states that contraction of skeletal muscles occur due to the sliding of thin filament over thick filament.

**6. Which compound provides energy for muscle contraction?**

**Ans.** The energy is derived from ATP present in muscles.

**7. What causes muscle fatigue?**

**Ans.** Accumulation of lactic acid causes muscle fatigue.

**8. Name the pigment concerned with storage of oxygen in vertebrate muscles.**

**Ans.** Myoglobin

**9. Give an example of white muscle fibre.**

**Ans.** Eye ball muscle

**10. What kind of muscle fibres are richly found in the extensor muscles of the back? What characteristics enable these fibres to serve their purpose?**

**Ans.** Red striated muscle fibres are found in extensor muscles of the back. The abundant myoglobin and mitochondria enable them to serve their purpose. (½ × ½)

**11. Name the protein present in cartilage.**

**Ans.** Chondrin.

**12. What is the difference between the matrix of bone and cartilage?** NCERT Exemplar

**Ans.** The matrix of bone is hard due to calcium salts, whereas, the cartilage has slightly pliable matrix due to chondroitin salts.

**13. How many total bones are there in human body? Name the largest and strongest bone.**

**Ans.** Human body contains 206 bones. Femur is the largest and strongest bone of human body. (½ × 2)

**14. The human endoskeleton consists of two parts. Name them with number of bones in each.**

**Ans.** Two parts of human endoskeleton are as follows

(i) Axial skeleton, it comprises of 80 bones.

(ii) Appendicular skeleton, it comprises of 126 bones. (½ × 2)

**15. Which bones help in hearing? Where are they found?**

**Ans.** Malleus, incus and stapes. They are found in internal ear.

**16. The three tiny bones present in middle ear are called ear ossicles. Write them in correct sequence beginning from ear drum.** Competency Based Que., NCERT Exemplar

**Ans.** Malleus, incus and stapes

**17. Name one animal that has seven cervical vertebrae.**

**Ans.** All mammals have seven cervical vertebrae.

**18. Where is acromion found?**

**Ans.** Scapula has slightly elevated ridge (spine) which projects as a flat, expanded process called the acromion.

**19. What are the points of articulation for pelvic and pectoral girdles?** NCERT Exemplar

**Ans.** Pelvic girdle articulates with femur through its acetabulum. Pectoral girdle by its glenoid cavity articulates with head of the humerus.

**20. Which type of movable joint makes the hip joint?**

**Ans.** Ball and socket joint

**21. Which substance is responsible for lubricating the freely movable joint at the shoulder?**

**Ans.** Synovial fluid.

**22. Give the location of ball and socket joint in a human body.** NCERT Exemplar

**Ans.** Shoulder joint (between pectoral girdle and head of humerus).

**23. Why is osteoporosis common in females?**

**Ans.** Females generally develop osteoarthritis because of the decline in oestrogen level after menopause.

## Short Answer Type Questions

**1. What are the different types of movements exhibited by the cells of human body?** NCERT

**Ans.** Refer to text on page no. 392.

**2. Mention and explain the special properties of muscle.**

**Ans.** Refer to text on page no. 392-393.

**3. Define the structure of smooth and cardiac muscle.**

**Ans.** Refer to text on page no. 393.

**4. How do you distinguish between a skeletal muscle and a cardiac muscle?** NCERT

**Ans.** Differences between skeletal muscle and cardiac muscle are as follow

| Skeletal Muscle | Cardiac Muscle |
|---|---|
| It is found in limbs, tongue, all parts in association with the skeleton of organism. | It is found in the walls of heart and large veins. |
| Fibres are unbranched. | Fibres are branched. |
| It is multinucleate. | It is uninucleate. |
| No oblique bridge and intercalated discs are present. | Oblique bridges and intercalated discs are present. |
| It gets fatigued soon. | It never gets fatigued |
| It is voluntary in nature. | It is involuntary. |

($\frac{1}{2} \times 6$)

**5. Give a brief account of visceral muscles. Mention their function.**

**Ans.** Refer to text on page no. 393.

**6. Sarcolemma, sarcoplasm and sarcoplasmic reticulum refer to a particular type of cell in our body. Which is this cell and to what parts of that cell do these names refer to?** Competency Based Que., NCERT Exemplar

**Ans.** The cell is muscle.

These names refer to the following parts

- **Sarcolemma**–Plasma membrane
- **Sarcoplasm**–Cytoplasm
- **Sarcoplasmic reticulum**–Endoplasmic reticulum ($\frac{1}{2} \times 4$)

**7. Why is muscle fibre a syncytium? How are myofilaments arranged in it?** NCERT Exemplar

**Ans.** Muscle fibre is a syncytium as the sarcoplasm contains many nuclei. Myofilaments are parallelly arranged within the muscle fibre, which is crucial for muscle contraction. (2)

**8. Draw the diagram of a sarcomere of skeletal muscle showing different regions.** NCERT

**Ans.** Refer to fig. no. 17.2 on page no. 394.

**9. Describe the important steps in muscle contraction.** NCERT

**Ans.** The important steps of muscle contraction are as follows

- Nerve impulse arrives at neuromuscular junction and release of acetylcholine.
- Spreading of action potential through muscle fibre.
- The release of $Ca^{2+}$ from sarcoplasmic reticulum to cytoplasm of muscle fibre.
- ATP joins to meromyosin head that hydrolyses it into ADP and Pi releasing energy. The mesomyosin uses the energy to raise the head to high energy state (the head joins active site on actin, forming cross-bridge).
- Actin filament is thus, pulled towards the centre of sarcomere. ADP and Pi are released and head returns to low energy state.
- And a new ATP joins head, detaching it from actin filament.
- Above mentioned steps are thus, repeated many times during one contraction to draw the thin myofilaments further inward.

**10. What is the role of calcium in muscle contraction?**

**Ans.** Calcium plays a key regulatory role in muscle contraction. The increase in $Ca^{2+}$ level in sarcoplasm leads to their binding to troponin subunit. Thus, exposing active sites on F-actin leading to cross-bridge formation.

**11. Explain the initiation of muscle contraction.**

**Ans.** Refer to mechanism of muscle contraction on page no. 395.

**12. Explain the formation of a cross-bridge during muscle contraction.**

**Ans.** Refer to text on page no. 395-396.

**13. Why do muscles fatigue?**

**Ans.** The continuous contraction and relaxation of muscles cause movement in organs. If it continues for longer time, then anaerobic conditions are created in muscle cells due to which lactic acid is formed. Thus, accumulation of lactic acid causes muscle fatigue. After taking some rest for some course of time, liver degrades the lactic acid and person is relieved from pain.

**14. Radha was running on a treadmill at a great speed for 15 minutes continuously. She stopped the treadmill and abruptly came out. For the next few minutes, she was breathing heavily/fast.**

Answer the following questions.

(i) What happened to her muscles when she strenuously exercised?

(ii) How did her breathing rate change? NCERT Exemplar

**Ans.** (i) By strenous exercise, the metabolism of the muscle increases, which leads to increased consumption of oxygen and ATP. To meet this demand, blood supply of muscle is also enhanced.

(ii) Increased consumption of oxygen and increased production of $CO_2$ stimulates the respiratory centres, which causes the change of breathing rate. (1½ × 2)

**15. Why are muscles rigidly locked in whatever position they are after death?** **Competency Based Que.**

**Ans.** Muscles require ATP to relax as well as to contract. On animal's death, its muscles soon exhaust ATP and lose the ability to contract or relax. They become rigidly locked in whatever position they were when ATP gets completely used up.

**16. How can a red muscle fibres work for prolonged period?** **Competency Based Que.**

**Ans.** Red muscle fibres can work for long periods because they have high myoglobin content for oxygen storage, a dense supply of mitochondria for production of energy through aerobic respiration and a rich blood supply for oxygen and nutrient delivery. Their slower contraction speed also makes them ideal for endurance activities. These characteristics help them resist fatigue during prolonged exercise.

**17. The axial skeleton comprises of ...*A*.... It includes ...*B*..., ...*C*... ribs and ...*D*.... .**

**Ans.** *A*– 80 bones, *B*– skull, *C*– vertebral column and *D*– sternum. (½ × 4)

**18. Give functions of sternum.**

**Ans.** Refer to text on page no. 398.

**19. (i) What do you mean by ear ossicles?**

**(ii) How many vertebrae are generally there in neck region of mammals?**

**Ans.** (i) The bones found in middle ear are called ear ossicles (malleus, incus and stapes) (1)

(ii) Mammals in general has seven cervical vertebrae in neck region. (1)

**20. What are floating ribs? How many of them are there in human body?**

**Ans.** The last two pairs of ribs are known as the floating ribs i.e. 11th and 12th pair. These are comparatively smaller and have cartilaginous tips. They are only connected to the thoracic vertebrae, there is no attachment present ventrally, hence the name floating ribs.

**21. How many bones are present in each human limb? Name these with their corresponding number in a forelimb.**

**Ans.** Refer to the limbs on page no. 398.

**22. Write the difference between**

**(i) Actin and myosin**

**(ii) Red and white muscles**

**(iii) Pectoral and pelvic girdle** **NCERT**

**Ans.** (i) The differences between actin and myosin are as follows

| Actin | Myosin |
|---|---|
| Actin is a globular protein (G-actin) that polymerises to form long filaments (F-actin). | Myosin is a motor protein that consists of a thick filament structure with a head region that binds to actin and uses ATP to generate force. |
| It primarily forms the thin filaments in muscle fibres. | It primarily forms the thick filaments in muscle fibres |

(½ × 2)

(ii) Refer to text on page no. 396 (½ × 2)

(iii) The differences between pectoral and pelvic girdle are as follows

| Pelvic Girdle | Pectoral Girdle |
|---|---|
| Composed of two hip bones (ilium, ischium and pubis) | Consists of the clavicles (collar bones) and scapula (shoulder blades) |
| Supports the weight of the upper body, protects reproductive organs and provides attachment for muscles of lower limbs. | Support the arms and allows for a wide range of motion, while facilitating upper limb movement. |

(½ × 2)

**23. What are the functions of girdles?**

**Ans.** Girdles connect limbs to the skeleton, providing support, facilitating movement, protecting vital organs and serving as attachment points for muscles.

(i) Pectoral girdles provide an attachment point for numerous muscles that allows shoulder and elbow joints to move.

(ii) Pelvic girdles provide articulations to the bones of legs. These support and protect abdominal visceral organs and provide attachment to certain leg muscles. (2 × 1)

**24. What are joints? Write their function?**

**Ans.** Refer to text on page no. 399 and 401.

**25. Name the joint, present between the vertebrae in the vertebral column. Also write in brief about the joint.**

**Ans.** Cartilaginous joint is present in between the vertebrae. It allows slight movement because of the elastic pads of fibrocartilage present between the ends of bones taking part in the joints.

**26. What makes the synovial joint freely movable? List the various types of synovial joints.**

**Ans.** Refer to text on page no. 400.

**27. Write true or false. Correct each false statement to make it true.**

**(i) Actin is present in thin filament.**

**(ii) H-zone of striated muscle fibre represents both thick and thin filaments.**

**(iii) In a muscle fibre, $Ca^{2+}$ is stored in nucleus.**

(iv) Thin filaments of myofibrils contain 2 F-actins.

(v) Sternum is present on the ventral side of the body. **NCERT**

**Ans.** (i) True.

(ii) False, H-zone of striated muscle fibre represents only thick filaments.

(iii) False, in a muscle fibre, $Ca^{2+}$ is stored in sarcoplasmic reticulum.

(iv) True

(v) True

**28. Name the type of joint between the following.**

**(i) Atlas/axis**

**(ii) Carpal/metacarpal of thumb**

**(iii) Between phalanges**

**(iv) Femur/acetabulum**

**(v) Between cranial bones**

**(vi) Between pubic bones in the pelvic girdle.** **NCERT**

**Ans.** (i) Pivot joint (ii) Saddle joint

(iii) Hinge joint (iv) Ball and socket joint

(v) Suture (vi) Cartilaginous joint (½ × 6)

**29. The following parts in our body has specific names in osteology write the name for each.**

**(i) Knee cap** **(ii) Collar bone**

**(iii) Skull** **(iv) Spine**

**(v) Shoulder bone**

**Ans.** (i) Patella (ii) Clavicle

(iii) Cranium (vi) Vertebral column

(v) Scapula

**30. Give the name of the major parts of human skeleton. Also mention the number of bones in each part.**

**Ans.**

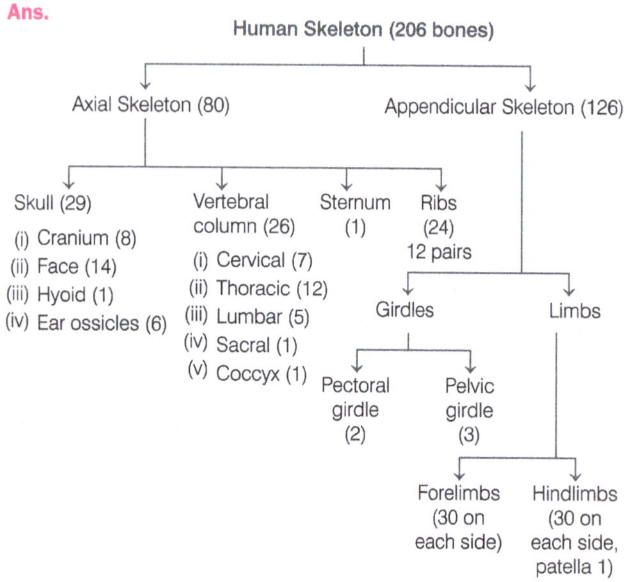


**31. Observe the diagram carefully and answer the following questions.** **Competency Based Que.**

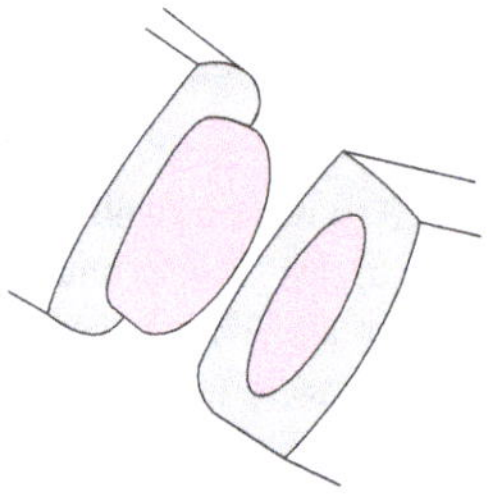

**(i) Which type of joint is shown in the diagram?**

**(ii) Where the joint is located?**

**Ans.** (i) Gliding joint (1)

(ii) Gliding joint is present between the carpel bones and the tarsal bones. (1)

**32. Which tissue is affected by myasthenia gravis? What is the underlying cause?**

**Ans.** Myasthenia gravis affects the skeletal muscles of the body. It is a chronic autoimmune neuromuscular disease characterised by varying degree of weakness in the skeletal muscles. (1+1)

**33. Write a few lines about gout.**

**Ans.** When metabolic waste like uric acid and urate crystals are present in excess in blood, they get accumulated in the joints causing gout or gouty arthritis. It is very painful, particularly at night and makes movement difficult.

## Long Answer Type Questions

**1. Define sliding filament theory of muscle contraction.** **NCERT**

**Ans.** Refer to text on page no. 395-396.

**2. Differentiate between**

**(i) Actin and myosin filaments**

**(ii) A-band and I-band.**

**(iii) Non-muscular and muscular movements**

**Ans.** . (i) Differences between actin and myosin filament are as follows

| Actin Filaments | Myosin Filaments |
|---|---|
| These are found in I-band. | These are found in A-band. |
| These are thin filaments. | These are thick filaments. |
| It does not directly form cross-bridges | It forms cross-bridges |
| It is a globular protein with low molecular weight. | It is a heavy molecular weight polymerised protein. |

(2)

(ii) Differences between A-band and I-band are as follows

| A-Band | I-Band |
|---|---|
| It is formed of myosin filaments. | It is formed of only actin filaments. |
| It gives dark appearance. | It gives light appearance. |
| It is anisotropic band which possesses two type of proteins. | It is isotropic band which possesses only one type of proteins. |

(2)

(iii) Differences between non-muscular and muscular movements are as follows

| Non-muscular Movements | Muscular Movements |
|---|---|
| These movements include pseudopodial and ciliary movements. | These movements are brought about by movement of myofilaments within muscle fibres. |
| They persist in the animals in some of their cells. | These are found in majority of animals. (1) |

**3. Write down the biochemical events in the mechanism of muscle contraction.**

**Ans.** Refer to text on page no. 395-396.

**4. (i) How does a muscle return to its original form during relaxation? Also draw a diagram showing relaxation of muscle.** **Competency Based Que.**

**(ii) Explain the formation of cross-bridge.**

**Ans.** (i) After contraction calcium ions are quickly pumped back to the sarcoplasmic cisternae. This leads to blocking of active sites on actin. The Z-line returns to the original position. Causing muscles to return to its original position, i.e. relaxation form.

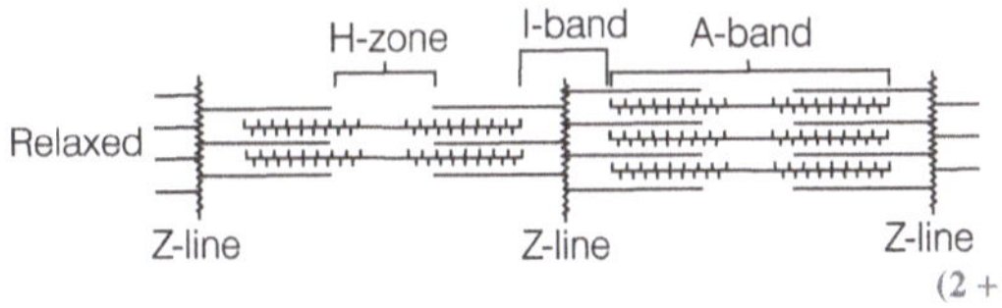


(2 + 1)

(ii) Refer to text on page no. 395-396.

**5. What is skeleton? Describe basic functions of human skeleton.**

**Ans.** Refer to text on page no. 396-397.

**6. (i) Write short note on pectoral and pelvic girdle.**

**(ii) Why 8th to 10th ribs are called as false ribs?**

**Ans.** (i) Pectoral and pelvic girdle help in the articulation of upper and lower limbs, respectively. Each girdle is made of two equal halves.

Each half of a pectoral girdle consists of clavicle and scapula. Scapula is a large triangular flat bone. There is glenoid cavity in the scapula, which articulates with the head of humerus to form the shoulder joint.

Each half of pelvic girdle is formed by three bones, i.e. ilium, ischium and pubis. At the point of their fusion there is a cavity called acetabulum to which the head of femur articulates. (3)

(ii) Refer to text on page no. 398. (2)

**7. Give classification of joints. Also give an example of each type. Explain the functions of joints.**

**Ans.** Refer to text on page no. 399-401.

**8. Write short note on**

**(i) Myasthenia gravis**

**(ii) Meromyosin**

**Ans.** (i) Refer to text on page no. 401. (2½)

(ii) Refer to text under the heading thick myofilament on page no. 394. (2½)

## Source Based/Case Based/Passage Based Questions

**1. A 75-year-old man named George visits the clinic after struggling with walking and experiencing frequent falls. He has a long-standing history of knee problems and has become increasingly inactive due to his limited mobility. During the examination, the doctor suggested a bone density test, which reveals low bone tissue mass.** **Competency Based Que.**

**(i) Based on George's symptoms, what condition might he be experiencing?**

**(ii) How do the principles of muscle contraction and joint mechanics play a role in George's difficulty with locomotion?**

**(iii) In what ways could George's lifestyle changes would impact his overall locomotion?**

**(iv) Describe two consequences if the mentioned disease remain untreated.**

**Ans.** (i) George is likely experiencing osteoporosis, particularly in his knees, which is contributing to his difficulty walking, joint stiffness and balance issues. (1)

(ii) George's difficulty with locomotion may stem from weakened muscle fibres and reduced joint flexibility, affecting his ability to generate force effectively. (1)

(iii) Increasing physical activity through regular, structured exercise can improve muscle strength, flexibility and balance, directly enhancing George's ability to walk and reducing fall risk. (1)

(iv) If osteoporosis remains untreated, it can lead to chronic pain and fractures. (1)

**2.** Refer to the given graph answer the following questions. **Competency Based Que.**

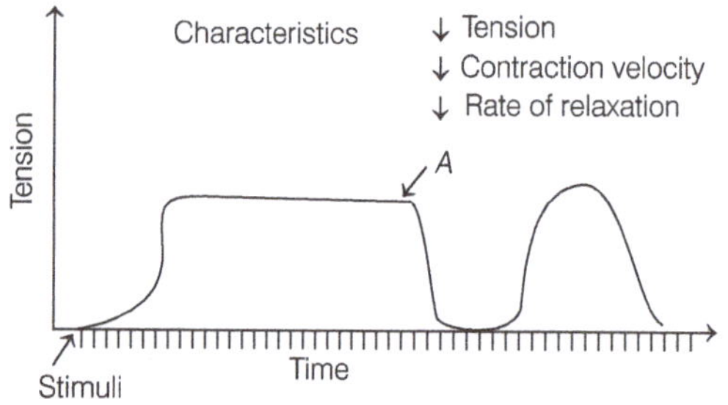


(i) What does *A* represents in the above graph?

(ii) What is the main cause of '*A*'?

(iii) What deficiency causes '*A*'?

*Or*

(iii) What are the symptoms associated with labelled '*A*'?

**Ans.** (i) *A* represents the muscle fatigue in above graph. (1)

(ii) Intracellular acidosis mainly due to lactic acid accumulation has been regarded as the most important causes of '*A*'. (1)

(iii) One possible reason is having low levels of iron, vitamin-D or vitamin $B_{12}$. (2)

*Or*

(iii) Symptoms associated with it include soreness, localised pain, shortness of breath, muscle twitching, trembling, weak grip, muscle cramps. (2)

**3.** Case: Alex, a 30-year-old individual, has recently taken up cycling as a form of exercise. Initially, Alex experienced significant fatigue and shortness of breath during long rides. After several weeks of dedicated training, Alex noticed improvements in stamina and endurance, supported by a fitness assessment showing increased aerobic capacity and a lower resting heart rate.

(i) What type of muscle fibres are likely in higher quantity in Alex's legs before starting the training?

(ii) How do Alex's muscle fibre types change as a result of consistent training?

(iii) What physiological adaptations occur in Alex's muscle fibres as a result of regular cycling?

(iv) How does the increase in aerobic capacity affect Alex's performance in long-distance cycling?

**Ans.** (i) Initially, Alex likely has a higher quantity of fast-twitch (white) muscle fibres. (1)

(ii) With consistent training, the proportion of slow-twitch (red) muscle fibres increases, enhancing endurance. (1)

(iii) Regular cycling leads to adaptations such as increased mitochondrial density, improved blood flow due to enhanced capillary networks and greater efficiency in oxygen utilisation. (1)

(iv) An increase in aerobic capacity allows Alex to sustain longer rides with less fatigue, improving overall endurance and performance during cycling. (1)

# SELF ASSESSMENT TEST

## Multiple Choice Questions

1. Choose the option that correctly represents the characteristics of visceral muscle.
   (a) Striated, branched and involuntary
   (b) Non-striated, unbranched and voluntary
   (c) Striated, unbranched and voluntary
   (d) Non-striated, unbranched and involuntary
2. The neuromuscular junction is a junction between
   (a) a sensory neuron and a muscle fibre
   (b) a motor neuron and a muscle fibre
   (c) a motor neuron and a sensory neuron
   (d) a sensory neuron and a gland
3. What role does calcium play in muscle contraction?
   (a) It provides energy for contraction
   (b) It binds to myosin
   (c) It binds to troponin, allowing myosin to bind to actin
   (d) It triggers the release of ATP
4. Arrange the following steps of muscle contraction in correct sequence.
   I. Shortening of sarcomere
   II. Release of $Ca^{2+}$ ions from sarcoplasmic reticulum
   III. Formation of cross bridge
   IV. Hydrolysis of ATP
   V. Release of ADP and Pi from myosin
   Choose the correct option.
   (a) II, IV, III, I and V
   (b) II, III, I, IV and V
   (c) IV, V, II, III and I
   (d) IV, V, III, I and II
5. Which of the following options correctly represents the formula of the vertebral column in an adult human?
   (a) 7 cervical, 12 thoracic, 5 lumbar, 5 sacral, 4 coccygeal
   (b) 8 cervical, 12 thoracic, 5 lumbar, 5 sacral, 3 coccygeal
   (c) 7 cervical, 11 thoracic, 6 lumbar, 5 sacral, 4 coccygeal
   (d) 7 cervical, 12 thoracic, 5 lumbar, 4 sacral, 5 coccygeal
6. Identify *A*, *B* and *C* from the diagram given below.

| | *A* | *B* | *C* |
|---|---|---|---|
| (a) | Clavicle | Radius | Ulna |
| (b) | Clavicle | Ulna | Radius |
| (c) | Scapula | Radius | Ulna |
| (d) | Scapula | Ulna | Radius |

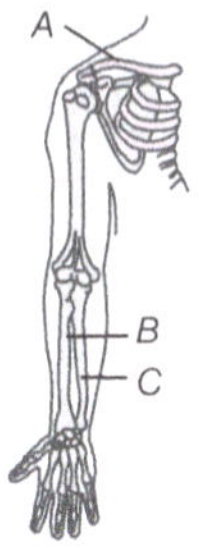


7. Choose the incorrect match-pair.
   (a) Saddle joint – Between carpal and metacarpal
   (b) Pivot joint – Between carpals
   (c) Hinge joint – Knee joint
   (d) Ball and socket Joint – Between humerus and pectoral girdle

## Assertion-Reason Questions

**Direction** (Q. Nos. 8-11) *In each of the following questions, a statement of Assertion (A) is given followed by corresponding statement of Reason (R). Of the statements, mark the correct answer*

(a) Both A and R are true and R is the correct explanation of A.
(b) Both A and R are true, but R is not the correct explanation of A.
(c) A is true, but R is false.
(d) A is false, but R is true.

8. **Assertion** (A) The A-band of a sarcomere is responsible for muscle relaxation.

**Reason** (R) The A-band consists of overlapping thick and thin filaments that facilitate contraction.

9. **Assertion** (A) Fatigue is the inability of muscles to relax.

**Reason** (R) It is due to lactic acid accumulation by repeated contractions.

10. **Assertion** (A) White fibres, in contrast to red fibres, are adapted for quick bursts of activity but fatigue more quickly.

**Reason** (R) White fibres contain fewer mitochondria and myoglobin, making them less efficient in utilising oxygen for ATP production.

11. **Assertion** (A) The human skeleton provides structural support, protects internal organs and enables movement.

**Reason** (R) Bones function as rigid supports and serve as attachment sites for muscles, enabling movement.

## Very Short Answer Type Questions

12. Differentiate between A-band and I-band.
13. Name the bones of hindlimb.
14. Why human skull is called dicondylic?
15. Give the location of hinge joint and glenoid joint in human body.

## Short Answer Type Questions

16. State the role of calcium ion and ATP in muscle contraction.
17. Write a short note on

(i) Knee cap (ii) Collar bone

18. What makes the synovial joint freely movable? List any four types of synovial joints.

## Long Answer Type Questions

19. Give a detailed account of bones of axial skeleton.
20. Explain the step-by-step process of sliding filament theory.
21. Explain the structure and functions of ribs.

## Case Based Question

22. The image depicts a girl and boy performing a bicep curl, a common weight lifting exercise. This exercise primarily targets the biceps brachii muscle, which is located in the upper arm. The bicep curl also engages other stabilising muscles. Observe the image given below and answer the following questions.

(i) Which type of movement is shown in the given figure?

(ii) Which type of joint is being used during a bicep curl?

(iii) Which type of proteins are present in the muscles used by the person?

(iv) How does muscle fatigue affect the performance of exercises like the bicep curl?

# Answers

1. (d) 2. (b) 3. (c) 4. (a) 5. (a) 6. (a) 7. (b) 8. (d)
9. (a) 10. (a) 11. (b)

# 18

CHAPTER

# Neural Control and Coordination

An essential feature of living things is their ability to detect changes in the environment and to exhibit response to **external stimuli**. This becomes possible only due to the presence of well-organised network of **neural system**, which provides point to point connections for quick coordination for receiving and responding to stimuli.

▼ **YOUR STUDY GOALS**



▼ **YOUR PRACTICE GOAL**

- Objective Type Questions (28 Qs ; MCQs, A-R) Case Based Questions (2)
- Subjective Type Questions
- (24 VSAs, 10 SAs, 11 LAs)

- The nervous system is responsible for coordinating and controlling all the functions of organs/organ system in the body to maintain homeostasis.
- In this chapter, we will learn about the neural system of human, mechanism of neural coordination and central nervous system.

## 18.1 Nervous System : An Overview

- **Coordination** is the process through which two or more organs of the body interact and complement the functions of each other.
- On the other hand, **integration** is a process, which makes two or more organs to work as a functional unit in harmony to carry out some vital functions of the body.
- For instance, during physical exercise, a significant increase in the rate of respiration, heartbeat, blood-flow, sweating, etc., is observed to meet enhanced need of oxygen and energy due to increased activities of lungs, heart, muscles and many other body organs.
- When physical exercise is stopped, the increased activities of lungs, heart, nerves, kidneys, muscles, etc., gradually return to normal.

- Thus, during exercise, the functions of various organs of the body are coordinated and integrated in a synchronised fashion.
- In higher animals (including human), two types of system have been developed for the control, coordination and integration of function of various organs, i.e. **nervous system** and **endocrine system.**
- The nervous system provides an organised network of point-to-point connections for a quick coordination.
- The endocrine system provides chemical coordination of organs and organ systems through hormones, which act as chemical messenger.

## 18.2 Neural System

- The neural system is the control system of the body. It consists of highly specialised cells called **neurons**, which can detect, receive and transmit different kinds of stimuli.
- It is present in most of the multicellular animals with increasing complexity from lower to higher forms of animals.
- The neural organisation is very simple in **lower invertebrates.** For example, in *Hydra* it is composed of only network of neurons.
- **In insects**, the brain is present along with the ganglia and neural tissue.
- The **vertebrates** have a more developed neural system.

### Functions of Neural System

The nervous system serves the following important functions

- **Control and Coordination** Nervous system controls and coordinates the working of all parts of the body, so that it function as an integrated unit. This is achieved by three overlapping processes, i.e. sensory input, integration and motor output.
- **Memory** Nervous system stores the impressions of previous stimuli and retrieves (recalls) these impressions in future. These impressions are referred to as the past experiences or memory.
- **Homeostasis** Nervous system helps in the maintenance of the body's internal environment, i.e. homeostasis.

### Human Neural System

- The nervous system of human being is derived from embryonic **ectoderm.**
- The human neural system is divided into two parts

#### 1. Central Neural System (CNS)

The CNS includes the **brain** and the **spinal cord** and is the site of information processing and control.

#### 2. Peripheral Neural System (PNS)

- The PNS comprises of all the nerves of the body associated with the CNS (brain and spinal cord).
- The nerve fibres of the PNS are of two types
  - **Afferent fibres** They transmit impulses from tissues/organs to the CNS.
  - **Efferent fibres** They transmit regulatory impulses from the CNS to the concerned peripheral tissues/organs.
- The PNS is divided into two divisions, i.e. somatic neural system and autonomic neural system.
  - The **somatic neural system** relays impulses from the CNS to skeletal muscles while, the autonomic neural system transmits impulses from the CNS to the involuntary organs and smooth muscles of the body.
  - The **autonomic neural system** is further classified into **sympathetic neural system** and **parasympathetic neural system.**
- **Visceral nervous system** is the part of the peripheral nervous system that comprises complex of nerves, fibres, ganglia and plexuses, by which impulses travel from the central nervous system to viscera and from viscera to the central nervous system.

## 18.3 Neuron

- It is a structural and functional unit of neural system.
- A neuron is a microscopic structure composed of the following three major parts

## 1. Cell Body (Cyton or Soma)

- Like a typical cell it consists of cytoplasm, nucleus and cell membrane.
- The cytoplasm has typical cell organelles like mitochondria, Golgi apparatus, rough endoplasmic reticulum, ribosomes, lysosomes, certain granular bodies and Nissl's granules.
- Presence of **Nissl's granules** (certain granular bodies) is the characteristic of all neurons.

## 2. Dendrites (Dendrons)

- These are short, tapering and branched processes that project out of the cell body.
- They also contain Nissl's granules and may be one to several in number.
- They conduct nerve impulses towards the neuron cell body.

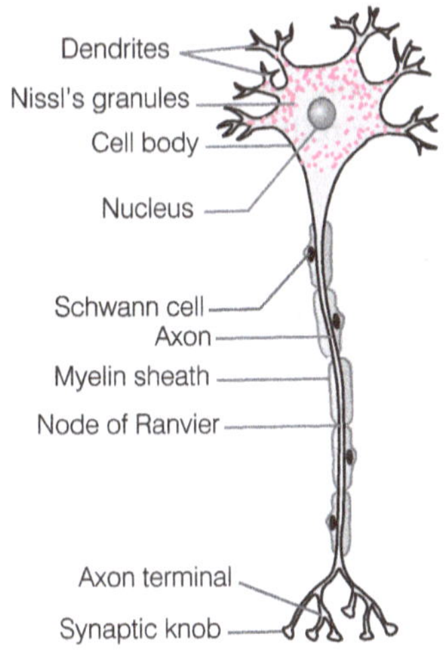


**Fig. 18.1** Structure of a neuron

## 3. Axon

- It is a single, usually very long process of uniform thickness and branched distal part.
- The part of cyton from where the axon arises is called **axon hillock** (most sensitive part of neuron).
- The axon does not have Nissl's granules, cell organelles and granular bodies.
- Each branch of axon terminates as a bulb-like structure called **synaptic knob,** which possesses synaptic vesicles (containing chemicals called **neurotransmitters**).
- The axons transmit nerve impulses away from the cell body to a synapse or to a neuromuscular junction.
- There are two types of axons

### (i) Myelinated

- In myelinated nerve fibres, Schwann cells form myelin sheath around the axon.
- The gaps between two adjacent myelin sheaths are called **nodes of Ranvier**.
- Myelinated nerve fibres are found in **cranial nerves** and **spinal nerves**.

### (ii) Non-myelinated

- In non-myelinated nerve fibres, Schwann cells do not form myelin sheath around the axon and are without nodes of Ranvier.
- They are commonly found in **autonomic** and **somatic neural systems**.

## Types of Neurons on the Basis of Structure

Based on the number of axon and dendrites, the neurons are divided into three types

- **Multipolar Neurons** These neurons have several dendrites and an axon. They are found in cerebral cortex.
- **Bipolar Neurons** These neurons have one dendrite and one axon. They are present in the retina of eye.
- **Unipolar Neurons** These neurons have cell body with one axon only. These are usually found in the embryonic stage.

> **TEACHER'S TIP**
> Based on their function and direction of impulse transmission, the neurons are divided into **sensory neurons** and **motor neurons.** The sensory neurons carry information from sensory receptors to the central nervous system, while motor neurons transmit commands from the central nervous system to muscles and glands.

### Main Properties of Neural Tissue

The neural tissue has two outstanding properties

- **Excitability** It is the ability of nerve cells to generate an electrical impulse in response to a stimulus, by altering the normal potential differences across their plasma membrane.

- **Conductivity** It is the ability of nerve cells to rapidly transmit the electrical impulses, as a wave, from the site of its origin along with their length in a particular direction.

**Quick Test 1**

1. When a man suddenly sees a dog running towards him, he experiences racing heart and sweaty palms, which part of nervous system get activated?
2. The '*X*' division of peripheral nervous system is responsible for picking a cup of coffee. Identify '*X*'.
3. After touching a hot object, which type of neuron carries the sensory information from the skin to the CNS?
4. The Schwann cells around the axon help to classify neurons in various types. Name them.
5. **State True or False.**
   The bipolar neurons are usually found in the embryonic stage.

## Generation and Conduction of Nerve Impulse

- Nerve impulse is a wave of bioelectric/ electrochemical disturbance that passes along a neuron during the conduction of an excitation.
- Impulse conduction depends upon
  - **Permeability of axon** membrane (axolemma).
  - **Electrical equivalence** between the axoplasm and Extracellular Fluid (ECF), present outside the axon.
- The generation of a nerve impulse is a temporary reversal of the resting potential in the neuron.
- It occurs in the following three steps

### 1. Polarisation (Resting Potential)

- The polarisation takes place due to the presence of different types of ion channels on the neural membrane.
- These ion channels are selectively permeable to different ions.
- When a neuron is not conducting any impulse, i.e. resting, the axonal membrane is comparatively more permeable to **potassium ions** ($K^+$) and nearly impermeable to **sodium ions** ($Na^+$).
- Similarly, the membrane is impermeable to negatively charged proteins present in the axoplasm.
- Consequently, in a resting nerve fibre (a nerve fibre that is not conducting an impulse), the axoplasm (neuroplasm of axon) contains high concentration of $K^+$ and negatively charged proteins and low concentration of $Na^+$.
- In contrast, the fluid outside axon contains low concentration of $K^+$ and a high concentration of $Na^+$ and thus forms a concentration gradient.
- These ionic gradients across the resting membrane are maintained by the active transport of ions by the **sodium-potassium pump**, which transports $3Na^+$ outwards and $2K^+$ inwards (into the cell).
- As a result, the outer surface of the axonal membrane becomes positively charged, while its inner surface becomes negatively charged and therefore is polarised.
- The electrical potential difference across the resting plasma membrane is called as the **resting potential.** The state of the resting membrane is called **polarised state**.

### 2. Depolarisation (Action Potential)

- When a stimulus of adequate strength (threshold stimulus) is applied to a polarised membrane, the permeability of the membrane to $Na^+$ ions is greatly increased at the point of stimulation (site *A*).
- This leads to a rapid influx of $Na^+$ followed by the reversal of the polarity at that site, i.e. the outer surface of the membrane becomes **negatively charged** and the inner side becomes **positively charged**.
- The polarity of the membrane at the site *A* is thus reversed and neuron at that point is said to be depolarised.
- The electrical potential difference across the plasma membrane at the site *A* is called the **action potential**, (another name of **nerve impulse**).
- At sites immediately ahead, e.g. site *B*, the axon membrane has **positive charge** (still polarised) on the outer surface and a **negative charge** on its inner surface.

- As a result, a current flows on the outer surface from site *B* to site *A*, while on the inner surface current flows from site *A* to site *B*.

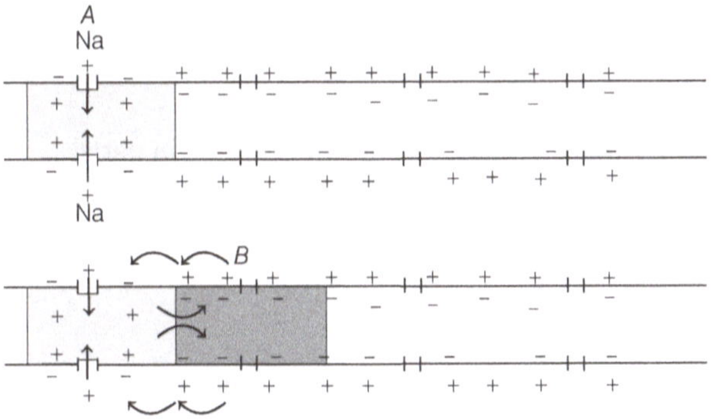


Fig. 18.2 Diagrammatic representation of impulse conduction through an axon (at point A adn B)

- Hence, the polarity at the site is reversed, and an action potential is generated at site *B*. Thus, the impulse (action potential) generated at site *A* arrives at site *B*.
- This process (reversal) repeats itself over and over again and a nerve impulse is conducted through the length of the neuron.

### 3. Repolarisation

- The rise in the stimulus-induced permeability to $Na^+$ is extremely short lived. It is quickly followed by a rise in membrane permeability to $K^+$.
- Within a fraction of a second, $Na^+$ influx stops and out flow of $K^+$ begins until the original resting state of ionic concentration is achieved.
- Thus, resting potential is restored at the site of excitation, which is called **repolarisation** of the membrane. This makes the fibre once more responsive to further stimulation.

## Transmission of Impulses

A nerve impulse is transmitted from one neuron to another through junctions called **synapses**. It is formed by the membranes of a pre-synaptic neuron and a post-synaptic neuron which may or may not be separated by a gap called **synaptic cleft**.

There are mainly two types of synapses as given below

### 1. Electrical Synapse

- The membranes of pre and post-synaptic neurons are in very close proximity (i.e. in continuity).
- In electrical synapse, there is minimal synaptic delay because of the **direct flow** of electrical current from one neuron to the other across these synapses.
- Thus, impulse transmission across an electrical synapse is always faster than that across a chemical synapse.
- In such synapses, transmission of impulse is very similar to impulse conduction along a single axon.
- The electrical synapses are rare in the human nervous system.

### 2. Chemical Synapses

The membranes of pre and post-synaptic neurons are separated by a fluid-filled space called **synaptic cleft.**

A brief description of the mechanism of synaptic transmission is given below

- When an impulse (action potential) arrives at a pre-synaptic knob, it causes the movement of the synaptic vesicles towards the surface of the pre-synaptic knob.
- The synaptic vesicles get fused with the pre-synaptic plasma membrane and get ruptured (exocytosis) to release their contents (neurotransmitter) into the synaptic cleft.
- The neurotransmitter in the synaptic cleft binds with specific protein receptor molecules, present on the post-synaptic membrane.
- This binding action changes the membrane potential of the post-synaptic membrane, opening channels in the neurolemma and sodium ions to enter the cell. This causes the depolarisation and generation of action potential in the post-synaptic membrane. Thus, the impulse is transferred to the next neuron.
- The new potential developed may be either excitatory or inhibitory.

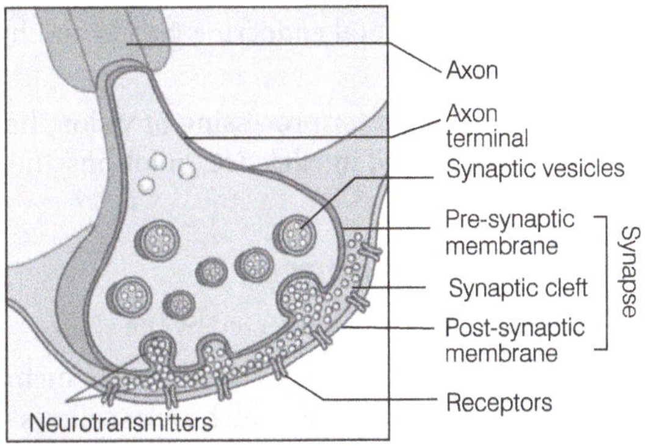


Fig. 18.3 Axon terminal and synapse

## Quick Test 2

1. In a condition where the sodium-potassium pump is inhibited, which phase of impulse transmission would be most affected?
2. Ion Y plays a crucial role in restoring the membrane potential of the axolemma after an action potential has occurred. Name Y.
3. **State True or False.**

   In humans, electrical synapses are frequently found in nervous system.
4. If the protein receptors on the post-synaptic neuron are damaged, what part of the synaptic transmission process would be affected?
5. Rearrange the following in the correct order of transmission in electrical impulse; movement synaptic knob, dendrites, cell body, axon terminal and axon.

# 18.4 Central Nervous System (CNS)

It is the integrating and command centre of the nervous system, which consists of the **brain** and **spinal cord**.

## Brain

- The brain is the central information processing organ of the body and acts as the 'command and control system'of all body activities.
- It controls the following activities
  - The voluntary movements and balance of the body.
  - Functioning of vital involuntary organs, e.g. lungs, heart, kidneys, etc.
  - Thermoregulation, hunger and thirst.
  - Circardian (24 hrs) rhythms of the body.
  - Activities of several endocrine glands and human behaviour.
  - It is also the site for processing of vision, hearing, speech, memory, intelligence, emotions and thoughts.

## Protective Coverings

The human brain is well-protected by the skull.

Inside the skull, the brain is covered by three membranes called the **cranial meninges**, which are as follows

- The outermost membrane is called **dura mater**.
- The middle membrane, is very thin layer and called as **arachnoid membrane**.
- The innermost membrane is **pia mater**. It is in contact with the brain tissue.

## Structure

The human brain is divisible into three main parts

### 1. Forebrain

It consists of cerebrum, thalamus and hypothalamus.

#### (i) Cerebrum

- It forms the major parts of the human brain.
- A deep cleft divides the cerebrum longitudinally into two equal halves. These are termed as the left and right **cerebral hemispheres.**
- These hemispheres are connected by a tract of nerve fibres, the **corpus callosum.**
- The layer of cells which covers the cerebral hemisphere is called **cerebral cortex.**
- The cerebral cortex is referred to as the grey matter due to its greyish appearance (as neuron cell bodies are concentrated here). The cerebral cortex has prominent folded.
- Beneath the grey matter, there are millions of myelinated nerve fibres, which constitute the inner part of the cerebral hemisphere.

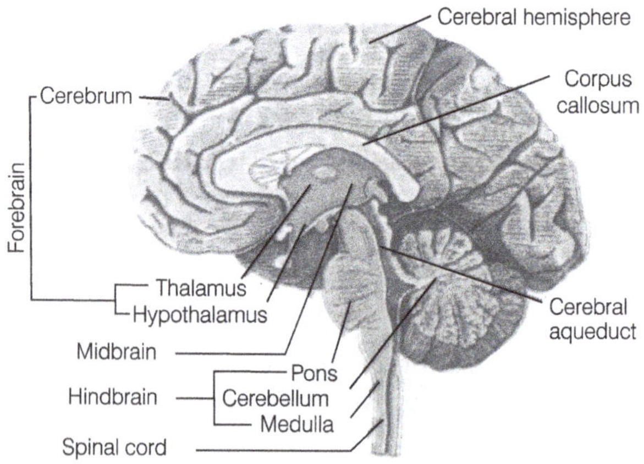


Fig. 18.4 Diagram showing sagital section of the human brain

- The large concentration of myelinated nerve fibres gives this tissue an opaque white appearance. Hence, it is called the **white matter.**
- In cerebral cortex, there are three types of functional areas as given below

- **Sensory Areas** It receives impulses from the receptors.
- **Motor Areas** Transmit impulses to the effectors.
- **Association Areas** These are large regions that are neither sensory nor motor in function. These areas are responsible for complex functions like memory, communication and other intersensory associations.

### (ii) Thalamus

The cerebrum wraps around a structure called thalamus, which is a major coordinating centre for sensory and motor signaling.

### (iii) Hypothalamus

- It lies at the base of thalamus.
- It contains a number of centres, which control body temperature, urge for eating and drinking.
- It also contains several groups of neurosecretory cells, which secrete hormones called **hypothalamic hormones.**
- The inner parts of cerebral hemispheres and a group of deeply associated structures like amygdala, hippocampus, etc., form a complex structure called **limbic lobe** or **limbic system**.
- Along with hypothalamus, it is involved in the regulation of sexual behaviour, expression of emotional reactions, e.g. excitement, pleasure, rage, fear and motivation.

### 2. Midbrain

- It is located between the thalamus, hypothalamus of the forebrain and pons of the hindbrain.
- A canal called the **cerebral aqueduct** passes through the midbrain.
- The dorsal portion of the midbrain mainly consists of four round swellings (lobes) called **corpora quadrigemina**.

### 3. Hindbrain

It consists of pons, cerebellum and medulla.

- **Pons** It consists of fibre tracts that interconnect different regions of the brain.
- **Cerebellum** It has very convoluted surface in order to provide the additional space for many more neurons.
- **Medulla** It is also called **medulla oblongata.** It is connected to the spinal cord and contains centres, which control respiratory rhythm, cardiovascular reflexes and gastric secretions.

The midbrain, pons and medulla oblongata together forms the brain stem. It serves as the connection between the brain and spinal cord.

## Spinal Cord

- It forms the posterior part of the CNS, running mid-dorsally within the neural canal of the vertebral column.
- Spinal cord conducts impulses to and from the brain as well as and controls most of the reflex activities.
- It also provides a means of communication between spinal nerves and the brain.

### Quick Test 3

1. If you were to closely examine a brain specimen, which layer of the cranial meninges would be in direct contact with the brain tissue?
2. A structure '*X*' connects the two hemispheres of the cerebrum. Identify *X*.
3. A person is experiencing difficulties with memory and communication following a head injury. Which part of the brain is likely to be affected?
4. Injury to which part of the hindbrain could be life-threatening? *NCERT*
5. Mention the parts of the hindbrain that make up the brain stem.

# Mind Map

## Neural Control and Coordination

### Neuron

Structural and functional unit of neural system.

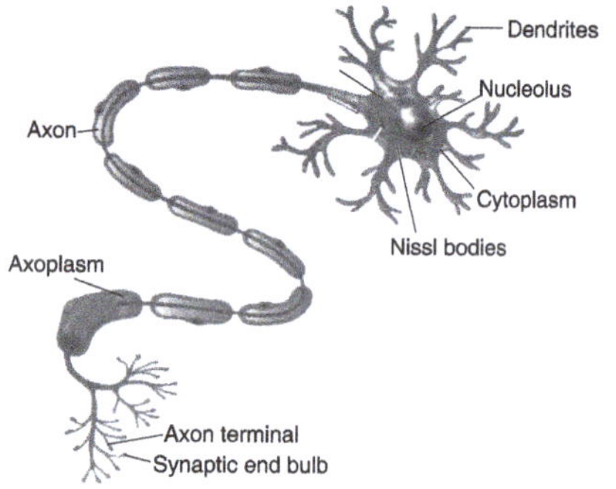


Each branch of axon terminates into synaptic which possess synaptic vesicles containing chemicals called **neurotransmitters.**

### Generation and Conduction of Nerve Impulse

- At the start, the membrane is completely polarised.
- When an action potential is initiated, a region of the membrane depolarised. As a result, the adjacent regions become depolarised.
- When the adjacent region is depolarised to its threshold, an action potential starts there.
- Repolarisation occurs due to the outward flow of $K^+$ ions. The depolarisation spreads forward, triggering and action potential.
- Depolarisation spreads forward, repeating the process.

### Neural System

- It is a network of specialised cells that coordinate and transmit signals between different parts of the body.
- Coordination is the process by which different organs and systems of the body work together to maintain balance and efficiency in bodily functions.
- In humans it primarily occurs through: Nervous and endocrine systems.

### Human Neural System

- **Central Nervous System** (CNS)
  - Brain
  - Spinal cord
- **Peripheral Nervous System** (PNS)
  - Somatic neural system
  - Autonomic neural system
    - Sympathetic neural system
    - Parasympathetic neural system

### Transmission of Nerve Impulse

- A nerve impulse is transmitted from one neuron to another through synapses.
- There are two types of synapse

1. **Electrical Synapse** Here, the membranes of pre and post-synaptic neurons are in very close proximity; quick transmission.
2. **Chemical Synapse** Here, the membrane of pre and post-synaptic neuron are separated by fluid filled space called **synaptic cleft**. Neurotransmitters are involved here.

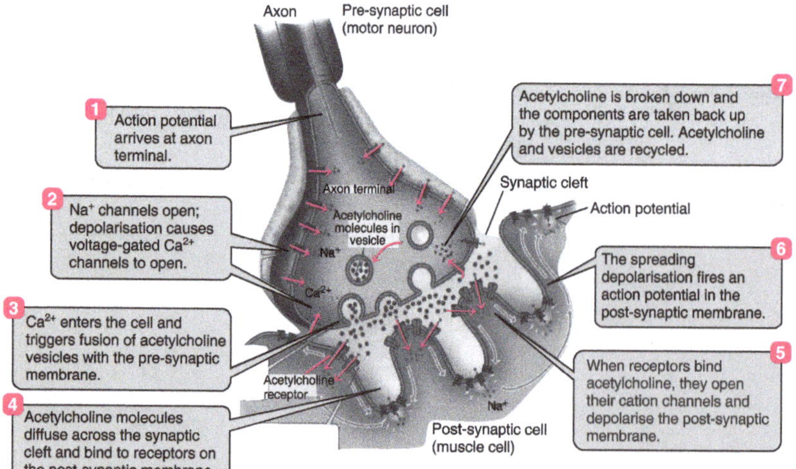


**Transmission of nerve impulse at a chemical synapse**

### Human Brain

- Major portion of central neural system which is well protected by the skull.

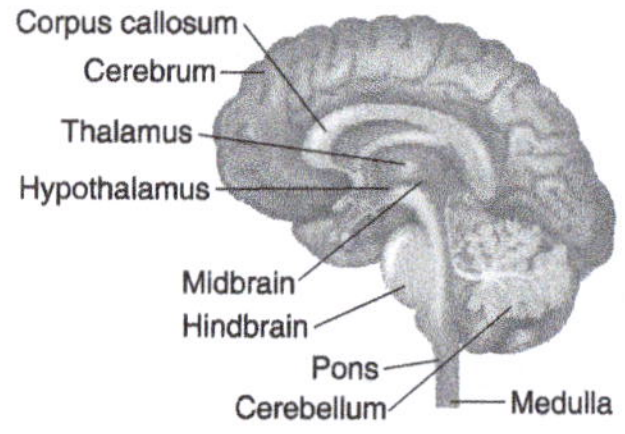


**Parts of brain**

**Forebrain**

- **Cerebrum** Controls memory and imagination, reasoning, judgement, expression of will power, etc.
- **Thalamus** acts as relay centre to receive and transmit general sensation of pain, touch and temperature.
- **Hypothalamus** centre for regulation of body temperature.

**Midbrain**

- Responsible to coordinate visual reflexes and auditory reflexes.

**Hindbrain**

- **Cerebellum** maintains posture and equilibrium of the body as well as coordinates and regulates voluntary movements.
- **Pons** relays impulse between medulla oblongata and cerebral hemisphere and between the hemisphere of cerebrum and cerebellum.
- **Medulla Oblongata** Centre that control respiration, cardiovascular reflexes and gastric secretion.

# EXAM PATTERN QUESTIONS

## Objective Type Questions

### Multiple Choice Questions

**1.** The neural system is composed of highly specialised cells called neurons that can

(a) detect stimuli
(b) receive stimuli
(c) transmit impulses
(d) All of the above

**Ans.** (*d*)

**2.** The neural organisation in given animal comprises of **Competency Based Que.**

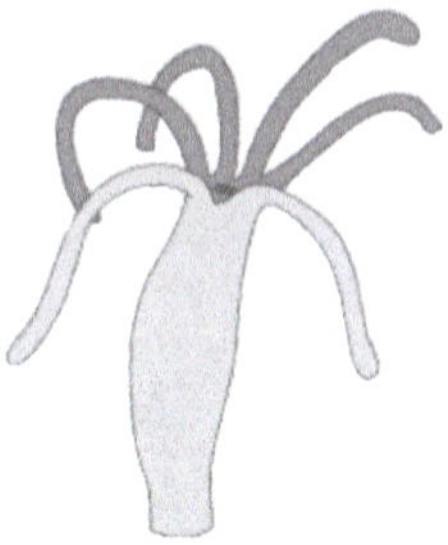

(a) network of neurons (b) CNS and PNS
(c) CNS (d) PNS

**Ans.** (*a*)

**3.** Visceral nervous system found in human body

(a) is a part of peripheral nervous system
(b) comprises the complex of nerves, ganglia and plexuses
(c) constitutes the connection between CNS and the viscera
(d) All of the above

**Ans.** (*d*)

**4.** The function of our visceral organs is controlled by **NCERT Exemplar**

(a) sympathetic and somatic neural system
(b) sympathetic and parasympathetic neural system
(c) central and somatic nervous system
(d) None of the above

**Ans.** (*b*) Sympathetic and parasympathetic neural system control all the visceral organs of the body. Whereas, somatic neural system is a part of peripheral nervous system that is not related to regulation of visceral organs. Similarly CNS is not concerned with it.

**5.** Refer to the given diagram of typical neurons.

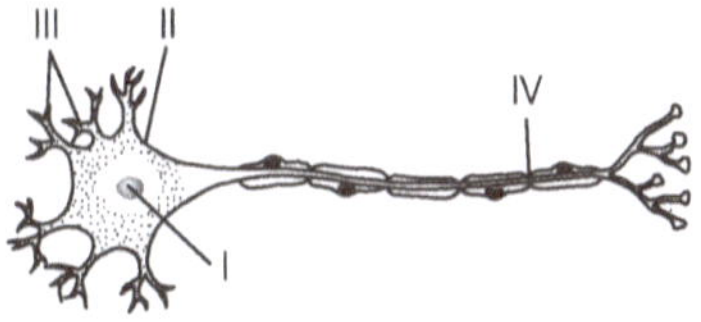


Identify the parts where Nissl's granules are likely to be found. **Competency Based Que.**

(a) Only I (b) II and III
(c) III and IV (d) I, II, III and IV

**Ans.** (*b*)

**6.** Match the Column I with Column II and identify the correct option from the codes given below.

| | Column I | | Column II |
|---|---|---|---|
| A. | Cell body | 1. | Tissue to CNS |
| B. | Synaptic vesicles | 2. | CNS to tissue |
| C. | Afferent fibres | 3. | Neurotransmitter |
| D. | Efferent fibres | 4. | Nissls's granules |

**Codes**

| | A | B | C | D | | A | B | C | D |
|---|---|---|---|---|---|---|---|---|---|
| (a) | 3 | 4 | 2 | 1 | (b) | 4 | 3 | 2 | 1 |
| (c) | 3 | 4 | 1 | 2 | (d) | 4 | 3 | 1 | 2 |

**Ans.** (*d*)

**7.** Myelinated nerve fibres are found in ....*A*..... and .....*B*..... nerves. Fill in the blanks *A* and *B* with correct options.

(a) *A*-cranial; *B*-sympathetic
(b) *A*-spinal; *B*-cranial
(c) *A*-spinal; *B*-parasympathetic
(d) *A*-sympathetic; *B*-parasympathetic

**Ans.** (*b*)

**8.** Potential difference across resting membrane is negatively charged. This is due to differential distribution of the following ions. **NCERT Exemplar**

(a) $Na^+$ and $K^+$ ions (b) $CO_3^{2-}$ and $Cl^-$ ions
(c) $Ca^{2+}$ and $Mg^{2+}$ ions (d) $Ca^{+4}$ and $Cl^-$ ions

**Ans.** (*a*) The ion gated channels on the neurolemma control the movement of $Na^+$ and $K^+$ maintaining a higher concentration of $Na^+$ outside and $K^+$ inside the nerve cell, leading to a negatively charged resting membrane potential.

$Ca^{2+}$, $CO_3^{2-}$, $Mg^{2+}$ and $Ca^{2+}$ ions are not related with nerve excitation rather are involved in other biological functions.

**9. During the transmission of nerve impluse through nerve fibre the potential on the inner side of the plasma membrane has which type of electric charge?** **Competency Based Que.**

(a) First positive then negative and continue to be negative
(b) First negative then positive and continue to be positive
(c) First positive then negative and again back to negative
(d) First negative then positive and again back to negative

**Ans.** *(d)*

**10. In the resting stage of a neuron, concentration gradient generates due to**

(a) high concentration of $K^+$ and low concentration of $Na^+$ inside the axon
(b) high concentration of $Na^+$ and low concentration of $K^+$ inside the axon
(c) low concentration of $Na^+$ outside the axon
(d) high concentration of $K^+$ outside the axon

**Ans.** *(a)*

**11. Depolarisation of axonal membrane during nerve conduction takes place because**

(a) equal amount of $Na^+$ and $K^+$ move out across axonal membrane
(b) Only $Na^+$ moves inside
(c) more $Na^+$ moves outside than $K^+$ moving outside
(d) None of the above

**Ans.** *(b)*

**12. Unidirectional transmission of a nerve impulse through nerve fibre occurs because**

(a) nerve fibre is insulated by a medullary sheath
(b) sodium pump starts operating only at the cyton and then continues into the nerve fibre
(c) neurotransmitter are released by dendrites and not by axon endings
(d) neurotransmitters are released by the axon endings and not by dendrites

**Ans.** *(d)*

**13. Association areas of the brain are**

(a) always sensory areas
(b) always motor areas
(c) Neither sensory nor motor areas
(d) None of the above

**Ans.** *(c)*

**14. Which part of the human brain controls the urge for eating and drinking?**

(a) Forebrain (b) Midbrain
(c) Hindbrain (d) Spinal cord

**Ans.** *(a)*

**15. Hypothalamus controls**

**I. Urge for eating and drinking.**
**II. Thermoregulation.**
**III. Hormones production.**

**Choose the correct option.**

(a) I and III (b) II and III
(c) I and II (d) I, II and III

**Ans.** *(d)*

**16. Match the following columns.**

| | Column I | | Column II |
|---|---|---|---|
| A. | Cerebral aqueduct | 1. | Forebrain |
| B. | Cerebral hemisphere | 2. | Midbrain |
| C. | Cerebellum | 3. | Cranial meninges |
| D. | Piamater | 4. | Hindbrain |

**Codes**

| | A | B | C | D | | A | B | C | D |
|---|---|---|---|---|---|---|---|---|---|
| (a) | 2 | 1 | 3 | 4 | (b) | 1 | 2 | 4 | 3 |
| (c) | 2 | 1 | 4 | 3 | (d) | 4 | 3 | 1 | 2 |

**Ans.** *(c)*

**17. Which of the following regions of the brain is incorrectly paired with its functions?**

(a) **Corpus callosum**–Communication between the left and right cerebral cortices.
(b) **Thalamus**–Coordinating centre for sensory and motor signalling
(c) **Medulla oblongata**–Memory and communication
(d) **Spinal cord**–controls most of the reflex activities

**Ans.** *(c)* The option (c) is incorrectly paired

Cerebrum is responsible for memory and communication..

## Assertion–Reason Questions

**Direction** (Q. Nos. 1-11) *In each of the following questions, a statement of Assertion (A) is given followed by corresponding statement of Reason (R). Of the statements, mark the correct answer.*

(a) Both A and R are true and R is the correct explanation of A
(b) Both A and R are true, but R is not the correct explanation of A
(c) A is true, but R is false
(d) A is false, but R is true

1. **Assertion** (A) Neurons are excitable cells.

   **Reason** (R) Membranes of the neurons are in a polarised state which is responsible for the excitability.

**Ans.** (*a*)

2. **Assertion** (A) The axoplasm inside the axon contains high concentration of $K^+$ and negatively charged proteins.

   **Reason** (R) The axonal membrane is impermeable to $Na^+$ and negatively charged proteins.

**Ans.** (*c*) A is true, but R is false. R can be corrected as The axonal membrane is impermeable to negatively charged proteins.

3. **Assertion** (A) The imbalance in concentration of $Na^+$, $K^+$ and proteins generate resting potential.

   **Reason** (R) To maintain the unequal distribution of $Na^+$ and $K^+$, the neurons use electrical energy.

**Ans.** (*c*)

4. **Assertion** (A) The membrane of a neuron remains in polarised state.

   **Reason** (R) Ion channels on the neural membrane are selectively permeable to different ions.

**Ans.** (*a*)

5. **Given below is the diagrammatic representation of impulse conduction through an axon (At points *A* and *B*). Study the diagram and comment upon the appropriateness of the Assertion and the Reason.** **CBQ**

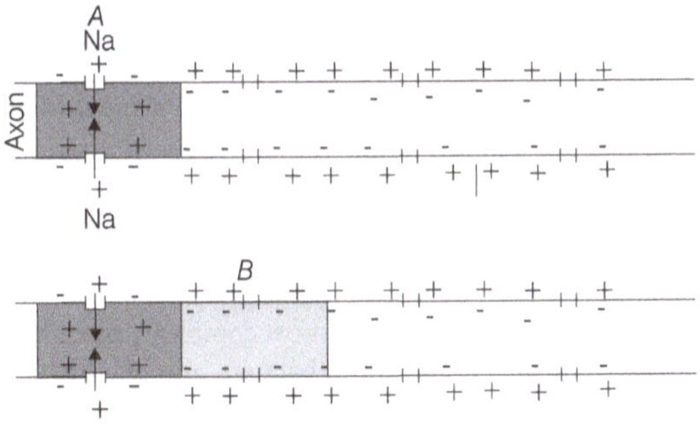


   **Assertion** (A) A nerve impulse is an electrochemical event.

   **Reason** (R) A current flows on the inner surface from site *A* to site *B* and on the outer surface, current flows from site *B* to site *A* to complete the circuit of current flow.

**Ans.** (*b*)

6. **Assertion** (A) Arrival of an impulse at the axon terminal, stimulates the release of neurotransmitters in the synaptic cleft.

   **Reason** (R) The neurotransmitters are responsible for the opening of ion channels.

**Ans.** (*b*)

7. **Assertion** (A) The pre-synaptic neuron transmits an impulse (action potential) across the synaptic cleft to the post-synaptic neuron.

   **Reason** (R) For the transmission of impulses at synapses, chemicals called neurotransmitters are responsible.

**Ans.** (*b*)

8. **Assertion** (A) The cerebral cortex is referred to as the white matter of the brain.

   **Reason** (R) There is high concentration of neuron cell bodies in the cerebral cortex.

**Ans.** (*d*) A is false, but R is true. A can be corrected as

The cerebral cortex is referred to as the grey matter of the brain.

9. **Assertion** (A) Midbrain is located above the thalamus and hypothalamus.

   **Reason** (R) Cerebral aqueduct passes through midbrain.

**Ans.** (*d*) A is false, but R is true. A can be corrected as Midbrain is located between the thalamus and hypothalamus.

10. **Given below is the diagramatic view of the human brain with a part labelled as *X*. Study the diagram and comment upon the appropriateness of the Assertion and the Reason.** **Competency Based Que.**

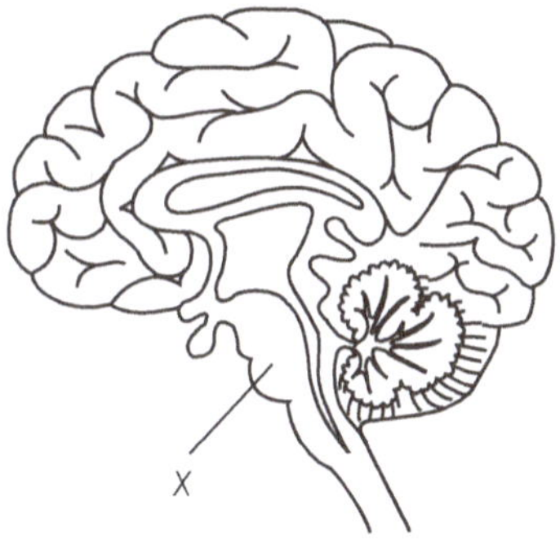


   **Assertion** (A) The part *X* is pons.

   **Reason** (R) Part *X* consists of fibre tract that interconnect different regions of brain.

**Ans.** (*b*)

11. **Assertion** (A) Injury to medulla could lead to death.

   **Reason** (R) Medulla control centres for respiration and cardiovascular reflexes.

**Ans.** (*a*)

# Subjective Questions

## Very Short Answer Type Questions

**1. What are the two types of system that have been developed for the control, coordination and integration?**

**Ans.** Nervous system and endocrine system. (½ × 2)

**2. Name the main division of nervous system in human.**

**Ans.** Central nervous (neural) system and peripheral nervous (neural) system. (½ × 2)

**3. Give the name of the part of human neural system that lies along the main axis of the body.**

**Ans.** Central neural (nervous) system, lies along the main central axis of the body.

**4. What is the role of afferent nerve fibres in the nervous system?**

**Ans.** It transmit impulses (sensory) from tissues/organs to the CNS.

**5. How do the efferent fibres work?**

**Ans.** The efferent nerve fibres transmit motor impulses from CNS to the concerned tissues/organs and form the motor or efferent pathway.

**6. How does the somatic nervous system work?** **Competency Based Que.**

**Ans.** The somatic nervous system controls the movements of the body by acting on the skeletal muscles (i.e. relays voluntary impulses from the CNS to skeletal muscles).

**7. The autonomic nervous system is considering involuntary nervous system. Why?** **Competency Based Que.**

**Ans.** This system transmits impulses from the CNS to the involuntary organs and smooth muscles of the body. So, it is also called involuntary nervous system.

**8. Write the location of Nissl's granules?**

**Ans.** Nissl's granules are present in the cytoplasm and dendrites of neurons. (½ × 2)

**9. Which part of the neuron is considered as afferent processes?**

**Ans.** Dendrites conduct nerve impulses towards the cell body and are called afferent processes (receiving processes).

**10. What do you understand by the polarised state of the nerve membrane?**

**Ans.** It is the state of the nerve membrane when its inner side is more electronegative than its outer side.

**11. How do the ionic gradients across the resting membrane can be maintained?** **Competency Based Que.**

**Ans.** The ionic gradients across the resting membrane are maintained by the active transport of ions by the sodium-potassium pump.

**12. State the role of sodium-potassium pump in the maintenance of ionic gradients.**

**Ans.** The sodium-potassium pump helps in the active transport of ions, 3 $Na^+$ are transported outwards and 2$K^+$ inwards through the neurolemma of neurons.

**13. What term is used for the stimulus of adequate strength to start an action potential.**

**Ans.** Threshold stimulus.

**14. Give the name of the central information processing organ of our body.**

**Ans.** Brain.

**15. Name the structure which protects the brain in vertebrate animals.**

**Ans.** Cranium

**16. Name the major divisions of the forebrain.**

**Ans.** Cerebrum, thalamus, hypothalamus.

**17. Give the name of the nervous tissues found in central nervous system.**

**Ans.** Grey matter and white matter. (½ × 2)

**18. Which parts of the CNS constitute the grey matter?**

**Ans.** Area that contains cell bodies of the neurons in cerebral cortex.

**19. Which is the largest and most complex of all the parts of the human brain?**

**Ans.** Forebrain, is the largest and most complex part of human brain. It includes cerebrum, thalamus and hypothalamus.

**20. Answer the following.**

**(i) Which part of the human brain is most developed?**

**(ii) Which part of the central nervous system acts as biological clock?** **NCERT**

**Ans.** (i) Cerebrum (ii) Pineal body of the brain (½ × 2)

**21. What are the two major parts of the limbic system?**

**Ans.** Amygdala and hippocampus. (½ × 2)

**22. Where is the emotional centre located in human brain?**

**Ans.** Hypothalamus and limbic system (forebrain). (½ × 2)

**23.** **Name the canal that passes through the midbrain.**

**Ans.** Cerebral aqueduct.

**24.** **Identify the part of the brain which is labelled as *X* in the given diagram and its respective function.**

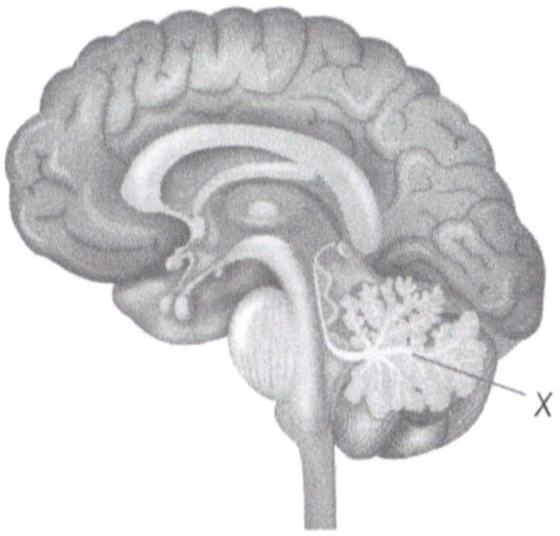


**Ans.** The *X* in the given image represents cerebellum, which provides additional space for several neurons. (½ × 2)

## Short Answer Type Questions

**1.** **The major parts of the human neural system is depicted below. Fill in the empty boxes with appropriate words.**

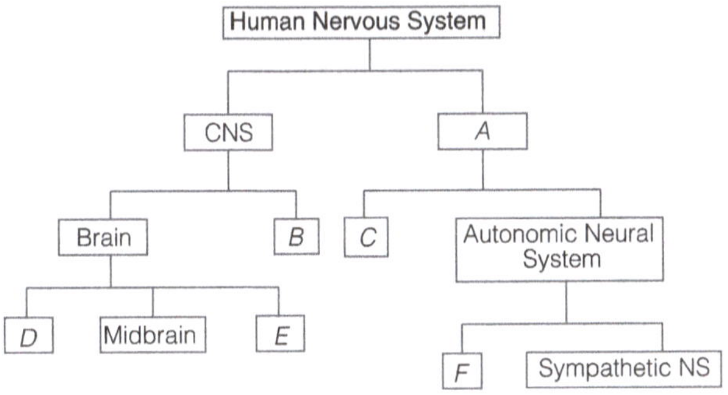


**Ans.**

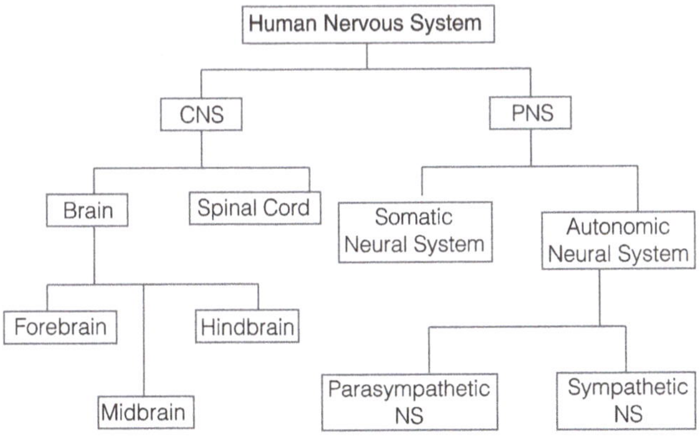


(½ × 6)

**2.** **Write a short note on *A* and *B*.**

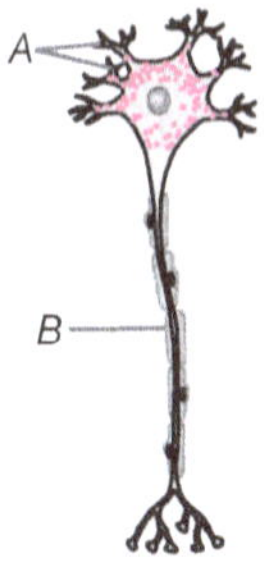


**Ans.** *A* in the given diagram represents dendrites. Refer to text on page no. 417

*B* in the given diagram represents axon. Refer to text on page no. 417. (½ × 2)

**3.** **Explain the factors on which the impulse conduction depends.**

**Ans.** Impulse conduction depends upon the following factors

(i) Permeability of axolemma (axon membrane)

(ii) Electrical potential difference between the axoplasm and extracellular fluid present outside the axon. (1 × 2)

**4.** **Explain the role of $Na^+$ in the generation of action potential.** **NCERT**

**Ans.** When a stimulus is applied to a nerve, the membrane of the nerve becomes freely permeable to $Na^+$.
This leads to a rapid influx of $Na^+$ followed by the reversal of the polarity at that site, i.e. the outer surface of the membrane becomes negatively charged and the inner side becomes positively charged.
The electrical potential difference across the plasma membrane is called the action potential, which is in fact termed as a nerve impulse.

Thus, this shows that $Na^+$ ions play an important role in the conduction of nerve impulse.

**5.** **Why nerve conduction in chemical synapse is slower as compared to electrical synapse?** **Competency Based Que.**

**Ans.** Nerve conduction in chemical synapse is slower because its pre-synaptic and post-synaptic membranes are separated by synaptic cleft, whereas in electrical synapse no such gaps are present.

**6.** **Compare the following.**

**(i) Central Nervous System (CNS) and Peripheral Nervous System (PNS).**

**(ii) Resting potential and action potential.** **NCERT**

**Ans.** (i) The CNS includes the brain and the spinal cord and is the site of information processing and control. The PNS comprises of all the nerves of the body associated with the CNS (brain and spinal cord).

(ii) Resting Potential is the electrical potential difference across the resting plasma membrane. Action Potential is another name of nerve impulse. The action potential is an electrical signal that travels along an axon. (1 × 2)

**7. Describe the protective coverings of the brain.**

**Ans.** Refer to text on page no. 420.

**8. Discuss the functional areas of the cerebrum.**

**Ans.** Refer to text on page no. 420-421.

**9. What do grey and white matter in the brain represent?**

**Ans.** Gray matter represents the area in central nervous system that contain mostly neuron cell bodies, dendrites and unmylinated axons, involved in processing and interpreting information while white matter represents areas that contain mostly myelinated axons, responsible for transmitting signals between different regions of the brain and spinal cord, facilitating communication.

**10. Describe the functions of limbic system?**

**Ans.** Along with the hypothalamus, it is involved in the regulation of sexual behaviour, expression of emotional reactions, e.g. pleasure, excitement, rage, fear and motivation.

## Long Answer Type Questions

**1. Give a brief account on the main properties and functions of neural system.**

**Ans.** Refer to text on page no. 416.

**2. Distinguish between**

**(i) afferent neurons and efferent neurons**

**(ii) impulse conduction in a myelinated nerve fibre and unmyelinated nerve fibre**

**(iii) cranial nerves and spinal nerves.** NCERT

**Ans.** (i) Differences between afferent neuron and efferent neuron is as follows

| Afferent Neurons | Efferent Neurons |
|---|---|
| Carry sensory information from tissue/organ to the Central Nervous System (CNS). | Transmit regulatory impulse from the CNS to effectors (muscles or glands). (1) |

(ii) Differences between impulse conduction in a myelinated nerve fibre and unmyelinated nerve fibre are as follows

| Impulse Conduction in a Myelinated Nerve Fibre | Impulse Conduction in an Unmyelinated Nerve Fibre |
|---|---|
| Conduct impulses faster due to saltatory conduction, where signals jump between nodes of Ranvier. | Conduct impulses more slowly through continuous conduction along the entire length of the axon. |
| The presence of the myelin sheath provides insulation and increases conduction efficiency. | Lack of myelin means that action potentials must propagate along the entire membrane. |

(2)

(iii) Differences between cranial nerve and spinal nerve are as follows

| Cranial Nerve | Spinal Nerve |
|---|---|
| The cranial nerves originate in the brain and terminate mostly in organs, head and upper body. | The spinal nerves originate in the spinal cord and extend to parts of the body below the head. |
| There are 12 pairs of cranial nerves. | There are 31 pairs of spinal nerves. (2) |

**3. Define nerve impulse. Differentiate between polarisation, depolarisation and repolarsation.**

**Ans.** Refer to text on page no. 418- 419.

**4. During resting potential, the axonal membrane is polarised. Explain the movement of positive and negative ions leading to polarisation.**

**Ans.** Refer to text on page no. 418.

**5. Explain the following processes** NCERT

**(i) Polarisation of the membrane of a nerve fibre.**

**(ii) Depolarisation of the membrane of a nerve fibre.**

**(iii) Conduction of a nerve impulse along a nerve fibre.**

**Ans.** (i) Refer to text on page no. 418.

(ii) Refer to text on page no. 418-419.

(iii) Refer to text on page no. 418-419.

**6. Give a brief account of mechanism of synaptic transmission.** NCERT

**Ans.** Refer to text on page no. 419.

**7. Explain the process of the transport and release of a neurotransmitter with the help of a labelled diagram showing a complete neuron, axon terminal and synapse.**

**Ans.** Refer to text on page no. 419.

**8. Draw labelled diagrams of the following:**

**(i) Neuron**

**(ii) Brain** NCERT

**Ans.** (i) Refer to fig. no. 18.1 on page no. 417.

(ii) Refer to fig. no. 18.4 on page no. 420.

**9. Briefly describe the structure of the brain.** **NCERT**

**Ans.** Refer to text on page no. 420-421.

**10. Write short notes on the following.** **NCERT**

(i) Neural coordination (ii) Forebrain
(iii) Midbrain (iv) Hindbrain
(v) Synapse

**Ans.** (i) The organised network of point-to-point connection for quick coordination provided by neural system is called neural coordination.

The mechanism of neural coordination involves transmission of nerve impulse, impulse conduction across a synapse and the physiology of reflex action.

(ii) Refer to text on page no. 420-421.
(iii) Refer to text on page no. 421.
(iv) Refer to text on page no. 421.
(v) Refer to text on page no. 419.

**11. Differentiate between:**

(i) Myelinated and non-myelinated axons
(ii) Dendrites and axons
(iii) Thalamus and Hypothalamus
(iv) Cerebrum and Cerebellum **NCERT**

**Ans.** (i) Differences between myelinated and non-myelinated axons are as follows

| Myelinated Axon | Non-myelinated Axon |
|---|---|
| The myelinated nerve fibres are enveloped with Schwann cells, which form a myelin sheath around the axon. | Non-myelinated nerve fibres are enclosed by a Schwann cells that do not form a myelin sheath around the axon. |
| Myelinated nerve fibres are found in spinal and cranial nerves. | These are commonly found in autonomous and the somatic nervous systems. |

(½ × 2)

(ii) Differences between dendrites and axons are as follows

| Dendrite | Axon |
|---|---|
| These are short fibres, which branch repeatedly and project out of the cell body and contain Nissl's granules. | The axon is a long branched fibre, which terminates as a bulb-like structure called synaptic knob. It possesses synaptic vesicles containing chemicals called neurotransmitters. |
| These fibres transmit impulses towards the cell body. | The axons transmit nerve impulses away from the cell body to a synapse. |

(½ × 2)

(iii) Differences between thalamus and hypothalamus are as follows

| Thalamus | Hypothalamus |
|---|---|
| The cerebrum wraps around a structural part of brain called thalamus. | It lies at the base of the thalamus. |
| All types of sensory input passes to the thalamus. | It contains neurosecretory cells that secrete hypothalamus hormones. |
| It is a major coordinating centre for sensory and motor signaling. | It regulates, sexual behaviour, expression of emotional reactions and motivation. |

(1½)

(iv) Differences between cerebrum and cerebellum are as follows

| Cerebrum | Cerebellum |
|---|---|
| Major part of the human brain forming the upper region. | Located beneath the cerebrum, at the back of the brain. |
| Divided into two hemispheres (left and right) connected by the corpus callosum; has a cerebral cortex with prominent folds. | Has a convoluted surface in order to provide the additional space for many more neurons. |
| Its functions are intelligence, learning, memory, speech, etc. | It contains centres for coordination and error checking during motor actions. |

(1½)

## Source Based/Case Based/Passage Based Questions

**1. The data below shows the working of various part of a student's brain during a three hours long exam.**

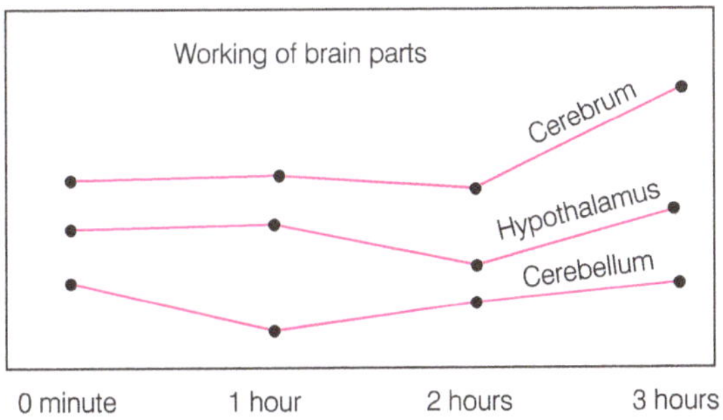

(i) With reference of the above graph explain which part of the brain is the most active during the examination?

(ii) Which is the least active among the three brain parts shown in the graph. What is its role in the body?

(iii) Human brain is divided into three main regions-forebrain, midbrain and hindbrain. Categorise the parts of the brain given in the graph into their respective region. **Competency Based Que.**

**Ans.** (i) The cerebrum is the most active region during the examination because it is the site for controlling thoughts, learning, intelligence, intellectual activities, translating perception and memories into plan actions, reasoning, decision-making, etc. (1)

(ii) Cerebellum is the least active among the three brain parts shown in the graph. It's main function is to maintain body posture, muscle toning, coordination and equilibrium of the body. (2)

(iii) Cerebrum and hypothalamus belong to forebrain. Cerebellum is a part of hindbrain (1)

**2.** A 35 year-old individual, Jordan, presents to a mental health clinic reporting difficulties with emotional regulation.

Over the past few months, Jordan has experienced intense feelings of anger and frustration, often triggered by minor events.

Additionally, there has been a noticeable decline in motivation to engage in previously enjoyed activities, including hobbies and social interactions.

(i) Which part of the brain is likely involved in the symptoms described?

(ii) Where is this region located within the brain?

(iii) What are other functions of this part of the brain?

(iv) How does this region interact with the endocrine system?

**Ans.** (i) The limbic system, including the hypothalamus, amygdala and hippocampus. (1)

(ii) It is located deep within the cerebral hemispheres, surrounding the thalamus and connected to various regions of the brain. (1)

(iii) In addition to regulating emotions and motivation, it is also involved in regulation of sexual behaviour. (1)

(iv) It influences the endocrine system by regulating the secretion of hormones, particularly through the hypothalamus, which controls the pituitary gland. (1)

# SELF ASSESSMENT TEST

## Multiple Choice Questions

1. The afferent nerve fibres transmit impulses from
   (a) tissues/organs to the CNS
   (b) the CNS to the concerned peripheral tissues/organs
   (c) the CNS to skeletal muscles
   (d) one tissue to another tissue

2. The system that transmits impulse from the CNS to the involuntary organs and smooth muscles of the body.
   (a) Sympathetic neural system
   (b) Parasympathetic neural system
   (c) Somatic neural system
   (d) Autonomic neural system

3. Which of the following is the differentiating factor between multipolar and bipolar neuron?
   (a) Number of axons
   (b) Presence or absence of Nissl's granules
   (c) Number of dendrites
   (d) Both (a) and (c)

4. Which of the following statements is/are correct about the resting state of neuron?
   I. Neuron do not conduct any impulse.
   II. Plasma membrane is electrically positive outside and negative inside.
   III. The nerve fibre is stimulated and conduct mechanical or electrical impulse.
   IV. Plasma membrane charge is negative outside and positive inside.

   Choose the correct option.
   (a) I and IV (b) II and IV (c) I and III (d) I and II

5. Select the correct statement for the thalamus part of forebrain.
   (a) It is a major coordinating centre for motor and sensory signaling
   (b) It is surrounded by cerebrum
   (c) It is found above the hypothalamus
   (d) All of the above

6. Which of the following statements are correct about the midbrain?
   I. Located between the hypothalamus and pons.
   II. Possesses a canal called cerebral aqueduct which passes through it.
   III. Dorsal part consists of four lobes.

   Choose the correct option.
   (a) I and II (b) I and III (c) I and II (d) All of these

## Assertion-Reason Questions

**Direction** (Q. Nos. 7-10) *In each of the following questions, a statement of Assertion (A) is given followed by corresponding statement of Reason (R). Of the statements, mark the correct answer*

(a) Both A and R are true and R is the correct explanation of A.
(b) Both A and R are true, but R is not the correct explanation of A.
(c) A is true, but R is false.
(d) A is false, but R is true.

7. **Assertion** (A) The neural system is better organised in insects.

   **Reason** (R) In insects, brain is present along with several ganglia and neural tissue.

8. **Assertion** (A) Electrical current can flow directly from one neuron into the other across the synapses.

   **Reason** (R) Impulse transmission across an electrical synapse is always faster than that across a chemical synapse.

9. **Assertion** (A) The dorsal portion of the midbrain consists mainly of two round swellings called corpora quadrigemina.

**Reason** (R) The midbrain is located between the thalamus/hypothalamus of the forebrain and pons of the hindbrain.

10. **Assertion** (A) The medulla of the brain is connected to the spinal cord.

**Reason** (R) The medulla contains centres which control respiration and cardiovascular reflexes

## Very Short Answer Type Questions

11. What is the term used for the gaps between two adjacent myelin sheaths?
12. Where can one find multipolar neurons?
13. Name the part of the brain which is responsible for thermoregulation.
14. Mention the different regions of the brain stem?

## Short Answer Type Questions

15. What are Nissl's granules? Where are they located?
16. Differentiate between unipolar and bipolar neuron.
17. Define synapse. Also, mention its two types.

## Long Answer Type Questions

18. Explain the structure of neuron with the help of a well labelled diagram.
19. During resting potential, the axonal membrane is polarised. Explain and indicate the movement of positive and negative ions leading to polarisation diagrammatically.
20. List the functions of the central information processing organ of the body.

## Case Based Question

21. Given below is the sagittal section of the human brain. Observe it carefully and answer the questions that follows.

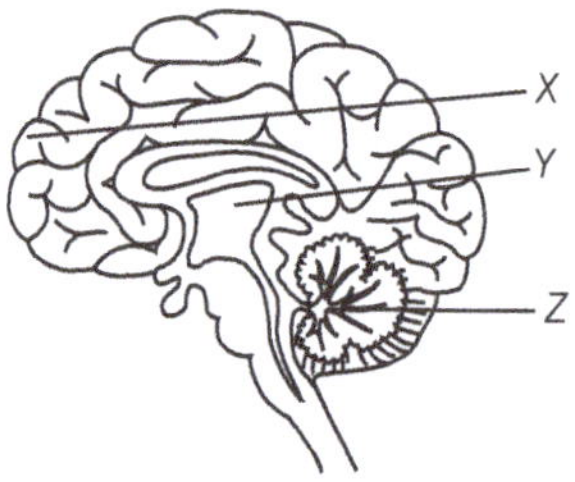


(i) Identify the structure *X*, *Y* and *Z*.

(ii) List any one function which is associated with *X*.

(iii) Mention any one similarity between *Y* and *Z*.

# Answers

| | | | | | | | |
|---|---|---|---|---|---|---|---|
| 1. (a) | 2. (d) | 3. (d) | 4. (d) | 5. (d) | 6. (d) | 7. (a) | 8. (b) |
| 9. (d) | 10. (b) | | | | | | |

19

CHAPTER

# Chemical Coordination and Integration

The nervous system and endocrine system are closely related to each other forming **neuroendocrine system**, which jointly coordinates and regulates the physiological functions of the body.

▼ **YOUR STUDY GOALS**



▼ **YOUR PRACTICE GOAL**

- Objective Type Questions (33 Qs ; MCQs, A-R) Case Based Questions (3)
- Subjective Type Questions
- (23 VSAs, 33 SAs, 14 LAs)

- In the previous chapter, you have already learnt that the nervous system in the body, provides point-to-point coordination among the organs.
- The neural coordination is rapid, but short lived in nature.
- As the nerve cells does not reach to each and every cell of the body. So, a special kind of coordination and integration is provided to each cell for continuous cellular functioning.
- This special function is performed by the chemical substances called **hormones**.
- In this chapter, we will discuss an overview of the endocrine system, major endocrine glands, hormones and their functions, regulation of hormone secretion and endocrine disorders.

## 19.1 Endocrine Glands and Hormones

- The endocrine glands are called **ductless glands** as they lack ducts.
- The endocrine glands pour their secretion into the surrounding blood which transport them to the site of action or distantly located target organ.
- Their secretions are called **hormones**.
- Endocrinology is the study of endocrine glands and hormones secreted by them.

## Hormones

- These are non-nutrient chemicals, which are produced in trace amounts and act as an **intercellular messengers**.
- These are responsible for regulating the biological processes in the body.
- The organised endocrine glands also secrete a number of new molecules in addition to the hormones.
- The hormones are transported by the blood stream from the endocrine cells to their respective target cells or organs.
- Vertebrates have large number of chemicals acting as hormones that provide coordination of various physiological processes. While invertebrates possess very simple endocrine system with few hormones.

# 19.2 Human Endocrine System

- The endocrine system in humans constitutes the endocrine glands and their hormones.
- The hormones produced from one gland may stimulate or inhibit the secretion of another endocrine gland.
- These glands also vary in structure.

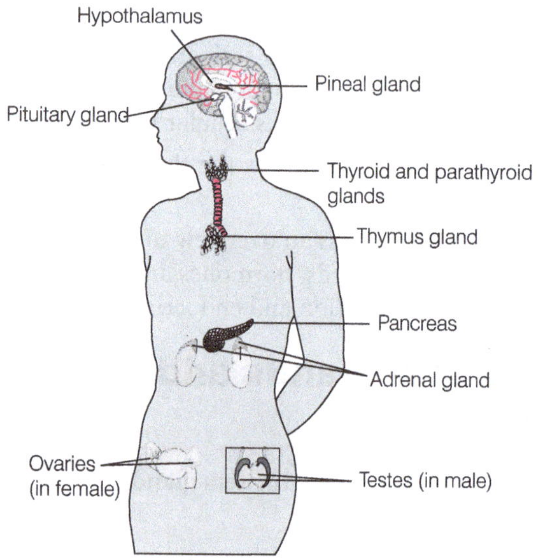


Fig. 19.1 Location of different endocrine glands

A brief account of the structure and functions of all major endocrine glands and hypothalamus is given in the following sections

## Hypothalamus

- In humans, the complete endocrine system works more or less under the influence of hypothalamus.
- **Location** Hypothalamus is located in the basal part of diencephalon (forebrain) and regulates a wide spectrum of functions in the body.
- **Structure** The hypothalamus provides the anatomical connection between the nervous and the endocrine system. It is mainly composed of nervous tissue connects with the anterior lobe of pituitary by hypophyseal portal blood vessels. However, it is also connected with the posterior lobe of pituitary by the axons of its neurons.

### Hormones of Hypothalamus

- Hypothalamus contains several groups of neurosecretory cells, known as **nuclei**, which synthesises hormones.
- The function of these hormones is to regulate the synthesis and secretion of pituitary hormones.
- Thus, the hypothalamus is often called the **control centre of the endocrine function**.
- Hormones produced by hypothalamus are of following two types

### 1. Releasing Hormones

These are the hormones that stimulate the secretion of pituitary hormones, e.g. Gonadotrophin Releasing Hormone (GnRH), which stimulates the gonadotroph cells of anterior pituitary gland to release gonadotrophins.

### 2. Inhibiting Hormone

- These are the hormones that inhibit the release of pituitary hormones, e.g. somatostatin, which inhibits the secretion of growth hormone from anterior lobe of pituitary gland.
- All these hormones originating in the hypothalamic neurons, pass through the axons and are released from their nerve endings.
- These hormones finally reach the pituitary gland through a **portal circulatory system** (hypophyseal portal system) and regulate the functions of anterior pituitary.
- The posterior pituitary, however is directly regulated by the hypothalamus.

## Pituitary Gland (Hypophysis)

- It is the **smallest endocrine gland**, but serves very important role in the human endocrine system.
- It directly or indirectly controls almost all other endocrine glands of the body. It is also known as **master gland**.
- **Location and Structure** It is about a size of a pea seed.
- The pituitary gland is located just below the hypothalamus in a small bony cavity called **sella tursica**.

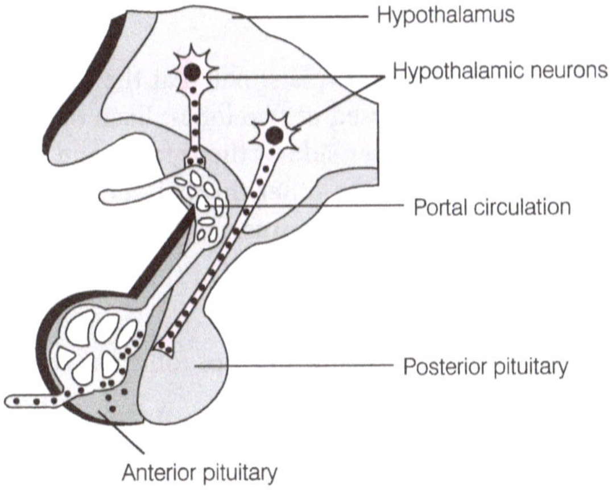


Fig. 19.2 Diagrammatic representation of pituitary gland and its relationship with hypothalamus

- The gland is attached to the brain by a stalk, called the **infundibulum** which is continuous with the hypothalamus above.

## Hormones of Pituitary Gland

The pituitary gland is anatomically divided into two major portions

### 1. Adenohypophysis

- It is the glandular anterior portion of the pituitary gland that covers 75% of the total pituitary.
- It further consists of two parts, i.e. **pars distalis** and **pars intermedia**.

### I. Pars Distalis

- It is also called **anterior pituitary**. It produces different hormones.
- These hormones and their functions are given below

#### (i) Growth Hormone (GH)

- GH stimulates body growth as well as regulate the metabolism of protein, fat and carbohydrate.
- **Oversecretion** of this hormone during childhood causes **gigantism** (excessive growth of bones), whereas in adulthood causes severe disfigurement (especially of the face) called **acromegaly.**
- Its **low secretion** results in stunted growth, i.e. pituitary **dwarfism**.

#### (ii) Prolactin (PRL)

PRL regulates the **growth of mammary glands** and formation of milk in them.

#### (iii) Thyroid Stimulating Hormone (TSH)

This TSH stimulates the synthesis and secretion of thyroid hormones from the thyroid gland.

#### (iv) Adrenocorticotropic Hormone (ACTH)

This stimulates the synthesis and secretion of steroid hormones called **glucocorticoids** from the adrenal cortex.

#### (v) Gonadotropin Hormone

- It includes Luteinizing Hormone (LH) and Follicle Stimulating Hormone (FSH).
- Both of these hormones stimulate the gonadal activity, hence called **gonadotropins.**
  - **Luteinizing Hormone** (LH) In males, it stimulates the synthesis and secretion of hormones called **androgens** from testis. While in females, it induces ovulation of fully mature follicles (Graafian follicles) and also helps in maintaining the corpus luteum formed from the remnants of the Graafian follicles after ovulation.
  - **Follicle Stimulating Hormone** (FSH) In males, the FSH and androgens together **regulate spermatogenesis.** In females, this hormone stimulates the **growth** and **development of the ovarian follicles.**

### II. Pars Intermedia or Intermediate Lobe

- This portion of adenohypophysis secretes only one hormone, i.e. **Melanocyte Stimulating Hormone** (MSH).
- The MSH acts on melanocytes (melanin containing cells) and regulates the pigmentation of the skin.
- In humans, the pars intermedia is almost merged with pars distalis.

## 2. Neurohypophysis

- Neurohypophysis forms the posterior lobe of pituitary gland. It is also known as **pars nervosa**.
- The posterior pituitary stores and releases two hormones which are actually synthesised by hypothalamus and are transported axonally to neurohypophysis.
- The hormones of posterior pituitary are given below

### (i) Oxytocin

- It acts on the smooth muscles and stimulates a vigorous contraction of uterus at the time of child birth.
- It also plays role in ejection of milk from the mammary glands in females.

### (ii) Vasopressin

- It is also known as **Antidiuretic Hormone** (ADH).
- This hormone acts mainly at the kidney, stimulating the reabsorption of water and electrolytes by the distal tubules.
- Thereby, reducing the loss of water through urine (diuresis).
- **Diabetes insipidus** is caused by lack of Antidiuretic Hormone (ADH), leading to water loss and dehydration.

### Quick Test 1

1. Decrease in the secretion of growth hormone during childhood cause '*X*', whereas during adulthood cause '*Y*'. Identify *X* and *Y*.
2. Identify the neurohormone that has its functioning in inhibiting the secretion of growth hormone from anterior lobe of pituitary.
3. Name the only hormone secreted by pars intermedia of pituitary glands.
4. **State True or False.**
   Oxytocin is produced in hypothalamus, but secreted through posterior pituitary.
5. A decrease in the secretion of which hormone causes intense thirst and heavy urination.

## Pineal Gland

- **Location** It is located on the dorsal side of the forebrain.
- **Structure** Pineal is a very small gland which is reddish grey in colour, conical in shape and has round solid body.

### Hormones of Pineal Gland

- It secretes a hormone called **melatonin** that plays a very important role in the regulation of a 24 hrs (diurnal) rhythm of our body.
- For example, it helps in maintaining the normal rhythms of sleep-wake cycle and body temperature.
- It addition, metabolism, pigmentation, menstrual cycle as well as our defence capability are also influenced by this hormone.

## Thyroid Gland

- The thyroid gland is known to be the largest endocrine gland.
- **Location and Structure** It is situated at the front of the larynx and composed of two lobes. Each of its lobe is located on either side of the trachea and are interconnected with each other through a thin flap of connective tissue called **isthmus**.
- It is composed of **follicles** (round in shape) and **stromal tissues**.
- Each thyroid follicle is composed of follicular cells, enclosing a cavity.

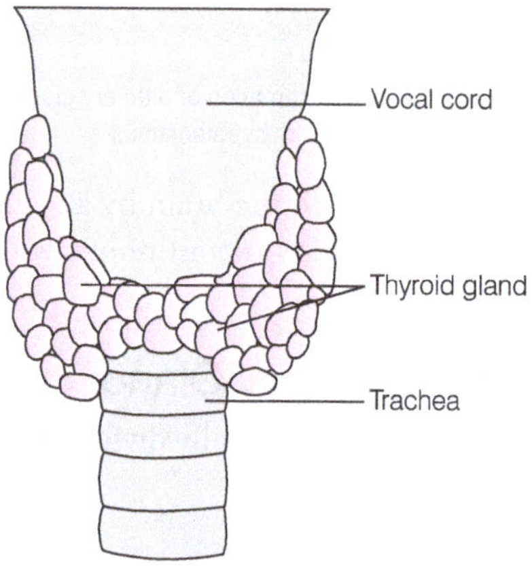


Fig. 19.3 Diagrammatic view of the position of thyroid gland (ventral side)

### Hormones of Thyroid Gland

- The follicular cells synthesises following two hormones
  - **Tetraiodothyronine** or **thyroxine** ($T_4$) hormone
  - **Triiodothyronine** ($T_3$) hormone.
- Iodine is essential for the synthesis of thyroid hormone at a normal rate in thyroid.

### Disorders of Thyroid Gland

Disorders of thyroid gland are as follows

#### 1. Hypothyroidism

This disorder occurs due to the deficiency of iodine in our diet. It leads to the enlargement of thyroid gland commonly known as **goitre**.

- **Hypothyroidism in pregnant women** affects the development and maturation of the growing baby and leads to stunted growth (**cretinism**), mental retardation, low intelligence quotient, abnormal skin, deaf-mutism, etc.
- **Hypothyroidism in adult women** may cause irregular menstrual cycle.

#### 2. Hyperthyroidism

- It is the condition during which rate of synthesis and secretion of thyroid hormones is increased to abnormal high levels.
- It may occur due to the cancer of the thyroid gland or due to development of nodules of the thyroid gland.
- It adversely affects the physiology of the body of an organism.
- **Exophthalmic Goitre** (**Grave's disease**) is a form of hyperthyroidism in which enlargement of thyroid gland takes place. Thus, thyroid secretion increases.
- It leads to protrusion of the eyeballs, increased basal metabolic rate and weight loss.

### Functions of Thyroid Hormones

Thyroid hormone serves several functions in the body, such as

- These hormones regulate and maintain the **Basal Metabolic Rate** (BMR), i.e. both $T_3$ and $T_4$ hormone, increases the overall metabolic rate of the body.
- They support the process of **formation of red blood cells**. Also helps in controlling the metabolism of carbohydrates, proteins and fats.
- Influences the maintenance of **water** and **electrolyte** in the body.
- Apart from the hormone $T_3$ and $T_4$, thyroid gland also secretes a protein hormone called **Thyrocalcitonin** (TCT). Its main function is to regulate the level of calcium in blood.

## Parathyroid Gland

- **Location** These glands are situated on the posterior side of the thyroid gland.
- **Structure** Parathyroid glands are four in number, i.e. each pair is situated in the two lobes of the thyroid gland on either side.

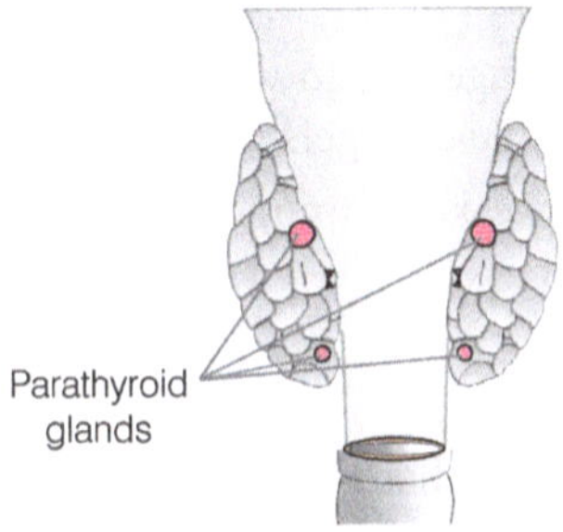


**Fig. 19.4** Diagrammatic view of the position of parathyroid glands (Dorsal side)

### Hormones of Parathyroid Gland

- Parathyroid glands secrete a single peptide hormone known as **Parathyroid Hormone** (PTH) (functions opposite to the thyrocalcitonin hormone).
- The secretion of PTH is regulated by the circulating level of calcium ions in the blood.

### Functions of Parathyroid Hormone

Parathyroid hormone serves several functions in the body, such as

- It increases the level of $Ca^{2+}$ in the blood.
- It stimulates the process of bone reabsorption (i.e. dissolution/demineralisation) by acting on bones.
- It also stimulates reabsorption of $Ca^{2+}$ by the renal tubules and absorption of $Ca^{2+}$ from the digested food, i.e. it acts as a hypercalcemic hormone i.e., it increase blood calcium level.
- Parathyroid glands are under the feedback control of blood calcium level. A fall in $Ca^{2+}$ in blood stimulates them to secrete PTH.
- Along with TCT, it plays a significant role in maintaining $Ca^{2+}$ balance in the body .

## Thymus

- It plays an important role in the development of the immune system.
- **Location** Thymus gland is a lobular structure located between lungs behind sternum on the ventral side of aorta.

## Hormones of Thymus Gland

- The thymus gland secretes a peptide hormone called **thymosin**, which plays a major role in the differentiation of **T-lymphocytes** to provide **cell-mediated immunity**.
- Thymosin also promotes production of antibodies to provide **humoral immunity**.
- It degenerates with age due to which the production of thymosin hormone also gets decreased.
- Thus, resulting in weaker immune responses inold people.

# Adrenal Gland

- **Location** Human body has a pair of adrenal glands, one at the anterior part of each kidney.

## Structure and Hormones of Adrenal Gland

Adrenal glands are conical yellowish bodies composed of two types of tissues. These are as follows

### 1. Adrenal Cortex

It is located on the outer layer of the adrenal gland.

- It is further divided into three concentric layers
  - **Zona Reticularis** It is the inner layer of the cortex.
  - **Zona Fasciculata** It is the middle layer of the cortex.
  - **Zona Glomerulosa** It is the outermost layer.

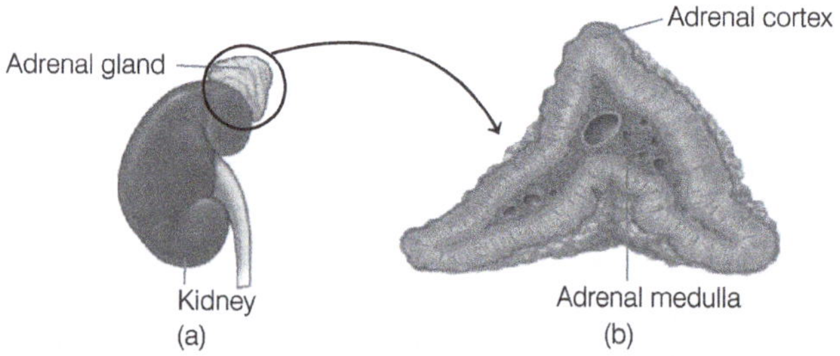


Fig. 19.5 Diagrammatic representation of : (a) Adrenal gland present above kidney, (b) Section showing two parts of adrenal gland

- Hormones secreted by these three layers of adrenal cortex are collectively known as **corticoids.**
- Three groups of steroid hormones are secreted by adrenal cortex, such as

#### (i) Mineralocorticoids

- They regulate the balance of water and electrolytes in our body.
- Aldosterone is the major mineralocorticoid found in the body.
- It mainly acts on renal tubules, stimulating the reabsorption of $Na^+$ and water.
- Also stimulates the excretion of $K^+$ and phosphate ions from the renal tubules.
- **Functions** Its main function is maintaining electrolytes, body fluid volume, osmotic pressure and blood pressure of the body.

#### (ii) Glucocorticoids

- These hormones regulate the metabolism of carbohydrates, in the body under production of this hormone alters carbohydrate. Metabolism causing acute weakness and fatigue leading to a disease called **Addison's disease.**
- Cortisol is the main glucocorticoid found in our body.
- Cortisol stimulates gluconeogenesis, aiding in carbohydrate synthesis for energy, while also playing a crucial role in maintaining the cardiovascular system, supporting kidney function and regulating inflammatory responses.
- Additionally, it suppresses the immune system to prevent excessive reactions and inflammation

**TEACHER'S TIP**

Cortisol, a stress hormone, promotes gluconeogenesis in the liver. This process involves synthesising glucose from non-carbohydrate sources like amino acids, glycerol and lactate. It helps to maintain the blood sugar level during fasting or stress, ensuring a continuous energy supply for vital functions.

#### (iii) Sexcorticoids

- Adrenal cortex also produces a small quantity of androgenic steroids both in males and females.
- **Function** It plays a major role in the growth of axial, pubic and facial hair during puberty in humans.

### 2. Adrenal Medulla

- The adrenal medulla lies in the centre of the adrenal gland.
- The adrenal medulla secretes two major hormones as below
  - **Adrenaline** (epinephrine)
  - **Nor-adrenaline** (nor-epinephrine)

- Both hormones belong to the category of compounds known as **catecholamines** and are secreted in response to any kind of stress, danger and during emergency situations.
- Thus, these are also known as **emergency hormones** or **hormones of fight** or **flight**.

### Functions of Adrenaline and Nor-adrenaline

These hormones serve following purposes

- Increase alertness.
- Dilation of pupil.
- Piloerection (raising of hairs of hands and legs).
- Sweating
- Increase in heartbeat strength of heart contraction and rate of respiration.
- They also stimulate the breakdown of glycogen due to which the concentration of glucose increases in the blood.
- Stimulate the breakdown of lipids and proteins.

### Quick Test 2

1. After a person undergoes night shift for several weeks, they begin to experience difficulty in sleeping and feel disoriented during the day. Which hormone is responsible for the given condition?
2. Name the hormone which can suppress the immune response?
3. Radha observed that her grandmother has an enlarged swelling in the neck. What is this condition called and which hormone is responsible for it?
4. A decreased cell-mediated immunity can result from the malfunction of which gland?
5. **State True or False.**
   Adrenaline hormone causes dilation of pupil, whereas nor-adrenaline hormone causes constriction of pupil.

## Pancreas

- It is a composite gland that acts as both exocrine and endocrine gland. Such glands are also called **heterocrine gland.**
- **Location** It lies below the stomach, in the loop of duodenum.
- **Structure** Pancreas consists of 1-2 million specialised cells called **islets of Langerhans.**
- In normal human pancreas, these cells represent only 1-2% of the pancreatic tissue.
- Each islet consists of two major types of cells as follows
  - **$\alpha$-cells** These cells secretes a peptide hormone called **glucagon**.
  - **$\beta$-cells** The cells secretes another peptide hormone called **insulin.**

## Hormones of Pancreas

- Glucagon and insulin have antagonistic effect on blood glucose level. This can be cleared from the functioning given below

### 1. Glucagon

- This peptide hormone plays an important role in maintaining the normal blood glucose levels in the body.
- Functions of glucagon are as follows
  - It acts mainly on liver cells (hepatocytes) and stimulates glycogenolysis, which results in an increased blood sugar level known as **hyperglycaemia.**
  - Apart from this, glucagon also stimulates the process of gluconeogenesis which also contributes to hyperglycaemia. Glucagon is known as hyperglycaemic hormone because it reduces the cellular glucose uptake and utilisation.

### 2. Insulin

- This peptide hormone plays a major role in **regulation of glucose level** in the blood.
- It mainly acts on **hepatocytes** and **adipocytes** (cells of adipose tissue) and increase the cellular glucose uptake and utilisation.
- As a result, there is a rapid movement of glucose from blood to liver cells and cells of adipose tissues resulting decreased in the blood glucose level (hypoglycaemia).
- Insulin stimulates the conversion of glucose to glycogen (glycogenesis) in the target cells.

#### Deficiency Disorder of Insulin

- **Diabetes mellitus** is the common complex disorder caused due to prolonged hyperglycaemia.
- This is associated with the loss of glucose (when complete glucose cannot be reabsorbed by the kidneys) through the urine and formation of harmful substances known as ketone bodies.
- Diabetic patients are successfully treated with insulin therapy.

## Testes

- These are the primary sex organ of males.
- They perform dual role, i.e. function as endocrine gland as well as male sex organ.
  - **Location** A pair of testis is located in the scrotal sac (outside abdomen) of male individuals.
  - **Structure** A testis is composed of many **seminiferous tubules**, which are lined by germinal epithelium and stromal or interstitial tissue.

### Hormone of Testes

- Androgens including testosterone are produced by the interstitial cells or Leydig cells.
- Androgens (mainly testosterone) performs a variety of functions as given below
  - They regulate the development, maturation and functions of male accessory sex organs like epididymis, vas deferens, seminal vesicles, prostate gland, urethra, etc.
  - These hormones also stimulate changes associated with **puberty in males**, i.e., muscular growth, growth of facial and axillary hair, aggressiveness, low pitch of voice, etc.
  - They stimulates the process of spermatogenesis, i.e. formation of spermatozoa.
  - Androgens also have **anabolic effects** (synthetic effects) on the metabolism of protein and carbohydrate.
  - These hormones acts on the central neural system and influence **male sexual behaviour** (libido).

## Ovaries

- These are the **primary sex organ** in females that helps to produce ova (female gametes) and female sex hormones.
- Ovary produces one ovum during each menstrual cycle.
- **Location** A pair of ovaries is located in the abdomen.
- **Structure** Internally, they are composed of ovarian follicles and stromal tissues.

### Hormones of Ovaries

- Ovary produces two groups of steroid hormones, i.e., **oestrogen** and **progesterone**.
- Oestrogens is synthesised and secreted by the growing ovarian follicle.
- After ovulation, the ruptured follicle is converted to another structure called **corpus luteum**, which is responsible for secretion of **progesterone.**
- Both oestrogen and progesterone play a vital role in various processes in female. These are as follows

#### Oestrogen

- It directly influences the **development of mammary glands**.
- **Regulates female sexual behaviour** and stimulates growth and activities of female secondary sex organs.
- Plays a role in the development of growing ovarian follicles.
- Appearance of female secondary sex characters high pitch of voice, etc.

#### Progesterone

- It supports pregnancy by forming placenta and preventing contractions in uterine wall.
- It also acts on mammary glands and stimulates the formation of alveoli (sac-like structures that store milk) and milk secretion.

### Quick Test 3

1. Identify, whether the given statement is correct or not, Glucagon and insulin have opposing functions in regulating blood glucose levels.
2. **State True or False.**
   β-cells of pancreas secretes a hormone that reduces the cellular glucose uptake and utilisation.
3. A medical report indicates an increased level of glucose in the urine. What condition is most likely responsible for this?
4. Name the hormone that is associated with appearance of facial and axillary hair in males.
5. There are many endocrine glands in the human body. Name the gland, which is absent in male and the one absent in female.

## 19.3 Hormones of Heart, Kidney and Gastrointestinal Tract

- Hormones are also secreted by some tissues which are not endocrine gland.
- Some examples of hormones secreted by various tissues are as follows

### Hormones of Heart

- A very important peptide hormone known as **Atrial Natriuretic Factor** (ANF) is secreted by the atrial walls of our heart.
- When blood pressure is increased, its secretion causes dilation of blood vessels thereby reducing the blood pressure.

### Hormones of Kidney

- A peptide hormone called **erythropoietin** is produced by the juxtaglomerular cells of kidney.
- This hormone stimulates formation of RBC, i.e. erythropoiesis.

### Hormones of Gastrointestinal Tract (GI)

- Endocrine cells that are present in different parts of GI tract secrete four major peptide hormones.
- These are as follows
  - **Gastrin** It acts on the gastric glands and stimulates the secretion of hydrochloric acid and pepsinogen.
  - **Secretin** It acts on the exocrine portion of pancreas and stimulate secretion of water and bicarbonate ions.
  - **Cholecystokinin** (CCK) This hormone acts on both pancreas and gall bladder, stimulating secretion of pancreatic enzymes and bile juice, respectively.
  - **Gastric Inhibitory Peptide** (GIP) Its function is to inhibit the secretion of gastric juice and its motility into the stomach.
- Apart from all these hormones, several other non-endocrine tissues secrete hormones known as **growth factors**. These factors are essential for normal growth, repair and regeneration of tissues.

## 19.4 Mechanism of Hormone Action

- Hormones produce their effect on target tissues by binding to the specific proteins known as **hormone receptors**, located in the target tissues only.

### Hormone-Receptor Complex

- Binding of a hormone to receptor leads to the formation of a **hormone receptor complex**. Formation of this complex leads to certain biochemical reactions or changes in the respective target tissue.
- Metabolism of target tissue and their physiological function are thus regulated by hormones.

### Types of Hormones

- On the basis of the chemical nature, hormones are divided into following four groups
  - **Peptide, Polypeptide, Protein, Hormones** (e.g. insulin, glucagon, pituitary hormones, hypothalamic hormones, etc).
  - **Steroids** (e.g. cortisol, testosterone, oestrogen and progesterone).
  - **Iodothyronines** (e.g. thyroid hormones).
  - **Amino acid derivatives** (e.g. epinephrine).

### Types of Hormone Receptors

Hormone receptors are of following two types

- **Membrane-Bound Receptors** Hormone receptors present in the cell membrane of the target cells.

- **Intracellular Receptors** Hormone receptors present inside the target cell, e.g. nuclear receptor (present in the nucleus of a cell).

**Mechanism of Hormone Action**

**Through membrane-bound receptor** (cAMP mediated)

Hormones, which interact with membrane-bound receptors and do not enter the target cell but generate second messengers like $IP_3$, $Ca^{2+}$, cAMP, etc. These secondary messengers inturn regulate cellular metabolism.

**Through intracellular receptors** (Transcription and translation effect)

The hormones which enter the cell and interact with intracellular receptors (e.g. steroid hormones, iodothyronines, etc.) mostly regulate gene expression or chromosome function by the interaction of hormone receptor complex with the genome. Cumulative biochemical actions result in physiological and developmental effects.

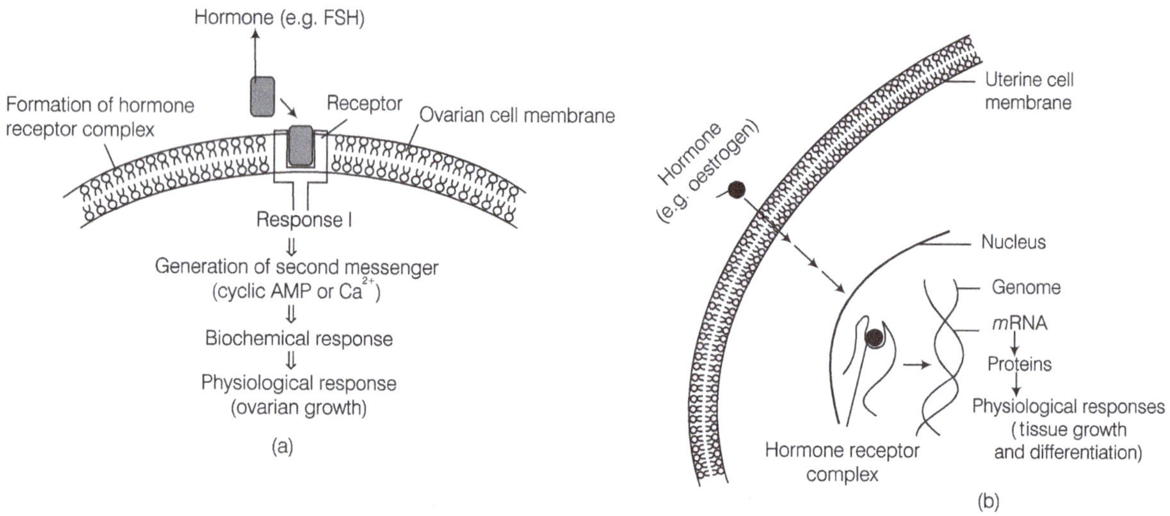


Fig. 19.6 Diagrammatic representation of the mechanism of hormone action: (a) Protein hormone, (b) Steroid hormone

## Quick Test 4

1. Give the name of the hormone, which has exactly opposite function to that of ANF.
2. Name the hormone which act on the exocrine part of pancreas and stimulates the secretion of water and bicarbonate ions.
3. **State True or False.**
   CCK hormone stimulates secretion of pancreatic enzyme and bile juice.
4. Among, insulin, cortisol, oestrogen and growth hormone, which hormone interacts with membrane-bound receptor.
5. Name one hormone whose function would be affected if the production of cAMP is blocked.

# Mind Map

## Chemical Coordination and Integration

### Endocrine Glands and Hormones

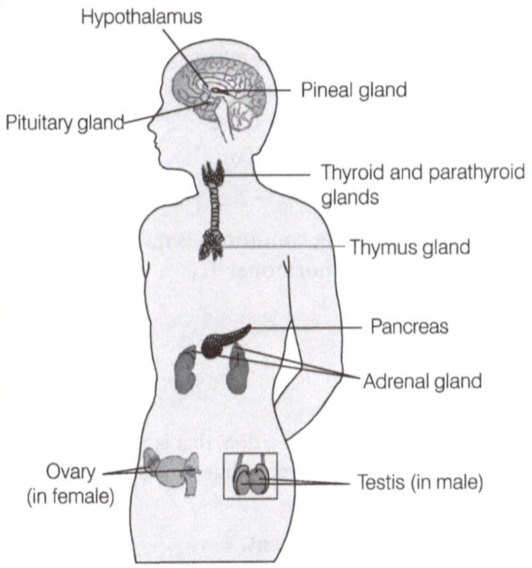


### Mechanism of Hormone Action

**Through membrane bound receptor**
↓
- Hormones interact with membrane bound receptors and do not enter the target cell.
- They generate second messengers, like $IP_3$, $Ca^{2+}$ cAMP etc. (e.g. peptide hormones).

**Through intracellular receptor**
↓
The hormones enter the cell and interact with intracellular receptors (e.g. steroid hormones iodothyronines, etc.)

### Parathyroid Gland

- Located on the back side of thyroid gland.
- Secretes peptide hormone, Parathyroid Hormone (PTH)

### Hypothalamus

- Major link between nervous and endocrine system.
- Neurosecretory cells secrete releasing and inhibiting hormones as well as oxytocin and vasopressin.

### Pineal Gland

- Located on dorsal side of forebrain.
- Secretes melatonin for regulation of 24 hrs rhythm.

### Pituitary Gland

**Pituitary Gland**

- Adenohypophysis
  - Pars distalis
    - → PRL
    - → GH
    - → TSH
    - → ACTH
    - → LH, FSH
  - Pars intermedia
- Neurohypophysis
  - → Oxytocin
  - → Vasopressin

### Thyroid Gland

- It has two lobes on either side of trachea.
- Secrete $T_3$ (tri-iodothyronine) and $T_4$ (thyroxine).

### Pancreas

- A composite glan, i.e. both exocrine and endocrine.
- Secretes glucagon (hyperglycemic hormone) and insulin (hypoglycemic hormone).

### Adrenal Gland

- Located on anterior part of each kidney.
- Adrenal medulla secrete adrenaline and nor-adrenaline.
- Adrenal cortex secrete as androgenic steroids, glucocorticoid and mineralocorticoids.

### Gonads

**Gonads**

**Testis** (Male)
- Leydig (interstitial) cells secrete androgens, mainly testosterone.

**Ovary** (Female)
- Ovarian follicles produce oestrogen (steroid hormone).

### Thymus

- Located on dorsal side of heart and aorta.
- Secretes peptide hormone thymosin.

# Exam Pattern Questions

## Objective Type Questions

### Multiple Choice Questions

**1. Which of the following statements is correct in relation to the endocrine system?**

(a) Organs in the body like gastrointestinal tract, heart, kidney and liver do not produce any hormones
(b) Non-nutrient chemicals produced by the body in trace amount that act as intercellular messenger are known as hormones
(c) Releasing and inhibitory hormones are produced by the pituitary gland
(d) Adenohypophysis is under direct neural regulation of the hypothalamus

**Ans.** (*b*)

**2. Hypothalamus releases two types of hormones mainly**

(a) stimulating hormones; releasing hormones
(b) stimulating hormones; inhibiting hormones
(c) exocrine hormones; inhibiting hormones
(d) exocrine hormones; stimulating hormones

**Ans.** (*b*)

**3. GnRH (Gonadotropin Releasing Hormone) stimulates the**

(a) pituitary to inhibit the gonadotropins
(b) pituitary for synthesis and release of gonadotropins
(c) testis to release the gonadotropins
(d) hypothalamus to release the gonadotropins

**Ans.** (*b*)

**4. Which of the following hormones is not secreted by anterior pituitary?** NCERT Exemplar

(a) Growth hormone
(b) Follicle stimulating hormone
(c) Oxytocin
(d) Adrenocorticotrophic hormone

**Ans.** (*c*)

**5. Gigantism and dwarfism are the diseases related to**

(a) prolactin hormone of mammary gland
(b) growth hormone of adenohypophysis
(c) luteinizing hormone of pituitary gland
(d) thyroid stimulating hormone of thyroid

**Ans.** (*b*)

**6. How many among the following given in the box are correspond to the functions of melatonin?**

**Diurnal rhythm, Body temperature, Pigmentation, Menstrual cycle, Defense capability**

(a) Five (b) Three
(c) Four (d) Two

**Ans.** (*a*)

**7. Which of the following conditions is not linked to deficiency of thyroid hormone?**

(a) Cretinism
(b) Goitre
(c) Myxoedema
(d) Exophthalmia

**Ans.** (*d*) **Exophthalmia,** is a condition, that is not linked to deficiency of thyroid hormone but to over secretion of thyroid hormone.

**8. Select the incorrect statement.**

(a) The thyroid gland plays a negligible role in the regulation of the basal metabolic rate
(b) The thyroid gland secretes thyroxine ($T_4$) and triiodothyronine ($T_3$)
(c) The lobes of thyroid gland are interconnected with a thin flap of connective tissue called isthmus
(d) The thyroid gland is composed of two lobes which are located on either side of the trachea

**Ans.** (*a*)

**9. Choose the statements which correctly indicates the functioning of thyroid hormones.** Competency Based Que.

**I. Regulation of the basal metabolic rate.**
**II. Stimulate the process of RBCs formation.**
**III. Regulating the blood phosphorus levels.**
**IV. Maintenance of pH and lipids balance.**

**The correct option is**

(a) I, II and IV
(b) I and II
(c) I, II, III and IV
(d) III and IV

**Ans.** (*b*)

**10.** **Identify *A*, *B*, *C* and *D* in the given diagrams and choose the correct combination.**

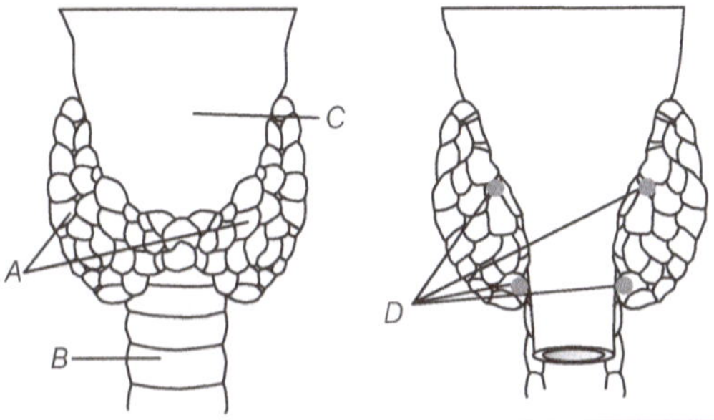


**Competency Based Que.**

(a) *A*–Thyroid, *B*–Trachea, *C*–Vocal cord, *D*–Parathyroid glands
(b) *A*–Trachea, *B*–Thyroid, *C*–Vocal cord, *D*–Parathyroid glands
(c) *A*–Trachea, *B*–Vocal cord, *C*–Thyroid, *D*–Parathyroid glands
(d) *A*–Parathyroid glands, *B*–Thyroid, *C*–Vocal cord, *D*–Trachea

**Ans.** (*a*)

**11.** **Cretinism, mental retardation, low intelligence quotient, abnormal skin, deaf-mutism, etc., are the results of**

(a) hyperthyroidism (b) goitre
(c) hypothyroidism (d) Both (b) and (c)

**Ans.** (*c*)

**12.** **Hormone that increases the blood calcium ($Ca^{2+}$) and decreases the excretion of $Ca^{2+}$ by increasing its reabsorption is**

(a) calcitonin (b) parathormone
(c) insulin (d) ACTH

**Ans.** (*b*)

**13.** **Which of the following do not play any role in calcium balance in the human body?** **NCERT Exemplar**

(a) Vitamin-D
(b) Parathyroid hormone
(c) Thyrocalcitonin
(d) Thymosin

**Ans.** (*d*) **Thymosin hormone** has no role in regulation of blood calcium homeostasis. It plays a major role in the differentiation of T-lymphocytes, which provides cell mediated immunity.

**14.** **Cortisol is involved in**

(a) maintaining cardiovascular system
(b) kidney functions
(c) RBCs production
(d) All of the above

**Ans.** (*d*)

**15.** **The steroid responsible for balance of water and electrolytes in our body is** **NCERT Exemplar**

(a) insulin
(b) melatonin
(c) testosterone
(d) aldosterone

**Ans.** (*d*) **Aldosterone** acts on the renal tubules, stimulating the reabsorption of $Na^+$ and water as well as the excretion of $K^+$ and phosphate ion. Thus, it helps maintain of electrolyte balance body fluid volume, osmotic pressure and blood pressure.

**16.** **Adrenal gland are the glands that are present on the top of the kidneys. Each gland is located at the anterior part of the kidney. Identify the correct function of the following hormones.**

| | Hormones | Function |
|---|---|---|
| (a) | Mineralocorticoids | Regulate balance of water and electrolytes |
| (b) | Glucocorticoids | Growth of hairs at puberty |
| (c) | Sexocorticoids | Stimulate liver for carbohydrate synthesis |
| (d) | Adrenaline and Nor-adrenaline | Produces insulin |

**Ans.** (*a*)

**17.** **Mary is about to face an interview. But during the first five minutes before the interview she experiences sweating, increased rate of heart beat, respiration, etc. Which hormone is responsible for her restlessness?** **NCERT Exemplar**

(a) Oestrogen and progesterone
(b) Oxytocin and vasopressin
(c) Adrenaline and nor-adrenaline
(d) Insulin and glucagon

**Ans.** (*c*) Mary, experiences sweating, increased heart rate and respiration during her first five minutes before interview because of stress which leads to release of **emergency hormones** or **hormones of flight** and **fight**, i.e. adrenaline and nor-adrenaline. These hormones stimulate the breakdown of glycogen resulting in increase concentration of glucose in blood.

**18.** **Given below in the list of glands and their hormones. Select the correct match.**

| S.No | Glands | S.No | Hormones |
|---|---|---|---|
| A. | Pituitary | 1. | Thyroid stimulating hormone |
| B. | Thyroid | 2. | Melatonin |
| C. | Pineal | 3. | Thyroxine |
| D. | Adrenal | 4. | Corticoids |

Codes

| | A | B | C | D |
|---|---|---|---|---|
| (a) | 1 | 3 | 2 | 4 |
| (b) | 2 | 4 | 1 | 3 |
| (c) | 1 | 3 | 4 | 2 |
| (d) | 2 | 4 | 3 | 1 |

**Ans.** (*a*)

**19. Which among the following is appropriate regarding the Islets of Langerhans?**

(a) Endocrine cells of adrenal medulla
(b) Exocrine cells of adrenal cortex
(c) Endocrine cells of pancreas
(d) Exocrine cells of pancreas

**Ans.** (*c*)

**20. Leydig cells produce a group of hormones called** **NCERT Exemplar**

(a) androgens
(b) oestrogens
(c) aldosterone
(d) gonadotropins

**Ans.** (*a*) The **Leydig cells** or **interstitial cells**, which are present in the interstitial spaces of testis produce a group of hormones called **androgens** mainly **testosterone**.

**21. Gastric Inhibitory Peptide (GIP)**

(a) inhibits the gastric secretion and motility
(b) inhibits the gastric secretion
(c) activate the gastric secretion and motility
(d) activate the gastric secretion

**Ans.** (*a*)

**22. Identify *A*, *B* and *C* in the diagrammatic representation of the mechanism of hormone action.**

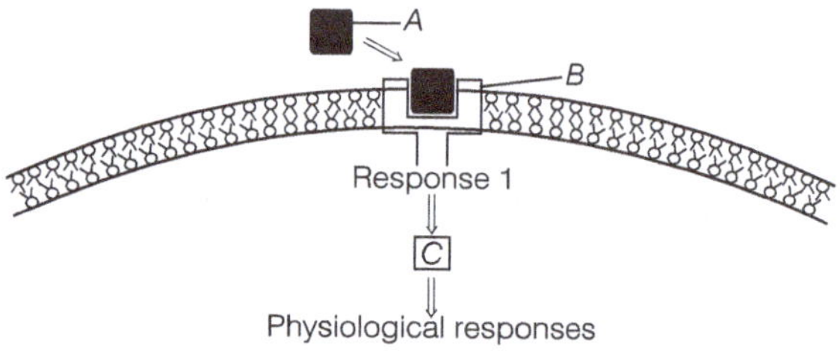


**Select the correct option from the following.** **Competency Based Que.**

(a) *A* – Steroid hormone, *B*–Hormone-receptor complex, *C* – Protein
(b) *A* – Protein hormone, *B* – Receptor, *C* – Cyclic AMP
(c) *A* – Steroid hormone, *B*–Receptor, *C*–Second messenger
(d) *A* – Protein hormone, *B* – Cyclic cAMP, *C* – Hormone-receptor complex

**Ans.** (*b*)

**23. Hormones are called chemical signals that stimulate specific target tissues. Which is the correct location of these receptors in protein hormones?** **NCERT Exemplar**

(a) Extra cellular matrix (b) Blood
(c) Plasma membrane (d) Nucleus

**Ans.** (*c*)

**24. Match the following columns.**

| | Column I (Types) | | Column II (Examples) |
|---|---|---|---|
| A. | Protein hormones | 1. | Epinephrine |
| B. | Steroid hormones | 2. | Testosterone, progesterone |
| C. | Iodothyronine hormones | 3. | Thyroid hormone |
| D. | Amino acid derivative hormones | 4. | Insulin and glucagon |

Codes

| | A | B | C | D | | A | B | C | D |
|---|---|---|---|---|---|---|---|---|---|
| (a) | 1 | 2 | 3 | 4 | (b) | 4 | 3 | 2 | 1 |
| (c) | 4 | 2 | 3 | 1 | (d) | 4 | 2 | 1 | 3 |

**Ans.** (*c*)

## Assertion-Reason Questions

**Direction** (Q. Nos. 1-9) *In each of the following questions, a statement of Assertion (A) is given followed by corresponding statement of Reason (R). Of the statements, mark the correct answer as*

(a) Both A and R are true and R is the correct explanation of A.
(b) Both A and R are true, but R is not the correct explanation of A.
(c) A is true, but R is false.
(d) A is false, but R is true.

**1. Assertion** (A) GnRH stimulates the pituitary synthesis and release of gonadotropins.

**Reason** (R) Hypothalamic hormones regulate the synthesis and secretion of pituitary hormones.

**Ans.** (*b*)

**2.** Given below is the structure of an endocrine gland. Study the figure and comment upon the correctness of both Assertion and Reason. **Competency Based Que.**

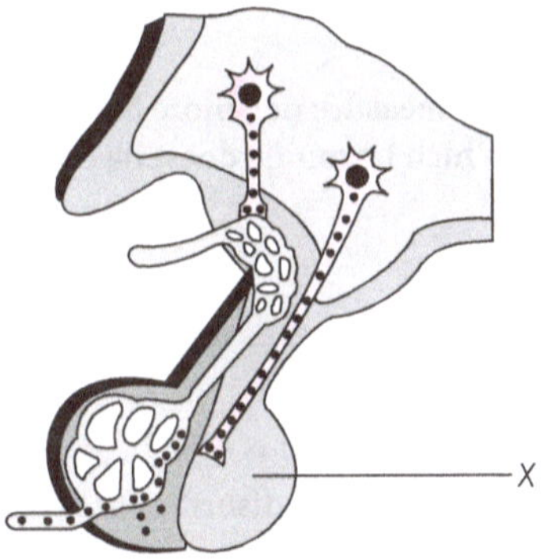


**Assertion** (A) The gland '*X*' releases oxytocin and vasopressin which are synthesised by the hypothalamus.

**Reason** (R) The gland '*X*' is located in the sella turcica.

**Ans.** (*b*)

**3. Assertion** (A) Hormone calcitonin has an antagonistic effect to that of parathormone.

**Reason** (R) Calcitonin decreases blood $Ca^{2+}$ level, while parathormone increases blood $Ca^{2+}$ level.

**Ans.** (*a*)

**4. Assertion** (A) ADH increases the volume of urine by increasing the reabsorption of water from the urine.

**Reason** (R) Failure of secretion of ADH causes diabetes insipidus.

**Ans.** (*d*) A is false, but R is true and A can be corrected as ADH (Antidiuretic Hormone) actually decreases the volume of urine by increasing the reabsorption of water in the kidneys, leading to more concentrated urine.

**5. Assertion** (A) Mineralocorticoids regulate the balance of water and electrolytes in the body.

**Reason** (R) Cortisol is the main mineralocorticoid.

**Ans.** (*c*) A is true, but R is false and R can be corrected as Cortisol is not the main mineralocorticoid, it is a glucocorticoid.

**6. Assertion** (A) Body secretes adrenaline in intense cold conditions.

**Reason** (R) Adrenaline raises the metabolic rate.

**Ans.** (*a*)

**7. Assertion** (A) Insulin and glucagon hormones are antagonistic to each other.

**Reason** (R) Insulin increases the blood glucose level whereas glucagon decreases the blood glucose level.

**Ans.** (*c*) A is true, but R is false and R can be corrected as

Insulin decreases blood glucose levels by promoting glucose uptake and storage, while glucagon increases blood glucose levels by stimulating the liver to release glucose into the bloodstream.

**8. Assertion** (A) Hormones are also secreted by some tissues which are not organised to form compact endocrine gland.

**Reason** (R) Heart, kidney, GIT and placenta also secrete hormones.

**Ans.** (*b*)

**9. Assertion** (A) Hormones interacting with membrane- bound receptors normally do not enter the target cells.

**Reason** (R) They generate second messengers like cyclic AMP, $IP_3$ and $Ca^{2+}$.

**Ans.** (*b*)

# Subjective Questions

## Very Short Answer Type Questions

**1. Why is chemical and hormonal coordination necessary?** **Competency Based Que.**

**Ans.** As the nerve fibres do not innervate all the cells of the body and cellular functions need to be regulated in a continuous manner. So, to regulate this coordination, endocrine system (chemical and hormonal coordination) is necessary. (½ × 2)

**2. State the reason for the occurrence of diabetes insipidus in an individual.**

**Ans.** Deficiency in the secretion of vasopressin (ADH) leads to the disorder known as diabetes insipidus.

**3. Which hormone is responsible for maintenance of diurnal rhythm of our body? Mention its source.**

**Ans.** The hormone responsible for diurnal rhythm of our body is melatonin. The source of its secretion is pineal gland.

**4. Mention the name of the largest and the smallest endocrine gland found in man.**

**Ans.** Thyroid gland is the largest endocrine gland and pituitary gland is the smallest endocrine gland. (½ × 2)

**5. Mention the differences between hypothyroidism and hyperthyroidism.** **NCERT Exemplar**

**Ans.** Hypothyroidism is low secretion of thyroxine hormone. Hyperthyroidism is over secretion of thyroid hormones. (½ × 2)

**6. Give the name of the endocrine gland that produces calcitonin and also mention the role played by this hormone.**

**Ans.** Calcitonin (CT) or thyrocalcitonin hormone is produced by thyroid glands. It is hypocalcemic peptide hormone, which regulate the level of calcium in blood.

**7. Which of the two adrenocortical layers, zona glomerulosa and zona reticularis lies outside, enveloping the other?** **NCERT Exemplar**

**Ans.** Zona glomerulosa (outer layer) envelops zona reticularis (inner layer) from the outside.

**8. Locate the hormone that controls $Na^+$ and $K^+$ metabolism in the body.**

**Ans.** Alodosterone is responsible for controlling $Na^+$ and $K^+$ metabolism in the body.

**9. A patient complains of constant thirst, excessive passing of urine and low blood pressure. When the doctor checked the patient's blood glucose and blood insulin level, the level were normal or slightly low. The doctor diagnosed the condition as diabetes insipidus. But he decided to measure one more hormone in patients blood. Which hormone does the doctor intend to measure?** **NCERT Exemplar**

**Ans.** Glucagon.

**10. How do catecholamines increase the level of blood glucose in body?**

**Ans.** Refer to text on page no. 439.

**11. Give the name of the disorder that is marked by the increased output of sugar in urine.**

**Ans.** Diabetes mellitus

**12. Which composite gland contains both exocrine and endocrine portions.**

**Ans.** Pancreas

**13. Identify the gland '*X*' and name the hormone it produces.** **Competency Based Que.**

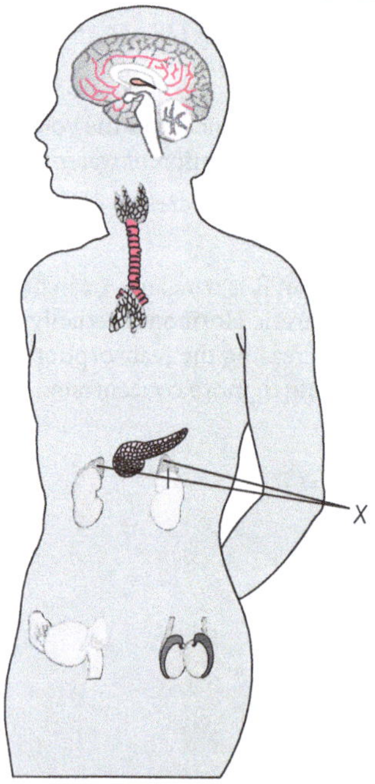


**Ans.** The '*X*' represents adrenal gland, which is responsible for the secretion of corticoids, adrenaline and nor-adrenaline.

**14. Which hormone induces spermatogenesis?**

**Ans.** Androgen (testosterone).

**15. Mention the name of the hormone that is responsible for urge of sex in males.**

**Ans.** Testosterone hormone is responsible for urge of sex in males.

**16. Mention two major functions performed by ovaries.**

**Ans.** Refer to text on page no. 440.

**17. Name the hormone and its source which produces change in secondary sex organs in human female to prepare for anticipated pregnancy?**

**Ans.** The hormone is progesterone and its source is the corpus luteum in the ovary. Progesterone prepares the secondary sex organs, particularly the uterus for implantation and supports pregnancy by maintaing the uterine lining.

**18. Mention the role of hormone secreted by the heart.**

**Ans.** Heart produces Atrial Natriuretic Factor (ANF) which promotes renal sodium excretion and lowers the blood pressure.

**19. Name the hormone that stimulates erythropoiesis.**

**Ans.** Erythropoiesis is the process of formation of RBCs. The juxtaglomerular cells of kidney produce a peptide hormone called erythropoietin, which stimulates it.

**20. Which two hormones are chemical steroids?**

**Ans.** Cortisol and testosterone are chemically steroid in nature. (½ × 2)

**21. Mention the name given to the hormones produced by some non-endocrine tissues.**

**Ans.** Hormones produced by some non-endocrine tissues are called growth factors.

**22. What act as the secondary messengers in hormone action?**

**Ans.** cAMP, DG, $Ca^{2+}$ and $IP_3$ act as secondary messengers in hormone action.

**23. Give an example of intracellular hormone receptor.**

**Ans.** Nuclear receptor (present inside the nucleus of a cell) acts as intracellular hormone receptor.

## Short Answer Type Questions

**1. Define the following**

**(i) Exocrine gland**

**(ii) Endocrine gland**

**(iii) Hormones** NCERT

**Ans.** (i) **Exocrine gland** is a gland that pours its secretion into a duct that carry it to specific location, for performing a metabolic activity, e.g. sebaceous glands, sweat glands, salivary glands, etc.

(ii) **Endocrine gland** is a gland that pours its secretion into the blood or lymph for reaching the target organ because the gland is not connected with the target organ by any duct. It is also known as ductless gland.

(iii) **Hormones** are non-nutrient chemicals which act as intercellular messengers and are produced in trace amount. (1 × 3)

**2. Diagrammatically indicate the location of the various endocrine glands in our body.** NCERT

**Ans.** Refer to fig. no. 19.1 on page no. 434.

**3. Hormones are called informational molecules. comment.**

**Ans.** Hormones are known as informational molecules because they transmit signals between different cells and organs. Their synthesis takes place in one part of the body, i.e. the endocrine cells and are carried by the blood to another part of the body, i.e. target organ or tissues where they stimulate or inhibit the specific physiological processes according to the need of the body.

**4. Hypothalamus is the master endocrine gland. Elaborate.**

**Ans.** Hypothalamus regulates a wide spectrum of body functions. It contains several groups of neurosecretory cells called nuclei, which produce hormones.

These hormones regulate the synthesis and secretion of pituitary hormones. However, the hormones produced by hypothalamus are of two types, the releasing hormones (which stimulate secretion of pituitary hormones) and the inhibiting hormones (which inhibit secretions of pituitary hormones).

The hormones reach the pituitary gland through a portal circulatory system and regulate the functions of the anterior pituitary.

The posterior pituitary is under the direct regulation of hypothalamus.

The oxytocin and vasopressin are the two hormones synthesised by hypothalamus that are transported to posterior pituitary.

**5. How are the hypothalamic hormones transported to target organs.**

**Ans.** The hypothalamic hormones secreted by the neurosecretory cells called nuclei, transport through their axons and released from their nerve endings and mixed with blood of hypophyseal portal vein.
These are then transported to anterior pituitary. The posterior pituitary hormones pass through the axons that reach the posterior pituitary and remain stored in the axon terminals, till they are stimulated for release.

**6. Which hormones are secreted by the posterior pituitary gland? What function does each serve? Where are these hormones actually produced? How are these hormones transported to the region from where they are released?** Competency Based Que.

**Ans.** Oxytocin and vasopressin are secreted by the posterior pituitary gland. (1)

(i) **Oxytocin**

It is released into the blood when hypothalamic neurons are stimulated by the widening of uterus at the time of delivery or by the sucking of breasts by an infant. It induces contraction of smooth muscles of the uterus, during the birth of a young one and of mammary glands to cause release of milk during breast feeding. (1)

(ii) **Vasopressin,**

It is also called Antidiuretic Hormone (ADH). It decreases the loss of water through urine by increasing reabsorption of water in distal convoluted tubules, collecting tubules and collecting ducts of kidneys. (1)

**7. A milkman is very upset one morning as his cow refuses to give any milk. The milkman's wife gets the calf from the shed. On feeding by the calf, the cow gave sufficient milk. Describe the role of endocrine gland and pathway associated with this response?**
**NCERT Exemplar**

**Ans.** The fonding by the calf stimulates the release of oxytocin from the posterior pituitary. Oxytocin brings about contraction of the smooth muscles of the mammary glands that causes ejection of milk.

**8. When does the secretion of adrenocorticotropin take place in the body? What is the purpose of its secretion?**

**Ans.** Adrenocorticotropin is secreted when adrenocorticotropin Releasing Hormone (ACRH) stimulates the corticotroph cells of the anterior lobe of pituitary gland.

It is released because its stimulation is responsible for the synthesis and secretion of glucocorticoid steroid hormone from the adrenal cortex of adrenal gland. (1 × 2)

**9. Name the gland that functions as a biological clock in our body where it is located? Name its one secretion.**
**DIKSHA**

**Ans.** Pineal gland functions as a biological clock in our body. It is located on the dorsal side of the forebrain. It secretes melatonin hormone.

**10. Explain the hormonal basis of diabetes insipidus.**

**Ans.** Refer to text on page no. 436.

**11. George comes on a vacation to India from US. The long journey disturbs his biological clock and he suffers from jet lag. What is the cause of his discomfort?**

**Ans.** Jet lag is caused by the disruption of the body clock as due to disturbance in synchronisation with the unfamiliar time zone of the two different parts of the world.

The body experiences different patterns of light and dark, than it is normally used to, which disrupts the natural sleep-wake cycle.

Melatonin is a hormone that plays a key role in body rhythms and jet lag. After the sun sets, the eyes perceive darkness and alert the hypothalamus.

In response to this, the pineal gland release melatonin, which promotes sleep. Conversely, when the eyes perceive sunlight, they send signals to the hypothalamus, which then sends signal to pineal gland to with-hold melatonin production. However, the hypothalamus cannot read just its schedule instantly, it takes several days.

**12. Study the figure and answer the questions that follows.**
**Competency Based Que.**

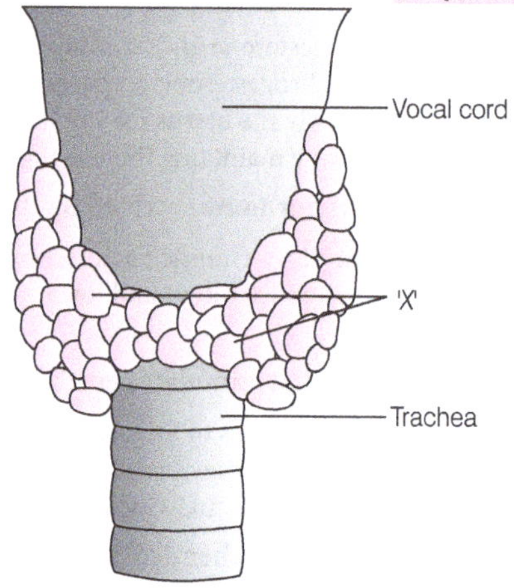


**(i) Explain the structure of a 'X' gland.**

**(ii) What are the two hormones produced by the 'X' gland?** **Competency Based Que.**

**Ans.** (i) The 'X' in the given figure represents. Thyroid gland which surrounds the front of the larynx and is composed of two lobes. Each of its lobe is located on either side of the trachea in the neck and is interconnected with the other through a flap called ishthmus. It contains thyroid follicles that has follicular cells enclosing a cavity. (2)

(ii) The two hormones produced are

(a) Tetraiodothyronine/Thyroxine ($T_4$) hormone

(b) Triiodothyronine ($T_3$) hormone (1)

**13. How does hypothyroidism affect adult women and pregnant women?**

**Ans.** Refer to text on page no. 437.

**14. In countries where dietary intake of iodine is low, goitre, enlargement of the thyroid are common. What would you say about the chain of events leading to the formation of goitre?** **Competency Based Que.**

**Ans.** In the absence of iodine, neither thyroxine nor triiodothyronine hormone is produced, due to which their concentration in the blood decreases.

To compensate this, the anterior pituitary secretes large amounts of TSH, which stimulate the growth of the thyroid gland, sometimes to gigantic proportions, leading to the formation of goitre.

However enlargement of the gland cannot increase the production of hormones, because of the deficiency of the of main ingredient i.e. iodine.

**15.** **On an educational trip to Uttarakhand, Ketki and her friends observed that many local people were having swollen necks. Please help Ketki and her friends to find out the solutions to the following questions.** **DIKSHA**

(i) **Which probable disease are these people suffering from?**

(ii) **How is it caused?**

(iii) **What effects does this condition have on pregnancy?**

**Ans.** (i) The people was suffering from the goitre disease.

(ii) Goitre is caused by the deficiency of iodine which leads to the hypothyroidism.

(iii) It leads to defective development of foetus and birth of child with cretinism. (1 × 3)

**16.** **Match the following columns.** **NCERT**

| | Column I | | Column II |
|---|---|---|---|
| A. | $T_4$ | 1. | Hypothalamus |
| B. | PTH | 2. | Thyroid |
| C. | GnRH | 3. | Pituitary |
| D. | LH | 4. | Parathyroid |

**Ans.** A–2, B–4, C–1, D–3. (½ × 4)

**17.** **Calcium plays a very important role in the formation of bones. Write about the role of endocrine glands and hormones responsible for maintaining calcium homeostasis.**

**Ans.** The secretion of Parathyroid Hormone (PTH) regulates the concentration of calcium ions ($Ca^{2+}$).

It acts on bones and stimulates the process of bone resorption (dissolution/ demineralisation). It also stimulates reabsorption of $Ca^{2+}$ by the renal tubules and increases $Ca^{2+}$ absorption from the digested food. It is thus clear that PTH is a hypercalcemic hormone, i.e. it increases the blood $Ca^{2+}$ levels. Along with TCT, it plays a significant role in calcium balance in the body.

**18.** **How do you justify the statement that hormones of adrenal medulla are emergency hormones?** **Competency Based Que.**

**Ans.** Hormones of adrenal medulla, i.e. adrenaline and nor-adrenaline (belong to the category of compounds called catecholamines) are secreted in response to any kind of stress, danger and during emergency situations like fall in blood pressure or sugar, increase respiratory rate and heartbeat.

CNS at the time of stress or danger stimulates adrenal medulla to release these hormones. All these conditions need more energy for their action. Thus, because these hormones prepare the body to face stress or danger hence are called emergency hormones.

**19.** **How does aldosterone function in our body?**

**Ans.** Refer to text on page no. 438.

**20.** **Name the gland of emergency. Give its role.**

**Ans.** Adrenal medulla. Refer to text on page no. 438-439.

**21.** **List the different groups of hormones secreted by adrenal cortex. Give specific region of secretion and one major function of each. Name the disorder that may occur in a human if the adrenal cortex is destroyed.**

**Ans.** Refer to text on page no. 438.

**22.** **Inflammatory responses can be controlled by a certain steroid. Name the steroid, its source and also its other important functions.** **NCERT Exemplar**

**Ans.** Inflammatory responses are controlled by steroid hormones called glucocorticoids. These are secreted by adrenal cortex. Its other functions are to stimulate gluconeogenesis, lipolysis and proteolysis and inhibit cellular uptake and utilisation of amino acids.

**23.** **Explain the structure of pancreas and also mention the roles of the hormone secreted by it.**

**Ans.** Refer to text on page no. 439.

**24.** **Write short notes on the functions of the following hormones.**

(i) **Adrenaline**

(ii) **Melatonin**

(iii) **Glucagon**

**Ans.** (i) Refer to text on page no. 439.

(ii) Refer to text on page no. 436.

(iii) Refer to text on page no. 439.

**25.** **Justify with examples that pancreas is a heterocrine gland.**

**Ans.** Refer to text on page no. 439.

**26.** **'Islets of Langerhans' are associated with which gland? What is its role?**

**Ans.** Islets of Langerhans are associated with pancreas. Refer to text on page no. 439.

**27.** **Differentiate between hyperglycaemia and hypoglycaemia.**

**Ans.** Differences between hyperglycaemia and hypoglycaemia are

| Hyperglycaemia | Hypoglycaemia |
|---|---|
| It results from hyposecretion of insulin. | It results from hypersecretion of insulin. |
| Its symptoms include high blood glucose level, breakdown of muscles tissues, loss of weight and tiredness. | Its symptoms include low blood glucose level, hunger, sweating, irritability, double vision. |

(1 × 2)

**28. Due to some physiological reasons the blood glucose level of an otherwise normal person has risen above normal. How will this condition be returned to normal through hormone action?** Competency Based Que.

**Ans.** Insulin will lowers blood glucose level by

(i) stimulating transport of glucose from blood to muscle and adipose cells and indirectly causing the liver to take up glucose.

(ii) promoting both oxidation of glucose and conversion of glucose into glycogen in muscles and liver cells.

(iii) inhibiting metabolic breakdown of stored glycogen in liver and muscle cells.

(iv) promoting synthesis of fats from glucose by adipose tissue and also inhibiting metabolic breakdown of fat. (½ × 4)

**29. Briefly mention the mechanism of action of FSH.** NCERT

**Ans.** In males, FSH and androgens regulate spermatogenesis. In females, FSH stimulates growth and development of the ovarian follicles. It stimulates the secretion of oestrogen in ovaries.

**30. How does progesterone function in a human female?**

**Ans.** Following are the functions performed by progesterone

(i) Helps in maintaining pregnancy by forming placenta and preventing uterine contraction.

(ii) Stimulates the development of secretory alveoli in mammary glands and secretion of milk. (1 × 2)

**31. Which hormonal deficiency is responsible for the following?** NCERT

**(i) Diabetes mellitus**

**(ii) Goitre**

**(iii) Cretinism**

**Ans.** (i) Diabetes mellitus is due to deficiency of insulin.

(ii) Goitre is due to deficiency of thyroxine ($T_4$) and triiodothyronine ($T_3$).

(iii) Cretinism is due to deficiency of thyroxine hormone. It mainly occurs in children. (1 × 3)

**32. Name the hormones that regulate the following.**

**(i) Control of skin colour**

**(ii) Release of sugar from liver**

**(iii) Appearance of secondary sexual character in females**

**(iv) Stimulate reabsorption of $Ca^{2+}$ by renal tubules.**

**(v) Maintain sleep-wake cycle.**

**Ans.** (i) MSH

(ii) Glucagon

(iii) Oestrogen

(iv) Parathyroid hormone

(v) Melatonin

**33. What is the role of second messenger in protein hormone action?** NCERT Exemplar

**Ans.** Hormones which do not enter the target cells, interact with specific receptors located on the surface of the target cell membranes and generates second messengers (e.g. *c*AMP) on the inner side of the plasma membrane. The second messenger, in turn, carries out all the hormonal functions.

## Long Answer Type Questions

**1. Give scientific reasons of the following statements.**

**(i) Adrenals are called glands of emergency.**

**(ii) The hormones released by the posterior lobe of pituitary are not its own products.**

**(iii) Endocrine glands directly release their products into the blood.**

**(iv) Hypothalamus is called control centre of the endocrine system.**

**Ans.** (i) The adrenal glands are called "glands of emergency" because they release adrenaline and nor-adrenaline during stress, preparing the body for the flight and fight response. They also produce cortisol to manage prolonged stress and aldosterone to regulate blood pressure. (2)

(ii) The hormones released by posterior lobe of pituitary gland are, in fact, synthesised by the neurons in the hypothalamus and sent to the former *via* axons for release. (1)

(iii) Endocrine glands are ductless glands and their products act at a target organ or tissue. (1)

(iv) The hypothalamus is so called becuase it regulates the release of hormones from the pituitary gland, which in turn control other endocrine glands. (1)

**2. A sample of urine was diagnosed to contain high content of glucose and ketone bodies. Based on this observation, answer the following.**

**(i) Which endocrine gland and hormone is related to this condition?**

**(ii) Name the cells on which this hormone acts.**

**(iii) What is the condition called and how can it be rectified?** Competency Based Que.

**Ans.** (i) Pancreas gland and insulin hormone is related to this condition. (1 × 2)

(ii) The β-cells of islets of Langerhans of pancreas. (1)

(iii) Prolonged hyperglycaemia leads to a complex disorder, called diabetes mellitus, which is associated with loss of glucose through urine and formation of harmful compounds known as ketone bodies. Diabetic patients are successfully treated with insulin therapy. (2)

**3. Explain the following by giving scientific reasons.**

**(i) Hypothalamus and pituitary function as an integrated and coordinated system.**

**(ii) Body growth is greatly accelerated at puberty in males.**

**Ans.** (i) The hypothalamus and pituitary function as an integrated and coordinated system because both of them are connected at the base of the brain.
They interact to each other in two ways

(a) By the hypophyseal portal system, which is a system of blood vessels that connects part of hypothalamus to the anterior lobe of pituitary gland. Hypothalamus secretes hormones into this portal system and the hormones act on the anterior pituitary, triggering the synthesis/secretion of pituitary hormone.

(b) The other is that they have direct anatomical connection between the hypothalamus and the posterior lobe of pituitary (posterior pituitary is actually are extension of hypothalamus). Thus, it is said that hormones released through posterior pituitary are actually released from the hypothalamus.

(ii) Puberty is the phenomenon of physical changes by which child's body matures into an adult male, capable of sexual reproduction and to enable fertilisation. It is initiated by the hormonal signals from the brain to the gonads, i.e. testes in a male. In response to the signals, gonads produce hormones that in turn stimulates bone growth and muscle development. An androgen called as testosterone in males, functions as principal sex hormone, producing all changes in male related to growth and development at puberty. ($2\frac{1}{2} \times 2$)

**4. What is meant by 'antagonistic effect? Illustrate your answer with an example.**

**Ans.** **Antagonistic effect** refers to the interaction between two substances (often hormones) that produce opposite effects on the same physiological process. When these substances act together, their effects cancel each other out or reduce each other's overall impact. In the context of **endocrinology**, antagonistic effects typically occur when two hormones exert opposite actions on the same target tissue or organ.

A classic example of antagonistic hormones is **insulin** and **glucagon**, both of which regulate blood glucose levels.

**Insulin** (produced by the pancreas) lowers blood glucose levels by promoting the uptake of glucose into cells and stimulating the conversion of glucose into **glycogen** (storage from of glucose) in the liver and muscles.

**Glucagon** (also produced by the pancreas) has the opposite effect. It raises blood glucose levels by stimulating the breakdown of glycogen into glucose (glycogenolysis) in the liver and promoting the production of new glucose (gluconeogenesis) from non-carbohydrate sources. (2 + 3)

**5. Differentiate between**

**(i) glucocorticoids and mineralocorticoids**

**(ii) vasopressin and oxytocin**

**(iii) oestrogen and progesterone**

**Ans.** (i) Refer to text on page no. 438.

(ii) Refer to text on page no. 436.

(iii) Refer to text on page no. 440.

**6. Fill in the blank spaces (i)-(vi) in the table given below.**

| Name of Endocrine Gland | Secreted Hormone | Functions of the Hormone |
|---|---|---|
| Pituitary | (i) | Reabsorption of water and electrolytes in kidney. |
| (ii) .......... | Insulin | (iii)..... |
| Thymus | Thymosins | (iv)..... |
| Ovary | (v) ..... and (vi) ..... | Development of growing ovarian follicles, controls metabolism of proteins, fats and carbohydrates. |

**Ans.** (i) Vasopressin

(ii) Pancreas

(iii) Reduces blood glucose level

(iv) Differentiation of T-lymphocytes

(v) Oestrogen

(vi) Progesterone

**7. Give examples of** **NCERT**

**(i) hyperglycaemic hormone and hypoglycaemic hormone**

**(ii) hypercalcaemic hormone**

**(iii) gonadotropic hormones**

**(iv) progestational hormone**

**(v) blood pressure lowering hormone**

**(vi) androgens and oestrogens**

**Ans.** (i) Glucagon and insulin, respectively

(ii) Parathyroid hormone

(iii) Follicle Stimulating Hormone (FSH) and Luteinizing Hormone (LH)

(iv) Progesterone

(v) Atrial Natriuretic Factor (ANF)
(vi) Androgens are mainly testosterone and oestrogens include oestriol, oestradiol and oestrone.

**8. Write short notes on the functions of the following hormones**
**(i) Parathyroid Hormone (PTH)**
**(ii) Thyroid hormone**
**(iii) Thymosins**
**(iv) Androgens**
**(v) Estrogens**
**(vi) Insulin and glucagon** NCERT

**Ans.** (i) **Parathyroid Hormone** (PTH) Increases blood calcium levels and decreases phosphate levels.

(ii) **Thyroid Hormones** The thyroid gland secretes thyroxine ($T_4$), triiodothyronine ($T_3$) and calcitonin. $T_4$ and $T_3$ regulate metabolism, promote growth, and stimulate tissue differentiation, while calcitonin helps to regulate blood calcium levels.

(iii) **Thymosin** Secreted by the thymus, it stimulates the development and differentiation of T-lymphocytes.

(iv) **Androgens** Secreted by the testes, androgens stimulate the development of the male reproductive system, promote sperm formation and influence male secondary sexual characteristics and sexual behaviour.

(v) **Estrogens** Secreted by the ovaries, estrogens stimulate the growth and functional maturation of the female reproductive tract and the development of secondary sexual characteristics.

(vi) **Insulin and glucagon**: Insulin is secreted by the β-cells of the pancreas; it lowers blood glucose levels and promotes protein and fat synthesis. Glucagon, secreted by a cells of the pancreas, increases blood glucose levels.

**9. List the hormones secreted by the following:**
**(i) Hypothalamus**
**(ii) Pituitary**
**(iii) Thyroid**
**(iv) Parathyroid**
**(v) Adrenal**
**(vi) Pancreas**
**(vii) Testis**
**(viii) Ovary**
**(ix) Thymus**
**(x) Atrium**
**(xi) Kidney**
**(xii) G I Tract** NCERT

**Ans.**

| | Gland | Hormones Secreted |
|---|---|---|
| (i) | Hypothalamus | Gonadotropin Releasing Hormone (GnRH) |
| | | Thyrotropin Releasing Hormone (TRH) |
| | | Corticotropin Releasing Hormone (CRH) |
| | | Growth Hormone Releasing Hormone (GHRH) |
| | | Somatostatin |
| (ii) | Pituitary | Growth Hormone (GH) |
| | | Prolactin (PRL) |
| | | Thyroid Stimulating Hormone (TSH) |
| | | Adrenocorticotropic Hormone (ACTH) |
| | | Luteinizing Hormone (LH) |
| | | Follicle Stimulating Hormone (FSH) |
| (iii) | Thyroid | Thyroxine ($T_4$) |
| | | Triiodothyronine ($T_3$) |
| | | Calcitonin |
| (iv) | Parathyroid | Parathyroid Hormone (PTH) |
| (v) | Adrenal | Cortisol |
| | | Aldosterone |
| | | Epinephrine (Adrenaline) |
| | | Nor-epinephrine |
| (vi) | Pancreas | Insulin |
| | | Glucagon |
| | | Somatostatin |
| (vii) | Testis | Testosterone |
| (viii) | Ovary | Oestrogen |

| | Gland | Hormones Secreted |
|---|---|---|
| | | Progesterone |
| (ix) | Thymus | Thymosin |
| (x) | Atrium | Atrial Natriuretic Factor (ANF) |
| (xi) | Kidney | Erythropoietin |
| | | Renin |
| (xii) | G I Tract | Gastrin |
| | | Secretin |
| | | Cholecystokinin (CCK) |

**10. Mention the major classes of hormones released in humans. Give examples of each.**

**Ans.** Although hormones are chemically diverse, they generally belong to one of four different chemical groups

(i) **Steroid Hormones** These hormones are manufactured by endocrine cells from cholesterol, an important type of lipid in the human body. Examples include cortisol are aldosterone, oestrogen, progesterone and testosterone. (1½)

(ii) **Amino Acid Derivatives** The thyroid hormones ($T_3$ and $T_4$) are synthesised from the amino acid tyrosine and iodide, respectively.
Adrenaline (also known as epinephrine) and nor-adrenaline (also known as nor-epinephrine) are produced by the medulla of the adrenal gland, are also derived from tyrosine.
Melatonin is synthesised from the amino acid tryptophan. (1½)

(iii) **Protein Hormones** These hormones are long, folded chains of amino acids. These hormones included are insulin, glucagons, parathyroid hormone, growth hormone, prolactin, etc. (1)

(iv) **Peptide Hormones** Hormones such as oxytocin and antidiuretic hormone are smaller than protein hormone. They are made up of a short chain of amino acids. (1)

**11. Write a note on hormone receptors.**

**Ans.** Refer to text on page no. 441-442.

**12. Explain the mechanism of steroid hormone action.**

**Ans.** Refer to text on page no. 442.

**13. (i) What is termed as first messenger and second messenger in the target cells?**

**(ii) How do protein hormones act on target cells?**

**Ans.** (i) The first messenger is the extracellular signaling molecule (e.g. hormone) that bind to a receptor on the target cell. Secondary messenger is the intracellular molecule (e.g. *c*AMP) that transmit and amplifies the signal within the cell, leading to physiological response.

(ii) Protein hormone is water-soluble, it binds to the extrinsic receptor present on the cell surface of the plasma membrane. Hormones when bind to them activates, a membrane-bound enzyme adenyl cyclase, which catalyses the conversion of ATP to *c*AMP.
The *c*AMP then activates one more enzyme known as protein kinases. After phosphorylation of protein, alteration of its function occurs which thereby, leads to some metabolic effect. (2 + 3)

**14. (i) Give a diagrammatic representation of the mechanism of protein hormone (e.g. FSH) action.**

**(ii) Illustrate the differences between the mechanism of action of a protein and a steroid hormone.**

**Ans.** (i)

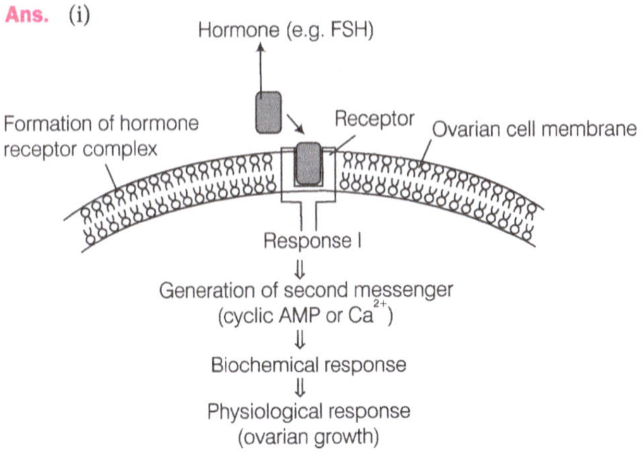


(ii) Differences between mechanism of action of a protein and a steroid hormones are as follows

| Protein Hormone | Steroid Hormone |
|---|---|
| They interact with membrane-bound receptors. | They interact with intracellular receptors. |
| They generate second messengers (cyclic AMP, $IP_3$, $Ca^{2+}$, etc). | They regulate gene expression or chromosome function by the interaction of hormone receptor complex with the genome. |
| The second messengers regulate cellular metabolism. | Cumulative biochemical action of hormone receptor complex results in physiological and developmental effects. |

(2 + 3)

## Source Based/Case Based/Passage Based Questions

**1.** The data below shows the levels of thyroid hormone production rate which can cause hypothyroidism and hyperthyroidism in the human. **Competency Based Que.**

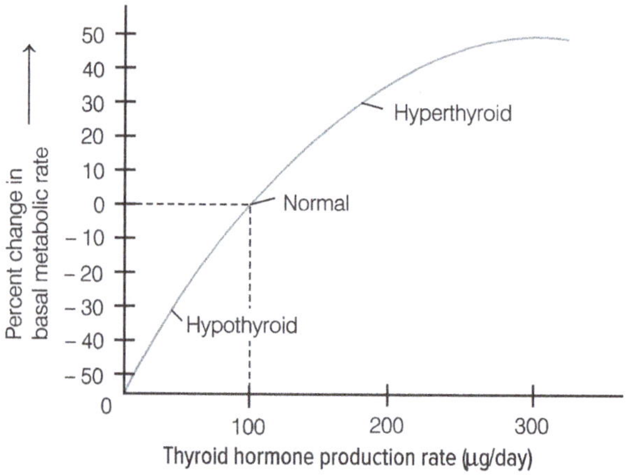


(i) With reference to the above graph what could be one of the reason behind hypothyroidism in the body?

(ii) What symptoms can be seen if hypothyroidism occurs during pregnancy?

*Or*

(ii) Give two important function of thyroid hormone.

(iii) Thyroid gland produces another hormone called thyrocalcitonin, what is its role in our body? **Competency Based Que.**

**Ans.** (i) Deficiency of iodine in our diet results in hypothyroidism and enlargement of thyroid gland. (1)

(ii) Hypothyroidism during pregnancy causes defective development and maturation of the growing baby leading to stunted growth, i.e. cretinism, mental retardation, low intelligence quotient, abnormal skin, deaf mutism, etc. (2)

*Or*

(ii) Thyroid hormones regulates the basal metabolic rate, support the process of red blood cell formation, control the metabolism of carbohydrates, protein and fats. (2)

(iii) Thyrocalcitonin (TCT) regulates the blood calcium levels in our body. (1)

**2.** Observe the given diagram and answer the questions that follows.

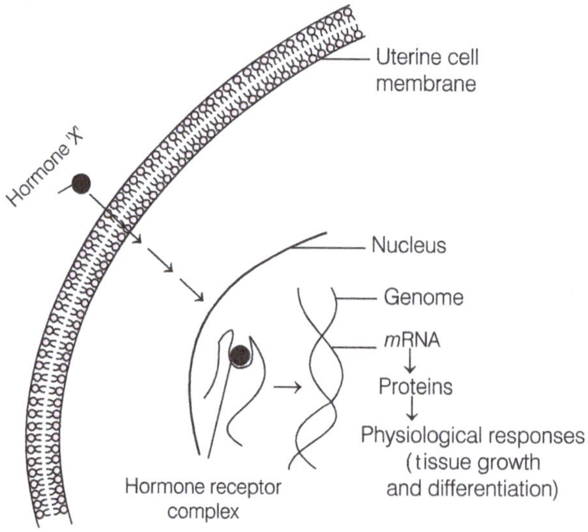

**Mechanism of hormone action is depicted in the above diagram. Study the diagram and answer the questions that follows.**

**(i) Which type of hormone is '*X*'?**

**(ii) Give two examples of hormone '*X*'.**

**(iii) What do you understand by hormone receptor complex?**

**(iv) Hormones interacting with membrane bound receptors play an indirect role in regulating cellular metabolism of the body. Justify.** **Competency Based Que.**

**Ans.** (i) Steroid hormone (1)

(ii) The two examples of hormone '*X*' are oestrogen and progesterone. (1)

(iii) It is the complex formed by hormone molecule in association with nuclear content. (1)

(iv) Hormones that interact with the membrane-bound receptors do not enter their target cell in normal condition but generate secondary messengers like *c*AMP which regulate cellular metabolism of the body. (1)

**3. Read the following passage and answer the questions that follows.**

**Radha's father who is a diabetic patient does not avoid food items that his doctor has advised him to restrict in his diet. He also feels too lazy to go for a walk. One day, his glucose level was checked by his doctor. The doctor advised him to take injections regularly, as he was not able to control his diabetes with diet and medication.** **Competency Based Que.**

**(i) What hormone does the doctor prescribe for Radha's father?**

**(ii) Which endocrine gland and its part is involved in the secretion of this hormone.**

**(iii) Why doctor preferred him to take these injections and what is the role of the prescribed hormone in controlling level of glucose in blood?**

*Or*

**(iii) What precaution he should take to protect himself from such disorder?**

**Ans.** (i) Doctor prescribed insulin hormone for Radha's father. (1)

(ii) Pancreas and its part, i.e. islets of Langerhans are related to the secretion of insulin. (1)

(iii) Doctor preferred him to take insulin in order to control the level of glucose in the blood. Insulin in the form of injection directly stimulates pancreas (in place of natural insulin produced by the body). It helps in transport of sugar from blood into other body tissues where it is used for energy. (2)

*Or*

(iii) Precautions that should be taken are as follows.

(a) Taking balanced good fibre diet is must,

(b) Regular exercise is also required. (2)

# SELF ASSESSMENT TEST

## Multiple Choice Questions

1. Which of the following is not a characteristic of hormones?
   (a) They act at a distance from their site of secretion.
   (b) They are always proteins.
   (c) They can be classified as steroids or non-steroids
   (d) They are secreted by glands.
2. The hypothalamus is involved in the regulation of which of the following?
   (a) Blood pressure (b) Body temperature
   (c) Sleep wake cycle (d) All of the above
3. Which hormone is secreted by the thyroid gland and increases metabolism?
   (a) Calcitonin
   (b) Parathyroid hormone
   (c) Triiodothyronine ($T_3$)
   (d) Thyroid Stimulating Hormone (TSH)
4. Which of the following hormones is primarily responsible for regulating metabolism?
   (a) Insulin (b) Thyroxine
   (c) Adrenaline (d) Cortisol
5. Which hormone is produced by the adrenal medulla?
   (a) Cortisol (b) Nor-epinephrine
   (c) Aldosterone (d) Insulin
6. Which of the following is a peptide hormone?
   (a) Oestrogen (b) Cortisol
   (c) Insulin (d) Testosterone
7. In the case of peptide hormones, which of the following is the primary mechanism by which they exert their effects on target cells?
   (a) They alter the transcription of DNA by interacting directly with the nucleus.
   (b) They initiate a signal transduction pathway through membrane-bound receptors, leading to a rapid cellular response.
   (c) They cross the plasma membrane and activate specific gene promoters.
   (d) They directly modify protein structure through phosphorylation.

## Assertion-Reason Questions

**Direction** (Q. Nos. 8-11) *In each of the following questions, a statement of Assertion (A) is given followed by corresponding statement of Reason (R). Of the statements, mark the correct answer as*

(a) Both A and R are true and R is the correct explanation of A.
(b) Both A and R are true, but R is not the correct explanation of A.
(c) A is true, but R is false.
(d) A is false, but R is true.

8. **Assertion** (A) Thyroxine deficiency leads to goitre.

   **Reason** (R) Goitre is caused by the overproduction of thyroid hormones due to iodine deficiency.
9. **Assertion** (A) Parathyroid hormone increases blood calcium levels.

   **Reason** (R) Parathyroid hormone promotes the absorption of calcium from the intestines and kidneys.

10. **Assertion** (A) Cortisol is known as the "stress hormone."

**Reason** (R) Cortisol helps to regulate metabolism and the immune response during stress.

11. **Assertion** (A) Oestrogen is primarily responsible for the development of male secondary sexual characteristics.

**Reason** (R) Testosterone is secreted by the testes in males.

## Very Short Answer Type Questions

12. What is the main function of thyroid hormones?
13. What is the primary function of Luteinizing Hormone (LH) in females?
14. What physiological role does oxytocin play during childbirth?
15. How does atrial natriuratic factor decrease blood pressure?

## Short Answer Type Questions

16. What are the consequences of excessive secretion of Growth Hormone (GH) in adults?
17. What is the primary function of vasopressin (Antidiuretic Hormone or ADH) in the kidneys?
18. The concentration of calcium ions in the blood is regulated by two antagonistic hormones. What are they? Which endocrine glands produced them and discuss their effects?

## Long Answer Type Questions

19. Discuss the effects of insulin and glucagon on blood glucose levels. How do these hormones work together and what are the consequences of their dysregulation?
20. Explain the role of the hypothalamus in the regulation of the endocrine system. How does it interact with pituitary gland?
21. Analyse the impact of sex hormones, such as oestrogen and testosterone, on human development and health. What roles do these hormones play during puberty and how can imbalances affect physical and psychological well-being?

## Case Based Question

22. A 28-year-old man experiences a sudden and intense stress response after narrowly avoiding a car accident. His heart rate increases, pupils dilate and he feels a surge of energy. A few minutes later, his body starts to return to normal. His doctor explains that the hormones responsible for these reactions were secreted by the adrenal glands.

(i) Which hormones are responsible for these physiological responses?

(ii) How do these hormones help in dealing with the stress of the upcoming presentation?

(iii) Why is it important for the body to quickly return to normal after such stress-induced reactions?

(iv) What could happen if these hormones are continually activated due to ongoing stress or anxiety?

# Answers

1.(b) 2. (d) 3. (c) 4. (b) 5. (b) 6. (c) 7. (b)

8.(c) 9. (a) 10. (a) 11. (d)

# 20
CHAPTER

All animals including humans are heterotrophs. They obtain food from plant and animal products. The macromolecules present in food cannot be utilised by our body in their original form. They are to be broken down into simpler forms, so that these can be utilised. This chapter deals with the simplification of complex food with the help of enzymes and digestive juices and their use by animal's body.

**YOUR STUDY GOALS**

20.1 Human Digestive System (Structure)
20.2 Digestion of Food
20.3 Absorption, Assimilation of Nutrients and Digestive Disorders.

**YOUR PRACTICE GOAL**

- Objective Type Questions (19 Qs ; MCQs, A-R)
  Case Based Question (1)
- Subjective Type Questions
- (22 VSAs, 45 SAs, 9 LAs)

# Digestion and Absorption

## Digestion : The System and Associated Glands

The digestion of food materials in digestive system is a complex process. The higher animals have holozoic type of nutrition. In this, food is taken inside well-developed digestive system and its digestion (breaking down of complex food materials into simpler one) takes place.

Digestive system in human beings is comprised of alimentary canal and digestive glands. Details of this system is discussed below in this chapter with suitable labelled diagram.

## 20.1 Human Digestive System (Structure)

The system that helps in the complete process of digestion by mechanical and biochemical methods is called **digestive system.**

The human digestive system consists of a long tubular structure called **alimentary canal** and its associated **digestive glands**.

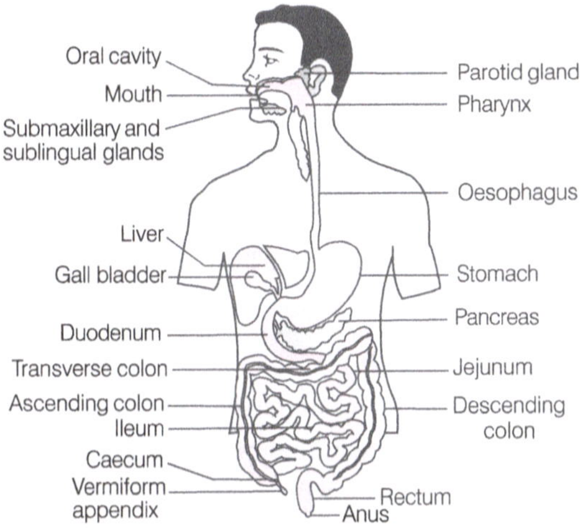


**Fig. 20.1** The human digestive system

## Alimentary Canal

It is a long tube (about 8-10 m in length) with muscular walls and varying diameter. It begins with an anterior opening, i.e. mouth and opens out posteriorly through the anus.

## Structure of Wall of Alimentary Canal

If a transverse section of an alimentary canal is viewed, the wall of alimentary canal from oesophagus to rectum (large intestine) in general shows following four concentric layers

(i) **Serosa** It is the outermost layer made up of a thin **mesothelium** (epithelium of visceral organs) with some connective tissues.

(ii) **Muscularis** It is the second layer present just below the serosa. It is very thick and contains muscle fibre. It is formed by smooth muscles. It consists of outer longitudinal and inner circular muscle fibres (both are unstriped, i.e. smooth).

**Note** In some regions like stomach an additional layer of oblique muscle is found inner to the circular muscle fibres.

(iii) **Submucosa** It lies below the muscular layer. It consists of loose connective tissues richly supplied with **nerves**, **blood** and **lymph vessels** and also with glands in some areas like duodenum.

(iv) **Mucosa** It is the innermost layer lining of the human gut or alimentary canal. It is named so because it has its major role in secreting mucus in order to lubricate inner lining of the gut.

This layer forms irregular folds (rugae) in the stomach and small finger-like foldings called **villi** in the small intestine. It also possesses gastric glands in the stomach.

**Note** All the four layers show modification in different parts of the alimentary canal.

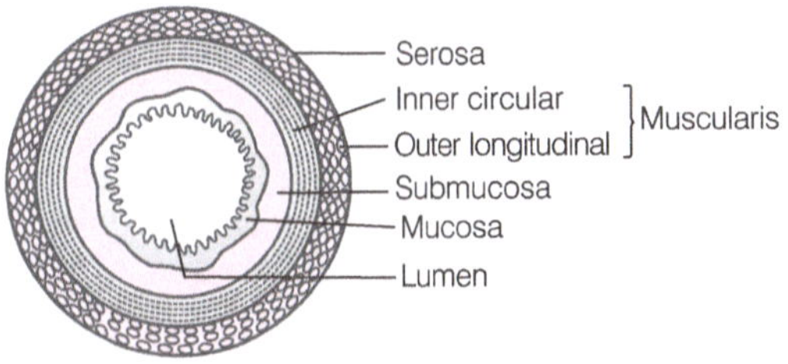


**Fig. 20.2** Diagrammatic representation of TS of a gut

Various parts of alimentary canal are discussed below

### 1. Mouth and Buccal Cavity

Mouth is a slit-like opening, bounded by two soft, movable **lips**. It opens into a small **vestibule** (space enclosed between lips and cheeks externally and gums and teeth internally), which in turn leads into the **buccal** or **oral cavity**.

Oral cavity further comprises of two main components

#### (i) Teeth

These are hard structures present in the mouth on both the jaws (i.e. upper and lower jaw). Each tooth is embedded in a socket of jaw bone.

Mammalian teeth are characterised by following three features

- **Thecodont** The teeth are fixed in sockets. They have very well-developed roots, which are implanted deeply in the jaw bone socket.
- **Diphyodont** Like other mammals, human beings also has two sets of teeth at different stages of their lifetime. The first set of teeth is **temporary** and is known as milk or **deciduous teeth**. Milk teeth are **20** in number.
- The milk set is replaced by the second set known as **permanent teeth** or **adult teeth**. Permanent teeth last for whole life, if lost, cannot be replaced.

- **Heterodont** An adult human has 32 permanent teeth, but they are of different size, shape and type.

They are of following four types

- Incisors (I) for cutting of food.
- Canine (C) for tearing the food.
- Premolars (Pm),
- Molars (M) for crushing, grinding and chewing the food.

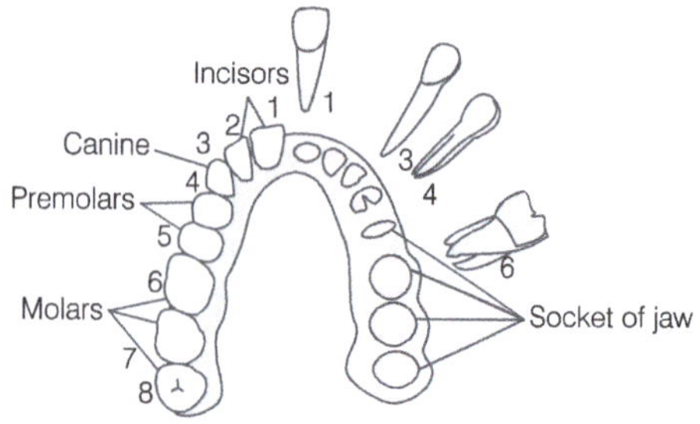


Fig. 20.3 Arrangement of different types of teeth in the jaws on one side and the sockets on the other side

**Dental Formula**

The number of each type of teeth can be expressed by a dental formula, which is the arrangement of teeth in each half of the upper and the lower jaw in the order I, C, Pm, M.

Dental formula of humans = $\frac{2, 1, 2, 3}{2, 1, 2, 3} \times 2 = 32$

Or $\frac{I, C, Pm, M}{I, C, Pm, M} \times 2 = 32$

### (ii) Tongue

It is a muscular organ, which is freely movable in the oral cavity. A fold called **frenulum** attaches the tongue to the floor of oral cavity. The upper surface of the tongue bears small projections (elevations) known as **papillae**. Some of the papillae bear taste buds. Human taste buds are sensitive to four basic tastes, i.e. sweet, bitter, salty and sour. These four taste buds are present at different locations of the tongue.

## 2. Pharynx

It is a small funnel-shaped structure located behind the oral cavity. It serves as a common passage for both food and air, i.e. it communicates with both **oesophagus** (food pipe) and **trachea** (wind pipe).

The opening of trachea or wind pipe is called **glottis**, which is guarded by a cartilaginous flap or lid called **epiglottis**. The glottis normally remains open, but during swallowing of food it gets covered by epiglottis to prevent the entry of food in trachea.

## 3. Oesophagus

It is the thin, long muscular tube that extend posteriorly passing through the neck, thorax and diaphragm and finally leads into a J-shaped bag- like structure called **stomach**. A muscular **gastro-oesophageal sphincter** regulates the opening of oesophagus into the stomach.

## 4. Stomach

It is the most dilated structure of alimentary canal situated between the oesophagus and small intestine. It lies below the diaphragm in the abdominal cavity towards the upper left side.

### Parts of Stomach

Stomach has three major parts as given below

(i) **Caloriac stomach**, the upper portion into which the oesophagus opens.

(ii) **Fundic stomach**, the middle portion.

(iii) **Pyloric stomach**, the lower portion, which opens into the first part of small intestine, i.e. duodenum. The terminal pylorus part of stomach (i.e. opening of stomach into duodenum) is guarded by a pyloric sphincter.

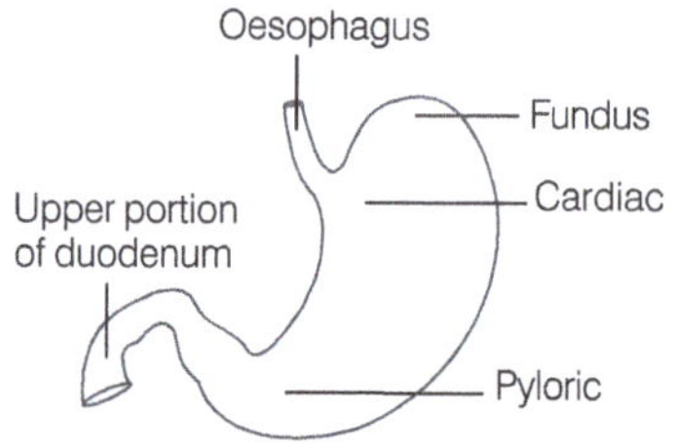


Fig. 20.4 Anatomical regions of human stomach

### Functions of Stomach

Stomach serves the following functions

(i) Acts as a short term food storage reservoir.

(ii) The substantial chemical and enzymatic digestion of protein takes place.

(iii) Gastric smooth muscles mix and grind the foodstuff by vigorous contractions with gastric secretions.

(iv) Food becomes liquified in the stomach and is released slowly in the small intestine.

## 5. Small Intestine

It is the longest part of the alimentary canal, which is about 6 m long in human beings.

It is divisible into three main regions

(i) **Duodenum** It is U-shaped, widest and shortest part of small intestine.

(ii) **Jejunum** It is the middle part of small intestine, which is about 2.5 m long and coiled.

(iii) **Ileum** It is highly coiled and the longest portion of the small intestine, which finally opens into large intestine on the right side of the abdominal cavity.

## Absorptive Surface Area of Small Intestine

The structure of small intestine is similar to all other regions of the alimentary canal. It possesses three important features, which contribute for its huge absorptive surface area.

These are as follows

(i) **Mucosal Folds** Inner surface of small intestine is thrown into circular folds, i.e. it is not flat.

(ii) **Villi** The inner mucosa layer of small intestine has, villi (about 1mm in height), covered with columnar epithelial cells.

(iii) **Microvilli** Numerous microscopic projections of microvilli are produced by the cells lining the villi. These microvilli give it a brush-border appearance and enormously increase the surface area of the intestine.

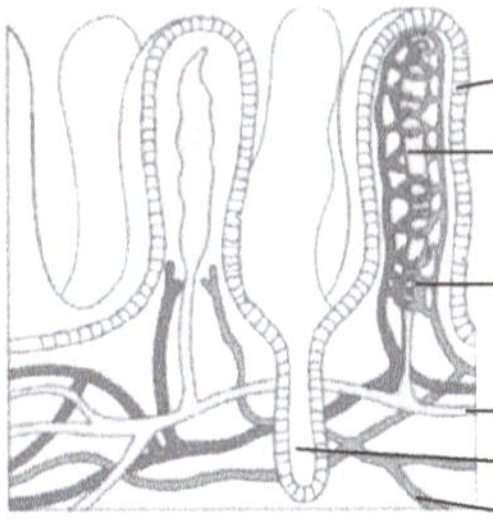


Fig. 20.5 A section of small intestinal mucosa showing villi

### Functions of Small Intestine

Following purposes are served by small intestine

(i) It acts as a major site for the digestion of food as it secretes most of the digestive enzymes and gastrointestinal hormones.

(ii) Maximum absorption of the end products of digestion takes place here, because it contains many villi that increase the surface area of absorption.

(iii) It also helps in absorption of fats.

### 6. Large Intestine

Although it is shorter in length, but is called **large intestine**, because it is wider in diameter than small intestine.

It is distinguishable into three main parts

(i) **Caecum** It is a small pouch-like structure connected to the terminal part of small intestine. It is a blind sac that functions as a host for various symbiotic microorganisms. **Vermiform appendix**, a narrow finger-like projection which is a vestigial organ arises from caecum.

> TEACHER'S TIP
> Both the structures are not well-developed in human beings, but in herbivores it is developed very well in order to digest cellulose whose digestion is difficult.

(ii) **Colon** It is the longest part of the large intestine. The caecum opens into colon, which is further divisible into three main parts, i.e. an **ascending colon**, **transverse colon** and **descending colon**.

(iii) **Rectum** It is the last part of the large intestine. The descending colon finally opens into rectum, which serves to store the **faecal matter** temporarily. It further leads to a short anal canal, which opens to outside through anus.

## Digestive Glands

These help in the chemical breakdown of food material. Digestive juices are secreted by the different glands. These are majorly **salivary glands**, the **liver** and **pancreas**.

## 1. Salivary Glands

These are exocrine glands that secrete **saliva**. There are three pairs of salivary glands in man. All three glands are situated just outside the buccal cavity and secrete salivary juice into the buccal cavity. These are as follows

(i) **Parotid Glands** These are largest of the three glands present one on either side of the cheek on the upper palate.

(ii) **Submaxillary or Submandibular Glands** These are present at the angle of the lower jaw.

(iii) **Sublingual Gland** These are situated beneath the tongue.

**Note** Each sublingual gland has about ten small ducts called **sub-ingual ducts** or **ducts of Rivinus**, which open into the floor of mouth.

## 2. Liver

It is the largest gland of the body. It is an exocrine gland. In adults, it weighs about 1.2-1.5 kg and lies in the abdominal cavity just below the diaphragm and has two lobes, i.e. left and right lobes.

Liver is a double membrane structure. Interiorly, it is divided into many small units called **hepatic** or **liver lobules** (structural and functional units of liver). It consists of many hepatic cells called **hepatocytes** that are arranged in the form of cords.

Each lobule is also covered by a thin connective tissue sheath called the **Glisson's capsule**. Hepatic cells secrete the bile juice, which passes through the hepatic duct into the gall bladder.

### Functions of Liver

Liver serves the following functions

(i) It helps in producing RBCs in embryo.

(ii) Bile secreted by the liver helps in emulsification of fats, i.e. breaking down of fats into very small micelles.

(iii) Bile also activates lipases.

(iv) It also produces heparin for preventing clotting of blood inside the blood vessels.

### Gall Bladder

It is a small pear-shaped, thin muscular sac-like organ situated just below the liver. It is attached by connective tissues to the liver. The duct of gall bladder, i.e. cystic duct along with the hepatic duct form a common bile duct, which regulates the amount of bile to be discharged into the duodenum.

After certain distance, the bile duct and pancreatic duct (duct of pancreas) form common **hepatopancreatic duct**, which opens into duodenum. It is guarded by a sphincter called the **sphincter of Oddi**.

The common hepatopancreatic duct carries both the bile (from liver) as well as pancreatic juice (from pancreas) into the duodenum.

## 3. Pancreas

It is a compound elongated heterocrine gland situated partly behind the stomach between the limbs of the **U-shaped duodenum**.

An alkaline pancreatic juice containing enzymes is secreted by its exocrine portion and the endocrine portion is responsible for the secretion of hormones, **insulin** and **glucagon**.

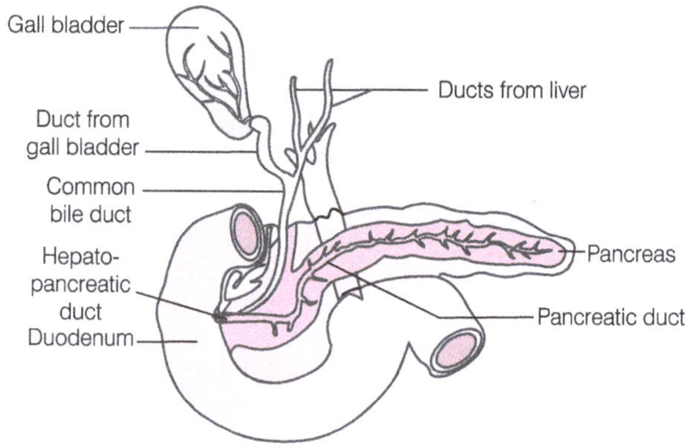


Fig. 20.6 Duct systems of liver, gall bladder and pancreas

## Other Glands

Apart from the above mentioned major glands, other glands also play an important role in completion of the process of digestion. These are mentioned below

### Gastric Glands

The glands of stomach are called **gastric glands**. These are present in the mucosa of the stomach. The gastric gland contains the following three types of secretory cells

(i) **Mucus** or **goblet cells**, secrete alkaline mucus.

(ii) **Peptic** or **chief or zymogenic** cells, secrete inactive precursors of gastric enzymes.

(iii) **Parietal** or **oxyntic cells**, secrete HCl and CIF (Castle's Intrinsic Factor).

### Intestinal Glands

The epithelium of intestine bears a large number of glands. Most of these glands are formed by the modification of the surface epithelial cells and are located in villi.

(i) **Brunner's glands** are present only in the submucosa of duodenum (not in ileum and jejunum).

(ii) The lamina propria of small intestine contains large masses of lymphocyte cells called **lymph nodules** or **Peyer's patches**. These help in destroying harmful bacteria of the region.

(iii) The mucus portion contains simple, tubular intestinal glands or **crypts of Leiberkuhn**.

These are pit-like glands with three types of cell, i.e.

- Undifferentiated epithelial cells.
- Zymogenic cells or cells of Paneth.
- Argentaffin or enterochromaffin cells.

In general intestinal juice is called **succus entericus** (secretion of cells of crypts of Lieberkuhn mainly, i.e. goblet cells and brush-bordered epithelial cells).

**TEACHER'S TIP**

- The estimated number of gastric glands in humans is about 35 millions (3.5 crore).
- The unicellular goblet cells are also present in small intestine. Infact, these glands are present throughout the alimentary canal and secrete mucus.

**Quick Test 1**

1. Out of the three types of dentition, which type provides separate socket for teeth in the jaw bone?
2. Give two anatomical adaptations of small intestine for increased absorption of nutrients.
3. Mention the functioning of mucous membrane of stomach.
4. HCl is secreted in the stomach. Give the name of the cells that secretes it.
5. If a person is suffering from reflux oesophagitis, which part of his alimentary canal is not functioning properly?

## 20.2 Digestion of Food : The Process and Control

The digestion of food involves breaking down of complex food into their simple forms. It occurs through the action of enzymes.

### Mobility of Gut

Alimentary canal allows the movement of food forward along its length. It occurs through peristaltic movements.

The alimentary canal or gut shows following movements

#### 1. In Buccal Cavity

The buccal cavity shows two major functions

(i) **Mastication of Food** The food substances are broken into smaller pieces by the movement of teeth. The tongue helps the food to mix thoroughly with saliva and mucus.

The mucus lubricates and adheres the masticated particles of food into a **bolus** and pushes it towards the pharynx for deglutition. The mastication of food is a voluntary process (in human being).

(ii) **Swallowing** (Deglutition) It is the process of passing bolus (mass of soft food) into the oesophagus from the buccal cavity through pharynx.

The food is pushed back against the epiglottis, at the same time epiglottis covers the glottis. Due to this, the oesophagial opening becomes wider and food enters into it easily.

The bolus further passes down through the oesophagus by a successive wave (peristalsis) as a reflex along with the constriction of the **oesophageal opening,** which takes the food down towards the stomach.

#### 2. Peristalsis

It is the reflex wave that comprises of a series of **muscle contraction** that passes through the whole digestive tract.

It pushes the food in the forward direction (away from the mouth).

### Mechanism of Digestion

In human being, the digestion of food starts in the buccal cavity itself. Then it continues till the anus of large intestine.

The mechanism of digestion continues in the following steps

#### 1. Digestion in Buccal or Oral Cavity

Digestion starts in the oral cavity by hydrolytic action of enzyme **salivary amylase**.

The saliva secreted into oral cavity contains electrolytes ($Na^+$, $K^+$, $Cl^-$, $HCO_3^-$, etc.) and two enzymes, i.e. salivary amylase and lysozyme. About 30% of the starch gets hydrolysed in the oral cavity by the action of salivary amylase (at optimum pH 6.8) into a disaccharide, i.e. maltose.

$$\text{Starch} \xrightarrow[\text{pH 6.8}]{\text{Salivary amylase}} \text{Maltose}$$

Lysozyme acts as an antibacterial agent. It kills bacteria thus prevents infections.

## 2. Digestion in Stomach

Food remains in the stomach for around 4-5 hours. Internal mucosa of stomach contains gastric glands, which mainly comprises of three types of cells

(a) **Mucus** or **neck cells** for secreting mucus.

(b) **Peptic** or **chief** or **zymogenic cells** for secreting proenzyme pepsinogen.

(c) **Parietal** or **oxyntic cells** for secreting HCl and intrinsic factor (essential for vitamin-$B_{12}$ absorption).

**Note** The gastro-oesophageal sphincter controls the passage of food into the stomach.

Food is slowly released from the stomach in small quantities into the small intestine, so that a slow process of digestion and absorption takes place.

The food mixes thoroughly with the acidic gastric juice secreted in the stomach by the **churning movements** of its muscles and becomes semidigested, acidic, pulpy mass called **chyme**.

The enzymes of stomach and their actions are given below

### (i) Pepsin

On exposure to HCl, the proenzyme pepsinogen gets converted into pepsin (proteolytic enzyme of the stomach) that further converts proteins into proteases and peptones (peptides).

$$\text{Pepsinogen} \xrightarrow{\text{HCl}} \text{Pepsin} \longrightarrow$$

$$\text{Proteins} \xrightarrow{\text{Pepsin (optimum pH 1-3)}} \text{Proteases} + \text{Peptones}$$

### (ii) Rennin

It is a proteolytic enzyme found in gastric juice of only infants, in its inactive form. Its secretion takes place in order to digest the milk proteins.

$$\text{Prorennin} \xrightarrow{\text{HCl}} \text{Rennin}$$

**Note** Rennin is the first enzyme isolated from calves stomach. It was used for making cheese in ancient times.

### (iii) Gastric Lipases

- Small amounts of lipases are also secreted by the gastric glands. Activity of this enzyme is inhibited in the stomach by the acidic condition. It acts on emulsified fats and also helps in digesting around 25% of milk fat (in infants).
- Apart from all these enzymes, the amount of **mucus** and **bicarbonates** present in the gastric juice play an important role in the lubrication and protection of mucosal epithelium from the action of highly acidic pH and getting destroyed.

## 3. Digestion in Small Intestine

- To further facilitate the digestion of food, muscularis layer of small intestine starts peristaltic movements. This allows a thorough mixing up of food with various secretions in the intestine.
- These contractions of muscles in the small intestine allows the further churning and kneading of the chyme and finally pushing it into the large intestine.
- The respective digestive juices from the liver (bile), pancreas (pancreatic juice) and small intestine (intestinal juices) are released into the small intestine to bring out the further chemical simplification of food. The pancreatic juice from the pancreas and the bile from the liver are released through the **hepatopancreatic duct**.

### Enzymes from Pancreas

The pancreatic juice secreted from the pancreas contains the various inactive enzymes.

These are as follows

(a) Trypsinogen

(b) Chymotrypsinogen

(c) Procarboxypeptidases

(d) Amylases

(e) Lipases

(f) Nucleases

Trypsinogen is activated by an enzyme **enterokinase** secreted by intestinal mucosa into active trypsin which in turn activates the other enzymes of pancreatic juice.

$$\text{Trypsinogen} \xrightarrow[\text{pH (7-9)}]{\text{Enterokinase}} \text{Trypsin}$$

- The **proteins, proteases** and **peptones** (partially hydrolysed form of proteins) present in the chyme (reaching the intestine) are acted upon by the proteolytic enzymes of pancreatic juice. These are given below as

$$\left.\begin{array}{l}\text{Proteins}\\ \text{Peptones}\\ \text{Proteoses}\end{array}\right\} \xrightarrow[\text{Carboxypeptidase}]{\text{Trypsin / Chymotrypsin}} \text{Dipeptides}$$

- **Carbohydrates** in the chyme are hydrolysed by pancreatic amylase into disaccharides.

  $$\text{Polysaccharides (starch)} \xrightarrow{\text{Amylase}} \text{Disaccharides}$$

- **Nucleases** in the pancreatic juice acts on nucleic acids to form nucleotides and nucleosides.

  $$\text{Nucleic acids} \longrightarrow \text{Nucleotides} \longrightarrow \text{Nucleosides}$$

## Digestive Juices from Liver

- The bile secreted from the liver is released into duodenum of small intestine. Bile contains the bile pigments, i.e. **bilirubin** and **biliverdin**, bile salts, cholesterol and phospholipids.
- Thus, fats are broken down into di and monoglycerides by the action of lipases secreted by pancreas.

  $$\text{Fats} \xrightarrow{\text{Lipases}} \text{Diglycerides} \xrightarrow{\text{Lipases}} \text{Monoglycerides}$$

- Bile does not contain any enzyme as gastric juice. It helps in emulsifying fats, i.e. in breakdown of fats into very small micelles which are kept suspended in an aqueous medium.
- The process of emulsification is basically carried out by the salts of bile. This increases the surface area of fat available for digestion by the lipase (as bile also activates lipases).

## Enzymes from Intestine

- Intestinal mucosal epithelium has **goblet cells** (secretes mucus). Thus, the secretions of the brush-border cells of mucosa together with the goblet cell secretions form the intestinal juice (also known as **succus entericus**).

The succus entericus, thus contains various enzymes

(a) Disaccharidases, e.g. maltase for digestion of maltose into glucose.

(b) Dipeptidases (c) Lipases

(d) Nucleosidases

**Note** Pancreatic and intestinal lipases together with bile salts help in the emulsification and digestion of big and complex fat molecules.

- The mucus along with the bicarbonates from the pancreas helps in protecting the mucosal layer of intestine from the action of acid and also provides an alkaline medium (pH-7.8) for enzymatic activities.
- Glands (Brunner's gland) from submucosal layer of intestine also help in this. Hence, all the enzymes in the succus entericus act on the end products of the above mentioned reactions in order to form their respective simpler forms.

$$\text{Dipeptides} \xrightarrow{\text{Dipeptidases}} \text{Amino acids}$$

$$\text{Maltose} \xrightarrow{\text{Maltase}} \text{Glucose} + \text{Glucose}$$

$$\text{Lactose} \xrightarrow{\text{Lactase}} \text{Glucose} + \text{Galactose}$$

$$\text{Sucrose} \xrightarrow{\text{Sucrase}} \text{Glucose} + \text{Fructose}$$

$$\text{Nucleotides} \xrightarrow{\text{Nucleotidases}} \text{Nucleosides} \xrightarrow{\text{Nucleosidases}} \text{Sugars} + \text{Nitrogenous bases}$$

$$\text{Di and Monoglycerides} \xrightarrow[\text{Lipolytic enzyme}]{\text{Lipases}} \text{Fatty acids} + \text{Glycerol}$$

All these final steps take place very close to mucosal epithelial cells of the intestine, which facilitate their absorption.

All the biomacromolecules mentioned above are broken down in the duodenum region of small intestine, while the simpler forms are absorbed in the other two regions of small intestine, i.e. jejunum and ileum.

## 4. Digestion in Large Intestine

- The last stage of chemical simplification of food occurs in the last part of the alimentary canal, i.e. large intestine. This is carried out by bacterial action. Glands of this region tends to secrete mucus. No enzyme is secreted into this part of the digestive system.
- The undigested and the unabsorbed substances are finally passed on to the large intestine.

**TEACHER'S TIP**

- There are more than 500 species of bacteria found in the colon region of the large intestine which are not usually harmful as long as they remain in the large intestine.
- Infact, all these bacteria synthesise vitamin-K and $B_{12}$, also help in absorption of calcium, magnesium and zinc (by increasing the acidity of colon region).

Following functions are performed by the large intestine

(i) Absorption of most of water, some minerals and certain drugs.

(ii) Secretion of mucus which helps in **adhering** the waste (undigested) particles together and **lubricating** it for an easy passage.

The undigested, unabsorbed substances called **faeces**, enter into the caecum region of the large intestine (through the **ileocaecal valve,** which prevents the backflow of faecel matter). It is temporarily stored in the rectum till defaecation (egestion) through the anus occurs.

## Neural and Hormonal Control of Digestion

For proper coordination and functioning of different parts of the **gastro intestinal tract**, it is always under a proper, neural and hormonal control.

### Neural Control

Secretion of saliva is stimulated by the sight, smell and the presence of food in the oral cavity. Similarly, the gastric and intestinal secretions are also under the control of neural signals. The muscular activities of different parts of the alimentary canal are also moderated by **neural mechanisms** (both local and through CNS).

### Hormonal Control

The major hormones that control the functions of digestive system are produced and released by the cells in the mucosa of the stomach and the large intestine.

**Quick Test 2**

1. How would non-secretion of saliva affect the digestion of food in the mouth?
2. Trypsin acts as an alkaline path what provides this alkalinity? Give the two action of trypsin.
3. How is the intestinal mucosa protected from the acidic food passing from the stomach?
4. Why does our mouth becomes water sometimes when we eat or think about the food loe like?

# 20.3 Absorption, Assimilation of Nutrients and Digestive Disorders

## Absorption of Digested Food Components

Absorption is the process by which end products of digestion pass through the intestinal mucosa into the blood or lymph. The site of absorption is mainly small intestine, where villi and microvilli are present. They play a major role in absorption of nutrients by the means of **diffusion**, **active**, **passive** or **facilitated transport** mechanisms.

### Absorption of Monosaccharides and Amino Acids

The carbohydrates are mainly absorbed in the form of monosaccharides (glucose, fructose, etc). The proteins are absorbed in the form of simple amino acids. Small amount of monosaccharides like glucose and amino acids are generally absorbed by simple diffusion. The passage of these substances into the blood depends upon their concentration gradients.

However, some other substances like fructose and some amino acids are absorbed with the help of the carrier molecules. This mechanism is known as the **facilitated transport.**

### Absorption of Water

Water absorption in the large intestine occurs by osmosis from the lumen of the large intestine through epithelial cells and blood capillaries in the villi. Transport of water depends upon the osmotic gradient. The absorption of water from the small intestine is associated with the absorption of electrolytes and digested food in order to maintain an osmotic balance with the blood.

### Absorption of Fats (Fatty Acids and Glycerol)

As fatty acids and glycerol are insoluble in water, these cannot be absorbed into the blood directly. Instead, these are first converted into small droplets called **micelles** with the help of bile salts and phospholipids (lecithin) and then, move into the intestinal mucosa.

The formation of micelle takes place due to the aggregation of many water molecules around fatty acid molecules. These can be absorbed into the intestinal cells by diffusion. These are reformed or resynthesised into very small protein coated fat globules called the **chylomicron.**

These chylomicrons are thus transported into the lymph vessels (lacteals) in the villi. These lymph vessels ultimately release the absorbed substances into the blood stream.

## Calorific Fuel Value and Physiological Fuel Value of Nutrients

The amount of energy liberated during complete combustion of 1 g of a substance in bomb calorimeter is its calorific fuel value.

The amount of energy made available during complete oxidation of 1g of a substance inside the body is its physiological fuel value.

Both the fuel values of macronutrients is given below

| Nutrients | Calorific Value | Physiological Value |
|---|---|---|
| Lipids | 9.45 kcal | 9 kcal |
| Carbohydrates | 4.1 kcal | 4 kcal |
| Proteins | 4.64 kcal | 4 kcal |

## Absorption of Salts (Electrolytes)

Electrolytes, mainly $Na^+$ are absorbed into the blood by the active transport through the mucosal cells. Chloride ions ($Cl^-$) are mainly absorbed by simple diffusion or active transport. Thus, absorption of various substances takes place by various mechanisms in different parts of the alimentary canal like mouth, stomach, small intestine and large intestine.

**Summary of Absorption in Different Parts of Digestive System**

| Mouth | Stomach | Small Intestine | Large Intestine |
|---|---|---|---|
| Certain drugs coming in contact with the mucosa of mouth and lower side of the tongue are absorbed into the blood capillaries lining them. | Absorption of water, simple sugars and alcohol, etc., takes place. | Principal organ for absorption of nutrient. The digestion is completed here and the final products of digestion such as glucose, fructose, fatty acids, glycerol and amino acids are absorbed through the mucosa into the blood stream and lymph. | Absorption of water, some minerals and drugs takes place. |

## Assimilation

It is the process by which absorbed nutrients or substances get distributed to various cells of the body. These ultimately utilise them for synthesis of materials for various metabolic activities. The assimilation of substances is an anabolic process, i.e., it requires energy for metabolic processes.

## Egestion

The digestive wastes are eliminated out of the body by the process called egestion. It is known to be the last step of the entire digestive process. The wastes gets solidified into **coherent faeces** in the rectum (part of large intestine), which initiate a neural reflex by causing an urge or desire for its removal. The egestion of faeces to the outside through the anal opening is a voluntary process.

The peristaltic movement gradually pushes the undigested slurry from small intestine to large intestine and finally to the outside.

**Note** About 70% of the faeces is water, rest 30% are solids. The large portion of solid is contributed by the dead bacteria, which are present in colon of large intestine.

## Disorders of Digestive System

The inflammation of the intestinal tract, is the most common ailment (a physical disorder or illness) caused due to the bacterial or viral infection.The infections may also be caused by the parasites of the intestine such as tapeworm, threadworm, roundworm, hookworm, pinworm, etc.

## Protein Energy Malnutrition (PEM)

It is also referred to as protein calorie malnutrition. It is a potentially fatal disorder, leading to death in children in developing countries. It develops in children and adults whose consumption of protein and energy (measured by calories) is insufficient to fulfil the body's nutritional needs. It is of following two types

(i) **Kwashiorkor** It is a form of severe protein energy malnutrition. It is characterised by irritability, oedema (swelling), dermatosis and an enlarged liver with thinning of hair and loss of teeth.

(ii) **Marasmus** It is caused by severe energy deficiency in the body. It is characterised by stunted growth, wasted appearance, loss of muscle mass, anaemia, etc. It usually develops in children between age group of six months to one year.

Some of the disorders of digestive system are given below

## Jaundice

It is the symptom of liver's malfunctioning. Bile pigments begin to excrete through other parts of the body due to their increased accumulation level in the blood. Thus, the skin and the white portion of sclera of the eyes turns yellow.

## Vomiting

It is the forceful throughing out of harmful contents of stomach through the mouth. It is not due to the reverse peristalsis of the stomach and oesophagus, instead the major thrust or force for expulsion is from the contraction of diaphragm and abdominal muscles.

The reflex action of vomiting is controlled by the vomit centre in the medulla.

The process of vomiting proceed as follows

Increased salivation → Sweating → Rapid heart rate → Discomfort → Nausea (feeling of vomit) → Vomiting (ejection of harmful contents).

## Diarrhoea

It is the condition of abnormal frequency of bowel movement (act of defecation) and increased liquidity of faeces, which is caused due to irritation in the lining of the colon.

During diarrhoea, the peristalsis movement gets increased due to which the contents of intestine pass through rapidly. Thus, reducing the absorption of food and water. It leads to dehydration and sometimes it is lethal if left untreated.

## Constipation

It is the condition of difficult or irregular defecation during which the faeces are retained within the rectum (large intestine) for a longer time than the normal. Due to this, more amount of water is absorbed from the faecal matter making it hard and dry to expel it out.

During constipation slowing down of peristaltic movements of alimentary canal is visible.

## Indigestion

In this condition, food is not properly digested by digestive system that leads to a feeling of fullness.

The incomplete digestion of food is due to one of the following causes, i.e. inadequate secretion of digestive enzymes and gastrointestinal hormones, anxiety, food poisoning, over eating, spicy food, etc.

### Quick Test 3

1. Name the type of vitamin and hormone respectively that may increase the absorption of cations in the body.
2. Unabsorbed fat droplets appear in faeces when the bile ducts are obstructed. State whether the given statement is true or false. If false, give reason.
3. List any two disorders, that affect the person's normal digestion mechanism. Explain in detail.
4. How are electrolyte (salts) absorbed into the blood?

# Exam Pattern Questions

## Objective Type Questions

### Multiple Choice Questions

**1.** **During swallowing food, the windpipe are closed by a flap like structure called**

(a) glottis (b) epiglottis
(c) sphincter (d) Both (a) and (b)

**Ans.** *(b)*

**2.** **The sigmoid colon is the part of**

(a) large intestine (b) small intestine
(c) pharynx (d) rectum

**Ans.** *(a)*

**3.** **Which out of the following is considered as the hardest part of the tooth?**

(a) Pulp (b) Enamel
(c) Dentine (d) Pulp cavity

**Ans.** *(b)*

**4.** **The chief function of bile juice is to**

(a) emulsify fats for digestion
(b) emulsify proteins for digestion
(c) regulate digestion of proteins
(d) digests fats by enzymes

**Ans.** *(a)*

**5.** **Which out of the following digestive gland secretes a digestive juice which does not contain enzymes?**

(a) Salivary (b) Pancreas
(c) Liver (d) None of these

**Ans.** *(c)*

**6.** **The correct parts of the small intestine are *P*, *Q* and *R*.**

| | *P* | *Q* | *R* |
|---|---|---|---|
| (a) | ileum | caecum | jejunum |
| (b) | duodenum | ileum | caecum |
| (c) | duodenum | jejunum | ileum |
| (d) | ileum | duodenum | caecum |

**Ans.** *(c)*

**7.** **Dental formula of adult human is**

(a) $\frac{2123}{2123}$ (b) $\frac{1223}{1223}$
(c) $\frac{2132}{2132}$ (d) $\frac{2213}{2213}$

**Ans.** *(a)*

**7.** **Choose from the following that correctly represents the enzyme composition of pancreatic juice.**

(a) Amylase, peptidase, trypsinogen, renin
(b) Lipase, amylase, trypsinogen, peptidase
(c) Lipase, amylase, pepsin and renin
(d) Peptidase, amylase, pepsin, renin

**Ans.** *(b)*

**8.** **The hepatic portal vein is located between the**

(a) hepatic vein and the vena cava
(b) small intestine and the liver
(c) mouth and the stomach
(d) pancreas and the small intestine

**Ans.** *(b)*

**9.** **Consider the following statements.**

**Statement I** Pharynx is a small funnel shaped structure located behind the oral cavity.

**Statement II** Pharynx acts as a common passage for both food and air.

**Choose the correct option.**

(a) Statement I is correct, but statement II is incorrect
(b) Statement I is incorrect, but statement II is correct
(c) Both statements I and II are correct
(d) Both statements I and II are incorrect

**Ans.** *(c)*

**10.** **What do *X*, *Y* and *Z* in the given diagram represent?**

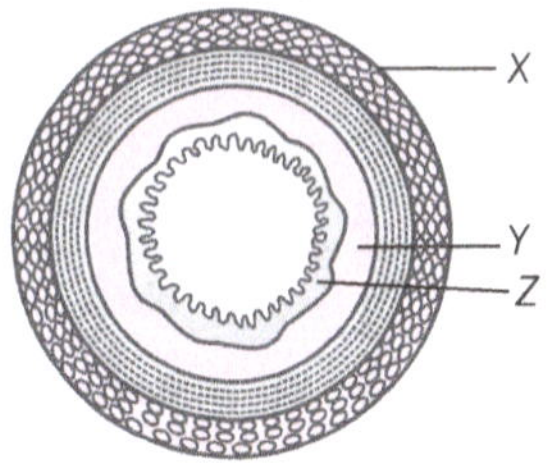


| | *X* | *Y* | *Z* |
|---|---|---|---|
| (a) | Serosa | Sub-mucosa | Mucosa |
| (b) | Sub-mucosa | Mucosa | Serosa |
| (c) | Mucosa | Serosa | Sub-mucosa |
| (d) | Serosa | Mucosa | Sub-mucosa |

**Ans.** *(a)*

**11.** What do we call the type of teeth attachment which each tooth is embedded in a socket of jaw bone?

(a) Thecodont (b) Phyodont
(c) Heterodont (d) None of these

**Ans.** *(a)*

**12.** Which sphincter is present in a form of a muscular ring in a digestive tract that regulate the opening of oesophagus into stomach?

(a) Pyloric sphincter
(b) Gastro-oesophagal sphincter
(c) Gastro-intestinal sphincter
(d) Sphincter of Oddi

**Ans.** *(c)*

**13.** Name the duct that brings secretion from gall bladder and pancreas to the duodenum.

(a) Bile duct (b) Pancreatic duct
(c) Hepato-pancreatic duct (d) Common bile duct

**Ans.** *(c)*

**14.** Match the enzymes with their respective substrates and choose the right one among the options given.

| Column I | | Column II | |
|---|---|---|---|
| A. | Lipase | 1. | Carbohydrates |
| B. | Nuclease | 2. | Fats |
| C. | Carboxypeptidase | 3. | Nucleic acids |
| D. | Glycosidases | 4. | Proteins, peptones, proteases |

**Codes** **NCERT Exemplar**

| | A | B | C | D | | A | B | C | D |
|---|---|---|---|---|---|---|---|---|---|
| (a) | 2 | 3 | 1 | 4 | (b) | 3 | 4 | 2 | 1 |
| (c) | 3 | 1 | 4 | 2 | (d) | 2 | 3 | 4 | 1 |

**Ans.** *(a)*

**15.** Match two columns and select the right one among the options given.

| Column I | | Column II | |
|---|---|---|---|
| A. | Duodenum | 1. | A cartilagenous flap |
| B. | Epiglottis | 2. | Small blind sac |
| C. | Glottis | 3. | U-shaped structure emerging from the stomach |
| D. | Caecum | 4. | Opening of wind pipe. |

**Codes**

| | A | B | C | D | | A | B | C | D |
|---|---|---|---|---|---|---|---|---|---|
| (a) | 1 | 2 | 3 | 4 | (b) | 4 | 3 | 2 | 1 |
| (c) | 3 | 1 | 4 | 2 | (d) | 2 | 4 | 1 | 3 |

**Ans.** *(c)*

## Assertion-Reason Questions

Direction (Q. Nos. 1-4) *In each of the following questions, a statement of Assertion (A) is given and followed by corresponding statement of Reason (R). Of the statements, mark the correct answer.*

(a) Both A and R are true and R is the correct explanation of A
(b) Both A and R are true, but R is not the correct explanation of A
(c) A is true, but R is false
(d) A is false, but R is true

**1. Assertion** (A) Human beings have two sets of teeth during their life.

**Reason** (R) Human beings have thecodont dentition.

**Ans.** *(b)* Both A and R are true, but R is not the correct explanation of A.

Majority of mammals including human beings possess two sets of teeth during their life, a set of permanent or adult teeth. This type of dentition is called diphyodont. Human beings also have a thecodont dentition, i.e. teeth are embedded with sockets of the jaw bones.

**2. Assertion** (A) Presence of HCl is the stomach is necessary for the process of digestion.

**Reason** (R) HCl kills and inhibits the growth of bacteria in the stomach.

**Ans.** *(b)*

**3. Assertion** (A) The main part of carbohydrate digestion takes place in small intestine.

**Reason** (R) Here, pancreatic amylase converts carbohydrate into lactose.

**Ans.** *(c)* A is true, but R is false. R can be corrected as

In small intestine, pancreatic amylase convert starch and dextrins into maltose and small intestine is the main site for digestion of carbohydrates.

**4. Assertion** (A) Bile salts of bile help in the emulsification of fats.

**Reason** (R) Lipases can break large fat droplets into small ones.

**Ans.** *(c)* A is true, but R is false R can be corrected as

lipases can digest fats in the significant amounts only when large fat droplets are broken into droplet to form a fine emulsion.

Emulsification of fats by bile salts, thus increases the lipase action of fats.

# Subjective Questions

## Very Short Answer Type Questions

**1. Out of the three types of dentition, which type provides separate socket for tooth in the jaw bone.**

**Ans.** In the thecodont type of dentition, separate sockets are provided for tooth in the jaw bone.

**2. Give the dental formula of human beings.** **[NCERT]**

**Ans.** The dental formula of human beings is $\frac{2123}{2123} \times 2$.

**3. Mention the name of different types of teeth and their number in an adult human.** **[NCERT]**

**Ans.** An adult human has 32 permanent teeth, which are of four different types (heterodont dentition), i.e. incisors (I), canine (C), premolars (Pm) and molars (M) and their numbers are 4, 2, 4, 6, respectively.

**4. In which portion of alimentary canal does oesophagus open?**

**Ans.** Oesophagus opens into the stomach.

**5. How the mucosa of the small intestine is adapted for the absorption of food?**

**Ans.** Mucosa of the small intestine is adapted for the absorption of food by having villi and brush-bordered epithelium.

**6. Out of the three types of salivary glands, which one is situated in the upper palate on either side of cheek?**

**Ans.** Parotid glands (a type of salivary gland) is situated in the upper palate on either side of the cheek.

**7. Crypts of Lieberkuhn are found in which part of the alimentary canal?**

**Ans.** These are found in small intestinal part of alimentary canal.

**8. HCl is secreted in stomach. Give the name of the cells that secrete it.**

**Ans.** Oxyntic cells (parietal cells) are present in the epithelial lining of stomach that secretes gastric acid, i.e. HCl.

**9. Mention the function of saliva other than digestion.**

**Ans.** Apart from taking part in digestion of starch, saliva also helps to lubricate the food for swallowing.

**10. The food mixes thoroughly with the acidic gastric juice of the stomach by the churning movements of its muscular wall. What do we call the food then?**

**Ans.** The food is known as chyme after mixing thoroughly with the acidic gastric juice of stomach by churning movement of its muscular wall.

**11. A chemical substance changes pepsinogen into pepsin. Identify it.**

**Pepsinogen ⟶ Pepsin**

**Ans.** Hydrochloric acid (HCl) is the chemical substance that changes pepsinogen into pepsin.

**12. State the indispensable protease of small intestine which does not directly take part in protein digestion.**

**Ans.** Enterokinase is protease enzyme of small intestine, which does not directly take part in the protein digestion.

**13. Trypsinogen is an inactive enzyme of pancreatic juice. An enzyme, enterokinase activates it. Which tissue/cells secrete this enzyme? How is it activated?** **[NCERT Exemplar]**

**Ans.** The cells of duodenum secrete enzyme enterokinase. It is activated by food in the duodenum.

**14. State the source of trypsin and the food constituent to which this enzyme hydrolyses.**

**Ans.** Pancreatic juice is the source of trypsin which hydrolyses proteins into peptides.

**15. Give the name of the enzymes involved in the breakdown of nucleotides into sugars and bases?** **[NCERT Exemplar]**

**Ans.** Nucleosidases break nucleotides into sugar and bases.

**16. Mention the important functioning of peristalsis movement that occurs throughout the alimentary canal.**

**Ans.** It is due to these waves of contraction of the circular muscle that passes along the stomach and oesophagus that the food is pushed into the relaxed portion.

**17. If a person is fasting for a prolonged period, what will be the sequence of organic food to be digested by the body.**

**Ans.** The sequence of organic food to be digested by the body after a prolonged fasting will be

Carbohydrates → Fats → Proteins.

**18. Name the mechanisms by which nutrients are absorbed in alimentary canal.**

**Ans.** Small nutrients are absorbed by active transport, some are absorbed by the facilitated transport and simple diffusion.

**19. As fatty acids and glycerol are not absorbed directly. Name the form in which fatty acids are converted to get absorbed.**

**Ans.** Fatty acids and glycerols are not absorbed directly into the blood stream. Thus, they are absorbed in the form of small droplets called micelles.

**20.** **Enumerate the condition when discolouration of skin and white portion of eye takes place.**

**Ans.** Condition is known as jaundice in which discolouration of the skin and white portion of eye takes place.

**21.** **What happens in the condition when bile from the liver crystalises?**

**Ans.** When bile from the liver get crystallised, person suffers because of the stone formation in kidney or urinary bladder in the body.

**22.** **State the conditions on which the transport of water depends.**

**Ans.** The transport of water depends on the osmotic grandient across the intestinal (large) wall.

## Short Answer Type Questions

**1.** **Explain the terms thecodont and diphyodont.** **[NCERT]**

**Ans.** Each tooth is embedded in a socket of jaw bone. This type of attachment is called thecodont.

Majority of mammals including human being forms two sets of teeth during their life, a set of temporary milk or deciduous teeth replaced by a set of permanent or adult teeth. This type of dentition is called diphyodont. [2]

**2.** **Stomach is located in upper left portion of the abdominal cavity and has three major parts. Name these three parts.** **[NCERT Exemplar]**

**Ans.** The stomach has three major parts as follows

(i) A cardiac portion into which the oesophagus opens.

(ii) A fundic portion which is a middle region.

(iii) A pyloric portion which opens into the first part of small intestine. [2]

**3.** **Mention the modification or structural features of ileum, which make it suitable for absorption of nutrients.**

**Ans.** The mucosa is folded into finger-like projections called villi. The cells lining the villi bear microvilli giving it a brush-bordered appearance. These two features increase the surface area of intestine for absorption. The villi are richly supplied with a network of blood capillaries and a large lymph vessel, lacteal, for easy absorption of nutrients. [2]

**4.** **Answer briefly**

**(i) Why are villi present in the intestine and not in the stomach?**

**(ii) What are the basic layers of the wall of alimentary canal?** **[NCERT]**

**Ans.** (i) Villi are present in the intestine to increase the surface area, so that absorption of digested food occurs efficiently.

(ii) The wall of alimentary canal from oesophagus to rectum possesses four layers, i.e. serosa, muscularis, submucosa and mucosa. Serosa is the outermost layer, followed by muscularis, submucosa and mucosa. [1+1]

**5.** **State the role of pancreas in human body. Also mention, what will happen to a person, if the pancreas does not work properly?**

**Ans.** Pancreas contributes in following functions in the body

(i) It contributes to the digestion of different components of food.

(ii) The absorption of food breaken down products from the digestive tract start taking place here.

(iii) The metabolism of blood sugar is regulated. [1]

Hence, if any malfunctioning happens to pancreas, it fails to perform these functions properly. [1]

**6.** **Give the name of the watery fluid secreted from Brunner's gland in the duodenum. Mention its any two characteristics. What role does it play inside the duodenum?**

**Ans.** The Brunner's gland secretes mucoid fluid. [1]

It has the following characteristics

(i) It is viscous and enzyme-free.

(ii) It is alkaline in nature and enables duodenum to withstand the acid chyme.

(iii) It also protects its wall from getting digested. [1]

**7.** **HCl is a strong acid. Yet it does not corrode the walls of the stomach. Why?**

**Ans.** The HCl produced in the stomach is not as strong as used for industrial purposes.

However, acidic behaviour of HCl does not corrode the stomach walls, because the gastric epithelium of stomach is secretory in nature, i.e. it produces mucus, which covers the stomach wall preventing it from corrosive action of gastric juice. [2]

**8.** **Give structural details about the wall of alimentary canal of human gut and all layers associated with it.**

**Ans.** Refer to text on page no. 461. [3]

**9.** **List the organs of human alimentary canal and name the major digestive glands with their location.**

**Ans.** Organs of human alimentary canal are mouth, oesophagus, stomach, small intestine and large intestine and anus. The major digestive glands and their location are as follows [1]

| Digestive Glands | Location |
|---|---|
| Salivary glands | Mouth cavity |
| Liver | In abdominal cavity, just below the diaphragm. |
| Pancreas | Between the limbs of U-shaped duodenum |

[2]

**10. Describe the accessory digestive glands in human.**

**Ans.** The accessory digestive glands include the salivary glands, the liver and the pancreas.

(i) Humans have three pairs of salivary glands, i.e. the parotids, submandibulars and sublinguals. They secrete major amount (about 1L) of the saliva, each day. The parotids are the largest glands in the cheek region near the ears. The submandibular glands are located towards the posterior end of the lower jaw. Sublingual glands are the smallest, present at the anterior part of the floor of the mouth.

(ii) The liver is the largest gland in the body. It weighs about 1.5 kg. It lies immediately under the diaphragm. The gall bladder is a small and elongated muscular sac situated below the liver.

(iii) The pancreas is an elongated gland, that is situated near the junction of the stomach and the duodenum. Both the liver and pancreas act as glands, whereas the gall bladder acts as a storing organ. [1× 3]

**11. Why is it so, that food does not pass through the digestive system by 'gravity', but still we are able to digest food even when we are lying down? Explain how food passes through our digestive system?**

**Ans.** The lining of the oesophagus, stomach and intestine is muscular, these help in pushing food through it easily by its own by peristalsis movements. These movements of muscles help the food to pass through along the whole alimentary canal. [2]

**12. Why does a piece of bread start tasting sweeter after it is chewed for some time?**

**Ans.** As bread is full of starch, the enzyme secreted in our mouth for digesting starch starts breaking down carbohydrates present in starch converting into simple sugars. Hence, it tastes sweeter after some time. [2]

**13. What is the action of salivary amylase?**

**Ans.** (i) Salivary amylase splits starch and glycogen first to dextrins and then into disaccharides like maltose, isomaltose and small dextrins called 'limit' dextrins.

$$\text{Starch} \xrightarrow[\text{amylase}]{\text{Salivary}} \text{Maltose} + \text{Isomaltose} + \alpha\text{-dextrins}$$

(ii) Bicarbonate ions in saliva neutralise the acids present in food. The thiocyanate ions of saliva act as anti-microbial agent. These prevent infection by the microbes. [1×2]

**14. Correct the following statements by deleting one of the options (given in bracket).**

**(i) Gastric glands of stomach mucosa have (oxyntic cell/chief cells) which secrete HCl.**

**(ii) Saliva contains enzymes that digest (starch/protein).**

**Ans.** (i) Gastric glands of stomach mucosa have oxyntic cells which secrete HCl.

(ii) Saliva contains enzymes that digest starch. [1+1]

**15. How our gut lining is protected from its own secretion of proteases?**

**Ans.** Gut lining is protected from its own secretion of proteases as

(i) Proteases are secreted in its inactive form called proenzymes so, that they do not act on gut lining.

(ii) Gut secretes mucus which thereby inactivates the proteases and protects the gut lining. [1+1]

**16. Answer briefly**

**(i) How does pepsinogen change into its active form?**

**(ii) How does bile help in the digestion of fats?**

**Ans.** (i) Inactive form of pepsinogen is activated by the action of HCl.

(ii) Bile salts help in emulsification of lipids and activate the lipases. [1+1]

**17. Correct the following statements by deleting one of the enzymes in bracket.**

**(i) Goblet cells are located in the intestinal mucosal epithelium and secrete (chymotrypsin /mucus).**

**(ii) Fats are broken down into di and monoglycerides with the help of (amylase /lipases).** **[NCERT Exemplar]**

**Ans.** (i) Goblet cells are located in the intestinal mucosal epithelium and secrete mucus.

(ii) Fats are broken down into di and monoglycerides with the help of lipases. [1+1]

**18. Describe the digestive role of chymotrypsin. Which two other digestive enzymes of the same category are secreted by its source gland?** **[NCERT]**

**Ans.** Chymotrypsin is the active form of chymotrypsinogen, it is activated by trypsin. It curdles milk. Nucleases like DNAse and RNAse and pancreatic lipase are other enzymes secreted by the pancreas. [2]

**19. Describe the enzymatic action on fats in the duodenum.**

**Ans.** Fats are broken down by lipases into di and monoglycerides in the duodenum of small intestine as

$$\text{Fats} \xrightarrow{\text{Lipase}} \text{Diglycerides} \longrightarrow \text{Monoglycerides}$$

[2]

**20. Match the Column I with Column II.**

| | Column I | | Column II |
|---|---|---|---|
| A. | Bilirubin and biliverdin | 1. | Parotid |
| B. | Hydrolysis of starch | 2. | Bile |
| C. | Digestion of fat | 3. | Lipase |
| D. | Salivary gland | 4. | Amylase |

**[NCERT]**

**Ans.** A–2, B–4, C–3, D–1 [½ × 4]

**21. Bile juice contains no digestive enzymes, yet it is important for digestion. Why?** **NCERT Exemplar]**

**Ans.** Bile is a yellowish green alkaline solution with 89-98% water, it has no digestive enzymes. The bile released into the duodenum contains bile pigments (bilirubin and biliverdin), bile salts, cholesterol and phospholipids, but no enzymes. Bile helps in emulsification of fats, i.e. breaking down of the fats into very small micelles. Bile also activates lipases. [2]

**22.** The diagram shows part of the human alimentary canal. Which two structures produce substances involved in the digestion of fats?

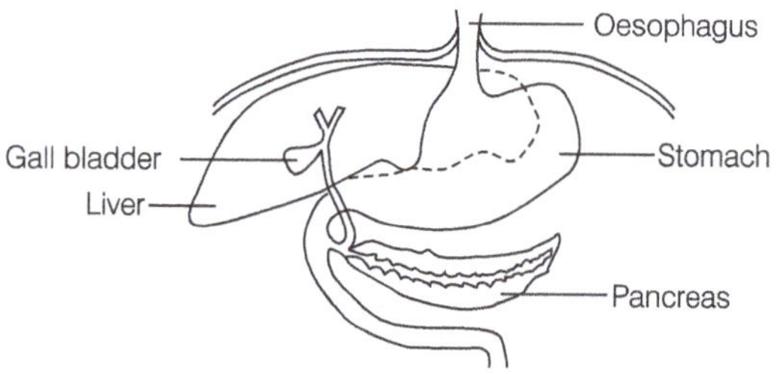


**Ans.** Bile is produced by the liver and pancreatic juice is secreted by pancreas. Liver and pancreas are the two glands of alimentary canal these produce substances (enzymes and bile free) involved in the digestion of fat. [1 + 1]

**23. Fill in the blanks with appropriate enzymes that bring the required changes in the following**

**(i) Trypsinogen $\xrightarrow{?}$ Trypsin**

**(ii) Caesin $\xrightarrow{?}$ Paracasein + Whey protein**

**(iii) RNA $\xrightarrow{?}$ Ribonucleotides**

**(iv) Triglycerides $\xrightarrow{?}$ Fatty acids + Glycerol**

**Ans.** (i) Enterokinase (ii) Rennin
(iii) Ribonuclease (iv) Lipase [½ × 4]

**24. 'Digestion of starch starts in the buccal cavity, but stops in the stomach'. Comment**

**Ans.** Starch is not digested in the stomach, because the enzyme ptyalin (salivary amylase) that is used in its digestion cannot survive in the acidic (low) pH of the stomach due to the presence of HCl. [2]

**25. Explain the process of digestion in the buccal cavity.**

**Ans.** The buccal cavity performs the following major functions.

(i) The teeth and the tongue with the help of saliva masticate and mix up the food thoroughly.

(ii) Mucus in saliva helps in lubricating and adhering the masticated food particles into bolus.

(iii) The bolus is then passed into the pharynx and then into oesophagus for further digestion. [3]

**26. How are polysaccharides and disaccharides digested?** **[NCERT]**

**Ans.** The chemical process of digestion of carbohydrates is initiated in the oral cavity by the hydrolytic action of the carbohydrate splitting enzyme, the salivary amylase. About 30% of starch is hydrolysed here by this enzyme (optimum pH 6.8) into a disaccharide maltose. Further, carbohydrates in the chyme are hydrolysed by pancreatic amylase into disaccharides. [2]

Polysaccharides (starch) $\xrightarrow{\text{Amylase}}$ Disaccharides [1]

**27. What would happen if HCl will not be secreted in the stomach?** **[NCERT]**

**Ans.** If HCl will not be secreted in the stomach, pepsinogen (proenzyme) and prorennin (proenzyme) will not be converted into pepsin and rennin, respectively. HCl provides acidic medium. So, that the enzyme can act on food in stomach. It also kills bacteria and other harmful organisms that may be present along with food. [3]

**28. Choose the correct answer among the following**

**(i) Gastric juice contains**

**(a) pepsin, lipase and rennin**

**(b) trypsin, lipase and rennin**

**(c) trypsin, pepsin and lipase**

**(d) trypsin, pepsin and rennin**

**(ii) Succus entericus is the name given to**

**(a) a junction between ileum and large intestine.**

**(b) intestinal juice.**

**(c) swelling in the gut.**

**(d) appendix.** **[NCERT]**

**Ans.** (i) (a) pepsin, lipase and rennin.

(ii) (b) intestinal juice. [1½ × 2]

**29. State the role of pancreatic juice in digestion of proteins.** **[NCERT]**

*Or* **Give the name of the three enzymes secreted by pancreas and their action on proteins, fats and starch.**

**Ans.** Trypsin, lipases and amylase are the three enzymes secreted by the pancreas.

Their action on proteins, fats and starch are as follows

(i) Trypsin acts on proteins, proteases and peptones and converts them into shorter peptides.

(ii) Lipase acts on triglycerides and converts them into diglycerides and monoglycerides along with the release of fatty acid.

(iii) Amylase acts on starch and converts it into maltose. [1×3]

**30. Explain the action of different enzymes in succus entericus.**

**Ans.** Dipeptides $\xrightarrow{\text{Dipeptidases}}$ Amino acids

Maltose $\xrightarrow{\text{Maltase}}$ Glucose + Glucose

Lactose $\xrightarrow{\text{Lactase}}$ Glucose + Galactose

Sucrose $\xrightarrow{\text{Sucrase}}$ Glucose + Fructose

Nucleotides $\xrightarrow{\text{Nucleotidase}}$ Nucleosides $\xrightarrow{\text{Nucleosidase}}$ Sugars + Bases

Di and monoglycerides $\xrightarrow{\text{Lipase}}$ Fatty acids + Glycerol [½ × 6]

**31. Indicate whether each of the following statements is true (T) or false (F).**

**(i) Bilirubin is derived from haemoglobin.**

**(ii) The stomach has the lowest pH.**

(iii) **The liver contains lipid emulsifier.**

(iv) **Large intestine secretes many enzymes.**

(v) **Insects have proteases to digest animal fibrous proteins.**

(vi) **All proteases function in the lumen of small intestine.**

**Ans.** True – (i), (ii), (iii), (v)

False – (iv), (vi) [½ × 6]

**32. Fill in the blanks *A-F* in the different columns of the table given below.**

| Enzymes | Site of Action | Substrates | Products of Action |
|---|---|---|---|
| Salivary amylase | Mouth and stomach | *A* | Maltose |
| *B* | Stomach | Proteins | Proteoses and peptones |
| Trypsin | *C* | Proteins, peptones and proteases | Dipeptides |
| Lipase | Small intestine | Fats | *D* |
| *E* | Small intestine | Nucleic acid | Nucleotides and nucleosides |
| Lactase | Small intestine | *F* | Glucose and galactose |

**Ans.** *A*– Starch, *B*– Pepsin, *C*– Duodenum, *D* – Fatty acids + Glycerol, *E* – Nucleases and *F*– Lactose. [½ × 6]

**33. Stomach is the right place where hydrochloric acid is required to be secreted in the gastric juice. Describe any three points to justify this statement.**

**Ans.** Stomach, serves as a right place due to the following reasons

(i) HCl inactivates the salivary amylase and prevents further breakdown of disaccharide carbohydrate.

(ii) It kills microorganisms and lower the pH of stomach between 1.5-2.5 (very acidic).

(iii) Pepsinogen (inactive precursor of pepsin) in the presence of HCl is converted into pepsin (principal protease of stomach). [1 × 3]

**34. Out of the parts labelled as *A*, *B*, *C* and *D* of alimentary canal in the diagram below. Where is the enzyme responsible for the first stage of protein digestion produced? Label all parts , i.e. *A-D*.**

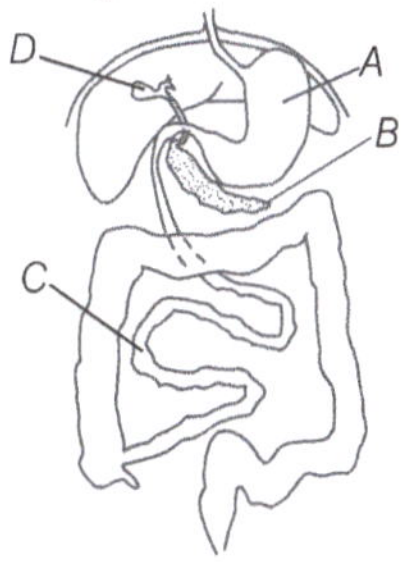


**Ans.** In the labelled part *A* (i.e. the stomach) the enzyme responsible for first stage of protein digestion is produced. *A*–Stomach, *B*–Pancrease, *C*–Small intestine, *D*–Gall bladder. [1 + 2]

**35. Which part of the alimentary canal produce local digestive hormones? What would happen if these hormones are not produced?**

**Ans.** The local digestive hormones are produced by gastric and intestinal mucosa, e.g. secretin, cholesyctokinine, etc. The hormones stimulate the activity of enzymes. If these are not produced, the process of digestion will be hindered and digestive system will not work properly. [3]

**36. Explain the phenomenon of absorption of water in the body of an organism.**

**Ans.** Absorption of water in the small intestine occurs by osmosis. The water passes the lumen of the small intestine through epithelial cells and then to blood capillaries in the villi. Water absorption in general is accompanied with the absorption of electrolytes and digested food in order to maintain an osmotic balance with the blood. [2]

**37. How do chylomicrons differ from micelles with regard to their structural components?**

**Ans.** Differences between chylomicrons and micelles are

| Chylomicrons | Micelles |
|---|---|
| Protein coated water soluble fat droplets of about 150 mm released into the lymph. | It is formed by combination of fatty acids, monoacylglycerols and the bile salts. |
| In this form fats/lipids are put into circulation. | In this form, digested fats are absorbed in intestinal cells in alimentary canal. |

**38.** The diagram shows a section through a villus. What is the function of structure *X*?

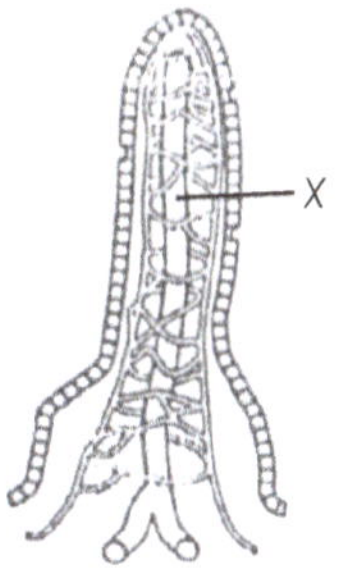


(i) **To absorb amino acids**

(ii) **To carry blood**

(iii) **To transport fats**

(iv) **To transport glucose**

**Ans.** (iii) The lacteal absorbs the end products of fat digestion, i.e. fatty acids and glycerol. This transports them to the lymphatic vessels that eventually empty these products into the blood circulation. [2]

**39. Name the part of the alimentary canal, where major absorption of digested food takes place. What are the absorbed forms of different kinds of food materials?**

Ans. The maximum absorption of digested food occurs in the small intestine of alimentary canal. The absorbed form of different food materials are

| Food Materials | Absorbed Form |
|---|---|
| Carbohydrate | Glucose |
| Protein | Amino acids |
| Fat | Fatty acids |

[1 + 1]

**40. Mention the causative factors for indigestion.**

Ans. Various causative factors for indigestion are

(i) Inadequate secretion of digestive enzymes and gastrointestinal hormones.

(ii) Anxiet

(iii) Food poisoning

(iv) Overeating and spicy food. [$\frac{1}{2}\times 4$]

**41. Why is the egestion process of food necessary?**

Ans. As the digestive waste reaches the rectum, it gets accumulated in rectum. If it is not excreted out through egestion process, it will intoxicate the whole body. [2]

**42. How is fat absorbed in the blood?**

Ans. Absorption of fat takes place in the following ways

(i) Digested fat is absorbed in the small intestine.

(ii) Bile salts break up bigger molecules of fat into small droplets called micelles that move into intestinal mucosa.

(iii) They are reformed into small protein coated fat globules called chylomicrons.

(iv) These are transported to lymph vessels (lacteales) in this villi.

(v) These lymph vessels ultimately release the absorbed substances into blood stream. [3]

**43. In which part of the alimentary canal major absorption of digested food takes place? What are the absorbed forms of different kinds of food materials?**

Ans Major absorption of food occurs in the ileum of small intestine.

Carbohydrates are absorbed as glucose, fructose and galactose, proteins as amino acids and lipids as fatty acids and glycerol. Mineral ions such as $Na^+$, $K^+$, $Ca^{2+}$, $Mg^{2+}$, $Cl^-$, etc., are also absorbed in this region and water is absorbed by osmosis. [1 + 2]

**44. Distinguish between constipation and indigestion. Mention their major causes.** [NCERT]

Ans. **Constipation** In this condition, the faeces are retained within the rectum as the bowel movements occur irregularly. The causes of constipation are water deficiency, lack of roughage in diet, etc. [1½]

**Indigestion** In this condition, the food is not properly digested leading to a feeling of fullness. The causes of indigestion are inadequate enzyme secretion, anxiety, food poisoning, over eating and spicy food. [1½]

**45. What would happen if the liver does not secrete bile?** [HOTS]

Ans. If the liver would stop secreting the bile, following may happen

(i) The fats in our diet would not be digested, it is because bile helps in emulsifying fats and breaks it down for the body to absorb.

(ii) The liver makes bile from cholesterol. Thus, higher levels of cholesterol in the body may occur.

(iii) Bilirubin is made from our dead red blood cells and is a type of a pigment, that also acts as a part of the bile. Hence, if the liver does not secrete bile, the bilirubin would stay in blood instead of being converted by the liver into a soluble form and flows with the bile.

(iv) This may make our skin, white of the eyes more yellow in colour (jaundice), darken our urine and the stools would be whiter in colour. [3]

## Long Answer Type Questions

**1. Draw a diagram of human digestive system. Label any five major parts and three glands associated with it .**

Ans. Refer to fig. no. 20.1.

**2. Name of the largest gland present in human body. Describe its role in digestion of food.**

Ans. Liver is the largest gland in human body which is mainly responsible for the digestion of food. [1]

Role of liver in digestion of food

(i) Its hepatic cells secrete bile juice which passes through the hepatic duct into the gall bladder.

(ii) It has its major role in processing of proteins, i.e. formation of urea.

(iii) Bile secreted by it is mainly responsible for digestion of fats for easy absorption in the body.

(iv) Also responsible for the removal of toxins from blood. [1×4]

**3. Discuss the main steps in the digestion of proteins as the food passes through different parts of the alimentary canal.** [NCERT]

Ans. **Digestion of Proteins in Stomach**

The proenzyme pepsinogen on exposure to HCl, gets converted into active enzyme pepsin.

Protein $\longrightarrow$ Proteoses + Peptones

Pepsin always acts in acidic medium (pH 1.8). In infants, milk proteins are digested by rennin.

**Digestion of Protein in Small Intestine**

Pancreatic juice contains proenzyme, i.e. trypsinogen that gets activated by an enterokinase, which is secreted by intestinal mucosa, into active trypsin. Trypsin acts in alkaline medium.

$$\text{Protein} \xrightarrow{\text{Trypsin / Chymotrypsin}} \text{Dipeptides}$$

The dipeptides are changed into amino acids by the enzyme succus entericus (intestinal juice).

$$\text{Dipeptides} \xrightarrow{\text{Dipeptidases}} \text{Amino acids}$$ [5]

**4. Distinguish between**

**(i) Peptic and oxyntic cells**

**(ii) Lipases and peptidases**

**(iii) Villi and microvilli**

**(iv) Sucrose and maltose**

**(v) Extracellular and intracellular digestion.**

**Ans.** (i) Peptic cells are glandular cells that are usually basal in location. These produce enzymes, while oxyntic cells are large, deep seated cells that secrete HCl.

(ii) Lipases are the type of enzymes found in digestive tract, which breaks fats into di and monoglycerides. Peptidases breaks proteins into their respective peptides.

(iii) Villi are the foldings of mucosa layer, whereas microvilli are the tiny finger-like projection present on the cells in mucosa layer. Both of them are meant to increase the area of absorption in small intestine.

(iv) Both enzymes are used in digestive tract to convert carbohydrate into its smaller units. Sucrase is the enzyme, which converts sucrose into glucose and fructose, while maltase enzyme converts maltose into glucose in small intestine.

(v) Extracellular digestion is the type of digestion (breaking down of macromolecules) which takes place outside the cell, while intracellular digestion is the type of digestion that takes place inside the cell. [1×5]

**5. A person had roti and dal in his lunch. Trace the changes that will take place during its complete passage through the alimentary canal.** **[NCERT Exemplar]**

**Ans.** Changes that will take place in food (roti and dal) through the passage of alimentary canal are

(i) The food substances are first masticated by the teeth in the mouth, where carbohydrate part of the food is digested by the action of salivary amylase enzyme secreted by the salivary glands.

(ii) This partially digested food reaches the stomach, where it receives acidic HCl and mainly the protein part of the food is digested by the action of proteolytic enzymes.

(iii) The lipid part of the food is digested by the bile secreted by the gall bladder.

(iv) In the small intestine, particularly in the duodenum this semidigested food is finally digested by the digestive enzymes present in the intestinal and pancreatic juices.

(v) After digestion, the broken down products of food, i.e. amino acids, glycerol, starch, etc., are absorbed mainly in the small intestine.

(vi) The undigested remains of food will finally pass through the anus in the form of faeces. [5]

**6. Correct the statements given below by choosing the right option shown in the bracket against them.**

**(i) Absorption of amino acids and glycerol takes place in the (small intestine/large intestine).**

**(ii) The faeces in the rectum initiate a reflex causing an urge for its removal (neural/hormonal).**

**(iii) Skin and eyes turn yellow in infection (liver/stomach).**

**(iv) Rennin is a proteolytic enzyme found in gastric juice in (infants/adults).**

**(v) Pancreatic juice and bile are released through (intestine pancreatic/hepato-pancreatic duct).**

**Ans.** (i) Absorption of amino acids and glycerol takes place in the small intestine.

(ii) The faeces in the rectum initiate a neural reflex causing an urge for its removal.

(iii) Skin and eyes turn yellow in infection of liver.

(iv) Rennin is a proteolytic enzyme found in gastric juice in infants.

(v) Pancreatic juice and bile are released through hepatopancreatic duct. [1×5]

**7. Describe the role played in the digestion and assimilation of food by the**

**(i) pancreas** **(ii) liver.**

**Ans.** (i) The pancreas secretes digestive enzymes into the duodenum. Pancreatic amylase digests starch to maltose, trypsin digests proteins to polypeptide and pancreatic lipase digests fats to fatty acids and glycerol. [2]

(ii) The liver produces bile, which is stored in the gall bladder. Bile is released into the duodenum for the emulsification of fats. This increases the surface area for digestion by enzyme lipase.

Amino acids and glucose are taken first into the liver by the hepatic portal vein. They are required by the body and transported out of the liver by the hepatic vein. Amino acids are used for growth and repair of worn out parts of the body and production of enzymes and hormones and glucose is utilised during cellular respiration to produce energy. In the liver, excess amino acids are deaminated, their amino groups are removed and converted to urea for excretion and glycogen for storage. [3]

**8. How does butter in your food get digested and absorbed in the body? Explain.** **[NCERT]**

**Ans.** (i) **Digestion of Butter** Butter is a fatty substance and is rich in neutral fats or triglycerides. It is hydrolysed by esterases most important of which is lipase. Digestion of butter starts in stomach and gets completed in small intestine.

(a) **In Stomach** Gastric juices contain a weak lipolytic gastric lipase, which hydrolyses only small amount of fats.

(b) **In Intestine** Bile salts of the bile juice emulsify the fats and increase the surface area for the action of lipases, while its sodium bicarbonate provides alkaline medium in small intestine.

Pancreatic lipase is strongest lipolytic enzyme that hydrolyses about two-third of triglycerides.

Intestinal lipase hydrolyses remaining triglycerides. But, fat digestion is never complete. Digestion products include glycerol, fatty acids, monoglycerides and small amount of diglycerides. [3]

(ii) **Absorption of Fat** Refer to text on page no. 468. [2]

**9. As a result of intestinal disease, parts of the alimentary canal are sometimes surgically removed. Discuss the effect of this removal on lifestyle and digestive function.**

**(i) Stomach (ii) Colon.**

**Ans.** (i) Removal of stomach, which is the main organ for digestion of protein, leads to a change in the patient's diet. It is the stomach where proteins are first broken down into polypeptides by pepsin in gastric juice before they can be acted up on by pancreatic enzymes and intestinal enzymes. The patient must lower down the in take of protein in his diet. Animal meat especially red meat, which is rich in proteins must be avoided.

(ii) Removal of the colon, which is responsible for absorption of water from undigested food, results in loss of water (dehydration) in patient. The patient needs to drink plenty of fluids to replace water loss. In most cases, where the whole colon is removed, a surgical procedure is done to attach the small intestine to the rectum to allow for recta elimination of liquid stools. A small pouch is created in the lower abdomen to collect the stool. The patient has to learn to regulate his bowel movements. [$2\frac{1}{2} \times 2$]

## Case Based Question

**1. Human digestive system is a tube that runs from mouth to anus. Its main function is to breakdown complex food molecules present in the food which cannot be absorbed as such into smaller molecules. These molecules are absorbed across the walls of the tube and the absorbed food reaches each and every cell of the body where it is utilised for obtaining energy.**

**(i) Name the glands present in the buccal cavity and write the components of food on which the secretions of these glands acts upon.**

**(ii) Name two organs that have a sphincter muscles at their exit.**

**(iii) What will happen if mucus is not secreted by gastric gland?**

*Or*

**(iii) Bile juice does not contain any enzyme. Yet it has impotant roles in digestion. Explain.**

**Ans.** (i) The glands present in buccal cavity are salivary glands. These glands secretes saliva, which contains enzyme amylase. The amylase acts on carbohydrates, breaking them down into simpler sugars.

(ii) The two organs that have a sphincter muscle at their exit are the stomach and anus.

(iii) If the mucus is not secreted by the gastric glands then the stomach lining would be exposed to the acidic environment created by hydrochloric acid. This could lead to the formation of ulcers and damage to the stomach lining.

*Or* (iii) Bile juice, although it does not contain any enzymes, plays a crucial role in digestion. It emulifies fats, breaking them into smaller droplets which increases the surface area for the action of lipase for an enzyme that digest fats. This process is essential for efficient digestion and absorption of fats.

# SAMPLE QUESTION PAPER 1

A Highly Simulated Sample Question Paper for CBSE Class XI Examination

## BIOLOGY

**Time : 3 Hours** **Max. Marks : 70**

### *General Instructions*

1. All questions are compulsory.
2. The question paper has five sections and 33 questions.
3. Section-A has 16 questions of 1 mark each; Section-B has 5 questions of 2 marks each; Section-C has 7 questions of 3 marks each; Section-D has 2 case-based questions of 4 marks each; and Section-E has 3 questions of 5 marks each.
4. There is no overall choice. However, internal choices have been provided in some questions. A student has to attempt only one of the alternatives in such questions.
5. Wherever necessary, neat and properly labelled diagrams should be drawn.

## SECTION-A

**1. Diagrams *A* and *B* indicate the shape of leaves in larkspur and buttercup, respectively. Choose the correct option.**

(a) The juvenile and adult leaf of larkspur differ in size due to genetic and plant growth regulator factors
(b) Both leaf of buttercup differ in size due to genetic and intercellular factors
(c) Both larkspur and buttercup leaf size variation is due to habitat plasticity
(d) None of the above

**2. Male frogs can croak louder than female frogs because of**

(a) vocal sacs
(b) strength
(c) large size
(d) large sound box

**3. 'Bakane' (foolish seedling) disease of rice seedlings, was caused by *Gibberella fujikuroi*, which is a**

(a) fungi (b) protozoans
(c) bacteria (d) virus

**4. Given below are some related pairs of bone.**

| | Column I | | Column II |
|---|---|---|---|
| A. | Flat bones | 1. | Sternum |
| B. | Irregular bones | 2. | Ear ossicles |
| C. | Glenoid cavity | 3. | Shoulder joint |
| D. | Clavicle | 4. | Collar bone |

**Observe them carefully and find how many of them are correctly match?**

(a) 3 (b) 2
(c) 1 (d) 4

**5. What happens when pacemaker is non-functional?**

(a) Only the auricle will contract rhythmically
(b) The cardiac muscle do not contract in a coordinated manner rhythmically
(c) Only ventricles will contract rhythmically
(d) Cardiac muscle will contract in a coordinated manner

**6.** Observe the diagram shown below and find out the parts labelled as *A*, *B*, *C* and *D* in the shown figure.

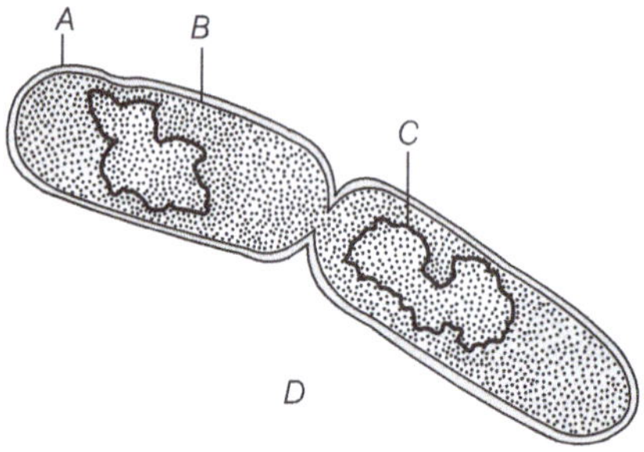


(a) *A*–Plasma membrane, *B*-Cell wall, *C*–RNA, *D*–Spore formation
(b) *A*–Cell wall, *B*-Cell membrane, *C*–DNA, *D*–Binary fission
(c) *A*–Plasma membrane, *B*–Mucilaginous, *C*–DNA, *D*–Transformation
(d) *A*–Mucilaginous, *B*–Cell membrane, *C*–RNA, *D*–Conjugation

**7.** Select the following statements carefully.
I. Aristotle divide plants into creepers and climbers.
II. Two kingdom classification was unable to distinguish between photosynthetic and non-photosynthetic.
III. Two kingdom classification used simple morphological characters to classify plants.
IV. Two kingdom classification was outdated as this system of classification fails to distinguish between plants and animals.

Choose the correct answer from the options given below.
(a) I and IV (b) II and III (c) I and IV (c) I and II

**8.** Which of the following is a non-hyphal unicellular fungus?
(a) Yeast (b) *Puccinia* (c) *Ustilago* (d) *Alternaria*

**9.** In an observation scientist kept two plates, one is of virus and other is of viroid. He forget to mark the plate and now he is confused which plate is of virus and viroids. Viroid differ from viruses in having
(a) DNA molecules with protein coat
(b) DNA molecules without protein coat
(c) RNA molecules with protein coat
(d) RNA molecules without protein coat

**10.** Name the blood cells, whose reduction in number can cause clotting disorder, leading to excessive loss of blood from the body
(a) erythrocytes (b) leucocytes
(c) neutrophils (d) thrombocytes

**11.** The contraction of the muscle continues in sliding filament theory
(a) till ATP binds to myosin head
(b) till ADP binds to myosin head
(c) till $Ca^{2+}$ present in sarcoplasm
(d) till polymerisation of myosin head is going on

**12.** Reflex action is controlled by
(a) ANS
(b) CNS
(c) Both (a) and (b)
(d) None of the above

**Direction** (Q. Nos. 13-16) *In each of the following questions, a statement of* ***Assertion*** *(A) is given followed by corresponding statement of* ***Reason*** *(R). Of the statements, mark the correct answer if*
(a) Both A and R are true and R is the correct explanation of A
(b) Both A and R are true, but R is not the correct explanation of A
(c) A is true, but R is false
(d) A is false, but R is true

**13.** Assertion (A) Starch is a polymer of glucose.
Reason (R) It is made up of several glucose units.

**14.** Assertion (A) Bryophytes are amphibians of plant kingdom.
Reason (R) They are found in swamps and the areas, where water and land meet.

**15.** Assertion (A) Vascular bundles in monocots are considered closed.
Reason (R) A bundle sheath surrounds each vascular bundle in monocots.

**16.** Assertion (A) Duck-billed platypus is a true mammal.
Reason (R) Mammals are all viviparous, while platypus lays eggs.

## SECTION-B

**17.** (i) Why does synapse act as a one way valves?
(ii) The Schwann cells around the axon helps to classify neurons in various types. Name them.

*Or*

(i) Name the major divisions of forebrain.
(ii) Arrange the following in accurate order in their association in electrical impulse movement-synaptic knob, axon terminal, axon dendrites, cell body.

**18.** Do amino acids exist as zwitter ion. Give its structure. Why is it formed?

**19.** The graphs given below shows the different growth curve.

A. Which of the following graphs shows the sigmoid growth curve?

B. Explain the reason behind this growth curve.

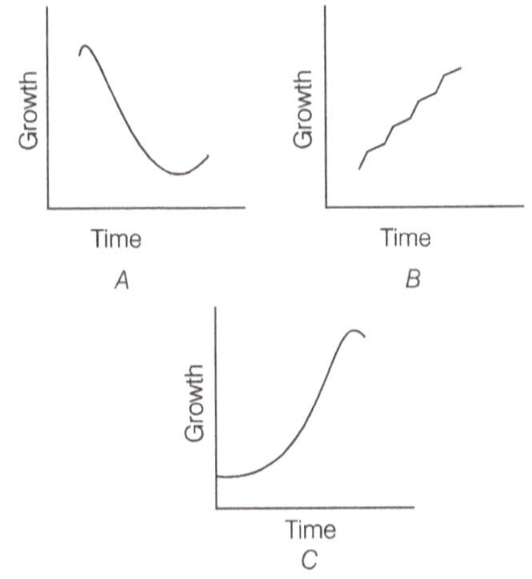


**20.** Given below are the experimentation of four coleoptiles for experiment.

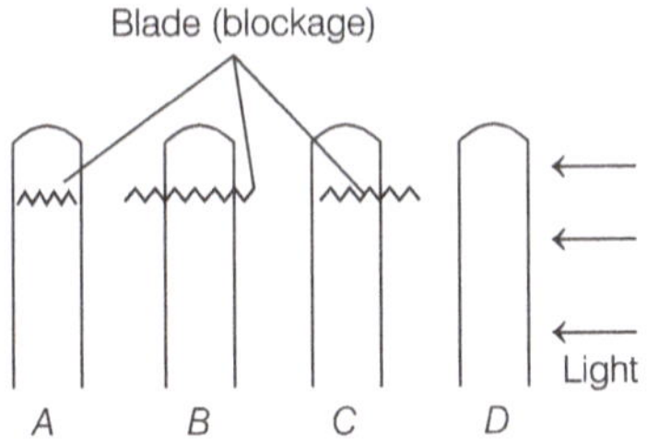


On the basis of your observation, answer the following questions.

(i) Which coleoptiles will bend towards the light?

(ii) Name the hormone responsible for bending of shoot tip towards the source of light.

*Or* The graph given below shows the effect of a plant growth regulator *X* on the rate of transpiration of a plant.

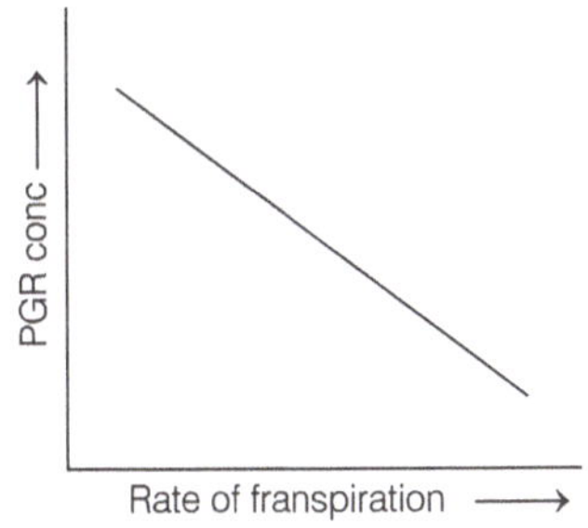


(i) Which hormone is responsible for the above condition?

(ii) Mention two functions performed by *X*.

**21.** Solanaceae consist of bisexual and actinomorphic flowers. The calyx and corolla have five united petal and sepals, respectively, with valvate aestivation . Stamens are five and epipetalous, ovary is bicarpellary, syncarpous and superior. Fruit are berry or capsule and seed are many and endospermic.

(i) Draw the floral diagram on the basis of above information.

(ii) Given two examples of plants that belongs to Solanaceae family.

*Or*

Use the information provided in the table given below to answer the following questions.

| Characters | Dicot Root | Monocot Root |
|---|---|---|
| Vascular bundles | 2 to 5 in number | More than 6 in number |
| Cambium | Present | *A* |
| Pith | Absent or poorly developed | Fully developed pith |
| Secondary growth | *B* | Does not takes place |

(i) Fill the appropriate answer in *A* and *B*.

(ii) What is the function of pericycle in roots?

## SECTION-C

**22.**

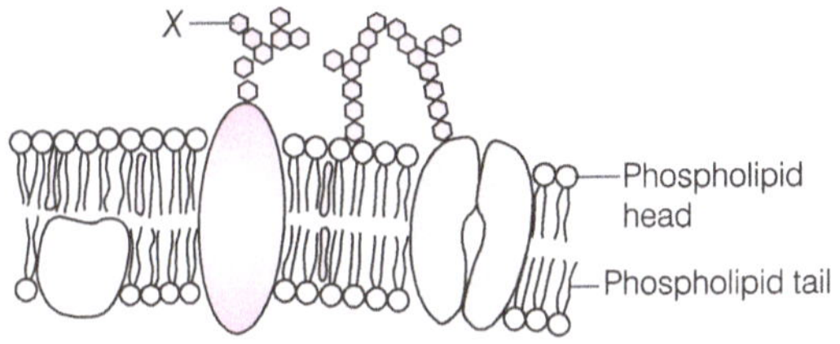


The above diagram shows the section of cell membrane observe the diagram and answer the following questions.

(i) State the function of cell membrane.

(ii) Mention the role of transmembrane protein in transport of materials across it.

(iii) Identify *X* in the given diagram.

**23.** Describe any two features of a newly discovered organism *X* for it to be classified as slime mould protist.

**24.** Differentiate between liverworts and mosses on the basis of following characteristics.

(i) Symmetry

(ii) Rhizoids

(iii) Differentiation of main body.

**25.** Golgi apparatus consist flat, disc-shaped, parallely stacked structure, possess *cis* (forming) and *trans* (maturation) faces. Observe the figure carefully and answer the following questions.

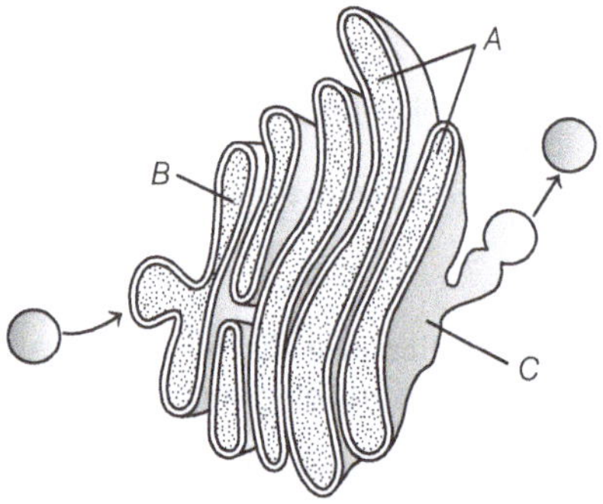


(i) Identify the labels *A*, *B* and *C*.
(ii) What is the function of Golgi apparatus?
(iii) Explain endomembrane system.

**26.** Photosynthesis and respiration are physiological processes which can be termed as mirror images. Justify.

**27.** Observe the following figure indicating the male reproductive system of frog.

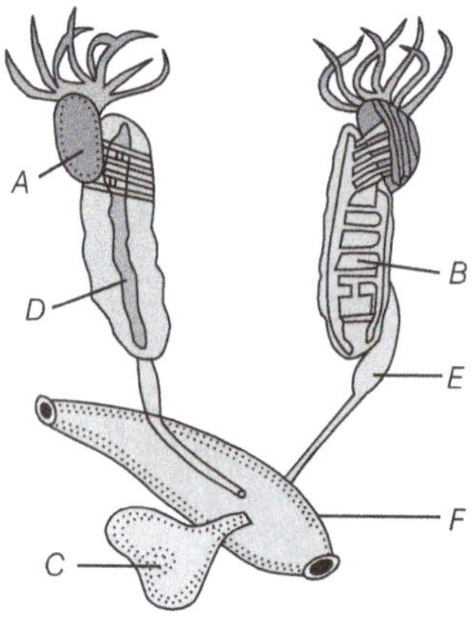


(i) Identify *A*, *B*, *C*, *D*, *E* and *F* in the given diagram.
(ii) Which of the labelled part (*A*, *B*, *C*, *D*) is responsible for producing sperm in the male frog?
(iii) Mention the functions of *B* and *D*.

*Or*

(iv) Which of the labelled part is representing urinogenital duct and cloaca.

**28.** Describe any three features of Phycomycetes also give two examples of this class.

## SECTION-D

**29.** Observe the given figure related to enzyme action and answer the questions that follows.

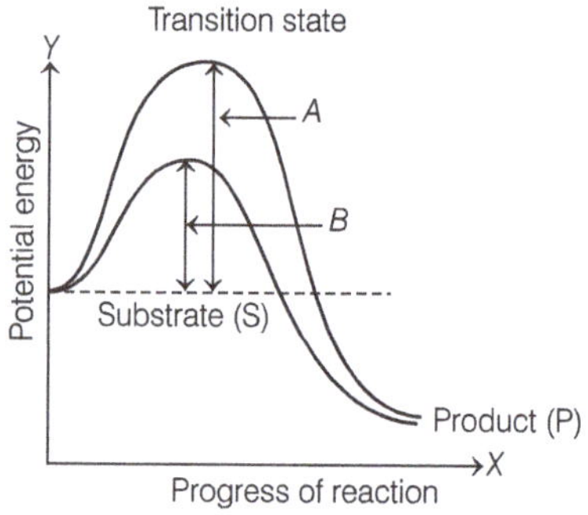


(i) What does the given graph illustrate? [1]
(ii) What does arrow *A* and *B* indicated? [1]
(iii) What happens when *P* is at a lower level than *S*? [2]

*Or*

(iii) Formation of Enzyme Substrate (ES) complex is the first step in catalysed reactions. Describe the other steps till the formation of product. [2]

**30.** The graph is showing the action spectra of the photosynthetic pigments. The first action spectrum was studied by Engelmann by using a green algae which liberated oxygen according to the rate of photosynthesis in different wavelength of light.

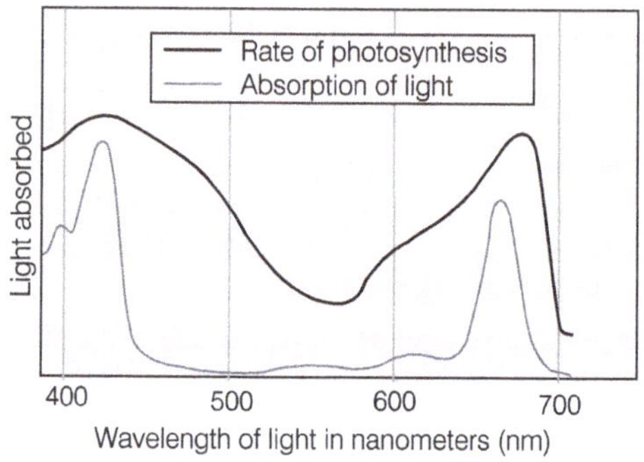


(i) What is the action spectrum? How is it related with the absorption of light at different wavelength? [1]
(ii) In which region, the rate of photosynthesis is maximum. [1]
(iii) Give one difference between action and absorption spectrum on the basis of the light energy. [2]

*Or*

(iii) **Study the graph below showing the absorbance of light by chloroplast pigments. Identify the labels *A*, *B* and *C*.** [2]

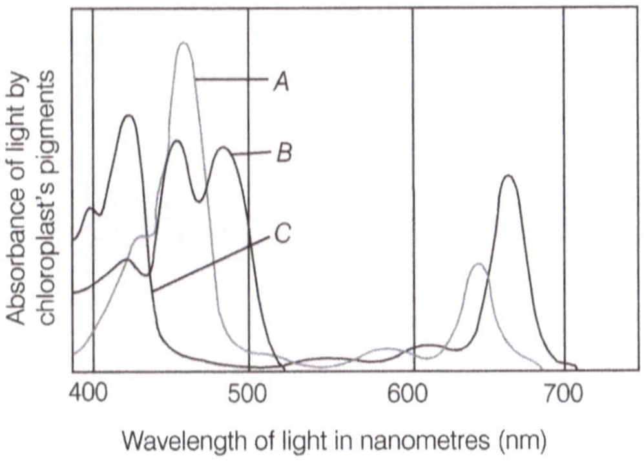


## SECTION-E

**31.** (A) **Observe the diagram given below and answer the questions that follows.**

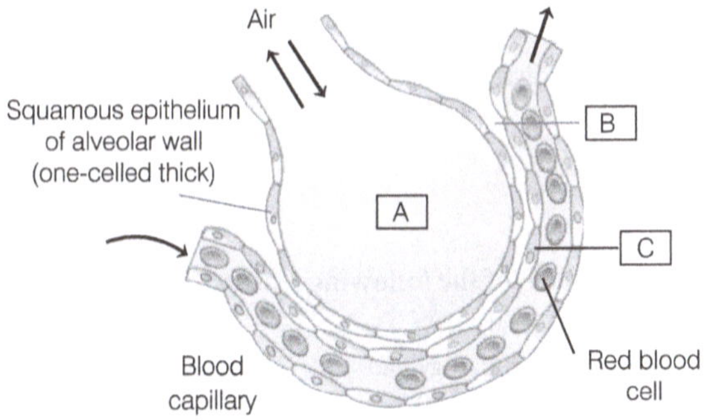


(i) **Identify *B* and write its feature and function.**

(ii) **How is oxygen carried from alveoli into the blood in pulmonary capillaries?**

(iii) **Which vein carry oxygenated blood in humans.**

(iv) **Diffusion of gases occurs in the alveolar region only and not in other parts of the respiratory system. Why?**

*Or*

(B) (i) **Explain how difference in the pressure of the blood in the pulmonary artery and in the aorta is related to**

(a) **the structure of the ventricles**

(b) **where blood is going?**

(ii) **Thrombocytes are essential for blood clotting. Comment.**

**32. Explain the structural division in a flowering plant using a suitable diagram.**

*Or*

**Briefly describe the circulatory system of frog.**

**33.** (A) (i) **List the waste products which can be eliminated by artificial kidney.**

(ii) **Discuss the role of anticoagulant used in this process.**

(iii) **Explain the tems uremia and renal calculi.**

*Or*

(B) (i) **Discuss the transport of oxygen and carbon dioxide in detail with the help of suitable labelled diagrams.**

(ii) **Give differences between oxyhaemoglobin and carboxyhaemoglobin.**

## Answers

1. (c) 2. (a) 3. (a) 4. (a) 5. (b) 6. (b) 7. (b) 8. (a) 9. (d) 10. (d)
11. (c) 12. (c) 13. (a) 14. (b) 15. (c) 16. (b)

# SAMPLE QUESTION PAPER 2

A Highly Simulated Sample Question Paper for CBSE Class XI Examination

## BIOLOGY

**Time : 3 Hours** **Max. Marks : 70**

### *General Instructions*

1. All questions are compulsory.
2. The question paper has five sections and 33 questions.
3. Section-A has 16 questions of 1 mark each; Section-B has 5 questions of 2 marks each; Section-C has 7 questions of 3 marks each; Section-D has 2 case-based questions of 4 marks each; and Section-E has 3 questions of 5 marks each.
4. There is no overall choice. However, internal choices have been provided in some questions. A student has to attempt only one of the alternatives in such questions.
5. Wherever necessary, neat and properly labelled diagrams should be drawn.

## SECTION-A

**1. Given below is the diagram of a stomatal apparatus. In which of the following all the four parts labelled as *A*, *B*, *C* and *D* are correctly identified? dran**

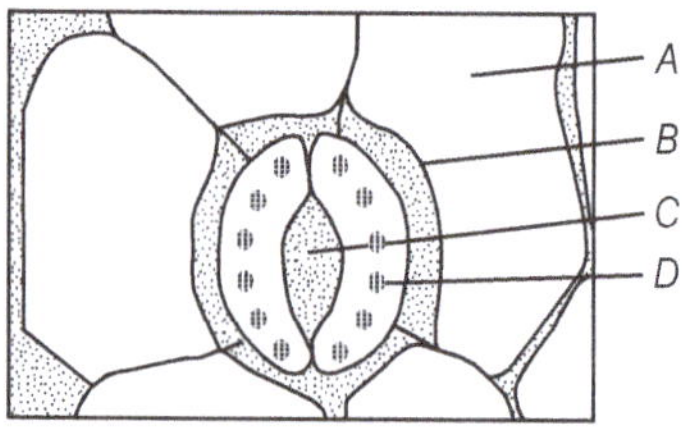


| | *A* | *B* | *C* | *D* |
|---|---|---|---|---|
| (a) | Subsidiary cell | Epidermal cell | Guard cell | Stomatal aperture |
| (b) | Guard cell | Stomatal aperture | Subsidiary cell | Epidermal cell |
| (c) | Epidermal cell | Guard cell | Stomatal aperture | Subsidiary cell |
| (d) | Epidermal cell | Subsidiary cell | Stomatal aperture | Guard cell |

**2. Which type of protein is present in human haemoglobin?**

(a) Secondary proteins (b) Tertiary proteins
(c) Quartenary proteins (d) None of the above

**3. Which of the following features distinguish a male frog?**

(a) Vocal sacs
(b) Copulatory pad
(c) Tympanum
(d) Both (a) and (b)

**4. Given below are some related pair of type of vertebrae with respect to their number. Find the incorrect one.**

| | Types of vertebrae | Number |
|---|---|---|
| (a) | Cervical vertebrae | 7 |
| (b) | Thoracic vertebrae | 12 |
| (c) | Lumbar vertebrae | 5 |
| (d) | Sacral vertebrae | 2 |

**5. Which of the following is correctly matched?**

(a) Basophils — Immunity
(b) Neutrophils — Phagocytes
(c) Eosinophils — Secrete histamine, serotonin and heparin
(d) Lymphocytes — Allergic reactions

**6.** **Which of the following statements are correct for the given bryophyte species?**

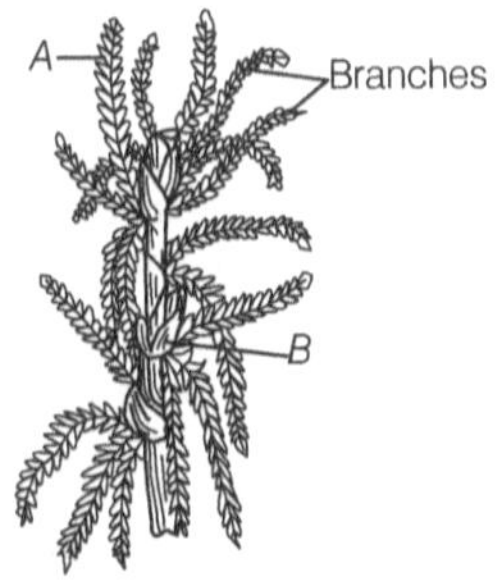


I. **The given diagram represent *Sphagnum* gametophyte.**
II. **The given species is a liverwort.**
III. **It provides peat.**
IV. **Scales and elaters are not found in it.**

**Codes**

(a) II and III (b) I and IV
(c) II, III and IV (d) I, III and IV

**7.** **A bryophyte found in dry habitat is**

(a) *Polytrichum* (b) *Marchantia*
(c) *Riccia* (d) All of these

**8.** **The thallus of bryophytes**

(a) possesses roots
(b) bears very small leaves
(c) is more differentiated than that of algae
(d) All of the above

**9.** **The female sex organ in bryophytes is**

(a) conspicous and reduced
(b) flask-shaped structure of thallus
(c) called sporophyll
(d) Both (a) and (b)

**10.** ***Marchantia* reproduce asexually with the help of**

(a) Gemmae
(b) Spores
(c) Buds
(d) Bulbils

**11.** **Refer to the given figure and select the correct option.**

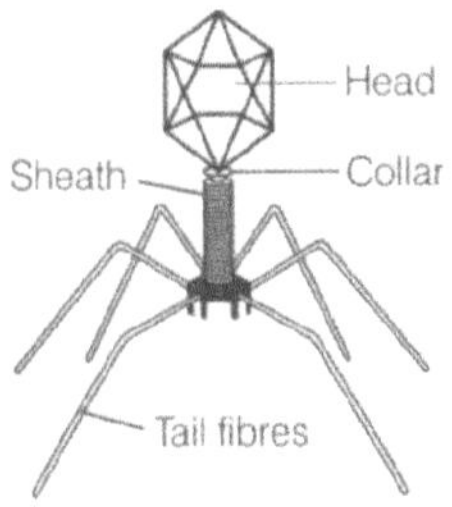


(a) It is a virus that infects plant
(b) It is virus that infects animals
(c) It is a virus that infects insects
(d) It is a virus that infects bacteria

**12.** **Substrate level phosphorylation occurs during which step of Krebs' cycle?**

(a) Succinyl Co-A $\rightarrow$ Succinic acid
(b) Isocitric acid $\rightarrow$ Oxalosuccinic acid
(c) Oxalosuccinic acid $\rightarrow$ $\alpha$-ketoglutaric acid
(d) Malic acid $\rightarrow$ OAA

**Direction** (Q. Nos. 13-16) *In each of the following questions, a statement of Assertion (A) is given followed by corresponding statement of Reason (R). Of the statements, mark the correct answer if*

(a) Both A and R are true and R is the correct explanation of A
(b) Both A and R are true, but R is not the correct explanation of A
(c) A is true, but R is false
(d) A is false, but R is true

**13.** **Assertion (A) In racemose type of inflorescence the main axis grows indefinitely.**

**Reason (R) Main axis is not terminated by flower.**

**14.** **Assertion (A) In prokaryotes, mitochondria are absent.**

**Reason (R) In prokaryotes, mesosomes are present which help in respiration.**

**15.** **Assertion (A) Bryophytes are a class of kingdom-Plantae.**

**Reason (R) Algae, fungi, lichens and mosses are included in bryophytes.**

**16.** **Assertion (A) The SA node acts as a pacemaker.**

**Reason (R) The SA node is located in the wall of the right atrium near the inter-atrial septum.**

## SECTION-B

**17.** (i) **How do auxins help in bending of stem towards light? Explain.**

(ii) **What is the principal physiological role of auxin in regulating plant growth and development?**

*Or*

**Name the groups of growth regulating plant hormones, which stimulate the following.**

(i) **Cell division even in non-meristematic tissues.**
(ii) **Elongation of stem and expansion of leaves.**

**18.** The diagrams below show chromosomes in a cell undergoing mitosis and in a cell undergoing meiosis.

Mitosis

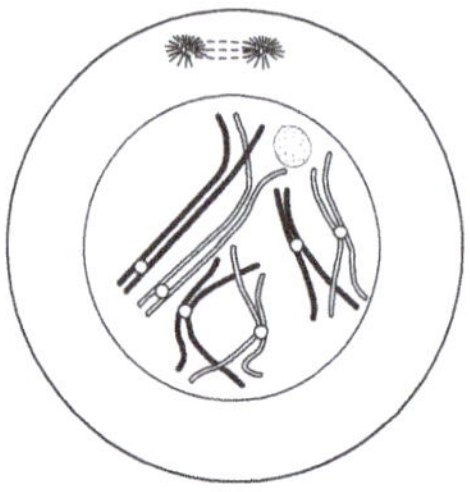

*A*

Meiosis

*B*

(i) Identify the stages shown in diagrams *A* and *B*.

(ii) Name the stage of meiosis in which formation of synaptonemal complex takes place.

*Or*

Study the diagram given below and answer the following questions.

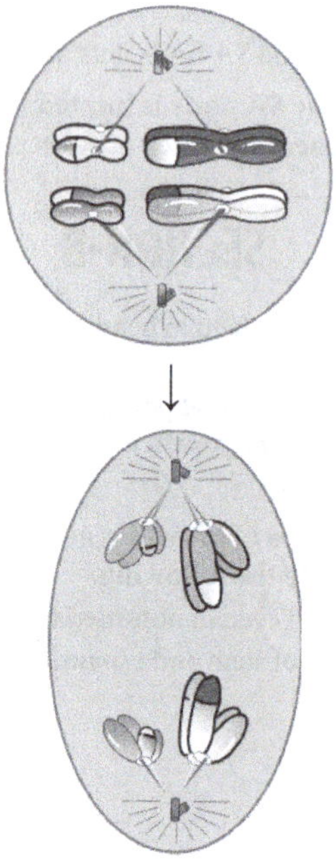

(i) Name the stages and type of cell division represented in *A* and *B*, respectively.

(ii) Explain any one stage that occurs before *A* and *B*.

**19.** The sequence of events by which a cell duplicates its genome, synthesise cell content and eventually divides into two daughter cells is termed as cell cycle.

(i) In the diagram depicting cell cycle name the phases *A*, *B*, *C* and *D*.

(ii) Also mention the phase in which DNA replication will takes place.

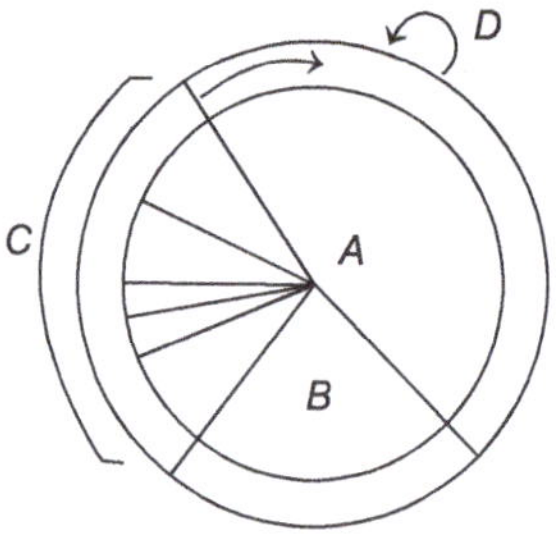


**20.** The given diagram represents the mechanism of protein hormone action. Study the mechanism carefully and then answer the following questions.

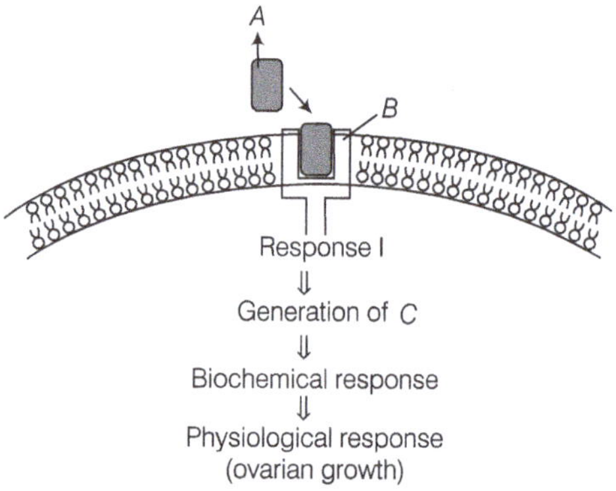


(i) Identify the labels *A*, *B* and *C*.

(ii) What is the role of secondary messenger?

**21.** The balance sheet for ATP production in glycolysis has been given below. Study the table given below and answer the following questions.

| | Steps | ATP utilisation | ATP production |
|---|---|---|---|
| 1. | Glucose → Glucose–6–phosphate | *P* | *X* |
| 2. | Fructose-6-phosphate → Fructose–1-6 bisphosphate | 1 | *Q* |
| 3. | 1, 3-bisphospho glyceric acid → 3-phosphoglyceric acid | *X* | *R* |
| 4. | 2 phosphoenol pyruvic acid and → Pyruvic acid | *S* | 2 |

(i) Fills up the blanks for *P*, *Q*, *R* and *S*.

(ii) Name the cellular metabolic processes can occur both in the presence or absence of $O_2$?

*Or*

The final product of glycolysis is pyruvic acid.

(i) Write the three metabolic fates of the pyruvic acid in anaerobic and aerobic conditions.

(ii) How is the pyruvic acid involved in the Krebs' cycle?

## SECTION-C

**22.** Name the cell that is found arrested in diplotene stage for months and years. Comment in 2-3 lines, how it completes cell cycle.

**23.** Observe the diagram shown below.

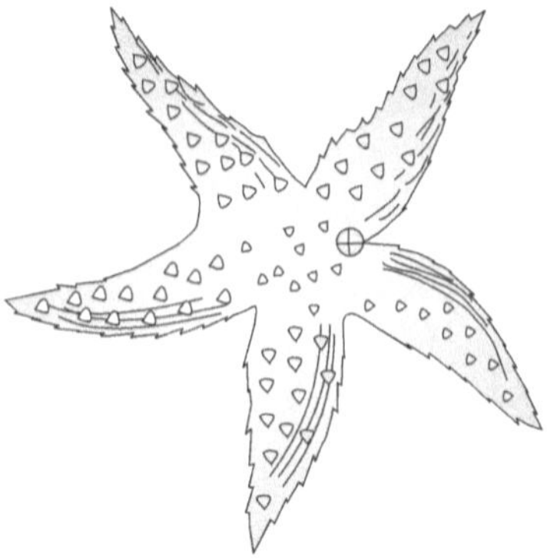

(i) Identify the organism shown in the diagram.

(ii) Name the phylum to which this organism belongs.

(iii) State two distinguishing charcteristics of this phylum.

**24.** Observe the diagram shown below and answer the following questions.

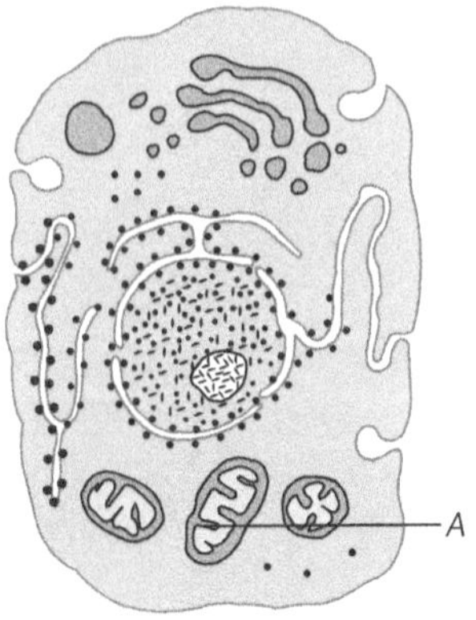


(i) Identify organelle *A* in the given diagram.

(ii) State any four functions of organelle *A*.

**25.** The graph below showing the effect of light intensity on the rate of photosynthesis. The point *D* represents the intensity of light at which some other factor became limiting.

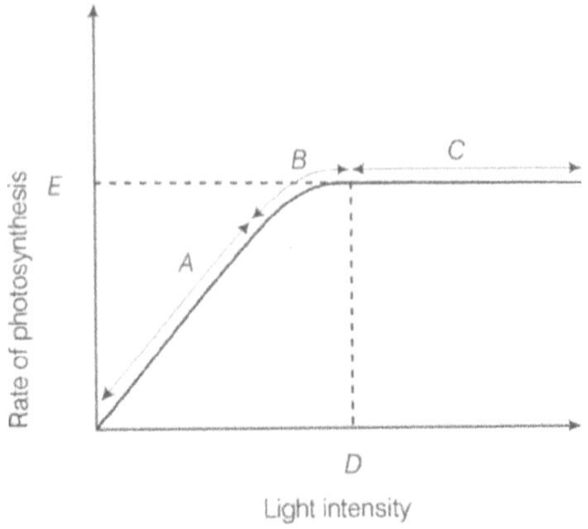


(i) What will be the limiting factor at region *C*?

(ii) Expand RuBisCO.

(iii) Define the law of limiting factor.

**26.** Cut a transverse section of a young plant stem from your school garden and observe it under the microscope. How would you determine whether it is a monocot stem or a dicot stem? Give reasons.

**27.** Why is it necessary to check the Rh-factor of the blood in a pregnant woman?

**28.** What do you understand by carbohydrates? Also give its classification.

## SECTION-D

**29.** Deuteromycetes is an artificial class of fungi which has been created to include all those fungi (imperfecti fungi) in which sexual stage is either absent or not known.

(i) Write two other important characteristics of this class. [1]

(ii) Name the organism which causes white spots on mustard leaves. [1]

(iii) Name the fruiting bodies of Zygomycetes, Ascomycetes and Basidiomycetes. [2]

*Or*

(iii) Plants are autotrophic, can you think of some plants that are partially heterotrophic? [2]

**30.** Observe the diagram given below and answer the questions that follows.

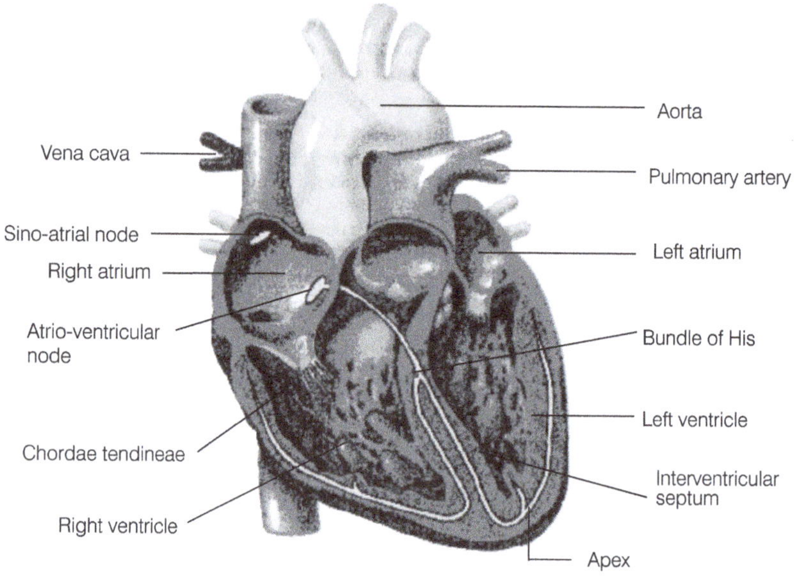


(i) Name the group/class of animals in which this type of heart is found. [1]

(ii) State the function of pulmonary artery and interventricular septum. [1]

(iii) What are the two heart sounds heard through stethoscope? How each of these produced? [2]

*Or*

(iii) Why is closed circulatory system more efficient than the open system? [2]

## SECTION-E

**31.** Mechanism of hormone action is depicted in the above diagram. Study the diagram and answer the following questions.

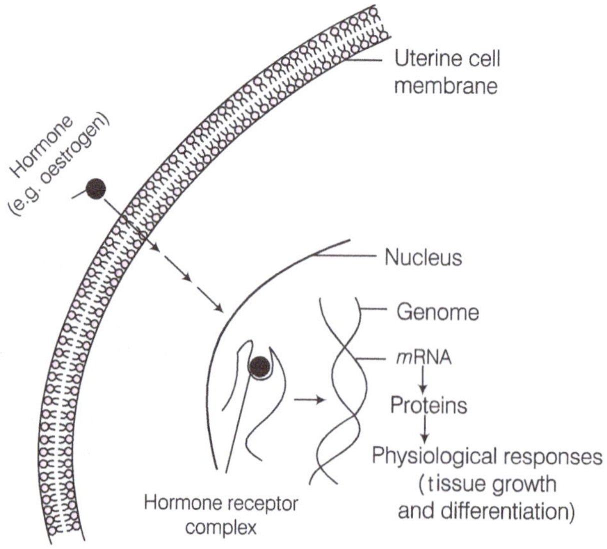

(i) Which type of hormone can be taken up by the cell membrane?

(ii) What do you understand by hormone receptor complex?

(iii) State the physiological response brought about this kind of hormone actions.

*Or* Hormone interacting with membrane-bound receptors play an indirect role in regulating cellular metabolism of the body. Justify.

**32.** (A) RuBisCO is an enzyme that acts both as a carboxylase and oxygenase. Why do you think RuBisCO carries out more carboxylation in $C_4$ plants?

*Or*

(B) A group of plants lacks photorespiration. Answer the following questions based on these plants.

(i) Which cells in the plant have RuBisCO?

(ii) In which cells, the $CO_2$ fixation initially occurs?

(iii) Name the first product found in $C_4$cycle.

(iv) Explain Kranz anatomy.

**33.** (A) (i) What is the role of second messenger in hormone action?

(ii) Name the hormones regulating the following.

(a) Control of skin colour

(b) Release of sugar from liver

(c) Widening of pelvis for childbirth

(d) Leydig's cells of testis

*Or*

(B) Explain the following by giving suitable scientific reasons.

(i) Hypothalamus and pituitary function as an integrated and coordinated system.

(ii) Body growth is greatly accelerated at puberty in males.

## Answers

1. (d) 2. (c) 3. (d) 4. (d) 5. (b) 6. (d) 7. (a) 8. (c) 9. (b) 10. (a)
11. (d) 12. (a) 13. (a) 14. (b) 15. (c) 16. (c)

# SAMPLE QUESTION PAPER 3

A Highly Simulated Sample Question Paper for CBSE Class XI Examination

## BIOLOGY

**Time : 3 Hours** **Max. Marks : 70**

### *General Instructions*

1. All questions are compulsory.
2. The question paper has five sections and 33 questions.
3. Section-A has 16 questions of 1 mark each; Section-B has 5 questions of 2 marks each; Section-C has 7 questions of 3 marks each; Section-D has 2 case-based questions of 4 marks each; and Section-E has 3 questions of 5 marks each.
4. There is no overall choice. However, internal choices have been provided in some questions. A student has to attempt only one of the alternatives in such questions.
5. Wherever necessary, neat and properly labelled diagrams should be drawn.

## SECTION-A

**1. Which of the following is the smallest region of the root?**

(a) Root cap
(b) Region of elongation
(c) Region of meristematic activity
(d) Region of maturation

**2. The joint present between the atlas and axis bone is**

(a) pivot (b) condyloid
(c) suture (d) gliding

**3. Match the Column I with Column II.**

| Column I (Categories) | Column II (Secondary metabolites) |
|---|---|
| A. Pigments | 1. Carotenoids, anthocyanins |
| B. Terpenoids | 2. Monoterpenes, diterpenes |
| C. Alkaloids | 3. Concanavalin-A |
| D. Lectins | 4. Morphine, codeine |

**How many pairs are correct?**

(a) 1 (b) 2 (c) 3 (d) 4

**4. In the figure given below, which of the following changes had occurred in the diaphragm and intercostal muscles when the movement of air takes place as shown.**

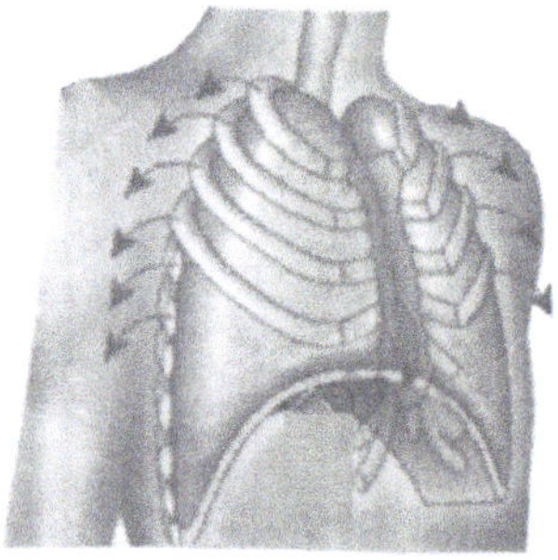

(a) External intercostal muscles relax and diaphragm contracts
(b) External intercostal muscles contract and diaphragm relaxes
(c) External intercostal muscles and diaphragm relax
(d) External intercostal muscles and diaphragm contract

**5. Which hormone was first isolated from human urine?**

(a) Auxin (b) ABA
(c) Ethylene (d) Gibberellic acid

**6.** Choose the incorrect characteristic about the lipid molecule shown below.

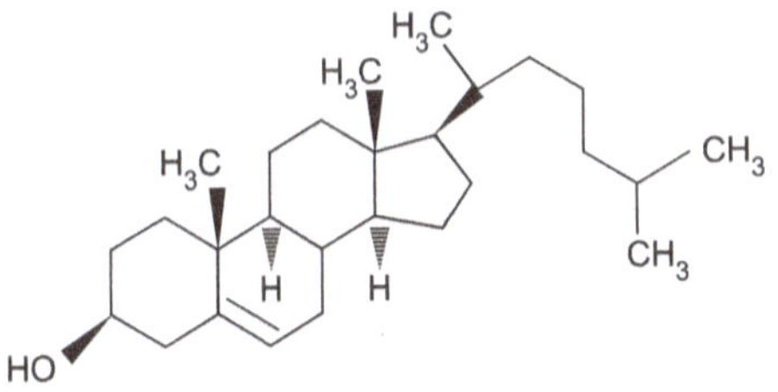


I. It is a common sterol molecule.
II. It is the precursor of steroid hormones.
III. The given molecule has a steroid nucleus, a hydrocarbon side chain and a hydroxyl group.
IV. Cholesterol is soluble in blood and thus transport through bloodstream easily.

(a) Only IV (b) III and IV
(c) I and II (d) Only II

**7.** Lipids mainly consist of
(a) Only carbon
(b) carbon, hydrogen and nitrogen
(c) carbon, hydrogen and oxygen
(d) Only hydrogen

**8.** Saturated fatty acids contain
(a) double bond
(b) carboxyl group
(c) Both (a) and (b)
(d) None of the above

**9.** An example of unsaturated fatty acid is
(a) oleic acid (b) stearic acid
(c) linoleic acid (d) Both (a) and (c)

**10.** Among the given options, non-polymeric molecule is
(a) nucleic acid (b) proteins
(c) lipids (d) polysaccharide

**11.** The characteristics and an example of a synovial joint in humans is

| | Characteristics | Examples |
|---|---|---|
| (a) | Fluid cartilage between two bones, limited movements | Knee joints |
| (b) | Fluid-filled between two joints provides cushion | Skull bones |
| (c) | Fluid-filled synovial cavity between two bones | Joint between atlas and axis |
| (d) | Lymph-filled between two bones, limited movement | Gliding joint between carpals |

**12.** Why terrestrial organism excrete lesser toxic nitrogenous waste?
(a) For conservation of water
(b) For maintaining osmolarity
(c) To facilitate simple diffusion
(d) It is easy to excrete less toxic substances

**Direction** (Q. Nos. 13-16) *In each of the following questions, a statement of Assertion (A) is given followed by corresponding statement of Reason (R). Of the statements, mark the correct answer if*
(a) Both A and R are true and R is the correct explanation of A
(b) Both A and R are true, but R is not the correct explanation of A
(c) A is true, but R is false
(d) A is false, but R is true

**13.** Assertion (A) The presence of accessory pigments increase the rate of photosynthesis.

Reason (R) These pigments absorb the light of different wavelength and transfer it to reaction centre.

**14.** Assertion (A) Diakinesis is final stage of prophase-I.

Reason (R) Terminalisation of chiasmata occurs in diakinesis.

**15.** Assertion (A) True fruits develop from ovary.

Reason (R) Leaves arise from the nodes of a stem.

**16.** Assertion (A) Ribosomes are considered as the most primitive cell organelles.

Reason (R) They occur in all eukaryotic organisms.

## SECTION-B

**17.** (i) Explain the process of formation of vascular cambium.
(ii) How does the vascular cambium contribute to secondary growth in plants?

*Or*

What part of the plant would show the following.
(i) Radial vascular bundle.
(ii) Polyarch xylem

**18.** (A)

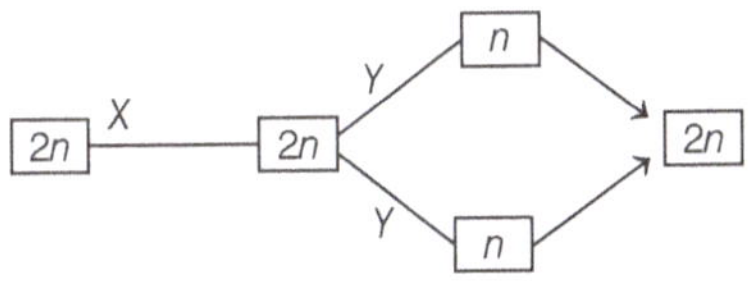


The diagram given above represents the changes in the number of chromosomes during several processes that occur in an animal cell.

(i) Name the processes of cell division occurring at *X* and *Y*.

(ii) State two differences in the behaviour of chromosomes between *X* and *Y*.

*Or*

(B) The cytokinesis in plant cell and animal cell during mitotic cell divison is depicted in the figure given below.

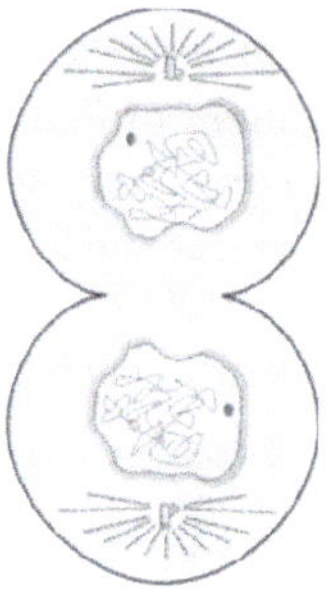

(i) At what stage of the cell cycle does cytokinesis occur in animal cells?

(ii) How does cytokinesis differ in animal cells compared to plant cells?

**19.** Where is cytochrome-*c* located? What is its function?

**20.** Observe the given figure related to enzyme action and answer the following questions.

(i) What does the *A* and *B* represents?

(ii) What does the arrows marked *C* to *E* indicate?

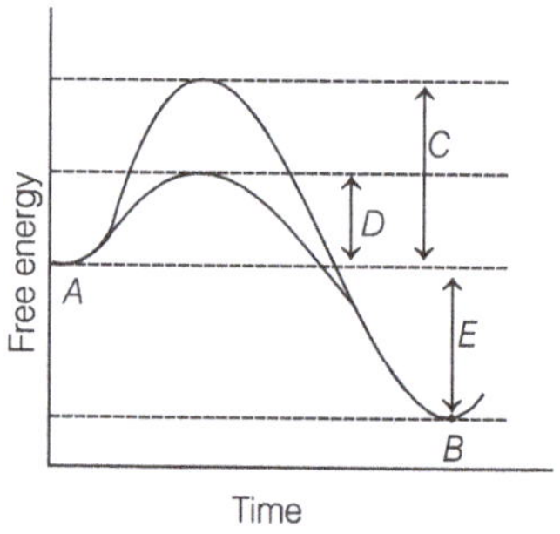


**21.** Respiration is an energy releasing and enzymatically controlled catabolic process, which involves a stepwise oxidative breakdown of organic substances inside living cells. In this statement about respiration explain the meaning of (i) stepwise oxidative breakdown (ii) organic substances (used as substrates).

*Or*

Succinic dehydrogenase is an enzyme that causes the substrate, succinate, to breakdown into fumarate.

Malonate is a substance that resembles succinate and inhibits the activity of succinic dehydrogenase.

(i) State the type of inhibition of succinic dehydrogenase by malonate.

(ii) Define the ferm inhibition.

## SECTION-C

**22.** (i) Study the given structure carefully and label the parts given as *A*, *B*, *C* and *D*.

(ii) Give one major function of any two of these.

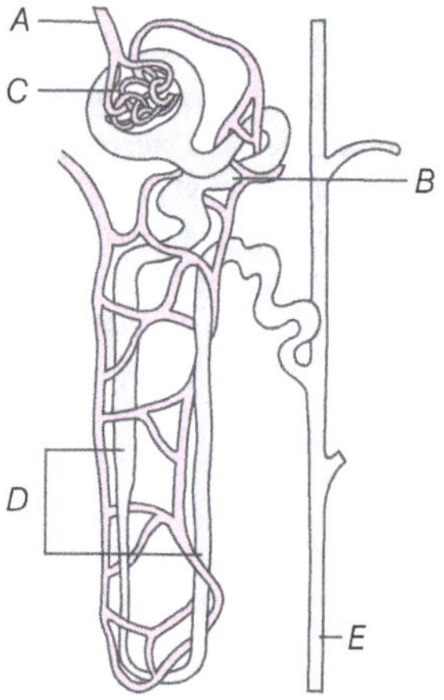


**23.** Explain the composition of triglyceride.

**24.** In old age, people often suffer from stiff and inflammed joints. What is this condition called? What are the possible reasons for these symptoms?

**25.** Oxygen dissociation curve is obtained by plotting percentage saturation of Hb with $O_2$ against $pO_2$.

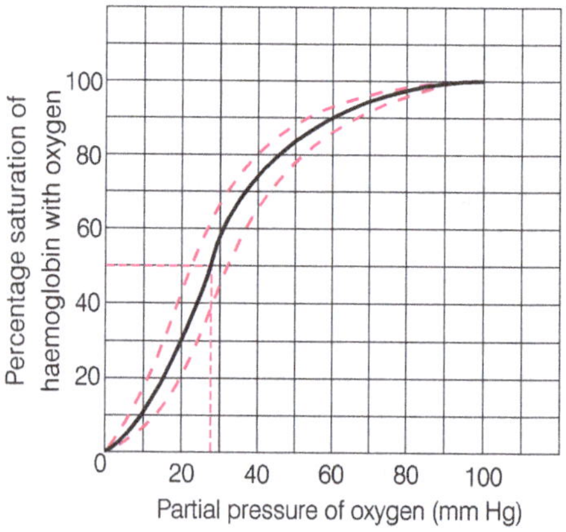


(i) How will an increase in temperature affect this curve?

(ii) When the curve shifts to left, what does it indicate?

(iii) Mention the significance of the curve.

**26.** Why the blood vascular system of leeches is also called haemocoelomic system? Write in detail.

**27.** Observe the organism in the image below and answer the questions that follows.

(i) Identify the organism in the image and the phylum it belongs to.

(ii) In the given animal, how do the sizes of males and females differ?

(iii) Give two examples of the animals that belong to same phylum.

**28.** Describe the vegetative characters of Solanaceae family. Also, write economic importance of Solanaceae.

## SECTION-D

**29.** John comes on a vacation to India from London. This long journey disturbed his biological clock and he suffers from jet lag.

(i) What is the cause of his discomfort? [1]

*Or*

(i) Which hormone is responsible for this jet lag? [1]

(ii) (a) Which gland secrete the hormone which is responsible for this discomfort?

(b) Mark the location of this gland in diagram. [2]

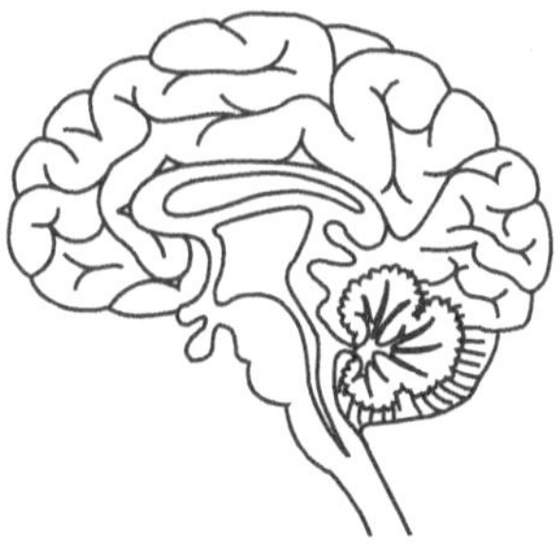

(iii) Write any two functions of this hormone. [1]

**30.** Plastids are cell organelles found in plant cell. Based on their function, they are of different types. Some contain specific pigments that impart colour to the plant while others store food. They are also considered semiautonomous organelles due to their own DNA and ability to replicate independently.

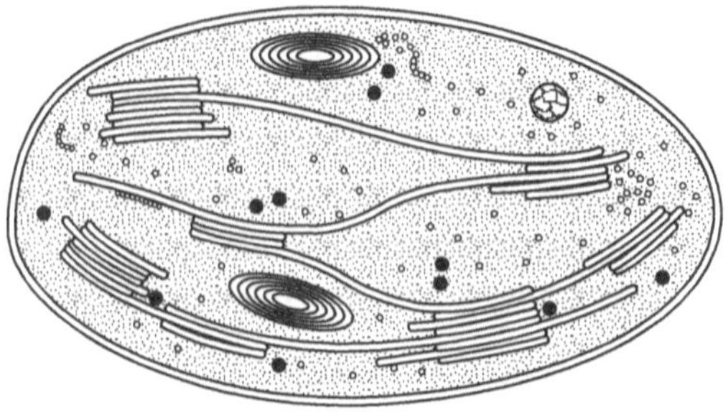

(i) Why plastids are called as semi-autonomous organelles? [1]

(ii) Write the types of plastids with their functions. [2]

(iii) Write the name of the space limited by inner membrane of chloroplast. [1]

*Or*

(iii) Why the lumen of thylakoids are acidic in nature, whereas the stroma is alkaline in nature? [1]

## SECTION-E

**31.** (A) The following image shows a specific organism belonging to the phylum-Chordata. Carefully observe the characteristics of the organism, answer the questions that follows.

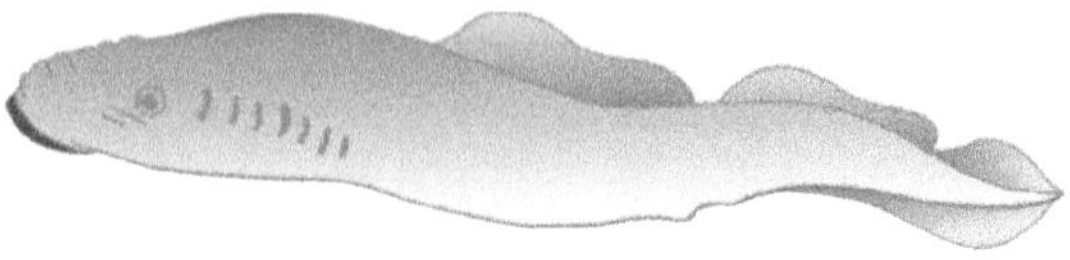

(i) Identify the given organism and mention the class it belongs to.

(ii) Give the examples of the animals belonging to this class.

(iii) Write a short note on migration seen in these animals

(iv) How do these animals differ from the members of class-Chondrichthyes.

*Or*

(B) Given below are some charactristic feature of Archaea and Eukarya domains.

| Characters | Archaea | Eukarya |
| --- | --- | --- |
| Cell type | Prokaryotic | Eukaryotic |
| Histones | *P* | Have histones |
| Ribosome size | *Q* | *R* |
| Cell wall composition | Made of protein (but lack peptidoglycan) | Not always present; Plants: Cellulose, Fungi: Chitin |

(i) Identify characteristic feature of *P*, *Q* and *R*.

(ii) Write the name of kingdom from which these domains belong.

(iii) Who introduced this system?

**32.** (A) (i) With the help of a diagram, depict Hatch and Slack pathway.

(ii) Briefly explain the factors that affect the rate of photosynthesis.

*Or* (B) (i) With the help of a flowchart, explain the various steps of glycolysis.

(ii) Explain the crucial events that take place in aerobic respiration.

**33.** (A) 'The glomerular filtrate in the loop of Henle gets concentrated in the descending limb and then gets diluted in the ascending limb'. Give the relative contribution of the parts of Henle's loop and explain the reason for the above given statement.

*Or* (B) Given below is a table depicting the blood groups and donor compatibility.

| Blood groups | Receive blood | Donate blood |
| --- | --- | --- |
| O | (*a*) | O, A, B, AB |
| (*b*) | A, B, AB, O | AB |

Name the (*a*) and (*b*) in the above table.

Justify giving reasons why blood groups and donor compatibility must be checked before blood transfusion?

## Answers

1. (c) 2. (a) 3. (b) 4. (c) 5. (a) 6. (a) 7. (c) 8. (b) 9. (d) 10. (c)
11. (c) 12. (a) 13. (a) 14. (b) 15. (b) 16. (b)